Collins
Spanish
Dictionary

Published by Collins
An imprint of HarperCollins
Publishers
Westerhill Road
Bishopbriggs
Glasgow G64 2QT
www.harpercollins.co.uk

This Edition 2014

10 9 8 7 6 5 4 3 2 1

© HarperCollins Publishers 2014

ISBN 978-0-00-794282-4
ISBN 978-0-00-794286-2
ISBN 978-0-00-758334-8
ISBN 978-0-00-794237-4

www.collins.co.uk
www.collinsdictionary.com

Printed in Great Britain by Clays Ltd,
St Ives plc

The contents of this publication
are believed correct at the time of
printing. Nevertheless the publisher
can accept no responsibility for
errors or omissions, changes in the
detail given or for any expense or loss
thereby caused.

HarperCollins does not warrant that
any website mentioned in this title
will be provided uninterrupted, that
any website will be error free, that
defects will be corrected, or that the
website or the server that makes it
available are free of viruses or bugs.
For full terms and conditions please
refer to the site terms provided on
the website.

A catalogue record for this book is
available from the British Library.

If you would like to comment on any
aspect of this book, please contact us
at the above address or online.
E-mail: dictionaries@harpercollins.
co.uk

Acknowledgements
We would like to thank those authors
and publishers who kindly gave
permission for copyright material
to be used in the Collins Corpus.
We would also like to thank Times
Newspapers Ltd for providing
valuable data.

ÍNDICE

CONTENTS

MARCAS REGISTRADAS

Las marcas que creemos que constituyen marcas registradas las denominamos como tales. Sin embargo, no debe considerarse que la presencia o la ausencia de esta designación tenga que ver con la situación legal de ninguna marca.

NOTE ON TRADEMARKS

Words which we have reason to believe constitute trademarks have been designated as such. However, neither the presence nor the absence of such designation should be regarded as affecting the legal status of any trademark.

INTRODUCCIÓN

Estamos muy satisfechos de que hayas decidido comprar este diccionario y esperamos que lo disfrutes y que te sirva de gran ayuda ya sea en el colegio, en el trabajo, en tus vacaciones o en casa.

INTRODUCTION

We are delighted that you have decided to buy this Spanish dictionary and hope you will enjoy and benefit from using it at school, at home, on holiday or at work.

ABREVIATURAS

ABBREVIATIONS

abreviatura	*ab(b)r*	abbreviation
adjetivo, locución adjetiva	*adj*	adjective, adjectival phrase
administración	*Admin*	administration
adverbio, locución adverbial	*adv*	adverb, adverbial phrase
agricultura	*Agr*	agriculture
anatomía	*Anat*	anatomy
Argentina	*Arg*	Argentina
arquitectura	*Arq, Arch*	architecture
el automóvil	*Aut(o)*	the motor car and motoring
aviación, viajes aéreos	*Aviac, Aviat*	flying, air travel
biología	*Bio(l)*	biology
botánica, flores	*Bot*	botany
inglés británico	BRIT	British English
Centroamérica	CAM	Central America
química	*Chem*	chemistry
comercio, finanzas, banca	*Com(m)*	commerce, finance, banking
informática	*Comput*	computing
conjunción	*conj*	conjunction
construcción	*Constr*	building
compuesto	*cpd*	compound element
Cono Sur	CS	Southern Cone
cocina	*Culin*	cookery
economía	*Econ*	economics
eletricidad, electrónica	*Elec*	electricity, electronics
enseñanza, sistema escolar y universitario	*Escol*	schooling, schools and universities
España	ESP	Spain
especialmente	*esp*	especially
exclamación, interjección	*excl*	exclamation, interjection
femenino	*f*	feminine
lengua familiar (! vulgar)	*fam(!)*	colloquial usage (! particularly offensive)
ferrocarril	*Ferro*	railways
uso figurado	*fig*	figurative use
fotografía	*Foto*	photography
(verbo inglés) del cual la partícula es inseparable	*fus*	(phrasal verb) where the particle is inseparable
generalmente	*gen*	generally
geografía, geología	*Geo*	geography, geology
geometría	*Geom*	geometry
historia	*Hist*	history
uso familiar (! vulgar)	*inf(!)*	colloquial usage (! particularly offensive)
infinitivo	*infin*	infinitive
informática	*Inform*	computing
invariable	*inv*	invariable
irregular	*irreg*	irregular
lo jurídico	*Jur*	law
América Latina	LAM	Latin America
gramática, lingüística	*Ling*	grammar, linguistics

ABREVIATURAS

ABBREVIATIONS

masculino	m	masculine
matemáticas	Mat(h)	mathematics
masculino/femenino	m/f	masculine/feminine
medicina	Med	medicine
México	MÉX, MEX	Mexico
lo militar, ejército	Mil	military matters
música	Mús, Mus	music
substantivo, nombre	n	noun
navegación, náutica	Náut, Naut	sailing, navigation
sustantivo numérico	num	numeral noun
complemento	obj	(grammatical) object
	o.s.	oneself
peyorativo	pey, pej	derogatory, pejorative
fotografía	Phot	photography
fisiología	Physiol	physiology
plural	pl	plural
política	Pol	politics
participio de pasado	pp	past participle
preposición	prep	preposition
pronombre	pron	pronoun
psicología, psiquiatría	Psico, Psych	psychology, psychiatry
tiempo pasado	pt	past tense
química	Quím	chemistry
ferrocarril	Rail	railways
religión	Rel	religion
Río de la Plata	RPL	River Plate
	sb	somebody
Cono Sur	SC	Southern Cone
enseñanza, sistema escolar y universitario	Scol	schooling, schools and universities
singular	sg	singular
España	SP	Spain
	sth	something
sujeto	su(b)j	(grammatical) subject
subjuntivo	subjun	subjunctive
tauromaquia	Taur	bullfighting
también	tb	also
técnica, tecnología	Tec(h)	technical term, technology
telecomunicaciones	Telec, Tel	telecommunications
imprenta, tipografía	Tip, Typ	typography, printing
televisión	TV	television
universidad	Univ	university
inglés norteamericano	US	American English
verbo	vb	verb
verbo intransitivo	vi	intransitive verb
verbo pronominal	vr	reflexive verb
verbo transitivo	vt	transitive verb
zoología	Zool	zoology
marca registrada	®	registered trademark
indica un equivalente cultural	≈	introduces a cultural equivalent

SPANISH PRONUNCIATION

VOWELS

a	[a]	pata	not as long as *a* in f*a*r. When followed by a consonant in the same syllable (i.e. in a closed syllable), as in *a*mante, the *a* is short, as in b*a*t
e	[e]	me	like *e* in th*ey*. In a closed syllable, as in g*e*nte, the *e* is short as in p*e*t
i	[i]	pino	as in m*ea*n or mach*i*ne
o	[o]	lo	as in l*o*cal. In a closed syllable, as in c*o*ntrol, the *o* is short as in c*o*t
u	[u]	lunes	as in r*u*le. It is silent after q, and in g*ue*, g*ui*, unless marked güe, güi e.g. antigüedad, when it is pronounced like *w* in *w*olf

SEMIVOWELS

i, y	[j]	bien hielo yunta	pronounced like *y* in *y*es
u	[w]	huevo fuento antigüedad	unstressed *u* between consonant and vowel is pronounced like *w* in *w*ell. See notes on *u* above.

DIPHTHONGS

ai, ay	[ai]	baile	as *i* in r*i*de
au	[au]	auto	as *ou* in sh*ou*t
ei, ey	[ei]	buey	as *ey* in gr*ey*
eu	[eu]	deuda	both elements pronounced independently [e] + [u]
oi, oy	[oi]	hoy	as *oy* in t*oy*

CONSONANTS

b	[b,β]	boda bomba labor	see notes on *v* below
c	[k]	caja	*c* before *a, o, u* is pronounced as in *c*at
ce, ci	[θe,θi]	cero cielo	*c* before *e* or *i* is pronounced as in *th*in
ch	[tʃ]	chiste	*ch* is pronounced as *ch* in *ch*air
d	[d,ð]	danés ciudad	at the beginning of a phrase or after *l* or *n*, *d* is pronounced as in English. In any other position it is pronounced like *th* in *th*e

g	[g, ɣ]	**g**afas pa**g**a	*g* before *a, o* or *u* is pronounced as in *g*ap, if at the beginning of a phrase or after *n*. In other positions the sound is softened
ge, gi	[xe, xi]	**g**ente **g**irar	*g* before *e* or *i* is pronounced similar to *ch* in Scottish lo*ch*
h		**h**aber	*h* is always silent in Spanish
j	[x]	**j**ugar	*j* is pronounced similar to *ch* in Scottish lo*ch*
ll	[ʎ]	ta**ll**e	*ll* is pronounced like the *y* in *y*et or the *lli* in mi*lli*on
ñ	[ʃ]	ni**ñ**o	*ñ* is pronounced like the *ni* in o*ni*on
q	[k]	**q**ue	*q* is pronounced as *k* in *k*ing
r, rr	[r, rr]	**q**uitar ga**rr**a	*r* is always pronounced in Spanish, unlike the silent *r* in dance*r*. *rr* is trilled, like a Scottish *r*
s	[s]	qui**z**ás i**s**la	*s* is usually pronounced as in pa*ss*, but before *b, d, g, l, m* or *n* it is pronounced as in ro*s*e
v	[b, β]	**v**ía	*v* is pronounced something like *b*. At the beginning of a phrase or after *m* or *n* it is pronounced as *b* in *b*oy. In any other position the sound is softened
z	[θ]	tena**z**	*z* is pronounced as *th* in *th*in

f, k, l, m, n, p, t and *x* are pronounced as in English.

STRESS

The rules of stress in Spanish are as follows:

(a) when a word ends in a vowel or in *n* or *s*, the second last syllable is stressed:
pa*ta*ta, pa*ta*tas; *co*me, *co*men
(b) when a word ends in a consonant other than *n* or *s*, the stress falls on the last syllable:
pa*red*, ha*blar*
(c) when the rules set out in (a) and (b) are not applied, an acute accent appears over the stressed vowel:
co*mún*, geogra*fía*, in*glés*

In the phonetic transcription, the symbol [¹] precedes the syllable on which the stress falls.

LA PRONUNCIACIÓN INGLESA

VOCALES

	Ejemplo inglés	Explicación
[ɑː]	father	Entre a de padre y o de noche
[ʌ]	but, come	a muy breve
[æ]	man, cat	Con los labios en la posición de e en pena y luego se pronuncia el sonido a parecido a la a de carro
[ə]	father, ago	Vocal neutra parecida a una e u o casi muda
[əː]	bird, heard	Entre e abierta y o cerrada, sonido alargado
[ɛ]	get, bed	Como en perro
[ɪ]	it, big	Más breve que en sí
[iː]	tea, see	Como en fíno
[ɔ]	hot, wash	Como en torre
[ɔː]	saw, all	Como en por
[u]	put, book	Sonido breve, más cerrado que burro
[uː]	too, you	Sonido largo, como en uno

DIPTONGOS

	Ejemplo inglés	Explicación
[aɪ]	fly, high	Como en fraile
[au]	how, house	Como en pausa
[ɛə]	there, bear	Casi como en vea, pero el sonido a se mezcla con el indistinto [ə]
[eɪ]	day, obey	e cerrada seguida por una i débil
[ɪə]	here, hear	Como en manía, mezclándose el sonido a con el indistinto [ə]
[əu]	go, note	[ə] seguido por una breve u
[əɪ]	boy, oil	Como en voy
[uə]	poor, sure	u bastante larga más el sonido indistinto [ə]

CONSONANTES

	Ejemplo inglés	Explicación
[b]	big, lobby	Como en tumban
[d]	mended	Como en conde, andar
[g]	go, get, big	Como en grande, gol
[dʒ]	gin, judge	Como en la ll andaluza y en Generalitat (catalán)
[ŋ]	sing	Como en vínculo
[h]	house, he	Como la jota hispanoamericana
[j]	young, yes	Como en ya
[k]	come, mock	Como en caña, Escocia
[r]	red, tread	Se pronuncia con la punta de la lengua hacia atrás y sin hacerla vibrar
[s]	sand, yes	Como en casa, sesión
[z]	rose, zebra	Como en desde, mismo
[ʃ]	she, machine	Como en chambre (francés), roxo (portugués)
[tʃ]	chin, rich	Como en chocolate
[v]	valley	Como f, pero se retiran los dientes superiores vibrándolos contra el labio inferior
[w]	water, which	Como la u de huevo, puede
[ʒ]	vision	Como en journal (francés)
[θ]	think, myth	Como en receta, zapato
[ð]	this, the	Como en hablado, verdad

f, l, m, n, p, t y x iguales que en español.

El signo [*] indica que la r final escrita apenas se pronuncia en inglés británico cuando la palabra siguiente empieza con vocal.
El signo [¹] indica la sílaba acentuada.

SPANISH VERB TABLES

1 Gerund 2 Imperative 3 Present 4 Preterite 5 Future 6 Present subjunctive 7 Imperfect subjunctive 8 Past participle 9 Imperfect

Etc indicates that the irregular root is used for all persons of the tense, e.g. **oír**: 6 oiga, oigas, oigamos, oigáis, oigan

agradecer 3 agradezco 6 agradezca *etc*

aprobar 2 aprueba 3 apruebo, apruebas, aprueba, aprueban 6 apruebe, apruebes, apruebe, aprueben

atravesar 2 atraviesa 3 atravieso, atraviesas, atraviesa, atraviesan 6 atraviese, atravieses, atraviese, atraviesen

caber 3 quepo 4 cupe, cupiste, cupo, cupimos, cupisteis, cupieron 5 cabré *etc* 6 quepa *etc* 7 cupiera *etc*

caer 1 cayendo 3 caigo 4 cayó, cayeron 6 caiga *etc* 7 cayera *etc*

cerrar 2 cierra 3 cierro, cierras, cierra, cierran 6 cierre, cierres, cierre, cierren

COMER 1 comiendo 2 come, comed 3 como, comes, come, comemos, coméis, comen 4 comí, comiste, comió, comimos, comisteis, comieron 5 comeré, comerás, comerá, comeremos, comeréis, comerán 6 coma, comas, coma, comamos, comáis, coman 7 comiera, comieras, comiera, comiéramos, comierais, comieran 8 comido 9 comía, comías, comía, comíamos, comíais, comían

conocer 3 conozco 6 conozca *etc*

contar 2 cuenta 3 cuento, cuentas, cuenta, cuentan 6 cuente, cuentes, cuente, cuenten

dar 3 doy 4 di, diste, dio, dimos, disteis, dieron 7 diera *etc*

decir 2 di 3 digo 4 dije, dijiste, dijo, dijimos, dijisteis, dijeron 5 diré *etc* 6 diga *etc* 7 dijera *etc* 8 dicho

despertar 2 despierta 3 despierto, despiertas, despierta, despiertan 6 despierte, despiertes, despierte, despierten

divertir 1 divirtiendo 2 divierte 3 divierto, diviertes, divierte, divierten 4 divirtió, divirtieron 6 divierta, diviertas, divierta, divirtamos, divirtáis, diviertan 7 divirtiera *etc*

dormir 1 durmiendo 2 duerme 3 duermo, duermes, duerme, duermen 4 durmió, durmieron 6 duerma, duermas, duerma, durmamos, durmáis, duerman 7 durmiera *etc*

empezar 2 empieza 3 empiezo, empiezas, empieza, empiezan 4 empecé 6 empiece, empieces, empiece, empecemos, empecéis, empiecen

entender 2 entiende 3 entiendo, entiendes, entiende, entienden 6 entienda, entiendas, entienda, entiendan

ESTAR 2 está 3 estoy, estás, está, están 4 estuve, estuviste,

estuvo, estuvimos, estuvisteis,
estuvieron **6** esté, estés, esté,
estén **7** estuviera *etc*
HABER 3 he, has, ha, hemos,
han **4** hube, hubiste, hubo,
hubimos, hubisteis, hubieron
5 habré *etc* **6** haya *etc* **7** hubiera
etc
HABLAR 1 hablando **2** habla,
hablad **3** hablo, hablas, habla,
hablamos, habláis, hablan
4 hablé, hablaste, habló,
hablamos, hablasteis,
hablaron **5** hablaré, hablarás,
hablará, hablaremos,
hablaréis, hablarán **6** hable,
hables, hable, hablemos,
habléis, hablen **7** hablara,
hablaras, hablara, habláramos,
hablarais, hablaran **8** hablado
9 hablaba, hablabas, hablaba,
hablábamos, hablabais,
hablaban
hacer 2 haz **3** hago **4** hice,
hiciste, hizo, hicimos,
hicisteis, hicieron **5** haré *etc*
6 haga *etc* **7** hiciera *etc* **8** hecho
instruir 1 instruyendo **2** instruye
3 instruyo, instruyes, instruye,
instruyen **4** instruyó,
instruyeron **6** instruya *etc*
7 instruyera *etc*
ir 1 yendo **2** ve **3** voy, vas, va,
vamos, vais, van **4** fui, fuiste,
fue, fuimos, fuisteis, fueron
6 vaya, vayas, vaya, vayamos,
vayáis, vayan **7** fuera *etc* **9** iba,
ibas, iba, íbamos, ibais, iban
jugar 2 juega **3** juego, juegas,
juega, juegan **4** jugué **6** juegue
etc
leer 1 leyendo **4** leyó, leyeron
7 leyera *etc*
morir 1 muriendo **2** muere
3 muero, mueres, muere,
mueren **4** murió, murieron

6 muera, mueras, muera,
muramos, muráis, mueran
7 muriera *etc* **8** muerto
mover 2 mueve **3** muevo,
mueves, mueve, mueven
6 mueva, muevas, mueva,
muevan
negar 2 niega **3** niego, niegas,
niega, niegan **4** negué
6 niegue, niegues, niegue,
neguemos, neguéis, nieguen
ofrecer 3 ofrezco **6** ofrezca *etc*
oír 1 oyendo **2** oye **3** oigo, oyes,
oye, oyen **4** oyó, oyeron **6** oiga
etc **7** oyera *etc*
oler 2 huele **3** huelo, hueles,
huele, huelen **6** huela, huelas,
huela, huelan
parecer 3 parezco **6** parezca *etc*
pedir 1 pidiendo **2** pide **3** pido,
pides, pide, piden **4** pidió,
pidieron **6** pida *etc* **7** pidiera *etc*
pensar 2 piensa **3** pienso,
piensas, piensa, piensan
6 piense, pienses, piense,
piensen
perder 2 pierde **3** pierdo, pierdes,
pierde, pierden **6** pierda,
pierdas, pierda, pierdan
poder 1 pudiendo **2** puede
3 puedo, puedes, puede,
pueden **4** pude, pudiste, pudo,
pudimos, pudisteis, pudieron
5 podré *etc* **6** pueda, puedas,
pueda, puedan **7** pudiera *etc*
poner 2 pon **3** pongo **4** puse,
pusiste, puso, pusimos,
pusisteis, pusieron **5** pondré *etc*
6 ponga *etc* **7** pusiera *etc*
8 puesto
preferir 1 prefiriendo **2** prefiere
3 prefiero, prefieres, prefiere,
prefieren **4** prefirió, prefirieron
6 prefiera, prefieras, prefiera,
prefiramos, prefiráis, prefieran
7 prefiriera *etc*

querer 2 quiere 3 quiero, quieres, quiere, quieren 4 quise, quisiste, quiso, quisimos, quisisteis, quisieron 5 querré *etc* 6 quiera, quieras, quiera, quieran 7 quisiera *etc*

reír 2 ríe 3 río, ríes, ríe, ríen 4 reí, rieron 6 ría, rías, ría, riamos, riáis, rían *etc*

repetir 1 repitiendo 2 repite 3 repito, repites, repite, repiten 4 repitió, repitieron 6 repita *etc* 7 repitiera *etc*

rogar 2 ruega 3 ruego, ruegas, ruega, ruegan 4 rogué 6 ruegue, ruegues, ruegue, roguemos, roguéis, rueguen

saber 3 sé 4 supe, supiste, supo, supimos, supisteis, supieron 5 sabré *etc* 6 sepa *etc* 7 supiera *etc*

salir 2 sal 3 salgo 5 saldré *etc* 6 salga *etc*

seguir 1 siguiendo 2 sigue 3 sigo, sigues, sigue, siguen 4 siguió, siguieron 6 siga *etc* 7 siguiera *etc*

sentar 2 sienta 3 siento, sientas, sienta, sientan 6 siente, sientes, siente, sienten

sentir 1 sintiendo 2 siente 3 siento, sientes, siente, sienten 4 sintió, sintieron 6 sienta, sientas, sienta, sintamos, sintáis, sientan 7 sintiera *etc*

SER 2 sé 3 soy, eres, es, somos, sois, son 4 fui, fuiste, fue, fuimos, fuisteis, fueron 6 sea *etc* 7 fuera *etc* 9 era, eras, era, éramos, erais, eran

servir 1 sirviendo 2 sirve 3 sirvo, sirves, sirve, sirven 4 sirvió, sirvieron 6 sirva *etc* 7 sirviera *etc*

soñar 2 sueña 3 sueño, sueñas, sueña, sueñan 6 sueñe, sueñes, sueñe, sueñen

tener 2 ten 3 tengo, tienes, tiene, tienen 4 tuve, tuviste, tuvo, tuvimos, tuvisteis, tuvieron 5 tendré *etc* 6 tenga *etc* 7 tuviera *etc*

traer 1 trayendo 3 traigo 4 traje, trajiste, trajo, trajimos, trajisteis, trajeron 6 traiga *etc* 7 trajera *etc*

valer 2 vale 3 valgo 5 valdré *etc* 6 valga *etc*

venir 2 ven 3 vengo, vienes, viene, vienen 4 vine, viniste, vino, vinimos, vinisteis, vinieron 5 vendré *etc* 6 venga *etc* 7 viniera *etc*

ver 3 veo 6 vea *etc* 8 visto 9 veía *etc*

vestir 1 vistiendo 2 viste 3 visto, vistes, viste, visten 4 vistió, vistieron 6 vista *etc* 7 vistiera *etc*

VIVIR 1 viviendo 2 vive, vivid 3 vivo, vives, vive, vivimos, vivís, viven 4 viví, viviste, vivió, vivimos, vivisteis, vivieron 5 viviré, vivirás, vivirá, viviremos, viviréis, vivirán 6 viva, vivas, viva, vivamos, viváis, vivan 7 viviera, vivieras, viviera, viviéramos, vivierais, vivieran 8 vivido 9 vivía, vivías, vivía, vivíamos, vivías, vivían

volver 2 vuelve 3 vuelvo, vuelves, vuelve, vuelven 6 vuelva, vuelvas, vuelva, vuelvan 8 vuelto

VERBOS IRREGULARES EN INGLÉS

PRESENTE	PASADO	PARTICIPIO	PRESENTE	PASADO	PARTICIPIO
arise	arose	arisen	fall	fell	fallen
awake	awoke	awoken	feed	fed	fed
be (am, is, are; being)	was, were	been	feel	felt	felt
			fight	fought	fought
bear	bore	born(e)	find	found	found
beat	beat	beaten	flee	fled	fled
become	became	become	fling	flung	flung
begin	began	begun	fly	flew	flown
bend	bent	bent	forbid	forbad(e)	forbidden
bet	bet, betted	bet, betted	forecast	forecast	forecast
			forget	forgot	forgotten
bid (at auction, cards)	bid	bid	forgive	forgave	forgiven
			forsake	forsook	forsaken
bid (say)	bade	bidden	freeze	froze	frozen
bind	bound	bound	get	got	got, (us) gotten
bite	bit	bitten			
bleed	bled	bled	give	gave	given
blow	blew	blown	go (goes)	went	gone
break	broke	broken	grind	ground	ground
breed	bred	bred	grow	grew	grown
bring	brought	brought	hang	hung	hung
build	built	built	hang (suspend) (execute)	hanged	hanged
burn	burnt, burned	burnt, burned	have	had	had
burst	burst	burst	hear	heard	heard
buy	bought	bought	hide	hid	hidden
can	could	(been able)	hit	hit	hit
cast	cast	cast	hold	held	held
catch	caught	caught	hurt	hurt	hurt
choose	chose	chosen	keep	kept	kept
cling	clung	clung	kneel	knelt, kneeled	knelt, kneeled
come	came	come			
cost (be valued at)	cost	cost	know	knew	known
			lay	laid	laid
cost (work out price of)	costed	costed	lead	led	led
			lean	leant, leaned	leant, leaned
creep	crept	crept			
cut	cut	cut	leap	leapt, leaped	leapt, leaped
deal	dealt	dealt			
dig	dug	dug	learn	learnt, learned	learnt, learned
do (does)	did	done			
draw	drew	drawn	leave	left	left
dream	dreamed, dreamt	dreamed, dreamt	lend	lent	lent
			let	let	let
drink	drank	drunk	lie (lying)	lay	lain
drive	drove	driven	light	lit, lighted	lit, lighted
dwell	dwelt	dwelt			
eat	ate	eaten	lose	lost	lost

XV

PRESENTE	PASADO	PARTICIPIO	PRESENTE	PASADO	PARTICIPIO
make	made	made	speed	sped,	sped,
may	might	–		speeded	speeded
mean	meant	meant	spell	spelt,	spelt,
meet	met	met		spelled	spelled
mistake	mistook	mistaken	spend	spent	spent
mow	mowed	mown,	spill	spilt,	spilt,
		mowed		spilled	spilled
must	(had to)	(had to)	spin	spun	spun
pay	paid	paid	spit	spat	spat
put	put	put	spoil	spoiled,	spoiled,
quit	quit,	quit,		spoilt	spoilt
	quitted	quitted	spread	spread	spread
read	read	read	spring	sprang	sprung
rid	rid	rid	stand	stood	stood
ride	rode	ridden	steal	stole	stolen
ring	rang	rung	stick	stuck	stuck
rise	rose	risen	sting	stung	stung
run	ran	run	stink	stank	stunk
saw	sawed	sawed,	stride	strode	stridden
		sawn	strike	struck	struck
say	said	said	strive	strove	striven
see	saw	seen	swear	swore	sworn
seek	sought	sought	sweep	swept	swept
sell	sold	sold	swell	swelled	swollen,
send	sent	sent			swelled
set	set	set	swim	swam	swum
sew	sewed	sewn	swing	swung	swung
shake	shook	shaken	take	took	taken
shear	sheared	shorn,	teach	taught	taught
		sheared	tear	tore	torn
shed	shed	shed	tell	told	told
shine	shone	shone	think	thought	thought
shoot	shot	shot	throw	threw	thrown
show	showed	shown	thrust	thrust	thrust
shrink	shrank	shrunk	tread	trod	trodden
shut	shut	shut	wake	woke,	woken,
sing	sang	sung		waked	waked
sink	sank	sunk	wear	wore	worn
sit	sat	sat	weave (on	wove	woven
slay	slew	slain	loom)		
sleep	slept	slept	weave (wind)	weaved	weaved
slide	slid	slid	wed	wedded,	wedded,
sling	slung	slung		wed	wed
slit	slit	slit	weep	wept	wept
smell	smelt,	smelt,	win	won	won
	smelled	smelled	wind	wound	wound
sow	sowed	sown,	wring	wrung	wrung
		sowed	write	wrote	written
speak	spoke	spoken			

a

abalanzarse [aβalanˈθarse] vr: **~ sobre** o **contra** to throw o.s. at

abanderado, -a [aβandeˈraðo] nm/f (portaestandarte) standard bearer; (de un movimiento) champion, leader; (MÉX: linier) linesman, assistant referee

abandonado, -a [aβandoˈnaðo, a] adj derelict; (desatendido) abandoned; (desierto) deserted; (descuidado) neglected

abandonar [aβandoˈnar] vt to leave; (persona) to abandon, desert; (cosa) to abandon, leave behind; (descuidar) to neglect; (renunciar a) to give up; (Inform) to quit; **abandonarse** vr: **~se a** to abandon o.s. to; **abandono** nm (acto) desertion, abandonment; (estado) abandon, neglect; (renuncia) withdrawal, retirement; **ganar por abandono** to win by default

abanico [aβaˈniko] nm fan; (Náut) derrick

abarcar [aβarˈkar] vt to include, embrace; (LAM: acaparar) to monopolize

abarrotado, -a [aβarroˈtaðo, a] adj packed

abarrotar [aβarroˈtar] vt (local, estadio, teatro) to fill, pack

abarrotero, -a [aβarroˈtero, a] (MÉX) nm/f grocer; **abarrotes** (MÉX) nmpl groceries; **tienda de abarrotes** (MÉX, CAM) grocery store

abastecer [aβasteˈθer] vt: **~ (de)** to supply (with); **abastecimiento** nm supply

abasto [aˈβasto] nm supply; **no dar ~ a** to be unable to cope with

abatible [aβaˈtiβle] adj: **asiento ~** tip-up seat; (Auto) reclining seat

abatido, -a [aβaˈtiðo, a] adj dejected, downcast

abatir [aβaˈtir] vt (muro) to demolish; (pájaro) to shoot o bring down; (fig) to depress

abdicar [aβðiˈkar] vi to abdicate

abdomen [aβˈðomen] nm abdomen; **abdominales** nmpl (tb: **ejercicios abdominales**) sit-ups

abecedario [aβeθeˈðarjo] nm alphabet

abedul [aβeˈðul] nm birch

abeja [aˈβexa] nf bee

abejorro [aβeˈxorro] nm bumblebee

abertura [aβerˈtura] nf = **apertura**

abeto [aˈβeto] nm fir

abierto, -a [aˈβjerto, a] pp de **abrir** ▷ adj open

abismal [aβisˈmal] adj (fig) vast, enormous

○ **PALABRA CLAVE**

a [a] (a + el = al) prep **1** (dirección) to; **fueron a Madrid/Grecia** they went to Madrid/Greece; **me voy a casa** I'm going home
2 (distancia): **está a 15 km de aquí** it's 15 kms from here
3 (posición): **estar a la mesa** to be at table; **al lado de** next to, beside; V tb **puerta**
4 (tiempo): **a las 10/a medianoche** at 10/midnight; **a la mañana siguiente** the following morning; **a los pocos días** after a few days; **estamos a 9 de julio** it's the ninth of July; **a los 24 años** at the age of 24; **al año/a la semana** a year/week later
5 (manera): **a la francesa** the French way; **a caballo** on horseback; **a oscuras** in the dark
6 (medio, instrumento): **a lápiz** in pencil; **a mano** by hand; **cocina a gas** gas stove
7 (razón): **a 30 céntimos el kilo** at 30 cents a kilo; **a más de 50 km/h** at more than 50 kms per hour
8 (dativo): **se lo di a él** I gave it to him; **vi al policía** I saw the policeman; **se lo compré a él** I bought it from him
9 (tras ciertos verbos): **voy a verle** I'm going to see him; **empezó a trabajar** he started working o to work
10 (+ infin): **al verlo, lo reconocí inmediatamente** when I saw him I recognized him at once; **el camino a recorrer** the distance we etc have to travel; **¡a callar!** keep quiet!; **¡a comer!** let's eat!

abad, esa [aˈβað, ˈðesa] nm/f abbot/abbess; **abadía** nf abbey

abajo [aˈβaxo] adv (situación) (down) below, underneath; (en edificio) downstairs; (dirección) down, downwards; **el piso de ~** the downstairs flat; **la parte de ~** the lower part; **¡~ el gobierno!** down with

abismo [a'βismo] nm abyss
ablandar [aβlan'dar] vt to soften;
 ablandarse vr to get softer
abocado, -a [aβo'kaðo, a] adj (vino)
 smooth, pleasant
abochornar [aβotʃor'nar] vt to
 embarrass
abofetear [aβofete'ar] vt to slap (in the
 face)
abogado, -a [aβo'ɣaðo, a] nm/f lawyer;
 (notario) solicitor; (en tribunal) barrister
 (BRIT), attorney (US); **abogado defensor**
 defence lawyer o (US) attorney
abogar [aβo'ɣar] vi: ~ **por** to plead for; (fig)
 to advocate
abolir [aβo'lir] vt to abolish; (cancelar) to
 cancel
abolladura [aβoʎa'ðura] nf dent
abollar [aβo'ʎar] vt to dent
abombarse [aβom'barse] (LAM) vr to
 go bad
abominable [aβomi'naβle] adj
 abominable
abonado, -a [aβo'naðo, a] adj (deuda)
 paid(-up) ▷ nm/f subscriber
abonar [aβo'nar] vt (deuda) to settle;
 (terreno) to fertilize; (idea) to endorse;
 abonarse vr to subscribe; **abono** nm
 payment; fertilizer; subscription
abordar [aβor'ðar] vt (barco) to board;
 (asunto) to broach
aborigen [aβo'rixen] nmf aborigine
aborrecer [aβorre'θer] vt to hate, loathe
abortar [aβor'tar] vi (malparir) to have
 a miscarriage; (deliberadamente) to have
 an abortion; **aborto** nm miscarriage;
 abortion
abovedado, -a [aβoβe'ðaðo, a] adj
 vaulted, domed
abrasar [aβra'sar] vt to burn (up); (Agr) to
 dry up, parch
abrazar [aβra'θar] vt to embrace, hug
abrazo [a'βraðo] nm embrace, hug; **un ~**
 (en carta) with best wishes
abrebotellas [aβreβo'teʎas] nm inv bottle
 opener
abrecartas [aβre'kartas] nm inv letter
 opener
abrelatas [aβre'latas] nm inv tin (BRIT) o
 can opener
abreviatura [aβreβja'tura] nf
 abbreviation
abridor [aβri'ðor] nm bottle opener; (de
 latas) tin (BRIT) o can opener
abrigador, a [aβriɣa'ðor, a] (MÉX) adj
 warm
abrigar [aβri'ɣar] vt (proteger) to shelter;
 (ropa) to keep warm; (fig) to cherish

abrigo [a'βriɣo] nm (prenda) coat,
 overcoat; (lugar protegido) shelter
abril [a'βril] nm April
abrillantador [aβriʎanta'ðor] nm polish
abrillantar [aβriʎan'tar] vt to polish
abrir [a'βrir] vt to open (up) ▷ vi to open;
 abrirse vr to open (up); (extenderse) to open
 out; (cielo) to clear; **~se paso** to find o force
 a way through
abrochar [aβro'tʃar] vt (con botones) to
 button (up); (zapato, con broche) to do up
abrupto, -a [a'βrupto, a] adj abrupt;
 (empinado) steep
absoluto, -a [aβso'luto, a] adj absolute;
 en ~ adv not at all
absolver [aβsol'βer] vt to absolve; (Jur) to
 pardon; (: acusado) to acquit
absorbente [aβsor'βente] adj absorbent;
 (interesante) absorbing
absorber [aβsor'βer] vt to absorb;
 (embeber) to soak up
absorción [aβsor'θjon] nf absorption;
 (Com) takeover
abstemio, -a [aβs'temjo, a] adj teetotal
abstención [aβsten'θjon] nf abstention
abstenerse [aβste'nerse] vr: ~ **(de)** to
 abstain o refrain (from)
abstinencia [aβsti'nenθja] nf
 abstinence; (ayuno) fasting
abstracto, -a [aβs'trakto, a] adj abstract
abstraer [aβstra'er] vt to abstract;
 abstraerse vr to be o become absorbed
abstraído, -a [aβstra'iðo, a] adj absent-
 minded
absuelto [aβ'swelto] pp de **absolver**
absurdo, -a [aβ'surðo, a] adj absurd
abuchear [aβutʃe'ar] vt to boo
abuelo, -a [a'βwelo, a] nm/f
 grandfather(-mother); **abuelos** nmpl
 grandparents
abultado, -a [aβul'taðo, a] adj bulky
abultar [aβul'tar] vi to be bulky
abundancia [aβun'danθja] nf: **una ~
 de** plenty of; **abundante** adj abundant,
 plentiful
abundar [aβun'dar] vi to abound, be
 plentiful
aburrido, -a [aβu'rriðo, a] adj (hastiado)
 bored; (que aburre) boring; **aburrimiento**
 nm boredom, tedium
aburrir [aβu'rrir] vt to bore; **aburrirse** vr
 to be bored, get bored
abusado, -a [aβu'saðo, a] (MÉX: fam) adj
 (astuto) sharp, cunning ▷ excl: **¡~!** (inv) look
 out!, careful!
abusar [aβu'sar] vi to go too far; **~ de** to
 abuse
abusivo, -a [aβu'siβo, a] adj (precio)

exorbitant

abuso [a'βuso] nm abuse

acá [a'ka] adv (lugar) here

acabado, -a [aka'βaðo, a] adj finished, complete; (perfecto) perfect; (agotado) worn out; (fig) masterly ▷ nm finish

acabar [aka'βar] vt (llevar a su fin) to finish, complete; (consumir) to use up; (rematar) to finish off ▷ vi to finish, end; **acabarse** vr to finish, stop; (terminarse) to be over; (agotarse) to run out; ~ **con** to put an end to; ~ **de llegar** to have just arrived; ~ **por hacer** to end (up) by doing; **¡se acabó!** it's all over!; (¡basta!) that's enough!

acabóse [aka'βose] nm: **esto es el** ~ this is the last straw

academia [aka'ðemja] nf academy; **academia de idiomas** language school; **académico, -a** adj academic

acalorado, -a [akalo'raðo, a] adj (discusión) heated

acampar [akam'par] vi to camp

acantilado [akanti'laðo] nm cliff

acaparar [akapa'rar] vt to monopolize; (acumular) to hoard

acariciar [akari'θjar] vt to caress; (esperanza) to cherish

acarrear [akarre'ar] vt to transport; (fig) to cause, result in

acaso [a'kaso] adv perhaps, maybe; **(por) si** ~ (just) in case

acatar [aka'tar] vt to respect; (ley) obey

acatarrarse [akata'rrarse] vr to catch a cold

acceder [akθe'ðer] vi: ~ **a** (petición etc) to agree to; (tener acceso a) to have access to; (Inform) to access

accesible [akθe'siβle] adj accessible

acceso [ak'θeso] nm access, entry; (camino) access, approach; (Med) attack, fit

accesorio, -a [akθe'sorjo, a] adj, nm accessory

accidentado, -a [akθiðen'taðo, a] adj uneven; (montañoso) hilly; (azaroso) eventful ▷ nm/f accident victim

accidental [akθiðen'tal] adj accidental

accidente [akθi'ðente] nm accident; **accidentes** nmpl (de terreno) unevenness sg; **accidente laboral** o **de trabajo/de tráfico** industrial/road o traffic accident

acción [ak'θjon] nf action; (acto) action, act; (Com) share; (Jur) action, lawsuit;

accionar vt to work, operate; (Inform) to drive

accionista [akθjo'nista] nmf shareholder, stockholder

acebo [a'θeβo] nm holly; (árbol) holly tree

acechar [aθe'tʃar] vt to spy on; (aguardar)

to lie in wait for; **acecho** nm: **estar al acecho (de)** to lie in wait (for)

aceite [a'θeite] nm oil; **aceite de girasol/oliva** olive/sunflower oil; **aceitera** nf oilcan; **aceitoso, -a** adj oily

aceituna [aθei'tuna] nf olive; **aceituna rellena** stuffed olive

acelerador [aθelera'ðor] nm accelerator

acelerar [aθele'rar] vt to accelerate

acelga [a'θelɣa] nf chard, beet

acento [a'θento] nm accent; (acentuación) stress

acentuar [aθen'twar] vt to accent; to stress; (fig) to accentuate

acepción [aθep'θjon] nf meaning

aceptable [aθep'taβle] adj acceptable

aceptación [aθepta'θjon] nf acceptance; (aprobación) approval

aceptar [aθep'tar] vt to accept; (aprobar) to approve; ~ **hacer algo** to agree to do sth

acequia [a'θekja] nf irrigation ditch

acera [a'θera] nf pavement (BRIT), sidewalk (US)

acerca [a'θerka]: ~ **de** prep about, concerning

acercar [aθer'kar] vt to bring o move nearer; **acercarse** vr to approach, come near

acero [a'θero] nm steel

acérrimo, -a [a'θerrimo, a] adj (partidario) staunch; (enemigo) bitter

acertado, -a [aθer'taðo, a] adj correct; (apropiado) apt; (sensato) sensible

acertar [aθer'tar] vt (blanco) to hit; (solución) to get right; (adivinar) to guess ▷ vi to get it right, be right; ~ **a** to manage to; ~ **con** to happen o hit on

acertijo [aθer'tixo] nm riddle, puzzle

achacar [atʃa'kar] vt to attribute

achacoso, -a [atʃa'koso, a] adj sickly

achicar [atʃi'kar] vt to reduce; (Náut) to bale out

achicharrar [atʃitʃa'rrar] vt to scorch, burn

achichincle [atʃi'tʃinkle] (MÉX: fam) nmf minion

achicoria [atʃi'korja] nf chicory

achuras [a'tʃuras] (RPL) nfpl offal sg

acicate [aθi'kate] nm spur

acidez [aθi'ðeθ] nf acidity

ácido, -a ['aθiðo, a] adj sour, acid ▷ nm acid

acierto etc [a'θjerto] vb V **acertar** ▷ nm success; (buen paso) wise move; (solución) solution; (habilidad) skill, ability

acitronar [aθitro'nar] (MÉX: fam) vt to brown

aclamar [akla'mar] vt to acclaim;

(*aplaudir*) to applaud

aclaración [aklara'θjon] nf clarification, explanation

aclarar [akla'rar] vt to clarify, explain; (*ropa*) to rinse ▷ vi to clear up; **aclararse** vr (*explicarse*) to understand; **~se la garganta** to clear one's throat

aclimatación [aklimata'θjon] nf acclimatization

aclimatar [aklima'tar] vt to acclimatize; **aclimatarse** vr to become acclimatized

acné [ak'ne] nm acne

acobardar [akoβar'ðar] vt to intimidate

acogedor, a [akoxe'ðor, a] adj welcoming; (*hospitalario*) hospitable

acoger [ako'xer] vt to welcome; (*abrigar*) to shelter

acogida [ako'xiða] nf reception; refuge

acomedido, -a [akome'ðiðo, a] (MÉX) adj helpful, obliging

acometer [akome'ter] vt to attack; (*emprender*) to undertake; **acometida** nf attack, assault

acomodado, -a [akomo'ðaðo, a] adj (*persona*) well-to-do

acomodador, a [akomoða'ðor, a] nm/f usher(ette)

acomodar [akomo'ðar] vt to adjust; (*alojar*) to accommodate; **acomodarse** vr to conform; (*instalarse*) to install o.s.; (*adaptarse*): **~se (a)** to adapt (to)

acompañar [akompa'ɲar] vt to accompany; (*documentos*) to enclose

acondicionar [akondiθjo'nar] vt to arrange, prepare; (*pelo*) to condition

aconsejar [akonse'xar] vt to advise, counsel; **~ a algn hacer** o **que haga algo** to advise sb to do sth

acontecer [akonte'θer] vi to happen, occur; **acontecimiento** nm event

acopio [a'kopjo] nm store, stock

acoplar [ako'plar] vt to fit; (*Elec*) to connect; (*vagones*) to couple

acorazado, -a [akora'θaðo, a] adj armour-plated, armoured ▷ nm battleship

acordar [akor'ðar] vt (*resolver*) to agree, resolve; (*recordar*) to remind; **acordarse** vr to agree; **~ hacer algo** to agree to do sth; **~se (de algo)** to remember (sth); **acorde** adj (*Mús*) harmonious; **acorde con** (*medidas etc*) in keeping with ▷ nm chord

acordeón [akorðe'on] nm accordion

acordonado, -a [akorðo'naðo, a] adj (*calle*) cordoned-off

acorralar [akorra'lar] vt to round up, corral

acortar [akor'tar] vt to shorten; (*duración*) to cut short; (*cantidad*) to reduce; **acortarse**

vr to become shorter

acosar [ako'sar] vt to pursue relentlessly; (*fig*) to hound, pester; **acoso** nm harassment; **acoso sexual** sexual harassment

acostar [akos'tar] vt (*en cama*) to put to bed; (*en suelo*) to lay down; **acostarse** vr to go to bed; to lie down; **~se con algn** to sleep with sb

acostumbrado, -a [akostum'braðo, a] adj usual; **~ a** used to

acostumbrar [akostum'brar] vt: **~ a algn a algo** to get sb used to sth ▷ vi: **~ (a) hacer** to be in the habit of doing; **acostumbrarse** vr: **~se a** to get used to

acotación [akota'θjon] nf marginal note; (*Geo*) elevation mark; (*de límite*) boundary mark; (*Teatro*) stage direction

acotamiento [akota'mjento] (MÉX) nm hard shoulder (BRIT), berm (US)

acre ['akre] adj (*olor*) acrid; (*fig*) biting ▷ nm acre

acreditar [akreði'tar] vt (*garantizar*) to vouch for, guarantee; (*autorizar*) to authorize; (*dar prueba de*) to prove; (*Com: abonar*) to credit; (*embajador*) to accredit

acreedor, a [akree'ðor, a] nm/f creditor

acribillar [akriβi'ʎar] vt: **~ a balazos** to riddle with bullets

acróbata [a'kroβata] nmf acrobat

acta ['akta] nf certificate; (*de comisión*) minutes pl, record; **acta de matrimonio/ nacimiento** (MÉX) marriage/birth certificate; **acta notarial** affidavit

actitud [akti'tuð] nf attitude; (*postura*) posture

activar [akti'βar] vt to activate; (*acelerar*) to speed up

actividad [aktiβi'ðað] nf activity

activo, -a [ak'tiβo, a] adj active; (*vivo*) lively ▷ nm (*Com*) assets pl

acto ['akto] nm act, action; (*ceremonia*) ceremony; (*Teatro*) act; **en el ~** immediately

actor [ak'tor] nm actor; (*Jur*) plaintiff ▷ adj: **parte ~a** prosecution

actriz [ak'triθ] nf actress

actuación [aktwa'θjon] nf action; (*comportamiento*) conduct, behaviour; (*Jur*) proceedings pl; (*desempeño*) performance

actual [ak'twal] adj present(-day), current

> No confundir **actual** con la palabra inglesa *actual*.

actualidad nf present; **actualidades** nfpl (*noticias*) news sg; **en la actualidad** at present; (*hoy día*) nowadays; **actualizar** [aktwali'θar] vt to update, modernize; **actualmente** [aktwal'mente] adv at present; (hoy día) nowadays

No confundir **actualmente** con la palabra inglesa *actually*.

actuar [ak'twar] vi (obrar) to work, operate; (actor) to act, perform ▷ vt to work, operate; **~ de** to act as

acuarela [akwa'rela] nf watercolour

acuario [a'kwarjo] nm aquarium; (Astrología): **A~** Aquarius

acuático, -a [a'kwatiko, a] adj aquatic

acudir [aku'ðir] vi (asistir) to attend; (ir) to go; **~ a** (fig) to turn to; **~ a una cita** to keep an appointment; **~ en ayuda de** to go to the aid of

acuerdo etc [a'kwerðo] vb V **acordar** ▷ nm agreement; **¡de ~!** agreed!; **de ~ con** (persona) in agreement with; (acción, documento) in accordance with; **estar de ~** to be agreed, agree

acumular [akumu'lar] vt to accumulate, collect

acuñar [aku'ɲar] vt (moneda) to mint; (frase) to coin

acupuntura [akupun'tura] nf acupuncture

acurrucarse [akurru'karse] vr to crouch; (ovillarse) to curl up

acusación [akusa'θjon] nf accusation

acusar [aku'sar] vt to accuse; (revelar) to reveal; (denunciar) to denounce

acuse [a'kuse] nm: **~ de recibo** acknowledgement of receipt

acústica [a'kustika] nf acoustics pl

acústico, -a [a'kustiko, a] adj acoustic

adaptación [aðapta'θjon] nf adaptation

adaptador [aðapta'ðor] nm (Elec) adapter, adaptor; **adaptador universal** universal adapter o adaptor

adaptar [aðap'tar] vt to adapt; (acomodar) to fit

adecuado, -a [aðe'kwaðo, a] adj (apto) suitable; (oportuno) appropriate

a. de J.C. abr (= antes de Jesucristo) B.C.

adelantado, -a [aðelan'taðo, a] adj advanced; (reloj) fast; **pagar por ~** to pay in advance

adelantamiento [aðelanta'mjento] nm (Auto) overtaking

adelantar [aðelan'tar] vt to move forward; (avanzar) to advance; (acelerar) to speed up; (Auto) to overtake ▷ vi to go forward, advance; **adelantarse** vr to go forward, advance

adelante [aðe'lante] adv forward(s), ahead ▷ excl come in!; **de hoy en ~** from now on; **más ~** later on; (más allá) further on

adelanto [aðe'lanto] nm advance; (mejora) improvement; (progreso) progress

adelgazar [aðelɣa'θar] vt to thin (down) ▷ vi to get thin; (con régimen) to slim down, lose weight

ademán [aðe'man] nm gesture; **ademanes** nmpl manners

además [aðe'mas] adv besides; (por otra parte) moreover; (también) also; **~ de** besides, in addition to

adentrarse [aðen'trarse] vr: **~ en** to go into, get inside; (penetrar) to penetrate (into)

adentro [a'ðentro] adv inside, in; **mar ~** out at sea; **tierra ~** inland

adepto, -a [a'ðepto, a] nm/f supporter

aderezar [aðere'θar] vt (ensalada) to dress; (comida) to season; **aderezo** nm dressing; seasoning

adeudar [aðeu'ðar] vt to owe

adherirse [aðe'rirse] vr: **~ a** to adhere to; (partido) to join

adhesión [aðe'sjon] nf adhesion; (fig) adherence

adicción [aðik'θjon] nf addiction

adición [aði'θjon] nf addition

adicto, -a [a'ðikto, a] adj: **~ a** addicted to; (dedicado) devoted to ▷ nm/f supporter, follower; (toxicómano) addict

adiestrar [aðjes'trar] vt to train, teach; (conducir) to guide, lead

adinerado, -a [aðine'raðo, a] adj wealthy

adiós [a'ðjos] excl (para despedirse) goodbye!, cheerio!; (al pasar) hello!

aditivo [aði'tiβo] nm additive

adivinanza [aðiβi'nanθa] nf riddle

adivinar [aðiβi'nar] vt to prophesy; (conjeturar) to guess; **adivino, -a** nm/f fortune-teller

adj abr (= adjunto) encl

adjetivo [aðxe'tiβo] nm adjective

adjudicar [aðxuði'kar] vt to award; **adjudicarse** vr: **~se algo** to appropriate sth

adjuntar [aðxun'tar] vt to attach, enclose; **adjunto, -a** adj attached, enclosed ▷ nm/f assistant

administración [aðministra'θjon] nf administration; (dirección) management; **administrador, a** nm/f administrator, manager(ess)

administrar [aðminis'trar] vt to administer; **administrativo, -a** adj administrative

admirable [aðmi'raβle] adj admirable

admiración [aðmira'θjon] nf admiration; (asombro) wonder; (Ling) exclamation mark

admirar [aðmi'rar] vt to admire; (extrañar) to surprise

admisible [aðmi'siβle] adj admissible

admisión [aðmi'sjon] nf admission; (reconocimiento) acceptance

admitir [aðmi'tir] vt to admit; (aceptar) to accept

adobar [aðo'βar] vt (Culin) to season

adobe [a'ðoβe] nm adobe, sun-dried brick

adolecer [aðole'θer] vi: ~ de to suffer from

adolescente [aðoles'θente] nmf adolescent, teenager

adonde [a'ðonde] conj (to) where

adónde [a'ðonde] adv = dónde

adopción [aðop'θjon] nf adoption

adoptar [aðop'tar] vt to adopt

adoptivo, -a [aðop'tiβo, a] adj (padres) adoptive; (hijo) adopted

adoquín [aðo'kin] nm paving stone

adorar [aðo'rar] vt to adore

adornar [aðor'nar] vt to adorn

adorno [a'ðorno] nm ornament; (decoración) decoration

adosado, -a [aðo'saðo, a] adj: **casa adosada** semi-detached house

adosar [aðo'sar] (MÉX) vt (adjuntar) to attach, enclose (with a letter)

adquiero etc vb V **adquirir**

adquirir [aðki'rir] vt to acquire, obtain

adquisición [aðkisi'θjon] nf acquisition

adrede [a'ðreðe] adv on purpose

ADSL nm abr broadband

aduana [a'ðwana] nf customs pl

aduanero, -a [aðwa'nero, a] adj customs cpd ▷ nm/f customs officer

adueñarse [aðwe'narse] vr: ~ de to take possession of

adular [aðu'lar] vt to flatter

adulterar [aðulte'rar] vt to adulterate

adulterio [aðul'terjo] nm adultery

adúltero, -a [a'ðultero, a] adj adulterous ▷ nm/f adulterer/adulteress

adulto, -a [a'ðulto, a] adj, nm/f adult

adverbio [að'βerβjo] nm adverb

adversario, -a [aðβer'sarjo, a] nm/f adversary

adversidad [aðβersi'ðað] nf adversity; (contratiempo) setback

adverso, -a [að'βerso, a] adj adverse

advertencia [aðβer'tenθja] nf warning; (prefacio) preface, foreword

advertir [aðβer'tir] vt to notice; (avisar): ~ a algn de to warn sb about o of

Adviento [að'βjento] nm Advent

advierto etc vb V **advertir**

aéreo, -a [a'ereo, a] adj aerial

aerobic [ae'roβik] nm aerobics sg; **aerobics** (MÉX) nmpl aerobics sg

aeromozo, -a [aero'moθo, a] (LAM) nm/f air steward(ess)

aeronáutica [aero'nautika] nf aeronautics sg

aeronave [aero'naβe] nm spaceship

aeroplano [aero'plano] nm aeroplane

aeropuerto [aero'pwerto] nm airport

aerosol [aero'sol] nm aerosol

afamado, -a [afa'maðo, a] adj famous

afán [a'fan] nm hard work; (deseo) desire

afanador, a [afana'ðor, a] (MÉX) nm/f (de limpieza) cleaner

afanar [afa'nar] vt to harass; (fam) to pinch

afear [afe'ar] vt to disfigure

afección [afek'θjon] nf (Med) disease

afectado, -a [afek'taðo, a] adj affected

afectar [afek'tar] vt to affect

afectísimo, -a [afek'tisimo, a] adj affectionate; **suyo ~** yours truly

afectivo, -a [afek'tiβo, a] adj (problema etc) emotional

afecto [a'fekto] nm affection; **tenerle ~ a algn** to be fond of sb

afectuoso, -a [afek'twoso, a] adj affectionate

afeitar [afei'tar] vt to shave; **afeitarse** vr to shave

afeminado, -a [afemi'naðo, a] adj effeminate

Afganistán [afɣanis'tan] nm Afghanistan

afianzar [afjan'θar] vt to strengthen; to secure; **afianzarse** vr to become established

afiche [a'fitʃe] (RPL) nm poster

afición [afi'θjon] nf fondness, liking; **la ~** the fans pl; **pinto por ~** I paint as a hobby;

aficionado, -a adj keen, enthusiastic; (no profesional) amateur ▷ nm/f enthusiast, fan; amateur; **ser aficionado a algo** to be very keen on o fond of sth

aficionar [afiθjo'nar] vt: ~ a algn a algo to make sb like sth; **aficionarse** vr: ~se a algo to grow fond of sth

afilado, -a [afi'laðo, a] adj sharp

afilar [afi'lar] vt to sharpen

afiliarse [afi'ljarse] vr to affiliate

afín [a'fin] adj (parecido) similar; (conexo) related

afinar [afi'nar] vt (Tec) to refine; (Mús) to tune ▷ vi (tocar) to play in tune; (cantar) to sing in tune

afincarse [afin'karse] vr to settle

afinidad [afini'ðað] nf affinity; (parentesco) relationship; **por ~** by marriage

afirmación [afirma'θjon] nf affirmation

afirmar [afir'mar] vt to affirm, state; **afirmativo, -a** adj affirmative

afligir [afli'xir] vt to afflict; (apenar) to distress

aflojar [aflo'xar] vt to slacken; (desatar) to loosen, undo; (relajar) to relax ▷ vi to drop; (bajar) to go down; **aflojarse** vr to relax

afluente [aflu'ente] adj flowing ▷ nm tributary

afmo, -a abr (= afectísimo(a) suyo(a)) Yours

afónico, -a [a'foniko, a] adj: **estar ~** to have a sore throat; to have lost one's voice

aforo [a'foro] nm (de teatro etc) capacity

afortunado, -a [afortu'naðo, a] adj fortunate, lucky

África ['afrika] nf Africa; **África del Sur** South Africa; **africano, -a** adj, nm/f African

afrontar [afron'tar] vt to confront; (poner cara a cara) to bring face to face

afrutado, -a [afru'taðo, a] adj fruity

after ['after] (pl ~s) nm after-hours club; **afterhours** [after'aurs] nm inv = **after**

afuera [a'fwera] adv out, outside; **afueras** nfpl outskirts

agachar [aɣa'tʃar] vt to bend, bow; **agacharse** vr to stoop, bend

agalla [a'ɣaʎa] nf (Zool) gill; **tener ~s** (fam) to have guts

agarradera [aɣarra'ðera] (MÉX) nf handle

agarrado, -a [aɣa'rraðo, a] adj mean, stingy

agarrar [aɣa'rrar] vt to grasp, grab; (LAM: tomar) to take, catch; (recoger) to pick up ▷ vi (planta) to take root; **agarrarse** vr to hold on (tightly)

agencia [a'xenθja] nf agency; **agencia de viajes** travel agency; **agencia inmobiliaria** estate (BRIT) o real estate (US) agent's (office)

agenciarse [axen'θjarse] vr to obtain, procure

agenda [a'xenda] nf diary; **~ electronica** PDA

> ❗ No confundir **agenda** con la palabra inglesa agenda.

agente [a'xente] nmf agent; (tb: **~ de policía**) policeman/policewoman; **agente de seguros** insurance agent; **agente de tránsito** (MÉX) traffic cop; **agente inmobiliario** estate agent (BRIT), realtor (US)

ágil ['axil] adj agile, nimble; **agilidad** nf agility, nimbleness

agilizar [axili'θar] vt (trámites) to speed up

agiotista [axjo'tista] (MÉX) nmf (usurero) usurer

agitación [axita'θjon] nf (de mano etc) shaking, waving; (de líquido etc) stirring; (fig) agitation

agitado, -a [axi'aðo, a] adj hectic; (viaje) bumpy

agitar [axi'tar] vt to wave, shake; (líquido) to stir; (fig) to stir up, excite; **agitarse** vr

to get excited; (inquietarse) to get worried o upset

aglomeración [aɣlomera'θjon] nf agglomeration; **aglomeración de gente/ tráfico** mass of people/traffic jam

agnóstico, -a [aɣ'nostiko, a] adj, nm/f agnostic

agobiar [aɣo'βjar] vt to weigh down; (oprimir) to oppress; (cargar) to burden

agolparse [aɣol'parse] vr to crowd together

agonía [aɣo'nia] nf death throes pl; (fig) agony, anguish

agonizante [aɣoni'θante] adj dying

agonizar [aɣoni'θar] vi to be dying

agosto [a'ɣosto] nm August

agotado, -a [aɣo'taðo, a] adj (persona) exhausted; (libros) out of print; (acabado) finished; (Com) sold out; **agotador, a** [aɣota'ðor, a] adj exhausting

agotamiento [aɣota'mjento] nm exhaustion

agotar [aɣo'tar] vt to exhaust; (consumir) to drain; (recursos) to use up, deplete; **agotarse** vr to be exhausted; (acabarse) to run out; (libro) to go out of print

agraciado, -a [aɣra'θjaðo, a] adj (atractivo) attractive; (en sorteo etc) lucky

agradable [aɣra'ðaβle] adj pleasant, nice

agradar [aɣra'ðar] vt: **él me agrada** I like him

agradecer [aɣraðe'θer] vt to thank; (favor etc) to be grateful for; **agradecido, -a** adj grateful; **¡muy agradecido!** thanks a lot!; **agradecimiento** nm thanks pl; gratitude

agradezco etc vb V **agradecer**

agrado [a'ɣraðo] nm: **ser de tu** etc **~** to be to your etc liking

agrandar [aɣran'dar] vt to enlarge; (fig) to exaggerate; **agrandarse** vr to get bigger

agrario, -a [a'ɣrarjo, a] adj agrarian, land cpd; (política) agricultural, farming

agravante [aɣra'βante] adj aggravating ▷ nm: **con el ~ de que ...** with the further difficulty that ...

agravar [aɣra'βar] vt (pesar sobre) to make heavier; (irritar) to aggravate; **agravarse** vr to worsen, get worse

agraviar [aɣra'βjar] vt to offend; (ser injusto con) to wrong

agredir [aɣre'ðir] vt to attack

agregado, -a [aɣre'ɣaðo, a] nm/f: **A- ≈** teacher (who is not head of department) ▷ nm aggregate; (persona) attaché

agregar [aɣre'ɣar] vt to gather; (añadir) to add; (persona) to appoint

agresión [aɣre'sjon] nf aggression

agresivo, -a [aɣre'siβo, a] adj aggressive

agriar [a'ɣrjar] vt to (turn) sour

agrícola [a'ɣrikola] adj farming cpd, agricultural

agricultor, a [aɣrikul'tor, a] nm/f farmer

agricultura [aɣrikul'tura] nf agriculture, farming

agridulce [aɣri'ðulθe] adj bittersweet; (Culin) sweet and sour

agrietarse [aɣrje'tarse] vr to crack; (piel) to chap

agrio, -a ['aɣrjo, a] adj bitter

agrupación [aɣrupa'θjon] nf group; (acto) grouping

agrupar [aɣru'par] vt to group

agua ['aɣwa] nf water; (Náut) wake; (Arq) slope of a roof; **aguas** nfpl (de piedra) water sg, sparkle sg; (Med) water sg, urine sg; (Náut) waters; **agua bendita/destilada/potable** holy/distilled/drinking water; **agua caliente** hot water; **agua corriente** running water; **agua de colonia** eau de cologne; **agua mineral (con/sin gas)** (sparkling/still) mineral water; **agua oxigenada** hydrogen peroxide; **aguas abajo/arriba** downstream/upstream; **aguas jurisdiccionales** territorial waters

aguacate [aɣwa'kate] nm avocado (pear)

aguacero [aɣwa'θero] nm (heavy) shower, downpour

aguado, -a [a'ɣwaðo, a] adj watery, watered down

aguafiestas [aɣwa'fjestas] nmf inv spoilsport, killjoy

aguamiel [aɣwa'mjel] (MÉX) nf fermented maguey o agave juice

aguanieve [aɣwa'njeβe] nf sleet

aguantar [aɣwan'tar] vt to bear, put up with; (sostener) to hold up ▷ vi to last; **aguantarse** vr to restrain o.s.; **aguante** nm (paciencia) patience; (resistencia) endurance

aguar [a'ɣwar] vt to water down

aguardar [aɣwar'ðar] vt to wait for

aguardiente [aɣwar'ðjente] nm brandy, liquor

aguarrás [aɣwa'rras] nm turpentine

aguaviva [aɣwa'βiβa] (RPL) nf jellyfish

agudeza [aɣu'ðeθa] nf sharpness; (ingenio) wit

agudo, -a [a'ɣuðo, a] adj sharp; (voz) high-pitched, piercing; (dolor, enfermedad) acute

agüero [a'ɣwero] nm: **buen/mal ~** good/bad omen

aguijón [aɣi'xon] nm sting; (fig) spur

águila ['aɣila] nf eagle; (fig) genius

aguileño, -a [aɣi'leɲo, a] adj (nariz) aquiline; (rostro) sharp-featured

aguinaldo [aɣi'naldo] nm Christmas box

aguja [a'ɣuxa] nf needle; (de reloj) hand; (Arq) spire; (Tec) firing-pin; **agujas** nfpl (Zool) ribs; (Ferro) points

agujerear [aɣuxere'ar] vt to make holes in

agujero [aɣu'xero] nm hole

agujetas [aɣu'xetas] nfpl stitch sg; (rigidez) stiffness sg

ahí [a'i] adv there; **de ~ que** so that, with the result that; **~ llega** here he comes; **por ~** that way; (allá) over there; **200 o por ~** 200 or so

ahijado, -a [ai'xaðo, a] nm/f godson/daughter

ahogar [ao'ɣar] vt to drown; (asfixiar) to suffocate, smother; (fuego) to put out; **ahogarse** vr (en el agua) to drown; (por asfixia) to suffocate

ahogo [a'oɣo] nm breathlessness; (fig) financial difficulty

ahondar [aon'dar] vt to deepen, make deeper; (fig) to study thoroughly ▷ vi: **~ en** to study thoroughly

ahora [a'ora] adv now; (hace poco) a moment ago, just now; (dentro de poco) in a moment; **~ voy** I'm coming; **~ mismo** right now; **~ bien** now then; **por ~** for the present

ahorcar [aor'kar] vt to hang

ahorita [ao'rita] (fam) adv (LAM: en este momento) right now; (MÉX: hace poco) just now; (: dentro de poco) in a minute

ahorrar [ao'rrar] vt (dinero) to save; (esfuerzos) to save, avoid; **ahorro** nm (acto) saving; **ahorros** nmpl (dinero) savings

ahuecar [awe'kar] vt to hollow (out); (voz) to deepen; **ahuecarse** vr to give o.s. airs

ahumar [au'mar] vt to smoke, cure; (llenar de humo) to fill with smoke ▷ vi to smoke; **ahumarse** vr to fill with smoke

ahuyentar [aujen'tar] vt to drive off, frighten off; (fig) to dispel

aire ['aire] nm air; (viento) wind; (corriente) draught; (Mús) tune; **al ~ libre** in the open air; **aire acondicionado** air conditioning; **airear** vt to air; **airearse** vr (persona) to go out for a breath of fresh air; **airoso, -a** adj windy; draughty; (fig) graceful

aislado, -a [ais'laðo, a] adj isolated; (incomunicado) cut-off; (Elec) insulated

aislar [ais'lar] vt to isolate; (Elec) to insulate

ajardinado, -a [axarði'naðo, a] adj landscaped

ajedrez [axe'ðreθ] nm chess

ajeno, -a [a'xeno, a] adj (que pertenece a otro) somebody else's; **~ a** foreign to

ajetreado, -a [axetre'aðo, a] adj busy

ajetreo [axe'treo] nm bustle

ají [a'xi] (cs) nm chil(l)i, red pepper; (salsa) chil(l)i sauce

ajillo [a'xiʎo] nm: **gambas al ~** garlic prawns

ajo ['axo] nm garlic

ajuar [a'xwar] nm household furnishings pl; (de novia) trousseau; (de niño) layette

ajustado, -a [axus'taðo, a] adj (tornillo) tight; (cálculo) right; (ropa) tight(-fitting); (resultado) close

ajustar [axus'tar] vt (adaptar) to adjust; (encajar) to fit; (Tec) to engage; (Imprenta) to make up; (apretar) to tighten; (concertar) to agree (on); (reconciliar) to reconcile; (cuentas, deudas) to settle ▷ vi to fit; **ajustarse** vr: **~se a** (precio etc) to be in keeping with, fit in with; **~ las cuentas a algn** to get even with sb

ajuste [a'xuste] nm adjustment; (Costura) fitting; (acuerdo) compromise; (de cuenta) settlement

al [al] = **a + el**; V **a**

ala ['ala] nf wing; (de sombrero) brim; winger; **ala delta** nf hang-glider

alabanza [ala'βanθa] nf praise

alabar [ala'βar] vt to praise

alacena [ala'θena] nf kitchen cupboard (BRIT) o closet (US)

alacrán [ala'kran] nm scorpion

alambrada [alam'braða] nf wire fence; (red) wire netting

alambre [a'lambre] nm wire; **alambre de púas** barbed wire

alameda [ala'meða] nf (plantío) poplar grove; (lugar de paseo) avenue, boulevard

álamo ['alamo] nm poplar

alarde [a'larðe] nm show, display; **hacer ~ de** to boast of

alargador [alarsa'ðor] nm (Elec) extension lead

alargar [alar'sar] vt to lengthen, extend; (paso) to hasten; (brazo) to stretch out; (cuerda) to pay out; (conversación) to spin out; **alargarse** vr to get longer

alarma [a'larma] nf alarm; **alarma de incendios** fire alarm; **alarmar** vt to alarm; **alarmarse** to get alarmed; **alarmante** [alar'mante] adj alarming

alba ['alβa] nf dawn

albahaca [al'βaka] nf basil

Albania [al'βanja] nf Albania

albañil [alβa'ɲil] nm bricklayer; (cantero) mason

albarán [alβa'ran] nm (Com) delivery note, invoice

albaricoque [alβari'koke] nm apricot

albedrío [alβe'ðrio] nm: **libre ~** free will

alberca [al'βerka] nf reservoir; (MÉX: piscina) swimming pool

albergar [alβer'sar] vt to shelter

albergue etc [al'βerxe] vb V **albergar** ▷ nm shelter, refuge; **albergue juvenil** youth hostel

albóndiga [al'βondisa] nf meatball

albornoz [alβor'noθ] nm (de los árabes) burnous; (para el baño) bathrobe

alborotar [alβoro'tar] vi to make a row ▷ vt to agitate, stir up; **alborotarse** vr to get excited; (mar) to get rough; **alboroto** nm row, uproar

álbum ['alβum] (pl **~s, ~es**) nm album; **álbum de recortes** scrapbook

albur [al'βur] (MÉX) nm (juego de palabras) pun; (doble sentido) double entendre

alcachofa [alka'tʃofa] nf artichoke

alcalde, -esa [al'kalde, esa] nm/f mayor(ess)

alcaldía [alkal'dia] nf mayoralty; (lugar) mayor's office

alcance etc [al'kanθe] vb V **alcanzar** ▷ nm reach; (Com) adverse balance; **al ~ de algn** available to sb

alcancía [alkan'θia] (LAM) nf (para ahorrar) money box; (para colectas) collection box

alcantarilla [alkanta'riʎa] nf (de aguas cloacales) sewer; (en la calle) gutter

alcanzar [alkan'θar] vt (algo: con la mano, el pie) to reach; (alguien: en el camino etc) to catch up (with); (autobús) to catch; (bala) to hit, strike ▷ vi (ser suficiente) to be enough; **~ a hacer** to manage to do

alcaparra [alka'parra] nf caper

alcayata [alka'jata] nf hook

alcázar [al'kaθar] nm fortress; (Náut) quarter-deck

alcoba [al'koβa] nf bedroom

alcohol [al'kol] nm alcohol; **alcohol metílico** methylated spirits pl (BRIT), wood alcohol (US); **alcohólico, -a** adj, nm/f alcoholic; **alcoholímetro** [alko'limetro] nm Breathalyser® (BRIT), drunkometer (US); **alcoholismo** [alko'lismo] nm alcoholism

alcornoque [alkor'noke] nm cork tree; (fam) idiot

aldea [al'dea] nf village; **aldeano, -a** adj village cpd ▷ nm/f villager

aleación [alea'θjon] nf alloy

aleatorio, -a [alea'torjo, a] adj random

aleccionar [alekθjo'nar] vt to instruct; (adiestrar) to train

alegar [ale'sar] vt to claim; (Jur) to plead ▷ vi (LAM: discutir) to argue

alegoría [aleso'ria] nf allegory

alegrar [ale'srar] vt (causar alegría) to cheer (up); (fuego) to poke; (fiesta) to liven up; **alegrarse** vr (fam) to get merry o tight; **~se de** to be glad about

alegre [a'leɣre] adj happy, cheerful; (fam) merry, tight; (chiste) risqué, blue; **alegría** nf happiness; merriment

alejar [ale'xar] vt to remove; (fig) to estrange; **alejarse** vr to move away

alemán, -ana [ale'man, ana] adj, nm/f German ▷ nm (Ling) German

Alemania [ale'manja] nf Germany

alentador, a [alenta'ðor, a] adj encouraging

alentar [alen'tar] vt to encourage

alergia [a'lerxja] nf allergy

alero [a'lero] nm (de tejado) eaves pl; (guardabarros) mudguard

alerta [a'lerta] adj, nm alert

aleta [a'leta] nf (de pez) fin; (ala) wing; (de foca, Deporte) flipper; (Auto) mudguard

aletear [alete'ar] vi to flutter

alevín [ale'ßin] nm fry, young fish

alevosía [aleßo'sia] nf treachery

alfabeto [alfa'ßeto] nm alphabet

alfalfa [al'falfa] nf alfalfa, lucerne

alfarería [alfare'ria] nf (de pez) pottery; (tienda) pottery shop; **alfarero, -a** nm/f potter

alféizar [al'feiθar] nm window-sill

alférez [al'fereθ] nm (Mil) second lieutenant; (Náut) ensign

alfil [al'fil] nm (Ajedrez) bishop

alfiler [alfi'ler] nm pin; (broche) clip

alfombra [al'fombra] nf carpet; (más pequeña) rug; **alfombrilla** nf rug, mat; (Inform) mouse mat o pad

alforja [al'forxa] nf saddlebag

algas ['alɣas] nfpl seaweed

álgebra ['alxeßra] nf algebra

algo ['alɣo] pron something; anything ▷ adv somewhat, rather; **¿~ más?** anything else?; (en tienda) is that all?; **por ~ será** there must be some reason for it

algodón [alɣo'ðon] nm cotton; (planta) cotton plant; **algodón de azúcar** candy floss (BRIT), cotton candy (US); **algodón hidrófilo** cotton wool (BRIT), absorbent cotton (US)

alguien ['alɣjen] pron someone, somebody; (en frases interrogativas) anyone, anybody

alguno, -a [al'ɣuno, a] adj (delante de nm): **algún** some; (después de n): **no tiene talento ~** he has no talent, he doesn't have any talent ▷ pron (alguien) someone, somebody; **algún que otro libro** some book or other; **algún día iré** I'll go one o some day; **sin interés ~** without the slightest interest; **~ que otro** an occasional one; **~s piensan** some (people) think

alhaja [a'laxa] nf jewel; (tesoro) precious object, treasure

alhelí [ale'li] nm wallflower, stock

aliado, -a [a'ljaðo, a] adj allied

alianza [a'ljanθa] nf alliance; (anillo) wedding ring

aliar [a'ljar] vt to ally; **aliarse** vr to form an alliance

alias ['aljas] adv alias

alicatado [alika'taðo] (ESP) nm tiling

alicates [ali'kates] nmpl pliers

aliciente [ali'θjente] nm incentive; (atracción) attraction

alienación [aljena'θjon] nf alienation

aliento [a'ljento] nm breath; (respiración) breathing; **sin ~** breathless

aligerar [alixe'rar] vt to lighten; (reducir) to shorten; (aliviar) to alleviate; (mitigar) to ease; (paso) to quicken

alijo [a'lixo] nm consignment

alimaña [ali'maɲa] nf pest

alimentación [alimenta'θjon] nf (comida) food; (acción) feeding; (tienda) grocer's (shop)

alimentar [alimen'tar] vt to feed; (nutrir) to nourish; **alimentarse** vr to feed

alimenticio, -a [alimen'tiθjo, a] adj food cpd; (nutritivo) nourishing, nutritious

alimento [ali'mento] nm food; (nutrición) nourishment

alineación [alinea'θjon] nf alignment; (Deporte) line-up

alinear [aline'ar] vt to align; (Deporte) to select, pick

aliñar [ali'ɲar] vt (Culin) to season; **aliño** nm (Culin) dressing

alioli [ali'oli] nm garlic mayonnaise

alisar [ali'sar] vt to smooth

alistarse [alis'tarse] vr to enlist; (inscribirse) to enrol

aliviar [ali'ßjar] vt (carga) to lighten; (persona) to relieve; (dolor) to relieve, alleviate

alivio [a'lißjo] nm alleviation, relief

aljibe [al'xiße] nm cistern

allá [a'ʎa] adv (lugar) there; (por ahí) over there; (tiempo) then; **~ abajo** down there; **más ~** further on; **más ~ de** beyond; **¡~ tú!** that's your problem!; **¡~ voy!** I'm coming!

allanamiento [aʎana'mjento] nm (LAM: de policía) raid; **allanamiento de morada** burglary

allanar [aʎa'nar] vt to flatten, level (out); (igualar) to smooth (out); (fig) to subdue; (Jur) to burgle, break into

allegado, -a [aʎe'ɣaðo, a] adj near, close ▷ nm/f relation

allí [a'ʎi] adv there; **~ mismo** right there;

por ~ over there; (*por ese camino*) that way

alma ['alma] *nf* soul; (*persona*) person

almacén [alma'θen] *nm* (*depósito*) warehouse, store; (*Mil*) magazine; (cs: *de comestibles*) grocer's (shop); **grandes almacenes** department store *sg*; **almacenaje** *nm* storage

almacenar [almaθe'nar] *vt* to store, put in storage; (*proveerse*) to stock up with

almanaque [alma'nake] *nm* almanac

almeja [al'mexa] *nf* clam

almendra [al'mendra] *nf* almond; **almendro** *nm* almond tree

almíbar [al'miβar] *nm* syrup

almidón [almi'ðon] *nm* starch

almirante [almi'rante] *nm* admiral

almohada [almo'aða] *nf* pillow; (*funda*) pillowcase; **almohadilla** *nf* cushion; (*para alfileres*) pincushion; (*Tec*) pad

almohadón [almoa'ðon] *nm* large pillow; bolster

almorranas [almo'rranas] *nfpl* piles, haemorrhoids

almorzar [almor'θar] *vt*: **~ una tortilla** to have an omelette for lunch ▷ *vi* to (have) lunch

almuerzo *etc* [al'mwerθo] *vb* V **almorzar** ▷ *nm* lunch

alocado, -a [alo'kaðo, a] *adj* crazy

alojamiento [aloxa'mjento] *nm* lodging(s) *pl*; (*viviendas*) housing

alojar [alo'xar] *vt* to lodge; **alojarse** *vr* to lodge, stay

alondra [a'londra] *nf* lark, skylark

alpargata [alpar'ɣata] *nf* rope-soled sandal, espadrille

Alpes ['alpes] *nmpl*: **los ~** the Alps

alpinismo [alpi'nismo] *nm* mountaineering, climbing; **alpinista** *nmf* mountaineer, climber

alpiste [al'piste] *nm* birdseed

alquilar [alki'lar] *vt* (*propietario: inmuebles*) to let, rent (out); (: *coche*) to hire out; (: *TV*) to rent (out); (*alquilador: inmuebles, TV*) to rent; (: *coche*) to hire; **"se alquila casa"** "house to let (BRIT) o for rent (US)"

alquiler [alki'ler] *nm* renting; letting; hiring; (*arriendo*) rent; hire charge; **de ~** for hire; **alquiler de automóviles** o **coches** car hire

alquimia [al'kimja] *nf* alchemy

alquitrán [alki'tran] *nm* tar

alrededor [alreðe'ðor] *adv* around, about; **~ de** around, about; **mirar a su ~** to look (round) about one; **alrededores** *nmpl* surroundings

alta ['alta] *nf* (certificate of) discharge

altar [al'tar] *nm* altar

altavoz [alta'βoθ] *nm* loudspeaker; (*amplificador*) amplifier

alteración [altera'θjon] *nf* alteration; (*alboroto*) disturbance

alterar [alte'rar] *vt* to alter; to disturb; **alterarse** *vr* (*persona*) to get upset

altercado [alter'kaðo] *nm* argument

alternar [alter'nar] *vt* to alternate ▷ *vi* to alternate; (*turnar*) to take turns; **alternarse** *vr* to alternate; to take turns; **~ con** to mix with; **alternativa** *nf* (*elección*) choice; **alternativo, -a** *adj* alternative; (*alterno*) alternating; **alterno, -a** *adj* alternate; (*Elec*) alternating

Alteza [al'teθa] *nf* (*tratamiento*) Highness

altibajos [alti'βaxos] *nmpl* ups and downs

altiplano [alti'plano] *nm* = **altiplanicie**

altisonante [altiso'nante] *adj* high-flown, high-sounding

altitud [alti'tuð] *nf* height; (*Aviac, Geo*) altitude

altivo, -a [al'tiβo, a] *adj* haughty, arrogant

alto, -a ['alto, a] *adj* high; (*persona*) tall; (*sonido*) high, sharp; (*noble*) high, lofty ▷ *nm* halt; (*Mús*) alto; (*Geo*) hill ▷ *adv* (*de sitio*) high; (*de sonido*) loud, loudly ▷ *excl* halt!; **la pared tiene 2 metros de ~** the wall is 2 metres high; **en alta mar** on the high seas; **en voz alta** in a loud voice; **las altas horas de la noche** the small o wee hours; **en lo ~ de** at the top of; **pasar por ~** to overlook; **altoparlante** [altopar'lante] (LAM) *nm* loudspeaker

altura [al'tura] *nf* height; (*Náut*) depth; (*Geo*) latitude; **la pared tiene 1.80 de ~** the wall is 1 metre 80cm high; **a estas ~s** at this stage; **a estas ~s del año** at this time of the year

alubia [a'luβja] *nf* bean

alucinación [aluθina'θjon] *nf* hallucination

alucinar [aluθi'nar] *vi* to hallucinate ▷ *vt* to deceive; (*fascinar*) to fascinate

alud [a'luð] *nm* avalanche; (*fig*) flood

aludir [alu'ðir] *vi*: **~ a** to allude to; **darse por aludido** to take the hint

alumbrado [alum'braðo] *nm* lighting

alumbrar [alum'brar] *vt* to light (up) ▷ *vi* (*Med*) to give birth

aluminio [alu'minjo] *nm* aluminium (BRIT), aluminum (US)

alumno, -a [a'lumno, a] *nm/f* pupil, student

alusión [alu'sjon] *nf* allusion

alusivo, -a [alu'siβo, a] *adj* allusive

aluvión [alu'βjon] *nm* alluvium; (*fig*) flood

alverja [al'βerxa] (LAM) *nf* pea

alza ['alθa] nf rise; (Mil) sight
alzamiento [alθa'mjento] nm (rebelión) rising
alzar [al'θar] vt to lift (up); (precio, muro) to raise; (cuello de abrigo) to turn up; (Agr) to gather in; (Imprenta) to gather; **alzarse** vr to get up, rise; (rebelarse) to revolt; (Com) to go fraudulently bankrupt; (Jur) to appeal
ama ['ama] nf lady of the house; (dueña) owner; (institutriz) governess; (madre adoptiva) foster mother; **ama de casa** housewife; **ama de llaves** housekeeper
amabilidad [amaβili'ðað] nf kindness; (simpatía) niceness; **amable** adj kind; nice; **es usted muy amable** that's very kind of you
amaestrado, -a [amaes'traðo, a] adj (animal: en circo etc) performing
amaestrar [amaes'trar] vt to train
amago [a'maxo] nm threat; (gesto) threatening gesture; (Med) symptom
amainar [amai'nar] vi (viento) to die down
amamantar [amaman'tar] vt to suckle, nurse
amanecer [amane'θer] vi to dawn ▷ nm dawn; **~ afiebrado** to wake up with a fever
amanerado, -a [amane'raðo, a] adj affected
amante [a'mante] adj: **~ de** fond of ▷ nmf lover
amapola [ama'pola] nf poppy
amar [a'mar] vt to love
amargado, -a [amar'xaðo, a] adj bitter
amargar [amar'xar] vt to make bitter; (fig) to embitter; **amargarse** vr to become embittered
amargo, -a [a'marxo, a] adj bitter
amarillento, -a [amari'ʎento, a] adj yellowish; (tez) sallow; **amarillo, -a** adj, nm yellow
amarrado, -a [ama'rraðo, a] (Méx: fam) adj mean, stingy
amarrar [ama'rrar] vt to moor; (sujetar) to tie up
amarras [a'marras] nfpl: **soltar ~** to set sail
amasar [ama'sar] vt (masa) to knead; (mezclar) to mix, prepare; (confeccionar) to concoct
amateur [ama'ter] nmf amateur
amazona [ama'θona] nf horsewoman; **Amazonas** nm: **el Amazonas** the Amazon
ámbar ['ambar] nm amber
ambición [ambi'θjon] nf ambition; **ambicionar** vt to aspire to; **ambicioso, -a** adj ambitious
ambidextro, -a [ambi'ðekstro, a] adj ambidextrous
ambientación [ambjenta'θjon] nf (Cine, Teatro etc) setting; (Radio) sound effects
ambiente [am'bjente] nm atmosphere; (medio) environment
ambigüedad [ambixwe'ðað] nf ambiguity; **ambiguo, -a** adj ambiguous
ámbito ['ambito] nm (campo) field; (fig) scope
ambos, -as ['ambos, as] adj pl, pron pl both
ambulancia [ambu'lanθja] nf ambulance
ambulante [ambu'lante] adj travelling cpd, itinerant
ambulatorio [ambula'torjo] nm state health-service clinic
amén [a'men] excl amen; **~ de** besides
amenaza [ame'naθa] nf threat; **amenazar** [amena'θar] vt to threaten ▷ vi: **amenazar con hacer** to threaten to do
ameno, -a [a'meno, a] adj pleasant
América [a'merika] nf America; **América Central/Latina** Central/Latin America; **América del Norte/del Sur** North/South America; **americana** nf coat, jacket; V tb americano; **americano, -a** adj, nm/f American
ametralladora [ametraʎa'ðora] nf machine gun
amigable [ami'xaβle] adj friendly
amígdala [a'mixðala] nf tonsil; **amigdalitis** nf tonsillitis
amigo, -a [a'mixo, a] adj friendly ▷ nm/f friend; (amante) lover; **ser ~ de algo** to be fond of sth; **ser muy ~s** to be close friends
aminorar [amino'rar] vt to diminish; (reducir) to reduce; **~ la marcha** to slow down
amistad [amis'tað] nf friendship; **amistades** nfpl (amigos) friends; **amistoso, -a** adj friendly
amnesia [am'nesja] nf amnesia
amnistía [amnis'tia] nf amnesty
amo ['amo] nm owner; (jefe) boss
amolar [amo'lar] (Méx: fam) vt to ruin, damage
amoldar [amol'dar] vt to mould; (adaptar) to adapt
amonestación [amonesta'θjon] nf warning; **amonestaciones** nfpl (Rel) marriage banns
amonestar [amones'tar] vt to warn; (Rel) to publish the banns of
amontonar [amonto'nar] vt to collect, pile up; **amontonarse** vr to crowd together; (acumularse) to pile up
amor [a'mor] nm love; (amante) lover;

hacer el ~ to make love; **amor propio** self-respect

amoratado, -a [amora'taðo, a] *adj* purple

amordazar [amorða'θar] *vt* to muzzle; *(fig)* to gag

amorfo, -a [a'morfo, a] *adj* amorphous, shapeless

amoroso, -a [amo'roso, a] *adj* affectionate, loving

amortiguador [amortigwa'ðor] *nm* shock absorber; *(parachoques)* bumper; **amortiguadores** *nmpl (Auto)* suspension *sg*

amortiguar [amorti'xwar] *vt* to deaden; *(ruido)* to muffle; *(color)* to soften

amotinar [amoti'nar] *vt* to stir up, incite (to riot); **amotinarse** *vr* to mutiny

amparar [ampa'rar] *vt* to protect; **ampararse** *vr* to seek protection; *(de la lluvia etc)* to shelter; **amparo** *nm* help, protection; **al amparo de** under the protection of

amperio [am'perjo] *nm* ampère, amp

ampliación [amplja'θjon] *nf* enlargement; *(extensión)* extension

ampliar [am'pljar] *vt* to enlarge; to extend

amplificador [amplifika'ðor] *nm* amplifier

amplificar [amplifi'kar] *vt* to amplify

amplio, -a ['ampljo, a] *adj* spacious; *(de falda etc)* full; *(extenso)* extensive; *(ancho)* wide; **amplitud** *nf* spaciousness; extent; *(fig)* amplitude

ampolla [am'poʎa] *nf* blister; *(Med)* ampoule

amputar [ampu'tar] *vt* to cut off, amputate

amueblar [amwe'βlar] *vt* to furnish

anales [a'nales] *nmpl* annals

analfabetismo [analfaβe'tismo] *nm* illiteracy; **analfabeto, -a** *adj, nm/f* illiterate

analgésico [anal'xesiko] *nm* painkiller, analgesic

análisis [a'nalisis] *nm inv* analysis

analista [ana'lista] *nmf (gen)* analyst

analizar [anali'θar] *vt* to analyse

analógico, -a [ana'loxiko, a] *adj (Inform)* analog; *(reloj)* analogue *(BRIT)*, analog *(US)*

análogo, -a [a'naloɣo, a] *adj* analogous, similar

ananá [ana'na] *(RPL) nm* pineapple

anarquía [anar'kia] *nf* anarchy; **anarquista** *nmf* anarchist

anatomía [anato'mia] *nf* anatomy

anca ['anka] *nf* rump, haunch; **ancas** *nfpl*

(fam) behind *sg*

ancho, -a ['antʃo, a] *adj* wide; *(falda)* full; *(fig)* liberal ▷ *nm* width; *(Ferro)* gauge; **ponerse ~** to get conceited; **estar a sus anchas** to be at one's ease

anchoa [an'tʃoa] *nf* anchovy

anchura [an'tʃura] *nf* width; *(extensión)* wideness

anciano, -a [an'θjano, a] *adj* old, aged ▷ *nm/f* old man/woman; elder

ancla ['ankla] *nf* anchor

Andalucía [andalu'θia] *nf* Andalusia; **andaluz, -a** *adj, nm/f* Andalusian

andamio [an'damjo] *nm* scaffold(ing)

andar [an'dar] *vt* to go, cover, travel ▷ *vi* to go, walk, travel; *(funcionar)* to go, work; *(estar)* to be ▷ *nm* walk, gait, pace; **andarse** *vr* to go away; **~ a pie/a caballo/ en bicicleta** to go on foot/on horseback/ by bicycle; **~ haciendo algo** to be doing sth; **¡anda!** *(sorpresa)* go on!; **anda por o en los 40** he's about 40

andén [an'den] *nm (Ferro)* platform; *(Náut)* quayside; *(CAM: de la calle)* pavement *(BRIT)*, sidewalk *(US)*

Andes ['andes] *nmpl:* **los ~** the Andes

andinismo [andi'nismo] *(LAM) nm* mountaineering, climbing

Andorra [an'dorra] *nf* Andorra

andrajoso, -a [andra'xoso, a] *adj* ragged

anduve *etc vb V* **andar**

anécdota [a'nekðota] *nf* anecdote, story

anegar [ane'ɣar] *vt* to flood; *(ahogar)* to drown

anemia [a'nemja] *nf* anaemia

anestesia [anes'tesja] *nf (sustancia)* anaesthetic; *(proceso)* anaesthesia; **anestesia general/local** general/local anaesthetic

anexar [anek'sar] *vt* to annex; *(documento)* to attach; **anexión** *nf* annexation; **anexo, -a** *adj* attached ▷ *nm* annexe

anfibio, -a [an'fiβjo, a] *adj* amphibious ▷ *nm* amphibian

anfiteatro [anfite'atro] *nm* amphitheatre; *(Teatro)* dress circle

anfitrión, -ona [anfi'trjon, ona] *nm/f* host(ess)

ánfora ['anfora] *nf (cántaro)* amphora; *(MÉX Pol)* ballot box

ángel ['anxel] *nm* angel; **ángel de la guarda** guardian angel

angina [an'xina] *nf (Med)* inflammation of the throat; **tener ~s** to have tonsillitis; **angina de pecho** angina

anglicano, -a [angli'kano, a] *adj, nm/f* Anglican

anglosajón, -ona [anglosa'xon, ona] *adj*

Anglo-Saxon
anguila [an'gila] nf eel
angula [an'gula] nf elver, baby eel
ángulo ['angulo] nm angle; (*esquina*) corner; (*curva*) bend
angustia [an'gustja] nf anguish
anhelar [ane'lar] vt to be eager for; (*desear*) to long for, desire ▷ vi to pant, gasp; **anhelo** nm eagerness; desire
anidar [ani'ðar] vi to nest
anillo [a'niʎo] nm ring; **anillo de boda/compromiso** wedding/engagement ring
animación [anima'θjon] nf liveliness; (*vitalidad*) life; (*actividad*) activity; bustle
animado, -a [ani'maðo, a] adj lively; (*vivaz*) animated; **animador, a** nm/f (TV) host(ess), compère; (*Deporte*) cheerleader
animal [ani'mal] adj animal; (*fig*) stupid ▷ nm animal; (*fig*) fool; (*bestia*) brute
animar [ani'mar] vt (Bio) to animate, give life to; (*fig*) to liven up, brighten up, cheer up; (*estimular*) to stimulate; **animarse** vr to cheer up; to feel encouraged; (*decidirse*) to make up one's mind
ánimo ['animo] nm (*alma*) soul; (*mente*) mind; (*valentía*) courage ▷ excl cheer up!
animoso, -a [ani'moso, a] adj brave; (*vivo*) lively
aniquilar [aniki'lar] vt to annihilate, destroy
anís [a'nis] nm aniseed; (*licor*) anisette
aniversario [aniβer'sarjo] nm anniversary
anoche [a'notʃe] adv last night; **antes de ~** the night before last
anochecer [anotʃe'θer] vi to get dark ▷ nm nightfall, dark; **al ~** at nightfall
anodino, -a [ano'ðino, a] adj dull, anodyne
anomalía [anoma'lia] nf anomaly
anonadado, -a [anona'ðaðo, a] adj: **estar ~** to be overwhelmed o amazed
anonimato [anoni'mato] nm anonymity
anónimo, -a [a'nonimo, a] adj anonymous; (Com) limited ▷ nm (*carta anónima*) anonymous letter; (: *maliciosa*) poison-pen letter
anormal [anor'mal] adj abnormal
anotación [anota'θjon] nf note; annotation
anotar [ano'tar] vt to note down; (*comentar*) to annotate
ansia ['ansja] nf anxiety; (*añoranza*) yearning; **ansiar** vt to long for
ansiedad [ansje'ðað] nf anxiety
ansioso, -a [an'sjoso, a] adj anxious; (*anhelante*) eager; **~ de** o **por algo** greedy for sth

antaño [an'taɲo] adv long ago, formerly
Antártico [an'tartiko] nm: **el ~** the Antarctic
ante ['ante] prep before, in the presence of; (*problema etc*) faced with ▷ nm (*piel*) suede; **~ todo** above all
anteanoche [antea'notʃe] adv the night before last
anteayer [antea'jer] adv the day before yesterday
antebrazo [ante'βraθo] nm forearm
antecedente [anteθe'ðente] adj previous ▷ nm antecedent; **antecedentes** nmpl (*historial*) record sg; **antecedentes penales** criminal record
anteceder [anteθe'ðer] vt to precede, go before
antecesor, a [anteθe'sor, a] nm/f predecessor
antelación [antela'θjon] nf: **con ~** in advance
antemano [ante'mano]: **de ~** adv beforehand, in advance
antena [an'tena] nf antenna; (*de televisión etc*) aerial; **antena parabólica** satellite dish
antenoche [ante'notʃe] (LAM) adv the night before last
anteojo [ante'oxo] nm eyeglass; **anteojos** nmpl (LAM: *gafas*) glasses, spectacles
antepasados [antepa'saðos] nmpl ancestors
anteponer [antepo'ner] vt to place in front; (*fig*) to prefer
anterior [ante'rjor] adj preceding, previous; **anterioridad** nf: **con anterioridad a** prior to, before
antes ['antes] adv (*con prioridad*) before ▷ prep: **~ de** before ▷ conj: **~ de ir/de que te vayas** before going/before you go; **~ bien** (but) rather; **dos días ~** two days before o previously; **no quiso venir ~** she didn't want to come any earlier; **tomo el avión ~ que el barco** I take the plane rather than the boat; **~ de** o **que nada** (*en el tiempo*) first of all; (*indicando preferencia*) above all; **~ que yo** before me; **lo ~ posible** as soon as possible; **cuanto ~ mejor** the sooner the better
antibalas [anti'βalas] adj inv: **chaleco ~** bullet-proof jacket
antibiótico [anti'βjotiko] nm antibiotic
anticaspa [anti'kaspa] adj inv anti-dandruff cpd
anticipación [antiθipa'θjon] nf anticipation; **con 10 minutos de ~** 10 minutes early
anticipado, -a [antiθi'paðo, a] adj (*pago*) advance; **por ~** in advance
anticipar [antiθi'par] vt to anticipate;

(adelantar) to bring forward; *(Com)* to advance; **anticiparse** *vr:* **~se a su época** to be ahead of one's time

anticipo [anti'θipo] *nm (Com)* advance

anticonceptivo, -a [antikonθep'tiβo, a] *adj, nm* contraceptive

anticongelante [antikonxe'lante] *nm* antifreeze

anticuado, -a [anti'kwaðo, a] *adj* out-of-date, old-fashioned; *(desusado)* obsolete

anticuario [anti'kwarjo] *nm* antique dealer

anticuerpo [anti'kwerpo] *nm (Med)* antibody

antidepresivo [antiðepre'siβo] *nm* antidepressant

antidóping [anti'dopin] *adj inv:* **control ~** drugs test

antídoto [an'tiðoto] *nm* antidote

antiestético, -a [anties'tetiko, a] *adj* unsightly

antifaz [anti'faθ] *nm* mask; *(velo)* veil

antiglobalización [antigloβaliθa'θjon] *nf* anti-globalization; **antiglobalizador, a** *adj* anti-globalization *cpd*

antiguamente [antixwa'mente] *adv* formerly; *(hace mucho tiempo)* long ago

antigüedad [antixwe'ðað] *nf* antiquity; *(artículo)* antique; *(rango)* seniority

antiguo, -a [an'tixwo, a] *adj* old, ancient; *(que fue)* former

Antillas [an'tiλas] *nfpl:* **las ~** the West Indies

antílope [an'tilope] *nm* antelope

antinatural [antinatu'ral] *adj* unnatural

antipatía [antipa'tia] *nf* antipathy, dislike; **antipático, -a** *adj* disagreeable, unpleasant

antirrobo [anti'rroβo] *adj inv (alarma etc)* anti-theft

antisemita [antise'mita] *adj* anti-Semitic ▷ *nmf* anti-Semite

antiséptico, -a [anti'septiko, a] *adj* antiseptic ▷ *nm* antiseptic

antivirus [anti'birus] *nm inv (Comput)* antivirus program

antojarse [anto'xarse] *vr (desear):* **se me antoja comprarlo** I have a mind to buy it; *(pensar):* **se me antoja que ...** I have a feeling that ...

antojitos [anto'xitos] *(MÉX) nmpl* snacks, nibbles

antojo [an'toxo] *nm* caprice, whim; *(rosa)* birthmark; *(lunar)* mole

antología [antolo'xia] *nf* anthology

antorcha [an'tortʃa] *nf* torch

antro ['antro] *nm* cavern

antropología [antropolo'xia] *nf* anthropology

anual [a'nwal] *adj* annual

anuario [a'nwarjo] *nm* yearbook

anulación [anula'θjon] *nf* annulment; *(cancelación)* cancellation

anular [anu'lar] *vt (contrato)* to annul, cancel; *(ley)* to revoke, repeal; *(suscripción)* to cancel ▷ *nm* ring finger

anunciar [anun'θjar] *vt* to announce; *(proclamar)* to proclaim; *(Com)* to advertise

anuncio [a'nunθjo] *nm* announcement; *(señal)* sign; *(Com)* advertisement; *(cartel)* poster

anzuelo [an'θwelo] *nm* hook; *(para pescar)* fish hook

añadidura [aɲaði'ðura] *nf* addition, extra; **por ~** besides, in addition

añadir [aɲa'ðir] *vt* to add

añejo, -a [a'ɲexo, a] *adj* old; *(vino)* mellow

añicos [a'ɲikos] *nmpl:* **hacer ~** to smash, shatter

año ['aɲo] *nm* year; **¡Feliz A~ Nuevo!** Happy New Year!; **tener 15 ~s** to be 15 (years old); **los ~s 90** the nineties; **el ~ que viene** next year; **año bisiesto/escolar/fiscal/sabático** leap/school/tax/sabbatical year

añoranza [aɲo'ranθa] *nf* nostalgia; *(anhelo)* longing

apa ['apa] *(MÉX) excl* goodness me!, good gracious!

apabullar [apaβu'ʎar] *vt* to crush, squash

apacible [apa'θiβle] *adj* gentle, mild

apaciguar [apaθi'ɣwar] *vt* to pacify, calm (down)

apadrinar [apaðri'nar] *vt* to sponsor, support; *(Rel)* to be godfather to

apagado, -a [apa'ɣaðo, a] *adj (volcán)* extinct; *(color)* dull; *(voz)* quiet; *(sonido)* muted, muffled; *(persona: apático)* listless; **estar ~** *(fuego, luz)* to be out; *(Radio, TV etc)* to be off

apagar [apa'ɣar] *vt* to put out; *(Elec, Radio, TV)* to turn off; *(sonido)* to silence, muffle; *(sed)* to quench

apagón [apa'ɣon] *nm* blackout; power cut

apalabrar [apala'βrar] *vt* to agree to; *(contratar)* to engage

apalear [apale'ar] *vt* to beat, thrash

apantallar [apanta'ʎar] *(MÉX) vt* to impress

apañar [apa'ɲar] *vt* to pick up; *(asir)* to take hold of, grasp; *(reparar)* to mend, patch up; **apañarse** *vr* to manage, get along

apapachar [apapa'tʃar] *(MÉX: fam) vt* to cuddle, hug

aparador [apara'ðor] *nm* sideboard; *(MÉX: escaparate)* shop window

aparato [apa'rato] *nm* apparatus;

(*máquina*) machine; (*doméstico*) appliance; (*boato*) ostentation; **aparato digestivo** (*Anat*) digestive system; **aparatoso, -a** *adj* showy, ostentatious

aparcamiento [aparka'mjento] *nm* car park (*BRIT*), parking lot (*US*)

aparcar [apar'kar] *vt, vi* to park

aparear [apare'ar] *vt* (*objetos*) to pair, match; (*animales*) to mate; **aparearse** *vr* to make a pair; to mate

aparecer [apare'θer] *vi* to appear; **aparecerse** *vr* to appear

aparejador, a [aparexa'ðor, a] *nm/f* (*Arq*) master builder

aparejo [apa'rexo] *nm* harness; rigging; (*de poleas*) block and tackle

aparentar [aparen'tar] *vt* (*edad*) to look; (*fingir*) ~ **tristeza** to pretend to be sad

aparente [apa'rente] *adj* apparent; (*adecuado*) suitable

aparezco *etc vb* V **aparecer**

aparición [apari'θjon] *nf* appearance; (*de libro*) publication; (*espectro*) apparition

apariencia [apa'rjenθja] *nf* (outward) appearance; **en ~** outwardly, seemingly

apartado, -a [apar'taðo, a] *adj* separate; (*lejano*) remote ▷ *nm* (*tipográfico*) paragraph; **apartado de correos** (*ESP*) post office box; **apartado postal** (*LAM*) post office box

apartamento [aparta'mento] *nm* apartment, flat (*BRIT*)

apartar [apar'tar] *vt* to separate; (*quitar*) to remove; **apartarse** *vr* to separate, part; (*irse*) to move away; to keep away

aparte [a'parte] *adv* (*separadamente*) separately; (*además*) besides ▷ *nm* aside; (*tipográfico*) new paragraph

aparthotel [aparto'tel] *nm* serviced apartments

apasionado, -a [apasjo'naðo, a] *adj* passionate

apasionar [apasjo'nar] *vt* to excite; **le apasiona el fútbol** she's crazy about football; **apasionarse** *vr* to get excited

apatía [apa'tia] *nf* apathy

apático, -a [a'patiko, a] *adj* apathetic

Apdo *abr* (= *Apartado (de Correos)*) PO Box

apeadero [apea'ðero] *nm* halt, stop, stopping place

apearse [ape'arse] *vr* (*jinete*) to dismount; (*bajarse*) to get down o out; (*Auto, Ferro*) to get off o out

apechugar [apetʃu'xar] *vr*: ~ **con algo** to face up to sth

apegarse [ape'xarse] *vr*: ~ **a** to become attached to; **apego** *nm* attachment, devotion

apelar [ape'lar] *vi* to appeal; ~ **a** (*fig*) to resort to

apellidar [apeʎi'ðar] *vt* to call, name; **apellidarse** *vr*: **se apellida Pérez** her (sur) name's Pérez

apellido [ape'ʎiðo] *nm* surname

apenar [ape'nar] *vt* to grieve, trouble; (*LAM*: *avergonzar*) to embarrass; **apenarse** *vr* to grieve; (*LAM*: *avergonzarse*) to be embarrassed

apenas [a'penas] *adv* scarcely, hardly ▷ *conj* as soon as, no sooner

apéndice [a'pendiθe] *nm* appendix; **apendicitis** *nf* appendicitis

aperitivo [aperi'tiβo] *nm* (*bebida*) aperitif; (*comida*) appetizer

apertura [aper'tura] *nf* opening; (*Pol*) liberalization

apestar [apes'tar] *vt* to infect ▷ *vi*: ~ **(a)** to stink (of)

apetecer [apete'θer] *vt*: **¿te apetece un café?** do you fancy a (cup of) coffee?; **apetecible** *adj* desirable; (*comida*) appetizing

apetito [ape'tito] *nm* appetite; **apetitoso, -a** *adj* appetizing; (*fig*) tempting

apiadarse [apja'ðarse] *vr*: ~ **de** to take pity on

ápice ['apiθe] *nm* whit, iota

apilar [api'lar] *vt* to pile o heap up

apiñarse [api'ɲarse] *vr* to crowd o press together

apio ['apjo] *nm* celery

apisonadora [apisona'ðora] *nf* steamroller

aplacar [apla'kar] *vt* to placate

aplastante [aplas'tante] *adj* overwhelming; (*lógica*) compelling

aplastar [aplas'tar] *vt* to squash (flat); (*fig*) to crush

aplaudir [aplau'ðir] *vt* to applaud

aplauso [a'plauso] *nm* applause; (*fig*) approval, acclaim

aplazamiento [aplaθa'mjento] *nm* postponement

aplazar [apla'θar] *vt* to postpone, defer

aplicación [aplika'θjon] *nf* application; (*esfuerzo*) effort

aplicado, -a [apli'kaðo, a] *adj* diligent, hard-working

aplicar [apli'kar] *vt* (*ejecutar*) to apply; **aplicarse** *vr* to apply o.s.

aplique *etc* [a'plike] *vb* V **aplicar** ▷ *nm* wall light

aplomo [a'plomo] *nm* aplomb, self-assurance

apodar [apo'ðar] *vt* to nickname

apoderado [apoðe'raðo] *nm* agent,

representative

apoderarse [apoðe'rarse] vr: ~ **de** to take possession of

apodo [a'poðo] nm nickname

apogeo [apo'xeo] nm peak, summit

apoquinar [apoki'nar] (fam) vt to fork out, cough up

aporrear [aporre'ar] vt to beat (up)

aportar [apor'tar] vt to contribute ▷ vi to reach port; **aportarse** vr (LAM: llegar) to arrive, come

aposta [a'posta] adv deliberately, on purpose

apostar [apos'tar] vt to bet, stake; (tropas etc) to station, post ▷ vi to bet

apóstol [a'postol] nm apostle

apóstrofo [a'postrofo] nm apostrophe

apoyar [apo'jar] vt to lean, rest; (fig) to support, back; **apoyarse** vr: ~**se en** to lean on; **apoyo** nm (gen) support; backing, help

apreciable [apre'θjaβle] adj considerable; (fig) esteemed

apreciar [apre'θjar] vt to evaluate, assess; (Com) to appreciate, value; (persona) to respect; (tamaño) to gauge, assess; (detalles) to notice

aprecio [a'preθjo] nm valuation, estimate; (fig) appreciation

aprehender [apreen'der] vt to apprehend, detain

apremio [a'premjo] nm urgency

aprender [apren'der] vt, vi to learn; ~ **algo de memoria** to learn sth (off) by heart

aprendiz, a [apren'diθ, a] nm/f apprentice; (principiante) learner; **aprendizaje** nm apprenticeship

aprensión [apren'sjon] nm apprehension, fear; **aprensivo, -a** adj apprehensive

apresar [apre'sar] vt to seize; (capturar) to capture

apresurado, -a [apresu'raðo, a] adj hurried, hasty

apresurar [apresu'rar] vt to hurry, accelerate; **apresurarse** vr to hurry, make haste

apretado, -a [apre'taðo, a] adj tight; (escritura) cramped

apretar [apre'tar] vt to squeeze; (Tec) to tighten; (presionar) to press together, pack ▷ vi to be too tight

apretón [apre'ton] nm squeeze; **apretón de manos** handshake

aprieto [a'prjeto] nm squeeze; (dificultad) difficulty; **estar en un** ~ to be in a fix

aprisa [a'prisa] adv quickly, hurriedly

aprisionar [aprisjo'nar] vt to imprison

aprobación [aproβa'θjon] nf approval

aprobar [apro'βar] vt to approve (of); (examen, materia) to pass ▷ vi to pass

apropiado, -a [apro'pjaðo, a] adj suitable

apropiarse [apro'pjarse] vr: ~ **de** to appropriate

aprovechado, -a [aproβe'tʃaðo, a] adj industrious, hard-working; (económico) thrifty; (pey) unscrupulous

aprovechar [aproβe'tʃar] vt to use; (explotar) to exploit; (experiencia) to profit from; (oferta, oportunidad) to take advantage of ▷ vi to progress, improve; **aprovecharse** vr: ~**se de** to make use of; to take advantage of; **¡que aproveche!** enjoy your meal!

aproximación [aproksima'θjon] nf approximation; (de lotería) consolation prize

aproximar [aproksi'mar] vt to bring nearer; **aproximarse** vr to come near, approach

apruebo etc vb V **aprobar**

aptitud [apti'tuð] nf aptitude

apto, -a ['apto, a] adj suitable

apuesta [a'pwesta] nf bet, wager

apuesto, -a [a'pwesto, a] adj neat, elegant

apuntar [apun'tar] vt (con arma) to aim at; (con dedo) to point at o to; (anotar) to note (down); (Teatro) to prompt; **apuntarse** vr (Deporte: tanto, victoria) to score; (Escol) to enrol

⎸ No confundir **apuntar** con la palabra inglesa appoint.

apunte [a'punte] nm note

apuñalar [apuɲa'lar] vt to stab

apurado, -a [apu'raðo, a] adj needy; (difícil) difficult; (peligroso) dangerous; (LAM: con prisa) hurried, rushed

apurar [apu'rar] vt (agotar) to drain; (recursos) to use up; (molestar) to annoy; **apurarse** vr (preocuparse) to worry; (LAM: darse prisa) to hurry

apuro [a'puro] nm (aprieto) fix, jam; (escasez) want, hardship; (vergüenza) embarrassment; (LAM: prisa) haste, urgency

aquejado, -a [ake'xaðo, a] adj: ~ **de** (Med) afflicted by

aquel, aquella [a'kel, a'keʎa] adj that; ~**los(as)** those

aquél, aquélla [a'kel, a'keʎa] pron that (one); ~**los(as)** those (ones)

aquello [a'keʎo] pron that, that business

aquí [a'ki] adv (lugar) here; (tiempo) now; ~ **arriba** up here; ~ **mismo** right here; ~ **yace** here lies; **de** ~ **a siete días** a week from now

ara ['ara] nf: **en** ~**s de** for the sake of

árabe ['araβe] adj, nmf Arab ▷ nm (Ling) Arabic

Arabia [a'raβja] nf Arabia; **Arabia Saudí**o
Saudita Saudi Arabia
arado [a'raðo] nm plough
Aragón [ara'ɣon] nm Aragon; **aragonés,**
-esa adj, nm/f Aragonese
arancel [aran'θel] nm tariff, duty
arandela [aran'dela] nf (Tec) washer
araña [a'raɲa] nf (Zool) spider; (lámpara)
chandelier
arañar [ara'ɲar] vt to scratch
arañazo [ara'ɲaθo] nm scratch
arbitrar [arβi'trar] vt to arbitrate in;
(Deporte) to referee ▷ vi to arbitrate
arbitrario, -a [arβi'trarjo, a] adj
arbitrary
árbitro ['arβitro] nm arbitrator; (Deporte)
referee; (Tenis) umpire
árbol ['arβol] nm (Bot) tree; (Náut)
mast; (Tec) axle, shaft; **árbol de Navidad**
Christmas tree
arboleda [arβo'leða] nf grove, plantation
arbusto [ar'βusto] nm bush, shrub
arca ['arka] nf chest, box
arcada [ar'kaða] nf arcade; (de puente)
arch, span; **arcadas** nfpl (náuseas) retching
sg
arcaico, -a [ar'kaiko, a] adj archaic
arce ['arθe] nm maple tree
arcén [ar'θen] nm (de autopista) hard
shoulder; (de carretera) verge
archipiélago [artʃi'pjelaɣo] nm
archipelago
archivador [artʃiβa'ðor] nm filing cabinet
archivar [artʃi'βar] vt to file (away);
archivo nm file, archive(s) pl; **archivo**
adjunto (Inform) attachment; **archivo de**
seguridad (Inform) backup file
arcilla [ar'θiʎa] nf clay
arco ['arko] nm arch; (Mat) arc; (Mil, Mús)
bow; **arco iris** rainbow
arder [ar'ðer] vi to burn; **estar que arde**
(persona) to fume
ardid [ar'ðið] nm ploy, trick
ardiente [ar'ðjente] adj burning, ardent
ardilla [ar'ðiʎa] nf squirrel
ardor [ar'ðor] nm (calor) heat; (fig) ardour;
ardor de estómago heartburn
arduo, -a ['arðwo, a] adj arduous
área ['area] nf area; (Deporte) penalty area
arena [a'rena] nf sand; (de una lucha)
arena; **arenas movedizas** quicksand sg;
arenal [are'nal] nm (terreno arenoso) sandy
spot
arenisca [are'niska] nf sandstone;
(cascajo) grit
arenoso, -a [are'noso, a] adj sandy
arenque [a'renke] nm herring
arete [a'rete] (MÉX) nm earring

Argel [ar'xel] n Algiers; **Argelia** nf Algeria;
argelino, -a adj, nm/f Algerian
Argentina [arxen'tina] nf (tb: **la ~**)
Argentina
argentino, -a [arxen'tino, a] adj
Argentinian; (de plata) silvery ▷ nm/f
Argentinian
argolla [ar'ɣoʎa] nf (large) ring
argot [ar'ɣo] (pl **~s**) nm slang
argucia [ar'ɣuθja] nf subtlety, sophistry
argumentar [arɣumen'tar] vt, vi to argue
argumento [arɣu'mento] nm argument;
(razonamiento) reasoning; (de novela etc) plot;
(Cine, TV) storyline
aria ['arja] nf aria
aridez [ari'ðeθ] nf aridity, dryness
árido, -a ['ariðo, a] adj arid, dry
Aries ['arjes] nm Aries
arisco, -a [a'risko, a] adj surly; (insociable)
unsociable
aristócrata [aris'tokrata] nmf aristocrat
arma ['arma] nf arm; **armas** nfpl arms;
arma blanca blade, knife; **arma de doble**
filo double-edged sword; **arma de fuego**
firearm; **armas de destrucción masiva**
weapons of mass destruction
armada [ar'maða] nf armada; (flota) fleet
armadillo [arma'ðiʎo] nm armadillo
armado, -a [ar'maðo, a] adj armed; (Tec)
reinforced
armadura [arma'ðura] nf (Mil) armour;
(Tec) framework; (Zool) skeleton; (Física)
armature
armamento [arma'mento] nm
armament; (Náut) fitting-out
armar [ar'mar] vt (soldado) to arm;
(máquina) to assemble; (navío) to fit out; **~la,**
~ un lío to start a row, kick up a fuss
armario [ar'marjo] nm wardrobe;
(de cocina, baño) cupboard; **armario**
empotrado built-in cupboard
armatoste [arma'toste] nm (mueble)
monstrosity; (máquina) contraption
armazón [arma'θon] nf o m body, chassis;
(de mueble etc) frame; (Arq) skeleton
armiño [ar'miɲo] nm stoat; (piel) ermine
armisticio [armis'tiθjo] nm armistice
armonía [armo'nia] nf harmony
armónica [ar'monika] nf harmonica
armonizar [armoni'θar] vt to harmonize;
(diferencias) to reconcile
aro ['aro] nm ring; (tejo) quoit;
(cs: pendiente) earring
aroma [a'roma] nm aroma, scent;
aromaterapia n aromatherapy;
aromático, -a [aro'matiko, a] adj
aromatic
arpa ['arpa] nf harp

arpía [ar'pia] *nf* shrew

arpón [ar'pon] *nm* harpoon

arqueología [arkeolo'xia] *nf* archaeology; **arqueólogo, -a** *nm/f* archaeologist

arquetipo [arke'tipo] *nm* archetype

arquitecto [arki'tekto] *nm* architect; **arquitectura** *nf* architecture

arrabal [arra'βal] *nm* poor suburb, slum; **arrabales** *nmpl* (*afueras*) outskirts

arraigar [arrai'ɣar] *vt* to establish ▷ *vi* to take root

arrancar [arran'kar] *vt* (*sacar*) to extract, pull out; (*arrebatar*) to snatch (away); (*Inform*) to boot; (*fig*) to extract ▷ *vi* (*Auto, máquina*) to start; (*ponerse en marcha*) to get going; **~ de** to stem from

arranque *etc* [a'rranke] *vb* V **arrancar** ▷ *nm* sudden start; (*Auto*) start; (*fig*) fit, outburst

arrasar [arra'sar] *vt* (*aplanar*) to level, flatten; (*destruir*) to demolish

arrastrar [arras'trar] *vt* to drag (along); (*fig*) to drag down, degrade; (*agua, viento*) to carry away ▷ *vi* to drag, trail on the ground; **arrastrarse** *vr* to crawl; (*fig*) to grovel; **llevar algo arrastrado** to drag sth along

arrear [arre'ar] *vt* to drive on, urge on ▷ *vi* to hurry along

arrebatar [arreβa'tar] *vt* to snatch (away), seize; (*fig*) to captivate

arrebato [arre'βato] *nm* fit of rage, fury; (*éxtasis*) rapture

arrecife [arre'θife] *nm* reef

arreglado, -a [arre'ɣlaðo, a] *adj* (*ordenado*) neat, orderly; (*moderado*) moderate, reasonable

arreglar [arre'ɣlar] *vt* (*poner orden*) to tidy up; (*algo roto*) to fix, repair; (*problema*) to solve; **arreglarse** *vr* to reach an understanding; **arreglárselas** (*fam*) to get by, manage

arreglo [a'rreɣlo] *nm* settlement; (*orden*) order; (*acuerdo*) agreement; (*Mús*) arrangement, setting

arremangar [arreman'gar] *vt* to roll up, turn up; **arremangarse** *vr* to roll up one's sleeves

arremeter [arreme'ter] *vi*: **~ contra** to attack, rush at

arrendamiento [arrenda'mjento] *nm* letting; (*alquiler*) hiring; (*contrato*) lease; (*alquiler*) rent; **arrendar** *vt* to let, lease; to rent; **arrendatario, -a** *nm/f* tenant

arreos [a'rreos] *nmpl* (*de caballo*) harness *sg*, trappings

arrepentimiento [arrepenti'mjento] *nm* regret, repentance

arrepentirse [arrepen'tirse] *vr* to repent; **~ de** to regret

arresto [a'rresto] *nm* arrest; (*Mil*) detention; (*audacia*) boldness, daring; **arresto domiciliario** house arrest

arriar [a'rrjar] *vt* (*velas*) to haul down; (*bandera*) to lower, strike; (*cable*) to pay out

○ **PALABRA CLAVE**

arriba [a'rriβa] *adv* **1** (*posición*) above; **desde arriba** from above; **arriba de todo** at the very top, right on top; **Juan está arriba** Juan is upstairs; **lo arriba mencionado** the aforementioned

2 (*dirección*): **calle arriba** up the street

3 de arriba abajo from top to bottom; **mirar a algn de arriba abajo** to look sb up and down

4 para arriba: de 5000 euros para arriba from 5000 euros up(wards)

▷ *adj*: **de arriba: el piso de arriba** the upstairs (BRIT) flat o apartment; **la parte de arriba** the top o upper part

▷ *prep*: **arriba de** (LAM: *por encima de*) above; **arriba de 200 dólares** more than 200 dollars

▷ *excl*: **¡arriba!** up!; **¡manos arriba!** hands up!; **¡arriba España!** long live Spain!

arribar [arri'βar] *vi* to put into port; (*llegar*) to arrive

arriendo *etc* [a'rrjendo] *vb* V **arrendar** ▷ *nm* = **arrendamiento**

arriesgado, -a [arrjes'ɣaðo, a] *adj* (*peligroso*) risky; (*audaz*) bold, daring

arriesgar [arrjes'ɣar] *vt* to risk; (*poner en peligro*) to endanger; **arriesgarse** *vr* to take a risk

arrimar [arri'mar] *vt* (*acercar*) to bring close; (*poner de lado*) to set aside; **arrimarse** *vr* to come close o closer; **~se a** to lean on

arrinconar [arrinko'nar] *vt* (*colocar*) to put in a corner; (*enemigo*) to corner; (*fig*) to put on one side; (*abandonar*) to push aside

arroba [a'rroβa] *nf* (*Internet*) at (sign)

arrodillarse [arroði'ʎarse] *vr* to kneel (down)

arrogante [arro'ɣante] *adj* arrogant

arrojar [arro'xar] *vt* to throw, hurl; (*humo*) to emit, give out; (*Com*) to yield, produce; **arrojarse** *vr* to throw o hurl o.s.

arrojo [a'rroxo] *nm* daring

arrollador, a [arroʎa'ðor, a] *adj* overwhelming

arrollar [arro'ʎar] *vt* (*Auto etc*) to run over, knock down; (*Deporte*) to crush

arropar [arro'par] *vt* to cover, wrap up;

arroparse vr to wrap o.s. up

arroyo [a'rrojo] nm stream; (de la calle) gutter

arroz [a'rroθ] nm rice; **arroz con leche** rice pudding

arruga [a'rruɣa] nf (de cara) wrinkle; (de vestido) crease; **arrugar** [arru'ɣar] vt to wrinkle; to crease; **arrugarse** vr to get creased

arruinar [arrwi'nar] vt to ruin, wreck; **arruinarse** vr to be ruined, go bankrupt

arsenal [arse'nal] nm naval dockyard; (Mil) arsenal

arte ['arte] (gen m en sg y siempre f en pl) nm art; (maña) skill, guile; **artes** nfpl (bellas artes) arts

artefacto [arte'fakto] nm appliance

arteria [ar'terja] nf artery

artesanía [artesa'nia] nf craftsmanship; (artículos) handicrafts pl; **artesano, -a** nm/f artisan, craftsman(-woman)

ártico, -a ['artiko, a] adj Arctic ▷ nm: **el Á~** the Arctic

articulación [artikula'θjon] nf articulation; (Med, Tec) joint

artículo [ar'tikulo] nm article; (cosa) thing, article; **artículos** nmpl (Com) goods; **artículos de escritorio** stationery

artífice [ar'tifiθe] nmf (fig) architect

artificial [artifi'θjal] adj artificial

artillería [artiʎe'ria] nf artillery

artilugio [arti'luxjo] nm gadget

artimaña [arti'maɲa] nf trap, snare; (astucia) cunning

artista [ar'tista] nmf (pintor) artist, painter; (Teatro) artist, artiste; **artista de cine** film actor/actress; **artístico, -a** adj artistic

artritis [ar'tritis] nf arthritis

arveja [ar'βexa] (LAM) nf pea

arzobispo [arθo'βispo] nm archbishop

as [as] nm ace

asa ['asa] nf handle; (fig) lever

asado [a'saðo] nm roast (meat); (LAM: barbacoa) barbecue

● **ASADO**
●
● Traditional Latin American barbecues,
● especially in the River Plate area, are
● celebrated in the open air around a large
● grill which is used to grill mainly beef
● and various kinds of spicy pork sausage.
● They are usually very common during
● the summer and can go on for several
● days. The head cook is nearly always
● a man.

asador [asa'ðor] nm spit

asadura [asa'ðura] nf entrails pl, offal

asalariado, -a [asala'rjaðo, a] adj paid, salaried ▷ nm/f wage earner

asaltar [asal'tar] vt to attack, assault; (fig) to assail; **asalto** nm attack, assault; (Deporte) round

asamblea [asam'blea] nf assembly; (reunión) meeting

asar [a'sar] vt to roast

ascendencia [asθen'denθja] nf ancestry; (LAM: influencia) ascendancy; **de ~ francesa** of French origin

ascender [asθen'der] vi (subir) to ascend, rise; (ser promovido) to gain promotion ▷ vt to promote; **~ a** to amount to; **ascendiente** nm influence ▷ nmf ancestor

ascensión [asθen'sjon] nf ascent; (Rel): **la A~** the Ascension

ascenso [as'θenso] nm ascent; (promoción) promotion

ascensor [asθen'sor] nm lift (BRIT), elevator (US)

asco ['asko] nm: **¡qué ~!** how revolting o disgusting; **el ajo me da ~** I hate o loathe garlic; **estar hecho un ~** to be filthy

ascua ['askwa] nf ember

aseado, -a [ase'aðo, a] adj clean; (arreglado) tidy; (pulcro) smart

asear [ase'ar] vt to clean, wash; to tidy (up)

asediar [ase'ðjar] vt (Mil) to besiege, lay siege to; (fig) to chase, pester; **asedio** nm siege; (Com) run

asegurado, -a [aseɣu'raðo, a] adj insured

asegurador, a [aseɣura'ðor, a] nm/f insurer

asegurar [aseɣu'rar] vt (consolidar) to secure, fasten; (dar garantía de) to guarantee; (preservar) to safeguard; (afirmar, dar por cierto) to assure, affirm; (tranquilizar) to reassure; (tomar un seguro) to insure; **asegurarse** vr to assure o.s., make sure

asemejarse [aseme'xarse] vr to be alike; **~ a** to be like, resemble

asentado, -a [asen'taðo, a] adj established, settled

asentar [asen'tar] vt (sentar) to seat, sit down; (poner) to place, establish; (alisar) to level, smooth down o out; (anotar) to note down ▷ vi to be suitable, suit

asentir [asen'tir] vi to assent, agree; **~ con la cabeza** to nod (one's head)

aseo [a'seo] nm cleanliness; **aseos** nmpl (servicios) toilet sg (BRIT), cloakroom sg (BRIT), restroom sg (US)

aséptico, -a [a'septiko, a] adj germ-free,

free from infection

asequible [ase'kiβle] *adj (precio)* reasonable; *(meta)* attainable; *(persona)* approachable

asesinar [asesi'nar] *vt* to murder; *(Pol)* to assassinate; **asesinato** *nm* murder; assassination

asesino, -a [ase'sino, a] *nm/f* murderer, killer; *(Pol)* assassin

asesor, a [ase'sor, a] *nm/f* adviser, consultant; **asesorar** [aseso'rar] *vt (Jur)* to advise, give legal advice to; *(Com)* to act as consultant to; **asesorarse** *vr:* **asesorarse con** *o* **de** to take advice from, consult; **asesoría** *nf (cargo)* consultancy; *(oficina)* consultant's office

asestar [ases'tar] *vt (golpe)* to deal, strike

asfalto [as'falto] *nm* asphalt

asfixia [as'fiksja] *nf* asphyxia, suffocation; **asfixiar** [asfik'sjar] *vt* to asphyxiate, suffocate; **asfixiarse** *vr* to be asphyxiated, suffocate

así [a'si] *adv (de esta manera)* in this way, like this, thus; *(aunque)* although; *(tan pronto como)* as soon as; **~ que** so; **~ como** as well as; **~ y todo** even so; **¿no es ~?** isn't it?, didn't you? *etc*; **~ de grande** this big

Asia ['asja] *nf* Asia; **asiático, -a** *adj, nm/f* Asian, Asiatic

asiduo, -a [a'siðwo, a] *adj* assiduous; *(frecuente)* frequent ▷ *nm/f* regular (customer)

asiento [a'sjento] *nm (mueble)* seat, chair; *(de coche, en tribunal etc)* seat; *(localidad)* seat, place; *(fundamento)* site; **asiento delantero/ trasero** front/back seat

asignación [asiɣna'θjon] *nf (atribución)* assignment; *(reparto)* allocation; *(sueldo)* salary; **asignación (semanal)** pocket money

asignar [asiɣ'nar] *vt* to assign, allocate

asignatura [asiɣna'tura] *nf* subject; course

asilo [a'silo] *nm (refugio)* asylum, refuge; *(establecimiento)* home, institution; **asilo político** political asylum

asimilar [asimi'lar] *vt* to assimilate

asimismo [asi'mismo] *adv* in the same way, likewise

asistencia [asis'tenθja] *nf* audience; *(Med)* attendance; *(ayuda)* assistance; **asistencia en carretera** roadside assistance; **asistente** *nmf* assistant; **los asistentes** those present; **asistente social** social worker

asistido, -a [asis'tiðo, a] *adj:* **~ por ordenador** computer-assisted

asistir [asis'tir] *vt* to assist, help ▷ *vi:* **~ a**

to attend, be present at

asma ['asma] *nf* asthma

asno ['asno] *nm* donkey; *(fig)* ass

asociación [asoθja'θjon] *nf* association; *(Com)* partnership; **asociado, -a** *adj* associate ▷ *nm/f* associate; *(Com)* partner

asociar [aso'θjar] *vt* to associate

asomar [aso'mar] *vt* to show, stick out ▷ *vi* to appear; **asomarse** *vr* to appear, show up; **~ la cabeza por la ventana** to put one's head out of the window

asombrar [asom'brar] *vt* to amaze, astonish; **asombrarse** *vr (sorprenderse)* to be amazed; *(asustarse)* to get a fright; **asombro** *nm* amazement, astonishment; *(susto)* fright; **asombroso, -a** *adj* astonishing, amazing

asomo [a'somo] *nm* hint, sign

aspa ['aspa] *nf (cruz)* cross; *(de molino)* sail; **en ~** X-shaped

aspaviento [aspa'βjento] *nm* exaggerated display of feeling; *(fam)* fuss

aspecto [as'pekto] *nm (apariencia)* look, appearance; *(fig)* aspect

áspero, -a ['aspero, a] *adj* rough; bitter; sour; harsh

aspersión [asper'sjon] *nf* sprinkling

aspiración [aspira'θjon] *nf* breath, inhalation; *(Mús)* short pause; **aspiraciones** *nfpl (ambiciones)* aspirations

aspirador [aspira'ðor] *nm* =**aspiradora**

aspiradora [aspira'ðora] *nf* vacuum cleaner, Hoover®

aspirante [aspi'rante] *nmf (candidato)* candidate; *(Deporte)* contender

aspirar [aspi'rar] *vt* to breathe in ▷ *vi:* **~ a** to aspire to

aspirina [aspi'rina] *nf* aspirin

asqueroso, -a [aske'roso, a] *adj* disgusting, sickening

asta ['asta] *nf* lance; *(arpón)* spear; *(mango)* shaft, handle; *(Zool)* horn; **a media ~** at half mast

asterisco [aste'risko] *nm* asterisk

astilla [as'tiʎa] *nf* splinter; *(pedacito)* chip; **astillas** *nfpl (leña)* firewood *sg*

astillero [asti'ʎero] *nm* shipyard

astro ['astro] *nm* star

astrología [astrolo'xia] *nf* astrology; **astrólogo, -a** *nm/f* astrologer

astronauta [astro'nauta] *nmf* astronaut

astronomía [astrono'mia] *nf* astronomy

astucia [as'tuθja] *nf* astuteness; *(ardid)* clever trick

asturiano, -a [astu'rjano, a] *adj, nm/f* Asturian

astuto, -a [as'tuto, a] *adj* astute; *(taimado)* cunning

asumir [asu'mir] vt to assume

asunción [asun'θjon] nf assumption; (Rel): **A~** Assumption

asunto [a'sunto] nm (tema) matter, subject; (negocio) business

asustar [asus'tar] vt to frighten; **asustarse** vr to be (o become) frightened

atacar [ata'kar] vt to attack

atadura [ata'ðura] nf bond, tie

atajar [ata'xar] vt (enfermedad, mal) to stop ▷ vi (persona) to take a short cut

atajo [a'taxo] nm short cut

atañer [ata'ɲer] vi: **~ a** to concern

ataque etc [a'take] vb V **atacar** ▷ nm attack; **ataque cardíaco** heart attack

atar [a'tar] vt to tie, tie up

atarantado, -a [ataran'taðo, a] (MÉX) adj (aturdido) dazed

atardecer [atarðe'θer] vi to get dark ▷ nm evening; (crepúsculo) dusk

atareado, -a [atare'aðo, a] adj busy

atascar [atas'kar] vt to clog up; (obstruir) to jam; (fig) to hinder; **atascarse** vr to stall; (cañería) to get blocked up; **atasco** nm obstruction; (Auto) traffic jam

ataúd [ata'uð] nm coffin

ataviar [ata'βjar] vt to deck, array

atemorizar [atemori'θar] vt to frighten, scare

Atenas [a'tenas] n Athens

atención [aten'θjon] nf attention; (bondad) kindness ▷ excl (be) careful!, look out!

atender [aten'der] vt to attend to, look after; (Tel) to answer ▷ vi to pay attention

atenerse [ate'nerse] vr: **~ a** to abide by, adhere to

atentado [aten'taðo] nm crime, illegal act; (asalto) assault; (tb: **~ terrorista**) terrorist attack; **~ contra la vida de algn** attempt on sb's life; **atentado suicida** suicide bombing

atentamente [atenta'mente] adv: **Le saluda ~** Yours faithfully

atentar [aten'tar] vi: **~ a o contra** to commit an outrage against

atento, -a [a'tento, a] adj attentive, observant; (cortés) polite, thoughtful; **estar ~ a** (explicación) to pay attention to

atenuar [ate'nwar] vt (disminuir) to lessen, minimize

ateo, -a [a'teo, a] adj atheistic ▷ nm/f atheist

aterrador, a [aterra'ðor, a] adj frightening

aterrizaje [aterri'θaxe] nm landing; **aterrizaje forzoso** emergency o forced landing

aterrizar [aterri'θar] vi to land

aterrorizar [aterrori'θar] vt to terrify

atesorar [ateso'rar] vt to hoard

atestar [ates'tar] vt to pack, stuff; (Jur) to attest, testify to

atestiguar [atesti'ɣwar] vt to testify to, bear witness to

atiborrar [atiβo'rrar] vt to fill, stuff; **atiborrarse** vr to stuff o.s.

ático ['atiko] nm (desván) attic; (apartamento) penthouse

atinado, -a [ati'naðo, a] adj (sensato) wise; (correcto) right, correct

atinar [ati'nar] vi (al disparar): **~ al blanco** to hit the target; (fig) to be right

atizar [ati'θar] vt to poke; (horno etc) to stoke; (fig) to stir up, rouse

atlántico, -a [at'lantiko, a] adj Atlantic ▷ nm: **el (océano) A~** the Atlantic (Ocean)

atlas ['atlas] nm inv atlas

atleta [at'leta] nm athlete; **atlético, -a** adj athletic; **atletismo** nm athletics sg

atmósfera [at'mosfera] nf atmosphere

atolladero [atoʎa'ðero] nm (fig) jam, fix

atómico, -a [a'tomiko, a] adj atomic

átomo ['atomo] nm atom

atónito, -a [a'tonito, a] adj astonished, amazed

atontado, -a [aton'taðo, a] adj stunned; (bobo) silly, daft

atormentar [atormen'tar] vt to torture; (molestar) to torment; (acosar) to plague, harass

atornillar [atorni'ʎar] vt to screw on o down

atosigar [atosi'ɣar] vt to harass, pester

atracador, a [atraka'ðor, a] nm/f robber

atracar [atra'kar] vt (Náut) to moor; (robar) to hold up, rob ▷ vi to moor; **atracarse** vr: **~se (de)** to stuff o.s. (with)

atracción [atrak'θjon] nf attraction

atraco [a'trako] nm holdup, robbery

atracón [atra'kon] nm: **darse o pegarse un ~ (de)** (fam) to stuff o.s. (with)

atractivo, -a [atrak'tiβo, a] adj attractive ▷ nm appeal

atraer [atra'er] vt to attract

atragantarse [atraɣan'tarse] vr: **~ (con)** to choke (on); **se me ha atragantado el chico** I can't stand the boy

atrancar [atran'kar] vt (puerta) to bar, bolt

atrapar [atra'par] vt to trap; (resfriado etc) to catch

atrás [a'tras] adv (movimiento) back(-wards); (lugar) behind; (tiempo) previously; **ir hacia ~** to go back(wards), to go to the rear; **estar ~** to be behind o at the back

atrasado, -a [atra'saðo, a] adj slow;

(*pago*) overdue, late; (*país*) backward
atrasar [atra'sar] *vi* to be slow; **atrasarse**
vr to remain behind; (*tren*) to be o run late;
atraso *nm* slowness; lateness, delay; (*de
país*) backwardness; **atrasos** *nmpl* (*Com*)
arrears
atravesar [atraβe'sar] *vt* (*cruzar*) to
cross (over); (*traspasar*) to pierce; to go
through; (*poner al través*) to lay o put across;
atravesarse *vr* to come in between;
(*intervenir*) to interfere
atravieso *etc vb* V **atravesar**
atreverse [atre'βerse] *vr* to dare;
(*insolentarse*) to be insolent; **atrevido, -a** *adj*
daring; insolent; **atrevimiento** *nm* daring;
insolence
atribución [atriβu'θjon] *nf* attribution;
atribuciones *nfpl* (*Pol*) powers; (*Admin*)
responsibilities
atribuir [atriβu'ir] *vt* to attribute;
(*funciones*) to confer
atributo [atri'βuto] *nm* attribute
atril [a'tril] *nm* (*para libro*) lectern; (*Mús*)
music stand
atropellar [atrope'ʎar] *vt* (*derribar*)
to knock over o down; (*empujar*) to push
(aside); (*Auto*) to run over, run down;
(*agraviar*) to insult; **atropello** *nm* (*Auto*)
accident; (*empujón*) push; (*agravio*) wrong;
(*atrocidad*) outrage
atroz [a'troθ] *adj* atrocious, awful
ATS *nmf abr* (= *Ayudante Técnico Sanitario*)
nurse
atuendo [a'twendo] *nm* attire
atún [a'tun] *nm* tuna
aturdir [atur'ðir] *vt* to stun; (*de ruido*) to
deafen; (*fig*) to dumbfound, bewilder
audacia [au'ðaθja] *nf* boldness, audacity;
audaz *adj* bold, audacious
audición [auði'θjon] *nf* hearing; (*Teatro*)
audition
audiencia [au'ðjenθja] *nf* audience;
(*Jur: tribunal*) court
audífono [au'ðifono] *nm* (*para sordos*)
hearing aid
auditor [auði'tor] *nm* (*Jur*) judge advocate;
(*Com*) auditor
auditorio [auði'torjo] *nm* audience; (*sala*)
auditorium
auge ['auxe] *nm* boom; (*clímax*) climax
augurar [auɣu'rar] *vt* to predict;
(*presagiar*) to portend
augurio [au'ɣurjo] *nm* omen
aula ['aula] *nf* classroom; (*en universidad
etc*) lecture room
aullar [au'ʎar] *vi* to howl, yell
aullido [au'ʎiðo] *nm* howl, yell
aumentar [aumen'tar] *vt* to increase;

(*precios*) to put up; (*producción*) to step up;
(*con microscopio, anteojos*) to magnify ▷ *vi* to
increase, be on the increase; **aumentarse**
vr to increase, be on the increase; **aumento**
nm increase; rise
aun [a'un] *adv* even; ~ **así** even so; ~ **más**
even o yet more
aún [a'un] *adv*: ~ **está aquí** he's still here; ~
no lo sabemos we don't know yet; **¿no ha
venido ~?** hasn't she come yet?
aunque [a'unke] *conj* though, although,
even though
aúpa [a'upa] *excl* come on!
auricular [auriku'lar] *nm* (*Tel*) receiver;
auriculares *nmpl* (*cascos*) headphones
aurora [au'rora] *nf* dawn
ausencia [au'senθja] *nf* absence
ausentarse [ausen'tarse] *vr* to go away;
(*por poco tiempo*) to go out
ausente [au'sente] *adj* absent
austero, -a [aus'tero, a] *adj* austere
austral [aus'tral] *adj* southern ▷ *nm*
monetary unit of Argentina
Australia [aus'tralja] *nf* Australia;
australiano, -a *adj, nm/f* Australian
Austria ['austrja] *nf* Austria; **austríaco,
-a** *adj, nm/f* Austrian
auténtico, -a [au'tentiko, a] *adj*
authentic
auto ['auto] *nm* (*Jur*) edict, decree;
(: *orden*) writ; (*Auto*) car; **autos** *nmpl* (*Jur*)
proceedings; (: *acta*) court record *sg*
autoadhesivo [autoaðe'siβo] *adj* self-
adhesive; (*sobre*) self-sealing
autobiografía [autoβjoɣra'fia] *nf*
autobiography
autobomba [auto'bomba] (*RPL*) *nm* fire
engine
autobronceador [autoβronθea'ðor] *adj*
self-tanning
autobús [auto'βus] *nm* bus; **autobús de
línea** long-distance coach
autocar [auto'kar] *nm* coach (*BRIT*),
(passenger) bus (*US*)
autóctono, -a [au'toktono, a] *adj* native,
indigenous
autodefensa [autoðe'fensa] *nf* self-
defence
autodidacta [autoði'ðakta] *adj* self-
taught
autoescuela [autoes'kwela] (*ESP*) *nf*
driving school
autógrafo [au'toɣrafo] *nm* autograph
autómata [au'tomata] *nm* automaton
automático, -a [auto'matiko, a] *adj*
automatic ▷ *nm* press stud
automóvil [auto'moβil] *nm* (motor) car
(*BRIT*), automobile (*US*); **automovilismo** *nm*

(*actividad*) motoring; (*Deporte*) motor racing;
automovilista *nmf* motorist, driver
autonomía [autono'mia] *nf* autonomy;
autónomo, -a (*ESP*), **autonómico, -a** (*ESP*)
adj (*Pol*) autonomous
autopista [auto'pista] *nf* motorway
(*BRIT*), freeway (*US*); **autopista de cuota**
(*ESP*) o **peaje** (*MÉX*) toll (*BRIT*) o turnpike
(*US*) road
autopsia [au'topsja] *nf* autopsy,
postmortem
autor, a [au'tor, a] *nm/f* author
autoridad [autori'ðað] *nf* authority;
autoritario, -a *adj* authoritarian
autorización [autoriθa'θjon] *nf*
authorization; **autorizado, -a** *adj*
authorized; (*aprobado*) approved
autorizar [autori'θar] *vt* to authorize;
(*aprobar*) to approve
autoservicio [autoser'βiθjo] *nm* (*tienda*)
self-service shop (*BRIT*) o store (*US*);
(*restaurante*) self-service restaurant
autostop [auto'stop] *nm* hitch-hiking;
hacer ~ to hitch-hike; **autostopista** *nmf*
hitch-hiker
autovía [auto'βia] *nf* ≈ A-road (*BRIT*), dual
carriageway (*BRIT*), ≈ state highway (*US*)
auxiliar [auksi'ljar] *vt* to help ▷ *nmf*
assistant; **auxilio** *nm* assistance, help;
primeros auxilios first aid *sg*
Av *abr* (= *Avenida*) Av(e)
aval [a'βal] *nm* guarantee; (*persona*)
guarantor
avalancha [aβa'lantʃa] *nf* avalanche
avance [a'βanθe] *nm* advance; (*pago*)
advance payment; (*Cine*) trailer
avanzar [aβan'θar] *vt, vi* to advance
avaricia [aβa'riθja] *nf* avarice, greed;
avaricioso, -a *adj* avaricious, greedy
avaro, -a [a'βaro, a] *adj* miserly, mean
▷ *nm/f* miser
Avda *abr* (= *Avenida*) Av(e)
AVE ['aβe] *nm abr* (= *Alta Velocidad Española*)
≈ bullet train
ave ['aβe] *nf* bird; **ave de rapiña** bird of
prey
avecinarse [aβeθi'narse] *vr* (*tormenta: fig*)
to be on the way
avellana [aβe'ʎana] *nf* hazelnut;
avellano *nm* hazel tree
avemaría [aβema'ria] *nm* Hail Mary,
Ave Maria
avena [a'βena] *nf* oats *pl*
avenida [aβe'niða] *nf* (*calle*) avenue
aventajar [aβenta'xar] *vt* (*sobrepasar*) to
surpass, outstrip
aventón [aβen'ton] (*MÉX: fam*) *nm* ride;
dar ~ a algn to give sb a ride

aventura [aβen'tura] *nf* adventure;
aventurero, -a *adj* adventurous
avergonzar [aβerxon'θar] *vt* to shame;
(*desconcertar*) to embarrass; **avergonzarse**
vr to be ashamed; to be embarrassed
avería [aβe'ria] *nf* (*Tec*) breakdown, fault
averiado, -a [aβe'rjaðo, a] *adj* broken
down; **"~"** "out of order"
averiguar [aβeri'ɣwar] *vt* to investigate;
(*descubrir*) to find out, ascertain
avestruz [aβes'truθ] *nm* ostrich
aviación [aβja'θjon] *nf* aviation; (*fuerzas
aéreas*) air force
aviador, a [aβja'ðor, a] *nm/f* aviator,
airman(-woman)
ávido, -a ['aβiðo, a] *adj* avid, eager
avinagrado, -a [aβina'ɣraðo, a] *adj*
sour, acid
avión [a'βjon] *nm* aeroplane; (*ave*) martin;
avión de reacción jet (plane)
avioneta [aβjo'neta] *nf* light aircraft
avisar [aβi'sar] *vt* (*advertir*) to warn,
notify; (*informar*) to tell; (*aconsejar*) to advise,
counsel; **aviso** *nm* warning; (*noticia*) notice
avispa [a'βispa] *nf* wasp
avispado, -a [aβis'paðo, a] *adj* sharp,
clever
avivar [aβi'βar] *vt* to strengthen, intensify
axila [ak'sila] *nf* armpit
ay [ai] *excl* (*dolor*) ow!, ouch!; (*aflicción*) oh!,
oh dear!; **¡~ de mí!** poor me!
ayer [a'jer] *adv, nm* yesterday; **antes de
~** the day before yesterday; **~ mismo** only
yesterday
ayote [a'jote] (*CAM*) *nm* pumpkin
ayuda [a'juða] *nf* help, assistance ▷ *nm*
page; **ayudante** *nmf* assistant, helper;
(*Escol*) assistant; (*Mil*) adjutant
ayudar [aju'ðar] *vt* to help, assist
ayunar [aju'nar] *vi* to fast; **ayunas**
nfpl: **estar en ayunas** to be fasting; **ayuno**
nm fast; fasting
ayuntamiento [ajunta'mjento] *nm*
(*consejo*) town (o city) council; (*edificio*) town
(o city) hall
azafata [aθa'fata] *nf* air stewardess
azafrán [aθa'fran] *nm* saffron
azahar [aθa'ar] *nm* orange/lemon
blossom
azar [a'θar] *nm* (*casualidad*) chance, fate;
(*desgracia*) misfortune, accident; **por ~** by
chance; **al ~** at random
Azores [a'θores] *nfpl*: **las ~** the Azores
azotar [aθo'tar] *vt* to whip, beat; (*pegar*)
to spank; **azote** *nm* (*látigo*) whip; (*latigazo*)
lash, stroke; (*en las nalgas*) spank; (*calamidad*)
calamity
azotea [aθo'tea] *nf* (flat) roof

azteca [aθ'teka] *adj*, *nmf* Aztec
azúcar [a'θukar] *nm* sugar; **azucarado, -a** *adj* sugary, sweet
azucarero, -a [aθuka'rero, a] *adj* sugar *cpd* ▷ *nm* sugar bowl
azucena [aθu'θena] *nf* white lily
azufre [a'θufre] *nm* sulphur
azul [a'θul] *adj*, *nm* blue; **azul celeste/ marino** sky/navy blue
azulejo [aθu'lexo] *nm* tile
azuzar [aθu'θar] *vt* to incite, egg on

B.A. *abr* (= *Buenos Aires*) B.A.
baba ['baβa] *nf* spittle, saliva; **babear** *vi* to drool, slaver
babero [ba'βero] *nm* bib
babor [ba'βor] *nm* port (side)
babosada [baβo'saða] (MÉX, CAM: *fam*) *nf* drivel; **baboso, -a** [ba'βoso, a] (LAM: *fam*) *adj* silly
baca ['baka] *nf* (*Auto*) luggage o roof rack
bacalao [baka'lao] *nm* cod(fish)
bache ['batʃe] *nm* pothole, rut; (*fig*) bad patch
bachillerato [batʃiʎe'rato] *nm* higher secondary school course
bacinica [baθi'nika] (LAM) *nf* potty
bacteria [bak'terja] *nf* bacterium, germ
Bahama [ba'ama]: **las (Islas) ~** *nfpl* the Bahamas
bahía [ba'ia] *nf* bay
bailar [bai'lar] *vt*, *vi* to dance; **bailarín, -ina** *nm/f* (*ballet*) dancer; **baile** *nm* dance; (*formal*) ball
baja ['baxa] *nf* drop, fall; (*Mil*) casualty; **dar de ~** (*soldado*) to discharge; (*empleado*) to dismiss
bajada [ba'xaða] *nf* descent; (*camino*) slope; (*de aguas*) ebb
bajar [ba'xar] *vi* to go down, come down; (*temperatura, precios*) to drop, fall ▷ *vt* (*cabeza*) to bow; (*escalera*) to go down, come down; (*precio, voz*) to lower; (*llevar abajo*) to take down; **bajarse** *vr* (*de coche*) to get out; (*de autobús, tren*) to get off; **~ de** (*coche*) to get out of; (*autobús, tren*) to get off; **~se algo de Internet** to download sth from the Internet
bajío [ba'xio] (LAM) *nm* lowlands *pl*
bajo, -a ['baxo] *adj* (*mueble, número, precio*) low; (*piso*) ground; (*de estatura*) small, short; (*color*) pale; (*sonido*) faint, soft, low; (*voz: en tono*) deep; (*metal*) base; (*humilde*) low, humble ▷ *adv* (*hablar*) softly, quietly; (*volar*)

low ▷ *prep* under, below, underneath ▷ *nm*
(*Mús*) bass; **~ la lluvia** in the rain
bajón [ba'xon] *nm* fall, drop
bakalao [baka'lao] (*ESP: fam*) *nm* rave
(music)
bala ['bala] *nf* bullet
balacear [balaθe'ar] (*MÉX, CAM*) *vt* to
shoot
balance [ba'lanθe] *nm* (*Com*) balance;
(: *libro*) balance sheet; (: *cuenta general*)
stocktaking
balancear [balanθe'ar] *vt* to balance ▷ *vi*
to swing (to and fro); (*vacilar*) to hesitate;
balancearse *vr* to swing (to and fro), to
hesitate
balanza [ba'lanθa] *nf* scales *pl*, balance;
balanza comercial balance of trade;
balanza de pagos balance of payments
balaustrada [balaus'traða] *nf*
balustrade; (*pasamanos*) banisters *pl*
balazo [ba'laθo] *nm* (*golpe*) shot; (*herida*)
bullet wound
balbucear [balβuθe'ar] *vi*, *vt* to stammer,
stutter
balcón [bal'kon] *nm* balcony
balde ['balde] *nm* bucket, pail; **de ~** (for)
free, for nothing; **en ~** in vain
baldosa [bal'dosa] *nf* (*azulejo*) floor tile;
(*grande*) flagstone; **baldosín** *nm* (small) tile
Baleares [bale'ares] *nfpl*: **las (Islas) ~** the
Balearic Islands
balero [ba'lero] (*LAM*) *nm* (*juguete*) cup-
and-ball toy
baliza [ba'liθa] *nf* (*Aviac*) beacon; (*Náut*)
buoy
ballena [ba'ʎena] *nf* whale
ballet [ba'le] (*pl* **~s**) *nm* ballet
balneario [balne'arjo] *nm* spa; (*cs: en la
costa*) seaside resort
balón [ba'lon] *nm* ball
baloncesto [balon'θesto] *nm* basketball
balonmano [balon'mano] *nm* handball
balsa ['balsa] *nf* raft; (*Bot*) balsa wood
bálsamo ['balsamo] *nm* balsam, balm
baluarte [ba'lwarte] *nm* bastion, bulwark
bambú [bam'bu] *nm* bamboo
banana [ba'nana] (*LAM*) *nf* banana;
banano *nm* (*LAM: árbol*) banana tree;
(*CAM: fruta*) banana
banca ['banka] *nf* (*Com*) banking
bancario, -a [ban'karjo, a] *adj* banking
cpd, bank *cpd*
bancarrota [banka'rrota] *nf* bankruptcy;
hacer ~ to go bankrupt
banco ['banko] *nm* bench; (*Escol*) desk;
(*Com*) bank; (*Geo*) stratum; **banco de arena**
sandbank; **banco de crédito** credit bank;
banco de datos databank

banda ['banda] *nf* band; (*pandilla*) gang;
(*Náut*) side, edge; **banda ancha** broadband;
banda sonora soundtrack
bandada [ban'daða] *nf* (*de pájaros*) flock;
(*de peces*) shoal
bandazo [ban'daθo] *nm*: **dar ~s** to sway
from side to side
bandeja [ban'dexa] *nf* tray
bandera [ban'dera] *nf* flag
banderilla [bande'riʎa] *nf* banderilla
bandido [ban'diðo] *nm* bandit
bando ['bando] *nm* (*edicto*) edict,
proclamation; (*facción*) faction; **bandos**
nmpl (*Rel*) banns
bandolera [bando'lera] *nf*: **llevar en ~** to
wear across one's chest
banquero [ban'kero] *nm* banker
banqueta [ban'keta] *nf* stool; (*MÉX: en
calle*) pavement (*BRIT*), sidewalk (*US*)
banquete [ban'kete] *nm* banquet; (*para
convidados*) formal dinner; **banquete de
boda(s)** wedding reception
banquillo [ban'kiʎo] *nm* (*Jur*) dock,
prisoner's bench; (*banco*) bench; (*para los
pies*) footstool
banquina [ban'kina] (*RPL*) *nf* hard
shoulder (*BRIT*), berm (*US*)
bañadera [baɲa'ðera] (*RPL*) *nf* bathtub
bañador [baɲa'ðor] (*ESP*) *nm* swimming
costume (*BRIT*), bathing suit (*US*)
bañar [ba'ɲar] *vt* to bath, bathe; (*objeto*)
to dip; (*de barniz*) to coat; **bañarse** *vr* (*en el
mar*) to bathe, swim; (*en la bañera*) to have
a bath
bañera [ba'ɲera] (*ESP*) *nf* bath(tub)
bañero, -a [ba'ɲero, a] (*cs*) *nm/f* lifeguard
bañista [ba'ɲista] *nmf* bather
baño ['baɲo] *nm* (*en bañera*) bath; (*en río*)
dip, swim; (*cuarto*) bathroom; (*bañera*)
bath(tub); (*capa*) coating; **darse** *o* **tomar
un ~** (*en bañera*) to have *o* take a bath; (*en
mar, piscina*) to have a swim; **baño María**
bain-marie
bar [bar] *nm* bar
barahúnda [bara'unda] *nf* uproar,
hubbub
baraja [ba'raxa] *nf* pack (of cards); **barajar**
vt (*naipes*) to shuffle; (*fig*) to jumble up
baranda [ba'randa] *nf* = **barandilla**
barandilla [baran'diʎa] *nf* rail, railing
barata [ba'rata] (*MÉX*) *nf* (*bargain*) sale
baratillo [bara'tiʎo] *nm* (*tienda*) junkshop;
(*subasta*) bargain sale; (*conjunto de cosas*)
secondhand goods *pl*
barato, -a [ba'rato, a] *adj* cheap ▷ *adv*
cheap, cheaply
barba ['barβa] *nf* (*mentón*) chin; (*pelo*)
beard

barbacoa [barβa'koa] nf (parrilla) barbecue; (carne) barbecued meat
barbaridad [barβari'ðað] nf barbarity; (acto) barbarism; (atrocidad) outrage; **una ~** (fam) loads; **¡qué ~!** (fam) how awful!
barbarie [bar'βarje] nf barbarism, savagery; (crueldad) barbarity
bárbaro, -a ['barβaro, a] adj barbarous, cruel; (grosero) rough, uncouth ▷ nm/f barbarian ▷ adv: **lo pasamos ~** (fam) we had a great time; **¡qué ~!** (fam) how marvellous!; **un éxito ~** (fam) a terrific success; **es un tipo ~** (fam) he's a great bloke
barbero [bar'βero] nm barber, hairdresser
barbilla [bar'βiʎa] nf chin, tip of the chin
barbudo, -a [bar'βuðo, a] adj bearded
barca ['barka] nf (small) boat; **barcaza** nf barge
Barcelona [barθe'lona] n Barcelona
barco ['barko] nm boat; (grande) ship; **barco de carga/pesca** cargo/fishing boat; **barco de vela** sailing ship
barda ['barða] nf (MÉX) nf (de madera) fence
baremo [ba'remo] nm (Mat: fig) scale
barítono [ba'ritono] nm baritone
barman ['barman] nm barman
barniz [bar'niθ] nm varnish; (en loza) glaze; (fig) veneer; **barnizar** vt to varnish; (loza) to glaze
barómetro [ba'rometro] nm barometer
barquillo [bar'kiʎo] nm cone, cornet
barra ['barra] nf bar, rod; (de un bar, café) bar; (de pan) French stick; (palanca) lever; **barra de labios** lipstick; **barra libre** free bar
barraca [ba'rraka] nf hut, cabin
barranco [ba'rranko] nm ravine; (fig) difficulty
barrena [ba'rrena] nf drill
barrer [ba'rrer] vt to sweep; (quitar) to sweep away
barrera [ba'rrera] nf barrier
barriada [ba'rrjaða] nf quarter, district
barricada [barri'kaða] nf barricade
barrida [ba'rriða] nf sweep, sweeping
barriga [ba'rriɣa] nf belly; (panza) paunch; **barrigón, -ona** adj potbellied; **barrigudo, -a** adj potbellied
barril [ba'rril] nm barrel, cask
barrio ['barrjo] nm (vecindad) area, neighborhood (us); (en afueras) suburb; **barrio chino** (ESP) red-light district
barro ['barro] nm (lodo) mud; (objetos) earthenware; (Med) pimple
barroco, -a [ba'rroko, a] adj, nm baroque
barrote [ba'rrote] nm (de ventana) bar
bartola [bar'tola] nf: **tirarse o tumbarse a la ~** to take it easy, be lazy
bártulos ['bartulos] nmpl things,

belongings
barullo [ba'ruʎo] nm row, uproar
basar [ba'sar] vt to base; **basarse** vr: **~se en** to be based on
báscula ['baskula] nf (platform) scales
base ['base] nf base; **a ~ de** on the basis of; (mediante) by means of; **base de datos** (Inform) database
básico, -a ['basiko, a] adj basic
basílica [ba'silika] nf basilica
básquetbol ['basketbol] (LAM) nm basketball

○ **PALABRA CLAVE**

bastante [bas'tante] adj 1 (suficiente) enough; **bastante dinero** enough o sufficient money; **bastantes libros** enough books
2 (valor intensivo): **bastante gente** quite a lot of people; **tener bastante calor** to be rather hot
▷ adv: **bastante bueno/malo** quite good/ rather bad; **bastante rico** pretty rich; **(lo) bastante inteligente (como) para hacer algo** clever enough o sufficiently clever to do sth

bastar [bas'tar] vi to be enough o sufficient; **bastarse** vr to be self-sufficient; **~ para** to be enough to; **¡basta!** (that's) enough!
bastardo, -a [bas'tarðo, a] adj, nm/f bastard
bastidor [basti'ðor] nm frame; (de coche) chassis; (Teatro) wing; **entre ~es** (fig) behind the scenes
basto, -a ['basto, a] adj coarse, rough; **bastos** nmpl (Naipes) ≈ clubs
bastón [bas'ton] nm stick, staff; (para pasear) walking stick
bastoncillo [baston'θiʎo] nm cotton bud
basura [ba'sura] nf rubbish (BRIT), garbage (us) ▷ adj: **comida/televisión ~** junk food/TV
basurero [basu'rero] nm (hombre) dustman (BRIT), garbage man (us); (lugar) dump; (cubo) (rubbish) bin (BRIT), trash can (us)
bata ['bata] nf (gen) dressing gown; (cubretodo) smock, overall; (Med, Tec etc) lab(oratory) coat
batalla [ba'taʎa] nf battle; **de ~** (fig) for everyday use; **batalla campal** pitched battle
batallón [bata'ʎon] nm battalion
batata [ba'tata] nf sweet potato
batería [bate'ria] nf battery; (Mús) drums;

batería de cocina kitchen utensils
batido, -a [ba'tiðo, a] *adj (camino)* beaten, well-trodden ▷ *nm (Culin: de leche)* milk shake
batidora [bati'ðora] *nf* beater, mixer; **batidora eléctrica** food mixer, blender
batir [ba'tir] *vt* to beat, strike; *(vencer)* to beat, defeat; *(revolver)* to beat, mix; **batirse** *vr* to fight; **~ palmas** to applaud
batuta [ba'tuta] *nf* baton; **llevar la ~** *(fig)* to be the boss, be in charge
baúl [ba'ul] *nm* trunk; *(Auto)* boot (BRIT), trunk (US)
bautismo [bau'tismo] *nm* baptism, christening
bautizar [bauti'θar] *vt* to baptize, christen; *(fam: diluir)* to water down; **bautizo** *nm* baptism, christening
bayeta [ba'jeta] *nf* floorcloth
baza ['baθa] *nf* trick; **meter ~** to butt in
bazar [ba'θar] *nm* bazaar
bazofia [ba'θofja] *nf* trash
be [be] *nf* name of the letter B; **be chica/grande** (MÉX) V/B; **be larga** (LAM) B
beato, -a [be'ato, a] *adj* blessed; *(piadoso)* pious
bebé [be'βe] *(pl ~s)* *nm* baby
bebedero, a [beβe'ðero, a] *(MÉX, CS)* *nm* drinking fountain
bebedor, a [beβe'ðor, a] *adj* hard-drinking
beber [be'βer] *vt, vi* to drink
bebida [be'βiða] *nf* drink; **bebido, -a** *adj* drunk
beca ['beka] *nf* grant, scholarship; **becario, -a** [be'karjo, a] *nm/f* scholarship holder, grant holder
bedel [be'ðel] *nm (Escol)* janitor; *(Univ)* porter
béisbol ['beisβol] *nm* baseball
Belén [be'len] *nm* Bethlehem; **belén** *nm (de Navidad)* nativity scene, crib
belga ['belɣa] *adj, nmf* Belgian
Bélgica ['belxika] *nf* Belgium
bélico, -a ['beliko, a] *adj (actitud)* warlike
belleza [be'ʎeθa] *nf* beauty
bello, -a ['beʎo, a] *adj* beautiful, lovely; **Bellas Artes** Fine Art
bellota [be'ʎota] *nf* acorn
bemol [be'mol] *nm (Mús)* flat; **esto tiene ~es** *(fam)* this is a tough one
bencina [ben'θina] *nf (Quím)* benzine
bendecir [bende'θir] *vt* to bless
bendición [bendi'θjon] *nf* blessing
bendito, -a [ben'dito, a] *pp de* **bendecir** ▷ *adj* holy; *(afortunado)* lucky; *(feliz)* happy; *(sencillo)* simple ▷ *nm/f* simple soul
beneficencia [benefi'θenθja] *nf* charity

beneficiario, -a [benefi'θjarjo, a] *nm/f* beneficiary
beneficio [bene'fiθjo] *nm (bien)* benefit, advantage; *(ganancia)* profit, gain; **a ~ de algn** in aid of sb; **beneficioso, -a** *adj* beneficial
benéfico, -a [be'nefiko, a] *adj* charitable
beneplácito [bene'plaθito] *nm* approval, consent
benévolo, -a [be'neβolo, a] *adj* benevolent, kind
benigno, -a [be'niɣno, a] *adj* kind; *(suave)* mild; *(Med: tumor)* benign, non-malignant
berberecho [berβe'retʃo] *nm (Zool, Culin)* cockle
berenjena [beren'xena] *nf* aubergine (BRIT), eggplant (US)
Berlín [ber'lin] *n* Berlin
berlinesa [berli'nesa] *(RPL)* *nf* doughnut, donut (US)
bermudas [ber'muðas] *nfpl* Bermuda shorts
berrido [be'rriðo] *nm* bellow(ing)
berrinche [be'rrintʃe] *(fam)* *nm* temper, tantrum
berro ['berro] *nm* watercress
berza ['berθa] *nf* cabbage
besamel [besa'mel] *nf (Culin)* white sauce, bechamel sauce
besar [be'sar] *vt* to kiss; *(fig: tocar)* to graze; **besarse** *vr* to kiss (one another); **beso** *nm* kiss
bestia ['bestja] *nf* beast, animal; *(fig)* idiot; **bestia de carga** beast of burden; **bestial** [bes'tjal] *adj* bestial; *(fam)* terrific; **bestialidad** *nf* bestiality; *(fam)* stupidity
besugo [be'suɣo] *nm* sea bream; *(fam)* idiot
besuquear [besuke'ar] *vt* to cover with kisses; **besuquearse** *vr* to kiss and cuddle
betabel [beta'bel] *(MÉX)* *nm* beetroot (BRIT), beet (US)
betún [be'tun] *nm* shoe polish; *(Quím)* bitumen
biberón [biβe'ron] *nm* feeding bottle
Biblia ['biβlja] *nf* Bible
bibliografía [biβljoɣra'fia] *nf* bibliography
biblioteca [biβljo'teka] *nf* library; *(mueble)* bookshelves; **biblioteca de consulta** reference library; **bibliotecario, -a** *nm/f* librarian
bicarbonato [bikarβo'nato] *nm* bicarbonate
bicho ['bitʃo] *nm (animal)* small animal; *(sabandija)* bug, insect; *(Taur)* bull
bici ['biθi] *(fam)* *nf* bike
bicicleta [biθi'kleta] *nf* bicycle, cycle; **ir**

en ~ to cycle
bidé [bi'ðe] (pl **~s**) nm bidet
bidón [bi'ðon] nm (de aceite) drum; (de gasolina) can

○ **PALABRA CLAVE**

bien [bjen] nm **1** (bienestar) good; **te lo digo por tu bien** I'm telling you for your own good; **el bien y el mal** good and evil
2 (posesión): **bienes** goods; **bienes de consumo** consumer goods; **bienes inmuebles** o **raíces/bienes muebles** real estate sg/personal property sg ▷ adv
1 (de manera satisfactoria, correcta etc) well; **trabaja/come bien** she works/eats well; **contestó bien** he answered correctly; **me siento bien** I feel fine; **no me siento bien** I don't feel very well; **se está bien aquí** it's nice here
2 (frases): **hiciste bien en llamarme** you were right to call me
3 (valor intensivo) very; **un cuarto bien caliente** a nice warm room; **bien se ve que ...** it's quite clear that ...
4 estar bien: **estoy muy bien aquí** I feel very happy here; **está bien que vengan** it's all right for them to come; **¡está bien! lo haré** oh all right, I'll do it
5 (de buena gana): **yo bien que iría pero ...** I'd gladly go but ... ▷ excl: **¡bien!** (aprobación) O.K.!; **¡muy bien!** well done! ▷ adj inv (matiz despectivo): **gente bien** posh people ▷ conj
1 bien ... bien: **bien en coche bien en tren** either by car or by train
2 (LAM) **no bien: no bien llegue te llamaré** as soon as I arrive I'll call you
3 **si bien** even though; V tb **más**

bienal [bje'nal] adj biennial
bienestar [bjenes'tar] nm well-being, welfare
bienvenida [bjembe'niða] nf welcome; **dar la ~ a algn** to welcome sb
bienvenido [bjembe'niðo] excl welcome!
bife ['bife] (cs) nm steak
bifurcación [bifurka'θjon] nf fork
bígamo, -a ['biɣamo, a] adj bigamous ▷ nm/f bigamist
bigote [bi'ɣote] nm moustache; **bigotudo, -a** adj with a big moustache
bikini [bi'kini] nm bikini; (Culin) toasted ham and cheese sandwich
bilingüe [bi'liŋgwe] adj bilingual
billar [bi'ʎar] nm billiards sg; **billares** nmpl (lugar) billiard hall; (sala de juegos) amusement arcade; **billar americano** pool
billete [bi'ʎete] nm ticket; (de banco) (bank)note (BRIT), bill (US); (carta) note; **~ de 20 libras** £20 note; **billete de ida y vuelta** return (BRIT) o round-trip (US) ticket; **billete sencillo** o **de ida** single (BRIT) o one-way (US) ticket; **billete electrónico** e-ticket
billetera [biʎe'tera] nf wallet
billón [bi'ʎon] nm billion
bimensual [bimen'swal] adj twice monthly
bingo ['biŋgo] nm bingo
biodegradable [bioðeɣra'ðaβle] adj biodegradable
biografía [bjoɣra'fia] nf biography
biología [bjolo'xia] nf biology; **biológico, -a** adj biological; (cultivo, producto) organic; **biólogo, -a** nm/f biologist
biombo ['bjombo] nm (folding) screen
bioterrorismo [bjoterro'rismo] nm bioterrorism
biquini [bi'kini] nm o (RPL) f bikini
birlar [bir'lar] vt to pinch
Birmania [bir'manja] nf Burma
birome [bi'rome] (RPL) nf ballpoint (pen)
birria ['birrja] nf: **ser una ~** (película, libro) to be rubbish
bis [bis] excl encore!
bisabuelo, -a [bisa'βwelo, a] nm/f great-grandfather(-mother)
bisagra [bi'saɣra] nf hinge
bisiesto [bi'sjesto] adj: **año ~** leap year
bisnieto, -a [bis'njeto, a] nm/f great-grandson/daughter
bisonte [bi'sonte] nm bison
bisté [bis'te] nm = bistec
bistec [bis'tek] nm steak
bisturí [bistu'ri] nm scalpel
bisutería [bisute'ria] nf imitation o costume jewellery
bit [bit] nm (Inform) bit
bizco, -a ['biθko, a] adj cross-eyed
bizcocho [biθ'kotʃo] nm (Culin) sponge cake
blanca ['blanka] nf (Mús) minim; **estar sin ~** (ESP: fam) to be broke; V tb **blanco**
blanco, -a ['blanko, a] adj white ▷ nm/f white man/woman, white ▷ nm (color) white; (en texto) blank; (Mil, fig) target; **en ~** blank; **noche en ~** sleepless night
blandir [blan'dir] vt to brandish
blando, -a ['blando, a] adj soft; (tierno) tender, gentle; (carácter) mild; (fam) cowardly
blanqueador [blankea'ðor] (MÉX) nm bleach
blanquear [blanke'ar] vt to whiten; (fachada) to whitewash; (paño) to bleach ▷ vi to turn white
blanquillo [blan'kiʎo] (MÉX, CAM) nm egg

blasfemar [blasfe'mar] vi to blaspheme, curse

bledo ['bleðo] nm: **me importa un ~** I couldn't care less

blindado, -a [blin'daðo, a] adj (Mil) armour-plated; (antibala) bullet-proof; **coche** (ESP) o **carro** (LAM) ~ armoured car

bloc [blok] (pl ~s) nm writing pad

blof [blof] (MÉX) nm bluff; **blofear** (MÉX) vi to bluff

blog [blox] (pl ~s) nm blog

bloque ['bloke] nm block; (Pol) bloc

bloquear [bloke'ar] vt to blockade; **bloqueo** nm blockade; (Com) freezing, blocking; **bloqueo mental** mental block

blusa ['blusa] nf blouse

bobada [bo'βaða] nf foolish action; foolish statement; **decir ~s** to talk nonsense

bobina [bo'βina] nf (Tec) bobbin; (Foto) spool; (Elec) coil

bobo, -a ['boβo, a] adj (tonto) daft, silly; (cándido) naôve ▷ nm/f fool, idiot ▷ nm (Teatro) clown, funny man

boca ['boka] nf mouth; (de crustáceo) pincer; (de cañón) muzzle; (entrada) mouth, entrance; **bocas** nfpl (de río) mouth sg; **~ abajo/arriba** face down/up; **se me hace la ~ agua** my mouth is watering; **boca de incendios** hydrant; **boca del estómago** pit of the stomach; **boca de metro** underground (BRIT) o subway (US) entrance

bocacalle [boka'kaʎe] nf (entrance to a) street; **la primera ~** the first turning o street

bocadillo [boka'ðiʎo] nm sandwich

bocado [bo'kaðo] nm mouthful, bite; (de caballo) bridle

bocajarro [boka'xarro]: **a ~** adv (disparar) point-blank

bocanada [boka'naða] nf (de vino) mouthful, swallow; (de aire) gust, puff

bocata [bo'kata] (fam) nm sandwich

bocazas [bo'kaθas] (fam) nm inv bigmouth

boceto [bo'θeto] nm sketch, outline

bochorno [bo'tʃorno] nm (vergüenza) embarrassment; (calor): **hace ~** it's very muggy

bocina [bo'θina] nf (Mús) trumpet; (Auto) horn; (para hablar) megaphone

boda ['boða] nf (tb: ~s) wedding, marriage; (fiesta) wedding reception; **bodas de oro/plata** golden/silver wedding sg

bodega [bo'ðexa] nf (de vino) (wine) cellar; (depósito) storeroom; (de barco) hold

bodegón [boðe'xon] nm (Arte) still life

bofetada [bofe'taða] nf slap (in the face)

boga ['boxa] nf: **en ~** (fig) in vogue

Bogotá [boxo'ta] n Bogotá

bohemio, -a [bo'emjo, a] adj, nm/f Bohemian

bohío [bo'io] (CAM) nm shack, hut

boicot [boi'kot] (pl ~s) nm boycott; **boicotear** vt to boycott

bóiler ['boiler] (MÉX) nm boiler

boina ['boina] nf beret

bola ['bola] nf ball; (canica) marble; (Naipes) (grand) slam; (betún) shoe polish; (mentira) tale, story; **bolas** nfpl (LAM: caza) bolas sg; **bola de billar** billiard ball; **bola de nieve** snowball

boleadoras [bolea'ðoras] nfpl bolas sg

bolear [bole'ar] (MÉX) vt (zapatos) to polish, shine

bolera [bo'lera] nf skittle o bowling alley

bolero, -a (MÉX) [bo'lero] nm/f (limpiabotas) shoeshine boy/girl

boleta [bo'leta] (LAM) nf (de rifa) ticket; (CS: recibo) receipt; **boleta de calificaciones** (MÉX) report card

boletería [bolete'ria] (LAM) nf ticket office

boletín [bole'tin] nm bulletin; (periódico) journal, review; **boletín de noticias** news bulletin

boleto [bo'leto] nm (LAM) ticket; **boleto de ida y vuelta** (LAM) round trip ticket; **boleto electrónico** (LAM) e-ticket; **boleto redondo** (MÉX) round trip ticket

boli ['boli] (fam) nm Biro®

bolígrafo [bo'lixrafo] nm ball-point pen, Biro®

bolilla [bo'liʎa] (RPL) nf topic

bolillo [bo'liʎo] (MÉX) nm (bread) roll

bolita [bo'lita] (CS) nf marble

bolívar [bo'liβar] nm monetary unit of Venezuela

Bolivia [bo'liβja] nf Bolivia; **boliviano, -a** adj, nm/f Bolivian

bollería [boʎe'ria] nf cakes pl and pastries pl

bollo ['boʎo] nm (pan) roll; (bulto) bump, lump; (abolladura) dent

bolo ['bolo] nm skittle; (píldora) (large) pill; **(juego de) bolos** nmpl skittles sg

bolsa ['bolsa] nf (para llevar algo) bag; (MÉX, CAM: bolsillo) pocket; (MÉX: de mujer) handbag; (Anat) cavity, sac; (Com) stock exchange; (Minería) pocket; **de ~** pocket cpd; **bolsa de agua caliente** hot water bottle; **bolsa de aire** air pocket; **bolsa de dormir** (MÉX, RPL) sleeping bag; **bolsa de la compra** shopping bag; **bolsa de papel/plástico** paper/plastic bag

bolsear [bolse'ar] (MÉX, CAM) vt: **~ a algn** to pick sb's pocket

bolsillo [bol'siʎo] nm pocket; (cartera) purse; **de ~** pocket(-size)

bolso ['bolso] nm (bolsa) bag; (de mujer)

handbag

bomba ['bomba] nf (Mil) bomb; (Tec) pump ▷ adj (fam): **noticia ~** bombshell ▷ adv (fam): **pasarlo ~** to have a great time; **bomba atómica/de efecto retardado/de humo** atomic/time/smoke bomb

bombacha [bom'batʃa] (RPL) nf panties pl

bombardear [bombarðe'ar] vt to bombard; (Mil) to bomb; **bombardeo** nm bombardment; bombing

bombazo [bom'baθo] (MÉX) nm (explosión) explosion; (fam: notición) bombshell; (: éxito) smash hit

bombear [bombe'ar] vt (agua) to pump (out o up)

bombero [bom'bero] nm fireman

bombilla [bom'biʎa] (ESP) nf (light) bulb

bombita [bom'bita] (RPL) nf (light) bulb

bombo ['bombo] nm (Mús) bass drum; (Tec) drum

bombón [bom'bon] nm chocolate; (MÉX: de caramelo) marshmallow

bombona [bom'bona] (ESP) nf (de butano, oxígeno) cylinder

bonachón, -ona [bona'tʃon, ona] adj good-natured, easy-going

bonanza [bo'nanθa] nf (Náut) fair weather; (fig) bonanza; (Minería) rich pocket o vein

bondad [bon'dað] nf goodness, kindness; **tenga la ~ de** (please) be good enough to

bonito, -a [bo'nito, a] adj pretty; (agradable) nice ▷ nm (atún) tuna (fish)

bono ['bono] nm voucher; (Finanzas) bond

bonobús [bono'βus] (ESP) nm bus pass

bonoloto [bono'loto] nf state-run weekly lottery

boquerón [boke'ron] nm (pez) (kind of) anchovy; (agujero) large hole

boquete [bo'kete] nm gap, hole

boquiabierto, -a [bokia'βjerto, a] adj: **quedarse ~** to be amazed o flabbergasted

boquilla [bo'kiʎa] nf (para riego) nozzle; (para cigarro) cigarette holder; (Mús) mouthpiece

borbotón [borβo'ton] nm: **salir a borbotones** to gush out

borda ['borða] nf (Náut) (ship's) rail; **tirar algo/caerse por la ~** to throw sth/fall overboard

bordado [bor'ðaðo] nm embroidery

bordar [bor'ðar] vt to embroider

borde ['borðe] nm edge, border; (de camino etc) side; (en la costura) hem; **al ~ de** (fig) on the verge o brink of; **ser ~** (ESP: fam) to be rude; **bordear** vt to border

bordillo [bor'ðiʎo] nm kerb (BRIT), curb (US)

bordo ['borðo] nm (Náut) side; **a ~** on board

borlote [bor'lote] (MÉX) nm row, uproar

borrachera [borra'tʃera] nf (ebriedad) drunkenness; (orgía) spree, binge

borracho, -a [bo'rratʃo, a] adj drunk ▷ nm/f (habitual) drunkard, drunk; (temporal) drunk, drunk man/woman

borrador [borra'ðor] nm (escritura) first draft, rough sketch; (goma) rubber (BRIT), eraser

borrar [bo'rrar] vt to erase, rub out

borrasca [bo'rraska] nf storm

borrego, -a [bo'rreɣo, a] nm/f (Zool: joven) (yearling) lamb; (adulto) sheep ▷ nm (MÉX: fam) false rumour

borrico, -a [bo'rriko, a] nm/f donkey/ she-donkey; (fig) stupid man/woman

borrón [bo'rron] nm (mancha) stain

borroso, -a [bo'rroso, a] adj vague, unclear; (escritura) illegible

bosque ['boske] nm wood; (grande) forest

bostezar [boste'θar] vi to yawn; **bostezo** nm yawn

bota ['bota] nf (calzado) boot; (para vino) leather wine bottle; **botas de agua** o **goma** Wellingtons

botana [bo'tana] (MÉX) nf snack, appetizer

botánica [bo'tanika] nf (ciencia) botany; V tb **botánico**

botánico, -a [bo'taniko, a] adj botanical ▷ nm/f botanist

botar [bo'tar] vt to throw, hurl; (Náut) to launch; (LAM: echar) to throw out ▷ vi (ESP: saltar) to bounce

bote ['bote] nm (salto) bounce; (golpe) thrust; (ESP: envase) tin, can; (embarcación) boat; (MÉX, CAM: pey: cárcel) jail; **de ~ en ~** packed, jammed full; **bote de la basura** (MÉX) dustbin (BRIT), trashcan (US); **bote salvavidas** lifeboat

botella [bo'teʎa] nf bottle; **botellín** nm small bottle; **botellón** nm (ESP: fam) outdoor drinking session

botijo [bo'tixo] nm (earthenware) jug

botín [bo'tin] nm (calzado) half boot; (polaina) spat; (Mil) booty

botiquín [boti'kin] nm (armario) medicine cabinet; (portátil) first-aid kit

botón [bo'ton] nm button; (Bot) bud

botones [bo'tones] nm inv bellboy (BRIT), bellhop (US)

bóveda ['boβeða] nf (Arq) vault

boxeador [boksea'ðor] nm boxer

boxeo [bok'seo] nm boxing

boya ['boja] nf (Náut) buoy; (de caña) float

boyante [bo'jante] adj prosperous

bozal [bo'θal] nm (para caballos) halter; (de

perro) muzzle

bragas ['braɣas] *nfpl (de mujer)* panties, knickers (BRIT)

bragueta [bra'ɣeta] *nf* fly, flies *pl*

braille [breil] *nm* braille

brasa ['brasa] *nf* live o hot coal

brasero [bra'sero] *nm* brazier

brasier [bra'sjer] (MÉX) *nm* bra

Brasil [bra'sil] *nm (tb: el ~)* Brazil; **brasileño, -a** *adj, nm/f* Brazilian

brassier [bra'sjer] (MÉX) *nm* V **brasier**

bravo, -a ['braβo, a] *adj (valiente)* brave; *(feroz)* ferocious; *(salvaje)* wild; *(mar etc)* rough, stormy ▷ *excl* bravo!; **bravura** *nf* bravery; ferocity

braza ['braθa] *nf* fathom; **nadar a ~** to swim breast-stroke

brazalete [braθa'lete] *nm (pulsera)* bracelet; *(banda)* armband

brazo ['braθo] *nm* arm; *(Zool)* foreleg; *(Bot)* limb, branch; **luchar a ~ partido** to fight hand-to-hand; **ir cogidos del ~** to walk arm in arm

brebaje [bre'βaxe] *nm* potion

brecha ['bretʃa] *nf (hoyo, vacío)* gap, opening; *(Mil, fig)* breach

brega ['breɣa] *nf (lucha)* struggle; *(trabajo)* hard work

breva ['breβa] *nf* early fig

breve ['breβe] *adj* short, brief ▷ *nf (Mús)* breve; **en ~** *(pronto)* shortly, before long; **brevedad** *nf* brevity, shortness

bribón, -ona [bri'βon, ona] *adj* idle, lazy ▷ *nm/f (pícaro)* rascal, rogue

bricolaje [briko'laxe] *nm* do-it-yourself, DIY

brida ['briða] *nf* bridle, rein; *(Tec)* clamp

bridge [britʃ] *nm* bridge

brigada [bri'ɣaða] *nf (unidad)* brigade; *(de trabajadores)* squad, gang ▷ *nm* ≈ staff-sergeant, sergeant-major

brillante [bri'ʎante] *adj* brilliant ▷ *nm* diamond

brillar [bri'ʎar] *vi* to shine; *(joyas)* to sparkle

brillo ['briʎo] *nm* shine; *(brillantez)* brilliance; *(fig)* splendour; **sacar ~ a** to polish

brincar [brin'kar] *vi* to skip about, hop about, jump about

brinco ['brinko] *nm* jump, leap

brindar [brin'dar] *vi*: **~ a o por** to drink (a toast) to ▷ *vt* to offer, present

brindis ['brindis] *nm inv* toast

brío ['brio] *nm* spirit, dash

brisa ['brisa] *nf* breeze

británico, -a [bri'taniko, a] *adj* British

▷ *nm/f* Briton, British person

brizna ['briθna] *nf (de hierba, paja)* blade; *(de tabaco)* leaf

broca ['broka] *nf (Tec)* drill, bit

brocha ['brotʃa] *nf (large)* paintbrush; **brocha de afeitar** shaving brush

broche ['brotʃe] *nm* brooch

broma ['broma] *nf* joke; **de o en ~** in fun, as a joke; **broma pesada** practical joke; **bromear** *vi* to joke

bromista [bro'mista] *adj* fond of joking ▷ *nmf* joker, wag

bronca ['bronka] *nf* row; **echar una ~ a algn** to tick sb off

bronce ['bronθe] *nm* bronze; **bronceado, -a** *adj* bronze; *(por el sol)* tanned ▷ *nm* (sun) tan; *(Tec)* bronzing

bronceador [bronθea'ðor] *nm* suntan lotion

broncearse [bronθe'arse] *vr* to get a suntan

bronquio ['bronkjo] *nm (Anat)* bronchial tube

bronquitis [bron'kitis] *nf inv* bronchitis

brotar [bro'tar] *vi (Bot)* to sprout; *(aguas)* to gush (forth); *(Med)* to break out

brote ['brote] *nm (Bot)* shoot; *(Med, fig)* outbreak

bruces ['bruθes]: **de bruces** *adv*: **caer o dar de ~** to fall headlong, fall flat

bruja ['bruxa] *nf* witch; **brujería** *nf* witchcraft

brujo ['bruxo] *nm* wizard, magician

brújula ['bruxula] *nf* compass

bruma ['bruma] *nf* mist

brusco, -a ['brusko, a] *adj (súbito)* sudden; *(áspero)* brusque

Bruselas [bru'selas] *n* Brussels

brutal [bru'tal] *adj* brutal; **brutalidad** [brutali'ðað] *nf* brutality

bruto, -a ['bruto, a] *adj (idiota)* stupid; *(bestial)* brutish; *(peso)* gross; **en ~** raw, unworked

Bs.As. *abr* (= *Buenos Aires*) B.A.

bucal [bu'kal] *adj* oral; **por vía ~** orally

bucear [buθe'ar] *vi* to dive ▷ *vt* to explore; **buceo** *nm* diving

bucle ['bukle] *nm* curl

budismo [bu'ðismo] *nm* Buddhism

buen [bwen] *adj m* V **bueno**

buenamente [bwena'mente] *adv (fácilmente)* easily; *(voluntariamente)* willingly

buenaventura [bwenaβen'tura] *nf (suerte)* good luck; *(adivinación)* fortune

buenmozo [bwen'moθo] (MÉX) *adj* handsome

○ PALABRA CLAVE

bueno, -a ['bweno, a] (antes de nmsg:
buen) adj 1 (excelente etc) good; **es un
libro bueno, es un buen libro** it's a good
book; **hace bueno, hace buen tiempo** the
weather is fine, it is fine; **el bueno de Paco**
good old Paco; **fue muy bueno conmigo** he
was very nice o kind to me
2 (apropiado): **ser bueno para** to be good for;
creo que vamos por buen camino I think
we're on the right track
3 (irónico): **le di un buen rapapolvo** I
gave him a good o real ticking off; **¡buen
conductor estás hecho!** some o a fine
driver you are!; **¡estaría bueno que ...!** a
fine thing it would be if ...!
4 (atractivo, sabroso): **está bueno este
bizcocho** this sponge is delicious; **Carmen
está muy buena** Carmen is gorgeous
5 (saludos): **¡buen día!, ¡buenos días!**
(good) morning!; **¡buenas (tardes)!** (good)
afternoon!; (más tarde) (good) evening!;
¡buenas noches! good night!
6 (otras locuciones): **estar de buenas** to be
in a good mood; **por las buenas o por las
malas** by hook or by crook; **de buenas a
primeras** all of a sudden ▷ excl: **¡bueno!** all
right!; **bueno, ¿y qué?** well, so what?

Buenos Aires [bweno'saires] nm Buenos
Aires
buey [bwei] nm ox
búfalo ['bufalo] nm buffalo
bufanda [bu'fanda] nf scarf
bufete [bu'fete] nm (despacho de abogado)
lawyer's office
bufón [bu'fon] nm clown
buhardilla [buar'ðiʎa] nf attic
búho ['buo] nm owl; (fig) hermit, recluse
buitre ['bwitre] nm vulture
bujía [bu'xia] nf (vela) candle; (Elec) candle
(power); (Auto) spark plug
bula ['bula] nf (papal) bull
bulbo ['bulβo] nm bulb
bulevar [bule'βar] nm boulevard
Bulgaria [bul'xarja] nf Bulgaria; **búlgaro,
-a** adj, nm/f Bulgarian
bulla ['buʎa] nf (ruido) uproar; (de gente)
crowd
bullicio [bu'ʎiθjo] nm (ruido) uproar;
(movimiento) bustle
bulto ['bulto] nm (paquete) package; (fardo)
bundle; (tamaño) size, bulkiness; (Med)
swelling, lump; (silueta) vague shape
buñuelo [bu'ɲwelo] nm ≈ doughnut
(BRIT), ≈ donut (US); (fruta de sartén) fritter
buque ['buke] nm ship, vessel; **buque de**

guerra warship
burbuja [bur'βuxa] nf bubble
burdel [bur'ðel] nm brothel
burgués, -esa [bur'ɣes, esa] adj middle-
class, bourgeois; **burguesía** nf middle
class, bourgeoisie
burla ['burla] nf (mofa) gibe; (broma) joke;
(engaño) trick; **burlar** [bur'lar] vt (engañar)
to deceive ▷ vi to joke; **burlarse** vr to joke;
burlarse de to make fun of
burlón, -ona [bur'lon, ona] adj mocking
buró [bu'ro] (MÉX) nm bedside table
burocracia [buro'kraθja] nf civil service
burrada [bu'rraða] nf: **decir** o **soltar ~s** to
talk nonsense; **hacer ~s** to act stupid; **una ~**
(ESP: mucho) a (hell of a) lot
burro, -a ['burro, a] nm/f donkey/she-
donkey; (fig) ass, idiot
bursátil [bur'satil] adj stock-exchange cpd
bus [bus] nm bus
busca ['buska] nf search, hunt ▷ nm (Tel)
bleeper; **en ~ de** in search of
buscador [buska'ðor] nm (Internet) search
engine
buscar [bus'kar] vt to look for, search for,
seek ▷ vi to look, search, seek; **se busca
secretaria** secretary wanted
busque etc vb V buscar
búsqueda ['buskeða] nf = busca
busto ['busto] nm (Anat, Arte) bust
butaca [bu'taka] nf armchair; (de cine,
teatro) stall, seat
butano [bu'tano] nm butane (gas)
buzo ['buθo] nm diver
buzón [bu'θon] nm (en puerta) letter box;
(en calle) pillar box

b

C

C. abr (= centígrado) C; (compañía) Co.

C/ abr (= calle) St

cabal [ka'βal] adj (exacto) exact; (correcto) right, proper; (acabado) finished, complete; **cabales** nmpl: **no está en sus cabales** she isn't in her right mind

cábalas ['kaβalas] nfpl: **hacer ~** to guess

cabalgar [kaβal'ɣar] vt, vi to ride

cabalgata [kaβal'ɣata] nf procession

caballa [ka'βaʎa] nf mackerel

caballería [kaβaʎe'ria] nf mount; (Mil) cavalry

caballero [kaβa'ʎero] nm gentleman; (de la orden de caballería) knight; (trato directo) sir

caballete [kaβa'ʎete] nm (Arte) easel; (Tec) trestle

caballito [kaβa'ʎito] nm (caballo pequeño) small horse, pony; **caballitos** nmpl (en verbena) roundabout, merry-go-round

caballo [ka'βaʎo] nm horse; (Ajedrez) knight; (Naipes) queen; **ir en ~** to ride; **caballo de carreras** racehorse; **caballo de fuerza** o **vapor** horsepower

cabaña [ka'βaɲa] nf (casita) hut, cabin

cabecear [kaβeθe'ar] vt, vi to nod

cabecera [kaβe'θera] nf head; (Imprenta) headline

cabecilla [kaβe'θiʎa] nm ringleader

cabellera [kaβe'ʎera] nf (head of) hair; (de cometa) tail

cabello [ka'βeʎo] nm (tb: **~s**) hair; **cabello de ángel** confectionery and pastry filling made of pumpkin and syrup

caber [ka'βer] vi (entrar) to fit, go; **caben 3 más** there's room for 3 more

cabestrillo [kaβes'triʎo] nm sling

cabeza [ka'βeθa] nf head; (Pol) chief, leader; **cabeza de ajo** bulb of garlic; **cabeza de familia** head of the household; **cabeza rapada** skinhead; **cabezada** nf (golpe) butt; **dar cabezadas** to nod off; **cabezón, -ona**

adj (vino) heady; (fam: persona) pig-headed

cabida [ka'βiða] nf space

cabina [ka'βina] nf cabin; (de avión) cockpit; (de camión) cab; **cabina telefónica** telephone (BRIT) box o booth

cabizbajo, -a [kaβiθ'βaxo, a] adj crestfallen, dejected

cable ['kaβle] nm cable

cabo ['kaβo] nm (de objeto) end, extremity; (Mil) corporal; (Náut) rope, cable; (Geo) cape; **al ~ de 3 días** after 3 days; **llevar a ~** to carry out

cabra ['kaβra] nf goat

cabré etc vb V **caber**

cabrear [kaβre'ar] (fam) vt to bug; **cabrearse** vr (enfadarse) to fly off the handle

cabrito [ka'βrito] nm kid

cabrón [ka'βron] nm cuckold; (fam!) bastard (!)

caca ['kaka] (fam) nf pooh

cacahuete [kaka'wete] (ESP) nm peanut

cacao [ka'kao] nm cocoa; (Bot) cacao

cacarear [kakare'ar] vi (persona) to boast; (gallina) to crow

cacería [kaθe'ria] nf hunt

cacarizo, -a [kaka'riθo, a] (MÉX) adj pockmarked

cacerola [kaθe'rola] nf pan, saucepan

cachalote [katʃa'lote] nm (Zool) sperm whale

cacharro [ka'tʃarro] nm earthenware pot; **cacharros** nmpl pots and pans

cachear [katʃe'ar] vt to search, frisk

cachemir [katʃe'mir] nm cashmere

cachetada [katʃe'taða] (LAM: fam) nf (bofetada) slap

cachete [ka'tʃete] nm (Anat) cheek; (ESP: bofetada) slap (in the face)

cachivache [katʃi'βatʃe] nm (trasto) piece of junk; **cachivaches** nmpl junk sg

cacho ['katʃo] nm (small) bit; (LAM: cuerno) horn

cachondeo [katʃon'deo] (ESP: fam) nm farce, joke

cachondo, -a [ka'tʃondo, a] adj (Zool) on heat; (fam: sexualmente) randy; (: gracioso) funny

cachorro, -a [ka'tʃorro, a] nm/f (perro) pup, puppy; (león) cub

cachucha [ka'tʃutʃa] (MÉX: fam) nf cap

cacique [ka'θike] nm chief, local ruler; (Pol) local party boss

cactus ['kaktus] nm inv cactus

cada ['kaða] adj inv each; (antes de número) every; **~ día** each day, every day; **~ dos días** every other day; **~ uno/a** each one, every one; **~ vez más/menos** more and more/ less and less; **~ vez que ...** whenever, every time (that) ...; **uno de ~ diez** one out of every ten

cadáver [ka'ðaβer] nm (dead) body, corpse

cadena [ka'ðena] nf chain; (TV) channel; **trabajo en ~** assembly line work; **cadena montañosa** mountain range; **cadena perpetua** (Jur) life imprisonment

cadera [ka'ðera] nf hip

cadete [ka'ðete] nm cadet

caducar [kaðu'kar] vi to expire; **caduco, -a** adj expired; (persona) very old

caer [ka'er] vi to fall (down); **caerse** vr to fall (down); **me cae bien/mal** I get on well with him/I can't stand him; **~ en la cuenta** to realize; **dejar ~** to drop; **su cumpleaños cae en viernes** her birthday falls on a Friday

café [ka'fe] (pl **~s**) nm (bebida, planta) coffee; (lugar) café ▷ adj (MÉX: color) brown, tan; **café con leche** white coffee; **café negro** (LAM) black coffee; **café solo** (ESP) black coffee

cafetera [kafe'tera] nf coffee pot

cafetería [kafete'ria] nf (gen) café

cafetero, -a [kafe'tero, a] adj coffee cpd; **ser muy ~** to be a coffee addict

cafishio [ka'fiʃjo] (cs) nm pimp

cagar [ka'ɣar] (fam!) vt to bungle, mess up ▷ vi to have a shit (!)

caída [ka'iða] nf fall; (declive) slope; (disminución) fall, drop

caído, -a [ka'iðo, a] adj drooping

caiga etc vb V **caer**

caimán [kai'man] nm alligator

caja ['kaxa] nf box; (para reloj) case; (de ascensor) shaft; (Com) cashbox; (donde se hacen los pagos) cashdesk; (: en supermercado) checkout, till; **caja de ahorros** savings bank; **caja de cambios** gearbox; **caja de fusibles** fuse box; **caja fuerte** o **de caudales** safe, strongbox

cajero, -a [ka'xero, a] nm/f cashier; **cajero automático** cash dispenser

cajetilla [kaxe'tiʎa] nf (de cigarrillos) packet

cajón [ka'xon] nm big box; (de mueble) drawer

cajuela (MÉX) nf (Auto) boot (BRIT), trunk (US)

cal [kal] nf lime

cala ['kala] nf (Geo) cove, inlet; (de barco) hold

calabacín [kalaβa'θin] nm (Bot) baby marrow; (: más pequeño) courgette (BRIT), zucchini (US)

calabacita [kalaβa'θita] (MÉX) nf courgette (BRIT), zucchini (US)

calabaza [kala'βaθa] nf (Bot) pumpkin

calabozo [kala'βoθo] nm (cárcel) prison; (celda) cell

calada [ka'laða] (ESP) nf (de cigarrillo) puff

calado, -a [ka'laðo, a] adj (prenda) lace cpd ▷ nm (Náut) draught

calamar [kala'mar] nm squid no pl

calambre [ka'lambre] nm (Elec) shock

calar [ka'lar] vt to soak, drench; (penetrar) to pierce, penetrate; (comprender) to see through; (vela) to lower; **calarse** vr (Auto) to stall; **~se las gafas** to stick one's glasses on

calavera [kala'βera] nf skull

calcar [kal'kar] vt (reproducir) to trace; (imitar) to copy

calcetín [kalθe'tin] nm sock

calcio ['kalθjo] nm calcium

calcomanía [kalkoma'nia] nf transfer

calculador, a [kalkula'ðor, a] adj (persona) calculating; **calculadora** [kalkula'ðora] nf calculator

calcular [kalku'lar] vt (Mat) to calculate, compute; **~ que ...** to reckon that ...

caldera [kal'dera] nf boiler

calderilla [kalde'riʎa] nf (moneda) small change

caldo ['kaldo] nm stock; (consomé) consommé

calefacción [kalefak'θjon] nf heating; **calefacción central** central heating

calefón [kale'fon] (RPL) nm boiler

calendario [kalen'darjo] nm calendar

calentador [kalenta'ðor] nm heater

calentamiento [kalenta'mjento] nm (Deporte) warm-up; **calentamiento global** global warming

calentar [kalen'tar] vt to heat (up); **calentarse** vr to heat up, warm up; (fig: discusión etc) to get heated

calentón [kalen'ton] (RPL: fam) adj (sexualmente) horny, randy (BRIT)

calentura [kalen'tura] nf (Med) fever, (high) temperature

calesita [kale'sita] (RPL) nf merry-go-round, carousel

calibre [ka'liβre] nm (de cañón) calibre, bore; (diámetro) diameter; (fig) calibre

calidad [kali'ðað] nf quality; **de ~** quality cpd; **en ~ de** in the capacity of, as

cálido, -a ['kaliðo, a] adj hot; (fig) warm

caliente etc [ka'ljente] vb V **calentar** ▷ adj hot; (fig) fiery; (disputa) heated; (fam: cachondo) randy

calificación [kalifika'θjon] nf qualification; (de alumno) grade, mark

calificado, -a [kalifi'kaðo, a] (LAM) adj (competente) qualified; (obrero) skilled

calificar [kalifi'kar] vt to qualify; (alumno) to grade, mark; **~ de** to describe as

calima [ka'lima] nf (cerca del mar) mist

cáliz ['kaliθ] nm chalice

caliza [ka'liθa] nf limestone

callado, -a [ka'ʎaðo, a] adj quiet

callar [ka'ʎar] vt (asunto delicado) to keep quiet about, say nothing about; (persona, opinión) to silence ▷ vi to keep quiet, be silent; **callarse** vr to keep quiet, be silent; **¡cállate!** be quiet!, shut up!

calle ['kaʎe] nf street; (Deporte) lane; **~ arriba/abajo** up/down the street; **calle de sentido único** one-way street; **calle mayor** (ESP) high (BRIT) o main (US) street; **calle peatonal** pedestrianized o pedestrian street; **calle principal** (LAM) high (BRIT) o main (US) street; **callejear** vi to wander (about) the streets; **callejero, -a** adj cpd ▷ nm street map; **callejón** nm alley, passage; **callejón sin salida** cul-de-sac; **callejuela** nf side-street, alley

callista [ka'ʎista] nmf chiropodist

callo ['kaʎo] nm callus; (en el pie) corn; **callos** nmpl (Culin) tripe sg

calma ['kalma] nf calm

calmante [kal'mante] nm sedative, tranquillizer

calmar [kal'mar] vt to calm, calm down ▷ vi (tempestad) to abate; (mente etc) to become calm

calor [ka'lor] nm heat; (agradable) warmth; **hace ~** it's hot; **tener ~** to be hot

caloría [kalo'ria] nf calorie

calumnia [ka'lumnja] nf calumny, slander

caluroso, -a [kalu'roso, a] adj hot; (sin exceso) warm; (fig) enthusiastic

calva ['kalβa] nf bald patch; (en bosque) clearing

calvario [kal'βarjo] nm stations pl of the cross

calvicie [kal'βiθje] nf baldness

calvo, -a ['kalβo, a] adj bald; (terreno) bare, barren; (tejido) threadbare

calza ['kalθa] nf wedge, chock

calzada [kal'θaða] nf roadway, highway

calzado, -a [kal'θaðo, a] adj shod ▷ nm footwear

calzador [kalθa'ðor] nm shoehorn

calzar [kal'θar] vt (zapatos etc) to wear; (mueble) to put a wedge under; **calzarse** vr: **~se los zapatos** to put on one's shoes; **¿qué (número) calza?** what size do you take?

calzón [kal'θon] nm (ESP: pantalón corto) shorts; (LAM: ropa interior: de hombre) underpants, pants (BRIT), shorts (US); (: de mujer) panties, knickers (BRIT)

calzoncillos [kalθon'θiʎos] nmpl underpants

cama ['kama] nf bed; **hacer la ~** to make the bed; **cama individual/de matrimonio** single/double bed

camaleón [kamale'on] nm chameleon

cámara ['kamara] nf chamber; (habitación) room; (sala) hall; (Cine) cine camera; (fotográfica) camera; **cámara de aire** (ESP) inner tube; **cámara de comercio** chamber of commerce; **cámara de gas** gas chamber; **cámara digital** digital camera; **cámara frigorífica** cold-storage room

camarada [kama'raða] nmf comrade, companion

camarera [kama'rera] nf (en restaurante) waitress; (en casa, hotel) maid

camarero [kama'rero] nm waiter

camarógrafo, -a [kama'rografo, a] (LAM) nm/f cameraman/camerawoman

camarón [kama'ron] nm shrimp

camarote [kama'rote] nm cabin

cambiable [kam'bjaβle] adj (variable) changeable, variable; (intercambiable) interchangeable

cambiante [kam'bjante] adj variable

cambiar [kam'bjar] vt to change; (dinero) to exchange ▷ vi to change; **cambiarse** vr (mudarse) to move; (de ropa) to change; **~ de idea** u **opinión** to change one's mind; **~se de ropa** to change (one's clothes)

cambio ['kambjo] nm change; (trueque) exchange; (Com) rate of exchange; (oficina) bureau de change; (dinero menudo) small change; **a ~ de** in return o exchange for; **en ~** on the other hand; (en lugar de) instead; **cambio climático** climate change; **cambio de divisas** foreign exchange; **cambio de marchas** o **velocidades** gear lever

camelar [kame'lar] vt to sweet-talk

camello [ka'meʎo] nm camel; (fam: traficante) pusher

camerino [kame'rino] nm dressing room

camilla [ka'miʎa] nf (Med) stretcher

caminar [kami'nar] vi (marchar) to walk, go ▷ vt (recorrer) to cover, travel

caminata [kami'nata] nf long walk; (por el campo) hike

camino [ka'mino] nm way, road; (sendero) track; **a medio ~** halfway (there); **en ~** on the way, en route; **~ de** on the way to; **Camino de Santiago** Way of St James; **camino particular** private road

● **CAMINO DE SANTIAGO**
●
● The **Camino de Santiago** is a medieval
● pilgrim route stretching from the
● Pyrenees to Santiago de Compostela

- in north-west Spain, where tradition
- has it the body of the Apostle James is
- buried. Nowadays it is a popular tourist
- route as well as a religious one.

camión [ka'mjon] nm lorry (BRIT), truck
(US); (MÉX: autobús) bus; **camión cisterna**
tanker; **camión de la basura** dustcart,
refuse lorry; **camión de mudanzas** removal
(BRIT) o moving (US) van; **camionero, -a**
nm/f lorry o truck driver

camioneta [kamjo'neta] nf van, light
truck

camisa [ka'misa] nf shirt; (Bot) skin;
camisa de fuerza straitjacket

camiseta [kami'seta] nf (prenda) tee-
shirt; (ropa interior) vest; (de deportista) top

camisón [kami'son] nm nightdress,
nightgown

camorra [ka'morra] nf: **buscar ~** to look
for trouble

camote [ka'mote] nm (MÉX, CS: batata)
sweet potato, yam; (MÉX: bulbo) tuber, bulb;
(CS: fam: enamoramiento) crush

campamento [kampa'mento] nm camp

campana [kam'pana] nf bell;
campanada nf peal; **campanario** nm belfry

campanilla [kampa'niʎa] nf small bell

campaña [kam'paɲa] nf (Mil, Pol)
campaign; **campaña electoral** election
campaign

campechano, -a [kampe'tʃano, a] adj
(franco) open

campeón, -ona [kampe'on, ona]
nm/f champion; **campeonato** nm
championship

cámper ['kamper] (LAM) nm o f caravan
(BRIT), trailer (US)

campera [kam'pera] (RPL) nf anorak

campesino, -a [kampe'sino, a] adj
country cpd, rural; (gente) peasant cpd
▷ nm/f countryman/woman; (agricultor)
farmer

campestre [kam'pestre] adj country
cpd, rural

camping ['kampin] (pl **~s**) nm camping;
(lugar) campsite; **ir** o **estar de ~** to go
camping

campo ['kampo] nm (fuera de la ciudad)
country, countryside; (Agr, Elec) field; (de
fútbol) pitch; (de golf) course; (Mil) camp;
campo de batalla battlefield; **campo
de concentración** concentration camp;
campo de deportes sports ground, playing
field; **campo visual** field of vision, visual
field

camuflaje [kamu'flaxe] nm camouflage

cana ['kana] nf white o grey hair; **tener ~s**

to be going grey

Canadá [kana'ða] nm Canada;
canadiense adj, nmf Canadian ▷ nf fur-
lined jacket

canal [ka'nal] nm canal; (Geo) channel,
strait; (de televisión) channel; (de tejado)
gutter; **canal de Panamá** Panama Canal

canaleta [kana'leta] (LAM) nf (de tejado)
gutter

canalizar [kanali'θar] vt to channel

canalla [ka'naʎa] nf rabble, mob ▷ nm
swine

canapé [kana'pe] (pl **~s**) nm sofa, settee;
(Culin) canapé

Canarias [ka'narjas] nfpl (tb: **las Islas ~**)
the Canary Islands, the Canaries

canario, -a [ka'narjo, a] adj, nm/f
(native) of the Canary Isles ▷ nm (Zool)
canary

canasta [ka'nasta] nf (round) basket

canasto [ka'nasto] nm large basket

cancela [kan'θela] nf gate

cancelación [kanθela'θjon] nf
cancellation

cancelar [kanθe'lar] vt to cancel; (una
deuda) to write off

cáncer ['kanθer] nm (Med) cancer; **C~**
(Astrología) Cancer

cancha ['kantʃa] nf (de baloncesto) court;
(LAM: campo) pitch; **cancha de tenis** (LAM)
tennis court

canciller [kanθi'ʎer] nm chancellor

canción [kan'θjon] nf song; **canción de
cuna** lullaby

candado [kan'daðo] nm padlock

candente [kan'dente] adj red-hot;
(fig: tema) burning

candidato, -a [kandi'ðato, a] nm/f
candidate

cándido, -a ['kandiðo, a] adj simple;
naive

> No confundir **cándido** con la palabra
> inglesa candid.

candil [kan'dil] nm oil lamp; **candilejas**
nfpl (Teatro) footlights

canela [ka'nela] nf cinnamon

canelones [kane'lones] nmpl cannelloni

cangrejo [kan'grexo] nm crab

canguro [kan'guro] nm kangaroo; **hacer
de ~** to babysit

caníbal [ka'niβal] adj, nmf cannibal

canica [ka'nika] nf marble

canijo, -a [ka'nixo, a] adj frail, sickly

canilla [ka'niʎa] (RPL) nf tap (BRIT), faucet
(US)

canjear [kanxe'ar] vt to exchange

canoa [ka'noa] nf canoe

canon ['kanon] nm canon; (pensión) rent;

(*Com*) tax

canonizar [kanoni'θar] *vt* to canonize

canoso, -a [ka'noso, a] *adj* grey-haired

cansado, -a [kan'saðo, a] *adj* tired, weary; (*tedioso*) tedious, boring

cansancio [kan'sanθjo] *nm* tiredness, fatigue

cansar [kan'sar] *vt* (*fatigar*) to tire, tire out; (*aburrir*) to bore; (*fastidiar*) to bother; **cansarse** *vr* to tire, get tired; (*aburrirse*) to get bored

cantábrico, -a [kan'taβriko, a] *adj* Cantabrian

cantante [kan'tante] *adj* singing ▷ *nmf* singer

cantar [kan'tar] *vt* to sing ▷ *vi* to sing; (*insecto*) to chirp ▷ *nm* (*acción*) singing; (*canción*) song; (*poema*) poem

cántaro ['kantaro] *nm* pitcher, jug; **llover a ~s** to rain cats and dogs

cante ['kante] *nm* (*Mús*) Andalusian folk song; **cante jondo** flamenco singing

cantera [kan'tera] *nf* quarry

cantero [kan'tero] (*RPL*) *nm* (*arriate*) border

cantidad [kanti'ðað] *nf* quantity, amount; **~ de** lots of

cantimplora [kantim'plora] *nf* (*frasco*) water bottle, canteen

cantina [kan'tina] *nf* canteen; (*de estación*) buffet; (*LAM: bar*) bar

cantinero, -a [kanti'nero, a] (*MÉX*) *nm/f* barman/barmaid, bartender (*US*)

canto ['kanto] *nm* singing; (*canción*) song; (*borde*) edge, rim; (*de cuchillo*) back; **canto rodado** boulder

cantor, a [kan'tor, a] *nm/f* singer

canturrear [kanturre'ar] *vi* to sing softly

canuto [ka'nuto] *nm* (*tubo*) small tube; (*fam: droga*) joint

caña ['kaɲa] *nf* (*Bot: tallo*) stem, stalk; (*carrizo*) reed; (*vaso*) tumbler; (*de cerveza*) glass of beer; (*Anat*) shinbone; **caña de azúcar** sugar cane; **caña de pescar** fishing rod

cañada [ka'ɲaða] *nf* (*entre dos montañas*) gully, ravine; (*camino*) cattle track

cáñamo ['kaɲamo] *nm* hemp

cañería [kaɲe'ria] *nf* (*tubo*) pipe

caño ['kaɲo] *nm* (*tubo*) tube, pipe; (*de albañal*) sewer; (*Mús*) pipe; (*de fuente*) jet

cañón [ka'ɲon] *nm* (*Mil*) cannon; (*de fusil*) barrel; (*Geo*) canyon, gorge

caoba [ka'oβa] *nf* mahogany

caos ['kaos] *nm* chaos

capa ['kapa] *nf* cloak, cape; (*Geo*) layer, stratum; **capa de ozono** ozone layer

capacidad [kapaθi'ðað] *nf* (*medida*)

capacity; (*aptitud*) capacity, ability

caparazón [kapara'θon] *nm* shell

capataz [kapa'taθ] *nm* foreman

capaz [ka'paθ] *adj* able, capable; (*amplio*) capacious, roomy

capellán [kape'ʎan] *nm* chaplain; (*sacerdote*) priest

capicúa [kapi'kua] *adj inv* (*número, fecha*) reversible

capilla [ka'piʎa] *nf* chapel

capital [kapi'tal] *adj* capital ▷ *nm* (*Com*) capital ▷ *nf* (*ciudad*) capital; **capital social** share o authorized capital

capitalismo [kapita'lismo] *nm* capitalism; **capitalista** *adj, nmf* capitalist

capitán [kapi'tan] *nm* captain

capítulo [ka'pitulo] *nm* chapter

capó [ka'po] *nm* (*Auto*) bonnet

capón [ka'pon] *nm* (*gallo*) capon

capota [ka'pota] *nf* (*de mujer*) bonnet; (*Auto*) hood (*BRIT*), top (*US*)

capote [ka'pote] *nm* (*abrigo: de militar*) greatcoat; (*de torero*) cloak

capricho [ka'pritʃo] *nm* whim, caprice; **caprichoso, -a** *adj* capricious

Capricornio [kapri'kornjo] *nm* Capricorn

cápsula ['kapsula] *nf* capsule

captar [kap'tar] *vt* (*comprender*) to understand; (*Radio*) to pick up; (*atención, apoyo*) to attract

captura [kap'tura] *nf* capture; (*Jur*) arrest; **capturar** *vt* to capture; to arrest

capucha [ka'putʃa] *nf* hood, cowl

capuchón [kapu'tʃon] (*ESP*) *nm* (*de bolígrafo*) cap

capullo [ka'puʎo] *nm* (*Bot*) bud; (*Zool*) cocoon; (*fam*) idiot

caqui ['kaki] *nm* khaki

cara ['kara] *nf* (*Anat: de moneda*) face; (*de disco*) side; (*descaro*) boldness; **~ a** facing; **de ~** opposite, facing; **dar la ~** to face the consequences; **¿~ o cruz?** heads or tails?; **¡qué ~ (más dura)!** what a nerve!

Caracas [ka'rakas] *n* Caracas

caracol [kara'kol] *nm* (*Zool*) snail; (*concha*) (sea) shell

carácter [ka'rakter] (*pl* **caracteres**) *nm* character; **tener buen/mal ~** to be good natured/bad tempered

característica [karakte'ristika] *nf* characteristic

característico, -a [karakte'ristiko, a] *adj* characteristic

caracterizar [karakteri'θar] *vt* to characterize, typify

caradura [kara'ðura] *nmf*: **es un ~** he's got a nerve

carajillo [kara'xiʎo] *nm* coffee with a dash

of brandy

carajo [ka'raxo] (fam!) nm: **¡~!** shit! (!)

caramba [ka'ramba] excl good gracious!

caramelo [kara'melo] nm (dulce) sweet; (azúcar fundida) caramel

caravana [kara'βana] nf caravan; (fig) group; (Auto) tailback

carbón [kar'βon] nm coal; **papel ~** carbon paper

carbono [kar'βono] nm carbon

carburador [karβura'ðor] nm carburettor

carburante [karβu'rante] nm (para motor) fuel

carcajada [karka'xaða] nf (loud) laugh, guffaw

cárcel ['karθel] nf prison, jail; (Tec) clamp

carcoma [kar'koma] nf woodworm

cardar [kar'ðar] vt (pelo) to backcomb

cardenal [karðe'nal] nm (Rel) cardinal; (Med) bruise

cardíaco, -a [kar'ðiako, a] adj cardiac, heart cpd

cardinal [karði'nal] adj cardinal

cardo ['karðo] nm thistle

carecer [kare'θer] vi: **~ de** to lack, be in need of

carencia [ka'renθja] nf lack; (escasez) shortage; (Med) deficiency

careta [ka'reta] nf mask

carga ['karɣa] nf (peso, Elec) load; (de barco) cargo, freight; (Mil) charge; (responsabilidad) duty, obligation

cargado, -a [kar'ɣaðo, a] adj loaded; (Elec) live; (café, té) strong; (cielo) overcast

cargamento [karɣa'mento] nm (acción) loading; (mercancías) load, cargo

cargar [kar'ɣar] vt (barco, arma) to load; (Elec) to charge; (Com: algo en cuenta) to charge; (Inform) to load ▷ vi (Mil) to charge; (Auto) to load (up); **~ con** to pick up, carry away; (peso: fig) to shoulder, bear; **cargarse** vr (fam: estropear) to break; (: matar) to bump off

cargo ['karɣo] nm (puesto) post, office; (responsabilidad) duty, obligation; (Jur) charge; **hacerse ~ de** to take charge of o responsibility for

carguero [kar'ɣero] nm freighter, cargo boat; (avión) freight plane

Caribe [ka'riβe] nm: **el ~** the Caribbean; **del ~** Caribbean; **caribeño, -a** [kari'βeɲo, a] adj Caribbean

caricatura [karika'tura] nf caricature

caricia [ka'riθja] nf caress

caridad [kari'ðað] nf charity

caries ['karjes] nf inv tooth decay

cariño [ka'riɲo] nm affection, love; (caricia) caress; (en carta) love ...; **tener ~ a** to be fond

of; **cariñoso, -a** adj affectionate

carisma [ka'risma] nm charisma

caritativo, -a [karita'tiβo, a] adj charitable

cariz [ka'riθ] nm: **tener o tomar buen/mal ~** to look good/bad

carmín [kar'min] nm lipstick

carnal [kar'nal] adj carnal; **primo ~** first cousin

carnaval [karna'βal] nm carnival

carne ['karne] nf flesh; (Culin) meat; **se me pone la ~ de gallina sólo verlo** I get the creeps just seeing it; **carne de cerdo/cordero/ternera/vaca** pork/lamb/veal/beef; **carne de gallina** (fig) gooseflesh; **carne molida** (LAM) mince (BRIT), ground meat (US); **carne picada** (ESP, RPL) mince (BRIT), ground meat (US)

carné [kar'ne] (ESP) (pl ~s) nm: **~ de conducir** driving licence (BRIT), driver's license (US); **~ de identidad** identity card; **~ de socio** membership card

carnero [kar'nero] nm sheep, ram; (carne) mutton

carnet [kar'ne] (ESP) (pl ~s) nm = **carné**

carnicería [karniθe'ria] nf butcher's (shop); (fig: matanza) carnage, slaughter

carnicero, -a [karni'θero, a] adj carnivorous ▷ nm/f butcher; (carnívoro) carnivore

carnívoro, -a [kar'niβoro, a] adj carnivorous

caro, -a ['karo, a] adj dear; (Com) dear, expensive ▷ adv dear, dearly

carpa ['karpa] nf (pez) carp; (de circo) big top; (LAM: tienda de campaña) tent

carpeta [kar'peta] nf folder, file; **carpeta de anillas** ring binder

carpintería [karpinte'ria] nf carpentry, joinery; **carpintero** nm carpenter

carraspear [karraspe'ar] vi to clear one's throat

carraspera [karras'pera] nf hoarseness

carrera [ka'rrera] nf (acción) run(ning); (espacio recorrido) run; (competición) race; (trayecto) course; (profesión) career; (licenciatura) degree; **a la ~** at (full) speed; **carrera de obstáculos** (Deporte) steeplechase

carrete [ka'rrete] nm reel, spool; (Tec) coil

carretera [karre'tera] nf (main) road, highway; **carretera de circunvalación** ring road; **carretera nacional** ≈ A road (BRIT), ≈ state highway (US)

carretilla [karre'tiʎa] nf trolley; (Agr) (wheel)barrow

carril [ka'rril] nm furrow; (de autopista) lane; (Ferro) rail; **carril-bici** cycle lane

carrito [ka'rrito] nm trolley

carro ['karro] nm cart, wagon; (Mil) tank; (LAM: coche) car; **carro patrulla** (LAM) patrol o panda (BRIT) car

carrocería [karroθe'ria] nf bodywork, coachwork

carroña [ka'rroɲa] nf carrion no pl

carroza [ka'rroθa] nf (carruaje) coach

carrusel [karru'sel] nm merry-go-round, roundabout

carta ['karta] nf letter; (Culin) menu; (naipe) card; (mapa) map; (Jur) document; **carta certificada/urgente** registered/special-delivery letter

cartabón [karta'βon] nm set square

cartel [kar'tel] nm (anuncio) poster, placard; (Escol) wall chart; (Com) cartel; **cartelera** nf hoarding, billboard; (en periódico etc) entertainments guide; **"en cartelera"** "showing"

cartera [kar'tera] nf (de bolsillo) wallet; (de colegial, cobrador) satchel; (de señora) handbag; (para documentos) briefcase; (Com) portfolio; **ocupa la ~ de Agricultura** she is Minister of Agriculture

carterista [karte'rista] nmf pickpocket

cartero [kar'tero] nm postman

cartilla [kar'tiʎa] nf primer, first reading book; **cartilla de ahorros** savings book

cartón [kar'ton] nm cardboard; **cartón piedra** papier-mâché

cartucho [kar'tutʃo] nm (Mil) cartridge

cartulina [kartu'lina] nf card

casa ['kasa] nf house; (hogar) home; (Com) firm, company; **en ~** at home; **casa consistorial** town hall; **casa de campo** country house; **casa de huéspedes** boarding house; **casa de socorro** first aid post; **casa rodante** (cs) caravan (BRIT), trailer (US)

casado, -a [ka'saðo, a] adj married ⊳ nm/f married man/woman

casar [ka'sar] vt to marry; (Jur) to quash,

annul; **casarse** vr to marry, get married

cascabel [kaska'βel] nm (small) bell

cascada [kas'kaða] nf waterfall

cascanueces [kaska'nweθes] nm inv nutcrackers pl

cascar [kas'kar] vt to crack, split, break (open); **cascarse** vr to crack, split, break (open)

cáscara ['kaskara] nf (de huevo, fruta seca) shell; (de fruta) skin; (de limón) peel

casco ['kasko] nm (de bombero, soldado) helmet; (Náut: de barco) hull; (Zool: de caballo) hoof; (botella) empty bottle; (de ciudad): **el ~ antiguo** the old part; **el ~ urbano** the town centre; **los ~s azules** the UN peace-keeping force, the blue berets

cascote [kas'kote] nm rubble

caserío [kase'rio] (ESP) nm farmhouse; (casa) country mansion

casero, -a [ka'sero, a] adj (pan etc) home-made ⊳ nm/f (propietario) landlord/lady; **ser muy ~** to be home-loving; **"comida casera"** "home cooking"

caseta [ka'seta] nf hut; (para bañista) cubicle; (de feria) stall

casete [ka'sete] nm o f cassette

casi ['kasi] adv almost, nearly; **~ nada** hardly anything; **~ nunca** hardly ever, almost never; **~ te caes** you almost fell

casilla [ka'siʎa] nf (casita) hut, cabin; (Ajedrez) square; (para cartas) pigeonhole; **casilla de correo** (LAM) P.O. Box; **casillero** nm (para cartas) pigeonholes pl

casino [ka'sino] nm club; (de juego) casino

caso ['kaso] nm case; **en ~ de** in case of; **en ~ de que ...** in case ...; **el ~ es que ...** the fact is that ...; **en ese/todo ~** in that/any case; **hacer ~ a** to pay attention to; **venir al ~** to be relevant

caspa ['kaspa] nf dandruff

cassette [ka'sete] nm o f = **casete**

castaña [kas'taɲa] nf chestnut

castaño, -a [kas'taɲo, a] adj chestnut(-coloured), brown ⊳ nm chestnut tree

castañuelas [kasta'ɲwelas] nfpl castanets

castellano, -a [kaste'ʎano, a] adj, nm/f Castilian ⊳ nm (Ling) Castilian, Spanish

castigar [kasti'ɣar] vt to punish; (Deporte) to penalize; **castigo** nm punishment; (Deporte) penalty

Castilla [kas'tiʎa] nf Castille

castillo [kas'tiʎo] nm castle

castizo, -a [kas'tiθo, a] adj (Ling) pure

casto, -a ['kasto, a] adj chaste, pure

castor [kas'tor] nm beaver

castrar [kas'trar] vt to castrate

casual [ka'swal] *adj* chance, accidental
▌No confundir **casual** con la palabra
inglesa *casual*.

casualidad *nf* chance, accident; (*combinación de circunstancias*) coincidence; **da la casualidad de que ...** it (just) so happens that ...; **¡qué casualidad!** what a coincidence!

cataclismo [kata'klismo] *nm* cataclysm

catador, a [kata'ðor, a] *nm/f* wine taster

catalán, -ana [kata'lan, ana] *adj, nm/f* Catalan ▷ *nm* (*Ling*) Catalan

catalizador [kataliθa'ðor] *nm* catalyst; (*Auto*) catalytic convertor

catalogar [katalo'ɣar] *vt* to catalogue; **~ a algn (de)** (*fig*) to categorize sb (as)

catálogo [ka'taloɣo] *nm* catalogue

Cataluña [kata'luɲa] *nf* Catalonia

catar [ka'tar] *vt* to taste, sample

catarata [kata'rata] *nf* (*Geo*) waterfall; (*Med*) cataract

catarro [ka'tarro] *nm* catarrh; (*constipado*) cold

catástrofe [ka'tastrofe] *nf* catastrophe

catear [kate'ar] (*fam*) *vt* (*examen, alumno*) to fail

cátedra ['kateðra] *nf* (*Univ*) chair, professorship

catedral [kate'ðral] *nf* cathedral

catedrático, -a [kate'ðratiko, a] *nm/f* professor

categoría [kateɣo'ria] *nf* category; (*rango*) rank, standing; (*calidad*) quality; **de ~** (*hotel*) top-class

cateto, -a ['kateto, a] (*ESP: pey*) *nm/f* peasant

catolicismo [katoli'θismo] *nm* Catholicism

católico, -a [ka'toliko, a] *adj, nm/f* Catholic

catorce [ka'torθe] *num* fourteen

cauce ['kauθe] *nm* (*de río*) riverbed; (*fig*) channel

caucho ['kautʃo] (*ESP*) *nm* rubber

caudal [kau'ðal] *nm* (*de río*) volume, flow; (*fortuna*) wealth; (*abundancia*) abundance

caudillo [kau'ðiʎo] *nm* leader, chief

causa ['kausa] *nf* cause; (*razón*) reason; (*Jur*) lawsuit, case; **a ~ de** because of; **causar** [kau'sar] *vt* to cause

cautela [kau'tela] *nf* caution, cautiousness; **cauteloso, -a** *adj* cautious, wary

cautivar [kauti'βar] *vt* to capture; (*atraer*) to captivate

cautiverio [kauti'βerjo] *nm* captivity

cautividad [kautiβi'ðað] *nf* = **cautiverio**

cautivo, -a [kau'tiβo, a] *adj, nm/f* captive

cauto, -a ['kauto, a] *adj* cautious, careful

cava ['kaβa] *nm* champagne-type wine

cavar [ka'βar] *vt* to dig

caverna [ka'βerna] *nf* cave, cavern

cavidad [kaβi'ðað] *nf* cavity

cavilar [kaβi'lar] *vt* to ponder

cayendo *etc vb* V **caer**

caza ['kaθa] *nf* (*acción: gen*) hunting; (: *con fusil*) shooting; (*una caza*) hunt, chase; (*de animales*) game ▷ *nm* (*Aviac*) fighter; **ir de ~** to go hunting; **caza mayor** game hunting; **cazador, a** [kaθa'ðor, a] *nm/f* hunter; **cazadora** *nf* jacket; **cazar** [ka'θar] *vt* to hunt; (*perseguir*) to chase; (*prender*) to catch

cazo ['kaθo] *nm* saucepan

cazuela [ka'θwela] *nf* (*vasija*) pan; (*guisado*) casserole

CD *nm abr* (= *compact disc*) CD

CD-ROM [θeðe'rom] *nm abr* CD-ROM

CE *nf abr* (= *Comunidad Europea*) EC

cebada [θe'βaða] *nf* barley

cebar [θe'βar] *vt* (*animal*) to fatten (up); (*anzuelo*) to bait; (*Mil, Tec*) to prime

cebo ['θeβo] *nm* (*para animales*) feed, food; (*para peces, fig*) bait; (*de arma*) charge

cebolla [θe'βoʎa] *nf* onion; **cebolleta** *nf* spring onion

cebra ['θeβra] *nf* zebra

cecear [θeθe'ar] *vi* to lisp

ceder [θe'ðer] *vt* to hand over, give up, part with ▷ *vi* (*renunciar*) to give in, yield; (*disminuir*) to diminish, decline; (*romperse*) to give way

cedro ['θeðro] *nm* cedar

cédula ['θeðula] *nf* certificate, document; **cédula de identidad** (*LAM*) identity card; **cédula electoral** (*LAM*) ballot

cegar [θe'ɣar] *vt* to blind; (*tubería etc*) to block up, stop up ▷ *vi* to go blind; **cegarse** *vr*: **~se (de)** to be blinded (by)

ceguera [θe'ɣera] *nf* blindness

ceja ['θexa] *nf* eyebrow

cejar [θe'xar] *vi* (*fig*) to back down

celada [θe'laða] *nf* cell

celador, a [θela'ðor, a] *nm/f* (*de edificio*) watchman; (*de museo etc*) attendant

celda ['θelda] *nf* cell

celebración [θeleβra'θjon] *nf* celebration

celebrar [θele'βrar] *vt* to celebrate; (*alabar*) to praise ▷ *vi* to be glad; **celebrarse** *vr* to occur, take place

célebre ['θelebre] *adj* famous

celebridad [θeleβri'ðað] *nf* fame; (*persona*) celebrity

celeste [θe'leste] *adj* (*azul*) sky-blue

celestial [θeles'tjal] *adj* celestial, heavenly

celo¹ ['θelo] *nm* zeal; (*Rel*) fervour; (*Zool*): **en ~** on heat; **celos** *nmpl* jealousy *sg*; **dar ~s a algn** to make sb jealous; **tener ~s** to be jealous

celo²® ['θelo] nm Sellotape®

celofán [θelo'fan] nm cellophane

celoso, -a [θe'loso, a] adj jealous; (trabajador) zealous

celta ['θelta] adj Celtic ▷ nmf Celt

célula ['θelula] nf cell

celulitis [θelu'litis] nf cellulite

cementerio [θemen'terjo] nm cemetery, graveyard

cemento [θe'mento] nm cement; (hormigón) concrete; (LAM: cola) glue

cena ['θena] nf evening meal, dinner; **cenar** [θe'nar] vt to have for dinner ▷ vi to have dinner

cenicero [θeni'θero] nm ashtray

ceniza [θe'niθa] nf ash, ashes pl

censo ['θenso] nm census; **censo electoral** electoral roll

censura [θen'sura] nf (Pol) censorship; **censurar** [θensu'rar] vt (idea) to censure; (cortar: película) to censor

centella [θen'teʎa] nf spark

centenar [θente'nar] nm hundred

centenario, -a [θente'narjo, a] adj centenary; hundred-year-old ▷ nm centenary

centeno [θen'teno] nm (Bot) rye

centésimo, -a [θen'tesimo, a] adj hundredth

centígrado [θen'tiɣraðo] adj centigrade

centímetro [θen'timetro] nm centimetre (BRIT), centimeter (US)

céntimo ['θentimo] nm cent

centinela [θenti'nela] nm sentry, guard

centollo [θen'toʎo] nm spider crab

central [θen'tral] adj central ▷ nf head office; (Tec) plant; (Tel) exchange; **central eléctrica** power station; **central nuclear** nuclear power station; **central telefónica** telephone exchange

centralita [θentra'lita] nf switchboard

centralizar [θentrali'θar] vt to centralize

centrar [θen'trar] vt to centre

céntrico, -a ['θentriko, a] adj central

centrifugar [θentrifu'ɣar] vt to spin-dry

centro ['θentro] nm centre; **centro comercial** shopping centre; **centro de atención al cliente** call centre; **centro de salud** health centre; **centro escolar** school; **centro juvenil** youth club; **centro turístico** (lugar muy visitado) tourist centre; **centro urbano** urban area, city

centroamericano, -a [θentroameri'kano, a] adj, nm/f Central American

ceñido, -a [θe'niðo, a] adj (chaqueta, pantalón) tight(-fitting)

ceñir [θe'nir] vt (rodear) to encircle, surround; (ajustar) to fit (tightly)

ceño ['θeno] nm frown, scowl; **fruncir el ~** to frown, knit one's brow

cepillar [θepi'ʎar] vt to brush; (madera) to plane (down)

cepillo [θe'piʎo] nm brush; (para madera) plane; **cepillo de dientes** toothbrush

cera ['θera] nf wax

cerámica [θe'ramika] nf pottery; (arte) ceramics

cerca ['θerka] nf fence ▷ adv near, nearby, close; **~ de** near, close to

cercanías [θerka'nias] nfpl (afueras) outskirts, suburbs

cercano, -a [θer'kano, a] adj close, near

cercar [θer'kar] vt to fence in; (rodear) to surround

cerco ['θerko] nm (Agr) enclosure; (LAM: valla) fence; (Mil) siege

cerdo, -a ['θerðo, a] nm/f pig/sow

cereal [θere'al] nm cereal; **cereales** nmpl cereals, grain sg

cerebro [θe'reβro] nm brain; (fig) brains pl

ceremonia [θere'monja] nf ceremony; **ceremonioso, -a** adj ceremonious

cereza [θe'reθa] nf cherry

cerilla [θe'riʎa] nf (fósforo) match

cerillo [θe'riʎo] (MÉX) nm match

cero ['θero] nm nothing, zero

cerquillo [θer'kiʎo] (CAM, RPL) nm fringe (BRIT), bangs pl (US)

cerrado, -a [θe'rraðo, a] adj closed, shut; (con llave) locked; (tiempo) cloudy, overcast; (curva) sharp; (acento) thick, broad

cerradura [θerra'ðura] nf (acción) closing; (mecanismo) lock

cerrajero [θerra'xero] nm locksmith

cerrar [θe'rrar] vt to close, shut; (paso, carretera) to close; (grifo) to turn off; (cuenta, negocio) to close ▷ vi to close, shut; (noche) to come down; **cerrarse** vr to close, shut; **~ con llave** to lock; **~ un trato** to strike a bargain

cerro ['θerro] nm hill

cerrojo [θe'rroxo] nm (herramienta) bolt; (de puerta) latch

certamen [θer'tamen] nm competition, contest

certero, -a [θer'tero, a] adj (gen) accurate

certeza [θer'teθa] nf certainty

certidumbre [θerti'ðumβre] nf = **certeza**

certificado, -a [θertifi'kaðo, a] adj (carta, paquete) registered; (aprobado) certified ▷ nm certificate; **certificado médico** medical certificate

certificar [θertifi'kar] vt (asegurar, atestar) to certify

cervatillo [θerβa'tiʎo] nm fawn

cervecería [θerβeθe'ria] nf (fábrica) brewery; (bar) public house, pub

cerveza [θer'βeθa] nf beer

cesar [θe'sar] vi to cease, stop ▷ vt (funcionario) to remove from office

cesárea [θe'sarea] nf (Med) Caesarean operation o section

cese ['θese] nm (de trabajo) dismissal; (de pago) suspension

césped ['θespeð] nm grass, lawn

cesta ['θesta] nf basket

cesto ['θesto] nm (large) basket, hamper

cfr abr (= confróntese) cf.

chabacano, -a [tʃaβa'kano, a] adj vulgar, coarse

chabola [tʃa'βola] (ESP) nf shack; **barrio de chabolas** shanty town

chacal [tʃa'kal] nm jackal

chacha ['tʃatʃa] (fam) nf maid

cháchara ['tʃatʃara] nf chatter; **estar de ~** to chatter away

chacra ['tʃakra] (CS) nf smallholding

chafa ['tʃafa] (MÉX: fam) adj useless, dud

chafar [tʃa'far] vt (aplastar) to crush; (plan etc) to ruin

chal [tʃal] nm shawl

chalado, -a [tʃa'lado, a] (fam) adj crazy

chalé [tʃa'le] (pl ~s) nm villa, ≈ detached house

chaleco [tʃa'leko] nm waistcoat, vest (US); **chaleco de seguridad** (Aut) reflective safety vest; **chaleco salvavidas** life jacket

chalet [tʃa'le] (pl ~s) nm = **chalé**

chamaco, -a (MÉX) [tʃa'mako, a] nm/f (niño) kid

chambear [tʃambe'ar] (MÉX: fam) vi to earn one's living

champán [tʃam'pan] nm champagne

champiñón [tʃampi'ɲon] nm mushroom

champú [tʃam'pu] (pl ~es, ~s) nm shampoo

chamuscar [tʃamus'kar] vt to scorch, sear, singe

chance ['tʃanθe] (LAM) nm chance

chancho, -a ['tʃantʃo, a] (LAM) nm/f pig

chanchullo [tʃan'tʃuʎo] (fam) nm fiddle

chandal [tʃan'dal] nm tracksuit

chantaje [tʃan'taxe] nm blackmail

chapa ['tʃapa] nf (de metal) plate, sheet; (de madera) board, panel; (RPL Auto) number (BRIT) o license (US) plate; **chapado, -a** adj: **chapado en oro** gold-plated

chaparrón [tʃapa'rron] (MÉX) nm downpour, cloudburst

chaperón [tʃape'ron] (MÉX) nm: **hacer de ~** to play gooseberry; **chaperona** (LAM) nf: **hacer de chaperona** to play gooseberry

chapopote [tʃapo'pote] (MÉX) nm tar

chapulín [tʃapu'lin] (MÉX, CAM) nm grasshopper

chapurrear [tʃapurre'ar] vt (idioma) to speak badly

chapuza [tʃa'puθa] nf botched job

chapuzón [tʃapu'θon] nm: **darse un ~** to go for a dip

chaqueta [tʃa'keta] nf jacket

chaquetón [tʃake'ton] nm long jacket

charca ['tʃarka] nf pond, pool

charco ['tʃarko] nm pool, puddle

charcutería [tʃarkute'ria] nf (tienda) shop selling chiefly pork meat products; (productos) cooked pork meats pl

charla ['tʃarla] nf talk, chat; (conferencia) lecture; **charlar** [tʃar'lar] vi to talk, chat; **charlatán, -ana** [tʃarla'tan, ana] nm/f (hablador) chatterbox; (estafador) trickster

charol [tʃa'rol] nm varnish; (cuero) patent leather

charola [tʃa'rola] (MÉX) nf tray

charro ['tʃarro, a] (MÉX) nm typical Mexican

chasco ['tʃasko] nm (desengaño) disappointment

chasis ['tʃasis] nm inv chassis

chasquido [tʃas'kiðo] nm crack; click

chat [tʃat] nm (Internet) chat room

chatarra [tʃa'tarra] nf scrap (metal)

chatear [tʃate'ar] vi (Internet) to chat

chato, -a ['tʃato, a] adj flat; (nariz) snub

chaucha ['tʃautʃa] (RPL) nf runner (BRIT) o pole (US) bean

chaval, a [tʃa'βal, a] (ESP) nm/f kid, lad/lass

chavo, -a ['tʃaβo] (MÉX: fam) nm/f guy/girl

checar [tʃe'kar] (MÉX) vt: **~ tarjeta** (al entrar) to clock in o on; (: al salir) to clock off o out

checo, -a ['tʃeko, a] adj, nm/f Czech ▷ nm (Ling) Czech

checoslovaco, -a [tʃekoslo'βako, a] adj, nm/f Czech, Czechoslovak

Checoslovaquia [tʃekoslo'βakja] nf (Hist) Czechoslovakia

cheque ['tʃeke] nm cheque (BRIT), check (US); **cobrar un ~** to cash a cheque; **cheque al portador** cheque payable to bearer; **cheque de viaje** traveller's cheque (BRIT), traveler's check (US); **cheque en blanco** blank cheque

chequeo [tʃe'keo] nm (Med) check-up; (Auto) service

chequera [tʃe'kera] (LAM) nf chequebook (BRIT), checkbook (US)

chévere ['tʃeβere] (LAM: fam) adj great

chícharo ['tʃitʃaro] (MÉX, CAM) nm pea

chichón [tʃi'tʃon] nm bump, lump

chicle ['tʃikle] nm chewing gum

chico, -a ['tʃiko, a] adj small, little ▷ nm/f (niño) child; (muchacho) boy/girl

chiflado, -a [tʃi'flaðo, a] adj crazy

chiflar [tʃi'flar] vt to hiss, boo

chilango, -a [tʃi'lango, a] (MÉX) adj of o from Mexico City

Chile ['tʃile] nm Chile; **chileno, -a** adj, nm/f Chilean

chile ['tʃile] nm chilli pepper

chillar [tʃi'ʎar] vi (persona) to yell, scream; (animal salvaje) to howl; (cerdo) to squeal

chillido [tʃi'ʎiðo] nm (de persona) yell, scream; (de animal) howl

chimenea [tʃime'nea] nf chimney; (hogar) fireplace

China ['tʃina] nf (tb: **la ~**) China

chinche ['tʃintʃe] nf (insecto) (bed)bug; (Tec) drawing pin (BRIT), thumbtack (US) ▷ nmf nuisance, pest

chincheta [tʃin'tʃeta] nf drawing pin (BRIT), thumbtack (US)

chingada [tʃin'gaða] (MÉX: fam!) nf: **hijo de la ~** bastard

chino, -a ['tʃino, a] adj, nm/f Chinese ▷ nm (Ling) Chinese

chipirón [tʃipi'ron] nm (Zool, Culin) squid

Chipre ['tʃipre] nf Cyprus; **chipriota** adj, nmf Cypriot

chiquillo, -a [tʃi'kiʎo, a] nm/f (fam) kid

chirimoya [tʃiri'moja] nf custard apple

chiringuito [tʃirin'ɣito] nm small open-air bar

chiripa [tʃi'ripa] nf fluke

chirriar [tʃi'rrjar] vi to creak, squeak

chirrido [tʃi'rriðo] nm creak(ing), squeak(ing)

chisme ['tʃisme] nm (habladurías) piece of gossip; (fam: objeto) thingummyjig

chismoso, -a [tʃis'moso, a] adj gossiping ▷ nm/f gossip

chispa ['tʃispa] nf spark; (fig) sparkle; (ingenio) wit; (fam) drunkenness

chispear [tʃispe'ar] vi (lloviznar) to drizzle

chiste ['tʃiste] nm joke, funny story

chistoso, -a [tʃis'toso, a] adj funny, amusing

chivo, -a ['tʃiβo, a] nm/f (billy-/nanny-) goat; **chivo expiatorio** scapegoat

chocante [tʃo'kante] adj startling; (extraño) odd; (ofensivo) shocking

chocar [tʃo'kar] vi (coches etc) to collide, crash ▷ vt to shock; (sorprender) to startle; **~ con** to collide with; (fig) to run into, run up against; **¡chócala!** (fam) put it there!

chochear [tʃotʃe'ar] vi to be senile

chocho, -a ['tʃotʃo, a] adj doddering, senile; (fig) soft, doting

choclo ['tʃoklo] (cs) nm (grano) sweet corn; (mazorca) corn on the cob

chocolate [tʃoko'late] adj, nm chocolate; **chocolatina** nf chocolate

chofer [tʃo'fer] nm = **chófer**

chófer ['tʃofer] nm driver

chollo ['tʃoʎo] (ESP: fam) nm bargain, snip

choque etc ['tʃoke] vb V **chocar** ▷ nm (impacto) impact; (golpe) jolt; (Auto) crash; (fig) conflict; **choque frontal** head-on collision

chorizo [tʃo'riθo] nm hard pork sausage, (type of) salami

chorrada [tʃo'rraða] (ESP: fam) nf: **¡es una ~!** that's crap! (!); **decir ~s** to talk crap (!)

chorrear [tʃorre'ar] vi to gush (out), spout (out); (gotear) to drip, trickle

chorro ['tʃorro] nm jet; (fig) stream

choza ['tʃoθa] nf hut, shack

chubasco [tʃu'βasko] nm squall

chubasquero [tʃuβas'kero] nm lightweight raincoat

chuchería [tʃutʃe'ria] nf trinket

chuleta [tʃu'leta] nf chop, cutlet

chulo ['tʃulo] nm (de prostituta) pimp

chupaleta [tʃupa'leta] (MÉX) nf lollipop

chupar [tʃu'par] vt to suck; (absorber) to absorb; **chuparse** vr to grow thin

chupete [tʃu'pete] (ESP, cs) nm dummy (BRIT), pacifier (US)

chupetín [tʃupe'tin] (RPL) nm lollipop

chupito [tʃu'pito] (fam) nm shot

chupón [tʃu'pon] nm (piruleta) lollipop; (LAM: chupete) dummy (BRIT), pacifier (US)

churro ['tʃurro] nm (type of) fritter

chusma ['tʃusma] nf rabble, mob

chutar [tʃu'tar] vi to shoot (at goal)

Cía abr (= compañía) Co.

cianuro [θja'nuro] nm cyanide

cibercafé [θiβerka'fe] nm cybercafé

cibernauta [θiβer'nauta] nmf web surfer, Internet user

ciberterrorista [θiβerterro'rista] nmf cyberterrorist

cicatriz [θika'triθ] nf scar; **cicatrizarse** vr to heal (up), form a scar

ciclismo [θi'klismo] nm cycling

ciclista [θi'klista] adj cycle cpd ▷ nmf cyclist

ciclo ['θiklo] nm cycle; **cicloturismo** nm touring by bicycle

ciclón [θi'klon] nm cyclone

ciego, -a ['θjeɣo, a] adj blind ▷ nm/f blind man/woman

cielo ['θjelo] nm sky; (Rel) heaven; **¡~s!** good heavens!

ciempiés [θjem'pjes] nm inv centipede

cien [θjen] *num* V **ciento**

ciencia ['θjenθja] *nf* science; **ciencias** *nfpl* (*Escol*) science *sg*; **ciencia-ficción** *nf* science fiction

científico, -a [θjen'tifiko, a] *adj* scientific ▷ *nm/f* scientist

ciento ['θjento] *num* hundred; **pagar al 10 por ~** to pay at 10 per cent; V *tb* **cien**

cierre *etc* ['θjerre] *vb* V **cerrar** ▷ *nm* closing, shutting; (*con llave*) locking; (*LAM: cremallera*) zip (fastener)

cierro *etc vb* V **cerrar**

cierto, -a ['θjerto, a] *adj* sure, certain; (*un tal*) a certain; (*correcto*) right, correct; **por ~** by the way; **~ hombre** a certain man; **ciertas personas** certain o some people; **sí, es ~** yes, that's correct

ciervo ['θjerβo] *nm* deer; (*macho*) stag

cifra ['θifra] *nf* number; (*secreta*) code; **cifrar** [θi'frar] *vt* to code, write in code

cigala [θi'xala] *nf* Norway lobster

cigarra [θi'xarra] *nf* cicada

cigarrillo [θixa'rriʎo] *nm* cigarette

cigarro [θi'xarro] *nm* cigarette; (*puro*) cigar

cigüeña [θi'xweɲa] *nf* stork

cilíndrico, -a [θi'lindriko, a] *adj* cylindrical

cilindro [θi'lindro] *nm* cylinder

cima ['θima] *nf* (*de montaña*) top, peak; (*de árbol*) top; (*fig*) height

cimentar [θimen'tar] *vt* to lay the foundations of; (*fig: fundar*) to found

cimiento [θi'mjento] *nm* foundation

cincel [θin'θel] *nm* chisel

cinco ['θinko] *num* five

cincuenta [θin'kwenta] *num* fifty

cine ['θine] *nm* cinema; **cinematográfico, -a** [θinemato'xrafiko, a] *adj* cine-, film *cpd*

cínico, -a ['θiniko, a] *adj* cynical ▷ *nm/f* cynic

cinismo [θi'nismo] *nm* cynicism

cinta ['θinta] *nf* band, strip; (*de tela*) ribbon; (*película*) reel; (*de máquina de escribir*) ribbon; **cinta adhesiva/aislante** sticky/ insulating tape; **cinta de vídeo** videotape; **cinta magnetofónica** tape; **cinta métrica** tape measure

cintura [θin'tura] *nf* waist

cinturón [θintu'ron] *nm* belt; **cinturón de seguridad** safety belt

ciprés [θi'pres] *nm* cypress (tree)

circo ['θirko] *nm* circus

circuito [θir'kwito] *nm* circuit

circulación [θirkula'θjon] *nf* circulation; (*Auto*) traffic

circular [θirku'lar] *adj*, *nf* circular ▷ *vi*, *vt* to circulate ▷ *vi* (*Auto*) to drive; **"circule por la derecha"** "keep (to the) right"

círculo ['θirkulo] *nm* circle; **círculo vicioso** vicious circle

circunferencia [θirkunfe'renθja] *nf* circumference

circunstancia [θirkuns'tanθja] *nf* circumstance

cirio ['θirjo] *nm* (wax) candle

ciruela [θi'rwela] *nf* plum; **ciruela pasa** prune

cirugía [θiru'xia] *nf* surgery; **cirugía estética** o **plástica** plastic surgery

cirujano [θiru'xano] *nm* surgeon

cisne ['θisne] *nm* swan

cisterna [θis'terna] *nf* cistern, tank

cita ['θita] *nf* appointment, meeting; (*de novios*) date; (*referencia*) quotation

citación [θita'θjon] *nf* (*Jur*) summons *sg*

citar [θi'tar] *vt* (*gen*) to make an appointment with; (*Jur*) to summons; (*un autor, texto*) to quote; **citarse** *vr*: **se ~on en el cine** they arranged to meet at the cinema

cítricos ['θitrikos] *nmpl* citrus fruit(s)

ciudad [θju'ðað] *nf* town; (*más grande*) city; **ciudadano, -a** *nm/f* citizen

cívico, -a ['θiβiko, a] *adj* civic

civil [θi'βil] *adj* civil ▷ *nm* (*guardia*) policeman; **civilización** [θiβiliθa'θjon] *nf* civilization; **civilizar** [θiβili'θar] *vt* to civilize

cizaña [θi'θaɲa] *nf* (*fig*) discord

cl. *abr* (= *centilitro*) cl.

clamor [kla'mor] *nm* clamour, protest

clandestino, -a [klandes'tino, a] *adj* clandestine; (*Pol*) underground

clara ['klara] *nf* (*de huevo*) egg white

claraboya [klara'βoja] *nf* skylight

clarear [klare'ar] *vi* (*el día*) to dawn; (*el cielo*) to clear up, brighten up; **clarearse** *vr* to be transparent

claridad [klari'ðað] *nf* (*de día*) brightness; (*de estilo*) clarity

clarificar [klarifi'kar] *vt* to clarify

clarinete [klari'nete] *nm* clarinet

claro, -a ['klaro, a] *adj* clear; (*luminoso*) bright; (*color*) light; (*evidente*) clear, evident; (*poco espeso*) thin ▷ *nm* (*en bosque*) clearing ▷ *adv* clearly ▷ *excl*: **¡~ que sí!** of course!; **¡~ que no!** of course not!

clase ['klase] *nf* class; **dar ~(s)** to teach; **clase alta/media/obrera** upper/middle/ working class; **clases particulares** private lessons o tuition *sg*

clásico, -a ['klasiko, a] *adj* classical

clasificación [klasifika'θjon] *nf* classification; (*Deporte*) league (table)

clasificar [klasifi'kar] *vt* to classify

claustro ['klaustro] *nm* cloister

cláusula ['klausula] nf clause
clausura [klau'sura] nf closing, closure
clavar [kla'βar] vt (clavo) to hammer in; (cuchillo) to stick, thrust
clave ['klaβe] nf key; (Mús) clef; **clave de acceso** password; **clave lada** (MÉX) dialling (BRIT) o area (US) code
clavel [kla'βel] nm carnation
clavícula [kla'βikula] nf collar bone
clavija [kla'βixa] nf peg, dowel, pin; (Elec) plug
clavo ['klaβo] nm (de metal) nail; (Bot) clove
claxon ['klakson] (pl ~s) nm horn
clérigo ['klerixo] nm priest
clero ['klero] nm clergy
clicar [kli'kar] vi (Internet) to click; ~ **en el icono** to click on an icon; ~ **dos veces** to double-click
cliché [kli'tʃe] nm cliché; (Foto) negative
cliente, -a ['kljente, a] nm/f client, customer; **clientela** [kljen'tela] nf clientele, customers pl
clima ['klima] nm climate; **climatizado, -a** [klimati'θaðo, a] adj air-conditioned
clímax ['klimaks] nm inv climax
clínica ['klinika] nf clinic; (particular) private hospital
clip [klip] (pl ~s) nm paper clip
clítoris ['klitoris] nm inv (Anat) clitoris
cloaca [klo'aka] nf sewer
clonar [klo'nar] vt to clone
cloro ['kloro] nm chlorine
clóset ['kloset] (MÉX) nm cupboard
club [klub] (pl ~s o ~es) nm club; **club nocturno** night club
cm abr (= centímetro, centímetros) cm
coágulo [ko'aɣulo] nm clot
coalición [koali'θjon] nf coalition
coartada [koar'taða] nf alibi
coartar [koar'tar] vt to limit, restrict
coba ['koβa] nf: **dar ~ a algn** (adular) to suck up to sb
cobarde [ko'βarðe] adj cowardly ▷ nm coward; **cobardía** nf cowardice
cobaya [ko'βaja] nf guinea pig
cobertizo [koβer'tiθo] nm shelter
cobertura [koβer'tura] nf cover; **aquí no hay ~** (Tel) I can't get a signal
cobija [ko'βixa] (LAM) nf blanket; **cobijar** [koβi'xar] vt (cubrir) to cover; (proteger) to shelter; **cobijo** nm shelter
cobra ['koβra] nf cobra
cobrador, a [koβra'ðor, a] nm/f (de autobús) conductor/conductress; (de impuestos, gas) collector
cobrar [ko'βrar] vt (cheque) to cash; (sueldo) to collect, draw; (objeto) to recover; (precio) to charge; (deuda) to collect ▷ vi to be paid;

cóbrese al entregar cash on delivery; **¿me cobra, por favor?** how much do I owe you?, can I have the bill, please?
cobre ['koβre] nm copper; **cobres** nmpl (Mús) brass instruments
cobro ['koβro] nm (de cheque) cashing; **presentar al ~** to cash
cocaína [koka'ina] nf cocaine
cocción [kok'θjon] nf (Culin) cooking; (en agua) boiling
cocer [ko'θer] vt, vi to cook; (en agua) to boil; (en horno) to bake
coche ['kotʃe] nm (Auto) car (BRIT), automobile (US); (de tren, de caballos) coach, carriage; (para niños) pram (BRIT), baby carriage (US); **ir en ~** to drive; **coche celular** police van; **coche de bomberos** fire engine; **coche de carreras** racing car; **coche fúnebre** hearse; **coche-cama** (pl coches-cama) nm (Ferro) sleeping car, sleeper
cochera [ko'tʃera] nf garage; (de autobuses, trenes) depot
coche restaurante (pl coches restaurante) nm (Ferro) dining car, diner
cochinillo [kotʃi'niʎo] nm (Culin) suckling pig, sucking pig
cochino, -a [ko'tʃino, a] adj filthy, dirty ▷ nm/f pig
cocido [ko'θiðo] nm stew
cocina [ko'θina] nf kitchen; (aparato) cooker, stove; (acto) cookery; **cocina eléctrica/de gas** electric/gas cooker; **cocina francesa** French cuisine; **cocinar** vt, vi to cook
cocinero, -a [koθi'nero, a] nm/f cook
coco ['koko] nm coconut
cocodrilo [koko'ðrilo] nm crocodile
cocotero [koko'tero] nm coconut palm
cóctel ['koktel] nm cocktail; **cóctel molotov** petrol bomb, Molotov cocktail
codazo [ko'ðaθo] nm: **dar un ~ a algn** to nudge sb
codicia [ko'ðiθja] nf greed; **codiciar** vt to covet
código ['koðixo] nm code; **código civil** common law; **código de barras** bar code; **código de circulación** highway code; **código de la zona** (LAM) dialling (BRIT) o area (US) code; **código postal** postcode
codillo [ko'ðiʎo] nm (Zool) knee; (Tec) elbow (joint)
codo ['koðo] nm (Anat, de tubo) elbow; (Zool) knee
codorniz [koðor'niθ] nf quail
coexistir [koe(k)sis'tir] vi to coexist
cofradía [kofra'ðia] nf brotherhood, fraternity
cofre ['kofre] nm (de joyas) case; (de dinero)

chest

coger [ko'xer] (ESP) vt to take (hold of); (objeto caído) to pick up; (frutas) to pick, harvest; (resfriado, ladrón, pelota) to catch ▷ vi: **~ por el buen camino** to take the right road; **cogerse** vr (el dedo) to catch; **~se a algo** to get hold of sth

cogollo [ko'ɣoʎo] nm (de lechuga) heart

cogote [ko'ɣote] nm back o nape of the neck

cohabitar [koaβi'tar] vi to live together, cohabit

coherente [koe'rente] adj coherent

cohesión [koe'sjon] nm cohesion

cohete [ko'ete] nm rocket

cohibido, -a [koi'βiðo, a] adj (Psico) inhibited; (tímido) shy

coincidencia [koinθi'ðenθja] nf coincidence

coincidir [koinθi'ðir] vi (en idea) to coincide, agree; (en lugar) to coincide

coito ['koito] nm intercourse, coitus

coja etc vb V **coger**

cojear [koxe'ar] vi (persona) to limp, hobble; (mueble) to wobble, rock

cojera [ko'xera] nf limp

cojín [ko'xin] nm cushion

cojo, -a etc ['koxo, a] vb V **coger** ▷ adj (que no puede andar) lame, crippled; (mueble) wobbly ▷ nm/f lame person, cripple

cojón [ko'xon] (fam!) nm: **¡cojones!** shit! (!); **cojonudo, -a** (fam) adj great, fantastic

col [kol] nf cabbage; **coles de Bruselas** Brussels sprouts

cola ['kola] nf tail; (de gente) queue; (lugar) end, last place; (para pegar) glue, gum; **hacer ~** to queue (up)

colaborador, a [kolaβora'ðor, a] nm/f collaborator

colaborar [kolaβo'rar] vi to collaborate

colada [ko'laða] (ESP) nf: **hacer la ~** to do the washing

colador [kola'ðor] nm (para líquidos) strainer; (para verduras etc) colander

colapso [ko'lapso] nm collapse

colar [ko'lar] vt (líquido) to strain off; (metal) to cast ▷ vi to ooze, seep (through); **colarse** vr to jump the queue; **~se en** to get into without paying; (fiesta) to gatecrash

colcha ['koltʃa] nf bedspread

colchón [kol'tʃon] nm mattress; **colchón inflable** air bed o mattress

colchoneta [koltʃo'neta] nf (en gimnasio) mat; (de playa) air bed

colección [kolek'θjon] nf collection; **coleccionar** vt to collect; **coleccionista** nmf collector

colecta [ko'lekta] nf collection

colectivo, -a [kolek'tiβo, a] adj collective, joint ▷ nm (ARG: autobús) (small) bus

colega [ko'leɣa] nmf colleague; (ESP: amigo) mate

colegial, a [kole'xjal, a] nm/f schoolboy(-girl)

colegio [ko'lexjo] nm college; (escuela) school; (de abogados etc) association; **colegio electoral** polling station; **colegio mayor** (ESP) hall of residence

---

COLEGIO

A **colegio** is normally a private primary or secondary school. In the state system it means a primary school although these are also called **escuelas**. State secondary schools are called **institutos**.

---

cólera ['kolera] nf (ira) anger; (Med) cholera

colesterol [koleste'rol] nm cholesterol

coleta [ko'leta] nf pigtail

colgante [kol'xante] adj hanging ▷ nm (joya) pendant

colgar [kol'xar] vt to hang (up); (ropa) to hang out ▷ vi (Tel) to hang up

cólico [ko'liko] nm colic

coliflor [koli'flor] nf cauliflower

colilla [ko'liʎa] nf cigarette end, butt

colina [ko'lina] nf hill

colisión [koli'sjon] nf collision; **colisión frontal** head-on crash

collar [ko'ʎar] nm necklace; (de perro) collar

colmar [kol'mar] vt to fill to the brim; (fig) to fulfil, realize

colmena [kol'mena] nf beehive

colmillo [kol'miʎo] nm (diente) eye tooth; (de elefante) tusk; (de perro) fang

colmo ['kolmo] nm: **¡es el ~!** it's the limit!

colocación [koloka'θjon] nf (acto) placing; (empleo) job, position

colocar [kolo'kar] vt to place, put, position; (dinero) to invest; (poner en empleo) to find a job for; **colocarse** vr to get a job

Colombia [ko'lombja] nf Colombia; **colombiano, -a** adj, nm/f Colombian

colonia [ko'lonja] nf colony; (agua de colonia) cologne; (MÉX: de casas) residential area; **colonia proletaria** (MÉX) shantytown

colonización [koloniθa'θjon] nf colonization; **colonizador, a** [koloniθa'ðor, a] adj colonizing ▷ nm/f colonist, settler

colonizar [koloni'θar] vt to colonize

coloquio [ko'lokjo] nm conversation; (congreso) conference

color [ko'lor] nm colour

colorado, -a [kolo'raðo, a] adj (rojo) red; (MÉX: chiste) smutty, rude

colorante [kolo'rante] nm colouring

colorear [kolore'ar] vt to colour

colorete [kolo'rete] nm blusher

colorido [kolo'riðo] nm colouring

columna [ko'lumna] nf column; (pilar) pillar; (apoyo) support; (tb: **~ vertebral**) spine, spinal column; (fig) backbone

columpiar [kolum'pjar] vt to swing; **columpiarse** vr to swing; **columpio** nm swing

coma ['koma] nf comma ▷ nm (Med) coma

comadre [ko'maðre] nf (madrina) godmother; (chismosa) gossip; **comadrona** nf midwife

comal [ko'mal] (MÉX, CAM) nm griddle

comandante [koman'dante] nm commandant

comarca [ko'marka] nf region

comba ['komba] (ESP) nf (cuerda) skipping rope; **saltar a la ~** to skip

combate [kom'bate] nm fight

combatir [komba'tir] vt to fight, combat

combinación [kombina'θjon] nf combination; (Quím) compound; (prenda) slip

combinar [kombi'nar] vt to combine

combustible [kombus'tiβle] nm fuel

comedia [ko'meðja] nf comedy; (Teatro) play, drama; **comediante** [kome'ðjante] nmf (comic) actor/actress

comedido, -a [kome'ðiðo, a] adj moderate

comedor, a [kome'ðor, a] nm (habitación) dining room; (cantina) canteen

comensal [komen'sal] nmf fellow guest (o diner)

comentar [komen'tar] vt to comment on; **comentario** [komen'tarjo] nm comment, remark; (literario) commentary; **comentarios** nmpl (chismes) gossip sg; **comentarista** [komenta'rista] nmf commentator

comenzar [komen'θar] vt, vi to begin, start; **~ a hacer algo** to begin o start doing sth

comer [ko'mer] vt to eat; (Damas, Ajedrez) to take, capture ▷ vi to eat; (ESP, MÉX: almorzar) to have lunch; **comerse** vr to eat up

comercial [komer'θjal] adj commercial; (relativo al negocio) business cpd; **comercializar** vt (producto) to market; (pey) to commercialize

comerciante [komer'θjante] nmf trader, merchant

comerciar [komer'θjar] vi to trade, do business

comercio [ko'merθjo] nm commerce, trade; (tienda) shop, store; (negocio) business; (fig) dealings pl; **comercio electrónico** e-commerce; **comercio exterior/interior** foreign/domestic trade

comestible [komes'tiβle] adj eatable, edible; **comestibles** nmpl food sg, foodstuffs

cometa [ko'meta] nm comet ▷ nf kite

cometer [kome'ter] vt to commit

cometido [kome'tiðo] nm task, assignment

cómic ['komik] nm comic

comicios [ko'miθjos] nmpl elections

cómico, -a [ko'miko, a] adj comic(al) ▷ nm/f comedian

comida [ko'miða] nf (alimento) food; (almuerzo, cena) meal; (de mediodía) lunch; **comida basura** junk food; **comida chatarra** (MÉX) junk food

comidilla [komi'ðiʎa] nf: **ser la ~ del barrio** o **pueblo** to be the talk of the town

comienzo etc [ko'mjenθo] vb V **comenzar** ▷ nm beginning, start

comillas [ko'miʎas] nfpl quotation marks

comilona [komi'lona] (fam) nf blow-out

comino [ko'mino] nm: **(no) me importa un ~** I don't give a damn

comisaría [komisa'ria] nf (de policía) police station; (Mil) commissariat

comisario [komi'sarjo] nm (Mil etc) commissary; (Pol) commissar

comisión [komi'sjon] nf commission; **Comisiones Obreras** (ESP) Communist trade union

comité [komi'te] (pl ~s) nm committee

comitiva [komi'tiβa] nf retinue

como ['komo] adv as; (tal ~) like; (aproximadamente) about, approximately ▷ conj (ya que, puesto que) as, since; **¡~ no!** of course!; **~ no lo haga hoy** unless he does it today; **~ si** as if; **es tan alto ~ ancho** it is as high as it is wide

cómo ['komo] adv how?, why? ▷ excl what?, I beg your pardon? ▷ nm: **el ~ y el porqué** the whys and wherefores

cómoda ['komoða] nf chest of drawers

comodidad [komoði'ðað] nf comfort

comodín [komo'ðin] nm joker

cómodo, -a ['komoðo, a] adj comfortable; (práctico, de fácil uso) convenient

compact [kom'pakt] (pl ~s) nm (tb: **~ disc**) compact disk player

compacto, -a [kom'pakto, a] adj

compact

compadecer [kompaðe'θer] vt to pity, be sorry for; **compadecerse** vr: **~se de** to pity, be o feel sorry for

compadre [kom'paðre] nm (padrino) godfather; (amigo) friend, pal

compañero, -a [kompa'ɲero, a] nm/f companion; (novio) boy/girlfriend; **compañero de clase** classmate

compañía [kompa'ɲia] nf company; **hacer ~ a algn** to keep sb company

comparación [kompara'θjon] nf comparison; **en ~ con** in comparison with

comparar [kompa'rar] vt to compare

comparecer [kompare'θer] vi to appear (in court)

comparsa [kom'parsa] nmf (Teatro) extra

compartimiento [komparti'mjento] nm (Ferro) compartment

compartir [kompar'tir] vt to share; (dinero, comida etc) to divide (up), share (out)

compás [kom'pas] nm (Mús) beat, rhythm; (Mat) compasses pl; (Náut etc) compass

compasión [kompa'sjon] nf compassion, pity

compasivo, -a [kompa'siβo, a] adj compassionate

compatible [kompa'tiβle] adj compatible

compatriota [kompa'trjota] nmf compatriot, fellow countryman/woman

compenetrarse [kompene'trarse] vr to be in tune

compensación [kompensa'θjon] nf compensation

compensar [kompen'sar] vt to compensate

competencia [kompe'tenθja] nf (incumbencia) domain, field; (Jur, habilidad) competence; (rivalidad) competition

competente [kompe'tente] adj competent

competición [kompeti'θjon] nf competition

competir [kompe'tir] vi to compete

compinche [kom'pintʃe] (LAM) nmf mate, buddy (US)

complacer [kompla'θer] vt to please; **complacerse** vr to be pleased

complaciente [kompla'θjente] adj kind, obliging, helpful

complejo, -a [kom'plexo, a] adj, nm complex

complementario, -a [komplemen'tarjo, a] adj complementary

completar [komple'tar] vt to complete

completo, -a [kom'pleto, a] adj complete; (perfecto) perfect; (lleno) full ▷ nm

full complement

complicado, -a [kompli'kaðo, a] adj complicated; **estar ~ en** to be mixed up in

cómplice ['kompliθe] nmf accomplice

complot [kom'plo(t)] (pl **~s**) nm plot

componer [kompo'ner] vt (Mús, Literatura, Imprenta) to compose; (algo roto) to mend, repair; (arreglar) to arrange; **componerse** vr: **~se de** to consist of

comportamiento [komporta'mjento] nm behaviour, conduct

comportarse [kompor'tarse] vr to behave

composición [komposi'θjon] nf composition

compositor, a [komposi'tor, a] nm/f composer

compostura [kompos'tura] nf (actitud) composure

compra ['kompra] nf purchase; **hacer la ~** to do the shopping; **ir de ~s** to go shopping; **comprador, a** nm/f buyer, purchaser; **comprar** [kom'prar] vt to buy, purchase

comprender [kompren'der] vt to understand; (incluir) to comprise, include

comprensión [kompren'sjon] nf understanding; **comprensivo, -a** adj (actitud) understanding

compresa [kom'presa] nf (para mujer) sanitary towel (BRIT) o napkin (US)

comprimido, -a [kompri'miðo, a] adj compressed ▷ nm (Med) pill, tablet

comprimir [kompri'mir] vt to compress; (Internet) to zip

comprobante [kompro'βante] nm proof; (Com) voucher; **comprobante de compra** proof of purchase

comprobar [kompro'βar] vt to check; (probar) to prove; (Tec) to check, test

comprometer [komprome'ter] vt to compromise; (poner en peligro) to endanger; **comprometerse** vr (involucrarse) to get involved

compromiso [kompro'miso] nm (obligación) obligation; (cometido) commitment; (convenio) agreement; (apuro) awkward situation

compuesto, -a [kom'pwesto, a] adj: **~ de** composed of, made up of ▷ nm compound

computadora [komputa'ðora] (LAM) nf computer; **computadora central** mainframe (computer); **computadora personal** personal computer

cómputo ['komputo] nm calculation

comulgar [komul'yar] vi to receive communion

común [ko'mun] adj common ▷ nm: **el ~** the community

comunicación [komunika'θjon] *nf* communication; (*informe*) report

comunicado [komuni'kaðo] *nm* announcement; **comunicado de prensa** press release

comunicar [komuni'kar] *vt, vi* to communicate; **comunicarse** *vr* to communicate; **está comunicando** (*Tel*) the line's engaged (BRIT) o busy (US); **comunicativo, -a** *adj* communicative

comunidad [komuni'ðað] *nf* community; **comunidad autónoma** (ESP) autonomous region; **Comunidad (Económica) Europea** European (Economic) Community; **comunidad de vecinos** residents' association

comunión [komu'njon] *nf* communion

comunismo [komu'nismo] *nm* communism; **comunista** *adj, nmf* communist

○ **PALABRA CLAVE**

con [kon] *prep* **1** (*medio, compañía*) with; **comer con cuchara** to eat with a spoon; **pasear con algn** to go for a walk with sb **2** (*a pesar de*): **con todo, merece nuestros respetos** all the same, he deserves our respect **3** (*para con*): **es muy bueno para con los niños** he's very good with (the) children **4** (+ *infin*): **con llegar a las seis estará bien** if you come by six it will be fine ▷ *conj*: **con que: será suficiente con que le escribas** it will be sufficient if you write to her

concebir [konθe'βir] *vt, vi* to conceive

conceder [konθe'ðer] *vt* to concede

concejal, a [konθe'xal, a] *nm/f* town councillor

concentración [konθentra'θjon] *nf* concentration

concentrar [konθen'trar] *vt* to concentrate; **concentrarse** *vr* to concentrate

concepto [kon'θepto] *nm* concept

concernir [konθer'nir] *vi* to concern; **en lo que concierne a ...** as far as ... is concerned; **en lo que a mí concierne** as far as I'm concerned

concertar [konθer'tar] *vt* (*Mús*) to harmonize; (*acordar: precio*) to agree; (: *tratado*) to conclude; (*trato*) to arrange, fix up; (*combinar: esfuerzos*) to coordinate ▷ *vi* to harmonize, be in tune

concesión [konθe'sjon] *nf* concession

concesionario [konθesjo'narjo] *nm* (licensed) dealer, agent

concha ['kontʃa] *nf* shell

conciencia [kon'θjenθja] *nf* conscience; **tomar ~ de** to become aware of; **tener la ~ tranquila** to have a clear conscience

concienciar [konθjen'θjar] *vt* to make aware; **concienciarse** *vr* to become aware

concienzudo, -a [konθjen'θuðo, a] *adj* conscientious

concierto *etc* [kon'θjerto] *vb* V **concertar** ▷ *nm* concert; (*obra*) concerto

conciliar [konθi'ljar] *vt* to reconcile; **~ el sueño** to get to sleep

concilio [kon'θiljo] *nm* council

conciso, -a [kon'θiso, a] *adj* concise

concluir [konklu'ir] *vt, vi* to conclude; **concluirse** *vr* to conclude

conclusión [konklu'sjon] *nf* conclusion

concordar [konkor'ðar] *vt* to reconcile ▷ *vi* to agree, tally

concordia [kon'korðja] *nf* harmony

concretar [konkre'tar] *vt* to make concrete, make more specific; **concretarse** *vr* to become more definite

concreto, -a [kon'kreto, a] *adj, nm* (LAM: *hormigón*) concrete; **en ~** (*en resumen*) to sum up; (*específicamente*) specifically; **no hay nada en ~** there's nothing definite

concurrido, -a [konku'rriðo, a] *adj* (*calle*) busy; (*local, reunión*) crowded

concursante [konkur'sante] *nmf* competitor

concurso [kon'kurso] *nm* (*de público*) crowd; (*Escol, Deporte, competencia*) competition; (*ayuda*) help, cooperation

condal [kon'dal] *adj*: **la Ciudad C~** Barcelona

conde ['konde] *nm* count

condecoración [kondekora'θjon] *nf* (*Mil*) medal

condena [kon'dena] *nf* sentence; **condenación** [kondena'θjon] *nf* condemnation; (*Rel*) damnation; **condenar** [konde'nar] *vt* to condemn; (*Jur*) to convict; **condenarse** *vr* (*Rel*) to be damned

condesa [kon'desa] *nf* countess

condición [kondi'θjon] *nf* condition; **a ~ de que ...** on condition that ...; **condicional** *adj* conditional

condimento [kondi'mento] *nm* seasoning

condominio [kondo'minjo] (LAM) *nm* condominium

condón [kon'don] *nm* condom

conducir [kondu'θir] *vt* to take, convey; (*Auto*) to drive ▷ *vi* to drive; (*fig*) to lead; **conducirse** *vr* to behave

conducta [kon'dukta] *nf* conduct,

behaviour

conducto [kon'dukto] nm pipe, tube; (fig) channel

conductor, a [konduk'tor, a] adj leading, guiding ▷ nm (Física) conductor; (de vehículo) driver

conduje etc vb V **conducir**

conduzco etc vb V **conducir**

conectado, -a [konek'taðo, a] adj (Inform) on-line

conectar [konek'tar] vt to connect (up); (enchufar) plug in

conejillo [kone'xiʎo] nm: **~ de Indias** guinea pig

conejo [ko'nexo] nm rabbit

conexión [konek'sjon] nf connection

confección [confe(k)'θjon] nf preparation; (industria) clothing industry

confeccionar [konfekθjo'nar] vt to make (up)

conferencia [konfe'renθja] nf conference; (lección) lecture; (ESP Tel) call; **conferencia de prensa** press conference

conferir [konfe'rir] vt to award

confesar [konfe'sar] vt to confess, admit

confesión [konfe'sjon] nf confession

confesionario [konfesjo'narjo] nm confessional

confeti [kon'feti] nm confetti

confiado, -a [kon'fjaðo, a] adj (crédulo) trusting; (seguro) confident

confianza [kon'fjanθa] nf trust; (seguridad) confidence; (familiaridad) intimacy, familiarity

confiar [kon'fjar] vt to entrust ▷ vi to trust; **~ en algn** to trust sb; **~ en que ...** to hope that ...

confidencial [konfiðen'θjal] adj confidential

confidente [konfi'ðente] nmf confidant/e; (policial) informer

configurar [konfiɣu'rar] vt to shape, form

confín [kon'fin] nm limit; **confines** nmpl confines, limits

confirmar [konfir'mar] vt to confirm

confiscar [konfis'kar] vt to confiscate

confite [kon'fite] nm sweet (BRIT), candy (US); **confitería** [konfite'ria] nf (tienda) confectioner's (shop)

confitura [konfi'tura] nf jam

conflictivo, -a [konflik'tiβo, a] adj (asunto, propuesta) controversial; (país, situación) troubled

conflicto [kon'flikto] nm conflict; (fig) clash

confluir [kon'flwir] vi (ríos) to meet; (gente) to gather

conformar [konfor'mar] vt to shape, fashion ▷ vi to agree; **conformarse** vr to conform; (resignarse) to resign o.s.; **~se con algo** to be happy with sth

conforme [kon'forme] adj (correspondiente): **~ con** in line with; (de acuerdo): **estar ~s (con algo)** to be in agreement (with sth) ▷ adv as ▷ excl agreed! ▷ prep: **~ a** in accordance with; **quedarse ~ (con algo)** to be satisfied (with sth)

confortable [konfor'taβle] adj comfortable

confortar [konfor'tar] vt to comfort

confrontar [konfron'tar] vt to confront; (dos personas) to bring face to face; (cotejar) to compare

confundir [konfun'dir] vt (equivocar) to mistake, confuse; (turbar) to confuse; **confundirse** vr (turbarse) to get confused; (equivocarse) to make a mistake; (mezclarse) to mix

confusión [konfu'sjon] nf confusion

confuso, -a [kon'fuso, a] adj confused

congelado, -a [konxe'laðo, a] adj frozen; **congelados** nmpl frozen food(s); **congelador** nm (aparato) freezer, deep freeze

congelar [konxe'lar] vt to freeze; **congelarse** vr (sangre, grasa) to congeal

congeniar [konxe'njar] vi to get on (BRIT) o along (US) well

congestión [konxes'tjon] nf congestion

congestionar [konxestjo'nar] vt to congest

congraciarse [kongra'θjarse] vr to ingratiate o.s.

congratular [kongratu'lar] vt to congratulate

congregar [kongre'ɣar] vt to gather together; **congregarse** vr to gather together

congresista [kongre'sista] nmf delegate, congressman/woman

congreso [kon'greso] nm congress

conjetura [konxe'tura] nf guess; **conjeturar** vt to guess

conjugar [konxu'ɣar] vt to combine, fit together; (Ling) to conjugate

conjunción [konxun'θjon] nf conjunction

conjunto, -a [kon'xunto, a] adj joint, united ▷ nm whole; (Mús) band; **en ~** as a whole

conmemoración [konmemora'θjon] nf commemoration

conmemorar [konmemo'rar] vt to commemorate

conmigo [kon'mixo] *pron* with me
conmoción [konmo'θjon] *nf* shock; (*fig*) upheaval; **conmoción cerebral** (*Med*) concussion
conmovedor, a [konmoβe'ðor, a] *adj* touching, moving; (*emocionante*) exciting
conmover [konmo'βer] *vt* to shake, disturb; (*fig*) to move
conmutador [konmuta'ðor] *nm* switch; (LAM: *centralita*) switchboard; (: *central*) telephone exchange
cono ['kono] *nm* cone; **Cono Sur** Southern Cone
conocedor, a [konoθe'ðor, a] *adj* expert, knowledgeable ▷ *nm/f* expert
conocer [kono'θer] *vt* to know; (*por primera vez*) to meet, get to know; (*entender*) to know about; (*reconocer*) to recognize; **conocerse** *vr* (*una persona*) to know o.s.; (*dos personas*) to (get to) know each other; ~ **a algn de vista** to know sb by sight
conocido, -a [kono'θiðo, a] *adj* (well-) known ▷ *nm/f* acquaintance
conocimiento [konoθi'mjento] *nm* knowledge; (*Med*) consciousness; **conocimientos** *nmpl* (*saber*) knowledge *sg*
conozco *etc vb* V **conocer**
conque ['konke] *conj* and so, so then
conquista [kon'kista] *nf* conquest; **conquistador, a** *adj* conquering ▷ *nm* conqueror; **conquistar** [konkis'tar] *vt* to conquer
consagrar [konsa'xrar] *vt* (*Rel*) to consecrate; (*fig*) to devote
consciente [kons'θjente] *adj* conscious
consecución [konseku'θjon] *nf* acquisition; (*de fin*) attainment
consecuencia [konse'kwenθja] *nf* consequence, outcome; (*coherencia*) consistency
consecuente [konse'kwente] *adj* consistent
consecutivo, -a [konseku'tiβo, a] *adj* consecutive
conseguir [konse'xir] *vt* to get, obtain; (*objetivo*) to attain
consejero, -a [konse'xero, a] *nm/f* adviser, consultant; (*Pol*) councillor
consejo [kon'sexo] *nm* advice; (*Pol*) council; **consejo de administración** (*Com*) board of directors; **consejo de guerra** court martial; **consejo de ministros** cabinet meeting
consenso [kon'senso] *nm* consensus
consentimiento [konsenti'mjento] *nm* consent
consentir [konsen'tir] *vt* (*permitir, tolerar*) to consent to; (*mimar*) to pamper, spoil;

(*aguantar*) to put up with ▷ *vi* to agree, consent; ~ **que algn haga algo** to allow sb to do sth
conserje [kon'serxe] *nm* caretaker; (*portero*) porter
conservación [konserβa'θjon] *nf* conservation; (*de alimentos, vida*) preservation
conservador, a [konserβa'ðor, a] *adj* (*Pol*) conservative ▷ *nm/f* conservative
conservante [konser'βante] *nm* preservative
conservar [konser'βar] *vt* to conserve, keep; (*alimentos, vida*) to preserve; **conservarse** *vr* to survive
conservas [kon'serβas] *nfpl* canned food(s) *pl*
conservatorio [konserβa'torjo] *nm* (*Mús*) conservatoire, conservatory
considerable [konsiðe'raβle] *adj* considerable
consideración [konsiðera'θjon] *nf* consideration; (*estimación*) respect
considerado, -a [konsiðe'raðo, a] *adj* (*atento*) considerate; (*respetado*) respected
considerar [konsiðe'rar] *vt* to consider
consigna [kon'sixna] *nf* (*orden*) order, instruction; (*para equipajes*) left-luggage office
consigo *etc* [kon'sixo] *vb* V **conseguir** ▷ *pron* (*m*) with him; (*f*) with her; (*Vd*) with you; (*reflexivo*) with o.s.
consiguiendo *etc vb* V **conseguir**
consiguiente [konsi'xjente] *adj* consequent; **por** ~ and so, therefore, consequently
consistente [konsis'tente] *adj* consistent; (*sólido*) solid, firm; (*válido*) sound
consistir [konsis'tir] *vi*: ~ **en** (*componerse de*) to consist of
consola [kon'sola] *nf* (*mueble*) console table; (*de videojuegos*) console
consolación [konsola'θjon] *nf* consolation
consolar [konso'lar] *vt* to console
consolidar [konsoli'ðar] *vt* to consolidate
consomé [konso'me] (*pl* ~**s**) *nm* consommé, clear soup
consonante [konso'nante] *adj* consonant, harmonious ▷ *nf* consonant
consorcio [kon'sorθjo] *nm* consortium
conspiración [konspira'θjon] *nf* conspiracy
conspirar [konspi'rar] *vi* to conspire
constancia [kon'stanθja] *nf* constancy; **dejar** ~ **de** to put on record
constante [kons'tante] *adj, nf* constant
constar [kons'tar] *vi* (*evidenciarse*) to be

clear o evident; **~ de** to consist of
constipado, -a [konsti'paðo, a]
adj: **estar ~** to have a cold ▷ nm cold

▌ No confundir **constipado** con la palabra
▌ inglesa *constipated*.

constitución [konstitu'θjon] nf
constitution
constituir [konstitu'ir] vt (formar,
componer) to constitute, make up; (fundar,
erigir, ordenar) to constitute, establish
construcción [konstruk'θjon] nf
construction, building
constructor, a [konstruk'tor, a] nm/f
builder
construir [konstru'ir] vt to build,
construct
construyendo etc vb V **construir**
consuelo [kon'swelo] nm consolation,
solace
cónsul ['konsul] nm consul; **consulado**
nm consulate
consulta [kon'sulta] nf consultation;
(Med): **horas de ~** surgery hours; **consultar**
[konsul'tar] vt to consult; **consultar
algo con algn** to discuss sth with sb;
consultorio [konsul'torjo] nm (Med)
surgery
consumición [konsumi'θjon] nf
consumption; (bebida) drink; (comida) food;
consumición mínima cover charge
consumidor, a [konsumi'ðor, a] nm/f
consumer
consumir [konsu'mir] vt to consume;
consumirse vr to be consumed; (persona)
to waste away
consumismo [konsu'mismo] nm
consumerism
consumo [kon'sumo] nm consumption
contabilidad [kontaβili'ðað] nf
accounting, book-keeping; (profesión)
accountancy; **contable** nmf accountant
contacto [kon'takto] nm contact; (Auto)
ignition; **estar/ponerse en ~ con algn** to
be/to get in touch with sb
contado, -a [kon'taðo, a] adj: **~s** (escasos)
numbered, scarce, few ▷ nm: **pagar al ~** to
pay (in) cash
contador [konta'ðor] nm (ESP: aparato)
meter ▷ nmf (LAM Com) accountant
contagiar [konta'xjar] vt (enfermedad)
to pass on, transmit; (persona) to infect;
contagiarse vr to become infected
contagio [kon'taxjo] nm infection;
contagioso, -a adj infectious; (fig)
catching
contaminación [kontamina'θjon] nf
contamination; (polución) pollution
contaminar [kontami'nar] vt to

contaminate; (aire, agua) to pollute
contante [kon'tante] adj: **dinero ~ (y
sonante)** cash
contar [kon'tar] vt (páginas, dinero) to
count; (anécdota, chiste etc) to tell ▷ vi to
count; **~ con** to rely on, count on
contemplar [kontem'plar] vt to
contemplate; (mirar) to look at
contemporáneo, -a [kontempo'raneo,
a] adj, nm/f contemporary
contenedor [kontene'ðor] nm container
contener [konte'ner] vt to contain, hold;
(retener) to hold back, contain; **contenerse**
vr to control o restrain o.s.
contenido, -a [konte'niðo, a] adj
(moderado) restrained; (risa etc) suppressed
▷ nm contents pl, content
contentar [konten'tar] vt (satisfacer) to
satisfy; (complacer) to please; **contentarse**
vr to be satisfied
contento, -a [kon'tento, a] adj (alegre)
pleased; (feliz) happy
contestación [kontesta'θjon] nf answer,
reply
contestador [kontesta'ðor] nm (tb: ~
automático) answering machine
contestar [kontes'tar] vt to answer, reply;
(Jur) to corroborate, confirm

▌ No confundir **contestar** con la palabra
▌ inglesa *contest*.

contexto [kon'te(k)sto] nm context
contigo [kon'tixo] pron with you
contiguo, -a [kon'tixwo, a] adj adjacent,
adjoining
continente [konti'nente] adj, nm
continent
continuación [kontinwa'θjon] nf
continuation; **a ~** then, next
continuar [konti'nwar] vt to continue,
go on with ▷ vi to continue, go on; **~
hablando** to continue talking o to talk
continuidad [kontinwi'ðað] nf
continuity
continuo, -a [kon'tinwo, a] adj (sin
interrupción) continuous; (acción perseverante)
continual
contorno [kon'torno] nm outline; (Geo)
contour; **contornos** nmpl neighbourhood
sg, surrounding area sg
contra ['kontra] prep, adv against ▷ nm inv
con ▷ nf: **la C~** (de Nicaragua) the Contras pl
contraataque [kontraa'take] nm
counter-attack
contrabajo [kontra'βaxo] nm double
bass
contrabandista [kontraβan'dista] nmf
smuggler
contrabando [kontra'βando] nm (acción)

smuggling; (*mercancías*) contraband
contracción [kontrak'θjon] *nf*
contraction
contracorriente [kontrako'rrjente] *nf*
cross-current
contradecir [kontraðe'θir] *vt* to
contradict
contradicción [kontraðik'θjon] *nf*
contradiction
contradictorio, -a [kontraðik'torjo, a]
adj contradictory
contraer [kontra'er] *vt* to contract;
(*limitar*) to restrict; **contraerse** *vr* to
contract; (*limitarse*) to limit o.s.
contraluz [kontra'luθ] *nm* view against
the light
contrapartida [kontrapar'tiða] *nf*: **como
~ (de)** in return (for)
contrapelo [kontra'pelo]: **a ~** *adv* the
wrong way
contrapeso [kontra'peso] *nm*
counterweight
contraportada [kontrapor'taða] *nf* (*de
revista*) back cover
contraproducente [kontraproðu'θente]
adj counterproductive
contrario, -a [kon'trarjo, a] *adj* contrary;
(*persona*) opposed; (*sentido, lado*) opposite
▷ *nm/f* enemy, adversary; (*Deporte*)
opponent; **al** o **por el ~** on the contrary; **de
lo ~** otherwise
contrarreloj [kontrarre'lo] *nf* (*tb:* **prueba
~**) time trial
contrarrestar [kontrarres'tar] *vt* to
counteract
contrasentido [kontrasen'tiðo] *nm*
(*contradicción*) contradiction
contraseña [kontra'seɲa] *nf* (*Inform*)
password
contrastar [kontras'tar] *vt, vi* to contrast
contraste [kon'traste] *nm* contrast
contratar [kontra'tar] *vt firmar un acuerdo
para*, to contract for; (*empleados, obreros*) to
hire, engage
contratiempo [kontra'tjempo] *nm*
setback
contratista [kontra'tista] *nmf* contractor
contrato [kon'trato] *nm* contract
contraventana [kontraβen'tana] *nf*
shutter
contribución [kontriβu'θjon] *nf*
(*municipal etc*) tax; (*ayuda*) contribution
contribuir [kontriβu'ir] *vt, vi* to
contribute; (*Com*) to pay (in taxes)
contribuyente [kontriβu'jente] *nmf*
(*Com*) taxpayer; (*que ayuda*) contributor
contrincante [kontrin'kante] *nmf*
opponent

control [kon'trol] *nm* control; (*inspección*)
inspection, check; **control de pasaportes**
passport inspection; **controlador, a** *nm/f*
controller; **controlador aéreo** air-traffic
controller; **controlar** [kontro'lar] *vt* to
control; (*inspeccionar*) to inspect, check
contundente [kontun'dente] *adj*
(*instrumento*) blunt; (*argumento, derrota*)
overwhelming
contusión [kontu'sjon] *nf* bruise
convalecencia [kombale'θenθja] *nf*
convalescence
convalecer [kombale'θer] *vi* to
convalesce, get better
convalidar [kombali'ðar] *vt* (*título*) to
recognize
convencer [komben'θer] *vt* to convince;
~ a algn (de o **para hacer algo)** to persuade
sb (to do sth)
convención [komben'θjon] *nf*
convention
conveniente [kombe'njente] *adj*
suitable; (*útil*) useful
convenio [kom'benjo] *nm* agreement,
treaty
convenir [kombe'nir] *vi* (*estar de acuerdo*)
to agree; (*venir bien*) to suit, be suitable
▌ No confundir **convenir** con la palabra
inglesa *convene*.
convento [kom'bento] *nm* convent
convenza *etc vb* V **convencer**
convergir [komber'xir] *vi* = **converger**
conversación [kombersa'θjon] *nf*
conversation
conversar [komber'sar] *vi* to talk,
converse
conversión [komber'sjon] *nf* conversion
convertir [komber'tir] *vt* to convert
convidar [kombi'ðar] *vt* to invite; **~ a
algn a una cerveza** to buy sb a beer
convincente [kombin'θente] *adj*
convincing
convite [kom'bite] *nm* invitation;
(*banquete*) banquet
convivencia [kombi'βenθja] *nf*
coexistence, living together
convivir [kombi'βir] *vi* to live together
convocar [kombo'kar] *vt* to summon, call
(together)
convocatoria [komboka'torja] *nf* (*de
oposiciones, elecciones*) notice; (*de huelga*) call
cónyuge ['konjuxe] *nmf* spouse
coñac [ko'ɲa(k)] (*pl* **-s**) *nm* cognac, brandy
coño ['koɲo] (*fam!*) *excl* (*enfado*) shit! (*!*);
(*sorpresa*) bloody hell! (*!*)
cool. [kul] *adj* (*fam*) cool
cooperación [koopera'θjon] *nf*
cooperation

cooperar [koope'rar] vi to cooperate

cooperativa [koopera'tiβa] nf cooperative

coordinadora [koorðina'ðora] nf (comité) coordinating committee

coordinar [koorði'nar] vt to coordinate

copa ['kopa] nf cup; (vaso) glass; (bebida): **tomar una ~** (to have a) drink; (de árbol) top; (de sombrero) crown; **copas** nfpl (Naipes) ≈ hearts

copia ['kopja] nf copy; **copia de respaldo** o **seguridad** (Inform) back-up copy; **copiar** vt to copy

copla ['kopla] nf verse; (canción) (popular) song

copo ['kopo] nm: **~ de nieve** snowflake; **~s de maíz** cornflakes

coqueta [ko'keta] adj flirtatious, coquettish; **coquetear** vi to flirt

coraje [ko'raxe] nm courage; (ánimo) spirit; (ira) anger

coral [ko'ral] adj choral ▷ nf (Mús) choir ▷ nm (Zool) coral

coraza [ko'raθa] nf (armadura) armour; (blindaje) armour-plating

corazón [kora'θon] nm heart

corazonada [koraθo'naða] nf impulse; (presentimiento) hunch

corbata [kor'βata] nf tie

corchete [kor'tʃete] nm catch, clasp

corcho ['kortʃo] nm cork; (Pesca) float

cordel [kor'ðel] nm cord, line

cordero [kor'ðero] nm lamb

cordial [kor'ðjal] adj cordial

cordillera [korði'ʎera] nf range (of mountains)

Córdoba ['korðoβa] n Cordova

cordón [kor'ðon] nm (cuerda) cord, string; (de zapatos) lace; (Mil etc) cordon; **cordón umbilical** umbilical cord

cordura [kor'ðura] nf: **con ~** (obrar, hablar) sensibly

corneta [kor'neta] nf bugle

cornisa [kor'nisa] nf (Arq) cornice

coro ['koro] nm chorus; (conjunto de cantores) choir

corona [ko'rona] nf crown; (de flores) garland

coronel [koro'nel] nm colonel

coronilla [koro'niʎa] nf (Anat) crown (of the head)

corporal [korpo'ral] adj corporal, bodily

corpulento, -a [korpu'lento, a] adj (persona) heavily-built

corral [ko'rral] nm farmyard

correa [ko'rrea] nf strap; (cinturón) belt; (de perro) lead, leash; **correa del ventilador** (Auto) fan belt

corrección [korrek'θjon] nf correction; (reprensión) rebuke; **correccional** nm reformatory

correcto, -a [ko'rrekto, a] adj correct; (persona) well-mannered

corredizo, -a [korre'ðiθo, a] adj (puerta etc) sliding

corredor, a [korre'ðor, a] nm (pasillo) corridor; (balcón corrido) gallery; (Com) agent, broker ▷ nm/f (Deporte) runner

corregir [korre'xir] vt (error) to correct; **corregirse** vr to reform

correo [ko'rreo] nm post, mail; (persona) courier; **Correos** nmpl (ESP) Post Office sg; **correo aéreo** airmail; **correo basura** (Inform) spam; **correo electrónico** e-mail, electronic mail; **correo web** webmail

correr [ko'rrer] vt to run; (cortinas) to draw; (cerrojo) to shoot ▷ vi to run; (líquido) to run, flow; **correrse** vr to slide, move; (colores) to run

correspondencia [korrespon'denθja] nf correspondence; (Ferro) connection

corresponder [korrespon'der] vi to correspond; (convenir) to be suitable; (pertenecer) to belong; (concernir) to concern; **corresponderse** vr (por escrito) to correspond; (amarse) to love one another

correspondiente [korrespon'djente] adj corresponding

corresponsal [korrespon'sal] nmf correspondent

corrida [ko'rriða] nf (de toros) bullfight

corrido, -a [ko'rriðo, a] adj (avergonzado) abashed; **un kilo ~** a good kilo

corriente [ko'rrjente] adj (agua) running; (dinero etc) current; (común) ordinary, normal ▷ nf current ▷ nm current month; **estar al ~ de** to be informed about; **corriente eléctrica** electric current

corrija etc vb V **corregir**

corro ['korro] nm ring, circle (of people)

corromper [korrom'per] vt (madera) to rot; (fig) to corrupt

corrosivo, -a [korro'siβo, a] adj corrosive

corrupción [korrup'θjon] nf rot, decay; (fig) corruption

corsé [kor'se] nm corset

cortacésped [korta'θespeð] nm lawn mower

cortado, -a [kor'taðo, a] adj (gen) cut; (leche) sour; (tímido) shy; (avergonzado) embarrassed ▷ nm coffee (with a little milk)

cortafuegos [korta'fweɣos] nm inv (en el bosque) firebreak, fire lane (US); (Internet) firewall

cortar [kor'tar] vt to cut; (suministro) to

cut off; (*un pasaje*) to cut out ▷ *vi* to cut;
cortarse *vr* (*avergonzarse*) to become
embarrassed; (*leche*) to turn, curdle; **~se el
pelo** to have one's hair cut

cortauñas [korta'uɲas] *nm inv* nail
clippers *pl*

corte ['korte] *nm* cut, cutting; (*de tela*)
piece, length ▷ *nf*: **las C~s** the Spanish
Parliament; **corte de luz** power cut; **corte y
confección** dressmaking

cortejo [kor'texo] *nm* entourage; **cortejo
fúnebre** funeral procession

cortés [kor'tes] *adj* courteous, polite

cortesía [korte'sia] *nf* courtesy

corteza [kor'teθa] *nf* (*de árbol*) bark; (*de
pan*) crust

cortijo [kor'tixo] (*ESP*) *nm* farm,
farmhouse

cortina [kor'tina] *nf* curtain

corto, -a ['korto, a] *adj* (*breve*) short;
(*tímido*) bashful; **~ de luces** not very bright;
~ de vista short-sighted; **estar ~ de fondos**
to be short of funds; **cortocircuito** *nm*
short circuit; **cortometraje** *nm* (*Cine*) short

cosa ['kosa] *nf* thing; **~ de** about; **eso es ~
mía** that's my business

coscorrón [kosko'rron] *nm* bump on
the head

cosecha [ko'setʃa] *nf* (*Agr*) harvest; (*de
vino*) vintage; **cosechar** [kose'tʃar] *vt* to
harvest, gather (in)

coser [ko'ser] *vt* to sew

cosmético, -a [kos'metiko, a] *adj, nm*
cosmetic

cosquillas [kos'kiʎas] *nfpl*: **hacer ~** to
tickle; **tener ~** to be ticklish

costa ['kosta] *nf* (*Geo*) coast; **a toda ~** at
all costs; **Costa Brava** Costa Brava; **Costa
Cantábrica** Cantabrian Coast; **Costa del
Sol** Costa del Sol

costado [kos'taðo] *nm* side

costanera [kosta'nera] (*cs*) *nf*
promenade, sea front

costar [kos'tar] *vt* (*valer*) to cost; **me
cuesta hablarle** I find it hard to talk to him

Costa Rica [kosta'rika] *nf* Costa Rica;
costarricense *adj, nmf* Costa Rican;
costarriqueño, -a *adj, nm/f* Costa Rican

coste ['koste] *nm* = **costo**

costear [koste'ar] *vt* to pay for

costero, -a [kos'tero, a] *adj* (*pueblecito,
camino*) coastal

costilla [kos'tiʎa] *nf* rib; (*Culin*) cutlet

costo ['kosto] *nm* cost, price; **costo de (la)
vida** cost of living; **costoso, -a** *adj* costly,
expensive

costra ['kostra] *nf* (*corteza*) crust; (*Med*)
scab

costumbre [kos'tumbre] *nf* custom,
habit

costura [kos'tura] *nf* sewing, needlework;
(*zurcido*) seam

costurera [kostu'rera] *nf* dressmaker

costurero [kostu'rero] *nm* sewing box
o case

cotidiano, -a [koti'ðjano, a] *adj* daily,
day to day

cotilla [ko'tiʎa] (*ESP: fam*) *nmf* gossip;
cotillear (*ESP*) *vi* to gossip; **cotilleo** (*ESP*)
nm gossip(ing)

cotizar [koti'θar] *vt* (*Com*) to quote, price;
cotizarse *vr*: **~se a** to sell at, fetch; (*Bolsa*) to
stand at, be quoted at

coto ['koto] *nm* (*terreno cercado*) enclosure;
(*de caza*) reserve

cotorra [ko'torra] *nf* parrot

coyote [ko'jote] *nm* coyote, prairie wolf

coz [koθ] *nf* kick

crack [krak] *nm* (*droga*) crack

cráneo ['kraneo] *nm* skull, cranium

cráter ['krater] *nm* crater

crayón [kra'jon] (*MÉX, RPL*) *nm* crayon,
chalk

creación [krea'θjon] *nf* creation

creador, a [krea'ðor, a] *adj* creative
▷ *nm/f* creator

crear [kre'ar] *vt* to create, make

crecer [kre'θer] *vi* to grow; (*precio*) to rise

creces ['kreθes]: **con ~** *adv* amply, fully

crecido, -a [kre'θiðo, a] *adj* (*persona,
planta*) full-grown; (*cantidad*) large

crecimiento [kreθi'mjento] *nm* growth;
(*aumento*) increase

credencial [kreðen'θjal] *nf* (*LAM: tarjeta*)
card; **credenciales** *nfpl* credentials;
credencial de socio (*LAM*) membership card

crédito ['kreðito] *nm* credit

credo ['kreðo] *nm* creed

creencia [kre'enθja] *nf* belief

creer [kre'er] *vt, vi* to think, believe;
creerse *vr* to believe o.s. (to be); **~ en** to
believe in; **creo que sí/no** I think/don't
think so; **¡ya lo creo!** I should think so!

creído, -a [kre'iðo, a] *adj* (*engreído*)
conceited

crema ['krema] *nf* cream; **crema batida**
(*LAM*) whipped cream; **crema pastelera**
(confectioner's) custard

cremallera [krema'ʎera] *nf* zip (fastener)

crepe ['krepe] (*ESP*) *nf* pancake

cresta ['kresta] *nf* (*Geo, Zool*) crest

creyendo *etc vb* V **creer**

creyente [kre'jente] *nmf* believer

creyó *etc vb* V **creer**

crezco *etc vb* V **crecer**

cría *etc* ['kria] *vb* V **criar** ▷ *nf* (*de animales*)

rearing, breeding; (*animal*) young; V tb **crío**
criadero [kria'ðero] nm (Zool) breeding place
criado, -a [kri'aðo, a] nm servant ▷ nf servant, maid
criador [kria'ðor] nm breeder
crianza [kri'anθa] nf rearing, breeding; (*fig*) breeding
criar [kri'ar] vt (*educar*) to bring up; (*producir*) to grow, produce; (*animales*) to breed
criatura [kria'tura] nf creature; (*niño*) baby, (*small*) child
cribar [kri'βar] vt to sieve
crimen ['krimen] nm crime
criminal [krimi'nal] adj, nmf criminal
crines ['krines] nfpl mane
crío, -a ['krio, a] (*fam*) nm/f (*niño*) kid
crisis ['krisis] nf inv crisis; **crisis nerviosa** nervous breakdown
crismas ['krismas] (ESP) nm inv Christmas card
cristal [kris'tal] nm crystal; (*de ventana*) glass, pane; (*lente*) lens; **cristalino, -a** adj crystalline; (*fig*) clear ▷ nm lens (of the eye)
cristianismo [kristja'nismo] nm Christianity
cristiano, -a [kris'tjano, a] adj, nm/f Christian
Cristo ['kristo] nm Christ; (*crucifijo*) crucifix
criterio [kri'terjo] nm criterion; (*juicio*) judgement
crítica ['kritika] nf criticism; V tb **crítico**
criticar [kriti'kar] vt to criticize
crítico, -a ['kritiko, a] adj critical ▷ nm/f critic
Croacia [kro'aθja] nf Croatia
cromo ['kromo] nm chrome
crónica ['kronika] nf chronicle, account
crónico, -a ['kroniko, a] adj chronic
cronómetro [kro'nometro] nm stopwatch
croqueta [kro'keta] nf croquette
cruce etc ['kruθe] vb V **cruzar** ▷ nm (*para peatones*) crossing; (*de carreteras*) crossroads
crucero [kru'θero] nm (*viaje*) cruise
crucificar [kruθifi'kar] vt to crucify
crucifijo [kruθi'fixo] nm crucifix
crucigrama [kruθi'ɣrama] nm crossword (puzzle)
cruda ['kruða] (MÉX, CAM: fam) nf hangover
crudo, -a ['kruðo, a] adj raw; (*no maduro*) unripe; (*petróleo*) crude; (*rudo, cruel*) cruel ▷ nm crude (oil)
cruel [krwel] adj cruel; **crueldad** nf cruelty
crujiente [kru'xjente] adj (*galleta etc*) crunchy
crujir [kru'xir] vi (*madera etc*) to creak; (*dedos*) to crack; (*dientes*) to grind; (*nieve, arena*) to crunch
cruz [kruθ] nf cross; (*de moneda*) tails sg; **cruz gamada** swastika
cruzada [kru'θaða] nf crusade
cruzado, -a [kru'θaðo, a] adj crossed ▷ nm crusader
cruzar [kru'θar] vt to cross; **cruzarse** vr (*líneas etc*) to cross; (*personas*) to pass each other
Cruz Roja nf Red Cross
cuaderno [kwa'ðerno] nm notebook; (*de escuela*) exercise book; (*Náut*) logbook
cuadra ['kwaðra] nf (*caballeriza*) stable; (LAM: entre calles) block
cuadrado, -a [kwa'ðraðo, a] adj square ▷ nm (Mat) square
cuadrar [kwa'ðrar] vt to square ▷ vi: ~ **con** to square with, tally with; **cuadrarse** vr (*soldado*) to stand to attention
cuadrilátero [kwaðri'latero] nm (Deporte) boxing ring; (Geom) quadrilateral
cuadrilla [kwa'ðriʎa] nf party, group
cuadro ['kwaðro] nm square; (Arte) painting; (Teatro) scene; (*diagrama*) chart; (Deporte, Med) team; **tela a ~s** checked (BRIT) o chequered (US) material
cuajar [kwa'xar] vt (*leche*) to curdle; (*sangre*) to congeal; (Culin) to set; **cuajarse** vr to curdle; to congeal; to set; (*llenarse*) to fill up
cuajo ['kwaxo] nm: **de ~** (*arrancar*) by the roots; (*cortar*) completely
cual [kwal] adv like, as ▷ pron: **el** etc ~ which; (*persona sujeto*) who; (: *objeto*) whom ▷ adj such as; **cada ~** each one; **déjalo tal ~** leave it just as it is
cuál [kwal] pron interr which (one)
cualesquier, a [kwales'kjer(a)] pl de **cualquier(a)**
cualidad [kwali'ðað] nf quality
cualquier [kwal'kjer] adj V **cualquiera**
cualquiera [kwal'kjera] (pl **cualesquiera**) adj (*delante de* nm y f **cualquier**) any ▷ pron anybody; **un coche ~ servirá** any car will do; **no es un hombre ~** he isn't just anybody; **cualquier día/libro** any day/book; **eso ~ lo sabe hacer** anybody can do that; **es un ~** he's a nobody
cuando ['kwando] adv when; (*aún si*) if, even if ▷ conj (*puesto que*) since ▷ prep: **yo, ~ niño ...** when I was a child ...; **~ no sea así** even if it is not so; **~ más** at (the) most; **~ menos** at least; **~ no** if not, otherwise; **de ~ en ~** from time to time
cuándo ['kwando] adv when; **¿desde ~?**

since when?
cuantía [kwan'tia] nf extent

○ **PALABRA CLAVE**

cuanto, -a ['kwanto, a] adj **1**(todo):
tiene todo cuanto desea he's got
everything he wants; **le daremos cuantos
ejemplares necesite** we'll give him as many
copies as o all the copies he needs; **cuantos
hombres la ven** all the men who see her
**2 unos cuantos: había unos cuantos
periodistas** there were a few journalists
3 (+ más): **cuanto más vino bebes peor te
sentirás** the more wine you drink the worse
you'll feel
▷ pron: **tiene cuanto desea** he has
everything he wants; **tome cuanto/
cuantos quiera** take as much/many as
you want
▷ adv: **en cuanto: en cuanto profesor** as
a teacher; **en cuanto a mí** as for me; V tb
antes
▷ conj **1 cuanto más gana menos gasta**
the more he earns the less he spends;
cuanto más joven más confiado the
younger you are the more trusting you are
2 en cuanto: en cuanto llegue/llegué as
soon as I arrive/arrived

cuánto, -a ['kwanto, a] adj (exclamación)
what a lot of; (interr: sg) how much?; (: pl)
how many? ▷ pron, adv how; (: interr: sg)
how much?; (: pl) how many?; **¡cuánta
gente!** what a lot of people!; **¿~ cuesta?**
how much does it cost?; **¿a ~s estamos?**
what's the date?
cuarenta [kwa'renta] num forty
cuarentena [kwaren'tena] nf quarantine
cuaresma [kwa'resma] nf Lent
cuarta ['kwarta] nf (Mat) quarter, fourth;
(palmo) span
cuartel [kwar'tel] nm (Mil) barracks pl;
cuartel de bomberos (RPL) fire station;
cuartel general headquarters pl
cuarteto [kwar'teto] nm quartet
cuarto, -a ['kwarto, a] adj fourth ▷ nm
(Mat) quarter, fourth; (habitación) room;
cuarto de baño bathroom; **cuarto de estar**
living room; **cuarto de hora** quarter (of an)
hour; **cuarto de kilo** quarter kilo; **cuartos
de final** quarter finals
cuatro ['kwatro] num four
Cuba ['kuβa] nf Cuba
cuba ['kuβa] nf cask, barrel
cubano, -a [ku'βano, a] adj, nm/f Cuban
cubata [ku'βata] nm (fam) large drink (of
rum and coke etc)

cubeta [ku'βeta] (ESP, MÉX) nf (balde)
bucket, tub
cúbico, -a ['kuβiko, a] adj cubic
cubierta [ku'βjerta] nf cover, covering;
(neumático) tyre; (Náut) deck
cubierto, -a [ku'βjerto, a] pp de **cubrir**
▷ adj covered ▷ nm cover; (lugar en la mesa)
place; **cubiertos** nmpl cutlery sg; **a ~** under
cover
cubilete [kuβi'lete] nm (en juegos) cup
cubito [ku'βito] nm (tb: ~ **de hielo**)
ice-cube
cubo ['kuβo] nm (Mat) cube; (ESP: balde)
bucket, tub; (Tec) drum; **cubo de (la) basura**
dustbin (BRIT), trash can (US)
cubrir [ku'βrir] vt to cover; **cubrirse** vr
(cielo) to become overcast
cucaracha [kuka'ratʃa] nf cockroach
cuchara [ku'tʃara] nf spoon; (Tec) scoop;
cucharada nf spoonful; **cucharadita** nf
teaspoonful
cucharilla [kutʃa'riʎa] nf teaspoon
cucharón [kutʃa'ron] nm ladle
cuchilla [ku'tʃiʎa] nf (large) knife; (de
arma blanca) blade; **cuchilla de afeitar**
razor blade
cuchillo [ku'tʃiʎo] nm knife
cuchitril [kutʃi'tril] nm hovel
cuclillas [ku'kliʎas] nfpl: **en ~** squatting
cuco, -a ['kuko, a] adj pretty; (astuto)
sharp ▷ nm cuckoo
cucurucho [kuku'rutʃo] nm cornet
cueca ['kweka] nf Chilean national dance
cuello ['kweʎo] nm (Anat) neck; (de vestido,
camisa) collar
cuenca ['kwenka] nf (Anat) eye socket;
(Geo) bowl, deep valley
cuenco ['kwenko] nm bowl
cuenta etc ['kwenta] vb V **contar**
▷ nf (cálculo) count, counting; (en café,
restaurante) bill (BRIT), check (US); (Com)
account; (de collar) bead; **a fin de ~** in the
end; **caer en la ~** to catch on; **darse ~ de** to
realize; **tener en ~** to bear in mind; **echar
~s** to take stock; **cuenta atrás** countdown;
cuenta corriente/de ahorros current/
savings account; **cuenta de correo
(electrónica)** (Inform) email account;
cuentakilómetros nm inv ~ milometer; (de
velocidad) speedometer
cuento etc ['kwento] vb V **contar** ▷ nm
story; **cuento chino** tall story; **cuento de
hadas** a fairy tale
cuerda ['kwerða] nf rope; (fina) string;
(de reloj) spring; **dar ~ a un reloj** to wind up
a clock; **cuerda floja** tightrope; **cuerdas
vocales** vocal cords
cuerdo, -a ['kwerðo, a] adj sane;

(prudente) wise, sensible

cuerno ['kwerno] nm horn

cuero ['kwero] nm leather; **en ~s** stark naked; **cuero cabelludo** scalp

cuerpo ['kwerpo] nm body

cuervo ['kwerβo] nm crow

cuesta etc ['kwesta] vb V **costar** ▷ nf slope; (en camino etc) hill; **~ arriba/abajo** uphill/downhill; **a ~s** on one's back

cueste etc vb V **costar**

cuestión [kwes'tjon] nf matter, question

cuete ['kwete] adj (MÉX: fam) drunk ▷ nm (LAM: cohete) rocket; (MÉX,RPL: fam: embriaguez) drunkenness; (MÉX: Culin) steak

cueva ['kweβa] nf cave

cuidado [kwi'ðaðo] nm care, carefulness; (preocupación) care, worry ▷ excl careful!, look out!; **eso me tiene sin ~** I'm not worried about that

cuidadoso, -a [kwiða'ðoso, a] adj careful; (preocupado) anxious

cuidar [kwi'ðar] vt (Med) to care for; (ocuparse de) to take care of, look after ▷ vi: **~ de** to take care of, look after; **cuidarse** vr to look after o.s.; **~se de hacer algo** to take care to do sth

culata [ku'lata] nf (de fusil) butt

culebra [ku'leβra] nf snake

culebrón [kule'βron] (fam) nm (TV) soap(-opera)

culo ['kulo] nm bottom, backside; (de vaso, botella) bottom

culpa ['kulpa] nf fault; (Jur) guilt; **por ~** because of; **echar la ~ a algn** to blame sb for sth; **tener la ~ (de)** to be to blame for sth; **culpable** adj guilty ▷ nmf culprit; **culpar** [kul'par] vt to blame; (acusar) to accuse

cultivar [kulti'βar] vt to cultivate

cultivo [kul'tiβo] nm (acto) cultivation; (plantas) crop

culto, -a ['kulto, a] adj (que tiene cultura) cultured, educated ▷ nm (homenaje) worship; (religión) cult

cultura [kul'tura] nf culture

culturismo [kultu'rismo] nm body-building

cumbia ['kumbja] nf popular Colombian dance

cumbre ['kumbre] nf summit, top

cumpleaños [kumple'aɲos] nm inv birthday

cumplido, -a [kum'pliðo, a] adj (abundante) plentiful; (cortés) courteous ▷ nm compliment; **visita de ~** courtesy call

cumplidor, a [kumpli'ðor, a] adj reliable

cumplimiento [kumpli'mjento] nm (de un deber) fulfilment; (acabamiento) completion

cumplir [kum'plir] vt (orden) to carry out, obey; (promesa) to carry out, fulfil; (condena) to serve ▷ vi: **~ con** (deber) to carry out, fulfil; **cumplirse** vr (plazo) to expire; **hoy cumple dieciocho años** he is eighteen today

cuna ['kuna] nf cradle, cot

cundir [kun'dir] vi (noticia, rumor, pánico) to spread; (rendir) to go a long way

cuneta [ku'neta] nf ditch

cuña ['kuɲa] nf wedge

cuñado, -a [ku'ɲaðo, a] nm/f brother-/ sister-in-law

cuota ['kwota] nf (parte proporcional) share; (cotización) fee, dues pl

cupe etc vb V **caber**

cupiera etc vb V **caber**

cupo ['kupo] vb V **caber** ▷ nm quota

cupón [ku'pon] nm coupon

cúpula ['kupula] nf dome

cura ['kura] nf (curación) cure; (método curativo) treatment ▷ nm priest

curación [kura'θjon] nf cure

curandero, -a [kuran'dero, a] nm/f quack

curar [ku'rar] vt (Med: herida) to treat, dress; (: enfermo) to cure; (Culin) to cure, salt; (cuero) to tan; **curarse** vr to get well, recover

curiosear [kurjose'ar] vt to glance at, look over ▷ vi to look round, wander round; (explorar) to poke about

curiosidad [kurjosi'ðað] nf curiosity

curioso, -a [ku'rjoso, a] adj curious ▷ nm/f bystander, onlooker

curita [ku'rita] (LAM) nf (sticking) plaster (BRIT), Bandaid® (US)

currante [ku'rrante] (ESP: fam) nmf worker

currar [ku'rrar] (ESP: fam) vi to work

currículo [ku'rrikulo] = **curriculum**

curriculum [ku'rrikulum] nm curriculum vitae

cursi ['kursi] (fam) adj affected

cursillo [kur'siʎo] nm short course

cursiva [kur'siβa] nf italics pl

curso ['kurso] nm course; **en ~** (año) current; (proceso) going on, under way

cursor [kur'sor] nm. (Inform) cursor

curul [ku'rul] (MÉX) nm (escaño) seat

curva ['kurβa] nf curve, bend

custodia [kus'toðja] nf safekeeping; custody

cutis ['kutis] nm inv skin, complexion

cutre ['kutre] (ESP: fam) adj (lugar) grotty

cuyo, -a ['kujo, a] pron (de quien) whose; (de que) whose, of which; **en ~ caso** in which case

C.V. abr (= caballos de vapor) H.P.

d

D. _abr_ (= _Don_) Esq

dado, -a ['daðo, a] _pp de_ **dar** ▷ _nm_ die; **dados** _nmpl_ dice; **~ que** given that

daltónico, -a [dal'toniko, a] _adj_ colour-blind

dama ['dama] _nf_ (_gen_) lady; (_Ajedrez_) queen; **damas** _nfpl_ (_juego_) draughts _sg_; **dama de honor** bridesmaid

damasco [da'masko] (_RPL_) _nm_ apricot

danés, -esa [da'nes, esa] _adj_ Danish ▷ _nm/f_ Dane

dañar [da'ɲar] _vt_ (_objeto_) to damage; (_persona_) to hurt; **dañarse** _vr_ (_objeto_) to get damaged

dañino, -a [da'ɲino, a] _adj_ harmful

daño ['daɲo] _nm_ (_objeto_) damage; (_persona_) harm, injury; **~s y perjuicios** (_Jur_) damages; **hacer ~ a** to damage; (_persona_) to hurt, injure; **hacerse ~** to hurt o.s.

○ **PALABRA CLAVE**

dar [dar] _vt_ **1** (_gen_) to give; (_obra de teatro_) to put on; (_film_) to show; (_fiesta_) to hold; **dar algo a algn** to give sb sth o sth to sb; **dar de beber a algn** to give sb a drink

2 (_producir: intereses_) to yield; (_fruta_) to produce

3 (_locuciones + n_): **da gusto escucharle** it's a pleasure to listen to him; V _tb_ **paseo**

4 (+ _n: = perífrasis de verbo_): **me da asco** it sickens me

5 (_considerar_): **dar algo por descontado/entendido** to take sth for granted/as read; **dar algo por concluido** to consider sth finished

6 (_hora_): **el reloj dio las 6** the clock struck 6 (o'clock)

7: **me da lo mismo** it's all the same to me; V _tb_ **igual, más**

▷ _vi_ **1 dar con: dimos con él dos horas**

más tarde we came across him two hours later; **al final di con la solución** I eventually came up with the answer

2: **dar en** (_blanco, suelo_) to hit; **el sol me da en la cara** the sun is shining (right) on my face

3: **dar de sí** (_zapatos etc_) to stretch, give

darse _vr_ **1**: **darse por vencido** to give up

2 (_ocurrir_): **se han dado muchos casos** there have been a lot of cases

3: **darse a: se ha dado a la bebida** he's taken to drinking

4: **se me dan bien/mal las ciencias** I'm good/bad at science

5: **dárselas de: se las da de experto** he fancies himself o poses as an expert

dardo ['darðo] _nm_ dart

dátil ['datil] _nm_ date

dato ['dato] _nm_ fact, piece of information; **datos personales** personal details

dcha. _abr_ (= _derecha_) r.h.

d. de C. _abr_ (= _después de Cristo_) A.D.

○ **PALABRA CLAVE**

de [de] (_de + el = del_) _prep_ **1** (_posesión_) of; **la casa de Isabel/mis padres** Isabel's/my parents' house; **es de ellos** it's theirs

2 (_origen, distancia, con números_) from; **soy de Gijón** I'm from Gijón; **de 8 a 20** from 8 to 20; **salir del cine** to go out of o leave the cinema; **de 2 en 2** 2 by 2, 2 at a time

3 (_valor descriptivo_): **una copa de vino** a glass of wine; **la mesa de la cocina** the kitchen table; **un billete de 10 euros** a 10 euro note; **un niño de tres años** a three-year-old (child); **una máquina de coser** a sewing machine; **ir vestido de gris** to be dressed in grey; **la niña del vestido azul** the girl in the blue dress; **trabaja de profesora** she works as a teacher; **de lado** sideways; **de atrás/delante** rear/front

4 (_hora, tiempo_): **a las 8 de la mañana** at 8 o'clock in the morning; **de día/noche** by day/night; **de hoy en ocho días** a week from now; **de niño era gordo** as a child he was fat

5 (_comparaciones_): **más/menos de cien personas** more/less than a hundred people; **el más caro de la tienda** the most expensive in the shop; **menos/más de lo pensado** less/more than expected

6 (_causa_): **del calor** from the heat

7 (_tema_) about; **clases de inglés** English classes; **¿sabes algo de él?** do you know anything about him?; **un libro de física** a physics book

8 (adj + de + infin): **fácil de entender** easy to understand

9 (oraciones pasivas): **fue respetado de todos** he was loved by all

10 (condicional + infin) if; **de ser posible** if possible; **de no terminarlo hoy** if I etc don't finish it today

dé [de] vb V **dar**

debajo [de'βaxo] adv underneath; **~ de** below, under; **por ~ de** beneath

debate [de'βate] nm debate; **debatir** vt to debate

deber [de'βer] nm duty ▷ vt to owe ▷ vi: **debe (de)** it must, it should; **deberes** nmpl (Escol) homework; **deberse** vr: **~se a** to be owing o due to; **debo hacerlo** I must do it; **debe de ir** he should go

debido, -a [de'βiðo, a] adj proper, just; **~ a** due to, because of

débil ['deβil] adj (persona, carácter) weak; (luz) dim; **debilidad** nf weakness; dimness

debilitar [deβili'tar] vt to weaken; **debilitarse** vr to grow weak

débito [de'βito] nm debit; **débito bancario** (LAM) direct debit (BRIT) o billing (US)

debutar [deβu'tar] vi to make one's debut

década ['dekaða] nf decade

decadencia [deka'ðenθja] nf (estado) decadence; (proceso) decline, decay

decaído, -a [deka'iðo, a] adj: **estar ~** (abatido) to be down

decano, -a [de'kano, a] nm/f (de universidad etc) dean

decena [de'θena] nf: **una ~** ten (or so)

decente [de'θente] adj decent

decepción [deθep'θjon] nf disappointment

No confundir **decepción** con la palabra inglesa deception.

decepcionar [deθepθjo'nar] vt to disappoint

decidir [deθi'ðir] vt, vi to decide; **decidirse** vr: **~se a** to make up one's mind to

décimo, -a ['deθimo, a] adj tenth ▷ nm tenth

decir [de'θir] vt to say; (contar) to tell; (hablar) to speak ▷ nm saying; **decirse** vr: **se dice que** it is said that; **es ~** that is (to say); **~ para sí** to say to o.s.; **querer ~** to mean; **¡dígame!** (Tel) hello!; (en tienda) can I help you?

decisión [deθi'sjon] nf (resolución) decision; (firmeza) decisiveness

decisivo, -a [deθi'siβo, a] adj decisive

declaración [deklara'θjon] nf (manifestación) statement; (de amor) declaration; **declaración fiscal** o **de la renta** income-tax return

declarar [dekla'rar] vt to declare ▷ vi to declare; (Jur) to testify; **declararse** vr to propose

decoración [dekora'θjon] nf decoration

decorado [deko'raðo] nm (Cine, Teatro) scenery, set

decorar [deko'rar] vt to decorate; **decorativo, -a** adj ornamental, decorative

decreto [de'kreto] nm decree

dedal [de'ðal] nm thimble

dedicación [deðika'θjon] nf dedication

dedicar [deði'kar] vt (libro) to dedicate; (tiempo, dinero) to devote; (palabras: decir, consagrar) to dedicate, devote; **dedicatoria** nf (de libro) dedication

dedo ['deðo] nm finger; **hacer ~** (fam) to hitch (a lift); **dedo anular** ring finger; **dedo corazón** middle finger; **dedo (del pie)** toe; **dedo gordo** (de la mano) thumb; (del pie) big toe; **dedo índice** index finger; **dedo meñique** little finger; **dedo pulgar** thumb

deducción [deðuk'θjon] nf deduction

deducir [deðu'θir] vt (concluir) to deduce, infer; (Com) to deduct

defecto [de'fekto] nm defect, flaw; **defectuoso, -a** adj defective, faulty

defender [defen'der] vt to defend; **defenderse** vr (desenvolverse) to get by

defensa [de'fensa] nf defence ▷ nm (Deporte) defender, back; **defensivo, -a** adj defensive; **a la defensiva** on the defensive

defensor, a [defen'sor, a] adj defending ▷ nm/f (abogado defensor) defending counsel; (protector) protector

deficiencia [defi'θjenθja] nf deficiency

deficiente [defi'θjente] adj (defectuoso) defective; **~ en** lacking o deficient in; **ser un ~ mental** to be mentally handicapped

déficit ['defiθit] (pl **~s**) nm deficit

definición [defini'θjon] nf definition

definir [defi'nir] vt (determinar) to determine, establish; (decidir) to define; (aclarar) to clarify; **definitivo, -a** adj definitive; **en definitiva** definitively; (en resumen) in short

deformación [deforma'θjon] nf (alteración) deformation; (Radio etc) distortion

deformar [defor'mar] vt (gen) to deform; **deformarse** vr to become deformed; **deforme** adj (informe) deformed; (feo) ugly; (malhecho) misshapen

defraudar [defrau'ðar] vt (decepcionar) to disappoint; (estafar) to defraud

defunción [defun'θjon] nf death, demise

degenerar [dexene'rar] vi to degenerate

degradar [deɣra'ðar] vt to debase,

degrade; **degradarse** vr to demean o.s.

degustación [deɣusta'θjon] nf sampling, tasting

dejar [de'xar] vt to leave; (permitir) to allow, let; (abandonar) to abandon, forsake; (beneficios) to produce, yield ▷ vi: ~ **de** (parar) to stop; (no hacer) to fail to; ~ **a un lado** to leave o set aside; ~ **entrar/salir** to let in/out; ~ **pasar** to let through

del [del] (= **de** + **el**) ∨ **de**

delantal [delan'tal] nm apron

delante [de'lante] adv in front; (enfrente) opposite; (adelante) ahead; ~ **de** in front of, before

delantera [delan'tera] nf (de vestido, casa etc) front part; (Deporte) forward line; **llevar la ~ (a algn)** to be ahead (of sb)

delantero, -a [delan'tero, a] adj front ▷ nm (Deporte) forward, striker

delatar [dela'tar] vt to inform on o against, betray; **delator, a** nm/f informer

delegación [deleɣa'θjon] nf (acción, delegados) delegation; (Com: oficina) office, branch; **delegación de policía** (MÉX) police station

delegado, -a [dele'ɣaðo, a] nm/f delegate; (Com) agent

delegar [dele'ɣar] vt to delegate

deletrear [deletre'ar] vt to spell (out)

delfín [del'fin] nm dolphin

delgado, -a [del'ɣaðo, a] adj thin; (persona) slim, thin; (tela etc) light, delicate

deliberar [deliβe'rar] vt to debate, discuss

delicadeza [delika'ðeθa] nf (gen) delicacy; (refinamiento, sutileza) refinement

delicado, -a [deli'kaðo, a] adj (gen) delicate; (sensible) sensitive; (quisquilloso) touchy

delicia [de'liθja] nf delight

delicioso, -a [deli'θjoso, a] adj (gracioso) delightful; (exquisito) delicious

delimitar [delimi'tar] vt (función, responsabilidades) to define

delincuencia [delin'kwenθja] nf delinquency; **delincuente** nmf delinquent; (criminal) criminal

delineante [deline'ante] nmf draughtsman/woman

delirante [deli'rante] adj delirious

delirar [deli'rar] vi to be delirious, rave

delirio [de'lirjo] nm (Med) delirium; (palabras insensatas) ravings pl

delito [de'lito] nm (gen) crime; (infracción) offence

delta ['delta] nm delta

demacrado, -a [dema'kraðo, a] adj: **estar ~** to look pale and drawn, be wasted away

demanda [de'manda] nf (pedido, Com) demand; (petición) request; (Jur) action, lawsuit; **demandar** [deman'dar] vt (gen) to demand; (Jur) to sue, file a lawsuit against

demás [de'mas] adj: **los ~ niños** the other o remaining children ▷ pron: **los/las ~** the others, the rest (of them); **lo ~** the rest (of it)

demasía [dema'sia] nf (exceso) excess, surplus; **comer en ~** to eat to excess

demasiado, -a [dema'sjaðo, a] adj: ~ **vino** too much wine ▷ adv (antes de adj, adv) too; **~s libros** too many books; **¡esto es ~!** that's the limit!; **hace ~ calor** it's too hot; ~ **despacio** too slowly; **~s** too many

demencia [de'menθja] nf (locura) madness

democracia [demo'kraθja] nf democracy

demócrata [de'mokrata] nmf democrat; **democrático, -a** adj democratic

demoler [demo'ler] vt to demolish; **demolición** nf demolition

demonio [de'monjo] nm devil, demon; **¡~s!** hell!, damn!; **¿cómo ~s?** how the hell?

demora [de'mora] nf delay

demos ['demos] vb ∨ **dar**

demostración [demostra'θjon] nf (Mat) proof; (de afecto) show, display

demostrar [demos'trar] vt (probar) to prove; (mostrar) to show; (manifestar) to demonstrate

den [den] vb ∨ **dar**

denegar [dene'ɣar] vt (rechazar) to refuse; (Jur) to reject

denominación [denomina'θjon] nf (acto) naming; **Denominación de Origen** see below

● **DENOMINACIÓN DE ORIGEN**
●
● The **Denominación de Origen**,
● abbreviated to **D.O.**, is a prestigious
● classification awarded to food products
● such as wines, cheeses, sausages
● and hams which meet the stringent
● quality and production standards of the
● designated region. **D.O.** labels serve as a
● guarantee of quality.

densidad [densi'ðað] nf density; (fig) thickness

denso, -a ['denso, a] adj dense; (espeso, pastoso) thick; (fig) heavy

dentadura [denta'ðura] nf (set of) teeth pl; **dentadura postiza** false teeth pl

dentera [den'tera] nf (grima): **dar ~ a algn** to set sb's teeth on edge

dentífrico, -a [den'tifriko, a] adj dental ▷ nm toothpaste

dentista [den'tista] *nmf* dentist

dentro ['dentro] *adv* inside ▷ *prep*: **~ de** in, inside, within; **por ~** (on the) inside; **mirar por ~** to look inside; **~ de tres meses** within three months

denuncia [de'nunθja] *nf* (*delación*) denunciation; (*acusación*) accusation; (*de accidente*) report; **denunciar** *vt* to report; (*delatar*) to inform on o against

departamento [departa'mento] *nm* sección administrativa, department, section; (LAM: *apartamento*) flat (BRIT), apartment

depender [depen'der] *vi*: **~ de** to depend on; **depende** it (all) depends

dependienta [depen'djenta] *nf* saleswoman, shop assistant

dependiente [depen'djente] *adj* dependent ▷ *nm* salesman, shop assistant

depilar [depi'lar] *vt* (*con cera*) to wax; (*cejas*) to pluck

deportar [depor'tar] *vt* to deport

deporte [de'porte] *nm* sport; **hacer ~** to play sports; **deportista** *adj* sports *cpd* ▷ *nmf* sportsman/woman; **deportivo, -a** *adj* (*club, periódico*) sports *cpd* ▷ *nm* sports car

depositar [deposi'tar] *vt* (*dinero*) to deposit; (*mercancías*) to put away, store; **depositarse** *vr* to settle

depósito [de'posito] *nm* (*gen*) deposit; (*almacén*) warehouse, store; (*de agua, gasolina etc*) tank; **depósito de cadáveres** mortuary

depredador, a [depreða'ðor, a] *adj* predatory ▷ *nm* predator

depresión [depre'sjon] *nf* depression; **depresión nerviosa** nervous breakdown

deprimido, -a [depri'miðo, a] *adj* depressed

deprimir [depri'mir] *vt* to depress; **deprimirse** *vr* (*persona*) to become depressed

deprisa [de'prisa] *adv* quickly, hurriedly

depurar [depu'rar] *vt* to purify; (*purgar*) to purge

derecha [de'retʃa] *nf* right(-hand) side; (Pol) right; **a la ~** (*estar*) on the right; (*torcer etc*) (to the) right

derecho, -a [de'retʃo, a] *adj* right, right-hand ▷ *nm* (*privilegio*) right; (*lado*) right(-hand) side; (*leyes*) law ▷ *adv* straight, directly; **derechos** *nmpl* (*de aduana*) duty *sg*; (*de autor*) royalties; **tener ~ a** to have a right to; **derechos de autor** royalties

deriva [de'riβa] *nf*: **ir** o **estar a la ~** to drift, be adrift

derivado [deri'βaðo] *nm* (Com) by-product

derivar [deri'βar] *vt* to derive; (*desviar*) to

direct ▷ *vi* to derive, be derived; (Náut) to drift; **derivarse** *vr* to derive, be derived; to drift

derramamiento [derrama'mjento] *nm* (*dispersión*) spilling; **derramamiento de sangre** bloodshed

derramar [derra'mar] *vt* to spill; (*verter*) to pour out; (*esparcir*) to scatter; **derramarse** *vr* to pour out

derrame [de'rrame] *nm* (*de líquido*) spilling; (*de sangre*) shedding; (*de tubo etc*) overflow; (*pérdida*) leakage; **derrame cerebral** brain haemorrhage

derredor [derre'ðor] *adv*: **al** o **en ~ de** around, about

derretir [derre'tir] *vt* (*gen*) to melt; (*nieve*) to thaw; **derretirse** *vr* to melt

derribar [derri'βar] *vt* to knock down; (*construcción*) to demolish; (*persona, gobierno, político*) to bring down

derrocar [derro'kar] *vt* (*gobierno*) to bring down, overthrow

derrochar [derro'tʃar] *vt* to squander; **derroche** *nm* (*despilfarro*) waste, squandering

derrota [de'rrota] *nf* (Náut) course; (Mil, Deporte etc) defeat, rout; **derrotar** *vt* (*gen*) to defeat; **derrotero** *nm* (*rumbo*) course

derrumbar [derrum'bar] *vt* (*edificio*) to knock down; **derrumbarse** *vr* to collapse

des etc *vb* V **dar**

desabrochar [desaβro'tʃar] *vt* (*botones, broches*) to undo, unfasten; **desabrocharse** *vr* (*ropa etc*) to come undone

desacato [desa'kato] *nm* (*falta de respeto*) disrespect; (Jur) contempt

desacertado, -a [desaθer'taðo, a] *adj* (*equivocado*) mistaken; (*inoportuno*) unwise

desacierto [desa'θjerto] *nm* mistake, error

desaconsejar [desakonse'xar] *vt* to advise against

desacreditar [desakreði'tar] *vt* (*desprestigiar*) to discredit, bring into disrepute; (*denigrar*) to run down

desacuerdo [desa'kwerðo] *nm* disagreement, discord

desafiar [desa'fjar] *vt* (*retar*) to challenge; (*enfrentarse a*) to defy

desafilado, -a [desafi'laðo, a] *adj* blunt

desafinado, -a [desafi'naðo, a] *adj*: **estar ~** to be out of tune

desafinar [desafi'nar] *vi* (*al cantar*) to be o go out of tune

desafío etc [desa'fio] *vb* V **desafiar** ▷ *nm* (*reto*) challenge; (*combate*) duel; (*resistencia*) defiance

desafortunado, -a [desafortu'naðo, a]

adj (desgraciado) unfortunate, unlucky

desagradable [desaɣra'ðaβle] *adj*
(fastidioso, enojoso) unpleasant; *(irritante)*
disagreeable

desagradar [desaɣra'ðar] *vi (disgustar)* to
displease; *(molestar)* to bother

desagradecido, -a [desaɣraðe'θiðo, a]
adj ungrateful

desagrado [desa'ɣraðo] *nm (disgusto)*
displeasure; *(contrariedad)* dissatisfaction

desagüe [des'aɣwe] *nm (de un líquido)*
drainage; *(cañería)* drainpipe; *(salida)* outlet,
drain

desahogar [desao'ɣar] *vt (aliviar)* to
ease, relieve; *(ira)* to vent; **desahogarse**
vr (relajarse) to relax; *(desfogarse)* to let off
steam

desahogo [desa'oɣo] *nm (alivio)* relief;
(comodidad) comfort, ease

desahuciar [desau'θjar] *vt (enfermo)* to
give up hope for; *(inquilino)* to evict

desairar [desai'rar] *vt (menospreciar)* to
slight, snub

desalentador, a [desalenta'ðor, a] *adj*
discouraging

desaliño [desa'liɲo] *nm* slovenliness

desalmado, -a [desal'maðo, a] *adj (cruel)*
cruel, heartless

desalojar [desalo'xar] *vt (expulsar, echar)*
to eject; *(abandonar)* to move out of ▷ *vi* to
move out

desamor [desa'mor] *nm (frialdad)*
indifference; *(odio)* dislike

desamparado, -a [desampa'raðo, a] *adj*
(persona) helpless; *(lugar: expuesto)* exposed;
(desierto) deserted

desangrar [desan'grar] *vt* to bleed;
(fig: persona) to bleed dry; **desangrarse** *vr*
to lose a lot of blood

desanimado, -a [desani'maðo, a] *adj*
(persona) downhearted; *(espectáculo, fiesta)*
dull

desanimar [desani'mar] *vt (desalentar)*
to discourage; *(deprimir)* to depress;
desanimarse *vr* to lose heart

desapacible [desapa'θiβle] *adj (gen)*
unpleasant

desaparecer [desapare'θer] *vi (gen)*
to disappear; *(el sol, el luz)* to vanish;
desaparecido, -a *adj* missing;
desaparición *nf* disappearance

desapercibido, -a [desaperθi'βiðo, a]
adj (desprevenido) unprepared; **pasar ~** to go
unnoticed

desaprensivo, -a [desapren'siβo, a] *adj*
unscrupulous

desaprobar [desapro'βar] *vt (reprobar)* to
disapprove of; *(condenar)* to condemn; *(no*

consentir) to reject

desaprovechado, -a [desaproβe'tʃaðo,
a] *adj (oportunidad, tiempo)* wasted;
(estudiante) slack

desaprovechar [desaproβe'tʃar] *vt* to
waste

desarmador [desarma'ðor] *(MÉX) nm*
screwdriver

desarmar [desar'mar] *vt (Mil, fig)* to
disarm; *(Tec)* to take apart, dismantle;
desarme *nm* disarmament

desarraigar [desarrai'ɣar] *vt* to uproot;
desarraigo *nm* uprooting

desarreglar [desarre'ɣlar] *vt (desordenar)*
to disarrange; *(trastocar)* to upset, disturb

desarrollar [desarro'ʎar] *vt (gen)* to
develop; **desarrollarse** *vr* to develop;
(ocurrir) to take place; *(Foto)* to develop;
desarrollo *nm* development

desarticular [desartiku'lar] *vt (hueso)*
to dislocate; *(objeto)* to take apart; *(fig)* to
break up

desasosegar [desasose'ɣar] *vt (inquietar)*
to disturb, make uneasy

desasosiego *etc* [desaso'sjeɣo] *vb* V
desasosegar ▷ *nm (intranquilidad)*
uneasiness, restlessness; *(ansiedad)* anxiety

desastre [de'sastre] *nm* disaster;
desastroso, -a *adj* disastrous

desatar [desa'tar] *vt (nudo)* to untie;
(paquete) to undo; *(separar)* to detach;
desatarse *vr (zapatos)* to come untied;
(tormenta) to break

desatascar [desatas'kar] *vt (cañería)* to
unblock, clear

desatender [desaten'der] *vt no prestar*
atención a, to disregard; *(abandonar)* to
neglect

desatino [desa'tino] *nm (idiotez)*
foolishness, folly; *(error)* blunder

desatornillar [desatorni'ʎar] *vt* to
unscrew

desatrancar [desatran'kar] *vt (puerta)* to
unbolt; *(cañería)* to clear, unblock

desautorizado, -a [desautori'θaðo, a]
adj unauthorized

desautorizar [desautori'θar] *vt (oficial)*
to deprive of authority; *(informe)* to deny

desayunar [desaju'nar] *vi* to have
breakfast ▷ *vt* to have for breakfast;
desayuno *nm* breakfast

desazón [desa'θon] *nf* anxiety

desbarajuste [desβara'xuste] *nm*
confusion, disorder

desbaratar [desβara'tar] *vt (deshacer,*
destruir) to ruin

desbloquear [desβloke'ar] *vt*
(negociaciónes, tráfico) to get going again;

(Com: *cuenta*) to unfreeze

desbordar [desβor'ðar] *vt* (*sobrepasar*) to go beyond; (*exceder*) to exceed; **desbordarse** *vr* (*río*) to overflow; (*entusiasmo*) to erupt

descabellado, -a [deskaβe'ʎaðo, a] *adj* (*disparatado*) wild, crazy

descafeinado, -a [deskafei'naðo, a] *adj* decaffeinated ▷ *nm* decaffeinated coffee

descalabro [deska'laβro] *nm* blow; (*desgracia*) misfortune

descalificar [deskalifi'kar] *vt* to disqualify; (*desacreditar*) to discredit

descalzar [deskal'θar] *vt* (*zapato*) to take off; **descalzo, -a** *adj* barefoot(ed)

descambiar [deskam'bjar] *vt* to exchange

descaminado, -a [deskami'naðo, a] *adj* (*equivocado*) on the wrong road; (*fig*) misguided

descampado [deskam'paðo] *nm* open space

descansado, -a [deskan'saðo, a] *adj* (*gen*) rested; (*que tranquiliza*) restful

descansar [deskan'sar] *vt* (*gen*) to rest ▷ *vi* to rest, have a rest; (*echarse*) to lie down

descansillo [deskan'siʎo] *nm* (*de escalera*) landing

descanso [des'kanso] *nm* (*reposo*) rest; (*alivio*) relief; (*pausa*) break; (*Deporte*) interval, half time

descapotable [deskapo'taβle] *nm* (*tb: coche ~*) convertible

descarado, -a [deska'raðo, a] *adj* shameless; (*insolente*) cheeky

descarga [des'karɣa] *nf* (*Arq, Elec, Mil*) discharge; (*Náut*) unloading; **descargar** [deskar'ɣar] *vt* to unload; (*golpe*) to let fly; **descargarse** *vr* to unburden o.s.; **descargarse algo de Internet** to download sth from the Internet

descaro [des'karo] *nm* nerve

descarriar [deska'rrjar] *vt* (*descaminar*) to misdirect; (*fig*) to lead astray; **descarriarse** *vr* (*perderse*) to lose one's way; (*separarse*) to stray; (*pervertirse*) to err, go astray

descarrilamiento [deskarrila'mjento] *nm* (*de tren*) derailment

descarrilar [deskarri'lar] *vi* to be derailed

descartar [deskar'tar] *vt* (*rechazar*) to reject; (*eliminar*) to rule out; **descartarse** *vr* (*Naipes*) to discard; **~se de** to shirk

descendencia [desθen'denθja] *nf* (*origen*) origin, descent; (*hijos*) offspring

descender [desθen'der] *vt* (*bajar: escalera*) to go down ▷ *vi* to descend; (*temperatura, nivel*) to fall, drop; **~ de** to be descended from

descendiente [desθen'djente] *nmf* descendant

descenso [des'θenso] *nm* descent; (*de temperatura*) drop

descifrar [desθi'frar] *vt* to decipher; (*mensaje*) to decode

descolgar [deskol'ɣar] *vt* (*bajar*) to take down; (*teléfono*) to pick up; **descolgarse** *vr* to let o.s. down

descolorido, -a [deskolo'riðo, a] *adj* faded; (*pálido*) pale

descompasado, -a [deskompa'saðo, a] *adj* (*sin proporción*) out of all proportion; (*excesivo*) excessive

descomponer [deskompo'ner] *vt* (*desordenar*) to disarrange, disturb; (*Tec*) to put out of order; (*dividir*) to break down (into parts); (*fig*) to provoke; **descomponerse** *vr* (*corromperse*) to rot, decompose; (*LAM Tec*) to break down

descomposición [deskomposi'θjon] *nf* (*de un objeto*) breakdown; (*de fruta etc*) decomposition; **descomposición de vientre** (ESP) stomach upset, diarrhoea

descompostura [deskompos'tura] *nf* (MÉx: *avería*) breakdown, fault; (LAM: *diarrea*) diarrhoea

descomprimir [deskompri'mir] (*Internet*) to unzip

descompuesto, -a [deskom'pwesto, a] *adj* (*corrompido*) decomposed; (*roto*) broken

desconcertado, -a [deskonθer'taðo, a] *adj* disconcerted, bewildered

desconcertar [deskonθer'tar] *vt* (*confundir*) to baffle; (*incomodar*) to upset, put out; **desconcertarse** *vr* (*turbarse*) to be upset

desconchado, -a [deskon'tʃaðo, a] *adj* (*pintura*) peeling

desconcierto *etc* [deskon'θjerto] *vb* V **desconcertar** ▷ *nm* (*gen*) disorder; (*desorientación*) uncertainty; (*inquietud*) uneasiness

desconectar [deskonek'tar] *vt* to disconnect

desconfianza [deskon'fjanθa] *nf* distrust

desconfiar [deskon'fjar] *vi* to be distrustful; **~ de** to distrust, suspect

descongelar [deskonxe'lar] *vt* to defrost; (*Com, Pol*) to unfreeze

descongestionar [deskonxestjo'nar] *vt* (*cabeza, tráfico*) to clear

desconocer [deskono'θer] *vt* (*ignorar*) not to know, be ignorant of

desconocido, -a [deskono'θiðo, a] *adj* unknown ▷ *nm/f* stranger

desconocimiento [deskonoθi'mjento]

nm falta de conocimientos, ignorance
desconsiderado, -a [deskonsiðeˈraðo, a]
adj inconsiderate; (*insensible*)
thoughtless
desconsuelo *etc* [deskonˈswelo] *vb* V
desconsolar ▷ *nm* (*tristeza*) distress;
(*desesperación*) despair
descontado, -a [deskonˈtaðo, a] *adj*:
dar por ~ (que) to take (it) for granted
(that)
descontar [deskonˈtar] *vt* (*deducir*) to take
away, deduct; (*rebajar*) to discount
descontento, -a [deskonˈtento, a]
adj dissatisfied ▷ *nm* dissatisfaction,
discontent
descorchar [deskorˈtʃar] *vt* to uncork
descorrer [deskoˈrrer] *vt* (*cortinas, cerrojo*)
to draw back
descortés [deskorˈtes] *adj* (*mal educado*)
discourteous; (*grosero*) rude
descoser [deskoˈser] *vt* to unstitch;
descoserse *vr* to come apart (at the
seams)
descosido, -a [deskoˈsiðo, a] *adj*
(*Costura*) unstitched
descreído, -a [deskreˈiðo, a] *adj*
(*incrédulo*) incredulous; (*falto de fe*)
unbelieving
descremado, -a [deskreˈmaðo, a] *adj*
skimmed
describir [deskriˈβir] *vt* to describe;
descripción [deskripˈθjon] *nf* description
descrito [desˈkrito] *pp de* **describir**
descuartizar [deskwartiˈθar] *vt* (*animal*)
to cut up
descubierto, -a [deskuˈβjerto, a] *pp de*
descubrir ▷ *adj* uncovered, bare; (*persona*)
bareheaded ▷ *nm* (*bancario*) overdraft; **al ~**
in the open
descubrimiento [deskuβriˈmjento] *nm*
(*hallazgo*) discovery; (*revelación*) revelation
descubrir [deskuˈβrir] *vt* to discover,
find; (*inaugurar*) to unveil; (*vislumbrar*) to
detect; (*revelar*) to reveal, show; (*destapar*)
to uncover; **descubrirse** *vr* to reveal o.s.;
(*quitarse sombrero*) to take off one's hat;
(*confesar*) to confess
descuento *etc* [desˈkwento] *vb* V
descontar ▷ *nm* discount
descuidado, -a [deskwiˈðaðo, a] *adj*
(*sin cuidado*) careless; (*desordenado*) untidy;
(*olvidadizo*) forgetful; (*dejado*) neglected;
(*desprevenido*) unprepared
descuidar [deskwiˈðar] *vt* (*dejar*) to
neglect; (*olvidar*) to overlook; **descuidarse**
vr (*distraerse*) to be careless; (*abandonarse*) to
let o.s. go; (*desprevenirse*) to drop one's guard;
¡descuida! don't worry!; **descuido** *nm*

(*dejadez*) carelessness; (*olvido*) negligence

○ **PALABRA CLAVE**

desde [ˈdesðe] *prep* **1** (*lugar*) from; **desde
Burgos hasta mi casa hay 30 km** it's 30 km
from Burgos to my house
2 (*posición*): **hablaba desde el balcón** she
was speaking from the balcony
3 (*tiempo: + adv, n*): **desde ahora** from now
on; **desde la boda** since the wedding;
desde niño since I *etc* was a child; **desde 3
años atrás** since 3 years ago
4 (*tiempo: + vb, fecha*) since; for; **nos
conocemos desde 1992/desde hace 20
años** we've known each other since 1992/
for 20 years; **no le veo desde 1997/desde
hace 5 años** I haven't seen him since 1997/
for 5 years
5 (*gama*): **desde los más lujosos hasta los
más económicos** from the most luxurious
to the most reasonably priced
6: **desde luego (que no)** of course (not)
▷ *conj*: **desde que**: **desde que recuerdo**
for as long as I can remember; **desde que
llegó no ha salido** he hasn't been out since
he arrived

desdén [desˈðen] *nm* scorn
desdeñar [desðeˈɲar] *vt* (*despreciar*) to
scorn
desdicha [desˈðitʃa] *nf* (*desgracia*)
misfortune; (*infelicidad*) unhappiness;
desdichado, -a *adj* (*sin suerte*) unlucky;
(*infeliz*) unhappy
desear [deseˈar] *vt* to want, desire, wish
for
desechar [deseˈtʃar] *vt* (*basura*) to throw
out o away; (*ideas*) to reject, discard;
desechos *nmpl* rubbish *sg*, waste *sg*
desembalar [desembaˈlar] *vt* to unpack
desembarazar [desembaraˈθar] *vt*
(*desocupar*) to clear; (*desenredar*) to free;
desembarazarse *vr*: **~se de** to free o.s. of,
get rid of
desembarcar [desembarˈkar] *vt*
(*mercancías etc*) to unload ▷ *vi* to disembark
desembocadura [desembokaˈðura] *nf*
(*de río*) mouth; (*de calle*) opening
desembocar [desemboˈkar] *vi* (*río*) to
flow into; (*fig*) to result in
desembolso [desemˈbolso] *nm* payment
desembrollar [desembroˈʎar] *vt* (*madeja*)
to unravel; (*asunto, malentendido*) to sort out
desemejanza [desemeˈxanθa] *nf*
dissimilarity
desempaquetar [desempakeˈtar] *vt*
(*regalo*) to unwrap; (*mercancía*) to unpack

desempate [desem'pate] nm (Fútbol) replay, play-off; (Tenis) tie-break(er)

desempeñar [desempe'ɲar] vt (cargo) to hold; (papel) to perform; (lo empeñado) to redeem; **~ un papel** (fig) to play (a role)

desempleado, -a [desemple'aðo, a] nm/f unemployed person; **desempleo** nm unemployment

desencadenar [desenkaðe'nar] vt to unchain; (ira) to unleash; **desencadenarse** vr to break loose; (tormenta) to burst; (guerra) to break out

desencajar [desenka'xar] vt (hueso) to dislocate; (mecanismo, pieza) to disconnect, disengage

desencanto [desen'kanto] nm disillusionment

desenchufar [desentʃu'far] vt to unplug

desenfadado, -a [desenfa'ðaðo, a] adj (desenvuelto) uninhibited; (descarado) forward; **desenfado** nm (libertad) freedom; (comportamiento) free and easy manner; (descaro) forwardness

desenfocado, -a [desenfo'kaðo, a] adj (Foto) out of focus

desenfreno [desen'freno] nm wildness; (de las pasiones) lack of self-control

desenganchar [desengan'tʃar] vt (gen) to unhook; (Ferro) to uncouple

desengañar [desenga'ɲar] vt to disillusion; **desengañarse** vr to become disillusioned; **desengaño** nm disillusionment; (decepción) disappointment

desenlace [desen'laθe] nm outcome

desenmascarar [desenmaska'rar] vt to unmask

desenredar [desenre'ðar] vt (pelo) to untangle; (problema) to sort out

desenroscar [desenros'kar] vt to unscrew

desentenderse [desenten'derse] vr: **~ de** to pretend not to know about; (apartarse) to have nothing to do with

desenterrar [desente'rrar] vt to exhume; (tesoro, fig) to unearth, dig up

desentonar [desento'nar] vi (Mús) to sing (o play) out of tune; (color) to clash

desentrañar [desentra'ɲar] vt (misterio) to unravel

desenvoltura [desenβol'tura] nf ease

desenvolver [desenβol'βer] vt (paquete) to unwrap; (fig) to perform; **desenvolverse** vr (desarrollarse) to unfold, develop; (arreglárselas) to cope

deseo [de'seo] nm desire, wish; **deseoso, -a** adj: **estar deseoso de** to be anxious to

desequilibrado, -a [desekili'βraðo, a] adj unbalanced

desertar [deser'tar] vi to desert

desértico, -a [de'sertiko, a] adj desert cpd

desesperación [desespera'θjon] nf (impaciencia) desperation, despair; (irritación) fury

desesperar [desespe'rar] vt to drive to despair; (exasperar) to drive to distraction ▷ vi: **~ de** to despair of; **desesperarse** vr to despair, lose hope

desestabilizar [desestaβili'θar] vt to destabilize

desestimar [desesti'mar] vt (menospreciar) to have a low opinion of; (rechazar) to reject

desfachatez [desfatʃa'teθ] nf (insolencia) impudence; (descaro) rudeness

desfalco [des'falko] nm embezzlement

desfallecer [desfaʎe'θer] vi (perder las fuerzas) to become weak; (desvanecerse) to faint

desfasado, -a [desfa'saðo, a] adj (anticuado) old-fashioned; **desfase** nm (diferencia) gap

desfavorable [desfaβo'raβle] adj unfavourable

desfigurar [desfiɣu'rar] vt (cara) to disfigure; (cuerpo) to deform

desfiladero [desfila'ðero] nm gorge

desfilar [desfi'lar] vi to parade; **desfile** nm procession; **desfile de modelos** fashion show

desgana [des'ɣana] nf (falta de apetito) loss of appetite; (apatía) unwillingness; **desganado, -a** adj: **estar desganado** (sin apetito) to have no appetite; (sin entusiasmo) to have lost interest

desgarrar [desɣa'rrar] vt to tear (up); (fig) to shatter; **desgarro** nm (en tela) tear; (aflicción) grief

desgastar [desɣas'tar] vt (deteriorar) to wear away o down; (estropear) to spoil; **desgastarse** vr to get worn out; **desgaste** nm wear (and tear)

desglosar [desɣlo'sar] vt (factura) to break down

desgracia [des'ɣraθja] nf misfortune; (accidente) accident; (vergüenza) disgrace; (contratiempo) setback; **por ~** unfortunately; **desgraciado, -a** [desɣra'θjaðo, a] adj (sin suerte) unlucky, unfortunate; (miserable) wretched; (infeliz) miserable

desgravar [desɣra'βar] vt (impuestos) to reduce the tax o duty on

desguace [des'ɣwaθe] (ESP) nm junkyard

deshabitado, -a [desaβi'taðo, a] adj uninhabited

deshacer [desa'θer] vt (casa) to break up; (Tec) to take apart; (enemigo) to defeat; (diluir) to melt; (contrato) to break; (intriga) to solve; **deshacerse** vr (disolverse) to melt; (despedazarse) to come apart o undone; **~se de** to get rid of; **~se en lágrimas** to burst into tears

deshecho, -a [des'etʃo, a] adj undone; (roto) smashed; (persona): **estar ~** to be shattered

desheredar [desere'ðar] vt to disinherit

deshidratar [desiðra'tar] vt to dehydrate

deshielo [des'jelo] nm thaw

deshonesto, -a [deso'nesto, a] adj indecent

deshonra [des'onra] nf (deshonor) dishonour; (vergüenza) shame

deshora [des'ora]: **a ~** adv at the wrong time

deshuesadero [deswesa'ðero] (MÉX) nm junkyard

deshuesar [deswe'sar] vt (carne) to bone; (fruta) to stone

desierto, -a [de'sjerto, a] adj (casa, calle, negocio) deserted ⊳ nm desert

designar [desix'nar] vt (nombrar) to designate; (indicar) to fix

desigual [desi'ɣwal] adj (terreno) uneven; (lucha etc) unequal

desilusión [desilu'sjon] nf disillusionment; (decepción) disappointment; **desilusionar** vt to disillusion; to disappoint; **desilusionarse** vr to become disillusioned

desinfectar [desinfek'tar] vt to disinfect

desinflar [desin'flar] vt to deflate

desintegración [desinteɣra'θjon] nf disintegration

desinterés [desinte'res] nm (desgana) lack of interest; (altruismo) unselfishness

desintoxicarse [desintoksi'karse] vr (drogadicto) to undergo detoxification

desistir [desis'tir] vi (renunciar) to stop, desist

desleal [desle'al] adj (infiel) disloyal; (Com: competencia) unfair; **deslealtad** nf disloyalty

desligar [desli'ɣar] vt (desatar) to untie, undo; (separar) to separate; **desligarse** vr (de un compromiso) to extricate o.s.

desliz [des'liθ] nm (fig) lapse; **deslizar** vt to slip, slide

deslumbrar [deslum'brar] vt to dazzle

desmadrarse [desma'ðrarse] (fam) vr (descontrolarse) to run wild; (divertirse) to let one's hair down; **desmadre** (fam) nm (desorganización) chaos; (jaleo) commotion

desmán [des'man] nm (exceso) outrage;

(abuso de poder) abuse

desmantelar [desmante'lar] vt (deshacer) to dismantle; (casa) to strip

desmaquillador [desmakiʎa'ðor] nm make-up remover

desmayar [desma'jar] vi to lose heart; **desmayarse** vr (Med) to faint; **desmayo** nm (Med: acto) faint; (: estado) unconsciousness

desmemoriado, -a [desmemo'rjado, a] adj forgetful

desmentir [desmen'tir] vt (contradecir) to contradict; (refutar) to deny

desmenuzar [desmenu'θar] vt (deshacer) to crumble; (carne) to chop; (examinar) to examine closely

desmesurado, -a [desmesu'raðo, a] adj disproportionate

desmontable [desmon'taβle] adj (que se quita: pieza) detachable; (plegable) collapsible, folding

desmontar [desmon'tar] vt (deshacer) to dismantle; (tierra) to level ⊳ vi to dismount

desmoralizar [desmorali'θar] vt to demoralize

desmoronar [desmoro'nar] vt to wear away, erode; **desmoronarse** vr (edificio, dique) to collapse; (economía) to decline

desnatado, -a [desna'taðo, a] adj skimmed

desnivel [desni'βel] nm (de terreno) unevenness

desnudar [desnu'ðar] vt (desvestir) to undress; (despojar) to strip; **desnudarse** vr (desvestirse) to get undressed; **desnudo, -a** adj naked ⊳ nm/f nude; **desnudo de** devoid o bereft of

desnutrición [desnutri'θjon] nf malnutrition; **desnutrido, -a** adj undernourished

desobedecer [desoβeðe'θer] vt, vi to disobey; **desobediencia** nf disobedience

desocupado, -a [desoku'paðo, a] adj at leisure; (desempleado) unemployed; (deshabitado) empty, vacant

desodorante [desoðo'rante] nm deodorant

desolación [desola'θjon] nf (de lugar) desolation; (fig) grief

desolar [deso'lar] vt to ruin, lay waste

desorbitado, -a [desorβi'taðo, a] adj (excesivo: ambición) boundless; (deseos) excessive; (: precio) exorbitant

desorden [des'orðen] nm confusion; (político) disorder, unrest

desorganización [desorɣaniθa'θjon] nf (de persona) disorganization; (en empresa, oficina) disorder, chaos

desorientar [desorjen'tar] vt (extraviar) to mislead; (confundir, desconcertar) to confuse; **desorientarse** vr (perderse) to lose one's way

despabilado, -a [despaβi'laðo, a] adj (despierto) wide-awake; (fig) alert, sharp

despachar [despa't∫ar] vt (negocio) to do, complete; (enviar) to send, dispatch; (vender) to sell, deal in; (billete) to issue; (mandar ir) to send away

despacho [des'pat∫o] nm (oficina) office; (de paquetes) dispatch; (venta) sale; (comunicación) message

despacio [des'paθjo] adv slowly

desparpajo [despar'paxo] nm self-confidence; (pey) nerve

desparramar [desparra'mar] vt (esparcir) to scatter; (líquido) to spill

despecho [des'pet∫o] nm spite

despectivo, -a [despek'tiβo, a] adj (despreciativo) derogatory; (Ling) pejorative

despedida [despe'ðiða] nf (adiós) farewell; (de obrero) sacking

despedir [despe'ðir] vt (visita) to see off, show out; (empleado) to dismiss; (inquilino) to evict; (objeto) to hurl; (color etc) to give out o off; **despedirse** vr: **~se de** to say goodbye to

despegar [despe'xar] vt to unstick ▷ vi (avión) to take off; **despegarse** vr to come loose, come unstuck; **despego** nm detachment

despegue etc [des'pexe] vb V **despegar** ▷ nm takeoff

despeinado, -a [despei'naðo, a] adj dishevelled, unkempt

despejado, -a [despe'xaðo, a] adj (lugar) clear, free; (cielo) clear; (persona) wide-awake, bright

despejar [despe'xar] vt (gen) to clear; (misterio) to clear up ▷ vi (el tiempo) to clear; **despejarse** vr (tiempo, cielo) to clear (up); (misterio) to become clearer; (cabeza) to clear

despensa [des'pensa] nf larder

despeñarse [despe'narse] vr to hurl o.s. down; (coche) to tumble over

desperdicio [desper'ðiθjo] nm (despilfarro) squandering; **desperdicios** nmpl (basura) rubbish sg (BRIT), garbage sg (US); (residuos) waste sg

desperezarse [despere'θarse] vr to stretch

desperfecto [desper'fekto] nm (deterioro) slight damage; (defecto) flaw, imperfection

despertador [desperta'ðor] nm alarm clock

despertar [desper'tar] nm awakening ▷ vt (persona) to wake up; (recuerdos) to revive; (sentimiento) to arouse ▷ vi to awaken, wake up; **despertarse** vr to awaken, wake up

despido etc [des'piðo] vb V **despedir** ▷ nm dismissal, sacking

despierto, -a etc [des'pjerto, a] vb V **despertar** ▷ adj awake; (fig) sharp, alert

despilfarro [despil'farro] nm (derroche) squandering; (lujo desmedido) extravagance

despistar [despis'tar] vt to throw off the track o scent; (confundir) to mislead, confuse; **despistarse** vr to take the wrong road; (confundirse) to become confused

despiste [des'piste] nm absent-mindedness; **un ~** a mistake o slip

desplazamiento [desplaθa'mjento] nm displacement

desplazar [despla'θar] vt to move; (Náut) to displace; (Inform) to scroll; (fig) to oust; **desplazarse** vr (persona) to travel

desplegar [desple'xar] vt (tela, papel) to unfold, open out; (bandera) to unfurl; **despliegue** etc [des'pleɣe] vb V **desplegar** ▷ nm display

desplomarse [desplo'marse] vr (edificio, gobierno, persona) to collapse

desplumar [desplu'mar] vt (ave) to pluck; (fam: estafar) to fleece

despoblado, -a [despo'βlaðo, a] adj (sin habitantes) uninhabited

despojar [despo'xar] vt (alguien: de sus bienes) to divest of, deprive of; (casa) to strip, leave bare; (alguien: de su cargo) to strip of

despojo [des'poxo] nm (acto) plundering; (objetos) plunder, loot; **despojos** nmpl (de ave, res) offal sg

desposado, -a [despo'saðo, a] adj, nm/f newly-wed

despreciar [despre'θjar] vt (desdeñar) to despise, scorn; (afrentar) to slight; **desprecio** nm scorn, contempt; slight

desprender [despren'der] vt (broche) to unfasten; (olor) to give off; **desprenderse** vr (botón: caerse) to fall off; (broche) to come unfastened; (olor, perfume) to be given off; **~se de algo que ...** to draw from sth that ...

desprendimiento [desprendi'mjento] nm (gen) loosening; (generosidad) disinterestedness; (de tierra, rocas) landslide; **desprendimiento de retina** detachment of the retina

despreocupado, -a [despreoku'paðo, a] adj (sin preocupación) unworried, nonchalant; (negligente) careless

despreocuparse [despreoku'parse] vr not to worry; **~ de** to have no interest in

desprestigiar [despresti'xjar] vt (criticar) to run down; (desacreditar) to discredit

desprevenido, -a [despreβe'niðo, a] *adj*
(*no preparado*) unprepared, unready
desproporcionado, -a
[desproporθjo'naðo, a] *adj*
disproportionate, out of proportion
desprovisto, -a [despro'βisto, a] *adj*: **~
de** devoid of
después [des'pwes] *adv* afterwards,
later; (*próximo paso*) next; **~ de comer** after
lunch; **un año ~** a year later; **~ se debatió el
tema** next the matter was discussed; **~ de
corregido el texto** after the text had been
corrected; **~ de todo** after all
desquiciado, -a [deski'θjaðo, a] *adj*
deranged
destacar [desta'kar] *vt* to emphasize,
point up; (*Mil*) to detach, detail ▷ *vi*
(*resaltarse*) to stand out; (*persona*) to be
outstanding *o* exceptional; **destacarse**
vr to stand out; to be outstanding *o*
exceptional
destajo [des'taxo] *nm*: **trabajar a ~** to do
piecework
destapar [desta'par] *vt* (*botella*) to open;
(*cacerola*) to take the lid off; (*descubrir*) to
uncover; **destaparse** *vr* (*revelarse*) to reveal
one's true character
destartalado, -a [destarta'laðo, a] *adj*
(*desordenado*) untidy; (*ruinoso*) tumbledown
destello [des'teʎo] *nm* (*de estrella*) twinkle;
(*de faro*) signal light
destemplado, -a [destem'plaðo, a] *adj*
(*Mús*) out of tune; (*voz*) harsh; (*Med*) out of
sorts; (*tiempo*) unpleasant, nasty
desteñir [deste'ɲir] *vt* to fade ▷ *vi* to
fade; **desteñirse** *vr* to fade; **esta tela no
destiñe** this fabric will not run
desternillarse [desterni'ʎarse] *vr*: **~ de
risa** to split one's sides laughing
desterrar [deste'rrar] *vt* (*exiliar*) to exile;
(*fig*) to banish, dismiss
destiempo [des'tjempo]: **a ~** *adv* out of
turn
destierro *etc* [des'tjerro] *vb* V **desterrar**
▷ *nm* exile
destilar [desti'lar] *vt* to distil; **destilería**
nf distillery
destinar [desti'nar] *vt* (*funcionario*) to
appoint, assign; (*fondos*): **~ (a)** to set aside
(for)
destinatario, -a [destina'tarjo, a] *nm/f*
addressee
destino [des'tino] *nm* (*suerte*) destiny; (*de
avión, viajero*) destination; **con ~ a Londres**
(*barco*) (bound) for London; (*avión, carta*) to
London
destituir [destitu'ir] *vt* to dismiss
destornillador [destorniʎa'ðor] *nm*

screwdriver
destornillar [destorni'ʎar] *vt* (*tornillo*) to
unscrew; **destornillarse** *vr* to unscrew
destreza [des'treθa] *nf* (*habilidad*) skill;
(*maña*) dexterity
destrozar [destro'θar] *vt* (*romper*) to
smash, break (up); (*estropear*) to ruin;
(*nervios*) to shatter
destrozo [des'troθo] *nm* (*acción*)
destruction; (*desastre*) smashing; **destrozos**
nmpl (*pedazos*) pieces; (*daños*) havoc *sg*
destrucción [destruk'θjon] *nf*
destruction
destruir [destru'ir] *vt* to destroy
desuso [des'uso] *nm* disuse; **caer en ~** to
become obsolete
desvalijar [desvali'xar] *vt* (*persona*) to rob;
(*casa, tienda*) to burgle; (*coche*) to break into
desván [des'βan] *nm* attic
desvanecer [desβane'θer] *vt* (*disipar*) to
dispel; (*borrar*) to blur; **desvanecerse** *vr*
(*humo etc*) to vanish, disappear; (*color*) to
fade; (*recuerdo, sonido*) to fade away; (*Med*) to
pass out; (*duda*) to be dispelled
desvariar [desβa'rjar] *vi* (*enfermo*) to be
delirious
desvelar [desβe'lar] *vt* to keep awake;
desvelarse *vr* (*no poder dormir*) to stay
awake; (*preocuparse*) to be vigilant *o*
watchful
desventaja [desβen'taxa] *nf*
disadvantage
desvergonzado, -a [desβerɣon'θaðo, a]
adj shameless
desvestir [desβes'tir] *vt* to undress;
desvestirse *vr* to undress
desviación [desβja'θjon] *nf* deviation;
(*Auto*) diversion, detour
desviar [des'βjar] *vt* to turn aside; (*río*)
to alter the course of; (*navío*) to divert, re-
route; (*conversación*) to sidetrack; **desviarse**
vr (*apartarse del camino*) to turn aside;
(: *barco*) to go off course
desvío *etc* [des'βio] *vb* V **desviar**
▷ *nm* (*desviación*) detour, diversion; (*fig*)
indifference
desvivirse [desβi'βirse] *vr*: **~ por** (*anhelar*)
to long for, crave for; (*hacer lo posible por*) to
do one's utmost for
detallar [deta'ʎar] *vt* to detail
detalle [de'taʎe] *nm* detail; (*gesto*) gesture,
token; **al ~** in detail; (*Com*) retail
detallista [deta'ʎista] *nmf* (*Com*) retailer
detective [detek'tiβe] *nmf* detective;
detective privado private detective
detener [dete'ner] *vt* (*gen*) to stop; (*Jur*)
to arrest; (*objeto*) to keep; **detenerse** *vr*
to stop; (*demorarse*): **~se en** to delay over,

linger over
detenidamente [deteni∂a'mente] *adv*
(*minuciosamente*) carefully; (*extensamente*) at
great length
detenido, -a [dete'ni∂o, a] *adj* (*arrestado*)
under arrest ▷ *nm/f* person under arrest,
prisoner
detenimiento [deteni'mjento] *nm*: **con ~**
thoroughly; (*observar, considerar*) carefully
detergente [deter'xente] *nm* detergent
deteriorar [deterjo'rar] *vt* to spoil,
damage; **deteriorarse** *vr* to deteriorate;
deterioro *nm* deterioration
determinación [determina'θjon] *nf*
(*empeño*) determination; (*decisión*) decision;
determinado, -a *adj* specific
determinar [determi'nar] *vt* (*plazo*) to
fix; (*precio*) to settle; **determinarse** *vr* to
decide
detestar [detes'tar] *vt* to detest
detractor, a [detrak'tor, a] *nm/f*
slanderer, libeller
detrás [de'tras] *adv* (*tb*: **por ~**) behind;
(*atrás*) at the back; **~ de** behind
detrimento [detri'mento] *nm*: **en ~ de** to
the detriment of
deuda ['deu∂a] *nf* debt; **deuda exterior/
pública** foreign/national debt
devaluación [deβalwa'θjon] *nf*
devaluation
devastar [deβas'tar] *vt* (*destruir*) to
devastate
deveras [de'βeras] (*MÉX*) *nf inv*: **un amigo
de (a) ~** a true o real friend
devoción [deβo'θjon] *nf* devotion
devolución [deβolu'θjon] *nf* (*reenvío*)
return, sending back; (*reembolso*)
repayment; (*Jur*) devolution
devolver [deβol'βer] *vt* to return; (*lo
extraviado, lo prestado*) to give back; (*carta al
correo*) to send back; (*Com*) to repay, refund
▷ *vi* (*vomitar*) to be sick
devorar [deβo'rar] *vt* to devour
devoto, -a [de'βoto, a] *adj* devout ▷ *nm/f*
admirer
devuelto *pp de* **devolver**
devuelva *etc vb* V **devolver**
di *etc vb* V **dar**; **decir**
día ['dia] *nm* day; **¿qué ~ es?** what's the
date?; **estar/poner al ~** to be/keep up
to date; **el ~ de hoy/de mañana** today/
tomorrow; **al ~ siguiente** (on) the following
day; **vivir al ~** to live from hand to mouth;
de ~ by day, in daylight; **en pleno ~** in
full daylight; **Día de la Independencia**
Independence Day; **Día de los Muertos**
(*MÉX*) All Souls' Day; **Día de Reyes** Epiphany;
día feriado (*LAM*) holiday; **día festivo** (*ESP*)

holiday; **día lectivo** teaching day; **día libre**
day off
diabetes [dja'βetes] *nf* diabetes
diablo ['djaβlo] *nm* devil; **diablura** *nf*
prank
diadema [dja'∂ema] *nf* tiara
diafragma [dja'fraɣma] *nm* diaphragm
diagnóstico [djaɣ'nostiko] *nm* =
diagnosis
diagonal [djaɣo'nal] *adj* diagonal
diagrama [dja'ɣrama] *nm* diagram
dial [djal] *nm* dial
dialecto [dja'lekto] *nm* dialect
dialogar [djalo'ɣar] *vi*: **~ con** (*Pol*) to hold
talks with
diálogo ['djaloɣo] *nm* dialogue
diamante [dja'mante] *nm* diamond
diana ['djana] *nf* (*Mil*) reveille; (*de blanco*)
centre, bull's-eye
diapositiva [djaposi'tiβa] *nf* (*Foto*) slide,
transparency
diario, -a ['djarjo, a] *adj* daily ▷ *nm*
newspaper; **a ~** daily; **de ~** everyday
diarrea [dja'rrea] *nf* diarrhoea
dibujar [diβu'xar] *vt* to draw, sketch;
dibujo *nm* drawing; **dibujos animados**
cartoons
diccionario [dikθjo'narjo] *nm* dictionary
dice *etc vb* V **decir**
dicho, -a ['dit∫o, a] *pp de* **decir** ▷ *adj*: **en
~s países** in the aforementioned countries
▷ *nm* saying
dichoso, -a [di't∫oso, a] *adj* happy
diciembre [di'θjembre] *nm* December
dictado [dik'ta∂o] *nm* dictation
dictador [dikta'∂or] *nm* dictator;
dictadura *nf* dictatorship
dictar [dik'tar] *vt* (*carta*) to dictate;
(*Jur: sentencia*) to pronounce; (*decreto*) to
issue; (*LAM: clase*) to give
didáctico, -a [di'∂aktiko, a] *adj*
educational
diecinueve [djeθi'nweβe] *num* nineteen
dieciocho [djeθi'ot∫o] *num* eighteen
dieciséis [djeθi'seis] *num* sixteen
diecisiete [djeθi'sjete] *num* seventeen
diente ['djente] *nm* (*Anat, Tec*) tooth; (*Zool*)
fang; (: *de elefante*) tusk; (*de ajo*) clove
diera *etc vb* V **dar**
diesel ['disel] *adj*: **motor ~** diesel engine
diestro, -a ['djestro, a] *adj* (*derecho*) right;
(*hábil*) skilful
dieta ['djeta] *nf* diet; **estar a ~** to be on
a diet
diez [djeθ] *num* ten
diferencia [dife'renθja] *nf* difference; **a
~ de** unlike; **diferenciar** *vt* to differentiate
between ▷ *vi* to differ; **diferenciarse**

vr to differ, be different; (*distinguirse*) to distinguish o.s.

diferente [dife'rente] *adj* different

diferido [dife'riðo] *nm*: **en ~** (*TV etc*) recorded

difícil [di'fiθil] *adj* difficult

dificultad [difikul'tað] *nf* difficulty; (*problema*) trouble

dificultar [difikul'tar] *vt* (*complicar*) to complicate, make difficult; (*estorbar*) to obstruct

difundir [difun'dir] *vt* (*calor, luz*) to diffuse; (*Radio, TV*) to broadcast; **~ una noticia** to spread a piece of news; **difundirse** *vr* to spread (out)

difunto, -a [di'funto, a] *adj* dead, deceased ▷ *nm/f* deceased (person)

difusión [difu'sjon] *nf* (*Radio, TV*) broadcasting

diga *etc vb* V **decir**

digerir [dixe'rir] *vt* to digest; (*fig*) to absorb; **digestión** *nf* digestion; **digestivo, -a** *adj* digestive

digital [dixi'tal] *adj* digital

dignarse [dix'narse] *vr* to deign to

dignidad [dixni'ðað] *nf* dignity

digno, -a ['dixno, a] *adj* worthy

digo *etc vb* V **decir**

dije *etc vb* V **decir**

dilatar [dila'tar] *vt* (*cuerpo*) to dilate; (*prolongar*) to prolong

dilema [di'lema] *nm* dilemma

diluir [dilu'ir] *vt* to dilute

diluvio [di'luβjo] *nm* deluge, flood

dimensión [dimen'sjon] *nf* dimension

diminuto, -a [dimi'nuto, a] *adj* tiny, diminutive

dimitir [dimi'tir] *vi* to resign

dimos *vb* V **dar**

Dinamarca [dina'marka] *nf* Denmark

dinámico, -a [di'namiko, a] *adj* dynamic

dinamita [dina'mita] *nf* dynamite

dínamo ['dinamo] *nf* dynamo

dineral [dine'ral] *nm* large sum of money, fortune

dinero [di'nero] *nm* money; **dinero en efectivo** *o* **metálico** cash; **dinero suelto** (loose) change

dio *vb* V **dar**

dios [djos] *nm* god; **¡D~ mío!** (oh,) my God!; **¡por D~!** for heaven's sake!; **diosa** ['djosa] *nf* goddess

diploma [di'ploma] *nm* diploma

diplomacia [diplo'maθja] *nf* diplomacy; (*fig*) tact

diplomado, -a [diplo'maðo, a] *adj* qualified

diplomático, -a [diplo'matiko, a] *adj* diplomatic ▷ *nm/f* diplomat

diputación [diputa'θjon] *nf* (*tb*: **~ provincial**) ≈ county council

diputado, -a [dipu'taðo, a] *nm/f* delegate; (*Pol*) ≈ member of parliament (*BRIT*) ≈ representative (*US*)

dique ['dike] *nm* dyke

diré *etc vb* V **decir**

dirección [direk'θjon] *nf* direction; (*señas*) address; (*Auto*) steering; (*gerencia*) management; (*Pol*) leadership; **dirección única/prohibida** one-way street/no entry

direccional [direkθjo'nal] (*MÉX*) *nf* (*Auto*) indicator

directa [di'rekta] *nf* (*Auto*) top gear

directiva [direk'tiβa] *nf* (*tb*: **junta ~**) board of directors

directo, -a [di'rekto, a] *adj* direct; (*Radio, TV*) live; **transmitir en ~** to broadcast live

director, a [direk'tor, a] *adj* leading ▷ *nm/f* director; (*Escol*) head (teacher) (*BRIT*), principal (*US*); (*gerente*) manager/ess; (*Prensa*) editor; **director de cine** film director; **director general** managing director

directorio [direk'torjo] (*MÉX*) *nm* (*telefónico*) phone book

dirigente [diri'xente] *nmf* (*Pol*) leader

dirigir [diri'xir] *vt* to direct; (*carta*) to address; (*obra de teatro, film*) to direct; (*Mús*) to conduct; (*negocio*) to manage; **dirigirse** *vr*: **~se a** to go towards, make one's way towards; (*hablar con*) to speak to

dirija *etc vb* V **dirigir**

disciplina [disθi'plina] *nf* discipline

discípulo, -a [dis'θipulo, a] *nm/f* disciple

Discman® ['diskman] *nm* Discman®

disco ['disko] *nm* disc; (*Deporte*) discus; (*Tel*) dial; (*Auto: semáforo*) light; (*Mús*) record; **disco compacto/de larga duración** compact disc/long-playing record; **disco de freno** brake disc; **disco flexible/duro** *o* **rígido** (*Inform*) floppy/hard disk

disconforme [diskon'forme] *adj* differing; **estar ~ (con)** to be in disagreement (with)

discordia [dis'korðja] *nf* discord

discoteca [disko'teka] *nf* disco(theque)

discreción [diskre'θjon] *nf* discretion; (*reserva*) prudence; **comer a ~** to eat as much as one wishes

discreto, -a [dis'kreto, a] *adj* discreet

discriminación [diskrimina'θjon] *nf* discrimination

disculpa [dis'kulpa] *nf* excuse; (*pedir perdón*) apology; **pedir ~s a/por** to apologize to/for; **disculpar** *vt* to excuse, pardon; **disculparse** *vr* to excuse o.s.; to apologize

discurso [dis'kurso] nm speech

discusión [disku'sjon] nf (diálogo) discussion; (riña) argument

discutir [disku'tir] vt (debatir) to discuss; (pelear) to argue about; (contradecir) to argue against ▷ vi (debatir) to discuss; (pelearse) to argue

disecar [dise'kar] vt (conservar: animal) to stuff; (: planta) to dry

diseñar [dise'ɲar] vt, vi to design

diseño [di'seɲo] nm design

disfraz [dis'fraθ] nm (máscara) disguise; (excusa) pretext; **disfrazar** vt to disguise; **disfrazarse** vr: **disfrazarse de** to disguise o.s. as

disfrutar [disfru'tar] vt to enjoy ▷ vi to enjoy o.s.; ~ **de** to enjoy, possess

disgustar [disɣus'tar] vt (no gustar) to displease; (contrariar, enojar) to annoy, upset; **disgustarse** vr (enfadarse) to get upset; (dos personas) to fall out

▌ No confundir **disgustar** con la palabra inglesa disgust.

disgusto [dis'ɣusto] nm (contrariedad) annoyance; (tristeza) grief; (riña) quarrel

disimular [disimu'lar] vt (ocultar) to hide, conceal ▷ vi to dissemble

dislocarse [dislo'karse] vr (articulación) to sprain, dislocate

disminución [disminu'θjon] nf decrease, reduction

disminuido, -a [disminu'iðo, a] nm/f: ~ **mental/físico** mentally/physically handicapped person

disminuir [disminu'ir] vt to decrease, diminish

disolver [disol'βer] vt (gen) to dissolve; **disolverse** vr to dissolve; (Com) to go into liquidation

dispar [dis'par] adj different

disparar [dispa'rar] vt, vi to shoot, fire

disparate [dispa'rate] nm (tontería) foolish remark; (error) blunder; **decir ~s** to talk nonsense

disparo [dis'paro] nm shot

dispersar [disper'sar] vt to disperse; **dispersarse** vr to scatter

disponer [dispo'ner] vt (arreglar) to arrange; (ordenar) to put in order; (preparar) to prepare, get ready ▷ vi: ~ **de** to have, own; **disponerse** vr: **~se a** o **para hacer** to prepare to do

disponible [dispo'niβle] adj available

disposición [disposi'θjon] nf arrangement, disposition; (voluntad) willingness; (Inform) layout; **a su ~** at your service

dispositivo [disposi'tiβo] nm device, mechanism

dispuesto, -a [dis'pwesto, a] pp de **disponer** ▷ adj (arreglado) arranged; (preparado) disposed

disputar [dispu'tar] vt (carrera) to compete in

disquete [dis'kete] nm floppy disk, diskette

distancia [dis'tanθja] nf distance; **distanciar** [distan'θjar] vt to space out; **distanciarse** vr to become estranged; **distante** [dis'tante] adj distant

diste vb V **dar**

disteis vb V **dar**

distinción [distin'θjon] nf distinction; (elegancia) elegance; (honor) honour

distinguido, -a [distin'giðo, a] adj distinguished

distinguir [distin'gir] vt to distinguish; (escoger) to single out; **distinguirse** vr to be distinguished

distintivo [distin'tiβo] nm badge; (fig) characteristic

distinto, -a [dis'tinto, a] adj different; (claro) clear

distracción [distrak'θjon] nf distraction; (pasatiempo) hobby, pastime; (olvido) absent-mindedness, distraction

distraer [distra'er] vt (atención) to distract; (divertir) to amuse; (fondos) to embezzle; **distraerse** vr (entretenerse) to amuse o.s.; (perder la concentración) to allow one's attention to wander

distraído, -a [distra'iðo, a] adj (gen) absent-minded; (entretenido) amusing

distribuidor, a [distriβui'ðor, a] nm/f distributor; **distribuidora** nf (Com) dealer, agent; (Cine) distributor

distribuir [distriβu'ir] vt to distribute

distrito [dis'trito] nm (sector, territorio) region; (barrio) district; **Distrito Federal** (MÉX) Federal District; **distrito postal** postal district

disturbio [dis'turβjo] nm disturbance; (desorden) riot

disuadir [diswa'ðir] vt to dissuade

disuelto [di'swelto] pp de **disolver**

DIU nm abr (= dispositivo intrauterino) IUD

diurno, -a ['djurno, a] adj day cpd

divagar [diβa'ɣar] vi (desviarse) to digress

diván [di'βan] nm divan

diversidad [diβersi'ðað] nf diversity, variety

diversión [diβer'sjon] nf (gen) entertainment; (actividad) hobby, pastime

diverso, -a [di'βerso, a] adj diverse; **~s libros** several books; **diversos** nmpl sundries

divertido, -a [diβer'tiðo, a] adj (chiste) amusing; (fiesta etc) enjoyable

divertir [diβer'tir] vt (entretener, recrear) to amuse; **divertirse** vr (pasarlo bien) to have a good time; (distraerse) to amuse o.s.

dividendos [diβi'ðendos] nmpl (Com) dividends

dividir [diβi'ðir] vt (gen) to divide; (distribuir) to distribute, share out

divierta etc vb V **divertir**

divino, -a [di'βino, a] adj divine

divirtiendo etc vb V **divertir**

divisa [di'βisa] nf (emblema) emblem, badge; **divisas** nfpl foreign exchange sg

divisar [diβi'sar] vt to make out, distinguish

división [diβi'sjon] nf (gen) division; (de partido) split; (de país) partition

divorciar [diβor'θjar] vt to divorce; **divorciarse** vr to get divorced; **divorcio** nm divorce

divulgar [diβul'ɣar] vt (ideas) to spread; (secreto) to divulge

DNI (ESP) nm abr (= Documento Nacional de Identidad) national identity card

- **DNI**
-
- The **Documento Nacional de**
- **Identidad** is a Spanish ID card
- which must be carried at all times
- and produced on request for the
- police. It contains the holder's photo,
- fingerprints and personal details. It
- is also known as the **DNI** or "carnet de
- identidad".

Dña. abr (= doña) Mrs

do [do] nm (Mús) do, C

dobladillo [doβla'ðiʎo] nm (de vestido) hem; (de pantalón: vuelta) turn-up (BRIT), cuff (US)

doblar [do'βlar] vt to double; (papel) to fold; (caño) to bend; (la esquina) to turn, go round; (film) to dub ▷ vi to turn; (campana) to toll; **doblarse** vr (plegarse) to fold (up), crease; (encorvarse) to bend; **~ a la derecha/izquierda** to turn right/left

doble ['doβle] adj double; (de dos aspectos) dual; (fig) two-faced ▷ nm double ▷ nmf (Teatro) double, stand-in; **dobles** nmpl (Deporte) doubles sg; **con ~ sentido** with a double meaning

doce ['doθe] num twelve; **docena** nf dozen

docente [do'θente] adj: **centro/personal ~** teaching establishment/staff

dócil ['doθil] adj (pasivo) docile; (obediente) obedient

doctor, a [dok'tor, a] nm/f doctor

doctorado [dokto'raðo] nm doctorate

doctrina [dok'trina] nf doctrine, teaching

documentación [dokumenta'θjon] nf documentation, papers pl

documental [dokumen'tal] adj, nm documentary

documento [doku'mento] nm (certificado) document; **documento adjunto** (Inform) attachment; **documento nacional de identidad** identity card

dólar ['dolar] nm dollar

doler [do'ler] vt, vi to hurt; (fig) to grieve; **dolerse** vr (de su situación) to grieve, feel sorry; (de las desgracias ajenas) to sympathize; **me duele el brazo** my arm hurts

dolor [do'lor] nm pain; (fig) grief, sorrow; **dolor de cabeza/estómago/muelas** headache/stomachache/toothache

domar [do'mar] vt to tame

domesticar [domesti'kar] vt = **domar**

doméstico, -a [do'mestiko, a] adj (vida, servicio) home; (tareas) household; (animal) tame, pet

domicilio [domi'θiljo] nm home; **servicio a ~** home delivery service; **sin ~ fijo** of no fixed abode; **domicilio particular** private residence

dominante [domi'nante] adj dominant; (persona) domineering

dominar [domi'nar] vt (gen) to dominate; (idiomas) to be fluent in ▷ vi to dominate, prevail

domingo [do'mingo] nm Sunday; **Domingo de Ramos/Resurrección** Palm/Easter Sunday

dominio [do'minjo] nm (tierras) domain; (autoridad) power, authority; (de las pasiones) grip, hold; (de idiomas) command

don [don] nm (talento) gift; **~ Juan Gómez** Mr Juan Gómez, Juan Gómez Esq (BRIT)

- **DON/DOÑA**
-
- The term **don/doña** often abbreviated
- to **D./Dña** is placed before the first
- name as a mark of respect to an older
- or more senior person – eg Don Diego,
- Doña Inés. Although becoming rarer
- in Spain it is still used with names and
- surnames on official documents and
- formal correspondence – eg "Sr. D. Pedro
- Rodríguez Hernández", "Sra. Dña. Inés
- Rodríguez Hernández".

dona ['dona] (MÉX) nf doughnut, donut (US)

donar [do'nar] vt to donate

donativo [dona'tiβo] nm donation

donde ['donde] adv where ▷ prep: **el coche está allí ~ el farol** the car is over there by the lamppost o where the lamppost is; **en ~** where, in which

dónde ['donde] adv where?; **¿a ~ vas?** where are you going (to)?; **¿de ~ vienes?** where have you been?; **¿por ~?** where?, whereabouts?

dondequiera [donde'kjera] adv anywhere; **por ~** everywhere, all over the place ▷ conj: **~ que** wherever

donut® [do'nut] (ESP) nm doughnut, donut (US)

doña ['dona] nf: **~ Alicia** Alicia; **~ Victoria Benito** Mrs Victoria Benito

dorado, -a [do'raðo, a] adj (color) golden; (Tec) gilt

dormir [dor'mir] vt: **~ la siesta** to have an afternoon nap ▷ vi to sleep; **dormirse** vr to fall asleep

dormitorio [dormi'torjo] nm bedroom

dorsal [dor'sal] nm (Deporte) number

dorso ['dorso] nm (de mano) back; (de hoja) other side

dos [dos] num two

dosis ['dosis] nf inv dose, dosage

dotado, -a [do'taðo, a] adj gifted; **~ de** endowed with

dotar [do'tar] vt to endow; **dote** nf dowry; **dotes** nfpl (talentos) gifts

doy [doj] vb V **dar**

drama ['drama] nm drama; **dramaturgo** [drama'turɣo] nm dramatist, playwright

drástico, -a ['drastiko, a] adj drastic

drenaje [dre'naxe] nm drainage

droga ['droɣa] nf drug; **drogadicto, -a** [droɣa'ðikto, a] nm/f drug addict

droguería [droɣe'ria] nf hardware shop (BRIT) o store (US)

ducha ['dutʃa] nf (baño) shower; (Med) douche; **ducharse** vr to take a shower

duda ['duða] nf doubt; **no cabe ~** there is no doubt about it; **dudar** vt, vi to doubt; **dudoso, -a** [du'ðoso, a] adj (incierto) hesitant; (sospechoso) doubtful

duela etc vb V **doler**

duelo ['dwelo] vb V **doler** ▷ nm (combate) duel; (luto) mourning

duende ['dwende] nm imp, goblin

dueño, -a ['dweno, a] nm/f (propietario) owner; (de pensión, taberna) landlord/lady; (empresario) employer

duermo etc vb V **dormir**

dulce ['dulθe] adj sweet ▷ adv gently, softly ▷ nm sweet

dulcería [dulθe'ria] (LAM) nf confectioner's (shop)

dulzura [dul'θura] nf sweetness; (ternura) gentleness

dúo ['duo] nm duet

duplicar [dupli'kar] vt (hacer el doble de) to duplicate

duque ['duke] nm duke; **duquesa** nf duchess

duración [dura'θjon] nf (de película, disco etc) length; (de pila etc) life; (curso: de acontecimientos etc) duration

duradero, -a [dura'ðero, a] adj (tela etc) hard-wearing; (fe, paz) lasting

durante [du'rante] prep during

durar [du'rar] vi to last; (recuerdo) to remain

durazno [du'raθno] (LAM) nm (fruta) peach; (árbol) peach tree

durex ['dureks] (MÉX, ARG) nm (tira adhesiva) Sellotape® (BRIT), Scotch tape® (US)

dureza [du'reθa] nf (calidad) hardness

duro, -a ['duro, a] adj hard; (carácter) tough ▷ adv hard ▷ nm (moneda) five-peseta coin o piece

DVD nm abr (= disco de vídeo digital) DVD

d

E *abr* (= *este*) E

e [e] *conj* and

ébano ['eβano] *nm* ebony

ebrio, -a ['eβrjo, a] *adj* drunk

ebullición [eβuʎi'θjon] *nf* boiling

echar [e'tʃar] *vt* to throw; (*agua, vino*) to pour (out); (*empleado: despedir*) to fire, sack; (*hojas*) to sprout; (*cartas*) to post; (*humo*) to emit, give out ▷ *vi*: **~ a correr** to run off; **echarse** *vr* to lie down; **~ llave a** to lock (up); **~ abajo** (*gobierno*) to overthrow; (*edificio*) to demolish; **~ mano a** to lay hands on; **~ una mano a algn** (*ayudar*) to give sb a hand; **~ de menos** to miss; **~se atrás** (*fig*) to back out

eclesiástico, -a [ekle'sjastiko, a] *adj* ecclesiastical

eco ['eko] *nm* echo; **tener ~** to catch on

ecología [ekolo'ɣia] *nf* ecology; **ecológico, -a** *adj* (*producto, método*) environmentally-friendly; (*agricultura*) organic; **ecologista** *adj* ecological, environmental ▷ *nmf* environmentalist

economía [ekono'mia] *nf* (*sistema*) economy; (*carrera*) economics

económico, -a [eko'nomiko, a] *adj* (*barato*) cheap, economical; (*ahorrativo*) thrifty; (*Com: año etc*) financial; (: *situación*) economic

economista [ekono'mista] *nmf* economist

Ecuador [ekwa'ðor] *nm* Ecuador; **ecuador** *nm* (*Geo*) equator

ecuatoriano, -a [ekwato'rjano, a] *adj, nm/f* Ecuadorian

ecuestre [e'kwestre] *adj* equestrian

edad [e'ðað] *nf* age; **¿qué ~ tienes?** how old are you?; **tiene ocho años de ~** he's eight (years old); **de ~ mediana/avanzada** middle-aged/advanced in years; **la E~ Media** the Middle Ages

edición [eði'θjon] *nf* (*acto*) publication; (*ejemplar*) edition

edificar [eðifi'kar] *vt, vi* to build

edificio [eði'fiθjo] *nm* building; (*fig*) edifice, structure

Edimburgo [eðim'burɣo] *nm* Edinburgh

editar [eði'tar] *vt* (*publicar*) to publish; (*preparar textos*) to edit

editor, a [eði'tor, a] *nm/f* (*que publica*) publisher; (*redactor*) editor ▷ *adj* publishing *cpd*; **editorial** *adj* editorial ▷ *nm* leading article, editorial; **casa editorial** publisher

edredón [eðre'ðon] *nm* duvet

educación [eðuka'θjon] *nf* education; (*crianza*) upbringing; (*modales*) (good) manners *pl*

educado, -a [eðu'kaðo, a] *adj*: **bien/mal ~** well/badly behaved

educar [eðu'kar] *vt* to educate; (*criar*) to bring up; (*voz*) to train

EE. UU. *nmpl abr* (= *Estados Unidos*) US(A)

efectivamente [efectiβa'mente] *adv* (*como respuesta*) exactly, precisely; (*verdaderamente*) really; (*de hecho*) in fact

efectivo, -a [efek'tiβo, a] *adj* effective; (*real*) actual, real ▷ *nm*: **pagar en ~** to pay (in) cash; **hacer ~ un cheque** to cash a cheque

efecto [e'fekto] *nm* effect, result; **efectos** *nmpl* (*efectos personales*) effects; (*bienes*) goods; (*Com*) assets; **en ~** in fact; (*respuesta*) exactly, indeed; **efecto invernadero** greenhouse effect; **efectos especiales/ secundarios/sonoros** special/side/sound effects

efectuar [efek'twar] *vt* to carry out; (*viaje*) to make

eficacia [efi'kaθja] *nf* (*de persona*) efficiency; (*de medicamento etc*) effectiveness

eficaz [efi'kaθ] *adj* (*persona*) efficient; (*acción*) effective

eficiente [efi'θjente] *adj* efficient

egipcio, -a [e'xipθjo, a] *adj, nm/f* Egyptian

Egipto [e'xipto] *nm* Egypt

egoísmo [eɣo'ismo] *nm* egoism

egoísta [eɣo'ista] *adj* egoistical, selfish ▷ *nmf* egoist

Eire ['eire] *nm* Eire

ej. *abr* (= *ejemplo*) eg

eje ['exe] *nm* (*Geo, Mat*) axis; (*de rueda*) axle; (*de máquina*) shaft, spindle

ejecución [exeku'θjon] *nf* execution; (*cumplimiento*) fulfilment; (*Mús*) performance; (*Jur: embargo de deudor*) attachment

ejecutar [exeku'tar] *vt* to execute, carry out; (*matar*) to execute; (*cumplir*) to fulfil;

(*Mús*) to perform; (*Jur: embargar*) to attach, distrain (on)

ejecutivo, -a [exeku'tiβo, a] *adj* executive; **el (poder)** ~ the executive (power)

ejemplar [exem'plar] *adj* exemplary ▷ *nm* example; (*Zool*) specimen; (*de libro*) copy; (*de periódico*) number, issue

ejemplo [e'xemplo] *nm* example; **por** ~ for example

ejercer [exer'θer] *vt* to exercise; (*influencia*) to exert; (*un oficio*) to practise ▷ *vi* (*practicar*): ~ **(de)** to practise (as)

ejercicio [exer'θiθjo] *nm* exercise; (*período*) tenure; **hacer** ~ to take exercise; **ejercicio comercial** financial year

ejército [e'xerθito] *nm* army; **entrar en el** ~ to join the army, join up; **ejército del aire/ de tierra** Air Force/Army

ejote [e'xote] (*MÉX*) *nm* green bean

○ **PALABRA CLAVE**

el [el] (*f* **la,** *pl* **los, las,** *neutro* **lo**) *art def* **1** the; **el libro/la mesa/los estudiantes** the book/table/students

2 (*con n abstracto: no se traduce*): **el amor/la juventud** love/youth

3 (*posesión: se traduce a menudo por adj posesivo*): **romperse el brazo** to break one's arm; **levantó la mano** he put his hand up; **se puso el sombrero** he put her hat on

4 (*valor descriptivo*): **tener la boca grande/ los ojos azules** to have a big mouth/blue eyes

5 (*con días*) on; **me iré el viernes** I'll leave on Friday; **los domingos suelo ir a nadar** on Sundays I generally go swimming

6 (*lo +adj*): **lo difícil/caro** what is difficult/ expensive; (*cuán*): **no se da cuenta de lo pesado que es** he doesn't realise how boring he is

▷ *pron demos* **1**: **mi libro y el de usted** my book and yours; **las de Pepe son mejores** Pepe's are better; **no la(s) blanca(s) sino la(s) gris(es)** not the white one(s) but the grey one(s)

2: **lo de: lo de ayer** what happened yesterday; **lo de las facturas** that business about the invoices

▷ *pron relativo* **1** (*indef*): **el que: el (los) que quiera(n) que se vaya(n)** anyone who wants to can leave; **llévese el que más le guste** take the one you like best

2 (*def*): **el que: el que compré ayer** the one I bought yesterday; **los que se van** those ~ who leave

3: **lo que: lo que pienso yo/más me gusta** what I think/like most

▷ *conj*: **el que: el que lo diga** the fact that he says so; **el que sea tan vago me molesta** his being so lazy bothers me

▷ *excl*: **¡el susto que me diste!** what a fright you gave me!

▷ *pron personal* **1** (*persona: m*) him; (*: f*) her; (*: pl*) them; **lo/las veo** I can see him/them

2 (*animal, cosa: sg*) it; (*: pl*) them; **lo (o la) veo** I can see it; **los (o la) veo** I can see them

3 (*como sustituto de frase*): **lo: no lo sabía** I didn't know; **ya lo entiendo** I understand now

él [el] *pron* (*persona*) he; (*cosa*) it; (*después de prep: persona*) him; (*: cosa*) it; **de** ~ his

elaborar [elaβo'rar] *vt* (*producto*) to make, manufacture; (*preparar*) to prepare; (*madera, metal etc*) to work; (*proyecto etc*) to work on *o* out

elástico, -a [e'lastiko, a] *adj* elastic; (*flexible*) flexible ▷ *nm* elastic; (*un elástico*) elastic band

elección [elek'θjon] *nf* election; (*selección*) choice, selection; **elecciones generales** general election *sg*

electorado [elekto'raðo] *nm* electorate, voters *pl*

electricidad [elektriθi'ðað] *nf* electricity

electricista [elektri'θista] *nmf* electrician

eléctrico, -a [e'lektriko, a] *adj* electric

electro... [elektro] *prefijo* electro...; **electrocardiograma** *nm* electrocardiogram; **electrocutar** *vt* to electrocute; **electrodo** *nm* electrode; **electrodomésticos** *nmpl* (electrical) household appliances

electrónica [elek'tronika] *nf* electronics *sg*

electrónico, -a [elek'troniko, a] *adj* electronic

elefante [ele'fante] *nm* elephant

elegancia [ele'γanθja] *nf* elegance, grace; (*estilo*) stylishness

elegante [ele'γante] *adj* elegant, graceful; (*estiloso*) stylish, fashionable

elegir [ele'xir] *vt* (*escoger*) to choose, select; (*optar*) to opt for; (*presidente*) to elect

elemental [elemen'tal] *adj* (*claro, obvio*) elementary; (*fundamental*) elemental, fundamental

elemento [ele'mento] *nm* element; (*fig*) ingredient; **elementos** *nmpl* elements, rudiments

elevación [eleβa'θjon] *nf* elevation; (*acto*) raising, lifting; (*de precios*) rise; (*Geo etc*) height, altitude

elevar [ele'βar] *vt* to raise, lift (up); (*precio*)

to put up; **elevarse** vr (edificio) to rise; (precios) to go up

eligiendo etc vb V **elegir**

elija etc vb V **elegir**

eliminar [elimi'nar] vt to eliminate, remove

eliminatoria [elimina'torja] nf heat, preliminary (round)

élite ['elite] nf elite

ella ['eʎa] pron (persona) she; (cosa) it; (después de prep: persona) her; (: cosa) it; **de ~** hers

ellas ['eʎas] pron (personas y cosas) they; (después de prep) them; **de ~** theirs

ello ['eʎo] pron it

ellos ['eʎos] pron they; (después de prep) them; **de ~** theirs

elogiar [elo'xjar] vt to praise; **elogio** nm praise

elote [e'lote] (MÉX) nm corn on the cob

eludir [elu'ðir] vt to avoid

email [i'mel] nm email; (dirección) email address; **mandar un ~ a algn** to email sb, send sb an email

embajada [emba'xaða] nf embassy

embajador, a [embaxa'ðor, a] nm/f ambassador/ambassadress

embalar [emba'lar] vt to parcel, wrap (up); **embalarse** vr to go fast

embalse [em'balse] nm (presa) dam; (lago) reservoir

embarazada [embara'θaða] adj pregnant ▷ nf pregnant woman

▌ No confundir **embarazada** con la palabra inglesa embarrassed.

embarazo [emba'raθo] nm (de mujer) pregnancy; (impedimento) obstacle, obstruction; (timidez) embarrassment; **embarazoso, -a** adj awkward, embarrassing

embarcación [embarka'θjon] nf (barco) boat, craft; (acto) embarkation, boarding

embarcadero [embarka'ðero] nm pier, landing stage

embarcar [embar'kar] vt (cargamento) to ship, stow; (persona) to embark, put on board; **embarcarse** vr to embark, go on board

embargar [embar'xar] vt (Jur) to seize, impound

embargo [em'barxo] nm (Jur) seizure; (Com, Pol) embargo

embargue etc vb V **embargar**

embarque etc [em'barke] vb V **embarcar** ▷ nm shipment, loading

embellecer [embeʎe'θer] vt to embellish, beautify

embestida [embes'tiða] nf attack,

onslaught; (carga) charge

embestir [embes'tir] vt to attack, assault; to charge, attack ▷ vi to attack

emblema [em'blema] nm emblem

embobado, -a [embo'βaðo, a] adj (atontado) stunned, bewildered

embolia [em'bolja] nf (Med) clot

émbolo ['embolo] nm (Auto) piston

emborrachar [emborra'tʃar] vt to make drunk, intoxicate; **emborracharse** vr to get drunk

emboscada [embos'kaða] nf ambush

embotar [embo'tar] vt to blunt, dull

embotellamiento [emboteʎa'mjento] nm (Auto) traffic jam

embotellar [embote'ʎar] vt to bottle

embrague [em'braxe] nm (tb: **pedal de ~**) clutch

embrión [em'brjon] nm embryo

embrollo [em'broʎo] nm (enredo) muddle, confusion; (aprieto) fix, jam

embrujado, -a [embru'xaðo, a] adj bewitched; **casa embrujada** haunted house

embrutecer [embrute'θer] vt (atontar) to stupefy

embudo [em'buðo] nm funnel

embuste [em'buste] nm (mentira) lie; **embustero, -a** adj lying, deceitful ▷ nm/f (mentiroso) liar

embutido [embu'tiðo] nm (Culin) sausage; (Tec) inlay

emergencia [emer'xenθja] nf emergency; (surgimiento) emergence

emerger [emer'xer] vi to emerge, appear

emigración [emixra'θjon] nf emigration; (de pájaros) migration

emigrar [emi'xrar] vi (personas) to emigrate; (pájaros) to migrate

eminente [emi'nente] adj eminent, distinguished; (elevado) high

emisión [emi'sjon] nf (acto) emission; (Com etc) issue; (Radio, TV: acto) broadcasting; (: programa) broadcast, programme (BRIT), program (US)

emisora [emi'sora] nf radio o broadcasting station

emitir [emi'tir] vt (olor etc) to emit, give off; (moneda etc) to issue; (opinión) to express; (Radio) to broadcast

emoción [emo'θjon] nf emotion; (excitación) excitement; (sentimiento) feeling

emocionante [emoθjo'nante] adj (excitante) exciting, thrilling

emocionar [emoθjo'nar] vt (excitar) to excite, thrill; (conmover) to move, touch; (impresionar) to impress

emoticón [emoti'kon], **emoticono**

[emoti'kono] nm smiley

emotivo, -a [emo'tiβo, a] adj emotional

empacho [em'patʃo] nm (Med)
indigestion; (fig) embarrassment

empalagoso, -a [empala'ɣoso, a] adj
cloying; (fig) tiresome

empalmar [empal'mar] vt to join,
connect ▷ vi (dos caminos) to meet, join;
empalme nm joint, connection; junction;
(de trenes) connection

empanada [empa'naða] nf pie, pasty

empañarse [empa'ɲarse] vr (cristales etc)
to steam up

empapar [empa'par] vt (mojar) to soak,
saturate; (absorber) to soak up, absorb;
empaparse vr: **~se de** to soak up

empapelar [empape'lar] vt (paredes) to
paper

empaquetar [empake'tar] vt to pack,
parcel up

empastar [empas'tar] vt (embadurnar) to
paste; (diente) to fill

empaste [em'paste] nm (de diente) filling

empatar [empa'tar] vi to draw, tie; **~on a
dos** they drew two-all; **empate** nm draw,
tie

empecé etc vb V **empezar**

empedernido, -a [empeðer'niðo, a] adj
hard, heartless; (fumador) inveterate

empeine [em'peine] nm (de pie, zapato)
instep

empeñado, -a [empe'ɲaðo, a] adj
(persona) determined; (objeto) pawned

empeñar [empe'ɲar] vt (objeto) to pawn,
pledge; (persona) to compel; **empeñarse** vr
(endeudarse) to get into debt; **~se en** to be
set on, be determined to

empeño [em'peɲo] nm (determinación,
insistencia) determination, insistence; **casa
de ~s** pawnshop

empeorar [empeo'rar] vt to make worse,
worsen ▷ vi to get worse, deteriorate

empezar [empe'θar] vt, vi to begin, start

empiece etc vb V **empezar**

empiezo etc vb V **empezar**

emplasto [em'plasto] nm (Med) plaster

emplazar [empla'θar] vt (ubicar) to site,
place, locate; (Jur) to summons; (convocar)
to summon

empleado, -a [emple'aðo, a] nm/f (gen)
employee; (de banco etc) clerk

emplear [emple'ar] vt (usar) to use,
employ; (dar trabajo a) to employ;
emplearse vr (conseguir trabajo) to be
employed; (ocuparse) to occupy o.s.

empleo [em'pleo] nm (puesto) job;
(puestos: colectivamente) employment; (uso)
use, employment

empollar [empo'ʎar] (ESP: fam) vt, vi to
swot (up); **empollón, -ona** (ESP: fam) nm/f
swot

emporio [em'porjo] (LAM) nm (gran
almacén) department store

empotrado, -a [empo'traðo, a] adj
(armario etc) built-in

emprender [empren'der] vt (empezar)
to begin, embark on; (acometer) to tackle,
take on

empresa [em'presa] nf (de espíritu
etc) enterprise; (Com) company,
firm; **empresariales** nfpl business
studies; **empresario, -a** nm/f (Com)
businessman(-woman)

empujar [empu'xar] vt to push, shove

empujón [empu'xon] nm push, shove

empuñar [empu'ɲar] vt (asir) to grasp,
take (firm) hold of

○ **PALABRA CLAVE**

en [en] prep **1** (posición) in; (: sobre) on;
está en el cajón it's in the drawer; **en
Argentina/La Paz** in Argentina/La Paz; **en
la oficina/el colegio** at the office/school;
está en el suelo/quinto piso it's on the
floor/the fifth floor

2 (dirección) into; **entró en el aula** she went
into the classroom; **meter algo en el bolso**
to put sth into one's bag

3 (tiempo) in; on; **en 1605/3 semanas/
invierno** in 1605/3 weeks/winter; **en (el
mes de) enero** in (the month of) January;
en aquella ocasión/época on that
occasion/at that time

4 (precio) for; **lo vendió en 20 dólares** he
sold it for 20 dollars

5 (diferencia) by; **reducir/aumentar en una
tercera parte/un 20 por ciento** to reduce/
increase by a third/20 per cent

6 (manera): **en avión/autobús** by plane/
bus; **escrito en inglés** written in English

7 (después de vb que indica gastar etc) on; **han
cobrado demasiado en dietas** they've
charged too much to expenses; **se le va la
mitad del sueldo en comida** he spends half
his salary on food

8 (tema, ocupación): **experto en la materia**
expert on the subject; **trabaja en la
construcción** he works in the building
industry

9 (adj + en + infin): **lento en reaccionar** slow
to react

---

enaguas [e'naɣwas] nfpl petticoat sg,
underskirt sg

enajenación [enaxena'θjon] nf (Psico: tb:

~ mental) mental derangement

enamorado, -a [enamo'raðo, a] *adj* in love ▷ *nm/f* lover; **estar ~ (de)** to be in love (with)

enamorar [enamo'rar] *vt* to win the love of; **enamorarse** *vr*: **~se de algn** to fall in love with sb

enano, -a [e'nano, a] *adj* tiny ▷ *nm/f* dwarf

encabezamiento [enkaβeθa'mjento] *nm* (*de carta*) heading; (*de periódico*) headline

encabezar [enkaβe'θar] *vt* (*movimiento, revolución*) to lead, head; (*lista*) to head, be at the top of; (*carta*) to put a heading to

encadenar [enkaðe'nar] *vt* to chain (together); (*poner grilletes a*) to shackle

encajar [enka'xar] *vt* (*ajustar*): **~ (en)** to fit (into); (*fam: golpe*) to take ▷ *vi* to fit (well); (*fig: corresponder a*) to match

encaje [en'kaxe] *nm* (*labor*) lace

encallar [enka'ʎar] *vi* (*Náut*) to run aground

encaminar [enkami'nar] *vt* to direct, send

encantado, -a [enkan'taðo, a] *adj* (*hechizado*) bewitched; (*muy contento*) delighted; **¡~!** how do you do, pleased to meet you

encantador, a [enkanta'ðor, a] *adj* charming, lovely ▷ *nm/f* magician, enchanter/enchantress

encantar [enkan'tar] *vt* (*agradar*) to charm, delight; (*hechizar*) to bewitch, cast a spell on; **me encanta eso** I love that; **encanto** *nm* (*hechizo*) spell, charm; (*fig*) charm, delight

encarcelar [enkarθe'lar] *vt* to imprison, jail

encarecer [enkare'θer] *vt* to put up the price of; **encarecerse** *vr* to get dearer

encargado, -a [enkar'ɣaðo, a] *adj* in charge ▷ *nm/f* agent, representative; (*responsable*) person in charge

encargar [enkar'ɣar] *vt* to entrust; (*recomendar*) to urge, recommend; **encargarse** *vr*: **~se de** to look after, take charge of; **~ algo a algn** to put sb in charge of sth; **~ a algn que haga algo** to ask sb to do sth

encargo [en'karɣo] *nm* (*tarea*) assignment, job; (*responsabilidad*) responsibility; (*Com*) order

encariñarse [enkari'ɲarse] *vr*: **~ con** to grow fond of, get attached to

encarnación [enkarna'θjon] *nf* incarnation, embodiment

encarrilar [enkarri'lar] *vt* (*tren*) to put back on the rails; (*fig*) to correct, put on the right track

encasillar [enkasi'ʎar] *vt* (*fig*) to pigeonhole; (*actor*) to typecast

encendedor [enθende'ðor] *nm* lighter

encender [enθen'der] *vt* (*con fuego*) to light; (*luz, radio*) to put on, switch on; (*avivar: pasión*) to inflame; **encenderse** *vr* to catch fire; (*excitarse*) to get excited; (*de cólera*) to flare up; (*el rostro*) to blush

encendido [enθen'diðo] *nm* (*Auto*) ignition

encerado [enθe'raðo] *nm* (*Escol*) blackboard

encerrar [enθe'rrar] *vt* (*confinar*) to shut in, shut up; (*comprender, incluir*) to include, contain

encharcado, -a [entʃar'kaðo, a] *adj* (*terreno*) flooded

encharcarse [entʃar'karse] *vr* to get flooded

enchufado, -a [entʃu'faðo, a] (*fam*) *nm/f* well-connected person

enchufar [entʃu'far] *vt* (*Elec*) to plug in; (*Tec*) to connect, fit together; **enchufe** *nm* (*Elec: clavija*) plug; (*: toma*) socket; (*de dos tubos*) joint, connection; (*fam: influencia*) contact, connection; (*: puesto*) cushy job

encía [en'θia] *nf* gum

encienda *etc vb* V **encender**

encierro *etc* [en'θjerro] *vb* V **encerrar** ▷ *nm* shutting in, shutting up; (*calabozo*) prison

encima [en'θima] *adv* (*sobre*) above, over; (*además*) besides; **~ de** (*en*) on, on top of; (*sobre*) above, over; (*además de*) besides, on top of; **por ~ de** over; **¿llevas dinero ~?** have you (got) any money on you?; **se me vino ~** it took me by surprise

encina [en'θina] *nf* holm oak

encinta [en'θinta] *adj* pregnant

enclenque [en'klenke] *adj* weak, sickly

encoger [enko'xer] *vt* to shrink, contract; **encogerse** *vr* to shrink, contract; (*fig*) to cringe; **~se de hombros** to shrug one's shoulders

encomendar [enkomen'dar] *vt* to entrust, commend; **encomendarse** *vr*: **~se a** to put one's trust in

encomienda *etc* [enko'mjenda] *vb* V **encomendar** ▷ *nf* (*encargo*) charge, commission; (*elogio*) tribute; **encomienda postal** (*LAM*) package

encontrar [enkon'trar] *vt* (*hallar*) to find; (*inesperadamente*) to meet, run into; **encontrarse** *vr* to meet (each other); (*situarse*) to be (situated); **~se con** to meet; **~se bien (de salud)** to feel well

encrucijada [enkruθi'xaða] *nf*

crossroads sg

encuadernación [enkwaðerna'θjon] nf
binding

encuadrar [enkwa'ðrar] vt (retrato) to
frame; (ajustar) to fit, insert; (contener) to
contain

encubrir [enku'βrir] vt (ocultar) to hide,
conceal; (criminal) to harbour, shelter

encuentro etc [en'kwentro] vb V
encontrar ▷ nm (de personas) meeting;
(Auto etc) collision, crash; (Deporte) match,
game; (Mil) encounter

encuerado, -a (MÉX) [enkwe'raðo, a] adj
nude, naked

encuesta [en'kwesta] nf inquiry,
investigation; (sondeo) (public) opinion poll

encumbrar [enkum'brar] vt (persona)
to exalt

endeble [en'deβle] adj (persona) weak;
(argumento, excusa, persona) weak

endemoniado, -a [endemo'njaðo, a] adj
possessed (of the devil); (travieso) devilish

enderezar [endere'θar] vt (poner derecho)
to straighten (out); (: verticalmente) to set
upright; (situación) to straighten o sort out;
(dirigir) to direct; **enderezarse** vr (persona
sentada) to straighten up

endeudarse [endeu'ðarse] vr to get
into debt

endiablado, -a [endja'βlaðo, a] adj
devilish, diabolical; (travieso) mischievous

endilgar [endil'yar] (fam) vt: ~**le algo a
algn** to lumber sb with sth

endiñar [endi'ɲar] (ESP: fam) vt (bofetón)
to land, belt

endosar [endo'sar] vt (cheque etc) to
endorse

endulzar [endul'θar] vt to sweeten;
(suavizar) to soften

endurecer [endure'θer] vt to harden;
endurecerse vr to harden, grow hard

enema [e'nema] nm (Med) enema

enemigo, -a [ene'miɣo, a] adj enemy,
hostile ▷ nm/f enemy

enemistad [enemis'tað] nf enmity

enemistar [enemis'tar] vt to make
enemies of, cause a rift between;
enemistarse vr to become enemies;
(amigos) to fall out

energía [ener'xia] nf (vigor) energy, drive;
(empuje) push; (Tec, Elec) energy, power;
energía eólica wind power; **energía solar**
solar energy o power

enérgico, -a [e'nerxiko, a] adj (gen)
energetic; (voz, modales) forceful

energúmeno, -a [ener'xumeno, a] (fam)
nm/f (fig) madman(-woman)

enero [e'nero] nm January

enfadado, -a [enfa'ðaðo, a] adj angry,
annoyed

enfadar [enfa'ðar] vt to anger, annoy;
enfadarse vr to get angry o annoyed

enfado [en'faðo] nm (enojo) anger,
annoyance; (disgusto) trouble, bother

énfasis ['enfasis] nm emphasis, stress

enfático, -a [en'fatiko, a] adj emphatic

enfermar [enfer'mar] vt to make ill ▷ vi
to fall ill, be taken ill

enfermedad [enferme'ðað] nf illness;
enfermedad venérea venereal disease

enfermera [enfer'mera] nf nurse

enfermería [enferme'ria] nf infirmary;
(de colegio etc) sick bay

enfermero [enfer'mero] nm (male) nurse

enfermizo, -a [enfer'miθo, a] adj
(persona) sickly, unhealthy; (fig) unhealthy

enfermo, -a [en'fermo, a] adj ill, sick
▷ nm/f invalid, sick person; (en hospital)
patient; **caer o ponerse ~** to fall ill

enfocar [enfo'kar] vt (foto etc) to focus;
(problema etc) to approach

enfoque etc [en'foke] vb V **enfocar** ▷ nm
focus

enfrentar [enfren'tar] vt (peligro) to face
(up to), confront; (oponer) to bring face to
face; **enfrentarse** vr (dos personas) to face o
confront each other; (Deporte: dos equipos) to
meet; ~**se a** o **con** to face up to, confront

enfrente [en'frente] adv opposite; **la casa
de** ~ the house opposite, the house across
the street; ~ **de** opposite, facing

enfriamiento [enfria'mjento] nm
chilling, refrigeration; (Med) cold, chill

enfriar [enfri'ar] vt (alimentos) to cool,
chill; (algo caliente) to cool down; **enfriarse**
vr to cool down; (Med) to catch a chill;
(amistad) to cool

enfurecer [enfure'θer] vt to enrage,
madden; **enfurecerse** vr to become
furious, fly into a rage; (mar) to get rough

enganchar [engan'tʃar] vt to hook;
(dos vagones) to hitch up; (Tec) to couple,
connect; (Mil) to recruit; **engancharse** vr
(Mil) to enlist, join up

enganche [en'gantʃe] nm hook; (ESP
Tec) coupling, connection; (acto) hooking
(up); (Mil) recruitment, enlistment;
(MÉX: depósito) deposit

engañar [enga'ɲar] vt to deceive;
(estafar) to cheat, swindle; **engañarse** vr
(equivocarse) to be wrong; (disimular la verdad)
to deceive o.s.

engaño [en'gaɲo] nm deceit; (estafa) trick,
swindle; (error) mistake, misunderstanding;
(ilusión) delusion; **engañoso, -a** adj
(tramposo) crooked; (mentiroso) dishonest,

deceitful; (*aspecto*) deceptive; (*consejo*)
misleading

engatusar [engatu'sar] (*fam*) vt to coax

engendro [en'xendro] nm (*Bio*) foetus;
(*fig*) monstrosity

englobar [englo'βar] vt to include,
comprise

engordar [engor'ðar] vt to fatten ▷ vi to
get fat, put on weight

engorroso, -a [engo'rroso, a] adj
bothersome, trying

engranaje [engra'naxe] nm (*Auto*) gear

engrasar [engra'sar] vt (*Tec: poner grasa*)
to grease; (: *lubricar*) to lubricate, oil;
(*manchar*) to make greasy

engreído, -a [engre'iðo, a] adj vain,
conceited

enhebrar [ene'βrar] vt to thread

enhorabuena [enora'βwena] excl: **¡~!**
congratulations! ▷ nf: **dar la ~ a** to
congratulate

enigma [e'niɣma] nm enigma; (*problema*)
puzzle; (*misterio*) mystery

enjambre [en'xambre] nm swarm

enjaular [enxau'lar] vt to (put in a) cage;
(*fam*) to jail, lock up

enjuagar [enxwa'xar] vt (*ropa*) to rinse
(out)

enjuague etc [en'xwaxe] vb V **enjuagar**
▷ nm (*Med*) mouthwash; (*de ropa*) rinse,
rinsing

enlace [en'laθe] nm link, connection;
(*relación*) relationship; (*tb:* **~ matrimonial**)
marriage; (*de carretera, trenes*) connection;
enlace sindical shop steward

enlatado, -a [enla'taðo, a] adj (*alimentos,
productos*) tinned, canned

enlazar [enla'θar] vt (*unir con lazos*) to
bind together; (*atar*) to tie; (*conectar*) to link,
connect; (*LAM: caballo*) to lasso

enloquecer [enloke'θer] vt to drive mad
▷ vi to go mad

enmarañar [enmara'ɲar] vt (*enredar*)
to tangle (up), entangle; (*complicar*) to
complicate; (*confundir*) to confuse

enmarcar [enmar'kar] vt (*cuadro*) to
frame

enmascarar [enmaska'rar] vt to mask;
enmascararse vr to put on a mask

enmendar [enmen'dar] vt to emend,
correct; (*constitución etc*) to amend;
(*comportamiento*) to reform; **enmendarse** vr
to reform, mend one's ways; **enmienda** nf
correction; amendment; reform

enmudecer [enmuðe'θer] vi (*perder
el habla*) to fall silent; (*guardar silencio*) to
remain silent

ennoblecer [ennoβle'θer] vt to ennoble

enojado, -a [eno'xaðo, a] (*LAM*) adj angry

enojar [eno'xar] vt (*encolerizar*) to anger;
(*disgustar*) to annoy, upset; **enojarse** vr to
get angry; to get annoyed

enojo [e'noxo] nm (*cólera*) anger; (*irritación*)
annoyance

enorme [e'norme] adj enormous, huge;
(*fig*) monstrous

enredadera [enreða'ðera] nf (*Bot*)
creeper, climbing plant

enredar [enre'ðar] vt (*cables, hilos etc*)
to tangle (up), entangle; (*situación*) to
complicate, confuse; (*meter cizaña*) to sow
discord among o between; (*implicar*) to
embroil, implicate; **enredarse** vr to get
entangled, get tangled (up); (*situación*) to
get complicated; (*persona*) to get embroiled;
(*LAM: fam*) to meddle

enredo [en'reðo] nm (*maraña*) tangle;
(*confusión*) mix-up, confusion; (*intriga*)
intrigue

enriquecer [enrike'θer] vt to make rich,
enrich; **enriquecerse** vr to get rich

enrojecer [enroxe'θer] vt to redden ▷ vi
(*persona*) to blush; **enrojecerse** vr to blush

enrollar [enro'ʎar] vt to roll (up), wind
(up)

ensalada [ensa'laða] nf salad; **ensaladilla
(rusa)** nf Russian salad

ensanchar [ensan'tʃar] vt (*hacer más
ancho*) to widen; (*agrandar*) to enlarge,
expand; (*Costura*) to let out; **ensancharse** vr
to get wider, expand

ensayar [ensa'jar] vt to test, try (out);
(*Teatro*) to rehearse

ensayo [en'sajo] nm test, trial; (*Quím*)
experiment; (*Teatro*) rehearsal; (*Deporte*) try;
(*Escol, Literatura*) essay

enseguida [ense'xiða] adv at once, right
away

ensenada [ense'naða] nf inlet, cove

enseñanza [ense'ɲanθa] nf (*educación*)
education; (*acción*) teaching; (*doctrina*)
teaching, doctrine; **enseñanza (de)
primaria/secundaria** elementary/
secondary education

enseñar [ense'ɲar] vt (*educar*) to teach;
(*mostrar, señalar*) to show

enseres [en'seres] nmpl belongings

ensuciar [ensu'θjar] vt (*manchar*) to dirty,
soil; (*fig*) to defile; **ensuciarse** vr to get
dirty; (*bebé*) to dirty one's nappy

entablar [enta'βlar] vt (*recubrir*) to board
(up); (*Ajedrez, Damas*) to set up; (*conversación*)
to strike up; (*Jur*) to file ▷ vi to draw

ente ['ente] nm (*organización*) body,
organization; (*fam: persona*) odd character

entender [enten'der] vt (*comprender*) to

understand; (*darse cuenta*) to realize ▷ *vi* to understand; (*creer*) to think, believe; **entenderse** *vr* (*comprenderse*) to be understood; (*ponerse de acuerdo*) to agree, reach an agreement; **~ de** to know all about; **~ algo de** to know a little about; **~ en** to deal with, have to do with; **~ mal** to misunderstand; **~se con algn** (*llevarse bien*) to get on o along with sb; **~se mal** (*dos personas*) to get on badly

entendido, -a [enten'diðo, a] *adj* (*comprendido*) understood; (*hábil*) skilled; (*inteligente*) knowledgeable ▷ *nm/f* (*experto*) expert ▷ *excl* agreed!; **entendimiento** *nm* (*comprensión*) understanding; (*inteligencia*) mind, intellect; (*juicio*) judgement

enterado, -a [ente'raðo, a] *adj* well-informed; **estar ~ de** to know about, be aware of

enteramente [entera'mente] *adv* entirely, completely

enterar [ente'rar] *vt* (*informar*) to inform, tell; **enterarse** *vr* to find out, get to know

enterito [ente'rito] (RPL) *nm* boiler suit (BRIT), overalls (US)

entero, -a [en'tero, a] *adj* (*total*) whole, entire; (*fig: honesto*) honest; (*: firme*) firm, resolute ▷ *nm* (Com: *punto*) point

enterrar [ente'rrar] *vt* to bury

entidad [enti'ðað] *nf* (*empresa*) firm, company; (*organismo*) body; (*sociedad*) society; (*Filosofía*) entity

entiendo *etc vb* V **entender**

entierro [en'tjerro] *nm* (*acción*) burial; (*funeral*) funeral

entonación [entona'θjon] *nf* (Ling) intonation

entonar [ento'nar] *vt* (*canción*) to intone; (*colores*) to tone; (Med) to tone up ▷ *vi* to be in tune

entonces [en'tonθes] *adv* then, at that time; **desde ~** since then; **en aquel ~** at that time; (**pues**) **~** and so

entornar [entor'nar] *vt* (*puerta, ventana*) to half-close, leave ajar; (*los ojos*) to screw up

entorpecer [entorpe'θer] *vt* (*entendimiento*) to dull; (*impedir*) to obstruct, hinder; (*: tránsito*) to slow down, delay

entrada [en'traða] *nf* (*acción*) entry, access; (*sitio*) entrance, way in; (Inform) input; (Com) receipts *pl*, takings *pl*; (Culin) starter; (Deporte) innings *sg*; (Teatro) house, audience; (*billete*) ticket; **~s y salidas** (Com) income and expenditure; **de ~** from the outset; **entrada de aire** (Tec) air intake o inlet

entrado, -a [en'traðo, a] *adj*: **~ en años** elderly; **una vez ~ el verano** in the summer(time), when summer comes

entramparse [entram'parse] *vr* to get into debt

entrante [en'trante] *adj* next, coming; **mes/año ~** next month/year; **entrantes** *nmpl* starters

entraña [en'traɲa] *nf* (*fig: centro*) heart, core; (*raíz*) root; **entrañas** *nfpl* (Anat) entrails; (*fig*) heart *sg*; **entrañable** *adj* close, intimate; **entrañar** *vt* to entail

entrar [en'trar] *vt* (*introducir*) to bring in; (Inform) to input ▷ *vi* (*meterse*) to go in, come in, enter; (*comenzar*): **~ diciendo** to begin by saying; **hacer ~** to show in; **me entró sed/sueño** I started to feel thirsty/ sleepy; **no me entra** I can't get the hang of it

entre ['entre] *prep* (*dos*) between; (*más de dos*) among(st)

entreabrir [entrea'βrir] *vt* to half-open, open halfway

entrecejo [entre'θexo] *nm*: **fruncir el ~** to frown

entredicho [entre'ðitʃo] *nm* (Jur) injunction; **poner en ~** to cast doubt on; **estar en ~** to be in doubt

entrega [en'treɣa] *nf* (*de mercancías*) delivery; (*de novela etc*) instalment; **entregar** [entre'ɣar] *vt* (*dar*) to hand (over), deliver; **entregarse** *vr* (*rendirse*) to surrender, give in, submit; (*dedicarse*) to devote o.s.

entremeses [entre'meses] *nmpl* hors d'œuvres

entremeter [entreme'ter] *vt* to insert, put in; **entremeterse** *vr* to meddle, interfere; **entremetido, -a** *adj* meddling, interfering

entremezclar [entremeθ'klar] *vt* to intermingle; **entremezclarse** *vr* to intermingle

entrenador, a [entrena'ðor, a] *nm/f* trainer, coach

entrenarse [entre'narse] *vr* to train

entrepierna [entre'pjerna] *nf* crotch

entresuelo [entre'swelo] *nm* mezzanine

entretanto [entre'tanto] *adv* meanwhile, meantime

entretecho [entre'tetʃo] (cs) *nm* attic

entretejer [entrete'xer] *vt* to interweave

entretener [entrete'ner] *vt* (*divertir*) to entertain, amuse; (*detener*) to hold up, delay; **entretenerse** *vr* (*divertirse*) to amuse o.s.; (*retrasarse*) to delay, linger; **entretenido, -a** *adj* entertaining, amusing; **entretenimiento** *nm* entertainment, amusement

entrever [entre'βer] *vt* to glimpse, catch a glimpse of

entrevista [entre'βista] *nf* interview;

entrevistar vt to interview; **entrevistarse** vr to have an interview

entristecer [entriste'θer] vt to sadden, grieve; **entristecerse** vr to grow sad

entrometerse [entrome'terse] vr: **~ (en)** to interfere (in o with)

entumecer [entume'θer] vt to numb, benumb; **entumecerse** vr (por el frío) to go o become numb

enturbiar [entur'βjar] vt (el agua) to make cloudy; (fig) to confuse; **enturbiarse** vr (oscurecerse) to become cloudy; (fig) to get confused, become obscure

entusiasmar [entusjas'mar] vt to excite, fill with enthusiasm; (gustar mucho) to delight; **entusiasmarse** vr: **~se con** o **por** to get enthusiastic o excited about

entusiasmo [entu'sjasmo] nm enthusiasm; (excitación) excitement

entusiasta [entu'sjasta] adj enthusiastic ▷ nmf enthusiast

enumerar [enume'rar] vt to enumerate

envainar [embai'nar] vt to sheathe

envalentonar [embalento'nar] vt to give courage to; **envalentonarse** vr (pey: jactarse) to boast, brag

envasar [emba'sar] vt (empaquetar) to pack, wrap; (enfrascar) to bottle; (enlatar) to can; (embolsar) to pocket

envase [em'base] nm (en paquete) packing, wrapping; (en botella) bottling; (en lata) canning; (recipiente) container; (paquete) package; (botella) bottle; (lata) tin (BRIT), can

envejecer [embexe'θer] vt to make old, age ▷ vi (volverse viejo) to grow old; (parecer viejo) to age

envenenar [embene'nar] vt to poison; (fig) to embitter

envergadura [emberɣa'ðura] nf (fig) scope, compass

enviar [em'bjar] vt to send; **~ un mensaje a algn** (por movil) to text sb, to send sb a text message

enviciarse [embi'θjarse] vr: **~ (con)** to get addicted (to)

envidia [em'biðja] nf envy; **tener ~ a** to envy, be jealous of; **envidiar** vt to envy

envío [em'bio] nm (acción) sending; (de mercancías) consignment; (de dinero) remittance

enviudar [embju'ðar] vi to be widowed

envoltura [embol'tura] nf (cobertura) cover; (embalaje) wrapper, wrapping; **envoltorio** nm package

envolver [embol'βer] vt to wrap (up); (cubrir) to cover; (enemigo) to surround; (implicar) to involve, implicate

envuelto [em'bwelto] pp de **envolver**

enyesar [enje'sar] vt (pared) to plaster; (Med) to put in plaster

enzarzarse [enθar'θarse] vr: **~ en** (pelea) to get mixed up in; (disputa) to get involved in

épica ['epika] nf epic

epidemia [epi'ðemja] nf epidemic

epilepsia [epi'lepsja] nf epilepsy

episodio [epi'soðjo] nm episode

época ['epoka] nf period, time; (Hist) age, epoch; **hacer ~** to be epoch-making

equilibrar [ekili'βrar] vt to balance; **equilibrio** nm balance, equilibrium; **mantener/perder el equilibrio** to keep/ lose one's balance; **equilibrista** nmf (funámbulo) tightrope walker; (acróbata) acrobat

equipaje [eki'paxe] nm luggage; (avíos): **hacer el ~** to pack; **equipaje de mano** hand luggage

equipar [eki'par] vt (proveer) to equip

equipararse [ekipa'rarse] vr: **~ con** to be on a level with

equipo [e'kipo] nm (conjunto de cosas) equipment; (Deporte) team; (de obreros) shift

equis ['ekis] nf inv (the letter) X

equitación [ekita'θjon] nf horse riding

equivalente [ekiβa'lente] adj, nm equivalent

equivaler [ekiβa'ler] vi to be equivalent o equal

equivocación [ekiβoka'θjon] nf mistake, error

equivocado, -a [ekiβo'kaðo, a] adj wrong, mistaken

equivocarse [ekiβo'karse] vr to be wrong, make a mistake; **~ de camino** to take the wrong road

era ['era] vb V **ser** ▷ nf era, age

erais vb V **ser**

éramos vb V **ser**

eran vb V **ser**

eras vb V **ser**

erección [erek'θjon] nf erection

eres vb V **ser**

erigir [eri'xir] vt to erect, build; **erigirse** vr: **~se en** to set o.s. up as

erizo [e'riθo] nm (Zool) hedgehog; **erizo de mar** sea-urchin

ermita [er'mita] nf hermitage; **ermitaño, -a** [ermi'taɲo, a] nm/f hermit

erosión [ero'sjon] nf erosion

erosionar [erosjo'nar] vt to erode

erótico, -a [e'rotiko, a] adj erotic; **erotismo** nm eroticism

errante [e'rrante] adj wandering, errant

erróneo, -a [e'rroneo, a] adj (equivocado) wrong, mistaken

error [e'rror] nm error, mistake; (Inform)

bug; **error de imprenta** misprint

eructar [eruk'tar] vt to belch, burp

erudito, -a [eru'ðito, a] adj erudite, learned

erupción [erup'θjon] nf eruption; (Med) rash

es vb V **ser**

esa ['esa] (pl ~**s**) adj demos V **ese**

ésa ['esa] (pl ~**s**) pron V **ése**

esbelto, -a [es'βelto, a] adj slim, slender

esbozo [es'βoθo] nm sketch, outline

escabeche [eska'βetʃe] nm brine; (de aceitunas etc) pickle; **en ~** pickled

escabullirse [eskaβu'ʎirse] vr to slip away, to clear out

escafandra [eska'fandra] nf (buzo) diving suit; (escafandra espacial) space suit

escala [es'kala] nf (proporción, Mús) scale; (de mano) ladder; (Aviac) stopover; **hacer ~ en** to stop o call in at

escalafón [eskala'fon] nm (escala de salarios) salary scale, wage scale

escalar [eska'lar] vt to climb, scale

escalera [eska'lera] nf stairs pl, staircase; (escala) ladder; (Naipes) run; **escalera de caracol** spiral staircase; **escalera de incendios** fire escape; **escalera mecánica** escalator

escalfar [eskal'far] vt (huevos) to poach

escalinata [eskali'nata] nf staircase

escalofriante [eskalo'frjante] adj chilling

escalofrío [eskalo'frio] nm (Med) chill; **escalofríos** nmpl (fig) shivers

escalón [eska'lon] nm step, stair; (de escalera) rung

escalope [eska'lope] nm (Culin) escalope

escama [es'kama] nf (de pez, serpiente) scale; (de jabón) flake; (fig) resentment

escampar [eskam'par] vb impers to stop raining

escandalizar [eskandali'θar] vt to scandalize, shock; **escandalizarse** vr to be shocked; (ofenderse) to be offended

escándalo [es'kandalo] nm scandal; (alboroto, tumulto) row, uproar; **escandaloso, -a** adj scandalous, shocking

escandinavo, -a [eskandi'naβo, a] adj, nm/f Scandinavian

escanear [eskane'ar] vt to scan

escaño [es'kaɲo] nm bench; (Pol) seat

escapar [eska'par] vi (gen) to escape, run away; (Deporte) to break away; **escaparse** vr to escape, get away; (agua, gas) to leak (out)

escaparate [eskapa'rate] nm shop window

escape [es'kape] nm (de agua, gas) leak; (de motor) exhaust

escarabajo [eskara'βaxo] nm beetle

escaramuza [eskara'muθa] nf skirmish

escarbar [eskar'βar] vt (tierra) to scratch

escarceos [eskar'θeos] nmpl: **en mis ~ con la política ...** in my dealings with politics ...; **escarceos amorosos** love affairs

escarcha [es'kartʃa] nf frost; **escarchado, -a** [eskar'tʃaðo, a] adj (Culin: fruta) crystallized

escarlatina [eskarla'tina] nf scarlet fever

escarmentar [eskarmen'tar] vt to punish severely ▷ vi to learn one's lesson

escarmiento etc [eskar'mjento] vb V **escarmentar** ▷ nm (ejemplo) lesson; (castigo) punishment

escarola [eska'rola] nf endive

escarpado, -a [eskar'paðo, a] adj (pendiente) sheer, steep; (rocas) craggy

escasear [eskase'ar] vi to be scarce

escasez [eska'seθ] nf (falta) shortage, scarcity; (pobreza) poverty

escaso, -a [es'kaso, a] adj (poco) scarce; (raro) rare; (ralo) thin, sparse; (limitado) limited

escatimar [eskati'mar] vt to skimp (on), be sparing with

escayola [eska'jola] nf plaster

escena [es'θena] nf scene

escenario [esθe'narjo] nm (Teatro) stage; (Cine) set; (fig) scene

▌ No confundir **escenario** con la palabra inglesa scenery.

escenografía nf set design

escéptico, -a [es'θeptiko, a] adj sceptical ▷ nm/f sceptic

esclarecer [esklare'θer] vt (misterio, problema) to shed light on

esclavitud [esklaβi'tuð] nf slavery

esclavizar [esklaβi'θar] vt to enslave

esclavo, -a [es'klaβo, a] nm/f slave

escoba [es'koβa] nf broom; **escobilla** nf brush

escocer [esko'θer] vi to burn, sting; **escocerse** vr to chafe, get chafed

escocés, -esa [esko'θes, esa] adj Scottish ▷ nm/f Scotsman(-woman), Scot

Escocia [es'koθja] nf Scotland

escoger [esko'xer] vt to choose, pick, select; **escogido, -a** adj chosen, selected

escolar [esko'lar] adj school cpd ▷ nmf schoolboy(-girl), pupil

escollo [es'koʎo] nm (obstáculo) pitfall

escolta [es'kolta] nf escort; **escoltar** vt to escort

escombros [es'kombros] nmpl (basura) rubbish sg; (restos) debris sg

esconder [eskon'der] vt to hide, conceal; **esconderse** vr to hide; **escondidas** (LAM) *nfpl*: **a escondidas** secretly; **escondite** *nm* hiding place; (*ESP*: *juego*) hide-and-seek; **escondrijo** *nm* hiding place, hideout

escopeta [esko'peta] *nf* shotgun

escoria [es'korja] *nf* (*de alto horno*) slag; (*fig*) scum, dregs *pl*

Escorpio [es'korpjo] *nm* Scorpio

escorpión [eskor'pjon] *nm* scorpion

escotado, -a [esko'taðo, a] *adj* low-cut

escote [es'kote] *nm* (*de vestido*) low neck; **pagar a ~** to share the expenses

escotilla [esko'tiʎa] *nf* (*Náut*) hatch(way)

escozor [esko'θor] *nm* (*dolor*) sting(ing)

escribible [eskri'βiβle] *adj* writable

escribir [eskri'βir] *vt, vi* to write; **~ a máquina** to type; **¿cómo se escribe?** how do you spell it?

escrito, -a [es'krito, a] *pp de* **escribir** ▷ *nm* (*documento*) document; (*manuscrito*) text, manuscript; **por ~** in writing

escritor, a [eskri'tor, a] *nm/f* writer

escritorio [eskri'torjo] *nm* desk

escritura [eskri'tura] *nf* (*acción*) writing; (*caligrafía*) (hand)writing; (*Jur*: *documento*) deed

escrúpulo [es'krupulo] *nm* scruple; (*minuciosidad*) scrupulousness; **escrupuloso, -a** *adj* scrupulous

escrutinio [eskru'tinjo] *nm* (*examen atento*) scrutiny; (*Pol*: *recuento de votos*) count(ing)

escuadra [es'kwaðra] *nf* (*Mil etc*) squad; (*Náut*) squadron; (*flota*: *de coches etc*) fleet; **escuadrilla** *nf* (*de aviones*) squadron; (*LAM*: *de obreros*) gang

escuadrón [eskwa'ðron] *nm* squadron

escuálido, -a [es'kwaliðo, a] *adj* skinny, scraggy; (*sucio*) squalid

escuchar [esku'tʃar] *vt* to listen to ▷ *vi* to listen

escudo [es'kuðo] *nm* shield

escuela [es'kwela] *nf* school; **escuela de artes y oficios** (*ESP*) ≈ technical college; **escuela de choferes** (*LAM*) driving school; **escuela de manejo** (*MÉX*) driving school

escueto, -a [es'kweto, a] *adj* plain; (*estilo*) simple

escuincle, -a [es'kwinkle, a] (*MÉX*: *fam*) *nm/f* kid

esculpir [eskul'pir] *vt* to sculpt; (*grabar*) to engrave; (*tallar*) to carve; **escultor, a** *nm/f* sculptor(-tress); **escultura** *nf* sculpture

escupidera [eskupi'ðera] *nf* spittoon

escupir [esku'pir] *vt, vi* to spit (out)

escurreplatos [eskurre'platos] (*ESP*) *nm inv* draining board (*BRIT*), drainboard (*US*)

escurridero [eskurri'ðero] (*LAM*) *nm* draining board (*BRIT*), drainboard (*US*)

escurridizo, -a [eskurri'ðiθo, a] *adj* slippery

escurridor [eskurri'ðor] *nm* colander

escurrir [esku'rrir] *vt* (*ropa*) to wring out; (*verduras, platos*) to drain ▷ *vi* (*líquidos*) to drip; **escurrirse** *vr* (*secarse*) to drain; (*resbalarse*) to slip, slide; (*escaparse*) to slip away

ese ['ese] (*f* **esa**, *pl* **esos, esas**) *adj demos* (*sg*) that; (*pl*) those

ése ['ese] (*f* **ésa**, *pl* **ésos, ésas**) *pron* (*sg*) that (one); (*pl*) those (ones); **~ ... éste ...** the former ... the latter ...; **no me vengas con ésas** don't give me any more of that nonsense

esencia [e'senθja] *nf* essence; **esencial** *adj* essential

esfera [es'fera] *nf* sphere; (*de reloj*) face; **esférico, -a** *adj* spherical

esforzarse [esfor'θarse] *vr* to exert o.s., make an effort

esfuerzo *etc* [es'fwerθo] *vb* V **esforzarse** ▷ *nm* effort

esfumarse [esfu'marse] *vr* (*apoyo, esperanzas*) to fade away

esgrima [es'ɣrima] *nf* fencing

esguince [es'ɣinθe] *nm* (*Med*) sprain

eslabón [esla'βon] *nm* link

eslip [ez'lip] *nm* pants *pl* (*BRIT*), briefs *pl*

eslovaco, -a [eslo'βako, a] *adj, nm/f* Slovak, Slovakian ▷ *nm* (*Ling*) Slovak, Slovakian

Eslovaquia [eslo'βakja] *nf* Slovakia

esmalte [es'malte] *nm* enamel; **esmalte de uñas** nail varnish *o* polish

esmeralda [esme'ralda] *nf* emerald

esmerarse [esme'rarse] *vr* (*aplicarse*) to take great pains, exercise great care; (*afanarse*) to work hard

esmero [es'mero] *nm* (great) care

esnob [es'nob] (*pl* **~s**) *adj* (*persona*) snobbish ▷ *nmf* snob

eso ['eso] *pron* that, that thing *o* matter; **~ de su coche** that business about his car; **~ de ir al cine** all that about going to the cinema; **a ~ de las cinco** at about five o'clock; **en ~** thereupon, at that point; **~ es** that's it; **¡~ sí que es vida!** now that is really living!; **por ~ te lo dije** that's why I told you; **y ~ que llovía** in spite of the fact it was raining

esos *adj demos* V **ese**

ésos *pron* V **ése**

espabilar *etc* [espaβi'lar] = **despabilar** *etc*

espacial [espa'θjal] *adj* (*del espacio*) space *cpd*

espaciar [espa'θjar] *vt* to space (out)

espacio [es'paθjo] *nm* space; (*Mús*)

interval; (*Radio, TV*) programme (*BRIT*), program (*US*); **el ~ space; espacio aéreo/exterior** air/outer space; **espacioso, -a** *adj* spacious, roomy

espada [es'paða] *nf* sword; **espadas** *nfpl* (*Naipes*) spades

espaguetis [espa'ɣetis] *nmpl* spaghetti *sg*

espalda [es'palda] *nf* (*gen*) back; **espaldas** *nfpl* (*hombros*) shoulders; **a ~s de algn** behind sb's back; **estar de ~s** to have one's back turned; **tenderse de ~s** to lie (down) on one's back; **volver la ~ a algn** to cold-shoulder sb

espantajo [espan'taxo] *nm* = **espantapájaros**

espantapájaros [espanta'paxaros] *nm inv* scarecrow

espantar [espan'tar] *vt* (*asustar*) to frighten, scare; (*ahuyentar*) to frighten off; (*asombrar*) to horrify, appal; **espantarse** *vr* to get frightened o scared; to be appalled

espanto [es'panto] *nm* (*susto*) fright; (*terror*) terror; (*asombro*) astonishment; **espantoso, -a** *adj* frightening; terrifying; astonishing

España [es'paɲa] *nf* Spain; **español, a** *adj* Spanish ▷*nm/f* Spaniard ▷*nm* (*Ling*) Spanish

esparadrapo [espara'ðrapo] *nm* (sticking) plaster (*BRIT*), adhesive tape (*US*)

esparcir [espar'θir] *vt* to spread; (*diseminar*) to scatter; **esparcirse** *vr* to spread (out); to scatter; (*divertirse*) to enjoy o.s.

espárrago [es'parraxo] *nm* asparagus

esparto [es'parto] *nm* esparto (grass)

espasmo [es'pasmo] *nm* spasm

espátula [es'patula] *nf* spatula

especia [es'peθja] *nf* spice

especial [espe'θjal] *adj* special; **especialidad** *nf* speciality (*BRIT*), specialty (*US*)

especie [es'peθje] *nf* (*Bio*) species; (*clase*) kind, sort; **en ~** in kind

especificar [espeθifi'kar] *vt* to specify; **específico, -a** *adj* specific

espécimen [es'peθimen] (*pl* **especímenes**) *nm* specimen

espectáculo [espek'takulo] *nm* (*gen*) spectacle; (*Teatro etc*) show

espectador, a [espekta'ðor, a] *nm/f* spectator

especular [espeku'lar] *vt, vi* to speculate

espejismo [espe'xismo] *nm* mirage

espejo [es'pexo] *nm* mirror; **(espejo) retrovisor** rear-view mirror

espeluznante [espeluθ'nante] *adj* horrifying, hair-raising

espera [es'pera] *nf* (*pausa, intervalo*) wait; (*Jur: plazo*) respite; **en ~ de** waiting for; (*con expectativa*) expecting

esperanza [espe'ranθa] *nf* (*confianza*) hope; (*expectativa*) expectation; **hay pocas ~s de que venga** there is little prospect of his coming; **esperanza de vida** life expectancy

esperar [espe'rar] *vt* (*aguardar*) to wait for; (*tener expectativa de*) to expect; (*desear*) to hope for ▷*vi* to wait; to expect; to hope; **hacer ~ a algn** to keep sb waiting; **~ un bebé** to be expecting (a baby)

esperma [es'perma] *nf* sperm

espeso, -a [es'peso, a] *adj* thick; **espesor** *nm* thickness

espía [es'pia] *nmf* spy; **espiar** *vt* (*observar*) to spy on

espiga [es'piɣa] *nf* (*Bot: de trigo etc*) ear

espigón [espi'ɣon] *nm* (*Bot*) ear; (*Náut*) breakwater

espina [es'pina] *nf* thorn; (*de pez*) bone; **espina dorsal** (*Anat*) spine

espinaca [espi'naka] *nf* spinach

espinazo [espi'naθo] *nm* spine, backbone

espinilla [espi'niʎa] *nf* (*Anat: tibia*) shin(bone); (*grano*) blackhead

espinoso, -a [espi'noso, a] *adj* (*planta*) thorny, prickly; (*asunto*) difficult

espionaje [espjo'naxe] *nm* spying, espionage

espiral [espi'ral] *adj, nf* spiral

espirar [espi'rar] *vt* to breathe out, exhale

espiritista [espiri'tista] *adj, nmf* spiritualist

espíritu [es'piritu] *nm* spirit; **Espíritu Santo** Holy Ghost o Spirit; **espiritual** *adj* spiritual

espléndido, -a [es'plendiðo, a] *adj* (*magnífico*) magnificent, splendid; (*generoso*) generous

esplendor [esplen'dor] *nm* splendour

espolvorear [espolβore'ar] *vt* to dust, sprinkle

esponja [es'ponxa] *nf* sponge; (*fig*) sponger; **esponjoso, -a** *adj* spongy

espontaneidad [espontanei'ðað] *nf* spontaneity; **espontáneo, -a** *adj* spontaneous

esposa [es'posa] *nf* wife; **esposas** *nfpl* handcuffs; **esposar** *vt* to handcuff

esposo [es'poso] *nm* husband

espray [es'prai] *nm* spray

espuela [es'pwela] *nf* spur

espuma [es'puma] *nf* foam; (*de cerveza*) froth, head; (*de jabón*) lather; **espuma de afeitar** shaving foam; **espumadera** *nf* (*utensilio*) skimmer; **espumoso, -a** *adj* frothy, foamy; (vino) sparkling

esqueleto [eske'leto] nm skeleton

esquema [es'kema] nm (diagrama)
diagram; (dibujo) plan; (Filosofía) schema

esquí [es'ki] (pl **~s**) nm (objeto) ski; (Deporte)
skiing; **esquí acuático** water-skiing;
esquiar vi to ski

esquilar [eski'lar] vt to shear

esquimal [eski'mal] adj, nmf Eskimo

esquina [es'kina] nf corner; **esquinazo**
[eski'naθo] nm: **dar esquinazo a algn** to
give sb the slip

esquirol [eski'rol] (ESP) nm strikebreaker,
scab

esquivar [eski'βar] vt to avoid

esta ['esta] adj demos V **este²**

está vb V **estar**

ésta pron V **éste**

estabilidad [estaβili'ðað] nf stability;
estable adj stable

establecer [estaβle'θer] vt to establish;
establecerse vr to establish o.s.; (echar
raíces) to settle (down); **establecimiento**
nm establishment

establo [es'taβlo] nm (Agr) stable

estaca [es'taka] nf stake, post; (de tienda de
campaña) peg

estacada [esta'kaða] nf (cerca) fence,
fencing; (palenque) stockade

estación [esta'θjon] nf station; (del
año) season; **estación balnearia** seaside
resort; **estación de autobuses** bus station;
estación de servicio service station

estacionamiento [estaθjona'mjento]
nm (Auto) parking; (Mil) stationing

estacionar [estaθjo'nar] vt (Auto) to park;
(Mil) to station

estadía [esta'ðia] (LAM) nf stay

estadio [es'taðjo] nm (fase) stage, phase;
(Deporte) stadium

estadista [esta'ðista] nm (Pol) statesman;
(Mat) statistician

estadística [esta'ðistika] nf figure,
statistic; (ciencia) statistics sg

estado [es'taðo] nm (Pol: condición) state;
estar en ~ to be pregnant; **estado civil**
marital status; **estado de ánimo** state of
mind; **estado de cuenta** bank statement;
estado de sitio state of siege; **estado
mayor** staff; **Estados Unidos** United States
(of America)

estadounidense [estaðouni'ðense]
adj United States cpd, American ▷ nmf
American

estafa [es'tafa] nf swindle, trick; **estafar**
vt to swindle, defraud

estáis vb V **estar**

estallar [esta'ʎar] vi to burst; (bomba) to

explode, go off; (epidemia, guerra, rebelión) to
break out; **~ en llanto** to burst into tears;
estallido nm explosion; (fig) outbreak

estampa [es'tampa] nf print, engraving;
estampado, -a [estam'paðo, a] adj
printed ▷ nm (impresión: acción) printing;
(: efecto) print; (marca) stamping

estampar [estam'par] vt (imprimir) to
print; (marcar) to stamp; (metal) to engrave;
(poner sello en) to stamp; (fig) to stamp,
imprint

estampida [estam'piða] nf stampede

estampido [estam'piðo] nm bang, report

estampilla [estam'piʎa] (LAM) nf
(postage) stamp

están vb V **estar**

estancado, -a [estan'kaðo, a] adj
stagnant

estancar [estan'kar] vt (aguas) to hold
up, hold back; (Com) to monopolize; (fig) to
block, hold up; **estancarse** vr to stagnate

estancia [es'tanθja] nf (ESP,
MÉX: permanencia) stay; (sala) room; (RPL: de
ganado) farm, ranch; **estanciero** (RPL) nm
farmer, rancher

estanco, -a [es'tanko, a] adj watertight
▷ nm tobacconist's (shop), cigar store (US)

estándar [es'tandar] adj, nm standard

estandarte [estan'darte] nm banner,
standard

estanque [es'tanke] nm (lago) pool, pond;
(Agr) reservoir

estanquero, -a [estan'kero, a] nm/f
tobacconist

estante [es'tante] nm (armario) rack,
stand; (biblioteca) bookcase; (anaquel) shelf;
estantería nf shelving, shelves pl

○ **PALABRA CLAVE**

estar [es'tar] vi **1** (posición) to be; **está en la
plaza** it's in the square; **¿está Juan?** is Juan
in?; **estamos a 30 km de Junín** we're 30 kms
from Junín

2 (+ adj: estado) to be; **estar enfermo** to be ill;
está muy elegante he's looking very smart;
¿cómo estás? how are you keeping?

3 (+ gerundio) to be; **estoy leyendo** I'm

reading

4 (uso pasivo): **está condenado a muerte** he's been condemned to death; **está envasado en ...** it's packed in ...

5 (con fechas): **¿a cuántos estamos?** what's the date today?; **estamos a 5 de mayo** it's the 5th of May

6 (locuciones): **¿estamos?** (¿de acuerdo?) okay?; (¿listo?) ready?

7: **estar de**: **estar de vacaciones/viaje** to be on holiday/away o on a trip; **está de camarero** he's working as a waiter

8: **estar para**: **está para salir** he's about to leave; **no estoy para bromas** I'm not in the mood for jokes

9: **estar por** (propuesta etc) to be in favour of; (persona etc) to support, side with; **está por limpiar** it still has to be cleaned

10: **estar sin**: **estar sin dinero** to have no money; **está sin terminar** it isn't finished yet

estarse vr: **se estuvo en la cama toda la tarde** he stayed in bed all afternoon

estas ['estas] adj demos V **este²**
éstas pron V **éste**
estatal [esta'tal] adj state cpd
estático, -a [es'tatiko, a] adj static
estatua [es'tatwa] nf statue
estatura [esta'tura] nf stature, height
este¹ ['este] nm east
este² ['este] (f **esta**, pl **estos, estas**) adj demos (sg) this; (pl) these
esté etc vb V **estar**
éste ['este] (f **ésta**, pl **éstos, éstas**) pron (sg) this (one); (pl) these (ones); **ése ... ~ ...** the former ... the latter ...
estén etc vb V **estar**
estepa [es'tepa] nf (Geo) steppe
estera [es'tera] nf mat(ting)
estéreo [es'tereo] adj inv, nm stereo; **estereotipo** nm stereotype
estéril [es'teril] adj sterile, barren; (fig) vain, futile; **esterilizar** vt to sterilize
esterlina [ester'lina] adj: **libra ~ pound** sterling
estés etc vb V **estar**
estética [es'tetika] nf aesthetics sg
estético, -a [es'tetiko, a] adj aesthetic
estiércol [es'tjerkol] nm dung, manure
estigma [es'tiɣma] nm stigma
estilo [es'tilo] nm style; (Tec) stylus; (Natación) stroke; **algo por el ~** something along those lines
estima [es'tima] nf esteem, respect; **estimación** [estima'θjon] nf (evaluación) estimation; (aprecio, afecto) esteem, regard; **estimado, a** adj esteemed; **E~ señor** Dear

Sir

estimar [esti'mar] vt (evaluar) to estimate; (valorar) to value; (apreciar) to esteem, respect; (pensar, considerar) to think, reckon
estimulante [estimu'lante] adj stimulating ⊳ nm stimulant
estimular [estimu'lar] vt to stimulate; (excitar) to excite
estímulo [es'timulo] nm stimulus; (ánimo) encouragement
estirar [esti'rar] vt to stretch; (dinero, suma etc) to stretch out; **estirarse** vr to stretch
estirón [esti'ron] nm pull, tug; (crecimiento) spurt, sudden growth; **dar o pegar un ~** (fam: niño) to shoot up (inf)
estirpe [es'tirpe] nf stock, lineage
estival [esti'ßal] adj summer cpd
esto ['esto] pron this, this thing o matter; **~ de la boda** this business about the wedding
Estocolmo [esto'kolmo] nm Stockholm
estofado [esto'faðo] nm stew
estómago [es'tomaxo] nm stomach; **tener ~** to be thick-skinned
estorbar [estor'ßar] vt to hinder, obstruct; (molestar) to bother, disturb ⊳ vi to be in the way; **estorbo** nm (molestia) bother, nuisance; (obstáculo) hindrance, obstacle
estornudar [estornu'ðar] vi to sneeze
estos ['estos] adj demos V **este²**
éstos pron V **éste**
estoy vb V **estar**
estrado [es'traðo] nm platform
estrafalario, -a [estrafa'larjo, a] adj odd, eccentric
estrago [es'traxo] nm ruin, destruction; **hacer ~s en** to wreak havoc among
estragón [estra'xon] nm tarragon
estrambótico, -a [estram'botiko, a] adj (persona) eccentric; (peinado, ropa) outlandish
estrangular [estrangu'lar] vt (persona) to strangle; (Med) to strangulate
estratagema [estrata'xema] nf (Mil) stratagem; (astucia) cunning
estrategia [estra'texja] nf strategy; **estratégico, -a** adj strategic
estrato [es'trato] nm stratum, layer
estrechar [estre'tʃar] vt (reducir) to narrow; (Costura) to take in; (abrazar) to hug, embrace; **estrecharse** vr (reducirse) to narrow, grow narrow; (abrazarse) to embrace; **~ la mano** to shake hands
estrechez [estre'tʃeθ] nf narrowness; (de ropa) tightness; **estrecheces** nfpl (dificultades económicas) financial difficulties
estrecho, -a [es'tretʃo, a] adj narrow; (apretado) tight; (íntimo) close, intimate; (miserable) mean ⊳ nm strait; **~ de miras**

narrow-minded

estrella [es'treʎa] nf star; **estrella de mar** (Zool) starfish; **estrella fugaz** shooting star

estrellar [estre'ʎar] vt (hacer añicos) to smash (to pieces); (huevos) to fry; **estrellarse** vr to smash; (chocarse) to crash; (fracasar) to fail

estremecer [estreme'θer] vt to shake; **estremecerse** vr to shake, tremble

estrenar [estre'nar] vt (vestido) to wear for the first time; (casa) to move into; (película, obra de teatro) to première; **estrenarse** vr (persona) to make one's début; **estreno** nm (Cine etc) première

estreñido, -a [estre'ɲiðo, a] adj constipated

estreñimiento [estreɲi'mjento] nm constipation

estrepitoso, -a [estrepi'toso, a] adj noisy; (fiesta) rowdy

estría [es'tria] nf groove

estribar [estri'βar] vi: ~ **en** to lie on

estribillo [estri'βiʎo] nm (Literatura) refrain; (Mús) chorus

estribo [es'triβo] nm (de jinete) stirrup; (de coche, tren) step; (de puente) support; (Geo) spur; **perder los ~s** to fly off the handle

estribor [estri'βor] nm (Náut) starboard

estricto, -a [es'trikto, a] adj (riguroso) strict; (severo) severe

estridente [estri'ðente] adj (color) loud; (voz) raucous

estropajo [estro'paxo] nm scourer

estropear [estrope'ar] vt to spoil; (dañar) to damage; **estropearse** vr (objeto) to get damaged; (persona, piel) to be ruined

estructura [estruk'tura] nf structure

estrujar [estru'xar] vt (apretar) to squeeze; (aplastar) to crush; (fig) to drain, bleed

estuario [es'twarjo] nm estuary

estuche [es'tutʃe] nm box, case

estudiante [estu'ðjante] nmf student; **estudiantil** adj student cpd

estudiar [estu'ðjar] vt to study

estudio [es'tuðjo] nm study; (Cine, Arte, Radio) studio; **estudios** nmpl studies; (erudición) learning sg; **estudioso, -a** adj studious

estufa [es'tufa] nf heater, fire

estupefaciente [estupefa'θjente] nm drug, narcotic

estupefacto, -a [estupe'fakto, a] adj speechless, thunderstruck

estupendo, -a [estu'pendo, a] adj wonderful, terrific; (fam) great; **¡~!** that's great!, fantastic!

estupidez [estupi'ðeθ] nf (torpeza) stupidity; (acto) stupid thing (to do)

estúpido, -a [es'tupiðo, a] adj stupid, silly

estuve etc vb V **estar**

ETA ['eta] (ESP) nf abr (= Euskadi ta Askatasuna) ETA

etapa [e'tapa] nf (de viaje) stage; (Deporte) leg; (parada) stopping place; (fase) stage, phase

etarra [e'tarra] nmf member of ETA

etc. abr (= etcétera) etc

etcétera [et'θetera] adv etcetera

eternidad [eterni'ðað] nf eternity; **eterno, -a** adj eternal, everlasting

ética ['etika] nf ethics pl

ético, -a ['etiko, a] adj ethical

etiqueta [eti'keta] nf (modales) etiquette; (rótulo) label, tag

Eucaristía [eukaris'tia] nf Eucharist

euforia [eu'forja] nf euphoria

euro ['euro] nm (moneda) euro

eurodiputado, -a [eurodipu'taðo, a] nm/f Euro MP, MEP

Europa [eu'ropa] nf Europe; **europeo, -a** adj, nm/f European

Euskadi [eus'kaði] nm the Basque Country o Provinces pl

euskera [eus'kera] nm (Ling) Basque

evacuación [eβakwa'θjon] nf evacuation

evacuar [eβa'kwar] vt to evacuate

evadir [eβa'ðir] vt to evade, avoid; **evadirse** vr to escape

evaluar [eβa'lwar] vt to evaluate

evangelio [eβan'xeljo] nm gospel

evaporar [eβapo'rar] vt to evaporate; **evaporarse** vr to vanish

evasión [eβa'sjon] nf escape, flight; (fig) evasion; **evasión de capitales** flight of capital

evasiva [eβa'siβa] nf (pretexto) excuse

evento [e'βento] nm event

eventual [eβen'twal] adj possible, conditional (upon circumstances); (trabajador) casual, temporary

No confundir **eventual** con la palabra inglesa eventual.

evidencia [eβi'ðenθja] nf evidence, proof

evidente [eβi'ðente] adj obvious, clear, evident

evitar [eβi'tar] vt (evadir) to avoid; (impedir) to prevent; ~ **hacer algo** to avoid doing sth

evocar [eβo'kar] vt to evoke, call forth

evolución [eβolu'θjon] nf (desarrollo) evolution, development; (cambio) change; (Mil) manoeuvre; **evolucionar** vi to evolve; to manoeuvre

ex [eks] adj ex-; **el ~ ministro** the former minister, the ex-minister

exactitud [eksakti'tuð] nf exactness;

(*precisión*) accuracy; (*puntualidad*) punctuality; **exacto, -a** *adj* exact; accurate; punctual; **¡exacto!** exactly!

exageración [eksaxera'θjon] *nf* exaggeration

exagerar [eksaxe'rar] *vt, vi* to exaggerate

exaltar [eksal'tar] *vt* to exalt, glorify; **exaltarse** *vr* (*excitarse*) to get excited *o* worked up

examen [ek'samen] *nm* examination; **examen de conducir** driving test; **examen de ingreso** entrance examination

examinar [eksami'nar] *vt* to examine; **examinarse** *vr* to be examined, take an examination

excavadora [ekskaβa'ðora] *nf* excavator

excavar [ekska'βar] *vt* to excavate

excedencia [eksθe'ðenθja] *nf*: **estar en ~** to be on leave; **pedir** *o* **solicitar la ~** to ask for leave

excedente [eksθe'ðente] *adj, nm* excess, surplus

exceder [eksθe'ðer] *vt* to exceed, surpass; **excederse** *vr* (*extralimitarse*) to go too far

excelencia [eksθe'lenθja] *nf* excellence; **su E~** his Excellency; **excelente** *adj* excellent

excéntrico, -a [eks'θentriko, a] *adj, nm/f* eccentric

excepción [eksθep'θjon] *nf* exception; **a ~ de** with the exception of, except for; **excepcional** *adj* exceptional

excepto [eks'θepto] *adv* excepting, except (for)

exceptuar [eksθep'twar] *vt* to except, exclude

excesivo, -a [eksθe'siβo, a] *adj* excessive

exceso [eks'θeso] *nm* (*gen*) excess; (*Com*) surplus; **exceso de equipaje/peso** excess luggage/weight; **exceso de velocidad** speeding

excitado, -a [eksθi'taðo, a] *adj* excited; (*emocciónes*) aroused

excitar [eksθi'tar] *vt* to excite; (*incitar*) to urge; **excitarse** *vr* to get excited

exclamación [eksklama'θjon] *nf* exclamation

exclamar [ekskla'mar] *vi* to exclaim

excluir [eksklu'ir] *vt* to exclude; (*dejar fuera*) to shut out; (*descartar*) to reject

exclusiva [eksklu'siβa] *nf* (*Prensa*) exclusive, scoop; (*Com*) sole right

exclusivo, -a [eksklu'siβo, a] *adj* exclusive; **derecho ~** sole *o* exclusive right

Excmo. *abr* = **excelentísimo**

excomulgar [ekskomul'xar] *vt* (*Rel*) to excommunicate

excomunión [ekskomu'njon] *nf* excommunication

excursión [ekskur'sjon] *nf* excursion, outing; **excursionista** *nmf* (*turista*) sightseer

excusa [eks'kusa] *nf* excuse; (*disculpa*) apology; **excusar** [eksku'sar] *vt* to excuse

exhaustivo, -a [eksaus'tiβo, a] *adj* (*análisis*) thorough; (*estudio*) exhaustive

exhausto, -a [ek'sausto, a] *adj* exhausted

exhibición [eksiβi'θjon] *nf* exhibition, display, show

exhibir [eksi'βir] *vt* to exhibit, display, show

exigencia [eksi'xenθja] *nf* demand, requirement; **exigente** *adj* demanding

exigir [eksi'xir] *vt* (*gen*) to demand, require; **~ el pago** to demand payment

exiliado, -a [eksi'ljaðo, a] *adj* exiled ▷ *nm/f* exile

exilio [ek'siljo] *nm* exile

eximir [eksi'mir] *vt* to exempt

existencia [eksis'tenθja] *nf* existence; **existencias** *nfpl* stock(s) *pl*

existir [eksis'tir] *vi* to exist, be

éxito ['eksito] *nm* (*triunfo*) success; (*Mús etc*) hit; **tener ~** to be successful

■ No confundir **éxito** con la palabra inglesa *exit*.

exorbitante [eksorβi'tante] *adj* (*precio*) exorbitant; (*cantidad*) excessive

exótico, -a [ek'sotiko, a] *adj* exotic

expandir [ekspan'dir] *vt* to expand

expansión [ekspan'sjon] *nf* expansion

expansivo, -a [ekspan'siβo, a] *adj*: **onda expansiva** shock wave

expatriarse [ekspa'trjarse] *vr* to emigrate; (*Pol*) to go into exile

expectativa [ekspekta'tiβa] *nf* (*espera*) expectation; (*perspectiva*) prospect

expedición [ekspeði'θjon] *nf* (*excursión*) expedition

expediente [ekspe'ðjente] *nm* expedient; (*Jur: procedimiento*) action, proceedings *pl*; (: *papeles*) dossier, file, record

expedir [ekspe'ðir] *vt* (*despachar*) to send, forward; (*pasaporte*) to issue

expensas [eks'pensas] *nfpl*: **a ~ de** at the expense of

experiencia [ekspe'rjenθja] *nf* experience

experimentado, -a [eksperimen'taðo, a] *adj* experienced

experimentar [eksperimen'tar] *vt* (*en laboratorio*) to experiment with; (*probar*) to test, try out; (*notar, observar*) to experience; (*deterioro, pérdida*) to suffer; **experimento** *nm* experiment

experto, -a [eks'perto, a] *adj* expert, skilled ▷ *nm/f* expert

expirar [ekspi'rar] *vi* to expire

explanada [ekspla'naða] *nf* (*llano*) plain

explayarse [ekspla'jarse] *vr* (*en discurso*) to speak at length; **~ con algn** to confide in sb

explicación [eksplika'θjon] *nf* explanation

explicar [ekspli'kar] *vt* to explain; **explicarse** *vr* to explain (o.s.)

explícito, -a [eks'pliθito, a] *adj* explicit

explique *etc vb V* **explicar**

explorador, a [eksplora'ðor, a] *nm/f* (*pionero*) explorer; (*Mil*) scout ▷ *nm* (*Med*) probe; (*Tec*) (*radar*) scanner

explorar [eksplo'rar] *vt* to explore; (*Med*) to probe; (*radar*) to scan

explosión [eksplo'sjon] *nf* explosion; **explosivo, -a** *adj* explosive

explotación [eksplota'θjon] *nf* exploitation; (*de planta etc*) running

explotar [eksplo'tar] *vt* to exploit to run, operate ▷ *vi* to explode

exponer [ekspo'ner] *vt* to expose; (*cuadro*) to display; (*vida*) to risk; (*idea*) to explain; **exponerse** *vr*: **~se a (hacer) algo** to run the risk of (doing) sth

exportación [eksporta'θjon] *nf* (*acción*) export; (*mercancías*) exports *pl*

exportar [ekspor'tar] *vt* to export

exposición [eksposi'θjon] *nf* (*gen*) exposure; (*de arte*) show, exhibition; (*explicación*) explanation; (*declaración*) account, statement

expresamente [ekspresa'mente] *adv* (*decir*) clearly; (*a propósito*) expressly

expresar [ekspre'sar] *vt* to express; **expresión** *nf* expression

expresivo, -a [ekspre'siβo, a] *adj* (*persona, gesto, palabras*) expressive; (*cariñoso*) affectionate

expreso, -a [eks'preso, a] *pp de* **expresar** ▷ *adj* (*explícito*) express; (*claro*) specific, clear; (*tren*) fast ▷ *adv*: **enviar ~** to send by express (delivery)

express [eks'pres] (*LAM*) *adv*: **enviar algo ~** to send sth special delivery

exprimidor [eksprimi'ðor] *nm* squeezer

exprimir [ekspri'mir] *vt* (*fruta*) to squeeze; (*zumo*) to squeeze out

expuesto, -a [eks'pwesto, a] *pp de* **exponer** ▷ *adj* exposed; (*cuadro etc*) on show, on display

expulsar [ekspul'sar] *vt* (*echar*) to eject, throw out; (*alumno*) to expel; (*despedir*) to sack, fire; (*Deporte*) to send off; **expulsión** *nf* expulsion; sending-off

exquisito, -a [ekski'sito, a] *adj* exquisite; (*comida*) delicious

éxtasis ['ekstasis] *nm* ecstasy

extender [eksten'der] *vt* to extend; (*los brazos*) to stretch out, hold out; (*mapa, tela*) to spread (out), open (out); (*mantequilla*) to spread; (*certificado*) to issue; (*cheque, recibo*) to make out; (*documento*) to draw up; **extenderse** *vr* (*gen*) to extend; (*persona: en el suelo*) to stretch out; (*epidemia*) to spread; **extendido, -a** *adj* (*abierto*) spread out, open; (*brazos*) outstretched; (*costumbre*) widespread

extensión [eksten'sjon] *nf* (*de terreno, mar*) expanse, stretch; (*de tiempo*) length, duration; (*Tel*) extension; **en toda la ~ de la palabra** in every sense of the word

extenso, -a [eks'tenso, a] *adj* extensive

exterior [ekste'rjor] *adj* (*de fuera*) external; (*afuera*) outside, exterior; (*apariencia*) outward; (*deuda, relaciónes*) foreign ▷ *nm* (*gen*) exterior, outside; (*aspecto*) outward appearance; (*Deporte*) wing(er); (*países extranjeros*) abroad; **en el ~** abroad; **al ~** outwardly, on the surface

exterminar [ekstermi'nar] *vt* to exterminate

externo, -a [eks'terno, a] *adj* (*exterior*) external, outside; (*superficial*) outward ▷ *nm/f* day pupil

extinguir [ekstin'gir] *vt* (*fuego*) to extinguish, put out; (*raza, población*) to wipe out; **extinguirse** *vr* (*fuego*) to go out; (*Bio*) to die out, become extinct

extintor [ekstin'tor] *nm* (*fire*) extinguisher

extirpar [ekstir'par] *vt* (*Med*) to remove (surgically)

extra ['ekstra] *adj inv* (*tiempo*) extra; (*chocolate, vino*) good-quality ▷ *nmf* extra ▷ *nm* extra; (*bono*) bonus

extracción [ekstrak'θjon] *nf* extraction; (*en lotería*) draw

extracto [eks'trakto] *nm* extract

extradición [ekstraði'θjon] *nf* extradition

extraer [ekstra'er] *vt* to extract, take out

extraescolar [ekstraesko'lar] *adj*: **actividad ~** extracurricular activity

extranjero, -a [ekstran'xero, a] *adj* foreign ▷ *nm/f* foreigner ▷ *nm* foreign countries *pl*; **en el ~** abroad

❚ No confundir **extranjero** con la palabra inglesa *stranger*.

extrañar [ekstra'ñar] *vt* (*sorprender*) to find strange o odd; (*echar de menos*) to miss; **extrañarse** *vr* (*sorprenderse*) to be amazed, be surprised; **me extraña** I'm surprised

extraño, -a [eks'traɲo, a] *adj (extranjero)* foreign; *(raro, sorprendente)* strange, odd

extraordinario, -a [ekstraorði'narjo, a] *adj* extraordinary; *(edición, número)* special ▷ *nm (de periódico)* special edition; **horas extraordinarias** overtime *sg*

extrarradio [ekstra'rraðjo] *nm* suburbs

extravagante [ekstraβa'ɣante] *adj (excéntrico)* eccentric; *(estrafalario)* outlandish

extraviado, -a [ekstra'βjaðo, a] *adj* lost, missing

extraviar [ekstra'βjar] *vt (persona: desorientar)* to mislead, misdirect; *(perder)* to lose, misplace; **extraviarse** *vr* to lose one's way, get lost

extremar [ekstre'mar] *vt* to carry to extremes

extremaunción [ekstremaun'θjon] *nf* extreme unction

extremidad [ekstremi'ðað] *nf (punta)* extremity; **extremidades** *nfpl (Anat)* extremities

extremo, -a [eks'tremo, a] *adj* extreme; *(último)* last ▷ *nm* end; *(límite, grado sumo)* extreme; **en último ~** as a last resort

extrovertido, -a [ekstroβer'tiðo, a] *adj, nm/f* extrovert

exuberante [eksuβe'rante] *adj* exuberant; *(fig)* luxuriant, lush

eyacular [ejaku'lar] *vt, vi* to ejaculate

fa [fa] *nm (Mús)* fa, F

fabada [fa'βaða] *nf* bean and sausage stew

fábrica ['faβrika] *nf* factory; **marca de ~** trademark; **precio de ~** factory price

⚠ No confundir **fábrica** con la palabra inglesa *fabric*.

fabricación [faβrika'θjon] *nf (manufactura)* manufacture; *(producción)* production; **de ~ casera** home-made; **fabricación en serie** mass production

fabricante [faβri'kante] *nmf* manufacturer

fabricar [faβri'kar] *vt (manufacturar)* to manufacture, make; *(construir)* to build; *(cuento)* to fabricate, devise

fábula ['faβula] *nf (cuento)* fable; *(chisme)* rumour; *(mentira)* fib

fabuloso, -a [faβu'loso, a] *adj (oportunidad, tiempo)* fabulous, great

facción [fak'θjon] *nf (Pol)* faction; **facciones** *nfpl (de rostro)* features

faceta [fa'θeta] *nf* facet

facha ['fatʃa] *(fam) nf (aspecto)* look; *(cara)* face

fachada [fa'tʃaða] *nf (Arq)* façade, front

fácil ['faθil] *adj (simple)* easy; *(probable)* likely

facilidad [faθili'ðað] *nf (capacidad)* ease; *(sencillez)* simplicity; *(de palabra)* fluency; **facilidades** *nfpl* facilities; **facilidades de pago** credit facilities

facilitar [faθili'tar] *vt (hacer fácil)* to make easy; *(proporcionar)* to provide

factor [fak'tor] *nm* factor

factura [fak'tura] *nf (cuenta)* bill; **facturación** *nf (de equipaje)* check-in; **facturar** *vt (Com)* to invoice, charge for; *(equipaje)* to check in

facultad [fakul'tað] *nf (aptitud, Escol etc)* faculty; *(poder)* power

faena [fa'ena] nf (trabajo) work; (quehacer) task, job

faisán [fai'san] nm pheasant

faja ['faxa] nf (para la cintura) sash; (de mujer) corset; (de tierra) strip

fajo ['faxo] nm (de papeles) bundle; (de billetes) wad

falda ['falda] nf (prenda de vestir) skirt; **falda pantalón** culottes pl, split skirt

falla ['faʎa] nf (defecto) fault, flaw; **falla humana** (LAM) human error

fallar [fa'ʎar] vt (Jur) to pronounce sentence on ▷ vi (memoria) to fail; (motor) to miss

Fallas ['faʎas] nfpl Valencian celebration of the feast of St Joseph

● **FALLAS**
●
● In the week of 19 March (the feast
● of San José), Valencia honours its
● patron saint with a spectacular fiesta
● called **Las Fallas**. The **Fallas** are huge
● papier-mâché, cardboard and wooden
● sculptures which are built by competing
● teams throughout the year. They depict
● politicians and well-known public
● figures and are thrown onto bonfires
● and set alight once a jury has judged
● them – only the best sculpture escapes
● the flames.

fallecer [faʎe'θer] vi to pass away, die; **fallecimiento** nm decease, demise

fallido, -a [fa'ʎiðo, a] adj (gen) frustrated, unsuccessful

fallo ['faʎo] nm (Jur) verdict, ruling; (fracaso) failure; **fallo cardíaco** heart failure; **fallo humano** (ESP) human error

falsificar [falsifi'kar] vt (firma etc) to forge; (moneda) to counterfeit

falso, -a ['falso, a] adj false; (documento, moneda etc) fake; **en ~** falsely

falta ['falta] nf (defecto) fault, flaw; (privación) lack, want; (ausencia) absence; (carencia) shortage; (equivocación) mistake; (Deporte) foul; **echar en ~** to miss; **hacer ~ hacer algo** to be necessary to do sth; **me hace ~ una pluma** I need a pen; **falta de educación** bad manners pl; **falta de ortografía** spelling mistake

faltar [fal'tar] vi (escasear) to be lacking, be wanting; (ausentarse) to be absent, be missing; **faltan 2 horas para llegar** there are 2 hours to go till arrival; **~ al respeto a algn** to be disrespectful to sb; **¡no faltaba más!** (no hay de qué) don't mention it

fama ['fama] nf (renombre) fame;

(reputación) reputation

familia [fa'milja] nf family; **familia numerosa** large family; **familia política** in-laws pl

familiar [fami'ljar] adj (relativo a la familia) family cpd; (conocido, informal) familiar ▷ nm relative, relation

famoso, -a [fa'moso, a] adj (renombrado) famous

fan [fan] (pl ~s) nmf fan

fanático, -a [fa'natiko, a] adj fanatical ▷ nm/f fanatic; (Cine, Deporte) fan

fanfarrón, -ona [fanfa'rron, ona] adj boastful

fango ['fango] nm mud

fantasía [fanta'sia] nf fantasy, imagination; **joyas de ~** imitation jewellery sg

fantasma [fan'tasma] nm (espectro) ghost, apparition; (fanfarrón) show-off

fantástico, -a [fan'tastiko, a] adj fantastic

farmacéutico, -a [farma'θeutiko, a] adj pharmaceutical ▷ nm/f chemist (BRIT), pharmacist

farmacia [far'maθja] nf chemist's (shop) (BRIT), pharmacy; **farmacia de guardia** all-night chemist

fármaco ['farmako] nm drug

faro ['faro] nm (Náut: torre) lighthouse; (Auto) headlamp; **faros antiniebla** fog lamps; **faros delanteros/traseros** headlights/rear lights

farol [fa'rol] nm lantern, lamp

farola [fa'rola] nf street lamp (BRIT) o light (US)

farra ['farra] (LAM: fam) nf party; **ir de ~** to go on a binge

farsa ['farsa] nf (gen) farce

farsante [far'sante] nmf fraud, fake

fascículo [fas'θikulo] nm (de revista) part, instalment

fascinar [fasθi'nar] vt (gen) to fascinate

fascismo [fas'θismo] nm fascism; **fascista** adj, nmf fascist

fase ['fase] nf phase

fashion ['faʃon] adj (fam) trendy

fastidiar [fasti'ðjar] vt (molestar) to annoy, bother; (estropear) to spoil; **fastidiarse** vr: **¡que se fastidie!** (fam) he'll just have to put up with it!

fastidio [fas'tiðjo] nm (molestia) annoyance; **fastidioso, -a** adj (molesto) annoying

fatal [fa'tal] adj (gen) fatal; (desgraciado) ill-fated; (fam: malo, pésimo) awful; **fatalidad** nf (destino) fate; (mala suerte) misfortune

fatiga [fa'tixa] nf (cansancio) fatigue,

weariness

fatigar [fati'ɣar] vt to tire, weary

fatigoso, -a [fati'ɣoso, a] adj (cansador) tiring

fauna ['fauna] nf fauna

favor [fa'βor] nm favour; **estar a ~ de** to be in favour of; **haga el ~ de ...** would you be so good as to ..., kindly ...; **por ~** please; **favorable** adj favourable

favorecer [faβore'θer] vt to favour; (vestido etc) to become, flatter; **este peinado le favorece** this hairstyle suits him

favorito, -a [faβo'rito, a] adj, nm/f favourite

fax [faks] nm inv fax; **mandar por ~** to fax

fe [fe] nf (Rel) faith; (documento) certificate; **actuar con buena/mala ~** to act in good/bad faith

febrero [fe'βrero] nm February

fecha ['fetʃa] nf date; **con ~ adelantada** postdated; **en ~ próxima** soon; **hasta la ~** to date, so far; **poner ~** to date; **fecha de caducidad** (de producto alimenticio) sell-by date; (de contrato etc) expiry date; **fecha de nacimiento** date of birth; **fecha límite** o **tope** deadline

fecundo, -a [fe'kundo, a] adj (fértil) fertile; (fig) prolific; (productivo) productive

federación [feðera'θjon] nf federation

felicidad [feliθi'ðað] nf happiness; **¡~es!** (deseos) best wishes, congratulations!; (en cumpleaños) happy birthday!

felicitación [feliθita'θjon] nf (tarjeta) greeting(s) card

felicitar [feliθi'tar] vt to congratulate

feliz [fe'liθ] adj happy

felpudo [fel'puðo] nm doormat

femenino, -a [feme'nino, a] adj, nm feminine

feminista [femi'nista] adj, nmf feminist

fenómeno [fe'nomeno] nm phenomenon; (fig) freak, accident ▷ adj great ▷ excl great!, marvellous!; **fenomenal** adj = **fenómeno**

feo, -a ['feo, a] adj (gen) ugly; (desagradable) bad, nasty

féretro ['feretro] nm (ataúd) coffin; (sarcófago) bier

feria ['ferja] nf (gen) fair; (descanso) holiday, rest day; (MÉX: cambio) small o loose change; (CS: mercado) village market

feriado [fe'rjaðo] nm holiday

fermentar [fermen'tar] vi to ferment

feroz [fe'roθ] adj (cruel) cruel; (salvaje) fierce

férreo, -a ['ferreo, a] adj iron

ferretería [ferrete'ria] nf (tienda) ironmonger's (shop) (BRIT), hardware

ferrocarril [ferroka'rril] nm railway

ferroviario, -a [ferro'βjarjo, a] adj rail cpd

ferry ['ferri] (pl **~s** o **ferries**) nm ferry

fértil ['fertil] adj (productivo) fertile; (rico) rich; **fertilidad** nf (gen) fertility; (productividad) fruitfulness

fervor [fer'βor] nm fervour

festejar [feste'xar] vt (celebrar) to celebrate

festejo [fes'texo] nm celebration; **festejos** nmpl (fiestas) festivals

festín [fes'tin] nm feast, banquet

festival [festi'βal] nm festival

festividad [festiβi'ðað] nf festivity

festivo, -a [fes'tiβo, a] adj (de fiesta) festive; (Cine, Literatura) humorous; **día ~** holiday

feto ['feto] nm foetus

fiable ['fjaβle] adj (persona) trustworthy; (máquina) reliable

fiambre ['fjambre] nm cold meat

fiambrera [fjam'brera] nf (para almuerzo) lunch box

fianza ['fjanθa] nf surety; (Jur): **libertad bajo ~** release on bail

fiar [fi'ar] vt (salir garante de) to guarantee; (vender a crédito) to sell on credit ▷ vi to trust; **fiarse** vr to trust (in), rely on; **~ a** (secreto) to confide (to); **~se de algn** to rely on sb

fibra ['fiβra] nf fibre; **fibra óptica** optical fibre

ficción [fik'θjon] nf fiction

ficha ['fitʃa] nf (Tel) token; (en juegos) counter, marker; (tarjeta) (index) card; **fichaje** nm (Deporte) signing; **fichar** vt (archivar) to file, index; (Deporte) to sign; **estar fichado** to have a record; **fichero** nm box file; (Inform) file

ficticio, -a [fik'tiθjo, a] adj (imaginario) fictitious; (falso) fabricated

fidelidad [fiðeli'ðað] nf (lealtad) fidelity, loyalty; **alta ~** high fidelity, hi-fi

fideos [fi'ðeos] nmpl noodles

fiebre ['fjeβre] nf (Med) fever; (fig) fever, excitement; **tener ~** to have a temperature; **fiebre aftosa** foot-and-mouth disease

fiel [fjel] adj (leal) faithful, loyal; (fiable) reliable; (exacto) accurate, faithful ▷ nm: **los ~es** the faithful

fieltro ['fjeltro] nm felt

fiera ['fjera] nf (animal feroz) wild animal o beast; (fig) dragon; V tb **fiero**

fiero, -a ['fjero, a] adj (cruel) cruel; (feroz) fierce; (duro) harsh

fierro ['fjerro] (LAM) nm (hierro) iron

fiesta ['fjesta] nf party; (de pueblo) festival; (vacaciones: tb: ~s) holiday sg; **fiesta mayor** annual festival; **fiesta patria** (LAM) independence day

● **FIESTAS**
●
● **Fiestas** can be official public holidays
● or holidays set by each autonomous
● region, many of which coincide with
● religious festivals. There are also
● many **fiestas** all over Spain for a local
● patron saint or the Virgin Mary. These
● often last several days and can include
● religious processions, carnival parades,
● bullfights and dancing.

figura [fi'ɣura] nf (gen) figure; (forma, imagen) shape, form; (Naipes) face card
figurar [fiɣu'rar] vt (representar) to represent; (fingir) to figure ▷ vi to figure; **figurarse** vr (imaginarse) to imagine; (suponer) to suppose
fijador [fixa'ðor] nm (Foto etc) fixative; (de pelo) gel
fijar [fi'xar] vt (gen) to fix; (estampilla) to affix, stick (on); **fijarse** vr: **~se en** to notice
fijo, -a ['fixo, a] adj (gen) fixed; (firme) firm; (permanente) permanent ▷ adv: **mirar ~** to stare
fila ['fila] nf row; (Mil) rank; **ponerse en ~** to line up, get into line; **fila india** single file
filatelia [fila'telja] nf philately, stamp collecting
filete [fi'lete] nm (de carne) fillet steak; (de pescado) fillet
filiación [filja'θjon] nf (Pol) affiliation
filial [fi'ljal] adj filial ▷ nf subsidiary
Filipinas [fili'pinas] nfpl: **las (Islas) ~** the Philippines; **filipino, -a** adj, nm/f Philippine
filmar [fil'mar] vt to film, shoot
filo ['filo] nm (gen) edge; **sacar ~ a** to sharpen; **al ~ del mediodía** at about midday; **de doble ~** double-edged
filología [filolo'xia] nf philology; **filología inglesa** (Univ) English Studies
filón [fi'lon] nm (Minería) vein, lode; (fig) goldmine
filosofía [filoso'fia] nf philosophy; **filósofo, -a** nm/f philosopher
filtrar [fil'trar] vt, vi to filter, strain; **filtrarse** vr to filter; **filtro** nm (Tec, utensilio) filter
fin [fin] nm end; (objetivo) aim, purpose; **al ~ y al cabo** when all's said and done; **a ~ de** in order to; **por ~** finally; **en ~** in short; **fin de semana** weekend

final [fi'nal] adj final ▷ nm end, conclusion ▷ nf final; **al ~** in the end; **a ~es de** at the end of; **finalidad** nf (propósito) purpose, intention; **finalista** nmf finalist; **finalizar** vt to end, finish; (Inform) to log out o off ▷ vi to end, come to an end
financiar [finan'θjar] vt to finance; **financiero, -a** adj financial ▷ nm/f financier
finca ['finka] nf (casa de campo) country house; (ESP: bien inmueble) property, land; (LAM: granja) farm
finde ['finde] nm abr (fam: fin de semana) weekend
fingir [fin'xir] vt (simular) to simulate, feign ▷ vi (aparentar) to pretend
finlandés, -esa [finlan'des, esa] adj Finnish ▷ nm/f Finn ▷ nm (Ling) Finnish
Finlandia [fin'landja] nf Finland
fino, -a ['fino, a] adj fine; (delgado) slender; (de buenas maneras) polite, refined; (jerez) fino, dry
firma ['firma] nf signature; (Com) firm, company
firmamento [firma'mento] nm firmament
firmar [fir'mar] vt to sign
firme ['firme] adj firm; (estable) stable; (sólido) solid; (constante) steady; (decidido) resolute ▷ nm road (surface); **firmeza** nf firmness; (constancia) steadiness; (solidez) solidity
fiscal [fis'kal] adj fiscal ▷ nmf public prosecutor; **año ~** tax o fiscal year
fisgonear [fisɣone'ar] vt to poke one's nose into ▷ vi to pry, spy
física ['fisika] nf physics sg; V tb **físico**
físico, -a ['fisiko, a] adj physical ▷ nm physique ▷ nm/f physicist
fisura [fi'sura] nf crack; (Med) fracture
flác(c)ido, -a ['fla(k)θiðo, a] adj flabby
flaco, -a ['flako, a] adj (muy delgado) skinny, thin; (débil) weak, feeble
flagrante [fla'ɣrante] adj flagrant
flama ['flama] (MÉX) nf flame; **flamable** (MÉX) adj flammable
flamante [fla'mante] (fam) adj brilliant; (nuevo) brand-new
flamenco, -a [fla'menko, a] adj (de Flandes) Flemish; (baile, música) flamenco ▷ nm (baile, música) flamenco; (Zool) flamingo
flamingo [fla'mingo] (MÉX) nm flamingo
flan [flan] nm creme caramel
 ▌No confundir **flan** con la palabra inglesa flan.
flash [flaʃ] (pl ~ o ~es) nm (Foto) flash
flauta ['flauta] nf (Mús) flute

flecha ['fletʃa] nf arrow
flechazo [fle'tʃaθo] nm love at first sight
fleco ['fleko] nm fringe
flema ['flema] nm phlegm
flequillo [fle'kiʎo] nm (pelo) fringe
flexible [flek'siβle] adj flexible
flexión [flek'sjon] nf press-up
flexo ['flekso] nm adjustable table-lamp
flirtear [flirte'ar] vi to flirt
flojera [flo'xera] (LAM: fam) nf: **me da ~** I can't be bothered
flojo, -a ['floxo, a] adj (gen) loose; (sin fuerzas) limp; (débil) weak
flor [flor] nf flower; **a ~ de** on the surface of; **flora** nf flora; **florecer** vi (Bot) to flower, bloom; (fig) to flourish; **florería** (LAM) nf florist's (shop); **florero** nm vase; **floristería** nf florist's (shop)
flota ['flota] nf fleet
flotador [flota'ðor] nm (gen) float; (para nadar) rubber ring
flotar [flo'tar] vi (gen) to float; **flote** nm: **a flote** afloat; **salir a flote** (fig) to get back on one's feet
fluidez [flui'ðeθ] nf fluidity; (fig) fluency
fluido, -a ['fluiðo, a] adj, nm fluid
fluir [flu'ir] vi to flow
flujo ['fluxo] nm flow; **flujo y reflujo** ebb and flow
flúor ['fluor] nm fluoride
fluorescente [flwores'θente] adj fluorescent ▷ nm fluorescent light
fluvial [fluβi'al] adj (navegación, cuenca) fluvial, river cpd
fobia ['fobja] nf phobia; **fobia a las alturas** fear of heights
foca ['foka] nf seal
foco ['foko] nm focus; (Elec) floodlight; (MÉx: bombilla) (light) bulb
fofo, -a ['fofo, a] adj soft, spongy; (carnes) flabby
fogata [fo'xata] nf bonfire
fogón [fo'xon] nm (de cocina) ring, burner
folio ['foljo] nm folio, page
follaje [fo'ʎaxe] nm foliage
folleto [fo'ʎeto] nm (Pol) pamphlet
follón [fo'ʎon] (ESP: fam) nm (lío) mess; (conmoción) fuss; **armar un ~** to kick up a row
fomentar [fomen'tar] vt (Med) to foment
fonda ['fonda] nf inn
fondo ['fondo] nm (de mar) bottom; (de coche, sala) back; (Arte etc) background; (reserva) fund; **fondos** nmpl (Com) funds, resources; **una investigación a ~** a thorough investigation; **en el ~** at bottom, deep down
fonobuzón [fonoβu'θon] nm voice mail

fontanería [fontane'ria] nf plumbing; **fontanero, -a** nm/f plumber
footing ['futin] nm jogging; **hacer ~** to jog, go jogging
forastero, -a [foras'tero, a] nm/f stranger
forcejear [forθexe'ar] vi (luchar) to struggle
forense [fo'rense] nmf pathologist
forma ['forma] nf (figura) form, shape; (Med) fitness; (método) way, means; **las ~s** the conventions; **estar en ~** to be fit; **de ~ que ...** so that ...; **de todas ~s** in any case
formación [forma'θjon] nf (gen) formation; (educación) education; **formación profesional** vocational training
formal [for'mal] adj (gen) formal; (fig: serio) serious; (: de fiar) reliable; **formalidad** nf formality; seriousness; **formalizar** vt (Jur) to formalize; (situación) to put in order, regularize; **formalizarse** vr (situación) to be put in order, be regularized
formar [for'mar] vt (componer) to form, shape; (constituir) to make up, constitute; (Escol) to train, educate; **formarse** vr (Escol) to be trained, educated; (cobrar forma) to form, take form; (desarrollarse) to develop
formatear [formate'ar] vt to format
formato [for'mato] nm format
formidable [formi'ðaβle] adj (temible) formidable; (estupendo) tremendous
fórmula ['formula] nf formula
formulario [formu'larjo] nm form
fornido, -a [for'niðo, a] adj well-built
foro ['foro] nm (Pol, Inform etc) forum
forrar [fo'rrar] vt (abrigo) to line; (libro) to cover; **forro** nm (de cuaderno) cover; (Costura) lining; (de sillón) upholstery; **forro polar** fleece
fortalecer [fortale'θer] vt to strengthen
fortaleza [forta'leθa] nf (Mil) fortress, stronghold; (fuerza) strength; (determinación) resolution
fortuito, -a [for'twito, a] adj accidental
fortuna [for'tuna] nf (suerte) fortune, (good) luck; (riqueza) fortune, wealth
forzar [for'θar] vt (puerta) to force (open); (compeler) to compel
forzoso, -a [for'θoso, a] adj necessary
fosa ['fosa] nf (sepultura) grave; (en tierra) pit; **fosas nasales** nostrils
fósforo ['fosforo] nm (Quím) phosphorus; (cerilla) match
fósil ['fosil] nm fossil
foso ['foso] nm ditch; (Teatro) pit; (Auto) inspection pit
foto ['foto] nf photo, snap(shot); **sacar una ~** to take a photo o picture; **foto (de)**

carné passport(-size) photo

fotocopia [foto'kopja] nf photocopy;
fotocopiadora nf photocopier; **fotocopiar**
vt to photocopy

fotografía [fotoɣra'fia] nf (Arte)
photography; (una fotografía) photograph;
fotografiar vt to photograph

fotógrafo, -a [fo'toɣrafo, a] nm/f
photographer

fotomatón [fotoma'ton] nm photo booth

FP (ESP) nf abr (= Formación Profesional)
vocational courses for 14- to 18-year-olds

fracasar [fraka'sar] vi (gen) to fail

fracaso [fra'kaso] nm failure

fracción [frak'θjon] nf fraction

fractura [frak'tura] nf fracture, break

fragancia [fra'ɣanθja] nf (olor) fragrance,
perfume

frágil ['fraxil] adj (débil) fragile; (Com)
breakable

fragmento [fraɣ'mento] nm (pedazo)
fragment

fraile ['fraile] nm (Rel) friar; (: monje) monk

frambuesa [fram'bwesa] nf raspberry

francés, -esa [fran'θes, esa] adj French
▷ nm/f Frenchman(-woman) ▷ nm (Ling)
French

Francia ['franθja] nf France

franco, -a ['franko, a] adj (cándido) frank,
open; (Com: exento) free ▷ nm (moneda) franc

francotirador, a [frankotira'ðor, a] nm/f
sniper

franela [fra'nela] nf flannel

franja ['franxa] nf fringe

franquear [franke'ar] vt (camino) to
clear; (carta, paquete postal) to frank, stamp;
(obstáculo) to overcome

franqueo [fran'keo] nm postage

franqueza [fran'keθa] nf (candor)
frankness

frasco ['frasko] nm bottle, flask

frase ['frase] nf sentence; **frase hecha** set
phrase; (pey) stock phrase

fraterno, -a [fra'terno, a] adj brotherly,
fraternal

fraude ['frauðe] nm (cualidad) dishonesty;
(acto) fraud

frazada [fra'saða] (LAM) nf blanket

frecuencia [fre'kwenθja] nf frequency;
con ~ frequently, often

frecuentar [frekwen'tar] vt to frequent

frecuente [fre'kwente] adj (gen) frequent

fregadero [freɣa'ðero] nm (kitchen) sink

fregar [fre'ɣar] vt (frotar) to scrub; (platos)
to wash (up); (LAM: fam: fastidiar) to annoy;
(: malograr) to screw up

fregona [fre'ɣona] nf mop

freír [fre'ir] vt to fry

frenar [fre'nar] vt to brake; (fig) to check

frenazo [fre'naθo] nm: **dar un ~** to brake
sharply

frenesí [frene'si] nm frenzy

freno ['freno] nm (Tec, Auto) brake; (de
cabalgadura) bit; (fig) check; **freno de mano**
handbrake

frente ['frente] nm (Arq, Pol) front; (de
objeto) front part ▷ nf forehead, brow; **~ a** in
front of; (en situación opuesta de) opposite; **al
~ de** (fig) at the head of; **chocar de ~** to crash
head-on; **hacer ~ a** to face up to

fresa ['fresa] (ESP) nf strawberry

fresco, -a ['fresko, a] adj (nuevo) fresh;
(frío) cool; (descarado) cheeky ▷ nm (aire)
fresh air; (Arte) fresco; (LAM: jugo) fruit drink
▷ nm/f (fam): **ser un ~** to have a nerve;
tomar el ~ to get some fresh air; **frescura**
nf freshness; (descaro) cheek, nerve

frialdad [frial'daθ] nf (gen) coldness;
(indiferencia) indifference

frigidez [frixi'ðeθ] nf frigidity

frigorífico [friɣo'rifiko] nm refrigerator

frijol [fri'xol] nm kidney bean

frío, -a etc ['frio, a] vb V **freír** ▷ adj
cold; (indiferente) indifferent ▷ nm cold;
indifference; **hace ~** it's cold; **tener ~** to
be cold

frito, -a ['frito, a] adj fried; **me trae ~
ese hombre** I'm sick and tired of that man;
fritos nmpl fried food

frívolo, -a ['friβolo, a] adj frivolous

frontal [fron'tal] adj frontal; **choque ~**
head-on collision

frontera [fron'tera] nf frontier;
fronterizo, -a adj frontier cpd; (contiguo)
bordering

frontón [fron'ton] nm (Deporte: cancha)
pelota court; (: juego) pelota

frotar [fro'tar] vt to rub; **frotarse** vr: **~se
las manos** to rub one's hands

fructífero, -a [fruk'tifero, a] adj fruitful

fruncir [frun'θir] vt to pucker; (Costura) to
pleat; **~ el ceño** to knit one's brow

frustrar [frus'trar] vt to frustrate

fruta ['fruta] nf fruit; **frutería** nf fruit
shop; **frutero, -a** adj fruit cpd ▷ nm/f
fruiterer ▷ nm fruit bowl

frutilla [fru'tiʎa] (CS) nf strawberry

fruto ['fruto] nm fruit; (fig: resultado) result;
(: beneficio) benefit; **frutos secos** nuts and
dried fruit pl

fucsia ['fuksja] nf fuchsia

fue [fwe] vb V **ser; ir**

fuego ['fweɣo] nm (gen) fire; **a ~ lento**
on a low heat; **¿tienes ~?** have you (got) a
light?; **fuego amigo** friendly fire; **fuegos
artificiales** fireworks

fuente ['fwente] nf fountain; (*manantial: fig*) spring; (*origen*) source; (*plato*) large dish

fuera etc ['fwera] vb V **ser; ir** ▷ adv out(side); (*en otra parte*) away; (*excepto, salvo*) except, save ▷ prep: **~ de** outside; (*fig*) besides; **~ de sí** beside o.s.; **por ~** (on the) outside

fuera-borda [fwera'βorða] nm speedboat

fuerte ['fwerte] adj strong; (*golpe*) hard; (*ruido*) loud; (*comida*) rich; (*lluvia*) heavy; (*dolor*) intense ▷ adv strongly; hard; loud(ly)

fuerza etc ['fwerθa] vb V **forzar** ▷ nf (*fortaleza*) strength; (*Tec, Elec*) power; (*coacción*) force; (*Mil, Pol*) force; **a ~ de** by dint of; **cobrar ~s** to recover one's strength; **tener ~s para** to have the strength to; **a la ~** forcibly, by force; **por ~** of necessity; **fuerza de voluntad** willpower; **fuerzas aéreas** air force sg; **fuerzas armadas** armed forces

fuga ['fuɣa] nf (*huida*) flight, escape; (*de gas etc*) leak

fugarse [fu'ɣarse] vr to flee, escape

fugaz [fu'ɣaθ] adj fleeting

fugitivo, a [fuxi'tiβo, a] adj, nm/f fugitive

fui [fwi] vb V **ser; ir**

fulano, -a [fu'lano, a] nm/f so-and-so, what's-his-name/what's-her-name

fulminante [fulmi'nante] adj (*fig: mirada*) fierce; (*Med: enfermedad, ataque*) sudden; (*fam: éxito, golpe*) sudden

fumador, a [fuma'ðor, a] nm/f smoker

fumar [fu'mar] vt, vi to smoke; **~ en pipa** to smoke a pipe

función [fun'θjon] nf function; (*en trabajo*) duties pl; (*espectáculo*) show; **entrar en funciones** to take up one's duties

funcionar [funθjo'nar] vi (*gen*) to function; (*máquina*) to work; **"no funciona"** "out of order"

funcionario, -a [funθjo'narjo, a] nm/f civil servant

funda ['funda] nf (*gen*) cover; (*de almohada*) pillowcase

fundación [funda'θjon] nf foundation

fundamental [fundamen'tal] adj fundamental, basic

fundamento [funda'mento] nm (*base*) foundation

fundar [fun'dar] vt to found; **fundarse** vr: **~se en** to be founded on

fundición [fundi'θjon] nf fusing; (*fábrica*) foundry

fundir [fun'dir] vt (*gen*) to fuse; (*metal*) to smelt, melt down; (*nieve etc*) to melt; (*Com*) to merge; (*estatua*) to cast; **fundirse** vr (*colores etc*) to merge, blend; (*unirse*) to fuse together; (*Elec: fusible, lámpara etc*) to fuse,

blow; (*nieve etc*) to melt

fúnebre ['funeβre] adj funeral cpd, funereal

funeral [fune'ral] nm funeral; **funeraria** nf undertaker's

funicular [funiku'lar] nm (*tren*) funicular; (*teleférico*) cable car

furgón [fur'ɣon] nm wagon; **furgoneta** nf (*Auto, Com*) (transit) van (BRIT), pick-up (truck) (US)

furia ['furja] nf (*ira*) fury; (*violencia*) violence; **furioso, -a** adj (*iracundo*) furious; (*violento*) violent

furtivo, -a [fur'tiβo, a] adj furtive ▷ nm poacher

fusible [fu'siβle] nm fuse

fusil [fu'sil] nm rifle; **fusilar** vt to shoot

fusión [fu'sjon] nf (*gen*) melting; (*unión*) fusion; (*Com*) merger

fútbol ['futβol] nm football (BRIT), soccer (US); **fútbol americano** American football (BRIT), football (US); **fútbol sala** indoor football (BRIT) o soccer (US); **futbolín** nm table football; **futbolista** nmf footballer

futuro, -a [fu'turo, a] adj, nm future

g

gabardina [gaβar'ðina] *nf* raincoat, gabardine

gabinete [gaβi'nete] *nm* (Pol) cabinet; (estudio) study; (de abogados etc) office

gachas ['gatʃas] *nfpl* porridge sg

gafas ['gafas] *nfpl* glasses; **gafas de sol** sunglasses

gafe ['gafe] (ESP) *nmf* jinx

gaita ['gaita] *nf* bagpipes pl

gajes ['gaxes] *nmpl*: **~ del oficio** occupational hazards

gajo ['gaxo] *nm* (de naranja) segment

gala ['gala] *nf* (traje de etiqueta) full dress; **galas** *nfpl* (ropa) finery sg; **estar de ~** to be in one's best clothes; **hacer ~ de** to display

galápago [ga'lapaɣo] *nm* (Zool) turtle

galardón [galar'ðon] *nm* award, prize

galaxia [ga'laksja] *nf* galaxy

galera [ga'lera] *nf* (nave) galley; (carro) wagon; (Imprenta) galley

galería [gale'ria] *nf* (gen) gallery; (balcón) veranda(h); (pasillo) corridor; **galería comercial** shopping mall

Gales ['gales] *nm* (tb: **País de ~**) Wales; **galés, -esa** *adj* Welsh ▷ *nm/f* Welshman(-woman) ▷ *nm* (Ling) Welsh

galgo, -a ['galɣo, a] *nm/f* greyhound

gallego, -a [ga'ʎeɣo, a] *adj, nm/f* Galician

galleta [ga'ʎeta] *nf* biscuit (BRIT), cookie (US)

gallina [ga'ʎina] *nf* hen ▷ *nmf* (fam: cobarde) chicken; **gallinero** *nm* henhouse; (Teatro) top gallery

gallo ['gaʎo] *nm* cock, rooster

galopar [galo'par] *vi* to gallop

gama ['gama] *nf* (fig) range

gamba ['gamba] *nf* prawn (BRIT), shrimp (US)

gamberro, -a [gam'berro, a] (ESP) *nm/f* hooligan, lout

gamuza [ga'muθa] *nf* chamois

gana ['gana] *nf* (deseo) desire, wish; (apetito) appetite; (voluntad) will; (añoranza) longing; **de buena ~** willingly; **de mala ~** reluctantly; **me da ~s de** I feel like, I want to; **no me da la ~** I don't feel like it; **tener ~s de** to feel like

ganadería [ganaðe'ria] *nf* (ganado) livestock; (ganado vacuno) cattle pl; (cría, comercio) cattle raising

ganadero, -a [gana'ðero, a] (ESP) *nm/f* (hacendado) rancher

ganado [ga'naðo] *nm* livestock; **ganado porcino** pigs pl

ganador, a [gana'ðor, a] *adj* winning ▷ *nm/f* winner

ganancia [ga'nanθja] *nf* (lo ganado) gain; (aumento) increase; (beneficio) profit; **ganancias** *nfpl* (ingresos) earnings; (beneficios) profit sg, winnings

ganar [ga'nar] *vt* (obtener) to get, obtain; (sacar ventaja) to gain; (salario etc) to earn; (Deporte, premio) to win; (derrotar a) to beat; (alcanzar) to reach ▷ *vi* (Deporte) to win; **ganarse** *vr*: **~se la vida** to earn one's living

ganchillo [gan'tʃiʎo] *nm* crochet

gancho ['gantʃo] *nm* (gen) hook; (colgador) hanger

gandul, a [gan'dul, a] *adj, nm/f* good-for-nothing, layabout

ganga ['ganga] *nf* bargain

gangrena [gan'grena] *nf* gangrene

ganso, -a ['ganso, a] *nm/f* (Zool) goose; (fam) idiot

ganzúa [gan'θua] *nf* skeleton key

garabato [gara'βato] *nm* (escritura) scrawl, scribble

garaje [ga'raxe] *nm* garage

garantía [garan'tia] *nf* guarantee

garantizar [garanti'θar] *vt* to guarantee

garbanzo [gar'βanθo] *nm* chickpea (BRIT), garbanzo (US)

garfio ['garfjo] *nm* grappling iron

garganta [gar'ɣanta] *nf* (Anat) throat; (de botella) neck; **gargantilla** *nf* necklace

gárgaras ['garɣaras] *nfpl*: **hacer ~** to gargle

gargarear [garɣare'ar] (LAM) *vi* to gargle

garita [ga'rita] *nf* cabin, hut; (Mil) sentry box

garra ['garra] *nf* (de gato, Tec) claw; (de ave) talon; (fam: mano) hand, paw

garrafa [ga'rrafa] *nf* carafe, decanter

garrapata [garra'pata] *nf* tick

gas [gas] *nm* gas; **gases lacrimógenos** tear gas sg

gasa ['gasa] *nf* gauze

gaseosa [gase'osa] *nf* lemonade

gaseoso, -a [gase'oso, a] *adj* gassy, fizzy

gasoil [ga'soil] nm diesel (oil)
gasóleo [ga'soleo] nm = **gasoil**
gasolina [gaso'lina] nf petrol (BRIT),
gas(oline) (US); **gasolinera** nf petrol (BRIT) o
gas (US) station
gastado, -a [gas'taðo, a] adj (dinero)
spent; (ropa) worn out; (usado: frase etc) trite
gastar [gas'tar] vt (dinero, tiempo) to
spend; (fuerzas) to use up; (desperdiciar) to
waste; (llevar) to wear; **gastarse** vr to wear
out; (estropearse) to waste; **~ en** to spend
on; **~ bromas** to crack jokes; **¿qué número
gastas?** what size (shoe) do you take?
gasto ['gasto] nm (desembolso)
expenditure, spending; (consumo, uso)
use; **gastos** nmpl (desembolsos) expenses;
(cargos) charges, costs
gastronomía [gastrono'mia] nf
gastronomy
gatear [gate'ar] vi (andar a gatas) to go on
all fours
gatillo [ga'tiʎo] nm (de arma de fuego)
trigger; (de dentista) forceps
gato, -a ['gato, a] nm/f cat ▷ nm (Tec)
jack; **andar a gatas** to go on all fours
gaucho ['gautʃo] nm gaucho

○ **GAUCHO**
○
○ **Gauchos** are the herdsmen or riders of
○ the Southern Cone plains. Although
○ popularly associated with Argentine
○ folklore, **gauchos** belong equally to the
○ cattle-raising areas of Southern Brazil
○ and Uruguay. **Gauchos'** traditions and
○ clothing reflect their mixed ancestry
○ and cultural roots. Their baggy trousers
○ are Arabic in origin, while the horse and
○ guitar are inherited from the Spanish
○ conquistadors; the poncho, maté and
○ **boleadoras** (strips of leather weighted
○ at either end with stones) form part of
○ the Indian tradition.

gaviota [ga'βjota] nf seagull
gay [ge] adj inv, nm gay, homosexual
gazpacho [gaθ'patʃo] nm gazpacho
gel [xel] nm: **~ de baño/ducha** bath/
shower gel
gelatina [xela'tina] nf jelly; (polvos etc)
gelatine
gema ['xema] nf gem
gemelo, -a [xe'melo, a] adj, nm/f twin;
gemelos nmpl (de camisa) cufflinks;
(prismáticos) field glasses, binoculars
gemido [xe'miðo] nm (quejido) moan,
groan; (aullido) howl
Géminis ['xeminis] nm Gemini

gemir [xe'mir] vi (quejarse) to moan,
groan; (aullar) to howl
generación [xenera'θjon] nf generation
general [xene'ral] adj general ▷ nm
general; **por lo** o **en ~** in general;
Generalitat nf Catalan parliament;
generalizar vt to generalize;
generalizarse vr to become generalized,
spread
generar [xene'rar] vt to generate
género ['xenero] nm (clase) kind, sort;
(tipo) type; (Bio) genus; (Ling) gender; (Com)
material; **género humano** human race
generosidad [xenerosi'ðað] nf
generosity; **generoso, -a** adj generous
genial [xe'njal] adj inspired; (idea)
brilliant; (estupendo) wonderful
genio ['xenjo] nm (carácter) nature,
disposition; (humor) temper; (facultad
creadora) genius; **de mal ~** bad-tempered
genital [xeni'tal] adj genital; **genitales**
nmpl genitals
genoma [xe'noma] nm genome
gente ['xente] nf (personas) people pl;
(parientes) relatives pl
gentil [xen'til] adj (elegante) graceful;
(encantador) charming
▐ No confundir **gentil** con la palabra
inglesa gentle.
genuino, -a [xe'nwino, a] adj genuine
geografía [xeoɣra'fia] nf geography
geología [xeolo'xia] nf geology
geometría [xeome'tria] nf geometry
gerente [xe'rente] nmf (supervisor)
manager; (jefe) director
geriatría [xeria'tria] nf (Med) geriatrics sg
germen ['xermen] nm germ
gesticular [xestiku'lar] vi to gesticulate;
(hacer muecas) to grimace; **gesticulación** nf
gesticulation; (mueca) grimace
gestión [xes'tjon] nf management;
(diligencia, acción) negotiation
gesto ['xesto] nm (mueca) grimace;
(ademán) gesture
Gibraltar [xiβral'tar] nm Gibraltar;
gibraltareño, -a adj, nm/f Gibraltarian
gigante [xi'xante] adj, nmf giant;
gigantesco, -a adj gigantic
gilipollas [xili'poʎas] (fam) adj inv daft
▷ nmf inv wally
gimnasia [xim'nasja] nf gymnastics pl;
gimnasio nm gymnasium; **gimnasta** nmf
gymnast
ginebra [xi'neβra] nf gin
ginecólogo, -a [xine'koloɣo, a] nm/f
gynaecologist
gira ['xira] nf tour, trip
girar [xi'rar] vt (dar la vuelta) to turn

(around); (: *rápidamente*) to spin; (*Com: giro postal*) to draw; (: *letra de cambio*) to issue ▷ vi to turn (round); (*rápido*) to spin

girasol [xira'sol] nm sunflower

giratorio, -a [xira'torjo, a] adj revolving

giro ['xiro] nm (*movimiento*) turn, revolution; (*Ling*) expression; (*Com*) draft; **giro bancario/postal** bank draft/money order

gis [xis] (*MÉx*) nm chalk

gitano, -a [xi'tano, a] adj, nm/f gypsy

glacial [gla'θjal] adj icy, freezing

glaciar [gla'θjar] nm glacier

glándula ['glandula] nf gland

global [glo'βal] adj global; **globalización** nf globalization

globo ['gloβo] nm (*esfera*) globe, sphere; (*aerostato, juguete*) balloon

glóbulo ['gloβulo] nm globule; (*Anat*) corpuscle

gloria ['glorja] nf glory

glorieta [glo'rjeta] nf (*de jardín*) bower, arbour; (*plazoleta*) roundabout (*BRIT*), traffic circle (*US*)

glorioso, -a [glo'rjoso, a] adj glorious

glotón, -ona [glo'ton, ona] adj gluttonous, greedy ▷ nm/f glutton

glucosa [glu'kosa] nf glucose

gobernador, a [goβerna'ðor, a] adj governing ▷ nm/f governor; **gobernante** adj governing

gobernar [goβer'nar] vt (*dirigir*) to guide, direct; (*Pol*) to rule, govern ▷ vi to govern; (*Náut*) to steer

gobierno etc [go'βjerno] vb V **gobernar** ▷ nm (*Pol*) government; (*dirección*) guidance, direction; (*Náut*) steering

goce etc ['goθe] vb V **gozar** ▷ nm enjoyment

gol [gol] nm goal

golf [golf] nm golf

golfa ['golfa] (*fam!*) nf (*mujer*) slut, whore

golfo, -a ['golfo, a] nm (*Geo*) gulf ▷ nm/f (*fam: niño*) urchin; (*gamberro*) lout

golondrina [golon'drina] nf swallow

golosina [golo'sina] nf (*dulce*) sweet; **goloso, -a** adj sweet-toothed

golpe ['golpe] nm blow; (*de puño*) punch; (*de mano*) smack; (*de remo*) stroke; (*fig: choque*) clash; **no dar ~** to be bone idle; **de un ~** with one blow; **de ~** suddenly; **golpe (de estado)** coup (d'état); **golpear** vt, vi to strike, knock; (*asestar*) to beat; (*de puño*) to punch; (*golpetear*) to tap

goma ['goma] nf (*caucho*) rubber; (*elástico*) elastic; (*una goma*) elastic band; **goma de borrar** eraser, rubber (*BRIT*); **goma espuma** foam rubber

gomina [go'mina] nf hair gel

gomita [go'mita] (*RPL*) nf rubber band

gordo, -a ['gorðo, a] adj (*gen*) fat; (*fam*) enormous; **el (premio) ~** (*en lotería*) first prize

gorila [go'rila] nm gorilla

gorra ['gorra] nf cap; (*de bebé*) bonnet; (*militar*) bearskin; **entrar de ~** (*fam*) to gatecrash; **ir de ~** to sponge

gorrión [go'rrjon] nm sparrow

gorro ['gorro] nm (*gen*) cap; (*de bebé, mujer*) bonnet

gorrón, -ona [go'rron, ona] nm/f scrounger; **gorronear** (*fam*) vi to scrounge

gota ['gota] nf (*gen*) drop; (*de sudor*) bead; (*Med*) gout; **gotear** vi to drip; (*lloviznar*) to drizzle; **gotera** nf leak

gozar [go'θar] vi to enjoy o.s.; **~ de** (*disfrutar*) to enjoy; (*poseer*) to possess

gr. abr (= *gramo, gramos*) g

grabación [graβa'θjon] nf recording

grabado [gra'βaðo] nm print, engraving

grabadora [graβa'ðora] nf tape-recorder; **grabadora de CD/DVD** CD/DVD writer

grabar [gra'βar] vt to engrave; (*discos, cintas*) to record

gracia ['graθja] nf (*encanto*) grace, gracefulness; (*humor*) humour, wit; **¡(muchas) ~s!** thanks (very much)!; **~s a** thanks to; **dar las ~s a algn por algo** to thank sb for sth; **tener ~** (*chiste etc*) to be funny; **no me hace ~** I am not keen; **gracioso, -a** adj (*divertido*) funny, amusing; (*cómico*) comical ▷ nm/f (*Teatro*) comic character

grada ['graða] nf (*de escalera*) step; (*de anfiteatro*) tier, row; **gradas** nfpl (*Deporte: de estadio*) terraces

grado ['graðo] nm degree; (*de aceite, vino*) grade; (*grada*) step; (*Mil*) rank; **de buen ~** willingly; **grado centígrado/Fahrenheit** degree centigrade/Fahrenheit

graduación [graðwa'θjon] nf (*del alcohol*) proof, strength; (*Escol*) graduation; (*Mil*) rank

gradual [gra'ðwal] adj gradual

graduar [gra'ðwar] vt (*gen*) to graduate; (*Mil*) to commission; **graduarse** vr to graduate; **~se la vista** to have one's eyes tested

gráfica ['grafika] nf graph

gráfico, -a ['grafiko, a] adj graphic ▷ nm diagram; **gráficos** nmpl (*Inform*) graphics

grajo ['graxo] nm rook

gramática [gra'matika] nf grammar

gramo ['gramo] nm gramme (*BRIT*), gram (*US*)

gran [gran] adj V **grande**

grana ['grana] nf (color, tela) scarlet

granada [gra'naða] nf pomegranate; (Mil) grenade

granate [gra'nate] adj deep red

Gran Bretaña [-bre'taɲa] nf Great Britain

grande ['grande] (antes de nmsg **gran**) adj (de tamaño) big, large; (alto) tall; (distinguido) great; (impresionante) grand ▷ nm grandee

granel [gra'nel]: **a ~** adv (Com) in bulk

granero [gra'nero] nm granary, barn

granito [gra'nito] nm (Agr) small grain; (roca) granite

granizado [grani'θaðo] nm iced drink

granizar [grani'θar] vi to hail; **granizo** nm hail

granja ['granxa] nf (gen) farm; **granjero, -a** nm/f farmer

grano ['grano] nm grain; (semilla) seed; (de café) bean; (Med) pimple, spot

granuja [gra'nuxa] nmf rogue; (golfillo) urchin

grapa ['grapa] nf staple; (Tec) clamp; **grapadora** nf stapler

grasa ['grasa] nf (gen) grease; (de cocinar) fat, lard; (sebo) suet; (mugre) filth; **grasiento, -a** adj greasy; (de aceite) oily; **graso, -a** adj (leche, queso, carne) fatty; (pelo, piel) greasy

gratinar [grati'nar] vt to cook au gratin

gratis ['gratis] adv free

grato, -a ['grato, a] adj (agradable) pleasant, agreeable

gratuito, -a [gra'twito, a] adj (gratis) free; (sin razón) gratuitous

grave ['graβe] adj heavy; (serio) grave, serious; **gravedad** nf gravity

Grecia ['greθja] nf Greece

gremio ['gremjo] nm trade, industry

griego, -a ['grjexo, a] adj, nm/f Greek

grieta ['grjeta] nf crack

grifo ['grifo] (ESP) nm tap (BRIT), faucet (US)

grillo ['griʎo] nm (Zool) cricket

gripa ['gripa] (MÉX) nf flu, influenza

gripe ['gripe] nf flu, influenza; **gripe aviar** bird flu

gris [gris] adj (color) grey

gritar [gri'tar] vt, vi to shout, yell; **grito** nm shout, yell; (de horror) scream

grosella [gro'seʎa] nf (red)currant

grosero, -a [gro'sero, a] adj (poco cortés) rude, bad-mannered; (ordinario) vulgar, crude

grosor [gro'sor] nm thickness

grúa ['grua] nf (Tec) crane; (de petróleo) derrick

grueso, -a ['grweso, a] adj thick; (persona) stout ▷ nm bulk; **el ~ de** the bulk of

grulla ['gruʎa] nf crane

grumo ['grumo] nm clot, lump

gruñido [gru'ɲiðo] nm grunt; (de persona) grumble

gruñir [gru'ɲir] vi (animal) to growl; (persona) to grumble

grupo ['grupo] nm group; (Tec) unit, set; **grupo de presión** pressure group; **grupo sanguíneo** blood group

gruta ['gruta] nf grotto

guacho, -a ['gwatʃo, a] (CS) nm/f homeless child

guajolote [gwaxo'lote] (MÉX) nm turkey

guante ['gwante] nm glove; **guantes de goma** rubber gloves; **guantera** nf glove compartment

guapo, -a ['gwapo, a] adj good-looking, attractive; (elegante) smart

guarda ['gwarða] nmf (persona) guard, keeper ▷ nf (acto) guarding; (custodia) custody; **guarda jurado** (armed) security guard; **guardabarros** nm inv mudguard (BRIT), fender (US); **guardabosques** nm inv gamekeeper; **guardacostas** nm inv coastguard vessel ▷ nmf guardian, protector; **guardaespaldas** nmf inv bodyguard; **guardameta** nmf goalkeeper; **guardar** vt (gen) to keep; (vigilar) to guard, watch over; (dinero: ahorrar) to save; **guardarse** vr (preservarse) to protect o.s.; (evitar) to avoid; **guardar cama** to stay in bed; **guardarropa** nm (armario) wardrobe; (en establecimiento público) cloakroom

guardería [gwarðe'ria] nf nursery

guardia ['gwarðja] nf (Mil) guard; (cuidado) care, custody ▷ nmf guard; (policía) policeman(-woman); **estar de ~** to be on guard; **montar a ~** to mount guard; **Guardia Civil** Civil Guard

guardián, -ana [gwar'ðjan, ana] nm/f (gen) guardian, keeper

guarida [gwa'riða] nf (de animal) den, lair; (refugio) refuge

guarnición [gwarni'θjon] nf (de vestimenta) trimming; (de piedra) mount; (Culin) garnish; (arneses) harness; (Mil) garrison

guarro, -a ['gwarro, a] nm/f pig

guasa ['gwasa] nf joke; **guasón, -ona** adj (bromista) joking ▷ nm/f wit; joker

Guatemala [gwate'mala] nf Guatemala

guay [gwai] (fam) adj super, great

güero, -a ['gwero, a] (MÉX) adj blond(e)

guerra ['gerra] nf war; **dar ~** to annoy; **guerra civil** civil war; **guerra fría** cold war; **guerrero, -a** adj fighting; (carácter) warlike ▷ nm/f warrior

guerrilla [ge'rriʎa] nf guerrilla warfare; (tropas) guerrilla band o group

guía etc ['gia] vb V **guiar** ▷ nmf (persona)

guide; (*nf: libro*) guidebook; **guía telefónica** telephone directory; **guía turística** tourist guide

guiar [gi'ar] *vt* to guide, direct; (*Auto*) to steer; **guiarse** *vr*: **~se por** to be guided by

guinda ['ginda] *nf* morello cherry

guindilla [gin'diʎa] *nf* chilli pepper

guiñar [gi'ɲar] *vt* to wink

guión [gi'on] *nm* (*Ling*) hyphen, dash; (*Cine*) script; **guionista** *nmf* scriptwriter

guiri ['giri] (*ESP: fam, pey*) *nmf* foreigner

guirnalda [gir'nalda] *nf* garland

guisado [gi'saðo] *nm* stew

guisante [gi'sante] *nm* pea

guisar [gi'sar] *vt*, *vi* to cook; **guiso** *nm* cooked dish

guitarra [gi'tarra] *nf* guitar

gula ['gula] *nf* gluttony, greed

gusano [gu'sano] *nm* worm; (*lombriz*) earthworm

gustar [gus'tar] *vt* to taste, sample ⊳ *vi* to please, be pleasing; **~ de algo** to like o enjoy sth; **me gustan las uvas** I like grapes; **le gusta nadar** she likes o enjoys swimming

gusto ['gusto] *nm* (*sentido, sabor*) taste; (*placer*) pleasure; **tiene ~ a menta** it tastes of mint; **tener buen ~** to have good taste; **coger el** o **tomar ~ a algo** to take a liking to sth; **sentirse a ~** to feel at ease; **mucho ~ (en conocerle)** pleased to meet you; **el ~ es mío** the pleasure is mine; **con ~** willingly, gladly

ha *vb* V **haber**

haba ['aβa] *nf* bean

Habana [a'βana] *nf*: **la ~** Havana

habano [a'βano] *nm* Havana cigar

habéis *vb* V **haber**

○ **PALABRA CLAVE**

haber [a'βer] *vb aux* **1** (*tiempos compuestos*) to have; **había comido** I had eaten; **antes/después de haberlo visto** before seeing/after seeing o having seen it

2: **¡haberlo dicho antes!** you should have said so before!

3: **haber de: he de hacerlo** I have to do it; **ha de llegar mañana** it should arrive tomorrow

⊳ *vb impers* **1** (*existencia: sg*) there is; (*: pl*) there are; **hay un hermano/dos hermanos** there is one brother/there are two brothers; **¿cuánto hay de aquí a Sucre?** how far is it from here to Sucre?

2 (*obligación*): **hay que hacer algo** something must be done; **hay que apuntarlo para acordarse** you have to write it down to remember

3: **¡hay que ver!** well I never!

4: **¡no hay de** o **por** (*LAM*) **qué!** don't mention it!, not at all!

5: **¿qué hay?** (*¿qué pasa?*) what's up?, what's the matter?; (*¿qué tal?*) how's it going?

⊳ *vt*: **he aquí unas sugerencias** here are some suggestions; **no hay cintas blancas pero sí las hay rojas** there aren't any white ribbons but there are some red ones

⊳ *nm* (*en cuenta*) credit side; **haberes** *nmpl* assets; **¿cuánto tengo en el haber?** how much do I have in my account?; **tiene varias novelas en su haber** he has several novels to his credit

haberse *vr*: **habérselas con algn** to have

it out with sb

habichuela [aβi'tʃwela] nf kidney bean
hábil ['aβil] adj (listo) clever, smart; (capaz)
fit, capable; (experto) expert; **día ~** working
day; **habilidad** nf skill, ability
habitación [aβita'θjon] nf (cuarto) room;
(Bio: morada) habitat; **habitación doble** o
de matrimonio double room; **habitación
individual** o **sencilla** single room
habitante [aβi'tante] nmf inhabitant
habitar [aβi'tar] vt (residir en) to inhabit;
(ocupar) to occupy ▷ vi to live
hábito ['aβito] nm habit
habitual [aβi'twal] adj usual
habituar [aβi'twar] vt to accustom;
habituarse vr: **~se a** to get used to
habla ['aβla] nf (capacidad de hablar)
speech; (idioma) language; (dialecto) dialect;
perder el ~ to become speechless; **de ~
francesa** French-speaking; **estar al ~** to be
in contact; (Tel) to be on the line; **¡González
al ~!** (Tel) González speaking!
hablador, a [aβla'ðor, a] adj talkative
▷ nm/f chatterbox
habladuría [aβlaðu'ria] nf rumour;
habladurías nfpl gossip sg
hablante [a'βlante] adj speaking ▷ nmf
speaker
hablar [a'βlar] vt to speak, talk ▷ vi to
speak; **hablarse** vr to speak to each other;
~ con to speak to; **~ de** to speak of o about;
¡ni ~! it's out of the question!; **"se habla
inglés"** "English spoken here"
habré etc [a'βre] vb V **haber**
hacendado [aθen'daðo] (LAM) nm
rancher, farmer
hacendoso, -a [aθen'doso, a] adj
industrious

○ **PALABRA CLAVE**

hacer [a'θer] vt 1 (fabricar, producir) to
make; (construir) to build; **hacer una
película/un ruido** to make a film/noise;
el guisado lo hice yo I made o cooked the
stew
2 (ejecutar: trabajo etc) to do; **hacer la colada**
to do the washing; **hacer la comida** to do
the cooking; **¿qué haces?** what are you
doing?; **hacer el malo** o **el papel del malo**
(Teatro) to play the villain
3 (estudios, algunos deportes) to do; **hacer
español/económicas** to do o study
Spanish/economics; **hacer yoga/
gimnasia** to do yoga/go to gym
4 (transformar, incidir en): **esto lo hará más
difícil** this will make it more difficult; **salir**

te hará sentir mejor going out will make
you feel better
5 (cálculo): **2 y 2 hacen 4** 2 and 2 make 4; **éste
hace 100** this one makes 100
6 (+ sub): **esto hará que ganemos** this will
make us win; **harás que no quiera venir**
you'll stop him wanting to come
7 (como sustituto de vb) to do; **él bebió y yo
hice lo mismo** he drank and I did likewise
8 no hace más que criticar all he does is
criticize
▷ vb semi-aux (directo): **hacer +infin: les
hice venir** I made o had them come; **hacer
trabajar a los demás** to get others to work
▷ vi 1 **haz como que no lo sabes** act as if
you don't know
2 (ser apropiado): **si os hace** if it's alright
with you
3 hacer de: hacer de Otelo to play Othello
▷ vb impers 1 **hace calor/frío** it's hot/cold;
V tb **bueno, sol, tiempo**
2 (tiempo): **hace 3 años** 3 years ago; **hace
un mes que voy/no voy** I've been going/I
haven't been for a month
**3 ¿cómo has hecho para llegar tan
rápido?** how did you manage to get here
so quickly?

hacerse vr 1 (volverse) to become; **se
hicieron amigos** they became friends
2 (acostumbrarse): **hacerse a** to get used to
3 se hace con huevos y leche it's made
out of eggs and milk; **eso no se hace** that's
not done
4 (obtener): **hacerse de** o **con algo** to get
hold of sth
5 (fingirse): **hacerse el sueco** to turn a deaf
ear

hacha ['atʃa] nf axe; (antorcha) torch
hachís [a'tʃis] nm hashish
hacia ['aθja] prep (en dirección de)
towards; (cerca de) near; (actitud) towards;
~ adelante/atrás forwards/backwards; **~
arriba/abajo** up(wards)/down(wards); **~
mediodía/las cinco** about noon/five
hacienda [a'θjenda] nf (propiedad)
property; (finca) farm; (LAM: rancho) ranch;
(Ministerio de) H~ Exchequer (BRIT),
Treasury Department (US); **hacienda
pública** public finance
hada ['aða] nf fairy
hago etc vb V **hacer**
Haití [ai'ti] nm Haiti
halagar [ala'ɣar] vt to flatter
halago [a'laɣo] nm flattery
halcón [al'kon] nm falcon, hawk
hallar [a'ʎar] vt (gen) to find; (descubrir) to
discover; (toparse con) to run into; **hallarse**

vr to be (situated)

halterofilia [altero'filja] *nf* weightlifting

hamaca [a'maka] *nf* hammock

hambre ['ambre] *nf* hunger; (*plaga*) famine; (*deseo*) longing; **tener ~** to be hungry; **¡me muero de ~!** I'm starving!;

hambriento, -a *adj* hungry, starving

hamburguesa [ambur'ɣesa] *nf* hamburger; **hamburguesería** *nf* burger bar

han *vb* V **haber**

harapos [a'rapos] *nmpl* rags

haré *vb* V **hacer**

harina [a'rina] *nf* flour; **harina de maíz** cornflour (BRIT), cornstarch (US); **harina de trigo** wheat flour

hartar [ar'tar] *vt* to satiate, glut; (*fig*) to tire, sicken; **hartarse** *vr* (*de comida*) to fill o.s., sicken; **hartarse** *vr* (*de comida*) to fill o.s., gorge o.s.; (*cansarse*): **~se (de)** to get fed up (with); **harto, -a** *adj* (*lleno*) full; (*cansado*) fed up ▷ *adv* (*bastante*) enough; (*muy*) very; **estar harto de hacer algo/de algn** to be fed up of doing sth/with sb

has *vb* V **haber**

hasta ['asta] *adv* even ▷ *prep* (*alcanzando a*) as far as; up to; down to; (*de tiempo: a tal hora*) till, until; (*antes de*) before ▷ *conj*: **~ que** ... until; **~ luego/el sábado** see you soon/ on Saturday; **~ ahora** (*al despedirse*) see you in a minute; **~ pronto** see you soon

hay *vb* V **haber**

Haya ['aja] *nf*: **la ~** The Hague

haya *etc* ['aja] *vb* V **haber** ▷ *nf* beech tree

haz [aθ] *vb* V **hacer** ▷ *nm* (*de luz*) beam

hazaña [a'θaɲa] *nf* feat, exploit

hazmerreír [aθmerre'ir] *nm inv* laughing stock

he *vb* V **haber**

hebilla [e'βiʎa] *nf* buckle, clasp

hebra ['eβra] *nf* thread; (*Bot: fibra*) fibre, grain

hebreo, -a [e'βreo, a] *adj*, *nm/f* Hebrew ▷ *nm* (*Ling*) Hebrew

hechizar [etʃi'θar] *vt* to cast a spell on, bewitch

hechizo [e'tʃiθo] *nm* witchcraft, magic; (*acto de magía*) spell, charm

hecho, -a ['etʃo, a] *pp de* **hacer** ▷ *adj* (*carne*) done; (*Costura*) ready-to-wear ▷ *nm* deed, act; (*dato*) fact; (*cuestión*) matter; (*suceso*) event ▷ *excl* agreed!, done!; **de ~** in fact, as a matter of fact; **el ~ es que** ... the fact is that ...; **¡bien ~!** well done!

hechura [e'tʃura] *nf* (*forma*) form, shape; (*de persona*) build

hectárea [ek'tarea] *nf* hectare

helada [e'laða] *nf* frost

heladera [ela'ðera] (LAM) *nf* (*refrigerador*) refrigerator

helado, -a [e'laðo, a] *adj* frozen; (*glacial*) icy; (*fig*) chilly, cold ▷ *nm* ice cream

helar [e'lar] *vt* to freeze, ice (up); (*dejar atónito*) to amaze; (*desalentar*) to discourage ▷ *vi* to freeze; **helarse** *vr* to freeze

helecho [e'letʃo] *nm* fern

hélice ['eliθe] *nf* (*Tec*) propeller

helicóptero [eli'koptero] *nm* helicopter

hembra ['embra] *nf* (*Bot, Zool*) female; (*mujer*) woman; (*Tec*) nut

hemorragia [emo'rraxja] *nf* haemorrhage

hemorroides [emo'rroiðes] *nfpl* haemorrhoids, piles

hemos *vb* V **haber**

heno ['eno] *nm* hay

heredar [ere'ðar] *vt* to inherit; **heredero, -a** *nm/f* heir(ess)

hereje [e'rexe] *nmf* heretic

herencia [e'renθja] *nf* inheritance

herida [e'riða] *nf* wound, injury; V tb **herido**

herido, -a [e'riðo, a] *adj* injured, wounded ▷ *nm/f* casualty

herir [e'rir] *vt* to wound, injure; (*fig*) to offend

hermanastro, -a [erma'nastro, a] *nm/f* stepbrother/sister

hermandad [erman'dað] *nf* brotherhood

hermano, -a [er'mano, a] *nm/f* brother/ sister; **hermano(-a) gemelo(-a)**, twin brother/sister; **hermano(-a) político(-a)**, brother-in-law/sister-in-law

hermético, -a [er'metiko, a] *adj* hermetic; (*fig*) watertight

hermoso, -a [er'moso, a] *adj* beautiful, lovely; (*estupendo*) splendid; (*guapo*) handsome; **hermosura** *nf* beauty

hernia ['ernja] *nf* hernia; **hernia discal** slipped disc

héroe ['eroe] *nm* hero

heroína [ero'ina] *nf* (*mujer*) heroine; (*droga*) heroin

herradura [erra'ðura] *nf* horseshoe

herramienta [erra'mjenta] *nf* tool

herrero [e'rrero] *nm* blacksmith

hervidero [erβi'ðero] *nm* (*fig*) swarm; (*Pol etc*) hotbed

hervir [er'βir] *vi* to boil; (*burbujear*) to bubble; **~ a fuego lento** to simmer; **hervor** *nm* boiling; (*fig*) ardour, fervour

heterosexual [eterosek'swal] *adj* heterosexual

hice *etc* *vb* V **hacer**

hidratante [iðra'tante] *adj*: **crema ~** moisturizing cream, moisturizer; **hidratar** *vt* (*piel*) to moisturize; **hidrato** *nm* hydrate;

hidratos de carbono carbohydrates

hidráulico, -a [i'ðrauliko, a] *adj* hydraulic

hidro... [iðro] *prefijo* hydro..., water-...; **hidroeléctrico, -a** *adj* hydroelectric; **hidrógeno** *nm* hydrogen

hiedra ['jeðra] *nf* ivy

hiel [jel] *nf* gall, bile; *(fig)* bitterness

hiela *etc vb V* **helar**

hielo ['jelo] *nm (gen)* ice; *(escarcha)* frost; *(fig)* coldness, reserve

hiena ['jena] *nf* hyena

hierba ['jerβa] *nf (pasto)* grass; *(Culin, Med: planta)* herb; **mala ~** weed; *(fig)* evil influence; **hierbabuena** *nf* mint

hierro ['jerro] *nm (metal)* iron; *(objeto)* iron object

hígado ['iɣaðo] *nm* liver

higiene [i'xjene] *nf* hygiene; **higiénico, -a** *adj* hygienic

higo ['iɣo] *nm* fig; **higo seco** dried fig; **higuera** *nf* fig tree

hijastro, -a [i'xastro, a] *nm/f* stepson/daughter

hijo, -a ['ixo, a] *nm/f* son/daughter, child; **hijos** *nmpl* children, sons and daughters; **hijo adoptivo** adopted child; **hijo de papá/mamá** daddy's/mummy's boy; **hijo de puta** *(fam!)* bastard (!), son of a bitch (!); **hijo/a político/a** son-/daughter-in-law

hilera [i'lera] *nf* row, file

hilo ['ilo] *nm* thread; *(Bot)* fibre; *(metal)* wire; *(de agua)* trickle, thin stream

hilvanar [ilβa'nar] *vt (Costura)* to tack (BRIT), baste (US); *(fig)* to do hurriedly

himno ['imno] *nm* hymn; **himno nacional** national anthem

hincapié [inka'pje] *nm*: **hacer ~ en** to emphasize

hincar [in'kar] *vt* to drive (in), thrust (in)

hincha ['intʃa] *(fam) nmf* fan

hinchado, -a [in'tʃaðo, a] *adj (gen)* swollen; *(persona)* pompous

hinchar [in'tʃar] *vt (gen)* to swell; *(inflar)* to blow up, inflate; *(fig)* to exaggerate; **hincharse** *vr (inflarse)* to swell up; *(fam: de comer)* to stuff o.s.; **hinchazón** *nf (Med)* swelling; *(altivez)* arrogance

hinojo [i'noxo] *nm* fennel

hipermercado [ipermer'kaðo] *nm* hypermarket, superstore

hípico, -a ['ipiko, a] *adj* horse *cpd*

hipnotismo [ipno'tismo] *nm* hypnotism; **hipnotizar** *vt* to hypnotize

hipo ['ipo] *nm* hiccups *pl*

hipocresía [ipokre'sia] *nf* hypocrisy; **hipócrita** *adj* hypocritical ▷ *nmf* hypocrite

hipódromo [i'poðromo] *nm* racetrack

hipopótamo [ipo'potamo] *nm* hippopotamus

hipoteca [ipo'teka] *nf* mortgage

hipótesis [i'potesis] *nf inv* hypothesis

hispánico, -a [is'paniko, a] *adj* Hispanic

hispano, -a [is'pano, a] *adj* Hispanic, Spanish, Hispano- ▷ *nm/f* Spaniard; **Hispanoamérica** *nf* Latin America; **hispanoamericano, -a** *adj, nm/f* Latin American

histeria [is'terja] *nf* hysteria

historia [is'torja] *nf* history; *(cuento)* story, tale; **historias** *nfpl (chismes)* gossip *sg*; **dejarse de ~s** to come to the point; **pasar a la ~** to go down in history; **historiador, a** *nm/f* historian; **historial** *nm (profesional)* curriculum vitae, C.V.; *(Med)* case history; **histórico, -a** *adj* historical; *(memorable)* historic

historieta [isto'rjeta] *nf* tale, anecdote; *(dibujos)* comic strip

hito ['ito] *nm (fig)* landmark

hizo *vb V* **hacer**

hocico [o'θiko] *nm* snout

hockey ['xokei] *nm* hockey; **hockey sobre hielo/patines** ice/roller hockey

hogar [o'ɣar] *nm* fireplace, hearth; *(casa)* home; *(vida familiar)* home life; **hogareño, -a** *adj* home *cpd*; *(persona)* home-loving

hoguera [o'ɣera] *nf (gen)* bonfire

hoja ['oxa] *nf (gen)* leaf; *(de flor)* petal; *(de papel)* sheet; *(página)* page; **hoja de afeitar** (LAM) razor blade; **hoja electrónica** *o* **de cálculo** spreadsheet; **hoja informativa** leaflet, handout

hojalata [oxa'lata] *nf* tin(plate)

hojaldre [o'xaldre] *nm (Culin)* puff pastry

hojear [oxe'ar] *vt* to leaf through, turn the pages of

hojuela [o'xwela] (MÉX) *nf* flake

hola ['ola] *excl* hello!

holá [o'la] (RPL) *excl* hello!

Holanda [o'landa] *nf* Holland; **holandés, -esa** *adj* Dutch ▷ *nm/f* Dutchman(-woman) ▷ *nm (Ling)* Dutch

holgado, -a [ol'ɣaðo, a] *adj (ropa)* loose, baggy; *(rico)* comfortable

holgar [ol'ɣar] *vi (descansar)* to rest; *(sobrar)* to be superfluous

holgazán, -ana [olɣa'θan, ana] *adj* idle, lazy ▷ *nm/f* loafer

hollín [o'ʎin] *nm* soot

hombre ['ombre] *nm (gen)* man; *(raza humana)*: **el ~** man(kind) ▷ *excl*: **¡sí ~!** *(claro)* of course!; *(para énfasis)* man, old boy; **hombre de negocios** businessman; **hombre de pro** honest man; **hombre-rana** frogman

hombrera [om'brera] nf shoulder strap

hombro ['ombro] nm shoulder

homenaje [ome'naxe] nm (gen) homage; (tributo) tribute

homicida [omi'θiða] adj homicidal ▷ nmf murderer; **homicidio** nm murder, homicide

homologar [omolo'ðar] vt (Com: productos, tamaños) to standardize

homólogo, -a [o'moloxo, a] nm/f: **su** etc ~ his etc counterpart o opposite number

homosexual [omosek'swal] adj, nmf homosexual

honda ['onda] (cs) nf catapult

hondo, -a ['ondo, a] adj deep; **lo ~ the** depth(s) pl, the bottom; **hondonada** nf hollow, depression; (cañón) ravine

Honduras [on'duras] nf Honduras

hondureño, -a [ondu'reɲo, a] adj, nm/f Honduran

honestidad [onesti'ðað] nf purity, chastity; (decencia) decency; **honesto, -a** adj chaste; decent; honest; (justo) just

hongo ['ongo] nm (Bot: gen) fungus; (: comestible) mushroom; (: venenoso) toadstool

honor [o'nor] nm (gen) honour; **en ~ a la verdad** to be fair; **honorable** adj honourable

honorario, -a [ono'rarjo, a] adj honorary; **honorarios** nmpl fees

honra ['onra] nf (gen) honour; (renombre) good name; **honradez** nf honesty; (de persona) integrity; **honrado, -a** adj honest, upright; **honrar** [on'rar] vt to honour

hora ['ora] nf (una hora) hour; (tiempo) time; ¿qué ~ es? what time is it?; ¿a qué ~? at what time?; **media ~** half an hour; **a la ~ de recreo** at playtime; **a primera ~** first thing (in the morning); **a última ~** at the last moment; **a altas ~s** in the small hours; **¡a buena ~!** about time too!; **pedir ~** to make an appointment; **dar la ~** to strike the hour; **horas de oficina/trabajo** office/working hours; **horas de visita** visiting times; **horas extras** o **extraordinarias** overtime sg; **horas pico** (LAM) rush o peak hours; **horas punta** (ESP) rush hours

horario, -a [o'rarjo, a] adj hourly, hour cpd ▷ nm timetable; **horario comercial** business hours pl

horca ['orka] nf gallows sg

horcajadas [orka'xaðas]: **a ~** adv astride

horchata [or'tʃata] nf cold drink made from tiger nuts and water, tiger nut milk

horizontal [oriθon'tal] adj horizontal

horizonte [ori'θonte] nm horizon

horma ['orma] nf mould

hormiga [or'miɣa] nf ant; **hormigas** nfpl (Med) pins and needles

hormigón [ormi'ɣon] nm concrete; **hormigón armado/pretensado** reinforced/prestressed concrete; **hormigonera** nf cement mixer

hormigueo [ormi'ɣeo] nm (comezón) itch

hormona [or'mona] nf hormone

hornillo [or'niʎo] nm (cocina) portable stove; **hornillo de gas** gas ring

horno ['orno] nm (Culin) oven; (Tec) furnace; **alto ~** blast furnace

horóscopo [o'roskopo] nm horoscope

horquilla [or'kiʎa] nf hairpin; (Agr) pitchfork

horrendo, -a [o'rrendo, a] adj horrendous, frightful

horrible [o'rriβle] adj horrible, dreadful

horripilante [orripi'lante] adj hair-raising, horrifying

horror [o'rror] nm horror, dread; (atrocidad) atrocity; **¡qué ~!** (fam) how awful!; **horrorizar** vt to horrify, frighten; **horrorizarse** vr to be horrified; **horroroso, -a** adj horrifying, ghastly

hortaliza [orta'liθa] nf vegetable

hortelano, -a [orte'lano, a] nm/f (market) gardener

hortera [or'tera] (fam) adj tacky

hospedar [ospe'ðar] vt to put up; **hospedarse** vr to stay, lodge

hospital [ospi'tal] nm hospital

hospitalario, -a [ospita'larjo, a] adj (acogedor) hospitable; **hospitalidad** nf hospitality

hostal [os'tal] nm small hotel

hostelería [ostele'ria] nf hotel business o trade

hostia ['ostja] nf (Rel) host, consecrated wafer; (fam!: golpe) whack, punch ▷ excl (fam!): **¡~(s)!** damn!

hostil [os'til] adj hostile

hotdog [ot'dog] (LAM) nm hot dog

hotel [o'tel] nm hotel; **hotelero, -a** adj hotel cpd ▷ nm/f hotelier

● **HOTEL**
●
●
● In Spain you can choose from
● the following categories of
● accommodation, in descending order of
● quality and price: **hotel** (from 5 stars to
● 1), **hostal, pensión, casa de huéspedes,**
● **fonda**. The State also runs luxury hotels
● called **paradores**, which are usually
● sited in places of particular historical
● interest and are often historic buildings
● themselves.

hoy [oi] adv (este día) today; (la actualidad) now(adays) ▷ nm present time; **~ (en) día** now(adays)

hoyo ['ojo] nm hole, pit

hoz [oθ] nf sickle

hube etc vb V **haber**

hucha ['utʃa] nf money box

hueco, -a ['weko, a] adj (vacío) hollow, empty; (resonante) booming ▷ nm hollow, cavity

huelga etc ['welɣa] vb V **holgar** ▷ nf strike; **declararse en ~** to go on strike, come out on strike; **huelga de hambre** hunger strike; **huelga general** general strike

huelguista [wel'ɣista] nmf striker

huella ['weʎa] nf (pisada) tread; (marca del paso) footprint, footstep; (: de animal, máquina) track; **huella dactilar** fingerprint

huelo etc vb V **oler**

huérfano, -a ['werfano, a] adj orphan(ed) ▷ nm/f orphan

huerta ['werta] nf market garden; (en Murcia y Valencia) irrigated region

huerto ['werto] nm kitchen garden; (de árboles frutales) orchard

hueso ['weso] nm (Anat) bone; (de fruta) stone

huésped ['wespeð] nmf guest

hueva ['weβa] nf roe

huevera [we'βera] nf eggcup

huevo ['weβo] nm egg; **huevo a la copa** (cs) soft-boiled egg; **huevo duro/escalfado** hard-boiled/poached egg; **huevo estrellado** (LAM) fried egg; **huevo frito** (ESP) fried egg; **huevo pasado por agua** soft-boiled egg; **huevos revueltos** scrambled eggs; **huevo tibio** (MÉX) soft-boiled egg

huida [u'iða] nf escape, flight

huir [u'ir] vi (escapar) to flee, escape; (evitar) to avoid

hule ['ule] nm oilskin; (MÉX: goma) rubber

hulera [u'lera] (MÉX) nf catapult

humanidad [umani'ðað] nf (género humano) man(kind); (cualidad) humanity

humanitario, -a [umani'tarjo, a] adj humanitarian

humano, -a [u'mano, a] adj (gen) human; (humanitario) humane ▷ nm human; **ser ~** human being

humareda [uma'reða] nf cloud of smoke

humedad [ume'ðað] nf (de clima) humidity; (de pared etc) dampness; **a prueba de ~** damp-proof; **humedecer** vt to moisten, wet; **humedecerse** vr to get wet

húmedo, -a ['umeðo, a] adj (mojado) damp, wet; (tiempo etc) humid

humilde [u'milde] adj humble, modest

humillación [umiʎa'θjon] nf humiliation; **humillante** adj humiliating

humillar [umi'ʎar] vt to humiliate

humo ['umo] nm (de fuego) smoke; (gas nocivo) fumes pl; (vapor) steam, vapour; **humos** nmpl (fig) conceit sg

humor [u'mor] nm (disposición) mood, temper; (lo que divierte) humour; **de buen/mal ~** in a good/bad mood; **humorista** nmf comic; **humorístico, -a** adj funny, humorous

hundimiento [undi'mjento] nm (gen) sinking; (colapso) collapse

hundir [un'dir] vt to sink; (edificio, plan) to ruin, destroy; **hundirse** vr to sink, collapse

húngaro, -a ['ungaro, a] adj, nm/f Hungarian

Hungría [un'gria] nf Hungary

huracán [ura'kan] nm hurricane

huraño, -a [u'raɲo, a] adj (antisocial) unsociable

hurgar [ur'ɣar] vt to poke, jab; (remover) to stir (up); **hurgarse** vr: **~se (las narices)** to pick one's nose

hurón, -ona [u'ron, ona] nm (Zool) ferret

hurtadillas [urta'ðiʎas]: **a ~** adv stealthily, on the sly

hurtar [ur'tar] vt to steal; **hurto** nm theft, stealing

husmear [usme'ar] vt (oler) to sniff out, scent; (fam) to pry into

huyo etc vb V **huir**

h

iba etc vb V **ir**

ibérico, -a [i'βeriko, a] adj Iberian

iberoamericano, -a [iβeroameri'kano, a] adj, nm/f Latin American

Ibiza [i'βiθa] nf Ibiza

iceberg [iθe'βer] nm iceberg

icono [i'kono] nm ikon, icon

ida ['iða] nf going, departure; ~ **y vuelta** round trip, return

idea [i'ðea] nf idea; **no tengo la menor** ~ I haven't a clue

ideal [iðe'al] adj, nm ideal; **idealista** nmf idealist; **idealizar** vt to idealize

ídem ['iðem] pron ditto

idéntico, -a [i'ðentiko, a] adj identical

identidad [iðenti'ðað] nf identity

identificación [iðentifika'θjon] nf identification

identificar [iðentifi'kar] vt to identify; **identificarse** vr: ~**se con** to identify with

ideología [iðeolo'xia] nf ideology

idilio [i'ðiljo] nm love-affair

idioma [i'ðjoma] nm (gen) language

⬛ No confundir **idioma** con la palabra inglesa *idiom*.

idiota [i'ðjota] adj idiotic ▷ nmf idiot

ídolo ['iðolo] nm (tb fig) idol

idóneo, -a [i'ðoneo, a] adj suitable

iglesia [i'ɣlesja] nf church

ignorante [iɣno'rante] adj ignorant, uninformed ▷ nmf ignoramus

ignorar [iɣno'rar] vt not to know, be ignorant of; (no hacer caso a) to ignore

igual [i'ɣwal] adj (gen) equal; (similar) like, similar; (mismo) (the) same; (constante) constant; (temperatura) even ▷ nmf equal; ~ **que** like, the same as; **me da** o **es** ~ I don't care; **son ~es** they're the same; **al ~ que** (prep, conj) like, just like

igualar [iɣwa'lar] vt (gen) to equalize, make equal; (allanar, nivelar) to level (off),

even (out); **igualarse** vr (platos de balanza) to balance out

igualdad [iɣwal'dað] nf equality; (similaridad) sameness; (uniformidad) uniformity

igualmente [iɣwal'mente] adv equally; (también) also, likewise ▷ excl the same to you!

ilegal [ile'ɣal] adj illegal

ilegítimo, -a [ile'xitimo, a] adj illegitimate

ileso, -a [i'leso, a] adj unhurt

ilimitado, -a [ilimi'taðo, a] adj unlimited

iluminación [ilumina'θjon] nf illumination; (alumbrado) lighting

iluminar [ilumi'nar] vt to illuminate, light (up); (fig) to enlighten

ilusión [ilu'sjon] nf illusion; (quimera) delusion; (esperanza) hope; **hacerse ilusiones** to build up one's hopes; **ilusionado, -a** adj excited; **ilusionar** vi: **le ilusiona ir de vacaciones** he's looking forward to going on holiday; **ilusionarse** vr: **ilusionarse (con)** to get excited (about)

iluso, -a [i'luso, a] adj easily deceived ▷ nm/f dreamer

ilustración [ilustra'θjon] nf illustration; (saber) learning, erudition; **la I~** the Enlightenment; **ilustrado, -a** adj illustrated; learned

ilustrar [ilus'trar] vt to illustrate; (instruir) to instruct; (explicar) to explain, make clear

ilustre [i'lustre] adj famous, illustrious

imagen [i'maxen] nf (gen) image; (dibujo) picture

imaginación [imaxina'θjon] nf imagination

imaginar [imaxi'nar] vt (gen) to imagine; (idear) to think up; (suponer) to suppose; **imaginarse** vr to imagine; **imaginario, -a** adj imaginary; **imaginativo, -a** adj imaginative

imán [i'man] nm magnet

imbécil [im'beθil] nmf imbecile, idiot

imitación [imita'θjon] nf imitation; **de ~** imitation cpd

imitar [imi'tar] vt to imitate; (parodiar, remedar) to mimic, ape

impaciente [impa'θjente] adj impatient; (nervioso) anxious

impacto [im'pakto] nm impact

impar [im'par] adj odd

imparcial [impar'θjal] adj impartial, fair

impecable [impe'kaβle] adj impeccable

impedimento [impeði'mento] nm impediment, obstacle

impedir [impe'ðir] vt (obstruir) to impede, obstruct; (estorbar) to prevent; ~ **a algn**

hacer o **que algn haga algo** to prevent sb (from) doing sth, stop sb doing sth

imperativo, -a [impera'tiβo, a] adj (urgente, Ling) imperative

imperdible [imper'ðiβle] nm safety pin

imperdonable [imperðo'naβle] adj unforgivable, inexcusable

imperfecto, -a [imper'fekto, a] adj imperfect

imperio [im'perjo] nm empire; (autoridad) rule, authority; (fig) pride, haughtiness

impermeable [imperme'aβle] adj waterproof ▷ nm raincoat, mac (BRIT)

impersonal [imperso'nal] adj impersonal

impertinente [imperti'nente] adj impertinent

ímpetu ['impetu] nm (impulso) impetus, impulse; (impetuosidad) impetuosity; (violencia) violence

implantar [implan'tar] vt to introduce

implemento [imple'mento] (LAM) nm tool, implement

implicar [impli'kar] vt to involve; (entrañar) to imply

implícito, -a [im'pliθito, a] adj (tácito) implicit; (sobreentendido) implied

imponente [impo'nente] adj (impresionante) impressive, imposing; (solemne) grand

imponer [impo'ner] vt (gen) to impose; (exigir) to exact; **imponerse** vr to assert o.s.; (prevalecer) to prevail; **imponible** adj (Com) taxable

impopular [impopu'lar] adj unpopular

importación [importa'θjon] nf (acto) importing; (mercancías) imports pl

importancia [impor'tanθja] nf importance; (valor) value, significance; (extensión) size, magnitude; **no tiene ~** it's nothing; **importante** adj important; valuable, significant

importar [impor'tar] vt (del extranjero) to import; (costar) to amount to ▷ vi to be important, matter; **me importa un rábano** I couldn't care less; **no importa** it doesn't matter; **¿le importa que fume?** do you mind if I smoke?

importe [im'porte] nm (total) amount; (valor) value

imposible [impo'siβle] adj (gen) impossible; (insoportable) unbearable, intolerable

imposición [imposi'θjon] nf imposition; (Com: impuesto) tax; (: inversión) deposit

impostor, a [impos'tor, a] nm/f impostor

impotencia [impo'tenθja] nf impotence; **impotente** adj impotent

impreciso, -a [impre'θiso, a] adj imprecise, vague

impregnar [impreɣ'nar] vt to impregnate; **impregnarse** vr to become impregnated

imprenta [im'prenta] nf (acto) printing; (aparato) press; (casa) printer's; (letra) print

imprescindible [impresθin'diβle] adj essential, vital

impresión [impre'sjon] nf (gen) impression; (Imprenta) printing; (edición) edition; (Foto) print; (marca) imprint; **impresión digital** fingerprint

impresionante [impresjo'nante] adj impressive; (tremendo) tremendous; (maravilloso) great, marvellous

impresionar [impresjo'nar] vt (conmover) to move; (afectar) to impress, strike; (película fotográfica) to expose; **impresionarse** vr to be impressed; (conmoverse) to be moved

impreso, -a [im'preso, a] pp de **imprimir** ▷ adj printed; **impresos** nmpl printed matter; **impresora** nf printer

imprevisto, -a [impre'βisto, a] adj (gen) unforeseen; (inesperado) unexpected

imprimir [impri'mir] vt to imprint, impress, stamp; (textos) to print; (Inform) to output, print out

improbable [impro'βaβle] adj improbable; (inverosímil) unlikely

impropio, -a [im'propjo, a] adj improper

improvisado, -a [improβi'saðo, a] adj improvised

improvisar [improβi'sar] vt to improvise

improviso, -a [impro'βiso, a] adj: **de ~** unexpectedly, suddenly

imprudencia [impru'ðenθja] nf imprudence; (indiscreción) indiscretion; (descuido) carelessness; **imprudente** adj unwise, imprudent; (indiscreto) indiscreet

impuesto, -a [im'pwesto, a] adj imposed ▷ nm tax; **impuesto al valor agregado** o **añadido** (LAM) value added tax (BRIT) ≈ sales tax (US); **impuesto sobre el valor añadido** (ESP) value added tax (BRIT) ≈ sales tax (US)

impulsar [impul'sar] vt to drive; (promover) to promote, stimulate

impulsivo, -a [impul'siβo, a] adj impulsive; **impulso** nm impulse; (fuerza, empuje) thrust, drive; (fig: sentimiento) urge, impulse

impureza [impu'reθa] nf impurity; **impuro, -a** adj impure

inaccesible [inakθe'siβle] adj inaccessible

inaceptable [inaθep'taβle] adj unacceptable

inactivo, -a [inak'tiβo, a] adj inactive

inadecuado, -a [inaðe'kwaðo, a] adj

(insuficiente) inadequate; *(inapto)* unsuitable

inadvertido, -a [inaðβer'tiðo, a] *adj (no visto)* unnoticed

inaguantable [inaɣwan'taβle] *adj* unbearable

inanimado, -a [inani'maðo, a] *adj* inanimate

inaudito, -a [inau'ðito, a] *adj* unheard-of

inauguración [inauɣura'θjon] *nf* inauguration; opening

inaugurar [inauɣu'rar] *vt* to inaugurate; *(exposición)* to open

inca ['inka] *nmf* Inca

incalculable [inkalku'laβle] *adj* incalculable

incandescente [inkandes'θente] *adj* incandescent

incansable [inkan'saβle] *adj* tireless, untiring

incapacidad [inkapaθi'ðað] *nf* incapacity; *(incompetencia)* incompetence; **incapacidad física/mental** physical/mental disability

incapacitar [inkapaθi'tar] *vt (inhabilitar)* to incapacitate, render unfit; *(descalificar)* to disqualify

incapaz [inka'paθ] *adj* incapable

incautarse [inkau'tarse] *vr*: ~ **de** to seize, confiscate

incauto, -a [in'kauto, a] *adj (imprudente)* incautious, unwary

incendiar [inθen'djar] *vt* to set fire to; *(fig)* to inflame; **incendiarse** *vr* to catch fire; **incendiario, -a** *adj* incendiary

incendio [in'θendjo] *nm* fire

incentivo [inθen'tiβo] *nm* incentive

incertidumbre [inθerti'ðumbre] *nf (inseguridad)* uncertainty; *(duda)* doubt

incesante [inθe'sante] *adj* incessant

incesto [in'θesto] *nm* incest

incidencia [inθi'ðenθja] *nf (Mat)* incidence

incidente [inθi'ðente] *nm* incident

incidir [inθi'ðir] *vi (influir)* to influence; *(afectar)* to affect

incienso [in'θjenso] *nm* incense

incierto, -a [in'θjerto, a] *adj* uncertain

incineración [inθinera'θjon] *nf* incineration; *(de cadáveres)* cremation

incinerar [inθine'rar] *vt* to burn; *(cadáveres)* to cremate

incisión [inθi'sjon] *nf* incision

incisivo, -a [inθi'siβo, a] *adj* sharp, cutting; *(fig)* incisive

incitar [inθi'tar] *vt* to incite, rouse

inclemencia [inkle'menθja] *nf (severidad)* harshness, severity; *(del tiempo)* inclemency

inclinación [inklina'θjon] *nf (gen)* inclination; *(de tierras)* slope, incline; *(de cabeza)* nod, bow; *(fig)* leaning, bent

inclinar [inkli'nar] *vt* to incline; *(cabeza)* to nod, bow ▷ *vi* to lean, slope; **inclinarse** *vr* to bow; *(encorvarse)* to stoop; ~**se a** *(parecerse a)* to take after, resemble; ~**se ante** to bow down to; **me inclino a pensar que ...** I'm inclined to think that ...

incluir [inklu'ir] *vt* to include; *(incorporar)* to incorporate; *(meter)* to enclose

inclusive [inklu'siβe] *adv* inclusive ▷ *prep* including

incluso [in'kluso] *adv* even

incógnita [in'koɣnita] *nf (Mat)* unknown quantity

incógnito [in'koɣnito] *nm*: **de** ~ incognito

incoherente [inkoe'rente] *adj* incoherent

incoloro, -a [inko'loro, a] *adj* colourless

incomodar [inkomo'ðar] *vt* to inconvenience; *(molestar)* to bother, trouble; *(fastidiar)* to annoy

incomodidad [inkomoði'ðað] *nf* inconvenience; *(fastidio, enojo)* annoyance; *(de vivienda)* discomfort

incómodo, -a [in'komoðo, a] *adj (inconfortable)* uncomfortable; *(molesto)* annoying; *(inconveniente)* inconvenient

incomparable [inkompa'raβle] *adj* incomparable

incompatible [inkompa'tiβle] *adj* incompatible

incompetente [inkompe'tente] *adj* incompetent

incompleto, -a [inkom'pleto, a] *adj* incomplete, unfinished

incomprensible [inkompren'siβle] *adj* incomprehensible

incomunicado, -a [inkomuni'kaðo, a] *adj (aislado)* cut off, isolated; *(confinado)* in solitary confinement

incondicional [inkondiθjo'nal] *adj* unconditional; *(apoyo)* wholehearted; *(partidario)* staunch

inconfundible [inkonfun'diβle] *adj* unmistakable

incongruente [inkon'grwente] *adj* incongruous

inconsciente [inkons'θjente] *adj* unconscious; thoughtless

inconsecuente [inkonse'kwente] *adj* inconsistent

inconstante [inkons'tante] *adj* inconstant

incontable [inkon'taβle] *adj* countless, innumerable

inconveniencia [inkombe'njenθja] *nf* unsuitability, inappropriateness;

(*descortesía*) impoliteness; **inconveniente** *adj* unsuitable; impolite ▷ *nm* obstacle; (*desventaja*) disadvantage; **el inconveniente es que ...** the trouble is that ...

incordiar [inkor'ðjar] (*fam*) *vt* to bug, annoy

incorporar [inkorpo'rar] *vt* to incorporate; **incorporarse** *vr* to sit up; **-se a** to join

incorrecto, -a [inko'rrekto, a] *adj* (*gen*) incorrect, wrong; (*comportamiento*) bad-mannered

incorregible [inkorre'xiβle] *adj* incorrigible

incrédulo, -a [in'kreðulo, a] *adj* incredulous, unbelieving; sceptical

increíble [inkre'iβle] *adj* incredible

incremento [inkre'mento] *nm* increment; (*aumento*) rise, increase

increpar [inkre'par] *vt* to reprimand

incruento, -a [in'krwento, a] *adj* bloodless

incrustar [inkrus'tar] *vt* to incrust; (*piedras: en joya*) to inlay

incubar [inku'βar] *vt* to incubate

inculcar [inkul'kar] *vt* to inculcate

inculto, -a [in'kulto, a] *adj* (*persona*) uneducated; (*grosero*) uncouth ▷ *nm/f* ignoramus

incumplimiento [inkumpli'mjento] *nm* non-fulfilment; **incumplimiento de contrato** breach of contract

incurrir [inku'rrir] *vi*: **~ en** to incur; (*crimen*) to commit

indagar [inda'xar] *vt* to investigate; to search; (*averiguar*) to ascertain

indecente [inde'θente] *adj* indecent, improper; (*lascivo*) obscene

indeciso, -a [inde'θiso, a] *adj* (*por decidir*) undecided; (*vacilante*) hesitant

indefenso, -a [inde'fenso, a] *adj* defenceless

indefinido, -a [indefi'niðo, a] *adj* indefinite; (*vago*) vague, undefined

indemne [in'demne] *adj* (*objeto*) undamaged; (*persona*) unharmed, unhurt

indemnizar [indemni'θar] *vt* to indemnify; (*compensar*) to compensate

independencia [indepen'denθja] *nf* independence

independiente [indepen'djente] *adj* (*libre*) independent; (*autónomo*) self-sufficient

indeterminado, -a [indetermi'naðo, a] *adj* indefinite; (*desconocido*) indeterminate

India ['indja] *nf*: **la ~** India

indicación [indika'θjon] *nf* indication;

(*señal*) sign; (*sugerencia*) suggestion, hint

indicado, -a [indi'kaðo, a] *adj* (*momento, método*) right; (*tratamiento*) appropriate; (*solución*) likely

indicador [indika'ðor] *nm* indicator; (*Tec*) gauge, meter

indicar [indi'kar] *vt* (*mostrar*) to indicate, show; (*termómetro etc*) to read, register; (*señalar*) to point to

índice ['indiθe] *nm* index; (*catálogo*) catalogue; (*Anat*) index finger, forefinger; **índice de materias** table of contents

indicio [in'diθjo] *nm* indication, sign; (*en pesquisa etc*) clue

indiferencia [indife'renθja] *nf* indifference; (*apatía*) apathy; **indiferente** *adj* indifferent

indígena [in'dixena] *adj* indigenous, native ▷ *nmf* native

indigestión [indixes'tjon] *nf* indigestion

indigesto, -a [indi'xesto, a] *adj* (*alimento*) indigestible; (*fig*) turgid

indignación [indixna'θjon] *nf* indignation

indignar [indix'nar] *vt* to anger, make indignant; **indignarse** *vr*: **-se por** to get indignant about

indigno, -a [in'dixno, a] *adj* (*despreciable*) low, contemptible; (*inmerecido*) unworthy

indio, -a ['indjo, a] *adj, nm/f* Indian

indirecta [indi'rekta] *nf* insinuation, innuendo; (*sugerencia*) hint

indirecto, -a [indi'rekto, a] *adj* indirect

indiscreción [indiskre'θjon] *nf* (*imprudencia*) indiscretion; (*irreflexión*) tactlessness; (*acto*) gaffe, faux pas

indiscreto, -a [indis'kreto, a] *adj* indiscreet

indiscutible [indisku'tiβle] *adj* indisputable, unquestionable

indispensable [indispen'saβle] *adj* indispensable, essential

indispuesto, -a [indis'pwesto, a] *adj* (*enfermo*) unwell, indisposed

indistinto, -a [indis'tinto, a] *adj* indistinct; (*vago*) vague

individual [indiβi'ðwal] *adj* individual; (*habitación*) single ▷ *nm* (*Deporte*) singles *sg*

individuo, -a [indi'βiðwo, a] *adj, nm* individual

índole ['indole] *nf* (*naturaleza*) nature; (*clase*) sort, kind

inducir [indu'θir] *vt* to induce; (*inferir*) to infer; (*persuadir*) to persuade

indudable [indu'ðaβle] *adj* undoubted; (*incuestionable*) unquestionable

indultar [indul'tar] *vt* (*perdonar*) to pardon, reprieve; (*librar de pago*) to exempt;

indulto nm pardon; exemption
industria [in'dustrja] nf industry;
(habilidad) skill; **industrial** adj industrial
▷ nm industrialist
inédito, -a [in'eðito, a] adj (texto)
unpublished; (nuevo) new
ineficaz [inefi'kaθ] adj (inútil) ineffective;
(ineficiente) inefficient
ineludible [inelu'ðiβle] adj inescapable,
unavoidable
ineptitud [inepti'tuð] nf ineptitude,
incompetence; **inepto, -a** adj inept,
incompetent
inequívoco, -a [ine'kiβoko, a] adj
unequivocal; (inconfundible) unmistakable
inercia [in'erθja] nf inertia; (pasividad)
passivity
inerte [in'erte] adj inert; (inmóvil)
motionless
inesperado, -a [inespe'raðo, a] adj
unexpected, unforeseen
inestable [ines'taβle] adj unstable
inevitable [ineβi'taβle] adj inevitable
inexacto, -a [inek'sakto, a] adj
inaccurate; (falso) untrue
inexperto, -a [inek'sperto, a] adj
(novato) inexperienced
infalible [infa'liβle] adj infallible; (plan)
foolproof
infame [in'fame] adj infamous; (horrible)
dreadful; **infamia** nf infamy; (deshonra)
disgrace
infancia [in'fanθja] nf infancy, childhood
infantería [infante'ria] nf infantry
infantil [infan'til] adj (pueril, aniñado)
infantile; (cándido) childlike; (literatura, ropa
etc) children's
infarto [in'farto] nm (tb: ~ de miocardio)
heart attack
infatigable [infati'ɣaβle] adj tireless,
untiring
infección [infek'θjon] nf infection;
infeccioso, -a adj infectious
infectar [infek'tar] vt to infect;
infectarse vr to become infected
infeliz [infe'liθ] adj unhappy, wretched
▷ nmf wretch
inferior [infe'rjor] adj inferior; (situación)
lower ▷ nmf inferior, subordinate
inferir [infe'rir] vt (deducir) to infer,
deduce; (causar) to cause
infidelidad [infiðeli'ðað] nf (gen)
infidelity, unfaithfulness
infiel [in'fjel] adj unfaithful, disloyal;
(erróneo) inaccurate ▷ nmf infidel,
unbeliever
infierno [in'fjerno] nm hell
infiltrarse [infil'trarse] vr: ~ en to

infiltrate in(to); (persona) to work one's
way in(to)
ínfimo, -a ['infimo, a] adj (más bajo)
lowest; (despreciable) vile, mean
infinidad [infini'ðað] nf infinity;
(abundancia) great quantity
infinito, -a [infi'nito, a] adj, nm infinite
inflación [infla'θjon] nf (hinchazón)
swelling; (monetaria) inflation; (fig) conceit
inflamable [infla'maβle] adj flammable
inflamar [infla'mar] vt (Med; fig) to
inflame; **inflamarse** vr to catch fire; to
become inflamed
inflar [in'flar] vt (hinchar) to inflate, blow
up; (fig) to exaggerate; **inflarse** vr to swell
(up); (fig) to get conceited
inflexible [inflek'siβle] adj inflexible; (fig)
unbending
influencia [influ'enθja] nf influence
influir [influ'ir] vt to influence
influjo [in'fluxo] nm influence
influya etc vb V **influir**
influyente [influ'jente] adj influential
información [informa'θjon] nf
information; (noticias) news sg; (Jur) inquiry;
I~ (oficina) Information Office; (mostrador)
Information Desk; (Tel) Directory Enquiries
informal [infor'mal] adj (gen) informal
informar [infor'mar] vt (gen) to inform;
(revelar) to reveal, make known ▷ vi (Jur) to
plead; (denunciar) to inform; (dar cuenta de)
to report on; **informarse** vr to find out; ~se
de to inquire into
informática [infor'matika] nf computer
science, information technology
informe [in'forme] adj shapeless ▷ nm
report
infracción [infrak'θjon] nf infraction,
infringement
infravalorar [infrabalo'rar] vt to
undervalue, underestimate
infringir [infrin'xir] vt to infringe,
contravene
infundado, -a [infun'daðo, a] adj
groundless, unfounded
infundir [infun'dir] vt to infuse, instil
infusión [infu'sjon] nf infusion; **infusión
de manzanilla** camomile tea
ingeniería [inxenje'ria] nf engineering;
ingeniería genética genetic engineering;
ingeniero, -a nm/f engineer; **ingeniero
civil** o **de caminos** civil engineer
ingenio [in'xenjo] nm (talento) talent;
(agudeza) wit; (habilidad) ingenuity,
inventiveness; **ingenio azucarero** (LAM)
sugar refinery; **ingenioso, -a** [inxe'njoso,
a] adj ingenious, clever; (divertido) witty;
ingenuo, -a adj ingenuous

ingerir [inxe'rir] vt to ingest; (tragar) to swallow; (consumir) to consume

Inglaterra [ingla'terra] nf England

ingle ['ingle] nf groin

inglés, -esa [in'gles, esa] adj English ▷ nm/f Englishman(-woman) ▷ nm (Ling) English

ingrato, -a [in'grato, a] adj (gen) ungrateful

ingrediente [ingre'ðjente] nm ingredient

ingresar [ingre'sar] vt (dinero) to deposit ▷ vi to come in; ~ **en el hospital** to go into hospital

ingreso [in'greso] nm (entrada) entry; (en hospital etc) admission; **ingresos** nmpl (dinero) income sg; (Com) takings pl

inhabitable [inaβi'taβle] adj uninhabitable

inhalar [ina'lar] vt to inhale

inhibir [ini'βir] vt to inhibit

inhóspito, -a [i'nospito, a] adj (región, paisaje) inhospitable

inhumano, -a [inu'mano, a] adj inhuman

inicial [ini'θjal] adj, nf initial

iniciar [ini'θjar] vt (persona) to initiate; (empezar) to begin, commence; (conversación) to start up

iniciativa [iniθja'tiβa] nf initiative; **iniciativa privada** private enterprise

ininterrumpido, -a [ininterrum'piðo, a] adj uninterrupted

injertar [inxer'tar] vt to graft; **injerto** nm graft

injuria [in'xurja] nf (agravio, ofensa) offence; (insulto) insult

▌No confundir **injuria** con la palabra inglesa injury.

injusticia [inxus'tiθja] nf injustice

injusto, -a [in'xusto, a] adj unjust, unfair

inmadurez [inmaðu'reθ] nf immaturity

inmediaciones [inmeðja'θjones] nfpl neighbourhood sg, environs

inmediato, -a [inme'ðjato, a] adj immediate; (contiguo) adjoining; (rápido) prompt; (próximo) neighbouring, next; **de ~** immediately

inmejorable [inmexo'raβle] adj unsurpassable; (precio) unbeatable

inmenso, -a [in'menso, a] adj immense, huge

inmigración [inmixra'θjon] nf immigration

inmobiliaria [inmoβi'ljarja] nf estate agency

inmolar [inmo'lar] vt to immolate, sacrifice

inmoral [inmo'ral] adj immoral

inmortal [inmor'tal] adj immortal; **inmortalizar** vt to immortalize

inmóvil [in'moβil] adj immobile

inmueble [in'mweβle] adj: **bienes ~s** real estate, landed property ▷ nm property

inmundo, -a [in'mundo, a] adj filthy

inmune [in'mune] adj: ~ **(a)** (Med) immune (to)

inmunidad [inmuni'ðað] nf immunity

inmutarse [inmu'tarse] vr to turn pale; **no se inmutó** he didn't turn a hair

innato, -a [in'nato, a] adj innate

innecesario, -a [inneθe'sarjo, a] adj unnecessary

innovación [innoβa'θjon] nf innovation

innovar [inno'βar] vt to introduce

inocencia [ino'θenθja] nf innocence

inocentada [inoθen'taða] nf practical joke

inocente [ino'θente] adj (ingenuo) naïve, innocent; (inculpable) innocent; (sin malicia) harmless ▷ nmf simpleton; **el día de los (Santos) I~s** ≈ April Fools' Day

> **DÍA DE LOS (SANTOS) INOCENTES**
>
> The 28th December, el **día de los (Santos) Inocentes**, is when the Church commemorates the story of Herod's slaughter of the innocent children of Judaea. On this day Spaniards play **inocentadas** (practical jokes) on each other, much like our April Fool's Day pranks.

inodoro [ino'ðoro] nm toilet, lavatory (BRIT)

inofensivo, -a [inofen'siβo, a] adj inoffensive, harmless

inolvidable [inolβi'ðaβle] adj unforgettable

inoportuno, -a [inopor'tuno, a] adj untimely; (molesto) inconvenient

inoxidable [inoksi'ðaβle] adj: **acero ~** stainless steel

inquietar [inkje'tar] vt to worry, trouble; **inquietarse** vr to worry, get upset; **inquieto, -a** adj anxious, worried; **inquietud** nf anxiety, worry

inquilino, -a [inki'lino, a] nm/f tenant

insaciable [insa'θjaβle] adj insatiable

inscribir [inskri'βir] vt to inscribe; ~ **a algn en** (lista) to put sb on; (censo) to register sb on

inscripción [inskrip'θjon] nf inscription; (Escol etc) enrolment; (en censo) registration

insecticida [insekti'θiða] nm insecticide

insecto [in'sekto] nm insect
inseguridad [insexuri'ðað] nf insecurity; **inseguridad ciudadana** lack of safety in the streets
inseguro, -a [inse'xuro, a] adj insecure; (inconstante) unsteady; (incierto) uncertain
insensato, -a [insen'sato, a] adj foolish, stupid
insensible [insen'siβle] adj (gen) insensitive; (movimiento) imperceptible; (sin sentido) numb
insertar [inser'tar] vt to insert
inservible [inser'βiβle] adj useless
insignia [in'sixnja] nf (señal distintiva) badge; (estandarte) flag
insignificante [insixnifi'kante] adj insignificant
insinuar [insi'nwar] vt to insinuate, imply
insípido, -a [in'sipiðo, a] adj insipid
insistir [insis'tir] vi to insist; **~ en algo** to insist on sth; (enfatizar) to stress sth
insolación [insola'θjon] nf (Med) sunstroke
insolente [inso'lente] adj insolent
insólito, -a [in'solito, a] adj unusual
insoluble [inso'luβle] adj insoluble
insomnio [in'somnjo] nm insomnia
insonorizado, -a [insonori'θaðo, a] adj (cuarto etc) soundproof
insoportable [insopor'taβle] adj unbearable
inspección [inspek'θjon] nf inspection, check; **inspeccionar** vt (examinar) to inspect, examine; (controlar) to check
inspector, a [inspek'tor, a] nm/f inspector
inspiración [inspira'θjon] nf inspiration
inspirar [inspi'rar] vt to inspire; (Med) to inhale; **inspirarse** vr: **~se en** to be inspired by
instalación [instala'θjon] nf (equipo) fittings pl, equipment; **instalación eléctrica** wiring
instalar [insta'lar] vt (establecer) to instal; (erguir) to set up, erect; **instalarse** vr to establish o.s.; (en una vivienda) to move into
instancia [ins'tanθja] nf (Jur) petition; (ruego) request; **en última ~** as a last resort
instantáneo, -a [instan'taneo, a] adj instantaneous; **café ~** instant coffee
instante [ins'tante] nm instant, moment; **al ~** right now
instar [ins'tar] vt to press, urge
instaurar [instau'rar] vt (costumbre) to establish; (normas, sistema) to bring in, introduce; (gobierno) to instal
instigar [insti'xar] vt to instigate

instinto [ins'tinto] nm instinct; **por ~** instinctively
institución [institu'θjon] nf institution, establishment
instituir [institu'ir] vt to establish; (fundar) to found; **instituto** nm (gen) institute; (ESP Escol) ≈ comprehensive (BRIT) o high (US) school
institutriz [institu'triθ] nf governess
instrucción [instruk'θjon] nf instruction
instruir [instru'ir] vt (gen) to instruct; (enseñar) to teach, educate
instrumento [instru'mento] nm (gen) instrument; (herramienta) tool, implement
insubordinarse [insuβorði'narse] vr to rebel
insuficiente [insufi'θjente] adj (gen) insufficient; (Escol: calificación) unsatisfactory
insular [insu'lar] adj insular
insultar [insul'tar] vt to insult; **insulto** nm insult
insuperable [insupe'raβle] adj (excelente) unsurpassable; (problema etc) insurmountable
insurrección [insurrek'θjon] nf insurrection, rebellion
intachable [inta'tʃaβle] adj irreproachable
intacto, -a [in'takto, a] adj intact
integral [inte'xral] adj integral; (completo) complete; **pan ~** wholemeal (BRIT) o wholewheat (US) bread
integrar [inte'xrar] vt to make up, compose; (Mat: fig) to integrate
integridad [intexri'ðað] nf wholeness; (carácter) integrity; **íntegro, -a** adj whole, entire; (honrado) honest
intelectual [intelek'twal] adj, nmf intellectual
inteligencia [inteli'xenθja] nf intelligence; (ingenio) ability; **inteligente** adj intelligent
intemperie [intem'perje] nf: **a la ~** out in the open, exposed to the elements
intención [inten'θjon] nf (gen) intention, purpose; **con segundas intenciones** maliciously; **con ~** deliberately
intencionado, -a [intenθjo'naðo, a] adj deliberate; **mal ~** ill-disposed, hostile
intensidad [intensi'ðað] nf (gen) intensity; (Elec, Tec) strength; **llover con ~** to rain hard
intenso, -a [in'tenso, a] adj intense; (sentimiento) profound, deep
intentar [inten'tar] vt (tratar) to try, attempt; **intento** nm attempt
interactivo, -a [interak'tiβo, a] adj

(*Inform*) interactive

intercalar [interka'lar] *vt* to insert

intercambio [inter'kambjo] *nm* exchange, swap

interceder [interθe'ðer] *vi* to intercede

interceptar [interθep'tar] *vt* to intercept

interés [inte'res] *nm* (*gen*) interest; (*parte*) share, part; (*pey*) self-interest; **intereses creados** vested interests

interesado, -a [intere'saðo, a] *adj* interested; (*prejuiciado*) prejudiced; (*pey*) mercenary, self-seeking

interesante [intere'sante] *adj* interesting

interesar [intere'sar] *vt, vi* to interest, be of interest to; **interesarse** *vr*: **~se en** o **por** to take an interest in

interferir [interfe'rir] *vt* to interfere with; (*Tel*) to jam ▷ *vi* to interfere

interfón [inter'fon] (*MÉX*) *nm* entry phone

interino, -a [inte'rino, a] *adj* temporary ▷ *nm/f* temporary holder of a post; (*Med*) locum; (*Escol*) supply teacher

interior [inte'rjor] *adj* inner, inside; (*Com*) domestic, internal ▷ *nm* interior, inside; (*fig*) soul, mind; **Ministerio del I~** ≈ Home Office (*BRIT*) ≈ Department of the Interior (*US*); **interiorista** (*ESP*) *nmf* interior designer

interjección [interxek'θjon] *nf* interjection

interlocutor, a [interloku'tor, a] *nm/f* speaker

intermedio, -a [inter'meðjo, a] *adj* intermediate ▷ *nm* interval

interminable [intermi'naβle] *adj* endless

intermitente [intermi'tente] *adj* intermittent ▷ *nm* (*Auto*) indicator

internacional [internaθjo'nal] *adj* international

internado [inter'naðo] *nm* boarding school

internar [inter'nar] *vt* to intern; (*en un manicomio*) to commit; **internarse** *vr* (*penetrar*) to penetrate

internauta [inter'nauta] *nmf* web surfer, Internet user

Internet, internet [inter'net] *nm* o *f* Internet

interno, -a [in'terno, a] *adj* internal, interior; (*Pol etc*) domestic ▷ *nm/f* (*alumno*) boarder

interponer [interpo'ner] *vt* to interpose, put in; **interponerse** *vr* to intervene

interpretación [interpreta'θjon] *nf* interpretation

interpretar [interpre'tar] *vt* to interpret; (*Teatro, Mús*) to perform, play; **intérprete** *nmf* (*Ling*) interpreter, translator; (*Mús, Teatro*) performer, artist(e)

interrogación [interroxa'θjon] *nf* interrogation; (*Ling*: tb: **signo de ~**) question mark

interrogar [interro'xar] *vt* to interrogate, question

interrumpir [interrum'pir] *vt* to interrupt

interrupción [interrup'θjon] *nf* interruption

interruptor [interrup'tor] *nm* (*Elec*) switch

intersección [intersek'θjon] *nf* intersection

interurbano, -a [interur'βano, a] *adj*: **llamada interurbana** long-distance call

intervalo [inter'βalo] *nm* interval; (*descanso*) break

intervenir [interβe'nir] *vt* (*controlar*) to control, supervise; (*Med*) to operate on ▷ *vi* (*participar*) to take part, participate; (*mediar*) to intervene

interventor, a [interβen'tor, a] *nm/f* inspector; (*Com*) auditor

intestino [intes'tino] *nm* (*Med*) intestine

intimar [inti'mar] *vi* to become friendly

intimidad [intimi'ðað] *nf* intimacy; (*familiaridad*) familiarity; (*vida privada*) private life; (*Jur*) privacy

íntimo, -a ['intimo, a] *adj* intimate

intolerable [intole'raβle] *adj* intolerable, unbearable

intoxicación [intoksika'θjon] *nf* poisoning; **intoxicación alimenticia** food poisoning

intranet [intra'net] *nf* intranet

intranquilo, -a [intran'kilo, a] *adj* worried

intransitable [intransi'taβle] *adj* impassable

intrépido, -a [in'trepiðo, a] *adj* intrepid

intriga [in'trixa] *nf* intrigue; (*plan*) plot; **intrigar** *vt, vi* to intrigue

intrínseco, -a [in'trinseko, a] *adj* intrinsic

introducción [introðuk'θjon] *nf* introduction

introducir [introðu'θir] *vt* (*gen*) to introduce; (*moneda etc*) to insert; (*Inform*) to input, enter

intromisión [intromi'sjon] *nf* interference, meddling

introvertido, -a [introβer'tiðo, a] *adj*, *nm/f* introvert

intruso, -a [in'truso, a] *adj* intrusive
▷ *nm/f* intruder
intuición [intwi'θjon] *nf* intuition
inundación [inunda'θjon] *nf* flood(ing);
inundar *vt* to flood; (*fig*) to swamp,
inundate
inusitado, -a [inusi'taðo, a] *adj* unusual,
rare
inútil [in'util] *adj* useless; (*esfuerzo*) vain,
fruitless
inutilizar [inutili'θar] *vt* to make o render
useless
invadir [imba'ðir] *vt* to invade
inválido, -a [im'baliðo, a] *adj* invalid
▷ *nm/f* invalid
invasión [imba'sjon] *nf* invasion
invasor, a [imba'sor, a] *adj* invading
▷ *nm/f* invader
invención [imben'θjon] *nf* invention
inventar [imben'tar] *vt* to invent
inventario [imben'tarjo] *nm* inventory
invento [im'bento] *nm* invention
inventor, a [imben'tor, a] *nm/f* inventor
invernadero [imberna'ðero] *nm*
greenhouse
inverosímil [imbero'simil] *adj*
implausible
inversión [imber'sjon] *nf* (*Com*)
investment
inverso, -a [im'berso, a] *adj* inverse,
opposite; **en el orden ~** in reverse order; **a la
inversa** inversely, the other way round
inversor, a [imber'sor, a] *nm/f* (*Com*)
investor
invertir [imber'tir] *vt* (*Com*) to invest;
(*volcar*) to turn upside down; (*tiempo etc*)
to spend
investigación [imbestiɣa'θjon]
nf investigation; (*Escol*) research;
investigación y desarrollo research and
development
investigar [imbesti'ɣar] *vt* to investigate;
(*Escol*) to do research into
invierno [im'bjerno] *nm* winter
invisible [imbi'siβle] *adj* invisible
invitado, -a [imbi'taðo, a] *nm/f* guest
invitar [imbi'tar] *vt* to invite; (*incitar*) to
entice; (*pagar*) to buy, pay for
invocar [imbo'kar] *vt* to invoke, call on
involucrar [imbolu'krar] *vt*: **~ en** to
involve in; **involucrarse** *vr* (*persona*): **~se
en** to get mixed up in
involuntario, -a [imbolun'tarjo, a]
adj (*movimiento, gesto*) involuntary; (*error*)
unintentional
inyección [injek'θjon] *nf* injection
inyectar [injek'tar] *vt* to inject
iPod® ['ipoð] (*pl* **~s**) *nm* iPod ®

○ **PALABRA CLAVE**

ir [ir] *vi* **1** to go; (*a pie*) to walk; (*viajar*) to
travel; **ir caminando** to walk; **fui en tren** I
went o travelled by train; **¡(ahora) voy!** (I'm
just) coming!

2: **ir (a) por**: **ir (a) por el médico** to fetch
the doctor

3 (*progresar: persona, cosa*) to go; **el trabajo
va muy bien** work is going very well; **¿cómo
te va?** how are things going?; **me va muy
bien** I'm getting on very well; **le fue fatal** it
went awfully badly for him

4 (*funcionar*): **el coche no va muy bien** the
car isn't running very well

5: **te va estupendamente ese color** that
colour suits you fantastically well

6 (*locuciones*): **¿vino? - ¡que va!** did he come?
– of course not!; **vamos, no llores** come on,
don't cry; **¡vaya coche!** what a car!, that's
some car!

7: **no vaya a ser: tienes que correr, no
vaya a ser que pierdas el tren** you'll have
to run so as not to miss the train

8 (+ *pp*): **iba vestido muy bien** he was very
well dressed

9: **ni me** *etc* **va ni me** *etc* **viene** I *etc* don't
care

▷ *vb aux* **1** **ir a**: **voy/iba a hacerlo hoy** I am/
was going to do it today

2 (+ *gerundio*): **iba anocheciendo** it was
getting dark; **todo se me iba aclarando**
everything was gradually becoming clearer
to me

3 (+ *pp*: = *pasivo*): **van vendidos 300
ejemplares** 300 copies have been sold so far
irse *vr* **1**: **¿por dónde se va al zoológico?**
which is the way to the zoo?

2 (*marcharse*) to leave; **ya se habrán ido** they
must already have left o gone

ira ['ira] *nf* anger, rage
Irak [i'rak] *nm* = **Iraq**
Irán [i'ran] *nm* Iran; **iraní** *adj, nmf* Iranian
Iraq [i'rak] *nm* Iraq; **iraquí** *adj, nmf* Iraqi
iris ['iris] *nm inv* (*tb*: **arco ~**) rainbow;
(*Anat*) iris
Irlanda [ir'landa] *nf* Ireland; **irlandés,
-esa** *adj* Irish ▷ *nm/f* Irishman(-woman);
los irlandeses the Irish
ironía [iro'nia] *nf* irony; **irónico, -a** *adj*
ironic(al)
IRPF *nm abr* (= *Impuesto sobre la Renta de las
Personas Físicas*) (personal) income tax
irreal [irre'al] *adj* unreal
irregular [irreɣu'lar] *adj* (*gen*) irregular;
(*situación*) abnormal
irremediable [irreme'ðjaβle] *adj*

irremediable; (vicio) incurable

irreparable [irrepa'raβle] adj (daños) irreparable; (pérdida) irrecoverable

irrespetuoso, -a [irrespe'twoso, a] adj disrespectful

irresponsable [irrespon'saβle] adj irresponsible

irreversible [irreβer'sible] adj irreversible

irrigar [irri'ɣar] vt to irrigate

irrisorio, -a [irri'sorjo, a] adj derisory, ridiculous

irritar [irri'tar] vt to irritate, annoy

irrupción [irrup'θjon] nf irruption; (invasión) invasion

isla ['isla] nf island

Islam [is'lam] nm Islam; **las enseñanzas del ~** the teachings of Islam; **islámico, -a** adj Islamic

islandés, -esa [islan'des, esa] adj Icelandic ▷ nm/f Icelander

Islandia [is'landja] nf Iceland

isleño, -a [is'leɲo, a] adj island cpd ▷ nm/f islander

Israel [isra'el] nm Israel; **israelí** adj, nmf Israeli

istmo ['istmo] nm isthmus

Italia [i'talja] nf Italy; **italiano, -a** adj, nm/f Italian

itinerario [itine'rarjo] nm itinerary, route

ITV (ESP) nf abr (= inspección técnica de vehículos) roadworthiness test, ≈ MOT (BRIT)

IVA ['iβa] nm abr (= impuesto sobre el valor añadido) VAT

izar [i'θar] vt to hoist

izdo, -a abr (= izquierdo, a) l

izquierda [iθ'kjerda] nf left; (Pol) left (wing); **a la ~** (estar) on the left; (torcer etc) (to the) left

izquierdo, -a [iθ'kjerðo, a] adj left

J

jabalí [xaβa'li] nm wild boar

jabalina [xaβa'lina] nf javelin

jabón [xa'βon] nm soap

jaca ['xaka] nf pony

jacal [xa'kal] (MÉX) nm shack

jacinto [xa'θinto] nm hyacinth

jactarse [xak'tarse] vr to boast, brag

jadear [xaðe'ar] vi to pant, gasp for breath

jaguar [xa'ɣwar] nm jaguar

jaiba ['xaiβa] (LAM) nf crab

jalar [xa'lar] (LAM) vt to pull

jalea [xa'lea] nf jelly

jaleo [xa'leo] nm racket, uproar; **armar un ~** to kick up a racket

jalón [xa'lon] (LAM) nm tug

jamás [xa'mas] adv never

jamón [xa'mon] nm ham; **jamón dulce** o **de York** cooked ham; **jamón serrano** cured ham

Japón [xa'pon] nm Japan; **japonés, -esa** adj, nm/f Japanese ▷ nm (Ling) Japanese

jaque ['xake] nm (Ajedrez) check; **jaque mate** checkmate

jaqueca [xa'keka] nf (very bad) headache, migraine

jarabe [xa'raβe] nm syrup

jardín [xar'ðin] nm garden; **jardín infantil** o **de infancia** nursery (school); **jardinería** nf gardening; **jardinero, -a** nm/f gardener

jarra ['xarra] nf jar; (jarro) jug

jarro ['xarro] nm jug

jarrón [xa'rron] nm vase

jaula ['xaula] nf cage

jauría [xau'ria] nf pack of hounds

jazmín [xaθ'min] nm jasmine

J.C. abr (= Jesucristo) J.C.

jeans [jins, dʒins] (LAM) nmpl jeans, denims; **unos ~** a pair of jeans

jefatura [xefa'tura] nf (tb: ~ de policía) police headquarters sg

jefe, -a ['xefe, a] nm/f (gen) chief, head;

(*patrón*) boss; **jefe de cocina** chef; **jefe de estación** stationmaster; **jefe de Estado** head of state; **jefe de estudios** (*Escol*) director of studies; **jefe de gobierno** head of government

jengibre [xen'xiβre] *nm* ginger

jeque ['xeke] *nm* sheik

jerárquico, -a [xe'rarkiko, a] *adj* hierarchic(al)

jerez [xe'reθ] *nm* sherry

jerga ['xerɣa] *nf* jargon

jeringa [xe'riŋga] *nf* syringe; (*LAM: molestia*) annoyance, bother; **jeringuilla** *nf* syringe

jeroglífico [xero'ɣlifiko] *nm* hieroglyphic

jersey [xer'sei] (*pl* ~**s**) *nm* jersey, pullover, jumper

Jerusalén [xerusa'len] *n* Jerusalem

Jesucristo [xesu'kristo] *nm* Jesus Christ

jesuita [xe'swita] *adj, nm* Jesuit

Jesús [xe'sus] *nm* Jesus; **¡~!** good heavens!; (*al estornudar*) bless you!

jinete [xi'nete] *nmf* horseman(-woman), rider

jipijapa [xipi'xapa] (*LAM*) *nm* straw hat

jirafa [xi'rafa] *nf* giraffe

jirón [xi'ron] *nm* rag, shred

jitomate [xito'mate] (*MÉX*) *nm* tomato

joder [xo'ðer] (*fam!*) *vt, vi* to fuck (!)

jogging ['joʝin] (*RPL*) *nm* tracksuit (*BRIT*), sweat suit (*US*)

jornada [xor'naða] *nf* (*viaje de un día*) day's journey; (*camino o viaje entero*) journey; (*día de trabajo*) working day

jornal [xor'nal] *nm* (day's) wage; **jornalero** *nm* (day) labourer

joroba [xo'roβa] *nf* hump, hunched back; **jorobado, -a** *adj* hunchbacked ▷ *nm/f* hunchback

jota ['xota] *nf* (the letter) J; (*danza*) Aragonese dance; **no saber ni ~** to have no idea

joven ['xoβen] (*pl* **jóvenes**) *adj* young ▷ *nm* young man, youth ▷ *nf* young woman, girl

joya ['xoja] *nf* jewel, gem; (*fig: persona*) gem; **joyas de fantasía** costume *o* imitation jewellery; **joyería** *nf* (*joyas*) jewellery; (*tienda*) jeweller's (shop); **joyero** *nm* (*persona*) jeweller; (*caja*) jewel case

juanete [xwa'nete] *nm* (*del pie*) bunion

jubilación [xuβila'θjon] *nf* (*retiro*) retirement

jubilado, -a [xuβi'laðo, a] *adj* retired ▷ *nm/f* pensioner (*BRIT*), senior citizen

jubilar [xuβi'lar] *vt* to pension off, retire; (*fam*) to discard; **jubilarse** *vr* to retire

júbilo ['xuβilo] *nm* joy, rejoicing; **jubiloso,**

-a *adj* jubilant

judía [xu'ðia] (*ESP*) *nf* (*Culin*) bean; **judía blanca/verde** haricot/French bean; V *tb* **judío**

judicial [xuði'θjal] *adj* judicial

judío, -a [xu'ðio, a] *adj* Jewish ▷ *nm/f* Jew(ess)

judo ['juðo] *nm* judo

juego *etc* ['xweɣo] *vb* V **jugar** ▷ *nm* (*gen*) play; (*pasatiempo, partido*) game; (*en casino*) gambling; (*conjunto*) set; **fuera de ~** (*Deporte: persona*) offside; (: *pelota*) out of play; **juego de palabras** pun, play on words; **Juegos Olímpicos** Olympic Games

juerga ['xwerɣa] (*ESP: fam*) *nf* binge; (*fiesta*) party; **ir de ~** to go out on a binge

jueves ['xweβes] *nm inv* Thursday

juez [xweθ] *nmf* judge; **juez de instrucción** examining magistrate; **juez de línea** linesman; **juez de salida** starter

jugada [xu'ɣaða] *nf* play; **buena ~** good move *o* shot *o* stroke *etc*

jugador, a [xuɣa'ðor, a] *nm/f* player; (*en casino*) gambler

jugar [xu'ɣar] *vt, vi* to play; (*en casino*) to gamble; (*apostar*) to bet; **~ al fútbol** to play football

juglar [xu'ɣlar] *nm* minstrel

jugo ['xuɣo] *nm* (*Bot*) juice; (*fig*) essence, substance; **jugo de naranja** (*LAM*) orange juice; **jugoso, -a** *adj* juicy; (*fig*) substantial, important

juguete [xu'ɣete] *nm* toy; **juguetear** *vi* to play; **juguetería** *nf* toyshop

juguetón, -ona [xuɣe'ton, ona] *adj* playful

juicio ['xwiθjo] *nm* judgement; (*razón*) sanity, reason; (*opinión*) opinion

julio ['xuljo] *nm* July

jumper ['dʒumper] (*LAM*) *nm* pinafore dress (*BRIT*), jumper (*US*)

junco ['xunko] *nm* rush, reed

jungla ['xuŋgla] *nf* jungle

junio ['xunjo] *nm* June

junta ['xunta] *nf* (*asamblea*) meeting, assembly; (*comité, consejo*) council, committee; (*Com, Finanzas*) board; (*Tec*) joint; **junta directiva** board of directors

juntar [xun'tar] *vt* to join, unite; (*maquinaria*) to assemble, put together; (*dinero*) to collect; **juntarse** *vr* to join, meet; (*reunirse: personas*) to meet, assemble; (*arrimarse*) to approach, draw closer; **~se con algn** to join sb

junto, -a ['xunto, a] *adj* joined; (*unido*) united; (*anexo*) near, close; (*contiguo, próximo*) next, adjacent ▷ *adv*: **todo ~** all at once; **~s** together; **~ a** near (to), next to; **~**

con (together) with

jurado [xu'raðo] *nm* (*Jur: individuo*) juror; (*: grupo*) jury; (*de concurso: grupo*) panel (of judges); (*: individuo*) member of a panel

juramento [xura'mento] *nm* oath; (*maldición*) oath, curse; **prestar ~** to take the oath; **tomar ~ a** to swear in, administer the oath to

jurar [xu'rar] *vt, vi* to swear; **~ en falso** to commit perjury; **tenérsela jurada a algn** to have it in for sb

jurídico, -a [xu'riðiko, a] *adj* legal

jurisdicción [xurisðik'θjon] *nf* (*poder, autoridad*) jurisdiction; (*territorio*) district

justamente [xusta'mente] *adv* justly, fairly; (*precisamente*) just, exactly

justicia [xus'tiθja] *nf* justice; (*equidad*) fairness, justice

justificación [xustifika'θjon] *nf* justification; **justificar** *vt* to justify

justo, -a ['xusto, a] *adj* (*equitativo*) just, fair, right; (*preciso*) exact, correct; (*ajustado*) tight ▷ *adv* (*precisamente*) exactly, precisely; (*LAM: apenas a tiempo*) just in time

juvenil [xuβe'nil] *adj* youthful

juventud [xuβen'tuð] *nf* (*adolescencia*) youth; (*jóvenes*) young people *pl*

juzgado [xuθ'ɣaðo] *nm* tribunal; (*Jur*) court

juzgar [xuθ'ɣar] *vt* to judge; **a ~ por ...** to judge by ..., judging by ...

k

kárate ['karate] *nm* karate

kg *abr* (= *kilogramo*) kg

kilo ['kilo] *nm* kilo; **kilogramo** *nm* kilogramme; **kilometraje** *nm* distance in kilometres ≈ mileage; **kilómetro** *nm* kilometre; **kilovatio** *nm* kilowatt

kiosco ['kjosko] *nm* = **quiosco**

kleenex® [kli'neks] *nm* paper handkerchief, tissue

Kosovo [ko'soβo] *nm* Kosovo

km *abr* (= *kilómetro*) km

kv *abr* (= *kilovatio*) kw

l abr (= litro) l

la [la] art def the ▷ pron her; (Ud.) you; (cosa) it ▷ nm (Mús) la; **~ del sombrero rojo** the girl in the red hat; V tb **el**

laberinto [laβe'rinto] nm labyrinth

labio ['laβjo] nm lip

labor [la'βor] nf labour; (Agr) farm work; (tarea) job, task; (Costura) needlework; **labores domésticas** o **del hogar** household chores; **laborable** adj (Agr) workable; **día laborable** working day; **laboral** adj (accidente) at work; (jornada) working

laboratorio [laβora'torjo] nm laboratory

laborista [laβo'rista] adj: **Partido L~** Labour Party

labrador, a [laβra'ðor, a] adj farming cpd ▷ nm/f farmer

labranza [la'βranθa] nf (Agr) cultivation

labrar [la'βrar] vt (gen) to work; (madera etc) to carve; (fig) to cause, bring about

laca ['laka] nf lacquer

lacio, -a ['laθjo, a] adj (pelo) straight

lacón [la'kon] nm shoulder of pork

lactancia [lak'tanθja] nf lactation

lácteo, -a ['lakteo, a] adj: **productos ~s** dairy products

ladear [laðe'ar] vt to tip, tilt ▷ vi to tilt; **ladearse** vr to lean

ladera [la'ðera] nf slope

lado ['laðo] nm (gen) side; (fig) protection; (Mil) flank; **al ~ de** beside; **poner de ~** to put on its side; **poner a un ~** to put aside; **por todos ~s** on all sides, all round (BRIT)

ladrar [la'ðrar] vi to bark; **ladrido** nm bark, barking

ladrillo [la'ðriʎo] nm (gen) brick; (azulejo) tile

ladrón, -ona [la'ðron, ona] nm/f thief

lagartija [laɣar'tixa] nf (Zool) (small) lizard

lagarto [la'ɣarto] nm (Zool) lizard

lago ['laɣo] nm lake

lágrima ['laɣrima] nf tear

laguna [la'ɣuna] nf (lago) lagoon; (hueco) gap

lamentable [lamen'taβle] adj lamentable, regrettable; (miserable) pitiful

lamentar [lamen'tar] vt (sentir) to regret; (deplorar) to lament; **lamentarse** vr to lament; **lo lamento mucho** I'm very sorry

lamer [la'mer] vt to lick

lámina ['lamina] nf (plancha delgada) sheet; (para estampar, estampa) plate

lámpara ['lampara] nf lamp; **lámpara de alcohol/gas** spirit/gas lamp; **lámpara de pie** standard lamp

lana ['lana] nf wool

lancha ['lantʃa] nf launch; **lancha motora** motorboat, speedboat

langosta [lan'gosta] nf (crustáceo) lobster; (: de río) crayfish; **langostino** nm Dublin Bay prawn

lanza ['lanθa] nf (arma) lance, spear

lanzamiento [lanθa'mjento] nm (gen) throwing; (Náut, Com) launch, launching; **lanzamiento de peso** putting the shot

lanzar [lan'θar] vt (gen) to throw; (Deporte: pelota) to bowl; (Náut, Com) to launch; (Jur) to evict; **lanzarse** vr to throw o.s.

lapa ['lapa] nf limpet

lapicero [lapi'θero] nm (CAM) (bolígrafo) ballpoint pen, Biro®

lápida ['lapiða] nf stone; **lápida mortuoria** headstone

lápiz ['lapiθ] nm pencil; **lápiz de color** coloured pencil; **lápiz de labios** lipstick; **lápiz de ojos** eyebrow pencil

largar [lar'ɣar] vt (soltar) to release; (aflojar) to loosen; (lanzar) to launch; (fam) to let fly; (velas) to unfurl; (LAM: lanzar) to throw; **largarse** vr (fam) to beat it; **~se a** (cs: empezar) to start to

largo, -a ['larɣo, a] adj (longitud) long; (tiempo) lengthy; (fig) generous ▷ nm length; (Mús) largo; **dos años ~s** two long years; **tiene 9 metros de ~** it is 9 metres long; **a la larga** in the long run; **a lo ~** along; (tiempo) all through, throughout

⎸ No confundir **largo** con la palabra inglesa *large*.

largometraje nm feature film

laringe [la'rinxe] nf larynx; **laringitis** nf laryngitis

las [las] art def the ▷ pron them; **~ que cantan** the ones o women o girls who sing; V tb **el**

lasaña [la'saɲa] nf lasagne, lasagna

láser ['laser] nm laser

lástima ['lastima] nf (pena) pity; **dar ~** to be pitiful; **es una ~ que ...** it's a pity that ...; **¡qué ~!** what a pity!; **está hecha una ~** she looks pitiful

lastimar [lasti'mar] vt (herir) to wound; (ofender) to offend; **lastimarse** vr to hurt o.s.

lata ['lata] nf (metal) tin; (caja) tin (BRIT), can; (fam) nuisance; **en ~** tinned (BRIT), canned; **dar la ~** to be a nuisance

latente [la'tente] adj latent

lateral [late'ral] adj side cpd, lateral ▷ nm (Teatro) wings

latido [la'tiðo] nm (de corazón) beat

latifundio [lati'fundjo] nm large estate

latigazo [lati'ɣaθo] nm (golpe) lash; (sonido) crack

látigo ['latiɣo] nm whip

latín [la'tin] nm Latin

latino, -a [la'tino, a] adj Latin; **latinoamericano, -a** adj, nm/f Latin-American

latir [la'tir] vi (corazón, pulso) to beat

latitud [lati'tuð] nf (Geo) latitude

latón [la'ton] nm brass

laurel [lau'rel] nm (Bot) laurel; (Culin) bay

lava ['laβa] nf lava

lavabo [la'βaβo] nm (pila) washbasin; (tb: ~s) toilet

lavado, -a [la'βaðo] nm washing; (de ropa) laundry; (Arte) wash; **lavado de cerebro** brainwashing; **lavado en seco** dry-cleaning

lavadora [laβa'ðora] nf washing machine

lavanda [la'βanda] nf lavender

lavandería [laβande'ria] nf laundry; (automática) launderette

lavaplatos [laβa'platos] nm inv dishwasher

lavar [la'βar] vt to wash; (borrar) to wipe away; **lavarse** vr to wash o.s.; **~se las manos** to wash one's hands; **~se los dientes** to brush one's teeth; **~ y marcar** (pelo) to shampoo and set; **~ en seco** to dry-clean; **~ los platos** to wash the dishes

lavarropas [laβa'rropas] (RPL) nm inv washing machine

lavavajillas [laβaβa'xiʎas] nm inv dishwasher

laxante [lak'sante] nm laxative

lazarillo [laθa'riʎo] nm (tb: **perro ~**) guide dog

lazo ['laθo] nm knot; (lazada) bow; (para animales) lasso; (trampa) snare; (vínculo) tie

le [le] pron (directo) him (o her); (: usted) you; (indirecto) to him (o her o it); (: usted) to you

leal [le'al] adj loyal; **lealtad** nf loyalty

lección [lek'θjon] nf lesson

leche ['letʃe] nf milk; **tiene mala ~** (fam!) he's a swine (!); **leche condensada** condensed milk; **leche desnatada** skimmed milk

lecho ['letʃo] nm (cama: de río) bed; (Geo) layer

lechón [le'tʃon] nm sucking (BRIT) o suckling (US) pig

lechoso, -a [le'tʃoso, a] adj milky

lechuga [le'tʃuɣa] nf lettuce

lechuza [le'tʃuθa] nf owl

lector, a [lek'tor, a] nm/f reader ▷ nm: **~ de discos compactos** CD player

lectura [lek'tura] nf reading

leer [le'er] vt to read

legado [le'ɣaðo] nm (don) bequest; (herencia) legacy; (enviado) legate

legajo [le'ɣaxo] nm file

legal [le'ɣal] adj (gen) legal; (persona) trustworthy; **legalizar** [leɣali'θar] vt to legalize; (documento) to authenticate

legaña [le'ɣaɲa] nf sleep (in eyes)

legión [le'xjon] nf legion; **legionario, -a** adj legionary ▷ nm legionnaire

legislación [lexisla'θjon] nf legislation

legislar [lexis'lar] vi to legislate

legislatura [lexisla'tura] nf (Pol) period of office

legítimo, -a [le'xitimo, a] adj (genuino) authentic; (legal) legitimate

legua ['leɣwa] nf league

legumbres [le'ɣumbres] nfpl pulses

leído, -a [le'iðo, a] adj well-read

lejanía [lexa'nia] nf distance; **lejano, -a** adj far-off; (en el tiempo) distant; (fig) remote

lejía [le'xia] nf bleach

lejos ['lexos] adv far, far away; **a lo ~** in the distance; **de o desde ~** from afar; **~ de** far from

lema ['lema] nm motto; (Pol) slogan

lencería [lenθe'ria] nf linen, drapery

lengua ['lengwa] nf tongue; (Ling) language; **morderse la ~** to hold one's tongue

lenguado [len'gwaðo] nm sole

lenguaje [len'gwaxe] nm language; **lenguaje de programación** program(m)-ing language

lengüeta [len'gweta] nf (Anat) epiglottis; (zapatos) tongue; (Mús) reed

lente ['lente] nf lens; (lupa) magnifying glass; **lentes** nfpl lenses ▷ nmpl (LAM: gafas) glasses; **lentes bifocales/de sol** (LAM) bifocals/sunglasses; **lentes de contacto** contact lenses

lenteja [len'texa] nf lentil; **lentejuela** nf sequin

lentilla [len'tiʎa] nf contact lens

lentitud [lenti'tuð] nf slowness; **con ~**

slowly

lento, -a ['lento, a] *adj* slow

leña ['leɲa] *nf* firewood; **leñador, a** *nm/f* woodcutter

leño ['leɲo] *nm* (*trozo de árbol*) log; (*madero*) timber; (*fig*) blockhead

Leo ['leo] *nm* Leo

león [le'on] *nm* lion; **león marino** sea lion

leopardo [leo'parðo] *nm* leopard

leotardos [leo'tarðos] *nmpl* tights

lepra ['lepra] *nf* leprosy; **leproso, -a** *nm/f* leper

les [les] *pron* (*directo*) them; (: *ustedes*) you; (*indirecto*) to them; (: *ustedes*) to you

lesbiana [les'βjana] *adj, nf* lesbian

lesión [le'sjon] *nf* wound, lesion; (*Deporte*) injury; **lesionado, -a** *adj* injured ▷ *nm/f* injured person

letal [le'tal] *adj* lethal

letanía [leta'nia] *nf* litany

letra ['letra] *nf* letter; (*escritura*) handwriting; (*Mús*) lyrics *pl*; **letra de cambio** bill of exchange; **letra de imprenta** print; **letrado, -a** *adj* learned ▷ *nm/f* lawyer; **letrero** *nm* (*cartel*) sign; (*etiqueta*) label

letrina [le'trina] *nf* latrine

leucemia [leu'θemja] *nf* leukaemia

levadura [leβa'ðura] *nf* (*para el pan*) yeast; (*de cerveza*) brewer's yeast

levantar [leβan'tar] *vt* (*gen*) to raise; (*del suelo*) to pick up; (*hacia arriba*) to lift (up); (*plan*) to make, draw up; (*mesa*) to clear; (*campamento*) to strike; (*fig*) to cheer up, hearten; **levantarse** *vr* to get up; (*enderezarse*) to straighten up; (*rebelarse*) to rebel; **~ el ánimo** to cheer up

levante [le'βante] *nm* east coast; **el L~** region of Spain extending from Castellón to Murcia

levar [le'βar] *vt* to weigh

leve ['leβe] *adj* light; (*fig*) trivial

levita [le'βita] *nf* frock coat

léxico ['leksiko] *nm* (*vocabulario*) vocabulary

ley [lei] *nf* (*gen*) law; (*metal*) standard

leyenda [le'jenda] *nf* legend

leyó *etc vb* V **leer**

liar [li'ar] *vt* to tie (up); (*unir*) to bind; (*envolver*) to wrap (up); (*enredar*) to confuse; (*cigarrillo*) to roll; **liarse** *vr* (*fam*) to get involved; **~se a palos** to get involved in a fight

Líbano ['liβano] *nm*: **el ~** the Lebanon

libélula [li'βelula] *nf* dragonfly

liberación [liβera'θjon] *nf* liberation; (*de la cárcel*) release

liberal [liβe'ral] *adj, nmf* liberal

liberar [liβe'rar] *vt* to liberate

libertad [liβer'tað] *nf* liberty, freedom; **libertad bajo fianza** bail; **libertad bajo palabra** parole; **libertad condicional** probation; **libertad de culto/de prensa/ de comercio** freedom of worship/of the press/of trade

libertar [liβer'tar] *vt* (*preso*) to set free; (*de una obligación*) to release; (*eximir*) to exempt

libertino, -a [liβer'tino, a] *adj* permissive ▷ *nm/f* permissive person

libra ['liβra] *nf* pound; **L~** (*Astrología*) Libra; **libra esterlina** pound sterling

libramiento [liβra'mjento] (*MÉX*) *nm* ring road (*BRIT*), beltway (*US*)

librar [li'βrar] *vt* (*de peligro*) to save; (*batalla*) to wage, fight; (*de impuestos*) to exempt; (*cheque*) to make out; (*Jur*) to exempt; **librarse** *vr*: **~se de** to escape from, free o.s. from

libre ['liβre] *adj* free; (*lugar*) unoccupied; (*asiento*) vacant; (*de deudas*) free of debts; **~ de impuestos** free of tax; **tiro ~** free kick; **los 100 metros ~s** the 100 metres free-style (race); **al aire ~** in the open air

librería [liβre'ria] *nf* (*tienda*) bookshop

┃ No confundir **librería** con la palabra
┃ inglesa *library*.

librero, -a *nm/f* bookseller

libreta [li'βreta] *nf* notebook

libro ['liβro] *nm* book; **libro de bolsillo** paperback; **libro de texto** textbook; **libro electrónico** e-book

Lic. *abr* = **licenciado, a**

licencia [li'θenθja] *nf* (*gen*) licence; (*permiso*) permission; **licencia de caza** game licence; **licencia por enfermedad** (*MÉX, RPL*) sick leave; **licenciado, -a** *adj* licensed ▷ *nm/f* graduate; **licenciar** *vt* (*empleado*) to dismiss; (*permitir*) to permit, allow; (*soldado*) to discharge; (*estudiante*) to confer a degree upon; **licenciarse** *vr*: **licenciarse en Derecho** to graduate in law

lícito, -a ['liθito, a] *adj* (*legal*) lawful; (*justo*) fair, just; (*permisible*) permissible

licor [li'kor] *nm* spirits *pl* (*BRIT*), liquor (*US*); (*de frutas etc*) liqueur

licuadora [likwa'ðora] *nf* blender

líder ['liðer] *nmf* leader; **liderato** *nm* leadership; **liderazgo** *nm* leadership

lidia ['liðja] *nf* bullfighting; (*una lidia*) bullfight; **toros de ~** fighting bulls; **lidiar** *vt, vi* to fight

liebre ['ljeβre] *nf* hare

lienzo ['ljenθo] *nm* linen; (*Arte*) canvas; (*Arq*) wall

liga ['liɣa] *nf* (*de medias*) garter, suspender; (*LAM: goma*) rubber band; (*confederación*)

league
ligadura [liɣaˈðura] nf bond, tie; (Med, Mús) ligature
ligamento [liɣaˈmento] nm ligament
ligar [liˈɣar] vt (atar) to tie; (unir) to join; (Med) to bind up; (Mús) to slur ▷ vi to mix, blend; (fam): **(él) liga mucho** he pulls a lot of women; **ligarse** vr to commit o.s.
ligero, -a [liˈɣero, a] adj (de peso) light; (tela) thin; (rápido) swift, quick; (ágil) agile, nimble; (de importancia) slight; (de carácter) flippant, superficial ▷ adv: **a la ligera** superficially
liguero [liˈɣero] nm suspender (BRIT) o garter (US) belt
lija [ˈlixa] nf (Zool) dogfish; (tb: **papel de ~**) sandpaper
lila [ˈlila] nf lilac
lima [ˈlima] nf file; (Bot) lime; **lima de uñas** nailfile; **limar** vt to file
limitación [limitaˈθjon] nf limitation, limit
limitar [limiˈtar] vt to limit; (reducir) to reduce, cut down ▷ vi: **~ con** to border on; **limitarse** vr: **~se a** to limit o.s. to
límite [ˈlimite] nm (gen) limit; (fin) end; (frontera) border; **límite de velocidad** speed limit
limítrofe [liˈmitrofe] adj neighbouring
limón [liˈmon] nm lemon ▷ adj: **amarillo ~** lemon-yellow; **limonada** nf lemonade
limosna [liˈmosna] nf alms pl; **vivir de ~** to live on charity
limpiador [limpjaˈðor] (MÉX) nm = **limpiaparabrisas**
limpiaparabrisas [limpjaparaˈβrisas] nm inv windscreen (BRIT) o windshield (US) wiper
limpiar [limˈpjar] vt to clean; (con trapo) to wipe; (quitar) to wipe away; (zapatos) to shine, polish; (fig) to clean up
limpieza [limˈpjeθa] nf (estado) cleanliness; (acto) cleaning; (: de las calles) cleansing; (: de zapatos) polishing; (habilidad) skill; (fig: Policía) clean-up; (pureza) purity; (Mil): **operación de ~** mopping-up operation; **limpieza en seco** dry cleaning
limpio, -a [ˈlimpjo, a] adj clean; (moralmente) pure; (Com) clear, net; (fam) honest ▷ adv: **jugar ~** to play fair; **pasar a (ESP) o en (LAM) ~** to make a clean copy of
lince [ˈlinθe] nm lynx
linchar [linˈtʃar] vt to lynch
lindar [linˈdar] vi to adjoin; **~ con** to border on
lindo, -a [ˈlindo, a] adj pretty, lovely ▷ adv: **nos divertimos de lo ~** we had a marvellous time; **canta muy ~** (LAM) he

sings beautifully
línea [ˈlinea] nf (gen) line; **en ~** (Inform) on line; **línea aérea** airline; **línea de meta** goal line; (en carrera) finishing line; **línea discontinua** (Auto) broken line; **línea recta** straight line
lingote [linˈgote] nm ingot
lingüista [linˈgwista] nmf linguist; **lingüística** nf linguistics sg
lino [ˈlino] nm linen; (Bot) flax
linterna [linˈterna] nf torch (BRIT), flashlight (US)
lío [ˈlio] nm bundle; (fam) fuss; (desorden) muddle, mess; **armar un ~** to make a fuss
liquen [ˈliken] nm lichen
liquidación [likiˈðaθjon] nf liquidation; **venta de ~** clearance sale
liquidar [likiˈðar] vt (mercancías) to liquidate; (deudas) to pay off; (empresa) to wind up
líquido, -a [ˈlikiðo, a] adj liquid; (ganancia) net ▷ nm liquid; **líquido imponible** net taxable income
lira [ˈlira] nf (Mús) lyre; (moneda) lira
lírico, -a [ˈliriko, a] adj lyrical
lirio [ˈlirjo] nm (Bot) iris
lirón [liˈron] nm (Zool) dormouse; (fig) sleepyhead
Lisboa [lisˈβoa] n Lisbon
lisiar [liˈsjar] vt to maim
liso, -a [ˈliso, a] adj (terreno) flat; (cabello) straight; (superficie) even; (tela) plain
lista [ˈlista] nf list; (de alumnos) school register; (de libros) catalogue; (de platos) menu; (de precios) price list; **pasar ~** to call the roll; **tela de ~s** striped material; **lista de espera** waiting list; **lista de precios** price list; **listín** nm (tb: **listín telefónico** o **de teléfonos**) telephone directory
listo, -a [ˈlisto, a] adj (perspicaz) smart, clever; (preparado) ready
listón [lisˈton] nm (de madera, metal) strip
litera [liˈtera] nf (en barco, tren) berth; (en dormitorio) bunk, bunk bed
literal [liteˈral] adj literal
literario, -a [liteˈrarjo, a] adj literary
literato, -a [liteˈrato, a] adj literary ▷ nm/f writer
literatura [literaˈtura] nf literature
litigio [liˈtixjo] nm (Jur) lawsuit; (fig): **en ~ con** in dispute with
litografía [litoɣraˈfia] nf lithography; (una litografía) lithograph
litoral [litoˈral] adj coastal ▷ nm coast, seaboard
litro [ˈlitro] nm litre
lívido, -a [ˈliβiðo, a] adj livid
llaga [ˈʎaɣa] nf wound

llama ['ʎama] nf flame; (Zool) llama
llamada [ʎa'maða] nf call; **llamada a
cobro revertido** reverse-charge (BRIT)
o collect (US) call; **llamada al orden** call
to order; **llamada de atención** warning;
llamada local (LAM) local call; **llamada
metropolitana** (ESP) local call; **llamada por
cobrar** (MÉX) reverse-charge (BRIT) o collect
(US) call
llamamiento [ʎama'mjento] nm call
llamar [ʎa'mar] vt to call; (atención) to
attract ▷ vi (por teléfono) to telephone; (a
la puerta) to knock (o ring); (por señas) to
beckon; (Mil) to call up; **llamarse** vr to be
called, be named; **¿cómo se llama (usted)?**
what's your name?
llamativo, -a [ʎama'tiβo, a] adj showy;
(color) loud
llano, -a ['ʎano, a] adj (superficie) flat;
(persona) straightforward; (estilo) clear ▷ nm
plain, flat ground
llanta ['ʎanta] nf (ESP) (wheel) rim; **llanta
(de goma)** (LAM: neumático) tyre; (: cámara)
inner (tube); **llanta de repuesto** (LAM)
spare tyre
llanto ['ʎanto] nm weeping
llanura [ʎa'nura] nf plain
llave ['ʎaβe] nf key; (del agua) tap;
(Mecánica) spanner; (de la luz) switch;
(Mús) key; **echar la ~ a** to lock up; **llave de
contacto** (ESP Auto) ignition key; **llave de
encendido** (LAM Auto) ignition key; **llave
de paso** stopcock; **llave inglesa** monkey
wrench; **llave maestra** master key; **llavero**
nm keyring
llegada [ʎe'ɣaða] nf arrival
llegar [ʎe'ɣar] vi to arrive; (alcanzar) to
reach; (bastar) to be enough; **llegarse**
vr: **~se a** to approach; **~ a** to manage to,
succeed in; **~ a saber** to find out; **~ a ser** to
become; **~ a las manos de** to come into the
hands of
llenar [ʎe'nar] vt to fill; (espacio) to cover;
(formulario) to fill in o up; (fig) to heap
lleno, -a ['ʎeno, a] adj full, filled; (repleto)
full up ▷ nm (Teatro) full house; **dar de ~
contra un muro** to hit a wall head-on
llevadero, -a [ʎeβa'ðero, a] adj bearable,
tolerable
llevar [ʎe'βar] vt to take; (ropa) to wear;
(cargar) to carry; (quitar) to take away; (en
coche) to drive; (transportar) to transport;
(traer: dinero) to carry; (conducir) to lead;
(Mat) to carry ▷ vi (suj: camino etc): **~ a** to
lead to; **llevarse** vr to carry off, take away;
llevamos dos días aquí we have been here
for two days; **él me lleva 2 años** he's 2 years
older than me; **~ los libros** (Com) to keep the

books; **~se bien** to get on well (together)
llorar [ʎo'rar] vt, vi to cry, weep; **~ de risa**
to cry with laughter
llorón, -ona [ʎo'ron, ona] adj tearful
▷ nm/f cry-baby
lloroso, -a [ʎo'roso, a] adj (gen) weeping,
tearful; (triste) sad, sorrowful
llover [ʎo'βer] vi to rain
llovizna [ʎo'βiθna] nf drizzle; **lloviznar**
vi to drizzle
llueve etc vb V **llover**
lluvia ['ʎuβja] nf rain; **lluvia radioactiva**
(radioactive) fallout; **lluvioso, -a** adj rainy
lo [lo] art def: **~ bel~** the beautiful, what is
beautiful, that which is beautiful ▷ pron
(persona) him; (cosa) it; **~ que sea** whatever;
V tb **el**
loable [lo'aβle] adj praiseworthy
lobo ['loβo] nm wolf; **lobo de mar** (fig)
sea dog
lóbulo ['loβulo] nm lobe
local [lo'kal] adj local ▷ nm place, site;
(oficinas) premises pl; **localidad** nf (barrio)
locality; (lugar) location; (Teatro) seat,
ticket; **localizar** vt to locate, find;
(restringir) to localize; (situar) to place
loción [lo'θjon] nf lotion
loco, -a ['loko, a] adj mad ▷ nm/f lunatic,
mad person; **estar ~ con** o **por algo/por
algn** to be mad about sth/sb
locomotora [lokomo'tora] nf engine,
locomotive
locuaz [lo'kwaθ] adj loquacious
locución [loku'θjon] nf expression
locura [lo'kura] nf madness; (acto) crazy
act
locutor, a [loku'tor, a] nm/f (Radio)
announcer; (comentarista) commentator;
(TV) newsreader
locutorio [loku'torjo] nm (en telefónica)
telephone booth
lodo ['loðo] nm mud
lógica ['loxika] nf logic
lógico, -a ['loxiko, a] adj logical
login ['loxin] nm login
logística [lo'xistika] nf logistics sg
logotipo [loðo'tipo] nm logo
logrado, -a [lo'ðraðo, a] adj
(interpretación, reproducción) polished,
excellent
lograr [lo'ɣrar] vt to achieve; (obtener) to
get, obtain; **~ hacer** to manage to do; **~ que
algn venga** to manage to get sb to come
logro ['loɣro] nm achievement, success
lóker ['loker] (LAM) nm locker
loma ['loma] nf hillock (BRIT), small hill
lombriz [lom'briθ] nf worm
lomo ['lomo] nm (de animal) back; (Culin: de

cerdo) pork loin; (: *de vaca*) rib steak; (*de libro*) spine

lona ['lona] *nf* canvas

loncha ['lontʃa] *nf* = **lonja**

lonchería [lontʃe'ria] (*LAM*) *nf* snack bar, diner (*US*)

Londres ['londres] *n* London

longaniza [longa'niθa] *nf* pork sausage

longitud [lonxi'tuð] *nf* length; (*Geo*) longitude; **tener 3 metros de ~** to be 3 metres long; **longitud de onda** wavelength

lonja ['lonxa] *nf* slice; (*de tocino*) rasher; **lonja de pescado** fish market

loro ['loro] *nm* parrot

los [los] *art def the* ▷ *pron* them; (*ustedes*) you; **mis libros y ~ tuyos** my books and yours; *V tb* **el**

losa ['losa] *nf* stone

lote ['lote] *nm* portion; (*Com*) lot

lotería [lote'ria] *nf* lottery; (*juego*) lotto

● **LOTERÍA**
●
● Millions of pounds are spent on lotteries
● each year in Spain, two of which are
● state-run: the **Lotería Primitiva** and
● the **Lotería Nacional**, with money
● raised going directly to the government.
● One of the most famous lotteries is run
● by the wealthy and influential society
● for the blind, "la ONCE".

loza ['loθa] *nf* crockery

lubina [lu'βina] *nf* sea bass

lubricante [luβri'kante] *nm* lubricant

lubricar [luβri'kar] *vt* to lubricate

lucha ['lutʃa] *nf* fight, struggle; **lucha de clases** class struggle; **lucha libre** wrestling; **luchar** *vi* to fight

lúcido, -a ['luθido, a] *adj* (*persona*) lucid; (*mente*) logical; (*idea*) crystal-clear

luciérnaga [lu'θjernaxa] *nf* glow-worm

lucir [lu'θir] *vt* to illuminate, light (up); (*ostentar*) to show off ▷ *vi* (*brillar*) to shine; **lucirse** *vr* (*irónico*) to make a fool of o.s.

lucro ['lukro] *nm* profit, gain

lúdico, -a ['ludiko, a] *adj* (*aspecto*, *actividad*) play *cpd*

luego ['lweɣo] *adv* (*después*) next; (*más tarde*) later, afterwards

lugar [lu'ɣar] *nm* place; (*sitio*) spot; **en primer ~** in the first place, firstly; **en ~ de** instead of; **hacer ~** to make room; **fuera de ~** out of place; **sin ~ a dudas** without doubt, undoubtedly; **dar ~ a** to give rise to; **tener ~** to take place; **yo en su ~** if I were him; **lugar común** commonplace

lúgubre ['luɣuβre] *adj* mournful

lujo ['luxo] *nm* luxury; (*fig*) profusion, abundance; **de ~** luxury *cpd*, de luxe; **lujoso, -a** *adj* luxurious

lujuria [lu'xurja] *nf* lust

lumbre ['lumbre] *nf* fire; (*para cigarrillo*) light

luminoso, -a [lumi'noso, a] *adj* luminous, shining

luna ['luna] *nf* moon; (*de un espejo*) glass; (*de gafas*) lens; (*fig*) crescent; **estar en la ~** to have one's head in the clouds; **luna de miel** honeymoon; **luna llena/nueva** full/new moon

lunar [lu'nar] *adj* lunar ▷ *nm* (*Anat*) mole; **tela de ~es** spotted material

lunes ['lunes] *nm inv* Monday

lupa ['lupa] *nf* magnifying glass

lustre ['lustre] *nm* polish; (*fig*) lustre; **dar ~ a** to polish

luto ['luto] *nm* mourning; **llevar el** *o* **vestirse de ~** to be in mourning

Luxemburgo [luksem'burxo] *nm* Luxembourg

luz [luθ] (*pl* **luces**) *nf* light; **dar a ~ un niño** to give birth to a child; **sacar a la ~** to bring to light; **dar** *o* **encender** (*ESP*) *o* **prender** (*LAM*)**/apagar la ~** to switch the light on/off; **tener pocas luces** to be dim *o* stupid; **traje de luces** bullfighter's costume; **luces de tráfico** traffic lights; **luz de freno** brake light; **luz roja/verde** red/green light

m

m *abr* (= *metro*) m; (= *minuto*) m

macana [ma'kana] (*MÉX*) *nf* truncheon (*BRIT*), billy club (*US*)

macarrones [maka'rrones] *nmpl* macaroni *sg*

macedonia [maθe'ðonja] *nf* (*tb*: ~ **de frutas**) fruit salad

maceta [ma'θeta] *nf* (*de flores*) pot of flowers; (*para plantas*) flowerpot

machacar [matʃa'kar] *vt* to crush, pound ▷ *vi* (*insistir*) to go on, keep on

machete [ma'tʃete] *nm* machete, (large) knife

machetear [matʃete'ar] (*MÉX*) *vt* to swot (*BRIT*), grind away (*US*)

machismo [ma'tʃismo] *nm* male chauvinism; **machista** *adj, nm* sexist

macho ['matʃo] *adj* male; (*fig*) virile ▷ *nm* male; (*fig*) he-man

macizo, -a [ma'θiθo, a] *adj* (*grande*) massive; (*fuerte, sólido*) solid ▷ *nm* mass, chunk

madeja [ma'ðexa] *nf* (*de lana*) skein, hank; (*de pelo*) mass, mop

madera [ma'ðera] *nf* wood; (*fig*) nature, character; **una** ~ a piece of wood

madrastra [ma'ðrastra] *nf* stepmother

madre ['maðre] *adj* mother *cpd* ▷ *nf* mother; (*de vino etc*) dregs *pl*; **madre política/soltera** mother-in-law/unmarried mother

Madrid [ma'ðrið] *n* Madrid

madriguera [maðri'ɣera] *nf* burrow

madrileño, -a [maðri'leɲo, a] *adj* of o from Madrid ▷ *nm/f* native of Madrid

madrina [ma'ðrina] *nf* godmother; (*Arq*) prop, shore; (*Tec*) brace; (*de boda*) bridesmaid

madrugada [maðru'ɣaða] *nf* early morning; (*alba*) dawn, daybreak

madrugador, a [maðruɣa'ðor, a] *adj* early-rising

madrugar [maðru'ɣar] *vi* to get up early; (*fig*) to get ahead

madurar [maðu'rar] *vt, vi* (*fruta*) to ripen; (*fig*) to mature; **madurez** *nf* ripeness; maturity; **maduro, -a** *adj* ripe; mature

maestra *nf* V **maestro**

maestría [maes'tria] *nf* mastery; (*habilidad*) skill, expertise

maestro, -a [ma'estro, a] *adj* masterly; (*principal*) main ▷ *nm/f* master/mistress; (*profesor*) teacher ▷ *nm* (*autoridad*) authority; (*Mús*) maestro; (*experto*) master; **maestro albañil** master mason

magdalena [maxða'lena] *nf* fairy cake

magia ['maxja] *nf* magic; **mágico, -a** *adj* magic(al) ▷ *nm/f* magician

magisterio [maxis'terjo] *nm* (*enseñanza*) teaching; (*profesión*) teaching profession; (*maestros*) teachers *pl*

magistrado [maxis'traðo] *nm* magistrate

magistral [maxis'tral] *adj* magisterial; (*fig*) masterly

magnate [max'nate] *nm* magnate, tycoon

magnético, -a [max'netiko, a] *adj* magnetic

magnetofón [maxneto'fon] *nm* tape recorder

magnetófono [maxne'tofono] *nm* = **magnetofón**

magnífico, -a [max'nifiko, a] *adj* splendid, magnificent

magnitud [maxni'tuð] *nf* magnitude

mago, -a ['maxo, a] *nm/f* magician; **los Reyes M~s** the Three Wise Men

magro, -a ['maxro, a] *adj* (*carne*) lean

mahonesa [mao'nesa] *nf* mayonnaise

maître ['metre] *nm* head waiter

maíz [ma'iθ] *nm* maize (*BRIT*), corn (*US*); sweet corn

majestad [maxes'tað] *nf* majesty

majo, -a ['maxo, a] *adj* nice; (*guapo*) attractive, good-looking; (*elegante*) smart

mal [mal] *adv* badly; (*equivocadamente*) wrongly ▷ *adj* = **malo** ▷ *nm* evil; (*desgracia*) misfortune; (*daño*) harm, damage; (*Med*) illness; ~ **que bien** rightly or wrongly; **ir de ~ en peor** to get worse and worse

malabarista [malaβa'rista] *nmf* juggler

malaria [ma'larja] *nf* malaria

malcriado, -a [mal'krjaðo, a] *adj* spoiled

maldad [mal'dað] *nf* evil, wickedness

maldecir [malde'θir] *vt* to curse

maldición [maldi'θjon] *nf* curse

maldito, -a [mal'dito, a] *adj* (*condenado*) damned; (*perverso*) wicked; **¡~ sea!** damn it!

malecón [male'kon] (*LAM*) *nm* sea front,

promenade

maleducado, -a [maleðu'kaðo, a] *adj* bad-mannered, rude

malentendido [malenten'diðo] *nm* misunderstanding

malestar [males'tar] *nm* (gen) discomfort; (fig: inquietud) uneasiness; (Pol) unrest

maleta [ma'leta] *nf* case, suitcase; (Auto) boot (BRIT), trunk (US); **hacer las ~s** to pack; **maletero** *nm* (Auto) boot (BRIT), trunk (US); **maletín** *nm* small case, bag

maleza [ma'leθa] *nf* (malas hierbas) weeds *pl*; (arbustos) thicket

malgastar [malɣas'tar] *vt* (tiempo, dinero) to waste; (salud) to ruin

malhechor, a [male'tʃor, a] *nm/f* delinquent

malhumorado, -a [malumo'raðo, a] *adj* bad-tempered

malicia [ma'liθja] *nf* (maldad) wickedness; (astucia) slyness, guile; (mala intención) malice, spite; (carácter travieso) mischievousness

maligno, -a [ma'liɣno, a] *adj* evil; (malévolo) malicious; (Med) malignant

malla ['maʎa] *nf* mesh; (de baño) swimsuit; (de ballet, gimnasia) leotard; **mallas** *nfpl* tights; **malla de alambre** wire mesh

Mallorca [ma'ʎorka] *nf* Majorca

malo, -a ['malo, a] *adj* bad, false ▷ *nm/f* villain; **estar ~** to be ill

malograr [malo'ɣrar] *vt* to spoil; (plan) to upset; (ocasión) to waste

malparado, -a [malpa'raðo, a] *adj*: **salir ~** to come off badly

malpensado, -a [malpen'saðo, a] *adj* nasty

malteada [malte'aða] (LAM) *nf* milkshake

maltratar [maltra'tar] *vt* to ill-treat, mistreat

malvado, -a [mal'βaðo, a] *adj* evil, villainous

Malvinas [mal'βinas] *nfpl* (tb: **Islas ~**) Falklands, Falkland Islands

mama ['mama] *nf* (de animal) teat; (de mujer) breast

mamá [ma'ma] (pl **~s**) (fam) *nf* mum, mummy

mamar [ma'mar] *vt, vi* to suck

mamarracho [mama'rratʃo] *nm* sight, mess

mameluco [mameluko] (RPL) *nm* dungarees *pl* (BRIT), overalls *pl* (US)

mamífero [ma'mifero] *nm* mammal

mampara [mam'para] *nf* (entre habitaciones) partition; (biombo) screen

mampostería [mamposte'ria] *nf* masonry

manada [ma'naða] *nf* (Zool) herd; (: de leones) pride; (: de lobos) pack

manantial [manan'tjal] *nm* spring

mancha ['mantʃa] *nf* stain, mark; (Zool) patch; **manchar** *vt* (gen) to stain, mark; (ensuciar) to soil, dirty

manchego, -a [man'tʃeɣo, a] *adj* of o from La Mancha

manco, -a ['manko, a] *adj* (de un brazo) one-armed; (de una mano) one-handed; (fig) defective, faulty

mancuernas [man'kwernas] (MÉX) *nfpl* cufflinks

mandado [man'daðo] (LAM) *nm* errand

mandamiento [manda'mjento] *nm* (orden) order, command; (Rel) commandment

mandar [man'dar] *vt* (ordenar) to order; (dirigir) to lead, command; (enviar) to send; (pedir) to order, ask for ▷ *vi* to be in charge; (pey) to be bossy; **¿mande?** (MÉX: ¿cómo dice?) pardon?, excuse me?; **~ hacer un traje** to have a suit made

mandarina [manda'rina] (ESP) *nf* tangerine, mandarin (orange)

mandato [man'dato] *nm* (orden) order; (Pol: período) term of office; (: territorio) mandate

mandíbula [man'diβula] *nf* jaw

mandil [man'dil] *nm* apron

mando ['mando] *nm* (Mil) command; (de país) rule; (el primer lugar) lead; (Pol) term of office; (Tec) control; **~ a la izquierda** left-hand drive; **mando a distancia** remote control

mandón, -ona [man'don, ona] *adj* bossy, domineering

manejar [mane'xar] *vt* to manage; (máquina) to work, operate; (caballo etc) to handle; (casa) to run, manage; (LAM: coche) to drive; **manejarse** *vr* (comportarse) to act, behave; (arreglárselas) to manage; **manejo** *nm* (de bicicleta) handling; (de negocio) management, running; (LAM Auto) driving; (facilidad de trato) ease, confidence; **manejos** *nmpl* (intrigas) intrigues

manera [ma'nera] *nf* way, manner, fashion; **maneras** *nfpl* (modales) manners; **su ~ de ser** the way he is; (aire) his manner; **de ninguna ~** no way, by no means; **de otra ~** otherwise; **de todas ~s** at any rate; **no hay ~ de persuadirle** there's no way of convincing him

manga ['manga] *nf* (de camisa) sleeve; (de riego) hose

mango ['mango] *nm* handle; (Bot) mango

manguera [man'gera] *nf* hose

maní [ma'ni] (LAM) *nm* peanut

manía [ma'nia] nf (Med) mania; (fig: moda) rage, craze; (disgusto) dislike; (malicia) spite; **coger ~ a algn** to take a dislike to sb; **tener ~ a algn** to dislike sb; **maníaco, -a** adj maniac(al) ▷ nm/f maniac

maniático, -a [ma'njatiko, a] adj maniac(al) ▷ nm/f maniac

manicomio [mani'komjo] nm mental hospital (BRIT), insane asylum (US)

manifestación [manifesta'θjon] nf (declaración) statement, declaration; (de emoción) show, display; (Pol: desfile) demonstration; (: concentración) mass meeting

manifestar [manifes'tar] vt to show, manifest; (declarar) to state, declare; **manifiesto, -a** adj clear, manifest ▷ nm manifesto

manillar [mani'ʎar] nm handlebars pl

maniobra [ma'njoβra] nf manoeuvre; **maniobras** nfpl (Mil) manoeuvres; **maniobrar** vt to manoeuvre

manipulación [manipula'θjon] nf manipulation

manipular [manipu'lar] vt to manipulate; (manejar) to handle

maniquí [mani'ki] nm dummy ▷ nmf model

manivela [mani'βela] nf crank

manjar [man'xar] nm (tasty) dish

mano ['mano] nf hand; (Zool) foot, paw; (de pintura) coat; (serie) lot, series; **a ~** by hand; **a ~ derecha/izquierda** on the right(-hand side)/left(-hand side); **de primera ~** (at) first hand; **de segunda ~** (at) second hand; **robo a ~ armada** armed robbery; **estrechar la ~ a algn** to shake sb's hand; **mano de obra** labour, manpower; **manos libres** adj inv (teléfono, dispositivo) hands-free ▷ nm inv hands-free kit

manojo [ma'noxo] nm handful, bunch; (de llaves) bunch

manopla [ma'nopla] nf mitten

manosear [manose'ar] vt (tocar) to handle, touch; (desordenar) to mess up, rumple; (insistir en) to overwork; (LAM: acariciar) to caress, fondle

manotazo [mano'taθo] nm slap, smack

mansalva [man'salβa]: **a ~** adv indiscriminately

mansión [man'sjon] nf mansion

manso, -a ['manso, a] adj gentle, mild; (animal) tame

manta ['manta] (ESP) nf blanket

manteca [man'teka] nf fat; (cs: mantequilla) butter; **manteca de cerdo** lard

mantecado [mante'kaðo] (ESP) nm Christmas sweet made from flour, almonds and lard

mantel [man'tel] nm tablecloth

mantendré etc vb V **mantener**

mantener [mante'ner] vt to support, maintain; (alimentar) to sustain; (conservar) to keep; (Tec) to maintain, service; **mantenerse** vr (seguir de pie) to be still standing; (no ceder) to hold one's ground; (subsistir) to sustain o.s., keep going; **mantenimiento** nm maintenance; sustenance; (sustento) support

mantequilla [mante'kiʎa] nf butter

mantilla [man'tiʎa] nf mantilla; **mantillas** nfpl (de bebé) baby clothes

manto ['manto] nm (capa) cloak; (de ceremonia) robe, gown

mantuve etc vb V **mantener**

manual [ma'nwal] adj manual ▷ nm manual, handbook

manuscrito, -a [manus'krito, a] adj handwritten ▷ nm manuscript

manutención [manuten'θjon] nf maintenance; (sustento) support

manzana [man'θana] nf apple; (Arq) block (of houses)

manzanilla [manθa'niʎa] nf (planta) camomile; (infusión) camomile tea

manzano [man'θano] nm apple tree

maña ['maɲa] nf (gen) skill, dexterity; (pey) guile; (destreza) trick, knack

mañana [ma'ɲana] adv tomorrow ▷ nm future ▷ nf morning; **de o por la ~** in the morning; **¡hasta ~!** see you tomorrow!; **~ por la** tomorrow morning

mapa ['mapa] nm map

maple ['maple] (LAM) nm maple

maqueta [ma'keta] nf (scale) model

maquiladora [makila'ðora] (MÉX) nf (Com) bonded assembly plant

maquillaje [maki'ʎaxe] nm make-up; (acto) making up

maquillar [maki'ʎar] vt to make up; **maquillarse** vr to put on (some) make-up

máquina ['makina] nf machine; (de tren) locomotive, engine; (Foto) camera; (fig) machinery; **escrito a ~** typewritten; **máquina de coser** sewing machine; **máquina de escribir** typewriter; **máquina fotográfica** camera

maquinaria [maki'narja] nf (máquinas) machinery; (mecanismo) mechanism, works pl

maquinilla [maki'niʎa] (ESP) nf (tb: ~ de afeitar) razor

maquinista [maki'nista] nmf (de tren) engine driver; (Tec) operator; (Náut) engineer

mar [mar] *nm of* sea; **~ adentro** out at sea; **en alta ~** on the high seas; **la ~ de** (*fam*) lots of; **el Mar Negro/Báltico** the Black/Baltic Sea

maraña [ma'raɲa] *nf* (*maleza*) thicket; (*confusión*) tangle

maravilla [mara'βiʎa] *nf* marvel, wonder; (*Bot*) marigold; **maravillar** *vt* to astonish, amaze; **maravillarse** *vr* to be astonished, be amazed; **maravilloso, -a** *adj* wonderful, marvellous

marca ['marka] *nf* (*gen*) mark; (*sello*) stamp; (*Com*) make, brand; **de ~** excellent, outstanding; **marca de fábrica** trademark; **marca registrada** registered trademark

marcado, -a [mar'kaðo, a] *adj* marked, strong

marcador [marka'ðor] *nm* (*Deporte*) scoreboard; (: *persona*) scorer

marcapasos [marka'pasos] *nm inv* pacemaker

marcar [mar'kar] *vt* (*gen*) to mark; (*número de teléfono*) to dial; (*gol*) to score; (*números*) to record, keep a tally of; (*pelo*) to set ▷ *vi* (*Deporte*) to score; (*Tel*) to dial

marcha ['martʃa] *nf* march; (*Tec*) running, working; (*Auto*) gear; (*velocidad*) speed; (*fig*) progress; (*dirección*) course; **poner en ~** to put into gear; (*fig*) to set in motion, get going; **dar ~ atrás** to reverse, put into reverse; **estar en ~** to be under way, be in motion

marchar [mar'tʃar] *vi* (*ir*) to go; (*funcionar*) to work, go; **marcharse** *vr* to go (away), leave

marchitar [martʃi'tar] *vt* to wither, dry up; **marchitarse** *vr* (*Bot*) to wither; (*fig*) to fade away; **marchito, -a** *adj* withered, faded; (*fig*) in decline

marciano, -a [mar'θjano, a] *adj, nm/f* Martian

marco ['marko] *nm* frame; (*moneda*) mark; (*fig*) framework

marea [ma'rea] *nf* tide; **marea negra** oil slick

marear [mare'ar] *vt* (*fig*) to annoy, upset; (*Med*): **~ a algn** to make sb feel sick; **marearse** *vr* (*tener náuseas*) to feel sick; (*desvanecerse*) to feel faint; (*aturdirse*) to feel dizzy; (*fam: emborracharse*) to get tipsy

maremoto [mare'moto] *nm* tidal wave

mareo [ma'reo] *nm* (*náusea*) sick feeling; (*en viaje*) travel sickness; (*aturdimiento*) dizziness; (*fam: lata*) nuisance

marfil [mar'fil] *nm* ivory

margarina [marɣa'rina] *nf* margarine

margarita [marɣa'rita] *nf* (*Bot*) daisy; (*Tip*) daisywheel

margen ['marxen] *nm* (*borde*) edge, border; (*fig*) margin, space ▷ *nf* (*de río etc*) bank; **dar ~ para** to give an opportunity for; **mantenerse al ~** to keep out (of things)

marginar [marxi'nar] *vt* (*socialmente*) to marginalize, ostracize

mariachi [ma'rjatʃi] *nm* (*persona*) mariachi musician; (*grupo*) mariachi band

marica [ma'rika] (*fam*) *nm* sissy

maricón [mari'kon] (*fam*) *nm* queer

marido [ma'riðo] *nm* husband

marihuana [mari'wana] *nf* marijuana, cannabis

marina [ma'rina] *nf* navy; **marina mercante** merchant navy

marinero, -a [mari'nero, a] *adj* sea *cpd* ▷ *nm* sailor, seaman

marino, -a [ma'rino, a] *adj* sea *cpd*, marine ▷ *nm* sailor

marioneta [marjo'neta] *nf* puppet

mariposa [mari'posa] *nf* butterfly

mariquita [mari'kita] *nf* ladybird (BRIT), ladybug (US)

marisco [ma'risko] (ESP) *nm* shellfish *inv*, seafood; **mariscos** (LAM) *nmpl* = **marisco**

marítimo, -a [ma'ritimo, a] *adj* sea *cpd*, maritime

mármol ['marmol] *nm* marble

marqués, -esa [mar'kes, esa] *nm/f* marquis/marchioness

marrón [ma'rron] *adj* brown

marroquí [marro'ki] *adj, nmf* Moroccan ▷ *nm* Morocco (leather)

Marruecos [ma'rrwekos] *nm* Morocco

martes ['martes] *nm inv* Tuesday; **~ y trece** ≈ Friday 13th

martillo [mar'tiʎo] nm hammer
mártir ['martir] nmf martyr; **martirio** nm
martyrdom; (fig) torture, torment
marxismo [mark'sismo] nm Marxism
marzo ['marθo] nm March

○ **PALABRA CLAVE**

más [mas] adj, adv 1: **más (que** o **de)**
(compar) more (than), ...+ er (than);
más grande/inteligente bigger/more
intelligent; **trabaja más (que yo)** he works
more (than me); V tb **cada**
2 (superl): **el más** the most, ...+ est; **el más
grande/inteligente (de)** the biggest/most
intelligent (in)
3 (negativo): **no tengo más dinero** I haven't
got any more money; **no viene más por
aquí** he doesn't come round here any more
4 (adicional): **no le veo más solución que
...** I see no other solution than to ...; **¿quién
más?** anybody else?
5 (+ adj: valor intensivo): **¡qué perro más
sucio!** what a filthy dog!; **¡es más tonto!**
he's so stupid!
6 (locuciones): **más o menos** more or less;
los más most people; **es más** furthermore;
más bien rather; **¡qué más da!** what does it
matter!; V tb **no**
7: **por más: por más que te esfuerces** no
matter how hard you try; **por más que
quisiera ...** much as I should like to ...
8: **de más: veo que aquí estoy de más** I can
see I'm not needed here; **tenemos uno de
más** we've got one extra ▷ prep: **2 más 2 son
4** 2 and o plus 2 are 4
▷ nm inv: **este trabajo tiene sus más y sus
menos** this job's got its good points and its
bad points

mas [mas] conj but
masa ['masa] nf (mezcla) dough; (volumen)
volume, mass; (Física) mass; **en ~** en masse;
las ~s (Pol) the masses
masacre [ma'sakre] nf massacre
masaje [ma'saxe] nm massage
máscara ['maskara] nf mask; **máscara
antigás/de oxígeno** gas/oxygen mask;
mascarilla nf (de belleza, Med) mask
masculino, -a [masku'lino, a] adj
masculine; (Bio) male
masía [ma'sia] nf farmhouse
masivo, -a [ma'siβo, a] adj mass cpd
masoquista [maso'kista] nmf masochist
máster ['master] (ESP) nm master
masticar [masti'kar] vt to chew
mástil ['mastil] nm (de navío) mast; (de
guitarra) neck

mastín [mas'tin] nm mastiff
masturbarse [mastur'βarse] vr to
masturbate
mata ['mata] nf (arbusto) bush, shrub; (de
hierba) tuft
matadero [mata'ðero] nm
slaughterhouse, abattoir
matamoscas [mata'moskas] nm inv
(pala) fly swat
matanza [ma'tanθa] nf slaughter
matar [ma'tar] vt, vi to kill; **matarse**
vr (suicidarse) to kill o.s., commit suicide;
(morir) to be o get killed; **~ el hambre** to
stave off hunger
matasellos [mata'seʎos] nm inv
postmark
mate ['mate] adj matt ▷ nm (en ajedrez)
(check)mate; (LAM: hierba) maté; (: vasija)
gourd
matemáticas [mate'matikas] nfpl
mathematics; **matemático, -a** adj
mathematical ▷ nm/f mathematician
materia [ma'terja] nf (gen) matter;
(Tec) material; (Escol) subject; **en ~ de**
on the subject of; **materia prima** raw
material; **material** adj material ▷ nm
material; (Tec) equipment; **materialista**
adj materialist(ic); **materialmente** adv
materially; (fig) absolutely
maternal [mater'nal] adj motherly,
maternal
maternidad [materni'ðað] nf
motherhood, maternity; **materno, -a** adj
maternal; (lengua) mother cpd
matinal [mati'nal] adj morning cpd
matiz [ma'tiθ] nm shade; **matizar** vt
(variar) to vary; (Arte) to blend; **matizar de**
to tinge with
matón [ma'ton] nm bully
matorral [mato'rral] nm thicket
matrícula [ma'trikula] nf (registro)
register; (Auto) registration number; (: placa)
number plate; **matrícula de honor** (Univ)
top marks in a subject at university with the
right to free registration the following year;
matricular vt to register, enrol
matrimonio [matri'monjo] nm (pareja)
(married) couple; (unión) marriage
matriz [ma'triθ] nf (Anat) womb; (Tec)
mould
matrona [ma'trona] nf (persona de edad)
matron; (comadrona) midwife
matufia [ma'tufja] (RPL: fam) nf put-up
job
maullar [mau'ʎar] vi to mew, miaow
maxilar [maksi'lar] nm jaw(bone)
máxima [ma'ksima] nf maxim
máximo, -a ['maksimo, a] adj

maximum; (*más alto*) highest; (*más grande*)
greatest ▷ *nm* maximum; **como ~** at most
mayo ['majo] *nm* May
mayonesa [majo'nesa] *nf* mayonnaise
mayor [ma'jor] *adj* main, chief; (*adulto*)
adult; (*de edad avanzada*) elderly; (*Mús*)
major; (*compar: de tamaño*) bigger; (: *de edad*)
older; (*superl: de tamaño*) biggest; (: *de edad*)
oldest ▷ *nm* (*adulto*) adult; **mayores** *nmpl*
(*antepasados*) ancestors; **al por ~** wholesale;
mayor de edad adult
mayoral [majo'ral] *nm* foreman
mayordomo [major'ðomo] *nm* butler
mayoría [majo'ria] *nf* majority, greater
part
mayorista [majo'rista] *nmf* wholesaler
mayoritario, -a [majori'tarjo, a] *adj*
majority *cpd*
mayúscula [ma'juskula] *nf* capital letter
mazapán [maθa'pan] *nm* marzipan
mazo ['maθo] *nm* (*martillo*) mallet; (*de
flores*) bunch; (*Deporte*) bat
me [me] *pron* (*directo*) me; (*indirecto*) (to)
me; (*reflexivo*) (to) myself; **¡dá~lo!** give it
to me!
mear [me'ar] (*fam*) *vi* to pee, piss (!)
mecánica [me'kanika] *nf* (*Escol*)
mechanics *sg*; (*mecanismo*) mechanism; *V tb*
mecánico
mecánico, -a [me'kaniko, a] *adj*
mechanical ▷ *nm/f* mechanic
mecanismo [meka'nismo] *nm*
mechanism; (*marcha*) gear
mecanografía [mekanovra'fia] *nf*
typewriting; **mecanógrafo, -a** *nm/f* typist
mecate [me'kate] (*MÉX, CAM*) *nm* rope
mecedora [meθe'ðora] *nf* rocking chair
mecer [me'θer] *vt* (*cuna*) to rock; **mecerse**
vr to rock; (*rama*) to sway
mecha ['metʃa] *nf* (*de vela*) wick; (*de bomba*)
fuse
mechero [me'tʃero] *nm* (*cigarette*) lighter
mechón [me'tʃon] *nm* (*gen*) tuft; (*de pelo*)
lock
medalla [me'ðaʎa] *nf* medal
media ['meðja] *nf* stocking; (*LAM: calcetín*)
sock; (*promedio*) average
mediado, -a [me'ðjaðo, a] *adj* half-full;
(*trabajo*) half-completed; **a ~s de** in the
middle of, halfway through
mediano, -a [me'ðjano, a] *adj* (*regular*)
medium, average; (*mediocre*) mediocre
medianoche [meðja'notʃe] *nf* midnight
mediante [me'ðjante] *adv* by (means of),
through
mediar [me'ðjar] *vi* (*interceder*) to mediate,
intervene
medicamento [meðika'mento] *nm*

medicine, drug
medicina [meði'θina] *nf* medicine
médico, -a ['meðiko, a] *adj* medical
▷ *nm/f* doctor
medida [me'ðiða] *nf* measure; (*medición*)
measurement; (*prudencia*) moderation,
prudence; **en cierta/gran ~** up to a point/
to a great extent; **un traje a la ~** a made-to-
measure suit; **~ de cuello** collar size; **a ~ de**
in proportion to; (*de acuerdo con*) in keeping
with; **a ~ que** (*conforme*) as; **medidor** (*LAM*)
nm meter
medio, -a ['meðjo, a] *adj* half (a); (*punto*)
mid, middle; (*promedio*) average ▷ *adv* half
▷ *nm* (*centro*) middle, centre; (*promedio*)
average; (*método*) means, way; (*ambiente*)
environment; **medios** *nmpl* means,
resources; **~ litro** half a litre; **las tres y
media** half past three; **a ~ terminar** half
finished; **pagar a medias** to share the
cost; **medio ambiente** environment;
medio de transporte means of transport;
Medio Oriente Middle East; **medios de
comunicación** media; **medioambiental**
adj (*política, efectos*) environmental
mediocre [me'ðjokre] *adj* mediocre
mediodía [meðjo'ðia] *nm* midday, noon
medir [me'ðir] *vt, vi* (*gen*) to measure
meditar [meði'tar] *vt* to ponder, think
over, meditate on; (*planear*) to think out
mediterráneo, -a [meðite'rraneo,
a] *adj* Mediterranean ▷ *nm*: **el M~** the
Mediterranean
médula ['meðula] *nf* (*Anat*) marrow;
médula espinal spinal cord
medusa [me'ðusa] (*ESP*) *nf* jellyfish
megáfono [me'ɣafono] *nm* megaphone
megapíxel [meɣa'piksel] (*pl* **megapixels**
or **~es**) *nm* megapixel
mejilla [me'xiʎa] *nf* cheek
mejillón [mexi'ʎon] *nm* mussel
mejor [me'xor] *adj, adv* (*compar*) better;
(*superl*) best; **a lo ~** probably; (*quizá*) maybe;
~ dicho rather; **tanto ~** so much the better
mejora [me'xora] *nf* improvement;
mejorar *vt* to improve, make better ▷ *vi*
to improve, get better; **mejorarse** *vr* to
improve, get better
melancólico, -a [melan'koliko, a] *adj*
(*triste*) sad, melancholy; (*soñador*) dreamy
melena [me'lena] *nf* (*de persona*) long hair;
(*Zool*) mane
mellizo, -a [me'ʎiθo, a] *adj, nm/f* twin
melocotón [meloko'ton] (*ESP*) *nm* peach
melodía [melo'ðia] *nf* melody, tune
melodrama [melo'ðrama] *nm*
melodrama; **melodramático, -a** *a* adj
melodramatic

m

melón [me'lon] nm melon

membrete [mem'brete] nm letterhead

membrillo [mem'briʎo] nm quince; **(carne de) ~** quince jelly

memoria [me'morja] nf (gen) memory; **memorias** nfpl (de autor) memoirs; **memorizar** vt to memorize

menaje [me'naxe] nm (tb: **artículos de ~**) household items

mencionar [menθjo'nar] vt to mention

mendigo, -a [men'diɣo, a] nm/f beggar

menear [mene'ar] vt to move; **menearse** vr to shake; (balancearse) to sway; (moverse) to move; (fig) to get a move on

menestra [me'nestra] nf (tb: **~ de verduras**) vegetable stew

menopausia [meno'pausja] nf menopause

menor [me'nor] adj (más pequeño: compar) smaller; (: superl) smallest; (más joven: compar) younger; (: superl) youngest; (Mús) minor ▷ nmf (joven) young person, juvenile; **no tengo la ~ idea** I haven't the faintest idea; **al por ~** retail; **menor de edad** person under age

Menorca [me'norka] nf Minorca

○ **PALABRA CLAVE**

menos [menos] adj 1: **menos (que o de)** (compar: cantidad) less (than); (: número) fewer (than); **con menos entusiasmo** with less enthusiasm; **menos gente** fewer people; V tb **cada**
2 (superl): **es el que menos culpa tiene** he is the least to blame
▷ adv 1 (compar): **menos (que o de)** less (than); **me gusta menos que el otro** I like it less than the other one
2 (superl): **es el menos listo (de su clase)** he's the least bright in his class; **de todas ellas es la que menos me agrada** out of all of them she's the one I like least
3 (locuciones): **no quiero verle y menos visitarle** I don't want to see him, let alone visit him; **tenemos siete de menos** we're seven short; **(por) lo menos** at (the very) least; **¡menos mal!** thank goodness!
▷ prep except; (cifras) minus; **todos menos él** everyone except (for) him; **5 menos 2** 5 minus 2
▷ conj: **a menos que: a menos que venga mañana** unless he comes tomorrow

menospreciar [menospre'θjar] vt to underrate, undervalue; (despreciar) to scorn, despise

mensaje [men'saxe] nm message; **enviar un ~ a algn** (por móvil) to text sb, send sb a text message; **mensaje de texto** text message; **mensajero, -a** nm/f messenger

menso, -a ['menso, a] (MÉX: fam) adj stupid

menstruación [menstrua'θjon] nf menstruation

mensual [men'swal] adj monthly; **100 euros ~es** 100 euros a month; **mensualidad** nf (salario) monthly salary; (Com) monthly payment, monthly instalment

menta ['menta] nf mint

mental [men'tal] adj mental; **mentalidad** nf mentality; **mentalizar** vt (sensibilizar) to make aware; (convencer) to convince; (padres) to prepare (mentally); **mentalizarse** vr (concienciarse) to become aware; **mentalizarse (de)** to get used to the idea (of); **mentalizarse de que ...** (convencerse) to get it into one's head that ...

mente ['mente] nf mind

mentir [men'tir] vi to lie

mentira [men'tira] nf (una mentira) lie; (acto) lying; (invención) fiction; **parece mentira que ...** it seems incredible that ..., I can't believe that ...; **mentiroso, -a** [menti'roso, a] adj lying ▷ nm/f liar

menú [me'nu] (pl **~s**) nm menu; **menú del día** set menu; **menú turístico** tourist menu

menudencias [menu'ðenθjas] (LAM) nfpl giblets

menudo, -a [me'nuðo, a] adj (pequeño) small, tiny; (sin importancia) petty, insignificant; **¡~ negocio!** (fam) some deal!; **a ~** often, frequently

meñique [me'ɲike] nm little finger

mercadillo [merka'ðiʎo] (ESP) nm flea market

mercado [mer'kaðo] nm market; **mercado de pulgas** (LAM) flea market

mercancía [merkan'θia] nf commodity; **mercancías** nfpl goods, merchandise sg

mercenario, -a [merθe'narjo, a] adj, nm mercenary

mercería [merθe'ria] nf haberdashery (BRIT), notions pl (US); (tienda) haberdasher's (BRIT), notions store (US)

mercurio [mer'kurjo] nm mercury

merecer [mere'θer] vt to deserve, merit ▷ vi to be deserving, be worthy; **merece la pena** it's worthwhile; **merecido, -a** adj (well) deserved; **llevar su merecido** to get one's deserts

merendar [meren'dar] vt to have for tea ▷ vi to have tea; (en el campo) to have a picnic; **merendero** nm open-air cafe

merengue [me'renge] nm meringue

meridiano [meri'ðjano] nm (Geo)

meridian

merienda [me'rjenda] *nf* (light) tea, afternoon snack; (*de campo*) picnic

mérito ['merito] *nm* merit; (*valor*) worth, value

merluza [mer'luθa] *nf* hake

mermelada [merme'laða] *nf* jam

mero, -a ['mero, a] *adj* mere; (*MÉX, CAM: fam*) very

merodear [meroðe'ar] *vi*: ~ **por** to prowl about

mes [mes] *nm* month

mesa ['mesa] *nf* table; (*de trabajo*) desk; (*Geo*) plateau; **poner/quitar la** ~ to lay/clear the table; **mesa electoral** officials in charge of a polling station; **mesa redonda** (*reunión*) round table; **mesero, -a** (*LAM*) *nm/f* waiter/waitress

meseta [me'seta] *nf* (*Geo*) plateau, tableland

mesilla [me'siʎa] *nf* (tb: ~ **de noche**) bedside table

mesón [me'son] *nm* inn

mestizo, -a [mes'tiθo, a] *adj* half-caste, of mixed race ▷ *nm/f* half-caste

meta ['meta] *nf* goal; (*de carrera*) finish

metabolismo [metaβo'lismo] *nm* metabolism

metáfora [me'tafora] *nf* metaphor

metal [me'tal] *nm* (*materia*) metal; (*Mús*) brass; **metálico, -a** *adj* metallic; (*de metal*) metal ▷ *nm* (*dinero contante*) cash

meteorología [meteorolo'xia] *nf* meteorology

meter [me'ter] *vt* (*colocar*) to put, place; (*introducir*) to put in, insert; (*involucrar*) to involve; (*causar*) to make, cause; **meterse** *vr*: ~**se en** to go into, enter; (*fig*) to interfere in, meddle in; ~**se a** to start; ~**se a escritor** to become a writer; ~**se con uno** to provoke sb, pick a quarrel with sb

meticuloso, -a [metiku'loso, a] *adj* meticulous, thorough

metódico, -a [me'toðiko, a] *adj* methodical

método [me'toðo] *nm* method

metralleta [metra'ʎeta] *nf* sub-machine-gun

métrico, -a ['metriko, a] *adj* metric

metro ['metro] *nm* metre; (*tren*) underground (*BRIT*), subway (*US*)

metrosexual [metrosek'swal] *adj, nm* metrosexual

mexicano, -a [mexi'kano, a] *adj, nm/f* Mexican

México ['mexiko] *nm* Mexico; **Ciudad de ~** Mexico City

mezcla ['meθkla] *nf* mixture; **mezcladora** (*MÉX*) *nf* (tb: **mezcladora de cemento**) cement mixer; **mezclar** *vt* to mix (up); **mezclarse** *vr* to mix, mingle; **mezclarse en** to get mixed up in, get involved in

mezquino, -a [meθ'kino, a] *adj* mean

mezquita [meθ'kita] *nf* mosque

mg. *abr* (= *miligramo*) mg

mi [mi] *adj pos* my ▷ *nm* (*Mús*) E

mí [mi] *pron* me; myself

mía *pron* V **mío**

michelín [mitʃe'lin] (*fam*) *nm* (*de grasa*) spare tyre

microbio [mi'kroβjo] *nm* microbe

micrófono [mi'krofono] *nm* microphone

microondas [mikro'ondas] *nm inv* (tb: **horno ~**) microwave (oven)

microscopio [mikro'skopjo] *nm* microscope

miedo ['mjeðo] *nm* fear; (*nerviosismo*) apprehension, nervousness; **tener** ~ to be afraid; **de** ~ wonderful, marvellous; **hace un frío de** ~ (*fam*) it's terribly cold; **miedoso, -a** *adj* fearful, timid

miel [mjel] *nf* honey

miembro ['mjembro] *nm* limb; (*socio*) member; **miembro viril** penis

mientras ['mjentras] *conj* while; (*duración*) as long as ▷ *adv* meanwhile; ~ **tanto** meanwhile

miércoles ['mjerkoles] *nm inv* Wednesday

mierda ['mjerða] (*fam!*) *nf* shit (!)

miga ['miɣa] *nf* crumb; (*fig: meollo*) essence; **hacer buenas ~s** (*fam*) to get on well

mil [mil] *num* thousand; **dos ~ libras** two thousand pounds

milagro [mi'laɣro] *nm* miracle; **milagroso, -a** *adj* miraculous

milésima [mi'lesima] *nf* (*de segundo*) thousandth

mili ['mili] (*ESP: fam*) *nf*: **hacer la ~** to do one's military service

milímetro [mi'limetro] *nm* millimetre

militante [mili'tante] *adj* militant

militar [mili'tar] *adj* military ▷ *nmf* soldier ▷ *vi* (*Mil*) to serve; (*en un partido*) to be a member

milla ['miʎa] *nf* mile

millar [mi'ʎar] *nm* thousand

millón [mi'ʎon] *num* million; **millonario, -a** *nm/f* millionaire

milusos [mi'lusos] (*MÉX*) *nm inv* odd-job man

mimar [mi'mar] *vt* to spoil, pamper

mimbre ['mimbre] *nm* wicker

mímica ['mimika] *nf* (*para comunicarse*) sign language; (*imitación*) mimicry

mimo ['mimo] *nm* (*caricia*) caress; (*de niño*)

spoiling; (*Teatro*) mime; (: *actor*) mime artist

mina ['mina] *nf* mine

mineral [mine'ral] *adj* mineral ▷ *nm* (*Geo*) mineral; (*mena*) ore

minero, -a [mi'nero, a] *adj* mining *cpd* ▷ *nm/f* miner

miniatura [minja'tura] *adj inv*, *nf* miniature

minidisco [mini'disko] *nm* MiniDisc®

minifalda [mini'falda] *nf* miniskirt

mínimo, -a ['minimo, a] *adj, nm* minimum

minino, -a [mi'nino, a] (*fam*) *nm/f* puss, pussy

ministerio [minis'terjo] *nm* Ministry; **Ministerio de Hacienda/de Asuntos Exteriores** Treasury (*BRIT*), Treasury Department (*US*)/Foreign Office (*BRIT*), State Department (*US*)

ministro, -a [mi'nistro, a] *nm/f* minister

minoría [mino'ria] *nf* minority

minúscula [mi'nuskula] *nf* small letter

minúsculo, -a [mi'nuskulo, a] *adj* tiny, minute

minusválido, -a [minus'βaliðo, a] *adj* (physically) handicapped ▷ *nm/f* (physically) handicapped person

minuta [mi'nuta] *nf* (*de comida*) menu

minutero [minu'tero] *nm* minute hand

minuto [mi'nuto] *nm* minute

mío, -a ['mio, a] *pron*: **el ~/la mía** mine; **un amigo ~** a friend of mine; **lo ~** what is mine

miope [mi'ope] *adj* short-sighted

mira ['mira] *nf* (*de arma*) sight(s) (*pl*); (*fig*) aim, intention

mirada [mi'raða] *nf* look, glance; (*expresión*) look, expression; **clavar la ~ en** to stare at; **echar una ~ a** to glance at

mirado, -a [mi'raðo, a] *adj* (*sensato*) sensible; (*considerado*) considerate; **bien/mal ~** (*estimado*) well/not well thought of; **bien ~ ...** all things considered ...

mirador [mira'ðor] *nm* viewpoint, vantage point

mirar [mi'rar] *vt* to look at; (*observar*) to watch; (*considerar*) to consider, think over; (*vigilar, cuidar*) to watch, look after ▷ *vi* to look; (*Arq*) to face; **mirarse** *vr* (*dos personas*) to look at each other; **~ bien/mal** to think highly of/have a poor opinion of; **~se al espejo** to look at o.s. in the mirror

mirilla [mi'riʎa] *nf* spyhole, peephole

mirlo ['mirlo] *nm* blackbird

misa ['misa] *nf* mass

miserable [mise'raβle] *adj* (*avaro*) mean, stingy; (*nimio*) miserable, paltry; (*lugar*) squalid; (*fam*) vile, despicable ▷ *nmf* (*malvado*) rogue

miseria [mi'serja] *nf* (*pobreza*) poverty; (*tacañería*) meanness, stinginess; (*condiciones*) squalor; **una ~** a pittance

misericordia [miseri'korðja] *nf* (*compasión*) compassion, pity; (*piedad*) mercy

misil [mi'sil] *nm* missile

misión [mi'sjon] *nf* mission; **misionero, -a** *nm/f* missionary

mismo, -a ['mismo, a] *adj* (*semejante*) same; (*después de pron*) -self; (*para énfasis*) very ▷ *adv*: **aquí/hoy ~** right here/this very day; **ahora ~** right now ▷ *conj*: **lo ~ que** just like *o* as; **el ~ traje** the same suit; **en ese ~ momento** at that very moment; **vino el ~ ministro** the minister himself came; **yo ~ lo vi** I saw it myself; **lo ~** the same (thing); **da lo ~** it's all the same; **quedamos en las mismas** we're no further forward; **por lo ~** for the same reason

misterio [mis'terjo] *nm* mystery; **misterioso, -a** *adj* mysterious

mitad [mi'tað] *nf* (*medio*) half; (*centro*) middle; **a ~ de precio** (at) half-price; **en** *o* **a ~ del camino** halfway along the road; **cortar por la ~** to cut through the middle

mitin ['mitin] (*pl* **mítines**) *nm* meeting

mito ['mito] *nm* myth

mixto, -a ['miksto, a] *adj* mixed

ml. *abr* (= *mililitro*) ml

mm. *abr* (= *milímetro*) mm

mobiliario [moβi'ljarjo] *nm* furniture

mochila [mo'tʃila] *nf* rucksack (*BRIT*), back-pack

moco ['moko] *nm* mucus; **mocos** *nmpl* (*fam*) snot; **limpiarse los ~s de la nariz** (*fam*) to wipe one's nose

moda ['moða] *nf* fashion; (*estilo*) style; **a la** *o* **de ~** in fashion, fashionable; **pasado de ~** out of fashion

modales [mo'ðales] *nmpl* manners

modelar [moðe'lar] *vt* to model

modelo [mo'ðelo] *adj inv*, *nmf* model

módem ['moðem] *nm* (*Inform*) modem

moderado, -a [moðe'raðo, a] *adj* moderate

moderar [moðe'rar] *vt* to moderate; (*violencia*) to restrain, control; (*velocidad*) to reduce; **moderarse** *vr* to restrain o.s., control o.s.

modernizar [moðerni'θar] *vt* to modernize

moderno, -a [mo'ðerno, a] *adj* modern; (*actual*) present-day

modestia [mo'ðestja] *nf* modesty; **modesto, -a** *adj* modest

modificar [moðifi'kar] *vt* to modify

modisto, -a [mo'ðisto, a] *nm/f* (*diseñador*) couturier, designer; (*que confecciona*) dressmaker

modo ['moðo] nm way, manner; (Mús) mode; **modos** nmpl manners; **de ningún ~** in no way; **de todos ~s** at any rate; **modo de empleo** directions pl (for use)

mofarse [mo'farse] vr: **~ de** to mock, scoff at

mofle ['mofle] (MÉX, CAM) nm silencer (BRIT), muffler (US)

mogollón [moɣo'ʎon] (ESP: fam) adv a hell of a lot

moho ['moo] nm mould, mildew; (en metal) rust

mojar [mo'xar] vt to wet; (humedecer) to damp(en), moisten; (calar) to soak; **mojarse** vr to get wet

molcajete [molka'xete] (MÉX) nm mortar

molde ['molde] nm mould; (Costura) pattern; (fig) model; **moldeado** nm soft perm; **moldear** vt to mould

mole ['mole] nf mass, bulk; (edificio) pile

moler [mo'ler] vt to grind, crush

molestar [moles'tar] vt to bother; (fastidiar) to annoy; (incomodar) to inconvenience, put out ▷ vi to be a nuisance; **molestarse** vr to bother; (incomodarse) to go to trouble; (ofenderse) to take offence; **¿(no) te molesta si ...?** do you mind if ...?

▌No confundir **molestar** con la palabra inglesa molest.

molestia [mo'lestja] nf bother, trouble; (incomodidad) inconvenience; (Med) discomfort; **es una ~** it's a nuisance; **molesto, -a** adj (que fastidia) annoying; (incómodo) inconvenient; (inquieto) uncomfortable, ill at ease; (enfadado) annoyed

molido, -a [mo'liðo, a] adj: **estar ~** (fig) to be exhausted o dead beat

molinillo [moli'niʎo] nm hand mill; **molinillo de café** coffee grinder

molino [mo'lino] nm (edificio) mill; (máquina) grinder

momentáneo, -a [momen'taneo, a] adj momentary

momento [mo'mento] nm moment; **de ~** at o for the moment

momia ['momja] nf mummy

monarca [mo'narka] nmf monarch, ruler; **monarquía** nf monarchy

monasterio [monas'terjo] nm monastery

mondar [mon'dar] vt to peel; **mondarse** vr (ESP): **~se de risa** (fam) to split one's sides laughing

mondongo [mon'dongo] (LAM) nm tripe

moneda [mo'neða] nf (tipo de dinero) currency, money; (pieza) coin; **una ~ de 2**

euros a 2 euro piece; **monedero** nm purse

monitor, a [moni'tor, a] nm/f instructor, coach ▷ nm (TV) set; (Inform) monitor

monja ['monxa] nf nun

monje ['monxe] nm monk

mono, -a ['mono, a] adj (bonito) lovely, pretty; (gracioso) nice, charming ▷ nm/f monkey, ape ▷ nm (overoles) dungarees pl; (overoles) overalls pl

monopatín [monopa'tin] nm skateboard

monopolio [mono'poljo] nm monopoly; **monopolizar** vt to monopolize

monótono, -a [mo'notono, a] adj monotonous

monstruo ['monstrwo] nm monster ▷ adj inv fantastic; **monstruoso, -a** adj monstrous

montaje [mon'taxe] nm assembly; (Teatro) décor; (Cine) montage

montaña [mon'taɲa] nf (monte) mountain; (sierra) mountains pl, mountainous area; **montaña rusa** roller coaster; **montañero, -a** nm/f mountaineer; **montañismo** nm mountaineering

montar [mon'tar] vt (subir a) to mount, get on; (Tec) to assemble, put together; (negocio) to set up; (arma) to cock; (colocar) to lift on to; (Culin) to beat ▷ vi to mount, get on; (sobresalir) to overlap; **~ en bicicleta** to ride a bicycle; **~ en cólera** to get angry; **~ a caballo** to ride, go horseriding

monte ['monte] nm (montaña) mountain; (bosque) woodland; (área sin cultivar) wild area, wild country; **monte de piedad** pawnshop

montón [mon'ton] nm heap, pile; (fig): **un ~ de** heaps o lots of

monumento [monu'mento] nm monument

moño ['moɲo] nm bun

moqueta [mo'keta] nf fitted carpet

mora ['mora] nf blackberry; V tb **moro**

morado, -a [mo'raðo, a] adj purple, violet ▷ nm bruise

moral [mo'ral] adj moral ▷ nf (ética) ethics pl; (moralidad) morals pl, morality; (ánimo) morale

moraleja [mora'lexa] nf moral

morboso, -a [mor'βoso, a] adj morbid

morcilla [mor'θiʎa] nf blood sausage ≈ black pudding (BRIT)

mordaza [mor'ðaθa] nf (para la boca) gag; (Tec) clamp

morder [mor'ðer] vt to bite; (fig: consumir) to eat away, eat into; **mordisco** nm bite

moreno, -a [mo'reno, a] adj (color) (dark) brown; (de tez) dark; (de pelo moreno) dark-

m

haired; (*negro*) black
morfina [mor'fina] *nf* morphine
moribundo, -a [mori'βundo, a] *adj*
dying
morir [mo'rir] *vi* to die; (*fuego*) to die
down; (*luz*) to go out; **morirse** *vr* to die;
(*fig*) to be dying; **murió en un accidente** he
was killed in an accident; **~se por algo** to be
dying for sth
moro, -a ['moro, a] *adj* Moorish ▷ *nm/f*
Moor
moroso, -a [mo'roso, a] *nm/f* bad debtor,
defaulter
morraña [mo'rraɲa] (*MÉX*) *nf* (*cambio*)
small *o* loose change
morro ['morro] *nm* (*Zool*) snout, nose;
(*Auto, Aviac*) nose
morsa ['morsa] *nf* walrus
mortadela [morta'ðela] *nf* mortadella
mortal [mor'tal] *adj* mortal; (*golpe*)
deadly; **mortalidad** *nf* mortality
mortero [mor'tero] *nm* mortar
mosca ['moska] *nf* fly
Moscú [mos'ku] *n* Moscow
mosquearse [moske'arse] (*fam*) *vr*
(*enojarse*) to get cross; (*ofenderse*) to take
offence
mosquitero [moski'tero] *nm* mosquito
net
mosquito [mos'kito] *nm* mosquito
mostaza [mos'taθa] *nf* mustard
mosto ['mosto] *nm* (unfermented) grape
juice
mostrador [mostra'ðor] *nm* (*de tienda*)
counter; (*de café*) bar
mostrar [mos'trar] *vt* to show; (*exhibir*)
to display, exhibit; (*explicar*) to explain;
mostrarse *vr*: **~se amable** to be kind;
to prove to be kind; **no se muestra muy
inteligente** he doesn't seem (to be) very
intelligent
mota ['mota] *nf* speck, tiny piece; (*en
diseño*) dot
mote ['mote] *nm* nickname
motín [mo'tin] *nm* (*del pueblo*) revolt,
rising; (*del ejército*) mutiny
motivar [moti'βar] *vt* (*causar*) to cause,
motivate; (*explicar*) to explain, justify;
motivo *nm* motive, reason
moto ['moto] (*fam*) *nf* = **motocicleta**
motocicleta [motoθi'kleta] *nf* motorbike
(*BRIT*), motorcycle
motoneta [moto'neta] (*cs*) *nf* scooter
motor [mo'tor] *nm* motor, engine; **motor
a chorro** *o* **de reacción/de explosión** jet
engine/internal combustion engine
motora [mo'tora] *nf* motorboat
movedizo, -a *adj* V **arena**

mover [mo'βer] *vt* to move; (*cabeza*) to
shake; (*accionar*) to drive; (*fig*) to cause,
provoke; **moverse** *vr* to move; (*fig*) to get
a move on
móvil ['moβil] *adj* mobile; (*pieza de
máquina*) moving; (*mueble*) movable ▷ *nm*
(*motivo*) motive; (*teléfono*) mobile
movimiento [moβi'mjento] *nm*
movement; (*Tec*) motion; (*actividad*) activity
mozo, -a ['moθo, a] *adj* (*joven*) young
▷ *nm/f* youth, young man/girl; (*cs: mesero*)
waiter/waitress
MP3 *nm* MP3; **reproductor (de) ~ MP3**
player
mucama [mu'kama] (*RPL*) *nf* maid
muchacho, -a [mu'tʃatʃo, a] *nm/f* (*niño*)
boy/girl; (*criado*) servant; (*criada*) maid
muchedumbre [mutʃe'ðumbre] *nf*
crowd

○ **PALABRA CLAVE**

mucho, -a ['mutʃo, a] *adj* **1** (*cantidad*) a
lot of, much; (*número*) lots of, a lot of, many;
mucho dinero a lot of money; **hace mucho
calor** it's very hot; **muchas amigas** lots *o* a
lot of friends
2 (*sg: grande*): **ésta es mucha casa para él**
this house is much too big for him
▷ *pron*: **tengo mucho que hacer** I've got
a lot to do; **muchos dicen que ...** a lot of
people say that ...; V *tb* **tener**
▷ *adv* **1** **me gusta mucho** I like it a lot; **lo
siento mucho** I'm very sorry; **come mucho**
he eats a lot; **¿te vas a quedar mucho?** are
you going to be staying long?
2 (*respuesta*) very; **¿estás cansado? –
¡mucho!** are you tired? – very!
3 (*locuciones*): **como mucho** at (the) most;
con mucho: el mejor con mucho by far
the best; **ni mucho menos: no es rico ni
mucho menos** he's far from being rich
4: **por mucho que: por mucho que le
creas** no matter how *o* however much you
believe her

muda ['muða] *nf* change of clothes
mudanza [mu'ðanθa] *nf* (*de casa*) move
mudar [mu'ðar] *vt* to change; (*Zool*) to
shed ▷ *vi* to change; **mudarse** *vr* (*ropa*) to
change; **~se de casa** to move house
mudo, -a ['muðo, a] *adj* dumb; (*callado,
Cine*) silent
mueble ['mweβle] *nm* piece of furniture;
muebles *nmpl* furniture *sg*
mueca ['mweka] *nf* face, grimace; **hacer
~s a** to make faces at
muela ['mwela] *nf* back tooth; **muela del**

juicio wisdom tooth
muelle ['mweʎe] nm spring; (Náut) wharf; (malecón) pier
muero etc vb V **morir**
muerte ['mwerte] nf death; (homicidio) murder; **dar ~ a** to kill
muerto, -a ['mwerto, a] pp de **morir** ▷ adj dead ▷ nm/f dead man/woman; (difunto) deceased; (cadáver) corpse; **estar ~ de cansancio** to be dead tired; **Día de los Muertos** (MÉX) All Souls' Day

● **DÍA DE LOS MUERTOS**
●
● All Souls' Day (or "Day of the Dead")
● in Mexico coincides with All Saints'
● Day, which is celebrated in the
● Catholic countries of Latin America on
● November 1st and 2nd. All Souls' Day
● is actually a celebration which begins
● in the evening of October 31st and
● continues until November 2nd. It is a
● combination of the Catholic tradition
● of honouring the Christian saints and
● martyrs, and the ancient Mexican or
● Aztec traditions, in which death was
● not something sinister. For this reason
● all the dead are honoured by bringing
● offerings of food, flowers and candles to
● the cemetery.

muestra ['mwestra] nf (señal) indication, sign; (demostración) demonstration; (prueba) proof; (estadística) sample; (modelo) model, pattern; (testimonio) token
muestro etc vb V **mostrar**
muevo etc vb V **mover**
mugir [mu'xir] vi (vaca) to moo
mugre ['muxre] nf dirt, filth
mujer [mu'xer] nf woman; (esposa) wife; **mujeriego** nm womanizer
mula ['mula] nf mule
muleta [mu'leta] nf (para andar) crutch; (Taur) stick with red cape attached
multa ['multa] nf fine; **poner una ~ a** to fine; **multar** vt to fine
multicines [multi'θines] nmpl multiscreen cinema sg
multinacional [multinaθjo'nal] nf multinational
múltiple ['multiple] adj multiple; (pl) many, numerous
multiplicar [multipli'kar] vt (Mat) to multiply; (fig) to increase; **multiplicarse** vr (Bio) to multiply; (fig) to be everywhere at once
multitud [multi'tuð] nf (muchedumbre) crowd; **~ de** lots of

mundial [mun'djal] adj world-wide, universal; (guerra, récord) world cpd
mundo ['mundo] nm world; **todo el ~** everybody; **tener ~** to be experienced, know one's way around
munición [muni'θjon] nf ammunition
municipal [muniθi'pal] adj municipal, local
municipio [muni'θipjo] nm (ayuntamiento) town council, corporation; (territorio administrativo) town, municipality
muñeca [mu'ɲeka] nf (Anat) wrist; (juguete) doll
muñeco [mu'ɲeko] nm (figura) figure; (marioneta) puppet; (fig) puppet, pawn
mural [mu'ral] adj mural, wall cpd ▷ nm mural
muralla [mu'raʎa] nf (city) wall(s) (pl)
murciélago [mur'θjelaxo] nm bat
murmullo [mur'muʎo] nm murmur(ing); (cuchicheo) whispering
murmurar [murmu'rar] vi to murmur, whisper; (cotillear) to gossip
muro ['muro] nm wall
muscular [musku'lar] adj muscular
músculo ['muskulo] nm muscle
museo [mu'seo] nm museum; **museo de arte** art gallery
musgo ['musxo] nm moss
música ['musika] nf music; V tb **músico**
músico, -a ['musiko, a] adj musical ▷ nm/f musician
muslo ['muslo] nm thigh
musulmán, -ana [musul'man, ana] nm/f Moslem
mutación [muta'θjon] nf (Bio) mutation; (cambio) (sudden) change
mutilar [muti'lar] vt to mutilate; (a una persona) to maim
mutuo, -a ['mutwo, a] adj mutual
muy [mwi] adv very; (demasiado) too; **M~ Señor mío** Dear Sir; **~ de noche** very late at night; **eso es ~ de él** that's just like him

m

n

N *abr* (= *norte*) N

nabo ['naβo] *nm* turnip

nacer [na'θer] *vi* to be born; (*de huevo*) to hatch; (*vegetal*) to sprout; (*río*) to rise; **nací en Barcelona** I was born in Barcelona; **nacido, -a** *adj* born; **recién nacido** newborn; **nacimiento** *nm* birth; (*de Navidad*) Nativity; (*de río*) source

nación [na'θjon] *nf* nation; **nacional** *adj* national; **nacionalismo** *nm* nationalism

nada ['naða] *pron* nothing ▷ *adv* not at all, in no way; **no decir ~** to say nothing, not to say anything; **~ más** nothing else; **de ~** don't mention it

nadador, a [naða'ðor, a] *nm/f* swimmer

nadar [na'ðar] *vi* to swim

nadie ['naðje] *pron* nobody, no-one; **~ habló** nobody spoke; **no había ~** there was nobody there, there wasn't anybody there

nado ['naðo] **a nado**: *adv*: **pasar a ~** to swim across

nafta ['nafta] (*RPL*) *nf* petrol (*BRIT*), gas (*US*)

naipe ['naipe] *nm* (playing) card; **naipes** *nmpl* cards

nalgas ['nalɣas] *nfpl* buttocks

nalguear [nalɣe'ar] (*MÉX, CAM*) *vt* to spank

nana ['nana] (*ESP*) *nf* lullaby

naranja [na'ranxa] *adj inv, nf* orange; **media ~** (*fam*) better half; **naranjada** *nf* orangeade; **naranjo** *nm* orange tree

narciso [nar'θiso] *nm* narcissus

narcótico, -a [nar'kotiko, a] *adj, nm* narcotic; **narcotizar** *vt* to drug; **narcotráfico** *nm* drug trafficking *o* running

nariz [na'riθ] *nf* nose; **nariz chata/respingona** snub/turned-up nose

narración [narra'θjon] *nf* narration

narrar [na'rrar] *vt* to narrate, recount; **narrativa** *nf* narrative

nata ['nata] *nf* cream; **nata montada** whipped cream

natación [nata'θjon] *nf* swimming

natal [na'tal] *adj*: **ciudad ~** home town; **natalidad** *nf* birth rate

natillas [na'tiʎas] *nfpl* custard *sg*

nativo, -a [na'tiβo, a] *adj, nm/f* native

natural [natu'ral] *adj* natural; (*fruta etc*) fresh ▷ *nmf* native ▷ *nm* (*disposición*) nature

naturaleza [natura'leθa] *nf* nature; (*género*) nature, kind; **naturaleza muerta** still life

naturalmente [natural'mente] *adv* (*de modo natural*) in a natural way; **¡~!** of course!

naufragar [naufra'ɣar] *vi* to sink; **naufragio** *nm* shipwreck

nauseabundo, -a [nausea'βundo, a] *adj* nauseating, sickening

náuseas ['nauseas] *nfpl* nausea *sg*; **me da ~** it makes me feel sick

náutico, -a ['nautiko, a] *adj* nautical

navaja [na'βaxa] *nf* knife; (*de barbero, peluquero*) razor

naval [na'βal] *adj* naval

Navarra [na'βarra] *n* Navarre

nave ['naβe] *nf* (*barco*) ship, vessel; (*Arq*) nave; **nave espacial** spaceship; **nave industrial** factory premises *pl*

navegador [naβeɣa'ðor] *nm* (*Inform*) browser

navegante [naβe'ɣante] *nmf* navigator

navegar [naβe'ɣar] *vi* (*barco*) to sail; (*avión*) to fly; **~ por Internet** to surf the Net

Navidad [naβi'ðað] *nf* Christmas; **Navidades** *nfpl* Christmas time; **¡Feliz ~!** Merry Christmas!; **navideño, -a** *adj* Christmas *cpd*

nazca *etc vb* V **nacer**

nazi ['naθi] *adj, nmf* Nazi

NE *abr* (= *nor(d)este*) NE

neblina [ne'βlina] *nf* mist

necesario, -a [neθe'sarjo, a] *adj* necessary

neceser [neθe'ser] *nm* toilet bag; (*bolsa grande*) holdall

necesidad [neθesi'ðað] *nf* need; (*lo inevitable*) necessity; (*miseria*) poverty; **en caso de ~** in case of need *o* emergency; **hacer sus ~es** to relieve o.s.

necesitado, -a [neθesi'taðo, a] *adj* needy, poor; **~ de** in need of

necesitar [neθesi'tar] *vt* to need, require

necio, -a ['neθjo, a] *adj* foolish

nectarina [nekta'rina] *nf* nectarine

nefasto, -a [ne'fasto, a] *adj* ill-fated, unlucky

negación [neɣa'θjon] *nf* negation;

(*rechazo*) refusal, denial

negar [ne'ɣar] *vt* (*renegar, rechazar*) to refuse; (*prohibir*) to refuse, deny; (*desmentir*) to deny; **negarse** *vr*: **~se a** to refuse to

negativa [neɣa'tiβa] *nf* negative; (*rechazo*) refusal, denial

negativo, -a [neɣa'tiβo, a] *adj, nm* negative

negociante [neɣo'θjante] *nmf* businessman/woman

negociar [neɣo'θjar] *vt, vi* to negotiate; **~ en** to deal o trade in

negocio [ne'ɣoθjo] *nm* (*Com*) business; (*asunto*) affair, business; (*operación comercial*) deal, transaction; (*lugar*) place of business; **los ~s** business *sg*; **hacer ~** to do business

negra ['neɣra] *nf* (*Mús*) crotchet; V tb **negro**

negro, -a ['neɣro, a] *adj* black; (*suerte*) awful ▷ *nm* black ▷ *nm/f* black man/ woman

nene, -a ['nene, a] *nm/f* baby, small child

neón [ne'on] *nm*: **luces/lámpara de ~** neon lights/lamp

neoyorquino, -a [neojor'kino, a] *adj* (of) New York

nervio ['nerβjo] *nm* nerve; **nerviosismo** *nm* nervousness, nerves *pl*; **nervioso, -a** *adj* nervous

neto, -a ['neto, a] *adj* net

neumático, -a [neu'matiko, a] *adj* pneumatic ▷ *nm* (*ESP*) tyre (*BRIT*), tire (*US*); **neumático de recambio** spare tyre

neurólogo, -a [neu'roloɣo, a] *nm/f* neurologist

neurona [neu'rona] *nf* nerve cell

neutral [neu'tral] *adj* neutral; **neutralizar** *vt* to neutralize; (*contrarrestar*) to counteract

neutro, -a ['neutro, a] *adj* (*Bio, Ling*) neuter

neutrón [neu'tron] *nm* neutron

nevada [ne'βaða] *nf* snowstorm; (*caída de nieve*) snowfall

nevar [ne'βar] *vi* to snow

nevera [ne'βera] (*ESP*) *nf* refrigerator (*BRIT*), icebox (*US*)

nevería [neβe'ria] (*MÉX*) *nf* ice-cream parlour

nexo ['nekso] *nm* link, connection

ni [ni] *conj* nor, neither; (*tb*: **~ siquiera**) not … even; **~ aunque que** not even if; **~ blanco ~ negro** neither white nor black

Nicaragua [nika'raɣwa] *nf* Nicaragua; **nicaragüense** *adj, nmf* Nicaraguan

nicho ['nitʃo] *nm* niche

nicotina [niko'tina] *nf* nicotine

nido ['niðo] *nm* nest

niebla ['njeβla] *nf* fog; (*neblina*) mist

niego *etc vb* V **negar**

nieto, -a ['njeto, a] *nm/f* grandson/ daughter; **nietos** *nmpl* grandchildren

nieve *etc* ['njeβe] *vb* V **nevar** ▷ *nf* snow; (*MÉX: helado*) ice cream

NIF *nm abr* (= *Número de Identificación Fiscal*) *personal identification number used for financial and tax purposes*

ninfa ['ninfa] *nf* nymph

ningún *adj* V **ninguno**

ninguno, -a [nin'guno, a] (*adj* **ningún**) no *pron* (*nadie*) nobody; (*ni uno*) none, not one; (*ni uno ni otro*) neither; **de ninguna manera** by no means, not at all

niña ['nina] *nf* (*Anat*) pupil; V tb **niño**

niñera [ni'nera] *nf* nursemaid, nanny

niñez [ni'neθ] *nf* childhood; (*infancia*) infancy

niño, -a ['nino, a] *adj* (*joven*) young; (*inmaduro*) immature ▷ *nm/f* child, boy/girl

nipón, -ona [ni'pon, ona] *adj, nm/f* Japanese

níquel ['nikel] *nm* nickel

níspero ['nispero] *nm* medlar

nítido, -a [ni'tiðo, a] *adj* clear; sharp

nitrato [ni'trato] *nm* nitrate

nitrógeno [ni'troxeno] *nm* nitrogen

nivel [ni'βel] *nm* (*Geo*) level; (*norma*) level, standard; (*altura*) height; **nivel de aceite** oil level; **nivel de aire** spirit level; **nivel de vida** standard of living; **nivelar** *vt* to level out; (*fig*) to even up; (*Com*) to balance

no [no] *adv* no; not; (*con verbo*) not ▷ *excl* no!; **~ tengo nada** I don't have anything, I have nothing; **~ es el mío** it's not mine; **ahora ~** not now; **¿~ lo sabes?** don't you know?; **~ mucho** not much; **~ bien termine, lo entregaré** as soon as I finish, I'll hand it over; **~ más: ayer ~** not yesterday; **¡pase ~ más!** come in!; **¡a que ~ lo sabes!** I bet you don't know!; **¡cómo ~!** of course!; **la ~ intervención** non-intervention

noble ['noβle] *adj, nmf* noble; **nobleza** *nf* nobility

noche ['notʃe] *nf* night, night-time; (*la tarde*) evening; **de ~, por la ~** at night; **es de ~** it's dark; **Noche de San Juan** *see below*

NOCHE DE SAN JUAN

The **Noche de San Juan** on the 24th June is a **fiesta** coinciding with the summer solstice and which has taken the place of other ancient pagan festivals. Traditionally fire plays a major part in these festivities with celebrations and dancing taking place around bonfires in towns and villages across the country.

nochebuena [notʃe'βwena] *nf* Christmas Eve

● **NOCHEBUENA**
●
● Traditional Christmas celebrations in
● Spanish-speaking countries mainly
● take place on the night of **Nochebuena**,
● Christmas Eve. Families gather together
● for a large meal and the more religiously
● inclined attend Midnight Mass. While
● presents are traditionally given by **los**
● **Reyes Magos** on the 6th January, more
● and more people are exchanging gifts
● on Christmas Eve.

nochevieja [notʃe'βjexa] *nf* New Year's Eve

nocivo, -a [no'θiβo, a] *adj* harmful

noctámbulo, -a [nok'tambulo, a] *nm/f* sleepwalker

nocturno, -a [nok'turno, a] *adj (de la noche)* nocturnal, night *cpd; (de la tarde)* evening *cpd* ▷ *nm* nocturne

nogal [no'ɣal] *nm* walnut tree

nómada ['nomaða] *adj* nomadic ▷ *nmf* nomad

nombrar [nom'brar] *vt (designar)* to name; *(mencionar)* to mention; *(dar puesto a)* to appoint

nombre ['nombre] *nm* name; *(sustantivo)* noun; **~ y apellidos** name in full; **poner ~ a** to call, name; **nombre común/propio** common/proper noun; **nombre de pila/de soltera** Christian/maiden name

nómina ['nomina] *nf (lista)* payroll; *(hoja)* payslip

nominal [nomi'nal] *adj* nominal

nominar [nomi'nar] *vt* to nominate

nominativo, -a [nomina'tiβo, a] *adj (Com)*: **cheque ~ a X** cheque made out to X

nordeste [nor'ðeste] *adj* north-east, north-eastern, north-easterly ▷ *nm* north-east

nórdico, -a ['norðiko, a] *adj* Nordic

noreste [no'reste] *adj, nm* = **nordeste**

noria ['norja] *nf (Agr)* waterwheel; *(de carnaval)* big (BRIT) o Ferris (US) wheel

norma ['norma] *nf* rule (of thumb)

normal [nor'mal] *adj (corriente)* normal; *(habitual)* usual, natural; **normalizarse** *vr* to return to normal; **normalmente** *adv* normally

normativa [norma'tiβa] *nf* (set of) rules *pl*, regulations *pl*

noroeste [noro'este] *adj* north-west, north-western, north-westerly ▷ *nm* north-west

norte ['norte] *adj* north, northern, northerly ▷ *nm* north; *(fig)* guide

norteamericano, -a [norteameri'kano, a] *adj, nm/f* (North) American

Noruega [no'rweɣa] *nf* Norway

noruego, -a [no'rweɣo, a] *adj, nm/f* Norwegian

nos [nos] *pron (directo)* us; *(indirecto)* us; to us; for us; from us; *(reflexivo)* (to) ourselves; *(recíproco)* (to) each other; **~ levantamos a las 7** we get up at 7

nosotros, -as [no'sotros, as] *pron (sujeto)* we; *(después de prep)* us

nostalgia [nos'talxja] *nf* nostalgia

nota ['nota] *nf* note; *(Escol)* mark

notable [no'taβle] *adj* notable; *(Escol)* outstanding

notar [no'tar] *vt* to notice, note; **notarse** *vr* to be obvious; **se nota que ...** one observes that ...

notario [no'tarjo] *nm* notary

noticia [no'tiθja] *nf (información)* piece of news; **las ~s** the news *sg;* **tener ~s de algn** to hear from sb

❚ No confundir **noticia** con la palabra inglesa *notice*.

noticiero [noti'θjero] (LAM) *nm* news bulletin

notificar [notifi'kar] *vt* to notify, inform

notorio, -a [no'torjo, a] *adj (público)* well-known; *(evidente)* obvious

novato, -a [no'βato, a] *adj* inexperienced ▷ *nm/f* beginner, novice

novecientos, -as [noβe'θjentos, as] *num* nine hundred

novedad [noβe'ðað] *nf (calidad de nuevo)* newness; *(noticia)* piece of news; *(cambio)* change, (new) development

novel [no'βel] *adj* new; *(inexperto)* inexperienced ▷ *nmf* beginner

novela [no'βela] *nf* novel

noveno, -a [no'βeno, a] *adj* ninth

noventa [no'βenta] *num* ninety

novia *nf* V **novio**

novicio, -a [no'βiθjo, a] *nm/f* novice

noviembre [no'βjembre] *nm* November

novillada [noβi'ʎaða] *nf (Taur)* bullfight with young bulls; **novillero** *nm* novice bullfighter; **novillo** *nm* young bull, bullock; **hacer novillos** *(fam)* to play truant

novio, -a ['noβjo, a] *nm/f* boyfriend/girlfriend; *(prometido)* fiancé/fiancée; *(recién casado)* bridegroom/bride; **los ~s** the newly-weds

nube ['nuβe] *nf* cloud

nublado, -a [nu'βlaðo, a] *adj* cloudy; **nublarse** *vr* to grow dark

nubosidad [nuβosi'ðað] *nf* cloudiness;

había mucha ~ it was very cloudy

nuca ['nuka] *nf* nape of the neck

nuclear [nukle'ar] *adj* nuclear

núcleo ['nukleo] *nm* (*centro*) core; (*Física*) nucleus; **núcleo urbano** city centre

nudillo [nu'ðiʎo] *nm* knuckle

nudista [nu'ðista] *adj* nudist

nudo ['nuðo] *nm* knot; (*de carreteras*) junction

nuera ['nwera] *nf* daughter-in-law

nuestro, -a ['nwestro, a] *adj pos* our ▷ *pron* ours; **~ padre** our father; **un amigo ~** a friend of ours; **es el ~** it's ours

Nueva York [-'jɔrk] *n* New York

Nueva Zelanda [-θe'landa] *nf* New Zealand

nueve ['nweβe] *num* nine

nuevo, -a ['nweβo, a] *adj* (*gen*) new; **de ~** again

nuez [nweθ] *nf* walnut; (*Anat*) Adam's apple; **nuez moscada** nutmeg

nulo, -a ['nulo, a] *adj* (*inepto, torpe*) useless; (*inválido*) (null and) void; (*Deporte*) drawn, tied

núm. *abr* (= *número*) no.

numerar [nume'rar] *vt* to number

número ['numero] *nm* (*gen*) number; (*tamaño: de zapato*) size; (*ejemplar: de diario*) number, issue; **sin ~** numberless, unnumbered; **número atrasado** back number; **número de matrícula/teléfono** registration/telephone number; **número impar/par** odd/even number; **número romano** Roman numeral

numeroso, -a [nume'roso, a] *adj* numerous

nunca ['nunka] *adv* (*jamás*) never; **~ lo pensé** I never thought it; **no viene ~** he never comes; **~ más** never again; **más que ~** more than ever

nupcias ['nupθjas] *nfpl* wedding *sg*, nuptials

nutria ['nutrja] *nf* otter

nutrición [nutri'θjon] *nf* nutrition

nutrir [nu'trir] *vt* (*alimentar*) to nourish; (*dar de comer*) to feed; (*fig*) to strengthen; **nutritivo, -a** *adj* nourishing, nutritious

nylon [ni'lon] *nm* nylon

ñango, -a ['ɲango, a] (*MÉX*) *adj* puny

ñapa ['ɲapa] (*LAM*) *nf* extra

ñata ['ɲata] (*LAM: fam*) *nf* nose; *V tb* **ñato**

ñato, -a ['ɲato, a] (*LAM*) *adj* snub-nosed

ñoñería [ɲoɲe'ria] *nf* insipidness

ñoño, -a ['ɲoɲo, a] *adj* (*fam: tonto*) silly, stupid; (*soso*) insipid; (*persona*) spineless; (*ESP: película, novela*) sentimental

ñ

O

O abr (=oeste) W

o [o] conj or

oasis [o'asis] nm inv oasis

obcecarse [oβθe'karse] vr to get o become stubborn

obedecer [oβeðe'θer] vt to obey; **obediente** adj obedient

obertura [oβer'tura] nf overture

obeso, -a [o'βeso, a] adj obese

obispo [o'βispo] nm bishop

obituario [oβɪ'twarjo] (LAM) nm obituary

objetar [oβxe'tar] vt, vi to object

objetivo, -a [oβxe'tiβo, a] adj, nm objective

objeto [oβ'xeto] nm (cosa) object; (fin) aim

objetor, a [oβxe'tor, a] nm/f objector

obligación [oβliɣa'θjon] nf obligation; (Com) bond

obligar [oβli'ɣar] vt to force; **obligarse** vr to bind o.s.; **obligatorio, -a** adj compulsory, obligatory

oboe [o'βoe] nm oboe

obra ['oβra] nf work; (Arq) construction, building; (Teatro) play; **por ~ de** thanks to (the efforts of); **obra maestra** masterpiece; **obras públicas** public works; **obrar** vt to work; (tener efecto) to have an effect on ▷ vi to act, behave; (tener efecto) to have an effect; **la carta obra en su poder** the letter is in his/her possession

obrero, -a [o'βrero, a] adj (clase) working; (movimiento) labour cpd ▷ nm/f (gen) worker; (sin oficio) labourer

obsceno, -a [oβs'θeno, a] adj obscene

obscu... = oscu...

obsequiar [oβse'kjar] vt (ofrecer) to present with; (agasajar) to make a fuss of, lavish attention on; **obsequio** nm (regalo) gift; (cortesía) courtesy, attention

observación [oβserβa'θjon] nf observation; (reflexión) remark

observador, a [oβserβa'ðor, a] nm/f observer

observar [oβser'βar] vt to observe; (anotar) to notice; **observarse** vr to keep to, observe

obsesión [oβse'sjon] nf obsession; **obsesivo, -a** adj obsessive

obstáculo [oβs'takulo] nm obstacle; (impedimento) hindrance, drawback

obstante [oβs'tante]: **no ~** adv nevertheless

obstinado, -a [oβsti'naðo, a] adj obstinate, stubborn

obstinarse [oβsti'narse] vr to be obstinate; **~ en** to persist in

obstruir [oβstru'ir] vt to obstruct

obtener [oβte'ner] vt (gen) to obtain; (premio) to win

obturador [oβtura'ðor] nm (Foto) shutter

obvio, -a ['oββjo, a] adj obvious

oca ['oka] nf (animal) goose; (juego) ≈ snakes and ladders

ocasión [oka'sjon] nf (oportunidad) opportunity, chance; (momento) occasion, time; (causa) cause; **de ~** secondhand; **ocasionar** vt to cause

ocaso [o'kaso] nm (fig) decline

occidente [okθi'ðente] nm west

OCDE nf abr (=Organización de Cooperación y Desarrollo Económico) OECD

océano [o'θeano] nm ocean; **Océano Índico** Indian Ocean

ochenta [o'tʃenta] num eighty

ocho ['otʃo] num eight; **dentro de ~ días** within a week

ocio ['oθjo] nm (tiempo) leisure; (pey) idleness

octavilla [okta'viʎa] nf leaflet, pamphlet

octavo, -a [ok'taβo, a] adj eighth

octubre [ok'tuβre] nm October

oculista [oku'lista] nmf oculist

ocultar [okul'tar] vt (esconder) to hide; (callar) to conceal; **oculto, -a** adj hidden; (fig) secret

ocupación [okupa'θjon] nf occupation

ocupado, -a [oku'paðo, a] adj (persona) busy; (plaza) occupied, taken; (teléfono) engaged; **ocupar** vt (gen) to occupy; **ocuparse** vr: **ocuparse de o en** (gen) to concern o.s. with; (cuidar) to look after

ocurrencia [oku'rrenθja] nf (idea) bright idea

ocurrir [oku'rrir] vi to happen; **ocurrirse** vr: **se me ocurrió que ...** it occurred to me that ...

odiar [o'ðjar] vt to hate; **odio** nm hate, hatred; **odioso, -a** adj (gen) hateful; (malo) nasty

odontólogo, -a [oðon'toloɣo, a] nm/f dentist, dental surgeon

oeste [o'este] nm west; **una película del ~** a western

ofender [ofen'der] vt (agraviar) to offend; (insultar) to insult; **ofenderse** vr to take offence; **ofensa** nf offence; **ofensiva** nf offensive; **ofensivo, -a** adj offensive

oferta [o'ferta] nf offer; (propuesta) proposal; **la ~ y la demanda** supply and demand; **artículos en ~** goods on offer

oficial [ofi'θjal] adj official ▷ nm (Mil) officer

oficina [ofi'θina] nf office; **oficina de correos** post office; **oficina de información** information bureau; **oficina de turismo** tourist office; **oficinista** nmf clerk

oficio [o'fiθjo] nm (profesión) profession; (puesto) post; (Rel) service; **ser del ~** to be an old hand; **tener mucho ~** to have a lot of experience; **oficio de difuntos** funeral service

ofimática [ofi'matika] nf office automation

ofrecer [ofre'θer] vt (dar) to offer; (proponer) to propose; **ofrecerse** vr (persona) to offer o.s., volunteer; (situación) to present itself; **¿qué se le ofrece?, ¿se le ofrece algo?** what can I do for you?, can I get you anything?

ofrecimiento [ofreθi'mjento] nm offer

oftalmólogo, -a [oftal'moloɣo, a] nm/f ophthalmologist

oída [o'iða] nf: **de ~s** by hearsay

oído [o'iðo] nm (Anat) ear; (sentido) hearing

oigo etc vb V **oír**

oír [o'ir] vt (gen) to hear; (atender a) to listen to; **¡oiga!** listen!; **~ misa** to attend mass

OIT nf abr (= Organización Internacional del Trabajo) ILO

ojal [o'xal] nm buttonhole

ojalá [oxa'la] excl if only (it were so)!, some hope! ▷ conj if only ...!, would that ...!; **~ (que) venga hoy** I hope he comes today

ojeada [oxe'aða] nf glance

ojera [o'xera] nf: **tener ~s** to have bags under one's eyes

ojo [o'xo] nm eye; (de puente) span; (de cerradura) keyhole ▷ excl careful!; **tener ~ para** to have an eye for; **ojo de buey** porthole

okey [o'kei] (LAM) excl O.K.

okupa [o'kupa] (ESP: fam) nmf squatter

ola [o'la] nf wave

olé [o'le] excl bravo!, olé!

oleada [ole'aða] nf big wave, swell; (fig) wave

oleaje [ole'axe] nm swell

óleo [o'leo] nm oil; **oleoducto** nm (oil) pipeline

oler [o'ler] vt (gen) to smell; (inquirir) to pry into; (fig: sospechar) to sniff out ▷ vi to smell; **~ a** to smell of

olfatear [olfate'ar] vt to smell; (inquirir) to pry into; **olfato** nm sense of smell

olimpiada [olim'piaða] nf: **las O~s** the Olympics; **olímpico, -a** [o'limpiko, a] adj Olympic

oliva [o'liβa] nf (aceituna) olive; **aceite de ~** olive oil; **olivo** nm olive tree

olla [o'ʎa] nf pan; (comida) stew; **olla exprés** o **a presión** (ESP) pressure cooker; **olla podrida** type of Spanish stew

olmo [o'lmo] nm elm (tree)

olor [o'lor] nm smell; **oloroso, -a** adj scented

olvidar [olβi'ðar] vt to forget; (omitir) to omit; **olvidarse** vr (fig) to forget o.s.; **se me olvidó** I forgot

olvido [ol'βiðo] nm oblivion; (despiste) forgetfulness

ombligo [om'bliɣo] nm navel

omelette [ome'lete] (LAM) nf omelet(te)

omisión [omi'sjon] nf (abstención) omission; (descuido) neglect

omiso, -a [o'miso, a] adj: **hacer caso ~ de** to ignore, pass over

omitir [omi'tir] vt to omit

omnipotente [omnipo'tente] adj omnipotent

omóplato [o'moplato] nm shoulder blade

OMS nf abr (= Organización Mundial de la Salud) WHO

once [on'θe] num eleven; **onces** (cs) nfpl tea break sg

onda [on'da] nf wave; **onda corta/larga/media** short/long/medium wave; **ondear** vt, vi to wave; (tener ondas) to be wavy; (agua) to ripple

ondulación [ondula'θjon] nf undulation; **ondulado, -a** adj wavy

ONG nf abr (= organización no gubernamental) NGO

ONU nf abr (= Organización de las Naciones Unidas) UNO

opaco, -a [o'pako, a] adj opaque

opción [op'θjon] nf (gen) option; (derecho) right, option

OPEP ['opep] nf abr (= Organización de Países Exportadores de Petróleo) OPEC

ópera ['opera] nf opera; **ópera bufa** o **cómica** comic opera

operación [opera'θjon] nf (gen) operation; (Com) transaction, deal

operador, a [opera'ðor, a] nm/f operator; (Cine: de proyección) projectionist; (: de rodaje) cameraman

operar [ope'rar] vt (*producir*) to produce, bring about; (*Med*) to operate on ▷ vi (*Com*) to operate, deal; **operarse** vr to occur; (*Med*) to have an operation

opereta [ope'reta] nf operetta

opinar [opi'nar] vt to think ▷ vi to give one's opinion; **opinión** nf (*creencia*) belief; (*criterio*) opinion

opio ['opjo] nm opium

oponer [opo'ner] vt (*resistencia*) to put up, offer; **oponerse** vr (*objetar*) to object; (*estar frente a frente*) to be opposed; (*dos personas*) to oppose each other; **~ A a B** to set A against B; **me opongo a pensar que ...** I refuse to believe o think that ...

oportunidad [oportuni'ðað] nf (*ocasión*) opportunity; (*posibilidad*) chance

oportuno, -a [opor'tuno, a] adj (*en su tiempo*) opportune, timely; (*respuesta*) suitable; **en el momento ~** at the right moment

oposición [oposi'θjon] nf opposition; **oposiciones** nfpl (*Escol*) public examinations

opositor, a [oposi'tor, a] nm/f (*adversario*) opponent; (*candidato*) **~ (a)** candidate (for)

opresión [opre'sjon] nf oppression; **opresor, a** nm/f oppressor

oprimir [opri'mir] vt to squeeze; (*fig*) to oppress

optar [op'tar] vi (*elegir*) to choose; **~ por** to opt for; **optativo, -a** adj optional

óptico, -a ['optiko, a] adj optic(al) ▷ nm/f optician; **óptica** nf optician's (shop); **desde esta óptica** from this point of view

optimismo [opti'mismo] nm optimism; **optimista** nmf optimist

opuesto, -a [o'pwesto, a] adj (*contrario*) opposite; (*antagónico*) opposing

oración [ora'θjon] nf (*Rel*) prayer; (*Ling*) sentence

orador, a [ora'ðor, a] nm/f (*conferenciante*) speaker, orator

oral [o'ral] adj oral

orangután [orangu'tan] nm orangutan

orar [o'rar] vi to pray

oratoria [ora'torja] nf oratory

órbita ['orβita] nf orbit

orden ['orðen] nm (*gen*) order ▷ nf (*gen*) order; (*Inform*) command; **en ~ de prioridad** in order of priority; **orden del día** agenda

ordenado, -a [orðe'naðo, a] adj (*metódico*) methodical; (*arreglado*) orderly

ordenador [orðena'ðor] nm computer; **ordenador central** mainframe computer

ordenar [orðe'nar] vt (*mandar*) to order; (*poner orden*) to put in order, arrange;

ordenarse vr (*Rel*) to be ordained

ordeñar [orðe'ɲar] vt to milk

ordinario, -a [orði'narjo, a] adj (*común*) ordinary, usual; (*vulgar*) vulgar, common

orégano [o'reɣano] nm oregano

oreja [o'rexa] nf ear; (*Mecánica*) lug, flange

orfanato [orfa'nato] nm orphanage

orfebrería [orfeβre'ria] nf gold/silver work

orgánico, -a [or'ɣaniko, a] adj organic

organismo [orɣa'nismo] nm (*Bio*) organism; (*Pol*) organization

organización [orɣaniθa'θjon] nf organization; **organizar** vt to organize

órgano ['orɣano] nm organ

orgasmo [or'ɣasmo] nm orgasm

orgía [or'xia] nf orgy

orgullo [or'ɣuʎo] nm pride; **orgulloso, -a** adj (*gen*) proud; (*altanero*) haughty

orientación [orjenta'θjon] nf (*posición*) position; (*dirección*) direction

oriental [orjen'tal] adj eastern; (*del Extremo Oriente*) oriental

orientar [orjen'tar] vt (*situar*) to orientate; (*señalar*) to point; (*dirigir*) to direct; (*guiar*) to guide; **orientarse** vr to get one's bearings

oriente [o'rjente] nm east; **el O~ Medio** the Middle East; **el Próximo/Extremo O~** the Near/Far East

origen [o'rixen] nm origin

original [orixi'nal] adj (*nuevo*) original; (*extraño*) odd, strange; **originalidad** nf originality

originar [orixi'nar] vt to start, cause; **originarse** vr to originate; **originario, -a** adj original; **originario de** native of

orilla [o'riʎa] nf (*borde*) border; (*de río*) bank; (*de bosque, tela*) edge; (*de mar*) shore

orina [o'rina] nf urine; **orinal** nm (*chamber*) pot; **orinar** vi to urinate; **orinarse** vr to wet o.s.

oro ['oro] nm gold; **oros** nmpl (*Naipes*) hearts

orquesta [or'kesta] nf orchestra; **orquesta sinfónica** symphony orchestra

orquídea [or'kiðea] nf orchid

ortiga [or'tiɣa] nf nettle

ortodoxo, -a [orto'ðokso, a] adj orthodox

ortografía [ortoɣra'fia] nf spelling

ortopedia [orto'peðja] nf orthopaedics sg; **ortopédico, -a** adj orthopaedic

oruga [o'ruɣa] nf caterpillar

orzuelo [or'θwelo] nm stye

os [os] pron (*gen*) you; (*a vosotros*) to you

osa ['osa] nf (she-)bear; **Osa Mayor/ Menor** Great/Little Bear

osadía [osa'ðia] nf daring
osar [o'sar] vi to dare
oscilación [osθila'θjon] nf (movimiento) oscillation; (fluctuación) fluctuation
oscilar [osθi'lar] vi to oscillate; to fluctuate
oscurecer [oskure'θer] vt to darken ▷ vi to grow dark; **oscurecerse** vr to grow o get dark
oscuridad [oskuri'ðað] nf obscurity; (tinieblas) darkness
oscuro, -a [os'kuro, a] adj dark; (fig) obscure; **a oscuras** in the dark
óseo, -a ['oseo, a] adj bone cpd
oso ['oso] nm bear; **oso de peluche** teddy bear; **oso hormiguero** anteater
ostentar [osten'tar] vt (gen) to show; (pey) to flaunt, show off; (poseer) to have, possess
ostión [os'tjon] (MÉX) nm = **ostra**
ostra ['ostra] nf oyster
OTAN ['otan] nf abr (= Organización del Tratado del Atlántico Norte) NATO
otitis [o'titis] nf earache
otoñal [oto'ɲal] adj autumnal
otoño [o'toɲo] nm autumn
otorgar [otor'ɣar] vt (conceder) to concede; (dar) to grant
otorrino, -a [oto'rrino, a], **otorrinolaringólogo, -a** [otorrinolarin'goloɣo, a] nm/f ear, nose and throat specialist

○ **PALABRA CLAVE**

otro, -a ['otro, a] adj **1** (distinto: sg) another; (: pl) other; **con otros amigos** with other o different friends
2 (adicional): **tráigame otro café (más), por favor** can I have another coffee please; **otros diez días más** another ten days
▷ pron **1** **el otro** the other one; **(los) otros** (the) others; **de otro** somebody else's; **que lo haga otro** let somebody else do it
2 (recíproco): **se odian (la) una a (la) otra** they hate one another o each other
3: **otro tanto: comer otro tanto** to eat the same o as much again; **recibió una decena de telegramas y otras tantas llamadas** he got about ten telegrams and as many calls

ovación [oβa'θjon] nf ovation
oval [o'βal] adj oval; **ovalado, -a** adj oval; **óvalo** nm oval
ovario [o'βario] nm ovary
oveja [o'βexa] nf sheep
overol [oβe'rol] (LAM) nm overalls pl
ovillo [o'βiʎo] nm (de lana) ball of wool
OVNI ['oβni] nm abr (= objeto volante no identificado) UFO
ovulación [oβula'θjon] nf ovulation; **óvulo** nm ovum
oxidación [oksiða'θjon] nf rusting
oxidar [oksi'ðar] vt to rust; **oxidarse** vr to go rusty
óxido ['oksiðo] nm oxide
oxigenado, -a [oksixe'naðo, a] adj (Quím) oxygenated; (pelo) bleached
oxígeno [ok'sixeno] nm oxygen
oyente [o'jente] nmf listener
oyes etc vb V **oír**
ozono [o'θono] nm ozone

o

P

pabellón [paβe'ʎon] *nm* bell tent; (*Arq*) pavilion; (*de hospital etc*) block, section; (*bandera*) flag
pacer [pa'θer] *vi* to graze
paciencia [pa'θjenθja] *nf* patience
paciente [pa'θjente] *adj, nmf* patient
pacificación [paθifika'θjon] *nf* pacification
pacífico, -a [pa'θifiko, a] *adj* (*persona*) peaceable; (*existencia*) peaceful; **el (Océano) P~** the Pacific (Ocean)
pacifista [paθi'fista] *nmf* pacifist
pacotilla [pako'tiʎa] *nf*: **de ~** (*actor, escritor*) third-rate
pactar [pak'tar] *vt* to agree to o on ▷ *vi* to come to an agreement
pacto ['pakto] *nm* (*tratado*) pact; (*acuerdo*) agreement
padecer [paðe'θer] *vt* (*sufrir*) to suffer; (*soportar*) to endure, put up with; **padecimiento** *nm* suffering
padrastro [pa'ðrastro] *nm* stepfather
padre ['paðre] *nm* father ▷ *adj* (*fam*): **un éxito ~** a tremendous success; **padres** *nmpl* parents; **padre político** father-in-law
padrino [pa'ðrino] *nm* (*Rel*) godfather; (*tb*: **~ de boda**) best man; (*fig*) sponsor, patron; **padrinos** *nmpl* godparents
padrón [pa'ðron] *nm* (*censo*) census, roll
padrote [pa'ðrote] (*MÉX: fam*) *nm* pimp
paella [pa'eʎa] *nf* paella, dish of rice with meat, shellfish etc
paga ['paɣa] *nf* (*pago*) payment; (*sueldo*) pay, wages *pl*
pagano, -a [pa'ɣano, a] *adj, nm/f* pagan, heathen
pagar [pa'ɣar] *vt* to pay; (*las compras, crimen*) to pay for; (*fig: favor*) to repay ▷ *vi* to pay; **~ al contado/a plazos** to pay (in) cash/ in instalments
pagaré [paɣa're] *nm* I.O.U.

página ['paxina] *nf* page; **página de inicio** (*Inform*) home page; **página web** (*Inform*) web page
pago ['paɣo] *nm* (*dinero*) payment; **en ~ de** in return for; **pago anticipado/a cuenta/ contra reembolso/en especie** advance payment/payment on account/cash on delivery/payment in kind
pág(s). *abr* (= *página(s)*) p(p).
pague *etc vb* V **pagar**
país [pa'is] *nm* (*gen*) country; (*región*) land; **los P~es Bajos** the Low Countries; **el P~ Vasco** the Basque Country
paisaje [pai'saxe] *nm* landscape, scenery
paisano, -a [pai'sano, a] *adj* of the same country ▷ *nm/f* (*compatriota*) fellow countryman/woman; **vestir de ~** (*soldado*) to be in civvies; (*guardia*) to be in plain clothes
paja ['paxa] *nf* straw; (*fig*) rubbish (*BRIT*), trash (*US*)
pajarita [paxa'rita] *nf* (*corbata*) bow tie
pájaro ['paxaro] *nm* bird; **pájaro carpintero** woodpecker
pajita [pa'xita] *nf* (*drinking*) straw
pala ['pala] *nf* spade, shovel; (*raqueta etc*) bat; (: *de tenis*) racquet; (*Culin*) slice; **pala mecánica** power shovel
palabra [pa'laβra] *nf* word; (*facultad*) (power of) speech; (*derecho de hablar*) right to speak; **tomar la ~** (*en mitin*) to take the floor
palabrota [pala'βrota] *nf* swearword
palacio [pa'laθjo] *nm* palace; (*mansión*) mansion, large house; **palacio de justicia** courthouse; **palacio municipal** town o city hall
paladar [pala'ðar] *nm* palate; **paladear** *vt* to taste
palanca [pa'lanka] *nf* lever; (*fig*) pull, influence
palangana [palan'gana] *nf* washbasin
palco ['palko] *nm* box
Palestina [pales'tina] *nf* Palestine; **palestino, -a** *nm/f* Palestinian
paleta [pa'leta] *nf* (*de pintor*) palette; (*de albañil*) trowel; (*de ping-pong*) bat; (*MÉX, CAM: helado*) ice lolly (*BRIT*), Popsicle® (*US*)
palidecer [paliðe'θer] *vi* to turn pale; **palidez** *nf* paleness; **pálido, -a** *adj* pale
palillo [pa'liʎo] *nm* (*mondadientes*) toothpick; (*para comer*) chopstick
palito [pa'lito] (*RPL*) *nm* (*helado*) ice lolly (*BRIT*), Popsicle® (*US*)
paliza [pa'liθa] *nf* beating, thrashing
palma ['palma] *nf* (*Anat*) palm; (*árbol*) palm tree; **batir o dar ~s** to clap, applaud; **palmada** *nf* slap; **palmadas** *nfpl* clapping

sg, applause *sg*

palmar [pal'mar] (*fam*) *vi* (*tb*: **~la**) to die, kick the bucket

palmear [palme'ar] *vi* to clap

palmera [pal'mera] *nf* (*Bot*) palm tree

palmo ['palmo] *nm* (*medida*) span; (*fig*) small amount; **~ a ~** inch by inch

palo ['palo] *nm* stick; (*poste*) post; (*de tienda de campaña*) pole; (*mango*) handle, shaft; (*golpe*) blow, hit; (*de golf*) club; (*de béisbol*) bat; (*Náut*) mast; (*Naipes*) suit

paloma [pa'loma] *nf* dove, pigeon

palomitas [palo'mitas] *nfpl* popcorn *sg*

palpar [pal'par] *vt* to touch, feel

palpitar [palpi'tar] *vi* to palpitate; (*latir*) to beat

palta ['palta] (*cs*) *nf* avocado

paludismo [palu'ðismo] *nm* malaria

pamela [pa'mela] *nf* picture hat, sun hat

pampa ['pampa] *nf* pampas, prairie

pan [pan] *nm* bread; (*una barra*) loaf; **pan integral** wholemeal (*BRIT*) o wholewheat (*US*) bread; **pan rallado** breadcrumbs *pl*; **pan tostado** (*MÉX*: *tostada*) toast

pana ['pana] *nf* corduroy

panadería [panaðe'ria] *nf* baker's (shop); **panadero, -a** *nm/f* baker

Panamá [pana'ma] *nm* Panama; **panameño, -a** *adj* Panamanian

pancarta [pan'karta] *nf* placard, banner

panceta [pan'θeta] (*ESP, RPL*) *nf* bacon

pancho ['pantʃo] (*RPL*) *nm* hot dog

pancito [pan'θito] *nm* (bread) roll

panda ['panda] *nm* (*Zool*) panda

pandereta [pande'reta] *nf* tambourine

pandilla [pan'diʎa] *nf* set, group; (*de criminales*) gang; (*pey*: *camarilla*) clique

panecillo [pane'θiʎo] (*ESP*) *nm* (bread) roll

panel [pa'nel] *nm* panel; **panel solar** solar panel

panfleto [pan'fleto] *nm* pamphlet

pánico ['paniko] *nm* panic

panorama [pano'rama] *nm* panorama; (*vista*) view

panqueque [pan'keke] (*LAM*) *nm* pancake

pantalla [pan'taʎa] *nf* (*de cine*) screen; (*de lámpara*) lampshade

pantalón [panta'lon] *nm* trousers; **pantalones** *nmpl* trousers; **pantalones cortes** shorts

pantano [pan'tano] *nm* (*ciénaga*) marsh, swamp; (*depósito: de agua*) reservoir; (*fig*) jam, difficulty

panteón [pante'on] *nm* (*monumento*) pantheon

pantera [pan'tera] *nf* panther

pantimedias [panti'meðjas] (*MÉX*) *nfpl*

= pantis

pantis ['pantis] *nmpl* tights (*BRIT*), pantyhose (*US*)

pantomima [panto'mima] *nf* pantomime

pantorrilla [panto'rriʎa] *nf* calf (of the leg)

pants [pants] (*MÉX*) *nmpl* tracksuit (*BRIT*), sweat suit (*US*)

pantufla [pan'tufla] *nf* slipper

panty(s) ['panti(s)] *nm(pl)* tights (*BRIT*), pantyhose (*US*)

panza ['panθa] *nf* belly, paunch

pañal [pa'ɲal] *nm* nappy (*BRIT*), diaper (*US*); **pañales** *nmpl* (*fig*) early stages, infancy *sg*

paño ['paɲo] *nm* (*tela*) cloth; (*pedazo de tela*) (piece of) cloth; (*trapo*) duster, rag; **paños menores** underclothes

pañuelo [pa'ɲwelo] *nm* handkerchief, hanky; (*fam*: *para la cabeza*) (head)scarf

papa ['papa] *nm*: **el P~** the Pope ▷ *nf* (*LAM*: *patata*) potato; **papas fritas** (*LAM*) French fries, chips (*BRIT*); (*de bolsa*) crisps (*BRIT*), potato chips (*US*)

papá [pa'pa] (*fam*) *nm* dad(dy), pa (*US*)

papada [pa'paða] *nf* double chin

papagayo [papa'xajo] *nm* parrot

papalote [papa'lote] (*MÉX, CAM*) *nm* kite

papanatas [papa'natas] (*fam*) *nm inv* simpleton

papaya [pa'paja] *nf* papaya

papear [pape'ar] (*fam*) *vt, vi* to scoff

papel [pa'pel] *nm* paper; (*hoja de papel*) sheet of paper; (*Teatro*: fig) role; **papel de aluminio** aluminium (*BRIT*) o aluminum (*US*) foil; **papel de arroz/envolver/fumar** rice/wrapping/cigarette paper; **papel de estaño** o **plata** tinfoil; **papel de lija** sandpaper; **papel higiénico** toilet paper; **papel moneda** paper money; **papel secante** blotting paper

papeleo [pape'leo] *nm* red tape

papelera [pape'lera] *nf* wastepaper basket; (*en la calle*) litter bin; **papelera (de reciclaje)** (*Inform*) wastebasket

papelería [papele'ria] *nf* stationer's (shop)

papeleta [pape'leta] (*ESP*) *nf* (*Pol*) ballot paper

paperas [pa'peras] *nfpl* mumps *sg*

papilla [pa'piʎa] *nf* (*de bebé*) baby food

paquete [pa'kete] *nm* (*de cigarrillos etc*) packet; (*Correos etc*) parcel

par [par] *adj* (*igual*) like, equal; (*Mat*) even ▷ *nm* equal; (*de guantes*) pair; (*de veces*) couple; (*Pol*) peer; (*Golf, Com*) par; **abrir de ~ en ~** to open wide

para ['para] *prep* for; **no es ~ comer** it's not for eating; **decir ~ sí** to say to o.s.; **¿~ qué lo quieres?** what do you want it for?; **se casaron ~ separarse otra vez** they married only to separate again; **lo tendré ~ mañana** I'll have it (for) tomorrow; **ir ~ casa** to go home, head for home; **~ profesor es muy estúpido** he's very stupid for a teacher; **¿quién es usted ~ gritar así?** who are you to shout like that?; **tengo bastante ~ vivir** I have enough to live on; *V tb* **con**

parabién [para'βjen] *nm* congratulations *pl*

parábola [pa'raβola] *nf* parable; (*Mat*) parabola; **parabólica** *nf* (*tb:* **antena parabólica**) satellite dish

parabrisas [para'βrisas] *nm inv* windscreen (*BRIT*), windshield (*US*)

paracaídas [paraka'iðas] *nm inv* parachute; **paracaidista** *nmf* parachutist; (*Mil*) paratrooper

parachoques [para'tʃokes] *nm inv* (*Auto*) bumper; (*Mecánica etc*) shock absorber

parada [pa'raða] *nf* stop; (*acto*) stopping; (*de industria*) shutdown, stoppage; (*lugar*) stopping place; **parada de autobús** bus stop; **parada de taxis** taxi stand *o* rank (*BRIT*)

paradero [para'ðero] *nm* stopping-place; (*situación*) whereabouts

parado, -a [pa'raðo, a] *adj* (*persona*) motionless, standing still; (*fábrica*) closed, at a standstill; (*coche*) stopped; (*LAM: de pie*) standing (up); (*ESP: sin empleo*) unemployed, idle

paradoja [para'ðoxa] *nf* paradox

parador [para'ðor] *nm* parador, state-run hotel

paragolpes [para'golpes] (*RPL*) *nm inv* (*Auto*) bumper, fender (*US*)

paraguas [pa'raxwas] *nm inv* umbrella

Paraguay [para'ɣwai] *nm* Paraguay; **paraguayo, -a** *adj, nm/f* Paraguayan

paraíso [para'iso] *nm* paradise, heaven

paraje [pa'raxe] *nm* place, spot

paralelo, -a [para'lelo, a] *adj* parallel

parálisis [pa'ralisis] *nf inv* paralysis; **paralítico, -a** *adj, nm/f* paralytic

paralizar [parali'θar] *vt* to paralyse; **paralizarse** *vr* to become paralysed; (*fig*) to come to a standstill

páramo ['paramo] *nm* bleak plateau

paranoico, -a [para'noiko, a] *nm/f* paranoiac

parapente [para'pente] *nm* (*deporte*) paragliding; (*aparato*) paraglider

parapléjico, -a [para'plexiko, a] *adj, nm/f* paraplegic

parar [pa'rar] *vt* to stop; (*golpe*) to ward off ▷ *vi* to stop; **pararse** *vr* to stop; (*LAM: ponerse de pie*) to stand up; **ha parado de llover** it has stopped raining; **van a ir a ~ a comisaría** they're going to end up in the police station; **~se en** to pay attention to

pararrayos [para'rrajos] *nm inv* lightning conductor

parásito, -a [pa'rasito, a] *nm/f* parasite

parcela [par'θela] *nf* plot, piece of ground

parche ['partʃe] *nm* (*gen*) patch

parchís [par'tʃis] *nm* ludo

parcial [par'θjal] *adj* (*pago*) part-; (*eclipse*) partial; (*Jur*) prejudiced, biased; (*Pol*) partisan

parecer [pare'θer] *nm* (*opinión*) opinion, view; (*aspecto*) looks *pl* ▷ *vi* (*tener apariencia*) to seem, look; (*asemejarse*) to look *o* seem like; (*aparecer, llegar*) to appear; **parecerse** *vr* to look alike, resemble each other; **al ~** apparently; **según parece** evidently, apparently; **~se a** to look like, resemble; **me parece que** I think (that), it seems to me that

parecido, -a [pare'θiðo, a] *adj* similar ▷ *nm* similarity, likeness, resemblance; **bien ~** good-looking, nice-looking

pared [pa'reð] *nf* wall

pareja [pa'rexa] *nf* (*par*) pair; (*dos personas*) couple; (*otro: de un par*) other one (of a pair); (*persona*) partner

parentesco [paren'tesko] *nm* relationship

paréntesis [pa'rentesis] *nm inv* parenthesis; (*en escrito*) bracket

parezco *etc vb V* **parecer**

pariente [pa'rjente] *nmf* relative, relation

▌ No confundir **pariente** con la palabra inglesa *parent*.

parir [pa'rir] *vt* to give birth to ▷ *vi* (*mujer*) to give birth, have a baby

París [pa'ris] *n* Paris

parka ['parka] (*LAM*) *nf* anorak

parking ['parkin] *nm* car park (*BRIT*), parking lot (*US*)

parlamentar [parlamen'tar] *vi* to parley

parlamentario, -a [parlamen'tarjo, a] *adj* parliamentary ▷ *nm/f* member of parliament

parlamento [parla'mento] *nm* parliament

parlanchín, -ina [parlan'tʃin, ina] *adj* indiscreet ▷ *nm/f* chatterbox

parlar [par'lar] *vi* to chatter (away)

paro ['paro] *nm* (*huelga*) stoppage (of work), strike; (*ESP: desempleo*) unemployment; (: *subsidio*) unemployment benefit; **estar en ~** (*ESP*) to be unemployed;

paro cardíaco cardiac arrest

parodia [pa'roðja] nf parody; **parodiar** vt to parody

parpadear [parpaðe'ar] vi (ojos) to blink; (luz) to flicker

párpado ['parpaðo] nm eyelid

parque ['parke] nm (lugar verde) park; (MÉX: munición) ammunition; **parque de atracciones** fairground; **parque de bomberos** (ESP) fire station; **parque infantil/temático/zoológico** playground/theme park/zoo

parqué [par'ke] nm parquet (flooring)

parquímetro [par'kimetro] nm parking meter

parra ['parra] nf (grape)vine

párrafo ['parrafo] nm paragraph; **echar un ~** (fam) to have a chat

parranda [pa'rranda] (fam) nf spree, binge

parrilla [pa'rriʎa] nf (Culin) grill; (de coche) grille; **(carne a la) ~** barbecue; **parrillada** nf barbecue

párroco ['parroko] nm parish priest

parroquia [pa'rrokja] nf parish; (iglesia) parish church; (Com) clientele, customers pl; **parroquiano, -a** nm/f parishioner; (Com) client, customer

parte ['parte] nm message; (informe) report ▷ nf part; (lado, cara) side; (de reparto) share; (Jur) party; **en alguna ~ de Europa** somewhere in Europe; **en o por todas ~s** everywhere; **en gran ~** to a large extent; **la mayor ~ de los españoles** most Spaniards; **de un tiempo a esta ~** for some time past; **de ~ de algn** on sb's behalf; **¿de ~ de quién?** (Tel) who is speaking?; **por ~ de** on the part of; **yo por mi ~** I for my part; **por otra ~** on the other hand; **dar ~** to inform; **tomar ~** to take part; **parte meteorológico** weather forecast o report

participación [partiθipa'θjon] nf (acto) participation, taking part; (parte, Com) share; (de lotería) shared prize; (aviso) notice, notification

participante [partiθi'pante] nmf participant

participar [partiθi'par] vt to notify, inform ▷ vi to take part, participate

partícipe [par'tiθipe] nmf participant

particular [partiku'lar] adj (especial) particular, special; (individual, personal) private, personal ▷ nm (punto, asunto) particular, point; (individuo) individual; **tiene coche ~** he has a car of his own

partida [par'tiða] nf (salida) departure; (Com) entry, item; (juego) game; (grupo de personas) band, group; **mala ~** dirty trick;

partida de nacimiento/matrimonio/defunción (ESP) birth/marriage/death certificate

partidario, -a [parti'ðarjo, a] adj partisan ▷ nm/f supporter, follower

partido [par'tiðo] nm (Pol) party; (Deporte) game, match; **sacar ~ de** to profit o benefit from; **tomar ~** to take sides

partir [par'tir] vt (dividir) to split, divide; (compartir, distribuir) to share (out), distribute; (romper) to break open, split open; (rebanada) to cut (off) ▷ vi (ponerse en camino) to set off o out; (comenzar) to start (off o out); **partirse** vr to crack o split o break (in two etc); **a ~ de** (starting) from

partitura [parti'tura] nf (Mús) score

parto ['parto] nm birth; (fig) product, creation; **estar de ~** to be in labour

parvulario [parβu'larjo] (ESP) nm nursery school, kindergarten

pasa ['pasa] nf raisin; **pasa de Corinto** currant

pasacintas [pasa'θintas] (LAM) nm cassette player

pasada [pa'saða] nf passing, passage; **de ~** in passing, incidentally; **una mala ~** a dirty trick

pasadizo [pasa'ðiθo] nm (pasillo) passage, corridor; (callejuela) alley

pasado, -a [pa'saðo, a] adj past; (malo: comida, fruta) bad; (muy cocido) overdone; (anticuado) out of date ▷ nm past; **~ mañana** the day after tomorrow; **el mes ~** last month

pasador [pasa'ðor] nm (cerrojo) bolt; (de pelo) hair slide; (horquilla) grip

pasaje [pa'saxe] nm passage; (pago de viaje) fare; (los pasajeros) passengers pl; (pasillo) passageway

pasajero, -a [pasa'xero, a] adj passing; (situación, estado) temporary; (amor, enfermedad) brief ▷ nm/f passenger

pasamontañas [pasamon'taɲas] nm inv balaclava helmet

pasaporte [pasa'porte] nm passport

pasar [pa'sar] vt (tiempo) to pass; (desgracias) to suffer, endure; (noticia) to give, pass on; (río) to cross; (barrera) to pass through; (falta) to overlook, tolerate; (contrincante) to surpass, do better than; (coche) to overtake; (Cine) to show; (enfermedad) to give, infect with ▷ vi (gen) to pass; (terminarse) to be over; (ocurrir) to happen; **pasarse** vr (flores) to fade; (comida) to go bad o off; (fig) to overdo it, go too far; **~ de** to go beyond, exceed; **~ por** (LAM) to fetch; **~lo bien/mal** to have a good/bad time; **¡pase!** come in!; **hacer ~** to show in;

P

lo que pasa es que ... the thing is ...; **~se al enemigo** to go over to the enemy; **se me pasó** I forgot; **no se le pasa nada** he misses nothing; **pase lo que pase** come what may; **¿qué pasa?** what's going on?, what's up?; **¿qué te pasa?** what's wrong?

pasarela [pasa'rela] nf footbridge; (en barco) gangway

pasatiempo [pasa'tjempo] nm pastime, hobby

Pascua ['paskwa] nf (en Semana Santa) Easter; **Pascuas** nfpl Christmas (time); **¡felices ~s!** Merry Christmas!

pase ['pase] nm pass; (Cine) performance, showing

pasear [pase'ar] vt to take for a walk; (exhibir) to parade, show off ▷ vi to walk, go for a walk; **pasearse** vr to walk, go for a walk; **~ en coche** to go for a drive; **paseo** nm (avenida) avenue; (distancia corta) walk, stroll; **dar un o ir de paseo** to go for a walk; **paseo marítimo** (ESP) promenade

pasillo [pa'siʎo] nm passage, corridor

pasión [pa'sjon] nf passion

pasivo, -a [pa'siβo, a] adj passive; (inactivo) inactive ▷ nm (Com) liabilities pl, debts pl

pasmoso, -a [pas'moso, a] adj amazing, astonishing

paso, -a ['paso, a] adj dried ▷ nm step; (modo de andar) walk; (huella) footprint; (rapidez) speed, pace, rate; (camino accesible) way through, passage; (cruce) crossing; (pasaje) passing, passage; (Geo) pass; (estrecho) strait; **a ese ~** (fig) at that rate; **salir al ~ de** o **a** to waylay; **estar de ~** to be passing through; **prohibido el ~** no entry; **ceda el ~** give way; **paso a nivel** (Ferro) level-crossing; **paso (de) cebra** (ESP) zebra crossing; **paso de peatones** pedestrian crossing; **paso elevado** flyover

pasota [pa'sota] (ESP: fam) adj, nmf ≈ dropout; **ser un ~** to be a bit of a dropout; (ser indiferente) not to care about anything

pasta ['pasta] nf paste; (Culin: masa) dough; (: de bizcochos etc) pastry; (fam) dough; **pastas** nfpl (bizcochos) pastries, small cakes; (fideos, espaguetis etc) pasta; **pasta dentífrica** o **de dientes** toothpaste

pastar [pas'tar] vi, vt to graze

pastel [pas'tel] nm (dulce) cake; (Arte) pastel; **pastel de carne** meat pie; **pastelería** nf cake shop

pastilla [pas'tiʎa] nf (de jabón, chocolate) bar; (píldora) tablet, pill

pasto ['pasto] nm (hierba) grass; (lugar) pasture, field; **pastor, a** [pas'tor, a] nm/f shepherd/ess ▷ nm (Rel) clergyman, pastor;

pastor alemán Alsatian

pata ['pata] nf (pierna) leg; (pie) foot; (de muebles) leg; **~s arriba** upside down; **metedura de ~** (fam) gaffe; **meter la ~** (fam) to put one's foot in it; **tener buena/mala ~** to be lucky/unlucky; **pata de cabra** (Tec) crowbar; **patada** nf kick; (en el suelo) stamp

patata [pa'tata] nf potato; **patatas fritas** chips, French fries; (de bolsa) crisps

paté [pa'te] nm pâté

patente [pa'tente] adj obvious, evident; (Com) patent ▷ nf patent

paternal [pater'nal] adj fatherly, paternal; **paterno, -a** adj paternal

patético, -a [pa'tetiko, a] adj pathetic, moving

patilla [pa'tiʎa] nf (de gafas) side (piece); **patillas** nfpl sideburns

patín [pa'tin] nm skate; (de trineo) runner; **patín de ruedas** roller skate; **patinaje** nm skating; **patinar** vi to skate; (resbalarse) to skid, slip; (fam) to slip up, blunder

patineta [pati'neta] nf (MÉX: patinete) scooter; (CS: monopatín) skateboard

patinete [pati'nete] nm scooter

patio ['patjo] nm (de casa) patio, courtyard; **patio de recreo** playground

pato ['pato] nm duck; **pagar el ~** (fam) to take the blame, carry the can

patoso, -a [pa'toso, a] (fam) adj clumsy

patotero [pato'tero] (cs) nm hooligan, lout

patraña [pa'traɲa] nf story, fib

patria ['patrja] nf native land, mother country

patrimonio [patri'monjo] nm inheritance; (fig) heritage

patriota [pa'trjota] nmf patriot

patrocinar [patroθi'nar] vt to sponsor

patrón, -ona [pa'tron, ona] nm/f (jefe) boss, chief, master (mistress); (propietario) landlord/lady; (Rel) patron saint ▷ nm (Tec, Costura) pattern

patronato [patro'nato] nm sponsorship; (acto) patronage; (fundación benéfica) trust, foundation

patrulla [pa'truʎa] nf patrol

pausa ['pausa] nf pause, break

pauta ['pauta] nf line, guide line

pava ['paβa] (RPL) nf kettle

pavimento [paβi'mento] nm (de losa) pavement, paving

pavo ['paβo] nm turkey; **pavo real** peacock

payaso, -a [pa'jaso, a] nm/f clown

payo, -a ['pajo, a] nm/f non-gipsy

paz [paθ] nf peace; (tranquilidad) peacefulness, tranquillity; **hacer las paces** to make peace; (fig) to make up; **¡déjame en**

~! leave me alone!

PC nm PC, personal computer

P.D. abr (= posdata) P.S., p.s.

peaje [pe'axe] nm toll

peatón [pea'ton] nm pedestrian; **peatonal** adj pedestrian

peca ['peka] nf freckle

pecado [pe'kaðo] nm sin; **pecador, a** adj sinful ▷ nm/f sinner

pecaminoso, -a [pekami'noso, a] adj sinful

pecar [pe'kar] vi (Rel) to sin; **peca de generoso** he is generous to a fault

pecera [pe'θera] nf fish tank; (redonda) goldfish bowl

pecho ['petʃo] nm (Anat) chest; (de mujer) breast; **dar el ~ a** to breast-feed; **tomar algo a ~** to take sth to heart

pechuga [pe'tʃuɣa] nf breast

peculiar [peku'ljar] adj special, peculiar; (característico) typical, characteristic

pedal [pe'ðal] nm pedal; **pedalear** vi to pedal

pedante [pe'ðante] adj pedantic ▷ nmf pedant

pedazo [pe'ðaθo] nm piece, bit; **hacerse ~s** to smash, shatter

pediatra [pe'ðjatra] nmf paediatrician

pedido [pe'ðiðo] nm (Com) order; (petición) request

pedir [pe'ðir] vt to ask for, request; (comida, Com: mandar) to order; (necesitar) to need, demand, require ▷ vi to ask; **me pidió que cerrara la puerta** he asked me to shut the door; **¿cuánto piden por el coche?** how much are they asking for the car?

pedo ['peðo] (fam!) nm fart

pega ['peɣa] nf snag; **poner ~s (a)** to complain (about)

pegadizo, -a [peɣa'ðiθo, a] adj (Mús) catchy

pegajoso, -a [peɣa'xoso, a] adj sticky, adhesive

pegamento [peɣa'mento] nm gum, glue

pegar [pe'ɣar] vt (papel, sellos) to stick (on); (cartel) to stick up; (coser) to sew (on); (unir: partes) to join, fix together; (Comput) to paste; (Med) to give, infect with; (dar: golpe) to give, deal ▷ vi (adherirse) to stick, adhere; (ir juntos: colores) to match, go together; (golpear) to hit; (quemar: el sol) to strike hot, burn; **pegarse** vr (gen) to stick; (dos personas) to hit each other, fight; (fam): **~ un grito** to let out a yell; **~ un salto** to jump (with fright); **~ en** to touch; **~se un tiro** to shoot o.s.

pegatina [peɣa'tina] nf sticker

pegote [pe'ɣote] (fam) nm eyesore, sight

peinado [pei'naðo] nm hairstyle

peinar [pei'nar] vt to comb; (hacer estilo) to style; **peinarse** vr to comb one's hair

peine ['peine] nm comb; **peineta** nf ornamental comb

p.ej. abr (= por ejemplo) e.g.

Pekín [pe'kin] n Pekin(g)

pelado, -a [pe'laðo, a] adj (fruta, patata etc) peeled; (cabeza) shorn; (campo, fig) bare; (fam: sin dinero) broke

pelar [pe'lar] vt (fruta, patatas etc) to peel; (cortar el pelo a) to cut the hair of; (quitar la piel: animal) to skin; **pelarse** vr (la piel) to peel off; **voy a ~me** I'm going to get my haircut

peldaño [pel'daɲo] nm step

pelea [pe'lea] nf (lucha) fight; (discusión) quarrel, row; **peleado, -a** [pele'aðo, a] adj: **estar peleado (con algn)** to have fallen out (with sb); **pelear** [pele'ar] vi to fight; **pelearse** vr to fight; (reñirse) to fall out, quarrel

pelela [pe'lela] (cs) nf potty

peletería [pelete'ria] nf furrier's, fur shop

pelícano [pe'likano] nm pelican

película [pe'likula] nf film; (cobertura ligera) thin covering; (Foto: rollo) roll o reel of film; **película de dibujos (animados)/del oeste** cartoon/western

peligro [pe'liɣro] nm danger; (riesgo) risk; **correr ~ de** to run the risk of; **peligroso, -a** adj dangerous; risky

pelirrojo, -a [peli'rroxo, a] adj red-haired, red-headed ▷ nm/f redhead

pellejo [pe'ʎexo] nm (de animal) skin, hide

pellizcar [peʎiθ'kar] vt to pinch, nip

pelma ['pelma] (ESP: fam) nmf pain (in the neck)

pelmazo [pel'maθo] (fam) nm = **pelma**

pelo ['pelo] nm (cabellos) hair; (de barba, bigote) whisker; (de animal: pellejo) hair, fur, coat; **venir al ~** to be exactly what one needs; **un hombre de ~ en pecho** a brave man; **por los ~s** by the skin of one's teeth; **no tener ~s en la lengua** to be outspoken, not to mince one's words; **con ~s y señales** in minute detail; **tomar el ~ a algn** to pull sb's leg

pelota [pe'lota] nf ball; **en ~** stark naked; **hacer la ~ (a algn)** (ESP: fam) to creep (to sb); **pelota vasca** pelota

pelotón [pelo'ton] nm (Mil) squad, detachment

peluca [pe'luka] nf wig

peluche [pe'lutʃe] nm: **oso/muñeco de ~** teddy bear/soft toy

peludo, -a [pe'luðo, a] adj hairy, shaggy

peluquería [peluke'ria] nf hairdresser's;

P

peluquero, -a nm/f hairdresser
pelusa [pe'lusa] nf (Bot) down; (en tela) fluff
pena ['pena] nf (congoja) grief, sadness; (remordimiento) regret; (dificultad) trouble; (dolor) pain; (Jur) sentence; **merecer** o **valer la ~** to be worthwhile; **a duras ~s** with great difficulty; **¡qué ~!** what a shame!; **pena capital** capital punishment; **pena de muerte** death penalty
penal [pe'nal] adj penal ▷ nm (cárcel) prison
penalidad [penali'ðað] nf (problema, dificultad) trouble, hardship; (Jur) penalty, punishment; **penalidades** nfpl trouble sg, hardship sg
penalti [pe'nalti] nm = **penalty**
penalty [pe'nalti] (pl ~s o **penalties**) nm penalty (kick)
pendiente [pen'djente] adj pending, unsettled ▷ nm earring ▷ nf hill, slope
pene ['pene] nm penis
penetrante [pene'trante] adj (herida) deep; (persona, arma) sharp; (sonido) penetrating, piercing; (mirada) searching; (viento, ironía) biting
penetrar [pene'trar] vt to penetrate, pierce; (entender) to grasp ▷ vi to penetrate, go in; (entrar) to enter, go in; (líquido) to soak in; (fig) to pierce
penicilina [peniθi'lina] nf penicillin
península [pe'ninsula] nf peninsula; **peninsular** adj peninsular
penique [pe'nike] nm penny
penitencia [peni'tenθja] nf penance
penoso, -a [pe'noso, a] adj (lamentable) distressing; (difícil) arduous, difficult
pensador, a [pensa'ðor, a] nm/f thinker
pensamiento [pensa'mjento] nm thought; (mente) mind; (idea) idea
pensar [pen'sar] vt to think; (considerar) to think over, think out; (proponerse) to intend, plan; (imaginarse) to think up, invent ▷ vi to think; **~ en** to aim at, aspire to; **pensativo, -a** adj thoughtful, pensive
pensión [pen'sjon] nf (casa) boarding o guest house; (dinero) pension; (cama y comida) board and lodging; **media ~** half-board; **pensión completa** full board; **pensionista** nmf (jubilado) (old-age) pensioner; (huésped) lodger
penúltimo, -a [pe'nultimo, a] adj penultimate, last but one
penumbra [pe'numbra] nf half-light
peña ['pena] nf (roca) rock; (cuesta) cliff, crag; (grupo) group, circle; (LAM: club) folk club
peñasco [pe'nasko] nm large rock, boulder

peñón [pe'non] nm wall of rock; **el P~** the Rock (of Gibraltar)
peón [pe'on] nm labourer; (LAM Agr) farm labourer, farmhand; (Ajedrez) pawn
peonza [pe'onθa] nf spinning top
peor [pe'or] adj (comparativo) worse; (superlativo) worst ▷ adv worse; worst; **de mal en ~** from bad to worse
pepinillo [pepi'niʎo] nm gherkin
pepino [pe'pino] nm cucumber; **(no) me importa un ~** I don't care one bit
pepita [pe'pita] nf (Bot) pip; (Minería) nugget
pepito [pe'pito] (ESP) nm (tb: ~ **de ternera**) steak sandwich
pequeño, -a [pe'keno, a] adj small, little
pera ['pera] nf pear; **peral** nm pear tree
percance [per'kanθe] nm setback, misfortune
percatarse [perka'tarse] vr: ~ **de** to notice, take note of
percebe [per'θeβe] nm barnacle
percepción [perθep'θjon] nf (vista) perception; (idea) notion, idea
percha ['pertʃa] nf (coat)hanger; (ganchos) coat hooks pl; (de ave) perch
percibir [perθi'βir] vt to perceive, notice; (Com) to earn, get
percusión [perku'sjon] nf percussion
perdedor, a [perðe'ðor, a] adj losing ▷ nm/f loser
perder [per'ðer] vt to lose; (tiempo, palabras) to waste; (oportunidad) to lose, miss; (tren) to miss ▷ vi to lose; **perderse** vr (extraviarse) to get lost; (desaparecer) to disappear, be lost to view; (arruinarse) to be ruined; **echar a ~** (comida) to spoil, ruin; (oportunidad) to waste
pérdida ['perðiða] nf loss; (de tiempo) waste; **pérdidas** nfpl (Com) losses
perdido, -a [per'ðiðo, a] adj lost
perdiz [per'ðiθ] nf partridge
perdón [per'ðon] nm (disculpa) pardon, forgiveness; (clemencia) mercy; **¡~!** sorry!, I beg your pardon!; **perdonar** vt to pardon, forgive; (la vida) to spare; (excusar) to exempt, excuse; **¡perdone (usted)!** sorry!, I beg your pardon!
perecedero, -a [pereθe'ðero, a] adj perishable
perecer [pere'θer] vi to perish, die
peregrinación [pereɣrina'θjon] nf (Rel) pilgrimage
peregrino, -a [pere'ɣrino, a] adj (idea) strange, absurd ▷ nm/f pilgrim
perejil [pere'xil] nm parsley
perenne [pe'renne] adj everlasting, perennial

pereza [pe'reθa] nf laziness, idleness; **perezoso, -a** adj lazy, idle
perfección [perfek'θjon] nf perfection; **perfeccionar** vt to perfect; (mejorar) to improve; (acabar) to complete, finish
perfecto, -a [per'fekto, a] adj perfect; (total) complete
perfil [per'fil] nm profile; (contorno) silhouette, outline; (Arq) (cross) section; **perfiles** nmpl features
perforación [perfora'θjon] nf perforation; (con taladro) drilling; **perforadora** nf punch
perforar [perfo'rar] vt to perforate; (agujero) to drill, bore; (papel) to punch a hole in ▷ vi to drill, bore
perfume [per'fume] nm perfume, scent
periferia [peri'ferja] nf periphery; (de ciudad) outskirts pl
periférico [peri'feriko] (LAM) nm ring road (BRIT), beltway (US)
perilla [pe'riʎa] nf (barba) goatee; (LAM: de puerta) doorknob, door handle
perímetro [pe'rimetro] nm perimeter
periódico, -a [pe'rjoðiko, a] adj periodic(al) ▷ nm newspaper
periodismo [perjo'ðismo] nm journalism; **periodista** nmf journalist
periodo [pe'rjoðo] nm period
período [pe'rioðo] nm = **periodo**
periquito [peri'kito] nm budgerigar, budgie
perito, -a [pe'rito, a] adj (experto) expert; (diestro) skilled, skilful ▷ nm/f expert; skilled worker; (técnico) technician
perjudicar [perxuði'kar] vt (gen) to damage, harm; **perjudicial** adj damaging, harmful; (en detrimento) detrimental; **perjuicio** nm damage, harm
perjurar [perxu'rar] vi to commit perjury
perla ['perla] nf pearl; **me viene de ~s** it suits me fine
permanecer [permane'θer] vi (quedarse) to stay, remain; (seguir) to continue to be
permanente [perma'nente] adj permanent, constant ▷ nf perm
permiso [per'miso] nm permission; (licencia) permit, licence; **con ~** excuse me; **estar de ~** (Mil) to be on leave; **permiso de conducir** driving licence (BRIT), driver's license (US); **permiso por enfermedad** (LAM) sick leave
permitir [permi'tir] vt to permit, allow
pernera [per'nera] nf trouser leg
pero ['pero] conj but; (aún) yet ▷ nm (defecto) flaw, defect; (reparo) objection
perpendicular [perpendiku'lar] adj perpendicular

perpetuo, -a [per'petwo, a] adj perpetual
perplejo, -a [per'plexo, a] adj perplexed, bewildered
perra ['perra] nf (Zool) bitch; **estar sin una ~** (ESP: fam) to be flat broke
perrera [pe'rrera] nf kennel
perrito [pe'rrito] nm (tb: ~ caliente) hot dog
perro ['perro] nm dog
persa ['persa] adj, nmf Persian
persecución [perseku'θjon] nf pursuit, chase; (Rel, Pol) persecution
perseguir [perse'ɣir] vt to pursue, hunt; (cortejar) to chase after; (molestar) to pester, annoy; (Rel, Pol) to persecute
persiana [per'sjana] nf (Venetian) blind
persistente [persis'tente] adj persistent
persistir [persis'tir] vi to persist
persona [per'sona] nf person; **persona mayor** elderly person
personaje [perso'naxe] nm important person, celebrity; (Teatro etc) character
personal [perso'nal] adj (particular) personal; (para una persona) single, for one person ▷ nm personnel, staff; **personalidad** nf personality
personarse [perso'narse] vr to appear in person
personificar [personifi'kar] vt to personify
perspectiva [perspek'tiβa] nf perspective; (vista, panorama) view, panorama; (posibilidad futura) outlook, prospect
persuadir [perswa'ðir] vt (gen) to persuade; (convencer) to convince; **persuadirse** vr to become convinced; **persuasión** nf persuasion
pertenecer [pertene'θer] vi to belong; (fig) to concern; **perteneciente** adj: **perteneciente a** belonging to; **pertenencia** nf ownership; **pertenencias** nfpl (bienes) possessions, property sg
pertenezca etc vb V **pertenecer**
pértiga ['pertiɣa] nf: **salto de ~** pole vault
pertinente [perti'nente] adj relevant, pertinent; (apropiado) appropriate; **~ a** concerning, relevant to
perturbación [perturβa'θjon] nf (Pol) disturbance; (Med) upset, disturbance
Perú [pe'ru] nm Peru; **peruano, -a** adj, nm/f Peruvian
perversión [perβer'sjon] nf perversion; **perverso, -a** adj perverse; (depravado) depraved
pervertido, -a [perβer'tiðo, a] adj perverted ▷ nm/f pervert
pervertir [perβer'tir] vt to pervert,

corrupt

pesa ['pesa] nf weight; (Deporte) shot

pesadez [pesa'ðeθ] nf (peso) heaviness; (lentitud) slowness; (aburrimiento) tediousness

pesadilla [pesa'ðiʎa] nf nightmare, bad dream

pesado, -a [pe'saðo, a] adj heavy; (lento) slow; (difícil, duro) tough, hard; (aburrido) boring, tedious; (tiempo) sultry

pésame ['pesame] nm expression of condolence, message of sympathy; **dar el ~** to express one's condolences

pesar [pe'sar] vt (tomar) to weigh ▷ vi to weigh; (ser pesado) to weigh a lot, be heavy; (fig: opinión) to carry weight; **no pesa mucho** it's not very heavy ▷ nm (arrepentimiento) regret; (pena) grief, sorrow; **a ~ de** o **pese a (que)** in spite of, despite

pesca ['peska] nf (acto) fishing; (lo pescado) catch; **ir de ~** to go fishing

pescadería [peskaðe'ria] nf fish shop, fishmonger's (BRIT)

pescadilla [peska'ðiʎa] nf whiting

pescado [pes'kaðo] nm fish

pescador, a [peska'ðor, a] nm/f fisherman/woman

pescar [pes'kar] vt (tomar) to catch; (intentar tomar) to fish for; (conseguir: trabajo) to manage to get ▷ vi to fish, go fishing

pesebre [pe'seβre] nm manger

peseta [pe'seta] nf (Hist) peseta

pesimista [pesi'mista] adj pessimistic ▷ nmf pessimist

pésimo, -a ['pesimo, a] adj awful, dreadful

peso ['peso] nm weight; (balanza) scales pl; (moneda) peso; **vender al ~** to sell by weight; **peso bruto/neto** gross/net weight; **peso pesado/pluma** heavyweight/ featherweight

pesquero, -a [pes'kero, a] adj fishing cpd

pestaña [pes'taɲa] nf (Anat) eyelash; (borde) rim

peste ['peste] nf plague; (mal olor) stink, stench

pesticida [pesti'θiða] nm pesticide

pestillo [pes'tiʎo] nm (cerrojo) bolt; (picaporte) door handle

petaca [pe'taka] nf (de cigarros) cigarette case; (de pipa) tobacco pouch; (MÉX: maleta) suitcase

pétalo ['petalo] nm petal

petardo [pe'tardo] nm firework, firecracker

petición [peti'θjon] nf (pedido) request, plea; (memorial) petition; (Jur) plea

peto ['peto] nm (ESP) dungarees pl, overalls pl (US)

petróleo [pe'troleo] nm oil, petroleum; **petrolero, -a** adj petroleum cpd ▷ nm (oil) tanker

peyorativo, -a [pejora'tiβo, a] adj pejorative

pez [peθ] nm fish; **pez espada** swordfish

pezón [pe'θon] nm teat, nipple

pezuña [pe'θuɲa] nf hoof

pianista [pja'nista] nmf pianist

piano ['pjano] nm piano

piar [pjar] vi to cheep

pibe, -a ['piβe, a] (RPL) nm/f boy/girl

picadero [pika'ðero] nm riding school

picadillo [pika'ðiʎo] nm mince, minced meat

picado, -a [pi'kaðo, a] adj pricked, punctured; (Culin) minced, chopped; (mar) choppy; (diente) bad; (tabaco) cut; (enfadado) cross

picador [pika'ðor] nm (Taur) picador; (minero) faceworker

picadura [pika'ðura] nf (pinchazo) puncture; (de abeja) sting; (de mosquito) bite; (tabaco picado) cut tobacco

picante [pi'kante] adj hot; (comentario) racy, spicy

picaporte [pika'porte] nm (manija) doorhandle; (pestillo) latch

picar [pi'kar] vt (agujerear, perforar) to prick, puncture; (abeja) to sting; (mosquito, serpiente) to bite; (Culin) to mince, chop; (incitar) to incite, goad; (dañar, irritar) to annoy, bother; (quemar: lengua) to burn, sting ▷ vi (pez) to bite, take the bait; (sol) to burn, scorch; (abeja, Med) to sting; (mosquito) to bite; **picarse** vr (agriarse) to turn sour, go off; (ofenderse) to take offence

picardía [pikar'ðia] nf villainy; (astucia) slyness, craftiness; (una picardía) dirty trick; (palabra) rude/bad word o expression

pícaro, -a ['pikaro, a] adj (malicioso) villainous; (travieso) mischievous ▷ nm (astuto) crafty sort; (sinvergüenza) rascal, scoundrel

pichi ['pitʃi] (ESP) nm pinafore dress (BRIT), jumper (US)

pichón [pi'tʃon] nm young pigeon

pico ['piko] nm (de ave) beak; (punta) sharp point; (Tec) pick, pickaxe; (Geo) peak, summit; **y ~** and a bit; **las seis y ~** six and a bit

picor [pi'kor] nm itch

picoso, -a [pi'koso, a] (MÉX) adj (comida) hot

picudo, -a [pi'kuðo, a] adj pointed, with a point

pidió etc vb V **pedir**

pido etc vb V **pedir**
pie [pje] (pl **-s**) nm foot; (fig: motivo) motive, basis; (: fundamento) foothold; **ir a -** to go on foot, walk; **estar de -** to be standing (up); **ponerse de -** to stand up; **de -s a cabeza** from top to bottom; **al - de la letra** (citar) literally, verbatim; (copiar) exactly, word for word; **en - de guerra** on a war footing; **dar - a** to give cause for; **hacer -** (en el agua) to touch (the) bottom
piedad [pje'ðað] nf (lástima) pity, compassion; (clemencia) mercy; (devoción) piety, devotion
piedra ['pjeðra] nf stone; (roca) rock; (de mechero) flint; (Meteorología) hailstone; **piedra preciosa** precious stone
piel [pjel] nf (Anat) skin; (Zool) skin, hide, fur; (cuero) leather; (Bot) skin, peel
pienso etc vb V **pensar**
pierdo etc vb V **perder**
pierna ['pjerna] nf leg
pieza ['pjeθa] nf piece; (habitación) room; **pieza de recambio** o **repuesto** spare (part)
pigmeo, -a [piɣ'meo, a] adj, nm/f pigmy
pijama [pi'xama] nm pyjamas pl (BRIT), pajamas pl (US)
pila ['pila] nf (Elec) battery; (montón) heap, pile; (lavabo) sink
píldora ['pildora] nf pill; **la - (anticonceptiva)** the (contraceptive) pill
pileta [pi'leta] (RPL) nf (fregadero) (kitchen) sink; (piscina) swimming pool
pillar [pi'ʎar] vt (saquear) to pillage, plunder; (fam: coger) to catch; (: agarrar) to grasp, seize; (: entender) to grasp, catch on to; **pillarse** vr: **~se un dedo con la puerta** to catch one's finger in the door
pillo, -a ['piʎo, a] adj villainous; (astuto) sly, crafty ▷ nm/f rascal, rogue, scoundrel
piloto [pi'loto] nm pilot; (de aparato) (pilot) light; (Auto: luz) tail o rear light; (: conductor) driver; **piloto automático** automatic pilot
pimentón [pimen'ton] nm paprika
pimienta [pi'mjenta] nf pepper
pimiento [pi'mjento] nm pepper, pimiento
pin [pin] (pl **-s**) nm badge
pinacoteca [pinako'teka] nf art gallery
pinar [pi'nar] nm pine forest (BRIT), pine grove (US)
pincel [pin'θel] nm paintbrush
pinchadiscos [pintʃa'ðiskos] (ESP) nmf inv disc-jockey, DJ
pinchar [pin'tʃar] vt (perforar) to prick, pierce; (neumático) to puncture; (fig) to prod; (Inform) to click
pinchazo [pin'tʃaθo] nm (perforación) prick; (de neumático) puncture; (fig) prod

pincho ['pintʃo] nm savoury (snack); **pincho de tortilla** small slice of omelette; **pincho moruno** shish kebab
ping-pong ['pin'pon] nm table tennis
pingüino [pin'gwino] nm penguin
pino ['pino] nm pine (tree)
pinta ['pinta] nf spot; (de líquidos) spot, drop; (aspecto) appearance, look(s) (pl); **pintado, -a** adj spotted; (de colores) colourful; **pintadas** nfpl graffiti sg
pintalabios [pinta'laβjos] (ESP) nm inv lipstick
pintar [pin'tar] vt to paint ▷ vi to paint; (fam) to count, be important; **pintarse** vr to put on make-up
pintor, a [pin'tor, a] nm/f painter
pintoresco, -a [pinto'resko, a] adj picturesque
pintura [pin'tura] nf painting; **pintura al óleo** oil painting
pinza ['pinθa] nf (Zool) claw; (para colgar ropa) clothes peg; (Tec) pincers pl; **pinzas** nfpl (para depilar etc) tweezers pl
piña ['piɲa] nf (de pino) pine cone; (fruta) pineapple; (fig) group
piñata [pi'ɲata] nf container hung up at parties to be beaten with sticks until sweets or presents fall out

○ **PIÑATA**
●
● **Piñata** is a very popular party game in
● Mexico. The **piñata** itself is a hollow
● figure made of papier maché, or,
● traditionally, from adobe, in the shape
● of an object, a star, a person or an
● animal. It is filled with either sweets
● and toys, or fruit and yam beans. The
● game consists of hanging the **piñata**
● from the ceiling, and beating it with a
● stick, blindfolded, until it breaks and the
● presents fall out.

piñón [pi'ɲon] nm (fruto) pine nut; (Tec) pinion
pío, -a ['pio, a] adj (devoto) pious, devout; (misericordioso) merciful
piojo ['pjoxo] nm louse
pipa ['pipa] nf pipe; **pipas** nfpl (Bot) (edible) sunflower seeds
pipí [pi'pi] (fam) nm: **hacer -** to have a wee(-wee) (BRIT), have to go (wee-wee) (US)
pique ['pike] nm (resentimiento) pique, resentment; (rivalidad) rivalry, competition; **irse a -** to sink; (esperanza, familia) to be ruined
piqueta [pi'keta] nf pick(axe)
piquete [pi'kete] nm (Mil) squad, party;

(*de obreros*) picket; (*MÉX: de insecto*) bite;
piquetear (*LAM*) *vt* to picket

pirado, -a [piˈraðo, a] (*fam*) *adj* round the
bend ▷ *nm/f* nutter

piragua [piˈraɣwa] *nf* canoe; **piragüismo**
nm canoeing

pirámide [piˈramiðe] *nf* pyramid

pirata [piˈrata] *adj, nmf* pirate; **pirata
informático** hacker

Pirineo(s) [piriˈneo(s)] *nm(pl)* Pyrenees *pl*

pirómano, -a [piˈromano, a] *nm/f* (*Med,
Jur*) arsonist

piropo [piˈropo] *nm* compliment, (piece
of) flattery

pirueta [piˈrweta] *nf* pirouette

piruleta [piruˈleta] (*ESP*) *nf* lollipop

pis [pis] (*fam*) *nm* pee, piss; **hacer ~** to have
a pee; (*para niños*) to wee-wee

pisada [piˈsaða] *nf* (*paso*) footstep; (*huella*)
footprint

pisar [piˈsar] *vt* (*caminar sobre*) to walk on,
tread on; (*apretar con el pie*) to press; (*fig*)
to trample on, walk all over ▷ *vi* to tread,
step, walk

piscina [pisˈθina] *nf* swimming pool

Piscis [ˈpisθis] *nm* Pisces

piso [ˈpiso] *nm* (*suelo, planta*) floor;
(*ESP: apartamento*) apartment; (*BRIT*)
primer ~ (*ESP*) first floor; (*LAM: planta baja*)
ground floor

pisotear [pisoteˈar] *vt* to trample (on o
underfoot)

pista [ˈpista] *nf* track, trail; (*indicio*) clue;
pista de aterrizaje runway; **pista de baile**
dance floor; **pista de hielo** ice rink; **pista de
tenis** (*ESP*) tennis court

pistola [pisˈtola] *nf* pistol; (*Tec*) spray-gun

pistón [pisˈton] *nm* (*Tec*) piston; (*Mús*) key

pitar [piˈtar] *vt* (*silbato*) to blow; (*rechiflar*)
to whistle at, boo ▷ *vi* to whistle; (*Auto*)
to sound o toot one's horn; (*LAM: fumar*) to
smoke

pitillo [piˈtiʎo] *nm* cigarette

pito [ˈpito] *nm* whistle; (*de coche*) horn

pitón [piˈton] *nm* (*Zool*) python

pitonisa [pitoˈnisa] *nf* fortune-teller

pitorreo [pitoˈrreo] *nm* joke; **estar de ~**
to be joking

píxel [ˈpiksel] (*pl* **pixels** *or* **-es**) *nm* pixel

piyama [piˈjama] (*LAM*) *nm* pyjamas *pl*
(*BRIT*), pajamas *pl* (*US*)

pizarra [piˈθarra] *nf* (*piedra*) slate;
(*ESP: encerado*) blackboard; **pizarra
blanca** whiteboard; **pizarra interactiva**
interactive whiteboard

pizarrón [piθaˈrron] (*LAM*) *nm* blackboard

pizca [ˈpiθka] *nf* pinch, spot; (*fig*) spot,
speck; **ni ~** not a bit

placa [ˈplaka] *nf* plate; (*distintivo*) badge,
insignia; **placa de matrícula** (*LAM*) number
plate

placard [plaˈkar] (*RPL*) *nm* cupboard

placer [plaˈθer] *nm* pleasure ▷ *vt* to please

plaga [ˈplaɣa] *nf* pest; (*Med*) plague;
(*abundancia*) abundance

plagio [ˈplaxjo] *nm* plagiarism

plan [plan] *nm* (*esquema, proyecto*) plan;
(*idea, intento*) idea, intention; **tener ~** (*fam*)
to have a date; **tener un ~** (*fam*) to have an
affair; **en ~ económico** (*fam*) on the cheap;
vamos en ~ de turismo we're going as
tourists; **si te pones en ese ~ ...** if that's
your attitude ...

plana [ˈplana] *nf* sheet (of paper), page;
(*Tec*) trowel; **en primera ~** on the front page

plancha [ˈplantʃa] *nf* (*para planchar*) iron;
(*rótulo*) plate, sheet; (*Náut*) gangway; **a la ~**
(*Culin*) grilled; **planchar** *vt* to iron ▷ *vi* to
do the ironing

planear [planeˈar] *vt* to plan ▷ *vi* to glide

planeta [plaˈneta] *nm* planet

plano, -a [ˈplano, a] *adj* flat, level, even
▷ *nm* (*Mat, Tec*) plane; (*Foto*) shot; (*Arq*) plan;
(*Geo*) map; (*de ciudad*) map, street plan;
primer ~ close-up

planta [ˈplanta] *nf* (*Bot, Tec*) plant;
(*Anat*) sole of the foot, foot; (*piso*) floor;
(*LAM: personal*) staff; **planta baja** ground
floor

plantar [planˈtar] *vt* (*Bot*) to plant;
(*levantar*) to erect, set up; **plantarse** *vr* to
stand firm; **~ a algn en la calle** to throw sb
out; **dejar plantado a algn** (*fam*) to stand
sb up

plantear [planteˈar] *vt* (*problema*) to pose;
(*dificultad*) to raise

plantilla [planˈtiʎa] *nf* (*de zapato*) insole;
(*ESP: personal*) personnel; **ser de ~** (*ESP*) to be
on the staff

plantón [planˈton] *nm* (*Mil*) guard, sentry;
(*fam*) long wait; **dar (un) ~ a algn** to stand
sb up

plasta [ˈplasta] (*ESP: fam*) *adj inv* boring
▷ *nmf* bore

plástico, -a [ˈplastiko, a] *adj* plastic ▷ *nm*
plastic

Plastilina® [plastiˈlina] *nf* Plasticine®

plata [ˈplata] *nf* (*metal*) silver; (*cosas hechas
de plata*) silverware; (*CS: dinero*) cash, dough

plataforma [plataˈforma] *nf* platform;
plataforma de lanzamiento/perforación
launch(ing) pad/drilling rig

plátano [ˈplatano] *nm* (*fruta*) banana;
(*árbol*) plane tree; banana tree

platea [plaˈtea] *nf* (*Teatro*) pit

plática [ˈplatika] *nf* talk, chat; **platicar** *vi*

to talk, chat

platillo [pla'tiʎo] nm saucer; **platillos** nmpl (Mús) cymbals; **platillo volante** flying saucer

platino [pla'tino] nm platinum; **platinos** nmpl (Auto) contact points

plato ['plato] nm plate, dish; (parte de comida) course; (comida) dish; **primer ~** first course; **plato combinado** set main course (served on one plate); **plato fuerte** main course

playa ['plaja] nf beach; (costa) seaside; **playa de estacionamiento** (cs) car park (BRIT), parking lot (US)

playera [pla'jera] nf (MÉX: camiseta) T-shirt; **playeras** nfpl (zapatos) canvas shoes

plaza ['plaθa] nf square; (mercado) market(place); (sitio) room, space; (de vehículo) seat, place; (colocación) post, job; **plaza de toros** bullring

plazo ['plaθo] nm (lapso de tiempo) time, period; (fecha de vencimiento) expiry date; (pago parcial) instalment; **a corto/largo ~** short-/long-term; **comprar algo a ~s** to buy sth on hire purchase (BRIT) o on time (US)

plazoleta [plaθo'leta] nf small square

plebeyo, -a [ple'βejo, a] adj plebeian; (pey) coarse, common

plegable [ple'xaβle] adj collapsible; (silla) folding

pleito ['pleito] nm (Jur) lawsuit, case; (fig) dispute, feud

plenitud [pleni'tuð] nf plenitude, fullness; (abundancia) abundance

pleno, -a ['pleno, a] adj full; (completo) complete ▷ nm plenum; **en ~ día** in broad daylight; **en ~ verano** at the height of summer; **en plena cara** full in the face

pliego etc ['pljexo] vb V plegar ▷ nm (hoja) sheet (of paper); (carta) sealed letter/ document; **pliego de condiciones** details pl, specifications pl

pliegue etc ['pljexe] vb V plegar ▷ nm fold, crease; (de vestido) pleat

plomería [plome'ria] (LAM) nf plumbing; **plomero** (LAM) nm plumber

plomo ['plomo] nm (metal) lead; (Elec) fuse; **sin ~** unleaded

pluma ['pluma] nf feather; (para escribir): **~ (estilográfica)** (LAM) ink pen; **~ fuente** (LAM) fountain pen

plumero [plu'mero] nm (para el polvo) feather duster

plumón [plu'mon] nm (de ave) down

plural [plu'ral] adj plural

pluriempleo [pluriem'pleo] nm having

more than one job

plus [plus] nm bonus

población [poβla'θjon] nf population; (pueblo, ciudad) town, city

poblado, -a [po'βlaðo, a] adj inhabited ▷ nm (aldea) village; (pueblo) (small) town; **densamente ~** densely populated

poblador, a [poβla'ðor, a] nm/f settler, colonist

pobre ['poβre] adj poor ▷ nmf poor person; **pobreza** nf poverty

pocilga [po'θilxa] nf pigsty

○ **PALABRA CLAVE**

poco, -a ['poko, a] adj **1** (sg) little, not much; **poco tiempo** little o not much time; **de poco interés** of little interest, not very interesting; **poca cosa** not much
2 (pl) few, not many; **unos pocos** a few, some; **pocos niños comen lo que les conviene** few children eat what they should ▷ adv **1** little, not much; **cuesta poco** it doesn't cost much
2 (+ adj: negativo, antónimo): **poco amable/ inteligente** not very nice/intelligent
3: **por poco me caigo** I almost fell
4: **a poco: a poco de haberse casado** shortly after getting married
5: **poco a poco** little by little ▷ nm a little, a bit; **un poco triste/de dinero** a little sad/money

podar [po'ðar] vt to prune

○ **PALABRA CLAVE**

poder [po'ðer] vi **1** (tener capacidad) can, be able to; **no puedo hacerlo** I can't do it, I'm unable to do it
2 (tener permiso) can, may, be allowed to; **¿se puede?** may I (o we)?; **puedes irte ahora** you may go now; **no se puede fumar en este hospital** smoking is not allowed in this hospital
3 (tener posibilidad) may, might, could; **puede llegar mañana** he may o might arrive tomorrow; **pudiste haberte hecho daño** you might o could have hurt yourself; **¡podías habérmelo dicho antes!** you might have told me before!
4: **puede ser** perhaps; **puede ser que lo sepa Tomás** Tomás may o might know
5: **¡no puedo más!** I've had enough!; **es tonto a más no poder** he's as stupid as they come
6: **poder con: no puedo con este crío** this kid's too much for me

P

▷ *nm* power; **detentar** *o* **ocupar** *o*
estar en el poder to be in power; **poder
adquisitivo/ejecutivo/legislativo**
purchasing/executive/legislative power;
poder judicial judiciary

poderoso, -a [poðeˈroso, a] *adj* (*político,
país*) powerful
podio [ˈpoðjo] *nm* (*Deporte*) podium
podium [ˈpoðjum] = **podio**
podrido, -a [poˈðriðo, a] *adj* rotten, bad;
(*fig*) rotten, corrupt
podrir [poˈðrir] = **pudrir**
poema [poˈema] *nm* poem
poesía [poeˈsia] *nf* poetry
poeta [poˈeta] *nmf* poet; **poético, -a** *adj*
poetic(al)
poetisa [poeˈtisa] *nf* (woman) poet
póker [ˈpoker] *nm* poker
polaco, -a [poˈlako, a] *adj* Polish ▷ *nm/f*
Pole
polar [poˈlar] *adj* polar
polea [poˈlea] *nf* pulley
polémica [poˈlemika] *nf* polemics *sg*; (*una
polémica*) controversy, polemic
polen [ˈpolen] *nm* pollen
policía [poliˈθia] *nmf* policeman/woman
▷ *nf* police; **policíaco, -a** *adj* police *cpd*;
novela policíaca detective story; **policial**
adj police *cpd*
polideportivo [poliðeporˈtiβo] *nm* sports
centre *o* complex
polígono [poˈliɣono] *nm* (*Mat*) polygon;
polígono industrial (*ESP*) industrial estate
polilla [poˈliʎa] *nf* moth
polio [ˈpoljo] *nf* polio
política [poˈlitika] *nf* politics *sg*;
(*económica, agraria etc*) policy; V *tb* **político**
político, -a [poˈlitiko, a] *adj* political;
(*discreto*) tactful; (*de familia*) ...-in-law ▷ *nm/f*
politician; **padre ~** father-in-law
póliza [ˈpoliθa] *nf* certificate, voucher;
(*impuesto*) tax stamp; **póliza de seguro(s)**
insurance policy
polizón [poliˈθon] *nm* stowaway
pollera [poˈʎera] (*cs*) *nf* skirt
pollo [ˈpoʎo] *nm* chicken
polo [ˈpolo] *nm* (*Geo, Elec*) pole; (*helado*) ice
lolly (*BRIT*), Popsicle® (*us*); (*Deporte*) polo;
(*suéter*) polo-neck; **polo Norte/Sur** North/
South Pole
Polonia [poˈlonja] *nf* Poland
poltrona [polˈtrona] *nf* easy chair
polución [poluˈθjon] *nf* pollution
polvera [polˈβera] *nf* powder compact
polvo [ˈpolβo] *nm* dust; (*Quím, Culin, Med*)
powder; **polvos** *nmpl* (*maquillaje*) powder
sg; **en ~** powdered; **quitar el ~** to dust; **estar**

hecho ~ (*fam*) to be worn out *o* exhausted;
polvos de talco talcum powder *sg*
pólvora [ˈpolβora] *nf* gunpowder
polvoriento, -a [polβoˈrjento, a] *adj*
(*superficie*) dusty; (*sustancia*) powdery
pomada [poˈmaða] *nf* cream, ointment
pomelo [poˈmelo] *nm* grapefruit
pómez [ˈpomeθ] *nf*: **piedra ~** pumice stone
pomo [ˈpomo] *nm* doorknob
pompa [ˈpompa] *nf* (*burbuja*) bubble;
(*bomba*) pump; (*esplendor*) pomp, splendour
pómulo [ˈpomulo] *nm* cheekbone
pon [pon] *vb* V **poner**
ponchadura [pontʃaˈdura] (*MÉX*) *nf*
puncture (*BRIT*), flat (*us*); **ponchar** (*MÉX*) *vt*
(*llanta*) to puncture
ponche [ˈpontʃe] *nm* punch
poncho [ˈpontʃo] *nm* poncho
pondré *etc vb* V **poner**

○ **PALABRA CLAVE**

poner [poˈner] *vt* **1** (*colocar*) to put;
(*telegrama*) to send; (*obra de teatro*) to put on;
(*película*) to show; **ponlo más fuerte** turn it
up; **¿qué ponen en el Excelsior?** what's on
at the Excelsior?
2 (*tienda*) to open; (*instalar: gas etc*) to put in;
(*radio, TV*) to switch *o* turn on
3 (*suponer*): **pongamos que ...** let's suppose
that ...
4 (*contribuir*): **el gobierno ha puesto otro
millón** the government has contributed
another million
5 (*Tel*): **póngame con el Sr. López** can you
put me through to Mr. López?
6: **poner de: le han puesto de director
general** they've appointed him general
manager
7 (+ *adj*) to make; **me estás poniendo
nerviosa** you're making me nervous
8 (*dar nombre*): **al hijo le pusieron Diego**
they called their son Diego
▷ *vi* (*gallina*) to lay
ponerse *vr* **1** (*colocarse*): **se puso a mi lado**
he came and stood beside me; **tú ponte en
esa silla** you go and sit on that chair
2 (*vestido, cosméticos*) to put on; **¿por qué no
te pones el vestido nuevo?** why don't you
put on *o* wear your new dress?
3 (+ *adj*) to turn; to get, become; **se puso
muy serio** he got very serious; **después de
lavarla la tela se puso azul** after washing
it the material turned blue
4: **ponerse a: se puso a llorar** he started
to cry; **tienes que ponerte a estudiar** you
must get down to studying

pongo etc vb V **poner**
poniente [po'njente] nm (occidente) west; (viento) west wind
pontífice [pon'tifiθe] nm pope, pontiff
popa ['popa] nf stern
popote [po'pote] (MÉX) nm straw
popular [popu'lar] adj popular; (cultura) of the people, folk cpd; **popularidad** nf popularity

○ **PALABRA CLAVE**

por [por] prep 1 (objetivo) for; **luchar por la patria** to fight for one's country
2 (+ infin): **por no llegar tarde** so as not to arrive late; **por citar unos ejemplos** to give a few examples
3 (causa) out of, because of; **por escasez de fondos** through o for lack of funds
4 (tiempo): **por la mañana/noche** in the morning/at night; **se queda por una semana** she's staying (for) a week
5 (lugar): **pasar por Madrid** to pass through Madrid; **ir a Guayaquil por Quito** to go to Guayaquil via Quito; **caminar por la calle** to walk along the street; V tb **todo**
6 (cambio, precio): **te doy uno nuevo por el que tienes** I'll give you a new one (in return) for the one you've got
7 (valor distributivo): **6 euros por hora/cabeza** 6 euros an o per hour/a o per head
8 (modo, medio) by; **por correo/avión** by post/air; **entrar por la entrada principal** to go in through the main entrance
9: **10 por 10 son 100** 10 times 10 is 100
10 (en lugar de): **vino él por su jefe** he came instead of his boss
11: **por mí que revienten** as far as I'm concerned they can drop dead
12: **¿por qué?** why?; **¿por qué no?** why not?

porcelana [porθe'lana] nf porcelain; (china) china
porcentaje [porθen'taxe] nm percentage
porción [por'θjon] nf (parte) portion, share; (cantidad) quantity, amount
porfiar [por'fjar] vi to persist, insist; (disputar) to argue stubbornly
pormenor [porme'nor] nm detail, particular
pornografía [pornoɣra'fia] nf pornography
poro ['poro] nm pore
pororó [poro'ro] (RPL) nm popcorn
poroso, -a [po'roso, a] adj porous
poroto [po'roto] (CS) nm bean
porque ['porke] conj (a causa de) because; (ya que) since; (con el fin de) so that, in order

that
porqué [por'ke] nm reason, cause
porquería [porke'ria] nf (suciedad) filth, dirt; (acción) dirty trick; (objeto) small thing, trifle; (fig) rubbish
porra ['porra] (ESP) nf (arma) stick, club
porrazo [po'rraθo] nm blow, bump
porro ['porro] (fam) nm (droga) joint (fam)
porrón [po'rron] nm glass wine jar with a long spout
portaaviones [porta'(a)βjones] nm inv aircraft carrier
portada [por'taða] nf (de revista) cover
portador, a [porta'ðor, a] nm/f carrier, bearer; (Com) bearer, payee
portaequipajes [portaeki'paxes] nm inv (Auto: maletero) boot; (: baca) luggage rack
portafolio [porta'foljo] (LAM) nm briefcase
portal [por'tal] nm (entrada) vestibule, hall; (portada) porch, doorway; (puerta de entrada) main door; (Internet) portal; **portales** nmpl (LAM) arcade sg
portamaletas [portama'letas] nm inv (Auto: maletero) boot; (: baca) roof rack
portarse [por'tarse] vr to behave, conduct o.s.
portátil [por'tatil] adj portable
portavoz [porta'βoθ] nmf spokesman/woman
portazo [por'taθo] nm: **dar un ~** to slam the door
porte ['porte] nm (Com) transport; (precio) transport charges pl
portentoso, -a [porten'toso, a] adj marvellous, extraordinary
porteño, -a [por'teɲo, a] adj of o from Buenos Aires
portería [porte'ria] nf (oficina) porter's office; (Deporte) goal
portero, -a [por'tero, a] nm/f porter; (conserje) caretaker; (ujier) doorman; (Deporte) goalkeeper; **portero automático** (ESP) entry phone
pórtico ['portiko] nm (patio) portico, porch; (fig) gateway; (arcada) arcade
portorriqueño, -a [portorri'keɲo, a] adj Puerto Rican
Portugal [portu'ɣal] nm Portugal; **portugués, -esa** adj, nm/f Portuguese ▷ nm (Ling) Portuguese
porvenir [porβe'nir] nm future
pos [pos] prep: **en ~ de** after, in pursuit of
posaderas [posa'ðeras] nfpl backside sg, buttocks
posar [po'sar] vt (en el suelo) to lay down, put down; (la mano) to place, put gently ▷ vi (modelo) to sit, pose; **posarse** vr to settle;

(*pájaro*) to perch; (*avión*) to land, come down
posavasos [posa'βasos] *nm inv* coaster;
(*para cerveza*) beermat
posdata [pos'ðata] *nf* postscript
pose ['pose] *nf* pose
poseedor, a [posee'ðor, a] *nm/f* owner,
possessor; (*de récord, puesto*) holder
poseer [pose'er] *vt* to possess, own;
(*ventaja*) to enjoy; (*récord, puesto*) to hold
posesivo, -a [pose'siβo, a] *adj* possessive
posibilidad [posiβili'ðað] *nf* possibility;
(*oportunidad*) chance; **posibilitar** *vt* to
make possible; (*hacer realizable*) to make
feasible
posible [po'siβle] *adj* possible; (*realizable*)
feasible; **de ser ~** if possible; **en lo ~** as far
as possible
posición [posi'θjon] *nf* position; (*rango
social*) status
positivo, -a [posi'tiβo, a] *adj* positive
poso ['poso] *nm* sediment; (*heces*) dregs *pl*
posponer [pospo'ner] *vt* (*relegar*) to put
behind/below; (*aplazar*) to postpone
posta ['posta] *nf*: **a ~** deliberately, on
purpose
postal [pos'tal] *adj* postal ▷ *nf* postcard
poste ['poste] *nm* (*de telégrafos etc*) post,
pole; (*columna*) pillar
póster [poster] (*pl* **~es, ~s**) *nm* poster
posterior [poste'rjor] *adj* back, rear;
(*siguiente*) following, subsequent; (*más
tarde*) later
postgrado [post'graðo] *nm* = **posgrado**
postizo, -a [pos'tiθo, a] *adj* false,
artificial ▷ *nm* hairpiece
postre ['postre] *nm* sweet, dessert
póstumo, -a ['postumo, a] *adj*
posthumous
postura [pos'tura] *nf* (*del cuerpo*) posture,
position; (*fig*) attitude, position
potable [po'taβle] *adj* drinkable; **agua ~**
drinking water
potaje [po'taxe] *nm* thick vegetable soup
potencia [po'tenθja] *nf* power; **potencial**
[poten'θjal] *adj, nm* potential
potente [po'tente] *adj* powerful
potro, -a ['potro, a] *nm/f* (*Zool*) colt/filly
▷ *nm* (*de gimnasia*) vaulting horse
pozo ['poθo] *nm* well; (*de río*) deep pool; (*de
mina*) shaft
PP (*ESP*) *nm abr* = **Partido Popular**
práctica ['praktika] *nf* practice; (*método*)
method; (*arte, capacidad*) skill; **en la ~** in
practice
practicable [prakti'kaβle] *adj*
practicable; (*camino*) passable
practicante [prakti'kante] *nmf*
(*Med: ayudante de doctor*) medical assistant;

(: *enfermero*) nurse; (*quien practica algo*)
practitioner ▷ *adj* practising
practicar [prakti'kar] *vt* to practise;
(*Deporte*) to play; (*realizar*) to carry out,
perform
práctico, -a ['praktiko, a] *adj* practical;
(*instruido: persona*) skilled, expert
practique *etc vb* V **practicar**
pradera [pra'ðera] *nf* meadow; (*us etc*)
prairie
prado ['praðo] *nm* (*campo*) meadow, field;
(*pastizal*) pasture
Praga ['praɣa] *n* Prague
pragmático, -a [praɣ'matiko, a] *adj*
pragmatic
precario, -a [pre'karjo, a] *adj* precarious
precaución [prekau'θjon] *nf* (*medida
preventiva*) preventive measure, precaution;
(*prudencia*) caution, wariness
precedente [preθe'ðente] *adj* preceding;
(*anterior*) former ▷ *nm* precedent
preceder [preθe'ðer] *vt, vi* to precede, go
before, come before
precepto [pre'θepto] *nm* precept
precinto [pre'θinto] *nm* (*tb: ~ de
garantía*) seal
precio ['preθjo] *nm* price; (*costo*) cost;
(*valor*) value, worth; (*de viaje*) fare; **precio al
contado/de coste/de oportunidad** cash/
cost/bargain price; **precio al por menor**
retail price; **precio de ocasión** bargain
price; **precio de venta al público** retail
price; **precio tope** top price
preciosidad [preθjosi'ðað] *nf* (*valor*)
(high) value, (great) worth; (*encanto*) charm;
(*cosa bonita*) beautiful thing; **es una ~** it's
lovely, it's really beautiful
precioso, -a [pre'θjoso, a] *adj* precious;
(*de mucho valor*) valuable; (*fam*) lovely,
beautiful
precipicio [preθi'pjθjo] *nm* cliff, precipice;
(*fig*) abyss
precipitación [preθipita'θjon] *nf* haste;
(*lluvia*) rainfall
precipitado, -a [preθipi'taðo, a] *adj*
(*conducta*) hasty, rash; (*salida*) hasty, sudden
precipitar [preθipi'tar] *vt* (*arrojar*) to hurl
down, throw; (*apresurar*) to hasten; (*acelerar*)
to speed up, accelerate; **precipitarse** *vr* to
throw o.s.; (*apresurarse*) to rush; (*actuar sin
pensar*) to act rashly
precisamente [preθisa'mente] *adv*
precisely; (*exactamente*) precisely, exactly
precisar [preθi'sar] *vt* (*necesitar*) to need,
require; (*fijar*) to determine exactly, fix;
(*especificar*) to specify
precisión [preθi'sjon] *nf* (*exactitud*)
precision

preciso, -a [pre'θiso, a] adj (exacto) precise; (necesario) necessary, essential

preconcebido, -a [prekonθe'βiðo, a] adj preconceived

precoz [pre'koθ] adj (persona) precocious; (calvicie etc) premature

predecir [preðe'θir] vt to predict, forecast

predestinado, -a [preðesti'naðo, a] adj predestined

predicar [preði'kar] vt, vi to preach

predicción [preðik'θjon] nf prediction

predilecto, -a [preði'lekto, a] adj favourite

predisposición [preðisposi'θjon] nf inclination; prejudice, bias

predominar [preðomi'nar] vt to dominate ▷ vi to predominate; (prevalecer) to prevail; **predominio** nm predominance; prevalence

preescolar [pre(e)sko'lar] adj preschool

prefabricado, -a [prefaβri'kaðo, a] adj prefabricated

prefacio [pre'faθjo] nm preface

preferencia [prefe'renθja] nf preference; **de ~** preferably, for preference

preferible [prefe'riβle] adj preferable

preferir [prefe'rir] vt to prefer

prefiero etc vb V **preferir**

prefijo [pre'fixo] nm (Tel) (dialling) code

pregunta [pre'ɣunta] nf question; **hacer una ~** to ask a question; **preguntas frecuentes** FAQs, frequently asked questions

preguntar [preɣun'tar] vt to ask; (cuestionar) to question ▷ vi to ask; **preguntarse** vr to wonder; **preguntar por algn** to ask for sb; **preguntón, -ona** [preɣun'ton, ona] adj inquisitive

prehistórico, -a [preis'toriko, a] adj prehistoric

prejuicio [pre'xwiθjo] nm (acto) prejudgement; (idea preconcebida) preconception; (parcialidad) prejudice, bias

preludio [pre'luðjo] nm prelude

prematuro, -a [prema'turo, a] adj premature

premeditar [premeði'tar] vt to premeditate

premiar [pre'mjar] vt to reward; (en un concurso) to give a prize to

premio ['premjo] nm reward; prize; (Com) premium

prenatal [prena'tal] adj antenatal, prenatal

prenda ['prenda] nf (ropa) garment, article of clothing; (garantía) pledge; **prendas** nfpl (talentos) talents, gifts

prender [pren'der] vt (captar) to catch, capture; (detener) to arrest; (Costura) to pin, attach; (sujetar) to fasten ▷ vi to catch; (arraigar) to take root; **prenderse** vr (encenderse) to catch fire

prendido, -a [pren'diðo, a] (LAM) adj (luz etc) on

prensa ['prensa] nf press; **la ~** the press

preñado, -a [pre'naðo, a] adj pregnant; **~ de** pregnant with, full of

preocupación [preokupa'θjon] nf worry, concern; (ansiedad) anxiety

preocupado, -a [preoku'paðo, a] adj worried, concerned; (ansioso) anxious

preocupar [preoku'par] vt to worry; **preocuparse** vr to worry; **~se de algo** (hacerse cargo) to take care of sth

preparación [prepara'θjon] nf (acto) preparation; (estado) readiness; (entrenamiento) training

preparado, -a [prepa'raðo, a] adj (dispuesto) prepared; (Culin) ready (to serve) ▷ nm preparation

preparar [prepa'rar] vt (disponer) to prepare, get ready; (Tec: tratar) to prepare, process; (entrenar) to teach, train; **prepararse** vr: **~se a o para** to prepare to o for, get ready to o for; **preparativo, -a** adj preparatory, preliminary; **preparativos** nmpl preparations; **preparatoria** (MÉX) nf sixth-form college (BRIT), senior high school (US)

presa ['presa] nf (cosa apresada) catch; (víctima) victim; (de animal) prey; (de agua) dam

presagiar [presa'xjar] vt to presage, forebode; **presagio** nm omen

prescindir [presθin'dir] vi: **~ de** (privarse de) to do o go without; (descartar) to dispense with

prescribir [preskri'βir] vt to prescribe

presencia [pre'senθja] nf presence; **presenciar** vt to be present at; (asistir a) to attend; (ver) to see, witness

presentación [presenta'θjon] nf presentation; (introducción) introduction

presentador, a [presenta'ðor, a] nm/f presenter, compère

presentar [presen'tar] vt to present; (ofrecer) to offer; (mostrar) to show, display; (a una persona) to introduce; **presentarse** vr (llegar inesperadamente) to appear, turn up; (ofrecerse: como candidato) to run, stand; (aparecer) to show, appear; (solicitar empleo) to apply

presente [pre'sente] adj present ▷ nm present; **hacer ~** to state, declare; **tener ~** to remember, bear in mind

presentimiento [presenti'mjento] nm

premonition, presentiment
presentir [presen'tir] vt to have a
premonition of
preservación [preserβa'θjon] nf
protection, preservation
preservar [preser'βar] vt to protect,
preserve; **preservativo** nm sheath,
condom
presidencia [presi'ðenθja] nf presidency;
(de comité) chairmanship
presidente [presi'ðente] nmf president;
(de comité) chairman/woman
presidir [presi'ðir] vt (dirigir) to preside at,
preside over; (: comité) to take the chair at;
(dominar) to dominate, rule ▷ vi to preside;
to take the chair
presión [pre'sjon] nf pressure; **presión
atmosférica** atmospheric o air pressure;
presionar vt to press; (fig) to press, put
pressure on ▷ vi: **presionar para** to press for
preso, -a ['preso, a] nm/f prisoner;
tomar o **llevar ~ a algn** to arrest sb, take
sb prisoner
prestación [presta'θjon] nf service;
(subsidio) benefit; **prestaciones** nfpl (Tec,
Auto) performance features
prestado, -a [pres'taðo, a] adj on loan;
pedir ~ to borrow
prestamista [presta'mista] nmf
moneylender
préstamo ['prestamo] nm loan;
préstamo hipotecario mortgage
prestar [pres'tar] vt to lend, loan;
(atención) to pay; (ayuda) to give
prestigio [pres'tixjo] nm prestige;
prestigioso, -a adj (honorable) prestigious;
(famoso, renombrado) renowned, famous
presumido, -a [presu'miðo, a] adj
(persona) vain
presumir [presu'mir] vt to presume ▷ vi
(tener aires) to be conceited; **presunto, -a**
adj (supuesto) supposed, presumed; (así
llamado) so-called; **presuntuoso, -a** adj
conceited, presumptuous
presupuesto [presu'pwesto] pp de
presuponer ▷ nm (Finanzas) budget;
(estimación: de costo) estimate
pretencioso, -a [preten'θjoso, a] adj
pretentious
pretender [preten'der] vt (intentar) to try
to, seek to; (reivindicar) to claim; (buscar) to
seek, try for; (cortejar) to woo, court; **~ que**
to expect that

▌ No confundir **pretender** con la palabra
inglesa pretend.

pretendiente nmf (amante) suitor; (al
trono) pretender; **pretensión** nf (aspiración)
aspiration; (reivindicación) claim; (orgullo)

pretension
pretexto [pre'teksto] nm pretext; (excusa)
excuse
prevención [preβen'θjon] nf prevention;
(precaución) precaution
prevenido, -a [preβe'niðo, a] adj
prepared, ready; (cauteloso) cautious
prevenir [preβe'nir] vt (impedir) to
prevent; (predisponer) to prejudice, bias;
(avisar) to warn; (preparar) to prepare,
get ready; **prevenirse** vr to get ready,
prepare; **~se contra** to take precautions
against; **preventivo, -a** adj preventive,
precautionary
prever [pre'βer] vt to foresee
previo, -a ['preβjo, a] adj (anterior)
previous; (preliminar) preliminary ▷ prep: **~
acuerdo de los otros** subject to the
agreement of the others
previsión [preβi'sjon] nf (perspicacia)
foresight; (predicción) forecast; **previsto, -a**
adj anticipated, forecast
prima ['prima] nf (Com) bonus; (de seguro)
premium; V tb **primo**
primario, -a [pri'marjo, a] adj primary
primavera [prima'βera] nf spring(-time)
primera [pri'mera] nf (Auto) first gear;
(Ferro: tb: **~ clase**) first class; **de ~** (fam) first-
class, first-rate
primero, -a [pri'mero, a] (adj **primer**) first;
(principal) prime adv first; (más bien) sooner,
rather; **primera plana** front page
primitivo, -a [primi'tiβo, a] adj
primitive; (original) original
primo, -a ['primo, a] adj prime ▷ nm/f
cousin; (fam) fool, idiot; **materias primas**
raw materials; **primo hermano** first cousin
primogénito, -a [primo'xenito, a] adj
first-born
primoroso, -a [primo'roso, a] adj
exquisite, delicate
princesa [prin'θesa] nf princess
principal [prinθi'pal] adj principal, main
▷ nm (jefe) chief, principal
príncipe ['prinθipe] nm prince
principiante [prinθi'pjante] nmf
beginner
principio [prin'θipjo] nm (comienzo)
beginning, start; (origen) origin; (primera
etapa) rudiment, basic idea; (moral)
principle; **desde el ~** from the first; **en un ~**
at first; **a ~s de** at the beginning of
pringue ['pringe] nm (grasa) grease, fat,
dripping
prioridad [priori'ðað] nf priority
prisa ['prisa] nf (apresuramiento) hurry,
haste; (rapidez) speed; (urgencia) (sense of)
urgency; **a** o **de ~** quickly; **correr ~** to be

urgent; **darse ~** to hurry up; **tener ~** to be
in a hurry

prisión [pri'sjon] nf (cárcel) prison; (período
de cárcel) imprisonment; **prisionero, -a**
nm/f prisoner

prismáticos [pris'matikos] nmpl
binoculars

privado, -a [pri'βaðo, a] adj private

privar [pri'βar] vt to deprive; **privativo, -a**
adj exclusive

privilegiar [priβile'xjar] vt to grant a
privilege to; (favorecer) to favour

privilegio [priβi'lexjo] nm privilege;
(concesión) concession

pro [pro] nm o f profit, advantage
▷ prep: **asociación ~ ciegos** association
for the blind ▷ prefijo: **~ americano** pro-
American; **en ~ de** on behalf of, for; **los ~s y
los contras** the pros and cons

proa ['proa] nf bow, prow; **de ~** bow cpd,
fore

probabilidad [proβaβili'ðað] nf
probability, likelihood; (oportunidad,
posibilidad) chance, prospect; **probable** adj
probable, likely

probador [proβa'ðor] nm (en tienda)
fitting room

probar [pro'βar] vt (demostrar) to prove;
(someter a prueba) to test, try out; (ropa) to try
on; (comida) to taste ▷ vi to try; **~se un traje**
to try on a suit

probeta [pro'βeta] nf test tube

problema [pro'βlema] nm problem

procedente [proθe'ðente] adj (razonable)
reasonable; (conforme a derecho) proper,
fitting; **~ de** coming from, originating in

proceder [proθe'ðer] vi (avanzar) to
proceed; (actuar) to act; (ser correcto) to
be right (and proper), be fitting ▷ nm
(comportamiento) behaviour, conduct; **~ de**
to come from, originate in; **procedimiento**
nm procedure; (proceso) process; (método)
means pl, method

procesador [proθesa'ðor] nm processor;
procesador de textos word processor

procesar [proθe'sar] vt to try, put on trial

procesión [proθe'sjon] nf procession

proceso [pro'θeso] nm process; (Jur) trial

proclamar [prokla'mar] vt to proclaim

procrear [prokre'ar] vt, vi to procreate

procurador, a [prokura'ðor, a] nm/f
attorney

procurar [proku'rar] vt (intentar) to
try, endeavour; (conseguir) to get, obtain;
(asegurar) to secure; (producir) to produce

prodigio [pro'ðixjo] nm prodigy; (milagro)
wonder, marvel; **prodigioso, -a** adj
prodigious, marvellous

pródigo, -a ['proðiχo, a] adj: **hijo ~**
prodigal son

producción [proðuk'θjon] nf (gen)
production; (producto) output; **producción
en serie** mass production

producir [proðu'θir] vt to produce;
(causar) to cause, bring about; **producirse**
vr (cambio) to come about; (accidente) to
take place; (problema etc) to arise; (hacerse) to
be produced, be made; (estallar) to break out

productividad [proðuktiβi'ðað]
nf productivity; **productivo, -a** adj
productive; (provechoso) profitable

producto [pro'ðukto] nm product

productor, a [proðuk'tor, a] adj
productive, producing ▷ nm/f producer

proeza [pro'eθa] nf exploit, feat

profano, -a [pro'fano, a] adj profane
▷ nm/f layman/woman

profecía [profe'θia] nf prophecy

profesión [profe'sjon] nf profession; (en
formulario) occupation; **profesional** adj
professional

profesor, a [profe'sor, a] nm/f teacher;
profesorado nm teaching profession

profeta [pro'feta] nmf prophet

prófugo, -a ['profuχo, a] nm/f fugitive;
(Mil: desertor) deserter

profundidad [profundi'ðað] nf depth;
profundizar vi: **profundizar en** to go
deeply into; **profundo, -a** adj deep;
(misterio, pensador) profound

progenitor [proxeni'tor] nm ancestor;
progenitores nmpl (padres) parents

programa [pro'xrama] nm programme
(BRIT), program (US); **programa de estudios**
curriculum, syllabus; **programación** nf
programming; **programador, a** nm/f
programmer; **programar** vt to program

progresar [proxre'sar] vi to progress,
make progress; **progresista** adj,
nmf progressive; **progresivo, -a** adj
progressive; (gradual) gradual; (continuo)
continuous; **progreso** nm progress

prohibición [proiβi'θjon] nf prohibition,
ban

prohibir [proi'βir] vt to prohibit, ban,
forbid; **prohibido o se prohibe fumar** no
smoking; **"prohibido el paso"** "no entry"

prójimo, -a ['proximo, a] nm/f fellow
man; (vecino) neighbour

prólogo ['proloχo] nm prologue

prolongar [prolon'xar] vt to extend;
(reunión etc) to prolong; (calle, tubo) to extend

promedio [pro'meðjo] nm average; (de
distancia) middle, mid-point

promesa [pro'mesa] nf promise

prometer [prome'ter] vt to promise ▷ vi

to show promise; **prometerse** vr (novios) to get engaged; **prometido, -a** adj promised; engaged ▷ nm/f fiancé/fiancée

prominente [promi'nente] adj prominent

promoción [promo'θjon] nf promotion

promotor [promo'tor] nm promoter; (instigador) instigator

promover [promo'βer] vt to promote; (causar) to cause; (instigar) to instigate, stir up

promulgar [promul'ɣar] vt to promulgate; (anunciar) to proclaim

pronombre [pro'nombre] nm pronoun

pronosticar [pronosti'kar] vt to predict, foretell, forecast; **pronóstico** nm prediction, forecast; **pronóstico del tiempo** weather forecast

pronto, -a ['pronto, a] adj (rápido) prompt, quick; (preparado) ready ▷ adv quickly, promptly; (en seguida) at once, right away; (dentro de poco) soon; (temprano) early ▷ nm: **tiene unos ~s muy malos** he gets ratty all of a sudden (inf); **de ~** suddenly; **por lo ~** meanwhile, for the present

pronunciación [pronunθja'θjon] nf pronunciation

pronunciar [pronun'θjar] vt to pronounce; (discurso) to make, deliver; **pronunciarse** vr to revolt, rebel; (declararse) to declare o.s.

propagación [propaɣa'θjon] nf propagation

propaganda [propa'ɣanda] nf (Pol) propaganda; (Com) advertising

propenso, -a [pro'penso, a] adj inclined to; **ser ~ a** to be inclined to, have a tendency to

propicio, -a [pro'piθjo, a] adj favourable, propitious

propiedad [propje'ðað] nf property; (posesión) possession, ownership; **propiedad particular** private property

propietario, -a [propje'tarjo, a] nm/f owner, proprietor

propina [pro'pina] nf tip

propio, -a ['propjo, a] adj own, of one's own; (característico) characteristic, typical; (debido) proper; (mismo) selfsame, very; **el ~ ministro** the minister himself; **¿tienes casa propia?** have you a house of your own?

proponer [propo'ner] vt to propose, put forward; (problema) to pose; **proponerse** vr to propose, intend

proporción [propor'θjon] nf proportion; (Mat) ratio; **proporciones** nfpl (dimensiones) dimensions; (fig) size sg; **proporcionado, -a** adj proportionate; (regular) medium,

middling; (justo) just right; **proporcionar** vt (dar) to give, supply, provide

proposición [proposi'θjon] nf proposition; (propuesta) proposal

propósito [pro'posito] nm purpose; (intento) aim, intention ▷ adv: **a ~** by the way, incidentally; (a posta) on purpose, deliberately; **a ~ de** about, with regard to

propuesta [pro'pwesta] vb V **proponer** ▷ nf proposal

propulsar [propul'sar] vt to drive, propel; (fig) to promote, encourage; **propulsión** nf propulsion; **propulsión a chorro** o **por reacción** jet propulsion

prórroga ['prorroɣa] nf extension; (Jur) stay; (Com) deferment; (Deporte) extra time; **prorrogar** vt (período) to extend; (decisión) to defer, postpone

prosa ['prosa] nf prose

proseguir [prose'ɣir] vt to continue, carry on ▷ vi to continue, go on

prospecto [pros'pekto] nm prospectus

prosperar [prospe'rar] vi to prosper, thrive, flourish; **prosperidad** nf prosperity; (éxito) success; **próspero, -a** adj prosperous, flourishing; (que tiene éxito) successful

prostíbulo [pros'tiβulo] nm brothel (BRIT), house of prostitution (US)

prostitución [prostitu'θjon] nf prostitution

prostituir [prosti'twir] vt to prostitute; **prostituirse** vr to prostitute o.s., become a prostitute

prostituta [prosti'tuta] nf prostitute

protagonista [protaɣo'nista] nmf protagonist

protección [protek'θjon] nf protection

protector, a [protek'tor, a] adj protective, protecting ▷ nm/f protector

proteger [prote'xer] vt to protect; **protegido, -a** nm/f protégé/protégée

proteína [prote'ina] nf protein

protesta [pro'testa] nf protest; (declaración) protestation

protestante [protes'tante] adj Protestant

protestar [protes'tar] vt to protest, declare ▷ vi to protest

protocolo [proto'kolo] nm protocol

prototipo [proto'tipo] nm prototype

provecho [pro'βetʃo] nm advantage, benefit; (Finanzas) profit; **¡buen ~!** bon appétit!; **en ~ de** to the benefit of; **sacar ~ de** to benefit from, profit by

provenir [proβe'nir] vi: **~ de** to come o stem from

proverbio [pro'βerβjo] nm proverb

providencia [proβiˈðenθja] nf providence
provincia [proˈβinθja] nf province
provisión [proβiˈsjon] nf provision; (abastecimiento) provision, supply; (medida) measure, step
provisional [proβisjoˈnal] adj provisional
provocar [proβoˈkar] vt to provoke; (alentar) to tempt, invite; (causar) to bring about, lead to; (promover) to promote; (estimular) to rouse, stimulate; **¿te provoca un café?** (CAM) would you like a coffee?; **provocativo, -a** adj provocative
proxeneta [prokseˈneta] nm pimp
próximamente [proksimaˈmente] adv shortly, soon
proximidad [proksimiˈðað] nf closeness, proximity; **próximo, -a** adj near, close; (vecino) neighbouring; (siguiente) next
proyectar [projekˈtar] vt (objeto) to hurl, throw; (luz) to cast, shed; (Cine) to screen, show; (planear) to plan
proyectil [projekˈtil] nm projectile, missile
proyecto [proˈjekto] nm plan; (estimación de costo) detailed estimate
proyector [projekˈtor] nm (Cine) projector
prudencia [pruˈðenθja] nf (sabiduría) wisdom; (cuidado) care; **prudente** adj sensible, wise; (conductor) careful
prueba etc [ˈprweβa] vb V **probar** ▷ nf proof; (ensayo) test, trial; (degustación) tasting, sampling; (de ropa) fitting; **a ~** on trial; **a ~ de** proof against; **a ~ de agua/fuego** waterproof/fireproof; **someter a ~ to** put to the test
psico... [siko] prefijo psycho...; **psicología** nf psychology; **psicológico, -a** adj psychological; **psicólogo, -a** nm/f psychologist; **psicópata** nmf psychopath; **psicosis** nf inv psychosis
psiquiatra [siˈkjatra] nmf psychiatrist; **psiquiátrico, -a** adj psychiatric
PSOE [peˈsoe] (ESP) nm abr = **Partido Socialista Obrero Español**
púa [ˈpua] nf (Bot, Zool) prickle, spine; (para guitarra) plectrum (BRIT), pick (US); **alambre de ~** barbed wire
pubertad [puβerˈtað] nf puberty
publicación [puβlikaˈθjon] nf publication
publicar [puβliˈkar] vt (editar) to publish; (hacer público) to publicize; (divulgar) to make public, divulge
publicidad [puβliθiˈðað] nf publicity; (Com: propaganda) advertising; **publicitario, -a** adj publicity cpd; advertising cpd
público, -a [ˈpuβliko, a] adj public ▷ nm public; (Teatro etc) audience

puchero [puˈtʃero] nm (Culin: guiso) stew; (: olla) cooking pot; **hacer ~s** to pout
pucho [ˈputʃo] (cs: fam) nm cigarette, fag (BRIT)
pude etc vb V **poder**
pudiente [puˈðjente] adj (rico) wealthy, well-to-do
pudiera etc vb V **poder**
pudor [puˈðor] nm modesty
pudrir [puˈðrir] vt to rot; **pudrirse** vr to rot, decay
pueblo [ˈpweβlo] nm people; (nación) nation; (aldea) village
puedo etc vb V **poder**
puente [ˈpwente] nm bridge; **hacer ~** (fam) to take extra days off work between 2 public holidays; to take a long weekend; **puente aéreo** shuttle service; **puente colgante** suspension bridge; **puente levadizo** drawbridge

● **HACER PUENTE**
●
● When a public holiday in Spain falls on
● a Tuesday or Thursday it is common
● practice for employers to make the
● Monday or Friday a holiday as well and
● to give everyone a four-day weekend.
● This is known as **hacer puente**. When
● a named public holiday such as the **Día
● de la Constitución** falls on a Tuesday
● or Thursday, people refer to the whole
● holiday period as e.g. the **puente de la
● Constitución**.

puerco, -a [ˈpwerko, a] nm/f pig/sow ▷ adj (sucio) dirty, filthy; (obsceno) disgusting; **puerco espín** porcupine
pueril [pweˈril] adj childish
puerro [ˈpwerro] nm leek
puerta [ˈpwerta] nf door; (de jardín) gate; (portal) doorway; (fig) gateway; (portería) goal; **a la ~** at the door; **a ~ cerrada** behind closed doors; **puerta giratoria** revolving door
puerto [ˈpwerto] nm port; (paso) pass; (fig) haven, refuge
Puerto Rico [pwertoˈriko] nm Puerto Rico; **puertorriqueño, -a** adj, nm/f Puerto Rican
pues [pwes] adv (entonces) then; (bueno) well, well then; (así que) so ▷ conj (ya que) since; **¡~ sí!** yes!, certainly!
puesta [ˈpwesta] nf (apuesta) bet, stake; **puesta al día** updating; **puesta a punto** fine tuning; **puesta de sol** sunset; **puesta en marcha** starting
puesto, -a [ˈpwesto, a] pp de **poner**

P

▷ adj: **tener algo ~** to have sth on, be wearing sth ▷ nm (lugar, posición) place; (trabajo) post, job; (Com) stall ▷ conj: **~ que** since, as

púgil ['puxil] nm boxer

pulga ['pulɣa] nf flea

pulgada [pul'ɣaða] nf inch

pulgar [pul'ɣar] nm thumb

pulir [pu'lir] vt to polish; (alisar) to smooth; (fig) to polish up, touch up

pulmón [pul'mon] nm lung; **pulmonía** nf pneumonia

pulpa ['pulpa] nf pulp; (de fruta) flesh, soft part

pulpería [pulpe'ria] (LAM) nf (tienda) small grocery store

púlpito ['pulpito] nm pulpit

pulpo ['pulpo] nm octopus

pulque ['pulke] nm pulque

● **PULQUE**
●
● **Pulque** is a thick, white, alcoholic
● drink which is very popular in Mexico.
● In ancient times it was considered
● sacred by the Aztecs. It is produced by
● fermenting the juice of the **maguey**,
● a Mexican cactus similar to the agave.
● It can be drunk by itself or mixed with
● fruit or vegetable juice.

pulsación [pulsa'θjon] nf beat; **pulsaciones** pulse rate

pulsar [pul'sar] vt (tecla) to touch, tap; (Mús) to play; (botón) to press, push ▷ vi to pulsate; (latir) to beat, throb

pulsera [pul'sera] nf bracelet

pulso ['pulso] nm (Anat) pulse; (fuerza) strength; (firmeza) steadiness, steady hand

pulverizador [pulβeriθa'ðor] nm spray, spray gun

pulverizar [pulβeri'θar] vt to pulverize; (líquido) to spray

puna ['puna] (CAM) nf mountain sickness

punta ['punta] nf point, tip; (extremo) end; (fig) touch, trace; **horas ~** peak o rush hours; **sacar ~ a** to sharpen

puntada [pun'taða] nf (Costura) stitch

puntal [pun'tal] nm prop, support

puntapié [punta'pje] nm kick

puntería [punte'ria] nf (de arma) aim, aiming; (destreza) marksmanship

puntero, -a [pun'tero, a] adj leading ▷ nm (palo) pointer

puntiagudo, -a [puntja'ɣuðo, a] adj sharp, pointed

puntilla [pun'tiʎa] nf (encaje) lace edging o trim; **(andar) de ~s** (to walk) on tiptoe

punto ['punto] nm (gen) point; (señal diminuta) spot, dot; (Costura, Med) stitch; (lugar) spot, place; (momento) point, moment; **a ~** ready; **estar a ~ de** to be on the point of o about to; **en ~** on the dot; **hasta cierto ~** to some extent; **hacer ~** (ESP: tejer) to knit; **dos ~s** (Ling) colon; **punto de interrogación** question mark; **punto de vista** point of view, viewpoint; **punto final** full stop (BRIT), period (US); **punto muerto** dead center; (Auto) neutral (gear); **punto y aparte** (en dictado) full stop, new paragraph; **punto y coma** semicolon

puntocom [punto'kom] adj inv, nf inv dotcom

puntuación [puntwa'θjon] nf punctuation; (puntos: en examen) mark(s) (pl); (Deporte) score

puntual [pun'twal] adj (a tiempo) punctual; (exacto) exact, accurate; **puntualidad** nf punctuality; exactness, accuracy

puntuar [pun'twar] vi (Deporte) to score, count

punzante [pun'θante] adj (dolor) shooting, sharp; (herramienta) sharp

puñado [pu'ɲaðo] nm handful

puñal [pu'ɲal] nm dagger; **puñalada** nf stab

puñetazo [puɲe'taθo] nm punch

puño ['puɲo] nm (Anat) fist; (cantidad) fistful, handful; (Costura) cuff; (de herramienta) handle

pupila [pu'pila] nf pupil

pupitre [pu'pitre] nm desk

puré [pu're] nm purée; (sopa) (thick) soup; **puré de papas** (LAM) mashed potatoes; **puré de patatas** (ESP) mashed potatoes

purga ['purɣa] nf purge; **purgante** adj, nm purgative

purgatorio [purɣa'torjo] nm purgatory

purificar [purifi'kar] vt to purify; (refinar) to refine

puritano, -a [puri'tano, a] adj (actitud) puritanical; (iglesia, tradición) puritan ▷ nm/f puritan

puro, -a ['puro, a] adj pure; (verdad) simple, plain ▷ nm cigar

púrpura ['purpura] nf purple

pus [pus] nm pus

puse etc vb V **poder**

pusiera etc vb V **poder**

puta ['puta] (fam!) nf whore, prostitute

putrefacción [putrefak'θjon] nf rotting, putrefaction

● **PVP** nm abr (= precio de venta al público) RRP

pyme, PYME ['pime] nf abr (= Pequeña y Mediana Empresa) SME

q

q

fraction

quebrantar [keβran'tar] *vt* (*infringir*) to violate, transgress

quebrar [ke'βrar] *vt* to break, smash ▷ *vi* to go bankrupt

quedar [ke'ðar] *vi* to stay, remain; (*encontrarse: sitio*) to be; (*haber aún*) to remain, be left; **quedarse** *vr* to remain, stay (behind); **~se (con)** algo to keep sth; **~ en** (*acordar*) to agree on/to; **~ en nada** to come to nothing; **~ por hacer** to be still to be done; **~ ciego/mudo** to be left blind/dumb; **no te queda bien ese vestido** that dress doesn't suit you; **eso queda muy lejos** that's a long way (away); **quedamos a las seis** we agreed to meet at six

quedo, -a ['keðo, a] *adj* still ▷ *adv* softly, gently

quehacer [kea'θer] *nm* task, job; **quehaceres (domésticos)** *nmpl* household chores

queja ['kexa] *nf* complaint; **quejarse** *vr* (*enfermo*) to moan, groan; (*protestar*) to complain; **quejarse de que** to complain that; **quejido** *nm* moan

quemado, -a [ke'maðo, a] *adj* burnt

quemadura [kema'ðura] *nf* burn, scald

quemar [ke'mar] *vt* to burn; (*fig: malgastar*) to burn up, squander ▷ *vi* to be burning hot; **quemarse** *vr* (*consumirse*) to burn (up); (*del sol*) to get sunburnt

quemarropa [kema'rropa]: **a ~** *adv* point-blank

quepo *etc vb* V **caber**

querella [ke'reʎa] *nf* (*Jur*) charge; (*disputa*) dispute

---

que [ke] *conj* **1** (*con oración subordinada: muchas veces no se traduce*) that; **dijo que vendría** he said (that) he would come; **espero que lo encuentres** I hope (that) you find it; V *tb* **el**

2 (*en oración independiente*): **¡que entre!** send him in; **¡que aproveche!** enjoy your meal!; **¡que se mejore tu padre!** I hope your father gets better

3 (*enfático*): **¿me quieres? - ¡que sí!** do you love me? - of course!

4 (*consecutivo: muchas veces no se traduce*) that; **es tan grande que no lo puedo levantar** it's so big (that) I can't lift it

5 (*comparaciones*) than; **yo que tú/él** if I were you/him; V *tb* **más, menos, mismo**

6 (*valor disyuntivo*): **que le guste o no** whether he likes it or not; **que venga o que no venga** whether he comes or not

7 (*porque*): **no puedo, que tengo que quedarme en casa** I can't, I've got to stay in ▷ *pron* **1** (*cosa*) that, which; (*+ prep*) which; **el sombrero que te compraste** the hat (that *o* which) you bought; **la cama en que dormí** the bed (that *o* which) I slept in

2 (*persona: suj*) that, who; (*: objeto*) that, whom; **el amigo que me acompañó al museo** the friend that *o* who went to the museum with me; **la chica que invité** the girl (that *o* whom) I invited

qué [ke] *adj* what?, which? ▷ *pron* what?; **¡~ divertido!** how funny!; **¿~ edad tienes?** how old are you?; **¿de ~ me hablas?** what are you saying to me?; **¿~ tal?** how are you?, how are things?; **¿~ hay (de nuevo)?** what's new?

quebrado, -a [ke'βraðo, a] *adj* (*roto*) broken ▷ *nm/f* bankrupt ▷ *nm* (*Mat*)

---

querer [ke'rer] *vt* **1** (*desear*) to want; **quiero más dinero** I want more money; **quisiera** *o* **querría un té** I'd like a tea; **sin querer** unintentionally; **quiero ayudar/que vayas** I want to help/you to go

2 (*preguntas: para pedir algo*): **¿quiere abrir la ventana?** could you open the window?; **¿quieres echarme una mano?** can you give me a hand?

3 (*amar*) to love; (*tener cariño a*) to be fond of; **te quiero** I love you; **quiere mucho a sus hijos** he's very fond of his children

4 le pedí que me dejara ir pero no quiso I asked him to let me go but he refused

querido, -a [ke'riðo, a] *adj* dear ▷ *nm/f* darling; (*amante*) lover

queso ['keso] *nm* cheese; **queso crema** (*LAM*) cream cheese; **queso de untar** (*ESP*) cream cheese; **queso manchego** *sheep's milk cheese made in La Mancha*

quicio ['kiθjo] *nm* hinge; **sacar a algn de ~** to get on sb's nerves

quiebra ['kjeβra] *nf* break, split; (Com) bankruptcy; (Econ) slump

quiebro ['kjeβro] *nm (del cuerpo)* swerve

quien [kjen] *pron* who; **hay ~ piensa que** there are those who think that; **no hay ~ lo haga** no-one will do it

quién [kjen] *pron* who, whom; **¿~ es?** who's there?

quienquiera [kjen'kjera] (*pl* **quienesquiera**) *pron* whoever

quiero *etc vb* V **querer**

quieto, -a ['kjeto, a] *adj* still; *(carácter)* placid

> ⚠ No confundir **quieto** con la palabra inglesa *quiet*.

quietud *nf* stillness

químico, -a ['kimiko, a] *adj* chemical ▷ *nm/f* chemist ▷ *nf* chemistry

quincalla [kin'kaʎa] *nf* hardware, ironmongery (BRIT)

quince ['kinθe] *num* fifteen; **~ días** a fortnight; **quinceañero, -a** *nm/f* teenager; **quincena** *nf* fortnight; *(pago)* fortnightly pay; **quincenal** *adj* fortnightly

quiniela [ki'njela] *nf* football pools *pl*; **quinielas** *nfpl (impreso)* pools coupon *sg*

quinientos, -as [ki'njentos, as] *adj, num* five hundred

quinto, -a ['kinto, a] *adj* fifth ▷ *nf* country house; *(Mil)* call-up, draft

quiosco ['kjosko] *nm (de música)* bandstand; *(de periódicos)* news stand

quirófano [ki'rofano] *nm* operating theatre

quirúrgico, -a [ki'rurxiko, a] *adj* surgical

quise *etc vb* V **querer**

quisiera *etc vb* V **querer**

quisquilloso, -a [kiski'ʎoso, a] *adj (susceptible)* touchy; *(meticuloso)* pernickety

quiste ['kiste] *nm* cyst

quitaesmalte [kitaes'malte] *nm* nail-polish remover

quitamanchas [kita'mantʃas] *nm inv* stain remover

quitanieves [kita'njeβes] *nm inv* snowplough (BRIT), snowplow (US)

quitar [ki'tar] *vt* to remove, take away; *(ropa)* to take off; *(dolor)* to relieve; **¡quita de ahí!** get away!; **quitarse** *vr* to withdraw; *(ropa)* to take off; **se quitó el sombrero** he took off his hat

Quito ['kito] *n* Quito

quizá(s) [ki'θa(s)] *adv* perhaps, maybe

rábano ['raβano] *nm* radish; **me importa un ~** I don't give a damn

rabia ['raβja] *nf (Med)* rabies *sg*; *(ira)* fury, rage; **rabiar** *vi* to have rabies; to rage, be furious; **rabiar por algo** to long for sth

rabieta [ra'βjeta] *nf* tantrum, fit of temper

rabino [ra'βino] *nm* rabbi

rabioso, -a [ra'βjoso, a] *adj* rabid; *(fig)* furious

rabo ['raβo] *nm* tail

racha ['ratʃa] *nf* gust of wind; **buena/mala ~** spell of good/bad luck

racial [ra'θjal] *adj* racial, race *cpd*

racimo [ra'θimo] *nm* bunch

ración [ra'θjon] *nf* portion; **raciones** *nfpl* rations

racional [raθjo'nal] *adj (razonable)* reasonable; *(lógico)* rational

racionar [raθjo'nar] *vt* to ration (out)

racismo [ra'θismo] *nm* racism; **racista** *adj, nm* racist

radar [ra'ðar] *nm* radar

radiador [raðja'ðor] *nm* radiator

radiante [ra'ðjante] *adj* radiant

radical [raði'kal] *adj, nmf* radical

radicar [raði'kar] *vi*: **~ en** *(dificultad, problema)* to lie in; *(solución)* to consist in

radio ['raðjo] *nf* radio; *(aparato)* radio (set) ▷ *nm (Mat)* radius; *(Quím)* radium; **radioactividad** *nf* radioactivity; **radioactivo, -a** *adj* radioactive; **radiografía** *nf* X-ray; **radioterapia** *nf* radiotherapy; **radioyente** *nmf* listener

ráfaga ['rafaɣa] *nf* gust; *(de luz)* flash; *(de tiros)* burst

raíz [ra'iθ] *nf* root; **a ~ de** as a result of; **raíz cuadrada** square root

raja ['raxa] *nf (de melón etc)* slice; *(grieta)* crack; **rajar** *vt* to split; *(fam)* to slash; **rajarse** *vr* to split, crack; **rajarse de** to back out of

rajatabla [raxa'taβla]: **a ~** adv (estrictamente) strictly, to the letter

rallador [raʎa'ðor] nm grater

rallar [ra'ʎar] vt to grate

rama ['rama] nf branch; **ramaje** nm branches pl, foliage; **ramal** nm (de cuerda) strand; (Ferro) branch line (BRIT); (Auto) branch (road) (BRIT)

rambla ['rambla] nf (avenida) avenue

ramo ['ramo] nm branch; (sección) department, section

rampa ['rampa] nf ramp; **rampa de acceso** entrance ramp

rana ['rana] nf frog; **salto de ~** leapfrog

ranchero [ran'tʃero] (MÉX) nm (hacendado) rancher; smallholder

rancho ['rantʃo] nm (grande) ranch; (pequeño) small farm

rancio, -a ['ranθjo, a] adj (comestibles) rancid; (vino) aged, mellow; (fig) ancient

rango ['rango] nm rank, standing

ranura [ra'nura] nf groove; (de teléfono etc) slot

rapar [ra'par] vt to shave; (los cabellos) to crop

rapaz [ra'paθ] (nf ~a) nmf young boy/girl ▷ adj (Zool) predatory

rape ['rape] nm (pez) monkfish; **al ~** cropped

rapé [ra'pe] nm snuff

rapidez [rapi'ðeθ] nf speed, rapidity; **rápido, -a** adj fast, quick ▷ adv quickly ▷ nm (Ferro) express; **rápidos** nmpl rapids

rapiña [ra'piɲa] nm robbery; **ave de ~** bird of prey

raptar [rap'tar] vt to kidnap; **rapto** nm kidnapping; (impulso) sudden impulse; (éxtasis) ecstasy, rapture

raqueta [ra'keta] nf racquet

raquítico, -a [ra'kitiko, a] adj stunted; (fig) poor, inadequate

rareza [ra'reθa] nf rarity; (fig) eccentricity

raro, -a ['raro, a] adj rare; (extraño) odd, strange; (excepcional) remarkable

ras [ras] nm: **a ~ de** level with; **a ~ de tierra** at ground level

rasar [ra'sar] vt (igualar) to level

rascacielos [raska'θjelos] nm inv skyscraper

rascar [ras'kar] vt (con las uñas etc) to scratch; (raspar) to scrape; **rascarse** vr to scratch (o.s.)

rasgar [ras'xar] vt to tear, rip (up)

rasgo ['rasxo] nm (con pluma) stroke; **rasgos** nmpl (facciones) features, characteristics; **a grandes ~s** in outline, broadly

rasguño [ras'xuɲo] nm scratch

raso, -a ['raso, a] adj (liso) flat, level; (a baja altura) very low ▷ nm satin; **cielo ~** clear sky

raspadura [raspa'ðura] nf (acto) scrape, scraping; (marca) scratch; **raspaduras** nfpl (de papel etc) scrapings

raspar [ras'par] vt to scrape; (arañar) to scratch; (limar) to file

rastra ['rastra] nf (Agr) rake; **a ~s** by dragging; (fig) unwillingly

rastrear [rastre'ar] vt (seguir) to track

rastrero, -a [ras'trero, a] adj (Bot, Zool) creeping; (fig) despicable, mean

rastrillo [ras'triʎo] nm rake

rastro ['rastro] nm (Agr) rake; (pista) track, trail; (vestigio) trace; **el R~** (ESP) the Madrid fleamarket

rasurado [rasu'raðo] (MÉX) nm shaving; **rasuradora** [rasura'ðora] (MÉX) nf electric shaver; **rasurar** [rasu'rar] (MÉX) vt to shave; **rasurarse** vr to shave

rata ['rata] nf rat

ratear [rate'ar] vt (robar) to steal

ratero, -a [ra'tero, a] adj light-fingered ▷ nm/f (carterista) pickpocket; (ladrón) petty thief

rato ['rato] nm while, short time; **a ~s** from time to time; **hay para ~** there's still a long way to go; **al poco ~** soon afterwards; **pasar el ~** to kill time; **pasar un buen/mal ~** to have a good/rough time; **en mis ~s libres** in my spare time

ratón [ra'ton] nm mouse; **ratonera** nf mousetrap

raudal [rau'ðal] nm torrent; **a ~es** in abundance

raya ['raja] nf line; (marca) scratch; (en tela) stripe; (de pelo) parting; (límite) boundary; (pez) ray; (puntuación) dash; **a ~s** striped; **pasarse de la ~** to go too far; **tener a ~** to keep in check; **rayar** vt to line; to scratch; (subrayar) to underline ▷ vi: **rayar en** o **con** to border on

rayo ['rajo] nm (del sol) ray, beam; (de luz) shaft; (en una tormenta) (flash of) lightning; **rayos X** X-rays

raza ['raθa] nf race; **raza humana** human race

razón [ra'θon] nf reason; (justicia) right, justice; (razonamiento) reasoning; (motivo) reason, motive; (Mat) ratio; **a ~ de 10 cada día** at the rate of 10 a day; **en ~ de** with regard to; **dar ~ a algn** to say that sb is right; **tener ~** to be right; **razón de ser** raison d'être; **razón directa/inversa** direct/inverse proportion; **razonable** adj reasonable; (justo, moderado) fair; **razonamiento** nm (juicio) judg(e)ment;

(*argumento*) reasoning; **razonar** vt, vi to reason, argue

re [re] nm (*Mús*) D

reacción [reak'θjon] nf reaction; **avión a ~** jet plane; **reacción en cadena** chain reaction; **reaccionar** vi to react

reacio, -a [re'aθjo, a] adj stubborn

reactivar [reakti'βar] vt to revitalize

reactor [reak'tor] nm reactor

real [re'al] adj real; (*del rey, fig*) royal

realidad [reali'ðað] nf reality, fact; (*verdad*) truth

realista [rea'lista] nmf realist

realización [realiθa'θjon] nf fulfilment

realizador, a [realiθa'ðor, a] nm/f film-maker

realizar [reali'θar] vt (*objetivo*) to achieve; (*plan*) to carry out; (*viaje*) to make, undertake; **realizarse** vr to come about, come true

realmente [real'mente] adv really, actually

realzar [real'θar] vt to enhance; (*acentuar*) to highlight

reanimar [reani'mar] vt to revive; (*alentar*) to encourage; **reanimarse** vr to revive

reanudar [reanu'ðar] vt (*renovar*) to renew; (*historia, viaje*) to resume

reaparición [reapari'θjon] nf reappearance

rearme [re'arme] nm rearmament

rebaja [re'βaxa] nf (*Com*) reduction; (: *descuento*) discount; **rebajas** nfpl (*Com*) sale; **rebajar** vt (*bajar*) to lower; (*reducir*) to reduce; (*disminuir*) to lessen; (*humillar*) to humble

rebanada [reβa'naða] nf slice

rebañar [reβa'ɲar] vt (*comida*) to scrape up; (*plato*) to scrape clean

rebaño [re'βaɲo] nm herd; (*de ovejas*) flock

rebatir [reβa'tir] vt to refute

rebeca [re'βeka] nf cardigan

rebelarse [reβe'larse] vr to rebel, revolt

rebelde [re'βelde] adj rebellious; (*niño*) unruly ▷ nmf rebel; **rebeldía** nf rebelliousness; (*desobediencia*) disobedience

rebelión [reβe'ljon] nf rebellion

reblandecer [reβlande'θer] vt to soften

rebobinar [reβoβi'nar] vt (*cinta, película de video*) to rewind

rebosante [reβo'sante] adj overflowing

rebosar [reβo'sar] vi (*líquido, recipiente*) to overflow; (*abundar*) to abound, be plentiful

rebotar [reβo'tar] vt to bounce; (*rechazar*) to repel ▷ vi (*pelota*) to bounce; (*bala*) to ricochet; **rebote** nm rebound; **de rebote** on the rebound

rebozado, -a [reβo'θaðo, a] adj fried in batter o breadcrumbs

rebozar [reβo'θar] vt to wrap up; (*Culin*) to fry in batter o breadcrumbs

rebuscado, -a [reβus'kaðo, a] adj (*amanerado*) affected; (*palabra*) recherché; (*idea*) far-fetched

rebuscar [reβus'kar] vi: **~ (en/por)** to search carefully (in/for)

recado [re'kaðo] nm (*mensaje*) message; (*encargo*) errand; **tomar un ~** (*Tel*) to take a message

recaer [reka'er] vi to relapse; **~ en** to fall to o on; (*criminal etc*) to fall back into, relapse into; **recaída** nf relapse

recalcar [rekal'kar] vt (*fig*) to stress, emphasize

recalentar [rekalen'tar] vt (*volver a calentar*) to reheat; (*calentar demasiado*) to overheat

recámara [re'kamara] (*MÉX*) nf bedroom

recambio [re'kambjo] nm spare; (*de pluma*) refill

recapacitar [rekapaθi'tar] vi to reflect

recargado, -a [rekar'ɣaðo, a] adj overloaded

recargar [rekar'ɣar] vt to overload; (*batería*) to recharge; **~ el saldo de** (*Tel*) to top up; **recargo** nm surcharge; (*aumento*) increase

recatado, -a [reka'taðo, a] adj (*modesto*) modest, demure; (*prudente*) cautious

recaudación [rekauða'θjon] nf (*acción*) collection; (*cantidad*) takings pl; (*en deporte*) gate; **recaudador, a** nm/f tax collector

recelar [reθe'lar] vt: **~ que ...** (*sospechar*) to suspect that ...; (*temer*) to fear that ... ▷ vi: **~ de** to distrust; **recelo** nm distrust, suspicion

recepción [reθep'θjon] nf reception; **recepcionista** nmf receptionist

receptor, a [reθep'tor, a] nm/f recipient ▷ nm (*Tel*) receiver

recesión [reθe'sjon] nf (*Com*) recession

receta [re'θeta] nf (*Culin*) recipe; (*Med*) prescription

No confundir **receta** con la palabra inglesa *receipt*.

rechazar [retʃa'θar] vt to reject; (*oferta*) to turn down; (*ataque*) to repel

rechazo [re'tʃaθo] nm rejection

rechinar [retʃi'nar] vi to creak; (*dientes*) to grind

rechistar [retʃis'tar] vi: **sin ~** without a murmur

rechoncho, -a [re'tʃontʃo, a] (*fam*) adj thickset (*BRIT*), heavy-set (*US*)

rechupete [retʃu'pete]: **de ~** adj (*comida*)

delicious, scrumptious

recibidor [reθiβi'ðor] nm entrance hall

recibimiento [reθiβi'mjento] nm reception, welcome

recibir [reθi'βir] vt to receive; (dar la bienvenida) to welcome ▷ vi to entertain; **recibo** receipt

reciclable [reθi'klaβle] adj recyclable

reciclar [reθi'klar] vt to recycle

recién [re'θjen] adv recently, newly; **los ~ casados** the newly-weds; **el ~ llegado** the newcomer; **el ~ nacido** the newborn child

reciente [re'θjente] adj recent; (fresco) fresh

recinto [re'θinto] nm enclosure; (área) area, place

recio, -a ['reθjo, a] adj strong, tough; (voz) loud ▷ adv hard, loud(ly)

recipiente [reθi'pjente] nm receptacle

recíproco, -a [re'θiproko, a] adj reciprocal

recital [reθi'tal] nm (Mús) recital; (Literatura) reading

recitar [reθi'tar] vt to recite

reclamación [reklama'θjon] nf claim, demand; (queja) complaint

reclamar [rekla'mar] vt to claim, demand ▷ vi: **~ contra** to complain about; **reclamo** nm (anuncio) advertisement; (tentación) attraction

reclinar [rekli'nar] vt to recline, lean; **reclinarse** vr to lean back

reclusión [reklu'sjon] nf (prisión) prison; (refugio) seclusion

recluta [re'kluta] nmf recruit ▷ nf recruitment; **reclutar** vt (datos) to collect; (dinero) to collect up; **reclutamiento** nm recruitment

recobrar [reko'βrar] vt (salud) to recover; (rescatar) to get back; **recobrarse** vr to recover

recodo [re'koðo] nm (de río, camino) bend

recogedor [rekoxe'ðor] nm dustpan

recoger [reko'xer] vt to collect; (Agr) to harvest; (levantar) to pick up; (juntar) to gather; (pasar a buscar) to come for, get; (dar asilo) to give shelter to; (faldas) to gather up; (pelo) to put up; **recogerse** vr (retirarse) to retire; **recogido, -a** adj (lugar) quiet, secluded; (pequeño) small ▷ nf (Correos) collection; (Agr) harvest

recolección [rekolek'θjon] nf (Agr) harvesting; (colecta) collection

recomendación [rekomenda'θjon] nf (sugerencia) suggestion, recommendation; (referencia) reference

recomendar [rekomen'dar] vt to suggest, recommend; (confiar) to entrust

recompensa [rekom'pensa] nf reward, recompense; **recompensar** vt to reward, recompense

reconciliación [rekonθilja'θjon] nf reconciliation

reconciliar [rekonθi'ljar] vt to reconcile; **reconciliarse** vr to become reconciled

recóndito, -a [re'kondito, a] adj (lugar) hidden, secret

reconocer [rekono'θer] vt to recognize; (registrar) to search; (Med) to examine; **reconocido, -a** adj recognized; (agradecido) grateful; **reconocimiento** nm recognition; search; examination; gratitude; (confesión) admission

reconquista [rekon'kista] nf reconquest; **la R~** the Reconquest (of Spain)

reconstituyente [rekonstitu'jente] nm tonic

reconstruir [rekonstru'ir] vt to reconstruct

reconversión [rekonβer'sjon] nf (reestructuración) restructuring; **reconversión industrial** industrial rationalization

recopilación [rekopila'θjon] nf (resumen) summary; (compilación) compilation; **recopilar** vt to compile

récord ['rekorð] (pl **~s**) adj inv, nm record

recordar [rekor'ðar] vt (acordarse de) to remember; (acordar a otro) to remind ▷ vi to remember

▌ No confundir **recordar** con la palabra inglesa record.

recorrer [reko'rrer] vt (país) to cross, travel through; (distancia) to cover; (registrar) to search; (repasar) to look over; **recorrido** nm run, journey; **tren de largo recorrido** main-line train

recortar [rekor'tar] vt to cut out; **recorte** nm (acción, de prensa) cutting; (de telas, chapas) trimming; **recorte presupuestario** budget cut

recostar [rekos'tar] vt to lean; **recostarse** vr to lie down

recoveco [reko'βeko] nm (de camino, río etc) bend; (en casa) cubby hole

recreación [rekrea'θjon] nf recreation

recrear [rekre'ar] vt (entretener) to entertain; (volver a crear) to recreate; **recreativo, -a** adj recreational; **recreo** nm recreation; (Escol) break, playtime

recriminar [rekrimi'nar] vt to reproach ▷ vi to recriminate; **recriminarse** vr to reproach each other

recrudecer [rekruðe'θer] vt, vi to worsen; **recrudecerse** vr to worsen

recta ['rekta] nf straight line

rectángulo, -a [rek'tangulo, a] *adj*
rectangular ▷ *nm* rectangle
rectificar [rektifi'kar] *vt* to rectify;
(*volverse recto*) to straighten ▷ *vi* to correct
o.s.
rectitud [rekti'tuð] *nf* straightness
recto, -a ['rekto, a] *adj* straight; (*persona*)
honest, upright; **siga todo ~** go straight on
▷ *nm* rectum
rector, a [rek'tor, a] *adj* governing
recuadro [re'kwaðro] *nm* box; (*Tip*) inset
recubrir [reku'βrir] *vt*: **~ (con)** (*pintura,
crema*) to cover (with)
recuento [re'kwento] *nm* inventory;
hacer el ~ de to count o reckon up
recuerdo [re'kwerðo] *nm* souvenir;
recuerdos *nmpl* (*memorias*) memories;
¡~s a tu madre! give my regards to your
mother!
recular [reku'lar] *vi* to back down
recuperación [rekupera'θjon] *nf*
recovery
recuperar [rekupe'rar] *vt* to recover;
(*tiempo*) to make up; **recuperarse** *vr* to
recuperate
recurrir [reku'rrir] *vi* (*Jur*) to appeal; **~ a**
to resort to; (*persona*) to turn to; **recurso**
nm resort; (*medios*) means *pl*, resources *pl*;
(*Jur*) appeal
red [reð] *nf* net, mesh; (*Ferro etc*) network;
(*trampa*) trap; **la R~** (*Internet*) the Net
redacción [reðak'θjon] *nf* (*acción*) editing;
(*personal*) editorial staff; (*Escol*) essay,
composition
redactar [reðak'tar] *vt* to draw up, draft;
(*periódico*) to edit
redactor, a [reðak'tor, a] *nm/f* editor
redada [re'ðaða] *nf* (*de policía*) raid,
round-up
rededor [reðe'ðor] *nm*: **al** o **en ~** around,
round about
redoblar [reðo'βlar] *vt* to redouble ▷ *vi*
(*tambor*) to roll
redonda [re'ðonda] *nf*: **a la ~** around,
round about
redondear [reðonde'ar] *vt* to round,
round off
redondel [reðon'del] *nm* (*círculo*) circle;
(*Taur*) bullring, arena
redondo, -a [re'ðondo, a] *adj* (*circular*)
round; (*completo*) complete
reducción [reðuk'θjon] *nf* reduction
reducido, -a [reðu'θiðo, a] *adj* reduced;
(*limitado*) limited; (*pequeño*) small
reducir [reðu'θir] *vt* to reduce; to limit;
reducirse *vr* to diminish
redundancia [reðun'danθja] *nf*
redundancy

reembolsar [re(e)mbol'sar] *vt* (*persona*)
to reimburse; (*dinero*) to repay, pay back;
(*depósito*) to refund; **reembolso** *nm*
reimbursement; refund
reemplazar [re(e)mpla'θar] *vt* to
replace; **reemplazo** *nm* replacement; **de
reemplazo** (*Mil*) reserve
reencuentro [re(e)n'kwentro] *nm*
reunion
reescribible [reeskri'βiβle] *adj* rewritable
refacción [refak'θjon] (*MÉX*) *nf* spare
(part)
referencia [refe'renθja] *nf* reference; **con
~ a** with reference to
referéndum [refe'rendum] (*pl* **~s**) *nm*
referendum
referente [refe'rente] *adj*: **~ a** concerning,
relating to
réferi ['referi] (*LAM*) *nmf* referee
referir [refe'rir] *vt* (*contar*) to tell, recount;
(*relacionar*) to refer, relate; **referirse** *vr*: **~se
a** to refer to
refilón [refi'lon]: **de ~** *adv* obliquely
refinado, -a [refi'naðo, a] *adj* refined
refinar [refi'nar] *vt* to refine; **refinería**
nf refinery
reflejar [refle'xar] *vt* to reflect; **reflejo,
-a** *adj* reflected; (*movimiento*) reflex ▷ *nm*
reflection; (*Anat*) reflex
reflexión [reflek'sjon] *nf* reflection;
reflexionar *vt* to reflect on ▷ *vi* to reflect;
(*detenerse*) to pause (to think)
reflexivo, -a [reflek'siβo, a] *adj*
thoughtful; (*Ling*) reflexive
reforma [re'forma] *nf* reform; (*Arq etc*)
repair; **reforma agraria** agrarian reform
reformar [refor'mar] *vt* to reform;
(*modificar*) to change, alter; (*Arq*) to repair;
reformarse *vr* to mend one's ways
reformatorio [reforma'torjo] *nm*
reformatory
reforzar [refor'θar] *vt* to strengthen; (*Arq*)
to reinforce; (*fig*) to encourage
refractario, -a [refrak'tarjo, a] *adj* (*Tec*)
heat-resistant
refrán [re'fran] *nm* proverb, saying
refregar [refre'xar] *vt* to scrub
refrescante [refres'kante] *adj* refreshing,
cooling
refrescar [refres'kar] *vt* to refresh ▷ *vi* to
cool down; **refrescarse** *vr* to get cooler;
(*tomar aire fresco*) to go out for a breath of
fresh air; (*beber*) to have a drink
refresco [re'fresko] *nm* soft drink, cool
drink; **"~s"** "refreshments"
refriega [re'frjexa] *nf* scuffle, brawl
refrigeración [refrixera'θjon] *nf*
refrigeration; (*de sala*) air-conditioning

refrigerador [refrixera'ðor] nm
refrigerator (BRIT), icebox (US)

refrigerar [refrixe'rar] vt to refrigerate;
(sala) to air-condition

refuerzo [re'fwerθo] nm reinforcement;
(Tec) support

refugiado, -a [refu'xjaðo, a] nm/f
refugee

refugiarse [refu'xjarse] vr to take refuge,
shelter

refugio [re'fuxjo] nm refuge; (protección)
shelter

refunfuñar [refunfu'ɲar] vi to grunt,
growl; (quejarse) to grumble

regadera [rexa'ðera] nf watering can

regadío [rega'ðio] nm irrigated land

regalado, -a [rexa'laðo, a] adj
comfortable, luxurious; (gratis) free, for
nothing

regalar [rexa'lar] vt (dar) to give (as a
present); (entregar) to give away; (mimar) to
pamper, make a fuss of

regaliz [rexa'liθ] nm liquorice

regalo [re'xalo] nm (obsequio) gift, present;
(gusto) pleasure

regañadientes [rexaɲa'ðjentes]: **a ~** adv
reluctantly

regañar [rexa'ɲar] vt to scold ▷ vi to
grumble; **regañón, -ona** adj nagging

regar [re'xar] vt to water, irrigate; (fig) to
scatter, sprinkle

regatear [rexate'ar] vt (Com) to bargain
over; (escatimar) to be mean with ▷ vi to
bargain, haggle; (Deporte) to dribble;
regateo nm bargaining; dribbling; (del
cuerpo) swerve, dodge

regazo [re'xaθo] nm lap

regenerar [rexene'rar] vt to regenerate

régimen ['reximen] (pl **regímenes**) nm
regime; (Med) diet

regimiento [rexi'mjento] nm regiment

regio, -a ['rexjo, a] adj royal, regal;
(fig: suntuoso) splendid; (cs: fam) great,
terrific

región [re'xjon] nf region

regir [re'xir] vt to govern, rule; (dirigir) to
manage, run ▷ vi to apply, be in force

registrar [rexis'trar] vt (buscar) to search;
(: en cajón) to look through; (inspeccionar) to
inspect; (anotar) to register, record; (Inform)
to log; **registrarse** vr to register; (ocurrir)
to happen

registro [re'xistro] nm (acto) registration;
(Mús, libro) register; (inspección) inspection,
search; **registro civil** registry office

regla ['rexla] nf (ley) rule, regulation; (de
medir) ruler, rule; (Med: período) period; **en
~** in order

reglamentación [rexlamenta'θjon] nf
(acto) regulation; (lista) rules pl

reglamentar [rexlamen'tar] vt to
regulate; **reglamentario, -a** adj statutory;
reglamento nm rules pl, regulations pl

regocijarse [rexoθi'xarse] vr (alegrarse) to
rejoice; **regocijo** nm joy, happiness

regrabadora [reɣraβa'ðora] nf rewriter;
regrabadora de DVD DVD rewriter

regresar [rexre'sar] vi to come back, go
back, return; **regreso** nm return

reguero [re'xero] nm (de sangre etc) trickle;
(de humo) trail

regulador [rexula'ðor] nm regulator; (de
radio etc) knob, control

regular [rexu'lar] adj regular; (normal)
normal, usual; (común) ordinary; (organizado)
regular, orderly; (mediano) average; (fam)
not bad, so-so ▷ adv so-so, alright ▷ vt
(controlar) to control, regulate; (Tec) to
adjust; **por lo ~** as a rule; **regularidad** nf
regularity; **regularizar** vt to regularize

rehabilitación [reaβilita'θjon] nf
rehabilitation; (Arq) restoration

rehabilitar [reaβili'tar] vt to rehabilitate;
(Arq) to restore; (reintegrar) to reinstate

rehacer [rea'θer] vt (reparar) to mend,
repair; (volver a hacer) to redo, repeat;
rehacerse vr (Med) to recover

rehén [re'en] nm hostage

rehuir [reu'ir] vt to avoid, shun

rehusar [reu'sar] vt, vi to refuse

reina ['reina] nf queen; **reinado** nm reign

reinar [rei'nar] vi to reign

reincidir [reinθi'ðir] vi to relapse

reincorporarse [reinkorpo'rarse] vr: **~
a** to rejoin

reino ['reino] nm kingdom; **reino animal/
vegetal** animal/plant kingdom; **el Reino
Unido** the United Kingdom

reintegrar [reinte'xrar] vt (reconstituir) to
reconstruct; (persona) to reinstate; (dinero)
to refund, pay back; **reintegrarse** vr: **~se a**
to return to

reír [re'ir] vi to laugh; **reírse** vr to laugh;
~se de to laugh at

reiterar [reite'rar] vt to reiterate

reivindicación [reiβindika'θjon] nf
(demanda) claim, demand; (justificación)
vindication

reivindicar [reiβindi'kar] vt to claim

reja ['rexa] nf (de ventana) grille, bars pl; (en
la calle) grating

rejilla [re'xiʎa] nf grating, grille; (muebles)
wickerwork; (de ventilación) vent; (de coche
etc) luggage rack

rejoneador [rexonea'ðor] nm mounted
bullfighter

r

rejuvenecer [rexuβene'θer] vt, vi to rejuvenate

relación [rela'θjon] nf relation, relationship; (Mat) ratio; (narración) report; **con ~ a, en ~ con** in relation to; **relaciones públicas** public relations; **relacionar** vt to relate, connect; **relacionarse** vr to be connected, be linked

relajación [relaxa'θjon] nf relaxation

relajar [rela'xar] vt to relax; **relajarse** vr to relax

relamerse [rela'merse] vr to lick one's lips

relámpago [re'lampaxo] nm flash of lightning; **visita ~** lightning visit

relatar [rela'tar] vt to tell, relate

relativo, -a [rela'tiβo, a] adj relative; **en lo ~ a** concerning

relato [re'lato] nm (narración) story, tale

relegar [rele'xar] vt to relegate

relevante [rele'βante] adj eminent, outstanding

relevar [rele'βar] vt (sustituir) to relieve; **relevarse** vr to relay; **~ a algn de un cargo** to relieve sb of his post

relevo [re'leβo] nm relief; **carrera de ~s** relay race

relieve [re'ljeβe] nm (Arte, Tec) relief; (fig) prominence, importance; **bajo ~** bas-relief

religión [reli'xjon] nf religion; **religioso, -a** adj religious ▷ nm/f monk/nun

relinchar [relin'tʃar] vi to neigh

reliquia [re'likja] nf relic; **reliquia de familia** heirloom

rellano [re'ʎano] nm (Arq) landing

rellenar [reʎe'nar] vt (llenar) to fill up; (Culin) to stuff; (Costura) to pad; **relleno, -a** adj full up; stuffed ▷ nm stuffing; (de tapicería) padding

reloj [re'lo(x)] nm clock; **poner el ~ (en hora)** to set one's watch (o the clock); **reloj (de pulsera)** wristwatch; **reloj despertador** alarm (clock); **reloj digital** digital watch; **relojero, -a** nm/f clockmaker; watchmaker

reluciente [relu'θjente] adj brilliant, shining

relucir [relu'θir] vi to shine; (fig) to excel

remachar [rema'tʃar] vt to rivet; (fig) to hammer home, drive home; **remache** nm rivet

remangar [reman'gar] vt to roll up

remanso [re'manso] nm pool

remar [re'mar] vi to row

rematado, -a [rema'taðo, a] adj complete, utter

rematar [rema'tar] vt to finish off; (Com) to sell off cheap ▷ vi to end, finish off; (Deporte) to shoot

remate [re'mate] nm end, finish; (punta) tip; (Deporte) shot; (Arq) top; **de o para ~** to crown it all (BRIT), to top it off

remedar [reme'ðar] vt to imitate

remediar [reme'ðjar] vt to remedy; (subsanar) to make good, repair; (evitar) to avoid

remedio [re'meðjo] nm remedy; (alivio) relief, help; (Jur) recourse, remedy; **poner ~ a** to correct, stop; **no tener más ~** to have no alternative; **¡qué ~!** there's no choice!; **sin ~** hopeless

remendar [remen'dar] vt to repair; (con parche) to patch

remiendo [re'mjendo] nm mend; (con parche) patch; (cosido) darn

remilgado, -a [remil'xaðo, a] adj prim; (afectado) affected

remiso, -a [re'miso, a] adj slack, slow

remite [re'mite] nm (en sobre) name and address of sender

remitir [remi'tir] vt to remit, send ▷ vi to slacken; (en carta): **remite: X** sender: X; **remitente** nmf sender

remo ['remo] nm (de barco) oar; (Deporte) rowing

remojar [remo'xar] vt to steep, soak; (galleta etc) to dip, dunk

remojo [re'moxo] nm: **dejar la ropa en ~** to leave clothes to soak

remolacha [remo'latʃa] nf beet, beetroot

remolcador [remolka'ðor] nm (Náut) tug; (Auto) breakdown lorry

remolcar [remol'kar] vt to tow

remolino [remo'lino] nm eddy; (de agua) whirlpool; (de viento) whirlwind; (de gente) crowd

remolque [re'molke] nm tow, towing; (cuerda) towrope; **llevar a ~** to tow

remontar [remon'tar] vt to mend; **remontarse** vr to soar; **~se a** (Com) to amount to; **~ el vuelo** to soar

remorder [remor'ðer] vt to distress, disturb; **~le la conciencia a algn** to have a guilty conscience; **remordimiento** nm remorse

remoto, -a [re'moto, a] adj remote

remover [remo'βer] vt to stir; (tierra) to turn over; (objetos) to move round

remuneración [remunera'θjon] nf remuneration

remunerar [remune'rar] vt to remunerate; (premiar) to reward

renacer [rena'θer] vi to be reborn; (fig) to revive; **renacimiento** nm rebirth; **el Renacimiento** the Renaissance

renacuajo [rena'kwaxo] nm (Zool) tadpole

renal [re'nal] *adj* renal, kidney *cpd*
rencilla [ren'θiʎa] *nf* quarrel
rencor [ren'kor] *nm* rancour, bitterness;
  rencoroso, -a *adj* spiteful
rendición [rendi'θjon] *nf* surrender
rendido, -a [ren'diðo, a] *adj* (*sumiso*)
  submissive; (*cansado*) worn-out, exhausted
rendija [ren'dixa] *nf* (*hendedura*) crack,
  cleft
rendimiento [rendi'mjento] *nm*
  (*producción*) output; (*Tec, Com*) efficiency
rendir [ren'dir] *vt* (*vencer*) to defeat;
  (*producir*) to produce; (*dar beneficio*) to yield;
  (*agotar*) to exhaust ▷ *vi* to pay; **rendirse**
  vr (*someterse*) to surrender; (*cansarse*) to
  wear o.s. out; **~ homenaje** o **culto a** to pay
  homage to
renegar [rene'xar] *vi* (*renunciar*) to
  renounce; (*blasfemar*) to blaspheme;
  (*quejarse*) to complain
RENFE ['renfe] *nf abr* (= *Red Nacional de los
  Ferrocarriles Españoles*)
renglón [ren'glon] *nm* (*línea*) line; (*Com*)
  item, article; **a ~ seguido** immediately after
renombre [re'nombre] *nm* renown
renovación [renoβa'θjon] *nf* (*de contrato*)
  renewal; (*Arq*) renovation
renovar [reno'βar] *vt* to renew; (*Arq*) to
  renovate
renta ['renta] *nf* (*ingresos*) income;
  (*beneficio*) profit; (*alquiler*) rent; **renta
  vitalicia** annuity; **rentable** *adj* profitable
renuncia [re'nunθja] *nf* resignation;
  renunciar [renun'θjar] *vt* to renounce;
  (*tabaco, alcohol etc*): **renunciar a** to give up;
  (*oferta, oportunidad*) to turn down; (*puesto*) to
  resign ▷ *vi* to resign
reñido, -a [re'niðo, a] *adj* (*batalla*) bitter,
  hard-fought; **estar ~ con algn** to be on bad
  terms with sb
reñir [re'nir] *vt* (*regañar*) to scold ▷ *vi*
  (*estar peleado*) to quarrel, fall out; (*combatir*)
  to fight
reo ['reo] *nmf* culprit, offender; (*acusado*)
  accused, defendant
reojo [re'oxo]: **de ~** *adv* out of the corner
  of one's eye
reparación [repara'θjon] *nf* (*acto*)
  mending, repairing; (*Tec*) repair; (*fig*)
  amends *pl*, reparation
reparar [repa'rar] *vt* to repair; (*fig*) to
  make amends for; (*observar*) to observe
  ▷ *vi*: **~ en** (*darse cuenta de*) to notice; (*prestar
  atención a*) to pay attention to
reparo [re'paro] *nm* (*advertencia*)
  observation; (*duda*) doubt; (*dificultad*)
  difficulty; **poner ~s (a)** to raise objections
  (to)

repartidor, a [reparti'ðor, a] *nm/f*
  distributor
repartir [repar'tir] *vt* to distribute,
  share out; (*Correos*) to deliver; **reparto** *nm*
  distribution; delivery; (*Teatro, Cine*) cast;
  (CAM: *urbanización*) housing estate (BRIT),
  real estate development (*us*)
repasar [repa'sar] *vt* (*Escol*) to revise;
  (*Mecánica*) to check, overhaul; (*Costura*)
  to mend; **repaso** *nm* revision; overhaul,
  checkup; mending
repecho [re'petʃo] *nm* steep incline
repelente [repe'lente] *adj* repellent,
  repulsive
repeler [repe'ler] *vt* to repel
repente [re'pente] *nm*: **de ~** suddenly
repentino, -a [repen'tino, a] *adj* sudden
repercusión [reperku'sjon] *nf*
  repercussion
repercutir [reperku'tir] *vi* (*objeto*) to
  rebound; (*sonido*) to echo; **~ en** (*fig*) to have
  repercussions on
repertorio [reper'torjo] *nm* list; (*Teatro*)
  repertoire
repetición [repeti'θjon] *nf* repetition
repetir [repe'tir] *vt* to repeat; (*plato*) to
  have a second helping of ▷ *vi* to repeat;
  (*sabor*) to come back; **repetirse** *vr* (*volver
  sobre un tema*) to repeat o.s.
repetitivo, -a [repeti'tiβo, a] *adj*
  repetitive, repetitious
repique [re'pike] *nm* pealing, ringing;
  repiqueteo *nm* pealing; (*de tambor*)
  drumming
repisa [re'pisa] *nf* ledge, shelf; (*de ventana*)
  windowsill; **la ~ de la chimenea** the
  mantelpiece
repito *etc vb* V **repetir**
replantearse [replante'arse] *vr*: **~ un
  problema** to reconsider a problem
repleto, -a [re'pleto, a] *adj* replete, full up
réplica ['replika] *nf* answer; (*Arte*) replica
replicar [repli'kar] *vi* to answer; (*objetar*)
  to argue, answer back
repliegue [re'pljexe] *nm* (*Mil*) withdrawal
repoblación [repoβla'θjon] *nf*
  repopulation; (*de río*) restocking;
  repoblación forestal reafforestation
repoblar [repo'βlar] *vt* to repopulate; (*con
  árboles*) to reafforest
repollito [repo'ʎito] (*cs*) *nm*: **~s de
  Bruselas** (Brussels) sprouts
repollo [re'poʎo] *nm* cabbage
reponer [repo'ner] *vt* to replace, put back;
  (*Teatro*) to revive; **reponerse** *vr* to recover;
  ~ que ... to reply that ...
reportaje [repor'taxe] *nm* report, article
reportero, -a [repor'tero, a] *nm/f*

reporter

reposacabezas [reposaka'βeθas] *nm inv* headrest

reposar [repo'sar] *vi* to rest, repose

reposera [repo'sera] (RPL) *nf* deck chair

reposición [reposi'θjon] *nf* replacement; (*Cine*) remake

reposo [re'poso] *nm* rest

repostar [repos'tar] *vt* to replenish; (*Auto*) to fill up (with petrol (BRIT) o gasoline (US))

repostería [reposte'ria] *nf* confectioner's (shop)

represa [re'presa] *nf* dam; (*lago artificial*) lake, pool

represalia [repre'salja] *nf* reprisal

representación [representa'θjon] *nf* representation; (*Teatro*) performance; **representante** *nmf* representative; performer

representar [represen'tar] *vt* to represent; (*Teatro*) to perform; (*edad*) to look; **representarse** *vr* to imagine; **representativo, -a** *adj* representative

represión [repre'sjon] *nf* repression

reprimenda [repri'menda] *nf* reprimand, rebuke

reprimir [repri'mir] *vt* to repress

reprobar [repro'βar] *vt* to censure, reprove

reprochar [repro'tʃar] *vt* to reproach; **reproche** *nm* reproach

reproducción [reproðuk'θjon] *nf* reproduction

reproducir [reproðu'θir] *vt* to reproduce; **reproducirse** *vr* to breed; (*situación*) to recur

reproductor, a [reproðuk'tor, a] *adj* reproductive ▷ *nm* player; **reproductor de CD** CD player

reptil [rep'til] *nm* reptile

república [re'puβlika] *nf* republic; **República Dominicana** Dominican Republic; **republicano, -a** *adj, nm* republican

repudiar [repu'ðjar] *vt* to repudiate; (*fe*) to renounce

repuesto [re'pwesto] *nm* (*pieza de recambio*) spare (part); (*abastecimiento*) supply; **rueda de ~** spare wheel

repugnancia [repuɣ'nanθja] *nf* repugnance; **repugnante** *adj* repugnant, repulsive

repugnar [repuɣ'nar] *vt* to disgust

repulsa [re'pulsa] *nf* rebuff

repulsión [repul'sjon] *nf* repulsion, aversion; **repulsivo, -a** *adj* repulsive

reputación [reputa'θjon] *nf* reputation

requerir [reke'rir] *vt* (*pedir*) to ask, request; (*exigir*) to require; (*llamar*) to send for, summon

requesón [reke'son] *nm* cottage cheese

requete... [re'kete] *prefijo* extremely

réquiem ['rekjem] (*pl* **~s**) *nm* requiem

requisito [reki'sito] *nm* requirement, requisite

res [res] *nf* beast, animal

resaca [re'saka] *nf* (*de mar*) undertow, undercurrent; (*fam*) hangover

resaltar [resal'tar] *vi* to project, stick out; (*fig*) to stand out

resarcir [resar'θir] *vt* to compensate; **resarcirse** *vr* to make up for

resbaladero [resβala'ðero] (MÉX) *nm* slide

resbaladizo, -a [resβala'ðiθo, a] *adj* slippery

resbalar [resβa'lar] *vi* to slip, slide; (*fig*) to slip (up); **resbalarse** *vr* to slip, slide; to slip (up); **resbalón** *nm* (*acción*) slip

rescatar [reska'tar] *vt* (*salvar*) to save, rescue; (*objeto*) to get back, recover; (*cautivos*) to ransom

rescate [res'kate] *nm* rescue; (*de objeto*) recovery; **pagar un ~** to pay a ransom

rescindir [resθin'dir] *vt* to rescind

rescisión [resθi'sjon] *nf* cancellation

resecar [rese'kar] *vt* to dry thoroughly; (*Med*) to cut out, remove; **resecarse** *vr* to dry up

reseco, -a [re'seko, a] *adj* very dry; (*fig*) skinny

resentido, -a [resen'tiðo, a] *adj* resentful

resentimiento [resenti'mjento] *nm* resentment, bitterness

resentirse [resen'tirse] *vr* (*debilitarse: persona*) to suffer; **~ de** (*consecuencias*) to feel the effects of; **~ de** (*o* **por**) **algo** to resent sth, be bitter about sth

reseña [re'seɲa] *nf* (*cuenta*) account; (*informe*) report; (*Literatura*) review

reseñar [rese'ɲar] *vt* to describe; (*Literatura*) to review

reserva [re'serβa] *nf* reserve; (*reservación*) reservation

reservado, -a [reser'βaðo, a] *adj* reserved; (*retraído*) cold, distant ▷ *nm* private room

reservar [reser'βar] *vt* (*guardar*) to keep; (*habitación, entrada*) to reserve; **reservarse** *vr* to save o.s.; (*callar*) to keep to o.s.

resfriado [resfri'aðo] *nm* cold; **resfriarse** *vr* to cool; (*Med*) to catch a cold

resguardar [resɣwar'ðar] *vt* to protect, shield; **resguardarse** *vr*: **~se de** to guard against; **resguardo** *nm* defence; (*vale*) voucher; (*recibo*) receipt, slip

residencia [resi'ðenθja] nf residence;
residencia de ancianos residential
home, old people's home; **residencia
universitaria** hall of residence; **residencial**
nf (urbanización) housing estate
residente [resi'ðente] adj, nmf resident
residir [resi'ðir] vi to reside, live; **~ en** to
reside in, lie in
residuo [re'siðwo] nm residue
resignación [resixna'θjon] nf
resignation; **resignarse** vr: **resignarse a** o
con to resign o.s. to, be resigned to
resina [re'sina] nf resin
resistencia [resis'tenθja] nf (dureza)
endurance, strength; (oposición, Elec)
resistance; **resistente** adj strong, hardy;
resistant
resistir [resis'tir] vt (soportar) to bear;
(oponerse a) to resist, oppose; (aguantar)
to put up with ▷ vi to resist; (aguantar) to
last, endure; **resistirse** vr: **~se a** to refuse
to, resist
resoluto, -a [reso'luto, a] adj resolute
resolver [resol'βer] vt to resolve;
(solucionar) to solve, resolve; (decidir) to
decide, settle; **resolverse** vr to make up
one's mind
resonar [reso'nar] vi to ring, echo
resoplar [reso'plar] vi to snort; **resoplido**
nm heavy breathing
resorte [re'sorte] nm spring; (fig) lever
resortera [resor'tera] (MÉX) nf catapult
respaldar [respal'dar] vt to back (up),
support; **respaldarse** vr to lean back;
~se con o **en** (fig) to take one's stand on;
respaldo nm (de sillón) back; (fig) support,
backing
respectivo, -a [respek'tiβo, a] adj
respective; **en lo ~ a** with regard to
respecto [res'pekto] nm: **al ~** on this
matter; **con ~ a, ~ de** with regard to, in
relation to
respetable [respe'taβle] adj respectable
respetar [respe'tar] vt to respect; **respeto**
nm respect; (acatamiento) deference;
respetos nmpl respects; **respetuoso, -a**
adj respectful
respingo [res'pingo] nm start, jump
respiración [respira'θjon] nf breathing;
(Med) respiration; (ventilación) ventilation;
respiración asistida artificial respiration
(by machine)
respirar [respi'rar] vi to breathe;
respiratorio, -a adj respiratory; **respiro**
nm breathing; (fig: descanso) respite
resplandecer [resplande'θer] vi to shine;
resplandeciente adj resplendent, shining;
resplandor nm brilliance, brightness; (de

luz, fuego) blaze
responder [respon'der] vt to answer ▷ vi
to answer; (fig) to respond; (pey) to answer
back; **~ de** o **por** to answer for; **respondón,
-ona** adj cheeky
responsabilidad [responsaβili'ðað] nf
responsibility
responsabilizarse [responsaβili'θarse]
vr to make o.s. responsible, take charge
responsable [respon'saβle] adj
responsible
respuesta [res'pwesta] nf answer, reply
resquebrajar [reskeβra'xar] vt to crack,
split; **resquebrajarse** vr to crack, split
resquicio [res'kiθjo] nm chink; (hendedura)
crack
resta ['resta] nf (Mat) remainder
restablecer [restaβle'θer] vt to re-
establish, restore; **restablecerse** vr to
recover
restante [res'tante] adj remaining; **lo ~**
the remainder
restar [res'tar] vt (Mat) to subtract; (fig) to
take away ▷ vi to remain, be left
restauración [restaura'θjon] nf
restoration
restaurante [restau'rante] nm
restaurant
restaurar [restau'rar] vt to restore
restituir [restitu'ir] vt (devolver) to return,
give back; (rehabilitar) to restore
resto ['resto] nm (residuo) rest, remainder;
(apuesta) stake; **restos** nmpl remains
restorán [resto'ran] nm (Lam) restaurant
restregar [restre'ɣar] vt to scrub, rub
restricción [restrik'θjon] nf restriction
restringir [restrin'xir] vt to restrict, limit
resucitar [resuθi'tar] vt, vi to resuscitate,
revive
resuelto, -a [re'swelto, a] pp de resolver
▷ adj resolute, determined
resultado [resul'taðo] nm result;
(conclusión) outcome; **resultante** adj
resulting, resultant
resultar [resul'tar] vi (ser) to be; (llegar a
ser) to turn out to be; (salir bien) to turn out
well; (Com) to amount to; **~ de** to stem from;
me resulta difícil hacerlo it's difficult for
me to do it
resumen [re'sumen] (pl **resúmenes**) nm
summary, résumé; **en ~** in short
resumir [resu'mir] vt to sum up; (cortar)
to abridge, cut down; (condensar) to
summarize

 ▌ No confundir **resumir** con la palabra
inglesa *resume*.

resurgir [resur'xir] vi (reaparecer) to
reappear

r

resurrección [resurre(k)'θjon] *nf*
resurrection
retablo [re'taβlo] *nm* altarpiece
retaguardia [reta'ɣwarðja] *nf* rearguard
retahíla [reta'ila] *nf* series, string
retal [re'tal] *nm* remnant
retar [re'tar] *vt* to challenge; (*desafiar*) to
defy, dare
retazo [re'taθo] *nm* snippet (BRIT),
fragment
retención [reten'θjon] *nf* (*tráfico*) hold-up;
retención fiscal deduction for tax purposes
retener [rete'ner] *vt* (*intereses*) to withhold
reticente [reti'θente] *adj* (*tono*)
insinuating; (*postura*) reluctant; **ser ~ a
hacer algo** to be reluctant *o* unwilling to
do sth
retina [re'tina] *nf* retina
retintín [retin'tin] *nm* jangle, jingle
retirada [reti'raða] *nf* (*Mil, refugio*) retreat;
(*de dinero*) withdrawal; (*de embajador*) recall;
retirado, -a *adj* (*lugar*) remote; (*vida*) quiet;
(*jubilado*) retired
retirar [reti'rar] *vt* to withdraw; (*quitar*)
to remove; (*jubilar*) to retire, pension off;
retirarse *vr* to retreat, withdraw; to retire;
(*acostarse*) to retire, go to bed; **retiro** *nm*
retreat; retirement; (*pago*) pension
reto [re'to] *nm* dare, challenge
retocar [reto'kar] *vt* (*fotografía*) to touch
up, retouch
retoño [re'toɲo] *nm* sprout, shoot; (*fig*)
offspring, child
retoque [re'toke] *nm* retouching
retorcer [retor'θer] *vt* to twist; (*manos,
lavado*) to wring; **retorcerse** *vr* to become
twisted; (*mover el cuerpo*) to writhe
retorcido, -a [retor'θiðo, a] *adj* (*persona*)
devious
retorcijón [retorθi'jon] (LAM) *nm* (*tb: ~ de
tripas*) stomach cramp
retórica [re'torika] *nf* rhetoric; (*pey*)
affectedness
retorno [re'torno] *nm* return
retortijón [retorti'xon] (ESP) *nm* (*tb: ~ de
tripas*) stomach cramp
retozar [reto'θar] *vi* (*juguetear*) to frolic,
romp; (*saltar*) to gambol
retracción [retrak'θjon] *nf* retraction
retraerse [retra'erse] *vr* to retreat,
withdraw; **retraído, -a** *adj* shy, retiring;
retraimiento *nm* retirement; (*timidez*)
shyness
retransmisión [retransmi'sjon] *nf*
repeat (broadcast)
retransmitir [retransmi'tir] *vt* (*mensaje*)
to relay; (*TV etc*) to repeat, retransmit; (: *en
vivo*) to broadcast live

retrasado, -a [retra'saðo, a] *adj* late;
(*Med*) mentally retarded; (*país etc*) backward,
underdeveloped
retrasar [retra'sar] *vt* (*demorar*) to
postpone, put off; (*retardar*) to slow down
▷ *vi* (*atrasarse*) to be late; (*reloj*) to be slow;
(*producción*) to fall (off); (*quedarse atrás*) to lag
behind; **retrasarse** *vr* to be late; to be slow;
to fall (off); to lag behind
retraso [re'traso] *nm* (*demora*) delay;
(*lentitud*) slowness; (*tardanza*) lateness;
(*atraso*) backwardness; **retrasos** *nmpl*
(*Finanzas*) arrears; **llegar con ~** to arrive late;
retraso mental mental deficiency
retratar [retra'tar] *vt* (*Arte*) to paint the
portrait of; (*fotografiar*) to photograph; (*fig*)
to depict, describe; **retrato** *nm* portrait;
(*fig*) likeness; **retrato-robot** (ESP) *nm*
Identikit®
retrete [re'trete] *nm* toilet
retribuir [retri'βwir] *vt* (*recompensar*) to
reward; (*pagar*) to pay
retro... [retro] *prefijo* retro...
retroceder [retroθe'ðer] *vi* (*echarse atrás*)
to move back(wards); (*fig*) to back down
retroceso [retro'θeso] *nm* backward
movement; (*Med*) relapse; (*fig*) backing
down
retrospectivo, -a [retrospek'tiβo, a] *adj*
retrospective
retrovisor [retroβi'sor] *nm* (*tb:* **espejo ~**)
rear-view mirror
retumbar [retum'bar] *vi* to echo, resound
reúma [re'uma], **reuma** ['reuma] *nm*
rheumatism
reunión [reu'njon] *nf* (*asamblea*) meeting;
(*fiesta*) party
reunir [reu'nir] *vt* (*juntar*) to reunite, join
(together); (*recoger*) to gather (together);
(*personas*) to get together; (*cualidades*)
to combine; **reunirse** *vr* (*personas: en
asamblea*) to meet, gather
revalidar [reβali'ðar] *vt* (*ratificar*) to
confirm, ratify
revalorizar [reβalori'θar] *vt* to revalue,
reassess
revancha [re'βantʃa] *nf* revenge
revelación [reβela'θjon] *nf* revelation
revelado [reβe'laðo] *nm* developing
revelar [reβe'lar] *vt* to reveal; (*Foto*) to
develop
reventa [re'βenta] *nf* (*de entradas: para
concierto*) touting
reventar [reβen'tar] *vt* to burst, explode
reventón [reβen'ton] *nm* (*Auto*) blow-out
(BRIT), flat (US)
reverencia [reβe'renθja] *nf* reverence;
reverenciar *vt* to revere

reverendo, -a [reβe'rendo, a] *adj* reverend

reverente [reβe'rente] *adj* reverent

reversa [re'βersa] (*MÉX, CAM*) *nf* reverse (gear)

reversible [reβer'siβle] *adj* (*prenda*) reversible

reverso [re'βerso] *nm* back, other side; (*de moneda*) reverse

revertir [reβer'tir] *vi* to revert

revés [re'βes] *nm* back, wrong side; (*fig*) reverse, setback; (*Deporte*) backhand; **al ~** the wrong way round; (*de arriba abajo*) upside down; (*ropa*) inside out; **volver algo del ~** to turn sth round; (*ropa*) to turn sth inside out

revisar [reβi'sar] *vt* (*examinar*) to check; (*texto etc*) to revise; **revisión** *nf* revision; **revisión salarial** wage review

revisor, a [reβi'sor, a] *nm/f* inspector; (*Ferro*) ticket collector

revista [re'βista] *nf* magazine, review; (*Teatro*) revue; (*inspección*) inspection; **pasar ~ a** to review, inspect; **revista del corazón** *magazine featuring celebrity gossip and real-life romance stories*

revivir [reβi'βir] *vi* to revive

revolcarse [reβol'karse] *vr* to roll about

revoltijo [reβol'tixo] *nm* mess, jumble

revoltoso, -a [reβol'toso, a] *adj* (*travieso*) naughty, unruly

revolución [reβolu'θjon] *nf* revolution; **revolucionario, -a** *adj, nm/f* revolutionary

revolver [reβol'βer] *vt* (*desordenar*) to disturb, mess up; (*mover*) to move about ▷ *vi*: **~ en** to go through, rummage (about) in; **revolverse** *vr* (*volver contra*) to turn on *o* against

revólver [re'βolβer] *nm* revolver

revuelo [re'βwelo] *nm* fluttering; (*fig*) commotion

revuelta [re'βwelta] *nf* (*motín*) revolt; (*agitación*) commotion

revuelto, -a [re'βwelto, a] *pp de* **revolver** ▷ *adj* (*mezclado*) mixed-up, in disorder

rey [rei] *nm* king; **Día de R~es** Twelfth Night; **los R~es Magos** the Three Wise Men, the Magi

● **REYES MAGOS**
●
●
● On the night before the 6th January (the
● Epiphany), children go to bed expecting
● **los Reyes Magos** (the Three Wise Men)
● to bring them presents. Twelfth Night
● processions, known as **cabalgatas**,
● take place that evening when 3 people
● dressed as **los Reyes Magos** arrive in

the town by land or sea to the delight of
the children.

reyerta [re'jerta] *nf* quarrel, brawl

rezagado, -a [reθa'ɣaðo, a] *nm/f* straggler

rezar [re'θar] *vi* to pray; **~ con** (*fam*) to concern, have to do with; **rezo** *nm* prayer

rezumar [reθu'mar] *vt* to ooze

ría ['ria] *nf* estuary

riada [ri'aða] *nf* flood

ribera [ri'βera] *nf* (*de río*) bank; (*: área*) riverside

ribete [ri'βete] *nm* (*de vestido*) border; (*fig*) addition

ricino [ri'θino] *nm*: **aceite de ~** castor oil

rico, -a ['riko, a] *adj* rich; (*adinerado*) wealthy, rich; (*lujoso*) luxurious; (*comida*) delicious; (*niño*) lovely, cute ▷ *nm/f* rich person

ridiculez [riðiku'leθ] *nf* absurdity

ridiculizar [riðikuli'θar] *vt* to ridicule

ridículo, -a [ri'ðikulo, a] *adj* ridiculous; **hacer el ~** to make a fool of o.s.; **poner a algn en ~** to make a fool of sb

riego ['rjexo] *nm* (*aspersión*) watering; (*irrigación*) irrigation; **riego sanguíneo** blood flow *o* circulation

riel [rjel] *nm* rail

rienda ['rjenda] *nf* rein; **dar ~ suelta a** to give free rein to

riesgo ['rjesxo] *nm* risk; **correr el ~ de** to run the risk of

rifa ['rifa] *nf* (*lotería*) raffle; **rifar** *vt* to raffle

rifle ['rifle] *nm* rifle

rigidez [rixi'ðeθ] *nf* rigidity, stiffness; (*fig*) strictness; **rígido, -a** *adj* rigid, stiff; strict, inflexible

rigor [ri'ɣor] *nm* strictness, rigour; (*inclemencia*) harshness; **de ~** de rigueur, essential; **riguroso, -a** *adj* rigorous; harsh; (*severo*) severe

rimar [ri'mar] *vi* to rhyme

rimbombante [rimbom'bante] *adj* pompous

rímel ['rimel] *nm* mascara

rímmel ['rimel] *nm* = **rímel**

rin [rin] (*MÉX*) *nm* (wheel) rim

rincón [rin'kon] *nm* corner (*inside*)

rinoceronte [rinoθe'ronte] *nm* rhinoceros

riña ['riɲa] *nf* (*disputa*) argument; (*pelea*) brawl

riñón [ri'ɲon] *nm* kidney

río *etc* ['rio] *vb V* **reír** ▷ *nm* river; (*fig*) torrent, stream; **río abajo/arriba** downstream/upstream; **Río de la Plata** River Plate

rioja [ri'oxa] nm (vino) rioja (wine)

rioplatense [riopla'tense] adj of o from the River Plate region

riqueza [ri'keθa] nf wealth, riches pl; (cualidad) richness

risa ['risa] nf laughter; (una risa) laugh; ¡qué ~! what a laugh!

risco ['risko] nm crag, cliff

ristra ['ristra] nf string

risueño, -a [ri'sweɲo, a] adj (sonriente) smiling; (contento) cheerful

ritmo ['ritmo] nm rhythm; **a ~ lento** slowly; **trabajar a ~ lento** to go slow; **ritmo cardíaco** heart rate

rito ['rito] nm rite

ritual [ri'twal] adj, nm ritual

rival [ri'βal] adj, nmf rival; **rivalidad** nf rivalry; **rivalizar** vi: **rivalizar con** to rival, vie with

rizado, -a [ri'θaðo, a] adj curly ▷ nm curls pl

rizar [ri'θar] vt to curl; **rizarse** vr (pelo) to curl; (agua) to ripple; **rizo** nm curl; ripple

RNE nf abr = **Radio Nacional de España**

robar [ro'βar] vt to rob; (objeto) to steal; (casa etc) to break into; (Naipes) to draw

roble ['roβle] nm oak; **robledal** nm oakwood

robo ['roβo] nm robbery, theft

robot [ro'βot] nm robot; **robot (de cocina)** (ESP) food processor

robustecer [roβuste'θer] vt to strengthen

robusto, -a [ro'βusto, a] adj robust, strong

roca ['roka] nf rock

roce ['roθe] nm (caricia) brush; (Tec) friction; (en la piel) graze; **tener ~ con** to be in close contact with

rociar [ro'θjar] vt to spray

rocín [ro'θin] nm nag, hack

rocío [ro'θio] nm dew

rocola [ro'kola] (LAM) nf jukebox

rocoso, -a [ro'koso, a] adj rocky

rodaballo [roða'baʎo] nm turbot

rodaja [ro'ðaxa] nf slice

rodaje [ro'ðaxe] nm (Cine) shooting, filming; (Auto): **en ~** running in

rodar [ro'ðar] vt (vehículo) to wheel (along); (escalera) to roll down; (viajar por) to travel (over) ▷ vi to roll; (coche) to go, run; (Cine) to shoot, film

rodear [roðe'ar] vt to surround ▷ vi to go round; **rodearse** vr: **~se de amigos** to surround o.s. with friends

rodeo [ro'ðeo] nm (ruta indirecta) detour; (evasión) evasion; (Deporte) rodeo; **hablar sin ~s** to come to the point, speak plainly

rodilla [ro'ðiʎa] nf knee; **de ~s** kneeling;

ponerse de ~s to kneel (down)

rodillo [ro'ðiʎo] nm roller; (Culin) rolling-pin

roedor, a [roe'ðor, a] adj gnawing ▷ nm rodent

roer [ro'er] vt (masticar) to gnaw; (corroer, fig) to corrode

rogar [ro'xar] vt, vi (pedir) to ask for; (suplicar) to beg, plead; **se ruega no fumar** please do not smoke

rojizo, -a [ro'xiθo, a] adj reddish

rojo, -a [ro'xo, a] adj, nm red; **al ~ vivo** red-hot

rol [rol] nm list, roll; (papel) role

rollito [ro'ʎito] nm (tb: ~ de primavera) spring roll

rollizo, -a [ro'ʎiθo, a] adj (objeto) cylindrical; (persona) plump

rollo ['roʎo] nm roll; (de cuerda) coil; (madera) log; (ESP: fam) bore; ¡qué ~! (ESP: fam) what a carry-on!

Roma ['roma] n Rome

romance [ro'manθe] nm (amoroso) romance; (Literatura) ballad

romano, -a [ro'mano, a] adj, nm/f Roman; **a la romana** in batter

romanticismo [romanti'θismo] nm romanticism

romántico, -a [ro'mantiko, a] adj romantic

rombo ['rombo] nm (Geom) rhombus

romería [rome'ria] nf (Rel) pilgrimage; (excursión) trip, outing

● **ROMERÍA**
●
● Originally a pilgrimage to a shrine or
● church to express devotion to the Virgin
● Mary or a local Saint, the **romería** has
● also become a rural festival which
● accompanies the pilgrimage. People
● come from all over to attend, bringing
● their own food and drink, and spend the
● day in celebration.

romero, -a [ro'mero, a] nm/f pilgrim ▷ nm rosemary

romo, -a ['romo, a] adj blunt; (fig) dull

rompecabezas [rompeka'βeθas] nm inv riddle, puzzle; (juego) jigsaw (puzzle)

rompehuelgas [rompe'welxas] (LAM) nm inv strikebreaker, scab

rompeolas [rompe'olas] nm inv breakwater

romper [rom'per] vt to break; (hacer pedazos) to smash; (papel, tela etc) to tear, rip ▷ vi (olas) to break; (sol, diente) to break through; **romperse** vr to break; **~ un**

contrato to break a contract; **~ a** (*empezar a*) to start (suddenly) to; **~ a llorar** to burst into tears; **~ con algn** to fall out with sb

ron [ron] *nm* rum

roncar [ron'kar] *vi* to snore

ronco, -a ['ronko, a] *adj* (*afónico*) hoarse; (*áspero*) raucous

ronda ['ronda] *nf* (*gen*) round; (*patrulla*) patrol; **rondar** *vt* to patrol ▷ *vi* to patrol; (*fig*) to prowl round

ronquido [ron'kiðo] *nm* snore, snoring

ronronear [ronrone'ar] *vi* to purr

roña ['roɲa] *nf* (*Veterinaria*) mange; (*mugre*) dirt, grime; (*óxido*) rust

roñoso, -a [ro'ɲoso, a] *adj* (*mugriento*) filthy; (*tacaño*) mean

ropa ['ropa] *nf* clothes *pl*, clothing; **ropa blanca** linen; **ropa de cama** bed linen; **ropa de color** coloureds *pl*; **ropa interior** underwear; **ropa sucia** dirty washing; **ropaje** *nm* gown, robes *pl*

ropero [ro'pero] *nm* linen cupboard; (*guardarropa*) wardrobe

rosa ['rosa] *adj* pink ▷ *nf* rose

rosado, -a [ro'saðo, a] *adj* pink ▷ *nm* rosé

rosal [ro'sal] *nm* rosebush

rosario [ro'sarjo] *nm* (*Rel*) rosary; **rezar el ~** to say the rosary

rosca ['roska] *nf* (*de tornillo*) thread; (*de humo*) coil, spiral; (*pan, postre*) ring-shaped roll/pastry

rosetón [rose'ton] *nm* rosette; (*Arq*) rose window

rosquilla [ros'kiʎa] *nf* doughnut-shaped fritter

rostro ['rostro] *nm* (*cara*) face

rotativo, -a [rota'tiβo, a] *adj* rotary

roto, -a ['roto, a] *pp de* **romper** ▷ *adj* broken

rotonda [ro'tonda] *nf* roundabout

rótula ['rotula] *nf* kneecap; (*Tec*) ball-and-socket joint

rotulador [rotula'ðor] *nm* felt-tip pen

rótulo ['rotulo] *nm* heading, title; label; (*letrero*) sign

rotundamente [rotunda'mente] *adv* (*negar*) flatly; (*responder, afirmar*) emphatically; **rotundo, -a** *adj* round; (*enfático*) emphatic

rotura [ro'tura] *nf* (*acto*) breaking; (*Med*) fracture

rozadura [roθa'ðura] *nf* abrasion, graze

rozar [ro'θar] *vt* (*frotar*) to rub; (*arañar*) to scratch; (*tocar ligeramente*) to shave, touch lightly; **rozarse** *vr* to rub (together); **~se con** (*fam*) to rub shoulders with

rte. *abr* (= *remite, remitente*) sender

RTVE *nf abr* = **Radiotelevisión Española**

rubí [ru'βi] *nm* ruby; (*de reloj*) jewel

rubio, -a ['ruβjo, a] *adj* fair-haired, blond(e) ▷ *nm/f* blond/blonde; **tabaco ~** Virginia tobacco

rubor [ru'βor] *nm* (*sonrojo*) blush; (*timidez*) bashfulness; **ruborizarse** *vr* to blush

rúbrica ['ruβrika] *nf* (*de la firma*) flourish; **rubricar** *vt* (*firmar*) to sign with a flourish; (*concluir*) to sign and seal

rudimentario, -a [ruðimen'tarjo, a] *adj* rudimentary

rudo, -a ['ruðo, a] *adj* (*sin pulir*) unpolished; (*grosero*) coarse; (*violento*) violent; (*sencillo*) simple

rueda ['rweða] *nf* wheel; (*círculo*) ring, circle; (*rodaja*) slice, round; **rueda de auxilio** (*RPL*) spare tyre; **rueda delantera/trasera/ de repuesto** front/back/spare wheel; **rueda de prensa** press conference; **rueda gigante** (*LAM*) big (*BRIT*) o Ferris (*US*) wheel

ruedo ['rweðo] *nm* (*círculo*) circle; (*Taur*) arena, bullring

ruego *etc* ['rweɣo] *vb* V **rogar** ▷ *nm* request

rugby ['ruɣβi] *nm* rugby

rugido [ru'xiðo] *nm* roar

rugir [ru'xir] *vi* to roar

rugoso, -a [ru'ɣoso, a] *adj* (*arrugado*) wrinkled; (*áspero*) rough; (*desigual*) ridged

ruido ['rwiðo] *nm* noise; (*sonido*) sound; (*alboroto*) racket, row; (*escándalo*) commotion, rumpus; **ruidoso, -a** *adj* noisy, loud; (*fig*) sensational

ruin [rwin] *adj* contemptible, mean

ruina ['rwina] *nf* ruin; (*colapso*) collapse; (*de persona*) ruin, downfall

ruinoso, -a [rwi'noso, a] *adj* ruinous; (*destartalado*) dilapidated, tumbledown; (*Com*) disastrous

ruiseñor [rwise'ɲor] *nm* nightingale

rulero [ru'lero] *nm* (*RPL*) roller

ruleta [ru'leta] *nf* roulette

rulo ['rulo] *nm* (*para el pelo*) curler

Rumanía [ruma'nia] *nf* Rumania

rumba ['rumba] *nf* rumba

rumbo ['rumbo] *nm* (*ruta*) route, direction; (*ángulo de dirección*) course, bearing; (*fig*) course of events; **ir con ~ a** to be heading for

rumiante [ru'mjante] *nm* ruminant

rumiar [ru'mjar] *vt* to chew; (*fig*) to chew over ▷ *vi* to chew the cud

rumor [ru'mor] *nm* (*ruido sordo*) low sound; (*murmuración*) murmur, buzz; **rumorearse** *vr*: **se rumorea que ...** it is rumoured that ...

rupestre [ru'pestre] *adj* rock *cpd*

ruptura [rup'tura] *nf* rupture

rural [ru'ral] *adj* rural

Rusia ['rusja] nf Russia; **ruso, -a** adj, nm/f
Russian
rústico, -a ['rustiko, a] adj rustic;
(ordinario) coarse, uncouth ▷ nm/f yokel
ruta ['ruta] nf route
rutina [ru'tina] nf routine

S

S abr (= santo, a) St; (= sur) S
s. abr (= siglo) C.; (= siguiente) foll
S.A. abr (= Sociedad Anónima) Ltd. (BRIT),
Inc. (US)
sábado ['saβaðo] nm Saturday
sábana ['saβana] nf sheet
sabañón [saβa'ɲon] nm chilblain
saber [sa'βer] vt to know; (llegar a conocer)
to find out, learn; (tener capacidad de) to
know how to ▷ vi: ~ **a** to taste of, taste like
▷ nm knowledge, learning; **a** ~ namely;
¿sabes conducir/nadar? can you drive/
swim?; **¿sabes francés?** do you speak
French?; ~ **de memoria** to know by heart;
hacer ~ **algo a algn** to inform sb of sth, let
sb know sth
sabiduría [saβiðu'ria] nf (conocimientos)
wisdom; (instrucción) learning
sabiendas [sa'βjendas]: **a** ~ adv knowingly
sabio, -a ['saβjo,a] adj (docto) learned;
(prudente) wise, sensible
sabor [sa'βor] nm taste, flavour; **saborear**
vt to taste, savour; (fig) to relish
sabotaje [saβo'taxe] nm sabotage
sabré etc vb V **saber**
sabroso, -a [sa'βroso, a] adj tasty;
(fig: fam) racy, salty
sacacorchos [saka'kortʃos] nm inv
corkscrew
sacapuntas [saka'puntas] nm inv pencil
sharpener
sacar [sa'kar] vt to take out; (fig: extraer)
to get (out); (quitar) to remove, get out;
(hacer salir) to bring out; (conclusión) to draw;
(novela etc) to publish, bring out; (ropa) to
take off; (obra) to make; (premio) to receive;
(entradas) to get; (Tenis) to serve; ~ **adelante**
(niño) to bring up; (negocio) to carry on, go on
with; ~ **a algn a bailar** to get sb up to dance;
~ **una foto** to take a photo; ~ **la lengua** to
stick out one's tongue; ~ **buenas/malas**

notas to get good/bad marks
sacarina [saka'rina] nf saccharin(e)
sacerdote [saθer'ðote] nm priest
saciar [sa'θjar] vt (hambre, sed) to satisfy;
 saciarse vr (de comida) to get full up
saco ['sako] nm bag; (grande) sack; (su
 contenido) bagful; (LAM: chaqueta) jacket;
 saco de dormir sleeping bag
sacramento [sakra'mento] nm
 sacrament
sacrificar [sakrifi'kar] vt to sacrifice;
 sacrificio nm sacrifice
sacristía [sakris'tia] nf sacristy
sacudida [saku'ðiða] nf (agitación)
 shake, shaking; (sacudimiento) jolt, bump;
 sacudida eléctrica electric shock
sacudir [saku'ðir] vt to shake; (golpear)
 to hit
Sagitario [saxi'tarjo] nm Sagittarius
sagrado, -a [sa'ɣraðo, a] adj sacred, holy
Sáhara ['saara] nm: **el ~** the Sahara (desert)
sal [sal] vb V **salir** ▷ nf salt; **sales de baño**
 bath salts
sala ['sala] nf room; (tb: ~ de estar)
 living room; (Teatro) house, auditorium;
 (de hospital) ward; **sala de espera** waiting
 room; **sala de estar** living room; **sala de
 fiestas** dance hall
salado, -a [sa'laðo, a] adj salty; (fig) witty,
 amusing; **agua salada** salt water
salar [sa'lar] vt to salt, add salt to
salario [sa'larjo] nm wage, pay
salchicha [sal'tʃitʃa] nf (pork) sausage;
 salchichón nm (salami-type) sausage
saldo ['saldo] nm (pago) settlement; (de una
 cuenta) balance; (lo restante) remnant(s) (pl),
 remainder; (de móvil) credit; **saldos** nmpl
 (en tienda) sale
saldré etc vb V **salir**
salero [sa'lero] nm salt cellar
salgo etc vb V **salir**
salida [sa'liða] nf (puerta etc) exit, way
 out; (acto) leaving, going out; (de tren,
 Aviac) departure; (Tec) output, production;
 (fig) way out; (Com) opening; (Geo, válvula)
 outlet; (de gas) leak; **calle sin ~** cul-de-sac;
 salida de baño (RPL) bathrobe; **salida de
 emergencia/incendios** emergency exit/
 fire escape

○ **PALABRA CLAVE**

salir [sa'lir] vi **1**(partir: tb: **salir de**) to
 leave; **Juan ha salido** Juan is out; **salió de la
 cocina** he came out of the kitchen
 2 (aparecer) to appear; (disco, libro) to come
 out; **anoche salió en la tele** she appeared
 o was on TV last night; **salió en todos los**

periódicos it was in all the papers
 3 (resultar): **la muchacha nos salió muy
 trabajadora** the girl turned out to be a
 very hard worker; **la comida te ha salido
 exquisita** the food was delicious; **sale muy
 caro** it's very expensive
 4: **salirle a uno algo: la entrevista que
 hice me salió bien/mal** the interview I did
 went o turned out well/badly
 5: **salir adelante: no sé como haré para
 salir adelante** I don't know how I'll get by
 salirse vr (líquido) to spill; (animal) to escape

saliva [sa'liβa] nf saliva
salmo ['salmo] nm psalm
salmón [sal'mon] nm salmon
salmonete [salmo'nete] nm red mullet
salón [sa'lon] nm (de casa) living room,
 lounge; (muebles) lounge suite; **salón de
 baile** dance hall; **salón de belleza** beauty
 parlour
salpicadera [salpika'ðera] (MÉX) nf
 mudguard (BRIT), fender (US)
salpicadero [salpika'ðero] nm (Auto)
 dashboard
salpicar [salpi'kar] vt (rociar) to sprinkle,
 spatter; (esparcir) to scatter
salpicón [salpi'kon] nm (tb: ~ de marisco)
 seafood salad
salsa ['salsa] nf sauce; (con carne asada)
 gravy; (fig) spice
saltamontes [salta'montes] nm inv
 grasshopper
saltar [sal'tar] vt to jump (over), leap
 (over); (dejar de lado) to skip, miss out ▷ vi to
 jump, leap; (pelota) to bounce; (al aire) to fly
 up; (quebrarse) to break; (al agua) to dive; (fig)
 to explode, blow up
salto ['salto] nm jump, leap; (al agua) dive;
 salto de agua waterfall; **salto de altura/
 longitud** high/long jump
salud [sa'luð] nf health; **¡(a su) ~!** cheers!,
 good health!; **saludable** adj (de buena salud)
 healthy; (provechoso) good, beneficial
saludar [salu'ðar] vt to greet; (Mil) to
 salute; **saludo** nm greeting; **"saludos"** (en
 carta) "best wishes", "regards"
salvación [salβa'θjon] nf salvation;
 (rescate) rescue
salvado [sal'βaðo] nm bran
salvaje [sal'βaxe] adj wild; (tribu) savage
salvamanteles [salβaman'teles] nm inv
 table mat
salvamento [salβa'mento] nm rescue
salvapantallas [salβapan'taʎas] nm inv
 screen saver
salvar [sal'βar] vt (rescatar) to save, rescue;
 (resolver) to overcome, resolve; (cubrir

distancias) to cover, travel; *(hacer excepción)* to except, exclude; *(barco)* to salvage

salvavidas [salβa'βiðas] *adj inv:* **bote/chaleco ~** lifeboat/life jacket

salvo, -a ['salβo, a] *adj* safe ▷ *adv* except (for), save; **a ~** out of danger; **~ que** unless

san [san] *adj* saint; **S~ Juan** St John

sanar [sa'nar] *vt (herida)* to heal; *(persona)* to cure ▷ *vi (persona)* to get well, recover; *(herida)* to heal

sanatorio [sana'torjo] *nm* sanatorium

sanción [san'θjon] *nf* sanction

sancochado, -a [sanko'tʃado, a] *(MÉX) adj (Culin)* underdone, rare

sandalia [san'dalja] *nf* sandal

sandía [san'dia] *nf* watermelon

sandwich ['sandwitʃ] *(pl* **~s, ~es)** *nm* sandwich

sanfermines [sanfer'mines] *nmpl festivities in celebration of San Fermín (Pamplona)*

sangrar [san'grar] *vt, vi* to bleed; **sangre** *nf* blood

sangría [san'gria] *nf* sangria, *sweetened drink of red wine with fruit*

sangriento, -a [san'grjento, a] *adj* bloody

sanguíneo, -a [san'gineo, a] *adj* blood *cpd*

sanidad [sani'ðað] *nf (tb:* **~ pública)** public health

San Isidro [sani'sidro] *nm patron saint of Madrid*

now include music, dance, a famous **romería**, theatre and bullfighting.

sanitario, -a [sani'tarjo, a] *adj* health *cpd*; **sanitarios** *nmpl* toilets *(BRIT)*, washroom *(US)*

sano, -a ['sano, a] *adj* healthy; *(sin daños)* sound; *(comida)* wholesome; *(entero)* whole, intact; **~ y salvo** safe and sound

▌No confundir **sano** con la palabra inglesa *sane.*

Santiago [san'tjaɣo] *nm:* **~ (de Chile)** Santiago

santiamén [santja'men] *nm:* **en un ~** in no time at all

santidad [santi'ðað] *nf* holiness, sanctity

santiguarse [santi'ɣwarse] *vr* to make the sign of the cross

santo, -a ['santo, a] *adj* holy; *(fig)* wonderful, miraculous ▷ *nm/f* saint ▷ *nm* saint's day; **~ y seña** password

santuario [san'twarjo] *nm* sanctuary, shrine

sapo ['sapo] *nm* toad

saque ['sake] *nm (Tenis)* service, serve; *(Fútbol)* throw-in; **saque de esquina** corner (kick)

saquear [sake'ar] *vt (Mil)* to sack; *(robar)* to loot, plunder; *(fig)* to ransack

sarampión [saram'pjon] *nm* measles *sg*

sarcástico, -a [sar'kastiko, a] *adj* sarcastic

sardina [sar'ðina] *nf* sardine

sargento [sar'xento] *nm* sergeant

sarmiento [sar'mjento] *nm (Bot)* vine shoot

sarna ['sarna] *nf* itch; *(Med)* scabies

sarpullido [sarpu'ʎiðo] *nm (Med)* rash

sarro ['sarro] *nm (en dientes)* tartar, plaque

sartén [sar'ten] *nf* frying pan

sastre ['sastre] *nm* tailor; **sastrería** *nf (arte)* tailoring; *(tienda)* tailor's (shop)

Satanás [sata'nas] *nm* Satan

satélite [sa'telite] *nm* satellite

sátira ['satira] *nf* satire

satisfacción [satisfak'θjon] *nf* satisfaction

satisfacer [satisfa'θer] *vt* to satisfy; *(gastos)* to meet; *(pérdida)* to make good; **satisfacerse** *vr* to satisfy o.s., be satisfied; *(vengarse)* to take revenge; **satisfecho, -a** *adj* satisfied; *(contento)* content(ed), happy; *(tb:* **satisfecho de sí mismo)** self-satisfied, smug

saturar [satu'rar] *vt* to saturate; **saturarse** *vr (mercado, aeropuerto)* to reach saturation point

sauce ['sauθe] *nm* willow; **sauce llorón**

weeping willow

sauna ['sauna] nf sauna

savia ['saβja] nf sap

saxofón [sakso'fon] nm saxophone

sazonar [saθo'nar] vt to ripen; (Culin) to flavour, season

scooter [e'skuter] (ESP) nf scooter

Scotch [skotʃ] (LAM) nm Sellotape® (BRIT), Scotch tape® (US)

SE abr (= sudeste) SE

O PALABRA CLAVE

se [se] pron 1 (reflexivo: sg: m) himself; (: f) herself; (: pl) themselves; (: cosa) itself; (: de Vd) yourself; (: deVds) yourselves; **se está preparando** she's preparing herself
2 (con complemento indirecto) to him; to her; to them; to it; to you; **a usted se lo dije ayer** I told you yesterday; **se compró un sombrero** he bought himself a hat; **se rompió la pierna** he broke his leg
3 (uso recíproco) each other, one another; **se miraron (el uno al otro)** they looked at each other o one another
4 (en oraciones pasivas): **se han vendido muchos libros** a lot of books have been sold
5 (impers): **se dice que ...** people say that ..., it is said that ...; **allí se come muy bien** the food there is very good, you can eat very well there

sé etc [se] vb V **saber; ser**

sea etc vb V **ser**

sebo ['seβo] nm fat, grease

secador [seka'ðor] nm: **~ de pelo** hairdryer

secadora [seka'ðora] nf tumble dryer

secar [se'kar] vt to dry; **secarse** vr to dry (off); (río, planta) to dry up

sección [sek'θjon] nf section

seco, -a ['seko, a] adj dry; (carácter) cold; (respuesta) sharp, curt; **parar en ~** to stop dead; **decir algo a secas** to say sth curtly

secretaría [sekreta'ria] nf secretariat

secretario, -a [sekre'tarjo, a] nm/f secretary

secreto, -a [se'kreto, a] adj secret; (persona) secretive ▷ nm secret; (calidad) secrecy

secta ['sekta] nf sect

sector [sek'tor] nm sector

secuela [se'kwela] nf consequence

secuencia [se'kwenθja] nf sequence

secuestrar [sekwes'trar] vt to kidnap; (bienes) to seize, confiscate; **secuestro** nm kidnapping; seizure, confiscation

secundario, -a [sekun'darjo, a] adj secondary

sed [seð] nf thirst; **tener ~** to be thirsty

seda ['seða] nf silk

sedal [se'ðal] nm fishing line

sedán [se'ðan] (LAM) nm saloon (BRIT), sedan (US)

sedante [se'ðante] nm sedative

sede ['seðe] nf (de gobierno) seat; (de compañía) headquarters pl; **Santa S~** Holy See

sedentario, -a [seðen'tario, a] adj sedentary

sediento, -a [se'ðjento, a] adj thirsty

sedimento [seði'mento] nm sediment

seducción [seðuk'θjon] nf seduction

seducir [seðu'θir] vt to seduce; (cautivar) to charm, fascinate; (atraer) to attract; **seductor, a** adj seductive; charming, fascinating; attractive ▷ nm/f seducer

segar [se'xar] vt (mies) to reap, cut; (hierba) to mow, cut

seglar [se'xlar] adj secular, lay

seguida [se'xiða] nf: **en ~** at once, right away

seguido, -a [se'xiðo, a] adj (continuo) continuous, unbroken; (recto) straight ▷ adv (directo) straight (on); (después) after; (LAM: a menudo) often; **~s** consecutive, successive; **5 días ~s** 5 days running, 5 days in a row

seguir [se'xir] vt to follow; (venir después) to follow on, come after; (proseguir) to continue; (perseguir) to chase, pursue ▷ vi (gen) to follow; (continuar) to continue, carry o go on; **seguirse** vr to follow; **sigo sin comprender** I still don't understand; **sigue lloviendo** it's still raining

según [se'xun] prep according to ▷ adv: **¿irás? – ~** are you going? – it all depends ▷ conj as; **~ caminamos** while we walk

segundo, -a [se'xundo, a] adj second ▷ nm second ▷ nf second meaning; **de segunda mano** second-hand; **segunda (clase)** second class; **segunda (marcha)** (Auto) second (gear)

seguramente [sexura'mente] adv surely; (con certeza) for sure, with certainty

seguridad [sexuri'ðað] nf safety; (del estado, de casa etc) security; (certidumbre) certainty; (confianza) confidence; (estabilidad) stability; **seguridad social** social security

seguro, -a [se'xuro, a] adj (cierto) sure, certain; (fiel) trustworthy; (libre de peligro) safe; (bien defendido, firme) secure ▷ adv for sure, certainly ▷ nm (Com) insurance; **seguro contra terceros/a todo riesgo** third party/comprehensive insurance;

s

seguros sociales social security *sg*
seis [seis] *num* six
seísmo [se'ismo] *nm* tremor, earthquake
selección [selek'θjon] *nf* selection;
  seleccionar *vt* to pick, choose, select
selectividad [selektiβi'ðað] (ESP) *nf*
  university entrance examination
selecto, -a [se'lekto, a] *adj* select, choice;
  (*escogido*) selected
sellar [se'ʎar] *vt* (*documento oficial*) to seal;
  (*pasaporte, visado*) to stamp
sello ['seʎo] *nm* stamp; (*precinto*) seal
selva ['selβa] *nf* (*bosque*) forest, woods *pl*;
  (*jungla*) jungle
semáforo [se'maforo] *nm* (*Auto*) traffic
  lights *pl*; (*Ferro*) signal
semana [se'mana] *nf* week; **entre ~**
  during the week; **Semana Santa** Holy
  Week; **semanal** *adj* weekly; **semanario** *nm*
  weekly magazine

⬤ **SEMANA SANTA**
⬤
⬤ In Spain celebrations for **Semana Santa**
⬤ (Holy Week) are often spectacular.
⬤ "Viernes Santo", "Sábado Santo" and
⬤ "Domingo de Resurrección" (Good
⬤ Friday, Holy Saturday, Easter Sunday)
⬤ are all national public holidays,
⬤ with additional days being given as
⬤ local holidays. There are fabulous
⬤ **procesiones** all over the country, with
⬤ members of "cofradías" (brotherhoods)
⬤ dressing in hooded robes and parading
⬤ their "pasos" (religious floats and
⬤ sculptures) through the streets. Seville
⬤ has the most famous Holy Week
⬤ processions.

sembrar [sem'brar] *vt* to sow; (*objetos*)
  to sprinkle, scatter about; (*noticias etc*) to
  spread
semejante [seme'xante] *adj* (*parecido*)
  similar ▷ *nm* fellow man, fellow creature;
  ~s alike, similar; **nunca hizo cosa ~** he
  never did any such thing; **semejanza** *nf*
  similarity, resemblance
semejar [seme'xar] *vi* to seem like,
  resemble; **semejarse** *vr* to look alike, be
  similar
semen ['semen] *nm* semen
semestral [semes'tral] *adj* half-yearly,
  bi-annual
semicírculo [semi'θirkulo] *nm* semicircle
semidesnatado, -a [semiðesna'taðo, a]
  adj semi-skimmed
semifinal [semifi'nal] *nf* semifinal
semilla [se'miʎa] *nf* seed

seminario [semi'narjo] *nm* (*Rel*)
  seminary; (*Escol*) seminar
sémola ['semola] *nf* semolina
senado [se'naðo] *nm* senate; **senador, a**
  nm/f senator
sencillez [senθi'ʎeθ] *nf* simplicity; (*de
  persona*) naturalness; **sencillo, -a** *adj*
  simple; natural, unaffected
senda ['senda] *nf* path, track
senderismo [sende'rismo] *nm* hiking
sendero [sen'dero] *nm* path, track
sendos, -as ['sendos, as] *adj pl*: **les dio ~
  golpes** he hit both of them
senil [se'nil] *adj* senile
seno ['seno] *nm* (*Anat*) bosom, bust; (*fig*)
  bosom; **~s** breasts
sensación [sensa'θjon] *nf* sensation;
  (*sentido*) sense; (*sentimiento*) feeling;
  sensacional *adj* sensational
sensato, -a [sen'sato, a] *adj* sensible
sensible [sen'sible] *adj* sensitive;
  (*apreciable*) perceptible, appreciable;
  (*pérdida*) considerable

▌ No confundir **sensible** con la palabra
  inglesa *sensible*.

sensiblero, -a *adj* sentimental
sensitivo, -a [sensi'tiβo, a] *adj* sense *cpd*
sensorial [senso'rjal] *adj* sensory
sensual [sen'swal] *adj* sensual
sentada [sen'taða] *nf* sitting; (*protesta*)
  sit-in
sentado, -a [sen'taðo, a] *adj*: **estar ~** to
  sit, be sitting (down); **dar por ~** to take for
  granted, assume
sentar [sen'tar] *vt* to sit, seat; (*fig*) to
  establish ▷ *vi* (*vestido*) to suit; (*alimento*): **~
  bien/mal a** to agree/disagree with;
  sentarse *vr* (*persona*) to sit, sit down; (*los
  depósitos*) to settle
sentencia [sen'tenθja] *nf* (*máxima*)
  maxim, saying; (*Jur*) sentence; **sentenciar**
  vt to sentence
sentido, -a [sen'tiðo, a] *adj* (*pérdida*)
  regrettable; (*carácter*) sensitive ▷ *nm* sense;
  (*sentimiento*) feeling; (*significado*) sense,
  meaning; (*dirección*) direction; **mi más ~
  pésame** my deepest sympathy; **tener ~**
  to make sense; **sentido común** common
  sense; **sentido del humor** sense of humour;
  sentido único one-way (street)
sentimental [sentimen'tal] *adj*
  sentimental; **vida ~** love life
sentimiento [senti'mjento] *nm* feeling
sentir [sen'tir] *vt* to feel; (*percibir*) to
  perceive, sense; (*lamentar*) to regret, be
  sorry for ▷ *vi* (*tener la sensación*) to feel;
  (*lamentarse*) to feel sorry ▷ *nm* opinion,
  judgement; **~se bien/mal** to feel well/ill; **lo**

siento I'm sorry

seña ['sɛɲa] nf sign; (Mil) password; **señas**
nfpl (dirección) address sg; **señas personales**
personal description sg

señal [se'ɲal] nf sign; (síntoma) symptom;
(Ferro, Tel) signal; (marca) mark; (Com)
deposit; **en ~ de** as a token o sign of; **señalar**
vt to mark; (indicar) to point out, indicate

señor [se'ɲor] nm (hombre) man; (caballero)
gentleman; (dueño) owner, master;
(trato: antes de nombre propio) Mr; (: hablando
directamente) sir; **muy ~ mío** Dear Sir; **el ~
alcalde/presidente** the mayor/president

señora [se'ɲora] nf (dama) lady;
(trato: antes de nombre propio) Mrs; (: hablando
directamente) madam; (esposa) wife; **Nuestra
S~** Our Lady

señorita [seɲo'rita] nf (con nombre y/o
apellido) Miss; (mujer joven) young lady

señorito [seɲo'rito] nm young gentleman;
(pey) rich kid

sepa etc vb V **saber**

separación [separa'θjon] nf separation;
(división) division; (hueco) gap

separar [sepa'rar] vt to separate; (dividir)
to divide; **separarse** vr (parte) to come
away; (partes) to come apart; (persona) to
leave, go away; (matrimonio) to separate;
separatismo nm separatism

sepia ['sepja] nf cuttlefish

septentrional [septentrjo'nal] adj
northern

septiembre [sep'tjembre] nm September

séptimo, -a ['septimo, a] adj, nm seventh

sepulcral [sepul'kral] adj (fig: silencio,
atmósfera) deadly; **sepulcro** nm tomb, grave

sepultar [sepul'tar] vt to bury; **sepultura**
nf (acto) burial; (tumba) grave, tomb

sequía [se'kia] nf drought

séquito ['sekito] nm (de rey etc) retinue;
(seguidores) followers pl

○ PALABRA CLAVE

ser [ser] vi **1** (descripción) to be; **es médica/
muy alta** she's a doctor/very tall; **la familia
es de Cuzco** his (o her etc) family is from
Cuzco; **soy Ana** (Tel) Ana speaking o here

2 (propiedad): **es de Joaquín** it's Joaquín's, it
belongs to Joaquín

3 (horas, fechas, números): **es la una** it's one
o'clock; **son las seis y media** it's half-past
six; **es el 1 de junio** it's the first of June;
somos/son seis there are six of us/them

4 (en oraciones pasivas): **ha sido descubierto
ya** it's already been discovered

5: **es de esperar que ...** it is to be hoped o I
etc hope that ...

6 (locuciones con sub): **o sea** that is to say; **sea
él sea su hermana** either him or his sister

7: **a no ser por él ...** but for him ...

8: **a no ser que: a no ser que tenga uno ya**
unless he's got one already ▷ nm being; **ser
humano** human being

sereno, -a [se'reno, a] adj (persona) calm,
unruffled; (el tiempo) fine, settled; (ambiente)
calm, peaceful ▷ nm night watchman

serial [ser'jal] nm serial

serie ['serje] nf series; (cadena) sequence,
succession; **fuera de ~** out of order; (fig)
special, out of the ordinary; **fabricación en
~** mass production

seriedad [serje'ðað] nf seriousness;
(formalidad) reliability; **serio, -a** adj serious;
reliable, dependable; grave, serious; **en
serio** adv seriously

serigrafía [serixra'fia] nf silk-screen
printing

sermón [ser'mon] nm (Rel) sermon

seropositivo, -a [seroposi'tiβo] adj HIV
positive

serpentear [serpente'ar] vi to wriggle;
(camino, río) to wind, snake

serpentina [serpen'tina] nf streamer

serpiente [ser'pjente] nf snake;
serpiente de cascabel rattlesnake

serranía [serra'nia] nf mountainous area

serrar [se'rrar] vt = **aserrar**

serrín [se'rrin] nm sawdust

serrucho [se'rrutʃo] nm saw

service ['serβis] (RPL) nm (Auto) service

servicio [ser'βiθjo] nm service; (LAM Auto)
service; **servicios** nmpl (ESP) toilet(s);
servicio incluido service charge included;
servicio militar military service

servidumbre [serβi'ðumbre] nf (sujeción)
servitude; (criados) servants pl, staff

servil [ser'βil] adj servile

servilleta [serβi'ʎeta] nf serviette, napkin

servir [ser'βir] vt to serve ▷ vi to serve;
(tener utilidad) to be of use, be useful;
servirse vr to serve o help o.s.; **~se de algo**
to make use of sth, use sth; **sírvase pasar**
please come in

sesenta [se'senta] num sixty

sesión [se'sjon] nf (Pol) session, sitting;
(Cine) showing

seso ['seso] nm brain; **sesudo, -a** adj
sensible, wise

seta ['seta] nf mushroom; **seta venenosa**
toadstool

setecientos, -as [sete'θjentos, as] adj,
num seven hundred

setenta [se'tenta] num seventy

seto ['seto] nm hedge

S

severo, -a [se'βero, a] *adj* severe
Sevilla [se'βiʎa] *n* Seville; **sevillano, -a** *adj* of o from Seville ▷ *nm/f* native o inhabitant of Seville
sexo ['sekso] *nm* sex
sexto, -a ['seksto, a] *adj, nm* sixth
sexual [sek'swal] *adj* sexual; **vida ~** sex life
si [si] *conj* if ▷ *nm* (Mús) B; **me pregunto ~ ...** I wonder if o whether ...
sí [si] *adv* yes ▷ *nm* consent ▷ *pron* (uso impersonal) oneself; (sg: m) himself; (: f) herself; (: de cosa) itself; (de usted) yourself; (pl) themselves; (de ustedes) yourselves; (recíproco) each other; **él no quiere pero yo ~** he doesn't want to but I do; **ella ~ vendrá** she will certainly come, she is sure to come; **claro que ~** of course; **creo que ~** I think so
siamés, -esa [sja'mes, esa] *adj, nm/f* Siamese
SIDA ['siða] *nm abr* (= Síndrome de Inmunodeficiencia Adquirida) AIDS
siderúrgico, -a [siðe'rurxico, a] *adj* iron and steel *cpd*
sidra ['siðra] *nf* cider
siembra ['sjembra] *nf* sowing
siempre ['sjempre] *adv* always; (todo el tiempo) all the time; **~ que** (cada vez) whenever; (dado que) provided that; **como ~** as usual; **para ~** for ever
sien [sjen] *nf* temple
siento *etc* ['sjento] *vb* V **sentar; sentir**
sierra ['sjerra] *nf* (Tec) saw; (cadena de montañas) mountain range
siervo, -a ['sjerβo, a] *nm/f* slave
siesta ['sjesta] *nf* siesta, nap; **echar la ~** to have an afternoon nap o a siesta
siete ['sjete] *num* seven
sifón [si'fon] *nm* syphon
sigla ['siɣla] *nf* abbreviation; acronym
siglo ['siɣlo] *nm* century; (fig) age
significado [siɣnifi'kaðo] *nm* (de palabra etc) meaning
significar [siɣnifi'kar] *vt* to mean, signify; (notificar) to make known, express
signo ['siɣno] *nm* sign; **signo de admiración** o **exclamación** exclamation mark; **signo de interrogación** question mark
sigo *etc* *vb* V **seguir**
siguiente [si'ɣjente] *adj* next, following
siguió *etc* *vb* V **seguir**
sílaba ['silaβa] *nf* syllable
silbar [sil'βar] *vt, vi* to whistle; **silbato** *nm* whistle; **silbido** *nm* whistle, whistling
silenciador [silenθja'ðor] *nm* silencer
silenciar [silen'θjar] *vt* (persona) to silence; (escándalo) to hush up; **silencio** *nm* silence, quiet; **silencioso, -a** *adj* silent, quiet

silla ['siʎa] *nf* (asiento) chair; (tb: **~ de montar**) saddle; **silla de ruedas** wheelchair
sillón [si'ʎon] *nm* armchair, easy chair
silueta [si'lweta] *nf* silhouette; (de edificio) outline; (figura) figure
silvestre [sil'βestre] *adj* wild
simbólico, -a [sim'boliko, a] *adj* symbolic(al)
simbolizar [simboli'θar] *vt* to symbolize
símbolo ['simbolo] *nm* symbol
similar [simi'lar] *adj* similar
simio ['simjo] *nm* ape
simpatía [simpa'tia] *nf* liking; (afecto) affection; (amabilidad) kindness; **simpático, -a** *adj* nice, pleasant; kind
No confundir **simpático** con la palabra inglesa *sympathetic*.
simpatizante [simpati'θante] *nmf* sympathizer
simpatizar [simpati'θar] *vi*: **~ con** to get on well with
simple ['simple] *adj* simple; (elemental) simple, easy; (mero) mere; (puro) pure, sheer ▷ *nmf* simpleton; **simpleza** *nf* simpleness; (necedad) silly thing; **simplificar** *vt* to simplify
simposio [sim'posjo] *nm* symposium
simular [simu'lar] *vt* to simulate
simultáneo, -a [simul'taneo, a] *adj* simultaneous
sin [sin] *prep* without; **la ropa está ~ lavar** the clothes are unwashed; **~ que** without; **~ embargo** however, still
sinagoga [sina'ɣoɣa] *nf* synagogue
sinceridad [sinθeri'ðað] *nf* sincerity; **sincero, -a** *adj* sincere
sincronizar [sinkroni'θar] *vt* to synchronize
sindical [sindi'kal] *adj* union *cpd*, trade-union *cpd*; **sindicalista** *adj, nmf* trade unionist
sindicato [sindi'kato] *nm* (de trabajadores) trade(s) union; (de negociantes) syndicate
síndrome ['sindrome] *nm* (Med) syndrome; **síndrome de abstinencia** (Med) withdrawal symptoms; **síndrome de la clase turista** (Med) economy-class syndrome
sinfín [sin'fin] *nm*: **un ~ de** a great many, no end of
sinfonía [sinfo'nia] *nf* symphony
singular [singu'lar] *adj* singular; (fig) outstanding, exceptional; (raro) peculiar, odd
siniestro, -a [si'njestro, a] *adj* sinister ▷ *nm* (accidente) accident
sinnúmero [sin'numero] *nm* = **sinfín**

sino ['sino] *nm* fate, destiny ▷ *conj* (*pero*) but; (*salvo*) except, save

sinónimo, -a [si'nonimo, a] *adj* synonymous ▷ *nm* synonym

síntesis ['sintesis] *nf* synthesis; **sintético, -a** *adj* synthetic

sintió *vb* V **sentir**

síntoma ['sintoma] *nm* symptom

sintonía [sinto'nia] *nf* (*Radio, Mús: de programa*) tuning; **sintonizar** *vt* (*Radio: emisora*) to tune (in)

sinvergüenza [simber'xwenθa] *nmf* rogue, scoundrel; **¡es un ~!** he's got a nerve!

siquiera [si'kjera] *conj* even if, even though ▷ *adv* at least; **ni ~** not even

Siria ['sirja] *nf* Syria

sirviente, -a [sir'βjente, a] *nm/f* servant

sirvo *etc vb* V **servir**

sistema [sis'tema] *nm* system; (*método*) method; **sistema educativo** education system; **sistemático, -a** *adj* systematic

○ **SISTEMA EDUCATIVO**
○
○
○ The reform of the Spanish **sistema**
○ **educativo** (education system) begun
○ in the early 90s has replaced the
○ courses EGB, BUP and COU with the
○ following: "Primaria" a compulsory 6
○ years; "Secundaria" a compulsory 4 years
○ and "Bachillerato" an optional 2-year
○ secondary school course, essential
○ for those wishing to go on to higher
○ education.

sitiar [si'tjar] *vt* to besiege, lay siege to

sitio ['sitjo] *nm* (*lugar*) place; (*espacio*) room, space; (*Mil*) siege; **sitio de taxis** (*MÉX: parada*) taxi stand o rank (*BRIT*); **sitio web** (*Inform*) website

situación [sitwa'θjon] *nf* situation, position; (*estatus*) status; (*posición*) position, standing

situado, -a [situ'aðo] *adj* situated, placed

situar [si'twar] *vt* to place, put; (*edificio*) to locate, situate

slip [slip] *nm* pants *pl*, briefs *pl*

smoking ['smokin, es'mokin] (*pl* **~s**) *nm* dinner jacket (*BRIT*), tuxedo (*US*)

▌ No confundir **smoking** con la palabra inglesa *smoking*.

SMS *nm* (*mensaje*) text message, SMS message

snob [es'nob] = **esnob**

SO *abr* (= *suroeste*) SW

sobaco [so'βako] *nm* armpit

sobar [so'βar] *vt* (*ropa*) to rumple; (*comida*) to play around with

soberanía [soβera'nia] *nf* sovereignty;

soberano, -a *adj* sovereign; (*fig*) supreme ▷ *nm/f* sovereign

soberbia [so'βerβja] *nf* pride; haughtiness, arrogance; magnificence

soberbio, -a [so'βerβjo, a] *adj* (*orgulloso*) proud; (*altivo*) arrogant; (*estupendo*) magnificent, superb

sobornar [soβor'nar] *vt* to bribe; **soborno** *nm* bribe

sobra ['soβra] *nf* excess, surplus; **sobras** *nfpl* left-overs, scraps; **de ~** surplus, extra; **tengo de ~** I've more than enough; **sobrado, -a** *adj* (*más que suficiente*) more than enough; (*superfluo*) excessive; **sobrante** *adj* remaining, extra ▷ *nm* surplus, remainder

sobrar [so'βrar] *vt* to exceed, surpass ▷ *vi* (*tener de más*) to be more than enough; (*quedar*) to remain, be left (over)

sobrasada [soβra'saða] *nf* pork sausage spread

sobre ['soβre] *prep* (*gen*) on; (*encima*) on (top of); (*por encima de, arriba de*) over, above; (*más que*) more than; (*además*) in addition to, besides; (*alrededor de*) about ▷ *nm* envelope; **~ todo** above all

sobrecama [soβre'kama] *nf* bedspread

sobrecargar [soβrekar'ɣar] *vt* (*camión*) to overload; (*Com*) to surcharge

sobredosis [soβre'ðosis] *nf inv* overdose

sobreentender [soβre(e)nten'der] *vt* to deduce, infer; **sobreentenderse** *vr*: **se sobreentiende que ...** it is implied that ...

sobrehumano, -a [soβreu'mano, a] *adj* superhuman

sobrellevar [soβreʎe'βar] *vt* to bear, endure

sobremesa [soβre'mesa] *nf*: **durante la ~** after dinner

sobrenatural [soβrenatu'ral] *adj* supernatural

sobrenombre [soβre'nombre] *nm* nickname

sobrepasar [soβrepa'sar] *vt* to exceed, surpass

sobreponerse [soβrepo'nerse] *vr*: **~ a** to overcome

sobresaliente [soβresa'ljente] *adj* outstanding, excellent

sobresalir [soβresa'lir] *vi* to project, jut out; (*fig*) to stand out, excel

sobresaltar [soβresal'tar] *vt* (*asustar*) to scare, frighten; (*sobrecoger*) to startle; **sobresalto** *nm* (*movimiento*) start; (*susto*) scare; (*turbación*) sudden shock

sobretodo [soβre'toðo] *nm* overcoat

sobrevenir [soβreβe'nir] *vi* (*ocurrir*) to happen (unexpectedly); (*resultar*) to follow, ensue

sobrevivir [soβreβi'βir] *vi* to survive

sobrevolar [soβreβo'lar] *vt* to fly over

sobriedad [soβrje'ðað] *nf* sobriety, soberness; (*moderación*) moderation, restraint

sobrino, -a [so'βrino, a] *nm/f* nephew/ niece

sobrio, -a ['soβrjo, a] *adj* sober; (*moderado*) moderate, restrained

socarrón, -ona [soka'rron, ona] *adj* (*sarcástico*) sarcastic, ironic(al)

socavón [soka'βon] *nm* (*hoyo*) hole

sociable [so'θjaβle] *adj* (*persona*) sociable, friendly; (*animal*) social

social [so'θjal] *adj* social; (*Com*) company *cpd*

socialdemócrata [soθjalde'mokrata] *nmf* social democrat

socialista [soθja'lista] *adj, nm* socialist

socializar [soθjali'θar] *vt* to socialize

sociedad [soθje'ðað] *nf* society; (*Com*) company; **sociedad anónima** limited company; **sociedad de consumo** consumer society

socio, -a ['soθjo, a] *nm/f* (*miembro*) member; (*Com*) partner

sociología [soθjolo'xia] *nf* sociology; **sociólogo, -a** *nm/f* sociologist

socorrer [soko'rrer] *vt* to help; **socorrista** *nmf* first aider; (*en piscina, playa*) lifeguard; **socorro** *nm* (*ayuda*) help, aid; (*Mil*) relief; **¡socorro!** help!

soda ['soða] *nf* (*sosa*) soda; (*bebida*) soda (water)

sofá [so'fa] (*pl* ~**s**) *nm* sofa, settee; **sofá-cama** *nm* studio couch; sofa bed

sofocar [sofo'kar] *vt* to suffocate; (*apagar*) to smother, put out; **sofocarse** *vr* to suffocate; (*fig*) to blush, feel embarrassed; **sofoco** *nm* suffocation; embarrassment

sofreír [sofre'ir] *vt* (*Culin*) to fry lightly

soga ['soxa] *nf* rope

sois *etc vb* V **ser**

soja ['soxa] *nf* soya

sol [sol] *nm* sun; (*luz*) sunshine, sunlight; (*Mús*) G; **hace ~** it's sunny

solamente [sola'mente] *adv* only, just

solapa [so'lapa] *nf* (*de chaqueta*) lapel; (*de libro*) jacket

solapado, -a [sola'paðo, a] *adj* (*intencíones*) underhand; (*gestos, movimiento*) sly

solar [so'lar] *adj* solar, sun *cpd*

soldado [sol'daðo] *nm* soldier; **soldado raso** private

soldador [solda'ðor] *nm* soldering iron; (*persona*) welder

soldar [sol'dar] *vt* to solder, weld

soleado, -a [sole'aðo, a] *adj* sunny

soledad [sole'ðað] *nf* solitude; (*estado infeliz*) loneliness

solemne [so'lemne] *adj* solemn

soler [so'ler] *vi* to be in the habit of, be accustomed to; **suele salir a las ocho** she usually goes out at eight o'clock

solfeo [sol'feo] *nm* solfa

solicitar [soliθi'tar] *vt* (*permiso*) to ask for, seek; (*puesto*) to apply for; (*votos*) to canvass for; (*atención*) to attract

solícito, -a [so'liθito, a] *adj* (*diligente*) diligent; (*cuidadoso*) careful; **solicitud** *nf* (*calidad*) great care; (*petición*) request; (*a un puesto*) application

solidaridad [soliðari'ðað] *nf* solidarity; **solidario, -a** *adj* (*participación*) joint, common; (*compromiso*) mutually binding

sólido, -a ['soliðo, a] *adj* solid

soliloquio [soli'lokjo] *nm* soliloquy

solista [so'lista] *nmf* soloist

solitario, -a [soli'tarjo, a] *adj* (*persona*) lonely, solitary; (*lugar*) lonely, desolate ▷ *nm/f* (*recluso*) recluse; (*en la sociedad*) loner ▷ *nm* solitaire

sollozar [soλo'θar] *vi* to sob; **sollozo** *nm* sob

solo, -a ['solo, a] *adj* (*único*) single, sole; (*sin compañía*) alone; (*solitario*) lonely; **hay una sola dificultad** there is just one difficulty; **a solas** alone, by oneself

sólo ['solo] *adv* only, just

solomillo [solo'miλo] *nm* sirloin

soltar [sol'tar] *vt* (*dejar ir*) to let go of; (*desprender*) to unfasten, loosen; (*librar*) to release, set free; (*risa etc*) to let out

soltero, -a [sol'tero, a] *adj* single, unmarried ▷ *nm/f* bachelor/single woman; **solterón, -ona** *nm/f* old bachelor/spinster

soltura [sol'tura] *nf* looseness, slackness; (*de los miembros*) agility, ease of movement; (*en el hablar*) fluency, ease

soluble [so'luβle] *adj* (*Quím*) soluble; (*problema*) solvable; **~ en agua** soluble in water

solución [solu'θjon] *nf* solution; **solucionar** *vt* (*problema*) to solve; (*asunto*) to settle, resolve

solventar [solβen'tar] *vt* (*pagar*) to settle, pay; (*resolver*) to resolve; **solvente** *adj* (*Econ: empresa, persona*) solvent

sombra ['sombra] *nf* shadow; (*como protección*) shade; **sombras** *nfpl* (*oscuridad*) darkness *sg*, shadows; **tener buena/mala ~** to be lucky/unlucky

sombrero [som'brero] *nm* hat

sombrilla [som'briλa] *nf* parasol,

sunshade

sombrío, -a [som'brio, a] *adj* (*oscuro*)
dark; (*triste*) sombre, sad; (*persona*) gloomy

someter [some'ter] *vt* (*país*) to conquer;
(*persona*) to subject to one's will; (*informe*) to
present, submit; **someterse** *vr* to give in,
yield, submit; **~ a** to subject to

somier [so'mjer] (*pl* **~s**) *n* spring mattress

somnífero [som'nifero] *nm* sleeping pill

somos *vb* V **ser**

son [son] *vb* V **ser** ▷ *nm* sound

sonaja [so'naxa] (*MÉX*) *nf* = **sonajero**

sonajero [sona'xero] *nm* (baby's) rattle

sonambulismo [sonambu'lismo]
nm sleepwalking; **sonámbulo, -a** *nm/f*
sleepwalker

sonar [so'nar] *vt* to ring ▷ *vi* to sound;
(*hacer ruido*) to make a noise; (*pronunciarse*)
to be sounded, be pronounced; (*ser conocido*)
to sound familiar; (*campana*) to ring; (*reloj*) to
strike, chime; **sonarse** *vr*: **~se (las narices)**
to blow one's nose; **me suena ese nombre**
that name rings a bell

sonda ['sonda] *nf* (*Náut*) sounding; (*Tec*)
bore, drill; (*Med*) probe

sondear [sonde'ar] *vt* to sound; to bore
(into), drill; to probe, sound; (*fig*) to sound
out; **sondeo** *nm* sounding; boring, drilling;
(*fig*) poll, enquiry

sonido [so'niðo] *nm* sound

sonoro, -a [so'noro, a] *adj* sonorous;
(*resonante*) loud, resonant

sonreír [sonre'ir] *vi* to smile; **sonreírse** *vr*
to smile; **sonriente** *adj* smiling; **sonrisa**
nf smile

sonrojarse [sonro'xarse] *vr* to blush, go
red; **sonrojo** *nm* blush

soñador, a [sona'ðor, a] *nm/f* dreamer

soñar [so'nar] *vt, vi* to dream; **~ con** to
dream about o of

soñoliento, -a [sono'ljento, a] *adj*
sleepy, drowsy

sopa ['sopa] *nf* soup

soplar [so'plar] *vt* (*polvo*) to blow away,
blow off; (*inflar*) to blow up; (*vela*) to blow
out ▷ *vi* to blow; **soplo** *nm* blow, puff; (*de
viento*) puff, gust

soplón, -ona [so'plon, ona] (*fam*) *nm/f*
(*niño*) telltale; (*de policía*) grass (*fam*)

soporífero [sopo'rifero] *nm* sleeping pill

soportable [sopor'taβle] *adj* bearable

soportar [sopor'tar] *vt* to bear, carry; (*fig*)
to bear, put up with

No confundir **soportar** con la palabra
inglesa *support*.

soporte *nm* support; (*fig*) pillar, support

soprano [so'prano] *nf* soprano

sorber [sor'βer] *vt* (*chupar*) to sip; (*absorber*)
to soak up, absorb

sorbete [sor'βete] *nm* iced fruit drink

sorbo ['sorβo] *nm* (*trago: grande*) gulp,
swallow; (*: pequeño*) sip

sordera [sor'ðera] *nf* deafness

sórdido, -a ['sorðiðo, a] *adj* dirty, squalid

sordo, -a ['sorðo, a] *adj* (*persona*) deaf
▷ *nm/f* deaf person; **sordomudo, -a** *adj*
deaf and dumb

sorna ['sorna] *nf* sarcastic tone

soroche [so'rotʃe] (*CAM*) *nm* mountain
sickness

sorprendente [sorpren'dente] *adj*
surprising

sorprender [sorpren'der] *vt* to surprise;
sorpresa *nf* surprise

sortear [sorte'ar] *vt* to draw lots for; (*rifar*)
to raffle; (*dificultad*) to avoid; **sorteo** *nm* (*en
lotería*) draw; (*rifa*) raffle

sortija [sor'tixa] *nf* ring; (*rizo*) ringlet, curl

sosegado, -a [sose'xaðo, a] *adj* quiet,
calm

sosiego [so'sjexo] *nm* quiet(ness),
calm(ness)

soso, -a ['soso, a] *adj* (*Culin*) tasteless;
(*aburrido*) dull, uninteresting

sospecha [sos'petʃa] *nf* suspicion;
sospechar *vt* to suspect; **sospechoso, -a**
adj suspicious; (*testimonio, opinión*) suspect
▷ *nm/f* suspect

sostén [sos'ten] *nm* (*apoyo*) support;
(*sujetador*) bra; (*alimentación*) sustenance,
food

sostener [soste'ner] *vt* to support;
(*mantener*) to keep up, maintain; (*alimentar*)
to sustain, keep going; **sostenerse** *vr* to
support o.s.; (*seguir*) to continue, remain;
sostenido, -a *adj* continuous, sustained;
(*prolongado*) prolonged

sotana [so'tana] *nf* (*Rel*) cassock

sótano ['sotano] *nm* basement

soy [soi] *vb* V **ser**

soya ['soja] (*LAM*) *nf* soya (*BRIT*), soy (*US*)

Sr. *abr* (= *Señor*) Mr

Sra. *abr* (= *Señora*) Mrs

Sres. *abr* (= *Señores*) Messrs

Srta. *abr* (= *Señorita*) Miss

Sta. *abr* (= *Santa*) St

Sto. *abr* (= *Santo*) St

su [su] *pron* (*de él*) his; (*de ella*) her; (*de
una cosa*) its; (*de ellos, ellas*) their; (*de usted,
ustedes*) your

suave ['swaβe] *adj* gentle; (*superficie*)
smooth; (*trabajo*) easy; (*música, voz*)
soft, sweet; **suavidad** *nf* gentleness;
smoothness; softness, sweetness;
suavizante *nm* (*de ropa*) softener; (*del pelo*)
conditioner; **suavizar** *vt* to soften; (*quitar*

la aspereza) to smooth (out)
subasta [su'βasta] *nf* auction; **subastar**
vt to auction (off)
subcampeón, -ona [suβkampe'on, ona]
nm/f runner-up
subconsciente [suβkon'sθjente] *adj, nm*
subconscious
subdesarrollado, -a [suβðesarro'ʎaðo,
a] *adj* underdeveloped
subdesarrollo [suβðesa'rroʎo] *nm*
underdevelopment
subdirector, a [suβðirek'tor, a] *nm/f*
assistant director
súbdito, a ['suβðito, a] *nm/f* subject
subestimar [suβesti'mar] *vt* to
underestimate, underrate
subida [su'βiða] *nf* (*de montaña etc*) ascent,
climb; (*de precio*) rise, increase; (*pendiente*)
slope, hill
subir [su'βir] *vt* (*objeto*) to raise, lift up;
(*cuesta, calle*) to go up; (*colina, montaña*) to
climb; (*precio*) to raise, put up ▷ *vi* to go up,
come up; (*a un coche*) to get in; (*a un autobús,
tren o avión*) to get on, board; (*precio*) to rise,
go up; (*río, marea*) to rise; **subirse** *vr* to get
up, climb
súbito, -a ['suβito, a] *adj* (*repentino*)
sudden; (*imprevisto*) unexpected
subjetivo, -a [suβxe'tiβo, a] *adj*
subjective
sublevar [suβle'βar] *vt* to rouse to revolt;
sublevarse *vr* to revolt, rise
sublime [su'βlime] *adj* sublime
submarinismo [suβmari'nismo] *nm*
scuba diving
submarino, -a [suβma'rino, a] *adj*
underwater ▷ *nm* submarine
subnormal [suβnor'mal] *adj* subnormal
▷ *nmf* subnormal person
subordinado, -a [suβorði'naðo, a] *adj,
nm/f* subordinate
subrayar [suβra'jar] *vt* to underline
subsanar [suβsa'nar] *vt* to rectify
subsidio [suβ'siðjo] *nm* (*ayuda*) aid,
financial help; (*subvención*) subsidy, grant;
(*de enfermedad, paro etc*) benefit, allowance
subsistencia [suβsis'tenθja] *nf*
subsistence
subsistir [suβsis'tir] *vi* to subsist;
(*sobrevivir*) to survive, endure
subte ['suβte] (*RPL*) *nm* underground
(*BRIT*), subway (*US*)
subterráneo, -a [suβte'rraneo, a]
adj underground, subterranean ▷ *nm*
underpass, underground passage
subtítulo [suβ'titulo] *nm* (*Cine*) subtitle
suburbio [su'βurβjo] *nm* (*barrio*) slum
quarter

subvención [suββen'θjon] *nf* (*Econ*)
subsidy, grant; **subvencionar** *vt* to
subsidize
sucedáneo, -a [suθe'ðaneo, a] *adj*
substitute ▷ *nm* substitute (food)
suceder [suθe'ðer] *vt, vi* to happen; (*seguir*)
to succeed, follow; **lo que sucede es que ...**
the fact is that ...; **sucesión** *nf* succession;
(*serie*) sequence, series
sucesivamente [suθesiβa'mente] *adv*: **y
así ~** and so on
sucesivo, -a [suθe'siβo, a] *adj* successive,
following; **en lo ~** in future, from now on
suceso [su'θeso] *nm* (*hecho*) event,
happening; (*incidente*) incident

▌ No confundir **suceso** con la palabra
inglesa *success*.

suciedad [suθje'ðað] *nf* (*estado*) dirtiness;
(*mugre*) dirt, filth
sucio, -a ['suθjo, a] *adj* dirty
suculento, -a [suku'lento, a] *adj*
succulent
sucumbir [sukum'bir] *vi* to succumb
sucursal [sukur'sal] *nf* branch (office)
sudadera [suða'ðera] *nf* sweatshirt
Sudáfrica [suð'afrika] *nf* South Africa
Sudamérica [suða'merika] *nf* South
America; **sudamericano, -a** *adj, nm/f*
South American
sudar [su'ðar] *vt, vi* to sweat
sudeste [su'ðeste] *nm* south-east
sudoeste [suðo'este] *nm* south-west
sudor [su'ðor] *nm* sweat; **sudoroso, -a** *adj*
sweaty, sweating
Suecia ['sweθja] *nf* Sweden; **sueco, -a** *adj*
Swedish ▷ *nm/f* Swede
suegro, -a ['sweɣro, a] *nm/f* father-/
mother-in-law
suela ['swela] *nf* sole
sueldo ['sweldo] *nm* pay, wage(s) (*pl*)
suele *etc vb* V **soler**
suelo ['swelo] *nm* (*tierra*) ground; (*de casa*)
floor
suelto, -a ['swelto, a] *adj* loose; (*libre*)
free; (*separado*) detached; (*ágil*) quick, agile
▷ *nm* (*loose*) change, small change
sueñito [swe'ɲito] (*LAM*) *nm* nap
sueño *etc* ['sweɲo] *vb* V **soñar** ▷ *nm* sleep;
(*somnolencia*) sleepiness, drowsiness; (*lo
soñado, fig*) dream; **tener ~** to be sleepy
suero ['swero] *nm* (*Med*) serum; (*de leche*)
whey
suerte ['swerte] *nf* (*fortuna*) luck; (*azar*)
chance; (*destino*) fate, destiny; (*especie*) sort,
kind; **tener ~** to be lucky
suéter ['sweter] *nm* sweater
suficiente [sufi'θjente] *adj* enough,
sufficient ▷ *nm* (*Escol*) pass

sufragio [su'fraxjo] nm (voto) vote; (derecho de voto) suffrage

sufrido, -a [su'friðo, a] adj (persona) tough; (paciente) long-suffering, patient

sufrimiento [sufri'mjento] nm (dolor) suffering

sufrir [su'frir] vt (padecer) to suffer; (soportar) to bear, put up with; (apoyar) to hold up, support ▷ vi to suffer

sugerencia [suxe'renθja] nf suggestion

sugerir [suxe'rir] vt to suggest; (sutilmente) to hint

sugestión [suxes'tjon] nf suggestion; (sutil) hint; **sugestionar** vt to influence

sugestivo, -a [suxes'tiβo, a] adj stimulating; (fascinante) fascinating

suicida [sui'θiða] adj suicidal ▷ nmf suicidal person; (muerto) suicide, person who has committed suicide; **suicidarse** vr to commit suicide, kill o.s.; **suicidio** nm suicide

Suiza ['swiθa] nf Switzerland; **suizo, -a** adj, nm/f Swiss

sujeción [suxe'θjon] nf subjection

sujetador [suxeta'ðor] nm (sostén) bra

sujetar [suxe'tar] vt (fijar) to fasten; (detener) to hold down; **sujetarse** vr to subject o.s.; **sujeto, -a** adj fastened, secure ▷ nm subject; (individuo) individual; **sujeto a** subject to

suma ['suma] nf (cantidad) total, sum; (de dinero) sum; (acto) adding (up), addition; **en ~** in short

sumamente [suma'mente] adv extremely, exceedingly

sumar [su'mar] vt to add (up) ▷ vi to add up

sumergir [sumer'xir] vt to submerge; (hundir) to sink

suministrar [sumini'strar] vt to supply, provide; **suministro** nm supply; (acto) supplying, providing

sumir [su'mir] vt to sink, submerge; (fig) to plunge

sumiso, -a [su'miso, a] adj submissive, docile

sumo, -a ['sumo, a] adj great, extreme; (autoridad) highest, supreme

suntuoso, -a [sun'twoso, a] adj sumptuous, magnificent

supe etc vb V **saber**

super... [super] prefijo super..., over...

superbueno, -a [super'bweno, a] adj great, fantastic

súper ['super] nf (gasolina) four-star (petrol)

superar [supe'rar] vt (sobreponerse a) to overcome; (rebasar) to surpass, do better than; (pasar) to go beyond; **superarse** vr to excel o.s.

superficial [superfi'θjal] adj superficial; (medida) surface cpd, of the surface

superficie [super'fiθje] nf surface; (área) area

superfluo, -a [su'perflwo, a] adj superfluous

superior [supe'rjor] adj (piso, clase) upper; (temperatura, número, nivel) higher; (mejor: calidad, producto) superior, better ▷ nmf superior; **superioridad** nf superiority

supermercado [supermer'kaðo] nm supermarket

superponer [superpo'ner] vt to superimpose

superstición [supersti'θjon] nf superstition; **supersticioso, -a** adj superstitious

supervisar [superβi'sar] vt to supervise

supervivencia [superβi'βenθja] nf survival

superviviente [superβi'βjente] adj surviving

supiera etc vb V **saber**

suplantar [suplan'tar] vt to supplant

suplemento [suple'mento] nm supplement

suplente [su'plente] adj, nm substitute

supletorio, -a [suple'torjo, a] adj supplementary ▷ nm supplement; **teléfono ~** extension

súplica ['suplika] nf request; (Jur) petition

suplicar [supli'kar] vt (cosa) to beg (for), plead for; (persona) to beg, plead with

suplicio [su'pliθjo] nm torture

suplir [su'plir] vt (compensar) to make good, make up for; (reemplazar) to replace, substitute ▷ vi: **~ a** to take the place of, substitute for

supo etc vb V **saber**

suponer [supo'ner] vt to suppose; **suposición** nf supposition

suprimir [supri'mir] vt to suppress; (derecho, costumbre) to abolish; (palabra etc) to delete; (restricción) to cancel, lift

supuesto, -a [su'pwesto, a] pp de **suponer** ▷ adj (hipotético) supposed ▷ nm assumption, hypothesis; **~ que** since; **por ~** of course

sur [sur] nm south

surcar [sur'kar] vt to plough; **surco** nm (en metal, disco) groove; (Agr) furrow

surgir [sur'xir] vi to arise, emerge; (dificultad) to come up, crop up

suroeste [suro'este] nm south-west

surtido, -a [sur'tiðo, a] adj mixed,

assorted ▷ *nm* (*selección*) selection, assortment; (*abastecimiento*) supply, stock; **surtidor** *nm* (*tb*: **surtidor de gasolina**) petrol pump (BRIT), gas pump (US)

surtir [sur'tir] *vt* to supply, provide ▷ *vi* to spout, spurt

susceptible [susθep'tiβle] *adj* susceptible; (*sensible*) sensitive; **~ de** capable of

suscitar [susθi'tar] *vt* to cause, provoke; (*interés, sospechas*) to arouse

suscribir [suskri'βir] *vt* (*firmar*) to sign; (*respaldar*) to subscribe to, endorse; **suscribirse** *vr* to subscribe; **suscripción** *nf* subscription

susodicho, -a [suso'ðitʃo, a] *adj* above-mentioned

suspender [suspen'der] *vt* (*objeto*) to hang (up), suspend; (*trabajo*) to stop, suspend; (*Escol*) to fail; (*interrumpir*) to adjourn; (*atrasar*) to postpone

suspense [sus'pense] (ESP) *nm* suspense; **película/novela de ~** thriller

suspensión [suspen'sjon] *nf* suspension; (*fig*) stoppage, suspension

suspenso, -a [sus'penso, a] *adj* hanging, suspended; (ESP *Escol*) failed ▷ *nm* (ESP *Escol*) fail; **película** *o* **novela de ~** (LAM) thriller; **quedar** *o* **estar en ~** to be pending

suspicaz [suspi'kaθ] *adj* suspicious, distrustful

suspirar [suspi'rar] *vi* to sigh; **suspiro** *nm* sigh

sustancia [sus'tanθja] *nf* substance

sustento [sus'tento] *nm* support; (*alimento*) sustenance, food

sustituir [sustitu'ir] *vt* to substitute, replace; **sustituto, -a** *nm/f* substitute, replacement

susto ['susto] *nm* fright, scare

sustraer [sustra'er] *vt* to remove, take away; (*Mat*) to subtract

susurrar [susu'rrar] *vi* to whisper; **susurro** *nm* whisper

sutil [su'til] *adj* (*aroma, diferencia*) subtle; (*tenue*) thin; (*inteligencia, persona*) sharp

suyo, -a ['sujo, a] (*con artículo o después del verbo* ser) *adj* (*de él*) his; (*de ella*) hers; (*de ellos, ellas*) theirs; (*de Ud, Uds*) yours; **un amigo ~** a friend of his (*o* hers *o* theirs *o* yours)

t

Tabacalera [taβaka'lera] *nf* Spanish state tobacco monopoly

tabaco [ta'βako] *nm* tobacco; (ESP: *fam*) cigarettes *pl*

tabaquería [tabake'ria] (LAM) *nf* tobacconist's (shop) (BRIT), smoke shop (US); **tabaquero, -a** (LAM) *nm/f* tobacconist

taberna [ta'βerna] *nf* bar, pub (BRIT)

tabique [ta'βike] *nm* partition (wall)

tabla ['taβla] *nf* (*de madera*) plank; (*estante*) shelf; (*de vestido*) pleat; (*Arte*) panel; **tablas** *nfpl*: **estar** *o* **quedar en ~** to draw; **tablado** *nm* (*plataforma*) platform; (*Teatro*) stage

tablao [ta'βlao] *nm* (*tb*: **~ flamenco**) flamenco show

tablero [ta'βlero] *nm* (*de madera*) plank, board; (*de ajedrez, damas*) board; **tablero de mandos** (LAM *Auto*) dashboard

tableta [ta'βleta] *nf* (*Med*) tablet; (*de chocolate*) bar

tablón [ta'βlon] *nm* (*de suelo*) plank; (*de techo*) beam; **tablón de anuncios** notice (BRIT) *o* bulletin (US) board

tabú [ta'βu] *nm* taboo

taburete [taβu'rete] *nm* stool

tacaño, -a [ta'kaɲo, a] *adj* mean

tacha ['tatʃa] *nf* flaw; (*Tec*) stud; **tachar** *vt* (*borrar*) to cross out; **tachar de** to accuse of

tacho ['tatʃo] (CS) *nm* (*balde*) bucket; **tacho de la basura** rubbish bin (BRIT), trash can (US)

taco ['tako] *nm* (*Billar*) cue; (*de billetes*) book; (CS: *de zapato*) heel; (*tarugo*) peg; (*palabrota*) swear word

tacón [ta'kon] *nm* heel; **de ~ alto** high-heeled

táctica ['taktika] *nf* tactics *pl*

táctico, -a ['taktiko, a] *adj* tactical

tacto ['takto] *nm* touch; (*fig*) tact

tajada [ta'xaða] *nf* slice

tajante [ta'xante] *adj* sharp

tajo ['taxo] nm (corte) cut; (Geo) cleft
tal [tal] adj such ▷ pron (persona) someone, such a one; (cosa) something, such a thing ▷ adv: **~ como** (igual) just as ▷ conj: **con ~ de que** provided that; **~ cual** (como es) just as it is; **~ vez** perhaps; **~ como** such as; **~ para cual** (dos iguales) two of a kind; **¿qué ~?** how are things?; **¿qué ~ te gusta?** how do you like it?
taladrar [tala'ðrar] vt to drill; **taladro** nm drill
talante [ta'lante] nm (humor) mood; (voluntad) will, willingness
talar [ta'lar] vt to fell, cut down; (devastar) to devastate
talco ['talko] nm (polvos) talcum powder
talento [ta'lento] nm talent; (capacidad) ability
TALGO ['talɣo] (ESP) nm abr (= tren articulado ligero Goicoechea-Oriol) ≈ HST (BRIT)
talismán [talis'man] nm talisman
talla ['taʎa] nf (estatura, fig, Med) height, stature; (palo) measuring rod; (Arte) carving; (medida) size
tallar [ta'ʎar] vt (madera) to carve; (metal etc) to engrave; (medir) to measure
tallarines [taʎa'rines] nmpl noodles
talle ['taʎe] nm (Anat) waist; (fig) appearance
taller [ta'ʎer] nm (Tec) workshop; (de artista) studio
tallo ['taʎo] nm (de planta) stem; (de hierba) blade; (brote) shoot
talón [ta'lon] nm (Anat) heel; (Com) counterfoil; (cheque) cheque (BRIT), check (US)
talonario [talo'narjo] nm (de cheques) chequebook (BRIT), checkbook (US); (de recibos) receipt book
tamaño, -a [ta'maɲo, a] adj (tan grande) such a big; (tan pequeño) such a small ▷ nm size; **de ~ natural** full-size
tamarindo [tama'rindo] nm tamarind
tambalearse [tambale'arse] vr (persona) to stagger; (vehículo) to sway
también [tam'bjen] adv (igualmente) also, too, as well; (además) besides
tambor [tam'bor] nm drum; (Anat) eardrum; **tambor del freno** brake drum
tamizar [tami'θar] vt to sieve
tampoco [tam'poko] adv nor, neither; **yo ~ lo compré** I didn't buy it either
tampón [tam'pon] nm tampon
tan [tan] adv so; **~ es así que ...** so much so that ...
tanda ['tanda] nf (gen) series; (turno) shift
tangente [tan'xente] nf tangent
tangerina [tanxe'rina] (LAM) nf tangerine
tangible [tan'xiβle] adj tangible
tanque ['tanke] nm (cisterna, Mil) tank; (Auto) tanker
tantear [tante'ar] vt (calcular) to reckon (up); (medir) to take the measure of; (probar) to test, try out; (tomar la medida: persona) to take the measurements of; (situación) to weigh up; (persona: opinión) to sound out ▷ vi (Deporte) to score; **tanteo** nm (cálculo) (rough) calculation; (prueba) test, trial; (Deporte) scoring
tanto, -a ['tanto, a] adj (cantidad) so much, as much ▷ adv (cantidad) so much, as much; (tiempo) so long, as long ▷ conj: **en ~ que** while ▷ nm (suma) certain amount; (proporción) so much; (punto) point; (gol) goal; **un ~ perezoso** somewhat lazy ▷ pron: **cada uno paga ~** each one pays so much; **~s** so many, as many; **20 y ~s** 20-odd; **hasta ~ (que)** until such time as; **~ tú como yo** both you and I; **~ como eso** as much as that; **~ más ... cuanto que** all the more ... because; **~ mejor/peor** so much the better/the worse; **~ si viene como si va** whether he comes or whether he goes; **~ es así que** so much so that; **por (lo) ~** therefore; **entre ~** meanwhile; **estar al ~** to be up to date; **me he vuelto ronco de o con ~ hablar** I have become hoarse with so much talking; **a ~s de agosto** on such and such a day in August
tapa ['tapa] nf (de caja, olla) lid; (de botella) top; (de libro) cover; (comida) snack
tapadera [tapa'ðera] nf lid, cover
tapar [ta'par] vt (cubrir) to cover; (envolver) to wrap o cover up; (la vista) to obstruct; (persona, falta) to conceal; (MÉX, CAM: diente) to fill; **taparse** vr to wrap o.s. up
taparrabo [tapa'rraβo] nm loincloth
tapete [ta'pete] nm table cover
tapia ['tapja] nf (garden) wall
tapicería [tapiθe'ria] nf tapestry; (para muebles) upholstery; (tienda) upholsterer's (shop)
tapiz [ta'piθ] nm (alfombra) carpet; (tela tejida) tapestry; **tapizar** vt (muebles) to upholster
tapón [ta'pon] nm (de botella) top; (de lavabo) plug; **tapón de rosca** screw-top
taquigrafía [takiɣra'fia] nf shorthand; **taquígrafo, -a** nm/f shorthand writer, stenographer
taquilla [ta'kiʎa] nf (donde se compra) booking office; (suma recogida) takings pl
tarántula [ta'rantula] nf tarantula
tararear [tarare'ar] vi to hum
tardar [tar'ðar] vi (tomar tiempo) to take a

long time; (*llegar tarde*) to be late; (*demorar*) to delay; **¿tarda mucho el tren?** does the train take (very) long?; **a más ~** at the latest; **no tardes en venir** come soon

tarde ['tarðe] *adv* late ▷ *nf* (*de día*) afternoon; (*al anochecer*) evening; **de ~ en ~** from time to time; **¡buenas ~s!** good afternoon!; **a** *o* **por la ~** in the afternoon; in the evening

tardío, -a [tar'ðio, a] *adj* (*retrasado*) late; (*lento*) slow (to arrive)

tarea [ta'rea] *nf* task; (*faena*) chore; (*Escol*) homework

tarifa [ta'rifa] *nf* (*lista de precios*) price list; (*precio*) tariff

tarima [ta'rima] *nf* (*plataforma*) platform

tarjeta [tar'xeta] *nf* card; **tarjeta de crédito/de Navidad/postal/telefónica** credit card/Christmas card/postcard/phonecard; **tarjeta de embarque** boarding pass; **tarjeta de memoria** memory card; **tarjeta prepago** top-up card; **tarjeta SIM** SIM card

tarro ['tarro] *nm* jar, pot

tarta ['tarta] *nf* (*pastel*) cake; (*de base dura*) tart

tartamudear [tartamuðe'ar] *vi* to stammer; **tartamudo, -a** *adj* stammering ▷ *nm/f* stammerer

tártaro, -a ['tartaro, a] *adj*: **salsa tártara** tartar(e) sauce

tasa ['tasa] *nf* (*precio*) (fixed) price, rate; (*valoración*) valuation; (*medida, norma*) measure, standard; **tasa de cambio/interés** exchange/interest rate; **tasas de aeropuerto** airport tax; **tasas universitarias** university fees

tasar [ta'sar] *vt* (*arreglar el precio*) to fix a price for; (*valorar*) to value, assess

tasca ['taska] (*fam*) *nf* pub

tatarabuelo, -a [tatara'βwelo, a] *nm/f* great-great-grandfather/mother

tatuaje [ta'twaxe] *nm* (*dibujo*) tattoo; (*acto*) tattooing

tatuar [ta'twar] *vt* to tattoo

taurino, -a [tau'rino, a] *adj* bullfighting *cpd*

Tauro ['tauro] *nm* Taurus

tauromaquia [tauro'makja] *nf* tauromachy, (art of) bullfighting

taxi ['taksi] *nm* taxi; **taxista** [tak'sista] *nmf* taxi driver

taza ['taθa] *nf* cup; (*de retrete*) bowl; **~ para café** coffee cup; **taza de café** cup of coffee; **tazón** *nm* (*taza grande*) mug, large cup; (*de fuente*) basin

te [te] *pron* (*complemento de objeto*) you; (*complemento indirecto*) (to) you; (*reflexivo*)

(to) yourself; **¿~ duele mucho el brazo?** does your arm hurt a lot?; **~ equivocas** you're wrong; **¡cálma~!** calm down!

té [te] *nm* tea

teatral [tea'tral] *adj* theatre *cpd*; (*fig*) theatrical

teatro [te'atro] *nm* theatre; (*Literatura*) plays *pl*, drama

tebeo [te'βeo] *nm* comic

techo ['tetʃo] *nm* (*externo*) roof; (*interno*) ceiling; **techo corredizo** sunroof

tecla ['tekla] *nf* key; **teclado** *nm* keyboard; **teclear** *vi* (*Mús*) to strum; (*con los dedos*) to tap ▷ *vt* (*Inform*) to key in

técnica ['teknika] *nf* technique; (*tecnología*) technology; *V tb* **técnico**

técnico, -a ['tekniko, a] *adj* technical ▷ *nm/f* technician; (*experto*) expert

tecnología [teknolo'xia] *nf* technology; **tecnológico, -a** *adj* technological

tecolote [teko'lote] (*MÉX*) *nm* owl

tedioso, -a [te'ðjoso, a] *adj* boring, tedious

teja ['texa] *nf* tile; (*Bot*) lime (tree); **tejado** *nm* (tiled) roof

tejemaneje [texema'nexe] *nm* (*lío*) fuss; (*intriga*) intrigue

tejer [te'xer] *vt* to weave; (*hacer punto*) to knit; (*fig*) to fabricate; **tejido** *nm* (*tela*) material, fabric; (*telaraña*) web; (*Anat*) tissue

tel [tel] *abr* (= *teléfono*) tel

tela ['tela] *nf* (*tejido*) material; (*telaraña*) web; (*en líquido*) skin; **telar** *nm* (*máquina*) loom

telaraña [tela'raɲa] *nf* cobweb

tele ['tele] (*fam*) *nf* telly (*BRIT*), tube (*US*)

tele... ['tele] *prefijo* tele...; **telebasura** *nf* trash TV; **telecomunicación** *nf* telecommunication; **telediario** *nm* television news; **teledirigido, -a** *adj* remote-controlled

teleférico [tele'feriko] *nm* (*de esquí*) ski-lift

telefonear [telefone'ar] *vi* to telephone

telefónico, -a [tele'foniko, a] *adj* telephone *cpd*

telefonillo [telefo'niʎo] *nm* (*de puerta*) intercom

telefonista [telefo'nista] *nmf* telephonist

teléfono [te'lefono] *nm* (tele)phone; **estar hablando al ~** to be on the phone; **llamar a algn por ~** to ring sb (up) *o* phone sb (up); **teléfono celular** (*LAM*) mobile phone; **teléfono con cámara** camera phone; **teléfono inalámbrico** cordless phone; **teléfono móvil** (*ESP*) mobile phone

telégrafo [te'leɣrafo] *nm* telegraph

telegrama [tele'ɣrama] *nm* telegram

tele: telenovela nf soap (opera);
teleobjetivo nm telephoto lens; **telepatía**
nf telepathy; **telepático, -a** adj telepathic;
telerrealidad nf reality TV; **telescopio**
nm telescope; **telesilla** nm chairlift;
telespectador, a nm/f viewer; **telesquí**
nm ski-lift; **teletarjeta** nf phonecard;
teletipo nm teletype; **teletrabajador,**
a nm/f teleworker; **teletrabajo** nm
teleworking; **televentas** nfpl telesales
televidente [teleβi'ðente] nmf viewer
televisar [teleβi'sar] vt to televise
televisión [teleβi'sjon] nf television;
televisión digital digital television
televisor [teleβi'sor] nm television set
télex ['teleks] nm inv telex
telón [te'lon] nm curtain; **telón de acero**
(Pol) iron curtain; **telón de fondo** backcloth,
background
tema ['tema] nm (asunto) subject, topic;
(Mús) theme; **temático, -a** adj thematic
temblar [tem'blar] vi to shake, tremble;
(por frío) to shiver; **temblor** nm trembling;
(de tierra) earthquake; **tembloroso, -a** adj
trembling
temer [te'mer] vt to fear ▷ vi to be afraid;
temo que llegue tarde I am afraid he may
be late
temible [te'miβle] adj fearsome
temor [te'mor] nm (miedo) fear; (duda)
suspicion
témpano ['tempano] nm (tb: ~ de hielo)
ice-floe
temperamento [tempera'mento] nm
temperament
temperatura [tempera'tura] nf
temperature
tempestad [tempes'tað] nf storm
templado, -a [tem'plaðo, a] adj
(moderado) moderate; (frugal) frugal; (agua)
lukewarm; (clima) mild; (Mús) well-tuned;
templanza nf moderation; mildness
templar [tem'plar] vt (moderar) to
moderate; (furia) to restrain; (calor) to
reduce; (afinar) to tune (up); (acero) to
temper; (tuerca) to tighten up; **temple**
nm (ajuste) tempering; (afinación) tuning;
(pintura) tempera
templo ['templo] nm (iglesia) church;
(pagano etc) temple
temporada [tempo'raða] nf time, period;
(estación) season
temporal [tempo'ral] adj (no permanente)
temporary ▷ nm storm
temprano, -a [tem'prano, a] adj early;
(demasiado pronto) too soon, too early
ten vb V **tener**
tenaces [te'naθes] adj pl V **tenaz**

tenaz [te'naθ] adj (material) tough;
(persona) tenacious; (creencia, resistencia)
stubborn
tenaza(s) [te'naθa(s)] nf(pl) (Med) forceps;
(Tec) pliers; (Zool) pincers
tendedero [tende'ðero] nm (para ropa)
drying place; (cuerda) clothes line
tendencia [ten'denθja] nf tendency;
tener ~ a to tend to, have a tendency to
tender [ten'der] vt (extender) to spread out;
(colgar) to hang out; (vía férrea, cable) to lay;
(estirar) to stretch ▷ vi: **~ a** to tend to, have
a tendency towards; **tenderse** vr to lie
down; **~ la cama/mesa** (LAM) to make the
bed/lay (BRIT) o set (US) the table
tenderete [tende'rete] nm (puesto) stall;
(exposición) display of goods
tendero, -a [ten'dero, a] nm/f
shopkeeper
tendón [ten'don] nm tendon
tendré etc vb V **tener**
tenebroso, -a [tene'βroso, a] adj (oscuro)
dark; (fig) gloomy
tenedor [tene'ðor] nm (Culin) fork
tenencia [te'nenθja] nf (de casa) tenancy;
(de oficio) tenure; (de propiedad) possession

○ **PALABRA CLAVE**

tener [te'ner] vt **1** (poseer, gen) to have; (en
la mano) to hold; **¿tienes un boli?** have you
got a pen?; **va a tener un niño** she's going
to have a baby; **¡ten** (o **tenga**)!, **¡aquí tienes**
(o **tiene**)!** here you are!

2 (edad, medidas) to be: **tiene 7 años** she's 7
(years old); **tiene 15 cm de largo** it's 15 cm
long; V **calor; hambre etc**

3 (considerar): **lo tengo por brillante** I
consider him to be brilliant; **tener en**
mucho a algn to think very highly of sb

4 (+ pp: = pretérito): **tengo terminada ya la**
mitad del trabajo I've done half the work
already

5: **tener que hacer algo** to have to do sth;
tengo que acabar este trabajo hoy I have
to finish this job today

6: **¿qué tienes, estás enfermo?** what's the
matter with you, are you ill?
tenerse vr **1**: **tenerse en pie** to stand up
2: **tenerse por** to think o.s.

tengo etc vb V **tener**
tenia ['tenja] nf tapeworm
teniente [te'njente] nm (rango)
lieutenant; (ayudante) deputy
tenis ['tenis] nm inv tennis; **tenis de mesa**
table tennis; **tenista** nmf tennis player
tenor [te'nor] nm (sentido) meaning; (Mús)

tenor; **a ~ de** on the lines of

tensar [ten'sar] vt to tighten; (arco) to draw

tensión [ten'sjon] nf tension; (Tec) stress; **tener la ~ alta** to have high blood pressure; **tensión arterial** blood pressure

tenso, -a ['tenso, a] adj tense

tentación [tenta'θjon] nf temptation

tentáculo [ten'takulo] nm tentacle

tentador, a [tenta'ðor, a] adj tempting

tentar [ten'tar] vt (seducir) to tempt; (atraer) to attract

tentempié [tentem'pje] nm snack

tenue ['tenwe] adj (delgado) thin, slender; (neblina) light; (lazo, vínculo) slight

teñir [te'ɲir] vt to dye; (fig) to tinge; **teñirse** vr to dye; **~se el pelo** to dye one's hair

teología [teolo'xia] nf theology

teoría [teo'ria] nf theory; **en ~** in theory; **teórico, -a** adj theoretic(al) ▷ nm/f theoretician, theorist; **teorizar** vi to theorize

terapéutico, -a [tera'peutiko, a] adj therapeutic

terapia [te'rapja] nf therapy

tercer adj V **tercero**

tercermundista [terθermun'dista] adj Third World cpd

tercero, -a [ter'θero, a] (delante de nmsg: **tercer**) adj third ▷ nm (Jur) third party

terceto [ter'θeto] nm trio

terciar [ter'θjar] vi (participar) to take part; (hacer de árbitro) to mediate; **terciario, -a** adj tertiary

tercio ['terθjo] nm third

terciopelo [terθjo'pelo] nm velvet

terco, -a ['terko, a] adj obstinate

tergal® [ter'ɣal] nm type of polyester

tergiversar [terxiβer'sar] vt to distort

termal [ter'mal] adj thermal

termas ['termas] nfpl hot springs

térmico, -a ['termiko, a] adj thermal

terminal [termi'nal] adj, nm, nf terminal

terminante [termi'nante] adj (final) final, definitive; (tajante) categorical; **terminantemente** adv: **terminantemente prohibido** strictly forbidden

terminar [termi'nar] vt (completar) to complete, finish; (concluir) to end ▷ vi (llegar a su fin) to end; (parar) to stop; (acabar) to finish; **terminarse** vr to come to an end; **~ por hacer algo** to end up (by) doing sth

término ['termino] nm end, conclusion; (parada) terminus; (límite) boundary; **en último ~** (a fin de cuentas) in the last analysis; (como último recurso) as a last resort; **término medio** average; (fig) middle way

termómetro [ter'mometro] nm thermometer

termo(s)® ['termo(s)] nm Thermos®

termostato [termo'stato] nm thermostat

ternero, -a [ter'nero, a] nm/f (animal) calf ▷ nf (carne) veal

ternura [ter'nura] nf (trato) tenderness; (palabra) endearment; (cariño) fondness

terrado [te'rraðo] nm terrace

terraplén [terra'plen] nm embankment

terrateniente [terrate'njente] nmf landowner

terraza [te'rraθa] nf (balcón) balcony; (tejado) (flat) roof; (Agr) terrace

terremoto [terre'moto] nm earthquake

terrenal [terre'nal] adj earthly

terreno [te'rreno] nm (tierra) land; (parcela) plot; (suelo) soil; (fig) field; **un ~** a piece of land

terrestre [te'rrestre] adj terrestrial; (ruta) land cpd

terrible [te'rriβle] adj terrible, awful

territorio [terri'torjo] nm territory

terrón [te'rron] nm (de azúcar) lump; (de tierra) clod, lump

terror [te'rror] nm terror; **terrorífico, -a** adj terrifying; **terrorista** adj, nmf terrorist; **terrorista suicida** suicide bomber

terso, -a ['terso, a] adj (liso) smooth; (pulido) polished

tertulia [ter'tulja] nf (reunión informal) social gathering; (grupo) group, circle

tesis ['tesis] nf inv thesis

tesón [te'son] nm (firmeza) firmness; (tenacidad) tenacity

tesorero, -a [teso'rero, a] nm/f treasurer

tesoro [te'soro] nm treasure; (Com, Pol) treasury

testamento [testa'mento] nm will

testarudo, -a [testa'ruðo, a] adj stubborn

testículo [tes'tikulo] nm testicle

testificar [testifi'kar] vt to testify; (fig) to attest ▷ vi to give evidence

testigo [tes'tixo] nmf witness; **testigo de cargo/descargo** witness for the prosecution/defence; **testigo ocular** eye witness

testimonio [testi'monjo] nm testimony

teta ['teta] nf (de biberón) teat; (Anat: fam) breast

tétanos ['tetanos] nm tetanus

tetera [te'tera] nf teapot

tétrico, -a ['tetriko, a] adj gloomy, dismal

textil [teks'til] adj textile

texto ['teksto] nm text; **textual** adj textual

textura [teks'tura] nf (de tejido) texture

tez [teθ] nf (cutis) complexion

ti [ti] pron you; (reflexivo) yourself

tía ['tia] nf (pariente) aunt; (fam) chick, bird

tibio, -a ['tiβjo, a] adj lukewarm

tiburón [tiβu'ron] nm shark

tic [tik] nm (ruido) click; (de reloj) tick; (Med): **~ nervioso** nervous tic

tictac [tik'tak] nm (de reloj) tick tock

tiempo ['tjempo] nm time; (época, período) age, period; (Meteorología) weather; (Ling) tense; (Deporte) half; **a ~ in** time; **a un o al mismo ~** at the same time; **al poco ~** very soon (after); **se quedó poco ~** he didn't stay very long; **hace poco ~** not long ago; **mucho ~** a long time; **de ~ en ~** from time to time; **hace buen/mal ~** the weather is fine/bad; **estar a ~** to be in time; **hace ~** some time ago; **hacer ~** to while away the time; **motor de 2 ~s** two-stroke engine; **primer ~** first half

tienda ['tjenda] nf shop, store; **tienda de abarrotes** (MÉX, CAM) grocer's (BRIT), grocery store (US); **tienda de alimentación o comestibles** grocer's (BRIT), grocery store (US); **tienda de campaña** tent

tienes etc vb V **tener**

tienta etc ['tjenta] vb V **tentar** ▷ nf: **andar a ~s** to grope one's way along

tiento etc ['tjento] vb V **tentar** ▷ nm (tacto) touch; (precaución) wariness

tierno, -a ['tjerno, a] adj (blando) tender; (fresco) fresh; (amable) sweet

tierra ['tjerra] nf earth; (suelo) soil; (mundo) earth, world; (país) country, land; **~ adentro** inland

tieso, -a ['tjeso, a] adj (rígido) rigid; (duro) stiff; (fam: orgulloso) conceited

tiesto ['tjesto] nm flowerpot

tifón [ti'fon] nm typhoon

tifus ['tifus] nm typhus

tigre ['tivre] nm tiger

tijera [ti'xera] nf scissors pl; (Zool) claw; **tijeras** nfpl scissors; (para plantas) shears

tila ['tila] nf lime blossom tea

tildar [til'dar] vt: **~ de** to brand as

tilde ['tilde] nf (Tip) tilde

tilín [ti'lin] nm tinkle

timar [ti'mar] vt (estafar) to swindle

timbal [tim'bal] nm small drum

timbre ['timbre] nm (sello) stamp; (campanilla) bell; (tono) timbre; (Com) stamp duty

timidez [timi'ðeθ] nf shyness; **tímido, -a** adj shy

timo ['timo] nm swindle

timón [ti'mon] nm helm, rudder; **timonel** nm helmsman

tímpano ['timpano] nm (Anat) eardrum; (Mús) small drum

tina ['tina] nf tub; (baño) bath(tub); **tinaja** nf large jar

tinieblas [ti'njeβlas] nfpl darkness sg; (sombras) shadows

tino ['tino] nm (habilidad) skill; (juicio) insight

tinta ['tinta] nf ink; (Tec) dye; (Arte) colour

tinte ['tinte] nm dye

tintero [tin'tero] nm inkwell

tinto ['tinto] nm red wine

tintorería [tintore'ria] nf dry cleaner's

tío ['tio] nm (pariente) uncle; (fam: individuo) bloke (BRIT), guy

tiovivo [tio'βiβo] nm merry-go-round

típico, -a ['tipiko, a] adj typical

tipo ['tipo] nm (clase) type, kind; (hombre) fellow; (Anat: de hombre) build; (: de mujer) figure; (Imprenta) type; **tipo bancario/de descuento/de interés/de cambio** bank/discount/interest/exchange rate

tipografía [tipoɣra'fia] nf printing cpd

tíquet ['tiket] (pl **~s**) nm ticket; (en tienda) cash slip

tiquismiquis [tikis'mikis] nm inv fussy person ▷ nmpl (querellas) squabbling sg; (escrúpulos) silly scruples

tira ['tira] nf strip; (fig) abundance; **tira y afloja** give and take

tirabuzón [tiraβu'θon] nm (rizo) curl

tirachinas [tira'tʃinas] nm inv catapult

tirada [ti'raða] nf (acto) cast, throw; (serie) series; (Tip) printing, edition; **de una ~** at one go

tirado, -a [ti'raðo, a] adj (barato) dirt-cheap; (fam: fácil) very easy

tirador [tira'ðor] nm (mango) handle

tirano, -a [ti'rano, a] adj tyrannical ▷ nm/f tyrant

tirante [ti'rante] adj (cuerda etc) tight, taut; (relaciones) strained ▷ nm (Arq) brace; (Tec) stay; **tirantes** nmpl (de pantalón) braces (BRIT), suspenders (US); **tirantez** nf tightness; (fig) tension

tirar [ti'rar] vt to throw; (dejar caer) to drop; (volcar) to upset; (derribar) to knock down o over; (desechar) to throw out o away; (dinero) to squander; (imprimir) to print ▷ vi (disparar) to shoot; (de la puerta etc) to pull; (fam: andar) to go; (tender a, buscar realizar) to tend to; (Deporte) to shoot; **tirarse** vr to throw o.s.; **~ abajo** to bring down, destroy; **tira más a su padre** he takes more after his father; **ir tirando** to manage

tirita [ti'rita] nf (sticking) plaster (BRIT), Bandaid® (US)

tiritar [tiri'tar] vi to shiver

tiro ['tiro] nm (lanzamiento) throw; (disparo) shot; (Deporte) shot; (Golf, Tenis) drive; (alcance) range; **caballo de ~** cart-horse; **tiro al blanco** target practice

tirón [ti'ron] nm (sacudida) pull, tug; **de un ~** in one go, all at once

tiroteo [tiro'teo] nm exchange of shots, shooting

tisis ['tisis] nf inv consumption, tuberculosis

títere ['titere] nm puppet

titubear [tituβe'ar] vi to stagger; to stammer; (fig) to hesitate; **titubeo** nm staggering; stammering; hesitation

titulado, -a [titu'laðo, a] adj (libro) entitled; (persona) titled

titular [titu'lar] adj titular ▷ nmf holder ▷ nm headline ▷ vt to title; **titularse** vr to be entitled; **título** nm title; (de diario) headline; (certificado) professional qualification; (universitario) (university) degree; **a título de** in the capacity of

tiza ['tiθa] nf chalk

toalla [to'aʎa] nf towel

tobillo [to'βiʎo] nm ankle

tobogán [toβo'ɣan] nm (montaña rusa) roller-coaster; (de niños) chute, slide

tocadiscos [toka'ðiskos] nm inv record player

tocado, -a [to'kaðo, a] adj (fam) touched ▷ nm headdress

tocador [toka'ðor] nm (mueble) dressing table; (cuarto) boudoir; (fam) ladies' toilet (BRIT) o room (US)

tocar [to'kar] vt to touch; (Mús) to play; (referirse a) to allude to; (timbre) to ring ▷ vi (a la puerta) to knock (on o at the door); (ser de turno) to fall to, be the turn of; (ser hora) to be due; **tocarse** vr (cubrirse la cabeza) to cover one's head; (tener contacto) to touch (each other); **por lo que a mí me toca** as far as I am concerned; **te toca a ti** it's your turn

tocayo, -a [to'kajo, a] nm/f namesake

tocino [to'θino] nm bacon

todavía [toða'βia] adv (aun) even; (aún) still, yet; **~ más** yet more; **~ no** not yet

○ **PALABRA CLAVE**

todo, -a ['toðo, a] adj **1** (con artículo sg) all; **toda la carne** all the meat; **toda la noche** all night, the whole night; **todo el libro** the whole book; **toda una botella** a whole bottle; **todo lo contrario** quite the opposite; **está toda sucia** she's all dirty; **por todo el país** throughout the whole country

2 (con artículo pl) all; every; **todos los libros** all the books; **todas las noches** every night; **todos los que quieran salir** all those who want to leave

▷ pron **1** everything, all; **todos** everyone, everybody; **lo sabemos todo** we know everything; **todos querían más tiempo** everybody o everyone wanted more time; **nos marchamos todos** all of us left

2: **con todo: con todo él me sigue gustando** even so I still like him

▷ adv all; **vaya todo seguido** keep straight on o ahead

▷ nm: **como un todo** as a whole; **del todo: no me agrada del todo** I don't entirely like it

todopoderoso, -a [toðopoðe'roso, a] adj all powerful; (Rel) almighty

todoterreno [toðote'rreno] sm inv four-wheel drive, SUV (ESP US)

toga ['toɣa] nf toga; (Escol) gown

Tokio ['tokjo] n Tokyo

toldo ['toldo] nm (para el sol) sunshade (BRIT), parasol; (tienda) marquee

tolerancia [tole'ranθja] nf tolerance; **tolerante** adj (sociedad) liberal; (persona) open-minded

tolerar [tole'rar] vt to tolerate; (resistir) to endure

toma ['toma] nf (acto) taking; (Med) dose; **toma de corriente** socket; **toma de tierra** earth (wire); **tomacorriente** (LAM) nm socket

tomar [to'mar] vt to take; (aspecto) to take on; (beber) to drink ▷ vi (LAM: beber) to drink; **tomarse** vr to take; **~se por** to consider o.s. to be; **~ a bien/mal** to take well/badly; **~ en serio** to take seriously; **~ el pelo a algn** to pull sb's leg; **~la con algn** to pick a quarrel with sb; **¡tome!** here you are!; **~ el sol** to sunbathe

tomate [to'mate] nm tomato

tomillo [to'miʎo] nm thyme

tomo ['tomo] nm (libro) volume

ton [ton] abr = tonelada ▷ nm: **sin ~ ni son** without rhyme or reason

tonalidad [tonali'ðað] nf tone

tonel [to'nel] nm barrel

tonelada [tone'laða] nf ton; **tonelaje** nm tonnage

tónica ['tonika] nf (Mús) tonic; (fig) keynote

tónico, -a ['toniko, a] adj tonic ▷ nm (Med) tonic

tono ['tono] nm tone; **fuera de ~** inappropriate

tontería [tonte'ria] nf (estupidez) foolishness; (cosa) stupid thing; (acto) foolish act; **tonterías** nfpl (disparates) rubbish sg, nonsense sg

tonto, -a ['tonto, a] adj stupid, silly ▷nm/f fool

topar [to'par] vi: **~ contra** o **en** to run into; **~ con** to run up against

tope ['tope] adj maximum ▷nm (fin) end; (límite) limit; (Ferro) buffer; (Auto) bumper; **al ~** end to end

tópico, -a ['topiko, a] adj topical ▷nm platitude

topo ['topo] nm (Zool) mole; (fig) blunderer

toque etc ['toke] vb V **tocar** ▷nm touch; (Mús) beat; (de campana) peal; **dar un ~ a** to warn; **toque de queda** curfew

toqué etc vb V **tocar**

toquetear [tokete'ar] vt to finger

toquilla [to'kiʎa] nf (pañuelo) headscarf; (chal) shawl

tórax ['toraks] nm thorax

torbellino [torbe'ʎino] nm whirlwind; (fig) whirl

torcedura [torθe'ðura] nf twist; (Med) sprain

torcer [tor'θer] vt to twist; (la esquina) to turn; (Med) to sprain ▷vi (desviar) to turn off; **torcerse** vr (ladearse) to bend; (desviarse) to go astray; (fracasar) to go wrong; **torcido, -a** adj twisted; (fig) crooked ▷nm curl

tordo, -a ['torðo, a] adj dappled ▷nm thrush

torear [tore'ar] vt (fig: evadir) to avoid; (jugar con) to tease ▷vi to fight bulls; **toreo** nm bullfighting; **torero, -a** nm/f bullfighter

tormenta [tor'menta] nf storm; (fig: confusión) turmoil

tormento [tor'mento] nm torture; (fig) anguish

tornar [tor'nar] vt (devolver) to return, give back; (transformar) to transform ▷vi to go back

tornasolado, -a [tornaso'laðo, a] adj (brillante) iridescent; (reluciente) shimmering

torneo [tor'neo] nm tournament

tornillo [tor'niʎo] nm screw

torniquete [torni'kete] nm (Med) tourniquet

torno ['torno] nm (Tec) winch; (tambor) drum; **en ~ (a)** round, about

toro ['toro] nm bull; (fam) he-man; **los ~s** bullfighting

toronja [to'ronxa] nf grapefruit

torpe ['torpe] adj (poco hábil) clumsy, awkward; (necio) dim; (lento) slow

torpedo [tor'peðo] nm torpedo

torpeza [tor'peθa] nf (falta de agilidad) clumsiness; (lentitud) slowness; (error) mistake

torre ['torre] nf tower; (de petróleo) derrick

torrefacto, -a [torre'fakto, a] adj roasted

torrente [to'rrente] nm torrent

torrija [to'rrixa] nf French toast

torsión [tor'sjon] nf twisting

torso ['torso] nm torso

torta ['torta] nf cake; (fam) slap

tortícolis [tor'tikolis] nm inv stiff neck

tortilla [tor'tiʎa] nf omelette; (LAM: de maíz) maize pancake; **tortilla de papas** (LAM) potato omelette; **tortilla de patatas** (ESP) potato omelette; **tortilla francesa** (ESP) plain omelette

tórtola ['tortola] nf turtledove

tortuga [tor'tuxa] nf tortoise

tortuoso, -a [tor'twoso, a] adj winding

tortura [tor'tura] nf torture; **torturar** vt to torture

tos [tos] nf cough; **tos ferina** whooping cough

toser [to'ser] vi to cough

tostada [tos'taða] nf piece of toast; **tostado, -a** adj toasted; (por el sol) dark brown; (piel) tanned

tostador [tosta'ðor] (ESP) nm toaster; **tostadora** (LAM) nf = **tostador**

tostar [tos'tar] vt to toast; (café) to roast; (persona) to tan; **tostarse** vr to get brown

total [to'tal] adj total ▷adv in short; (al fin y al cabo) when all is said and done ▷nm total; **en ~** in all; **~ que ...** to cut (BRIT) o make (US) a long story short ...

totalidad [totali'ðað] nf whole

totalitario, -a [totali'tarjo, a] adj totalitarian

tóxico, -a ['toksiko, a] adj toxic ▷nm poison; **toxicómano, -a** nm/f drug addict

toxina [to'ksina] nf toxin

tozudo, -a [to'θuðo, a] adj obstinate

trabajador, a [traβaxa'ðor, a] adj hard-working ▷nm/f worker; **trabajador autónomo** o **por cuenta propia** self-employed person

trabajar [traβa'xar] vt to work; (Agr) to till; (empeñarse en) to work at; (convencer) to persuade ▷vi to work; (esforzarse) to strive; **trabajo** nm work; (tarea) task; (Pol) labour; (fig) effort; **tomarse el trabajo de** to take the trouble to; **trabajo a destajo** piecework; **trabajo en equipo** teamwork; **trabajo por turnos** shift work; **trabajos forzados** hard labour sg

trabalenguas [traβa'lengwas] nm inv tongue twister

tracción [trak'θjon] nf traction; **tracción delantera/trasera** front-wheel/rear-wheel drive

t

tractor [trak'tor] nm tractor
tradición [traði'θjon] nf tradition; **tradicional** adj traditional
traducción [traðuk'θjon] nf translation
traducir [traðu'θir] vt to translate; **traductor, a** nm/f translator
traer [tra'er] vt to bring; (llevar) to carry; (llevar puesto) to wear; (incluir) to carry; (causar) to cause; **traerse** vr: **~se algo** to be up to sth
traficar [trafi'kar] vi to trade
tráfico ['trafiko] nm (Com) trade; (Auto) traffic
tragaluz [traɣa'luθ] nm skylight
tragamonedas [traɣamo'neðas] (LAM) nf inv slot machine
tragaperras [traɣa'perras] (ESP) nf inv slot machine
tragar [tra'ɣar] vt to swallow; (devorar) to devour, bolt down; **tragarse** vr to swallow
tragedia [tra'xeðja] nf tragedy; **trágico, -a** adj tragic
trago ['traɣo] nm (líquido) drink; (bocado) gulp; (fam: de bebida) swig; (desgracia) blow; **echar un ~** to have a drink
traición [trai'θjon] nf treachery; (Jur) treason; (una traición) act of treachery; **traicionar** vt to betray
traidor, a [trai'ðor, a] adj treacherous ▷ nm/f traitor
traigo etc vb V **traer**
traje ['traxe] vb V **traer** ▷ nm (de hombre) suit; (de mujer) dress; (vestido típico) costume; **traje de baño/chaqueta** swimsuit/suit; **traje de etiqueta** dress suit; **traje de luces** bullfighter's costume
trajera etc vb V **traer**
trajín [tra'xin] nm (fam: movimiento) bustle; **trajinar** vi (moverse) to bustle about
trama ['trama] nf (intriga) plot; (de tejido) weft (BRIT), woof (US); **tramar** vt to plot; (Tec) to weave
tramitar [trami'tar] vt (asunto) to transact; (negociar) to negotiate
trámite ['tramite] nm (paso) step; (Jur) transaction; **trámites** nmpl (burocracia) procedure sg; (Jur) proceedings
tramo ['tramo] nm (de tierra) plot; (de escalera) flight; (de vía) section
trampa ['trampa] nf trap; (en el suelo) trapdoor; (truco) trick; (engaño) fiddle; **trampear** vt, vi to cheat
trampolín [trampo'lin] nm (de piscina etc) diving board
tramposo, -a [tram'poso, a] adj crooked, cheating ▷ nm/f crook, cheat
tranca ['tranka] nf (palo) stick; (de puerta, ventana) bar; **trancar** vt to bar

trance ['tranθe] nm (momento difícil) difficult moment o juncture; (estado hipnotizado) trance
tranquilidad [trankili'ðað] nf (calma) calmness, stillness; (paz) peacefulness
tranquilizar [trankili'θar] vt (calmar) to calm (down); (asegurar) to reassure; **tranquilizarse** vr to calm down; **tranquilo, -a** adj (calmado) calm; (apacible) peaceful; (mar) calm; (mente) untroubled
transacción [transak'θjon] nf transaction
transbordador [transβorða'ðor] nm ferry
transbordo [trans'βorðo] nm transfer; **hacer ~** to change (trains etc)
transcurrir [transku'rrir] vi (tiempo) to pass; (hecho) to take place
transcurso [trans'kurso] nm: **~ del tiempo** lapse (of time)
transeúnte [transe'unte] nmf passer-by
transferencia [transfe'renθja] nf transference; (Com) transfer
transferir [transfe'rir] vt to transfer
transformador [transforma'ðor] nm (Elec) transformer
transformar [transfor'mar] vt to transform; (convertir) to convert
transfusión [transfu'sjon] nf transfusion
transgénico, -a [trans'xeniko, a] adj genetically modified, GM
transición [transi'θjon] nf transition
transigir [transi'xir] vi to compromise, make concessions
transitar [transi'tar] vi to go (from place to place); **tránsito** nm transit; (Auto) traffic; **transitorio, -a** adj transitory
transmisión [transmi'sjon] nf (Tec) transmission; (transferencia) transfer; **transmisión exterior/en directo** outside/ live broadcast
transmitir [transmi'tir] vt to transmit; (Radio, TV) to broadcast
transparencia [transpa'renθja] nf transparency; (claridad) clearness, clarity; (foto) slide
transparentar [transparen'tar] vt to reveal ▷ vi to be transparent; **transparente** adj transparent; (claro) clear
transpirar [transpi'rar] vi to perspire
transportar [transpor'tar] vt to transport; (llevar) to carry; **transporte** nm transport; (Com) haulage
transversal [transβer'sal] adj transverse, cross
tranvía [tram'bia] nm tram
trapeador [trapea'ðor] (LAM) nm mop; **trapear** (LAM) vt to mop

trapecio [tra'peθjo] nm trapeze; **trapecista** nmf trapeze artist
trapero, -a [tra'pero, a] nm/f ragman
trapicheo [trapi'tʃeo] (fam) nm scheme, fiddle
trapo ['trapo] nm (tela) rag; (de cocina) cloth
tráquea ['trakea] nf windpipe
traqueteo [trake'teo] nm rattling
tras [tras] prep (detrás) behind; (después) after
trasatlántico [trasat'lantiko] nm (barco) (cabin) cruiser
trascendencia [trasθen'denθja] nf (importancia) importance; (Filosofía) transcendence
trascendental [trasθenden'tal] adj important; (Filosofía) transcendental
trasero, -a [tra'sero, a] adj back, rear ▷ nm (Anat) bottom
trasfondo [tras'fondo] nm background
trasgredir [trasɣre'ðir] vt to contravene
trashumante [trasu'mante] adj (animales) migrating
trasladar [trasla'ðar] vt to move; (persona) to transfer; (postergar) to postpone; (copiar) to copy; **trasladarse** vr (mudarse) to move; **traslado** nm move; (mudanza) move, removal
traslucir [traslu'θir] vt to show
trasluz [tras'luθ] nm reflected light; **al ~** against o up to the light
trasnochador, a [trasnotʃa'ðor, a] nm/f night owl
trasnochar [trasno'tʃar] vi (acostarse tarde) to stay up late
traspapelar [traspape'lar] vt (documento, carta) to mislay, misplace
traspasar [traspa'sar] vt (suj: bala etc) to pierce, go through; (propiedad) to sell, transfer; (calle) to cross over; (límites) to go beyond; (ley) to break; **traspaso** nm (venta) transfer, sale
traspatio [tras'patjo] (LAM) nm backyard
traspié [tras'pje] nm (tropezón) trip; (error) blunder
trasplantar [trasplan'tar] vt to transplant
traste ['traste] nm (Mús) fret; **dar al ~ con algo** to ruin sth
trastero [tras'tero] nm storage room
trastienda [tras'tjenda] nf back of shop
trasto ['trasto] (pey) nm (cosa) piece of junk; (persona) dead loss
trastornado, -a [trastor'naðo, a] adj (loco) mad, crazy
trastornar [trastor'nar] vt (fig: planes) to disrupt; (: nervios) to shatter; (: persona) to drive crazy; **trastornarse** vr (volverse loco) to go mad o crazy; **trastorno** nm (acto) overturning; (confusión) confusion
tratable [tra'taβle] adj friendly
tratado [tra'taðo] nm (Pol) treaty; (Com) agreement
tratamiento [trata'mjento] nm treatment; **tratamiento de textos** (Inform) word processing cpd
tratar [tra'tar] vt (ocuparse de) to treat; (manejar, Tec) to handle; (Med) to treat; (dirigirse a: persona) to address ▷ vi: **~ de** (hablar sobre) to deal with, be about; (intentar) to try to; **tratarse** vr to treat each other; **~ con** (Com) to trade in; (negociar) to negotiate with; (tener contactos) to have dealings with; **¿de qué se trata?** what's it about?; **trato** nm dealings pl; (relaciónes) relationship; (comportamiento) manner; (Com) agreement
trauma ['trauma] nm trauma
través [tra'βes] nm (fig) reverse; **al ~** across, crossways; **a ~ de** across; (sobre) over; (por) through
travesaño [traβe'saɲo] nm (Arq) crossbeam; (Deporte) crossbar
travesía [traβe'sia] nf (calle) cross-street; (Náut) crossing
travesura [traβe'sura] nf (broma) prank; (ingenio) wit
travieso, -a [tra'βjeso, a] adj (niño) naughty
trayecto [tra'jekto] nm (ruta) road, way; (viaje) journey; (tramo) stretch; **trayectoria** nf trajectory; (fig) path
traza ['traθa] nf (aspecto) looks pl; (señal) sign; **trazado, -a** adj: **bien trazado** shapely, well-formed ▷ nm (Arq) plan, design; (fig) outline
trazar [tra'θar] vt (Arq) to plan; (Arte) to sketch; (fig) to trace; (plan) to draw up; **trazo** nm (línea) line; (bosquejo) sketch
trébol ['treβol] nm (Bot) clover
trece ['treθe] num thirteen
trecho ['tretʃo] nm (distancia) distance; (tiempo) while
tregua ['treɣwa] nf (Mil) truce; (fig) respite
treinta ['treinta] num thirty
tremendo, -a [tre'mendo, a] adj (terrible) terrible; (imponente: cosa) imposing; (fam: fabuloso) tremendous
tren [tren] nm train; **tren de aterrizaje** undercarriage; **tren de cercanías** suburban train
trenca ['trenka] nf duffel coat
trenza ['trenθa] nf (de pelo) plait (BRIT), braid (US)
trepadora [trepa'ðora] nf (Bot) climber
trepar [tre'par] vt, vi to climb

tres [tres] num three

tresillo [tre'siʎo] nm three-piece suite; (Mús) triplet

treta ['treta] nf trick

triángulo ['trjangulo] nm triangle

tribu ['triβu] nf tribe

tribuna [tri'βuna] nf (plataforma) platform; (Deporte) (grand)stand

tribunal [triβu'nal] nm (Jur) court; (comisión, fig) tribunal; ~ **popular** jury

tributo [tri'βuto] nm (Com) tax

trigal [tri'xal] nm wheat field

trigo ['trixo] nm wheat

trigueño, -a [tri'xeɲo, a] adj (pelo) corn-coloured

trillar [tri'ʎar] vt (Agr) to thresh

trimestral [trimes'tral] adj quarterly; (Escol) termly

trimestre [tri'mestre] nm (Escol) term

trinar [tri'nar] vi (pájaros) to sing; (rabiar) to fume, be angry

trinchar [trin'tʃar] vt to carve

trinchera [trin'tʃera] nf (fosa) trench

trineo [tri'neo] nm sledge

trinidad [trini'ðað] nf trio; (Rel): **la T~** the Trinity

tripa ['tripa] nf (Anat) intestine; (fam: tb: ~s) insides pl

triple ['triple] adj triple

triplicado, -a [tripli'kaðo, a] adj: **por ~** in triplicate

triplicación [tripula'θjon] nf crew

tripulante [tripu'lante] nmf crewman/woman

tripular [tripu'lar] vt (barco) to man; (Auto) to drive

triquiñuela [triki'ŋwela] nf trick

tris [tris] nm inv crack

triste ['triste] adj sad; (lamentable) sorry, miserable; **tristeza** nf (aflicción) sadness; (melancolía) melancholy

triturar [tritu'rar] vt (moler) to grind; (mascar) to chew

triunfar [trjun'far] vi (tener éxito) to triumph; (ganar) to win; **triunfo** nm triumph

trivial [tri'βjal] adj trivial

triza ['triθa] nf: **hacer ~s** to smash to bits; (papel) to tear to shreds

trocear [troθe'ar] vt (carne, manzana) to cut up, cut into pieces

trocha ['trotʃa] nf short cut

trofeo [tro'feo] nm (premio) trophy; (éxito) success

tromba ['tromba] nf downpour

trombón [trom'bon] nm trombone

trombosis [trom'bosis] nf inv thrombosis

trompa ['trompa] nf horn; (trompo) humming top; (hocico) snout; (fam): **cogerse una ~** to get tight

trompazo [trom'paθo] nm bump, bang

trompeta [trom'peta] nf trumpet; (clarín) bugle

trompicón [trompi'kon]: **a trompicones** adv in fits and starts

trompo ['trompo] nm spinning top

trompón [trom'pon] nm bump

tronar [tro'nar] vt (MÉX, CAM: fusilar) to shoot; (MÉX: examen) to flunk ▷ vi to thunder; (fig) to rage

tronchar [tron'tʃar] vt (árbol) to chop down; (fig: vida) to cut short; (: esperanza) to shatter; (persona) to tire out; **troncharse** vr to fall down

tronco ['tronko] nm (de árbol, Anat) trunk

trono ['trono] nm throne

tropa ['tropa] nf (Mil) troop; (soldados) soldiers pl

tropezar [trope'θar] vi to trip, stumble; (errar) to slip up; ~ **con** to run into; (topar con) to bump into; **tropezón** nm trip; (fig) blunder

tropical [tropi'kal] adj tropical

trópico ['tropiko] nm tropic

tropiezo [tro'pjeθo] vb V **tropezar** ▷ nm (error) slip, blunder; (desgracia) misfortune; (obstáculo) snag

trotamundos [trota'mundos] nm inv globetrotter

trotar [tro'tar] vi to trot; **trote** nm trot; (fam) travelling; **de mucho trote** hard-wearing

trozar [tro'θar] (LAM) vt to cut up, cut into pieces

trozo ['troθo] nm bit, piece

trucha ['trutʃa] nf trout

truco ['truko] nm (habilidad) knack; (engaño) trick

trueno ['trweno] nm thunder; (estampido) bang

trueque etc ['trweke] vb V **trocar** ▷ nm exchange; (Com) barter

trufa ['trufa] nf (Bot) truffle

truhán, -ana [tru'an, ana] nm/f rogue

truncar [trun'kar] vt (cortar) to truncate; (fig: la vida etc) to cut short; (: el desarrollo) to stunt

tu [tu] adj your

tú [tu] pron you

tubérculo [tu'βerkulo] nm (Bot) tuber

tuberculosis [tuβerku'losis] nf inv tuberculosis

tubería [tuβe'ria] nf pipes pl; (conducto) pipeline

tubo ['tuβo] nm tube, pipe; **tubo de ensayo** test tube; **tubo de escape** exhaust

(pipe)

tuerca ['twerka] nf nut

tuerto, -a ['twerto, a] adj blind in one eye ▷ nm/f one-eyed person

tuerza etc vb V **torcer**

tuétano ['twetano] nm marrow; (Bot) pith

tufo ['tufo] nm (hedor) stench

tul [tul] nm tulle

tulipán [tuli'pan] nm tulip

tullido, -a [tu'ʎiðo, a] adj crippled

tumba ['tumba] nf (sepultura) tomb

tumbar [tum'bar] vt to knock down; **tumbarse** vr (echarse) to lie down; (extenderse) to stretch out

tumbo ['tumbo] nm: **dar ~s** to stagger

tumbona [tum'bona] nf (butaca) easy chair; (de playa) deckchair (BRIT), beach chair (US)

tumor [tu'mor] nm tumour

tumulto [tu'multo] nm turmoil

tuna ['tuna] nf (Mús) student music group; V tb **tuno**

tunante [tu'nante] nmf rascal

tunear [tune'ar] vt (Auto) to style, mod (inf)

túnel ['tunel] nm tunnel

tuning ['tunin] nm (Auto) car styling, modding (inf)

tuno, -a ['tuno, a] nm/f (fam) rogue ▷ nm member of student music group

tupido, -a [tu'piðo, a] adj (denso) dense; (tela) close-woven

turbante [tur'βante] nm turban

turbar [tur'βar] vt (molestar) to disturb; (incomodar) to upset

turbina [tur'βina] nf turbine

turbio, -a ['turβjo, a] adj cloudy; (tema etc) confused

turbulencia [turβu'lenθja] nf turbulence; (fig) restlessness; **turbulento, -a** adj turbulent; (fig: intranquilo) restless; (: ruidoso) noisy

turco, -a ['turko, a] adj Turkish ▷ nm/f Turk

turismo [tu'rismo] nm tourism; (coche) car; **turista** nmf tourist; **turístico, -a** adj tourist cpd

turnar [tur'nar] vi to take (it in) turns; **turnarse** vr to take (it in) turns; **turno** nm (de trabajo) shift; (en juegos etc) turn

turquesa [tur'kesa] nf turquoise

Turquía [tur'kia] nf Turkey

turrón [tu'rron] nm (dulce) nougat

tutear [tute'ar] vt to address as familiar "tú"; **tutearse** vr to be on familiar terms

tutela [tu'tela] nf (legal) guardianship; **tutelar** adj tutelary ▷ vt to protect

tutor, a [tu'tor, a] nm/f (legal) guardian; (Escol) tutor

tuve etc vb V **tener**

tuviera etc vb V **tener**

tuyo, -a ['tujo, a] adj yours, of yours ▷ pron yours; **un amigo ~** a friend of yours; **los ~s** (fam) your relations o family

TV nf abr (= televisión) TV

TVE nf abr = **Televisión Española**

u

u [u] *conj* or
ubicar [uβi'kar] *vt* to place, situate; (*LAM: encontrar*) to find; **ubicarse** *vr* (*LAM: encontrarse*) to lie, be located
ubre ['uβre] *nf* udder
UCI *nf abr* (= *Unidad de Cuidados Intensivos*) ICU
Ud(s) *abr* = **usted(es)**
UE *nf abr* (= *Unión Europea*) EU
ufanarse [ufa'narse] *vr* to boast; **ufano, -a** *adj* (*arrogante*) arrogant; (*presumido*) conceited
UGT (*ESP*) *nf abr* = **Unión General de Trabajadores**
úlcera ['ulθera] *nf* ulcer
ulterior [ulte'rjor] *adj* (*más allá*) farther, further; (*subsecuente, siguiente*) subsequent
últimamente ['ultimamente] *adv* (*recientemente*) lately, recently
ultimar [ulti'mar] *vt* to finish; (*finalizar*) to finalize; (*LAM: matar*) to kill
ultimátum [ulti'matum] (*pl* **~s**) *nm* ultimatum
último, -a ['ultimo, a] *adj* last; (*más reciente*) latest, most recent; (*más bajo*) bottom; (*más alto*) top; **en las últimas** on one's last legs; **por ~** finally
ultra ['ultra] *adj* ultra ▷ *nmf* extreme right-winger
ultraje [ul'traxe] *nm* outrage; insult
ultramar [ultra'mar] *nm*: **de** *o* **en ~** abroad, overseas
ultramarinos [ultrama'rinos] *nmpl* groceries; **tienda de ~** grocer's (shop)
ultranza [ul'tranθa]: **a ~** *adv* (*a todo trance*) at all costs; (*completo*) outright
umbral [um'bral] *nm* (*gen*) threshold

○ **PALABRA CLAVE**

un, una [un, 'una] *art indef* a; (*antes de vocal*) an; **una mujer/naranja** a woman/ an orange
▷ *adj*: **unos** (*o* **unas**): **hay unos regalos para ti** there are some presents for you; **hay unas cervezas en la nevera** there are some beers in the fridge

unánime [u'nanime] *adj* unanimous; **unanimidad** *nf* unanimity
undécimo, -a [un'deθimo, a] *adj* eleventh
ungir [un'xir] *vt* to anoint
ungüento [un'gwento] *nm* ointment
único, -a ['uniko, a] *adj* only, sole; (*sin par*) unique
unidad [uni'ðað] *nf* unity; (*Com, Tec etc*) unit
unido, -a [u'niðo, a] *adj* joined, linked; (*fig*) united
unificar [unifi'kar] *vt* to unite, unify
uniformar [unifor'mar] *vt* to make uniform, level up; (*persona*) to put into uniform
uniforme [uni'forme] *adj* uniform, equal; (*superficie*) even ▷ *nm* uniform
unilateral [unilate'ral] *adj* unilateral
unión [u'njon] *nf* union; (*acto*) uniting, joining; (*unidad*) unity; (*Tec*) joint; **Unión Europea** European Union
unir [u'nir] *vt* (*juntar*) to join, unite; (*atar*) to tie, fasten; (*combinar*) to combine; **unirse** *vr* to join together, unite; (*empresas*) to merge
unísono [u'nisono] *nm*: **al ~** in unison
universal [uniβer'sal] *adj* universal; (*mundial*) world *cpd*
universidad [uniβersi'ðað] *nf* university
universitario, -a [uniβersi'tarjo, a] *adj* university *cpd* ▷ *nm/f* (*profesor*) lecturer; (*estudiante*) (university) student; (*graduado*) graduate
universo [uni'βerso] *nm* universe

○ **PALABRA CLAVE**

uno, -a ['uno, a] *adj* one; **unos pocos** a few; **unos cien** about a hundred ▷ *pron*
1 one; **quiero sólo uno** I only want one; **uno de ellos** one of them
2 (*alguien*) somebody, someone; **conozco a uno que se te parece** I know somebody *o* someone who looks like you; **uno mismo** oneself; **unos querían quedarse** some (people) wanted to stay
3 (**los**) **unos ... (los) otros ...** some ... others
▷ *nf* one; **es la una** it's one o'clock
▷ *nm* (*number*) one

untar [un'tar] vt (mantequilla) to spread; (engrasar) to grease, oil

uña ['uɲa] nf (Anat) nail; (garra) claw; (casco) hoof; (arrancaclavos) claw

uranio [u'ranjo] nm uranium

urbanización [urβaniθa'θjon] nf (barrio, colonia) housing estate

urbanizar [urβani'θar] vt (zona) to develop, urbanize

urbano, -a [ur'βano, a] adj (de ciudad) urban; (cortés) courteous, polite

urbe ['urβe] nf large city

urdir [ur'ðir] vt to warp; (complot) to plot, contrive

urgencia [ur'xenθja] nf urgency; (prisa) haste, rush; (emergencia) emergency; **servicios de ~** emergency services; **"U~s"** "Casualty"; **urgente** adj urgent

urgir [ur'xir] vi to be urgent; **me urge** I'm in a hurry for it

urinario, -a [uri'narjo, a] adj urinary ▷ nm urinal

urna ['urna] nf urn; (Pol) ballot box

urraca [u'rraka] nf magpie

URSS [urs] nf (Hist): **la URSS** the USSR

Uruguay [uru'ɣwai] nm (tb: **el ~**) Uruguay; **uruguayo, -a** adj, nm/f Uruguayan

usado, -a [u'saðo, a] adj used; (de segunda mano) secondhand

usar [u'sar] vt to use; (ropa) to wear; (tener costumbre) to be in the habit of; **usarse** vr to be used; **uso** nm use; wear; (costumbre) usage, custom; (moda) fashion; **al uso** in keeping with custom; **al uso de** in the style of; **de uso externo** (Med) for external use

usted [us'teð] pron (sg) you sg; (pl): **~es** you pl

usual [u'swal] adj usual

usuario, -a [usu'arjo, a] nm/f user

usurpar [usur'par] vt to usurp

utensilio [uten'siljo] nm tool; (Culin) utensil

útero ['utero] nm uterus, womb

útil ['util] adj useful ▷ nm tool; **utilidad** nf usefulness; (Com) profit; **utilizar** vt to use, utilize

uva ['uβa] nf grape

● **LAS UVAS**
●
●
● In Spain **Las uvas** play a big part on
● New Year's Eve (**Nochevieja**), when on
● the stroke of midnight people gather
● at home, in restaurants or in the **plaza
● mayor** and eat a grape for each stroke
● of the clock of the **Puerta del Sol** in
● Madrid. It is said to bring luck for the
● following year.

---

v abr (= voltio) v

va vb V **ir**

vaca ['baka] nf (animal) cow; **carne de ~** beef

vacaciones [baka'θjones] nfpl holidays

vacante [ba'kante] adj vacant, empty ▷ nf vacancy

vaciar [ba'θjar] vt to empty out; (ahuecar) to hollow out; (moldear) to cast; **vaciarse** vr to empty

vacilar [baθi'lar] vi to be unsteady; (al hablar) to falter; (dudar) to hesitate, waver; (memoria) to fail

vacío, -a [ba'θio, a] adj empty; (puesto) vacant; (desocupado) idle; (vano) vain ▷ nm emptiness; (Física) vacuum; (un vacío) (empty) space

vacuna [ba'kuna] nf vaccine; **vacunar** vt to vaccinate

vacuno, -a [ba'kuno, a] adj cow cpd; **ganado ~** cattle

vadear [baðe'ar] vt (río) to ford; **vado** nm ford

vagabundo, -a [baɣa'βundo, a] adj wandering ▷ nm tramp

vagancia [ba'ɣanθja] nf (pereza) idleness, laziness

vagar [ba'ɣar] vi to wander; (no hacer nada) to idle

vagina [ba'xina] nf vagina

vago, -a ['baɣo, a] adj vague; (perezoso) lazy ▷ nm/f (vagabundo) tramp; (flojo) lazybones sg, idler

vagón [ba'ɣon] nm (Ferro: de pasajeros) carriage; (: de mercancías) wagon

vaho ['bao] nm (vapor) vapour, steam; (respiración) breath

vaina ['baina] nf sheath

vainilla [bai'niʎa] nf vanilla

vais vb V **ir**

vaivén [bai'βen] nm to-and-fro

movement; (*de tránsito*) coming and going;
vaivenes *nmpl* (*fig*) ups and downs

vajilla [ba'xiʎa] *nf* crockery, dishes *pl*;
(*juego*) service, set

valdré *etc vb* V **valer**

vale ['bale] *nm* voucher; (*recibo*) receipt;
(*pagaré*) IOU

valedero, -a [bale'ðero, a] *adj* valid

valenciano, -a [balen'θjano, a] *adj*
Valencian

valentía [balen'tia] *nf* courage, bravery

valer [ba'ler] *vt* to be worth; (*Mat*) to
equal; (*costar*) to cost ▷ *vi* (*ser útil*) to be
useful; (*ser válido*) to be valid; **valerse** *vr*
to take care of oneself; **~se de** to make
use of, take advantage of; **~ la pena** to be
worthwhile; **¿vale?** (*ESP*) OK?; **más vale que
nos vayamos** we'd better go; **¡eso a mí no
me vale!** (*MÉX: fam: no importar*) I couldn't
care less about that

valeroso, -a [bale'roso, a] *adj* brave,
valiant

valgo *etc vb* V **valer**

valía [ba'lia] *nf* worth, value

validar [bali'ðar] *vt* to validate; **validez** *nf*
validity; **válido, -a** *adj* valid

valiente [ba'ljente] *adj* brave, valiant
▷ *nm* hero

valija [ba'lixa] (*cs*) *nf* (suit)case

valioso, -a [ba'ljoso, a] *adj* valuable

valla ['baʎa] *nf* fence; (*Deporte*) hurdle;
valla publicitaria hoarding; **vallar** *vt* to
fence in

valle ['baʎe] *nm* valley

valor [ba'lor] *nm* value, worth; (*precio*)
price; (*valentía*) valour, courage; (*importancia*)
importance; **valores** *nmpl* (*Com*) securities;
valorar *vt* to value

vals [bals] *nm inv* waltz

válvula ['balβula] *nf* valve

vamos *vb* V **ir**

vampiro, -resa [bam'piro, 'resa] *nm/f*
vampire

van *vb* V **ir**

vanguardia [ban'gwardja] *nf* vanguard;
(*Arte etc*) avant-garde

vanidad [bani'ðað] *nf* vanity; **vanidoso,
-a** *adj* vain, conceited

vano, -a ['bano, a] *adj* vain

vapor [ba'por] *nm* vapour; (*vaho*) steam;
al ~ (*Culin*) steamed; **vapor de agua** water
vapour; **vaporizador** *nm* atomizer;
vaporizar *vt* to vaporize; **vaporoso, -a** *adj*
vaporous

vaquero, -a [ba'kero, a] *adj* cattle *cpd*
▷ *nm* cowboy; **vaqueros** *nmpl* (*pantalones*)
jeans

vaquilla [ba'kiʎa] *nf* (*Zool*) heifer

vara ['bara] *nf* stick; (*Tec*) rod

variable [ba'rjaβle] *adj, nf* variable

variación [barja'θjon] *nf* variation

variar [bar'jar] *vt* to vary; (*modificar*) to
modify; (*cambiar de posición*) to switch
around ▷ *vi* to vary

varicela [bari'θela] *nf* chickenpox

varices [ba'riθes] *nfpl* varicose veins

variedad [barje'ðað] *nf* variety

varilla [ba'riʎa] *nf* stick; (*Bot*) twig; (*Tec*)
rod; (*de rueda*) spoke

vario, -a ['barjo, a] *adj* varied; **~s** various,
several

varita [ba'rita] *nf* (*tb: ~ mágica*) magic
wand

varón [ba'ron] *nm* male, man; **varonil** *adj*
manly, virile

Varsovia [bar'soβja] *n* Warsaw

vas *vb* V **ir**

vasco, -a ['basko, a] *adj, nm/f* Basque;
vascongado, -a [baskon'gaðo, a] *adj*
Basque; **las Vascongadas** the Basque
Country

vaselina [base'lina] *nf* Vaseline®

vasija [ba'sixa] *nf* container, vessel

vaso ['baso] *nm* glass, tumbler; (*Anat*)
vessel

> No confundir **vaso** con la palabra inglesa
> *vase*.

vástago ['bastaxo] *nm* (*Bot*) shoot; (*Tec*)
rod; (*fig*) offspring

vasto, -a ['basto, a] *adj* vast, huge

Vaticano [bati'kano] *nm*: **el ~** the Vatican

vatio ['batjo] *nm* (*Elec*) watt

vaya *etc vb* V **ir**

Vd(s) *abr* = **usted(es)**

ve [be] *vb* V **ir; ver**

vecindad [beθin'dað] *nf* neighbourhood;
(*habitantes*) residents *pl*

vecindario [beθin'darjo] *nm*
neighbourhood; residents *pl*

vecino, -a [be'θino, a] *adj* neighbouring
▷ *nm/f* neighbour; (*residente*) resident

veda ['beða] *nf* prohibition; **vedar**
[be'ðar] *vt* (*prohibir*) to ban, prohibit;
(*impedir*) to stop, prevent

vegetación [bexeta'θjon] *nf* vegetation

vegetal [bexe'tal] *adj, nm* vegetable

vegetariano, -a [bexeta'rjano, a] *adj,
nm/f* vegetarian

vehículo [be'ikulo] *nm* vehicle; (*Med*)
carrier

veía *etc vb* V **ver**

veinte ['beinte] *num* twenty

vejar [be'xar] *vt* (*irritar*) to annoy, vex;
(*humillar*) to humiliate

vejez [be'xeθ] *nf* old age

vejiga [be'xixa] *nf* (*Anat*) bladder

vela ['bela] nf (de cera) candle; (Náut) sail; (insomnio) sleeplessness; (vigilia) vigil; (Mil) sentry duty; **estar a dos ~s** (fam: sin dinero) to be skint

velado, -a [be'laðo, a] adj veiled; (sonido) muffled; (Foto) blurred ▷ nf soirée

velar [be'lar] vt (vigilar) to keep watch over ▷ vi to stay awake; **~ por** to watch over, look after

velatorio [bela'torjo] nm (funeral) wake

velero [be'lero] nm (Náut) sailing ship; (Aviac) glider

veleta [be'leta] nf weather vane

veliz [be'lis] (MÉX) nm (suit)case

vello ['beʎo] nm down, fuzz

velo ['belo] nm veil

velocidad [beloθi'ðað] nf speed; (Tec, Auto) gear

velocímetro [belo'θimetro] nm speedometer

velorio [be'lorjo] (LAM) nm (funeral) wake

veloz [be'loθ] adj fast

ven vb V **venir**

vena ['bena] nf vein

venado [be'naðo] nm deer

vencedor, a [benθe'ðor, a] adj victorious ▷ nm/f victor, winner

vencer [ben'θer] vt (dominar) to defeat, beat; (derrotar) to vanquish; (superar, controlar) to overcome, master ▷ vi (triunfar) to win (through), triumph; (plazo) to expire; **vencido, -a** adj (derrotado) defeated, beaten; (Com) due ▷ adv: **pagar vencido** to pay in arrears

venda ['benda] nf bandage; **vendaje** nm bandage, dressing; **vendar** vt to bandage; **vendar los ojos** to blindfold

vendaval [benda'βal] nm (viento) gale

vendedor, a [bende'ðor, a] nm/f seller

vender [ben'der] vt to sell; **venderse** vr (estar a la venta) to be on sale; **~ al contado/ al por mayor/al por menor** to sell for cash/ wholesale/retail; **"se vende"** "for sale"

vendimia [ben'dimja] nf grape harvest

vendré etc vb V **venir**

veneno [be'neno] nm poison; (de serpiente) venom; **venenoso, -a** adj poisonous; venomous

venerable [bene'raβle] adj venerable; **venerar** vt (respetar) to revere; (adorar) to worship

venéreo, -a [be'nereo, a] adj: **enfermedad venérea** venereal disease

venezolano, -a [beneθo'lano, a] adj Venezuelan

Venezuela [bene'θwela] nf Venezuela

venganza [ben'ganθa] nf vengeance, revenge; **vengar** vt to avenge; **vengarse** vr to take revenge; **vengativo, -a** adj (persona) vindictive

vengo etc vb V **venir**

venia ['benja] nf (perdón) pardon; (permiso) consent

venial [be'njal] adj venial

venida [be'niða] nf (llegada) arrival; (regreso) return

venidero, -a [beni'ðero, a] adj coming, future

venir [be'nir] vi to come; (llegar) to arrive; (ocurrir) to happen; (fig): **~ de** to stem from; **~ bien/mal** to be suitable/unsuitable; **el año que viene** next year; **~se abajo** to collapse

venta ['benta] nf (Com) sale; **"en ~"** "for sale"; **estar a la** o **en ~** to be (up) for sale o on the market; **venta a domicilio** door-to-door selling; **venta a plazos** hire purchase; **venta al contado/al por mayor/al por menor** cash sale/wholesale/retail

ventaja [ben'taxa] nf advantage; **ventajoso, -a** adj advantageous

ventana [ben'tana] nf window; **ventanilla** nf (de taquilla) window (of booking office etc)

ventilación [bentila'θjon] nf ventilation; (corriente) draught

ventilador [bentila'ðor] nm fan

ventilar [benti'lar] vt to ventilate; (para secar) to put out to dry; (asunto) to air, discuss

ventisca [ben'tiska] nf blizzard

ventrílocuo, -a [ben'trilokwo, a] nm/f ventriloquist

ventura [ben'tura] nf (felicidad) happiness; (buena suerte) luck; (destino) fortune; **a la (buena) ~** at random; **venturoso, -a** adj happy; (afortunado) lucky, fortunate

veo etc vb V **ver**

ver [ber] vt to see; (mirar) to look at, watch; (entender) to understand; (investigar) to look into ▷ vi to see; to understand; **verse** vr (encontrarse) to meet; (dejarse ver) to be seen; (hallarse: en un apuro) to find o.s., be; **(vamos) a ~** let's see; **no tener nada que ~ con** to have nothing to do with; **a mi modo de ~** as I see it; **ya ~emos** we'll see

vera ['bera] nf edge, verge; (de río) bank

veranear [berane'ar] vi to spend the summer; **veraneo** nm summer holiday; **veraniego, -a** adj summer cpd

verano [be'rano] nm summer

veras ['beras] nfpl truth sg; **de ~** really, truly

verbal [ber'βal] adj verbal

verbena [ber'βena] nf (baile) open-air dance

verbo ['berβo] nm verb
verdad [ber'ðað] nf truth; (fiabilidad) reliability; **de ~** real, proper; **a decir ~** to tell the truth; **verdadero, -a** adj (veraz) true, truthful; (fiable) reliable; (fig) real
verde ['berðe] adj green; (chiste) blue, dirty ▷ nm green; **viejo ~** dirty old man; **verdear** vi to turn green; **verdor** nm greenness
verdugo [ber'ðuxo] nm executioner
verdulero, -a [berðu'lero, a] nm/f greengrocer
verduras [ber'ðuras] nfpl (Culin) greens
vereda [be'reða] nf path; (cs: acera) pavement (BRIT), sidewalk (US)
veredicto [bere'ðikto] nm verdict
vergonzoso, -a [berxon'θoso, a] adj shameful; (tímido) timid, bashful
vergüenza [ber'xwenθa] nf shame, sense of shame; (timidez) bashfulness; (pudor) modesty; **me da ~** I'm ashamed
verídico, -a [be'riðiko, a] adj true, truthful
verificar [berifi'kar] vt to check; (corroborar) to verify; (llevar a cabo) to carry out; **verificarse** vr (predicción) to prove to be true
verja ['berxa] nf (cancela) iron gate; (valla) iron railings pl; (de ventana) grille
vermut [ber'mut] (pl ~s) nm vermouth
verosímil [bero'simil] adj likely, probable; (relato) credible
verruga [be'rruxa] nf wart
versátil [ber'satil] adj versatile
versión [ber'sjon] nf version
verso ['berso] nm verse; **un ~** a line of poetry
vértebra ['berteβra] nf vertebra
verter [ber'ter] vt (líquido: adrede) to empty, pour (out); (: sin querer) to spill; (basura) to dump ▷ vi to flow
vertical [berti'kal] adj vertical
vértice ['bertiθe] nm vertex, apex
vertidos [ber'tiðos] nmpl waste sg
vertiente [ber'tjente] nf slope; (fig) aspect
vértigo ['bertixo] nm vertigo; (mareo) dizziness
vesícula [be'sikula] nf blister
vespino® [bes'pino] nm o nf moped
vestíbulo [bes'tiβulo] nm hall; (de teatro) foyer
vestido [bes'tiðo] nm (ropa) clothes pl, clothing; (de mujer) dress, frock ▷ pp de **vestir**; **~ de azul/marinero** dressed in blue/as a sailor
vestidor [besti'ðor] (MÉX) nm (Deporte) changing (BRIT) o locker (US) room
vestimenta [besti'menta] nf clothing
vestir [bes'tir] vt (poner: ropa) to put on;

(llevar: ropa) to wear; (proveer de ropa a) to clothe; (sastre) to make clothes for ▷ vi to dress; (verse bien) to look good; **vestirse** vr to get dressed, dress o.s.
vestuario [bes'twarjo] nm clothes pl, wardrobe; (Teatro: cuarto) dressing room; (Deporte) changing (BRIT) o locker (US) room
vetar [be'tar] vt to veto
veterano, -a [bete'rano, a] adj, nm veteran
veterinaria [beteri'narja] nf veterinary science; V tb **veterinario**
veterinario, -a [beteri'narjo, a] nm/f vet(erinary surgeon)
veto ['beto] nm veto
vez [beθ] nf time; (turno) turn; **a la ~ que** at the same time as; **a su ~** in its turn; **otra ~** again; **una ~** once; **de una ~** in one go; **de una ~ para siempre** once and for all; **en ~ de** instead of; **a o algunas veces** sometimes; **una y otra ~** repeatedly; **de ~ en cuando** from time to time; **7 veces 9** 7 times 9; **hacer las veces de** to stand in for; **tal ~** perhaps
vía ['bia] nf track, route; (Ferro) line; (fig) way; (Anat) passage, tube ▷ prep via, by way of; **por ~ judicial** by legal means; **en ~s de** in the process of; **vía aérea** airway; **Vía Láctea** Milky Way; **vía pública** public road o thoroughfare
viable ['bjaβle] adj (solución, plan, alternativa) feasible
viaducto [bja'ðukto] nm viaduct
viajante [bja'xante] nm commercial traveller
viajar [bja'xar] vi to travel; **viaje** nm journey; (gira) tour; (Náut) voyage; **estar de viaje** to be on a trip; **viaje de ida y vuelta** round trip; **viaje de novios** honeymoon; **viajero, -a** adj travelling; (Zool) migratory ▷ nm/f (quien viaja) traveller; (pasajero) passenger
víbora ['biβora] nf (Zool) viper; (: (MÉX: venenoso) poisonous snake
vibración [biβra'θjon] nf vibration
vibrar [bi'βrar] vt, vi to vibrate
vicepresidente [biθepresi'ðente] nmf vice-president
viceversa [biθe'βersa] adv vice versa
vicio ['biθjo] nm vice; (mala costumbre) bad habit; **vicioso, -a** adj (muy malo) vicious; (corrompido) depraved ▷ nm/f depraved person
víctima ['biktima] nf victim
victoria [bik'torja] nf victory; **victorioso, -a** adj victorious
vid [bið] nf vine
vida ['biða] nf (gen) life; (duración) lifetime;

de por ~ for life; **en la** o **mi ~** never; **estar con ~** to be still alive; **ganarse la ~** to earn one's living

vídeo ['biðeo] nm video ▷ adj inv: **película de ~** video film; **videocámara** nf camcorder; **videocasete** nm video cassette, videotape; **videoclub** nm video club; **videojuego** nm video game; **videollamada** nf video call; **videoteléfono** nf videophone

vidrio ['biðrjo] nm glass

vieira ['bjeira] nf scallop

viejo, -a ['bjexo, a] adj old ▷ nm/f old man/woman; **hacerse ~** to get old

Viena ['bjena] n Vienna

vienes etc vb V **venir**

vienés, -esa [bje'nes, esa] adj Viennese

viento ['bjento] nm wind; **hacer ~** to be windy

vientre ['bjentre] nm belly; (matriz) womb

viernes ['bjernes] nm inv Friday; **Viernes Santo** Good Friday

Vietnam [bjet'nam] nm Vietnam; **vietnamita** adj Vietnamese

viga ['biɣa] nf beam, rafter; (de metal) girder

vigencia [bi'xenθja] nf validity; **estar en ~** to be in force; **vigente** adj valid, in force; (imperante) prevailing

vigésimo, -a [bi'xesimo, a] adj twentieth

vigía [bi'xia] nm look-out

vigilancia [bixi'lanθja] nf: **tener a algn bajo ~** to keep watch on sb

vigilar [bixi'lar] vt to watch over ▷ vi (gen) to be vigilant; (hacer guardia) to keep watch; **~ por** to take care of

vigilia [vi'xilja] nf wakefulness, being awake; (Rel) fast

vigor [bi'ɣor] nm vigour, vitality; **en ~** in force; **entrar/poner en ~** to come/put into effect; **vigoroso, -a** adj vigorous

VIH nm abr (= virus de la inmunodeficiencia humana) HIV; **VIH negativo/positivo** HIV-negative/-positive

vil [bil] adj vile, low

villa ['biʎa] nf (casa) villa; (pueblo) small town; (municipalidad) municipality

villancico [biʎan'θiko] nm (Christmas) carol

vilo ['bilo]: **en ~** adv in the air, suspended; (fig) on tenterhooks, in suspense

vinagre [bi'naɣre] nm vinegar

vinagreta [bina'ɣreta] nf vinaigrette, French dressing

vinculación [binkula'θjon] nf (lazo) link, bond; (acción) linking

vincular [binku'lar] vt to link, bind;

vínculo nm link, bond

vine etc vb V **venir**

vinicultura [binikul'tura] nf wine growing

viniera etc vb V **venir**

vino ['bino] vb V **venir** ▷ nm wine; **vino blanco/tinto** white/red wine

viña ['biɲa] nf vineyard; **viñedo** nm vineyard

viola ['bjola] nf viola

violación [bjola'θjon] nf violation; (sexual) rape

violar [bjo'lar] vt to violate; (sexualmente) to rape

violencia [bjo'lenθja] nf violence, force; (incomodidad) embarrassment; (acto injusto) unjust act; **violentar** vt to force; (casa) to break into; (agredir) to assault; (violar) to violate; **violento, -a** adj violent; (furioso) furious; (situación) embarrassing; (acto) forced, unnatural

violeta [bjo'leta] nf violet

violín [bjo'lin] nm violin

violón [bjo'lon] nm double bass

virar [bi'rar] vi to change direction

virgen ['birxen] adj, nf virgin

Virgo ['birɣo] nm Virgo

viril [bi'ril] adj virile; **virilidad** nf virility

virtud [bir'tuð] nf virtue; **en ~ de** by virtue of; **virtuoso, -a** adj virtuous ▷ nm/f virtuoso

viruela [bi'rwela] nf smallpox

virulento, -a [biru'lento, a] adj virulent

virus ['birus] nm inv virus

visa ['bisa] (LAM) nf = **visado**

visado [bi'saðo] (ESP) nm visa

víscera ['bisθera] nf (Anat, Zool) gut, bowel; **vísceras** nfpl entrails

visceral [bisθe'ral] adj (odio) intense; **reacción ~** gut reaction

visera [bi'sera] nf visor

visibilidad [bisiβili'ðað] nf visibility; **visible** adj visible; (fig) obvious

visillos [bi'siʎos] nmpl lace curtains

visión [bi'sjon] nf (Anat) vision, (eye)sight; (fantasía) vision, fantasy

visita [bi'sita] nf call, visit; (persona) visitor; **hacer una ~** to pay a visit; **visitar** [bisi'tar] vt to visit, call on

visón [bi'son] nm mink

visor [bi'sor] nm (Foto) viewfinder

víspera ['bispera] nf: **la ~ de ...** the day before ...

vista ['bista] nf sight, vision; (capacidad de ver) (eye)sight; (mirada) look(s) (pl); **a primera ~** at first glance; **hacer la ~ gorda** to turn a blind eye; **volver la ~** to look back; **está a la ~ que** it's obvious that; **en ~ de** in view of; **en ~ de que** in view of the fact that; **¡hasta la ~!** so long!, see you!; **con ~s a** with a view to; **vistazo** nm glance; **dar** o **echar un vistazo a** to glance at

visto, -a ['bisto, a] pp de **ver** ▷ vb V tb **vestir** ▷ adj seen; (considerado) considered ▷ nm: **~ bueno** approval; **por lo ~** apparently; **está ~ que** it's clear that; **está bien/mal ~** it's acceptable/unacceptable; **~ que** since, considering that

vistoso, -a [bis'toso, a] adj colourful

visual [bi'swal] adj visual

vital [bi'tal] adj life cpd, living cpd; (fig) vital; (persona) lively, vivacious; **vitalicio, -a** adj for life; **vitalidad** nf (de persona, negocio) energy; (de ciudad) liveliness

vitamina [bita'mina] nf vitamin

vitorear [bitore'ar] vt to cheer, acclaim

vitrina [bi'trina] nf show case; (LAM: escaparate) shop window

viudo, -a ['bjuðo, a] nm/f widower/widow

viva ['biβa] excl hurrah!; **¡~ el rey!** long live the king!

vivaracho, -a [biβa'ratʃo, a] adj jaunty, lively; (ojos) bright, twinkling

vivaz [bi'βaθ] adj lively

víveres ['biβeres] nmpl provisions

vivero [bi'βero] nm (para plantas) nursery; (para peces) fish farm; (fig) hotbed

viveza [bi'βeθa] nf liveliness; (agudeza: mental) sharpness

vivienda [bi'βjenda] nf housing; (una vivienda) house; (piso) flat (BRIT), apartment (US)

viviente [bi'βjente] adj living

vivir [bi'βir] vt, vi to live ▷ nm life, living

vivo, -a ['biβo, a] adj living, alive; (fig: descripción) vivid; (persona: astuto) smart, clever; **en ~** (transmisión etc) live

vocablo [bo'kaβlo] nm (palabra) word; (término) term

vocabulario [bokaβu'larjo] nm vocabulary

vocación [boka'θjon] nf vocation; **vocacional** (LAM) nf = technical college

vocal [bo'kal] adj vocal ▷ nf vowel; **vocalizar** vt to vocalize

vocero [bo'θero] (LAM) nmf spokesman/woman

voces ['boθes] pl de **voz**

vodka ['boðka] nm o f vodka

vol abr = **volumen**

volado [bo'laðo] (MÉX) adv in a rush, hastily

volador, a [bola'ðor, a] adj flying

volandas [bo'landas]: **en ~** adv in the air

volante [bo'lante] adj flying ▷ nm (de

coche) steering wheel; (de reloj) balance

volar [bo'lar] vt (edificio) to blow up ▷ vi to fly

volátil [bo'latil] adj volatile

volcán [bol'kan] nm volcano; **volcánico, -a** adj volcanic

volcar [bol'kar] vt to upset, overturn; (tumbar, derribar) to knock over; (vaciar) to empty out ▷ vi to overturn; **volcarse** vr to tip over

voleibol [bolei'βol] nm volleyball

volqué etc vb V **volcar**

voltaje [bol'taxe] nm voltage

voltear [bolte'ar] vt to turn over; (volcar) to turn upside down

voltereta [bolte'reta] nf somersault

voltio ['boltjo] nm volt

voluble [bo'luβle] adj fickle

volumen [bo'lumen] (pl volúmenes) nm volume; **voluminoso, -a** adj voluminous; (enorme) massive

voluntad [bolun'tað] nf will; (resolución) willpower; (deseo) desire, wish

voluntario, -a [bolun'tarjo, a] adj voluntary ▷ nm/f volunteer

volver [bol'βer] vt (gen) to turn; (dar vuelta a) to turn (over); (voltear) to turn round, turn upside down; (poner al revés) to turn inside out; (devolver) to return ▷ vi to return, go back, come back; **volverse** vr to turn round; **~ la espalda** to turn one's back; **~ triste** etc **a algn** to make sb sad etc; **~ a hacer** to do again; **~ en sí** to come to; **~se insoportable/muy caro** to get o become unbearable/very expensive; **~se loco** to go mad

vomitar [bomi'tar] vt, vi to vomit; **vómito** nm vomit

voraz [bo'raθ] adj voracious

vos [bos] (LAM) pron you

vosotros, -as [bo'sotros, as] (ESP) pron you; (reflexivo): **entre/para ~** among/for yourselves

votación [bota'θjon] nf (acto) voting; (voto) vote

votar [bo'tar] vi to vote; **voto** nm vote; (promesa) vow; **votos** nmpl (good) wishes

voy vb V **ir**

voz [boθ] nf voice; (grito) shout; (rumor) rumour; (Ling) word; **dar voces** to shout, yell; **de viva ~** verbally; **en ~ alta** aloud; **en ~ baja** in a low voice, in a whisper; **voz de mando** command

vuelco ['bwelko] vb V **volcar** ▷ nm spill, overturning

vuelo ['bwelo] vb V **volar** ▷ nm flight; (encaje) lace, frill; **coger al ~** to catch in flight; **vuelo chárter/regular** charter/

scheduled flight; **vuelo libre** (*Deporte*) hang-gliding

vuelque *etc vb V* **volcar**

vuelta ['bwelta] *nf* (*gen*) turn; (*curva*) bend, curve; (*regreso*) return; (*revolución*) revolution; (*de circuito*) lap; (*de papel, tela*) reverse; (*cambio*) change; **a la ~** on one's return; **a la ~ (de la esquina)** round the corner; **a ~ de correo** by return of post; **dar ~s** (*cabeza*) to spin; **dar(se) la ~** (*volverse*) to turn round; **dar ~s a una idea** to turn over an idea (in one's head); **estar de ~** to be back; **dar una ~** to go for a walk; (*en coche*) to go for a drive; **vuelta ciclista** (*Deporte*) (cycle) tour

vuelto ['bwelto] *pp de* **volver**

vuelvo *etc vb V* **volver**

vuestro, -a ['bwestro, a] *adj pos* your; **un amigo ~** a friend of yours ▷ *pron*: **el ~/la vuestra, los ~s/las vuestras** yours

vulgar [bul'ɣar] *adj* (*ordinario*) vulgar; (*común*) common; **vulgaridad** *nf* commonness; (*acto*) vulgarity; (*expresión*) coarse expression

vulnerable [bulne'raβle] *adj* vulnerable

vulnerar [bulne'rar] *vt* (*ley, acuerdo*) to violate, breach; (*derechos, intimidad*) to violate; (*reputación*) to damage

walkie-talkie [walki-'talki] (*pl ~s*) *nm* walkie-talkie

Walkman® ['walkman] *nm* Walkman®

wáter ['bater] *nm* (*taza*) toilet; (*LAM: lugar*) toilet (*BRIT*), rest room (*US*)

web [web] *nm o f* (*página*) website; (*red*) (World Wide) Web; **webcam** *nf* webcam; **webmaster** *nmf* webmaster; **website** *nm* website

western ['western] (*pl ~s*) *nm* western

whisky ['wiski] *nm* whisky, whiskey

windsurf ['winsurf] *nm* windsurfing; **hacer ~** to go windsurfing

X Y

xenofobia [kseno'foβja] *nf* xenophobia
xilófono [ksi'lofono] *nm* xylophone
xocoyote, -a [ksoko'yote, a] (*MÉx*) *nm/f* baby of the family, youngest child

y [i] *conj* and
ya [ja] *adv* (*gen*) already; (*ahora*) now; (*en seguida*) at once; (*pronto*) soon ▷ *excl* all right! ▷ *conj* (*ahora que*) now that; **~ lo sé** I know; **~ que** ... since; **¡~ está bien!** that's (quite) enough!; **¡~ voy!** coming!
yacaré [jaka're] (*cs*) *nm* cayman
yacer [ja'θer] *vi* to lie
yacimiento [jaθi'mjento] *nm* (*de mineral*) deposit; (*arqueológico*) site
yanqui ['janki] *adj, nmf* Yankee
yate ['jate] *nm* yacht
yazco *etc vb* V **yacer**
yedra ['jeðra] *nf* ivy
yegua ['jeɣwa] *nf* mare
yema ['jema] *nf* (*del huevo*) yolk; (*Bot*) leaf bud; (*fig*) best part; **yema del dedo** fingertip
yerno ['jerno] *nm* son-in-law
yeso ['jeso] *nm* plaster
yo [jo] *pron* I; **soy ~** it's me
yodo ['joðo] *nm* iodine
yoga ['joɣa] *nm* yoga
yogur(t) [jo'ɣur(t)] *nm* yoghurt
yuca ['juka] *nf* (*alimento*) cassava, manioc root
Yugoslavia [juɣos'laβja] *nf* (*Hist*) Yugoslavia
yugular [juɣu'lar] *adj* jugular
yunque ['junke] *nm* anvil
yuyo ['jujo] (*RPL*) *nm* (*mala hierba*) weed

Z

zafar [θa'far] vt (soltar) to untie; (superficie) to clear; **zafarse** vr (escaparse) to escape; (Tec) to slip off
zafiro [θa'firo] nm sapphire
zaga ['θaxa] nf: **a la ~** behind
zaguán [θa'ɣwan] nm hallway
zalamero, -a [θala'mero, a] adj flattering; (cobista) suave
zamarra [θa'marra] nf (chaqueta) sheepskin jacket
zambullirse [θambu'ʎirse] vr to dive
zampar [θam'par] vt to gobble down
zanahoria [θana'orja] nf carrot
zancadilla [θanka'ðiʎa] nf trip
zanco ['θanko] nm stilt
zanja ['θanxa] nf ditch; **zanjar** vt (resolver) to resolve
zapata [θa'pata] nf (Mecánica) shoe
zapatería [θapate'ria] nf (oficio) shoemaking; (tienda) shoe shop; (fábrica) shoe factory; **zapatero, -a** nm/f shoemaker
zapatilla [θapa'tiʎa] nf slipper; **zapatilla de deporte** training shoe
zapato [θa'pato] nm shoe
zapping ['θapin] nm channel-hopping; **hacer ~** to channel-hop
zar [θar] nm tsar, czar
zarandear [θarande'ar] (fam) vt to shake vigorously
zarpa ['θarpa] nf (garra) claw
zarpar [θar'par] vi to weigh anchor
zarza ['θarθa] nf (Bot) bramble; **zarzamora** nf blackberry
zarzuela [θar'θwela] nf Spanish light opera
zigzag [θix'θax] nm zigzag
zinc [θink] nm zinc
zíper ['θiper] (MÉX, CAM) nm zip (fastener) (BRIT), zipper (US)
zócalo ['θokalo] nm (Arq) plinth, base; (de pared) skirting board (BRIT), baseboard (US);

(MÉX: plaza) main o public square
zoclo ['θoklo] (MÉX) nm skirting board (BRIT), baseboard (US)
zodíaco [θo'ðiako] nm zodiac
zona ['θona] nf zone; **zona fronteriza** border area; **zona roja** (LAM) red-light district
zonzo, -a (LAM: fam) ['θonθo, a] adj silly ▷ nm/f fool
zoo ['θoo] nm zoo
zoología [θoolo'xia] nf zoology; **zoológico, -a** adj zoological ▷ nm (tb: **parque zoológico**) zoo; **zoólogo, -a** nm/f zoologist
zoom [θum] nm zoom lens
zopilote [θopi'lote] (MÉX, CAM) nm buzzard
zoquete [θo'kete] nm (fam) blockhead
zorro, -a ['θorro, a] adj crafty ▷ nm/f fox/ vixen
zozobrar [θoθo'βrar] vi (hundirse) to capsize; (fig) to fail
zueco ['θweko] nm clog
zumbar [θum'bar] vt (golpear) to hit ▷ vi to buzz; **zumbido** nm buzzing
zumo ['θumo] nm juice
zurcir [θur'θir] vt (coser) to darn
zurdo, -a ['θurðo, a] adj left-handed
zurrar [θu'rrar] (fam) vt to wallop

a

A [eɪ] *n* (*Mus*) la *m*

○ **KEYWORD**

a [ə] (*before vowel or silent h: an*) *indef art*
1 un(a); **a book** un libro; **an apple** una
manzana; **she's a doctor** (ella) es médica
2 (*instead of the number "one"*) un(a); **a year
ago** hace un año; **a hundred/thousand** *etc*
pounds cien/mil *etc* libras
3 (*in expressing ratios, prices etc*): **3 a day/
week** 3 al día/a la semana; **10 km an hour**
10 km por hora; **£5 a person** £5 por persona;
30p a kilo 30p el kilo

A2 (*BRIT: Scol*) *n* segunda parte de los "A levels"
A.A. *n abbr* (*BRIT:* = *Automobile Association*)
≈ RACE *m* (*SP*); (= *Alcoholics Anonymous*)
Alcohólicos Anónimos
A.A.A. (*US*) *n abbr* (= *American Automobile
Association*) ≈ RACE *m* (*SP*)
aback [ə'bæk] *adv*: **to be taken ~** quedar
desconcertado
abandon [ə'bændən] *vt* abandonar; (*give
up*) renunciar a
abattoir ['æbətwɑ:*] (*BRIT*) *n* matadero
abbey ['æbɪ] *n* abadía
abbreviation [ə'bri:vɪ'eɪʃən] *n* (*short form*)
abreviatura
abdomen ['æbdəmən] *n* abdomen *m*
abduct [æb'dʌkt] *vt* raptar, secuestrar
abide [ə'baɪd] *vt*: **I can't ~ it/him** no lo/le
puedo ver; **abide by** *vt fus* atenerse a
ability [ə'bɪlɪtɪ] *n* habilidad *f*, capacidad *f*;
(*talent*) talento
able ['eɪbl] *adj* capaz; (*skilled*) hábil; **to be ~
to do sth** poder hacer algo
abnormal [æb'nɔ:məl] *adj* anormal
aboard [ə'bɔ:d] *adv* a bordo ▷ *prep* a
bordo de
abolish [ə'bɔlɪʃ] *vt* suprimir, abolir

abolition [æbəu'lɪʃən] *n* supresión *f*,
abolición *f*
abort [ə'bɔ:t] *vt*, *vi* abortar; **abortion**
[ə'bɔ:ʃən] *n* aborto; **to have an abortion**
abortar, hacerse abortar

○ **KEYWORD**

about [ə'baut] *adv* **1** (*approximately*) más
o menos, aproximadamente; **about a
hundred/thousand** *etc* unos(unas) cien/
mil *etc*; **it takes about 10 hours** se tarda
unas o más o menos 10 horas; **at about
2 o'clock** sobre las dos; **I've just about
finished** casi he terminado
2 (*referring to place*) por todas partes; **to
leave things lying about** dejar las cosas
(tiradas) por ahí; **to run about** correr por
todas partes; **to walk about** pasearse, ir
y venir
3: **to be about to do sth** estar a punto de
hacer algo
▷ *prep* **1** (*relating to*) de, sobre, acerca de; **a
book about London** un libro sobre *or* acerca
de Londres; **what is it about?** ¿de qué se
trata?; **we talked about it** hablamos de eso
or ello; **what** *or* **how about doing this?** ¿qué
tal si hacemos esto?
2 (*referring to place*) por; **to walk about the
town** caminar por la ciudad

above [ə'bʌv] *adv* encima, por encima,
arriba ▷ *prep* encima de; (*greater than: in
number*) más de; (: *in rank*) superior a;
mentioned ~ susodicho; **~ all** sobre todo
abroad [ə'brɔ:d] *adv* (*to be*) en el
extranjero; (*to go*) al extranjero
abrupt [ə'brʌpt] *adj* (*sudden*) brusco; (*curt*)
áspero
abscess ['æbsɪs] *n* absceso
absence ['æbsəns] *n* ausencia
absent ['æbsənt] *adj* ausente; **absent-
minded** *adj* distraído
absolute ['æbsəlu:t] *adj* absoluto;
absolutely [-'lu:tlɪ] *adv* (*totally*)
totalmente; (*certainly!*) ¡por supuesto (que
sí)!
absorb [əb'zɔ:b] *vt* absorber; **to be ~ed in
a book** estar absorto en un libro; **absorbent
cotton** (*US*) *n* algodón *m* hidrófilo;
absorbing *adj* absorbente
abstain [əb'steɪn] *vi*: **to ~ (from)**
abstenerse (de)
abstract ['æbstrækt] *adj* abstracto
absurd [əb'sə:d] *adj* absurdo
abundance [ə'bʌndəns] *n* abundancia
abundant [ə'bʌndənt] *adj* abundante
abuse [*n* ə'bju:s, *vb* ə'bju:z] *n* (*insults*)

insultos *mpl*, injurias *fpl*; (*ill-treatment*) malos tratos *mpl*; (*misuse*) abuso ▷ *vt* insultar; maltratar; abusar de; **abusive** *adj* ofensivo

abysmal [ə'bɪzməl] *adj* pésimo; (*failure*) garrafal; (*ignorance*) supino

academic [ækə'dɛmɪk] *adj* académico, universitario; (*pej: issue*) puramente teórico ▷ *n* estudioso/a, profesor(a) *m/f* universitario/a; **academic year** *n* (*Univ*) año *m* académico; (*Scol*) año *m* escolar

academy [ə'kædəmɪ] *n* (*learned body*) academia; (*school*) instituto, colegio; **~ of music** conservatorio

accelerate [æk'sɛləreɪt] *vt, vi* acelerar; **acceleration** [æksɛlə'reɪʃən] *n* aceleración *f*; **accelerator** *n* acelerador *m*

accent ['æksɛnt] *n* acento; (*fig*) énfasis *m*

accept [ək'sɛpt] *vt* aceptar; (*responsibility, blame*) admitir; **acceptable** *adj* aceptable; **acceptance** *n* aceptación *f*

access ['æksɛs] *n* acceso; **to have ~ to** tener libre acceso a; **accessible** [-'sɛsəbl] *adj* (*place, person*) accesible; (*knowledge etc*) asequible

accessory [æk'sɛsərɪ] *n* accesorio; (*Law*): **~ to** cómplice de

accident ['æksɪdənt] *n* accidente *m*; (*chance event*) casualidad *f*; **by ~** (*unintentionally*) sin querer; (*by chance*) por casualidad; **accidental** [-'dɛntl] *adj* accidental, fortuito; **accidentally** [-'dɛntəlɪ] *adv* sin querer; por casualidad; **Accident and Emergency Department** *n* (*BRIT*) Urgencias *fpl*; **accident insurance** *n* seguro contra accidentes

acclaim [ə'kleɪm] *vt* aclamar, aplaudir ▷ *n* aclamación *f*, aplausos *mpl*

accommodate [ə'kɔmədeɪt] *vt* (*person*) alojar, hospedar; (*: car, hotel etc*) tener cabida para; (*oblige, help*) complacer

accommodation [əkɔmə'deɪʃən] (*us* **accommodations**) *n* alojamiento

accompaniment [ə'kʌmpənɪmənt] *n* acompañamiento

accompany [ə'kʌmpənɪ] *vt* acompañar

accomplice [ə'kʌmplɪs] *n* cómplice *mf*

accomplish [ə'kʌmplɪʃ] *vt* (*finish*) concluir; (*achieve*) lograr; **accomplishment** *n* (*skill: gen pl*) talento; (*completion*) realización *f*

accord [ə'kɔ:d] *n* acuerdo ▷ *vt* conceder; **of his own ~** espontáneamente; **accordance** *n*: **in accordance with** de acuerdo con; **according** ▷ **according to** *prep* según; (*in agreement with*) conforme a; **accordingly** *adv* (*appropriately*) de acuerdo con esto; (*as a result*) en consecuencia

account [ə'kaunt] *n* (*Comm*) cuenta; (*report*) informe *m*; **accounts** *npl* (*Comm*) cuentas *fpl*; **of no ~** de ninguna importancia; **on ~** a cuenta; **on no ~** bajo ningún concepto; **on ~ of** a causa de, por motivo de; **to take into ~, take ~ of** tener en cuenta; **account for** *vt fus* (*explain*) explicar; (*represent*) representar; **accountable** *adj*: **accountable (to)** responsable (ante); **accountant** *n* contable *mf*, contador(a) *m/f*; **account number** *n* (*at bank etc*) número de cuenta

accumulate [ə'kju:mjuleɪt] *vt* acumular ▷ *vi* acumularse

accuracy ['ækjurəsɪ] *n* (*of total*) exactitud *f*; (*of description etc*) precisión *f*

accurate ['ækjurɪt] *adj* (*total*) exacto; (*description*) preciso; (*person*) cuidadoso; (*device*) de precisión; **accurately** *adv* con precisión

accusation [ækju'zeɪʃən] *n* acusación *f*

accuse [ə'kju:z] *vt*: **to ~ sb (of sth)** acusar a algn (de algo); **accused** *n* (*Law*) acusado/a

accustomed [ə'kʌstəmd] *adj*: **~ to** acostumbrado a

ace [eɪs] *n* as *m*

ache [eɪk] *n* dolor *m* ▷ *vi* doler; **my head ~s** me duele la cabeza

achieve [ə'tʃi:v] *vt* (*aim, result*) alcanzar; (*success*) lograr, conseguir; **achievement** *n* (*completion*) realización *f*; (*success*) éxito

acid ['æsɪd] *adj* ácido; (*taste*) agrio ▷ *n* (*Chem, inf: LSD*) ácido

acknowledge [ək'nɔlɪdʒ] *vt* (*letter: also: ~ receipt of*) acusar recibo de; (*fact, situation, person*) reconocer; **acknowledgement** *n* acuse *m* de recibo

acne ['æknɪ] *n* acné *m*

acorn ['eɪkɔ:n] *n* bellota

acoustic [ə'ku:stɪk] *adj* acústico

acquaintance [ə'kweɪntəns] *n* (*person*) conocido/a; (*with person, subject*) conocimiento

acquire [ə'kwaɪə*] *vt* adquirir; **acquisition** [ækwɪ'zɪʃən] *n* adquisición *f*

acquit [ə'kwɪt] *vt* absolver, exculpar; **to ~ o.s. well** salir con éxito

acre ['eɪkə*] *n* acre *m*

acronym ['ækrənɪm] *n* siglas *fpl*

across [ə'krɔs] *prep* (*on the other side of*) al otro lado de, del otro lado de; (*crosswise*) a través de ▷ *adv* de un lado a otro, de una parte a otra; a través, al través; (*measurement*): **the road is 10m ~** la carretera tiene 10m de ancho; **to run/swim ~** atravesar corriendo/nadando; **~ from** enfrente de

acrylic [ə'krɪlɪk] *adj* acrílico ▷ *n* acrílica

act [ækt] n acto, acción f; (of play) acto; (in music hall etc) número; (Law) decreto, ley f ▷ vi (behave) comportarse; (have effect: drug, chemical) hacer efecto; (Theatre) actuar; (pretend) fingir; (take action) obrar ▷ vt (part) hacer el papel de; **in the ~ of: to catch sb in the ~ of ...** pillar a algn en el momento en que ...; **to ~ as** actuar or hacer de; **act up** (inf) vi (person) portarse mal; **acting** adj suplente ▷ n (activity) actuación f; (profession) profesión f de actor

action ['ækʃən] n acción f, acto; (Mil) acción f, batalla; (Law) proceso, demanda; **out of ~** (person) fuera de combate; (thing) estropeado; **to take ~** tomar medidas; **action replay** n. (TV) repetición f

activate ['æktɪveɪt] vt activar

active ['æktɪv] adj activo, enérgico; (volcano) en actividad; **actively** adv (participate) activamente; (discourage, dislike) enérgicamente

activist ['æktɪvɪst] n activista m/f

activity [-'tɪvɪtɪ] n actividad f; **activity holiday** n vacaciones con actividades organizadas

actor ['æktə*] n actor m, actriz f

actress ['æktrɪs] n actriz f

actual ['æktjuəl] adj verdadero, real; (emphatic use) propiamente dicho

> Be careful not to translate **actual** by the Spanish word actual.

actually ['æktjuəlɪ] adv realmente, en realidad; (even) incluso

> Be careful not to translate **actually** by the Spanish word actualmente.

acupuncture ['ækjupʌŋktʃə*] n acupuntura

acute [ə'kju:t] adj agudo

ad [æd] n abbr = **advertisement**

A.D. adv abbr (= anno Domini) DC

adamant ['ædəmənt] adj firme, inflexible

adapt [ə'dæpt] vt adaptar ▷ vi: **to ~ (to)** adaptarse (a), ajustarse (a); **adapter** (us **adaptor**) n (Elec) adaptador m; (for several plugs) ladrón m

add [æd] vt añadir, agregar; **add up** vt (figures) sumar ▷ vi (fig): **it doesn't add up** no tiene sentido; **add up to** vt fus (Math) sumar, ascender a; (fig: mean) querer decir, venir a ser

addict ['ædɪkt] n adicto/a; (enthusiast) entusiasta mf; **addicted** [ə'dɪktɪd] adj: **to be addicted to** ser adicto a, ser fanático de; **addiction** [ə'dɪkʃən] n (to drugs etc) adicción f; **addictive** [ə'dɪktɪv] adj que causa adicción

addition [ə'dɪʃən] n (adding up) adición f; (thing added) añadidura, añadido; **in ~**

además, por añadidura; **in ~ to** además de; **additional** adj adicional

additive ['ædɪtɪv] n aditivo

address [ə'drɛs] n dirección f, señas fpl; (speech) discurso ▷ vt (letter) dirigir; (speak to) dirigirse a, dirigir la palabra a; (problem) tratar; **address book** n agenda (de direcciones)

adequate ['ædɪkwət] adj (satisfactory) adecuado; (enough) suficiente

adhere [əd'hɪə*] vi: **to ~ to** (stick to) pegarse a; (fig: abide by) observar; (: belief etc) ser partidario de

adhesive [əd'hi:zɪv] n adhesivo; **adhesive tape** n (BRIT) cinta adhesiva; (us Med) esparadrapo

adjacent [ə'dʒeɪsənt] adj: **~ to** contiguo a, inmediato a

adjective ['ædʒɛktɪv] n adjetivo

adjoining [ə'dʒɔɪnɪŋ] adj contiguo, vecino

adjourn [ə'dʒə:n] vt aplazar ▷ vi suspenderse

adjust [ə'dʒʌst] vt (change) modificar; (clothing) arreglar; (machine) ajustar ▷ vi: **to ~ (to)** adaptarse (a); **adjustable** adj ajustable; **adjustment** n adaptación f; (to machine, prices) ajuste m

administer [əd'mɪnɪstə*] vt administrar; **administration** [-'treɪʃən] n (management) administración f; (government) gobierno; **administrative** [-trətɪv] adj administrativo

administrator [əd'mɪnɪstreɪtə*] n administrador(a) m/f

admiral ['ædmərəl] n almirante m

admiration [ædmə'reɪʃən] n admiración f

admire [əd'maɪə*] vt admirar; **admirer** n (fan) admirador(a) m/f

admission [əd'mɪʃən] n (to university, club) ingreso; (entry fee) entrada; (confession) confesión f

admit [əd'mɪt] vt (confess) confesar; (permit to enter) dejar entrar, dar entrada a; (to club, organization) admitir; (accept: defeat) reconocer; **to be ~ted to hospital** ingresar en el hospital; **admit to** vt fus confesarse culpable de; **admittance** n entrada; **admittedly** adv es cierto or verdad que

adolescent [ædəu'lɛsnt] adj, n adolescente mf

adopt [ə'dɔpt] vt adoptar; **adopted** adj adoptivo; **adoption** [ə'dɔpʃən] n adopción f

adore [ə'dɔ:*] vt adorar

adorn [ə'dɔ:n] vt adornar

Adriatic [eɪdrɪ'ætɪk] n: **the ~ (Sea)** el (Mar) Adriático

adrift [ə'drɪft] adv a la deriva
adult ['ædʌlt] n adulto/a ▷ adj (grown-up) adulto; (for adults) para adultos; **adult education** n educación f para adultos
adultery [ə'dʌltərɪ] n adulterio
advance [əd'vɑ:ns] n (progress) adelanto, progreso; (money) anticipo, préstamo; (Mil) avance m ▷ adj: **~ booking** venta anticipada; **~ notice, ~ warning** previo aviso ▷ vt (money) anticipar; (theory, idea) proponer (para la discusión) ▷ vi avanzar, adelantarse; **to make ~s (to sb)** hacer proposiciones (a algn); **in ~** por adelantado; **advanced** adj avanzado; (Scol: studies) adelantado
advantage [əd'vɑ:ntɪdʒ] n (also Tennis) ventaja; **to take ~ of** (person) aprovecharse de; (opportunity) aprovechar
advent ['ædvənt] n advenimiento; **A~** Adviento
adventure [əd'ventʃə*] n aventura; **adventurous** [-tʃərəs] adj atrevido; aventurero
adverb ['ædvə:b] n adverbio
adversary ['ædvəsərɪ] n adversario, contrario
adverse ['ædvə:s] adj adverso, contrario
advert ['ædvə:t] (BRIT) n abbr = **advertisement**
advertise ['ædvətaɪz] vi (in newspaper etc) anunciar, hacer publicidad; **to ~ for** (staff, accommodation etc) buscar por medio de anuncios ▷ vt anunciar; **advertisement** [əd'və:tɪsmənt] n (Comm) anuncio; **advertiser** n anunciante mf; **advertising** n publicidad f, anuncios mpl; (industry) industria publicitaria
advice [əd'vaɪs] n consejo, consejos mpl; (notification) aviso; **a piece of ~** un consejo; **to take legal ~** consultar con un abogado
advisable [əd'vaɪzəbl] adj aconsejable, conveniente
advise [əd'vaɪz] vt aconsejar; (inform): **to ~ sb of sth** informar a algn de algo; **to ~ sb against sth/doing sth** desaconsejar algo a algn/aconsejar a algn que no haga algo; **adviser, advisor** n consejero/a; (consultant) asesor(a) m/f; **advisory** adj consultivo
advocate [vb 'ædvəkeɪt, n -kɪt] vt abogar por ▷ n (lawyer) abogado/a; (supporter): **~ of** defensor(a) m/f de
Aegean [i:'dʒi:ən] n: **the ~ (Sea)** el (Mar) Egeo
aerial ['ɛərɪəl] n antena ▷ adj aéreo
aerobics [ɛə'rəubɪks] n aerobic m
aeroplane ['ɛərəpleɪn] (BRIT) n avión m
aerosol ['ɛərəsɔl] n aerosol m

affair [ə'fɛə*] n asunto; (also: **love ~**) aventura (amorosa)
affect [ə'fɛkt] vt (influence) afectar, influir en; (afflict, concern) afectar; (move) conmover; **affected** adj afectado; **affection** n afecto, cariño; **affectionate** adj afectuoso, cariñoso
afflict [ə'flɪkt] vt afligir
affluent ['æfluənt] adj (wealthy) acomodado; **the ~ society** la sociedad opulenta
afford [ə'fɔ:d] vt (provide) proporcionar; **can we ~ (to buy) it?** ¿tenemos bastante dinero para comprarlo?; **affordable** adj asequible
Afghanistan [æf'gænɪstæn] n Afganistán m
afraid [ə'freɪd] adj: **to be ~ of** (person) tener miedo a; (thing) tener miedo de; **to be ~ to** tener miedo de, temer; **I am ~ that** me temo que; **I am ~ not/so** lo siento, pero no/es así
Africa ['æfrɪkə] n África; **African** adj, n africano/a m/f; **African-American** adj, n afroamericano/a
after ['ɑ:ftə*] prep (time) después de; (place, order) detrás de, tras ▷ adv después ▷ conj después (de) que; **what/who are you ~?** ¿qué/a quién buscas usted?; **~ having done/he left** después de haber hecho/después de que se marchó; **to name sb ~ sb** llamar a algn por algn; **it's twenty ~ eight** (US) son las ocho y veinte; **to ask ~ sb** preguntar por algn; **~ all** después de todo, al fin y al cabo; **~ you!** ¡pase usted!; **after-effects** npl consecuencias fpl, efectos mpl; **aftermath** n consecuencias fpl, resultados mpl; **afternoon** n tarde f; **after-shave (lotion)** n aftershave m; **aftersun (lotion/cream)** n loción f/crema para después del sol, aftersun m; **afterwards** (US **afterward**) adv después, más tarde
again [ə'gɛn] adv otra vez, de nuevo; **to do sth ~** volver a hacer algo; **~ and ~** una y otra vez
against [ə'gɛnst] prep (in opposition to) en contra de; (leaning on, touching) contra, junto a
age [eɪdʒ] n edad f; (period) época ▷ vi envejecer(se) ▷ vt envejecer; **she is 20 years of ~** tiene 20 años; **to come of ~** llegar a la mayoría de edad; **it's been ~s since I saw you** hace siglos que no te veo; **~d 10** de 10 años de edad; **age group** n: **to be in the same age group** tener la misma edad; **age limit** n edad f mínima (or máxima)
agency ['eɪdʒənsɪ] n agencia
agenda [ə'dʒɛndə] n orden m del día
■ Be careful not to translate **agenda** by the

▧ Spanish word *agenda*.

agent ['eɪdʒənt] *n* agente *mf*; (*Comm: holding concession*) representante *mf*, delegado/a; (*Chem, fig*) agente *m*

aggravate ['ægrəveɪt] *vt* (*situation*) agravar; (*person*) irritar

aggression [ə'greʃən] *n* agresión *f*

aggressive [ə'gresɪv] *adj* (*belligerent*)· agresivo; (*assertive*) enérgico

agile ['ædʒaɪl] *adj* ágil

agitated ['ædʒɪteɪtɪd] *adj* agitado

AGM *n abbr* (= *annual general meeting*) asamblea anual

ago [ə'gəu] *adv*: **2 days ~** hace 2 días; **not long ~** hace poco; **how long ~?** ¿hace cuánto tiempo?

agony ['ægənɪ] *n* (*pain*) dolor *m* agudo; (*distress*) angustia; **to be in ~** retorcerse de dolor

agree [ə'griː] *vt* (*price, date*) acordar, quedar en ▷ *vi* (*have same opinion*): **to ~ (with/that)** estar de acuerdo (con/que); (*correspond*) coincidir, concordar; (*consent*) acceder; **to ~ with** (*person*) estar de acuerdo con, ponerse de acuerdo con; (: *food*) sentar bien a; (*Ling*) concordar con; **to ~ to sth/ to do sth** consentir en algo/aceptar hacer algo; **to ~ that** (*admit*) estar de acuerdo en que; **agreeable** *adj* (*sensation*) agradable; (*person*) simpático; (*willing*) de acuerdo, conforme; **agreed** *adj* (*time, place*) convenido; **agreement** *n* acuerdo; (*contract*) contrato; **in agreement** de acuerdo, conforme

agricultural [ægrɪ'kʌltʃərəl] *adj* agrícola

agriculture ['ægrɪkʌltʃə*] *n* agricultura

ahead [ə'hed] *adv* (*in front*) delante; (*into the future*): **she had no time to think ~** no tenía tiempo de hacer planes para el futuro; **~ of** delante de; (*in advance of*) antes de; **~ of time** antes de la hora; **go right** *or* **straight ~** (*direction*) siga adelante; (*permission*) hazlo (*or* hágalo)

aid [eɪd] *n* ayuda, auxilio; (*device*) aparato ▷ *vt* ayudar, auxiliar; **in ~ of** a beneficio de

aide [eɪd] *n* (*person, also Mil*) ayudante *mf*

AIDS [eɪdz] *n abbr* (= *acquired immune deficiency syndrome*) SIDA *m*

ailing ['eɪlɪŋ] *adj* (*person, economy*) enfermizo

ailment ['eɪlmənt] *n* enfermedad *f*, achaque *m*

aim [eɪm] *vt* (*gun, camera*) apuntar; (*missile, remark*) dirigir; (*blow*) asestar ▷ *vi* (*also:* **take ~**) apuntar ▷ *n* (*in shooting: skill*) puntería; (*objective*) propósito, meta; **to ~ at** (*with weapon*) apuntar a; (*objective*) aspirar a, pretender; **to ~ to do** tener la intención

de hacer

ain't [eɪnt] (*inf*) = **am not; aren't; isn't**

air [ɛə*] *n* aire *m*; (*appearance*) aspecto ▷ *vt* (*room*) ventilar; (*clothes, ideas*) airear ▷ *cpd* aéreo; **to throw sth into the ~** (*ball etc*) lanzar algo al aire; **by ~** (*travel*) en avión; **to be on the ~** (*Radio, TV*) estar en antena; **airbag** *n* airbag *m inv*; **airbed** (BRIT) *n* colchón *m* neumático; **airborne** *adj* (*in the air*) en el aire; **as soon as the plane was airborne** tan pronto como el avión estuvo en el aire; **air-conditioned** *adj* climatizado; **air conditioning** *n* aire acondicionado; **aircraft** *n inv* avión *m*; **airfield** *n* campo de aviación; **Air Force** *n* fuerzas *fpl* aéreas, aviación *f*; **air hostess** (BRIT) *n* azafata; **airing cupboard** (BRIT) *n* armario *m* para oreo; **airlift** *n* puente *m* aéreo; **airline** *n* línea aérea; **airliner** *n* avión *m* de pasajeros; **airmail** *n*: **by airmail** por avión; **airplane** (US) *n* avión *m*; **airport** *n* aeropuerto; **air raid** *n* ataque *m* aéreo; **airsick** *adj*: **to be airsick** marearse (en avión); **airspace** *n* espacio aéreo; **airstrip** *n* pista de aterrizaje; **air terminal** *n* terminal *f*; **airtight** *adj* hermético; **air-traffic controller** *n* controlador(a) *m/f* aéreo/a; **airy** *adj* (*room*) bien ventilado; (*fig: manner*) desenfadado

aisle [aɪl] *n* (*of church*) nave *f*; (*of theatre, supermarket*) pasillo; **aisle seat** *n* (*on plane*) asiento de pasillo

ajar [ə'dʒɑː*] *adj* entreabierto

à la carte [ælæ'kɑːt] *adv* a la carta

alarm [ə'lɑːm] *n* (*in shop, bank*) alarma; (*anxiety*) inquietud *f* ▷ *vt* asustar, inquietar; **alarm call** *n* (*in hotel etc*) alarma; **alarm clock** *n* despertador *m*; **alarmed** *adj* (*person*) alarmado, asustado; (*house, car etc*) con alarma; **alarming** *adj* alarmante

Albania [æl'beɪnɪə] *n* Albania

albeit [ɔːl'biːɪt] *conj* aunque

album ['ælbəm] *n* álbum *m*; (L.P.) elepé *m*

alcohol ['ælkəhɔl] *n* alcohol *m*; **alcohol-free** *adj* sin alcohol; **alcoholic** [-'hɔlɪk] *adj*, *n* alcohólico/a *m/f*

alcove ['ælkəuv] *n* nicho, hueco

ale [eɪl] *n* cerveza

alert [ə'ləːt] *adj* (*attentive*) atento; (*to danger, opportunity*) alerta ▷ *n* alerta *m*, alarma ▷ *vt* poner sobre aviso; **to be on the ~** (*also Mil*) estar alerta *or* sobre aviso

algebra ['ældʒɪbrə] *n* álgebra

Algeria [æl'dʒɪərɪə] *n* Argelia

alias ['eɪlɪəs] *adv* alias, conocido por ▷ *n* (*of criminal*) apodo; (*of writer*) seudónimo

alibi ['ælɪbaɪ] *n* coartada

alien ['eɪlɪən] *n* (*foreigner*) extranjero/a;

(extraterrestrial) extraterrestre mf ▷ adj: **~ to** ajeno a; **alienate** vt enajenar, alejar

alight [ə'laɪt] adj ardiendo; (eyes) brillante ▷ vi (person) apearse, bajar; (bird) posarse

align [ə'laɪn] vt alinear

alike [ə'laɪk] adj semejantes, iguales ▷ adv igualmente, del mismo modo; **to look ~** parecerse

alive [ə'laɪv] adj vivo; (lively) alegre

O **KEYWORD**

all [ɔ:l] adj (sg) todo/a; (pl) todos/as; **all day** todo el día; **all night** toda la noche; **all men** todos los hombres; **all five came** vinieron los cinco; **all the books** todos los libros; **all his life** toda su vida
▷ pron 1 todo; **I ate it all, I ate all of it** me lo comí todo; **all of us went** fuimos todos; **all the boys went** fueron todos los chicos; **is that all?** ¿eso es todo?, ¿algo más?; (in shop) ¿algo más?, ¿alguna cosa más?
2 (in phrases): **above all** sobre todo; por encima de todo; **after all** después de todo; **at all: not at all** (in answer to question) en absoluto; (in answer to thanks) ¡de nada!, ¡no hay de qué!; **I'm not at all tired** no estoy nada cansado/a; **anything at all will do** cualquier cosa viene bien; **all in all** a fin de cuentas
▷ adv: **all alone** completamente solo/a; **it's not as hard as all that** no es tan difícil como lo pintas; **all the more/the better** tanto más/mejor; **all but** casi; **the score is 2 all** están empatados a 2

Allah [ˈælə] n Alá m

allegation [ælɪˈɡeɪʃən] n alegato

alleged [əˈlɛdʒd] adj supuesto, presunto; **allegedly** adv supuestamente, según se afirma

allegiance [əˈliːdʒəns] n lealtad f

allergic [əˈləːdʒɪk] adj: **~ to** alérgico a

allergy [ˈælədʒɪ] n alergia

alleviate [əˈliːvɪeɪt] vt aliviar

alley [ˈælɪ] n callejuela

alliance [əˈlaɪəns] n alianza

allied [ˈælaɪd] adj aliado

alligator [ˈælɪɡeɪtə*] n (Zool) caimán m

all-in (BRIT) [ˈɔ:lɪn] adj, adv (charge) todo incluido

allocate [ˈæləkeɪt] vt (money etc) asignar

allot [əˈlɔt] vt asignar

all-out [ˈɔ:laʊt] adj (effort etc) supremo

allow [əˈlaʊ] vt permitir, dejar; (a claim) admitir; (sum, time etc) dar, conceder; (concede): **to ~ that** reconocer que; **to ~ sb to do** permitir a algn hacer; **he is ~ed to**

... se le permite ...; **allow for** vt fus tener en cuenta; **allowance** n subvención f; (welfare payment) subsidio, pensión f; (pocket money) dinero de bolsillo; (tax allowance) desgravación f; **to make allowances for** (person) disculpar a; (thing) tener en cuenta

all right adv bien; (as answer) ¡conforme!, ¡está bien!

ally [ˈælaɪ] n aliado/a ▷ vt: **to ~ o.s. with** aliarse con

almighty [ɔ:lˈmaɪtɪ] adj todopoderoso; (row etc) imponente

almond [ˈɑːmənd] n almendra

almost [ˈɔ:lməʊst] adv casi

alone [əˈləʊn] adj, adv solo; **to leave sb ~** dejar a algn en paz; **to leave sth ~** no tocar algo, dejar algo sin tocar; **let ~ ...** y mucho menos ...

along [əˈlɒŋ] prep a lo largo de, por ▷ adv: **is he coming ~ with us?** ¿viene con nosotros?; **he was limping ~** iba cojeando; **~ with** junto con; **all ~** (all the time) desde el principio; **alongside** prep al lado de ▷ adv al lado

aloof [əˈluːf] adj reservado ▷ adv: **to stand ~** mantenerse apartado

aloud [əˈlaʊd] adv en voz alta

alphabet [ˈælfəbɛt] n alfabeto

Alps [ælps] npl: **the ~** los Alpes

already [ɔ:lˈrɛdɪ] adv ya

alright [ˈɔ:lˈraɪt] (BRIT) adv = **all right**

also [ˈɔ:lsəʊ] adv también, además

altar [ˈɔltə*] n altar m

alter [ˈɔltə*] vt cambiar, modificar ▷ vi cambiar; **alteration** [ɔltəˈreɪʃən] n cambio; (to clothes) arreglo; (to building) arreglos mpl

alternate [adj ɔlˈtəːnɪt, vb ˈɔltəːneɪt] adj (actions etc) alternativo; (events) alterno; (US) = **alternative** ▷ vi: **to ~ (with)** alternar (con); **on ~ days** un día sí y otro no

alternative [ɔlˈtəːnətɪv] adj alternativo ▷ n alternativa; **~ medicine** medicina alternativa; **alternatively** adv: **alternatively one could ...** por otra parte se podría ...

although [ɔ:lˈðəʊ] conj aunque

altitude [ˈæltɪtjuːd] n altura

altogether [ɔ:ltəˈɡɛðə*] adv completamente, del todo; (on the whole) en total, en conjunto

aluminium [æljuˈmɪnɪəm] (BRIT), **aluminum** [əˈluːmɪnəm] (US) n aluminio

always [ˈɔ:lweɪz] adv siempre

Alzheimer's (disease) [ˈæltshaɪməz-] n enfermedad f de Alzheimer

am [æm] vb see **be**

amalgamate [əˈmælɡəmeɪt] vi

amalgamarse ▷ vt amalgamar, unir

amass [ə'mæs] vt amontonar, acumular

amateur ['æmətə*] n aficionado/a,
amateur mf

amaze [ə'meɪz] vt asombrar, pasmar; **to
be ~d (at)** quedar pasmado (de); **amazed**
adj asombrado; **amazement** n asombro,
sorpresa; **amazing** adj extraordinario;
(fantastic) increíble

Amazon ['æməzən] n (Geo) Amazonas m

ambassador [æm'bæsədə*] n
embajador(a) m/f

amber ['æmbə*] n ámbar m; **at ~** (BRIT Aut)
en el amarillo

ambiguous [æm'bɪgjuəs] adj ambiguo

ambition [æm'bɪʃən] n ambición f;
ambitious [-ʃəs] adj ambicioso

ambulance ['æmbjuləns] n ambulancia

ambush ['æmbuʃ] n emboscada ▷ vt
tender una emboscada a

amen [ɑː'mɛn] excl amén

amend [ə'mɛnd] vt enmendar; **to make
~s** dar cumplida satisfacción; **amendment**
n enmienda

amenities [ə'miːnɪtɪz] npl comodidades
fpl

America [ə'mɛrɪkə] n (USA) Estados mpl
Unidos; **American** adj, n norteamericano/a;
estadounidense mf; **American football** n
(BRIT) fútbol m americano

amicable ['æmɪkəbl] adj amistoso,
amigable

amid(st) [ə'mɪd(st)] prep entre, en medio
de

ammunition [æmju'nɪʃən] n municiones
fpl

amnesty ['æmnɪstɪ] n amnistía

among(st) [ə'mʌŋ(st)] prep entre, en
medio de

amount [ə'maunt] n (gen) cantidad f; (of
bill etc) suma, importe m ▷ vi: **to ~ to** sumar;
(be same as) equivaler a, significar

amp(ère) ['æmp(ɛə*)] n amperio

ample ['æmpl] adj (large) grande;
(abundant) abundante; (enough) bastante,
suficiente

amplifier ['æmplɪfaɪə*] n amplificador m

amputate ['æmpjuteɪt] vt amputar

Amtrak ['æmtræk] (US) n empresa nacional
de ferrocarriles de los EEUU

amuse [ə'mjuːz] vt divertir; (distract)
distraer, entretener; **amusement** n
diversión f; (pastime) pasatiempo; (laughter)
risa; **amusement arcade** n salón m de
juegos; **amusement park** n parque m de
atracciones

amusing [ə'mjuːzɪŋ] adj divertido

an [æn] indef art see **a**

anaemia [ə'niːmɪə] (US **anemia**) n
anemia

anaemic [ə'niːmɪk] (US **anemic**) adj
anémico; (fig) soso, insípido

anaesthetic [ænɪs'θɛtɪk] (US **anesthetic**)
n anestesia

analog(ue) ['ænəlɔg] adj (computer,
watch) analógico

analogy [ə'nælədʒɪ] n analogía

analyse ['ænəlaɪz] (US **analyze**) vt
analizar; **analysis** [ə'næləsɪs] (pl **analyses**)
n análisis m inv; **analyst** [-lɪst] n (political
analyst, psychoanalyst) analista mf

analyze ['ænəlaɪz] (US) vt = **analyse**

anarchy ['ænəkɪ] n anarquía, desorden m

anatomy [ə'nætəmɪ] n anatomía

ancestor ['ænsɪstə*] n antepasado

anchor ['æŋkə*] n ancla, áncora ▷ vi
(also: **to drop ~**) anclar ▷ vt anclar; **to
weigh ~** levar anclas

anchovy ['æntʃəvɪ] n anchoa

ancient ['eɪnʃənt] adj antiguo

and [ænd] conj y; (before i-, hi- + consonant)
e; **men ~ women** hombres y mujeres;
father ~ son padre e hijo; **trees ~ grass**
árboles y hierba; **~ so on** etcétera, y así
sucesivamente; **try ~ come** procura venir;
he talked ~ talked habló sin parar; **better ~
better** cada vez mejor

Andes ['ændiːz] npl: **the ~** los Andes

Andorra [æn'dɔːrə] n Andorra

anemia etc [ə'niːmɪə] (US) = **anaemia** etc

anesthetic [ænɪs'θɛtɪk] (US) =
anaesthetic

angel ['eɪndʒəl] n ángel m

anger ['æŋgə*] n cólera

angina [æn'dʒaɪnə] n angina (del pecho)

angle ['æŋgl] n ángulo; **from their ~** desde
su punto de vista

angler ['æŋglə*] n pescador(a) m/f (de
caña)

Anglican ['æŋglɪkən] adj, n anglicano/a
m/f

angling ['æŋglɪŋ] n pesca con caña

angrily ['æŋgrɪlɪ] adv coléricamente,
airadamente

angry ['æŋgrɪ] adj enfadado, airado;
(wound) inflamado; **to be ~ with sb/at sth**
estar enfadado con algn/por algo; **to get ~**
enfadarse, enojarse

anguish ['æŋgwɪʃ] n (physical) tormentos
mpl; (mental) angustia

animal ['ænɪməl] n animal m; (pej: person)
bestia ▷ adj animal

animated [-meɪtɪd] adj animado

animation [ænɪ'meɪʃən] n animación f

aniseed ['ænɪsiːd] n anís m

ankle ['æŋkl] n tobillo

annex [n 'ænɛks, vb æ'nɛks] n (BRIT: also: ~e: building) edificio anexo ▷ vt (territory) anexionar

anniversary [ænɪ'vəːsərɪ] n aniversario

announce [ə'naʊns] vt anunciar; **announcement** n anuncio; (official) declaración f; **announcer** n (Radio) locutor(a) m/f; (TV) presentador(a) m/f

annoy [ə'nɔɪ] vt molestar, fastidiar; **don't get ~ed!** ¡no se enfade!; **annoying** adj molesto, fastidioso; (person) pesado

annual ['ænjuəl] adj anual ▷ n (Bot) anual m; (book) anuario; **annually** adv anualmente, cada año

annum ['ænəm] n see **per**

anonymous [ə'nɒnɪməs] adj anónimo

anorak ['ænəræk] n anorak m

anorexia [ænə'rɛksɪə] n (Med: also: ~ nervosa) anorexia

anorexic [ænə'rɛksɪk] adj, n anoréxico/a m/f

another [ə'nʌðə*] adj (one more, a different one) otro ▷ pron otro; see **one**

answer ['ɑːnsə*] n contestación f, respuesta; (to problem) solución f ▷ vi contestar, responder ▷ vt (reply to) contestar a, responder a; (problem) resolver; (prayer) escuchar; **in ~ to your letter** contestando or en contestación a su carta; **to ~ the phone** contestar or coger el teléfono; **to ~ the bell** or **the door** acudir a la puerta; **answer back** vi replicar, ser respondón/ona; **answerphone** n (esp BRIT) contestador m (automático)

ant [ænt] n hormiga

Antarctic [ænt'ɑːktɪk] n: **the ~** el Antártico

antelope ['æntɪləʊp] n antílope m

antenatal ['æntɪ'neɪtl] adj antenatal, prenatal

antenna [æn'tɛnə, pl -niː] (pl **antennae**) n antena

anthem ['ænθəm] n: **national ~** himno nacional

anthology [æn'θɒlədʒɪ] n antología

anthrax ['ænθræks] n ántrax m

anthropology [ænθrə'pɒlədʒɪ] n antropología

anti [æntɪ] prefix anti; **antibiotic** [-baɪ'ɒtɪk] n antibiótico; **antibody** ['æntɪbɒdɪ] n anticuerpo

anticipate [æn'tɪsɪpeɪt] vt prever; (expect) esperar, contar con; (look forward to) esperar con ilusión; (do first) anticiparse a, adelantarse a; **anticipation** [-'peɪʃən] n (expectation) previsión f; (eagerness) ilusión f, expectación f

anticlimax [æntɪ'klaɪmæks] n decepción f

anticlockwise [æntɪ'klɒkwaɪz] (BRIT) adv en dirección contraria a la de las agujas del reloj

antics ['æntɪks] npl gracias fpl

anti: antidote ['æntɪdəʊt] n antídoto; **antifreeze** ['æntɪfriːz] n anticongelante m; **antihistamine** [-'hɪstəmiːn] n antihistamínico; **antiperspirant** ['æntɪpə:spɪrənt] n antitranspirante m

antique [æn'tiːk] n antigüedad f ▷ adj antiguo; **antique shop** n tienda de antigüedades

antiseptic [æntɪ'sɛptɪk] adj, n antiséptico

antisocial [æntɪ'səʊʃəl] adj antisocial

antivirus [æntɪ'vaɪərəs] adj (program, software) antivirus inv

antlers ['æntləz] npl cuernas fpl, cornamenta sg

anxiety [æŋ'zaɪətɪ] n inquietud f; (Med) ansiedad f; **~ to do** deseo de hacer

anxious ['æŋkʃəs] adj inquieto, preocupado; (worrying) preocupante; (keen): **to be ~ to do** tener muchas ganas de hacer

○ **KEYWORD**

any ['ɛnɪ] adj **1** (in questions etc) algún/alguna; **have you any butter/children?** ¿tienes mantequilla/hijos?; **if there are any tickets left** si quedan billetes, si queda algún billete

2 (with negative): **I haven't any money/books** no tengo dinero/libros

3 (no matter which) cualquier; **any excuse will do** valdrá or servirá cualquier excusa; **choose any book you like** escoge el libro que quieras

4 (in phrases): **in any case** de todas formas, en cualquier caso; **any day now** cualquier día (de estos); **at any moment** en cualquier momento, de un momento a otro; **at any rate** en todo caso; **any time: come (at) any time** ven cuando quieras; **he might come (at) any time** podría llegar de un momento a otro

▷ pron **1** (in questions etc): **have you got any?** ¿tienes alguno(s)/a(s)?; **can any of you sing?** ¿sabe cantar alguno de vosotros/ustedes?

2 (with negative): **I haven't any (of them)** no tengo ninguno

3 (no matter which one(s)): **take any of those books (you like)** toma el libro que quieras de ésos

▷ adv **1** (in questions etc): **do you want any**

more soup/sandwiches? ¿quieres más sopa/bocadillos?; **are you feeling any better?** ¿te sientes algo mejor? **2** (with negative): **I can't hear him any more** ya no le oigo; **don't wait any longer** no esperes más

any: anybody pron cualquiera; (in interrogative sentences) alguien; (in negative sentences): **I don't see anybody** no veo a nadie; **if anybody should phone …** si llama alguien …; **anyhow** adv (at any rate) de todos modos, de todas formas; (haphazard): **do it anyhow you like** hazlo como quieras; **she leaves things just anyhow** deja las cosas como quiera or de cualquier modo; **I shall go anyhow** de todos modos iré; **anyone** pron = **anybody**; **anything** pron (in questions etc) algo, alguna cosa; (with negative) nada; **can you see anything?** ¿ves algo?; **if anything happens to me …** si algo me ocurre …; (no matter what): **you can say anything you like** puedes decir lo que quieras; **anything will do** vale todo or cualquier cosa; **he'll eat anything** come de todo or lo que sea; **anytime** adv (at any moment) en cualquier momento, de un momento a otro; (whenever) no importa cuándo, cuando quiera; **anyway** adv (at any rate) de todos modos, de todas formas; **I shall go anyway** iré de todos modos; (besides): **anyway, I couldn't come even if I wanted to** además, no podría venir aunque quisiera; **why are you phoning, anyway?** ¿entonces, por qué llamas?, ¿por qué llamas, pues?; **anywhere** adv (in questions etc): **can you see him anywhere?** ¿le ves por algún lado?; **are you going anywhere?** ¿vas a algún sitio?; (with negative): **I can't see him anywhere** no le veo por ninguna parte; **anywhere in the world** (no matter where) en cualquier parte (del mundo); **put the books down anywhere** deja los libros donde quieras

apart [əˈpɑːt] adv (aside) aparte; (situation): **~ (from)** separado (de); (movement): **to pull ~** separar; **10 miles ~** separados por 10 millas; **to take ~** desmontar; **~ from** prep aparte de

apartment [əˈpɑːtmənt] n (US) piso (SP), departamento (LAM), apartamento; (room) cuarto; **apartment building** (US) n edificio de apartamentos

apathy [ˈæpəθɪ] n apatía, indiferencia

ape [eɪp] n mono ▷ vt imitar, remedar

aperitif [əˈperɪtɪf] n aperitivo

aperture [ˈæpətʃjuə*] n rendija,

resquicio; (Phot) abertura

APEX [ˈeɪpɛks] n abbr (=Advanced Purchase Excursion Fare) tarifa f APEX

apologize [əˈpɒlədʒaɪz] vi: **to ~ (for sth to sb)** disculparse (con algn de algo)

apology [əˈpɒlədʒɪ] n disculpa, excusa
> Be careful not to translate **apology** by the Spanish word *apología*.

apostrophe [əˈpɒstrəfɪ] n apóstrofo

appal [əˈpɔːl] (US **appall**) vt horrorizar, espantar; **appalling** adj espantoso; (awful) pésimo

apparatus [æpəˈreɪtəs] n (equipment) equipo; (organization) aparato; (in gymnasium) aparatos mpl

apparent [əˈpærənt] adj aparente; (obvious) evidente; **apparently** adv por lo visto, al parecer

appeal [əˈpiːl] vi (Law) apelar ▷ n (Law) apelación f; (request) llamamiento; (plea) petición f; (charm) atractivo; **to ~ for** reclamar; **to ~ to** (be attractive to) atraer; **it doesn't ~ to me** no me atrae, no me llama la atención; **appealing** adj (attractive) atractivo

appear [əˈpɪə*] vi aparecer, presentarse; (Law) comparecer; (publication) salir (a luz), publicarse; (seem) parecer; **to ~ on TV/in "Hamlet"** salir por la tele/hacer un papel en "Hamlet"; **it would ~ that** parecería que; **appearance** n aparición f; (look) apariencia, aspecto

appendices [əˈpɛndɪsiːz] npl of **appendix**

appendicitis [əpɛndɪˈsaɪtɪs] n apendicitis f

appendix [əˈpɛndɪks] (pl **appendices**) n apéndice m

appetite [ˈæpɪtaɪt] n apetito; (fig) deseo, anhelo

appetizer [ˈæpɪtaɪzə*] n (drink) aperitivo; (food) tapas fpl (SP)

applaud [əˈplɔːd] vt, vi aplaudir

applause [əˈplɔːz] n aplausos mpl

apple [ˈæpl] n manzana; **apple pie** n pastel m de manzana, pay m de manzana (LAM)

appliance [əˈplaɪəns] n aparato

applicable [əˈplɪkəbl] adj (relevant): **to be ~ (to)** referirse (a)

applicant [ˈæplɪkənt] n candidato/a; solicitante mf

application [æplɪˈkeɪʃən] n aplicación f; (for a job etc) solicitud f, petición f; **application form** n solicitud f

apply [əˈplaɪ] vt (paint etc) poner; (law etc: put into practice) poner en vigor ▷ vi: **to ~ to** (ask) dirigirse a; (be applicable) ser aplicable a; **to ~ for** (permit, grant, job)

solicitar; **to ~ o.s. to** aplicarse a, dedicarse a
appoint [ə'pɔɪnt] vt (to post) nombrar a

▌Be careful not to translate **appoint** by the
Spanish word *apuntar*.

appointment n (with client) cita; (act)
nombramiento; (post) puesto; (at hairdresser
etc): **to have an appointment** tener hora;
to make an appointment (with sb) citarse
(con algn)
appraisal [ə'preɪzl] n valoración f
appreciate [ə'priːʃɪeɪt] vt apreciar,
tener en mucho; (be grateful for) agradecer;
(be aware) comprender ▷ vi (Comm)
aumentar(se) en valor; **appreciation**
[-'eɪʃən] n apreciación f; (gratitude)
reconocimiento, agradecimiento; (Comm)
aumento en valor
apprehension [æprɪ'henʃən] n (fear)
aprensión f
apprehensive [æprɪ'hensɪv] adj
aprensivo
apprentice [ə'prentɪs] n aprendiz(a) m/f
approach [ə'prəʊtʃ] vi acercarse
▷ vt acercarse a; (ask, apply to) dirigirse
a; (situation, problem) abordar ▷ n
acercamiento; (access) acceso; (to problem,
situation): **~ (to)** actitud f (ante)
appropriate [adj ə'prəʊprɪɪt,
vb ə'prəʊprɪeɪt] adj apropiado,
conveniente ▷ vt (take) apropiarse de
approval [ə'pruːvəl] n aprobación f, visto
bueno; (permission) consentimiento; **on ~**
(Comm) a prueba
approve [ə'pruːv] vt aprobar; **approve of**
vt fus (thing) aprobar; (person): **they don't
approve of her** (ella) no les parece bien
approximate [ə'prɔksɪmɪt] adj
aproximado; **approximately** adv
aproximadamente, más o menos
Apr. abbr (=April) abr
apricot ['eɪprɪkɔt] n albaricoque m,
chabacano (MEX), damasco (RPL)
April ['eɪprəl] n abril m; **April Fools' Day** n
el primero de abril, ≈ día m de los Inocentes
(28 December)
apron ['eɪprən] n delantal m
apt [æpt] adj acertado, apropiado;
(likely): **~ to do** propenso a hacer
aquarium [ə'kwɛərɪəm] n acuario
Aquarius [ə'kwɛərɪəs] n Acuario
Arab ['ærəb] adj, n árabe mf
Arabia [ə'reɪbɪə] n Arabia; **Arabian**
adj árabe; **Arabic** ['ærəbɪk] adj árabe;
(numerals) arábigo ▷ n árabe m
arbitrary ['ɑːbɪtrərɪ] adj arbitrario
arbitration [ɑːbɪ'treɪʃən] n arbitraje m
arc [ɑːk] n arco
arcade [ɑː'keɪd] n (round a square)

soportales mpl; (shopping mall) galería
comercial
arch [ɑːtʃ] n arco; (of foot) arco del pie ▷ vt
arquear
archaeology [ɑːkɪ'ɔlədʒɪ] (US **archeology**)
n arqueología
archbishop [ɑːtʃ'bɪʃəp] n arzobispo
archeology [ɑːkɪ'ɔlədʒɪ] (US) =
archaeology
architect ['ɑːkɪtekt] n arquitecto/a;
architectural [ɑːkɪ'tektʃərəl] adj
arquitectónico; **architecture** n
arquitectura
archive ['ɑːkaɪv] n (often pl: also Comput)
archivo
Arctic ['ɑːktɪk] adj ártico ▷ n: **the ~** el
Ártico
are [ɑː*] vb see be
area ['ɛərɪə] n área, región f; (part of
place) zona; (Math etc) área, superficie f; (in
room: e.g. dining area) parte f; (of knowledge,
experience) campo; **area code** (US) n (Tel)
prefijo
arena [ə'riːnə] n estadio; (of circus) pista
aren't [ɑːnt] = are not
Argentina [ɑːdʒən'tiːnə] n Argentina;
Argentinian [-'tɪnɪən] adj, n argentino/a
m/f
arguably ['ɑːgjuəblɪ] adv posiblemente
argue ['ɑːgjuː] vi (quarrel) discutir,
pelearse; (reason) razonar, argumentar; **to ~
that** sostener que
argument ['ɑːgjumənt] n discusión f,
pelea; (reasons) argumento
Aries ['ɛərɪz] n Aries m
arise [ə'raɪz] (pt arose, pp arisen) vi surgir,
presentarse
arithmetic [ə'rɪθmətɪk] n aritmética
arm [ɑːm] n brazo ▷ vt armar; **arms**
npl armas fpl; **~ in ~** cogidos del brazo;
armchair ['ɑːmtʃɛə*] n sillón m, butaca
armed [ɑːmd] adj armado; **armed
robbery** n robo a mano armada
armour ['ɑːmə*] (US **armor**) n armadura;
(Mil: tanks) blindaje m
armpit ['ɑːmpɪt] n sobaco, axila
armrest ['ɑːmrest] n apoyabrazos m inv
army ['ɑːmɪ] n ejército; (fig) multitud f
A road n (BRIT) ≈ carretera f nacional
aroma [ə'rəʊmə] n aroma m, fragancia;
aromatherapy n aromaterapia
arose [ə'rəʊz] pt of arise
around [ə'raʊnd] adv alrededor; (in the
area): **there is no one else ~** no hay nadie
más por aquí ▷ prep alrededor de
arouse [ə'raʊz] vt despertar; (anger)
provocar
arrange [ə'reɪndʒ] vt arreglar, ordenar;

(*organize*) organizar; **to ~ to do sth** quedar en hacer algo; **arrangement** *n* arreglo; (*agreement*) acuerdo; **arrangements** *npl* (*preparations*) preparativos *mpl*

array [ə'reɪ] *n*: **~ of** (*things*) serie *f* de; (*people*) conjunto de

arrears [ə'rɪəz] *npl* atrasos *mpl*; **to be in ~ with one's rent** estar retrasado en el pago del alquiler

arrest [ə'rɛst] *vt* detener; (*sb's attention*) llamar ▷ *n* detención *f*; **under ~** detenido

arrival [ə'raɪvəl] *n* llegada; **new ~** recién llegado/a; (*baby*) recién nacido

arrive [ə'raɪv] *vi* llegar; (*baby*) nacer; **arrive at** *vt fus* (*decision, solution*) llegar a

arrogance ['ærəgəns] *n* arrogancia, prepotencia (LAM)

arrogant ['ærəgənt] *adj* arrogante

arrow ['ærəu] *n* flecha

arse [ɑːs] (BRIT: *infl*) *n* culo, trasero

arson ['ɑːsn] *n* incendio premeditado

art [ɑːt] *n* arte *m*; (*skill*) destreza; **art college** *n* escuela *f* de Bellas Artes

artery ['ɑːtərɪ] *n* arteria

art gallery *n* pinacoteca; (*saleroom*) galería de arte

arthritis [ɑː'θraɪtɪs] *n* artritis *f*

artichoke ['ɑːtɪtʃəuk] *n* alcachofa; **Jerusalem ~** aguaturma

article ['ɑːtɪkl] *n* artículo

articulate [*adj* ɑː'tɪkjulɪt, *vb* ɑː'tɪkjuleɪt] *adj* claro, bien expresado ▷ *vt* expresar

artificial [ɑːtɪ'fɪʃəl] *adj* artificial; (*affected*) afectado

artist ['ɑːtɪst] *n* artista *mf*; (*Mus*) intérprete *mf*; **artistic** [ɑː'tɪstɪk] *adj* artístico

art school *n* escuela de bellas artes

○ KEYWORD

as [æz] *conj* **1** (*referring to time*) cuando, mientras; a medida que; **as the years went by** con el paso de los años; **he came in as I was leaving** entró cuando me marchaba; **as from tomorrow** desde *or* a partir de mañana

2 (*in comparisons*): **as big as** tan grande como; **twice as big as** el doble de grande que; **as much money/many books as** tanto dinero/tantos libros como; **as soon as** en cuanto

3 (*since, because*) como, ya que; **he left early as he had to be home by 10** se fue temprano ya que tenía que estar en casa a las 10

4 (*referring to manner, way*): **do as you wish** haz lo que quieras; **as she said** como dijo;

he gave it to me as a present me lo dio de regalo

5 (*in the capacity of*): **he works as a barman** trabaja de barman; **as chairman of the company, he ...** como presidente de la compañía ...

6 (*concerning*): **as for** *or* **to that** por *or* en lo que respecta a eso

7: **as if** *or* **though** como si; **he looked as if he was ill** parecía como si estuviera enfermo, tenía aspecto de enfermo; *see also* **long; such; well**

a.s.a.p. *abbr* (= *as soon as possible*) cuanto antes

asbestos [æz'bɛstəs] *n* asbesto, amianto

ascent [ə'sɛnt] *n* subida; (*slope*) cuesta, pendiente *f*

ash [æʃ] *n* ceniza; (*tree*) fresno

ashamed [ə'ʃeɪmd] *adj* avergonzado, apenado (LAM); **to be ~ of** avergonzarse de

ashore [ə'ʃɔː*] *adv* en tierra; (*swim etc*) a tierra

ashtray ['æʃtreɪ] *n* cenicero

Ash Wednesday *n* miércoles *m* de Ceniza

Asia ['eɪʃə] *n* Asia; **Asian** *adj, n* asiático/a *m/f*

aside [ə'saɪd] *adv* a un lado ▷ *n* aparte *m*

ask [ɑːsk] *vt* (*question*) preguntar; (*invite*) invitar; **to ~ sb sth/to do sth** preguntar algo a algn/pedir a algn que haga algo; **to ~ sb about sth** preguntar algo a algn; **to ~ (sb) a question** hacer una pregunta (a algn); **to ~ sb out to dinner** invitar a cenar a algn; **ask for** *vt fus* pedir; (*trouble*) buscar

asleep [ə'sliːp] *adj* dormido; **to fall ~** dormirse, quedarse dormido

asparagus [əs'pærəgəs] *n* (*plant*) espárrago; (*food*) espárragos *mpl*

aspect ['æspɛkt] *n* aspecto, apariencia; (*direction in which a building etc faces*) orientación *f*

aspirations [æspə'reɪʃənz] *npl* aspiraciones *fpl*; (*ambition*) ambición *f*

aspire [əs'paɪə*] *vi*: **to ~ to** aspirar a, ambicionar

aspirin ['æsprɪn] *n* aspirina

ass [æs] *n* asno, burro; (*inf: idiot*) imbécil *mf*; (*US: infl*) culo, trasero

assassin [ə'sæsɪn] *n* asesino/a; **assassinate** *vt* asesinar

assault [ə'sɔːlt] *n* asalto; (*Law*) agresión *f* ▷ *vt* asaltar, atacar; (*sexually*) violar

assemble [ə'sɛmbl] *vt* reunir, juntar; (*Tech*) montar ▷ *vi* reunirse, juntarse

assembly [ə'sɛmblɪ] *n* reunión *f*, asamblea; (*parliament*) parlamento; (*construction*) montaje *m*

assert [ə'sə:t] vt afirmar; (*authority*) hacer valer; **assertion** [-fən] n afirmación f

assess [ə'sɛs] vt valorar, calcular; (*tax, damages*) fijar; (*for tax*) gravar; **assessment** n valoración f; (*for tax*) gravamen m

asset ['æsɛt] n ventaja; **assets** npl (*Comm*) activo; (*property, funds*) fondos mpl

assign [ə'saɪn] vt: **to ~ (to)** (*date*) fijar (para); (*task*) asignar (a); (*resources*) destinar (a); **assignment** n tarea

assist [ə'sɪst] vt ayudar; **assistance** n ayuda, auxilio; **assistant** n ayudante mf; (BRIT: also: **shop assistant**) dependiente/a m/f

associate [*adj, n* ə'səʊʃɪɪt, *vb* ə'səʊʃɪeɪt] adj asociado ▷ n (*at work*) colega mf ▷ vt asociar; (*ideas*) relacionar ▷ vi: **to ~ with sb** tratar con algn

association [əsəʊsɪ'eɪʃən] n asociación f

assorted [ə'sɔ:tɪd] adj surtido, variado

assortment [ə'sɔ:tmənt] n (*of shapes, colours*) surtido; (*of books*) colección f; (*of people*) mezcla

assume [ə'sju:m] vt suponer; (*responsibilities*) asumir; (*attitude*) adoptar, tomar

assumption [ə'sʌmpʃən] n suposición f, presunción f; (*of power etc*) toma

assurance [ə'fʊərəns] n garantía, promesa; (*confidence*) confianza, aplomo; (*insurance*) seguro

assure [ə'fʊə*] vt asegurar

asterisk ['æstərɪsk] n asterisco

asthma ['æsmə] n asma

astonish [ə'stɒnɪʃ] vt asombrar, pasmar; **astonished** adj estupefacto, pasmado; **to be astonished (at)** asombrarse (de); **astonishing** adj asombroso, pasmoso; **I find it astonishing that ...** me asombra or pasma que ...; **astonishment** n asombro, sorpresa

astound [ə'staund] vt asombrar, pasmar

astray [ə'streɪ] adv: **to go ~** extraviarse; **to lead ~** (*morally*) llevar por mal camino

astrology [æs'trɒlədʒɪ] n astrología

astronaut ['æstrənɔ:t] n astronauta mf

astronomer [əs'trɒnəmə*] n astrónomo/a

astronomical [æstrə'nɒmɪkəl] adj astronómico

astronomy [əs'trɒnəmɪ] n astronomía

astute [əs'tju:t] adj astuto

asylum [ə'saɪləm] n (*refuge*) asilo; (*mental hospital*) manicomio

○ **KEYWORD**

at [æt] prep **1** (*referring to position*) en; (*direction*) a; **at the top** en lo alto; **at home/school** en casa/la escuela; **to look at sth/sb** mirar algo/a algn

2 (*referring to time*): **at 4 o'clock** a las 4; **at night** por la noche; **at Christmas** en Navidad; **at times** a veces

3 (*referring to rates, speed etc*): **at £1 a kilo** a una libra el kilo; **two at a time** de dos en dos; **at 50 km/h** a 50 km/h

4 (*referring to manner*): **at a stroke** de un golpe; **at peace** en paz

5 (*referring to activity*): **to be at work** estar trabajando; (*in the office etc*) estar en el trabajo; **to play at cowboys** jugar a los vaqueros; **to be good at sth** ser bueno en algo

6 (*referring to cause*): **shocked/surprised/annoyed at sth** asombrado/sorprendido/fastidiado por algo; **I went at his suggestion** fui a instancias suyas

7 (*symbol*) arroba

ate [eɪt] pt of **eat**

atheist ['eɪθɪɪst] n ateo/a

Athens ['æθɪnz] n Atenas

athlete ['æθli:t] n atleta mf

athletic [æθ'lɛtɪk] adj atlético; **athletics** n atletismo

Atlantic [ət'læntɪk] adj atlántico ▷ n: **the ~ (Ocean)** el (Océano) Atlántico

atlas ['ætləs] n atlas m inv

A.T.M. n abbr (= *automated telling machine*) cajero automático

atmosphere ['ætməsfɪə*] n atmósfera; (*of place*) ambiente m

atom ['ætəm] n átomo; **atomic** [ə'tɒmɪk] adj atómico; **atom(ic) bomb** n bomba atómica

A to Z® n (*map*) callejero

atrocity [ə'trɒsɪtɪ] n atrocidad f

attach [ə'tætʃ] vt (*fasten*) atar; (*join*) unir, sujetar; (*document, letter*) adjuntar; (*importance etc*) dar, conceder; **to be ~ed to sb/sth** (*to like*) tener cariño a algn/algo; **attachment** n (*tool*) accesorio; (*Comput*) archivo, documento adjunto; (*love*): **attachment (to)** apego (a)

attack [ə'tæk] vt (*Mil*) atacar; (*criminal*) agredir, asaltar; (*criticize*) criticar; (*task*) emprender ▷ n ataque m, asalto; (*on sb's life*) atentado; (*fig: criticism*) crítica; (*of illness*) ataque m; **heart ~** infarto (de miocardio); **attacker** n agresor(a) m/f, asaltante mf

attain [ə'teɪn] vt (*also*: **~ to**) alcanzar; (*achieve*) lograr, conseguir

attempt [ə'tɛmpt] n tentativa, intento; (*attack*) atentado ▷ vt intentar

attend [ə'tɛnd] vt asistir a; (*patient*)

atender; **attend to** *vt fus* ocuparse de; (*customer, patient*) atender a; **attendance** *n* asistencia, presencia; (*people present*) concurrencia; **attendant** *n* ayudante *mf*; (*in garage etc*) encargado/a ▷ *adj* (*dangers*) concomitante

attention [əˈtɛnʃən] *n* atención *f*; (*care*) atenciones *fpl* ▷ *excl* (*Mil*) ¡firme(s)!; **for the ~ of ...** (*Admin*) atención ...

attic [ˈætɪk] *n* desván *m*

attitude [ˈætɪtjuːd] *n* actitud *f*; (*disposition*) disposición *f*

attorney [əˈtɜːnɪ] *n* (*lawyer*) abogado/a; **Attorney General** *n* (*BRIT*) ≈ Presidente *m* del Consejo del Poder Judicial (*SP*); (*US*) ≈ ministro de Justicia

attract [əˈtrækt] *vt* atraer; (*sb's attention*) llamar; **attraction** [əˈtrækʃən] *n* encanto; (*gen pl: amusements*) diversiones *fpl*; (*Physics*) atracción *f*; (*fig: towards sb, sth*) atractivo; **attractive** *adj* guapo; (*interesting*) atrayente

attribute [*n* ˈætrɪbjuːt, *vb* əˈtrɪbjuːt] *n* atributo ▷ *vt*: **to ~ sth to** atribuir algo a

aubergine [ˈəubəʒiːn] (*BRIT*) *n* berenjena; (*colour*) morado

auburn [ˈɔːbən] *adj* color castaño rojizo

auction [ˈɔːkʃən] *n* (*also*: **sale by ~**) subasta ▷ *vt* subastar

audible [ˈɔːdɪbl] *adj* audible, que se puede oír

audience [ˈɔːdɪəns] *n* público; (*Radio*) radioescuchas *mpl*; (*TV*) telespectadores *mpl*; (*interview*) audiencia

audit [ˈɔːdɪt] *vt* revisar, intervenir

audition [ɔːˈdɪʃən] *n* audición *f*

auditor [ˈɔːdɪtə*] *n* interventor(a) *m/f*, censor(a) *m/f* de cuentas

auditorium [ɔːdɪˈtɔːrɪəm] *n* auditorio

Aug. *abbr* (= *August*) ag

August [ˈɔːgəst] *n* agosto

aunt [ɑːnt] *n* tía; **auntie** *n diminutive of* **aunt**; **aunty** *n diminutive of* **aunt**

au pair [ˈəuˈpɛə*] *n* (*also*: **~ girl**) (chica) au pair *f*

aura [ˈɔːrə] *n* aura; (*atmosphere*) ambiente *m*

austerity [ɔˈstɛrɪtɪ] *n* austeridad *f*

Australia [ɔsˈtreɪlɪə] *n* Australia; **Australian** *adj, n* australiano/a *m/f*

Austria [ˈɔstrɪə] *n* Austria; **Austrian** *adj, n* austríaco/a *m/f*

authentic [ɔːˈθɛntɪk] *adj* auténtico

author [ˈɔːθə*] *n* autor(a) *m/f*

authority [ɔːˈθɔrɪtɪ] *n* autoridad *f*; (*official permission*) autorización *f*; **the authorities** *npl* las autoridades

authorize [ˈɔːθəraɪz] *vt* autorizar

auto [ˈɔːtəu] (*US*) *n* coche *m* (*SP*), carro (*LAM*), automóvil *m*

auto: autobiography [ɔːtəbaɪˈɔgrəfɪ] *n* autobiografía; **autograph** [ˈɔːtəgrɑːf] *n* autógrafo ▷ *vt* (*photo etc*) dedicar; (*programme*) firmar; **automatic** [ɔːtəˈmætɪk] *adj* automático ▷ *n* (*gun*) pistola automática; (*car*) coche *m* automático; **automatically** *adv* automáticamente; **automobile** [ˈɔːtəməbiːl] (*US*) *n* coche *m* (*SP*), carro (*LAM*), automóvil *m*; **autonomous** [ɔːˈtɔnəməs] *adj* autónomo; **autonomy** [ɔːˈtɔnəmɪ] *n* autonomía

autumn [ˈɔːtəm] *n* otoño

auxiliary [ɔːgˈzɪlɪərɪ] *adj, n* auxiliar *mf*

avail [əˈveɪl] *vt*: **to ~ o.s. of** aprovechar(se) de ▷ *n*: **to no ~** en vano, sin resultado

availability [əveɪləˈbɪlɪtɪ] *n* disponibilidad *f*

available [əˈveɪləbl] *adj* disponible; (*unoccupied*) libre; (*person: unattached*) soltero y sin compromiso

avalanche [ˈævəlɑːnʃ] *n* alud *m*, avalancha

Ave. *abbr* = **avenue**

avenue [ˈævənjuː] *n* avenida; (*fig*) camino

average [ˈævərɪdʒ] *n* promedio, término medio ▷ *adj* medio, de término medio; (*ordinary*) regular, corriente ▷ *vt* sacar un promedio de; **on ~** por regla general

avert [əˈvɜːt] *vt* prevenir; (*blow*) desviar; (*one's eyes*) apartar

avid [ˈævɪd] *adj* ávido

avocado [ævəˈkɑːdəu] *n* (*also BRIT*: **~ pear**) aguacate *m*, palta (*SC*)

avoid [əˈvɔɪd] *vt* evitar, eludir

await [əˈweɪt] *vt* esperar, aguardar

awake [əˈweɪk] (*pt* **awoke**, *pp* **awoken** *or* **awaked**) *adj* despierto ▷ *vt* despertar ▷ *vi* despertarse; **to be ~** estar despierto

award [əˈwɔːd] *n* premio; (*Law: damages*) indemnización *f* ▷ *vt* otorgar, conceder; (*Law: damages*) adjudicar

aware [əˈwɛə*] *adj*: **~ (of)** consciente (de); **to become ~ of/that** (*realize*) darse cuenta de/de que; (*learn*) enterarse de/de que; **awareness** *n* conciencia; (*knowledge*) conocimiento

away [əˈweɪ] *adv* fuera; (*movement*): **she went ~** se marchó; **far ~** lejos; **two kilometres ~** a dos kilómetros de distancia; **two hours ~ by car** a dos horas en coche; **the holiday was two weeks ~** faltaban dos semanas para las vacaciones; **he's ~ for a week** estará ausente una semana; **to take ~ (from)** quitar (a); (*subtract*) substraer (de); **to work/pedal ~** seguir trabajando/pedaleando; **to fade ~** (colour) desvanecerse; (sound) apagarse

awe [ɔ:] n admiración f respetuosa; **awesome** ['ɔ:səm] (us) adj (excellent) formidable

awful ['ɔ:fəl] adj horroroso; (quantity): **an ~ lot (of)** cantidad (de); **awfully** adv (very) terriblemente

awkward ['ɔ:kwəd] adj desmañado, torpe; (shape) incómodo; (embarrassing) delicado, difícil

awoke [ə'wəuk] pt of **awake**

awoken [ə'wəukən] pp of **awake**

axe [æks] (us **ax**) n hacha ▷ vt (project) cortar; (jobs) reducir

axle ['æksl] n eje m, árbol m

ay(e) [aɪ] excl sí

azalea [ə'zeɪlɪə] n azalea

B [bi:] n (Mus) si m

B.A. abbr = **Bachelor of Arts**

baby ['beɪbɪ] n bebé mf; (us: inf: darling) mi amor; **baby carriage** (us) n cochecito; **baby-sit** vi hacer de canguro; **baby-sitter** n canguro/a; **baby wipe** n toallita húmeda (para bebés)

bachelor ['bætʃələ*] n soltero; **B~ of Arts/ Science** licenciado/a en Filosofía y Letras/ Ciencias

back [bæk] n (of person) espalda; (of animal) lomo; (of hand) dorso; (as opposed to front) parte f de atrás; (of chair) respaldo; (of page) reverso; (of book) final m; (Football) defensa m; (of crowd): **the ones at the ~** los del fondo ▷ vt (candidate: also: **~ up**) respaldar, apoyar; (horse: at races) apostar a; (car) dar marcha atrás a or con ▷ vi (car etc) ir (or salir or entrar) marcha atrás ▷ adj (payment, rent) atrasado; (seats, wheels) de atrás ▷ adv (not forward) (hacia) atrás; (returned): **he's ~** está de vuelta, ha vuelto; **he ran ~** volvió corriendo; (restitution): **throw the ball ~** devuelve la pelota; **can I have it ~?** ¿me lo devuelve?; (again): **he called ~** llamó de nuevo; **back down** vi echarse atrás; **back out** vi (of promise) volverse atrás; **back up** vt (person) apoyar, respaldar; (theory) defender; (Comput) hacer una copia preventiva or de reserva; **backache** n dolor m de espalda; **backbencher** (BRIT) n miembro del parlamento sin cargo relevante; **backbone** n columna vertebral; **back door** n puerta f trasera; **backfire** vi (Aut) petardear; (plans) fallar, salir mal; **backgammon** n backgammon m; **background** n fondo; (of events) antecedentes mpl; (basic knowledge) bases fpl; (experience) conocimientos mpl, educación f; **family background** origen m, antecedentes mpl; **backing** n (fig) apoyo, respaldo; **backlog** n: **backlog of work** trabajo atrasado; **backpack** n mochila; **backpacker** n mochilero/a; **backslash** n pleca, barra inversa; **backstage** adv entre bastidores; **backstroke** n espalda; **backup** adj suplementario; (*Comput*) de reserva ▷n (*support*) apoyo; (*also:* **backup file**) copia preventiva or de reserva; **backward** adj (*person, country*) atrasado; **backwards** adv hacia atrás; (*read a list*) al revés; (*fall*) de espaldas; **backyard** n traspatio

bacon ['beɪkən] n tocino, beicon m

bacteria [bæk'tɪərɪə] npl bacterias fpl

bad [bæd] adj malo; (*mistake, accident*) grave; (*food*) podrido, pasado; **his ~ leg** su pierna lisiada; **to go ~** (*food*) pasarse

badge [bædʒ] n insignia; (*policeman's*) chapa, placa

badger ['bædʒə*] n tejón m

badly ['bædlɪ] adv mal; **to reflect ~ on sb** influir negativamente en la reputación de algn; **~ wounded** gravemente herido; **he needs it ~** le hace gran falta; **to be ~ off (for money)** andar mal de dinero

bad-mannered ['bæd'mænəd] adj mal educado

badminton ['bædmɪntən] n bádminton m

bad-tempered ['bæd'tempəd] adj de mal genio or carácter; (*temporarily*) de mal humor

bag [bæg] n bolsa; (*handbag*) bolso; (*satchel*) mochila; (*case*) maleta; **~s of** (*inf*) un montón de; **baggage** n equipaje m; **baggage allowance** n límite m de equipaje; **baggage reclaim** n recogida de equipajes; **baggy** adj amplio; **bagpipes** npl gaita

bail [beɪl] n fianza ▷vt (*prisoner: gen: grant bail to*) poner en libertad bajo fianza; (*boat: also:* **~ out**) achicar; **on ~** (*prisoner*) bajo fianza; **to ~ sb out** obtener la libertad de algn bajo fianza

bait [beɪt] n cebo ▷vt poner cebo en; (*tease*) tomar el pelo a

bake [beɪk] vt cocer (al horno) ▷vi cocerse; **baked beans** npl judías fpl en salsa de tomate; **baked potato** n patata al horno; **baker** n panadero; **bakery** n panadería; (*for cakes*) pastelería; **baking** n (*act*) amasar m; (*batch*) hornada; **baking powder** n levadura (en polvo)

balance ['bæləns] n equilibrio; (*Comm: sum*) balance m; (*remainder*) resto; (*scales*) balanza ▷vt equilibrar; (*budget*) nivelar; (*account*) saldar; (*make equal*) equilibrar; **~ of trade/payments** balanza de comercio/pagos; **balanced** adj (*personality, diet*) equilibrado; (*report*) objetivo; **balance sheet** n balance m

balcony ['bælkənɪ] n (*open*) balcón m; (*closed*) galería; (*in theatre*) anfiteatro

bald [bɔːld] adj calvo; (*tyre*) liso

Balearics [bælɪ'ærɪks] npl: **the ~** las Baleares

ball [bɔːl] n pelota; (*football*) balón m; (*of wool, string*) ovillo; (*dance*) baile m; **to play ~** (*fig*) cooperar

ballerina [bælə'riːnə] n bailarina

ballet ['bæleɪ] n ballet m; **ballet dancer** n bailarín/ina m/f

balloon [bə'luːn] n globo

ballot ['bælət] n votación f

ballpoint (pen) ['bɔːlpɔɪnt-] n bolígrafo

ballroom ['bɔːlrum] n salón m de baile

Baltic ['bɔːltɪk] n: **the ~ (Sea)** el (Mar) Báltico

bamboo [bæm'buː] n bambú m

ban [bæn] n prohibición f, proscripción f ▷vt prohibir, proscribir

banana [bə'nɑːnə] n plátano, banana (*LAM*), banano (*CAM*)

band [bænd] n grupo; (*strip*) faja, tira; (*stripe*) lista; (*Mus: jazz*) orquesta; (: *rock*) grupo; (*Mil*) banda

bandage ['bændɪdʒ] n venda, vendaje m ▷vt vendar

Band-Aid® ['bændeɪd] (*US*) n tirita

bandit ['bændɪt] n bandido

bang [bæŋ] n (*of gun, exhaust*) estallido, detonación f; (*of door*) portazo; (*blow*) golpe m ▷vt (*door*) cerrar de golpe; (*one's head*) golpear ▷vi estallar; (*door*) cerrar de golpe

Bangladesh [bɑːŋɡlə'deʃ] n Bangladesh m

bangle ['bæŋɡl] n brazalete m, ajorca

bangs [bæŋz] (*US*) npl flequillo

banish ['bænɪʃ] vt desterrar

banister(s) ['bænɪstə(z)] n(pl) barandilla, pasamanos m inv

banjo ['bændʒəu] (*pl* **~es** or **~s**) n banjo

bank [bæŋk] n (*Comm*) banco; (*of river, lake*) ribera, orilla; (*of earth*) terraplén m ▷vi (*Aviat*) ladearse; **bank on** vt fus contar con; **bank account** n cuenta de banco; **bank balance** n saldo; **bank card** n tarjeta bancaria; **bank charges** npl comisión fsg; **banker** n banquero; **bank holiday** n (*BRIT*) día m festivo or de fiesta; **banking** n banca; **bank manager** n director(a) m/f (de sucursal) de banco; **banknote** n billete m de banco

● **BANK HOLIDAY**
●
● El término **bank holiday** se aplica en el
● Reino Unido a todo día festivo oficial
● en el que cierran bancos y comercios.

● Los más importantes son en Navidad,
● Semana Santa, finales de mayo y
● finales de agosto y, al contrario que
● en los países de tradición católica, no
● coinciden necesariamente con una
● celebración religiosa.

bankrupt ['bæŋkrʌpt] *adj* quebrado,
insolvente; **to go ~** hacer bancarrota; **to be
~** estar en quiebra; **bankruptcy** *n* quiebra
bank statement *n* balance *m* or detalle
m de cuenta
banner ['bænə*] *n* pancarta
bannister(s) ['bænɪstə(z)] *n(pl)* =
banister(s)
banquet ['bæŋkwɪt] *n* banquete *m*
baptism ['bæptɪzəm] *n* bautismo; *(act)*
bautizo
baptize [bæp'taɪz] *vt* bautizar
bar [ba:*] *n* *(pub)* bar *m*; *(counter)* mostrador
m; *(rod)* barra; *(of window, cage)* reja; *(of soap)*
pastilla; *(of chocolate)* tableta; *(fig: hindrance)*
obstáculo; *(prohibition)* proscripción *f*; *(Mus)*
barra ▷ *vt* *(road)* obstruir; *(person)* excluir;
(activity) prohibir; **the B~** *(Law)* la abogacía;
behind ~s entre rejas; **~ none** sin excepción
barbaric [ba:'bærɪk] *adj* bárbaro
barbecue ['ba:bɪkju:] *n* barbacoa
barbed wire ['ba:bd-] *n* alambre *m* de
púas
barber ['ba:bə*] *n* peluquero, barbero;
barber's (shop) *(US* **barber (shop))** *n*
peluquería
bar code *n* código de barras
bare [bɛə*] *adj* desnudo; *(trees)* sin hojas;
(necessities etc) básico ▷ *vt* desnudar; *(teeth)*
enseñar; **barefoot** *adj, adv* descalzo; **barely**
adv apenas
bargain ['ba:gɪn] *n* pacto, negocio; *(good
buy)* ganga ▷ *vi* negociar; *(haggle)* regatear;
into the ~ además, por añadidura; **bargain
for** *vt fus*: **he got more than he bargained
for** le resultó peor de lo que esperaba
barge [ba:dʒ] *n* barcaza; **barge in**
vi irrumpir; *(interrupt: conversation)*
interrumpir
bark [ba:k] *n* *(of tree)* corteza; *(of dog)*
ladrido ▷ *vi* ladrar
barley ['ba:lɪ] *n* cebada
barmaid ['ba:meɪd] *n* camarera
barman ['ba:mən] *(irreg)* *n* camarero,
barman *m*
barn [ba:n] *n* granero
barometer [bə'rɔmɪtə*] *n* barómetro
baron ['bærən] *n* barón *m*; *(press baron etc)*
magnate *m*; **baroness** *n* baronesa
barracks ['bærəks] *npl* cuartel *m*
barrage ['bæra:ʒ] *n* *(Mil)* descarga,

bombardeo; *(dam)* presa; *(of criticism)* lluvia,
aluvión *m*
barrel ['bærəl] *n* barril *m*; *(of gun)* cañón *m*
barren ['bærən] *adj* estéril
barrette [bə'ret] *(US)* *n* pasador *m* *(LAM,
SP)*, broche *m* *(MEX)*
barricade [bærɪ'keɪd] *n* barricada
barrier ['bærɪə*] *n* barrera
barring ['ba:rɪŋ] *prep* excepto, salvo
barrister ['bærɪstə*] *(BRIT)* *n* abogado/a
barrow ['bærəu] *n* *(cart)* carretilla *(de
mano)*
bartender ['ba:tendə*] *(US)* *n* camarero,
barman *m*
base [beɪs] *n* base *f* ▷ *vt*: **to ~ sth on** basar
or fundar algo en ▷ *adj* bajo, infame
baseball ['beɪsbɔ:l] *n* béisbol *m*; **baseball
cap** *n* gorra *f* de béisbol
basement ['beɪsmənt] *n* sótano
bases¹ ['beɪsi:z] *npl of* **basis**
bases² ['beɪsɪz] *npl of* **base**
bash [bæʃ] *(inf)* *vt* golpear
basic ['beɪsɪk] *adj* básico; **basically** *adv*
fundamentalmente, en el fondo; *(simply)*
sencillamente; **basics** *npl*: **the basics** los
fundamentos
basil ['bæzl] *n* albahaca
basin ['beɪsn] *n* cuenco, tazón *m*; *(Geo)*
cuenca; *(also:* **wash~**) lavabo
basis ['beɪsɪs] *(pl* **bases**) *n* base *f*; **on a
part-time/trial ~** a tiempo parcial/a
prueba
basket ['ba:skɪt] *n* cesta, cesto; canasta;
basketball *n* baloncesto
bass [beɪs] *n* *(Mus: instrument)* bajo; *(double
bass)* contrabajo; *(singer)* bajo
bastard ['ba:stəd] *n* bastardo; *(inf!)* hijo
de puta *(!)*
bat [bæt] *n* *(Zool)* murciélago; *(for ball
games)* palo; *(BRIT: for table tennis)* pala
▷ *vt*: **he didn't ~ an eyelid** ni pestañeó
batch [bætʃ] *n* *(of bread)* hornada; *(of letters
etc)* lote *m*
bath [ba:θ, pl ba:ðz] *n* *(action)* baño;
(bathtub) bañera *(SP)*, tina *(LAM)*, bañadera
(RPL) ▷ *vt* bañar; **to have a ~** bañarse,
tomar un baño; *see also* **baths**
bathe [beɪð] *vi* bañarse ▷ *vt* *(wound)* lavar
bathing ['beɪðɪŋ] *n* el bañarse; **bathing
costume** *(US* **bathing suit)** *n* traje *m* de
baño
bath: **bathrobe** *n* *(man's)* batín *m*;
(woman's) bata; **bathroom** *n* *(cuarto de)*
baño; **baths** [ba:ðz] *npl* *(also:* **swimming
baths)** piscina; **bath towel** *n* toalla de
baño; **bathtub** *n* bañera
baton ['bætən] *n* *(Mus)* batuta; *(Athletics)*
testigo; *(weapon)* porra

batter ['bætə*] *vt* maltratar; (*rain etc*) azotar ▷ *n* masa (para rebozar); **battered** *adj* (*hat, pan*) estropeado

battery ['bætərɪ] *n* (*Aut*) batería; (*of torch*) pila; **battery farming** *n* cría intensiva

battle ['bætl] *n* batalla; (*fig*) lucha ▷ *vi* luchar; **battlefield** *n* campo *m* de batalla

bay [beɪ] *n* (*Geo*) bahía; **B~ of Biscay** ≈ mar Cantábrico; **to hold sb at ~** mantener a algn a raya

bazaar [bə'zɑ:*] *n* bazar *m*; (*fete*) venta con fines benéficos

B. & B. *n abbr* = **bed and breakfast**; (*place*) pensión *f*; (*terms*) cama y desayuno

BBC *n abbr* (= *British Broadcasting Corporation*) cadena de radio y televisión estatal británica

B.C. *adv abbr* (= *before Christ*) a. de C.

○ **KEYWORD**

be [bi:] (*pt* **was, were**, *pp* **been**) *aux vb*
1 (*with present participle: forming continuous tenses*): **what are you doing?** ¿qué estás haciendo?, ¿qué haces?; **they're coming tomorrow** vienen mañana; **I've been waiting for you for hours** llevo horas esperándote
2 (*with pp: forming passives*): ser (*but often replaced by active or reflexive constructions*); **to be murdered** ser asesinado; **the box had been opened** habían abierto la caja; **the thief was nowhere to be seen** no se veía al ladrón por ninguna parte
3 (*in tag questions*): **it was fun, wasn't it?** fue divertido, ¿no? *or* ¿verdad?; **he's good-looking, isn't he?** es guapo, ¿no te parece?; **she's back again, is she?** entonces, ¿ha vuelto?
4 (*+to +infin*): **the house is to be sold** (*necessity*) hay que vender la casa; (*future*) van a vender la casa; **he's not to open it** no tiene que abrirlo ▷ *vb +complement*
1 (*with n or num complement, but see also 3, 4, 5 and impers vb below*): ser; **he's a doctor** es médico; **2 and 2 are 4** 2 y 2 son 4
2 (*with adj complement: expressing permanent or inherent quality*) ser; (: *expressing state seen as temporary or reversible*) estar; **I'm English** soy inglés/esa; **she's tall/pretty** es alta/bonita; **he's young** es joven; **be careful/good/quiet** ten cuidado/pórtate bien/cállate; **I'm tired** estoy cansado/a; **it's dirty** está sucio/a
3 (*of health*) estar; **how are you?** ¿cómo estás?; **he's very ill** está muy enfermo; **I'm better now** ya estoy mejor
4 (*of age*) tener; **how old are you?** ¿cuántos

años tienes?; **I'm sixteen (years old)** tengo dieciséis años
5 (*cost*) costar; ser; **how much was the meal?** ¿cuánto fue *or* costó la comida?; **that'll be £5.75, please** son £5.75, por favor; **this shirt is £17** esta camisa cuesta £17 ▷ *vi* **1** (*exist, occur etc*) existir, haber; **the best singer that ever was** el mejor cantante que existió jamás; **is there a God?** ¿hay un Dios?, ¿existe Dios?; **be that as it may** sea como sea; **so be it** así sea
2 (*referring to place*) estar; **I won't be here tomorrow** no estaré aquí mañana
3 (*referring to movement*): **where have you been?** ¿dónde has estado?
▷ *impers vb* **1** (*referring to time*): **it's 5 o'clock** son las 5; **it's the 28th of April** estamos a 28 de abril
2 (*referring to distance*): **it's 10 km to the village** el pueblo está a 10 km
3 (*referring to the weather*): **it's too hot/cold** hace demasiado calor/frío; **it's windy today** hace viento hoy
4 (*emphatic*): **it's me** soy yo; **it was Maria who paid the bill** fue María la que pagó la cuenta

beach [bi:tʃ] *n* playa ▷ *vt* varar

beacon ['bi:kən] *n* (*lighthouse*) faro; (*marker*) guía

bead [bi:d] *n* cuenta; (*of sweat etc*) gota; **beads** *npl* (*necklace*) collar *m*

beak [bi:k] *n* pico

beam [bi:m] *n* (*Arch*) viga, travesaño; (*of light*) rayo, haz *m* de luz ▷ *vi* brillar; (*smile*) sonreír

bean [bi:n] *n* judía; **runner/broad ~** habichuela/haba; **coffee ~** grano de café; **beansprouts** *npl* brotes *mpl* de soja

bear [beə*] (*pt* **bore**, *pp* **borne**) *n* oso ▷ *vt* (*weight etc*) llevar; (*cost*) pagar; (*responsibility*) tener; (*endure*) soportar, aguantar; (*children*) parir, tener; (*fruit*) dar ▷ *vi*: **to ~ right/left** torcer a la derecha/izquierda

beard [bɪəd] *n* barba

bearer ['beərə*] *n* portador(a) *m/f*

bearing ['beərɪŋ] *n* porte *m*, comportamiento; (*connection*) relación *f*

beast [bi:st] *n* bestia; (*inf*) bruto, salvaje *m*

beat [bi:t] (*pt* **~**, *pp* **beaten**) *n* (*of heart*) latido; (*Mus*) ritmo, compás *m*; (*of policeman*) ronda ▷ *vt* pegar, golpear; (*eggs*) batir; (*defeat: opponent*) vencer, derrotar; (: *record*) sobrepasar ▷ *vi* (*heart*) latir; (*drum*) redoblar; (*rain, wind*) azotar; **off the ~ track** aislado; **to ~ it** (*inf*) largarse; **beat up** *vt* (*attack*) dar una paliza a; **beating** *n* paliza

beautiful ['bju:tɪful] *adj* precioso,

hermoso, bello; **beautifully** adv
maravillosamente

beauty ['bjuːtɪ] n belleza; **beauty parlour**
(us **beauty parlor**) n salón m de belleza;
beauty salon n salón m de belleza; **beauty
spot** n (Tourism) lugar m pintoresco

beaver ['biːvə*] n castor m

became [bɪ'keɪm] pt of **become**

because [bɪ'kɔz] conj porque; **~ of** debido
a, a causa de

beckon ['bɛkən] vt (also: **~ to**) llamar con
señas

become [bɪ'kʌm] (pt **became**, pp **~**)
vt (suit) favorecer, sentar bien a ▷ vi (+
n) hacerse, llegar a ser; (+ adj) ponerse,
volverse; **to ~ fat** engordar

bed [bɛd] n cama; (of flowers) macizo; (of
coal, clay) capa; (of river) lecho; (of sea) fondo;
to go to ~ acostarse; **bed and breakfast** n
(place) pensión f; (terms) cama y desayuno;
bedclothes npl ropa de cama; **bedding**
n ropa de cama; **bed linen** n (BRIT) ropa f
de cama

● **BED AND BREAKFAST**
●
● Se llama **bed and breakfast** a una forma
● de alojamiento, en el campo o la ciudad,
● que ofrece cama y desayuno a precios
● inferiores a los de un hotel. El servicio
● se suele anunciar con carteles en los
● que a menudo se usa únicamente la
● abreviatura **B. & B.**

bed: bedroom n dormitorio; **bedside** n: **at
the bedside of** a la cabecera de; **bedside
lamp** n lámpara de noche; **bedside
table** n mesilla de noche; **bedsit(ter)**
(BRIT) n cuarto de alquiler; **bedspread** n
cubrecama m, colcha; **bedtime** n hora de
acostarse

bee [biː] n abeja

beech [biːtʃ] n haya

beef [biːf] n carne f de vaca; **roast ~** rosbif
m; **beefburger** n hamburguesa; **Beefeater**
n alabardero de la Torre de Londres

been [biːn] pp of **be**

beer [bɪə*] n cerveza; **beer garden** n
(BRIT) terraza f de verano, jardín m (de un
bar)

beet [biːt] (us) n (also: **red ~**) remolacha

beetle ['biːtl] n escarabajo

beetroot ['biːtruːt] (BRIT) n remolacha

before [bɪ'fɔː*] prep (of time) antes de;
(of space) delante de ▷ conj antes (de)
que ▷ adv antes, anteriormente; delante,
adelante; **~ going** antes de marcharse; **~
she goes** antes de que se vaya; **the week**

~ la semana anterior; I've never seen it ~
no lo he visto nunca; **beforehand** adv de
antemano, con anticipación

beg [bɛg] vi pedir limosna ▷ vt pedir,
rogar; (entreat) suplicar; **to ~ sb to do sth**
rogar a algn que haga algo; see also **pardon**

began [bɪ'gæn] pt of **begin**

beggar ['bɛgə*] n mendigo/a

begin [bɪ'gɪn] (pt **began**, pp **begun**) vt,
vi empezar, comenzar; **to ~ doing** or **to
do sth** empezar a hacer algo; **beginner** n
principiante mf; **beginning** n principio,
comienzo

begun [bɪ'gʌn] pp of **begin**

behalf [bɪ'hɑːf] n: **on ~ of** en nombre de,
por; (for benefit of) en beneficio de; **on my/
his ~** por mí/él

behave [bɪ'heɪv] vi (person) portarse,
comportarse; (well: also: **~ o.s.**) portarse
bien; **behaviour** (us **behavior**) n
comportamiento, conducta

behind [bɪ'haɪnd] prep detrás de;
(supporting): **to be ~ sb** apoyar a algn ▷ adv
detrás, por detrás, atrás ▷ n trasero; **to be
~ (schedule)** ir retrasado; **~ the scenes** (fig)
entre bastidores

beige [beɪʒ] adj color beige

Beijing ['beɪ'dʒɪŋ] n Pekín m

being ['biːɪŋ] n ser m; (existence): **in ~**
existente; **to come into ~** aparecer

belated [bɪ'leɪtɪd] adj atrasado, tardío

belch [bɛltʃ] vi eructar ▷ vt (gen: **belch
out**: smoke etc) arrojar

Belgian ['bɛldʒən] adj, n belga mf

Belgium ['bɛldʒəm] n Bélgica

belief [bɪ'liːf] n opinión f; (faith) fe f

believe [bɪ'liːv] vt, vi creer; **to ~ in** creer
en; **believer** n partidario/a; (Rel) creyente
mf, fiel mf

bell [bɛl] n campana; (small) campanilla;
(on door) timbre m

bellboy ['bɛlbɔɪ] (BRIT) n botones m inv

bellhop ['bɛlhɔp] (us) n = **bellboy**

bellow ['bɛləu] vi bramar; (person) rugir

bell pepper n (esp us) pimiento, pimentón
m (LAM)

belly ['bɛlɪ] n barriga, panza; **belly button**
(inf) n ombligo

belong [bɪ'lɔŋ] vi: **to ~ to** pertenecer a;
(club etc) ser socio de; **this book ~s here** este
libro va aquí; **belongings** npl pertenencias
fpl

beloved [bɪ'lʌvɪd] adj querido/a

below [bɪ'ləu] prep bajo, debajo de; (less
than) inferior a ▷ adv abajo, (por) debajo;
see ~ véase más abajo

belt [bɛlt] n cinturón m; (Tech) correa, cinta
▷ vt (thrash) pegar con correa; **beltway** (us)

n (Aut) carretera de circunvalación
bemused [bɪˈmjuːzd] adj perplejo
bench [bentʃ] n banco; (BRIT Pol): **the Government/Opposition ~es** (los asientos de) los miembros del Gobierno/ de la Oposición; **the B~** (Law: judges) magistratura
bend [bend] (pt, pp **bent**) vt doblar ▷ vi inclinarse ▷ n (BRIT: in road, river) curva; (in pipe) codo; **bend down** vi inclinarse, doblarse; **bend over** vi inclinarse
beneath [bɪˈniːθ] prep bajo, debajo de; (unworthy) indigno de ▷ adv abajo, (por) debajo
beneficial [benɪˈfɪʃəl] adj beneficioso
benefit [ˈbenɪfɪt] n beneficio; (allowance of money) subsidio ▷ vt beneficiar ▷ vi: **he'll ~ from it** le sacará provecho
benign [bɪˈnaɪn] adj benigno; (smile) afable
bent [bent] pt, pp of **bend** ▷ n inclinación f ▷ adj: **to be ~ on** estar empeñado en
bereaved [bɪˈriːvd] npl: **the ~** los íntimos de una persona afligidos por su muerte
beret [ˈbereɪ] n boina
Berlin [bɜːˈlɪn] n Berlín
Bermuda [bɜːˈmjuːdə] n las Bermudas
berry [ˈberɪ] n baya
berth [bɜːθ] n (bed) litera; (cabin) camarote m; (for ship) amarradero ▷ vi atracar, amarrar
beside [bɪˈsaɪd] prep junto a, al lado de; **to be ~ o.s. with anger** estar fuera de sí; **that's ~ the point** eso no tiene nada que ver; **besides** adv además ▷ prep además de
best [best] adj (el/la) mejor ▷ adv (lo) mejor; **the ~ part of** (quantity) la mayor parte de; **at ~** en el mejor de los casos; **to make the ~ of sth** sacar el mejor partido de algo; **to do one's ~** hacer todo lo posible; **to the ~ of my knowledge** que yo sepa; **to the ~ of my ability** como mejor puedo; **best-before date** n fecha de consumo preferente; **best man** (irreg) n padrino de boda; **bestseller** n éxito de librería, bestseller m
bet [bet] (pt, pp **~** or **-ted**) n apuesta ▷ vt: **to ~ money on** apostar dinero por ▷ vi apostar; **to ~ sb sth** apostar algo a algn
betray [bɪˈtreɪ] vt traicionar; (trust) faltar a
better [ˈbetə*] adj, adv mejor ▷ vt superar ▷ n: **to get the ~ of** quedar por encima de algn; **you had ~ do it** más vale que lo hagas; **he thought ~ of it** cambió de parecer; **to get ~** (Med) mejorar(se)
betting [ˈbetɪŋ] n juego, el apostar; **betting shop** (BRIT) n agencia de apuestas
between [bɪˈtwiːn] prep entre ▷ adv

(time) mientras tanto; (place) en medio
beverage [ˈbevərɪdʒ] n bebida
beware [bɪˈweə*] vi: **to ~ (of)** tener cuidado (con); **"~ of the dog"** "perro peligroso"
bewildered [bɪˈwɪldəd] adj aturdido, perplejo
beyond [bɪˈjɒnd] prep más allá de; (past: understanding) fuera de; (after: date) después de, más allá de; (above) superior a ▷ adv (in space) más allá; (in time) posteriormente; **~ doubt** fuera de toda duda; **~ repair** irreparable
bias [ˈbaɪəs] n (prejudice) prejuicio, pasión f; (preference) predisposición f; **bias(s)ed** adj parcial
bib [bɪb] n babero
Bible [ˈbaɪbl] n Biblia
bicarbonate of soda [baɪˈkɑːbənɪt-] n bicarbonato sódico
biceps [ˈbaɪseps] n bíceps m
bicycle [ˈbaɪsɪkl] n bicicleta; **bicycle pump** n bomba de bicicleta
bid [bɪd] (pt **bade** or **~**, pp **bidden** or **~**) n oferta, postura; (in tender) licitación f; (attempt) tentativa, conato ▷ vi hacer una oferta ▷ vt (offer) ofrecer; **to ~ sb good day** dar a algn los buenos días; **bidder** n: **the highest bidder** el mejor postor
bidet [ˈbiːdeɪ] n bidet m
big [bɪg] adj grande; (brother, sister) mayor; **bigheaded** adj engreído; **big toe** n dedo gordo (del pie)
bike [baɪk] n bici f; **bike lane** n carril-bici m
bikini [bɪˈkiːnɪ] n bikini m
bilateral [baɪˈlætərl] adj (agreement) bilateral
bilingual [baɪˈlɪŋgwəl] adj bilingüe
bill [bɪl] n cuenta; (invoice) factura; (Pol) proyecto de ley; (US: banknote) billete m; (of bird) pico; (of show) programa m; **"post no ~s"** "prohibido fijar carteles"; **to fit** or **fill the ~** (fig) cumplir con los requisitos; **billboard** (US) n cartelera; **billfold** [ˈbɪlfəuld] (US) n cartera
billiards [ˈbɪljədz] n billar m
billion [ˈbɪljən] n (BRIT) billón m (millón de millones); (US) mil millones mpl
bin [bɪn] n (for rubbish) cubo or bote m (MEX) or tacho (SC) de la basura; (container) recipiente m
bind [baɪnd] (pt, pp **bound**) vt atar; (book) encuadernar; (oblige) obligar ▷ n (inf: nuisance) lata
binge [bɪndʒ] (inf) n: **to go on a ~** ir de juerga
bingo [ˈbɪŋgəu] n bingo m

binoculars [bɪˈnɔkjuləz] npl prismáticos mpl
bio... [baɪə'] prefix: **biochemistry** n bioquímica; **biodegradable** [baɪə udɪ'greɪdəbl] adj biodegradable; **biography** [baɪˈɔgrəfɪ] n biografía; **biological** adj biológico; **biology** [baɪˈɔlədʒɪ] n biología; **biometric** [baɪəˈmɛtrɪk] adj biométrico
birch [bəːtʃ] n (tree) abedul m
bird [bəːd] n ave f, pájaro; (BRIT: inf: girl) chica; **bird flu** n gripe f aviar; **bird of prey** n ave f de presa; **birdwatching** n: he likes to go birdwatching on Sundays los domingos le gusta ir a ver pájaros
Biro® [ˈbaɪrəu] n boli
birth [bəːθ] n nacimiento; **to give ~ to** parir, dar a luz; **birth certificate** n partida de nacimiento; **birth control** n (policy) control m de natalidad; (methods) métodos mpl anticonceptivos; **birthday** n cumpleaños m inv ▷ cpd (cake, card etc) de cumpleaños; **birthmark** n antojo, marca de nacimiento; **birthplace** n lugar m de nacimiento
biscuit [ˈbɪskɪt] (BRIT) n galleta
bishop [ˈbɪʃəp] n obispo; (Chess) alfil m
bistro [ˈbiːstrəu] n café-bar m
bit [bɪt] pt of **bite** ▷ n trozo, pedazo, pedacito; (Comput) bit m, bitio; (for horse) freno, bocado; **a ~ of** un poco de; **a ~ mad** un poco loco; **~ by ~** poco a poco
bitch [bɪtʃ] n perra; (infl: woman) zorra (!)
bite [baɪt] (pt **bit**, pp **bitten**) vt, vi morder; (insect etc) picar ▷ n (insect bite) picadura; (mouthful) bocado; **to ~ one's nails** comerse las uñas; **let's have a ~ (to eat)** (inf) vamos a comer algo
bitten [ˈbɪtn] pp of **bite**
bitter [ˈbɪtə*] adj amargo; (wind) cortante, penetrante; (battle) encarnizado ▷ n (BRIT: beer) cerveza típica británica a base de lúpulos
bizarre [bɪˈzɑː*] adj raro, extraño
black [blæk] adj negro; (tea, coffee) solo ▷ n color m negro; (person): **B~** negro/a ▷ vt (BRIT Industry) boicotear; **to give sb a ~ eye** ponerle a algn el ojo morado; **~ and blue** (bruised) amoratado; **to be in the ~** (bank account) estar en números negros; **black out** vi (faint) desmayarse; **blackberry** n zarzamora; **blackbird** n mirlo; **blackboard** n pizarra; **black coffee** n café m solo; **blackcurrant** n grosella negra; **black ice** n hielo invisible en la carretera; **blackmail** n chantaje m ▷ vt chantajear; **black market** n mercado negro; **blackout** n (Mil) oscurecimiento; (power cut) apagón

m; (TV, Radio) interrupción f de programas; (fainting) desvanecimiento; **black pepper** n pimienta f negra; **black pudding** n morcilla; **Black Sea** n: **the Black Sea** el Mar Negro
bladder [ˈblædə*] n vejiga
blade [bleɪd] n hoja; (of propeller) paleta; **a ~ of grass** una brizna de hierba
blame [bleɪm] n culpa ▷ vt: **to ~ sb for sth** echar la culpa de algo; **to be to ~ (for)** tener la culpa (de)
bland [blænd] adj (music, taste) soso
blank [blæŋk] adj en blanco; (look) sin expresión ▷ n (of memory): **my mind is a ~** no puedo recordar nada; (on form) blanco, espacio en blanco; (cartridge) cartucho sin bala or de fogueo
blanket [ˈblæŋkɪt] n manta (sp), cobija (LAM); (of snow) capa; (of fog) manto
blast [blɑːst] n (of wind) ráfaga, soplo; (of explosive) explosión f ▷ vt (blow up) volar
blatant [ˈbleɪtənt] adj descarado
blaze [bleɪz] n (fire) fuego; (fig: of colour) despliegue m; (: of glory) esplendor m ▷ vi arder en llamas; (fig) brillar ▷ vt: **to ~ a trail** (fig) abrir (un) camino; **in a ~ of publicity** con gran publicidad
blazer [ˈbleɪzə*] n chaqueta de uniforme de colegial o de socio de club
bleach [bliːtʃ] n (also: **household ~**) lejía ▷ vt blanquear; **bleachers** (us) npl (Sport) gradas fpl al sol
bleak [bliːk] adj (countryside) desierto; (prospect) poco prometedor(a); (weather) crudo; (smile) triste
bled [blɛd] pt, pp of **bleed**
bleed [bliːd] (pt, pp **bled**) vt, vi sangrar; **my nose is ~ing** me está sangrando la nariz
blemish [ˈblɛmɪʃ] n marca, mancha; (on reputation) tacha
blend [blɛnd] n mezcla ▷ vt mezclar; (colours etc) combinar, mezclar ▷ vi (colours etc: also: **~ in**) combinarse, mezclarse; **blender** n (Culin) batidora
bless [blɛs] (pt, pp **~ed** or **blest**) vt bendecir; **~ you!** (after sneeze) ¡Jesús!; **blessing** n (approval) aprobación f; (godsend) don m del cielo, bendición f; (advantage) beneficio, ventaja
blew [bluː] pt of **blow**
blight [blaɪt] vt (hopes etc) frustrar, arruinar
blind [blaɪnd] adj ciego; (fig): **~ (to)** ciego (a) ▷ n (for window) persiana ▷ vt cegar; (dazzle) deslumbrar; (deceive): **to ~ sb to ...** cegar a algn a ...; **the blind** npl los ciegos; **blind alley** n callejón m sin salida; **blindfold** n venda ▷ adv con los ojos

vendados ▷vt vendar los ojos a
blink [blɪŋk] vi parpadear, pestañear;
(light) oscilar
bliss [blɪs] n felicidad f
blister ['blɪstə*] n ampolla ▷vi (paint)
ampollarse
blizzard ['blɪzəd] n ventisca
bloated ['bləʊtɪd] adj hinchado;
(person: full) ahíto
blob [blɔb] n (drop) gota; (indistinct object)
bulto
block [blɔk] n bloque m; (in pipes)
obstáculo; (of buildings) manzana (SP),
cuadra (LAM) ▷vt obstruir, cerrar; (progress)
estorbar; **~ of flats** (BRIT) bloque m de pisos;
mental ~ bloqueo mental; **block up** vt
tapar, obstruir; (pipe) atascar; **blockade**
[-'keɪd] n bloqueo ▷vt bloquear; **blockage**
n estorbo, obstrucción f; **blockbuster** n
(book) bestseller m; (film) éxito de público;
block capitals npl mayúsculas fpl; **block
letters** npl mayúsculas fpl
blog [blɔg] n blog m
bloke [bləʊk] (BRIT: inf) n tipo, tío
blond(e) [blɔnd] adj, n rubio/a m/f
blood [blʌd] n sangre f; **blood donor**
n donante mf de sangre; **blood group**
n grupo sanguíneo; **blood poisoning**
n envenenamiento de la sangre; **blood
pressure** n presión f sanguínea;
bloodshed n derramamiento de sangre;
bloodshot adj inyectado en sangre;
bloodstream n corriente f sanguínea;
blood test n análisis m inv de sangre;
blood transfusion n transfusión f de
sangre; **blood type** n grupo sanguíneo;
blood vessel n vaso sanguíneo; **bloody**
adj sangriento; (fig: inf!) lleno de sangre;
(BRIT: inf!): **this bloody ...** este condenado o
puñetero ... (!) ▷adv: **bloody strong/good**
(BRIT: inf!) terriblemente fuerte/bueno
bloom [bluːm] n flor f ▷vi florecer
blossom ['blɔsəm] n flor f ▷vi florecer
blot [blɔt] n borrón m; (fig) mancha ▷vt
(stain) manchar
blouse [blauz] n blusa
blow [bləʊ] (pt blew, pp blown) n golpe
m; (with sword) espadazo ▷vi soplar; (dust,
sand etc) volar; (fuse) fundirse ▷vt (wind)
llevarse; (fuse) quemar; (instrument) tocar;
to ~ one's nose sonarse; **blow away** vt
llevarse, arrancar; **blow out** vi apagarse;
blow up vi estallar ▷vt volar; (tyre) inflar;
(Phot) ampliar; **blow-dry** n moldeado (con
secador)
blown [bləʊn] pp of **blow**
blue [bluː] adj azul; (depressed) deprimido;
~ film/joke película/chiste m verde;

out of the ~ (fig) de repente; **bluebell** n
campanilla, campánula azul; **blueberry**
n arándano; **blue cheese** n queso azul;
blues npl: **the blues** (Mus) el blues; **to have
the blues** estar triste; **bluetit** n herrerillo
m (común)
bluff [blʌf] vi tirarse un farol, farolear ▷n
farol m; **to call sb's ~** coger a algn la palabra
blunder ['blʌndə*] n patinazo, metedura
de pata ▷vi cometer un error, meter la pata
blunt [blʌnt] adj (pencil) despuntado;
(knife) desafilado, romo; (person) franco,
directo
blur [bləː*] n (shape): **to become a ~**
hacerse borroso ▷vt (vision) enturbiar;
(distinction) borrar; **blurred** adj borroso
blush [blʌʃ] vi ruborizarse, ponerse
colorado ▷n rubor m; **blusher** n colorete
m
board [bɔːd] n (cardboard) cartón m;
(wooden) tabla, tablero; (on wall) tablón
m; (for chess etc) tablero; (committee)
junta, consejo; (in firm) mesa or junta
directiva; (Naut, Aviat): **on ~** a bordo ▷vt
(ship) embarcarse en; (train) subir a; **full
~** (BRIT) pensión completa; **half ~** (BRIT)
media pensión; **to go by the ~** (fig) ser
abandonado or olvidado; **board game** n
juego de tablero; **boarding card** (BRIT) n
tarjeta de embarque; **boarding pass** (US)
n = **boarding card**; **boarding school** n
internado; **board room** n sala de juntas
boast [bəʊst] vi: **to ~ (about or of)** alardear
(de)
boat [bəʊt] n barco, buque m; (small)
barca, bote m
bob [bɔb] vi (also: **~ up and down**)
menearse, balancearse
bobby pin ['bɔbɪ-] (US) n horquilla
body ['bɔdɪ] n cuerpo; (corpse) cadáver m;
(of car) caja, carrocería; (fig: group) grupo;
(: organization) organismo; **body-building** n
culturismo; **bodyguard** n guardaespaldas
m inv; **bodywork** n carrocería
bog [bɔg] n pantano, ciénaga ▷vt: **to get
~ged down** (fig) empantanarse, atascarse
bogus ['bəʊgəs] adj falso, fraudulento
boil [bɔɪl] vt (water) hervir; (eggs) pasar
por agua, cocer ▷vi hervir; (fig: with anger)
estar furioso; (: with heat) asfixiarse ▷n
(Med) furúnculo, divieso; **to come to the
~, to come to a ~** (US) comenzar a hervir;
to ~ down to (fig) reducirse a; **boil over** vi
salirse, rebosar; (anger etc) llegar al colmo;
boiled egg n (soft) huevo tibio (MEX) or
pasado por agua o a la copa (SC); (hard)
huevo duro; **boiled potatoes** npl patatas
fpl (SP) or papas fpl (LAM) cocidas; **boiler** n

caldera; **boiling** ['bɔɪlɪŋ] *adj*: **I'm boiling (hot)** (*inf*) estoy asado; **boiling point** *n* punto de ebullición

bold [bəʊld] *adj* valiente, audaz; (*pej*) descarado; (*colour*) llamativo

Bolivia [bə'lɪvɪə] *n* Bolivia; **Bolivian** *adj, n* boliviano/a *m/f*

bollard ['bɒləd] (*BRIT*) *n* (*Aut*) poste *m*

bolt [bəʊlt] *n* (*lock*) cerrojo; (*with nut*) perno, tornillo ▷ *adv*: **~ upright** rígido, erguido ▷ *vt* (*door*) echar el cerrojo a; (*also*: **~ together**) sujetar con tornillos; (*food*) engullir ▷ *vi* fugarse; (*horse*) desbocarse

bomb [bɒm] *n* bomba ▷ *vt* bombardear; **bombard** [bɒm'bɑːd] *vt* bombardear; (*fig*) asediar; **bomber** *n* (*Aviat*) bombardero; **bomb scare** *n* amenaza de bomba

bond [bɒnd] *n* (*promise*) fianza; (*Finance*) bono; (*link*) vínculo, lazo; (*Comm*): **in ~** en depósito bajo fianza; **bonds** *npl* (*chains*) cadenas *fpl*

bone [bəʊn] *n* hueso; (*of fish*) espina ▷ *vt* deshuesar; quitar las espinas a

bonfire ['bɒnfaɪə*] *n* hoguera, fogata

bonnet ['bɒnɪt] *n* gorra; (*BRIT*: *of car*) capó *m*

bonus ['bəʊnəs] *n* (*payment*) paga extraordinaria, plus *m*; (*fig*) bendición *f*

boo [buː] *excl* ¡uh! ▷ *vt* abuchear, rechiflar

book [bʊk] *n* libro; (*of tickets*) taco; (*of stamps etc*) librito ▷ *vt* (*ticket*) sacar; (*seat, room*) reservar; **books** *npl* (*Comm*) cuentas *fpl*, contabilidad *f*; **book in** *vi* (*at hotel*) registrarse; **book up** *vt*: **to be booked up** (*hotel*) estar completo; **bookcase** *n* librería, estante *m* para libros; **booking** *n* reserva; **booking office** *n* (*BRIT Rail*) despacho de billetes (*SP*) or boletos (*LAM*); (*Theatre*) taquilla (*SP*), boletería (*LAM*); **book-keeping** *n* contabilidad *f*; **booklet** *n* folleto; **bookmaker** *n* corredor *m* de apuestas; **bookmark** *n* (*also Comput*) marcador; **bookseller** *n* librero; **bookshelf** *n* estante *m* (para libros); **bookshop, book store** *n* librería

boom [buːm] *n* (*noise*) trueno, estampido; (*in prices etc*) alza rápida; (*Econ, in population*) boom *m* ▷ *vi* (*cannon*) hacer gran estruendo, retumbar; (*Econ*) estar en alza

boost [buːst] *n* estímulo, empuje *m* ▷ *vt* estimular, empujar

boot [buːt] *n* bota; (*BRIT*: *of car*) maleta, maletero ▷ *vt* (*Comput*) arrancar; **to ~** (*in addition*) además, por añadidura

booth [buːð] *n* (*telephone booth, voting booth*) cabina

booze [buːz] (*inf*) *n* bebida

border ['bɔːdə*] *n* borde *m*, margen *m*; (*of a*

country) frontera; (*for flowers*) arriate *m* ▷ *vt* (*road*) bordear; (*another country*: *also*: **~ on**) lindar con; **borderline** *n*: **on the borderline** en el límite

bore [bɔː*] *pt of* **bear** ▷ *vt* (*hole*) hacer un agujero en; (*well*) perforar; (*person*) aburrir ▷ *n* (*person*) pelmazo, pesado; (*of gun*) calibre *m*; **bored** *adj* aburrido; **he's bored to tears** *or* **to death** *or* **stiff** está aburrido como una ostra, está muerto de aburrimiento; **boredom** *n* aburrimiento

boring ['bɔːrɪŋ] *adj* aburrido

born [bɔːn] *adj*: **to be ~** nacer; **I was ~ in 1960** nací en 1960

borne [bɔːn] *pp of* **bear**

borough ['bʌrə] *n* municipio

borrow ['bɒrəʊ] *vt*: **to ~ sth (from sb)** tomar algo prestado (a algn)

Bosnia(-Herzegovina) ['bɒzˈnɪə(hɜːzəˈgəʊviːnə)] *n* Bosnia(-Herzegovina); **Bosnian** ['bɒznɪən] *adj, n* bosnio/a

bosom ['bʊzəm] *n* pecho

boss [bɒs] *n* jefe *m* ▷ *vt* (*also*: **~ about or around**) mangonear; **bossy** *adj* mandón/ona

both [bəʊθ] *adj, pron* ambos/as, los dos (las dos); **~ of us went, we ~ went** fuimos los dos, ambos fuimos ▷ *adv*: **~ A and B** tanto A como B

bother ['bɒðə*] *vt* (*worry*) preocupar; (*disturb*) molestar, fastidiar ▷ *vi* (*also*: **~ o.s.**) molestarse ▷ *n* (*trouble*) dificultad *f*; (*nuisance*) molestia, lata; **to ~ doing** tomarse la molestia de hacer

bottle ['bɒtl] *n* botella; (*small*) frasco; (*baby's*) biberón *m* ▷ *vt* embotellar; **bottle bank** *n* contenedor *m* de vidrio; **bottle-opener** *n* abrebotellas *m inv*

bottom ['bɒtəm] *n* (*of box, sea*) fondo; (*buttocks*) trasero, culo; (*of page*) pie *m*; (*of list*) final *m*; (*of class*) último/a ▷ *adj* (*lowest*) más bajo; (*last*) último

bought [bɔːt] *pt, pp of* **buy**

boulder ['bəʊldə*] *n* canto rodado

bounce [baʊns] *vi* (*ball*) (re)botar; (*cheque*) ser rechazado ▷ *vt* hacer (re)botar ▷ *n* (*rebound*) (re)bote *m*; **bouncer** (*inf*) *n* gorila *m* (*que echa a los alborotadores de un bar, club etc*)

bound [baʊnd] *pt, pp of* **bind** ▷ *n* (*leap*) salto; (*gen pl*: *limit*) límite *m* ▷ *vi* (*leap*) saltar ▷ *vt* (*border*) rodear ▷ *adj*: **~ by** rodeado de; **to be ~ to do sth** (*obliged*) tener el deber de hacer algo; **he's ~ to come** es seguro que vendrá; **out of ~s** prohibido el paso; **~ for** con destino a

boundary ['baʊndrɪ] *n* límite *m*

bouquet ['buːkeɪ] n (of flowers) ramo
bourbon ['buǝbǝn] (US) n (also: ~
whiskey) whisky m americano, bourbon m
bout [baut] n (of malaria etc) ataque m; (of
activity) período; (Boxing etc) combate m,
encuentro
boutique [buː'tiːk] n boutique f, tienda
de ropa
bow¹ [bǝu] n (knot) lazo; (weapon, Mus) arco
bow² [bau] n (of the head) reverencia;
(Naut: also: ~s) proa ▷vi inclinarse, hacer
una reverencia
bowels [bauǝlz] npl intestinos mpl,
vientre m; (fig) entrañas fpl
bowl [bǝul] n tazón m, cuenco; (ball) bola
▷vi (Cricket) arrojar la pelota; see also **bowls**;
bowler n (Cricket) lanzador m (de la pelota);
(BRIT: also: **bowler hat**) hongo, bombín m;
bowling n (game) bochas fpl, bolos mpl;
bowling alley n bolera; **bowling green**
n pista para bochas; **bowls** n juego de las
bochas, bolos mpl
bow tie ['bǝu-] n corbata de lazo, pajarita
box [bɔks] n (also: **cardboard ~**) caja,
cajón m; (Theatre) palco ▷vt encajonar ▷vi
(Sport) boxear; **boxer** n ['bɔksǝ*] n (person)
boxeador m; **boxer shorts** ['bɔksǝfɔːts]
pl n bóxers; **a pair of boxer shorts** unos
bóxers; **boxing** ['bɔksɪn] n (Sport) boxeo;
Boxing Day (BRIT) n día en que se dan los
aguinaldos, 26 de diciembre; **boxing gloves**
npl guantes mpl de boxeo; **boxing ring**
n ring m, cuadrilátero; **box office** n taquilla
(SP), boletería (LAM)
boy [bɔɪ] n (young) niño; (older) muchacho,
chico; (son) hijo; **boy band** n boy band m
(grupo musical de chicos)
boycott ['bɔɪkɔt] n boicot m ▷vt
boicotear
boyfriend ['bɔɪfrɛnd] n novio
bra [braː] n sostén m, sujetador m
brace [breɪs] n (BRIT: also: ~s: on teeth)
corrector m, aparato; (tool) berbiquí m ▷vt
(knees, shoulders) tensionar; **braces** npl
(BRIT) tirantes mpl; **to ~ o.s.** (fig) prepararse
bracelet ['breɪslɪt] n pulsera, brazalete m
bracket ['brækɪt] n (Tech) soporte m,
puntal m; (group) clase f, categoría; (also:
brace ~) soporte m, abrazadera; (also: **round
~**) paréntesis m inv; (also: **square ~**) corchete
m ▷vt (word etc) poner entre paréntesis
brag [bræg] vi jactarse
braid [breɪd] n (trimming) galón m; (of hair)
trenza
brain [breɪn] n cerebro; **brains** npl sesos
mpl; **she's got ~s** es muy lista
braise [breɪz] vt cocer a fuego lento
brake [breɪk] n (on vehicle) freno ▷vi

frenar; **brake light** n luz f de frenado
bran [bræn] n salvado
branch [braːntʃ] n rama; (Comm) sucursal
f; **branch off** vi: **a small road branches off
to the right** hay una carretera pequeña que
sale hacia la derecha; **branch out** vi (fig)
extenderse
brand [brænd] n marca; (fig: type) tipo ▷vt
(cattle) marcar con hierro candente; **brand
name** n marca; **brand-new** adj flamante,
completamente nuevo
brandy ['brændɪ] n coñac m
brash [bræʃ] adj descarado
brass [braːs] n latón m; **the ~** (Mus) los
cobres; **brass band** n banda de metal
brat [bræt] (pej) n mocoso/a
brave [breɪv] adj valiente, valeroso ▷vt
(face up to) desafiar; **bravery** n valor m,
valentía
brawl [brɔːl] n pelea, reyerta
Brazil [brǝ'zɪl] n (el) Brasil; **Brazilian** adj, n
brasileño/a m/f
breach [briːtʃ] vt abrir brecha en ▷n (gap)
brecha; (breaking): **~ of contract** infracción
f de contrato; **~ of the peace** perturbación f
del órden público
bread [brɛd] n pan m; **breadbin** n panera;
breadbox (US) n panera; **breadcrumbs** npl
migajas fpl; (Culin) pan rallado
breadth [brɛtθ] n anchura; (fig) amplitud f
break [breɪk] (pt broke, pp broken) vt
romper; (promise) faltar a; (law) violar,
infringir; (record) batir ▷vi romperse,
quebrarse; (storm) estallar; (weather)
cambiar; (dawn) despuntar; (news etc) darse
a conocer ▷n (gap) abertura; (fracture)
fractura; (time) intervalo; (: at school)
(período de) recreo; (chance) oportunidad f;
to ~ the news to sb comunicar la noticia a
algn; **break down** vt (figures, data) analizar,
descomponer ▷vi (machine) estropearse;
(Aut) averiarse; (person) romper a llorar;
(talks) fracasar; **break in** vt (horse etc)
domar ▷vi (burglar) forzar una entrada;
(interrupt) interrumpir; **break into** vt
fus (house) forzar; **break off** vi (speaker)
pararse, detenerse; (branch) partir; **break
out** vi estallar; (prisoner) escaparse; **to
break out in spots** salirle a algn granos;
break up vi (ship) hacerse pedazos; (crowd,
meeting) disolverse; (marriage) deshacerse;
(Scol) terminar (el curso); (line) cortarse ▷vt
(rocks etc) partir; (journey) partir; (fight etc)
acabar con; **the line's** or **you're breaking
up** se corta; **breakdown** n (Aut) avería; (in
communications) interrupción f; (Med: also:
nervous breakdown) colapso, crisis f
nerviosa; (of marriage, talks) fracaso; (of

statistics) análisis *m inv*; **breakdown truck, breakdown van** *n* (camión *m*) grúa

breakfast ['brɛkfəst] *n* desayuno

break: break-in *n* robo con allanamiento de morada; **breakthrough** *n* (*also fig*) avance *m*

breast [brɛst] *n* (*of woman*) pecho, seno; (*chest*) pecho; (*of bird*) pechuga; **breast-feed** (*pt, pp* **breast-fed**) *vt, vi* amamantar, criar a los pechos; **breast-stroke** *n* braza (de pecho)

breath [brɛθ] *n* aliento, respiración *f*; **to take a deep ~** respirar hondo; **out of ~** sin aliento, sofocado

Breathalyser® ['brɛθəlaɪzə*] (*BRIT*) *n* alcoholímetro

breathe [briːð] *vt, vi* respirar; **breathe in** *vt, vi* aspirar; **breathe out** *vt, vi* espirar; **breathing** *n* respiración *f*

breath: breathless *adj* sin aliento, jadeante; **breathtaking** *adj* imponente, pasmoso; **breath test** *n* prueba de la alcoholemia

bred [brɛd] *pt, pp* *of* **breed**

breed [briːd] (*pt, pp* **bred**) *vt* criar ▷ *vi* reproducirse, procrear ▷ *n* (*Zool*) raza, casta; (*type*) tipo

breeze [briːz] *n* brisa

breezy ['briːzɪ] *adj* de mucho viento, ventoso; (*person*) despreocupado

brew [bruː] *vt* (*tea*) hacer; (*beer*) elaborar ▷ *vi* (*fig: trouble*) prepararse; (*storm*) amenazar; **brewery** *n* fábrica de cerveza, cervecería

bribe [braɪb] *n* soborno ▷ *vt* sobornar, cohechar; **bribery** *n* soborno, cohecho

bric-a-brac ['brɪkəbræk] *n inv* baratijas *fpl*

brick [brɪk] *n* ladrillo; **bricklayer** *n* albañil *m*

bride [braɪd] *n* novia; **bridegroom** *n* novio; **bridesmaid** *n* dama de honor

bridge [brɪdʒ] *n* puente *m*; (*Naut*) puente *m* de mando; (*of nose*) caballete *m*; (*Cards*) bridge *m* ▷ *vt* (*fig*): **to ~ a gap** llenar un vacío

bridle ['braɪdl] *n* brida, freno

brief [briːf] *adj* breve, corto ▷ *n* (*Law*) escrito; (*task*) cometido, encargo ▷ *vt* informar; **briefs** *npl* (*for men*) calzoncillos *mpl*; (*for women*) bragas *fpl*; **briefcase** *n* cartera (*SP*), portafolio (*LAM*); **briefing** *n* (*Press*) informe *m*; **briefly** *adv* (*glance*) fugazmente; (*say*) en pocas palabras

brigadier [brɪgə'dɪə*] *n* general *m* de brigada

bright [braɪt] *adj* brillante; (*room*) luminoso; (*day*) de sol; (*person: clever*) listo,

inteligente; (*: lively*) alegre; (*colour*) vivo; (*future*) prometedor(a)

brilliant ['brɪljənt] *adj* brillante; (*inf*) fenomenal

brim [brɪm] *n* borde *m*; (*of hat*) ala

brine [braɪn] *n* (*Culin*) salmuera

bring [brɪŋ] (*pt, pp* **brought**) *vt* (*thing, person: with you*) traer; (*: to sb*) llevar, conducir; (*trouble, satisfaction*) causar; **bring about** *vt* ocasionar, producir; **bring back** *vt* volver a traer; (*return*) devolver; **bring down** *vt* (*government, plane*) derribar; (*price*) rebajar; **bring in** *vt* (*harvest*) recoger; (*person*) hacer entrar or pasar; (*object*) traer; (*Pol: bill, law*) presentar; (*produce: income*) producir, rendir; **bring on** *vt* (*illness, attack*) producir, causar; (*player, substitute*) sacar (de la reserva), hacer salir; **bring out** *vt* sacar; (*book etc*) publicar; (*meaning*) subrayar; **bring up** *vt* subir; (*person*) educar, criar; (*question*) sacar a colación; (*food: vomit*) devolver, vomitar

brink [brɪŋk] *n* borde *m*

brisk [brɪsk] *adj* (*abrupt: tone*) brusco; (*person*) enérgico, vigoroso; (*pace*) rápido; (*trade*) activo

bristle ['brɪsl] *n* cerda ▷ *vi*: **to ~ in anger** temblar de rabia

Brit [brɪt] *n abbr* (*inf: = British person*) británico/a

Britain ['brɪtən] *n* (*also*: **Great ~**) Gran Bretaña

British ['brɪtɪʃ] *adj* británico ▷ *npl*: **the ~** los británicos; **British Isles** *npl*: **the British Isles** las Islas Británicas

Briton ['brɪtən] *n* británico/a

brittle ['brɪtl] *adj* quebradizo, frágil

broad [brɔːd] *adj* ancho; (*range*) amplio; (*smile*) abierto; (*general: outlines etc*) general; (*accent*) cerrado; **in ~ daylight** en pleno día; **broadband** *n* banda ancha; **broad bean** *n* haba; **broadcast** (*pt, pp* **~**) *n* emisión *f* ▷ *vt* (*Radio*) emitir; (*TV*) transmitir ▷ *vi* emitir; transmitir; **broaden** *vt* ampliar ▷ *vi* ensancharse; **to broaden one's mind** hacer más tolerante a algn; **broadly** *adv* en general; **broad-minded** *adj* tolerante, liberal

broccoli ['brɔkəlɪ] *n* brécol *m*

brochure ['brəuʃjuə*] *n* folleto

broil [brɔɪl] *vt* (*Culin*) asar a la parrilla

broiler ['brɔɪlə*] *n* (*grill*) parrilla

broke [brəuk] *pt* of **break** ▷ *adj* (*inf*) pelado, sin blanca

broken ['brəukən] *pp* of **break** ▷ *adj* roto; (*machine: also*: **~ down**) averiado; **~ leg** pierna rota; **in ~ English** en un inglés imperfecto

broker ['brəukə*] n agente mf, bolsista mf; (insurance broker) agente de seguros

bronchitis [brɔŋ'kaɪtɪs] n bronquitis f

bronze [brɔnz] n bronce m

brooch [brəutʃ] n prendedor m, broche m

brood [bru:d] n camada, cría ⊳ vi (person) dejarse obsesionar

broom [brum] n escoba; (Bot) retama

Bros. abbr (= Brothers) Hnos

broth [brɔθ] n caldo

brothel ['brɔθl] n burdel m

brother ['brʌðə*] n hermano; **brother-in-law** n cuñado

brought [brɔ:t] pt, pp of **bring**

brow [brau] n (forehead) frente m; (eyebrow) ceja; (of hill) cumbre f

brown [braun] adj (colour) marrón; (hair) castaño; (tanned) bronceado, moreno ⊳ n (colour) color m marrón or pardo ⊳ vt (Culin) dorar; **brown bread** n pan integral

Brownie ['brauni] n niña exploradora

brown rice n arroz m integral

brown sugar n azúcar m terciado

browse [brauz] vi (through book) hojear; (in shop) mirar; **browser** n (Comput) navegador m

bruise [bru:z] n cardenal m (sp), moretón m ⊳ vt magullar

brunette [bru:'net] n morena

brush [brʌʃ] n cepillo; (for painting, shaving etc) brocha; (artist's) pincel m; (with police etc) roce m ⊳ vt (sweep) barrer; (groom) cepillar; (also: ~ against) rozar al pasar

Brussels ['brʌslz] n Bruselas

Brussels sprout n col f de Bruselas

brutal ['bru:tl] adj brutal

B.Sc. abbr (= Bachelor of Science) licenciado en Ciencias

BSE n abbr (= bovine spongiform encephalopathy) encefalopatía espongiforme bovina

bubble ['bʌbl] n burbuja ⊳ vi burbujear, borbotar; **bubble bath** n espuma para el baño; **bubble gum** n chicle m de globo; **bubblejet printer** ['bʌbldʒet-] n impresora de inyección por burbujas

buck [bʌk] n (rabbit) conejo macho; (deer) gamo; (us: inf) dólar m ⊳ vi corcovear; **to pass the ~ (to sb)** echar (a algn) el muerto

bucket ['bʌkɪt] n cubo, balde m

buckle ['bʌkl] n hebilla ⊳ vt abrochar con hebilla ⊳ vi combarse

bud [bʌd] n (of plant) brote m, yema; (of flower) capullo ⊳ vi brotar, echar brotes

Buddhism ['budɪzm] n Budismo

Buddhist ['budɪst] adj, n budista m/f

buddy ['bʌdɪ] (us) n compañero, compinche m

budge [bʌdʒ] vt mover; (fig) hacer ceder ⊳ vi moverse, ceder

budgerigar ['bʌdʒərɪɡɑ:*] n periquito

budget ['bʌdʒɪt] n presupuesto ⊳ vi: **to ~ for sth** presupuestar algo

budgie ['bʌdʒɪ] n = **budgerigar**

buff [bʌf] adj (colour) color de ante ⊳ n (inf: enthusiast) entusiasta mf

buffalo ['bʌfələu] (pl ~ or ~es) n (BRIT) búfalo; (us: bison) bisonte m

buffer ['bʌfə*] n (Comput) memoria intermedia; (Rail) tope m

buffet¹ ['bʌfɪt] vt golpear

buffet² ['bufeɪ] n (BRIT: in station) bar m, cafetería; (food) buffet m; **buffet car** (BRIT) n (Rail) coche-comedor m

bug [bʌg] n (esp us: insect) bicho, sabandija; (Comput) error m; (germ) microbio, bacilo; (spy device) micrófono oculto ⊳ vt (inf: annoy) fastidiar; (room) poner micrófono oculto en

buggy ['bʌgɪ] n cochecito de niño

build [bɪld] (pt, pp **built**) n (of person) tipo ⊳ vt construir, edificar; **build up** vt (morale, forces, production) acrecentar; (stocks) acumular; **builder** n (contractor) contratista mf; **building** n construcción f; (structure) edificio; **building site** n obra; **building society** (BRIT) n sociedad f inmobiliaria

built [bɪlt] pt, pp of **build**; **built-in** adj (cupboard) empotrado; (device) interior, incorporado; **built-up** adj (area) urbanizado

bulb [bʌlb] n (Bot) bulbo; (Elec) bombilla, foco (MEX), bujía (CAM), bombita (RPL)

Bulgaria [bʌl'ɡeərɪə] n Bulgaria; **Bulgarian** adj, n búlgaro/a m/f

bulge [bʌldʒ] n bulto, protuberancia ⊳ vi bombearse, pandearse; (pocket etc): **to ~ (with)** rebosar (de)

bulimia [bə'lɪmɪə] n bulimia

bulimic [bju:'lɪmɪk] adj, n bulímico/a m/f

bulk [bʌlk] n masa, mole f; **in ~** (Comm) a granel; **the ~ of** la mayor parte de; **bulky** adj voluminoso, abultado

bull [bul] n toro; (male elephant, whale) macho

bulldozer ['buldəuzə*] n bulldozer m

bullet ['bulɪt] n bala

bulletin ['bulɪtɪn] n anuncio, parte m; (journal) boletín m; **bulletin board** n (us) tablón m de anuncios; (Comput) tablero de noticias

bullfight ['bulfaɪt] n corrida de toros; **bullfighter** n torero; **bullfighting** n los toros, el toreo

bully ['bulɪ] n valentón m, matón m ⊳ vt

intimidar, tiranizar

bum [bʌm] n (inf: backside) culo; (esp US: tramp) vagabundo

bumblebee ['bʌmblbiː] n abejorro

bump [bʌmp] n (blow) tope m, choque m; (jolt) sacudida; (on road etc) bache m; (on head etc) chichón m ▷ vt (strike) chocar contra; **bump into** vt fus chocar contra, tropezar con; (person) topar con; **bumper** n (Aut) parachoques m inv ▷ adj: **bumper crop** or **harvest** cosecha abundante; **bumpy** adj (road) lleno de baches

bun [bʌn] n (BRIT: cake) pastel m; (US: bread) bollo; (of hair) moño

bunch [bʌntʃ] n (of flowers) ramo; (of keys) manojo; (of bananas) piña; (of people) grupo; **bunches** npl (in hair) coletas fpl

bundle ['bʌndl] n bulto, fardo; (of sticks) haz m; (of papers) legajo ▷ vt (also: ~ up) atar, envolver; **to ~ sth/sb into** meter algo/a algn precipitadamente en

bungalow ['bʌŋgələu] n bungalow m, chalé m

bungee jumping ['bʌndʒiː'dʒʌmpɪŋ] n puenting m, banyi m

bunion ['bʌnjən] n juanete m

bunk [bʌŋk] n litera; **bunk beds** npl literas fpl

bunker ['bʌŋkə*] n (coal store) carbonera; (Mil) refugio; (Golf) bunker m

bunny ['bʌnɪ] n (inf: also: ~ rabbit) conejito

buoy [bɔɪ] n boya; **buoyant** adj (ship) capaz de flotar; (economy) boyante; (person) optimista

burden ['bəːdn] n carga ▷ vt cargar

bureau [bjuə'rəu] (pl ~x) n (BRIT: writing desk) escritorio, buró m; (US: chest of drawers) cómoda; (office) oficina, agencia

bureaucracy [bjuə'rɔkrəsɪ] n burocracia

bureaucrat ['bjuərəkræt] n burócrata m/f

bureau de change [-də'ʃɑ̃ʒ] (pl **bureaux de change**) n caja f de cambio

bureaux ['bjuərəuz] npl of **bureau**

burger ['bəːgə*] n hamburguesa

burglar ['bəːglə*] n ladrón/ona m/f; **burglar alarm** n alarma f antirrobo; **burglary** n robo con allanamiento, robo de una casa

burial ['berɪəl] n entierro

burn [bəːn] (pt, pp **~ed** or **~t**) vt quemar; (house) incendiar ▷ vi quemarse, arder; incendiarse; (sting) escocer ▷ n quemadura; **burn down** vt incendiar; **burn out** vt (writer etc): **to burn o.s. out** agotarse; **burning** adj (building etc) en llamas; (hot: sand etc) abrasador(a); (ambition) ardiente

Burns' Night [bəːnz-] n ver abajo

burnt [bəːnt] pt, pp of **burn**

burp [bəːp] (inf) n eructo ▷ vi eructar

burrow ['bʌrəu] n madriguera ▷ vi hacer una madriguera; (rummage) hurgar

burst [bəːst] (pt, pp **~**) vt reventar; (river: banks etc) romper ▷ vi reventarse; (tyre) pincharse ▷ n (of gunfire) ráfaga; (also: **~ pipe**) reventón m; **a ~ of energy/speed/ enthusiasm** una explosión de energía/ un ímpetu de velocidad/un arranque de entusiasmo; **to ~ into flames** estallar en llamas; **to ~ into tears** deshacerse en lágrimas; **to ~ out laughing** soltar la carcajada; **to ~ open** abrirse de golpe; **to be ~ing with** (container) estar lleno a rebosar de; (: person) reventar por or de; **burst into** vt fus (room etc) irrumpir en

bury ['berɪ] vt enterrar; (body) enterrar, sepultar

bus [bʌs] (pl **~es**) n autobús m

bush [buʃ] n arbusto; (scrub land) monte m; **to beat about the ~** andar(se) con rodeos

business ['bɪznɪs] n (matter) asunto; (trading) comercio, negocios mpl; (firm) empresa, casa; (occupation) oficio; **to be away on ~** estar en viaje de negocios; **it's my ~ to ...** me toca or corresponde ...; **it's none of my ~** yo no tengo nada que ver; **he means ~** habla en serio; **business class** n (Aer) clase f preferente; **businesslike** adj eficiente; **businessman** (irreg) n hombre m de negocios; **business trip** n viaje m de negocios; **businesswoman** (irreg) n mujer f de negocios

busker ['bʌskə*] (BRIT) n músico/a ambulante

bus: bus pass n bonobús; **bus shelter** n parada cubierta; **bus station** n estación f de autobuses; **bus stop** n parada de autobús

bust [bʌst] n (Anat) pecho; (sculpture) busto

▷ adj (inf: broken) roto, estropeado; **to go ~** quebrar

bustling ['bʌslɪŋ] adj (town) animado, bullicioso

busy ['bɪzɪ] adj ocupado, atareado; (shop, street) concurrido, animado; (Tel: line) comunicando ▷ vt: **to ~ o.s. with** ocuparse en; **busy signal** (US) n (Tel) señal f de comunicando

but [bʌt] conj **1** pero; **he's not very bright, but he's hard-working** no es muy inteligente, pero es trabajador

2 (in direct contradiction) sino; **he's not English but French** no es inglés sino francés; **he didn't sing but he shouted** no cantó sino que gritó

3 (showing disagreement, surprise etc) but **that's far too expensive!** ¡pero eso es carísimo!; **but it does work!** ¡(pero) sí que funciona!

▷ prep (apart from, except) menos, salvo; **we've had nothing but trouble** no hemos tenido más que problemas; **no-one but him can do it** nadie más que él puede hacerlo; **who but a lunatic would do such a thing?** ¡sólo un loco haría una cosa así!; **but for you/your help** si no fuera por ti/tu ayuda; **anything but that** cualquier cosa menos eso

▷ adv (just, only) **she's but a child** no es más que una niña; **had I but known** si lo hubiera sabido; **I can but try** al menos lo puedo intentar; **it's all but finished** está casi acabado

butcher ['bʊtʃə*] n carnicero ▷ vt hacer una carnicería con; (cattle etc) matar; **butcher's (shop)** n carnicería

butler ['bʌtlə*] n mayordomo

butt [bʌt] n (barrel) tonel m; (of gun) culata; (of cigarette) colilla; (BRIT: fig: target) blanco ▷ vt dar cabezadas contra, top(et)ar

butter ['bʌtə*] n mantequilla ▷ vt untar con mantequilla; **buttercup** n botón m de oro

butterfly ['bʌtəflaɪ] n mariposa; (Swimming: also: ~ **stroke**) braza de mariposa

buttocks ['bʌtəks] npl nalgas fpl

button ['bʌtn] n botón m; (US) placa, chapa ▷ vt (also: ~ **up**) abotonar, abrochar ▷ vi abrocharse

buy [baɪ] (pt, pp bought) vt comprar ▷ n compra; **to ~ sb sth/sth from sb** comprarle algo a algn; **to ~ sb a drink** invitar a algn a tomar algo; **buy out** vt (partner) comprar la parte de; **buy up** vt (property) acaparar; (stock) comprar todas las existencias de; **buyer** n comprador(a) m/f

buzz [bʌz] n zumbido; (inf: phone call) llamada (por teléfono) ▷ vi zumbar; **buzzer** n timbre m

by [baɪ] prep **1** (referring to cause, agent) por; de; **killed by lightning** muerto por un relámpago; **a painting by Picasso** un cuadro de Picasso

2 (referring to method, manner, means): **by bus/car/train** en autobús/coche/tren; **to pay by cheque** pagar con un cheque; **by moonlight/candlelight** a la luz de la luna/ una vela; **by saving hard he ...** ahorrando ...

3 (via, through) por; **we came by Dover** vinimos por Dover

4 (close to, past): **the house by the river** la casa junto al río; **she rushed by me** pasó a mi lado como una exhalación; **I go by the post office every day** paso por delante de Correos todos los días

5 (time: not later than) para; (: during): **by daylight** de día; **by 4 o'clock** para las cuatro; **by this time tomorrow** mañana a estas horas; **by the time I got here it was too late** cuando llegué ya era demasiado tarde

6 (amount): **by the metre/kilo** por metro/ kilo; **paid by the hour** pagado por hora

7 (Math, measure): **to divide/multiply by 3** dividir/multiplicar por 3; **a room 3 metres by 4** una habitación de 3 metros por 4; **it's broader by a metre** es un metro más ancho

8 (according to) según, de acuerdo con; **it's 3 o'clock by my watch** según mi reloj, son las tres; **it's all right by me** por mí, está bien

9: **(all) by oneself** etc todo solo; **he did it (all) by himself** lo hizo él solo; **he was standing (all) by himself in a corner** estaba de pie solo en un rincón

10: **by the way** a propósito, por cierto; **this wasn't my idea, by the way** pues, no fue idea mía

▷ adv **1** see **go; pass** etc

2: **by and by** finalmente; **they'll come back by and by** acabarán volviendo; **by and large** en líneas generales, en general

bye(-bye) ['baɪ('baɪ)] excl adiós, hasta luego

by-election (BRIT) n elección f parcial

bypass ['baɪpɑːs] n carretera de circunvalación; (Med) (operación f de) by-pass f ▷ vt evitar

byte [baɪt] n (Comput) byte m, octeto

C

C [si:] n (Mus) do m

cab [kæb] n taxi m; (of truck) cabina

cabaret ['kæbəreɪ] n cabaret m

cabbage ['kæbɪdʒ] n col f, berza

cabin ['kæbɪn] n cabaña; (on ship) camarote m; (on plane) cabina; **cabin crew** n tripulación f de cabina

cabinet ['kæbɪnɪt] n (Pol) consejo de ministros; (furniture) armario; (also: **display** ~) vitrina; **cabinet minister** n ministro/a (del gabinete)

cable ['keɪbl] n cable m ▷ vt cablegrafiar; **cable car** n teleférico; **cable television** n televisión f por cable

cactus ['kæktəs] (pl **cacti**) n cacto

café ['kæfeɪ] n café m

cafeteria [kæfɪ'tɪərɪə] n cafetería

caffein(e) ['kæfi:n] n cafeína

cage [keɪdʒ] n jaula

cagoule [kə'gu:l] n chubasquero

cake [keɪk] n (Culin: large) tarta; (: small) pastel m; (of soap) pastilla

calcium ['kælsɪəm] n calcio

calculate ['kælkjuleɪt] vt calcular; **calculation** [-'leɪʃən] n cálculo, cómputo; **calculator** n calculadora

calendar ['kæləndə*] n calendario

calf [kɑ:f] (pl **calves**) n (of cow) ternero, becerro; (of other animals) cría; (also: ~**skin**) piel f de becerro; (Anat) pantorrilla

calibre ['kælɪbə*] (US **caliber**) n calibre m

call [kɔ:l] vt llamar; (meeting) convocar ▷ vi (shout) llamar; (Tel) llamar (por teléfono); (visit: also: ~ **in**, ~ **round**) hacer una visita ▷ n (of bird) canto; (of person) llamada; **to be** ~**ed** llamarse; **on** ~ (on duty) de guardia; **call back** vi (return) volver; (Tel) volver a llamar; **call for** vt fus (demand) pedir, exigir; (fetch) pasar a recoger; **call in** vt (doctor, expert, police) llamar; **call off** vt (cancel: meeting, race) cancelar; (: deal) anular; (: strike)

desconvocar; **call on** vt fus (visit) visitar; (turn to) acudir a; **call out** vi gritar; **call up** vt (Mil) llamar al servicio militar; (Tel) llamar; **callbox** (BRIT) n cabina telefónica; **call centre** (US **call center**) n centro de atención al cliente; **caller** n visita; (Tel) usuario/a

callous ['kæləs] adj insensible, cruel

calm [kɑ:m] adj tranquilo; (sea) liso, en calma, tranquilidad f ▷ vt calmar, tranquilizar; **calm down** vi calmarse, tranquilizarse ▷ vt calmar, tranquilizar; **calmly** ['kɑ:mlɪ] adv tranquilamente, con calma

Calor gas® ['kælə*-] n butano

calorie ['kælərɪ] n caloría

calves [kɑ:vz] npl of **calf**

camcorder ['kæmkɔ:də*] n videocámara

came [keɪm] pt of **come**

camel ['kæməl] n camello

camera ['kæmərə] n máquina fotográfica; (Cinema, TV) cámara; **in** ~ (Law) a puerta cerrada; **cameraman** (irreg) n cámara m; **camera phone** n teléfono con cámara

camouflage ['kæməflɑ:ʒ] n camuflaje m ▷ vt camuflar

camp [kæmp] n campamento, camping m; (Mil) campamento; (for prisoners) campo; (fig: faction) bando ▷ vi acampar ▷ adj afectado, afeminado

campaign [kæm'peɪn] n (Mil, Pol etc) campaña ▷ vi hacer campaña; **campaigner** n: **campaigner for** defensor(a) m/f de

camp: **campbed** (BRIT) n cama de campaña; **camper** n campista mf; (vehicle) caravana; **campground** (US) n camping m, campamento; **camping** n camping m; **to go camping** hacer camping; **campsite** n camping m

campus ['kæmpəs] n ciudad f universitaria

can¹ [kæn] n (of oil, water) bidón m; (tin) lata, bote m ▷ vt enlatar

○ KEYWORD

can² [kæn] (negative **cannot**, **can't**, conditional and pt **could**) aux vb **1** (be able to) poder; **you can do it if you try** puedes hacerlo si lo intentas; **I can't see you** no te veo

2 (know how to) saber; **I can swim/play tennis/drive** sé nadar/jugar al tenis/ conducir; **can you speak French?** ¿hablas or sabes hablar francés?

3 (may) poder; **can I use your phone?** ¿me dejas or puedo usar tu teléfono?

4 (expressing disbelief, puzzlement etc): **it can't**

be true! ¡no puede ser (verdad)!; **what CAN he want?** ¿qué querrá?
5 (expressing possibility, suggestion etc): **he could be in the library** podría estar en la biblioteca; **she could have been delayed** pudo haberse retrasado

Canada ['kænədə] n (el) Canadá; **Canadian** [kə'neɪdɪən] adj, n canadiense mf
canal [kə'næl] n canal m
canary [kə'nɛərɪ] n canario
Canary Islands [kə'nɛərɪ'aɪləndz] npl: **the ~** las (Islas) Canarias
cancel ['kænsəl] vt cancelar; (train) suprimir; (cross out) tachar, borrar; **cancellation** [-'leɪʃən] n cancelación f; supresión f
Cancer ['kænsə*] n (Astrology) Cáncer m
cancer ['kænsə*] n cáncer m
candidate ['kændɪdeɪt] n candidato/a
candle ['kændl] n vela; (in church) cirio; **candlestick** n (single) candelero; (low) palmatoria; (bigger, ornate) candelabro
candy ['kændɪ] n azúcar m cande; (US) caramelo; **candy bar** (US) n barrita (dulce); **candyfloss** (BRIT) n algodón m (azucarado)
cane [keɪn] n (Bot) caña; (stick) vara, palmeta; (for furniture) mimbre f ▷ vt (BRIT: Scol) castigar (con vara)
canister ['kænɪstə*] n bote m, lata; (of gas) bombona
cannabis ['kænəbɪs] n marijuana
canned [kænd] adj en lata, de lata
cannon ['kænən] (pl ~ or ~s) n cañón m
cannot ['kænɔt] = **can not**
canoe [kə'nuː] n canoa; (Sport) piragua; **canoeing** n piragüismo
canon ['kænən] n (clergyman) canónigo; (standard) canon m
can-opener ['kænəupnə*] n abrelatas m inv
can't [kænt] = **can not**
canteen [kæn'tiːn] n (eating place) cantina; (BRIT: of cutlery) juego
canter ['kæntə*] vi ir a medio galope
canvas ['kænvəs] n (material) lona; (painting) lienzo; (Naut) velas fpl
canvass ['kænvəs] vi (Pol): **to ~ for** solicitar votos por ▷ vt (Comm) sondear
canyon ['kænjən] n cañón m
cap [kæp] n (hat) gorra; (of pen) capuchón m; (of bottle) tapa, tapón m; (contraceptive) diafragma m; (for toy gun) cápsula ▷ vt (outdo) superar; (limit) recortar
capability [keɪpə'bɪlɪtɪ] n capacidad f
capable ['keɪpəbl] adj capaz
capacity [kə'pæsɪtɪ] n capacidad f;

(position) calidad f
cape [keɪp] n capa; (Geo) cabo
caper ['keɪpə*] n (Culin: gen pl) alcaparra; (prank) broma
capital ['kæpɪtl] n (also: ~ city) capital f; (money) capital m; (also: ~ letter) mayúscula; **capitalism** n capitalismo; **capitalist** adj, n capitalista mf; **capital punishment** n pena de muerte
Capitol ['kæpɪtl] n ver abajo

● **CAPITOL**
●
● El Capitolio **(Capitol)** es el edificio del
● Congreso **(Congress)** de los Estados
● Unidos, situado en la ciudad de
● Washington. Por extensión, también
● se suele llamar así al edificio en el que
● tienen lugar las sesiones parlamentarias
● de la cámara de representantes de
● muchos de los estados.

Capricorn ['kæprɪkɔːn] n Capricornio
capsize [kæp'saɪz] vt volcar, hacer zozobrar ▷ vi volcarse, zozobrar
capsule ['kæpsjuːl] n cápsula
captain ['kæptɪn] n capitán m
caption ['kæpʃən] n (heading) título; (to picture) leyenda
captivity [kæp'tɪvɪtɪ] n cautiverio
capture ['kæptʃə*] vt prender, apresar; (animal, Comput) capturar; (place) tomar; (attention) captar, llamar ▷ n apresamiento; captura; toma; (data capture) formulación f de datos
car [kɑː*] n coche m, carro (LAM), automóvil m; (US Rail) vagón m
carafe [kə'ræf] n jarra
caramel ['kærəməl] n caramelo
carat ['kærət] n quilate m
caravan ['kærəvæn] n (BRIT) caravana, ruló f; (in desert) caravana; **caravan site** (BRIT) n camping m para caravanas
carbohydrate [kɑːbəu'haɪdreɪt] n hidrato de carbono; (food) fécula
carbon ['kɑːbən] n carbono; **carbon dioxide** n dióxido de carbono, anhídrido carbónico; **carbon monoxide** n monóxido de carbono
car boot sale n mercadillo organizado en un aparcamiento, en el que se exponen las mercancías en el maletero del coche
carburettor [kɑːbju'rɛtə*] (US **carburetor**) n carburador m
card [kɑːd] n (material) cartulina; (index card etc) ficha; (playing card) carta, naipe m; (visiting card, greetings card etc) tarjeta; **cardboard** n cartón m; **card game** n

juego de naipes *or* cartas
cardigan ['kɑːdɪgən] *n* rebeca
cardinal ['kɑːdɪnl] *adj* cardinal;
(*importance, principal*) esencial ▷ *n* cardenal
m
cardphone ['kɑːdfəun] *n* cabina que
funciona con tarjetas telefónicas
care [kɛə*] *n* cuidado; (*worry*) inquietud
f; (*charge*) cargo, custodia ▷ *vi*: **to ~ about**
(*person, animal*) tener cariño a; (*thing, idea*)
preocuparse por; **~ of** en casa de, al cuidado
de; **in sb's ~** a cargo de algn; **to take ~ to**
cuidarse de, tener cuidado de; **to take ~ of**
cuidar; (*problem etc*) ocuparse de; **I don't**
~ no me importa; **I couldn't ~ less** eso me
trae sin cuidado; **care for** *vt fus* cuidar a;
(*like*) querer
career [kə'rɪə*] *n* profesión *f*; (*in work,
school*) carrera ▷ *vi* (*also:* **~ along**) correr a
toda velocidad
care: carefree *adj* despreocupado; **careful**
adj cuidadoso; (*cautious*) cauteloso; **(be)**
careful! ¡tenga cuidado!; **carefully** *adv* con
cuidado, cuidadosamente; con cautela;
caregiver (*us*) *n* (*professional*) enfermero/a
m/f; (*unpaid*) persona que cuida a un pariente o
vecino; **careless** *adj* descuidado; (*heedless*)
poco atento; **carelessness** *n* descuido,
falta de atención; **carer** ['kɛərə*] *n*
(*professional*) enfermero/a *m/f*; (*unpaid*)
persona que cuida a un pariente o vecino;
caretaker *n* portero/a, conserje *mf*
car-ferry ['kɑːfɛrɪ] *n* transbordador *m*
para coches
cargo ['kɑːgəu] (*pl* **~es**) *n* cargamento,
carga
car hire *n* alquiler *m* de automóviles
Caribbean [kærɪ'biːən] *n*: **the ~ (Sea)** el
(Mar) Caribe
caring ['kɛərɪŋ] *adj* humanitario;
(*behaviour*) afectuoso
carnation [kɑː'neɪʃən] *n* clavel *m*
carnival ['kɑːnɪvəl] *n* carnaval *m*;
(*us: funfair*) parque *m* de atracciones
carol ['kærəl] *n*: **(Christmas) ~** villancico
carousel [kærə'sɛl] (*us*) *n* tiovivo,
caballitos *mpl*
car park (*BRIT*) *n* aparcamiento, parking *m*
carpenter ['kɑːpɪntə*] *n* carpintero/a
carpet ['kɑːpɪt] *n* alfombra; (*fitted*)
moqueta ▷ *vt* alfombrar
car rental (*us*) *n* alquiler *m* de coches
carriage ['kærɪdʒ] *n* (*BRIT Rail*) vagón *m*;
(*horse-drawn*) coche *m*; (*of goods*) transporte
m; (*: cost*) porte *m*, flete *m*; **carriageway**
(*BRIT*) *n* (*part of road*) calzada
carrier ['kærɪə*] *n* (*transport company*)
transportista, empresa de transportes;

(*Med*) portador(a) *m/f*; **carrier bag** (*BRIT*) *n*
bolsa de papel *or* plástico
carrot ['kærət] *n* zanahoria
carry ['kærɪ] *vt* (*person*) llevar; (*transport*)
transportar; (*involve: responsibilities etc*)
entrañar, implicar; (*Med*) ser portador de
▷ *vi* (*sound*) oírse; **to get carried away**
(*fig*) entusiasmarse; **carry on** *vi* (*continue*)
seguir (adelante), continuar ▷ *vt* proseguir,
continuar; **carry out** *vt* (*orders*) cumplir;
(*investigation*) llevar a cabo, realizar
cart [kɑːt] *n* carro, carreta ▷ *vt*
(*inf: transport*) acarrear
carton ['kɑːtən] *n* (*box*) caja (de cartón); (*of
milk etc*) bote *m*; (*of yogurt*) tarrina
cartoon [kɑː'tuːn] *n* (*Press*) caricatura;
(*comic strip*) tira cómica; (*film*) dibujos *mpl*
animados
cartridge ['kɑːtrɪdʒ] *n* cartucho; (*of pen*)
recambio
carve [kɑːv] *vt* (*meat*) trinchar; (*wood,
stone*) cincelar, esculpir; (*initials etc*) grabar;
carving *n* (*object*) escultura; (*design*) talla;
(*art*) tallado
car wash *n* lavado de coches
case [keɪs] *n* (*container*) caja; (*Med*) caso;
(*for jewels etc*) estuche *m*; (*Law*) causa,
proceso; (*BRIT: also:* **suit~**) maleta; **in ~ of**
en caso de; **in any ~** en todo caso; **just in ~**
por si acaso
cash [kæʃ] *n* dinero en efectivo, dinero
contante ▷ *vt* cobrar, hacer efectivo; **to**
pay (in) ~ pagar al contado; **~ on delivery**
cóbrese al entregar; **cashback** *n* (*discount*)
devolución *f*; (*at supermarket etc*) retirada de
dinero en efectivo de un establecimiento donde se
ha pagado con tarjeta; también dinero retirado;
cash card *n* tarjeta *f* dinero; **cash desk**
(*BRIT*) *n* caja; **cash dispenser** *n* cajero
automático
cashew [kæ'fuː] *n* (*also:* **~ nut**) anacardo
cashier [kæ'fɪə*] *n* cajero/a
cashmere ['kæʃmɪə*] *n* cachemira
cash point *n* cajero automático
cash register *n* caja
casino [kə'siːnəu] *n* casino
casket ['kɑːskɪt] *n* cofre *m*, estuche *m*;
(*us: coffin*) ataúd *m*
casserole ['kæsərəul] *n* (*food, pot*) cazuela
cassette [kæ'sɛt] *n* casete *f*; **cassette**
player, cassette recorder *n* casete *m*
cast [kɑːst] (*pt, pp* **~**) *vt* (*throw*) echar,
arrojar, lanzar; (*glance, eyes*) dirigir;
(*Theatre*): **to ~ sb as Othello** dar a algn el
papel de Otelo ▷ *vi* (*Fishing*) lanzar ▷ *n*
(*Theatre*) reparto; (*also: plaster ~*) vaciado;
to ~ one's vote votar; **to ~ doubt on**
suscitar dudas acerca de; **cast off** *vi* (*Naut*)

desamarrar; (Knitting) cerrar (los puntos)
castanets [kæstə'nɛts] npl castañuelas fpl
caster sugar ['kɑːstə*-] (BRIT) n azúcar m extrafino
Castile [kæs'tiːl] n Castilla; **Castilian** adj, n castellano/a m/f
cast-iron ['kɑːstaɪən] adj (lit) (hecho) de hierro fundido; (fig: case) irrebatible
castle ['kɑːsl] n castillo; (Chess) torre f
casual ['kæʒjul] adj fortuito; (irregular: work etc) eventual, temporero; (unconcerned) despreocupado; (clothes) informal

▌Be careful not to translate **casual** by the Spanish word casual.

casualty ['kæʒjultɪ] n víctima, herido/a; (dead) muerto/a; (Med: department) urgencias fpl
cat [kæt] n gato; (big cat) felino
Catalan ['kætəlæn] adj, n catalán/ana m/f
catalogue ['kætəlɒg] (us **catalog**) n catálogo ▷ vt catalogar
Catalonia [kætə'ləunɪə] n Cataluña
catalytic converter [kætə'lɪtɪkkən'vəːtə*] n catalizador m
cataract ['kætərækt] n (Med) cataratas fpl
catarrh [kə'tɑː*] n catarro
catastrophe [kə'tæstrəfɪ] n catástrofe f
catch [kætʃ] (pt, pp **caught**) vt coger (SP), agarrar (LAM); (arrest) detener; (grasp) asir; (breath) contener; (surprise: person) sorprender; (attract: attention) captar; (hear) oír; (Med) contagiarse de, coger; (also: ~ **up**) alcanzar ▷ vi (fire) encenderse; (in branches etc) enredarse ▷ n (fish etc) pesca; (act of catching) cogida; (hidden problem) dificultad f; (game) pilla-pilla; (of lock) pestillo, cerradura; **to ~ fire** encenderse; **to ~ sight of** divisar; **catch up** vi (fig) ponerse al día; **catching** ['kætʃɪŋ] adj (Med) contagioso
category ['kætɪgərɪ] n categoría, clase f
cater ['keɪtə*] vi: **to ~ for** (BRIT) abastecer a; (needs) atender a; (Comm: parties etc) proveer comida a
caterpillar ['kætəpɪlə*] n oruga, gusano
cathedral [kə'θiːdrəl] n catedral f
Catholic ['kæθəlɪk] adj, n (Rel) católico/a m/f
Catseye® ['kæts'aɪ] (BRIT) n (Aut) catafoto
cattle ['kætl] npl ganado
catwalk ['kætwɔːk] n pasarela
caught [kɔːt] pt, pp of **catch**
cauliflower ['kɒlɪflauə*] n coliflor f
cause [kɔːz] n causa, motivo, razón f; (principle: also Pol) causa ▷ vt causar
caution ['kɔːʃən] n cautela, prudencia; (warning) advertencia, amonestación f

▷ vt amonestar; **cautious** adj cauteloso, prudente, precavido
cave [keɪv] n cueva, caverna; **cave in** vi (roof etc) derrumbarse, hundirse
caviar(e) ['kævɪɑː*] n caviar m
cavity ['kævɪtɪ] n hueco, cavidad f
cc abbr (= cubic centimetres) c.c.; (= carbon copy) copia hecha con papel del carbón
CCTV n abbr (= closed-circuit television) circuito cerrado de televisión
CD n abbr (= compact disc) CD m; (player) (reproductor m de) CD; **CD player** n reproductor m de CD; **CD-ROM** [siːdiː'rɒm] n abbr CD-ROM m; **CD writer** n grabadora de CD
cease [siːs] vt, vi cesar; **ceasefire** n alto m el fuego
cedar ['siːdə*] n cedro
ceilidh ['keɪlɪ] n baile con música y danzas tradicionales escocesas o irlandesas
ceiling ['siːlɪŋ] n techo; (fig) límite m
celebrate ['sɛlɪbreɪt] vt celebrar ▷ vi divertirse; **celebration** [-'breɪʃən] n fiesta, celebración f
celebrity [sɪ'lɛbrɪtɪ] n celebridad f
celery ['sɛlərɪ] n apio
cell [sɛl] n celda; (Biol) célula; (Elec) elemento
cellar ['sɛlə*] n sótano; (for wine) bodega
cello ['tʃɛləu] n violoncelo
Cellophane® ['sɛləfeɪn] n celofán m
cellphone ['sɛlfəun] n teléfono celular
Celsius ['sɛlsɪəs] adj centígrado
Celtic ['kɛltɪk] adj celta
cement [sə'mɛnt] n cemento
cemetery ['sɛmɪtrɪ] n cementerio
censor ['sɛnsə*] n censor m ▷ vt (cut) censurar; **censorship** n censura
census ['sɛnsəs] n censo
cent [sɛnt] n (unit of dollar) centavo, céntimo; (unit of euro) céntimo; see also **per**
centenary [sɛn'tiːnərɪ] n centenario
centennial [sɛn'tɛnɪəl] (us) n centenario
center ['sɛntə*] (us) = **centre**
centi... [sɛntɪ] prefix: **centigrade** adj centígrado; **centimetre** (us **centimeter**) n centímetro; **centipede** ['sɛntɪpiːd] n ciempiés m inv
central ['sɛntrəl] adj central; (of house etc) céntrico; **Central America** n Centroamérica; **central heating** n calefacción f central; **central reservation** n (BRIT Aut) mediana
centre ['sɛntə*] (us **center**) n centro; (fig) núcleo ▷ vt centrar; **centre-forward** n (Sport) delantero centro; **centre-half** n (Sport) medio centro
century ['sɛntjurɪ] n siglo; **20th ~** siglo

veinte

CEO n abbr = **chief executive officer**

ceramic [sɪˈræmɪk] adj cerámico

cereal [ˈsiːrɪəl] n cereal m

ceremony [ˈsɛrɪmənɪ] n ceremonia; **to stand on ~** hacer ceremonias, estar de cumplido

certain [ˈsəːtən] adj seguro; (person): **a ~ Mr Smith** un tal Sr. Smith; (particular, some) cierto; **for ~** a ciencia cierta; **certainly** adv (undoubtedly) ciertamente; (of course) desde luego, por supuesto; **certainty** n certeza, certidumbre f, seguridad f; (inevitability) certeza

certificate [səˈtɪfɪkɪt] n certificado

certify [ˈsəːtɪfaɪ] vt certificar; (award diploma to) conceder un diploma a; (declare insane) declarar loco

cf. abbr (= compare) cfr

CFC n abbr (= chlorofluorocarbon) CFC m

chain [tʃeɪn] n cadena; (of mountains) cordillera; (of events) sucesión f ▷ vt (also: ~ up) encadenar; **chain-smoke** vi fumar un cigarrillo tras otro

chair [tʃeə*] n silla; (armchair) sillón m, butaca; (of university) cátedra; (of meeting etc) presidencia ▷ vt (meeting) presidir; **chairlift** n telesilla; **chairman** (irreg) n presidente m; **chairperson** n presidente/a m/f; **chairwoman** (irreg) n presidenta

chalet [ˈʃæleɪ] n chalet m (de madera)

chalk [tʃɔːk] n (Geo) creta; (for writing) tiza, gis m (MEX); **chalkboard** (US) n pizarrón (LAM), pizarra (SP)

challenge [ˈtʃælɪndʒ] n desafío, reto ▷ vt desafiar, retar; (statement, right) poner en duda; **to ~ sb to do sth** retar a algn a que haga algo; **challenging** adj exigente; (tone) de desafío

chamber [ˈtʃeɪmbə*] n cámara, sala; (Pol) cámara; (BRIT Law: gen pl) despacho; **~ of commerce** cámara de comercio; **chambermaid** n camarera

champagne [ʃæmˈpeɪn] n champaña m, champán m

champion [ˈtʃæmpɪən] n campeón/ona m/f; (of cause) defensor(a) m/f; **championship** n campeonato

chance [tʃɑːns] n (opportunity) ocasión f, oportunidad f; (likelihood) posibilidad f; (risk) riesgo ▷ vt arriesgar, probar ▷ adj fortuito, casual; **to ~ it** arriesgarse, intentarlo; **to take a ~** arriesgarse; **by ~** por casualidad

chancellor [ˈtʃɑːnsələ*] n canciller m; **Chancellor of the Exchequer** (BRIT) n Ministro de Hacienda

chandelier [ʃændəˈlɪə*] n araña (de luces)

change [tʃeɪndʒ] vt cambiar; (replace)

cambiar, reemplazar; (gear, clothes, job) cambiar de; (transform) transformar ▷ vi cambiar(se); (change trains) hacer transbordo; (traffic lights) cambiar de color; (be transformed): **to ~ into** transformarse en ▷ n cambio; (alteration) modificación f; (transformation) transformación f; (of clothes) muda; (coins) suelto, sencillo; (money returned) vuelta; **to ~ gear** (Aut) cambiar de marcha; **to ~ one's mind** cambiar de opinión o idea; **for a ~** para variar; **change over** vi (from sth to sth) cambiar; (players etc) cambiar(se) ▷ vt cambiar; **changeable** adj (weather) cambiable; **change machine** n máquina de cambio; **changing room** (BRIT) n vestuario

channel [ˈtʃænl] n (TV) canal m; (of river) cauce m; (groove) conducto; (fig: medium) medio ▷ vt (river etc) encauzar; **the (English) C~** el Canal (de la Mancha); **the C~ Islands** las Islas Normandas; **Channel Tunnel** n: **the Channel Tunnel** el túnel del Canal de la Mancha, el Eurotúnel

chant [tʃɑːnt] n (of crowd) gritos mpl; (Rel) canto ▷ vt (slogan, word) repetir a gritos

chaos [ˈkeɪɔs] n caos m

chaotic [keɪˈɔtɪk] adj caótico

chap [tʃæp] (BRIT: inf) n (man) tío, tipo

chapel [ˈtʃæpəl] n capilla

chapped [tʃæpt] adj agrietado

chapter [ˈtʃæptə*] n capítulo

character [ˈkærɪktə*] n carácter m, naturaleza, índole f; (moral strength, personality) carácter; (in novel, film) personaje m; **characteristic** [-ˈrɪstɪk] adj característico ▷ n característica; **characterize** [ˈkærɪktəraɪz] vt caracterizar

charcoal [ˈtʃɑːkəul] n carbón m vegetal; (Art) carboncillo

charge [tʃɑːdʒ] n (Law) cargo, acusación f; (cost) precio, coste m; (responsibility) cargo ▷ vt (Law): **to ~ (with)** acusar (de); (battery) cargar; (price) pedir; (customer) cobrar ▷ vi precipitarse; (Mil) cargar, atacar; **charge card** n tarjeta de cuenta; **charger** n (also: **battery charger**) cargador m (de baterías)

charismatic [kærɪzˈmætɪk] adj carismático

charity [ˈtʃærɪtɪ] n caridad f; (organization) sociedad f benéfica; (money, gifts) limosnas fpl; **charity shop** n (BRIT) tienda de artículos de segunda mano que dedica su recaudación a causas benéficas

charm [tʃɑːm] n encanto, atractivo; (talisman) hechizo; (on bracelet) dije m ▷ vt encantar; **charming** adj encantador(a)

chart [tʃɑːt] n (diagram) cuadro; (graph) gráfica; (map) carta de navegación ▷ vt (course) trazar; (progress) seguir; **charts** npl (Top 40): **the ~s** = los 40 principales (SP)

charter ['tʃɑːtəʳ] vt (plane) alquilar; (ship) fletar ▷ n (document) carta; (of university, company) estatutos mpl; **chartered accountant** (BRIT) n contable m/f diplomado/a; **charter flight** n vuelo chárter

chase [tʃeɪs] vt (pursue) perseguir; (also: ~ away) ahuyentar ▷ n persecución f

chat [tʃæt] vi (also: have a ~) charlar; (on Internet) chatear ▷ n charla; **chat up** vt (inf: girl) ligar con, enrollarse con; **chat room** n (Internet) chat m, canal m de charla; **chat show** (BRIT) n programa m de entrevistas

chatter ['tʃætəʳ] vi (person) charlar; (teeth) castañetear ▷ n (of birds) parloteo; (of people) charla, cháchara

chauffeur ['ʃəʊfəʳ] n chófer m

chauvinist ['ʃəʊvɪnɪst] n (male chauvinist) machista m; (nationalist) chovinista mf

cheap [tʃiːp] adj barato; (joke) de mal gusto; (poor quality) de mala calidad ▷ adv barato; **cheap day return** n billete de ida y vuelta el mismo día; **cheaply** adv barato, a bajo precio

cheat [tʃiːt] vi hacer trampa ▷ vt: **to ~ sb (out of sth)** estafar (algo) a algn ▷ n (person) tramposo/a; **cheat on** vt fus engañar

Chechnya [tʃɪtʃˈnjɑː] n Chechenia

check [tʃek] vt (examine) controlar; (facts) comprobar; (halt) parar, detener; (restrain) refrenar, restringir ▷ n (inspection) control m, inspección f; (curb) freno; (us: bill) nota, cuenta; (us) = **cheque**; (pattern: gen pl) cuadro; **check in** vi (at hotel) firmar el registro; (at airport) facturar el equipaje ▷ vt (luggage) facturar; **check off** vt (esp us: luggage) comprobar; (cross off) tachar; **check out** vi (of hotel) marcharse; **check up** vi: **to check up on sth** comprobar algo; **to check up on sb** investigar a algn; **checkbook** (us) = **chequebook**; **checked** adj a cuadros; **checkers** (us) n juego de damas; **check-in** n (also: **check-in desk**: at airport) mostrador m de facturación; **checking account** (us) n cuenta corriente; **checklist** n lista (de control); **checkmate** n jaque m mate; **checkout** n caja; **checkpoint** n (punto de) control m; **checkroom** (us) n consigna; **checkup** n (Med) reconocimiento general

cheddar ['tʃedəʳ] n (also: ~ cheese) queso m cheddar

cheek [tʃiːk] n mejilla; (impudence)

descaro; **what a ~!** ¡qué cara! **cheekbone** n pómulo; **cheeky** adj fresco, descarado

cheer [tʃɪəʳ] vt vitorear, aplaudir; (gladden) alegrar, animar ▷ vi dar vivas ▷ n viva m; **cheer up** vi animarse ▷ vt alegrar, animar; **cheerful** adj alegre

cheerio [tʃɪərɪˈəʊ] (BRIT) excl ¡hasta luego!

cheerleader ['tʃɪəliːdəʳ] n animador(a) m/f

cheese [tʃiːz] n queso; **cheeseburger** n hamburguesa con queso; **cheesecake** n pastel m de queso

chef [ʃef] n jefe/a m/f de cocina

chemical ['kemɪkəl] adj químico ▷ n producto químico

chemist ['kemɪst] n (BRIT: pharmacist) farmacéutico/a; (scientist) químico/a; **chemistry** n química; **chemist's (shop)** (BRIT) n farmacia

cheque [tʃek] (us **check**) n cheque m; **chequebook** n talonario de cheques (SP), chequera (LAM); **cheque card** n tarjeta de cheque

cherry ['tʃerɪ] n cereza; (also: ~ tree) cerezo

chess [tʃes] n ajedrez m

chest [tʃest] n (Anat) pecho; (box) cofre m, cajón m

chestnut ['tʃesnʌt] n castaña; (also: ~ tree) castaño

chest of drawers n cómoda

chew [tʃuː] vt mascar, masticar; **chewing gum** n chicle m

chic [ʃiːk] adj elegante

chick [tʃɪk] n pollito, polluelo; (inf: girl) chica

chicken ['tʃɪkɪn] n gallina, pollo; (food) pollo; (inf: coward) gallina mf; **chicken out** (inf) vi rajarse; **chickenpox** n varicela

chickpea ['tʃɪkpiː] n garbanzo

chief [tʃiːf] n jefe/a m/f ▷ adj principal; **chief executive (officer)** n director(a) m/f general; **chiefly** adv principalmente

child [tʃaɪld] (pl **-ren**) n niño/a; (offspring) hijo/a; **child abuse** n (with violence) malos tratos mpl a niños; (sexual) abuso m sexual de niños; **child benefit** n (BRIT) subsidio por cada hijo pequeño; **childbirth** n parto; **childcare** n cuidado de los niños; **childhood** n niñez f, infancia; **childish** adj pueril, aniñado; **child minder** (BRIT) n madre f de día; **children** ['tʃɪldrən] npl of **child**

Chile ['tʃɪlɪ] n Chile m; **Chilean** adj, n chileno/a m/f

chill [tʃɪl] n frío; (Med) resfriado ▷ vt enfriar; (Culin) congelar; **chill out** vi (esp us: inf) tranquilizarse

chil(l)i ['tʃɪlɪ] (BRIT) n chile m, ají m (SC)

chilly ['tʃɪlɪ] adj frío

chimney ['tʃɪmnɪ] n chimenea
chimpanzee [tʃɪmpæn'ziː] n chimpancé m
chin [tʃɪn] n mentón m, barbilla
China ['tʃaɪnə] n China
china ['tʃaɪnə] n porcelana; (crockery) loza
Chinese [tʃaɪ'niːz] adj chino ▷ n inv chino/a m/f; (Ling) chino
chip [tʃɪp] n (gen pl: Culin: BRIT) patata (SP) or papa (LAM) frita; (: US: also: **potato ~**) patata or papa frita; (of wood) astilla; (of glass, stone) lasca; (at poker) ficha; (Comput) chip m ▷ vt (cup, plate) desconchar; **chip shop** n pescadería (donde se vende principalmente pescado rebozado y patatas fritas)
chiropodist [kɪ'rɔpədɪst] (BRIT) n pedicuro/a, callista m/f
chisel ['tʃɪzl] n (for wood) escoplo; (for stone) cincel m
chives [tʃaɪvz] npl cebollinos mpl
chlorine ['klɔːriːn] n cloro
choc-ice ['tʃɔkaɪs] n (BRIT) helado m cubierto de chocolate
chocolate ['tʃɔklɪt] n chocolate m; (sweet) bombón m
choice [tʃɔɪs] n elección f, selección f; (option) opción f; (preference) preferencia ▷ adj escogido
choir ['kwaɪə*] n coro
choke [tʃəʊk] vi ahogarse; (on food) atragantarse ▷ vt estrangular, ahogar; (block): **to be ~d with** estar atascado de ▷ n (Aut) estárter m
cholesterol [kə'lɛstərɒl] n colesterol m
choose [tʃuːz] (pt **chose**, pp **chosen**) vt escoger, elegir; (team) seleccionar; **to ~ to do sth** optar por hacer algo
chop [tʃɔp] vt (wood) cortar, tajar; (Culin: also: **~ up**) picar ▷ n (Culin) chuleta; **chop down** vt (tree) talar; **chop off** vt cortar (de un tajo); **chopsticks** ['tʃɔpstɪks] npl palillos mpl
chord [kɔːd] n (Mus) acorde m
chore [tʃɔː*] n faena, tarea; (routine task) trabajo rutinario
chorus ['kɔːrəs] n coro; (repeated part of song) estribillo
chose [tʃəʊz] pt of **choose**
chosen ['tʃəʊzn] pp of **choose**
Christ [kraɪst] n Cristo
christen ['krɪsn] vt bautizar; **christening** n bautizo
Christian ['krɪstɪən] adj, n cristiano/a m/f; **Christianity** [-'ænɪtɪ] n cristianismo; **Christian name** n nombre m de pila
Christmas ['krɪsməs] n Navidad f; **Merry ~!** ¡Felices Pascuas!; **Christmas**

card n crismas m inv, tarjeta de Navidad; **Christmas carol** n villancico m; **Christmas Day** n día m de Navidad; **Christmas Eve** n Nochebuena; **Christmas pudding** n (esp BRIT) pudin m de Navidad; **Christmas tree** n árbol m de Navidad
chrome [krəʊm] n cromo
chronic ['krɒnɪk] adj crónico
chrysanthemum [krɪ'sænθəməm] n crisantemo
chubby ['tʃʌbɪ] adj regordete
chuck [tʃʌk] (inf) vt lanzar, arrojar; (BRIT: also: **~ up**) abandonar; **chuck out** vt (person) echar (fuera); (rubbish etc) tirar
chuckle ['tʃʌkl] vi reírse entre dientes
chum [tʃʌm] n compañero/a
chunk [tʃʌŋk] n pedazo, trozo
church [tʃəːtʃ] n iglesia; **churchyard** n cementerio
churn [tʃəːn] n (for butter) mantequera; (for milk) lechera
chute [ʃuːt] n (also: **rubbish ~**) vertedero; (for coal etc) rampa de caída
chutney ['tʃʌtnɪ] n condimento a base de frutas de la India
CIA (US) n abbr (= Central Intelligence Agency) CIA f
CID (BRIT) n abbr (= Criminal Investigation Department) ≈ B.I.C. f (SP)
cider ['saɪdə*] n sidra
cigar [sɪ'ɡɑː*] n puro
cigarette [sɪɡə'rɛt] n cigarrillo; **cigarette lighter** n mechero
cinema ['sɪnəmə] n cine m
cinnamon ['sɪnəmən] n canela
circle ['səːkl] n círculo; (in theatre) anfiteatro ▷ vi dar vueltas ▷ vt (surround) rodear, cercar; (move round) dar la vuelta a
circuit ['səːkɪt] n circuito; (tour) gira; (track) pista; (lap) vuelta
circular ['səːkjulə*] adj circular ▷ n circular f
circulate ['səːkjuleɪt] vi circular; (person: at party etc) hablar con los invitados ▷ vt poner en circulación; **circulation** [-'leɪʃən] n circulación f; (of newspaper) tirada
circumstances ['səːkəmstənsɪz] npl circunstancias fpl; (financial condition) situación f económica
circus ['səːkəs] n circo
cite [saɪt] vt citar
citizen ['sɪtɪzn] n (Pol) ciudadano/a; (of city) vecino/a, habitante mf; **citizenship** n ciudadanía; (BRIT: Scol) civismo
citrus fruits ['sɪtrəs-] npl agrios mpl
city ['sɪtɪ] n ciudad f; **the C~** centro financiero de Londres; **city centre** (BRIT)

n centro de la ciudad; **city technology college** *n* centro de formación profesional (*centro de enseñanza secundaria que da especial importancia a la ciencia y tecnología.*)

civic ['sɪvɪk] *adj* cívico; (*authorities*) municipal

civil ['sɪvɪl] *adj* civil; (*polite*) atento, cortés; **civilian** [sɪ'vɪlɪən] *adj* civil (*no militar*) ▷ *n* civil *mf*, paisano/a

civilization [sɪvɪlaɪ'zeɪʃən] *n* civilización *f*

civilized ['sɪvɪlaɪzd] *adj* civilizado

civil: civil law *n* derecho civil; **civil rights** *npl* derechos *mpl* civiles; **civil servant** *n* funcionario/a del Estado; **Civil Service** *n* administración *f* pública; **civil war** *n* guerra civil

CJD *n abbr* (= *Creutzfeldt-Jakob disease*) enfermedad de Creutzfeldt-Jakob

claim [kleɪm] *vt* exigir, reclamar; (*rights etc*) reivindicar; (*assert*) pretender ▷ *vi* (*for insurance*) reclamar ▷ *n* reclamación *f*; pretensión *f*; **claim form** *n* solicitud *f*

clam [klæm] *n* almeja

clamp [klæmp] *n* abrazadera, grapa ▷ *vt* (*two things together*) cerrar fuertemente; (*one thing on another*) afianzar (con abrazadera); (*Aut: wheel*) poner el cepo a

clan [klæn] *n* clan *m*

clap [klæp] *vi* aplaudir

claret ['klærət] *n* burdeos *m inv*

clarify ['klærɪfaɪ] *vt* aclarar

clarinet [klærɪ'nɛt] *n* clarinete *m*

clarity ['klærɪtɪ] *n* claridad *f*

clash [klæʃ] *n* enfrentamiento; choque *m*; desacuerdo; estruendo ▷ *vi* (*fight*) enfrentarse; (*beliefs*) chocar; (*disagree*) estar en desacuerdo; (*colours*) desentonar; (*two events*) coincidir

clasp [klɑːsp] *n* (*hold*) apretón *m*; (*of necklace, bag*) cierre *m* ▷ *vt* apretar; abrazar

class [klɑːs] *n* clase *f* ▷ *vt* clasificar

classic ['klæsɪk] *adj, n* clásico; **classical** *adj* clásico

classification [klæsɪfɪ'keɪʃən] *n* clasificación *f*

classify ['klæsɪfaɪ] *vt* clasificar

classmate ['klɑːsmeɪt] *n* compañero/a de clase

classroom ['klɑːsrum] *n* aula; **classroom assistant** *n* profesor(a) *m/f* de apoyo

classy ['klɑːsɪ] *adj* (*inf*) elegante, con estilo

clatter ['klætə*] *n* estrépito ▷ *vi* hacer ruido *or* estrépito

clause [klɔːz] *n* cláusula; (*Ling*) oración *f*

claustrophobic [klɔːstrə'fəubɪk] *adj* claustrofóbico; **I feel ~** me entra claustrofobia

claw [klɔː] *n* (*of cat*) uña; (*of bird of prey*)

garra; (*of lobster*) pinza

clay [kleɪ] *n* arcilla

clean [kliːn] *adj* limpio; (*record, reputation*) bueno, intachable; (*joke*) decente ▷ *vt* limpiar; (*hands etc*) lavar; **clean up** *vt* limpiar, asear; **cleaner** *n* (*person*) asistenta; (*substance*) producto para la limpieza; **cleaner's** *n* tintorería; **cleaning** *n* limpieza

cleanser ['klɛnzə*] *n* (*for face*) crema limpiadora

clear [klɪə*] *adj* claro; (*road, way*) libre; (*conscience*) limpio, tranquilo; (*skin*) terso; (*sky*) despejado ▷ *vt* (*space*) despejar, limpiar; (*Law: suspect*) absolver; (*obstacle*) salvar, saltar por encima de; (*cheque*) aceptar ▷ *vi* (*fog etc*) despejarse ▷ *adv*: **~ of** a distancia de; **to ~ the table** recoger *or* levantar la mesa; **clear away** *vt* (*things, clothes etc*) quitar (de en medio); (*dishes*) retirar; **clear up** *vt* (*mystery*) aclarar, resolver; **clearance** *n* (*removal*) despeje *m*; (*permission*) acreditación *f*; **clear-cut** *adj* bien definido, nítido; **clearing** *n* (*in wood*) claro; **clearly** *adv* claramente; (*evidently*) sin duda; **clearway** (*BRIT*) *n* carretera donde no se puede parar

clench [klɛntʃ] *vt* apretar, cerrar

clergy ['klɜːdʒɪ] *n* clero

clerk [klɑːk, (*US*) klɜːrk] *n* (*BRIT*) oficinista *mf*; (*US*) dependiente/a *m/f*

clever ['klɛvə*] *adj* (*intelligent*) inteligente, listo; (*skilful*) hábil; (*device, arrangement*) ingenioso

cliché ['kliːʃeɪ] *n* cliché *m*, frase *f* hecha

click [klɪk] *vt* (*tongue*) chasquear; (*heels*) taconear ▷ *vi* (*Comput*) hacer clic; **to ~ on an icon** hacer clic en un icono

client ['klaɪənt] *n* cliente *m/f*

cliff [klɪf] *n* acantilado

climate ['klaɪmɪt] *n* clima *m*; **climate change** *n* cambio climático

climax ['klaɪmæks] *n* (*of battle, career*) apogeo; (*of film, book*) punto culminante; (*sexual*) orgasmo

climb [klaɪm] *vi* subir; (*plant*) trepar; (*move with effort*): **to ~ over a wall/into a car** trepar a una tapia/subir a un coche ▷ *vt* (*stairs*) subir; (*tree*) trepar a; (*mountain*) escalar ▷ *n* subida; **climb down** *vi* (*fig*) volverse atrás; **climber** *n* alpinista *mf* (*SP, MEX*), andinista *mf* (*LAM*); **climbing** *n* alpinismo (*SP, MEX*), andinismo (*LAM*)

clinch [klɪntʃ] *vt* (*deal*) cerrar; (*argument*) remachar

cling [klɪŋ] (*pt, pp clung*) *vi*: **to ~ to** agarrarse a; (*clothes*) pegarse a

Clingfilm® ['klɪŋfɪlm] *n* plástico

adherente

clinic ['klɪnɪk] n clínica

clip [klɪp] n (for hair) horquilla; (also:
paper ~) sujetapapeles m inv, clip m; (TV,
Cinema) fragmento ▷ vt (cut) cortar; (also:
~ together) unir; **clipping** n (newspaper)
recorte m

cloak [kləuk] n capa, manto ▷ vt (fig)
encubrir, disimular; **cloakroom** n
guardarropa; (BRIT: WC) lavabo (SP), aseos
mpl (SP), baño (LAM)

clock [klɔk] n reloj m; **clock in** or **on** vi
(with card) fichar, picar; (start work) entrar
a trabajar; **clock off** or **out** vi (with card)
fichar or picar la salida; (leave work) salir del
trabajar; **clockwise** adv en el sentido de las
agujas del reloj; **clockwork** n aparato de
relojería ▷ adj (toy) de cuerda

clog [klɔg] n zueco, chanclo ▷ vt atascar
▷ vi (also: **~ up**) atascarse

clone [kləun] n clon m ▷ vt clonar

close¹ [kləus] adj (near): **~ (to)** cerca
(de); (friend) íntimo; (connection) estrecho;
(examination) detallado, minucioso;
(weather) bochornoso ▷ adv cerca; **~ by**, **~
at hand** muy cerca; **to have a ~ shave** (fig)
escaparse por un pelo

close² [kləuz] vt (shut) cerrar; (end)
concluir, terminar ▷ vi (shop etc) cerrarse;
(end) concluirse, terminarse ▷ n (end) fin
m, final m, conclusión f; **close down** vi
cerrarse definitivamente; **closed** adj (shop
etc) cerrado

closely ['kləuslɪ] adv (study) con detalle;
(watch) de cerca; (resemble) estrechamente

closet ['klɔzɪt] n armario

close-up ['kləusʌp] n primer plano

closing time n hora de cierre

closure ['kləuʒə*] n cierre m

clot [klɔt] n (gen) coágulo; (inf: idiot)
imbécil m/f ▷ vi (blood) coagularse

cloth [klɔθ] n (material) tela, paño; (rag)
trapo

clothes [kləuðz] npl ropa; **clothes line** n
cuerda (para tender la ropa); **clothes peg**
(US **clothes pin**) n pinza

clothing ['kləuðɪŋ] n = **clothes**

cloud [klaud] n nube f; **cloud over** vi (also
fig) nublarse; **cloudy** adj nublado, nubloso;
(liquid) turbio

clove [kləuv] n clavo; **~ of garlic** diente
m de ajo

clown [klaun] n payaso ▷ vi (also: **~
about**, **~ around**) hacer el payaso

club [klʌb] n (society) club m; (weapon)
porra, cachiporra; (also: **golf ~**) palo ▷ vt
aporrear ▷ vi: **to ~ together** (for gift)
comprar entre todos; **clubs** npl (Cards)

tréboles mpl; **club class** n (Aviat) clase f
preferente

clue [kluː] n pista; (in crosswords)
indicación f; **I haven't a ~** no tengo ni idea

clump [klʌmp] n (of trees) grupo

clumsy ['klʌmzɪ] adj (person) torpe,
desmañado; (tool) difícil de manejar;
(movement) desgarbado

clung [klʌŋ] pt, pp of **cling**

cluster ['klʌstə*] n grupo ▷ vi agruparse,
apiñarse

clutch [klʌtʃ] n (Aut) embrague m;
(grasp): **~es** garras fpl ▷ vt asir; agarrar

cm abbr (= centimetre) cm

Co. abbr = **county; company**

c/o abbr (= care of) c/a, a/c

coach [kəutʃ] n autocar m (SP), coche m
de línea; (horse-drawn) coche m; (of train)
vagón m, coche m; (Sport) entrenador(a) m/f,
instructor(a) m/f; (tutor) profesor(a) m/f
particular ▷ vt (Sport) entrenar; (student)
preparar, enseñar; **coach station** n (BRIT)
estación f de autobuses etc; **coach trip** n
excursión f en autocar

coal [kəul] n carbón m

coalition [kəuə'lɪʃən] n coalición f

coarse [kɔːs] adj basto, burdo; (vulgar)
grosero, ordinario

coast [kəust] n costa, litoral m ▷ vi (Aut)
ir en punto muerto; **coastal** adj costero,
costanero; **coastguard** n guardacostas m
inv; **coastline** n litoral m

coat [kəut] n abrigo; (of animal) pelaje
m, lana; (of paint) mano f, capa ▷ vt cubrir,
revestir; **coat hanger** n percha (SP),
gancho (LAM); **coating** n capa, baño

coax [kəuks] vt engatusar

cob [kɔb] n see **corn**

cobbled ['kɔbld] adj: **~ street** calle f
empedrada, calle f adoquinada

cobweb ['kɔbweb] n telaraña

cocaine [kə'keɪn] n cocaína

cock [kɔk] n (rooster) gallo; (male bird)
macho ▷ vt (gun) amartillar; **cockerel** n
gallito

cockney ['kɔknɪ] n habitante de ciertos
barrios de Londres

cockpit ['kɔkpɪt] n cabina

cockroach ['kɔkrəutʃ] n cucaracha

cocktail ['kɔkteɪl] n coctel m, cóctel m

cocoa ['kəukəu] n cacao; (drink) chocolate
m

coconut ['kəukənʌt] n coco

cod [kɔd] n bacalao

C.O.D. abbr (= cash on delivery) C.A.E.

code [kəud] n código; (cipher) clave f;
(dialling code) prefijo; (post code) código
postal

coeducational [kəʊedju'keɪʃənl] *adj* mixto

coffee ['kɒfɪ] *n* café *m*; **coffee bar** (BRIT) *n* cafetería; **coffee bean** *n* grano de café; **coffee break** *n* descanso (para tomar café); **coffee maker** *n* máquina de hacer café, cafetera; **coffeepot** *n* cafetera; **coffee shop** *n* café *m*; **coffee table** *n* mesita (para servir el café)

coffin ['kɒfɪn] *n* ataúd *m*

cog [kɒg] *n* (*wheel*) rueda dentada; (*tooth*) diente *m*

cognac ['kɒnjæk] *n* coñac *m*

coherent [kəʊ'hɪərənt] *adj* coherente

coil [kɔɪl] *n* rollo; (*Elec*) bobina, carrete *m*; (*contraceptive*) espiral *f* ▷ *vt* enrollar

coin [kɔɪn] *n* moneda ▷ *vt* (*word*) inventar, idear

coincide [kəʊɪn'saɪd] *vi* coincidir; (*agree*) estar de acuerdo; **coincidence** [kəʊ'ɪnsɪdəns] *n* casualidad *f*

Coke® [kəʊk] *n* Coca-Cola®

coke [kəʊk] *n* (*coal*) coque *m*

colander ['kɒləndə*] *n* colador *m*, escurridor *m*

cold [kəʊld] *adj* frío ▷ *n* frío; (*Med*) resfriado; **it's ~** hace frío; **to be ~** (*person*) tener frío; **to catch (a) ~** resfriarse; **in ~ blood** a sangre fría; **cold sore** *n* herpes *mpl or fpl*

coleslaw ['kəʊlslɔ:] *n* especie de ensalada de col

colic ['kɒlɪk] *n* cólico

collaborate [kə'læbəreɪt] *vi* colaborar

collapse [kə'læps] *vi* hundirse, derrumbarse; (*Med*) sufrir un colapso ▷ *n* hundimiento, derrumbamiento; (*Med*) colapso

collar ['kɒlə*] *n* (*of coat, shirt*) cuello; (*of dog etc*) collar; **collarbone** *n* clavícula

colleague ['kɒli:g] *n* colega *mf*; (*at work*) compañero/a

collect [kə'lekt] *vt* (*litter, mail etc*) recoger; (*as a hobby*) coleccionar; (BRIT: *call and pick up*) recoger; (*debts, subscriptions etc*) recaudar ▷ *vi* reunirse; (*dust*) acumularse; **to call ~** (US *Tel*) llamar a cobro revertido; **collection** [kə'lekʃən] *n* colección *f*; (*of mail, for charity*) recogida; **collective** [kə'lektɪv] *adj* colectivo; **collector** *n* coleccionista *mf*

college ['kɒlɪdʒ] *n* colegio mayor; (*of agriculture, technology*) escuela universitaria

collide [kə'laɪd] *vi* chocar

collision [kə'lɪʒən] *n* choque *m*

cologne [kə'ləʊn] *n* (*also:* **eau de ~**) (agua de) colonia

Colombia [kə'lɒmbɪə] *n* Colombia; **Colombian** *adj, n* colombiano/a

colon ['kəʊlən] *n* (*sign*) dos puntos; (*Med*) colon *m*

colonel ['kɜ:nl] *n* coronel *m*

colonial [kə'ləʊnɪəl] *adj* colonial

colony ['kɒlənɪ] *n* colonia

colour *etc* ['kʌlə*] (US **color** *etc*) *n* color *m* ▷ *vt* color(e)ar; (*dye*) teñir; (*fig: account*) adornar; (: *judgement*) distorsionar ▷ *vi* (*blush*) sonrojarse; **colour in** *vt* colorear; **colour-blind** *adj* daltónico; **coloured** *adj* de color; (*photo*) en color; **colour film** *n* película en color; **colourful** *adj* lleno de color; (*story*) fantástico; (*person*) excéntrico; **colouring** *n* (*complexion*) tez *f*; (*in food*) colorante *m*; **colour television** *n* televisión *f* en color

column ['kɒləm] *n* columna

coma ['kəʊmə] *n* coma *m*

comb [kəʊm] *n* peine *m*; (*ornamental*) peineta ▷ *vt* (*hair*) peinar; (*area*) registrar a fondo

combat ['kɒmbæt] *n* combate *m* ▷ *vt* combatir

combination [kɒmbɪ'neɪʃən] *n* combinación *f*

combine [*vb* kəm'baɪn, *n* 'kɒmbaɪn] *vt* combinar; (*qualities*) reunir ▷ *vi* combinarse ▷ *n* (*Econ*) cartel *m*

○ **KEYWORD**

come [kʌm] (*pt* **came**, *pp* **come**) *vi*
1 (*movement towards*) venir; **to come running** venir corriendo
2 (*arrive*) llegar; **he's come here to work** ha venido aquí para trabajar; **to come home** volver a casa
3 (*reach*): **to come to** llegar a; **the bill came to £40** la cuenta ascendía a cuarenta libras
4 (*occur*): **an idea came to me** se me ocurrió una idea
5 (*be, become*): **to come loose/undone** *etc* aflojarse/desabrocharse/desatarse *etc*; **I've come to like him** por fin ha llegado a gustarme

come across *vt fus* (*person*) topar con; (*thing*) dar con

come along *vi* (BRIT: *progress*) ir

come back *vi* (*return*) volver

come down *vi* (*price*) bajar; (*tree, building*) ser derribado

come from *vt fus* (*place, source*) ser de

come in *vi* (*visitor*) entrar; (*train, report*) llegar; (*fashion*) ponerse de moda; (*on deal etc*) entrar

come off *vi* (*button*) soltarse, desprenderse; (*attempt*) salir bien

come on *vi* (*pupil*) progresar; (*work, project*)

desarrollarse; (lights) encenderse; (electricity)
volver; **come on!** ¡vamos!
come out vi (fact) salir a la luz; (book, sun)
salir; (stain) quitarse
come round vi (after faint, operation) volver
en sí
come to vi (wake) volver en sí
come up vi (sun) salir; (problem) surgir;
(event) aproximarse; (in conversation)
mencionarse
come up with vt fus (idea) sugerir; (money)
conseguir

comeback ['kʌmbæk] n: **to make a ~**
(Theatre) volver a las tablas
comedian [kə'miːdiən] n humorista mf
comedy ['kɒmɪdɪ] n comedia; (humour)
comicidad f
comet ['kɒmɪt] n cometa m
comfort ['kʌmfət] n bienestar m; (relief)
alivio ▷ vt consolar; **comfortable** adj
cómodo; (financially) acomodado; (easy)
fácil; **comfort station** (US) n servicios mpl
comic ['kɒmɪk] adj (also: **~al**) cómico ▷ n
(comedian) cómico; (BRIT: for children) tebeo;
(BRIT: for adults) comic m; **comic book** (US)
n libro m de cómics; **comic strip** n tira
cómica
comma ['kɒmə] n coma
command [kə'mɑːnd] n orden f,
mandato; (Mil: authority) mando; (mastery)
dominio ▷ vt (troops) mandar; (give orders
to): **to ~ sb to do** mandar or ordenar a algn
hacer; **commander** n (Mil) comandante
mf, jefe/a m/f
commemorate [kə'mɛməreɪt] vt
conmemorar
commence [kə'mɛns] vt, vi comenzar,
empezar; **commencement** (US) n (Univ)
(ceremonia de) graduación f
commend [kə'mɛnd] vt elogiar, alabar;
(recommend) recomendar
comment ['kɒmɛnt] n comentario
▷ vi: **to ~ on** hacer comentarios sobre; **"no
~"** (written) "sin comentarios"; (spoken)
"no tengo nada que decir"; **commentary**
['kɒməntərɪ] n comentario; **commentator**
['kɒmənteɪtə*] n comentarista mf
commerce ['kɒmɜːs] n comercio
commercial [kə'mɜːʃəl] adj comercial ▷ n
(TV, Radio) anuncio; **commercial break** n
intermedio para publicidad
commission [kə'mɪʃən] n (committee,
fee) comisión f ▷ vt (work of art) encargar;
out of ~ fuera de servicio; **commissioner** n
(Police) comisario de policía
commit [kə'mɪt] vt (act) cometer;
(resources) dedicar; (to sb's care) entregar;

to ~ o.s. (to do) comprometerse (a hacer);
to ~ suicide suicidarse; **commitment** n
compromiso; (to ideology etc) entrega
committee [kə'mɪtɪ] n comité m
commodity [kə'mɒdɪtɪ] n mercancía
common ['kɒmən] adj común; (pej)
ordinario ▷ n campo común; **commonly**
adv comúnmente; **commonplace** adj de lo
más común; **Commons** (BRIT) npl (Pol): **the
Commons** (la Cámara de) los Comunes;
common sense n sentido común;
Commonwealth n: **the Commonwealth**
la Commonwealth
communal ['kɒmjuːnl] adj (property)
comunal; (kitchen) común
commune [n 'kɒmjuːn, vb kə'mjuːn] n
(group) comuna ▷ vi: **to ~ with** comulgar or
conversar con
communicate [kə'mjuːnɪkeɪt] vt
comunicar ▷ vi: **to ~ (with)** comunicarse
(con); (in writing) estar en contacto (con)
communication [kəmjuːnɪ'keɪʃən] n
comunicación f
communion [kə'mjuːnɪən] n (also: **Holy
~**) comunión f
communism ['kɒmjunɪzəm] n
comunismo; **communist** adj, n comunista
mf
community [kə'mjuːnɪtɪ] n comunidad
f; (large group) colectividad f; **community
centre** (US **community center**) n centro
social; **community service** n trabajo m
comunitario (prestado en lugar de cumplir una
pena de prisión)
commute [kə'mjuːt] vi viajar a diario de la
casa al trabajo ▷ vt conmutar; **commuter** n
persona que viaja a diario de la casa al trabajo
compact [adj kəm'pækt, n 'kɒmpækt] adj
compacto ▷ n (also: **powder ~**) polvera;
compact disc n compact disc m; **compact
disc player** n reproductor m de disco
compacto, compact disc m
companion [kəm'pænɪən] n
compañero/a
company ['kʌmpənɪ] n compañía;
(Comm) sociedad f, compañía; **to keep sb ~**
acompañar a algn; **company car** n coche
m de la empresa; **company director** n
director(a) m/f de empresa
comparable ['kɒmpərəbl] adj
comparable
comparative [kəm'pærətɪv] adj relativo;
(study) comparativo; **comparatively** adv
(relatively) relativamente
compare [kəm'pɛə*] vt: **to ~ sth/sb with**
or **to** comparar algo/a algn con ▷ vi: **to
~ (with)** compararse (con); **comparison**
[-'pærɪsn] n comparación f

compartment [kəm'pɑ:tmənt] n (also: Rail) compartim(i)ento

compass ['kʌmpəs] n brújula; **compasses** npl (Math) compás m

compassion [kəm'pæʃən] n compasión f

compatible [kəm'pætɪbl] adj compatible

compel [kəm'pɛl] vt obligar; **compelling** adj (fig: argument) convincente

compensate ['kɔmpənseɪt] vt compensar ⊳ vi: **to ~ for** compensar; **compensation** [-'seɪʃən] n (for loss) indemnización f

compete [kəm'pi:t] vi (take part) tomar parte, concurrir; (vie with): **to ~ with** competir con, hacer competencia a

competent ['kɔmpɪtənt] adj competente, capaz

competition [kɔmpɪ'tɪʃən] n (contest) concurso; (rivalry) competencia

competitive [kəm'pɛtɪtɪv] adj (Econ, Sport) competitivo

competitor [kəm'pɛtɪtə*] n (rival) competidor(a) m/f; (participant) concursante mf

complacent [kəm'pleɪsənt] adj autocomplaciente

complain [kəm'pleɪn] vi quejarse; (Comm) reclamar; **complaint** n queja; reclamación f; (Med) enfermedad f

complement [n 'kɔmplɪmənt, vb 'kɔmplɪmɛnt] n complemento; (esp of ship's crew) dotación f ⊳ vt (enhance) complementar; **complementary** [kɔmplɪ'mɛntərɪ] adj complementario

complete [kəm'pli:t] adj (full) completo; (finished) acabado ⊳ vt (fulfil) completar; (finish) acabar; (a form) llenar; **completely** adv completamente; **completion** [-'pli:ʃən] n terminación f; (of contract) realización f

complex ['kɔmplɛks] adj, n complejo

complexion [kəm'plɛkʃən] n (of face) tez f, cutis m

compliance [kəm'plaɪəns] n (submission) sumisión f; (agreement) conformidad f; **in ~ with** de acuerdo con

complicate ['kɔmplɪkeɪt] vt complicar; **complicated** adj complicado; **complication** [-'keɪʃən] n complicación f

compliment n ['kɔmplɪmənt] n (formal) cumplido ⊳ vt felicitar; **complimentary** [-'mɛntərɪ] adj lisonjero; (free) de favor

comply [kəm'plaɪ] vi: **to ~ with** cumplir con

component [kəm'pəunənt] adj componente ⊳ n (Tech) pieza

compose [kəm'pəuz] vt: **to be ~d of** componerse de; (music etc) componer;

to ~ o.s. tranquilizarse; **composer** n (Mus) compositor(a) m/f; **composition** [kɔmpə'zɪʃən] n composición f

composure [kəm'pəuʒə*] n serenidad f, calma

compound ['kɔmpaund] n (Chem) compuesto; (Ling) palabra compuesta; (enclosure) recinto ⊳ adj compuesto; (fracture) complicado

comprehension [-'hɛnʃən] n comprensión f

comprehensive [kɔmprɪ'hɛnsɪv] adj exhaustivo; (Insurance) contra todo riesgo; **comprehensive (school)** n centro estatal de enseñanza secundaria ≈ Instituto Nacional de Bachillerato (sp)

compress [vb kəm'prɛs, n 'kɔmprɛs] vt comprimir; (information) condensar ⊳ n (Med) compresa

comprise [kəm'praɪz] vt (also: **be ~d of**) comprender, constar de; (constitute) constituir

compromise ['kɔmprəmaɪz] n (agreement) arreglo ⊳ vt comprometer ⊳ vi transigir

compulsive [kəm'pʌlsɪv] adj compulsivo; (viewing, reading) obligado

compulsory [kəm'pʌlsərɪ] adj obligatorio

computer [kəm'pju:tə*] n ordenador m, computador m, computadora; **computer game** n juego para ordenador; **computer-generated** adj realizado por ordenador, creado por ordenador; **computerize** vt (data) computerizar; (system) informatizar; **we're computerized now** ya nos hemos informatizado; **computer programmer** n programador(a) m/f; **computer programming** n programación f; **computer science** n informática; **computer studies** npl informática fsg, computación fsg (LAM); **computing** [kəm-'pju:tɪŋ] n (activity, science) informática

con [kɔn] vt (deceive) engañar; (cheat) estafar ⊳ n estafa

conceal [kən'si:l] vt ocultar

concede [kən'si:d] vt (point, argument) reconocer; (territory) ceder; **to ~ (defeat)** darse por vencido; **to ~ that** admitir que

conceited [kən'si:tɪd] adj presumido

conceive [kən'si:v] vt, vi concebir

concentrate ['kɔnsəntreɪt] vi concentrarse ⊳ vt concentrar

concentration [kɔnsən'treɪʃən] n concentración f

concept ['kɔnsɛpt] n concepto

concern [kən'sə:n] n (matter) asunto; (Comm) empresa; (anxiety) preocupación *f* ▷ *vt* (*worry*) preocupar; (*involve*) afectar; (*relate to*) tener que ver con; **to be ~ed (about)** interesarse (por), preocuparse (por); **concerning** *prep* sobre, acerca de

concert ['kɔnsət] *n* concierto; **concert hall** *n* sala de conciertos

concerto [kən'tʃə:təu] *n* concierto

concession [kən'seʃən] *n* concesión *f*; **tax ~** privilegio fiscal

concise [kən'saɪs] *adj* conciso

conclude [kən'klu:d] *vt* concluir; (*treaty etc*) firmar; (*agreement*) llegar a; (*decide*) llegar a la conclusión de; **conclusion** [-'klu:ʒən] *n* conclusión *f*; firma

concrete ['kɔnkri:t] *n* hormigón *m* ▷ *adj* de hormigón; (*fig*) concreto

concussion [kən'kʌʃən] *n* conmoción *f* cerebral

condemn [kən'dem] *vt* condenar; (*building*) declarar en ruina

condensation [kɔnden'seɪʃən] *n* condensación *f*

condense [kən'dens] *vi* condensarse ▷ *vt* condensar, abreviar

condition [kən'dɪʃən] *n* condición *f*, estado; (*requirement*) condición *f* ▷ *vt* condicionar; **on ~ that** a condición (de) que; **conditional** [kən'dɪʃənl] *adj* condicional; **conditioner** *n* suavizante

condo ['kɔndəu] (*US*) *n* (*inf*) = **condominium**

condom ['kɔndəm] *n* condón *m*

condominium [kɔndə'mɪnɪəm] (*US*) *n* (*building*) bloque *m* de pisos or apartamentos (*propiedad de quienes lo habitan*), condominio (*LAM*); (*apartment*) piso or apartamento (en propiedad), condominio (*LAM*)

condone [kən'dəun] *vt* condonar

conduct [*n* 'kɔndʌkt, *vb* kən'dʌkt] *n* conducta, comportamiento ▷ *vt* (*lead*) conducir; (*manage*) llevar a cabo, dirigir; (*Mus*) dirigir; **to ~ o.s.** comportarse; **conducted tour** (*BRIT*) *n* visita acompañada; **conductor** *n* (*of orchestra*) director *m*; (*US: on train*) revisor(a) *m/f*; (*on bus*) cobrador *m*; (*Elec*) conductor *m*

cone [kəun] *n* cono; (*pine cone*) piña; (*on road*) pivote *m*; (*for ice-cream*) cucurucho

confectionery [kən'fekʃənrɪ] *n* dulces *mpl*

confer [kən'fə:*] *vt*: **to ~ sth on** otorgar algo a ▷ *vi* conferenciar

conference ['kɔnfərns] *n* (*meeting*) reunión *f*; (*convention*) congreso

confess [kən'fes] *vt* confesar ▷ *vi* admitir; **confession** [-'feʃən] *n* confesión *f*

confide [kən'faɪd] *vi*: **to ~ in** confiar en

confidence ['kɔnfɪdns] *n* (*also*: **self-~**)

confianza; (*secret*) confidencia; **in ~** (*speak, write*) en confianza; **confident** *adj* seguro de sí mismo; (*certain*) seguro; **confidential** [kɔnfɪ'denʃəl] *adj* confidencial

confine [kən'faɪn] *vt* (*limit*) limitar; (*shut up*) encerrar; **confined** *adj* (*space*) reducido

confirm [kən'fə:m] *vt* confirmar; **confirmation** [kɔnfə'meɪʃən] *n* confirmación *f*

confiscate ['kɔnfɪskeɪt] *vt* confiscar

conflict [*n* 'kɔnflɪkt, *vb* kən'flɪkt] *n* conflicto ▷ *vi* (*opinions*) chocar

conform [kən'fɔ:m] *vi* conformarse; **to ~ to** ajustarse a

confront [kən'frʌnt] *vt* (*problems*) hacer frente a; (*enemy, danger*) enfrentarse con; **confrontation** [kɔnfrən'teɪʃən] *n* enfrentamiento

confuse [kən'fju:z] *vt* (*perplex*) aturdir, desconcertar; (*mix up*) confundir; (*complicate*) complicar; **confused** *adj* confuso; (*person*) perplejo; **confusing** *adj* confuso; **confusion** [-'fju:ʒən] *n* confusión *f*

congestion [kən'dʒestʃən] *n* congestión *f*

congratulate [kən'grætjuleɪt] *vt*: **to ~ sb (on)** felicitar a algn (por); **congratulations** [-'leɪʃənz] *npl* felicitaciones *fpl*; **congratulations!** ¡enhorabuena!

congregation [-'geɪʃən] *n* (*of a church*) feligreses *mpl*

congress ['kɔŋgres] *n* congreso; (*US*): **C~** Congreso; **congressman** (*irreg: US*) *n* miembro del Congreso; **congresswoman** (*irreg: US*) *n* diputada, miembro *f* del Congreso

conifer ['kɔnɪfə*] *n* conífera

conjugate ['kɔndʒugeɪt] *vt* conjugar

conjugation [kɔndʒə'geɪʃən] *n* conjugación *f*

conjunction [kən'dʒʌŋkʃən] *n* conjunción *f*; **in ~ with** junto con

conjure ['kʌndʒə*] *vi* hacer juegos de manos

connect [kə'nekt] *vt* juntar, unir; (*Elec*) conectar; (*Tel: subscriber*) poner; (: *caller*) poner al habla; (*fig*) relacionar, asociar ▷ *vi*: **to ~ with** (*train*) enlazar con; **to be ~ed with** (*associated*) estar relacionado con; **connecting flight** *n* vuelo *m* de enlace; **connection** [-ʃən] *n* juntura, unión *f*; (*Elec*) conexión *f*; (*Rail*) enlace *m*; (*Tel*) comunicación *f*; (*fig*) relación *f*

conquer ['kɔŋkə*] *vt* (*territory*) conquistar; (*enemy, feelings*) vencer

conquest ['kɔŋkwest] *n* conquista

cons [kɔnz] *npl see* **convenience; pro; mod**

conscience ['kɒnʃəns] n conciencia
conscientious [kɒnʃɪˈenʃəs] adj
concienzudo; (objection) de conciencia
conscious ['kɒnʃəs] adj (deliberate)
deliberado; (awake, aware) consciente;
consciousness n conciencia; (Med)
conocimiento
consecutive [kənˈsekjutɪv] adj
consecutivo; **on 3 ~ occasions** en 3
ocasiones consecutivas
consensus [kənˈsensəs] n consenso
consent [kənˈsent] n consentimiento
▷ vi: **to ~ (to)** consentir (en)
consequence ['kɒnsɪkwəns] n
consecuencia; (significance) importancia
consequently ['kɒnsɪkwəntlɪ] adv por
consiguiente
conservation [kɒnsəˈveɪʃən] n
conservación f
conservative [kənˈsɜːvətɪv] adj
conservador(a); (estimate etc) cauteloso;
Conservative (BRIT) adj, n (Pol)
conservador(a) m/f
conservatory [kənˈsɜːvətrɪ] n
invernadero; (Mus) conservatorio
consider [kənˈsɪdə*] vt considerar;
(take into account) tener en cuenta;
(study) estudiar, examinar; **to ~ doing
sth** pensar en (la posibilidad de) hacer
algo; **considerable** adj considerable;
considerably adv notablemente;
considerate adj considerado;
consideration [-ˈreɪʃən] n consideración
f; (factor) factor m; **to give sth further
consideration** estudiar algo más a fondo;
considering prep teniendo en cuenta
consignment [kənˈsaɪnmənt] n envío
consist [kənˈsɪst] vi: **to ~ of** consistir en
consistency [kənˈsɪstənsɪ] n (of argument
etc) coherencia; consecuencia; (thickness)
consistencia
consistent [kənˈsɪstənt] adj (person)
consecuente; (argument etc) coherente
consolation [kɒnsəˈleɪʃən] n consuelo
console¹ [kənˈsəul] vt consolar
console² ['kɒnsəul] n consola
consonant ['kɒnsənənt] n consonante f
conspicuous [kənˈspɪkjuəs] adj (visible)
visible
conspiracy [kənˈspɪrəsɪ] n conjura,
complot m
constable ['kʌnstəbl] (BRIT) n policía mf;
chief ~ = jefe m de policía
constant ['kɒnstənt] adj constante;
constantly adv constantemente
constipated ['kɒnstɪpeɪtəd] adj
estreñido

▌ Be careful not to translate **constipated**

▌ by the Spanish word constipado.
constipation [kɒnstɪˈpeɪʃən] n
estreñimiento
constituency [kənˈstɪtjuənsɪ] n
(Pol: area) distrito electoral; (: electors)
electorado
constitute ['kɒnstɪtjuːt] vt constituir
constitution [kɒnstɪˈtjuːʃən] n
constitución f
constraint [kənˈstreɪnt] n obligación f;
(limit) restricción f
construct [kənˈstrʌkt] vt construir;
construction [-ʃən] n construcción f;
constructive adj constructivo
consul ['kɒnsl] n cónsul mf; **consulate**
['kɒnsjulɪt] n consulado
consult [kənˈsʌlt] vt consultar;
consultant n (BRIT Med) especialista mf;
(other specialist) asesor(a) m/f; **consultation**
[kɒnsəlˈteɪʃən] n consulta; **consulting
room** (BRIT) n consultorio
consume [kənˈsjuːm] vt (eat) comerse;
(drink) beberse; (fire etc, Comm) consumir;
consumer n consumidor(a) m/f
consumption [kənˈsʌmpʃən] n consumo
cont. abbr (= continued) sigue
contact ['kɒntækt] n contacto; (person)
contacto; (: pej) enchufe m ▷ vt ponerse en
contacto con; **contact lenses** npl lentes fpl
de contacto
contagious [kənˈteɪdʒəs] adj contagioso
contain [kənˈteɪn] vt contener; **to ~ o.s.**
contenerse; **container** n recipiente m; (for
shipping etc) contenedor m
contaminate [kənˈtæmɪneɪt] vt
contaminar
cont'd abbr (= continued) sigue
contemplate ['kɒntəmpleɪt] vt
contemplar; (reflect upon) considerar
contemporary [kənˈtempərərɪ] adj, n
contemporáneo/a m/f
contempt [kənˈtempt] n desprecio; **~ of
court** (Law) desacato (a los tribunales)
contend [kənˈtend] vt (argue) afirmar
▷ vi: **to ~ with/for** luchar contra/por
content [adj, vb kənˈtent, n ˈkɒntent]
adj (happy) contento; (satisfied) satisfecho
▷ vt contentar; satisfacer ▷ n contenido;
contents npl contenido; **(table of) ~s**
índice m de materias; **contented** adj
contento; satisfecho
contest [n ˈkɒntest, vb kənˈtest] n lucha;
(competition) concurso ▷ vt (dispute)
impugnar; (Pol) presentarse como
candidato/a en

▌ Be careful not to translate **contest** by the
▌ Spanish word contestar.

contestant [kənˈtestənt] n concursante

mf; (*in fight*) contendiente *mf*

context ['kɒntɛkst] *n* contexto

continent ['kɒntɪnənt] *n* continente
m; **the C~** (BRIT) el continente europeo;
continental [-'nɛntl] *adj* continental;
continental breakfast *n* desayuno
estilo europeo; **continental quilt** (BRIT) *n*
edredón *m*

continual [kən'tɪnjuəl] *adj* continuo;
continually *adv* constantemente

continue [kən'tɪnju:] *vi, vt* seguir,
continuar

continuity [kɒntɪ'nju:ɪtɪ] *n* (*also Cine*)
continuidad *f*

continuous [kən'tɪnjuəs] *adj* continuo;
continuous assessment *n* (BRIT)
evaluación *f* continua; **continuously** *adv*
continuamente

contour ['kɒntuə*] *n* contorno; (*also: ~
line*) curva de nivel

contraception [kɒntrə'sɛpʃən] *n*
contracepción *f*

contraceptive [kɒntrə'sɛptɪv] *adj, n*
anticonceptivo

contract [*n* 'kɒntrækt, *vb* kən'trækt]
n contrato ▷ *vi* (*Comm*): **to ~ to do sth**
comprometerse por contrato a hacer algo;
(*become smaller*) contraerse, encogerse ▷ *vt*
contraer; **contractor** *n* contratista *mf*

contradict [kɒntrə'dɪkt] *vt* contradecir;
contradiction [-ʃən] *n* contradicción *f*

contrary¹ ['kɒntrərɪ] *adj* contrario ▷ *n*
lo contrario; **on the ~** al contrario; **unless
you hear to the ~** a no ser que le digan lo
contrario

contrary² [kən'trɛərɪ] *adj* (*perverse*) terco

contrast [*n* 'kɒntrɑːst, *vt* kən'trɑːst] *n*
contraste *m* ▷ *vt* comparar; **in ~ to** en
contraste con

contribute [kən'trɪbjuːt] *vi* contribuir
▷ *vt*: **to ~ £10/an article to** contribuir con 10
libras/un artículo a; **to ~ to** (*charity*) donar
a; (*newspaper*) escribir para; (*discussion*)
intervenir en; **contribution** [kɒntrɪ'bjuː-
ʃən] *n* (*donation*) donativo; (BRIT: *for
social security*) cotización *f*; (*to debate*)
intervención *f*; (*to journal*) colaboración
f; **contributor** *n* contribuyente *mf*; (*to
newspaper*) colaborador(a) *m/f*

control [kən'trəul] *vt* controlar; (*process
etc*) dirigir; (*machinery*) manejar; (*temper*)
dominar; (*disease*) contener ▷ *n* control
m; **controls** *npl* (*of vehicle*) instrumentos
mpl de mando; (*of radio*) controles *mpl*;
(*governmental*) medidas *fpl* de control; **under
~** bajo control; **to be in ~ of** tener el mando
de; **the car went out of ~** se perdió el
control del coche; **control tower** *n* (*Aviat*)

torre *f* de control

controversial [kɒntrə'vəːʃl] *adj* polémico

controversy ['kɒntrəvəːsɪ] *n* polémica

convenience [kən'viːnɪəns] *n* (*easiness*)
comodidad *f*; (*suitability*) idoneidad *f*;
(*advantage*) ventaja; **at your ~** cuando le sea
conveniente; **all modern ~s, all mod cons**
(BRIT) todo confort

convenient [kən'viːnɪənt] *adj* (*useful*)
útil; (*place, time*) conveniente

convent ['kɒnvənt] *n* convento

convention [kən'vɛnʃən] *n* convención
f; (*meeting*) asamblea; (*agreement*) convenio;
conventional *adj* convencional

conversation [kɒnvə'seɪʃən] *n*
conversación *f*

conversely [-'vəːslɪ] *adv* a la inversa

conversion [kən'vəːʃən] *n* conversión *f*

convert [*vb* kən'vəːt, *n* 'kɒnvəːt] *vt* (*Rel,
Comm*) convertir; (*alter*): **to ~ sth into/to**
transformar algo en/convertir algo a ▷ *n*
converso/a; **convertible** *adj* convertible
▷ *n* descapotable *m*

convey [kən'veɪ] *vt* llevar; (*thanks*)
comunicar; (*idea*) expresar; **conveyor belt** *n*
cinta transportadora

convict [*vb* kən'vɪkt, *n* 'kɒnvɪkt] *vt* (*find
guilty*) declarar culpable a ▷ *n* presidiario/a;
conviction [-ʃən] *n* condena; (*belief,
certainty*) convicción *f*

convince [kən'vɪns] *vt* convencer;
convinced *adj*: **convinced of/that**
convencido de/de que; **convincing** *adj*
convincente

convoy ['kɒnvɔɪ] *n* convoy *m*

cook [kuk] *vt* (*stew etc*) guisar; (*meal*)
preparar ▷ *vi* cocer; (*person*) cocinar ▷ *n*
cocinero/a; **cook book** *n* libro de cocina;
cooker *n* cocina; **cookery** *n* cocina;
cookery book (BRIT) *n* = **cook book**; **cookie**
(US) *n* galleta; **cooking** *n* cocina

cool [kuːl] *adj* fresco; (*not afraid*) tranquilo;
(*unfriendly*) frío ▷ *vt* enfriar ▷ *vi* enfriarse;
cool down *vi* enfriarse; (*fig: person,
situation*) calmarse; **cool off** *vi* (*become
calmer*) calmarse, apaciguarse; (*lose
enthusiasm*) perder (el) interés, enfriarse

cop [kɒp] (*inf*) *n* poli *mf* (SP), tira *mf* (MEX)

cope [kəup] *vi*: **to ~ with** (*problem*) hacer
frente a

copper ['kɒpə*] *n* (*metal*) cobre *m*; (BRIT: *inf*)
poli *mf*, tira *mf* (MEX)

copy ['kɒpɪ] *n* copia; (*of book etc*) ejemplar
m ▷ *vt* copiar; **copyright** *n* derechos *mpl*
de autor

coral ['kɒrəl] *n* coral *m*

cord [kɔːd] *n* cuerda; (*Elec*) cable *m*; (*fabric*)
pana; **cords** *npl* (*trousers*) pantalones *mpl* de

pana; **cordless** adj sin hilos
corduroy ['kɔːdərɔɪ] n pana
core [kɔː*] n centro, núcleo; (of fruit) corazón m; (of problem) meollo ▷ vt quitar el corazón de
coriander [kɒrɪ'ændə*] n culantro
cork [kɔːk] n corcho; (tree) alcornoque m; **corkscrew** n sacacorchos m inv
corn [kɔːn] n (BRIT: cereal crop) trigo; (US: maize) maíz m; (on foot) callo; ~ **on the cob** (Culin) mazorca, elote m (MEX), choclo (SC)
corned beef ['kɔːnd-] n carne f acecinada (en lata)
corner ['kɔːnə*] n (outside) esquina; (inside) rincón m; (in road) curva; (Football) córner m; (Boxing) esquina ▷ vt (trap) arrinconar; (Comm) acaparar ▷ vi (in car) tomar las curvas; **corner shop** (BRIT) tienda de la esquina
cornflakes ['kɔːnfleɪks] npl copos mpl de maíz, cornflakes mpl
cornflour ['kɔːnflauə*] (BRIT) n harina de maíz
cornstarch ['kɔːnstɑːtʃ] (US) n = **cornflour**
Cornwall ['kɔːnwəl] n Cornualles m
coronary ['kɔrənərɪ] n (also: ~ **thrombosis**) infarto
coronation [kɔrə'neɪʃən] n coronación f
coroner ['kɔrənə*] n juez mf de instrucción
corporal ['kɔːpərl] n cabo ▷ adj: ~ **punishment** castigo corporal
corporate ['kɔːpərɪt] adj (action, ownership) colectivo; (finance, image) corporativo
corporation [kɔːpə'reɪʃən] n (of town) ayuntamiento; (Comm) corporación f
corps [kɔː*, pl kɔːz] n inv cuerpo; **diplomatic** ~ cuerpo diplomático; **press** ~ gabinete m de prensa
corpse [kɔːps] n cadáver m
correct [kə'rɛkt] adj justo, exacto; (proper) correcto ▷ vt corregir; (exam) corregir, calificar; **correction** [-ʃən] n (act) corrección f; (instance) rectificación f
correspond [kɔrɪs'pɔnd] vi (write): **to ~ (with)** escribirse (con); (be equivalent to): **to ~ (to)** corresponder (a); (be in accordance): **to ~ (with)** corresponder (con); **correspondence** n correspondencia; **correspondent** n corresponsal mf; **corresponding** adj correspondiente
corridor ['kɔrɪdɔː*] n pasillo
corrode [kə'rəud] vt corroer ▷ vi corroerse
corrupt [kə'rʌpt] adj (person) corrupto; (Comput) corrompido ▷ vt corromper;

(Comput) degradar; **corruption** n corrupción f; (of data) alteración f
Corsica ['kɔːsɪkə] n Córcega
cosmetic [kɒz'mɛtɪk] adj, n cosmético; **cosmetic surgery** n cirugía f estética
cosmopolitan [kɒzmə'pɔlɪtn] adj cosmopolita
cost [kɒst] (pt, pp ~) n (price) precio ▷ vi costar, valer ▷ vt preparar el presupuesto de; **how much does it ~?** ¿cuánto cuesta?; **to ~ sb time/effort** costarle a algn tiempo/esfuerzo; **it ~ him his life** le costó la vida; **at all ~s** cueste lo que cueste; **costs** npl (Comm) costes mpl; (Law) costas fpl
co-star ['kəustɑː*] n coprotagonista mf
Costa Rica ['kɒstə'riːkə] n Costa Rica; **Costa Rican** adj, n costarriqueño/a
costly ['kɒstlɪ] adj costoso
cost of living n costo or coste m (Sp) de la vida
costume ['kɒstjuːm] n traje m; (BRIT: also: **swimming** ~) traje de baño
cosy ['kəuzɪ] (US **cozy**) adj (person) cómodo; (room) acogedor(a)
cot [kɒt] n (BRIT: child's) cuna; (US: campbed) cama de campaña
cottage ['kɒtɪdʒ] n casita de campo; (rustic) barraca; **cottage cheese** n requesón m
cotton ['kɒtn] n algodón m; (thread) hilo; **cotton on** vi (inf): **to cotton on (to sth)** caer en la cuenta (de algo); **cotton bud** n (BRIT) bastoncillo m de algodón; **cotton candy** (US) n algodón m (azucarado); **cotton wool** (BRIT) n algodón m (hidrófilo)
couch [kautʃ] n sofá m; (doctor's etc) diván m
cough [kɒf] vi toser ▷ n tos f; **cough mixture** n jarabe m para la tos
could [kud] pt of **can²**; **couldn't** = **could not**
council ['kaunsl] n consejo; **city or town ~** consejo municipal; **council estate** (BRIT) n urbanización de viviendas municipales de alquiler; **council house** (BRIT) n vivienda municipal de alquiler; **councillor** (US **councilor**) n concejal(a) m/f; **council tax** n (BRIT) contribución f municipal (dependiente del valor de la vivienda)
counsel ['kaunsl] n (advice) consejo; (lawyer) abogado/a ▷ vt aconsejar; **counselling** (US **counseling**) n (Psych) asistencia f psicológica; **counsellor** (US **counselor**) n consejero/a, abogado/a
count [kaunt] vt contar; (include) incluir ▷ vi contar ▷ n cuenta; (of votes) escrutinio; (level) nivel m; (nobleman) conde m; **count in** (inf) vt: **to count sb in on sth** contar con

algn para algo; **count on** *vt fus* contar con;
countdown *n* cuenta atrás

counter ['kauntə*] *n* (*in shop*) mostrador
m; (*in games*) ficha ▷ *vt* contrarrestar
▷ *adv*: **to run ~ to** ser contrario a, ir en
contra de; **counter clockwise** (*us*) *adv* en
sentido contrario al de las agujas del reloj

counterfeit ['kauntəfɪt] *n* falsificación
f, simulación *f* ▷ *vt* falsificar ▷ *adj* falso,
falsificado

counterpart ['kauntəpɑːt] *n*
homólogo/a

countess ['kauntɪs] *n* condesa

countless ['kauntlɪs] *adj* innumerable

country ['kʌntrɪ] *n* país *m*; (*native land*)
patria; (*as opposed to town*) campo; (*region*)
región *f*, tierra; **country and western
(music)** *n* música country; **country house**
n casa de campo; **countryside** *n* campo

county ['kauntɪ] *n* condado

coup [kuː] (*pl* **~s**) *n* (*also*: **~ d'état**) golpe *m*
(de estado); (*achievement*) éxito

couple ['kʌpl] *n* (*of things*) par *m*; (*of people*)
pareja; (*married couple*) matrimonio; **a ~ of**
un par de

coupon ['kuːpɔn] *n* cupón *m*; (*voucher*)
valé *m*

courage ['kʌrɪdʒ] *n* valor *m*, valentía;
courageous [kə'reɪdʒəs] *adj* valiente

courgette [kuə'ʒet] (*BRIT*) *n* calabacín *m*,
calabacita (*MEX*)

courier ['kurɪə*] *n* mensajero/a; (*for
tourists*) guía *mf* (de turismo)

course [kɔːs] *n* (*direction*) dirección *f*;
(*of river, Scol*) curso; (*process*) transcurso;
(*Med*): **~ of treatment** tratamiento; (*of ship*)
rumbo; (*part of meal*) plato; (*Golf*) campo; **of
~ desde luego**, naturalmente; **of ~!** ¡claro!

court [kɔːt] *n* (*royal*) corte *f*; (*Law*) tribunal
m, juzgado; (*Tennis etc*) pista, cancha ▷ *vt*
(*woman*) cortejar a; **to take to ~** demandar

courtesy ['kəːtəsɪ] *n* cortesía; **(by) ~ of**
por cortesía de; **courtesy bus, courtesy
coach** *n* autobús *m* gratuito

court-: court-house ['kɔːthaus] (*us*) *n*
palacio de justicia; **courtroom** ['kɔːtrum]
n sala de justicia; **courtyard** ['kɔːtjɑːd]
n patio

cousin ['kʌzn] *n* primo/a; **first ~** primo/a
carnal, primo/a hermano/a

cover ['kʌvə*] *vt* cubrir; (*feelings, mistake*)
ocultar; (*with lid*) tapar; (*book etc*) forrar;
(*distance*) recorrer; (*include*) abarcar;
(*protect: also: Insurance*) cubrir; (*Press*)
investigar; (*discuss*) tratar ▷ *n* cubierta; (*lid*)
tapa; (*for chair etc*) funda; (*envelope*) sobre
m; (*for book*) forro; (*of magazine*) portada;
(*shelter*) abrigo; (*Insurance*) cobertura; (*of

spy) cobertura; **covers** *npl* (*on bed*) sábanas;
mantas; **to take ~** (*shelter*) protegerse,
resguardarse; **under ~** (*indoors*) bajo techo;
under ~ of darkness al amparo de la
oscuridad; **under separate ~** (*Comm*) por
separado; **cover up** *vi*: **to cover up for sb**
encubrir a algn; **coverage** *n* (*TV, Press*)
cobertura; **cover charge** *n* precio del
cubierto; **cover-up** *n* encubrimiento

cow [kau] *n* vaca; (*infl: woman*) bruja ▷ *vt*
intimidar

coward ['kauəd] *n* cobarde *mf*; **cowardly**
adj cobarde

cowboy ['kaubɔɪ] *n* vaquero

cozy ['kəuzɪ] (*us*) *adj* =**cosy**

crab [kræb] *n* cangrejo

crack [kræk] *n* grieta; (*noise*) crujido; (*drug*)
crack *m* ▷ *vt* agrietar, romper; (*nut*) cascar;
(*solve: problem*) resolver; (: *code*) descifrar;
(*whip etc*) chasquear; (*knuckles*) crujir; (*joke*)
contar ▷ *adj* (*expert*) de primera; **crack
down on** *vt fus* adoptar fuertes medidas
contra; **cracked** *adj* (*cup, window*) rajado;
(*wall*) resquebrajado; **cracker** *n* (*biscuit*)
cráquer *m*; (*Christmas cracker*) petardo
sorpresa

crackle ['krækl] *vi* crepitar

cradle ['kreɪdl] *n* cuna

craft [krɑːft] *n* (*skill*) arte *m*; (*trade*) oficio;
(*cunning*) astucia; (*boat: pl inv*) barco;
(*plane: pl inv*) avión *m*; **craftsman** (*irreg*)
n artesano; **craftsmanship** *n* (*quality*)
destreza

cram [kræm] *vt* (*fill*): **to ~ sth with** llenar
algo (a reventar) de; (*put*): **to ~ sth into**
meter algo a la fuerza en ▷ *vi* (*for exams*)
empollar

cramp [kræmp] *n* (*Med*) calambre *m*;
cramped *adj* apretado, estrecho

cranberry ['krænbərɪ] *n* arándano agrio

crane [kreɪn] *n* (*Tech*) grúa; (*bird*) grulla

crap [kræp] *n* (*infl*) mierda (!)

crash [kræʃ] *n* (*noise*) estrépito; (*of cars
etc*) choque *m*; (*of plane*) accidente *m* de
aviación; (*Comm*) quiebra ▷ *vt* (*car, plane*)
estrellar ▷ *vi* (*car, plane*) estrellarse; (*two
cars*) chocar; (*Comm*) quebrar; **crash course**
n curso acelerado; **crash helmet** *n* casco
(protector)

crate [kreɪt] *n* cajón *m* de embalaje; (*for
bottles*) caja

crave [kreɪv] *vt, vi*: **to ~ (for)** ansiar,
anhelar

crawl [krɔːl] *vi* (*drag o.s.*) arrastrarse; (*child*)
andar a gatas, gatear; (*vehicle*) avanzar
(lentamente) ▷ *n* (*Swimming*) crol *m*

crayfish ['kreɪfɪʃ] *n inv* (*freshwater*)
cangrejo de río; (*saltwater*) cigala

crayon ['kreɪən] n lápiz m de color
craze [kreɪz] n (fashion) moda
crazy ['kreɪzɪ] adj (person) loco; (idea)
disparatado; (inf: keen): **~ about sb/sth** loco
por algn/algo
creak [kriːk] vi (floorboard) crujir; (hinge etc)
chirriar, rechinar
cream [kriːm] n (of milk) nata, crema;
(lotion) crema; (fig) flor f y nata ▷ adj (colour)
color crema; **cream cheese** n queso
blanco; **creamy** adj cremoso; (colour) color
crema
crease [kriːs] n (fold) pliegue m; (in trousers)
raya; (wrinkle) arruga ▷ vt (wrinkle) arrugar
▷ vi (wrinkle up) arrugarse
create [kriːˈeɪt] vt crear; **creation** [-ʃən] n
creación f; **creative** adj creativo; **creator** n
creador(a) m/f
creature ['kriːtʃə*] n (animal) animal m,
bicho; (person) criatura
crèche [kreʃ] n guardería (infantil)
credentials [krɪˈdɛnʃlz] npl (references)
referencias fpl; (identity papers) documentos
mpl de identidad
credibility [krɛdɪˈbɪlɪtɪ] n credibilidad f
credible ['krɛdɪbl] adj creíble; (trustworthy)
digno de confianza
credit ['krɛdɪt] n crédito; (merit) honor m,
mérito ▷ vt (Comm) abonar; (believe: also:
give ~ to) creer, prestar fe a ▷ adj crediticio;
credits npl (Cinema) fichas fpl técnicas; **to
be in ~** (person) tener saldo a favor; **to ~ sb
with** (fig) reconocer a algn el mérito de;
credit card n tarjeta de crédito
creek [kriːk] n cala, ensenada; (us)
riachuelo
creep [kriːp] (pt, pp **crept**) vi arrastrarse
cremate [krɪˈmeɪt] vt incinerar
crematorium [krɛməˈtɔːrɪəm] (pl
crematoria) n crematorio
crept [krɛpt] pt, pp of **creep**
crescent ['krɛsnt] n media luna; (street)
calle f (en forma de semicírculo)
cress [krɛs] n berro
crest [krɛst] n (of bird) cresta; (of hill) cima,
cumbre f; (of coat of arms) blasón m
crew [kruː] n (of ship etc) tripulación f;
(TV, Cinema) equipo; **crew-neck** n cuello
a la caja
crib [krɪb] n cuna ▷ vt (inf) plagiar
cricket ['krɪkɪt] n (insect) grillo; (game)
críquet m; **cricketer** n jugador(a) m/f de
críquet
crime [kraɪm] n (no pl: illegal activities)
crimen m; (illegal action) delito; **criminal**
['krɪmɪnl] n criminal mf, delincuente mf
▷ adj criminal; (illegal) delictivo; (law) penal
crimson ['krɪmzn] adj carmesí

cringe [krɪndʒ] vi agacharse, encogerse
cripple ['krɪpl] n lisiado/a, cojo/a ▷ vt
lisiar, mutilar
crisis ['kraɪsɪs] (pl **crises**) n crisis f inv
crisp [krɪsp] adj fresco; (vegetables etc)
crujiente; (manner) seco; **crispy** adj
crujiente
criterion [kraɪˈtɪərɪən] (pl **criteria**) n
criterio
critic ['krɪtɪk] n crítico/a; **critical** adj
crítico; (illness) grave; **criticism** ['krɪtɪsɪzm]
n crítica; **criticize** ['krɪtɪsaɪz] vt criticar
Croat ['krəuæt] adj, n = **Croatian**
Croatia [krəuˈeɪʃə] n Croacia; **Croatian**
adj, n croata m/f ▷ n (Ling) croata m
crockery ['krɔkərɪ] n loza, vajilla
crocodile ['krɔkədaɪl] n cocodrilo
crocus ['krəukəs] n croco, crocus m
croissant ['krwasŋ] n croissant m,
medialuna (esp LAM)
crook [kruk] n ladrón/ona m/f; (of
shepherd) cayado; **crooked** ['krukɪd] adj
torcido; (dishonest) nada honrado
crop [krɔp] n (produce) cultivo; (amount
produced) cosecha; (riding crop) látigo de
montar ▷ vt cortar, recortar; **crop up** vi
surgir, presentarse
cross [krɔs] n cruz f; (hybrid) cruce m ▷ vt
(street etc) cruzar, atravesar ▷ adj de mal
humor, enojado; **cross off** vt tachar;
cross out vt tachar; **cross over** vi cruzar;
cross-Channel ferry ['krɔsˈtʃænl-] n
transbordador m que cruza el Canal de la
Mancha; **crosscountry (race)** n carrera
a campo traviesa, cross m; **crossing** n
(sea passage) travesía; (also: **pedestrian
crossing**) paso para peatones; **crossing
guard** (us) n persona encargada de ayudar a
los niños a cruzar la calle; **crossroads** n cruce
m, encrucijada; **crosswalk** (us) n paso de
peatones; **crossword** n crucigrama m
crotch [krɔtʃ] n (Anat, of garment)
entrepierna
crouch [krautʃ] vi agacharse, acurrucarse
crouton ['kruːtɔn] n cubito de pan frito
crow [krəu] n (bird) cuervo; (of cock) canto,
cacareo ▷ vi (cock) cantar
crowd [kraud] n muchedumbre f,
multitud f ▷ vt (fill) llenar ▷ vi (gather): **to
~ round** reunirse en torno a; (cram): **to
~ in** entrar en tropel; **crowded** adj (full)
atestado; (densely populated) superpoblado
crown [kraun] n corona; (of head)
coronilla; (for tooth) funda; (of hill) cumbre
f ▷ vt coronar; (fig) completar, rematar;
crown jewels npl joyas fpl reales
crucial ['kruːʃl] adj decisivo
crucifix ['kruːsɪfɪks] n crucifijo

crude [kruːd] *adj* (*materials*) bruto; (*fig: basic*) tosco; (: *vulgar*) ordinario; **crude (oil)** *n* (*petróleo*) crudo

cruel ['kruəl] *adj* cruel; **cruelty** *n* crueldad *f*

cruise [kruːz] *n* crucero ▷ *vi* (*ship*) hacer un crucero; (*car*) ir a velocidad de crucero

crumb [krʌm] *n* miga, migaja

crumble ['krʌmbl] *vt* desmenuzar ▷ *vi* (*building, also fig*) desmoronarse

crumpet ['krʌmpɪt] *n* ≈ bollo para tostar

crumple ['krʌmpl] *vt* (*paper*) estrujar; (*material*) arrugar

crunch [krʌntʃ] *vt* (*with teeth*) mascar; (*underfoot*) hacer crujir ▷ *n* (*fig*) hora or momento de la verdad; **crunchy** *adj* crujiente

crush [krʌʃ] *n* (*crowd*) aglomeración *f*; (*infatuation*): **to have a ~ on sb** estar loco por algn; (*drink*): **lemon ~** limonada ▷ *vt* aplastar; (*paper*) estrujar; (*cloth*) arrugar; (*fruit*) exprimir; (*opposition*) aplastar; (*hopes*) destruir

crust [krʌst] *n* corteza; (*of snow, ice*) costra; **crusty** *adj* (*bread*) crujiente; (*person*) de mal carácter

crutch [krʌtʃ] *n* muleta

cry [kraɪ] *vi* llorar ▷ *n* (*shriek*) chillido; (*shout*) grito; **cry out** *vi* (*call out, shout*) lanzar un grito, echar un grito ▷ *vt* gritar

crystal ['krɪstl] *n* cristal *m*

cub [kʌb] *n* cachorro; (*also*: **~ scout**) niño explorador

Cuba ['kjuːbə] *n* Cuba; **Cuban** *adj, n* cubano/a *m/f*

cube [kjuːb] *n* cubo ▷ *vt* (*Math*) cubicar

cubicle ['kjuːbɪkl] *n* (*at pool*) caseta; (*for bed*) cubículo

cuckoo [kukuː] *n* cuco

cucumber ['kjuːkʌmbə*] *n* pepino

cuddle ['kʌdl] *vt* abrazar ▷ *vi* abrazarse

cue [kjuː] *n* (*snooker cue*) taco; (*Theatre etc*) señal *f*

cuff [kʌf] *n* (*of sleeve*) puño; (*us: of trousers*) vuelta; (*blow*) bofetada ▷ **off the ~** *adv* de improviso; **cufflinks** *npl* gemelos *mpl*

cuisine [kwɪˈziːn] *n* cocina

cul-de-sac ['kʌldəsæk] *n* callejón *m* sin salida

cull [kʌl] *vt* (*idea*) sacar ▷ *n* (*of animals*) matanza selectiva

culminate ['kʌlmɪneɪt] *vi*: **to ~ in** terminar en

culprit ['kʌlprɪt] *n* culpable *mf*

cult [kʌlt] *n* culto

cultivate ['kʌltɪveɪt] *vt* cultivar

cultural ['kʌltʃərəl] *adj* cultural

culture ['kʌltʃə*] *n* (*also fig*) cultura; (*Biol*) cultivo

cumin ['kʌmɪn] *n* (*spice*) comino

cunning ['kʌnɪŋ] *n* astucia ▷ *adj* astuto

cup [kʌp] *n* taza; (*as prize*) copa

cupboard ['kʌbəd] *n* armario; (*in kitchen*) alacena

cup final *n* (*Football*) final *f* de copa

curator [kjuˈreɪtə*] *n* director(a) *m/f*

curb [kəːb] *vt* refrenar; (*person*) reprimir ▷ *n* freno; (*us*) bordillo

curdle ['kəːdl] *vi* cuajarse

cure [kjuə*] *vt* curar ▷ *n* cura, curación *f*; (*fig: solution*) remedio

curfew ['kəːfjuː] *n* toque *m* de queda

curiosity [kjuərɪˈɔsɪtɪ] *n* curiosidad *f*

curious ['kjuərɪəs] *adj* curioso; (*person: interested*): **to be ~** sentir curiosidad

curl [kəːl] *n* rizo ▷ *vt* (*hair*) rizar ▷ *vi* rizarse; **curl up** *vi* (*person*) hacerse un ovillo; **curler** *n* rulo; **curly** *adj* rizado

currant ['kʌrnt] *n* pasa (de Corinto); (*blackcurrant, redcurrant*) grosella

currency ['kʌrnsɪ] *n* moneda; **to gain ~** (*fig*) difundirse

current ['kʌrnt] *n* corriente *f* ▷ *adj* (*accepted*) corriente; (*present*) actual; **current account** (*BRIT*) *n* cuenta corriente; **current affairs** *npl* noticias *fpl* de actualidad; **currently** *adv* actualmente

curriculum [kəˈrɪkjuləm] (*pl ~s* or **curricula**) *n* plan *m* de estudios; **curriculum vitae** *n* currículum *m*

curry ['kʌrɪ] *n* curry *m* ▷ *vt*: **to ~ favour with** buscar favores con; **curry powder** *n* curry *m* en polvo

curse [kəːs] *vi* soltar tacos ▷ *vt* maldecir ▷ *n* maldición *f*; (*swearword*) palabrota, taco

cursor ['kəːsə*] *n* (*Comput*) cursor *m*

curt [kəːt] *adj* corto, seco

curtain ['kəːtn] *n* cortina; (*Theatre*) telón *m*

curve [kəːv] *n* curva ▷ *vi* (*road*) hacer una curva; (*line etc*) curvarse; **curved** *adj* curvo

cushion ['kuʃən] *n* cojín *m*; (*of air*) colchón *m* ▷ *vt* (*shock*) amortiguar

custard ['kʌstəd] *n* natillas *fpl*

custody ['kʌstədɪ] *n* custodia; **to take into ~** detener

custom ['kʌstəm] *n* costumbre *f*; (*Comm*) clientela

customer ['kʌstəmə*] *n* cliente *m/f*

customized ['kʌstəmaɪzd] *adj* (*car etc*) hecho a encargo

customs ['kʌstəmz] *npl* aduana; **customs officer** *n* aduanero/a

cut [kʌt] (*pt, pp ~*) *vt* cortar; (*price*) rebajar; (*text, programme*) acortar; (*reduce*) reducir ▷ *vi* cortar ▷ *n* (*of garment*) corte *m*; (*in skin*) cortadura; (*in salary etc*) rebaja; (*in spending*) reducción f, recorte m; (slice of meat) tajada; **to ~ a tooth** echar un diente; **to ~ and paste** (Comput) cortar y pegar; **cut back** vt (plants) podar; (production, expenditure) reducir; **cut down** vt (tree) derribar; (reduce) reducir; **cut off** vt (person, place) aislar; (Tel) desconectar; **cut out** vt (shape) recortar; (stop: activity etc) dejar; (remove) quitar; **cut up** vt cortar (en pedazos); **cutback** n reducción f

cute [kju:t] adj mono

cutlery ['kʌtlərɪ] n cubiertos mpl

cutlet ['kʌtlɪt] n chuleta; (nut etc cutlet) plato vegetariano hecho con nueces y verdura en forma de chuleta

cut-price ['kʌt'praɪs] (BRIT) adj a precio reducido

cut-rate ['kʌt'reɪt] (US) adj = cut-price

cutting ['kʌtɪŋ] adj (remark) mordaz ▷ n (BRIT: from newspaper) recorte m; (from plant) esqueje m

CV n abbr = curriculum vitae

cwt abbr = hundredweight(s)

cybercafé ['saɪbəkæfeɪ] n cibercafé m

cyberspace ['saɪbəspeɪs] n ciberespacio

cycle ['saɪkl] n ciclo; (bicycle) bicicleta ▷ vi ir en bicicleta; **cycle hire** n alquiler m de bicicletas; **cycle lane** n carril-bici m; **cycle path** n carril-bici m; **cycling** n ciclismo; **cyclist** n ciclista mf

cyclone ['saɪkləun] n ciclón m

cylinder ['sɪlɪndə*] n cilindro; (of gas) bombona

cymbal ['sɪmbl] n címbalo, platillo

cynical ['sɪnɪkl] adj cínico

Cypriot ['sɪprɪət] adj, n chipriota m/f

Cyprus ['saɪprəs] n Chipre f

cyst [sɪst] n quiste m; **cystitis** [-'taɪtɪs] n cistitis f

czar [zɑː*] n zar m

Czech [tʃɛk] adj, n checo/a m/f; **Czech Republic** n: **the Czech Republic** la República Checa

d

D [diː] n (Mus) re m

dab [dæb] vt (eyes, wound) tocar (ligeramente); (paint, cream) poner un poco de

dad [dæd] n = **daddy**

daddy ['dædɪ] n papá m

daffodil ['dæfədɪl] n narciso

daft [dɑːft] adj tonto

dagger ['dægə*] n puñal m, daga

daily ['deɪlɪ] adj diario, cotidiano ▷ adv todos los días, cada día

dairy ['dɛərɪ] n (shop) lechería; (on farm) vaquería; **dairy produce** n productos mpl lácteos

daisy ['deɪzɪ] n margarita

dam [dæm] n presa ▷ vt construir una presa sobre, represar

damage ['dæmɪdʒ] n lesión f; daño; (dents etc) desperfectos mpl; (fig) perjuicio ▷ vt dañar, perjudicar; (spoil, break) estropear; **damages** npl (Law) daños mpl y perjuicios

damn [dæm] vt condenar; (curse) maldecir ▷ n (inf): **I don't give a ~** me importa un pito ▷ adj (inf: also: **~ed**) maldito; **~ (it)!** ¡maldito sea!

damp [dæmp] adj húmedo, mojado ▷ n humedad f ▷ vt (also: **~en**: cloth, rag) mojar; (: enthusiasm) enfriar

dance [dɑːns] n baile m ▷ vi bailar; **dance floor** n pista f de baile; **dancer** n bailador(a) m/f; (professional) bailarín/ina m/f; **dancing** n baile m

dandelion ['dændɪlaɪən] n diente m de león

dandruff ['dændrəf] n caspa

Dane [deɪn] n danés/esa m/f

danger ['deɪndʒə*] n peligro; (risk) riesgo; **~!** (on sign) ¡peligro de muerte!; **to be in ~ of** correr riesgo de; **dangerous** adj peligroso

dangle ['dæŋgl] vt colgar ▷ vi pender, colgar

Danish ['deɪnɪʃ] adj danés/esa ▷ n (Ling) danés m

dare [dɛə*] vt: **to ~ sb to do** desafiar a algn a hacer ▷ vi: **to ~ (to) do sth** atreverse a hacer algo; **I ~ say** (I suppose) puede ser (que); **daring** adj atrevido, osado ▷ n atrevimiento, osadía

dark [dɑːk] adj oscuro; (hair, complexion) moreno ▷ n: **in the ~** a oscuras; **to be in the ~ about** (fig) no saber nada de; **after ~** después del anochecer; **darken** vt (colour) hacer más oscuro ▷ vi oscurecerse; **darkness** n oscuridad f; **darkroom** n cuarto oscuro

darling ['dɑːlɪŋ] adj, n querido/a m/f

dart [dɑːt] n dardo; (in sewing) sisa ▷ vi precipitarse; **dartboard** n diana; **darts** n (game) dardos mpl

dash [dæʃ] n (small quantity: of liquid) gota, chorrito; (sign) raya ▷ vt (throw) tirar; (hopes) defraudar ▷ vi precipitarse, ir de prisa

dashboard ['dæʃbɔːd] n (Aut) salpicadero

data ['deɪtə] npl datos mpl; **database** n base f de datos; **data processing** n proceso de datos

date [deɪt] n (day) fecha; (with friend) cita; (fruit) dátil m ▷ vt fechar; (person) salir con; **~ of birth** fecha de nacimiento; **to ~** adv hasta la fecha; **dated** adj anticuado

daughter ['dɔːtə*] n hija; **daughter-in-law** n nuera, hija política

daunting ['dɔːntɪŋ] adj desalentador(a)

dawn [dɔːn] n alba, amanecer m; (fig) nacimiento ▷ vi (day) amanecer; (fig): **it ~ed on him that ...** cayó en la cuenta de que ...

day [deɪ] n día m; (working day) jornada; (heyday) tiempos mpl, días mpl; **the ~ before/after** el día anterior/siguiente; **the ~ after tomorrow** pasado mañana; **the ~ before yesterday** anteayer; **the following ~** el día siguiente; **by ~** de día; **day-care centre** ['deɪkɛə-] n centro de día; (for children) guardería infantil; **daydream** vi soñar despierto; **daylight** n luz f (del día); **day return** (BRIT) n billete m de ida y vuelta (en un día); **daytime** n día m; **day-to-day** adj cotidiano; **day trip** n excursión f (de un día)

dazed [deɪzd] adj aturdido

dazzle ['dæzl] vt deslumbrar; **dazzling** adj (light, smile) deslumbrante; (colour) fuerte

DC abbr (= direct current) corriente f continua

dead [dɛd] adj muerto; (limb) dormido; (telephone) cortado; (battery) agotado ▷ adv (completely) exactamente; (exactly) exactamente; **to shoot sb ~** matar a algn a tiros; **~ tired** muerto (de cansancio); **to**

stop ~ parar en seco; **dead end** n callejón m sin salida; **deadline** n fecha (or hora) tope; **deadly** adj mortal, fatal; **Dead Sea** n: **the Dead Sea** el Mar Muerto

deaf [dɛf] adj sordo; **deafen** vt ensordecer; **deafening** adj ensordecedor/a

deal [diːl] n (pt, pp ~t) n (agreement) pacto, convenio; (business deal) trato ▷ vt dar; (card) repartir; **a great ~ (of)** bastante, mucho; **deal with** vt fus (people) tratar con; (problem) ocuparse de; (subject) tratar de; **dealer** n comerciante m/f; (Cards) mano f; **dealings** npl (Comm) transacciones fpl; (relations) relaciones fpl

dealt [dɛlt] pt, pp of **deal**

dean [diːn] n (Rel) deán m; (Scol: BRIT) decano; (: US) decano; rector m

dear [dɪə*] adj caro; (expensive) caro ▷ n: **my ~** mi querido/a ▷ excl: **~ me!** ¡Dios mío!; **D~ Sir/Madam** (in letter) Muy Señor Mío, Estimado Señor/Estimada Señora; **D~ Mr/Mrs X** Estimado/a Señor(a) X; **dearly** adv (love) mucho; (pay) caro

death [dɛθ] n muerte f; **death penalty** n pena de muerte; **death sentence** n condena a muerte

debate [dɪ'beɪt] n debate m ▷ vt discutir

debit ['dɛbɪt] n debe m ▷ vt: **to ~ a sum to sb** or **to sb's account** cargar una suma en cuenta a algn; **debit card** n tarjeta f de débito

debris ['dɛbriː] n escombros mpl

debt [dɛt] n deuda; **to be in ~** tener deudas

debut [deɪ'bjuː] n presentación f

Dec. abbr (= December) dic

decade ['dɛkeɪd] n decenio, década

decaffeinated [dɪ'kæfɪneɪtɪd] adj descafeinado

decay [dɪ'keɪ] n (of building) desmoronamiento; (of tooth) caries f inv ▷ vi (rot) pudrirse

deceased [dɪ'siːst] n: **the ~** el(la) difunto/a

deceit [dɪ'siːt] n engaño; **deceive** [dɪ'siːv] vt engañar

December [dɪ'sɛmbə*] n diciembre m

decency ['diːsənsɪ] n decencia

decent ['diːsənt] adj (proper) decente; (person: kind) amable, bueno

deception [dɪ'sɛpʃən] n engaño

deceptive [dɪ'sɛptɪv] adj engañoso

▌ Be careful not to translate **deception** by the Spanish word decepción.

decide [dɪ'saɪd] vt (person) decidir; (question, argument) resolver ▷ vi decidir; **to ~ to do/that** decidir hacer/que; **to ~ on sth** decidirse por algo

decimal ['dɛsɪməl] adj decimal ▷ n decimal m

decision [dɪˈsɪʒən] n decisión f
decisive [dɪˈsaɪsɪv] adj decisivo; (person) decidido
deck [dɛk] n (Naut) cubierta f; (of bus) piso; (record deck) platina; (of cards) baraja; **deckchair** n tumbona
declaration [dɛkləˈreɪʃən] n declaración f
declare [dɪˈklɛəˈ] vt declarar
decline [dɪˈklaɪn] n disminución f, descenso ▷ vt rehusar ▷ vi (person, business) decaer; (strength) disminuir
decorate [ˈdɛkəreɪt] vt (adorn): **to ~ (with)** adornar (de), decorar (de); (paint) pintar; (paper) empapelar; **decoration** [-ˈreɪʃən] n adorno; (act) decoración f; (medal) condecoración f; **decorator** n (workman) pintor m (decorador)
decrease [n ˈdiːkriːs, vb dɪˈkriːs] n: **~ (in)** disminución f (de) ▷ vt disminuir, reducir ▷ vi reducirse
decree [dɪˈkriː] n decreto
dedicate [ˈdɛdɪkeɪt] vt dedicar; **dedicated** adj dedicado; (Comput) especializado; **dedicated word processor** procesador m de textos especializado or dedicado; **dedication** [-ˈkeɪʃən] n (devotion) dedicación f; (in book) dedicatoria
deduce [dɪˈdjuːs] vt deducir
deduct [dɪˈdʌkt] vt restar; descontar; **deduction** [dɪˈdʌkʃən] n (amount deducted) descuento; (conclusion) deducción f, conclusión f
deed [diːd] n hecho, acto; (feat) hazaña; (Law) escritura
deem [diːm] vt (formal) juzgar, considerar
deep [diːp] adj profundo; (expressing measurements) de profundidad; (voice) bajo; (breath) profundo; (colour) intenso ▷ adv: **the spectators stood 20 ~** los espectadores se formaron de 20 en fondo; **to be 4 metres ~** tener 4 metros de profundidad; **deep-fry** vt freír en aceite abundante; **deeply** adv (breathe) a pleno pulmón; (interested, moved, grateful) profundamente, hondamente
deer [dɪəˈ] n inv ciervo
default [dɪˈfɔːlt] n: **by ~ (win)** por incomparecencia ▷ adj (Comput) por defecto
defeat [dɪˈfiːt] n derrota ▷ vt derrotar, vencer
defect [n ˈdiːfɛkt, vb dɪˈfɛkt] n defecto ▷ vi: **to ~ to the enemy** pasarse al enemigo; **defective** [dɪˈfɛktɪv] adj defectuoso
defence [dɪˈfɛns] (us **defense**) n defensa
defend [dɪˈfɛnd] vt defender; **defendant** n acusado/a; (in civil case) demandado/a; **defender** n defensor(a) m/f; (Sport) defensa mf

defense [dɪˈfɛns] (us) = **defence**
defensive [dɪˈfɛnsɪv] adj defensivo ▷ n: **on the ~** a la defensiva
defer [dɪˈfəːˈ] vt aplazar
defiance [dɪˈfaɪəns] n desafío; **in ~ of** en contra de; **defiant** [dɪˈfaɪənt] adj (challenging) desafiante, retador(a)
deficiency [dɪˈfɪʃənsɪ] n (lack) falta; (defect) defecto; **deficient** [dɪˈfɪʃənt] adj deficiente
deficit [ˈdɛfɪsɪt] n déficit m
define [dɪˈfaɪn] vt (word etc) definir; (limits etc) determinar
definite [ˈdɛfɪnɪt] adj (fixed) determinado; (obvious) claro; (certain) indudable; **he was ~ about it** no dejó lugar a dudas (sobre ello); **definitely** adv desde luego, por supuesto
definition [dɛfɪˈnɪʃən] n definición f; (clearness) nitidez f
deflate [diːˈfleɪt] vt desinflar
deflect [dɪˈflɛkt] vt desviar
defraud [dɪˈfrɔːd] vt: **to ~ sb of sth** estafar algo a algn
defrost [diːˈfrɔst] vt descongelar
defuse [diːˈfjuːz] vt desactivar; (situation) calmar
defy [dɪˈfaɪ] vt (resist) oponerse a; (challenge) desafiar; (fig): **it defies description** resulta imposible describirlo
degree [dɪˈɡriː] n grado; (Scol) título; **to have a ~ in maths** tener una licenciatura en matemáticas; **by ~s** (gradually) poco a poco, por etapas; **to some ~** hasta cierto punto
dehydrated [diːhaɪˈdreɪtɪd] adj deshidratado; (milk) en polvo
de-icer [diːˈaɪsəˈ] n descongelador m
delay [dɪˈleɪ] vt demorar, aplazar; (person) entretener; (train) retrasar ▷ vi tardar ▷ n demora, retraso; **to be ~ed** retrasarse; **without ~** en seguida, sin tardar
delegate [n ˈdɛlɪɡɪt, vb ˈdɛlɪɡeɪt] n delegado/a ▷ vt (person) delegar en; (task) delegar
delete [dɪˈliːt] vt suprimir, tachar
deli [ˈdɛlɪ] n = **delicatessen**
deliberate [adj dɪˈlɪbərɪt, vb dɪˈlɪbəreɪt] adj (intentional) intencionado; (slow) pausado, lento ▷ vi deliberar; **deliberately** adv (on purpose) a propósito
delicacy [ˈdɛlɪkəsɪ] n delicadeza; (choice food) manjar m
delicate [ˈdɛlɪkɪt] adj delicado; (fragile) frágil
delicatessen [dɛlɪkəˈtɛsn] n ultramarinos mpl finos
delicious [dɪˈlɪʃəs] adj delicioso
delight [dɪˈlaɪt] n (feeling) placer m, deleite m; (person, experience etc) encanto,

delicia ▷ vt encantar, deleitar; **to take ~ in**
deleitarse en; **delighted** adj: **delighted (at**
or **with/to do)** encantado (con/de hacer);
delightful adj encantador(a), delicioso
delinquent [dɪ'lɪŋkwənt] adj, n
delincuente mf
deliver [dɪ'lɪvə*] vt (distribute) repartir;
(hand over) entregar; (message) comunicar;
(speech) pronunciar; (Med) asistir al parto
de; **delivery** n reparto; entrega; (of
speaker) modo de expresarse; (Med) parto,
alumbramiento; **to take delivery of** recibir
delusion [dɪ'luːʒən] n ilusión f, engaño
de luxe [də'lʌks] adj de lujo
delve [dɛlv] vi: **to ~ into** hurgar en
demand [dɪ'mɑːnd] vt (gen) exigir; (rights)
reclamar ▷ n exigencia; (claim) reclamación
f; (Econ) demanda; **to be in ~** ser muy
solicitado; **on ~** a solicitud; **demanding** adj
(boss) exigente; (work) absorbente
demise [dɪ'maɪz] n (death) fallecimiento
demo ['dɛməʊ] (inf) n abbr (= demonstration)
manifestación f
democracy [dɪ'mɔkrəsɪ] n democracia;
democrat ['dɛməkræt] n demócrata
mf; **democratic** [dɛmə'krætɪk] adj
democrático; (us) demócrata
demolish [dɪ'mɔlɪʃ] vt derribar, demoler;
(fig: argument) destruir
demolition [dɛmə'lɪʃən] n derribo,
demolición f
demon ['diːmən] n (evil spirit) demonio
demonstrate ['dɛmənstreɪt] vt
demostrar; (skill, appliance) mostrar ▷ vi
manifestarse; **demonstration**
[-'streɪʃən] n (Pol) manifestación f; (proof,
exhibition) demostración f; **demonstrator**
n (Pol) manifestante mf; (Comm)
demostrador(a) m/f; vendedor(a) m/f
demote [dɪ'məʊt] vt degradar
den [dɛn] n (of animal) guarida; (room)
habitación f
denial [dɪ'naɪəl] n (refusal) negativa; (of
report etc) negación f
denim ['dɛnɪm] n tela vaquera; **denims**
npl vaqueros mpl
Denmark ['dɛnmɑːk] n Dinamarca
denomination [dɪnɔmɪ'neɪʃən] n valor
m; (Rel) confesión f
denounce [dɪ'naʊns] vt denunciar
dense [dɛns] adj (crowd) denso; (thick)
espeso; (: foliage etc) tupido; (inf: stupid)
torpe
density ['dɛnsɪtɪ] n densidad f ▷ **single/**
double-~ disk n (Comput) disco de densidad
sencilla/de doble densidad
dent [dɛnt] n abolladura ▷ vt (also: **make**
a ~ in) abollar

dental ['dɛntl] adj dental; **dental floss**
[-flɔs] n seda dental; **dental surgery** n
clínica f dental, consultorio m dental
dentist ['dɛntɪst] n dentista mf
dentures ['dɛntʃəz] npl dentadura
(postiza)
deny [dɪ'naɪ] vt negar; (charge) rechazar
deodorant [diː'əʊdərənt] n desodorante
m
depart [dɪ'pɑːt] vi irse, marcharse; (train)
salir; **to ~ from** (fig: differ from) apartarse de
department [dɪ'pɑːtmənt] n (Comm)
sección f; (Scol) departamento; (Pol)
ministerio; **department store** n gran
almacén m
departure [dɪ'pɑːtʃə*] n partida, ida; (of
train) salida; (of employee) marcha; **a new ~**
un nuevo rumbo; **departure lounge** n (at
airport) sala de embarque
depend [dɪ'pɛnd] vi: **to ~ on** depender de;
(rely on) contar con; **it ~s** depende, según;
~ing on the result según el resultado;
dependant n dependiente mf; **dependent**
adj: **to be dependent on** depender de ▷ n =
dependant
depict [dɪ'pɪkt] vt (in picture) pintar;
(describe) representar
deport [dɪ'pɔːt] vt deportar
deposit [dɪ'pɔzɪt] n depósito; (Chem)
sedimento; (of ore, oil) yacimiento ▷ vt
(gen) depositar; **deposit account** (BRIT) n
cuenta de ahorros
depot ['dɛpəʊ] n (storehouse) depósito; (for
vehicles) parque m; (us) estación f
depreciate [dɪ'priːʃɪeɪt] vi depreciarse,
perder valor
depress [dɪ'prɛs] vt deprimir; (wages
etc) hacer bajar; (press down) apretar;
depressed adj deprimido; **depressing**
adj deprimente; **depression** [dɪ'prɛʃən] n
depresión f
deprive [dɪ'praɪv] vt: **to ~ sb of** privar a
algn de; **deprived** adj necesitado
dept. abbr (= department) dto
depth [dɛpθ] n profundidad f; (of cupboard)
fondo; **to be in the ~s of despair** sentir la
mayor desesperación; **to be out of one's**
~ (in water) no hacer pie; (fig) sentirse
totalmente perdido
deputy ['dɛpjʊtɪ] adj: **~ head**
subdirector(a) m/f ▷ n sustituto/a,
suplente mf; (us Pol) diputado/a; (us: also: **~**
sheriff) agente m del sheriff
derail [dɪ'reɪl] vt: **to be ~ed** descarrilarse
derelict ['dɛrɪlɪkt] adj abandonado
derive [dɪ'raɪv] vt (benefit etc) obtener
▷ vi: **to ~ from** derivarse de
descend [dɪ'sɛnd] vt, vi descender, bajar;

to ~ from descender de; **to ~ to** rebajarse a;
descendant n descendiente mf
descent [dɪˈsɛnt] n descenso; (origin)
descendencia
describe [dɪsˈkraɪb] vt describir;
description [-ˈkrɪpʃən] n descripción f;
(sort) clase f, género
desert [n ˈdɛzət, vb dɪˈzəːt] n desierto ▷ vt
abandonar ▷ vi (Mil) desertar; **deserted**
[dɪˈzəːtɪd] adj desierto
deserve [dɪˈzəːv] vt merecer, ser digno de
design [dɪˈzaɪn] n (sketch) bosquejo;
(layout, shape) diseño; (pattern) dibujo;
(intention) intención f ▷ vt diseñar; **design
and technology** (BRIT: Scol) n = dibujo y
tecnología
designate [vb ˈdɛzɪgneɪt, adj ˈdɛzɪgnɪt] vt
(appoint) nombrar; (destine) designar ▷ adj
designado
designer [dɪˈzaɪnə*] n diseñador(a) m/f;
(fashion designer) modisto/a, diseñador(a)
m/f de moda
desirable [dɪˈzaɪərəbl] adj (proper)
deseable; (attractive) atractivo
desire [dɪˈzaɪə*] n deseo ▷ vt desear
desk [dɛsk] n (in office) escritorio; (for pupil)
pupitre m; (in hotel, at airport) recepción
f; (BRIT: in shop, restaurant) caja; **desk-top
publishing** [ˈdɛsktɔp-] n autoedición f
despair [dɪsˈpɛə*] n desesperación f
▷ vi: **to ~ of** perder la esperanza de
despatch [dɪsˈpætʃ] n, vt = **dispatch**
desperate [ˈdɛspərɪt] adj desesperado;
(fugitive) peligroso; **to be ~ for sth/to
do** necesitar urgentemente algo/hacer;
desperately adv desesperadamente; (very)
terriblemente, gravemente
desperation [dɛspəˈreɪʃən]
n desesperación f; **in (sheer) ~**
(absolutamente) desesperado
despise [dɪsˈpaɪz] vt despreciar
despite [dɪsˈpaɪt] prep a pesar de, pese a
dessert [dɪˈzəːt] n postre m;
dessertspoon n cuchara (de postre)
destination [dɛstɪˈneɪʃən] n destino
destined [ˈdɛstɪnd] adj: **~ for London** con
destino a Londres
destiny [ˈdɛstɪnɪ] n destino
destroy [dɪsˈtrɔɪ] vt destruir; (animal)
sacrificar
destruction [dɪsˈtrʌkʃən] n destrucción f
destructive [dɪsˈtrʌktɪv] adj destructivo,
destructor(a)
detach [dɪˈtætʃ] vt separar; (unstick)
despegar; **detached** adj (attitude) objetivo,
imparcial; **detached house** n = chalé m,
= chalet m
detail [ˈdiːteɪl] n detalle m; (no pl; (: in

picture etc) detalles mpl; (trifle) pequeñez
f ▷ vt detallar; (Mil) destacar; **in ~**
detalladamente; **detailed** adj detallado
detain [dɪˈteɪn] vt retener; (in captivity)
detener
detect [dɪˈtɛkt] vt descubrir; (Med, Police)
identificar; (Mil, Radar, Tech) detectar;
detection [dɪˈtɛkʃən] n descubrimiento;
identificación f; **detective** n detective mf;
detective story n novela policíaca
detention [dɪˈtɛnʃən] n detención f,
arresto; (Scol) castigo
deter [dɪˈtəː*] vt (dissuade) disuadir
detergent [dɪˈtəːdʒənt] n detergente m
deteriorate [dɪˈtɪərɪəreɪt] vi deteriorarse
determination [dɪtəːmɪˈneɪʃən] n
resolución f
determine [dɪˈtəːmɪn] vt determinar;
determined adj (person) resuelto, decidido;
determined to do resuelto a hacer
deterrent [dɪˈtɛrənt] n (Mil) fuerza de
disuasión
detest [dɪˈtɛst] vt aborrecer
detour [ˈdiːtuə*] n (gen, US Aut) desviación
f
detract [dɪˈtrækt] vt: **to ~ from** quitar
mérito a, desvirtuar
detrimental [dɛtrɪˈmɛntl] adj: **~ (to)**
perjudicial (a)
devastating [ˈdɛvəsteɪtɪŋ] adj
devastador(a); (fig) arrollador(a)
develop [dɪˈvɛləp] vt desarrollar; (Phot)
revelar; (disease) coger; (habit) adquirir;
(fault) empezar a tener ▷ vi desarrollarse;
(advance) progresar; (facts, symptoms)
aparecer; **developing country** n país m
en (vías de) desarrollo; **development** n
desarrollo; (advance) progreso; (of affair, case)
desenvolvimiento; (of land) urbanización f
device [dɪˈvaɪs] n (apparatus) aparato,
mecanismo
devil [ˈdɛvl] n diablo, demonio
devious [ˈdiːvɪəs] adj taimado
devise [dɪˈvaɪz] vt idear, inventar
devote [dɪˈvəut] vt: **to ~ sth to** dedicar
algo a; **devoted** adj (loyal) leal, fiel; **to be
devoted to sb** querer con devoción a algn;
the book is devoted to politics el libro
trata de la política; **devotion** n dedicación
f; (Rel) devoción f
devour [dɪˈvauə*] vt devorar
devout [dɪˈvaut] adj devoto
dew [djuː] n rocío
diabetes [daɪəˈbiːtiːz] n diabetes f
diabetic [daɪəˈbɛtɪk] adj, n diabético/a
m/f
diagnose [ˈdaɪəgnəuz] vt diagnosticar
diagnosis [daɪəgˈnəusɪs] (pl **-ses**) n

diagnóstico

diagonal [daɪˈægənl] *adj, n* diagonal *f*

diagram [ˈdaɪəgræm] *n* diagrama *m*, esquema *m*

dial [ˈdaɪəl] *n* esfera (SP), cara (LAM); *(on radio etc)* dial *m; (of phone)* disco ▷ *vt (number)* marcar

dialect [ˈdaɪəlɛkt] *n* dialecto

dialling code [ˈdaɪəlɪŋ-] *n* prefijo

dialling tone (US **dial tone**) *n* (BRIT) señal *f or* tono de marcar

dialogue [ˈdaɪəlɒg] (US **dialog**) *n* diálogo

diameter [daɪˈæmɪtə*] *n* diámetro

diamond [ˈdaɪəmənd] *n* diamante *m; (shape)* rombo; **diamonds** *npl (Cards)* diamantes *mpl*

diaper [ˈdaɪəpə*] (US) *n* pañal *m*

diarrhoea [daɪəˈriːə] (US **diarrhea**) *n* diarrea

diary [ˈdaɪərɪ] *n (daily account)* diario; *(book)* agenda

dice [daɪs] *n inv* dados *mpl* ▷ *vt (Culin)* cortar en cuadritos

dictate [dɪkˈteɪt] *vt* dictar; *(conditions)* imponer; **dictation** [-ˈteɪʃən] *n* dictado; *(giving of orders)* órdenes *fpl*

dictator [dɪkˈteɪtə*] *n* dictador *m*

dictionary [ˈdɪkʃənrɪ] *n* diccionario

did [dɪd] *pt of* **do**

didn't [ˈdɪdənt] = **did not**

die [daɪ] *vi* morir; (fig: fade) desvanecerse, desaparecer; **to be dying for sth/to do sth** morirse por algo/de ganas de hacer algo; **die down** *vi* apagarse; (wind) amainar; **die out** *vi* desaparecer

diesel [ˈdiːzəl] *n* vehículo con motor Diesel

diet [ˈdaɪət] *n* dieta; *(restricted food)* régimen *m* ▷ *vi (also:* **be on a ~**) estar a dieta, hacer régimen

differ [ˈdɪfə*] *vi:* **to ~ (from)** *(be different)* ser distinto (a), diferenciarse (de); *(disagree)* discrepar (de); **difference** *n* diferencia; *(disagreement)* desacuerdo; **different** *adj* diferente, distinto; **differentiate** [-ˈrɛnʃɪeɪt] *vi:* **to differentiate (between)** distinguir (entre); **differently** *adv* de otro modo, en forma distinta

difficult [ˈdɪfɪkəlt] *adj* difícil; **difficulty** *n* dificultad *f*

dig [dɪg] *(pt, pp* **dug**) *vt (hole, ground)* cavar ▷ *n (prod)* empujón *m; (archaeological)* excavación *f; (remark)* indirecta; **to ~ one's nails into** clavar las uñas en; **dig up** *vt (information)* desenterrar; *(plant)* desarraigar

digest [*vb* daɪˈdʒɛst, *n* ˈdaɪdʒɛst] *vt (food)* digerir; *(facts)* asimilar ▷ *n* resumen *m*; **digestion** [dɪˈdʒɛstʃən] *n* digestión *f*

digit [ˈdɪdʒɪt] *n (number)* dígito; *(finger)*

dedo; **digital** *adj* digital; **digital camera** *n* cámara digital; **digital TV** *n* televisión *f* digital

dignified [ˈdɪgnɪfaɪd] *adj* grave, solemne

dignity [ˈdɪgnɪtɪ] *n* dignidad *f*

digs [dɪgz] (BRIT: *inf*) *npl* pensión *f*, alojamiento

dilemma [daɪˈlɛmə] *n* dilema *m*

dill [dɪl] *n* eneldo

dilute [daɪˈluːt] *vt* diluir

dim [dɪm] *adj (light)* débil; *(outline)* indistinto; *(room)* oscuro; *(inf: stupid)* lerdo ▷ *vt (light)* bajar

dime [daɪm] (US) *n* moneda de diez centavos

dimension [dɪˈmɛnʃən] *n* dimensión *f*

diminish [dɪˈmɪnɪʃ] *vt, vi* disminuir

din [dɪn] *n* estruendo, estrépito

dine [daɪn] *vi* cenar; **diner** *n (person)* comensal *mf*

dinghy [ˈdɪŋgɪ] *n* bote *m; (also:* **rubber ~**) lancha (neumática)

dingy [ˈdɪndʒɪ] *adj (room)* sombrío; *(colour)* sucio

dining car [ˈdaɪnɪŋ-] (BRIT) *n (Rail)* coche-comedor *m*

dining room [ˈdaɪnɪŋ-] *n* comedor *m*

dining table *n* mesa *f* de comedor

dinner [ˈdɪnə*] *n (evening meal)* cena; *(lunch)* comida; *(public)* cena, banquete *m*; **dinner jacket** *n* smoking *m*; **dinner party** *n* cena; **dinner time** *n (evening)* hora de cenar; *(midday)* hora de comer

dinosaur [ˈdaɪnəsɔː*] *n* dinosaurio

dip [dɪp] *n (slope)* pendiente *m; (in sea)* baño; *(Culin)* salsa ▷ *vt (in water)* mojar; *(ladle etc)* meter; *(BRIT Aut):* **to ~ one's lights** poner luces de cruce ▷ *vi (road etc)* descender, bajar

diploma [dɪˈpləumə] *n* diploma *m*

diplomacy [dɪˈpləuməsɪ] *n* diplomacia

diplomat [ˈdɪpləmæt] *n* diplomático/a; **diplomatic** [dɪpləˈmætɪk] *adj* diplomático

dipstick [ˈdɪpstɪk] (BRIT) *n (Aut)* varilla de nivel (del aceite)

dire [daɪə*] *adj* calamitoso

direct [daɪˈrɛkt] *adj* directo; *(challenge)* claro; *(person)* franco ▷ *vt* dirigir; *(order):* **to ~ sb to do sth** mandar a algn hacer algo ▷ *adv* derecho; **can you ~ me to ...?** ¿puede indicarme dónde está ...?; **direct debit** (BRIT) *n* domiciliación *f* bancaria de recibos

direction [dɪˈrɛkʃən] *n* dirección *f; sense of ~* sentido de la dirección; **directions** *npl (instructions)* instrucciones *fpl*; **~s for use** modo de empleo

directly [dɪˈrɛktlɪ] *adv (in straight line)* directamente; *(at once)* en seguida

director [dɪˈrɛktə*] *n* director(a) *m/f*

directory [dɪˈrɛktərɪ] n (Tel) guía
(telefónica); (Comput) directorio; **directory
enquiries** (us **directory assistance**) n
(servicio de) información f
dirt [dəːt] n suciedad f; (earth) tierra; **dirty**
adj sucio; (joke) verde, colorado (MEX) ▷ vt
ensuciar; (stain) manchar
disability [dɪsəˈbɪlɪtɪ] n incapacidad f
disabled [dɪsˈeɪbld] adj: **to be physically
~** ser minusválido/a; **to be mentally ~** ser
deficiente mental
disadvantage [dɪsədˈvɑːntɪdʒ] n
desventaja, inconveniente m
disagree [dɪsəˈɡriː] vi (differ) discrepar;
to ~ (with) no estar de acuerdo (con);
disagreeable adj desagradable; (person)
antipático; **disagreement** n desacuerdo
disappear [dɪsəˈpɪə*] vi desaparecer;
disappearance n desaparición f
disappoint [dɪsəˈpɔɪnt] vt decepcionar,
defraudar; **disappointed** adj
decepcionado; **disappointing** adj
decepcionante; **disappointment** n
decepción f
disapproval [dɪsəˈpruːvəl] n
desaprobación f
disapprove [dɪsəˈpruːv] vi: **to ~ of** ver mal
disarm [dɪsˈɑːm] vt desarmar;
disarmament [dɪsˈɑːməmənt] n desarme
m
disaster [dɪˈzɑːstə*] n desastre m
disastrous [dɪˈzɑːstrəs] adj desastroso
disbelief [dɪsbəˈliːf] n incredulidad f
disc [dɪsk] n disco; (Comput) = **disk**
discard [dɪsˈkɑːd] vt (old things) tirar; (fig)
descartar
discharge [vb dɪsˈtʃɑːdʒ, n ˈdɪstʃɑːdʒ] vt
(task, duty) cumplir; (waste) verter; (patient)
dar de alta; (employee) despedir; (soldier)
licenciar; (defendant) poner en libertad
▷ n (Elec) descarga; (Med) supuración f;
(dismissal) despedida; (of duty) desempeño;
(of debt) pago, descargo
discipline [ˈdɪsɪplɪn] n disciplina ▷ vt
disciplinar; (punish) castigar
disc jockey n pinchadiscos mf inv
disclose [dɪsˈkləuz] vt revelar
disco [ˈdɪskəu] n abbr discoteca
discoloured [dɪsˈkʌləd] (us **discolored**)
adj descolorido
discomfort [dɪsˈkʌmfət] n incomodidad
f; (unease) inquietud f; (physical) malestar m
disconnect [dɪskəˈnɛkt] vt separar; (Elec
etc) desconectar
discontent [dɪskənˈtɛnt] n descontento
discontinue [dɪskənˈtɪnjuː] vt
interrumpir; (payments) suspender; **"~d"**
(Comm) "ya no se fabrica"

discount [n ˈdɪskaunt, vb dɪsˈkaunt] n
descuento ▷ vt descontar
discourage [dɪsˈkʌrɪdʒ] vt desalentar;
(advise against): **to ~ sb from doing** disuadir
a algn de hacer
discover [dɪsˈkʌvə*] vt descubrir;
(error) darse cuenta de; **discovery** n
descubrimiento
discredit [dɪsˈkrɛdɪt] vt desacreditar
discreet [dɪsˈkriːt] adj (tactful) discreto;
(careful) prudente
discrepancy [dɪsˈkrɛpənsɪ] n diferencia
discretion [dɪsˈkrɛʃən] n (tact) discreción
f; **at the ~ of** a criterio de
discriminate [dɪsˈkrɪmɪneɪt] vi: **to ~
between** distinguir entre; **to ~ against**
discriminar contra; **discrimination**
[-ˈneɪʃən] n (discernment) perspicacia; (bias)
discriminación f
discuss [dɪsˈkʌs] vt discutir; (a theme)
tratar; **discussion** [dɪsˈkʌʃən] n discusión f
disease [dɪˈziːz] n enfermedad f
disembark [dɪsɪmˈbɑːk] vt, vi
desembarcar
disgrace [dɪsˈɡreɪs] n ignominia; (shame)
vergüenza, escándalo ▷ vt deshonrar;
disgraceful adj vergonzoso
disgruntled [dɪsˈɡrʌntld] adj disgustado,
descontento
disguise [dɪsˈɡaɪz] n disfraz m ▷ vt
disfrazar; **in ~** disfrazado
disgust [dɪsˈɡʌst] n repugnancia ▷ vt
repugnar, dar asco a
> Be careful not to translate **disgust** by the
> Spanish word disgustar.
disgusted [dɪsˈɡʌstɪd] adj indignado
> Be careful not to translate **disgusted** by
> the Spanish word disgustado.
disgusting [dɪsˈɡʌstɪŋ] adj repugnante,
asqueroso; (behaviour etc) vergonzoso
dish [dɪʃ] n (gen) plato; **to do** or **wash the
~es** fregar los platos; **dishcloth** n estropajo
dishonest [dɪsˈɔnɪst] adj (person) poco
honrado, tramposo; (means) fraudulento
dishtowel [ˈdɪʃtauəl] (us) n estropajo
dishwasher [ˈdɪʃwɔʃə*] n lavaplatos m inv
disillusion [dɪsɪˈluːʒən] vt desilusionar
disinfectant [dɪsɪnˈfɛktənt] n
desinfectante m
disintegrate [dɪsˈɪntɪɡreɪt] vi
disgregarse, desintegrarse
disk [dɪsk] n (esp us) = **disc**; (Comput) disco,
disquete m; **single-/double-sided ~** disco
de una cara/dos caras; **disk drive** n disc
drive m; **diskette** n = **disk**
dislike [dɪsˈlaɪk] n antipatía, aversión f
▷ vt tener antipatía a
dislocate [ˈdɪsləkeɪt] vt dislocar

disloyal [dɪsˈlɔɪəl] *adj* desleal
dismal [ˈdɪzml] *adj* (*gloomy*) deprimente,
triste; (*very bad*) malísimo, fatal
dismantle [dɪsˈmæntl] *vt* desmontar,
desarmar
dismay [dɪsˈmeɪ] *n* consternación *f* ▷ *vt*
consternar
dismiss [dɪsˈmɪs] *vt* (*worker*) despedir;
(*pupils*) dejar marchar; (*soldiers*) dar permiso
para irse; (*idea, Law*) rechazar; (*possibility*)
descartar; **dismissal** *n* despido
disobedient [dɪsəˈbiːdɪənt] *adj*
desobediente
disobey [dɪsəˈbeɪ] *vt* desobedecer
disorder [dɪsˈɔːdə*] *n* desorden *m*; (*rioting*)
disturbios *mpl*; (*Med*) trastorno
disorganized [dɪsˈɔːɡənaɪzd] *adj*
desorganizado
disown [dɪsˈəʊn] *vt* (*action*) renegar de;
(*person*) negar cualquier tipo de relación con
dispatch [dɪsˈpætʃ] *vt* enviar ▷ *n* (*sending*)
envío; (*Press*) informe *m*; (*Mil*) parte *m*
dispel [dɪsˈpel] *vt* disipar
dispense [dɪsˈpens] *vt* (*medicines*)
preparar; **dispense with** *vt fus* prescindir
de; **dispenser** *n* (*container*) distribuidor *m*
automático
disperse [dɪsˈpəːs] *vt* dispersar ▷ *vi*
dispersarse
display [dɪsˈpleɪ] *n* (*in shop window*)
escaparate *m*; (*exhibition*) exposición
f; (*Comput*) visualización *f*; (*of feeling*)
manifestación *f* ▷ *vt* exponer; manifestar;
(*ostentatiously*) lucir
displease [dɪsˈpliːz] *vt* (*offend*) ofender;
(*annoy*) fastidiar
disposable [dɪsˈpəʊzəbl] *adj* desechable;
(*income*) disponible
disposal [dɪsˈpəʊzl] *n* (*of rubbish*)
destrucción *f*; **at one's ~** a su disposición
dispose [dɪsˈpəʊz] *vi*: **to ~ of** (*unwanted
goods*) deshacerse de; (*problem etc*) resolver;
disposition [dɪspəˈzɪʃən] *n* (*nature*)
temperamento; (*inclination*) propensión *f*
disproportionate [dɪsprəˈpɔːʃənət] *adj*
desproporcionado
dispute [dɪsˈpjuːt] *n* disputa; (*also*:
industrial ~) conflicto (laboral) ▷ *vt* (*argue*)
disputar, discutir; (*question*) cuestionar
disqualify [dɪsˈkwɒlɪfaɪ] *vt* (*Sport*)
desclasificar; **to ~ sb for sth/from doing
sth** incapacitar a algn para algo/hacer algo
disregard [dɪsrɪˈɡɑːd] *vt* (*ignore*) no hacer
caso de
disrupt [dɪsˈrʌpt] *vt* (*plans*) desbaratar,
trastornar; (*conversation*) interrumpir;
disruption [dɪsˈrʌpʃən] *n* trastorno,
desbaratamiento; interrupción *f*

dissatisfaction [dɪssætɪsˈfækʃən] *n*
disgusto, descontento
dissatisfied [dɪsˈsætɪsfaɪd] *adj*
insatisfecho
dissect [dɪˈsekt] *vt* disecar
dissent [dɪˈsent] *n* disensión *f*
dissertation [dɪsəˈteɪʃən] *n* tesina
dissolve [dɪˈzɒlv] *vt* disolver ▷ *vi*
disolverse; **to ~ in(to) tears** deshacerse en
lágrimas
distance [ˈdɪstəns] *n* distancia; **in the ~**
a lo lejos
distant [ˈdɪstənt] *adj* lejano; (*manner*)
reservado, frío
distil [dɪsˈtɪl] (*us* **distill**) *vt* destilar;
distillery *n* destilería
distinct [dɪsˈtɪŋkt] *adj* (*different*) distinto;
(*clear*) claro; (*unmistakeable*) inequívoco;
as ~ from a diferencia de; **distinction**
[dɪsˈtɪŋkʃən] *n* distinción *f*; (*honour*) honor
m; (*in exam*) sobresaliente *m*; **distinctive** *adj*
distintivo
distinguish [dɪsˈtɪŋɡwɪʃ] *vt* distinguir;
to ~ o.s. destacarse; **distinguished** *adj*
(*eminent*) distinguido
distort [dɪsˈtɔːt] *vt* distorsionar; (*shape,
image*) deformar
distract [dɪsˈtrækt] *vt* distraer;
distracted *adj* distraído; **distraction**
[dɪsˈtrækʃən] *n* distracción *f*; (*confusion*)
aturdimiento
distraught [dɪsˈtrɔːt] *adj* loco de
inquietud
distress [dɪsˈtres] *n* (*anguish*) angustia,
aflicción *f* ▷ *vt* afligir; **distressing** *adj*
angustioso; doloroso
distribute [dɪsˈtrɪbjuːt] *vt* distribuir;
(*share out*) repartir; **distribution** [-ˈbjuːʃən]
n distribución *f*, reparto; **distributor** *n*
(*Aut*) distribuidor *m*; (*Comm*) distribuidora
district [ˈdɪstrɪkt] *n* (*of country*) zona,
región *f*; (*of town*) barrio; (*Admin*) distrito;
district attorney (*us*) *n* fiscal *mf*
distrust [dɪsˈtrʌst] *n* desconfianza ▷ *vt*
desconfiar de
disturb [dɪsˈtəːb] *vt* (*person: bother,
interrupt*) molestar; (: *upset*) perturbar,
inquietar; (*disorganize*) alterar; **disturbance**
n (*upheaval*) perturbación *f*; (*political etc: gen
pl*) disturbio; (*of mind*) trastorno; **disturbed**
adj (*worried, upset*) preocupado, angustiado;
emotionally disturbed trastornado;
disturbing *adj* inquietante, perturbador(a)
ditch [dɪtʃ] *n* zanja; (*irrigation ditch*)
acequia *f* ▷ *vt* (*inf: partner*) deshacerse de;
(: *plan, car etc*) abandonar
ditto [ˈdɪtəʊ] *adv* ídem, lo mismo

dive [daɪv] n (from board) salto; (underwater) buceo; (of submarine) sumersión f ▷ vi (swimmer: into water) saltar; (: under water) zambullirse, bucear; (fish, submarine) sumergirse; (bird) lanzarse en picado; **to ~ into** (bag etc) meter la mano en; (place) meterse de prisa en; **diver** n (underwater) buzo

diverse [daɪ'vɜːs] adj diversos/as, varios/as

diversion [daɪ'vɜːʃən] n (BRIT Aut) desviación f; (distraction, Mil) diversión f; (of funds) distracción f

diversity [daɪ'vɜːsɪtɪ] n diversidad f

divert [daɪ'vɜːt] vt (turn aside) desviar

divide [dɪ'vaɪd] vt dividir; (separate) separar ▷ vi dividirse; (road) bifurcarse; **divided highway** (US) n carretera de doble calzada

divine [dɪ'vaɪn] adj (also fig) divino

diving ['daɪvɪŋ] n (Sport) salto; (underwater) buceo; **diving board** n trampolín m

division [dɪ'vɪʒən] n división f; (sharing out) reparto; (disagreement) diferencias fpl; (Comm) sección f

divorce [dɪ'vɔːs] n divorcio ▷ vt divorciarse de; **divorced** adj divorciado; **divorcee** [-'siː] n divorciado/a

D.I.Y. (BRIT) adj, n abbr = **do-it-yourself**

dizzy ['dɪzɪ] adj (spell) de mareo; **to feel ~** marearse

DJ n abbr = **disc jockey**

DNA n abbr (= deoxyribonucleic acid) ADN m

○ **KEYWORD**

do [duː] (pt **did**, pp **done**) n (inf: party etc): **we're having a little do on Saturday** damos una fiestecita el sábado; **it was rather a grand do** fue un acontecimiento a lo grande

▷ aux vb **1** (in negative constructions: not translated): **I don't understand** no entiendo

2 (to form questions: not translated): **didn't you know?** ¿no lo sabías?; **what do you think?** ¿qué opinas?

3 (for emphasis, in polite expressions): **people do make mistakes sometimes** sí que se cometen errores a veces; **she does seem rather late** a mí también me parece que se ha retrasado; **do sit down/help yourself** siéntate/sírvete por favor; **do take care!** ¡ten cuidado(, te pido)!

4 (used to avoid repeating vb): **she sings better than I do** canta mejor que yo; **do you agree? – yes, I do/no, I don't** ¿estás de acuerdo? – sí (lo estoy)/no (lo estoy); **she lives in Glasgow – so do I** vive en Glasgow

– yo también; **he didn't like it and neither did we** no le gustó y a nosotros tampoco; **who made this mess? – I did** ¿quién hizo esta chapuza? – yo; **he asked me to help him and I did** me pidió que le ayudara y lo hice

5 (in question tags): **you like him, don't you?** te gusta, ¿verdad? or ¿no?; **I don't know him, do I?** creo que no le conozco

▷ vt **1** (gen, carry out, perform etc): **what are you doing tonight?** ¿qué haces esta noche?; **what can I do for you?** ¿en qué puedo servirle?; **to do the washing-up/cooking** fregar los platos/cocinar; **to do one's teeth/hair/nails** lavarse los dientes/arreglarse el pelo/arreglarse las uñas

2 (Aut etc): **the car was doing 100** el coche iba a 100; **we've done 200 km already** ya hemos hecho 200 km; **he can do 100 in that car** puede ir a 100 en ese coche

▷ vi **1** (act, behave): **do as I do** haz como yo

2 (get on, fare): **he's doing well/badly at school** va bien/mal en la escuela; **the firm is doing well** la empresa anda or va bien; **how do you do?** mucho gusto; (less formal) ¿qué tal?

3 (suit): **will it do?** ¿sirve?, ¿está or va bien?

4 (be sufficient) bastar; **will £10 do?** ¿será bastante con £10?; **that'll do** así está bien; **that'll do!** (in annoyance) ¡ya está bien!, ¡basta ya!; **to make do (with)** arreglárselas (con)

do up vt (laces) atar; (zip, dress, shirt) abrochar; (renovate: room, house) renovar

do with vt fus (need): **I could do with a drink/some help** no me vendría mal un trago/un poco de ayuda; (be connected) tener que ver con; **what has it got to do with you?** ¿qué tiene que ver contigo?

do without vi pasar sin; **if you're late for tea then you'll do without** si llegas tarde tendrás que quedarte sin cenar

▷ vt fus pasar sin; **I can do without a car** puedo pasar sin coche

dock [dɔk] n (Naut) muelle m; (Law) banquillo (de los acusados) ▷ vi (enter dock) atracar (la) muelle; (Space) acoplarse; **docks** npl (Naut) muelles mpl, puerto sg

doctor ['dɔktə*] n médico/a; (Ph.D. etc) doctor(a) m/f ▷ vt (drink etc) adulterar; **Doctor of Philosophy** n Doctor en Filosofía y Letras

document ['dɔkjumənt] n documento; **documentary** [-'mɛntərɪ] adj documental ▷ n documental m; **documentation** [-mɛn'teɪʃən] n documentación f

dodge [dɔdʒ] n (fig) truco ▷ vt evadir; (blow) esquivar

dodgy ['dɔdʒɪ] adj (inf: uncertain) dudoso; (suspicious) sospechoso; (risky) arriesgado

does [dʌz] vb see **do**

doesn't ['dʌznt] = **does not**

dog [dɔg] n perro ▷ vt seguir los pasos de; (bad luck) perseguir; **doggy bag** ['dɔgɪ-] n bolsa para llevarse las sobras de la comida

do-it-yourself ['duːɪtjɔːˈsɛlf] n bricolaje m

dole [dəul] (BRIT) n (payment) subsidio de paro; **on the ~** parado

doll [dɔl] n muñeca; (US: inf: woman) muñeca, gachí f

dollar ['dɔlə*] n dólar m

dolphin ['dɔlfɪn] n delfín m

dome [dəum] n (Arch) cúpula

domestic [dəˈmɛstɪk] adj (animal, duty) doméstico; (flight, policy) nacional; **domestic appliance** n aparato m doméstico, aparato m de uso doméstico

dominant ['dɔmɪnənt] adj dominante

dominate ['dɔmɪneɪt] vt dominar

domino ['dɔmɪnəu] (pl ~es) n ficha de dominó; **dominoes** n (game) dominó

donate [dəˈneɪt] vt donar; **donation** [dəˈneɪʃən] n donativo

done [dʌn] pp of **do**

donkey ['dɔŋkɪ] n burro

donor ['dəunə*] n donante mf; **donor card** n carnet m de donante

don't [dəunt] = **do not**

donut ['dəunʌt] (US) n = **doughnut**

doodle ['duːdl] vi hacer dibujitos or garabatos

doom [duːm] n (fate) suerte f ▷ vt: **to be ~ed to failure** estar condenado al fracaso

door [dɔː*] n puerta; **doorbell** n timbre m; **door handle** n tirador m; (of car) manija; **doorknob** n pomo m de la puerta, manilla f (LAM); **doorstep** n peldaño; **doorway** n entrada, puerta

dope [dəup] n (inf: illegal drug) droga; (: person) imbécil mf ▷ vt (horse etc) drogar

dormitory ['dɔːmɪtrɪ] n (BRIT) dormitorio; (US) colegio mayor

DOS n abbr (= disk operating system) DOS m

dosage ['dəusɪdʒ] n dosis f inv

dose [dəus] n dosis f inv

dot [dɔt] n punto ▷ vi: **~ted with** salpicado de; **on the ~** en punto; **dotcom** [dɔt'kɔm] n punto.com f inv; **dotted line** ['dɔtɪd-] n: **to sign on the dotted line** firmar

double ['dʌbl] adj doble ▷ adv (twice): **to cost ~** costar el doble ▷ n doble m ▷ vt doblar ▷ vi doblarse; **on the ~, at the ~** (BRIT) corriendo; **double back** vi (person)

volver sobre sus pasos; **double bass** n contrabajo; **double bed** n cama de matrimonio; **double-check** vt volver a revisar ▷ vi: **I'll double-check** voy a revisarlo otra vez; **double-click** vi (Comput) hacer doble clic; **double-cross** vt (trick) engañar; (betray) traicionar; **doubledecker** n autobús m de dos pisos; **double glazing** (BRIT) n doble acristalamiento; **double room** n habitación f doble; **doubles** n (Tennis) juego de dobles; **double yellow lines** npl (BRIT: Aut) línea doble amarilla de prohibido aparcar, ≈ línea fsg amarilla continua

doubt [daut] n duda ▷ vt dudar; (suspect) dudar de; **to ~ that** dudar que; **doubtful** adj dudoso; (person): **to be doubtful about sth** tener dudas sobre algo; **doubtless** adv sin duda

dough [dəu] n masa, pasta; **doughnut** (US **donut**) n ≈ rosquilla

dove [dʌv] n paloma

down [daun] n (feathers) plumón m, flojel m ▷ adv (downwards) abajo, hacia abajo; (on the ground) por o en tierra ▷ prep abajo ▷ vt (inf: drink) beberse; **~ with X!** ¡abajo X!; **down-and-out** n vagabundo/a; **downfall** n caída, ruina; **downhill** adv: **to go downhill** (also fig) ir cuesta abajo

Downing Street ['daunɪŋ-] n (BRIT) Downing Street f

down: download vt (Comput) bajar; **downright** adj (nonsense, lie) manifiesto; (refusal) terminante

Down's syndrome ['daunz-] n síndrome m de Down

down: downstairs adv (below) (en el piso de) abajo; (downwards) escaleras abajo; **down-to-earth** adj práctico; **downtown** adv en el centro de la ciudad; **down under** adv en Australia (or Nueva Zelanda); **downward** [-wəd] adj, adv hacia abajo; **downwards** [-wədz] adv hacia abajo

doz. abbr = **dozen**

doze [dəuz] vi dormitar

dozen ['dʌzn] n docena; **a ~ books** una docena de libros; **~s of** cantidad de

Dr. abbr = **doctor; drive**

drab [dræb] adj gris, monótono

draft [drɑːft] n (first copy) borrador m; (Pol: of bill) anteproyecto; (US: call-up) quinta ▷ vt (plan) preparar; (write roughly) hacer un borrador de; see also **draught**

drag [dræg] vt arrastrar; (river) dragar, rastrear ▷ vi (time) pasar despacio; (play, film etc) hacerse pesado ▷ n (inf) lata; (women's clothing): **in ~** vestido de travesti; **to ~ and drop** (Comput) arrastrar y soltar

dragon ['drægən] n dragón m

dragonfly ['drægənflaɪ] n libélula

drain [dreɪn] n desaguadero; (in street) sumidero; (source of loss): **to be a ~ on** consumir, agotar ▷ vt (land, marshes) desaguar; (reservoir) desecar; (vegetables) escurrir ▷ vi escurrirse; **drainage** n (act) desagüe m; (Med, Agr) drenaje m; (sewage) alcantarillado; **drainpipe** n tubo de desagüe

drama ['drɑːmə] n (art) teatro; (play) drama m; (excitement) emoción f; **dramatic** [drə'mætɪk] adj dramático; (sudden, marked) espectacular

drank [dræŋk] pt of **drink**

drape [dreɪp] vt (cloth) colocar; (flag) colgar; **drapes** npl (US) cortinas fpl

drastic ['dræstɪk] adj (measure) severo; (change) radical, drástico

draught [drɑːft] (US **draft**) n (of air) corriente f de aire; (Naut) calado; **on ~** (beer) de barril; **draught beer** n cerveza de barril; **draughts** (BRIT) n (game) juego de damas

draw [drɔː] (pt **drew**, pp **drawn**) vt (picture) dibujar; (cart) tirar de; (curtain) correr; (take out) sacar; (attract) atraer; (money) retirar; (wages) cobrar ▷ vi (Sport) empatar ▷ n (Sport) empate m; (lottery) sorteo; **draw out** vi (lengthen) alargarse ▷ vt sacar; **draw up** vi (stop) pararse ▷ vt (chair) acercar; (document) redactar; **drawback** n inconveniente m, desventaja

drawer [drɔː*] n cajón m

drawing ['drɔːɪŋ] n dibujo; **drawing pin** (BRIT) n chincheta; **drawing room** n salón m

drawn [drɔːn] pp of **draw**

dread [dred] n pavor m, terror m ▷ vt temer, tener miedo or pavor a; **dreadful** adj horroroso

dream [driːm] (pt, pp **~ed** or **~t**) n sueño ▷ vt, vi soñar; **dreamer** n soñador(a) m/f

dreamt [dremt] pt, pp of **dream**

dreary ['drɪərɪ] adj monótono

drench [drentʃ] vt empapar

dress [dres] n vestido; (clothing) ropa ▷ vt vestir; (wound) vendar ▷ vi vestirse; **to get ~ed** vestirse; **dress up** vi vestirse de etiqueta; (in fancy dress) disfrazarse; **dress circle** (BRIT) n principal m; **dresser** n (furniture) aparador m; (: US) cómoda (con espejo); **dressing** n (Med) vendaje m; (Culin) aliño; **dressing gown** (BRIT) n bata; **dressing room** n (Theatre) camarín m; (Sport) vestuario; **dressing table** n tocador m; **dressmaker** n modista, costurera

drew [druː] pt of **draw**

dribble ['drɪbl] vi (baby) babear ▷ vt (ball)

regatear

dried [draɪd] adj (fruit) seco; (milk) en polvo

drier ['draɪə*] n = **dryer**

drift [drɪft] n (of current etc) flujo; (of snow) ventisquero; (meaning) significado ▷ vi (boat) ir a la deriva; (sand, snow) amontonarse

drill [drɪl] n (drill bit) broca; (tool for DIY etc) taladro; (of dentist) fresa; (for mining etc) perforadora, barrena; (Mil) instrucción f ▷ vt perforar, taladrar; (troops) enseñar la instrucción a ▷ vi (for oil) perforar

drink [drɪŋk] (pt **drank**, pp **drunk**) n bebida; (sip) trago ▷ vt, vi beber; **to have a ~** tomar algo; tomar una copa or un trago; **a ~ of water** un trago de agua; **drink-driving** n: **to be charged with drink-driving** ser acusado de conducir borracho or en estado de embriaguez; **drinker** n bebedor(a) m/f; **drinking water** n agua potable

drip [drɪp] n (act) goteo; (one drip) gota; (Med) gota a gota m ▷ vi gotear

drive [draɪv] (pt **drove**, pp **driven**) n (journey) viaje m (en coche); (also: **~way**) entrada; (energy) energía, vigor m; (Comput: also: **disk ~**) drive m ▷ vt (car) conducir (SP), manejar (LAM); (nail) clavar; (push) empujar; (Tech: motor) impulsar ▷ vi (Aut: at controls) conducir; (: travel) pasearse en coche; **left-/right-hand ~** conducción f a la izquierda/derecha; **to ~ sb mad** volverle loco a algn; **drive out** vt (force out) expulsar, echar; **drive-in** adj (esp US): **drive-in cinema** autocine m

driven ['drɪvn] pp of **drive**

driver ['draɪvə*] n conductor(a) m/f (SP), chofer mf (LAM); (of taxi, bus) chófer mf (SP), chofer mf (LAM); **driver's license** (US) n carnet m de conducir

driveway ['draɪvweɪ] n entrada

driving ['draɪvɪŋ] n el conducir (SP), el manejar (LAM); **driving instructor** n profesor(a) m/f de autoescuela (SP), instructor(a) m/f de manejo (LAM); **driving lesson** n clase f de conducir (SP) or manejar (LAM); **driving licence** (BRIT) n licencia de manejo (LAM), carnet m de conducir (SP); **driving test** n examen m de conducir (SP) or manejar (LAM)

drizzle ['drɪzl] n llovizna

droop [druːp] vi (flower) marchitarse; (shoulders) encorvarse; (head) inclinarse

drop [drɒp] n (of water) gota; (lessening) baja; (fall) caída ▷ vt dejar caer; (voice, eyes, price) bajar; (passenger) dejar; (omit) omitir ▷ vi (object) caer; (wind) amainar; **drop in** vi (inf: visit): **to drop in (on)** pasar por casa (de); **drop off** vi (sleep) dormirse ▷ vt

(*passenger*) dejar; **drop out** vi (*withdraw*)
retirarse
drought [draut] n sequía
drove [drəʊv] pt of **drive**
drown [draun] vt ahogar ▷vi ahogarse
drowsy ['drauzı] adj soñoliento; **to be ~**
tener sueño
drug [drʌg] n medicamento; (*narcotic*)
droga ▷vt drogar; **to be on ~s** drogarse;
drug addict n drogadicto/a; **drug dealer**
n traficante mf de drogas; **druggist** (us)
n farmacéutico; **drugstore** (us) n farmacia
drum [drʌm] n tambor m; (*for oil, petrol*)
bidón m; **drums** npl batería; **drummer** n
tambor m
drunk [drʌŋk] pp of **drink** ▷adj borracho
▷n (*also*: **~ard**) borracho/a; **drunken** adj
borracho; (*laughter, party*) de borrachos
dry [draı] adj seco; (*day*) sin lluvia; (*climate*)
árido, seco ▷vt secar; (*tears*) enjugarse
▷vi secarse; **dry off** vi secarse ▷vt secar;
dry up vi (*river*) secarse; **dry-cleaner's** n
tintorería; **dry-cleaning** n lavado en seco;
dryer n (*for hair*) secador m; (*us: for clothes*)
secadora
DSS n abbr = **Department of Social
Security**
D & T (*BRIT: Scol*) n abbr (= *design and
technology*) ≈ dibujo y tecnología
DTP n abbr (= *desk-top publishing*)
autoedición f
dual ['djuəl] adj doble; **dual carriageway**
(*BRIT*) n carretera de doble calzada
dubious ['djuːbıəs] adj indeciso;
(*reputation, company*) sospechoso
duck [dʌk] n pato ▷vi agacharse
due [djuː] adj (*owed*): **he is ~ £10** se le deben
10 libras; (*expected: event*): **the meeting is ~
on Wednesday** la reunión tendrá lugar el
miércoles; (: *arrival*): **the train is ~ at 8am**
el tren tiene su llegada para las 8; (*proper*)
debido ▷n: **to give sb his** (*or* **her**) **~** ser
justo con algn ▷adv: **~ north** derecho al
norte
duel ['djuəl] n duelo
duet [djuːˈɛt] n dúo
dug [dʌg] pt, pp of **dig**
duke [djuːk] n duque m
dull [dʌl] adj (*light*) débil; (*stupid*) torpe;
(*boring*) pesado; (*sound, pain*) sordo; (*weather,
day*) gris ▷vt (*pain, grief*) aliviar; (*mind,
senses*) entorpecer
dumb [dʌm] adj mudo; (*pej: stupid*)
estúpido
dummy ['dʌmı] n (*tailor's dummy*) maniquí
m; (*mock-up*) maqueta; (*BRIT: for baby*)
chupete m ▷adj falso, postizo
dump [dʌmp] n (*also*: **rubbish ~**) basurero,

vertedero; (*inf: place*) cuchitril m ▷vt (*put
down*) dejar; (*get rid of*) deshacerse de;
(*Comput: data*) transferir
dumpling ['dʌmplıŋ] n bola de masa
hervida
dune [djuːn] n duna
dungarees [dʌŋgəˈriːz] npl mono
dungeon ['dʌndʒən] n calabozo
duplex ['djuːplɛks] n dúplex m
duplicate [n 'djuːplıkət, vb 'djuːplıkeıt]
n duplicado ▷vt duplicar; (*photocopy*)
fotocopiar; (*repeat*) repetir; **in ~** por
duplicado
durable ['djuərəbl] adj duradero
duration [djuəˈreıʃən] n duración f
during ['djuərıŋ] prep durante
dusk [dʌsk] n crepúsculo, anochecer m
dust [dʌst] n polvo ▷vt quitar el polvo
a, desempolvar; (*cake etc*): **to ~ with**
espolvorear de; **dustbin** (*BRIT*) n cubo
or bote m (*MEX*) or tacho (*SC*) de la basura;
duster n paño, trapo; **dustman** (*BRIT: irreg*)
n basurero; **dustpan** n cogedor m; **dusty**
adj polvoriento
Dutch [dʌtʃ] adj holandés/esa ▷n
(*Ling*) holandés m; **the Dutch** npl los
holandeses; **to go ~** (*inf*) pagar cada uno
lo suyo; **Dutchman** (*irreg*) n holandés m;
Dutchwoman (*irreg*) n holandésa
duty ['djuːtı] n deber m; (*tax*) derechos mpl
de aduana; **on ~** de servicio; (*at night etc*) de
guardia; **off ~** libre (de servicio); **duty-free**
adj libre de impuestos
duvet ['duːveı] (*BRIT*) n edredón m
DVD n abbr (= *digital versatile or video disc*)
DVD m; **DVD player** n lector m de DVD;
DVD writer n grabadora de DVD
dwarf [dwɔːf] (*pl* **dwarves**) n enano/a
▷vt empequeñecer
dwell [dwɛl] (*pt, pp* **dwelt**) vi morar; **dwell
on** vt fus explayarse en
dwelt [dwɛlt] pt, pp of **dwell**
dwindle ['dwındl] vi disminuir
dye [daı] n tinte m ▷vt teñir
dying ['daııŋ] adj moribundo
dynamic [daıˈnæmık] adj dinámico
dynamite ['daınəmaıt] n dinamita
dyslexia [dısˈlɛksıə] n dislexia
dyslexic [dısˈlɛksık] adj, n disléxico/a m/f

e

E [iː] n (Mus) mi m

E111 n abbr (= form E111) impreso E111

each [iːtʃ] adj cada inv ▷ pron cada uno; **~ other** el uno al otro; **they hate ~ other** se odian (entre ellos or mutuamente); **they have 2 books ~** tienen 2 libros por persona

eager ['iːgə*] adj (keen) entusiasmado; **to be ~ to do sth** tener muchas ganas de hacer algo, impacientarse por hacer algo; **to be ~ for** tener muchas ganas de

eagle ['iːgl] n águila

ear [ɪə*] n oreja; oído; (of corn) espiga; **earache** n dolor m de oídos; **eardrum** n tímpano

earl [əːl] n conde m

earlier ['əːlɪə*] adj anterior ▷ adv antes

early ['əːlɪ] adv temprano; (before time) con tiempo, con anticipación ▷ adj temprano; (settlers etc) primitivo; (death, departure) prematuro; (reply) pronto; **to have an ~ night** acostarse temprano; **in the ~** or **~ in the spring/19th century** a principios de primavera/del siglo diecinueve; **early retirement** n jubilación f anticipada

earmark ['ɪəmɑːk] vt: **to ~ (for)** reservar (para), destinar (a)

earn [əːn] vt (salary) percibir; (interest) devengar; (praise) merecerse

earnest ['əːnɪst] adj (wish) fervoroso; (person) serio, formal; **in ~** en serio

earnings ['əːnɪŋz] npl (personal) sueldo, ingresos mpl; (company) ganancias fpl

ear: earphones npl auriculares mpl; **earplugs** npl tapones mpl para los oídos; **earring** n pendiente m, arete m

earth [əːθ] n tierra; (BRIT Elec) cable m de toma de tierra ▷ vt (BRIT Elec) conectar a tierra; **earthquake** n terremoto

ease [iːz] n facilidad f; (comfort) comodidad f ▷ vt (lessen: problem) mitigar; (: pain) aliviar; (: tension) reducir; **to ~ sth in/out**

meter/sacar algo con cuidado; **at ~!** (Mil) ¡descansen!

easily ['iːzɪlɪ] adv fácilmente

east [iːst] n este m ▷ adj del este, oriental; (wind) este ▷ adv al este, hacia el este; **the E~** el Oriente; (Pol) los países del Este; **eastbound** adj en dirección este

Easter ['iːstə*] n Pascua (de Resurrección); **Easter egg** n huevo de Pascua

eastern ['iːstən] adj del este, oriental; (oriental) oriental

Easter Sunday n Domingo de Resurrección

easy ['iːzɪ] adj fácil; (simple) sencillo; (comfortable) holgado, cómodo; (relaxed) tranquilo ▷ adv: **to take it** or **things ~** (not worry) tomarlo con calma; (rest) descansar; **easy-going** adj acomodadizo

eat [iːt] (pt ate, pp eaten) vt comer; **eat out** vi comer fuera

eavesdrop ['iːvzdrɔp] vi: **to ~ (on)** escuchar a escondidas

e-book ['iːbuk] n libro electrónico

e-business ['iːbɪznɪs] n (company) negocio electrónico; (commerce) comercio electrónico

EC n abbr (= European Community) CE f

eccentric [ɪk'sɛntrɪk] adj, n excéntrico/a m/f

echo ['ɛkəu] (pl ~es) n eco ▷ vt (sound) repetir ▷ vi resonar, hacer eco

eclipse [ɪ'klɪps] n eclipse m

eco-friendly ['iːkəufrɛndlɪ] adj ecológico

ecological [iːkə'lɔdʒɪkl] adj ecológico

ecology [ɪ'kɔlədʒɪ] n ecología

e-commerce n abbr comercio electrónico

economic [iːkə'nɔmɪk] adj económico; (business etc) rentable; **economical** adj económico; **economics** n (Scol) economía ▷ npl (of project etc) rentabilidad f

economist [ɪ'kɔnəmɪst] n economista m/f

economize [ɪ'kɔnəmaɪz] vi economizar, ahorrar

economy [ɪ'kɔnəmɪ] n economía; **economy class** n (Aviat) clase f económica; **economy class syndrome** n síndrome m de la clase turista

ecstasy ['ɛkstəsɪ] n éxtasis m inv; (drug) éxtasis m inv; **ecstatic** [ɛks'tætɪk] adj extático

eczema ['ɛksɪmə] n eczema m

edge [ɛdʒ] n (of knife) filo; (of object) borde m; (of lake) orilla ▷ vt (Sewing) ribetear; **on ~** (fig) = **edgy**; **to ~ away from** alejarse poco a poco de

edgy ['ɛdʒɪ] adj nervioso, inquieto

edible ['ɛdɪbl] adj comestible

Edinburgh ['edɪnbərə] n Edimburgo
edit ['edɪt] vt (be editor of) dirigir; (text, report) corregir, preparar; **edition** [ɪ'dɪʃən] n edición f; **editor** n (of newspaper) director(a) m/f; (of column): **foreign/political editor** encargado de la sección de extranjero/política; (of book) redactor(a) m/f; **editorial** [-'tɔ:rɪəl] adj editorial ▷ n editorial m
educate ['edjukeɪt] vt (gen) educar; (instruct) instruir; **educated** ['edjukeɪtɪd] adj culto
education [edju'keɪʃən] n educación f; (schooling) enseñanza; (Scol) pedagogía; **educational** adj (policy etc) educacional; (experience) docente; (toy) educativo
eel [i:l] n anguila
eerie ['ɪərɪ] adj misterioso
effect [ɪ'fekt] n efecto ▷ vt efectuar, llevar a cabo; **to take ~** (law) entrar en vigor or vigencia; (drug) surtir efecto; **in ~** en realidad; **effects** npl (property) efectos mpl; **effective** adj eficaz; (actual) verdadero; **effectively** adv eficazmente; (in reality) efectivamente
efficiency [ɪ'fɪʃənsɪ] n eficiencia; rendimiento
efficient [ɪ'fɪʃənt] adj eficiente; (machine) de buen rendimiento; **efficiently** adv eficientemente, de manera eficiente
effort ['efət] n esfuerzo; **effortless** adj sin ningún esfuerzo; (style) natural
e.g. adv abbr (= exempli gratia) p. ej.
egg [eg] n huevo; **hard-boiled/soft-boiled ~** huevo duro/pasado por agua; **eggcup** n huevera; **eggplant** (esp US) n berenjena; **eggshell** n cáscara de huevo; **egg white** n clara de huevo; **egg yolk** n yema de huevo
ego ['i:gəu] n ego
Egypt ['i:dʒɪpt] n Egipto; **Egyptian** [ɪ'dʒɪpʃən] adj, n egipcio/a m/f
eight [eɪt] num ocho; **eighteen** num diez y ocho, dieciocho; **eighteenth** adj decimoctavo; **the eighteenth floor** la planta dieciocho; **the eighteenth of August** el dieciocho de agosto; **eighth** num octavo; **eightieth** ['eɪtɪɪθ] adj octogésimo
eighty ['eɪtɪ] num ochenta
Eire ['eərə] n Eire m
either ['aɪðə*] adj cualquiera de los dos; (both, each) cada ▷ pron: **~ (of them)** cualquiera (de los dos) ▷ adv tampoco ▷ conj: **~ yes or no** o sí o no; **on ~ side** en ambos lados; **I don't like ~** no me gusta ninguno/a de los(las) dos; **no, I don't ~** no, yo tampoco
eject [ɪ'dʒekt] vt echar, expulsar; (tenant) desahuciar
elaborate [adj ɪ'læbərɪt, vb ɪ'læbəreɪt] adj (complex) complejo ▷ vt (expand) ampliar; (refine) refinar ▷ vi explicar con más detalles
elastic [ɪ'læstɪk] n elástico ▷ adj elástico; (fig) flexible; **elastic band** (BRIT) n gomita
elbow ['elbəu] n codo
elder ['eldə*] adj mayor ▷ n (tree) saúco; (person) mayor; **elderly** adj de edad, mayor ▷ npl: **the elderly** los mayores
eldest ['eldɪst] adj, n el/la mayor
elect [ɪ'lekt] vt elegir ▷ adj: **the president ~** el presidente electo; **to ~ to do** optar por hacer; **election** n elección f; **electoral** adj electoral; **electorate** n electorado
electric [ɪ'lektrɪk] adj eléctrico; **electrical** adj eléctrico; **electric blanket** n manta eléctrica; **electric fire** n estufa eléctrica; **electrician** [ɪlek'trɪʃən] n electricista mf; **electricity** [ɪlek'trɪsɪtɪ] n electricidad f; **electric shock** n electrochoque m; **electrify** [ɪ'lektrɪfaɪ] vt (Rail) electrificar; (fig: audience) electrizar
electronic [ɪlek'trɒnɪk] adj electrónico; **electronic mail** n correo electrónico; **electronics** n electrónica
elegance ['elɪgəns] n elegancia
elegant ['elɪgənt] adj elegante
element ['elɪmənt] n elemento; (of kettle etc) resistencia
elementary [elɪ'mentərɪ] adj elemental; (primitive) rudimentario; **elementary school** (US) n escuela de enseñanza primaria
elephant ['elɪfənt] n elefante m
elevate ['elɪveɪt] vt (gen) elevar; (in rank) ascender
elevator ['elɪveɪtə*] (US) n ascensor m; (in warehouse etc) montacargas m inv
eleven [ɪ'levn] num once; **eleventh** num undécimo
eligible ['elɪdʒəbl] adj: **an ~ young man/woman** un buen partido; **to be ~ for sth** llenar los requisitos para algo
eliminate [ɪ'lɪmɪneɪt] vt (suspect, possibility) descartar
elm [elm] n olmo
eloquent ['eləkwənt] adj elocuente
else [els] adv: **something ~** otra cosa; **somewhere ~** en otra parte; **everywhere ~** en todas partes menos aquí; **where ~?** ¿dónde más?, ¿en qué otra parte?; **there was little ~ to do** apenas quedaba otra cosa que hacer; **nobody ~ spoke** no habló nadie más; **elsewhere** adv (be) en otra parte; (go) a otra parte
elusive [ɪ'lu:sɪv] adj esquivo; (quality) difícil de encontrar
e-mail ['i:meɪl] n abbr (= electronic mail) correo electrónico, e-mail m; **e-mail**

address n dirección f electrónica, email m
embankment [ɪm'bæŋkmənt] n
terraplén m
embargo [ɪm'bɑːɡəʊ] (pl **~es**) n (Comm,
Naut) embargo; (prohibition) prohibición f; **to
put an ~ on sth** poner un embargo en algo
embark [ɪm'bɑːk] vi embarcarse ▷vt
embarcar; **to ~ on** (journey) emprender;
(course of action) lanzarse a
embarrass [ɪm'bærəs] vt avergonzar;
(government etc) dejar en mal lugar;
embarrassed adj (laugh, silence)
embarazoso

▌ Be careful not to translate **embarrassed**
by the Spanish word embarazada.

embarrassing adj (situation) violento;
(question) embarazoso; **embarrassment**
n (shame) vergüenza; (problem): **to be an
embarrassment for sb** poner en un aprieto
a algn
embassy ['embəsɪ] n embajada
embrace [ɪm'breɪs] vt abrazar, dar un
abrazo a; (include) abarcar ▷vi abrazarse
▷n abrazo
embroider [ɪm'brɔɪdə*] vt bordar;
embroidery n bordado
embryo ['embrɪəʊ] n embrión m
emerald ['emərəld] n esmeralda
emerge [ɪ'mɜːdʒ] vi salir; (arise) surgir
emergency [ɪ'mɜːdʒənsɪ] n crisis f inv;
in an ~ en caso de urgencia; **state of ~**
estado de emergencia; **emergency brake**
(us) n freno de mano; **emergency exit** n
salida de emergencia; **emergency landing**
n aterrizaje m forzoso; **emergency room**
(us: Med) n sala f de urgencias; **emergency
services** npl (fire, police, ambulance)
servicios mpl de urgencia or emergencia
emigrate ['emɪɡreɪt] vi emigrar;
emigration [emɪ'ɡreɪʃən] n emigración f
eminent ['emɪnənt] adj eminente
emissions [ɪ'mɪʃənz] npl emisión f
emit [ɪ'mɪt] vt emitir; (smoke) arrojar;
(smell) despedir; (sound) producir
emotion [ɪ'məʊʃən] n emoción f;
emotional adj (needs) emocional; (person)
sentimental; (scene) conmovedor(a),
emocionante; (speech) emocionado
emperor ['empərə*] n emperador m
emphasis ['emfəsɪs] (pl **-ses**) n énfasis
m inv
emphasize ['emfəsaɪz] vt (word, point)
subrayar, recalcar; (feature) hacer resaltar
empire ['empaɪə*] n imperio
employ [ɪm'plɔɪ] vt emplear; **employee**
[-'iː] n empleado/a; **employer** n patrón/
ona m/f; empresario; **employment** n
(work) trabajo; **employment agency** n

agencia de colocaciones
empower [ɪm'paʊə*] vt: **to ~ sb to do sth**
autorizar a algn para hacer algo
empress ['empris] n emperatriz f
emptiness ['emptɪnɪs] n vacío; (of life etc)
vaciedad f
empty ['emptɪ] adj vacío; (place) desierto;
(house) desocupado; (threat) vano ▷vt
vaciar; (place) dejar vacío ▷vi vaciarse;
(house etc) quedar desocupado; **empty-
handed** adj con las manos vacías
EMU n abbr (= European Monetary Union)
UME f
emulsion [ɪ'mʌlʃən] n emulsión f; (also: ~
paint) pintura emulsión
enable [ɪ'neɪbl] vt: **to ~ sb to do sth**
permitir a algn hacer algo
enamel [ɪ'næməl] n esmalte m; (also: ~
paint) pintura esmaltada
enchanting [ɪn'tʃɑːntɪŋ] adj
encantador(a)
encl. abbr (= enclosed) adj
enclose [ɪn'kləʊz] vt (land) cercar; (letter
etc) adjuntar; **please find ~d** le mandamos
adjunto
enclosure [ɪn'kləʊʒə*] n cercado, recinto
encore [ɔŋ'kɔː*] excl ¡otra!, ¡bis! ▷n bis m
encounter [ɪn'kaʊntə*] n encuentro
▷vt encontrar, encontrarse con; (difficulty)
tropezar con
encourage [ɪn'kʌrɪdʒ] vt alentar, animar;
(activity) fomentar; (growth) estimular;
encouragement n estímulo; (of industry)
fomento
encouraging [ɪn'kʌrɪdʒɪŋ] adj
alentador(a)
encyclop(a)edia [ensaɪkləʊ'piːdɪə] n
enciclopedia
end [end] n fin m; (of table) extremo; (of
street) final m; (Sport) lado ▷vt terminar,
acabar; (also: **bring to an ~**, **put an ~ to**)
acabar con ▷vi terminar, acabar; **in the
~** al fin; **on ~** (object) de punta, de cabeza;
to stand on ~ (hair) erizarse; **for hours on
~** hora tras hora; **end up** vi: **to end up in**
terminar en; (place) ir a parar en
endanger [ɪn'deɪndʒə*] vt poner en
peligro; **an ~ed species** una especie en
peligro de extinción
endearing [ɪn'dɪərɪŋ] adj simpático,
atractivo
endeavour [ɪn'devə*] (us **endeavor**) n
esfuerzo; (attempt) tentativa ▷vi: **to ~ to do**
esforzarse por hacer; (try) procurar hacer
ending ['endɪŋ] n (of book) desenlace m;
(Ling) terminación f
endless ['endlɪs] adj interminable,
inacabable

endorse [ɪn'dɔːs] vt (cheque) endosar; (approve) aprobar; **endorsement** n (on driving licence) nota de inhabilitación

endurance [ɪn'djuərəns] n resistencia

endure [ɪn'djuə*] vt (bear) aguantar, soportar ▷ vi (last) durar

enemy ['ɛnəmɪ] adj, n enemigo/a m/f

energetic [ɛnə'dʒɛtɪk] adj enérgico

energy ['ɛnədʒɪ] n energía

enforce [ɪn'fɔːs] vt (Law) hacer cumplir

engaged [ɪn'geɪdʒd] adj (BRIT: busy, in use) ocupado; (betrothed) prometido; **to get ~** prometerse; **engaged tone** (BRIT) n (Tel) señal f de comunicando

engagement [ɪn'geɪdʒmənt] n (appointment) compromiso, cita; (booking) contratación f; (to marry) compromiso; (period) noviazgo; **engagement ring** n anillo de prometida

engaging [ɪn'geɪdʒɪŋ] adj atractivo

engine ['ɛndʒɪn] n (Aut) motor m; (Rail) locomotora

engineer [ɛndʒɪ'nɪə*] n ingeniero; (BRIT: for repairs) mecánico; (on ship, US Rail) maquinista m; **engineering** n ingeniería

England ['ɪŋglənd] n Inglaterra

English ['ɪŋglɪʃ] adj inglés/esa ▷ n (Ling) inglés m; **the English** npl los ingleses mpl; **English Channel** n: **the English Channel** (el Canal de) la Mancha; **Englishman** (irreg) n inglés m; **Englishwoman** (irreg) n inglésa

engrave [ɪn'greɪv] vt grabar

engraving [ɪn'greɪvɪŋ] n grabado

enhance [ɪn'hɑːns] vt (gen) aumentar; (beauty) realzar

enjoy [ɪn'dʒɔɪ] vt (health, fortune) disfrutar de, gozar de; (like) gustarle a algn; **to ~ o.s.** divertirse; **enjoyable** adj agradable; (amusing) divertido; **enjoyment** n (joy) placer m; (activity) diversión f

enlarge [ɪn'lɑːdʒ] vt aumentar; (broaden) extender; (Phot) ampliar ▷ vi: **to ~ on** (subject) tratar con más detalles; **enlargement** n (Phot) ampliación f

enlist [ɪn'lɪst] vt alistar; (support) conseguir ▷ vi alistarse

enormous [ɪ'nɔːməs] adj enorme

enough [ɪ'nʌf] adj: **~ time/books** bastante tiempo/bastantes libros ▷ pron bastante(s) ▷ adv: **big ~** bastante grande; **he has not worked ~** no ha trabajado bastante; **have you got ~?** ¿tiene usted bastante(s)?; **~ to eat** (lo) suficiente or (lo) bastante para comer; **~!** ¡basta ya!; **that's ~, thanks** con eso basta, gracias; **I've had ~ of him** estoy harto de él; **... which, funnily or oddly ~ ...** ... lo que, por extraño que parezca ...

enquire [ɪn'kwaɪə*] vt, vi = **inquire**

enquiry [ɪn'kwaɪərɪ] n (official investigation) investigación

enrage [ɪn'reɪdʒ] vt enfurecer

enrich [ɪn'rɪtʃ] vt enriquecer

enrol [ɪn'rəul] (US **enroll**) vt (members) inscribir; (Scol) matricular ▷ vi inscribirse; matricularse; **enrolment** (US **enrollment**) n inscripción f; matriculación f

en route [ɒn'ruːt] adv durante el viaje

en suite [ɒn'swiːt] adj: **with ~ bathroom** con baño

ensure [ɪn'ʃuə*] vt asegurar

entail [ɪn'teɪl] vt suponer

enter ['ɛntə*] vt (room) entrar en; (club) hacerse socio de; (army) alistarse en; (sb for a competition) inscribir; (write down) anotar, apuntar; (Comput) meter ▷ vi entrar

enterprise ['ɛntəpraɪz] n empresa; (spirit) iniciativa; **free ~** la libre empresa; **private ~** la iniciativa privada; **enterprising** adj emprendedor(a)

entertain [ɛntə'teɪn] vt (amuse) divertir; (invite: guest) invitar (a casa); (idea) abrigar; **entertainer** n artista m/f; **entertaining** adj divertido, entretenido; **entertainment** n (amusement) diversión f; (show) espectáculo

enthusiasm [ɪn'θuːzɪæzəm] n entusiasmo

enthusiast [ɪn'θuːzɪæst] n entusiasta m/f; **enthusiastic** [-'æstɪk] adj entusiasta; **to be enthusiastic about** entusiasmarse por

entire [ɪn'taɪə*] adj entero; **entirely** adv totalmente

entitle [ɪn'taɪtl] vt: **to ~ sb to sth** dar a algn derecho a algo; **entitled** adj (book) titulado; **to be entitled to do** tener derecho a hacer

entrance [n 'ɛntrəns, vb ɪn'trɑːns] n entrada ▷ vt encantar, hechizar; **to gain ~ to** (university etc) ingresar en; **entrance examination** n examen m de ingreso; **entrance fee** n cuota; **entrance ramp** (US) n (Aut) rampa de acceso

entrant ['ɛntrənt] n (in race, competition) participante m/f; (in examination) candidato/a

entrepreneur [ɒntrəprə'nɜː] n empresario

entrust [ɪn'trʌst] vt: **to ~ sth to sb** confiar algo a algn

entry ['ɛntrɪ] n entrada; (in competition) participación f; (in register) apunte m; (in account) partida; (in reference book) artículo; **"no ~"** "prohibido el paso"; (Aut) "dirección prohibida"; **entry phone** n portero automático

envelope ['ɛnvələup] n sobre m

envious ['ɛnvɪəs] adj envidioso; (look) de

envidia
environment [ɪnˈvaɪərnmənt] *n*
(*surroundings*) entorno; (*natural world*):
the ~ el medio ambiente; **environmental**
[-ˈmɛntl] *adj* ambiental; medioambiental;
environmentally [-ˈmɛntəlɪ]
adv: **environmentally sound/friendly**
ecológico
envisage [ɪnˈvɪzɪdʒ] *vt* prever
envoy [ˈɛnvɔɪ] *n* enviado
envy [ˈɛnvɪ] *n* envidia ▷*vt* tener envidia a;
to ~ sb sth envidiar algo a algn
epic [ˈɛpɪk] *n* épica ▷*adj* épico
epidemic [ɛpɪˈdɛmɪk] *n* epidemia
epilepsy [ˈɛpɪlɛpsɪ] *n* epilepsia
epileptic [ɛpɪˈlɛptɪk] *adj*, *n* epiléptico/a
m/f; **epileptic fit** [ɛpɪˈlɛptɪk-] *n* ataque *m*
de epilepsia, acceso *m* epiléptico
episode [ˈɛpɪsəud] *n* episodio
equal [ˈiːkwl] *adj* igual; (*treatment*)
equitativo ▷*n* igual *mf* ▷*vt* ser igual a;
(*fig*) igualar; **to be ~ to** (*task*) estar a la altura
de; **equality** [iːˈkwɔlɪtɪ] *n* igualdad *f*;
equalize *vi* (*Sport*) empatar; **equally** *adv*
igualmente; (*share etc*) a partes iguales
equation [ɪˈkweɪʒən] *n* (*Math*) ecuación *f*
equator [ɪˈkweɪtə*] *n* ecuador *m*
equip [ɪˈkwɪp] *vt* equipar; (*person*) proveer;
to be well ~ped estar bien equipado;
equipment *n* equipo; (*tools*) avíos *mpl*
equivalent [ɪˈkwɪvələnt] *adj*: **~ (to)**
equivalente (a) ▷*n* equivalente *m*
ER *abbr* (*BRIT*: = *Elizabeth Regina*) la reina
Isabel; (*US*: *Med*) = **emergency room**
era [ˈɪərə] *n* era, época
erase [ɪˈreɪz] *vt* borrar; **eraser** *n* goma
de borrar
erect [ɪˈrɛkt] *adj* erguido ▷*vt* erigir,
levantar; (*assemble*) montar; **erection** [-ʃən]
n construcción *f*; (*assembly*) montaje *m*;
(*Physiol*) erección *f*
ERM *n abbr* (= *Exchange Rate Mechanism*) tipo
de cambio europeo
erode [ɪˈrəud] *vt* (*Geo*) erosionar; (*metal*)
corroer, desgastar; (*fig*) desgastar
erosion [ɪˈrəuʒən] *n* erosión *f*; desgaste *m*
erotic [ɪˈrɔtɪk] *adj* erótico
errand [ˈɛrnd] *n* recado (*SP*), mandado
(*LAM*)
erratic [ɪˈrætɪk] *adj* desigual, poco
uniforme
error [ˈɛrə*] *n* error *m*, equivocación *f*
erupt [ɪˈrʌpt] *vi* entrar en erupción; (*fig*)
estallar; **eruption** [ɪˈrʌpʃən] *n* erupción *f*;
(*of war*) estallido
escalate [ˈɛskəleɪt] *vi* extenderse,
intensificarse
escalator [ˈɛskəleɪtə*] *n* escalera móvil

escape [ɪˈskeɪp] *n* fuga ▷*vi* escaparse;
(*flee*) huir, evadirse; (*leak*) fugarse
▷*vt* (*responsibility etc*) evitar, eludir;
(*consequences*) escapar a; (*elude*): **his name
~s me** no me sale su nombre; **to ~ from**
(*place*) escaparse de; (*person*) escaparse a
escort [*n* ˈɛskɔːt, *vb* ɪˈskɔːt] *n*
acompañante *mf*; (*Mil*) escolta *mf* ▷*vt*
acompañar
especially [ɪˈspɛʃlɪ] *adv* (*above all*)
sobre todo; (*particularly*) en particular,
especialmente
espionage [ˈɛspɪɑːnɑːʒ] *n* espionaje *m*
essay [ˈɛseɪ] *n* (*Literature*) ensayo;
(*Scol*: *short*) redacción *f*; (: *long*) trabajo
essence [ˈɛsns] *n* esencia
essential [ɪˈsɛnʃl] *adj* (*necessary*)
imprescindible; (*basic*) esencial; **essentially**
adv esencialmente; **essentials** *npl* lo
imprescindible, lo esencial
establish [ɪˈstæblɪʃ] *vt* establecer;
(*prove*) demostrar; (*relations*) entablar;
(*reputation*) ganarse; **establishment** *n*
establecimiento; **the Establishment** la
clase dirigente
estate [ɪˈsteɪt] *n* (*land*) finca, hacienda;
(*inheritance*) herencia; (*BRIT*: *also*: **housing
~**) urbanización *f*; **estate agent** (*BRIT*) *n*
agente *mf* inmobiliario/a; **estate car** (*BRIT*)
n furgoneta
estimate [*n* ˈɛstɪmət, *vb* ˈɛstɪmeɪt] *n*
estimación *f*, apreciación *f*; (*assessment*)
tasa, cálculo; (*Comm*) presupuesto ▷*vt*
estimar, tasar; calcular
etc *abbr* (= *et cetera*) etc
eternal [ɪˈtəːnl] *adj* eterno
eternity [ɪˈtəːnɪtɪ] *n* eternidad *f*
ethical [ˈɛθɪkl] *adj* ético; **ethics** [ˈɛθɪks] *n*
ética ▷*npl* moralidad *f*
Ethiopia [iːθɪˈəupɪə] *n* Etiopía
ethnic [ˈɛθnɪk] *adj* étnico; **ethnic
minority** *n* minoría étnica
e-ticket [ˈiːtɪkɪt] *n* billete *m* electrónico
(*SP*), boleto electrónico (*LAM*)
etiquette [ˈɛtɪkɛt] *n* etiqueta
EU *n abbr* (= *European Union*) UE *f*
euro *n* euro
Europe [ˈjuərəp] *n* Europa; **European**
[-ˈpiːən] *adj*, *n* europeo/a *m/f*; **European
Community** *n* Comunidad *f* Europea;
European Union *n* Unión *f* Europea
Eurostar® [ˈjuərəustɑː*] *n* Eurostar® *m*
evacuate [ɪˈvækjueɪt] *vt* (*people*) evacuar;
(*place*) desocupar
evade [ɪˈveɪd] *vt* evadir, eludir
evaluate [ɪˈvæljueɪt] *vt* evaluar; (*value*)
tasar; (*evidence*) interpretar
evaporate [ɪˈvæpəreɪt] *vi* evaporarse; (*fig*)

desvanecerse

eve [iːv] n: **on the ~ of** en vísperas de

even ['iːvn] adj (level) llano; (smooth) liso; (speed, temperature) uniforme; (number) par ▷ adv hasta, incluso; (introducing a comparison) aún, todavía; **~ if, ~ though** aunque +subjun; **~ more** aun más; **~ so** aun así; **not ~** ni siquiera; **~ he was there** hasta él estuvo allí; **~ on Sundays** incluso los domingos; **to get ~ with sb** ajustar cuentas con algn

evening ['iːvnɪŋ] n tarde f; (late) noche f; **in the ~** por la tarde; **evening class** n clase f nocturna; **evening dress** n (no pl: formal clothes) traje m de etiqueta; (woman's) traje m de noche

event [ɪ'vent] n suceso, acontecimiento; (Sport) prueba; **in the ~ of** en caso de; **eventful** adj (life) activo; (day) ajetreado

eventual [ɪ'ventʃuəl] adj final

▌ Be careful not to translate **eventual** by the Spanish word eventual.

eventually adv (finally) finalmente; (in time) con el tiempo

ever ['evə*] adv (at any time) nunca, jamás; (at all times) siempre; (in question): **why ~ not?** ¿y por qué no?; **the best ~** lo nunca visto; **have you ~ seen it?** ¿lo ha visto usted alguna vez?; **better than ~** mejor que nunca; **~ since** adv desde entonces ▷ conj después de que; **evergreen** n árbol m de hoja perenne

○ **KEYWORD**

every ['evrɪ] adj **1** (each) cada; **every one of them** (persons) todos ellos/as; (objects) cada uno de ellos/as; **every shop in the town was closed** todas las tiendas de la ciudad estaban cerradas **2** (all possible) todo/a; **I gave you every assistance** te di toda la ayuda posible; **I have every confidence in him** tiene toda mi confianza; **we wish you every success** te deseamos toda suerte de éxitos **3** (showing recurrence) todo/a; **every day/ week** todos los días/todas las semanas; **every other car had been broken into** habían forzado uno de cada dos coches; **she visits me every other/third day** me visita cada dos/tres días; **every now and then** de vez en cuando

every: everybody pron = **everyone**; **everyday** adj (daily) cotidiano, de todos los días; (usual) acostumbrado; **everyone** pron todos/as, todo el mundo; **everything** pron todo; **this shop sells everything**

esta tienda vende de todo; **everywhere** adv: **I've been looking for you everywhere** te he estado buscando por todas partes; **everywhere you go you meet ...** en todas partes encuentras ...

evict [ɪ'vɪkt] vt desahuciar

evidence ['evɪdəns] n (proof) prueba; (of witness) testimonio; (sign) indicios mpl; **to give ~** prestar declaración, dar testimonio

evident ['evɪdənt] adj evidente, manifiesto; **evidently** adv por lo visto

evil ['iːvl] adj malo; (influence) funesto ▷ n mal m

evoke [ɪ'vəuk] vt evocar

evolution [iːvə'luːʃən] n evolución f

evolve [ɪ'vɔlv] vt desarrollar ▷ vi evolucionar, desarrollarse

ewe [juː] n oveja

ex [eks] (inf) n: **my ~** mi ex

ex- [eks] prefix ex

exact [ɪg'zækt] adj exacto; (person) meticuloso ▷ vt: **to ~ sth (from)** exigir algo (de); **exactly** adv exactamente; (indicating agreement) exacto

exaggerate [ɪg'zædʒəreit] vt, vi exagerar; **exaggeration** [-'reɪʃən] n exageración f

exam [ɪg'zæm] n abbr (Scol) = **examination**

examination [ɪgzæmɪ'neɪʃən] n examen m; (Med) reconocimiento

examine [ɪg'zæmɪn] vt examinar; (inspect) inspeccionar, escudriñar; (Med) reconocer; **examiner** n examinador(a) m/f

example [ɪg'zɑːmpl] n ejemplo; **for ~** por ejemplo

exasperated [ɪg'zɑːspəreɪtɪd] adj exasperado

excavate ['ekskəveit] vt excavar

exceed [ɪk'siːd] vt (amount) exceder; (number) pasar de; (speed limit) sobrepasar; (powers) excederse en; (hopes) superar; **exceedingly** adv sumamente, sobremanera

excel [ɪk'sel] vi sobresalir; **to ~ o.s** lucirse

excellence ['eksələns] n excelencia

excellent ['eksələnt] adj excelente

except [ɪk'sept] prep (also: **~ for, ~ing**) excepto, salvo ▷ vt exceptuar, excluir; **~ if/when** excepto si/cuando; **~ that** salvo que; **exception** [ɪk'sepʃən] n excepción f; **to take exception to** ofenderse por; **exceptional** [ɪk'sepʃənl] adj excepcional; **exceptionally** [ɪk'sepʃənəlɪ] adv excepcionalmente, extraordinariamente

excerpt ['eksɔːpt] n extracto

excess [ɪk'ses] n exceso; **excess baggage** n exceso de equipaje; **excessive** adj excesivo

exchange [ɪks'tʃeɪndʒ] n intercambio; (conversation) diálogo; (also: **telephone ~**)

central f (telefónica) ▷ vt: **to ~ (for)** cambiar
(por); **exchange rate** n tipo de cambio
excite [ɪkˈsaɪt] vt (stimulate) estimular;
(arouse) excitar; **excited** adj: **to get excited**
emocionarse; **excitement** n (agitation)
excitación f; (exhilaration) emoción f;
exciting adj emocionante
exclaim [ɪkˈskleɪm] vi exclamar;
exclamation [ɛkskləˈmeɪʃən] n
exclamación f; **exclamation mark** n punto
de admiración; **exclamation point** (US) =
exclamation mark
exclude [ɪkˈskluːd] vt excluir; exceptuar
excluding [ɪksˈkluːdɪŋ] prep: **~ VAT** IVA
no incluido
exclusion [ɪkˈskluːʒən] n exclusión f; **to
the ~ of** con exclusión de
exclusive [ɪkˈskluːsɪv] adj exclusivo;
(club, district) selecto; **~ of tax** excluyendo
impuestos; **exclusively** adv únicamente
excruciating [ɪkˈskruːʃɪeɪtɪŋ] adj (pain)
agudísimo, atroz; (noise, embarrassment)
horrible
excursion [ɪkˈskjuːʃən] n (tourist excursion)
excursión f
excuse [n ɪkˈskjuːs, vb ɪkˈskjuːz] n
disculpa, excusa; (pretext) pretexto ▷ vt
(justify) justificar; (forgive) disculpar,
perdonar; **to ~ sb from doing sth** dispensar
a algn de hacer algo; **~ me!** (attracting
attention) ¡por favor!; (apologizing) ¡perdón!; **if
you will ~ me** con su permiso
ex-directory [ˈɛksdɪˈrɛktərɪ] (BRIT) adj
que no consta en la guía
execute [ˈɛksɪkjuːt] vt (plan) realizar;
(order) cumplir; (person) ajusticiar, ejecutar;
execution [-ˈkjuːʃən] n realización f;
cumplimiento; ejecución f
executive [ɪgˈzɛkjutɪv] n (person,
committee) ejecutivo; (Pol: committee) poder
m ejecutivo ▷ adj ejecutivo
exempt [ɪgˈzɛmpt] adj: **~ from** exento de
▷ vt: **to ~ sb from** eximir a algn de
exercise [ˈɛksəsaɪz] n ejercicio ▷ vt
(patience) usar de; (right) valerse de; (dog)
llevar de paseo; (mind) preocupar ▷ vi
(also: **to take ~**) hacer ejercicio(s); **exercise
book** n cuaderno
exert [ɪgˈzəːt] vt ejercer; **to ~ o.s.**
esforzarse; **exertion** [-ʃən] n esfuerzo
exhale [eksˈheɪl] vt despedir ▷ vi exhalar
exhaust [ɪgˈzɔːst] n (Aut: also: **~ pipe**)
escape m; (: fumes) gases mpl de escape
▷ vt agotar; **exhausted** adj agotado;
exhaustion [ɪgˈzɔːstʃən] n agotamiento;
nervous exhaustion postración f nerviosa
exhibit [ɪgˈzɪbɪt] n (Art) obra expuesta;
(Law) objeto expuesto ▷ vt (show: emotions)

manifestar; (: courage, skill) demostrar;
(paintings) exponer; **exhibition** [ɛksɪˈbɪʃən]
n exposición f; (of talent etc) demostración f
exhilarating [ɪgˈzɪləreɪtɪŋ] adj
estimulante, tónico
exile [ˈɛksaɪl] n exilio; (person) exiliado/a
▷ vt desterrar, exiliar
exist [ɪgˈzɪst] vi existir; (live) vivir;
existence n existencia; **existing** adj
existente, actual
exit [ˈɛksɪt] n salida ▷ vi (Theatre) hacer
mutis; (Comput) salir (del sistema)
▌ Be careful not to translate **exit** by the
Spanish word éxito.
exit ramp (US) n (Aut) vía de acceso
exotic [ɪgˈzɔtɪk] adj exótico
expand [ɪkˈspænd] vt ampliar; (number)
aumentar ▷ vi (population) aumentar; (trade
etc) expandirse; (gas, metal) dilatarse
expansion [ɪkˈspænʃən] n (of population)
aumento; (of trade) expansión f
expect [ɪkˈspɛkt] vt esperar; (require)
contar con; (suppose) suponer ▷ vi: **to be
~ing** (pregnant woman) estar embarazada;
expectation [ɛkspɛkˈteɪʃən] n (hope)
esperanza; (belief) expectativa
expedition [ɛkspəˈdɪʃən] n expedición f
expel [ɪkˈspɛl] vt arrojar; (from place)
expulsar
expenditure [ɪksˈpɛndɪtʃə*] n gastos mpl,
desembolso; consumo
expense [ɪkˈspɛns] n gasto, gastos mpl;
(high cost) costa; **expenses** npl (Comm)
gastos mpl; **at the ~ of** a costa de; **expense
account** n cuenta de gastos
expensive [ɪkˈspɛnsɪv] adj caro, costoso
experience [ɪkˈspɪərɪəns] n experiencia
▷ vt experimentar; (suffer) sufrir;
experienced adj experimentado
experiment [ɪkˈspɛrɪmənt] n
experimento ▷ vi hacer experimentos;
experimental [-ˈmɛntl] adj experimental;
**the process is still at the experimental
stage** el proceso está todavía en prueba
expert [ˈɛkspəːt] adj experto, perito ▷ n
experto/a, perito/a; (specialist) especialista
mf; **expertise** [-ˈtiːz] n pericia
expire [ɪkˈspaɪə*] vi caducar, vencer;
expiry n vencimiento; **expiry date** n (of
medicine, food item) fecha de caducidad
explain [ɪkˈspleɪn] vt explicar;
explanation [ɛkspləˈneɪʃən] n explicación
f
explicit [ɪkˈsplɪsɪt] adj explícito
explode [ɪkˈspləud] vi estallar, explotar;
(population) crecer rápidamente; (with anger)
reventar
exploit [n ˈɛksplɔɪt, vb ɪkˈsplɔɪt] n hazaña

▷ vt explotar; **exploitation** [-'teɪʃən] n explotación f

explore [ɪk'splɔ:*] vt explorar; (fig) examinar; investigar; **explorer** n explorador(a) m/f

explosion [ɪk'spləʊʒən] n explosión f; **explosive** [ɪks'pləʊsɪv] adj, n explosivo

export [vb ɛk'spɔ:t, n, cpd 'ekspɔ:t] vt exportar ▷ n (process) exportación f; (product) producto de exportación ▷ cpd de exportación; **exporter** n exportador m

expose [ɪk'spəʊz] vt exponer; (unmask) desenmascarar; **exposed** adj expuesto

exposure [ɪk'spəʊʒə*] n exposición f; (publicity) publicidad f; (Phot: speed) velocidad f de obturación; (: shot) fotografía; **to die from ~** (Med) morir de frío

express [ɪk'sprɛs] adj (definite) expreso, explícito; (BRIT: letter etc) urgente ▷ n (train) rápido ▷ vt expresar; **expression** [ɪk'sprɛʃən] n expresión f; (of actor etc) sentimiento; **expressway** (US) n (urban motorway) autopista

exquisite [ɛk'skwɪzɪt] adj exquisito

extend [ɪk'stɛnd] vt (visit, street) prolongar; (building) ampliar; (invitation) ofrecer ▷ vi (land) extenderse; (period of time) prolongarse

extension [ɪk'stɛnʃən] n extensión f; (building) ampliación f; (of time) prolongación f; (Tel: in private house) línea derivada; (: in office) extensión f; **extension lead** n alargador m, alargadera

extensive [ɪk'stɛnsɪv] adj extenso; (damage) importante; (knowledge) amplio

extent [ɪk'stɛnt] n (breadth) extensión f; (scope) alcance m; **to some ~** hasta cierto punto; **to the ~ of ...** hasta el punto de ...; **to such an ~ that ...** hasta tal punto que ...; **to what ~?** ¿hasta qué punto?

exterior [ɛk'stɪərɪə*] adj exterior, externo ▷ n exterior m

external [ɛk'stə:nl] adj externo

extinct [ɪk'stɪŋkt] adj (volcano) extinguido; (race) extinto; **extinction** n extinción f

extinguish [ɪk'stɪŋgwɪʃ] vt extinguir, apagar

extra ['ɛkstrə] adj adicional ▷ adv (in addition) de más ▷ n (luxury, addition) extra m; (Cinema, Theatre) extra m/f, comparsa m/f

extract [vb ɪk'strækt, n 'ɛkstrækt] vt sacar; (tooth) extraer; (money, promise) obtener ▷ n extracto

extradite ['ɛkstrədaɪt] vt extraditar

extraordinary [ɪk'strɔ:dnrɪ] adj extraordinario; (odd) raro

extravagance [ɪk'strævəgəns] n derroche m, despilfarro; (thing bought) extravagancia

extravagant [ɪk'strævəgənt] adj (lavish: person) pródigo; (: gift) (demasiado) caro; (wasteful) despilfarrador(a)

extreme [ɪk'stri:m] adj extremo, extremado ▷ n extremo; **extremely** adv sumamente, extremadamente

extremist [ɪk'stri:mɪst] adj, n extremista m/f

extrovert ['ɛkstrəvə:t] n extrovertido/a

eye [aɪ] n ojo ▷ vt mirar de soslayo, ojear; **to keep an ~ on** vigilar; **eyeball** n globo ocular; **eyebrow** n ceja; **eyedrops** npl gotas fpl para los ojos, colino; **eyelash** n pestaña; **eyelid** n párpado; **eyeliner** n delineador m (de ojos); **eyeshadow** n sombreador m de ojos; **eyesight** n vista; **eye witness** n testigo m/f presencial

f

F [ɛf] n (Mus) fa m

fabric ['fæbrɪk] n tejido, tela

▌ Be careful not to translate **fabric** by the Spanish word *fábrica*.

fabulous ['fæbjuləs] adj fabuloso

face [feɪs] n (Anat) cara, rostro; (of clock) esfera (SP), cara (LAM); (of mountain) cara, ladera; (of building) fachada ▷ vt (direction) estar de cara a; (situation) hacer frente a; (facts) aceptar; **~ down** (person, card) boca abajo; **to lose ~** desprestigiarse; **to make or pull a ~** hacer muecas; **in the ~ of** (difficulties etc) ante; **on the ~ of it** a primera vista; **~ to ~** cara a cara; **face up to** vt fus hacer frente a, arrostrar; **face cloth** (BRIT) n manopla; **face pack** n (BRIT) mascarilla

facial ['feɪʃəl] adj de la cara ▷ n (also: **beauty ~**) tratamiento facial, limpieza

facilitate [fə'sɪlɪteɪt] vt facilitar

facilities [fə'sɪlɪtɪz] npl (buildings) instalaciones fpl; (equipment) servicios mpl; **credit ~** facilidades fpl de crédito

fact [fækt] n hecho; **in ~** en realidad

faction ['fækʃən] n facción f

factor ['fæktə*] n factor m

factory ['fæktərɪ] n fábrica

factual ['fæktjuəl] adj basado en los hechos

faculty ['fækəltɪ] n facultad f; (US: teaching staff) personal m docente

fad [fæd] n novedad f, moda

fade [feɪd] vi destenirse; (sound, smile) desvanecerse; (light) apagarse; (flower) marchitarse; (hope, memory) perderse; **fade away** vi (sound) apagarse

fag [fæg] (BRIT: inf) n (cigarette) pitillo (SP), cigarro

Fahrenheit ['fɑːrənhaɪt] n Fahrenheit m

fail [feɪl] vt (candidate, test) suspender (SP), reprobar (LAM); (memory etc) fallar a ▷ vi suspender (SP), reprobar (LAM); (be unsuccessful) fracasar; (strength, brakes) fallar; (light) acabarse; **to ~ to do sth** (neglect) dejar de hacer algo; (be unable) no poder hacer algo; **without ~** sin falta; **failing** n falta, defecto ▷ prep a falta de; **failure** ['feɪljə*] n fracaso; (person) fracasado/a; (mechanical etc) fallo

faint [feɪnt] adj débil; (recollection) vago; (mark) apenas visible ▷ n desmayo ▷ vi desmayarse; **to feel ~** estar mareado, marearse; **faintest** adj: **I haven't the faintest idea** no tengo la más remota idea; **faintly** adv débilmente; (vaguely) vagamente

fair [fɛə*] adj justo; (hair, person) rubio; (weather) bueno; (good enough) regular; (considerable) considerable ▷ adv (play) limpio ▷ n feria; (BRIT: funfair) parque m de atracciones; **fairground** n recinto ferial; **fair-haired** adj (person) rubio; **fairly** adv (justly) con justicia; (quite) bastante; **fair trade** n comercio justo; **fairway** n (Golf) calle f

fairy ['fɛərɪ] n hada; **fairy tale** n cuento de hadas

faith [feɪθ] n fe f; (trust) confianza; (sect) religión f; **faithful** adj (loyal: troops etc) leal; (spouse) fiel; (account) exacto; **faithfully** adv fielmente; **yours faithfully** (BRIT: in letters) le saluda atentamente

fake [feɪk] n (painting etc) falsificación f; (person) impostor(a) m/f ▷ adj falso ▷ vt fingir; (painting etc) falsificar

falcon ['fɔːlkən] n halcón m

fall [fɔːl] (pt fell, pp fallen) n caída; (in price etc) descenso; (US) otoño ▷ vi caer(se); (price) bajar, descender; **falls** npl (waterfall) cascada, salto de agua; **to ~ flat** (on one's face) caerse (boca abajo); (plan) fracasar; (joke, story) no hacer gracia; **fall apart** vi deshacerse; **fall down** vi (person) caerse; (building, hopes) derrumbarse; **fall for** vt fus (trick) dejarse engañar por; (person) enamorarse de; **fall off** vi caerse; (diminish) disminuir; **fall out** vi (friends etc) reñir; (hair, teeth) caerse; **fall over** vi caer(se); **fall through** vi (plan, project) fracasar

fallen ['fɔːlən] pp of **fall**

fallout ['fɔːlaut] n lluvia radioactiva

false [fɔːls] adj falso; **under ~ pretences** con engaños; **false alarm** n falsa alarma; **false teeth** (BRIT) npl dentadura postiza

fame [feɪm] n fama

familiar [fə'mɪlɪə*] adj conocido, familiar; (tone) de confianza; **to be ~ with** (subject) conocer (bien); **familiarize** [fə'mɪlɪəraɪz] vt: **to familiarize o.s. with** familiarizarse con

family ['fæmɪlɪ] n familia; **family doctor** n médico/a de cabecera; **family planning** n planificación f familiar

famine ['fæmɪn] n hambre f, hambruna

famous ['feɪməs] adj famoso, célebre

fan [fæn] n abanico; (Elec) ventilador m; (of pop star) fan mf; (Sport) hincha mf ▷ vt abanicar; (fire, quarrel) atizar

fanatic [fə'nætɪk] n fanático/a

fan belt n correa del ventilador

fan club n club m de fans

fancy ['fænsɪ] n (whim) capricho, antojo; (imagination) imaginación f ▷ adj (luxury) lujoso, de lujo ▷ vt (feel like, want) tener ganas de; (imagine) imaginarse; (think) creer; **to take a ~ to sb** tomar cariño a algn; **he fancies her** (inf) le gusta (ella) mucho; **fancy dress** n disfraz m

fan heater n calefactor m de aire

fantasize ['fæntəsaɪz] vi fantasear, hacerse ilusiones

fantastic [fæn'tæstɪk] adj (enormous) enorme; (strange, wonderful) fantástico

fantasy ['fæntəzɪ] n (dream) sueño; (unreality) fantasía

fanzine ['fænziːn] n fanzine m

FAQs abbr (= frequently asked questions) preguntas frecuentes

far [fɑː*] adj (distant) lejano ▷ adv lejos; (much, greatly) mucho; **~ away, ~ off** (a lo) lejos; **~ better** mucho mejor; **~ from** lejos de; **by ~** con mucho; **go as ~ as the farm** vaya hasta la granja; **as ~ as I know** que yo sepa; **how ~?** ¿hasta dónde?; (fig) ¿hasta qué punto?

farce [fɑːs] n farsa

fare [fɛə*] n (on trains, buses) precio (del billete); (in taxi: cost) tarifa; (food) comida; **half ~** medio pasaje m; **full ~** pasaje completo

Far East n: **the ~** el Extremo Oriente

farewell [fɛə'wɛl] excl, n adiós m

farm [fɑːm] n cortijo (SP), hacienda (LAM), rancho (MEX), estancia (RPL) ▷ vt cultivar; **farmer** n granjero, hacendado (LAM), ranchero (MEX), estanciero (RPL); **farmhouse** n granja, casa del hacendado (LAM), rancho (MEX), casco de la estancia (RPL); **farming** n agricultura; (of crops) cultivo; (of animals) cría; **farmyard** n corral m

far-reaching [fɑː'riːtʃɪŋ] adj (reform, effect) de gran alcance

fart [fɑːt] (inf!) vi tirarse un pedo (!)

farther ['fɑːðə*] adv más lejos, más allá ▷ adj más lejano

farthest ['fɑːðɪst] superlative of **far**

fascinate ['fæsɪneɪt] vt fascinar;

fascinated adj fascinado

fascinating ['fæsɪneɪtɪŋ] adj fascinante

fascination [-'neɪʃən] n fascinación f

fascist ['fæʃɪst] adj, n fascista m/f

fashion ['fæʃən] n moda; (fashion industry) industria de la moda; (manner) manera ▷ vt formar; **in ~** a la moda; **out of ~** pasado de moda; **fashionable** adj de moda; **fashion show** n desfile m de modelos

fast [fɑːst] adj rápido; (dye, colour) resistente; (clock): **to be ~** estar adelantado ▷ adv rápidamente, de prisa; (stuck, held) firmemente ▷ n ayuno ▷ vi ayunar; **~ asleep** profundamente dormido

fasten ['fɑːsn] vt atar, sujetar; (coat, belt) abrochar ▷ vi atarse; abrocharse

fast food n comida rápida, platos mpl preparados

fat [fæt] adj gordo; (book) grueso; (profit) grande, pingüe ▷ n grasa; (on person) carnes fpl; (lard) manteca

fatal ['feɪtl] adj (mistake) fatal; (injury) mortal; **fatality** [fə'tælɪtɪ] n (road death etc) víctima f; **fatally** adv fatalmente; mortalmente

fate [feɪt] n destino; (of person) suerte f

father ['fɑːðə*] n padre m; **Father Christmas** n Papá m Noel; **father-in-law** n suegro

fatigue [fə'tiːg] n fatiga, cansancio

fattening ['fætnɪŋ] adj (food) que hace engordar

fatty ['fætɪ] adj (food) graso ▷ n (inf) gordito/a, gordinflón/ona m/f

faucet ['fɔːsɪt] (US) n grifo (SP), llave f, canilla (RPL)

fault [fɔːlt] n (blame) culpa; (defect: in person, machine) defecto; (Geo) falla ▷ vt criticar; **it's my ~** es culpa mía; **to find ~ with** criticar, poner peros a; **at ~** culpable; **faulty** adj defectuoso

fauna ['fɔːnə] n fauna

favour etc ['feɪvə*] (US favor etc) n favor m; (approval) aprobación f ▷ vt (proposition) estar a favor de, aprobar; (assist) ser propicio a; **to do sb a ~** hacer un favor a algn; **to find ~ with sb** caer en gracia a algn; **in ~ of** a favor de; **favourable** adj favorable; **favourite** ['feɪvrɪt] adj, n favorito/a, preferido

fawn [fɔːn] n cervato ▷ adj (also: **~-coloured**) color de cervato, leonado ▷ vi: **to ~ (up)on** adular

fax [fæks] n (document) fax m; (machine) telefax m ▷ vt mandar por telefax

FBI (US) n abbr (= Federal Bureau of Investigation) ≈ BIC f (SP)

fear [fɪə*] n miedo, temor m ▷ vt tener

miedo de, temer; **for ~ of** por si; **fearful**
adj temeroso, miedoso; *(awful)* terrible;
fearless *adj* audaz
feasible ['fiːzəbl] *adj* factible
feast [fiːst] *n* banquete *m*; *(Rel: also: ~ day)*
fiesta ⊳ *vi* festejar
feat [fiːt] *n* hazaña
feather ['feðə*] *n* pluma
feature ['fiːtʃə*] *n* característica; *(article)*
artículo de fondo ⊳ *vt* *(film)* presentar
⊳ *vi*: **to ~ in** tener un papel destacado en;
features *npl* *(of face)* facciones *fpl*; **feature**
film *n* largometraje *m*
Feb. *abbr* (= *February*) feb
February ['februəri] *n* febrero
fed [fed] *pt, pp* of **feed**
federal ['fedərəl] *adj* federal
federation [fedə'reiʃən] *n* federación *f*
fed up [fed'ʌp] *adj*: **to be ~ (with)** estar
harto (de)
fee [fiː] *n* pago; *(professional)* derechos *mpl*,
honorarios *mpl*; *(of club)* cuota; **school ~s**
matrícula
feeble ['fiːbl] *adj* débil; *(joke)* flojo
feed [fiːd] *(pt, pp* **fed)** *n* comida; *(of*
animal) pienso; *(on printer)* dispositivo
de alimentación ⊳ *vt* alimentar;
(BRIT: baby: breastfeed) dar el pecho a; *(animal)*
dar de comer a; *(data, information)*: **to ~**
into meter en; **feedback** *n* reacción *f*,
feedback *m*
feel [fiːl] *(pt, pp* **felt)** *n* *(sensation)* sensación
f; *(sense of touch)* tacto; *(impression)*: **to have**
the ~ of parecerse a ⊳ *vt* tocar; *(pain etc)*
sentir; *(think, believe)* creer; **to ~ hungry/**
cold tener hambre/frío; **to ~ lonely/**
better sentirse solo/mejor; **I don't ~ well**
no me siento bien; **it ~s soft** es suave al
tacto; **to ~ like** *(want)* tener ganas de;
feeling *n* *(physical)* sensación *f*; *(foreboding)*
presentimiento; *(emotion)* sentimiento
feet [fiːt] *npl* of **foot**
fell [fel] *pt* of **fall** ⊳ *vt* *(tree)* talar
fellow ['feləu] *n* tipo, tío *(SP)*; *(comrade)*
compañero; *(of learned society)* socio/a;
fellow citizen *n* conciudadano/a; **fellow**
countryman *(irreg)* *n* compatriota
m; **fellow men** *npl* semejantes *mpl*;
fellowship *n* compañerismo; *(grant)* beca
felony ['feləni] *n* crimen *m*
felt [felt] *pt, pp* of **feel** ⊳ *n* fieltro; **felt-tip**
n *(also:* **felt-tip pen)** rotulador *m*
female ['fiːmeil] *n* *(pej: woman)* mujer *f*,
tía; *(Zool)* hembra ⊳ *adj* femenino; hembra
feminine ['feminin] *adj* femenino
feminist ['feminist] *n* feminista
fence [fens] *n* valla, cerca ⊳ *vt* *(also:* **~ in)**
cercar ⊳ *vi* *(Sport)* hacer esgrima; **fencing**

n esgrima
fend [fend] *vi*: **to ~ for o.s.** valerse por
sí mismo; **fend off** *vt* *(attack)* rechazar;
(questions) evadir
fender ['fendə*] *(US)* *n* guardafuego; *(Aut)*
parachoques *m inv*
fennel ['fenl] *n* hinojo
ferment [*vb* fə'ment, *n* 'fɜːment] *vi*
fermentar ⊳ *n* *(fig)* agitación *f*
fern [fɜːn] *n* helecho
ferocious [fə'rəuʃəs] *adj* feroz
ferret ['ferit] *n* hurón *m*
ferry ['feri] *n* *(small)* barca (de pasaje),
balsa; *(large: also:* **~boat)** transbordador *m*,
ferry *m* ⊳ *vt* transportar
fertile ['fɜːtail] *adj* fértil; *(Biol)* fecundo;
fertilize ['fɜːtilaiz] *vt* *(Biol)* fecundar; *(Agr)*
abonar; **fertilizer** *n* abono
festival ['festivəl] *n* *(Rel)* fiesta; *(Art, Mus)*
festival *m*
festive ['festiv] *adj* festivo; **the ~ season**
(BRIT: Christmas) las Navidades
fetch [fetʃ] *vt* ir a buscar; *(sell for)* venderse
por
fête [feit] *n* fiesta
fetus ['fiːtəs] *(US)* *n* = **foetus**
feud [fjuːd] *n* *(hostility)* enemistad *f*;
(quarrel) disputa
fever ['fiːvə*] *n* fiebre *f*; **feverish** *adj* febril
few [fjuː] *adj* *(not many)* pocos ⊳ *pron*
pocos; algunos; **a ~** *adj* unos pocos,
algunos; **fewer** *adj* menos; **fewest** *adj*
los(las) menos
fiancé [fi'ɑ̃:ŋsei] *n* novio, prometido;
fiancée *n* novia, prometida
fiasco [fi'æskəu] *n* fiasco
fib [fib] *n* mentirilla
fibre ['faibə*] *(us* **fiber)** *n* fibra; **fibreglass**
(us **Fiberglass®)** *n* fibra de vidrio
fickle ['fikl] *adj* inconstante
fiction ['fikʃən] *n* ficción *f*; **fictional** *adj*
novelesco
fiddle ['fidl] *n* *(Mus)* violín *m*; *(cheating)*
trampa ⊳ *vt* *(BRIT: accounts)* falsificar; **fiddle**
with *vt fus* juguetear con
fidelity [fi'deliti] *n* fidelidad *f*
field [fiːld] *n* campo; *(fig)* campo, esfera;
(Sport) campo *(SP)*, cancha *(LAM)*; **field**
marshal *n* mariscal *m*
fierce [fiəs] *adj* feroz; *(wind, heat)* fuerte;
(fighting, enemy) encarnizado
fifteen [fif'tiːn] *num* quince; **fifteenth** *adj*
decimoquinto; **the fifteenth floor** la planta
quince; **the fifteenth of August** el quince
de agosto
fifth [fifθ] *num* quinto
fiftieth ['fiftiiθ] *adj* quincuagésimo
fifty ['fifti] *num* cincuenta; **fifty-fifty** *adj*

fig | 288

(*deal, split*) a medias ▷ *adv* a medias, mitad por mitad

fig [fɪg] *n* higo

fight [faɪt] (*pt, pp* **fought**) *n* (*gen*) pelea; (*Mil*) combate *m*; (*struggle*) lucha ▷ *vt* luchar contra; (*cancer, alcoholism*) combatir; (*election*) intentar ganar; (*emotion*) resistir ▷ *vi* pelear, luchar; **fight back** *vi* defenderse; (*after illness*) recuperarse ▷ *vt* (*tears*) contener; **fight off** *vt* (*attack, attacker*) rechazar; (*disease, sleep, urge*) luchar contra; **fighting** *n* combate *m*, pelea

figure ['fɪgə*] *n* (*Drawing, Geom*) figura, dibujo; (*number, cipher*) cifra; (*body, outline*) tipo; (*personality*) figura ▷ *vt* (*esp us*) imaginar ▷ *vi* (*appear*) figurar; **figure out** *vt* (*work out*) resolver

file [faɪl] *n* (*tool*) lima; (*dossier*) expediente *m*; (*folder*) carpeta; (*Comput*) fichero; (*row*) fila ▷ *vt* limar; (*Law: claim*) presentar; (*store*) archivar; **filing cabinet** *n* fichero, archivador *m*

Filipino [fɪlɪ'piːnəu] *adj* filipino ▷ *n* (*person*) filipino/a *m/f*; (*Ling*) tagalo

fill [fɪl] *vt* (*space*): **to ~ (with)** llenar (de); (*vacancy, need*) cubrir ▷ *n*: **to eat one's ~** llenarse; **fill in** *vt* rellenar; **fill out** *vt* (*form, receipt*) rellenar; **fill up** *vt* llenar (hasta el borde) ▷ *vi* (*Aut*) poner gasolina

fillet ['fɪlɪt] *n* filete *m*; **fillet steak** *n* filete *m* de ternera

filling ['fɪlɪŋ] *n* (*Culin*) relleno; (*for tooth*) empaste *m*; **filling station** *n* estación *f* de servicio

film [fɪlm] *n* película ▷ *vt* (*scene*) filmar ▷ *vi* rodar (una película); **film star** *n* astro, estrella de cine

filter ['fɪltə*] *n* filtro ▷ *vt* filtrar; **filter lane** (*BRIT*) *n* carril *m* de selección

filth [fɪlθ] *n* suciedad *f*; **filthy** *adj* sucio; (*language*) obsceno

fin [fɪn] *n* (*gen*) aleta

final ['faɪnl] *adj* (*last*) final, último; (*definitive*) definitivo, terminante ▷ *n* (*BRIT Sport*) final *f*; **finals** *npl* (*Scol*) examen *m* final; (*US Sport*) final *f*

finale [fɪ'nɑːlɪ] *n* final *m*

final: finalist *n* (*Sport*) finalista *mf*; **finalize** *vt* concluir, completar; **finally** *adv* (*lastly*) por último, finalmente; (*eventually*) por fin

finance [faɪ'næns] *n* (*money*) fondos *mpl* ▷ *vt* financiar; **finances** *npl* finanzas *fpl*; (*personal finances*) situación *f* económica; **financial** [-'nænʃəl] *adj* financiero; **financial year** *n* ejercicio (financiero)

find [faɪnd] (*pt, pp* **found**) *vt* encontrar, hallar; (*come upon*) descubrir ▷ *n* hallazgo; descubrimiento; **to ~ sb guilty** (*Law*)

declarar culpable a algn; **find out** *vt* averiguar; (*truth, secret*) descubrir; **to find out about** (*subject*) informarse sobre; (*by chance*) enterarse de; **findings** *npl* (*Law*) veredicto, fallo; (*of report*) recomendaciones *fpl*

fine [faɪn] *adj* excelente; (*thin*) fino ▷ *adv* (*well*) bien ▷ *n* (*Law*) multa ▷ *vt* (*Law*) multar; **to be ~** (*person*) estar bien; (*weather*) hacer buen tiempo; **fine arts** *npl* bellas artes *fpl*

finger ['fɪŋgə*] *n* dedo ▷ *vt* (*touch*) manosear; **little/index** ~ (dedo) meñique *m*/índice *m*; **fingernail** *n* uña; **fingerprint** *n* huella dactilar; **fingertip** *n* yema del dedo

finish ['fɪnɪʃ] *n* (*end*) fin *m*; (*Sport*) meta; (*polish etc*) acabado ▷ *vt*, *vi* terminar; **to ~ doing sth** acabar de hacer algo; **to ~ third** llegar el tercero; **finish off** *vt* acabar, terminar; (*kill*) acabar con; **finish up** *vt* acabar, terminar ▷ *vi* ir a parar, terminar

Finland ['fɪnlənd] *n* Finlandia

Finn [fɪn] *n* finlandés/esa *m/f*; **Finnish** *adj* finlandés/esa ▷ *n* (*Ling*) finlandés *m*

fir [fəː*] *n* abeto

fire ['faɪə*] *n* fuego; (*in hearth*) lumbre *f*; (*accidental*) incendio; (*heater*) estufa ▷ *vt* (*gun*) disparar; (*interest*) despertar; (*inf: dismiss*) despedir ▷ *vi* (*shoot*) disparar; **on ~** ardiendo, en llamas; **fire alarm** *n* alarma de incendios; **firearm** *n* arma de fuego; **fire brigade** (*us* **fire department**) *n* (cuerpo de) bomberos *mpl*; **fire engine** (*BRIT*) *n* coche *m* de bomberos; **fire escape** *n* escalera de incendios; **fire exit** *n* salida de incendios; **fire extinguisher** *n* extintor *m* (de incendios); **fireman** (*irreg*) *n* bombero; **fireplace** *n* chimenea; **fire station** *n* parque *m* de bomberos; **firetruck** (*us*) *n* = **fire engine**; **firewall** *n* (*Internet*) firewall *m*; **firewood** *n* leña; **fireworks** *npl* fuegos *mpl* artificiales

firm [fəːm] *adj* firme; (*look, voice*) resuelto ▷ *n* firma, empresa; **firmly** *adv* firmemente; resueltamente

first [fəːst] *adj* primero ▷ *adv* (*before others*) primero; (*when listing reasons etc*) en primer lugar, primeramente ▷ *n* (*person: in race*) primero/a; (*Aut*) primera; (*BRIT Scol*) título de licenciado con calificación de sobresaliente; **at ~** al principio; **~ of all** ante todo; **first aid** *n* primera ayuda, primeros auxilios *mpl*; **first-aid kit** *n* botiquín *m*; **first-class** *adj* (*excellent*) de primera (categoría); (*ticket etc*) de primera clase; **first-hand** *adj* de primera mano; **first lady** *n* (*esp us*) primera dama; **firstly** *adv* en primer lugar; **first**

name n nombre m (de pila); **first-rate** adj estupendo

fiscal ['fɪskəl] adj fiscal; **fiscal year** n año fiscal, ejercicio

fish [fɪʃ] n inv pez m; (food) pescado ▷ vt, vi pescar; **to go ~ing** ir de pesca; **~ and chips** pescado frito con patatas fritas; **fisherman** (irreg) n pescador m; **fish fingers** (BRIT) npl croquetas fpl de pescado; **fishing** n pesca; **fishing boat** n barca de pesca; **fishing line** n sedal m; **fishmonger** n (BRIT) pescadero/a; **fishmonger's (shop)** (BRIT) n pescadería; **fish sticks** (US) npl =**fish fingers**; **fishy** (inf) adj sospechoso

fist [fɪst] n puño

fit [fɪt] adj (healthy) en (buena) forma; (proper) adecuado, apropiado ▷ vt (clothes) estar or sentar bien a; (instal) poner; (equip) proveer, dotar; (facts) cuadrar or corresponder con ▷ vi (clothes) sentar bien; (in space, gap) caber; (facts) coincidir ▷ n (Med) ataque m; **~ to** (ready) a punto de; **~ for** apropiado para; **a ~ of anger/pride** un arranque de cólera/orgullo; **this dress is a good ~** este vestido me sienta bien; **by ~s and starts** a rachas; **fit in** vi (fig: person) llevarse bien (con todos); **fitness** n (Med) salud f; **fitted** adj (jacket, shirt) entallado; (sheet) de cuatro picos; **fitted carpet** n moqueta; **fitted kitchen** n cocina amueblada; **fitting** adj apropiado ▷ n (of dress) prueba; (of piece of equipment) instalación f; **fitting room** n probador m; **fittings** npl instalaciones fpl

five [faɪv] num cinco; **fiver** (inf) n (BRIT) billete m de cinco libras; (US) billete m de cinco dólares

fix [fɪks] vt (secure) fijar, asegurar; (mend) arreglar; (prepare) preparar ▷ n: **to be in a ~** estar en un aprieto; **fix up** vt (meeting) arreglar; **to fix sb up with sth** proveer a algn de algo; **fixed** adj (prices etc) fijo; **fixture** n (Sport) encuentro

fizzy ['fɪzɪ] adj (drink) gaseoso

flag [flæg] n bandera; (stone) losa ▷ vi decaer ▷ vt: **to ~ sb down** hacer señas a algn para que se pare; **flagpole** n asta de bandera

flair [flɛə*] n aptitud f especial

flak [flæk] n (Mil) fuego antiaéreo; (inf: criticism) lluvia de críticas

flake [fleɪk] n (of rust, paint) escama; (of snow, soap powder) copo ▷ vi (also: **~ off**) desconcharse

flamboyant [flæm'bɔɪənt] adj (dress) vistoso; (person) extravagante

flame [fleɪm] n llama

flamingo [flə'mɪŋɡəu] n flamenco

flammable ['flæməbl] adj inflamable

flan [flæn] (BRIT) n tarta

▌ Be careful not to translate **flan** by the Spanish word flan.

flank [flæŋk] n (of animal) ijar m; (of army) flanco ▷ vt flanquear

flannel ['flænl] n (BRIT: also: **face ~**) manopla; (fabric) franela

flap [flæp] n (of pocket, envelope) solapa ▷ vt (wings, arms) agitar ▷ vi (sail, flag) ondear

flare [flɛə*] n llamarada; (Mil) bengala; (in skirt etc) vuelo; **flares** npl (trousers) pantalones mpl de campana; **flare up** vi encenderse; (fig: person) encolerizarse; (: revolt) estallar

flash [flæʃ] n relámpago; (also: **news ~**) noticias fpl de última hora; (Phot) flash m ▷ vt (light, headlights) lanzar un destello con; (news, message) transmitir; (smile) lanzar ▷ vi brillar; (hazard light etc) lanzar destellos; **in a ~** en un instante; **he ~ed by** or **past** pasó como un rayo; **flashback** n (Cinema) flashback m; **flashbulb** n bombilla fusible; **flashlight** n linterna

flask [flɑːsk] n frasco; (also: **vacuum ~**) termo

flat [flæt] adj llano; (smooth) liso; (tyre) desinflado; (battery) descargado; (beer) muerto; (refusal etc) rotundo; (Mus) desafinado; (rate) fijo ▷ n (BRIT: apartment) piso (sp), departamento (LAM), apartamento; (Aut) pinchazo; (Mus) bemol m; **to work ~ out** trabajar a toda mecha; **flatten** vt (also: **flatten out**) allanar; (smooth out) alisar; (building, plants) arrasar

flatter ['flætə*] vt adular, halagar; **flattering** adj halagüeño; (dress) que favorece

flaunt [flɔːnt] vt ostentar, lucir

flavour etc ['fleɪvə*] (US **flavor** etc) n sabor m, gusto ▷ vt sazonar, condimentar; **strawberry-flavoured** con sabor a fresa; **flavouring** n (in product) aromatizante m

flaw [flɔː] n defecto; **flawless** adj impecable

flea [fliː] n pulga; **flea market** n rastro, mercadillo

flee [fliː] (pt, pp **fled**) vt huir de ▷ vi huir, fugarse

fleece [fliːs] n vellón m; (wool) lana; (top) forro polar ▷ vt (inf) desplumar

fleet [fliːt] n flota; (of lorries etc) escuadra

fleeting ['fliːtɪŋ] adj fugaz

Flemish ['flemɪʃ] adj flamenco

flesh [fleʃ] n carne f; (skin) piel f; (of fruit) pulpa

flew [fluː] pt of **fly**

flex [fleks] n cordón m ▷ vt (muscles)

tensar; **flexibility** n flexibilidad f; **flexible** adj flexible; **flexitime** (us **flextime**) n horario flexible

flick [flɪk] n capirotazo; chasquido ▷ vt (with hand) dar un capirotazo a; (whip etc) chasquear; (switch) accionar; **flick through** vt fus hojear

flicker ['flɪkə*] vi (light) parpadear; (flame) vacilar

flies [flaɪz] npl of **fly**

flight [flaɪt] n vuelo; (escape) huida, fuga; (also: **~ of steps**) tramo (de escaleras); **flight attendant** n auxiliar mf de vuelo

flimsy ['flɪmzɪ] adj (thin) muy ligero; (building) endeble; (excuse) flojo

flinch [flɪntʃ] vi encogerse; **to ~ from** retroceder ante

fling [flɪŋ] (pt, pp **flung**) vt arrojar

flint [flɪnt] n pedernal m; (in lighter) piedra

flip [flɪp] vt dar la vuelta a; (switch: turn on) encender; (turn) apagar; (coin) echar a cara o cruz

flip-flops ['flɪpflɔps] npl (esp BRIT) chancletas fpl

flipper ['flɪpə*] n aleta

flirt [flɜːt] vi coquetear, flirtear ▷ n coqueta

float [fləut] n flotador m; (in procession) carroza; (money) reserva ▷ vi flotar; (swimmer) hacer la plancha

flock [flɔk] n (of sheep) rebaño; (of birds) bandada ▷ vi: **to ~ to** acudir en tropel a

flood [flʌd] n inundación f; (of letters, imports etc) avalancha ▷ vt inundar ▷ vi (place) inundarse; (people): **to ~ into** inundar; **flooding** n inundaciones fpl; **floodlight** n foco

floor [flɔː*] n suelo; (storey) piso; (of sea) fondo ▷ vt (question) dejar sin respuesta; (: blow) derribar; **ground ~, first ~** (us) planta baja; **first ~, second ~** (us) primer piso; **floorboard** n tabla; **flooring** n suelo; (material) solería; **floor show** n cabaret m

flop [flɔp] n fracaso ▷ vi (fail) fracasar; (fall) derrumbarse; **floppy** adj flojo ▷ n (Comput: also: **floppy disk**) floppy m

flora ['flɔːrə] n flora

floral ['flɔːrl] adj (pattern) floreado

florist ['flɔrɪst] n florista mf; **florist's (shop)** n floristería

flotation f [fləu'teɪʃən] n (of shares) emisión f; (of company) lanzamiento

flour ['flauə*] n harina

flourish ['flʌrɪʃ] vi florecer ▷ n ademán m, movimiento (ostentoso)

flow [fləu] n (movement) flujo; (of traffic) circulación f; (tide) corriente f ▷ vi (river, blood) fluir; (traffic) circular

flower ['flauə*] n flor f ▷ vi florecer; **flower bed** n macizo; **flowerpot** n tiesto

flown [fləun] pp of **fly**

fl. oz. abbr (= fluid ounce)

flu [fluː] n: **to have ~** tener la gripe

fluctuate ['flʌktjueɪt] vi fluctuar

fluent ['fluːənt] adj (linguist) que habla perfectamente; (speech) elocuente; **he speaks ~ French, he's ~ in French** domina el francés

fluff [flʌf] n pelusa; **fluffy** adj de pelo suave

fluid ['fluːɪd] adj (movement) fluido, líquido; (situation) inestable ▷ n fluido, líquido; **fluid ounce** n onza f líquida

fluke [fluːk] (inf) n chiripa

flung [flʌŋ] pt, pp of **fling**

fluorescent [fluə'rɛsnt] adj fluorescente

fluoride ['fluəraɪd] n fluoruro

flurry ['flʌrɪ] n (of snow) temporal m; **~ of activity** frenesí m de actividad

flush [flʌʃ] n rubor m; (fig: of youth etc) resplandor m ▷ vt limpiar con agua ▷ vi ruborizarse ▷ adj: **~ with** a ras de; **to ~ the toilet** hacer funcionar la cisterna

flute [fluːt] n flauta

flutter ['flʌtə*] n (of wings) revoloteo, aleteo; (fig): **a ~ of panic/excitement** una oleada de pánico/excitación ▷ vi revolotear

fly [flaɪ] (pt **flew**, pp **flown**) n mosca; (on trousers: also: **flies**) bragueta ▷ vt (plane) pilot(e)ar; (cargo) transportar (en avión); (distances) recorrer (en avión) ▷ vi volar; (passengers) ir en avión; (escape) evadirse; (flag) ondear; **fly away, fly off** vi emprender el vuelo; **fly-drive** n: **fly-drive holiday** vacaciones que incluyen vuelo y alquiler de coche; **flying** n (activity) (el) volar; (action) vuelo ▷ adj: **flying visit** visita relámpago; **with flying colours** con lucimiento; **flying saucer** n platillo volante; **flyover** (BRIT) n paso a desnivel o superior

FM abbr (Radio) (= frequency modulation) FM

foal [fəul] n potro

foam [fəum] n espuma ▷ vi hacer espuma

focus ['fəukəs] (pl **~es**) n foco; (centre) centro ▷ vt (field glasses etc) enfocar ▷ vi: **to ~ (on)** enfocar (a); (issue etc) centrarse en; **in/out of ~** enfocado/desenfocado

foetus ['fiːtəs] (us **fetus**) n feto

fog [fɔg] n niebla; **foggy** adj: **it's foggy** hay niebla, está brumoso; **fog lamp** (us **fog light**) n (Aut) faro de niebla

foil [fɔɪl] vt frustrar ▷ n hoja; (kitchen foil) papel m (de) aluminio; (complement) complemento; (Fencing) florete m

fold [fəuld] n (bend, crease) pliegue m; (Agr)

redil m ▷ vt doblar; (arms) cruzar; **fold up**
vi plegarse, doblarse; (business) quebrar
▷ vt (map etc) plegar; **folder** n (for papers)
carpeta; (Comput) directorio; **folding** adj
(chair, bed) plegable

foliage ['fəʊlɪɪdʒ] n follaje m

folk [fəʊk] npl gente f ▷ adj popular,
folklórico; **folks** npl (family) familia sg,
parientes mpl; **folklore** ['fəʊklɔː*] n
folklore m; **folk music** n música folk; **folk
song** n canción f popular

follow ['fɒləʊ] vt seguir ▷ vi seguir;
(result) resultar; **to ~ suit** hacer lo mismo;
follow up vt (letter, offer) responder a; (case)
investigar; **follower** n (of person, belief)
partidario/a; **following** adj siguiente
▷ n afición f, partidarios mpl; **follow-up** n
continuación f

fond [fɒnd] adj (memory, smile etc) cariñoso;
(hopes) ilusorio; **to be ~ of** tener cariño a;
(pastime, food) ser aficionado a

food [fuːd] n comida; **food mixer** n
batidora; **food poisoning** n intoxicación
f alimenticia; **food processor** n robot m
de cocina; **food stamp** (US) n vale m para
comida

fool [fuːl] n tonto/a; (Culin) puré m de
frutas con nata ▷ vt engañar ▷ vi (gen)
bromear; **fool about, fool around** vi
hacer el tonto; **foolish** adj tonto; (careless)
imprudente; **foolproof** adj (plan etc)
infalible

foot [fʊt] (pl feet) n pie m; (measure) pie m
(= 304 mm); (of animal) pata ▷ vt (bill) pagar;
on ~ a pie; footage n (Cinema) imágenes
fpl; **foot-and-mouth (disease)**
['fʊtənd'maʊθ-] n fiebre f aftosa; **football**
n balón m; (game: BRIT) fútbol m; (: US) fútbol
m americano; **footballer** n (BRIT) = **football
player**; **football match** n partido de
fútbol; **football player** n (BRIT) futbolista
mf; (US) jugador m de fútbol americano;
footbridge n puente m para peatones;
foothills npl estribaciones fpl; **foothold**
n pie m firme; **footing** n (fig) posición f; **to
lose one's footing** perder el pie; **footnote**
n nota (al pie de la página); **footpath**
n sendero; **footprint** n huella, pisada;
footstep n paso; **footwear** n calzado

○ **KEYWORD**

for [fɔː] prep **1** (indicating destination,
intention) para; **the train for London** el
tren con destino a or de Londres; **he went for
Rome** marchó para Roma; **he went for the
paper** fue por el periódico; **is this for me?**
¿es esto para mí?; **it's time for lunch** es la

hora de comer

2 (indicating purpose) para; **what('s it) for?**
¿para qué (es)?; **to pray for peace** rezar
por la paz

3 (on behalf of, representing): **the MP for Hove**
el diputado por Hove; **he works for the
government/a local firm** trabaja para el
gobierno/en una empresa local; **I'll ask him
for you** se
lo pediré por ti; **G for George** G de Gerona

4 (because of) por esta razón; **for fear of
being criticized** por temor a ser criticado

5 (with regard to) para; **it's cold for July** hace
frío para julio; **he has a gift for languages**
tiene don de lenguas

6 (in exchange for) por; **I sold it for £5** lo vendí
por £5; **to pay 50 pence for a ticket** pagar
50 peniques por un billete

7 (in favour of): **are you for or against us?**
¿estás con nosotros o contra nosotros?; **I'm
all for it** estoy totalmente a favor; **vote for
X** vote (a) X

8 (referring to distance): **there are roadworks
for 5 km** hay obras en 5 km; **we walked for
miles** caminamos kilómetros y kilómetros

9 (referring to time): **he was away for two
years** estuvo fuera (durante) dos años; **it
hasn't rained for 3 weeks** no ha llovido
durante or en 3 semanas; **I have known her
for years** la conozco desde hace años; **can
you do it for tomorrow?** ¿lo podrás hacer
para mañana?

10 (with infinitive clauses): **it is not for me to
decide** la decisión no es cosa mía; **it would
be best for you to leave** sería mejor que
te fueras; **there is still time for you to do
it** todavía te queda tiempo para hacerlo;
for this to be possible ... para que esto sea
posible ...

11 (in spite of) a pesar de; **for all his
complaints** a pesar de sus quejas ▷ conj
(since, as: rather formal) puesto que

forbid [fə'bɪd] (pt forbad(e), pp forbidden)
vt prohibir; **to ~ sb to do sth** prohibir a algn
hacer algo; **forbidden** pt of forbid ▷ adj
(food, area) prohibido; (word, subject) tabú

force [fɔːs] n fuerza ▷ vt forzar; (push)
meter a la fuerza; **to ~ o.s. to do** hacer un
esfuerzo por hacer; **forced** adj forzado;
forceful adj enérgico

ford [fɔːd] n vado

fore [fɔː*] n: **to come to the ~** empezar
a destacar; **forearm** n antebrazo;
forecast (pt, pp forecast) n pronóstico
▷ vt pronosticar; **forecourt** n patio;
forefinger n (dedo) índice m; **forefront**
n: **in the forefront of** en la vanguardia de;

foreground n primer plano; **forehead** ['fɔrɪd] n frente f

foreign ['fɔrɪn] adj extranjero; (trade) exterior; (object) extraño; **foreign currency** n divisas fpl; **foreigner** n extranjero/a; **foreign exchange** n divisas fpl; **Foreign Office** (BRIT) n Ministerio de Asuntos Exteriores; **Foreign Secretary** (BRIT) n Ministro de Asuntos Exteriores

fore: foreman (irreg) n capataz m; (in construction) maestro de obras; **foremost** adj principal ▷ adv: **first and foremost** ante todo; **forename** n nombre m (de pila)

forensic [fə'rɛnsɪk] adj forense

foresee [fɔː'siː] (pt **foresaw**, pp **foreseen**) vt prever; **foreseeable** adj previsible

forest ['fɔrɪst] n bosque m; **forestry** n silvicultura

forever [fə'rɛvə*] adv para siempre; (endlessly) constantemente

foreword ['fɔːwəːd] n prefacio

forfeit ['fɔːfɪt] vt perder

forgave [fə'geɪv] pt of **forgive**

forge [fɔːdʒ] n herrería ▷ vt (signature, money) falsificar; (metal) forjar; **forger** n falsificador(a) m/f; **forgery** n falsificación f

forget [fə'gɛt] (pt **forgot**, pp **forgotten**) vt olvidar ▷ vi olvidarse; **forgetful** adj despistado

forgive [fə'gɪv] (pt **forgave**, pp **forgiven**) vt perdonar; **to ~ sb for sth** perdonar algo a algn

forgot [fə'gɔt] pt of **forget**

forgotten [fə'gɔtn] pp of **forget**

fork [fɔːk] n (for eating) tenedor m; (for gardening) horca; (of roads) bifurcación f ▷ vi (road) bifurcarse

forlorn [fə'lɔːn] adj (person) triste, melancólico; (place) abandonado; (attempt, hope) desesperado

form [fɔːm] n forma; (BRIT Scol) clase f; (document) formulario ▷ vt formar; (idea) concebir; (habit) adquirir; **in top ~** en plena forma; **to ~ a queue** hacer cola

formal ['fɔːməl] adj (offer, receipt) por escrito; (person etc) correcto; (occasion, dinner) de etiqueta; (dress) correcto; (garden) (de estilo) clásico; **formality** [-'mælɪtɪ] n (procedure) trámite m; corrección f; etiqueta

format ['fɔːmæt] n formato ▷ vt (Comput) formatear

formation [fɔː'meɪʃən] n formación f

former ['fɔːmə*] adj anterior; (earlier) antiguo; (ex) ex; **the ~ ... the latter ...** aquél ... éste ...; **formerly** adv antes

formidable ['fɔːmɪdəbl] adj formidable

formula ['fɔːmjulə] n fórmula

fort [fɔːt] n fuerte m

forthcoming [fɔː'θkʌmɪŋ] adj próximo, venidero; (help, information) disponible; (character) comunicativo

fortieth ['fɔːtɪɪθ] adj cuadragésimo

fortify ['fɔːtɪfaɪ] vt (city) fortificar; (person) fortalecer

fortnight ['fɔːtnaɪt] (BRIT) n quince días mpl; quincena; **fortnightly** adj de cada quince días, quincenal ▷ adv cada quince días, quincenalmente

fortress ['fɔːtrɪs] n fortaleza

fortunate ['fɔːtʃənɪt] adj afortunado; **it is ~ that ...** (es una) suerte que ...; **fortunately** adv afortunadamente

fortune ['fɔːtʃən] n suerte f; (wealth) fortuna; **fortune-teller** n adivino/a

forty ['fɔːtɪ] num cuarenta

forum ['fɔːrəm] n foro

forward ['fɔːwəd] adj (movement, position) avanzado; (front) delantero; (in time) adelantado; (not shy) atrevido ▷ n (Sport) delantero ▷ vt (letter) remitir; (career) promocionar; **to move ~** avanzar; **forwarding address** n destinatario; **forward(s)** adv (hacia) adelante; **forward slash** n barra diagonal

fossil ['fɔsl] n fósil m

foster ['fɔstə*] vt (child) acoger en una familia; fomentar; **foster child** n hijo/a adoptivo/a; **foster mother** n madre f adoptiva

fought [fɔːt] pt, pp of **fight**

foul [faul] adj sucio, puerco; (weather, smell etc) asqueroso; (language) grosero; (temper) malísimo ▷ n (Sport) falta ▷ vt (dirty) ensuciar; **foul play** n (Law) muerte f violenta

found [faund] pt, pp of **find** ▷ vt fundar; **foundation** [-'deɪʃən] n (act) fundación f; (basis) base f; (also: **foundation cream**) crema base; **foundations** npl (of building) cimientos mpl

founder ['faundə*] n fundador(a) m/f ▷ vi hundirse

fountain ['fauntɪn] n fuente f; **fountain pen** n (pluma) estilográfica (SP), pluma-fuente f (LAM)

four [fɔː*] num cuatro; **on all ~s** a gatas; **four-letter word** n taco; **four-poster** n (also: **four-poster bed**) cama de columnas; **fourteen** num catorce; **fourteenth** adj decimocuarto; **fourth** num cuarto; **four-wheel drive** n tracción f a las cuatro ruedas

fowl [faul] n ave f (de corral)

fox [fɔks] n zorro ▷ vt confundir

foyer ['fɔɪeɪ] n vestíbulo

fraction ['frækʃən] n fracción f

fracture ['fræktʃə*] n fractura

fragile ['frædʒaɪl] adj frágil
fragment ['frægmənt] n fragmento
fragrance ['freɪɡrəns] n fragancia
frail [freɪl] adj frágil; (person) débil
frame [freɪm] n (Tech) armazón m; (of person) cuerpo; (of picture, door etc) marco; (of spectacles: also: **~s**) montura ▷ vt enmarcar; **framework** n marco
France [frɑːns] n Francia
franchise ['fræntʃaɪz] n (Pol) derecho de votar, sufragio; (Comm) licencia, concesión f
frank [fræŋk] adj franco ▷ vt (letter) franquear; **frankly** adv francamente
frantic ['fræntɪk] adj (distraught) desesperado; (hectic) frenético
fraud [frɔːd] n fraude m; (person) impostor(a) m/f
fraught [frɔːt] adj: **~ with** lleno de
fray [freɪ] vi deshilacharse
freak [friːk] n (person) fenómeno; (event) suceso anormal
freckle ['frɛkl] n peca
free [friː] adj libre; (gratis) gratuito ▷ vt (prisoner etc) poner en libertad; (jammed object) soltar; **~ (of charge), for ~** gratis; **freedom** n libertad f; **Freefone®** n número gratuito; **free gift** n prima; **free kick** n tiro libre; **freelance** adj independiente ▷ adv por cuenta propia; **freely** adv libremente; (liberally) generosamente; **Freepost®** n porte m pagado; **free-range** adj (hen, eggs) de granja; **freeway** (us) n autopista; **free will** n libre albedrío; **of one's own free will** por su propia voluntad
freeze [friːz] (pt froze, pp frozen) vi (weather) helar; (liquid, pipe, person) helarse, congelarse ▷ vt helar; (food, prices, salaries) congelar ▷ n helada; (on arms, wages) congelación f; **freezer** n congelador m, freezer m (sc)
freezing ['friːzɪŋ] adj helado; **three degrees below ~** tres grados bajo cero; **freezing point** n punto de congelación
freight [freɪt] n (goods) carga; (money charged) flete m; **freight train** (us) n tren m de mercancías
French [frɛntʃ] adj francés/esa ▷ n (Ling) francés m; **the French** npl los franceses; **French bean** n judía verde; **French bread** n pan m francés; **French dressing** n (Culin) vinagreta; **French fries** (us) npl patatas fpl (sp) or papas fpl (LAM) fritas; **Frenchman** (irreg) n francés m; **Frenchwoman** (irreg) n francésa; **French stick** n barra de pan; **French window** n puerta de cristal
frenzy ['frɛnzɪ] n frenesí m

frequency ['friːkwənsɪ] n frecuencia
frequent [adj 'friːkwənt, vb frɪ'kwɛnt] adj frecuente ▷ vt frecuentar; **frequently** [-əntlɪ] adv frecuentemente, a menudo
fresh [frɛʃ] adj fresco; (bread) tierno; (new) nuevo; **freshen** vi (wind, air) soplar más recio; **freshen up** vi (person) arreglarse, lavarse; **fresher** (BRIT: inf) n (Univ) estudiante mf de primer año; **freshly** adv (made, painted etc) recién; **freshman** (us: irreg) n = **fresher**; **freshwater** adj (fish) de agua dulce
fret [frɛt] vi inquietarse
Fri abbr (= Friday) vier
friction ['frɪkʃən] n fricción f
Friday ['fraɪdɪ] n viernes m inv
fridge [frɪdʒ] (BRIT) n frigorífico (SP), nevera (SP), refrigerador m (LAM), heladera (RPL)
fried [fraɪd] adj frito
friend [frɛnd] n amigo/a; **friendly** adj simpático; (government) amigo; (place) acogedor(a); (match) amistoso; **friendship** n amistad f
fries [fraɪz] (esp us) npl = **French fried potatoes**
frigate ['frɪɡɪt] n fragata
fright [fraɪt] n (terror) terror m; (scare) susto; **to take ~** asustarse; **frighten** vt asustar; **frightened** adj asustado; **frightening** adj espantoso; **frightful** adj espantoso, horrible
frill [frɪl] n volante m
fringe [frɪndʒ] n (BRIT: of hair) flequillo; (on lampshade etc) flecos mpl; (of forest etc) borde m, margen m
Frisbee® ['frɪzbɪ] n frisbee® m
fritter ['frɪtə*] n buñuelo
frivolous ['frɪvələs] adj frívolo
fro [frəu] see **to**
frock [frɔk] n vestido
frog [frɔɡ] n rana; **frogman** (irreg) n hombre-rana m

O KEYWORD

from [frɔm] prep **1** (indicating starting place) de, desde; **where do you come from?** ¿de dónde eres?; **from London to Glasgow** de Londres a Glasgow; **to escape from sth/sb** escaparse de algo/algn
2 (indicating origin etc) de; **a letter/ telephone call from my sister** una carta/ llamada de mi hermana; **tell him from me that ...** dígale de mi parte que ...
3 (indicating time): **from one o'clock to** or **until** or **till two** (de)sde la una a or hasta las dos; **from January (on)** a partir de enero

4 (*indicating distance*) de; **the hotel is 1 km from the beach** el hotel está a 1 km de la playa

5 (*indicating price, number etc*) de; **prices range from £10 to £50** los precios van desde £10 a *or* hasta £50; **the interest rate was increased from 9% to 10%** el tipo de interés fue incrementado de un 9% a un 10%

6 (*indicating difference*) de; **he can't tell red from green** no sabe distinguir el rojo del verde; **to be different from sb/sth** ser diferente a algn/algo

7 (*because of, on the basis of*): **from what he says** por lo que dice; **weak from hunger** debilitado por el hambre

front [frʌnt] n (*foremost part*) parte f delantera; (*of house*) fachada; (*of dress*) delantero; (*promenade: also:* **sea ~**) paseo marítimo; (*Mil, Pol, Meteorology*) frente m; (*fig: appearances*) apariencias fpl ▷ adj (*wheel, leg*) delantero; (*row, line*) primero; **in ~ (of)** delante (de); **front door** n puerta principal; **frontier** [ˈfrʌntɪə*] n frontera; **front page** n primera plana; **front-wheel drive** n tracción f delantera

frost [frɔst] n helada; (*also:* **hoar~**) escarcha; **frostbite** n congelación f; **frosting** n (*esp us: icing*) glaseado; **frosty** adj (*weather*) de helada; (*welcome etc*) glacial

froth [frɔθ] n espuma

frown [fraun] vi fruncir el ceño

froze [frəuz] pt of **freeze**

frozen [ˈfrəuzn] pp of **freeze**

fruit [fru:t] n inv fruta; fruto; (*fig*) fruto; resultados mpl; **fruit juice** n zumo (SP) or jugo (LAM) de fruta; **fruit machine** (BRIT) n máquina f tragaperras; **fruit salad** n macedonia (SP) or ensalada (LAM) de frutas

frustrate [frʌsˈtreit] vt frustrar; **frustrated** adj frustrado

fry [frai] (*pt, pp* **fried**) vt freír; **small ~** gente f menuda; **frying pan** n sartén f

ft. abbr =**foot; feet**

fudge [fʌdʒ] n (*Culin*) caramelo blando

fuel [fjuəl] n (*for heating*) combustible m; (*coal*) carbón m; (*wood*) leña; (*for engine*) carburante m; **fuel tank** n depósito (de combustible)

fulfil [fulˈfil] vt (*function*) cumplir con; (*condition*) satisfacer; (*wish, desire*) realizar

full [ful] adj lleno; (*fig*) pleno; (*complete*) completo; (*maximum*) máximo; (*information*) detallado; (*price*) íntegro; (*skirt*) amplio ▷ adv: **to know ~ well that** saber perfectamente que; **I'm ~ (up)** no puedo más; **~ employment** pleno empleo; **a ~ two hours** dos horas completas; **at ~ speed** a

máxima velocidad; **in ~** (*reproduce, quote*) íntegramente; **full-length** adj (*novel etc*) entero; (*coat*) largo; (*portrait*) de cuerpo entero; **full moon** n luna llena; **full-scale** adj (*attack, war*) en gran escala; (*model*) de tamaño natural; **full stop** n punto; **full-time** adj (*work*) de tiempo completo ▷ adv: **to work full-time** trabajar a tiempo completo; **fully** adv completamente; (*at least*) por lo menos

fumble [ˈfʌmbl] vi: **to ~ with** manejar torpemente

fume [fju:m] vi (*rage*) estar furioso; **fumes** npl humo, gases mpl

fun [fʌn] n (*amusement*) diversión f; **to have ~** divertirse; **for ~** en broma; **to make ~ of** burlarse de

function [ˈfʌŋkʃən] n función f ▷ vi funcionar

fund [fʌnd] n fondo; (*reserve*) reserva; **funds** npl (*money*) fondos mpl

fundamental [fʌndəˈmentl] adj fundamental

funeral [ˈfju:nərəl] n (*burial*) entierro; (*ceremony*) funerales mpl; **funeral director** n director(a) m/f de pompas fúnebres; **funeral parlour** (BRIT) n funeraria

funfair [ˈfʌnfeə*] (BRIT) n parque m de atracciones

fungus [ˈfʌŋgəs] (*pl* **fungi**) n hongo; (*mould*) moho

funnel [ˈfʌnl] n embudo; (*of ship*) chimenea

funny [ˈfʌni] adj gracioso, divertido; (*strange*) curioso, raro

fur [fə:*] n piel f; (BRIT: *in kettle etc*) sarro; **fur coat** n abrigo de pieles

furious [ˈfjuəriəs] adj furioso; (*effort*) violento

furnish [ˈfə:niʃ] vt amueblar; (*supply*) suministrar; (*information*) facilitar; **furnishings** npl muebles mpl

furniture [ˈfə:nitʃə*] n muebles mpl; **piece of ~** mueble m

furry [ˈfə:ri] adj peludo

further [ˈfə:ðə*] adj (*new*) nuevo, adicional ▷ adv más lejos; (*more*) más; (*moreover*) además ▷ vt promover, adelantar; **further education** n educación f superior; **furthermore** adv además

furthest [ˈfə:ðist] superlative of **far**

fury [ˈfjuəri] n furia

fuse [fju:z] (US **fuze**) n fusible m; (*for bomb etc*) mecha ▷ vt (*metal*) fundir; (*fig*) fusionar ▷ vi fundirse; fusionarse; (BRIT *Elec*): **to ~ the lights** fundir los plomos; **fuse box** n caja de fusibles

fusion [ˈfju:ʒən] n fusión f

fuss [fʌs] n (*excitement*) conmoción f; (*trouble*) alboroto; **to make a ~** armar un lío or jaleo; **to make a ~ of sb** mimar a algn; **fussy** adj (*person*) exigente; (*too ornate*) recargado

future ['fjuːtʃə*] adj futuro; (*coming*) venidero ▷ n futuro; (*prospects*) porvenir m; **in ~** de ahora en adelante; **futures** npl (Comm) operaciones fpl a término, futuros mpl

fuze [fjuːz] (US) = **fuse**

fuzzy ['fʌzɪ] adj (Phot) borroso; (*hair*) muy rizado

g

G [dʒiː] n (Mus) sol m

g. abbr (= gram(s)) gr.

gadget ['gædʒɪt] n aparato

Gaelic ['geɪlɪk] adj, n (Ling) gaélico

gag [gæg] n (*on mouth*) mordaza; (*joke*) chiste m ▷ vt amordazar

gain [geɪn] n: **~ (in)** aumento (de); (*profit*) ganancia ▷ vt ganar ▷ vi (*watch*) adelantarse; **to ~ from/by sth** sacar provecho de algo; **to ~ on sb** ganar terreno a algn; **to ~ 3 lbs (in weight)** engordar 3 libras

gal. abbr = **gallon**

gala ['gɑːlə] n fiesta

galaxy ['gæləksɪ] n galaxia

gale [geɪl] n (*wind*) vendaval m

gall bladder ['gɔːl-] n vesícula biliar

gallery ['gælərɪ] n (*also*: **art ~**: *public*) pinacoteca; (: *private*) galería de arte; (*for spectators*) tribuna

gallon ['gæln] n galón m (BRIT = 4,546 litros, US = 3,785 litros)

gallop ['gæləp] n galope m ▷ vi galopar

gallstone ['gɔːlstəun] n cálculo biliario

gamble ['gæmbl] n (*risk*) riesgo ▷ vt jugar, apostar ▷ vi (*take a risk*) jugárselas; (*bet*) apostar; **to ~ on** apostar a; (*success etc*) contar con; **gambler** n jugador(a) m/f; **gambling** n juego

game [geɪm] n juego; (*match*) partido; (*of cards*) partida; (Hunting) caza ▷ adj (*willing*): **to be ~ for anything** atreverse a todo; **big ~** caza mayor (*contest*) juegos; (BRIT: Scol) deportes mpl; **games console** [geɪmz-] n consola de juegos; **game show** n programa m concurso m, concurso

gammon ['gæmən] n (*bacon*) tocino ahumado; (*ham*) jamón m ahumado

gang [gæŋ] n (*of criminals*) pandilla; (*of friends etc*) grupo; (*of workmen*) brigada

gangster ['gæŋstə*] n gángster m

gap [gæp] n vacío (SP), hueco (LAM);

(in trees, traffic) claro; (in time) intervalo; (difference): **~ (between)** diferencia (entre)
gape [ɡeɪp] vi mirar boquiabierto; (shirt etc) abrirse (completamente)
gap year n año sabático (antes de empezar a estudiar en la universidad)
garage ['ɡærɑːʒ] n garaje m; (for repairs) taller m; **garage sale** n venta de objetos usados (en el jardín de una casa particular)
garbage ['ɡɑːbɪdʒ] (US) n basura; (inf: nonsense) tonterías fpl; **garbage can** n cubo or bote m (MEX) or tacho (SC) de la basura; **garbage collector** (US) n basurero/a
garden ['ɡɑːdn] n jardín m; **gardens** npl (park) parque m; **garden centre** (BRIT) n centro de jardinería; **gardener** n jardinero/a; **gardening** n jardinería
garlic ['ɡɑːlɪk] n ajo
garment ['ɡɑːmənt] n prenda (de vestir)
garnish ['ɡɑːnɪʃ] vt (Culin) aderezar
garrison ['ɡærɪsn] n guarnición f
gas [ɡæs] n gas m; (fuel) combustible m; (US: gasoline) gasolina ⊳ vt asfixiar con gas; **gas cooker** (BRIT) n cocina de gas; **gas cylinder** n bombona de gas; **gas fire** n estufa de gas
gasket ['ɡæskɪt] n (Aut) junta de culata
gasoline ['ɡæsəliːn] (US) n gasolina
gasp [ɡɑːsp] n boqueada; (of shock etc) grito sofocado ⊳ vi (pant) jadear
gas: gas pedal n (esp US) acelerador m; **gas station** (US) n gasolinera; **gas tank** (US) n (Aut) depósito (de gasolina)
gate [ɡeɪt] n puerta; (iron gate) verja
gateau ['ɡætəu] (pl **~x**) n tarta
gatecrash ['ɡeɪtkræʃ] (BRIT) vt colarse en
gateway ['ɡeɪtweɪ] n puerta
gather ['ɡæðə*] vt (flowers, fruit) coger (SP), recoger; (assemble) reunir; (pick up) recoger; (Sewing) fruncir; (understand) entender ⊳ vi (assemble) reunirse; **to ~ speed** ganar velocidad; **gathering** n reunión f, asamblea
gauge [ɡeɪdʒ] n (instrument) indicador m ⊳ vt medir; (fig) juzgar
gave [ɡeɪv] pt of **give**
gay [ɡeɪ] adj (homosexual) gay; (joyful) alegre; (colour) vivo
gaze [ɡeɪz] n mirada fija ⊳ vi: **to ~ at sth** mirar algo fijamente
GB abbr = **Great Britain**
GCSE (BRIT) n abbr (= General Certificate of Secondary Education) examen de reválida que se hace a los 16 años
gear [ɡɪə*] n equipo, herramientas fpl; (Tech) engranaje m; (Aut) velocidad f, marcha ⊳ vt (fig: adapt): **to ~ sth to** adaptar

or ajustar algo a; **top** or **high** (US)**/low ~** cuarta/primera velocidad; **in ~** en marcha; **gear up** vi prepararse; **gear box** n caja de cambios; **gear lever** n palanca de cambio; **gear shift** (US) n = **gear lever**; **gear stick** n (BRIT) palanca de cambios
geese [ɡiːs] npl of **goose**
gel [dʒɛl] n gel m
gem [dʒɛm] n piedra preciosa
Gemini ['dʒɛmɪnaɪ] n Géminis m, Gemelos mpl
gender ['dʒɛndə*] n género
gene [dʒiːn] n gen(e)m
general ['dʒɛnərl] n general m ⊳ adj general; **in ~** en general; **general anaesthetic** (US **general anesthetic**) n anestesia general; **general election** n elecciones fpl generales; **generalize** vi generalizar; **generally** adv generalmente, en general; **general practitioner** n médico general; **general store** n tienda (que vende de todo) (LAM, SP), almacén m (SC, SP)
generate ['dʒɛnəreɪt] vt (Elec) generar; (jobs, profits) producir
generation [dʒɛnə'reɪʃən] n generación f
generator ['dʒɛnəreɪtə*] n generador m
generosity [dʒɛnə'rɔsɪtɪ] n generosidad f
generous ['dʒɛnərəs] adj generoso
genetic [dʒɪ'nɛtɪk] adj: **~ engineering** ingeniería genética; **~ fingerprinting** identificación f genética; **genetically modified** adj transgénico; **genetics** n genética
genitals ['dʒɛnɪtlz] npl (órganos mpl) genitales mpl
genius ['dʒiːnɪəs] n genio
genome ['ɡiːnəum] n genoma m
gent [dʒɛnt] n abbr (BRIT inf)= **gentleman**
gentle ['dʒɛntl] adj apacible, dulce; (animal) manso; (breeze, curve etc) suave

▌Be careful not to translate **gentle** by the Spanish word **gentil**.

gentleman ['dʒɛntlmən] (irreg) n señor m; (well-bred man) caballero
gently ['dʒɛntlɪ] adv dulcemente; suavemente
gents [dʒɛnts] n aseos mpl (de caballeros)
genuine ['dʒɛnjuɪn] adj auténtico; (person) sincero; **genuinely** adv sinceramente
geographic(al) [dʒɪə'ɡræfɪk(l)] adj geográfico
geography [dʒɪ'ɔɡrəfɪ] n geografía
geology [dʒɪ'ɔlədʒɪ] n geología
geometry [dʒɪ'ɔmətrɪ] n geometría
geranium [dʒɪ'reɪnjəm] n geranio
geriatric [dʒɛrɪ'ætrɪk] adj, n geriátrico/a m/f

germ [dʒɜːm] n (microbe) microbio,
bacteria; (seed, fig) germen m
German ['dʒɜːmən] adj alemán/ana ▷ n
alemán/ana m/f; (Ling) alemán m; **German
measles** n rubéola
Germany ['dʒɜːmənɪ] n Alemania
gesture ['dʒɛstjə*] n gesto; (symbol)
muestra

○ **KEYWORD**

get [ɡɛt] (pt, pp **got**, pp **gotten** (US)) vi
1 (become, be) ponerse, volverse; **to get old/
tired** envejecer/cansarse; **to get drunk**
emborracharse; **to get dirty** ensuciarse;
to get married casarse; **when do I get
paid?** ¿cuándo me pagan or se me paga?; **it's
getting late** se está haciendo tarde
2 (go): **to get to/from** llegar a/de; **to get
home** llegar a casa
3 (begin) empezar a; **to get to know sb**
(llegar a) conocer a algn; **I'm getting to like
him** me está empezando a gustar; **let's get
going** or **started** ¡vamos (a empezar)!
4 (modal aux vb): **you've got to do it** tienes
que hacerlo
▷ vt **1**: **to get sth done** (finish) terminar
algo; (have done) mandar hacer algo; **to get
one's hair cut** cortarse el pelo; **to get the
car going** or **to go** arrancar el coche; **to get
sb to do sth** conseguir or hacer que algn
haga algo; **to get sth/sb ready** preparar
algo/a algn
2 (obtain: money, permission, results)
conseguir; (find: job, flat) encontrar;
(fetch: person, doctor) buscar; (object) ir a
buscar, traer; **to get sth for sb** conseguir
algo para algn; **get me Mr Jones, please**
(Tel) póngame (SP) or comuníqueme (LAM)
con el Sr. Jones, por favor; **can I get you a
drink?** ¿quieres algo de beber?
3 (receive: present, letter) recibir;
(acquire: reputation) alcanzar; (: prize) ganar;
what did you get for your birthday?
¿qué te regalaron por tu cumpleaños?;
how much did you get for the painting?
¿cuánto sacaste por el cuadro?
4 (catch) coger (SP), agarrar (LAM); (hit: target
etc) dar en; **to get sb by the arm/throat**
coger or agarrar a algn por el brazo/cuello;
get him! ¡cógelo! (SP), ¡atrápalo! (LAM); **the
bullet got him in the leg** la bala le dio en
la pierna
5 (take, move) llevar; **to get sth to sb** hacer
llegar algo a algn; **do you think we'll get it
through the door?** ¿crees que lo podremos
meter por la puerta?
6 (catch, take: plane, bus etc) coger (SP),

tomar (LAM); **where do I get the train for
Birmingham?** ¿dónde se coge or se toma el
tren para Birmingham?
7 (understand) entender; (hear) oír; **I've got
it!** ¡ya lo tengo!, ¡eureka!; **I don't get your
meaning** no te entiendo; **I'm sorry, I didn't
get your name** lo siento, no cogí tu nombre
8 (have, possess): **to have got** tener
get away vi marcharse; (escape) escaparse
get away with vt fus hacer impunemente
get back vi (return) volver ▷ vt recobrar
get in vi entrar; (train) llegar; (arrive home)
volver a casa, regresar
get into vt fus entrar en; (vehicle) subir a; **to
get into a rage** enfadarse
get off vi (from train etc) bajar;
(depart: person, car) marcharse ▷ vt (remove)
quitar ▷ vt fus (train, bus) bajar de
get on vi (at exam etc): **how are you
getting on?** ¿cómo te va?; (agree): **to get on
(with)** llevarse bien (con) ▷ vt fus subir a
get out vi salir; (of vehicle) bajar ▷ vt sacar
get out of vt fus salir de; (duty etc)
escaparse de
get over vt fus (illness) recobrarse de
get through vi (Tel) (lograr) comunicarse
get up vi (rise) levantarse ▷ vt fus subir

getaway ['ɡɛtəweɪ] n fuga
Ghana ['ɡɑːnə] n Ghana
ghastly ['ɡɑːstlɪ] adj horrible
ghetto ['ɡɛtəʊ] n gueto
ghost [ɡəʊst] n fantasma m
giant ['dʒaɪənt] n gigante mf ▷ adj
gigantesco, gigante
gift [ɡɪft] n regalo; (ability) talento; **gifted**
adj dotado; **gift shop** (US **gift store**) n
tienda de regalos; **gift token**, **gift voucher**
n vale m canjeable por un regalo
gig [ɡɪɡ] n (inf: concert) actuación f
gigabyte ['dʒɪɡəbaɪt] n gigabyte m
gigantic [dʒaɪ'ɡæntɪk] adj gigantesco
giggle ['ɡɪɡl] vi reírse tontamente
gills [ɡɪlz] npl (of fish) branquias fpl, agallas
fpl
gilt [ɡɪlt] adj, n dorado
gimmick ['ɡɪmɪk] n truco
gin [dʒɪn] n ginebra
ginger ['dʒɪndʒə*] n jengibre m
gipsy ['dʒɪpsɪ] n = **gypsy**
giraffe [dʒɪ'rɑːf] n jirafa
girl [ɡɜːl] n (small) niña; (young woman)
chica, joven f, muchacha; (daughter) hija;
an English ~ una (chica) inglesa; **girl band**
n girl band m (grupo musical de chicas);
girlfriend n (of girl) amiga; (of boy) novia;
Girl Scout (US) n = **Girl Guide**
gist [dʒɪst] n lo esencial

g

give [gɪv] (*pt* **gave**, *pp* **given**) *vt* dar;
(*deliver*) entregar; (*as gift*) regalar ▷ *vi* (*break*)
romperse; (*stretch: fabric*) dar de sí; **to ~ sb
sth**, **~ sth to sb** dar algo a algn; **give away**
vt (*give free*) regalar; (*betray*) traicionar;
(*disclose*) revelar; **give back** *vt* devolver;
give in *vi* ceder ▷ *vt* entregar; **give out**
vt distribuir; **give up** *vi* rendirse, darse
por vencido ▷ *vt* renunciar a; **to give up
smoking** dejar de fumar; **to give o.s. up**
entregarse

given ['gɪvn] *pp of* **give** ▷ *adj* (*fixed: time,
amount*) determinado ▷ *conj*: **~ (that)** ...
dado (que) ...; **~ the circumstances** ...
dadas las circunstancias ...

glacier ['glæsɪə*] *n* glaciar *m*

glad [glæd] *adj* contento; **gladly** ['-lɪ] *adv*
con mucho gusto

glamour ['glæmər] (*US* **glamor**) *n*
encanto, atractivo; **glamorous** *adj*
encantador(a), atractivo

glance [glɑːns] *n* ojeada, mirada ▷ *vi*: **to ~
at** echar una ojeada a

gland [glænd] *n* glándula

glare [gleə*] *n* (*of anger*) mirada feroz; (*of
light*) deslumbramiento, brillo; **to be in
the ~ of publicity** ser el foco de la atención
pública ▷ *vi* deslumbrar; **to ~ at** mirar con
odio a; **glaring** *adj* (*mistake*) manifiesto

glass [glɑːs] *n* vidrio, cristal *m*; (*for
drinking*) vaso; (: *with stem*) copa; **glasses** *npl*
(*spectacles*) gafas *fpl*

glaze [gleɪz] *vt* (*window*) poner cristales a;
(*pottery*) vidriar ▷ *n* vidriado

gleam [gliːm] *vi* brillar

glen [glɛn] *n* cañada

glide [glaɪd] *vi* deslizarse; (*Aviat: birds*)
planear; **glider** *n* (*Aviat*) planeador *m*

glimmer ['glɪmə*] *n* luz *f* tenue; (*of
interest*) muestra; (*of hope*) rayo

glimpse [glɪmps] *n* vislumbre *m* ▷ *vt*
vislumbrar, entrever

glint [glɪnt] *vi* centellear

glisten ['glɪsn] *vi* relucir, brillar

glitter ['glɪtə*] *vi* relucir, brillar

global ['gləʊbl] *adj* mundial;
globalization *n* globalización *f*; **global
warming** *n* (re)calentamiento global *or*
de la tierra

globe [gləʊb] *n* globo; (*model*) globo
terráqueo

gloom [gluːm] *n* oscuridad *f*; (*sadness*)
tristeza; **gloomy** *adj* (*dark*) oscuro; (*sad*)
triste; (*pessimistic*) pesimista

glorious ['glɔːrɪəs] *adj* glorioso; (*weather
etc*) magnífico

glory ['glɔːrɪ] *n* gloria

gloss [glɔs] *n* (*shine*) brillo; (*paint*) pintura
de aceite

glossary ['glɔsərɪ] *n* glosario

glossy ['glɔsɪ] *adj* lustroso; (*magazine*)
de lujo

glove [glʌv] *n* guante *m*; **glove
compartment** *n* (*Aut*) guantera

glow [gləʊ] *vi* brillar

glucose ['gluːkəʊs] *n* glucosa

glue [gluː] *n* goma (de pegar), cemento
▷ *vt* pegar

GM *adj abbr* (= *genetically modified*)
transgénico

gm *abbr* (= *gram*) g

GMO *n abbr* (= *genetically modified organism*)
organismo transgénico

GMT *abbr* (= *Greenwich Mean Time*) GMT

gnaw [nɔː] *vt* roer

go [gəʊ] (*pt* **went**, *pp* **gone**, *pl* **~es**) *vi* ir;
(*travel*) viajar; (*depart*) irse, marcharse; (*work*)
funcionar, marchar; (*be sold*) venderse;
(*time*) pasar; (*fit, suit*): **to ~ with** hacer
juego con; (*become*) ponerse; (*break etc*)
estropearse, romperse ▷ *n*: **to have a ~
(at)** probar suerte (con); **to be on the ~** no
parar; **whose ~ is it?** ¿a quién le toca?; **he's
~ing to do it** va a hacerlo; **to ~ for a walk**
ir de paseo; **to ~ dancing** ir a bailar; **how
did it ~?** ¿qué tal salió or resultó?, ¿cómo ha
ido?; **to ~ round the back** pasar por detrás;
go ahead *vi* seguir adelante; **go away**
vi irse, marcharse; **go back** *vi* volver; **go
by** *vi* (*time*) pasar ▷ *vt fus* guiarse por;
go down *vi* bajar; (*ship*) hundirse; (*sun*)
ponerse ▷ *vt fus* bajar; **go for** *vt fus* (*fetch*)
ir por; (*attack*) atacar; **go in** *vi* entrar;
entrar; **go into** *vt fus* entrar en; (*investigate*)
investigar; (*embark on*) dedicarse a; **go off**
vi irse, marcharse; (*food*) pasarse; (*explode*)
estallar; (*event*) realizarse ▷ *vt fus* dejar
de gustar; **I'm going off him/the idea**
ya no me gusta tanto él/la idea; **go on** *vi*
(*continue*) seguir, continuar; (*happen*) pasar,
ocurrir; **to go on doing sth** seguir haciendo
algo; **go out** *vi* salir; (*fire, light*) apagarse;
go over *vi* (*ship*) zozobrar ▷ *vt fus* (*check*)
revisar; **go past** *vi, vt fus* pasar; **go round**
vi (*circulate: news, rumour*) correr; (*suffice*)
alcanzar, bastar; (*revolve*) girar, dar vueltas;
(*visit*): **to go round (to sb's)** pasar a ver (a
algn); **to go round (by)** (*make a detour*) dar
la vuelta (por); **go through** *vt fus* (*town etc*)
atravesar; **go up** *vi, vt fus* subir; **go with**
vt fus (*accompany*) ir con, acompañar a; **go
without** *vt fus* pasarse sin

go-ahead ['gəʊəhɛd] *adj* (*person*)
dinámico; (*firm*) innovador(a) ▷ *n* luz *f*
verde

goal [gəʊl] *n* meta; (*score*) gol *m*;

goalkeeper n portero; **goal-post** n poste m (de la portería)

goat [gəʊt] n cabra

gobble ['gɔbl] vt (also: ~ down, ~ up) tragarse, engullir

God [gɔd] n Dios m; **godchild** n ahijado/a; **goddaughter** n ahijada; **goddess** n diosa; **godfather** n padrino; **godmother** n madrina; **godson** n ahijado

goggles ['gɔglz] npl gafas fpl

going ['gəʊɪŋ] n (conditions) estado del terreno ▷ adj: **the ~ rate** la tarifa corriente or en vigor

gold [gəʊld] n oro ▷ adj de oro; **golden** adj (made of gold) de oro; (gold in colour) dorado; **goldfish** n pez m de colores; **goldmine** n (also fig) mina de oro; **gold-plated** adj chapado en oro

golf [gɔlf] n golf m; **golf ball** n (for game) pelota de golf; (on typewriter) esfera; **golf club** n club m de golf; (stick) palo (de golf); **golf course** n campo de golf; **golfer** n golfista mf

gone [gɔn] pp of **go**

gong [gɔŋ] n gong m

good [gʊd] adj bueno; (pleasant) agradable; (kind) bueno, amable; (well-behaved) educado ▷ n bien m, provecho; **goods** npl (Comm) mercancías fpl; **~!** ¡qué bien!; **to be ~ at** tener aptitud para; **to be ~ for** servir para; **it's ~ for you** te hace bien; **would you be ~ enough to ...?** ¿podría hacerme el favor de ...?, ¿sería tan amable de ...?; **a ~ deal (of)** mucho; **a ~ many** muchos; **to make ~** reparar; **it's no ~ complaining** no vale la pena (de) quejarse; **for ~** para siempre, definitivamente; **~ morning/afternoon!** ¡buenos días/buenas tardes!; **~ evening!** ¡buenas noches!; **~ night!** ¡buenas noches!

goodbye [gʊd'baɪ] excl ¡adiós!; **to say ~ (to)** (person) despedirse (de)

good: Good Friday n Viernes m Santo; **good-looking** adj guapo; **good-natured** adj amable, simpático; **goodness** n (of person) bondad f; **for goodness sake!** ¡por Dios!; **goodness gracious!** ¡Dios mío!; **goods train** (BRIT) n tren m de mercancías; **goodwill** n buena voluntad f

Google® ['gu:gəl] n Google ® m ▷ vi hacer búsquedas en Internet ▷ vt buscar información en Internet sobre

goose [gu:s] (pl geese) n ganso, oca

gooseberry ['gʊzbəri] n grosella espinosa; **to play ~** hacer de carabina

goose bumps, goose pimples npl carne f de gallina

gorge [gɔːdʒ] n barranco ▷ vr: **to ~ o.s. (on)** atracarse (de)

gorgeous ['gɔːdʒəs] adj (thing) precioso; (weather) espléndido; (person) guapísimo

gorilla [gə'rɪlə] n gorila m

gosh [gɔʃ] (inf) excl ¡cielos!

gospel ['gɔspl] n evangelio

gossip ['gɔsɪp] n (scandal) cotilleo, chismes mpl; (chat) charla; (scandalmonger) cotilla m/f, chismoso/a ▷ vi cotillear; **gossip column** n ecos mpl de sociedad

got [gɔt] pt, pp of **get**

gotten (us) ['gɔtn] pp of **get**

gourmet ['gʊəmeɪ] n gastrónomo/a m/f

govern ['gʌvən] vt gobernar; (influence) dominar; **government** n gobierno; **governor** n gobernador(a) m/f; (of school etc) miembro del consejo; (of jail) director(a) m/f

gown [gaʊn] n traje m; (of teacher, BRIT: of judge) toga

G.P. n abbr = **general practitioner**

grab [græb] vt coger (SP), agarrar (LAM), arrebatar ▷ vi: **to ~ at** intentar agarrar

grace [greɪs] n gracia ▷ vt honrar; (adorn) adornar; **5 days' ~** un plazo de 5 días; **graceful** adj grácil, ágil; (style, shape) elegante, gracioso; **gracious** ['greɪʃəs] adj amable

grade [greɪd] n (quality) clase f, calidad f; (in hierarchy) grado; (Scol: mark) nota; (us: school class) curso ▷ vt clasificar; **grade crossing** (us) n paso a nivel; **grade school** (us) n escuela primaria

gradient ['greɪdɪənt] n pendiente f

gradual ['grædjuəl] adj paulatino; **gradually** adv paulatinamente

graduate [n 'grædjuɪt, vb 'grædjueɪt] n (us: of high school) graduado/a; (of university) licenciado/a ▷ vi graduarse; licenciarse; **graduation** [-'eɪʃən] n (ceremony) entrega del título

graffiti [grə'fi:tɪ] n pintadas fpl

graft [grɑːft] n (Agr, Med) injerto; (BRIT: inf) trabajo duro; (bribery) corrupción f ▷ vt injertar

grain [greɪn] n (single particle) grano; (corn) granos mpl, cereales mpl; (of wood) fibra

gram [græm] n gramo

grammar ['græmə*] n gramática; **grammar school** (BRIT) n ≈ instituto de segunda enseñanza, liceo (SP)

gramme [græm] n = **gram**

gran [græn] (inf) n (BRIT) abuelita

grand [grænd] adj magnífico, imponente; (wonderful) estupendo; (gesture etc) grandioso; **grandad** (inf) n = **granddad**; **grandchild** (pl grandchildren) n nieto/a m/f; **granddad** (inf) n yayo, abuelito;

granddaughter *n* nieta; **grandfather** *n* abuelo; **grandma** (*inf*) *n* yaya, abuelita; **grandmother** *n* abuela; **grandpa** (*inf*) *n* = **granddad**; **grandparents** *npl* abuelos *mpl*; **grand piano** *n* piano de cola; **Grand Prix** ['grã:'pri:] *n* (*Aut*) gran premio, Grand Prix *m*; **grandson** *n* nieto

granite ['grænɪt] *n* granito

granny ['grænɪ] (*inf*) *n* abuelita, yaya

grant [grɑːnt] *vt* (*concede*) conceder; (*admit*) reconocer ▷ *n* (*Scol*) beca; (*Admin*) subvención *f*; **to take sth/sb for ~ed** dar algo por sentado/no hacer ningún caso a algn

grape [greɪp] *n* uva

grapefruit ['greɪpfruːt] *n* pomelo (*SP*, *SC*), toronja (*LAM*)

graph [grɑːf] *n* gráfica; **graphic** ['græfɪk] *adj* gráfico; **graphics** *n* artes *fpl* gráficas ▷ *npl* (*drawings*) dibujos *mpl*

grasp [grɑːsp] *vt* agarrar, asir; (*understand*) comprender ▷ *n* (*grip*) asimiento; (*understanding*) comprensión *f*

grass [grɑːs] *n* hierba; (*lawn*) césped *m*; **grasshopper** *n* saltamontes *m inv*

grate [greɪt] *n* parrilla de chimenea ▷ *vi*: **to ~ (on)** chirriar (sobre) ▷ *vt* (*Culin*) rallar

grateful ['greɪtful] *adj* agradecido

grater ['greɪtə*] *n* rallador *m*

gratitude ['grætɪtjuːd] *n* agradecimiento

grave [greɪv] *n* tumba ▷ *adj* serio, grave

gravel ['grævl] *n* grava

gravestone ['greɪvstəun] *n* lápida

graveyard ['greɪvjɑːd] *n* cementerio

gravity ['grævɪtɪ] *n* gravedad *f*

gravy ['greɪvɪ] *n* salsa de carne

gray [greɪ] *adj* = **grey**

graze [greɪz] *vi* pacer ▷ *vt* (*touch lightly*) rozar; (*scrape*) raspar ▷ *n* (*Med*) abrasión *f*

grease [griːs] *n* (*fat*) grasa; (*lubricant*) lubricante *m* ▷ *vt* engrasar; lubrificar; **greasy** *adj* grasiento

great [greɪt] *adj* grande; (*inf*) magnífico, estupendo; **Great Britain** *n* Gran Bretaña; **great-grandfather** *n* bisabuelo; **great-grandmother** *n* bisabuela; **greatly** *adv* muy; (*with verb*) mucho

Greece [griːs] *n* Grecia

greed [griːd] *n* (*also*: **~iness**) codicia, avaricia; (*for food*) gula; (*for power etc*) avidez *f*; **greedy** *adj* avaro; (*for food*) glotón/ona

Greek [griːk] *adj* griego ▷ *n* griego/a; (*Ling*) griego

green [griːn] *adj* (*also Pol*) verde; (*inexperienced*) novato ▷ *n* verde *m*; (*stretch of grass*) césped *m*; (*Golf*) green; *m* **greens** *npl* (*vegetables*) verduras *fpl*; **green card**

n (*Aut*) carta verde; (*us*: *work permit*) permiso de trabajo para los extranjeros en EE. UU.; **greengage** *n* ciruela claudia; **greengrocer** (*BRIT*) *n* verdulero/a; **greenhouse** *n* invernadero; **greenhouse effect** *n* efecto invernadero

Greenland ['griːnlənd] *n* Groenlandia

green salad *n* ensalada *f* (*de lechuga, pepino, pimiento verde, etc*)

greet [griːt] *vt* (*welcome*) dar la bienvenida a; (*receive*: *news*) recibir; **greeting** *n* (*welcome*) bienvenida; **greeting(s) card** *n* tarjeta de felicitación

grew [gruː] *pt of* **grow**

grey [greɪ] (*us* **gray**) *adj* gris; (*weather*) sombrío; **grey-haired** *adj* canoso; **greyhound** *n* galgo

grid [grɪd] *n* reja; (*Elec*) red *f*; **gridlock** *n* (*traffic jam*) retención *f*

grief [griːf] *n* dolor *m*, pena

grievance ['griːvəns] *n* motivo de queja, agravio

grieve [griːv] *vi* afligirse, acongojarse ▷ *vt* dar pena a; **to ~ for** llorar por

grill [grɪl] *n* (*on cooker*) parrilla; (*also*: **mixed ~**) parrillada ▷ *vt* (*BRIT*) asar a la parrilla; (*inf*: *question*) interrogar

grille [grɪl] *n* reja; (*Aut*) rejilla

grim [grɪm] *adj* (*place*) sombrío; (*situation*) triste; (*person*) ceñudo

grime [graɪm] *n* mugre *f*, suciedad *f*

grin [grɪn] *n* sonrisa abierta ▷ *vi* sonreír abiertamente

grind [graɪnd] (*pt*, *pp* **ground**) *vt* (*coffee, pepper etc*) moler; (*us*: *meat*) picar; (*make sharp*) afilar ▷ *n* (*work*) rutina

grip [grɪp] *n* (*hold*) asimiento; (*control*) control *m*, dominio; (*of tyre etc*) to **have a good/bad ~** agarrarse bien/mal; (*handle*) asidero; (*holdall*) maletín *m* ▷ *vt* agarrar; (*viewer, reader*) fascinar; **to get to ~s with** enfrentarse con; **gripping** *adj* absorbente

grit [grɪt] *n* gravilla; (*courage*) valor *m* ▷ *vt* (*road*) poner gravilla en; **to ~ one's teeth** apretar los dientes

grits [grɪts] (*us*) *npl* maíz *msg* a medio moler

groan [grəun] *n* gemido; quejido ▷ *vi* gemir; quejarse

grocer ['grəusə*] *n* tendero (*de ultramarinos* (*SP*)); **groceries** *npl* comestibles *mpl*; **grocer's (shop)** *n* tienda de comestibles *or* (*MEX, CAM*) abarrotes, almacén (*SC*); **grocery** *n* (*shop*) tienda de ultramarinos

groin [grɔɪn] *n* ingle *f*

groom [gruːm] *n* mozo/a de cuadra; (*also*: **bride~**) novio ▷ *vt* (*horse*) almohazar;

(fig): **to ~ sb for** preparar a algn para; **well-~ed** de buena presencia

groove [gru:v] n ranura, surco

grope [grəup] vi: **to ~ for** buscar a tientas

gross [grəus] adj (neglect, injustice) grave; (vulgar: behaviour) grosero; (: appearance) de mal gusto; (Comm) bruto; **grossly** adv (greatly) enormemente

grotesque [grə'tɛsk] adj grotesco

ground [graund] pt, pp of **grind** ▷ n suelo, tierra; (Sport) campo, terreno; (reason: gen pl) causa, razón f; (us: also: ~ **wire**) tierra ▷ vt (plane) mantener en tierra; (us Elec) conectar con tierra; **grounds** npl (of coffee etc) poso; (gardens etc) jardines mpl, parque m; **on the ~** en el suelo; **to the ~** al suelo; **to gain/lose ~** ganar/perder terreno; **ground floor** n (BRIT) planta baja; **groundsheet** (BRIT) n tela impermeable; suelo; **groundwork** n preparación f

group [gru:p] n grupo; (musical) conjunto ▷ vt (also: ~ **together**) agrupar ▷ vi (also: ~ **together**) agruparse

grouse [graus] n inv (bird) urogallo ▷ vi (complain) quejarse

grovel ['grɔvl] vi (fig): **to ~ before** humillarse ante

grow [grəu] (pt **grew**, pp **grown**) vi crecer; (increase) aumentar; (expand) desarrollarse; (become) volverse; **to ~ rich/weak** enriquecerse/debilitarse ▷ vt cultivar; (hair, beard) dejar crecer; **grow on** vt fus: **that painting is growing on me** ese cuadro me gusta cada vez más; **grow up** vi crecer, hacerse hombre/mujer

growl [graul] vi gruñir

grown [grəun] pp of **grow**; **grown-up** n adulto/a, mayor mf

growth [grəuθ] n crecimiento, desarrollo; (what has grown) brote m; (Med) tumor m

grub [grʌb] n larva, gusano; (inf: food) comida

grubby ['grʌbɪ] adj sucio, mugriento

grudge [grʌdʒ] n (motivo de) rencor m ▷ vt: **to ~ sb sth** dar algo a algn de mala gana; **to bear sb a ~** guardar rencor a algn

gruelling ['gruəlɪŋ] (us **grueling**) adj penoso, duro

gruesome ['gru:səm] adj horrible

grumble ['grʌmbl] vi refunfuñar, quejarse

grumpy ['grʌmpɪ] adj gruñón/ona

grunt [grʌnt] vi gruñir

guarantee [gærən'ti:] n garantía ▷ vt garantizar

guard [gɑ:d] n (squad) guardia; (one man) guardia mf; (BRIT Rail) jefe m de tren; (on machine) dispositivo de seguridad; (also: **fire~**) rejilla de protección ▷ vt guardar;

(prisoner) vigilar; **to be on one's ~** estar alerta; **guardian** n guardián/ana m/f; (of minor) tutor(a) m/f

guerrilla [gə'rɪlə] n guerrillero/a

guess [gɛs] vi adivinar; (us) suponer ▷ vt adivinar; suponer ▷ n suposición f, conjetura; **to take** or **have a ~** tratar de adivinar

guest [gɛst] n invitado/a; (in hotel) huésped mf; **guest house** n casa de huéspedes, pensión f; **guest room** n cuarto de huéspedes

guidance ['gaɪdəns] n (advice) consejos mpl

guide [gaɪd] n (person) guía mf; (book, fig) guía; (also: **Girl ~**) guía ▷ vt (round museum etc) guiar; (lead) conducir; (direct) orientar; **guidebook** n guía; **guide dog** n perro m guía; **guided tour** n visita f con guía; **guidelines** npl (advice) directrices fpl

guild [gɪld] n gremio

guilt [gɪlt] n culpabilidad f; **guilty** adj culpable

guinea pig ['gɪnɪ-] n cobaya; (fig) conejillo de Indias

guitar [gɪ'tɑ:*] n guitarra; **guitarist** n guitarrista m/f

gulf [gʌlf] n golfo; (abyss) abismo

gull [gʌl] n gaviota

gulp [gʌlp] vi tragar saliva ▷ vt (also: ~ **down**) tragarse

gum [gʌm] n (Anat) encía; (glue) goma, cemento; (sweet) caramelo de goma; (also: **chewing-~**) chicle m ▷ vt pegar con goma

gun [gʌn] n (small) pistola, revólver m; (shotgun) escopeta; (rifle) fusil m; (cannon) cañón m; **gunfire** n disparos mpl; **gunman** (irreg) n pistolero; **gunpoint** n: **at gunpoint** a mano armada; **gunpowder** n pólvora; **gunshot** n escopetazo

gush [gʌʃ] vi salir a raudales; (person) deshacerse en efusiones

gust [gʌst] n (of wind) ráfaga

gut [gʌt] n intestino; **guts** npl (Anat) tripas fpl; (courage) valor m

gutter ['gʌtə*] n (of roof) canalón m; (in street) cuneta

guy [gaɪ] n (also: ~**rope**) cuerda; (inf: man) tío (sp); (figure) monigote m

Guy Fawkes' Night [gaɪ'fɔ:ks-] n ver abajo

fallido de volar el parlamento de Jaime
I en 1605. Esa noche se lanzan fuegos
artificiales y se hacen hogueras en las
que se queman unos muñecos de trapo
que representan a **Guy Fawkes**, uno
de los cabecillas de la revuelta. Días
antes, los niños tienen por costumbre
pedir a los transeúntes "a penny for the
guy", dinero que emplean en comprar
cohetes y petardos.

gym [dʒɪm] n gimnasio; **gymnasium** n
gimnasio mf; **gymnast** n gimnasta mf;
gymnastics n gimnasia; **gym shoes** npl
zapatillas fpl (de deporte)
gynaecologist [gaɪnɪ'kɔlədʒɪst] (US
gynecologist) n ginecólogo/a
gypsy ['dʒɪpsɪ] n gitano/a

haberdashery [hæbə'dæʃərɪ] (BRIT) n
mercería
habit ['hæbɪt] n hábito, costumbre f; (drug
habit) adicción f; (costume) hábito
habitat ['hæbɪtæt] n hábitat m
hack [hæk] vt (cut) cortar; (slice) tajar ⊳ n
(pej: writer) escritor(a) m/f a sueldo; **hacker**
n (Comput) pirata mf informático/a
had [hæd] pt, pp of **have**
haddock ['hædək] (pl ~ or ~s) n especie de
merluza
hadn't ['hædnt] = **had not**
haemorrhage ['hɛmərɪdʒ] (US
hemorrhage) n hemorragia
haemorrhoids ['hɛmərɔɪdz] (US
hemorrhoids) npl hemorroides fpl
haggle ['hægl] vi regatear
Hague [heɪg] n: **The ~** La Haya
hail [heɪl] n granizo; (fig) lluvia ⊳ vt
saludar; (taxi) llamar a; (acclaim) aclamar
⊳ vi granizar; **hailstone** n (piedra de)
granizo
hair [hɛə*] n pelo, cabellos mpl; (one hair)
pelo, cabello; (on legs etc) vello; **to do one's**
~ arreglarse el pelo; **to have grey ~** tener
canas fpl; **hairband** n cinta; **hairbrush** n
cepillo (para el pelo); **haircut** n corte m (de
pelo); **hairdo** n peinado; **hairdresser** n
peluquero/a; **hairdresser's** n peluquería;
hair dryer n secador m de pelo; **hair gel**
n fijador; **hair spray** n laca; **hairstyle**
n peinado; **hairy** adj peludo; velludo;
(inf: frightening) espeluznante
hake [heɪk] (pl ~ or ~s) n merluza
half [hɑːf] (pl **halves**) n mitad f; (of beer)
≈ caña (SP), media pinta; (Rail, Bus) billete
m de niño ⊳ adj medio ⊳ adv medio, a
medias; **two and a ~** dos y media; **~ a dozen**
media docena; **~ a pound** media libra; **to**
cut sth in ~ cortar algo por la mitad; **half**
board n (BRIT: in hotel) media pensión; **half-**

brother n hermanastro; **half day** n medio día m, media jornada; **half fare** n medio pasaje m; **half-hearted** adj indiferente, poco entusiasta; **half-hour** n media hora; **half-price** adj, adv a mitad de precio; **half term** (BRIT) n (Scol) vacaciones de mediados del trimestre; **half-time** n descanso; **halfway** adv a medio camino; **halfway through** a mitad de

hall [hɔːl] n (for concerts) sala; (entrance way) hall m; vestíbulo

hallmark ['hɔːlmɑːk] n sello

hallo [hə'ləu] excl = hello

hall of residence (BRIT) n residencia

Hallowe'en [hæləu'iːn] n víspera de Todos los Santos

● **HALLOWE'EN**
●
● La tradición anglosajona dice que en
● la noche del 31 de octubre, **Hallowe'en**,
● víspera de Todos los Santos, es posible
● ver a brujas y fantasmas. En este día los
● niños se disfrazan y van de puerta en
● puerta llevando un farol hecho con una
● calabaza en forma de cabeza humana.
● Cuando se les abre la puerta gritan "trick
● or treat", amenazando con gastar una
● broma a quien no les dé golosinas o algo
● de calderilla.

hallucination [həluːsɪ'neɪʃən] n alucinación f

hallway ['hɔːlweɪ] n vestíbulo

halo ['heɪləu] n (of saint) halo, aureola

halt [hɔːlt] n (stop) alto, parada ▷ vt parar, interrumpir ▷ vi pararse

halve [hɑːv] vt partir por la mitad

halves [hɑːvz] npl of half

ham [hæm] n jamón m (cocido)

hamburger ['hæmbəːgə*] n hamburguesa

hamlet ['hæmlɪt] n aldea

hammer ['hæmə*] n martillo ▷ vt (nail) clavar; (force): **to ~ an idea into sb/a message home** meter una idea en la cabeza a algn/machacar una idea ▷ vi dar golpes

hammock ['hæmək] n hamaca

hamper ['hæmpə*] vt estorbar ▷ n cesto

hamster ['hæmstə*] n hámster m

hamstring ['hæmstrɪŋ] n (Anat) tendón m de la corva

hand [hænd] n mano f; (of clock) aguja; (writing) letra; (worker) obrero ▷ vt dar, pasar; **to give** or **lend sb a ~** echar una mano a algn, ayudar a algn; **at ~** a mano; **in ~** (time) libre; (job etc) entre manos; **on ~** (person, services) a mano, al alcance; **to ~** (information

etc) a mano; **on the one ~ ...**, **on the other ~ ...** por una parte ... por otra (parte) ...; **hand down** vt pasar, bajar; (tradition) transmitir; (heirloom) dejar en herencia; (US: sentence, verdict) imponer; **hand in** vt entregar; **hand out** vt distribuir; **hand over** vt (deliver) entregar; **handbag** n bolso (SP), cartera (LAM), bolsa (MEX); **hand baggage** n = **hand luggage**; **handbook** n manual m; **handbrake** n freno de mano; **handcuffs** npl esposas fpl; **handful** n puñado

handicap ['hændɪkæp] n minusvalía; (disadvantage) desventaja; (Sport) handicap m ▷ vt estorbar; **to be mentally ~ped** ser mentalmente m/f discapacitado; **to be physically ~ped** ser minusválido/a

handkerchief ['hæŋkətʃɪf] n pañuelo

handle ['hændl] n (of door etc) tirador m; (of cup etc) asa; (of knife etc) mango; (for winding) manivela ▷ vt (touch) tocar; (deal with) encargarse de; (treat: people) manejar; **"~ with care"** "(manéjese) con cuidado"; **to fly off the ~** perder los estribos; **handlebar(s)** n(pl) manillar m

hand: hand luggage n equipaje m de mano; **handmade** adj hecho a mano; **handout** n (money etc) limosna; (leaflet) folleto; **hands-free** adj (phone) manos libres inv; **hands-free kit** n manos libres m inv

handsome ['hænsəm] adj guapo; (building) bello; (fig: profit) considerable

handwriting ['hændraɪtɪŋ] n letra

handy ['hændɪ] adj (close at hand) a la mano; (tool etc) práctico; (skilful) hábil, diestro

hang [hæŋ] (pt, pp hung) vt colgar; (criminal: pt, pp hanged) ahorcar ▷ vi (painting, coat etc) colgar; (hair, drapery) caer; **to get the ~ of sth** (inf) lograr dominar algo; **hang about** or **around** vi haraganear; **hang down** vi colgar, pender; **hang on** vi (wait) esperar; **hang out** vt (washing) tender, colgar ▷ vi (inf: live) vivir; (spend time) pasar el rato; **to hang out of sth** colgar fuera de algo; **hang round** vi = **hang around**; **hang up** vi (Tel) colgar ▷ vt colgar

hanger ['hæŋə*] n percha

hang-gliding ['-glaɪdɪŋ] n vuelo libre

hangover ['hæŋəuvə*] n (after drinking) resaca

hankie, hanky ['hæŋkɪ] n abbr = **handkerchief**

happen ['hæpən] vi suceder, ocurrir; (chance): **he ~ed to hear/see** dió la casualidad de que oyó/vió; **as it ~s** da la casualidad de que

happily ['hæpɪlɪ] adv (luckily)

h

afortunadamente; (*cheerfully*) alegremente

happiness ['hæpɪnɪs] n felicidad f;
(*cheerfulness*) alegría

happy ['hæpɪ] adj feliz; (*cheerful*) alegre; **to
be ~ (with)** estar contento (con); **to be ~ to
do** estar encantado de hacer; **~ birthday!**
¡feliz cumpleaños!

harass ['hærəs] vt acosar, hostigar;
harassment n persecución f

harbour ['hɑ:bə*] (*us* **harbor**) n puerto
▷ vt (*fugitive*) dar abrigo a; (*hope etc*) abrigar

hard [hɑ:d] adj duro; (*difficult*) difícil; (*work*)
arduo; (*person*) severo; (*fact*) innegable ▷ adv
(*work*) mucho, duro; (*think*) profundamente;
to look ~ at clavar los ojos en; **to try ~**
esforzarse; **no ~ feelings!** ¡sin rencor(es)!;
to be ~ of hearing ser duro de oído; **to
be ~ done by** ser tratado injustamente;
hardback n libro en cartoné; **hardboard**
n aglomerado m (*de madera*); **hard disk** n
(*Comput*) disco duro or rígido; **harden** vt
endurecer; (*fig*) curtir ▷ vi endurecerse;
curtirse

hardly ['hɑ:dlɪ] adv apenas; **~ ever** casi
nunca

hard: hardship n privación f; **hard
shoulder** (*BRIT*) n (*Aut*) arcén m; **hard-up**
(*inf*) adj sin un duro (*SP*), pelado, sin un
centavo (*MEX*), pato (*SC*); **hardware** n
ferretería; (*Comput*) hardware m; (*Mil*)
armamento; **hardware shop** (*us* **hardware
store**) ferretería; **hard-working** adj
trabajador(a)

hardy ['hɑ:dɪ] adj fuerte; (*plant*) resistente

hare [hɛə*] n liebre f

harm [hɑ:m] n daño, mal m ▷ vt (*person*)
hacer daño a; (*health, interests*) perjudicar;
(*thing*) dañar; **out of ~'s way** a salvo;
harmful adj dañino; **harmless** adj (*person*)
inofensivo; (*joke etc*) inocente

harmony ['hɑ:mənɪ] n armonía

harness ['hɑ:nɪs] n arreos mpl; (*for child*)
arnés m; (*safety harness*) arneses mpl ▷ vt
(*horse*) enjaezar; (*resources*) aprovechar

harp [hɑ:p] n arpa ▷ vi: **to ~ on (about)**
machacar (con)

harsh [hɑ:ʃ] adj (*cruel*) duro, cruel;
(*severe*) severo; (*sound*) áspero; (*light*)
deslumbrador(a)

harvest ['hɑ:vɪst] n (*harvest time*) siega;
(*of cereals etc*) cosecha; (*of grapes*) vendimia
▷ vt cosechar

has [hæz] vb see **have**

hasn't ['hæznt] = **has not**

hassle ['hæsl] (*inf*) n lata

haste [heɪst] n prisa; **hasten** ['heɪsn]
vt acelerar ▷ vi darse prisa; **hastily** adv
de prisa; precipitadamente; **hasty** adj

apresurado; (*rash*) precipitado

hat [hæt] n sombrero

hatch [hætʃ] n (*Naut: also*: **~way**) escotilla;
(*also*: **service ~**) ventanilla ▷ vi (*bird*) salir
del cascarón ▷ vt incubar; (*plot*) tramar; **5
eggs have ~ed** han salido 5 pollos

hatchback ['hætʃbæk] n (*Aut*) tres or
cinco puertas m

hate [heɪt] vt odiar, aborrecer ▷ n odio;
hatred ['heɪtrɪd] n odio

haul [hɔ:l] vt tirar ▷ n (*of fish*) redada; (*of
stolen goods etc*) botín m

haunt [hɔ:nt] vt (*ghost*) aparecerse en;
(*obsess*) obsesionar ▷ n guarida; **haunted**
adj (*castle etc*) embrujado; (*look*) de angustia

○ **KEYWORD**

have [hæv] (*pt, pp* **had**) *aux vb* **1** (*gen*)
haber; **to have arrived/eaten** haber
llegado/comido; **having finished** or **when
he had finished, he left** cuando hubo
acabado, se fue

2 (*in tag questions*): **you've done it, haven't
you?** lo has hecho, ¿verdad? *or* ¿no?

3 (*in short answers and questions*): **I haven't**
no; **so I have** pues, es verdad; **we haven't
paid – yes we have!** no hemos pagado –
¡sí que hemos pagado!; **I've been there
before, have you?** he estado allí antes,
¿y tú?

▷ *modal aux vb* (*be obliged*): **to have (got) to
do sth** tener que hacer algo; **you haven't to
tell her** no hay que or no debes decírselo

▷ *vt* **1** (*possess*): **he has (got) blue eyes/
dark hair** tiene los ojos azules/el pelo negro

2 (*referring to meals etc*): **to have breakfast/
lunch/dinner** desayunar/comer/cenar;
to have a drink/a cigarette tomar algo/
fumar un cigarrillo

3 (*receive*) recibir; (*obtain*) obtener; **may
I have your address?** ¿puedes darme tu
dirección?; **you can have it for £5** te lo
puedes quedar por £5; **I must have it by
tomorrow** lo necesito para mañana; **to
have a baby** tener un niño *or* bebé

4 (*maintain, allow*): **I won't have it/this
nonsense!** ¡no lo permitiré!/¡no permitiré
estas tonterías!; **we can't have that** no
podemos permitir eso

5 to have sth done hacer *or* mandar hacer
algo; **to have one's hair cut** cortarse el
pelo; **to have sb do sth** hacer que algn
haga algo

6 (*experience, suffer*): **to have a cold/flu**
tener un resfriado/la gripe; **she had her
bag stolen/her arm broken** le robaron
el bolso/se rompió un brazo; **to have an**

operation operarse
7 (+ *noun*): **to have a swim/walk/bath/
rest** nadar/dar un paseo/darse un baño/
descansar; **let's have a look** vamos a ver;
to have a meeting/party celebrar una
reunión/una fiesta; **let me have a try**
déjame intentarlo

haven ['heɪvn] *n* puerto; (*fig*) refugio
haven't ['hævnt] = **have not**
havoc ['hævək] *n* estragos *mpl*
Hawaii [hə'waɪiː] *n* (Islas *fpl*) Hawai *fpl*
hawk [hɔːk] *n* halcón *m*
hawthorn ['hɔːθɔːn] *n* espino
hay [heɪ] *n* heno; **hay fever** *n* fiebre *f* del
heno; **haystack** *n* almiar *m*
hazard ['hæzəd] *n* peligro ▷ *vt* aventurar;
hazardous *adj* peligroso; **hazard warning
lights** *npl* (*Aut*) señales *fpl* de emergencia
haze [heɪz] *n* neblina
hazel ['heɪzl] *n* (*tree*) avellano ▷ *adj* (*eyes*)
color *m* de avellano; **hazelnut** *n* avellana
hazy ['heɪzɪ] *adj* brumoso; (*idea*) vago
he [hiː] *pron* él; **~ who ...** él que ..., quien ...
head [hɛd] *n* cabeza; (*leader*) jefe/a *m/f*; (*of
school*) director(a) *m/f* ▷ *vt* (*list*) encabezar;
(*group*) capitanear; (*company*) dirigir; **~s
(or tails)** cara (o cruz); **~ first** de cabeza;
~ over heels (*in love*) perdidamente; **to ~
the ball** cabecear (la pelota); **head for** *vt
fus* dirigirse a; (*disaster*) ir camino de; **head
off** *vt* (*threat, danger*) evitar; **headache**
n dolor *m* de cabeza; **heading** *n* título;
headlamp (*BRIT*) *n* = **headlight**; **headlight**
n faro; **headline** *n* titular *m*; **head office** *n*
oficina central, central *f*; **headphones** *npl*
auriculares *mpl*; **headquarters** *npl* sede *f*
central; (*Mil*) cuartel *m* general; **headroom**
n (*in car*) altura interior; (*under bridge*)
(límite *m* de) altura; **headscarf** *n* pañuelo;
headset *n* cascos *mpl*; **headteacher** *n*
director (directora) *m*; **head waiter** *n* maître
m
heal [hiːl] *vt* curar ▷ *vi* cicatrizarse
health [hɛlθ] *n* salud *f*; **health care** *n*
asistencia sanitaria; **health centre** (*BRIT*) *n*
ambulatorio, centro médico; **health food**
n alimentos *mpl* orgánicos; **Health Service**
(*BRIT*) *n* el servicio de salud pública, ≈ el
Insalud (*SP*); **healthy** *adj* sano, saludable
heap [hiːp] *n* montón *m* ▷ *vt*: **to ~ (up)**
amontonar; **to ~ sth with** llenar algo hasta
arriba de; **~s of** un montón de
hear [hɪə*] (*pt, pp* **~d**) *vt* (*also Law*) oír;
(*news*) saber ▷ *vi* oír; **to ~ about** oír hablar
de; **to ~ from sb** tener noticias de algn
heard [hɜːd] *pt, pp of* **hear**
hearing ['hɪərɪŋ] *n* (*sense*) oído; (*Law*) vista;

hearing aid *n* audífono
hearse [hɜːs] *n* coche *m* fúnebre
heart [hɑːt] *n* corazón *m*; (*fig*) valor
m; (*of lettuce*) cogollo; **hearts** *npl*
(*Cards*) corazones *mpl*; **to lose/take ~**
descorazonarse/cobrar ánimo; **at ~** en
el fondo; **by ~** (*learn, know*) de memoria;
heart attack *n* infarto (de miocardio);
heartbeat *n* latido (del corazón);
heartbroken *adj*: **she was heartbroken
about it** esto le partió el corazón;
heartburn *n* acedía; **heart disease** *n*
enfermedad *f* cardíaca
hearth [hɑːθ] *n* (*fireplace*) chimenea
heartless ['hɑːtlɪs] *adj* despiadado
hearty ['hɑːtɪ] *adj* (*person*) campechano;
(*laugh*) sano; (*dislike, support*) absoluto
heat [hiːt] *n* calor *m*; (*Sport: also:*
qualifying ~) prueba eliminatoria ▷ *vt*
calentar; **heat up** *vi* calentarse ▷ *vt*
calentar; **heated** *adj* caliente; (*fig*)
acalorado; **heater** *n* estufa; (*in car*)
calefacción *f*
heather ['hɛðə*] *n* brezo
heating ['hiːtɪŋ] *n* calefacción *f*
heatwave ['hiːtweɪv] *n* ola de calor
heaven ['hɛvn] *n* cielo; (*fig*) una maravilla;
heavenly *adj* celestial; (*fig*) maravilloso
heavily ['hɛvɪlɪ] *adv* pesadamente;
(*drink, smoke*) con exceso; (*sleep, sigh*)
profundamente; (*depend*) mucho
heavy ['hɛvɪ] *adj* pesado; (*work, blow*)
duro; (*sea, rain, meal*) fuerte; (*drinker, smoker*)
grande; (*responsibility*) grave; (*schedule*)
ocupado; (*weather*) bochornoso
Hebrew ['hiːbruː] *adj, n* (*Ling*) hebreo
hectare ['hɛktɑː*] *n* (*BRIT*) hectárea
hectic ['hɛktɪk] *adj* agitado
he'd [hiːd] = **he would; he had**
hedge [hɛdʒ] *n* seto ▷ *vi* contestar con
evasivas; **to ~ one's bets** (*fig*) cubrirse
hedgehog ['hɛdʒhɔg] *n* erizo
heed [hiːd] *vt* (*also:* **take ~**: *pay attention to*)
hacer caso de
heel [hiːl] *n* talón *m*; (*of shoe*) tacón *m* ▷ *vt*
(*shoe*) poner tacón a
hefty ['hɛftɪ] *adj* (*person*) fornido; (*parcel,
profit*) gordo
height [haɪt] *n* (*of person*) estatura; (*of
building*) altura; (*high ground*) cerro; (*altitude*)
altitud *f*; (*fig: of season*): **at the ~ of summer**
en los días más calurosos del verano; (*: of
power etc*) cúspide *f*; (*: of stupidity etc*) colmo;
heighten *vt* elevar; (*fig*) aumentar
heir [ɛə*] *n* heredero; **heiress** *n* heredera
held [hɛld] *pt, pp of* **hold**
helicopter ['hɛlɪkɔptə*] *n* helicóptero
hell [hɛl] *n* infierno; **~!** (*inf*) ¡demonios!

h

he'll [hiːl] = **he will; he shall**

hello [hə'ləʊ] excl ¡hola!; (to attract attention) ¡oiga!; (surprise) ¡caramba!

helmet ['hɛlmɪt] n casco

help [hɛlp] n ayuda; (cleaner etc) criada, asistenta ▷ vt ayudar; **~!** ¡socorro!; **~ yourself** sírvete; **he can't ~ it** no es culpa suya; **help out** vi ayudar, echar una mano ▷ vt: **to help sb out** ayudar a algn, echar una mano a algn; **helper** n ayudante mf; **helpful** adj útil; (person) servicial; (advice) útil; **helping** n ración f; **helpless** adj (incapable) incapaz; (defenceless) indefenso; **helpline** n teléfono de asistencia al público

hem [hɛm] n dobladillo ▷ vt poner or coser el dobladillo de

hemisphere ['hɛmɪsfɪə*] n hemisferio

hemorrhage ['hɛmərɪdʒ] (US) n = **haemorrhage**

hemorrhoids ['hɛmərɔɪdz] (US) npl = **haemorrhoids**

hen [hɛn] n gallina; (female bird) hembra

hence [hɛns] adv (therefore) por lo tanto; **2 years ~** de aquí a 2 años

hen night, hen party n (inf) despedida de soltera

hepatitis [hɛpə'taɪtɪs] n hepatitis f

her [həː*] pron (direct) la; (indirect) le; (stressed, after prep) ella ▷ adj su; see also **me; my**

herb [həːb] n hierba; **herbal** adj de hierbas; **herbal tea** n infusión f de hierbas

herd [həːd] n rebaño

here [hɪə*] adv aquí; (at this point) en este punto; **~!** (present) ¡presente!; **~ is/are** aquí está/están; **~ she is** aquí está

hereditary [hɪ'rɛdɪtrɪ] adj hereditario

heritage ['hɛrɪtɪdʒ] n patrimonio

hernia ['həːnɪə] n hernia

hero ['hɪərəʊ] (pl **~es**) n héroe m; (in book, film) protagonista m; **heroic** [hɪ'rəʊɪk] adj heroico

heroin ['hɛrəʊɪn] n heroína

heroine ['hɛrəʊɪn] n heroína; (in book, film) protagonista

heron ['hɛrən] n garza

herring ['hɛrɪŋ] n arenque m

hers [həːz] pron (el) suyo/(la) suya) etc; see also **mine¹**

herself [həː'sɛlf] pron (reflexive) se; (emphatic) ella misma; (after prep) sí (misma); see also **oneself**

he's [hiːz] = **he is; he has**

hesitant ['hɛzɪtənt] adj vacilante

hesitate ['hɛzɪteɪt] vi vacilar; (in speech) titubear; (be unwilling) resistirse a; **hesitation** ['-teɪʃən] n indecisión f; titubeo; dudas fpl

heterosexual [hɛtərəʊ'sɛksjʊəl] adj heterosexual

hexagon ['hɛksəgən] n hexágono

hey [heɪ] excl ¡oye!, ¡oiga!

heyday ['heɪdeɪ] n: **the ~ of** el apogeo de

HGV n abbr (= heavy goods vehicle) vehículo pesado

hi [haɪ] excl ¡hola!; (to attract attention) ¡oiga!

hibernate ['haɪbəneɪt] vi invernar

hiccough ['hɪkʌp] = **hiccup**

hiccup ['hɪkʌp] vi hipar

hid [hɪd] pt of **hide**

hidden ['hɪdn] pp of **hide** ▷ adj: **~ agenda** plan m encubierto

hide [haɪd] (pt **hid**, pp **hidden**) n (skin) piel f ▷ vt esconder, ocultar ▷ vi: **to ~ (from sb)** esconderse or ocultarse (de algn)

hideous ['hɪdɪəs] adj horrible

hiding ['haɪdɪŋ] n (beating) paliza; **to be in ~** (concealed) estar escondido

hi-fi ['haɪfaɪ] n estéreo, hifi m ▷ adj de alta fidelidad

high [haɪ] adj alto; (speed, number) grande; (price) elevado; (wind) fuerte; (voice) agudo ▷ adv alto, a gran altura; **it is 20 m ~** tiene 20 m de altura; **~ in the air** en las alturas; **highchair** n silla alta; **high-class** adj (hotel) de lujo; (person) distinguido, de categoría; (food) de alta categoría; **higher education** n educación f or enseñanza superior; **high heels** npl (heels) tacones mpl altos; (shoes) zapatos mpl de tacón; **high jump** n (Sport) salto de altura; **highlands** ['haɪləndz] npl tierras fpl altas; **the Highlands** (in Scotland) las Tierras Altas de Escocia; **highlight** n (fig: of event) punto culminante ▷ vt subrayar; **highlights** npl (in hair) reflejos mpl; **highlighter** n rotulador; **highly** adv (paid) muy bien; (critical, confidential) sumamente; (a lot): **to speak/think highly of** hablar muy bien de/tener en mucho a; **highness** n altura; **Her/His Highness** Su Alteza; **high-rise** n (also: **high-rise block, high-rise building**) torre f de pisos; **high school** n ≈ Instituto Nacional de Bachillerato (SP); **high season** (BRIT) n temporada alta; **high street** (BRIT) n calle f mayor; **high-tech** (inf) adj al-tec (inf), de alta tecnología; **highway** n carretera; (US) carretera nacional; autopista; **Highway Code** (BRIT) n código de la circulación

hijack ['haɪdʒæk] vt secuestrar; **hijacker** n secuestrador(a) m/f

hike [haɪk] vi (go walking) ir de excursión (a pie) ▷ n caminata; **hiker** n excursionista mf; **hiking** n senderismo

hilarious [hɪ'lɛərɪəs] *adj* divertidísimo
hill [hɪl] *n* colina; (*high*) montaña; (*slope*) cuesta; **hillside** *n* ladera; **hill walking** *n* senderismo (de montaña); **hilly** *adj* montañoso
him [hɪm] *pron* (*direct*) le, lo; (*indirect*) le; (*stressed, after prep*) él; *see also* **me**; **himself** *pron* (*reflexive*) se; (*emphatic*) él mismo; (*after prep*) sí (mismo); *see also* **oneself**
hind [haɪnd] *adj* posterior
hinder ['hɪndə*] *vt* estorbar, impedir
hindsight ['haɪndsaɪt] *n*: **with ~** en retrospectiva
Hindu ['hɪnduː] *n* hindú *mf*; **Hinduism** *n* (*Rel*) hinduismo
hinge [hɪndʒ] *n* bisagra, gozne *m* ▷ *vi* (*fig*): **to ~ on** depender de
hint [hɪnt] *n* indirecta; (*advice*) consejo; (*sign*) dejo ▷ *vt*: **to ~ that** insinuar que ▷ *vi*: **to ~ at** hacer alusión a
hip [hɪp] *n* cadera
hippie ['hɪpɪ] *n* hippie *m/f*, jipi *m/f*
hippo ['hɪpəu] (*pl* **~s**) *n* hipopótamo
hippopotamus [hɪpə'pɔtəməs] (*pl* **~es** *or* **hippopotami**) *n* hipopótamo
hippy ['hɪpɪ] *n* = **hippie**
hire ['haɪə*] *vt* (*BRIT: car, equipment*) alquilar; (*worker*) contratar ▷ *n* alquiler *m*; **for ~** se alquila; (*taxi*) libre; **hire(d) car** (*BRIT*) *n* coche *m* de alquiler; **hire purchase** (*BRIT*) *n* compra a plazos
his [hɪz] *pron* (el) suyo ((la) suya) *etc* ▷ *adj* su; *see also* **mine**[1]; **my**
Hispanic [hɪs'pænɪk] *adj* hispánico
hiss [hɪs] *vi* silbar
historian [hɪ'stɔːrɪən] *n* historiador(a) *m/f*
historic(al) [hɪ'stɔrɪk(l)] *adj* histórico
history ['hɪstərɪ] *n* historia
hit [hɪt] (*pt, pp* **~**) *vt* (*strike*) golpear, pegar; (*reach: target*) alcanzar; (*collide with: car*) chocar contra; (*fig: affect*) afectar ▷ *n* golpe *m*; (*success*) éxito; (*on website*) visita; (*in web search*) correspondencia; **to ~ it off with sb** llevarse bien con algn; **hit back** *vi* defenderse; (*fig*) devolver golpe por golpe
hitch [hɪtʃ] *vt* (*fasten*) atar, amarrar; (*also: ~ up*) remangar ▷ *n* (*difficulty*) dificultad *f*; **to ~ a lift** hacer autostop
hitch-hike ['hɪtʃhaɪk] *vi* hacer autostop; **hitch-hiker** *n* autostopista *m/f*; **hitch-hiking** *n* autostop *m*
hi-tech [haɪ'tɛk] *adj* de alta tecnología
hitman ['hɪtmæn] (*irreg*) *n* asesino a sueldo
HIV *n abbr* (= human immunodeficiency virus) VIH *m*; **~-negative/positive** VIH negativo/positivo

hive [haɪv] *n* colmena
hoard [hɔːd] *n* (*treasure*) tesoro; (*stockpile*) provisión *f* ▷ *vt* acumular; (*goods in short supply*) acaparar
hoarse [hɔːs] *adj* ronco
hoax [həuks] *n* trampa
hob [hɔb] *n* quemador *m*
hobble ['hɔbl] *vi* cojear
hobby ['hɔbɪ] *n* pasatiempo, afición *f*
hobo ['həubəu] (*US*) *n* vagabundo
hockey ['hɔkɪ] *n* hockey *m*; **hockey stick** *n* palo *m* de hockey
hog [hɔg] *n* cerdo, puerco ▷ *vt* (*fig*) acaparar; **to go the whole ~** poner toda la carne en el asador
Hogmanay [hɔgmə'neɪ] *n* ver abajo

> ● **HOGMANAY**
> ●
> ● La Nochevieja o "New Year's Eve" se
> ● conoce como "Hogmanay" en Escocia,
> ● donde se festeje de forma especial. La
> ● familia y los amigos se suelen juntar
> ● para oír las campanadas del reloj y luego
> ● se hace el "first-footing", costumbre que
> ● consiste en visitar a los amigos y vecinos
> ● llevando algo de beber (generalmente
> ● whisky) y un trozo de carbón que se
> ● supone que traerá buena suerte para el
> ● año entrante.

hoist [hɔɪst] *n* (*crane*) grúa ▷ *vt* levantar, alzar; (*flag, sail*) izar
hold [həuld] (*pt, pp* **held**) *vt* sostener; (*contain*) contener; (*have: power, qualification*) tener; (*keep back*) retener; (*believe*) sostener; (*consider*) considerar; (*keep in position*): **to ~ one's head up** mantener la cabeza alta; (*meeting*) celebrar ▷ *vi* (*withstand pressure*) resistir; (*be valid*) valer ▷ *n* (*grasp*) asimiento; (*fig*) dominio; **~ the line!** (*Tel*) ¡no cuelgue!; **to ~ one's own** (*fig*) defenderse; **to catch** *or* **get (a) ~ of** agarrarse *or* asirse de; **hold back** *vt* retener; (*secret*) ocultar; **hold on** *vi* agarrarse bien; (*wait*) esperar; **hold on!** (*Tel*) ¡(espere) un momento!; **hold out** *vt* ofrecer ▷ *vi* (*resist*) resistir; **hold up** *vt* (*raise*) levantar; (*support*) apoyar; (*delay*) retrasar; (*rob*) asaltar; **holdall** (*BRIT*) *n* bolsa; **holder** *n* (*container*) receptáculo; (*of ticket, record*) poseedor(a) *m/f*; (*of office, title etc*) titular *mf*
hole [həul] *n* agujero
holiday ['hɔlədɪ] *n* vacaciones *fpl*; (*public holiday*) (día *m* de) fiesta, día *m* feriado; **on ~** de vacaciones; **holiday camp** *n* (*BRIT: also:* **holiday centre**) centro de vacaciones; **holiday job** *n* (*BRIT*) trabajillo extra para las

vacaciones; **holiday-maker** (*BRIT*) n turista
mf; **holiday resort** n centro turístico
Holland ['hɔlənd] n Holanda
hollow ['hɔləʊ] adj hueco; (*claim*) vacío;
(*eyes*) hundido; (*sound*) sordo ▷ n hueco; (*in
ground*) hoyo ▷ vt: **to ~ out** excavar
holly ['hɔlɪ] n acebo
Hollywood ['hɔlɪwʊd] n Hollywood *m*
holocaust ['hɔləkɔːst] n holocausto
holy ['həʊlɪ] adj santo, sagrado; (*water*)
bendito
home [həʊm] n casa; (*country*) patria;
(*institution*) asilo ▷ cpd (*domestic*) casero, de
casa; (*Econ, Pol*) nacional ▷ adv (*direction*)
a casa; (*right in: nail etc*) a fondo; **at ~** en
casa; (*in country*) en el país; (*fig*) como pez
en el agua; **to go/come ~** ir/volver a casa;
make yourself at ~ ¡estás en tu casa!; **home
address** n domicilio; **homeland** n tierra
natal; **homeless** adj sin hogar, sin casa;
homely adj (*simple*) sencillo; **home-made**
adj casero; **home match** n partido en
casa; **Home Office** (*BRIT*) n Ministerio del
Interior; **home owner** n propietario/a
m/f de una casa; **home page** n página de
inicio; **Home Secretary** (*BRIT*) n Ministro
del Interior; **homesick** adj: **to be homesick**
tener morriña, sentir nostalgia; **home
town** n ciudad *f* natal; **homework** n
deberes *mpl*
homicide ['hɔmɪsaɪd] (*US*) n homicidio
homoeopathic [həʊmɪə'pæθɪk] (*US
homeopathic*) adj homeopático
homoeopathy [həʊmɪ'ɔpəθɪ] (*US
homeopathy*) n homeopatía
homosexual [hɔməʊ'sɛksjuəl] adj, n
homosexual *mf*
honest ['ɔnɪst] adj honrado;
(*sincere*) franco, sincero; **honestly** adv
honradamente; francamente; **honesty** n
honradez *f*
honey ['hʌnɪ] n miel *f*; **honeymoon** n
luna de miel; **honeysuckle** n madreselva
Hong Kong ['hɔŋ'kɔŋ] n Hong-Kong *m*
honorary ['ɔnərərɪ] adj (*member, president*)
de honor; (*title*) honorífico; **~ degree**
doctorado honoris causa
honour ['ɔnə*] (*US* **honor**) vt honrar;
(*commitment, promise*) cumplir con ▷ n
honor *m*, honra; **to graduate with ~s**
≈ licenciarse con matrícula (de honor);
honourable (*US* **honorable**) adj honorable;
honours degree n (*Scol*) título de licenciado
con calificación alta
hood [hʊd] n capucha; (*BRIT Aut*) capota;
(*US Aut*) capó *m*; (*of cooker*) campana de
humos; **hoodie** n (*top*) jersey *m* con
capucha

hoof [huːf] (*pl* **hooves**) n pezuña
hook [hʊk] n gancho; (*on dress*) corchete
m, broche *m*; (*for fishing*) anzuelo ▷ vt
enganchar; (*fish*) pescar
hooligan ['huːlɪɡən] n gamberro
hoop [huːp] n aro
hooray [huː'reɪ] excl = **hurray**
hoot [huːt] (*BRIT*) vi (*Aut*) tocar el pito,
pitar; (*siren*) (hacer) sonar; (*owl*) ulular
Hoover® ['huːvə*] (*BRIT*) n aspiradora
▷ vt: **to hoover** pasar la aspiradora por
hooves [huːvz] *npl of* **hoof**
hop [hɔp] vi saltar, brincar; (*on one foot*)
saltar con un pie
hope [həʊp] vt, vi esperar ▷ n esperanza;
I ~ so/not espero que sí/no; **hopeful**
adj (*person*) optimista; (*situation*)
prometedor(a); **hopefully** adv con
esperanza; (*one hopes*): **hopefully he will
recover** esperamos que se recupere;
hopeless adj desesperado; (*person*): **to be
hopeless** ser un desastre
hops [hɔps] *npl* lúpulo
horizon [hə'raɪzn] n horizonte *m*;
horizontal [hɔrɪ'zɔntl] adj horizontal
hormone ['hɔːməʊn] n hormona
horn [hɔːn] n cuerno; (*Mus: also:* **French ~**)
trompa; (*Aut*) pito, claxon *m*
horoscope ['hɔrəskəʊp] n horóscopo
horrendous [hɔ'rɛndəs] adj horrendo
horrible ['hɔrɪbl] adj horrible
horrid ['hɔrɪd] adj horrible, horroroso
horrific [hɔ'rɪfɪk] adj (*accident*) horroroso;
(*film*) horripilante
horrifying ['hɔrɪfaɪɪŋ] adj horroroso
horror ['hɔrə*] n horror *m*; **horror film** n
película de horror
hors d'œuvre [ɔː'dəːvrə] n entremeses
mpl
horse [hɔːs] n caballo; **horseback** n: **on
horseback** a caballo; **horse chestnut** n
(*tree*) castaño de Indias; (*nut*) castaña de
Indias; **horsepower** n caballo (de fuerza);
horse-racing n carreras *fpl* de caballos;
horseradish n rábano picante; **horse
riding** n (*BRIT*) equitación *f*
hose [həʊz] n manguera; **hosepipe** n
manguera
hospital ['hɔspɪtl] n hospital *m*
hospitality [hɔspɪ'tælɪtɪ] n hospitalidad *f*
host [həʊst] n anfitrión *m*; (*TV, Radio*)
presentador *m*; (*Rel*) hostia; (*large number*): **a
~ of** multitud de
hostage ['hɔstɪdʒ] n rehén *m*
hostel ['hɔstl] n hostal *m*; (**youth**) **~**
albergue *m* juvenil
hostess ['həʊstɪs] n anfitriona; (*BRIT: air
hostess*) azafata; (*TV, Radio*) presentadora

hostile ['hɒstaɪl] *adj* hostil
hostility [hɒ'stɪlɪtɪ] *n* hostilidad*f*
hot [hɒt] *adj* caliente; (*weather*) caluroso, de calor; (*as opposed to warm*) muy caliente; (*spicy*) picante; **to be ~** (*person*) tener calor; (*object*) estar caliente; (*weather*) hacer calor; **hot dog** *n* perro caliente
hotel [hau'tel] *n* hotel *m*
hot-water bottle [hɒt'wɔːtə*-] *n* bolsa de agua caliente
hound [haund] *vt* acosar ▷ *n* perro (de caza)
hour ['auə*] *n* hora; **hourly** *adj* (de) cada hora
house [*n* haus, *pl* 'hauzɪz, *vb* hauz] *n* (*gen*, *firm*) casa; (*Pol*) cámara; (*Theatre*) sala ▷ *vt* (*person*) alojar; (*collection*) albergar; **on the ~** (*fig*) la casa invita; **household** *n* familia; (*home*) casa; **householder** *n* propietario/a; (*head of house*) cabeza de familia; **housekeeper** *n* ama de llaves; **housekeeping** *n* (*work*) trabajos *mpl* domésticos; **housewife** (*irreg*) *n* ama de casa; **house wine** *n* vino *m* de la casa; **housework** *n* faenas *fpl* (de la casa)
housing ['hauzɪŋ] *n* (*act*) alojamiento; (*houses*) viviendas *fpl*; **housing development, housing estate** (BRIT) *n* urbanización*f*
hover ['hɒvə*] *vi* flotar (en el aire); **hovercraft** *n* aerodeslizador *m*
how [hau] *adv* (*in what way*) cómo; **~ are you?** ¿cómo estás?; **~ much milk/many people?** ¿cuánta leche/gente?; **~ much does it cost?** ¿cuánto cuesta?; **~ long have you been here?** ¿cuánto hace que estás aquí?; **~ old are you?** ¿cuántos años tienes?; **~ tall is he?** ¿cómo es de alto?; **~ is school?** ¿cómo (te) va (en) la escuela?; **~ was the film?** ¿qué tal la película?; **~ lovely/awful!** ¡qué bonito/horror!
however [hau'evə*] *adv*: **~ I do it** lo haga como lo haga; **~ cold it is** por mucho frío que haga; **~ fast he runs** por muy rápido que corra; **~ did you do it?** ¿cómo lo hiciste? ▷ *conj* sin embargo, no obstante
howl [haul] *n* aullido ▷ *vi* aullar; (*person*) dar alaridos; (*wind*) ulular
H.P. *n abbr* = **hire purchase**
h.p. *abbr* = **horsepower**
HQ *n abbr* = **headquarters**
hr(s) *abbr* (= *hour(s)*) h
HTML *n abbr* (= *hypertext markup language*) lenguaje *m* de hipertexto
hubcap ['hʌbkæp] *n* tapacubos *m inv*
huddle ['hʌdl] *vi*: **to ~ together** acurrucarse
huff [hʌf] *n*: **in a ~** enojado

hug [hʌg] *vt* abrazar; (*thing*) apretar con los brazos
huge [hjuːdʒ] *adj* enorme
hull [hʌl] *n* (*of ship*) casco
hum [hʌm] *vt* tararear, canturrear ▷ *vi* tararear, canturrear; (*insect*) zumbar
human ['hjuːmən] *adj*, *n* humano
humane [hjuː'meɪn] *adj* humano, humanitario
humanitarian [hjuːmænɪ'tɛərɪən] *adj* humanitario
humanity [hjuː'mænɪtɪ] *n* humanidad*f*
human rights *npl* derechos *mpl* humanos
humble ['hʌmbl] *adj* humilde
humid ['hjuːmɪd] *adj* húmedo; **humidity** [-'mɪdɪtɪ] *n* humedad*f*
humiliate [hjuː'mɪlɪeɪt] *vt* humillar
humiliating [hjuː'mɪlɪeɪtɪŋ] *adj* humillante, vergonzoso
humiliation [hjuːmɪlɪ'eɪʃən] *n* humillación*f*
hummus ['huməs] *n* paté de garbanzos
humorous ['hjuːmərəs] *adj* gracioso, divertido
humour ['hjuːmə*] (*us* **humor**) *n* humorismo, sentido del humor; (*mood*) humor *m* ▷ *vt* (*person*) complacer
hump [hʌmp] *n* (*in ground*) montículo; (*camel's*) giba
hunch [hʌntʃ] *n* (*premonition*) presentimiento
hundred ['hʌndrəd] *num* ciento; (*before n*) cien; **~s of** centenares de; **hundredth** [-ɪdθ] *adj* centésimo
hung [hʌŋ] *pt*, *pp of* **hang**
Hungarian [hʌŋ'gɛərɪən] *adj*, *n* húngaro/a *m/f*
Hungary ['hʌŋgərɪ] *n* Hungría
hunger ['hʌŋgə*] *n* hambre *f* ▷ *vi*: **to ~ for** (*fig*) tener hambre de, anhelar
hungry ['hʌŋgrɪ] *adj*: **~ (for)** hambriento (de); **to be ~** tener hambre
hunt [hʌnt] *vt* (*seek*) buscar; (*Sport*) cazar ▷ *vi* (*search*): **to ~ (for)** buscar; (*Sport*) cazar ▷ *n* búsqueda; caza, cacería; **hunter** *n* cazador(a) *m/f*; **hunting** *n* caza
hurdle ['həːdl] *n* (*Sport*) valla; (*fig*) obstáculo
hurl [həːl] *vt* lanzar, arrojar
hurrah [hu'rɑː] *excl* = **hurray**
hurray [hu'reɪ] *excl* ¡viva!
hurricane ['hʌrɪkən] *n* huracán *m*
hurry ['hʌrɪ] *n* prisa ▷ *vt* (*also*: **~ up**: *person*) dar prisa a; (: *work*) apresurar, hacer de prisa; **to be in a ~** tener prisa; **hurry up** *vi* darse prisa, apurarse (LAM)
hurt [həːt] (*pt*, *pp* **~**) *vt* hacer daño a ▷ *vi* doler ▷ *adj* lastimado

husband ['hʌzbənd] n marido
hush [hʌʃ] n silencio ▷ vt hacer callar; **~!**
¡chitón!, ¡cállate!
husky ['hʌskɪ] adj ronco ▷ n perro
esquimal
hut [hʌt] n cabaña; (shed) cobertizo
hyacinth ['haɪəsɪnθ] n jacinto
hydrangea [haɪ'dreɪnʒə] n hortensia
hydrofoil ['haɪdrəfɔɪl] n aerodeslizador m
hydrogen ['haɪdrədʒən] n hidrógeno
hygiene ['haɪdʒi:n] n higiene f; **hygienic**
[-'dʒi:nɪk] adj higiénico
hymn [hɪm] n himno
hype [haɪp] (inf) n bombardeo publicitario
hyphen ['haɪfn] n guión m
hypnotize ['hɪpnətaɪz] vt hipnotizar
hypocrite ['hɪpəkrɪt] n hipócrita mf
hypocritical [hɪpə'krɪtɪkl] adj hipócrita
hypothesis [haɪ'pɔθɪsɪs] (pl **hypotheses**)
n hipótesis f inv
hysterical [hɪ'stɛrɪkl] adj histérico;
(funny) para morirse de risa
hysterics [hɪ'stɛrɪks] npl histeria; **to be in
~** (fig) morirse de risa

I

I [aɪ] pron yo
ice [aɪs] n hielo; (ice cream) helado ▷ vt
(cake) alcorzar ▷ vi (also: **~ over**, **~ up**)
helarse; **iceberg** n iceberg m; **ice cream**
n helado; **ice cube** n cubito de hielo; **ice
hockey** n hockey m sobre hielo
Iceland ['aɪslənd] n Islandia; **Icelander**
n islandés/esa m/f; **Icelandic** [aɪs'lændɪk]
adj islandés/esa ▷ n (Ling) islandés m
ice: **ice lolly** (BRIT) n polo; **ice rink** n pista
de hielo; **ice skating** n patinaje m sobre
hielo
icing ['aɪsɪŋ] n (Culin) alcorza; **icing sugar**
(BRIT) n azúcar m glas(eado)
icon ['aɪkɔn] n icono
ICT (BRIT: Scol) n abbr (= information and
communications technology) informática
icy ['aɪsɪ] adj helado
I'd [aɪd] = **I would**; **I had**
ID card n (identity card) DNI m
idea [aɪ'dɪə] n idea
ideal [aɪ'dɪəl] n ideal m ▷ adj ideal; **ideally**
[-dɪəlɪ] adv idealmente; **they're ideally
suited** hacen una pareja ideal
identical [aɪ'dɛntɪkl] adj idéntico
identification [aɪdɛntɪfɪ'keɪʃən] n
identificación f; **(means of) ~** documentos
mpl personales
identify [aɪ'dɛntɪfaɪ] vt identificar
identity [aɪ'dɛntɪtɪ] n identidad f;
identity card n carnet m de identidad;
identity theft n robo de identidad
ideology [aɪdɪ'ɔlədʒɪ] n ideología
idiom ['ɪdɪəm] n modismo; (style of
speaking) lenguaje m

  Be careful not to translate **idiom** by the
  Spanish word idioma.

idiot ['ɪdɪət] n idiota mf
idle ['aɪdl] adj (inactive) ocioso; (lazy)
holgazán/ana; (unemployed) parado,
desocupado; (machinery etc) parado; (talk etc)

frívolo ▷ vi (*machine*) marchar en vacío
idol ['aɪdl] n ídolo
idyllic [ɪ'dɪlɪk] adj idílico
i.e. abbr (= *that is*) esto es
if [ɪf] conj si; ~ **necessary** si fuera
necesario, si hiciese falta; ~ **I were you** yo
en tu lugar; ~ **so/not** de ser así/si no; ~ **only
I could!** ¡ojalá pudiera!; *see also* **as; even**
ignite [ɪg'naɪt] vt (*set fire to*) encender ▷ vi
encenderse
ignition [ɪg'nɪʃən] n (Aut: *process*) ignición
f; (: *mechanism*) encendido; **to switch on/off
the** ~ arrancar/apagar el motor
ignorance ['ɪgnərəns] n ignorancia
ignorant ['ɪgnərənt] adj ignorante; **to be
~ of** ignorar
ignore [ɪg'nɔː*] vt (*person, advice*) no hacer
caso de; (*fact*) pasar por alto
I'll [aɪl] = **I will; I shall**
ill [ɪl] adj enfermo, malo ▷ n mal m ▷ adv
mal; **to be taken ~** ponerse enfermo
illegal [ɪ'liːgl] adj ilegal
illegible [ɪ'lɛdʒɪbl] adj ilegible
illegitimate [ɪlɪ'dʒɪtɪmət] adj ilegítimo
ill health n mala salud f; **to be in ~** estar
mal de salud
illiterate [ɪ'lɪtərət] adj analfabeto
illness ['ɪlnɪs] n enfermedad f
illuminate [ɪ'luːmɪneɪt] vt (*room, street*)
iluminar, alumbrar
illusion [ɪ'luːʒən] n ilusión f; (*trick*) truco
illustrate ['ɪləstreɪt] vt ilustrar
illustration [ɪlə'streɪʃən] n (*act of
illustrating*) ilustración f; (*example*) ejemplo,
ilustración f; (*in book*) lámina
I'm [aɪm] = **I am**
image ['ɪmɪdʒ] n imagen f
imaginary [ɪ'mædʒɪnərɪ] adj imaginario
imagination [ɪmædʒɪ'neɪʃən] n
imaginación f; (*inventiveness*) inventiva
imaginative [ɪ'mædʒɪnətɪv] adj
imaginativo
imagine [ɪ'mædʒɪn] vt imaginarse
imbalance [ɪm'bæləns] n desequilibrio
imitate ['ɪmɪteɪt] vt imitar; **imitation**
[ɪmɪ'teɪʃən] n imitación f; (*copy*) copia
immaculate [ɪ'mækjulət] adj
inmaculado
immature [ɪmə'tjuə*] adj (*person*)
inmaduro
immediate [ɪ'miːdɪət] adj inmediato;
(*pressing*) urgente, apremiante;
(*nearest: family*) próximo; (: *neighbourhood*)
inmediato; **immediately** adv (*at once*)
en seguida; (*directly*) inmediatamente;
immediately next to muy junto a
immense [ɪ'mɛns] adj inmenso, enorme;
(*importance*) enorme; **immensely** adv

enormemente
immerse [ɪ'mɜːs] vt (*submerge*) sumergir;
to be ~d in (*fig*) estar absorto en
immigrant ['ɪmɪgrənt] n inmigrante mf;
immigration [ɪmɪ'greɪʃən] n inmigración
f
imminent ['ɪmɪnənt] adj inminente
immoral [ɪ'mɔrl] adj inmoral
immortal [ɪ'mɔːtl] adj inmortal
immune [ɪ'mjuːn] adj: ~ **(to)** inmune (a);
immune system n sistema m inmunitario
immunize ['ɪmjunaɪz] vt inmunizar
impact ['ɪmpækt] n impacto
impair [ɪm'pɛə*] vt perjudicar
impartial [ɪm'pɑːʃl] adj imparcial
impatience [ɪm'peɪʃəns] n impaciencia
impatient [ɪm'peɪʃənt] adj impaciente;
to get or **grow ~** impacientarse
impeccable [ɪm'pɛkəbl] adj impecable
impending [ɪm'pɛndɪŋ] adj inminente
imperative [ɪm'pɛrətɪv] adj (*tone*)
imperioso; (*need*) imprescindible
imperfect [ɪm'pɜːfɪkt] adj (*goods etc*)
defectuoso ▷ n (Ling: *also:* ~ **tense**)
imperfecto
imperial [ɪm'pɪərɪəl] adj imperial
impersonal [ɪm'pɜːsənl] adj impersonal
impersonate [ɪm'pɜːsəneɪt] vt hacerse
pasar por; (*Theatre*) imitar
impetus ['ɪmpətəs] n ímpetu m; (*fig*)
impulso
implant [ɪm'plɑːnt] vt (*Med*) injertar,
implantar; (*fig: idea, principle*) inculcar
implement [n 'ɪmplɪmənt, vb 'ɪmplɪmɛnt]
n herramienta; (*for cooking*) utensilio ▷ vt
(*regulation*) hacer efectivo; (*plan*) realizar
implicate ['ɪmplɪkeɪt] vt (*compromise*)
comprometer; **to ~ sb in sth** comprometer
a algn en algo
implication [ɪmplɪ'keɪʃən] n
consecuencia; **by ~** indirectamente
implicit [ɪm'plɪsɪt] adj implícito; (*belief,
trust*) absoluto
imply [ɪm'plaɪ] vt (*involve*) suponer; (*hint*)
dar a entender que
impolite [ɪmpə'laɪt] adj mal educado
import [vb ɪm'pɔːt, n 'ɪmpɔːt] vt importar
▷ n (Comm) importación f; (: *article*)
producto importado; (*meaning*) significado,
sentido
importance [ɪm'pɔːtəns] n importancia
important [ɪm'pɔːtənt] adj importante;
it's not ~ no importa, no tiene importancia
importer [ɪm'pɔːtə*] n importador(a) m/f
impose [ɪm'pəuz] vt imponer ▷ vi: **to
~ on sb** abusar de algn; **imposing** adj
imponente, impresionante
impossible [ɪm'pɔsɪbl] adj imposible;

(person) insoportable
impotent ['ɪmpətənt] adj impotente
impoverished [ɪm'pɒvərɪʃt] adj
necesitado
impractical [ɪm'præktɪkl] adj (person,
plan) poco práctico
impress [ɪm'prɛs] vt impresionar; (mark)
estampar; **to ~ sth on sb** hacer entender
algo a algn
impression [ɪm'prɛʃən] n impresión f;
(imitation) imitación f; **to be under the ~
that** tener la impresión de que
impressive [ɪm'prɛsɪv] adj
impresionante
imprison [ɪm'prɪzn] vt encarcelar;
imprisonment n encarcelamiento; (term of
imprisonment) cárcel f
improbable [ɪm'prɒbəbl] adj improbable,
inverosímil
improper [ɪm'prɒpə*] adj
(unsuitable: conduct etc) incorrecto;
(: activities) deshonesto
improve [ɪm'pruːv] vt mejorar; (foreign
language) perfeccionar ▷ vi mejorarse;
improvement n mejoramiento;
perfección f; progreso
improvise ['ɪmprəvaɪz] vt, vi improvisar
impulse ['ɪmpʌls] n impulso; **to act on ~**
obrar sin reflexión; **impulsive** [ɪm'pʌlsɪv]
adj irreflexivo

○ **KEYWORD**

in [ɪn] prep **1** (indicating place, position, with
place names) en; **in the house/garden** en
(la) casa/el jardín; **in here/there** aquí/
ahí or allí dentro; **in London/England** en
Londres/Inglaterra
2 (indicating time) en; **in spring** en (la)
primavera; **in the afternoon** por la tarde;
at 4 o'clock in the afternoon a las 4 de la
tarde; **I did it in 3 hours/days** lo hice en 3
horas/días; **I'll see you in 2 weeks** or **in 2
weeks' time** te veré dentro de 2 semanas
3 (indicating manner etc) en; **in a loud/soft
voice** en voz alta/baja; **in pencil/ink** a
lápiz/bolígrafo; **the boy in the blue shirt** el
chico de la camisa azul
4 (indicating circumstances): **in the sun/
shade/rain** al sol/a la sombra/bajo la
lluvia; **a change in policy** un cambio de
política
5 (indicating mood, state): **in tears** en
lágrimas, llorando; **in anger/despair**
enfadado/desesperado; **to live in luxury**
vivir lujosamente
6 (with ratios, numbers): **1 in 10 households,
1 household in 10** una de cada 10 familias;

20 pence in the pound 20 peniques por
libra; **they lined up in twos** se alinearon de
dos en dos
7 (referring to people, works) en; entre;
the disease is common in children la
enfermedad es común entre los niños; **in
(the works of) Dickens** en (las obras de)
Dickens
8 (indicating profession etc): **to be in teaching**
estar en la enseñanza
9 (after superlative) de; **the best pupil in the
class** el(la) mejor alumno/a de la clase
10 (with present participle): **in saying this** al
decir esto
▷ adv: **to be in** (person: at home) estar en
casa; (at work) estar; (train, ship, plane) haber
llegado; (in fashion) estar de moda; **she'll be
in later today** llegará más tarde hoy; **to ask
sb in** hacer pasar a algn; **to run/limp etc in**
entrar corriendo/cojeando etc
▷ n: **the ins and outs** (of proposal, situation
etc) los detalles

inability [ɪnə'bɪlɪtɪ] n: **~ (to do)**
incapacidad f (de hacer)
inaccurate [ɪn'ækjurət] adj inexacto,
incorrecto
inadequate [ɪn'ædɪkwət] adj (income,
reply etc) insuficiente; (person) incapaz
inadvertently [ɪnəd'vəːtntlɪ] adv por
descuido
inappropriate [ɪnə'prəuprɪət] adj
inadecuado; (improper) poco oportuno
inaugurate [ɪ'nɔːgjureɪt] vt inaugurar;
(president, official) investir
Inc. (us) abbr (= incorporated) S.A.
incapable [ɪn'keɪpəbl] adj incapaz
incense [n 'ɪnsɛns, vb ɪn'sɛns] n incienso
▷ vt (anger) indignar, encolerizar
incentive [ɪn'sɛntɪv] n incentivo,
estímulo
inch [ɪntʃ] n pulgada; **to be within an ~ of**
estar a dos dedos de; **he didn't give an ~** no
dio concesión alguna
incidence ['ɪnsɪdns] n (of crime, disease)
incidencia
incident ['ɪnsɪdnt] n incidente m
incidentally [ɪnsɪ'dɛntəlɪ] adv (by the
way) a propósito
inclination [ɪnklɪ'neɪʃən] n (tendency)
tendencia, inclinación f; (desire) deseo;
(disposition) propensión f
incline [n 'ɪnklaɪn, vb ɪn'klaɪn] n
pendiente m, cuesta ▷ vt (head) poner de
lado ▷ vi inclinarse; **to be ~d to** (tend) tener
tendencia a hacer algo
include [ɪn'kluːd] vt (incorporate) incluir;
(in letter) adjuntar; **including** prep incluso,

inclusive

inclusion [ɪnˈkluːʒən] n inclusión f

inclusive [ɪnˈkluːsɪv] adj inclusivo; **~ of tax** incluidos los impuestos

income [ˈɪŋkʌm] n (earned) ingresos mpl; (from property etc) renta; (from investment etc) rédito; **income support** n (BRIT) ≈ ayuda familiar; **income tax** n impuesto sobre la renta

incoming [ˈɪnkʌmɪŋ] adj (flight, government etc) entrante

incompatible [ɪnkəmˈpætɪbl] adj incompatible

incompetence [ɪnˈkɔmpɪtəns] n incompetencia

incompetent [ɪnˈkɔmpɪtənt] adj incompetente

incomplete [ɪnkəmˈpliːt] adj (partial: achievement etc) incompleto; (unfinished: painting etc) inacabado

inconsistent [ɪnkənˈsɪstənt] adj inconsecuente; (contradictory) incongruente; **~ with** (que) no concuerda con

inconvenience [ɪnkənˈviːnjəns] n inconvenientes mpl; (trouble) molestia, incomodidad f ▷ vt incomodar

inconvenient [ɪnkənˈviːnjənt] adj incómodo, poco práctico; (time, place, visitor) inoportuno

incorporate [ɪnˈkɔːpəreɪt] vt incorporar; (contain) comprender; (add) agregar

incorrect [ɪnkəˈrɛkt] adj incorrecto

increase [n ˈɪnkriːs, vb ɪnˈkriːs] n aumento ▷ vi aumentar; (grow) crecer; (price) subir ▷ vt aumentar; (price) subir; **increasingly** adv cada vez más, más y más

incredible [ɪnˈkrɛdɪbl] adj increíble; **incredibly** adv increíblemente

incur [ɪnˈkəː*] vt (expenditure) incurrir; (loss) sufrir; (anger, disapproval) provocar

indecent [ɪnˈdiːsnt] adj indecente

indeed [ɪnˈdiːd] adv efectivamente, en realidad; (in fact) en efecto; (furthermore) es más; **yes ~!** ¡claro que sí!

indefinitely [ɪnˈdɛfɪnɪtlɪ] adv (wait) indefinidamente

independence [ɪndɪˈpɛndns] n independencia; **Independence Day** (US) n Día m de la Independencia

● En ella se proclamaba la independencia
● total de Gran Bretaña de las trece
● colonias americanas que serían el origen
● de los Estados Unidos de América.

independent [ɪndɪˈpɛndənt] adj independiente; **independent school** n (BRIT) escuela f privada, colegio m privado

index [ˈɪndɛks] (pl **~es**) n (in book) índice m; (: in library etc) catálogo; (pl **indices**: ratio, sign) exponente m

India [ˈɪndɪə] n la India; **Indian** adj, n indio/a; **Red Indian** piel roja mf

indicate [ˈɪndɪkeɪt] vt indicar; **indication** [-ˈkeɪʃən] n indicio, señal f; **indicative** [ɪnˈdɪkətɪv] adj: **to be indicative of** indicar; **indicator** n indicador m; (Aut) intermitente m

indices [ˈɪndɪsiːz] npl of **index**

indict [ɪnˈdaɪt] vt acusar; **indictment** n acusación f

indifference [ɪnˈdɪfrəns] n indiferencia

indifferent [ɪnˈdɪfrənt] adj indiferente; (mediocre) regular

indigenous [ɪnˈdɪdʒɪnəs] adj indígena

indigestion [ɪndɪˈdʒɛstʃən] n indigestión f

indignant [ɪnˈdɪgnənt] adj: **to be ~ at sth/ with sb** indignarse por algo/con algn

indirect [ɪndɪˈrɛkt] adj indirecto

indispensable [ɪndɪˈspɛnsəbl] adj indispensable, imprescindible

individual [ɪndɪˈvɪdjuəl] n individuo ▷ adj individual; (personal) personal; (particular) particular; **individually** adv (singly) individualmente

Indonesia [ɪndəˈniːzɪə] n Indonesia

indoor [ˈɪndɔː*] adj (swimming pool) cubierto; (plant) de interior; (sport) bajo cubierta; **indoors** [ɪnˈdɔːz] adv dentro

induce [ɪnˈdjuːs] vt inducir, persuadir; (bring about) producir; (labour) provocar

indulge [ɪnˈdʌldʒ] vt (whim) satisfacer; (person) complacer; (child) mimar ▷ vi: **to ~ in** darse el gusto de; **indulgent** adj indulgente

industrial [ɪnˈdʌstrɪəl] adj industrial; **industrial estate** (BRIT) n polígono (SP) or zona (LAM) industrial; **industrialist** n industrial mf; **industrial park** (US) n = **industrial estate**

industry [ˈɪndəstrɪ] n industria; (diligence) aplicación f

inefficient [ɪnɪˈfɪʃənt] adj ineficaz, ineficiente

inequality [ɪnɪˈkwɔlɪtɪ] n desigualdad f

inevitable [ɪnˈɛvɪtəbl] adj inevitable; **inevitably** adv inevitablemente

inexpensive [ɪnɪk'spɛnsɪv] *adj*
económico
inexperienced [ɪnɪk'spɪərɪənst] *adj*
inexperto
inexplicable [ɪnɪk'splɪkəbl] *adj*
inexplicable
infamous ['ɪnfəməs] *adj* infame
infant ['ɪnfənt] *n* niño/a; (*baby*) niño/a
pequeño/a, bebé *mf*; (*pej*) aniñado
infantry ['ɪnfəntrɪ] *n* infantería
infant school (*BRIT*) *n* parvulario
infect [ɪn'fɛkt] *vt* (*wound*) infectar; (*food*)
contaminar; (*person, animal*) contagiar;
infection [ɪn'fɛkʃən] *n* infección *f*; (*fig*)
contagio; **infectious** [ɪn'fɛkʃəs] *adj* (*also
fig*) contagioso
infer [ɪn'fə:*] *vt* deducir, inferir
inferior [ɪn'fɪərɪə*] *adj, n* inferior *mf*
infertile [ɪn'fə:taɪl] *adj* estéril; (*person*)
infecundo
infertility [ɪnfə:'tɪlɪtɪ] *n* esterilidad *f*;
infecundidad *f*
infested [ɪn'fɛstɪd] *adj*: ~ **with** plagado de
infinite ['ɪnfɪnɪt] *adj* infinito; **infinitely**
adv infinitamente
infirmary [ɪn'fə:mərɪ] *n* hospital *m*
inflamed [ɪn'fleɪmd] *adj*: **to become** ~
inflamarse
inflammation [ɪnflə'meɪʃən] *n*
inflamación *f*
inflatable [ɪn'fleɪtəbl] *adj* (*ball, boat*)
inflable
inflate [ɪn'fleɪt] *vt* (*tyre, price etc*) inflar;
(*fig*) hinchar; **inflation** [ɪn'fleɪʃən] *n* (*Econ*)
inflación *f*
inflexible [ɪn'flɛksəbl] *adj* (*rule*) rígido;
(*person*) inflexible
inflict [ɪn'flɪkt] *vt*: **to ~ sth on sb** infligir
algo en algn
influence ['ɪnfluəns] *n* influencia
▷ *vt* influir en, influenciar; **under the**
~ **of alcohol** en estado de embriaguez;
influential [-'ɛnʃl] *adj* influyente
influx ['ɪnflʌks] *n* afluencia
info (*inf*) ['ɪnfəu] *n* =**information**
inform [ɪn'fɔ:m] *vt*: **to ~ sb of sth** informar
a algn sobre *or* de algo ▷ *vi*: **to ~ on sb**
delatar a algn
informal [ɪn'fɔ:məl] *adj* (*manner, tone*)
familiar; (*dress, interview, occasion*) informal;
(*visit, meeting*) extraoficial
information [ɪnfə'meɪʃən] *n* información
f; (*knowledge*) conocimientos *mpl*; **a piece
of** ~ un dato; **information office** *n*
información *f*; **information technology** *n*
informática
informative [ɪn'fɔ:mətɪv] *adj*
informativo

infra-red [ɪnfrə'rɛd] *adj* infrarrojo
infrastructure ['ɪnfrəstrʌktʃə*] *n* (*of
system etc*) infraestructura
infrequent [ɪn'fri:kwənt] *adj* infrecuente
infuriate [ɪn'fjuərɪeɪt] *vt*: **to become ~d**
ponerse furioso
infuriating [ɪn'fjuərɪeɪtɪŋ] *adj* (*habit,
noise*) enloquecedor(a)
ingenious [ɪn'dʒi:nɪəs] *adj* ingenioso
ingredient [ɪn'gri:dɪənt] *n* ingrediente *m*
inhabit [ɪn'hæbɪt] *vt* vivir en; **inhabitant**
n habitante *mf*
inhale [ɪn'heɪl] *vt* inhalar ▷ *vi* (*breathe
in*) aspirar; (*in smoking*) tragar; **inhaler** *n*
inhalador *m*
inherent [ɪn'hɪərənt] *adj*: ~ **in** *or* **to**
inherente a
inherit [ɪn'hɛrɪt] *vt* heredar; **inheritance**
n herencia; (*fig*) patrimonio
inhibit [ɪn'hɪbɪt] *vt* inhibir, impedir;
inhibition [-'bɪʃən] *n* cohibición *f*
initial [ɪ'nɪʃl] *adj* primero ▷ *n* inicial *f*
▷ *vt* firmar con las iniciales; **initials** *npl* (*as
signature*) iniciales *fpl*; (*abbreviation*) siglas
fpl; **initially** *adv* al principio
initiate [ɪ'nɪʃɪeɪt] *vt* iniciar; **to ~
proceedings against sb** (*Law*) entablar
proceso contra algn
initiative [ɪ'nɪʃətɪv] *n* iniciativa
inject [ɪn'dʒɛkt] *vt* inyectar; **to ~ sb
with sth** inyectar algo a algn; **injection**
[ɪn'dʒɛkʃən] *n* inyección *f*
injure ['ɪndʒə*] *vt* (*hurt*) herir, lastimar;
(*fig: reputation etc*) perjudicar; **injured** *adj*
(*person, arm*) herido, lastimado; **injury** *n*
herida, lesión *f*; (*wrong*) perjuicio, daño
    Be careful not to translate **injury** by the
    Spanish word *injuria*.
injustice [ɪn'dʒʌstɪs] *n* injusticia
ink [ɪŋk] *n* tinta; **ink-jet printer**
['ɪŋkdʒɛt-] *n* impresora de chorro de tinta
inland [*adj* 'ɪnlənd, *adv* ɪn'lænd] *adj*
(*waterway, port etc*) interior ▷ *adv* tierra
adentro; **Inland Revenue** (*BRIT*) *n*
departamento de impuestos ≈ Hacienda
(*SP*)
in-laws ['ɪnlɔ:z] *npl* suegros *mpl*
inmate ['ɪnmeɪt] *n* (*in prison*) preso/a,
presidiario/a; (*in asylum*) internado/a
inn [ɪn] *n* posada, mesón *m*
inner ['ɪnə*] *adj* (*courtyard, calm*) interior;
(*feelings*) íntimo; **inner-city** *adj* (*schools,
problems*) de las zonas céntricas pobres, de
los barrios céntricos pobres
inning ['ɪnɪŋ] *n* (*US: Baseball*) inning *m*,
entrada; ~**s** (*Cricket*) entrada, turno
innocence ['ɪnəsns] *n* inocencia
innocent ['ɪnəsnt] *adj* inocente

innovation [ɪnəʊˈveɪʃən] n novedad f
innovative [ˈɪnəʊveɪtɪv] adj innovador
in-patient [ˈɪnpeɪʃənt] n paciente m/f
interno/a
input [ˈɪnpʊt] n entrada; (of resources)
inversión f; (Comput) entrada de datos
inquest [ˈɪnkwɛst] n (coroner's) encuesta
judicial
inquire [ɪnˈkwaɪə*] vi preguntar ▷ vt: **to
~ whether** preguntar si; **to ~ about** (person)
preguntar por; (fact) informarse de; **inquiry**
n pregunta; (investigation) investigación f,
pesquisa; **"Inquiries"** "Información"
ins. abbr = **inches**
insane [ɪnˈseɪn] adj loco; (Med) demente
insanity [ɪnˈsænɪtɪ] n demencia, locura
insect [ˈɪnsɛkt] n insecto; **insect
repellent** n loción f contra insectos
insecure [ɪnsɪˈkjʊə*] adj inseguro
insecurity [ɪnsɪˈkjʊərɪtɪ] n inseguridad f
insensitive [ɪnˈsɛnsɪtɪv] adj insensible
insert [vb ɪnˈsəːt, n ˈɪnsəːt] vt (into sth)
introducir ▷ n encarte m
inside [ˈɪnˈsaɪd] n interior m ▷ adj interior,
interno ▷ adv (be) (por) dentro; (go) hacia
dentro ▷ prep dentro de; (of time): **~ 10
minutes** en menos de 10 minutos; **inside
lane** n (Aut: in Britain) carril m izquierdo;
(: in US, Europe etc) carril m derecho; **inside
out** adv (turn) al revés; (know) a fondo
insight [ˈɪnsaɪt] n perspicacia
insignificant [ɪnsɪgˈnɪfɪkənt] adj
insignificante
insincere [ɪnsɪnˈsɪə*] adj poco sincero
insist [ɪnˈsɪst] vi insistir; **to ~ on** insistir
en; **to ~ that** insistir en que; (claim) exigir
que; **insistent** adj insistente; (noise, action)
persistente
insomnia [ɪnˈsɒmnɪə] n insomnio
inspect [ɪnˈspɛkt] vt inspeccionar,
examinar; (troops) pasar revista a;
inspection [ɪnˈspɛkʃən] n inspección f,
examen m; (of troops) revista; **inspector**
n inspector(a) m/f; (BRIT: on buses, trains)
revisor(a) m/f
inspiration [ɪnspəˈreɪʃən] n inspiración
f; **inspire** [ɪnˈspaɪə*] vt inspirar; **inspiring**
adj inspirador(a)
instability [ɪnstəˈbɪlɪtɪ] n inestabilidad f
install [ɪnˈstɔːl] (us **instal**) vt instalar;
(official) nombrar; **installation** [ɪnstəˈleɪʃən]
n instalación f
installment [ɪnˈstɔːlmənt] (us
installment) n plazo; (of story) entrega;
(of TV serial etc) capítulo; **in ~s** (pay, receive)
a plazos
instance [ˈɪnstəns] n ejemplo, caso; **for ~**
por ejemplo; **in the first ~** en primer lugar

instant [ˈɪnstənt] n instante m, momento
▷ adj inmediato; (coffee etc) instantáneo;
instantly adv en seguida; **instant
messaging** n mensajería instantánea
instead [ɪnˈstɛd] adv en cambio; **~ of** en
lugar de, en vez de
instinct [ˈɪnstɪŋkt] n instinto; **instinctive**
adj instintivo
institute [ˈɪnstɪtjuːt] n instituto;
(professional body) colegio ▷ vt (begin)
iniciar, empezar; (proceedings) entablar;
(system, rule) establecer
institution [ɪnstɪˈtjuːʃən] n institución
f; (Med: home) asilo; (: asylum) manicomio;
(of system etc) establecimiento; (of custom)
iniciación f
instruct [ɪnˈstrʌkt] vt: **to ~ sb in sth**
instruir a algn en or sobre algo; **to ~ sb to
do sth** dar instrucciones a algn de hacer
algo; **instruction** [ɪnˈstrʌkʃən] n (teaching)
instrucción f; **instructions** npl (orders)
órdenes fpl; **instructions (for use)** modo de
empleo; **instructor** n instructor(a) m/f
instrument [ˈɪnstrəmənt] n
instrumento; **instrumental** [-ˈmɛntl] adj
(Mus) instrumental; **to be instrumental in**
ser (el) artífice de
insufficient [ɪnsəˈfɪʃənt] adj insuficiente
insulate [ˈɪnsjuleɪt] vt aislar; **insulation**
[-ˈleɪʃən] n aislamiento
insulin [ˈɪnsjulɪn] n insulina
insult [n ˈɪnsʌlt, vb ɪnˈsʌlt] n insulto ▷ vt
insultar; **insulting** adj insultante
insurance [ɪnˈʃʊərəns] n seguro; **fire/
life ~** seguro contra incendios/sobre la
vida; **insurance company** n compañía f
de seguros; **insurance policy** n póliza (de
seguros)
insure [ɪnˈʃʊə*] vt asegurar
intact [ɪnˈtækt] adj íntegro; (unharmed)
intacto
intake [ˈɪnteɪk] n (of food) ingestión f; (of
air) consumo; (BRIT Scol): **an ~ of 200 a year**
200 matriculados al año
integral [ˈɪntɪgrəl] adj (whole) íntegro;
(part) integrante
integrate [ˈɪntɪgreɪt] vt integrar ▷ vi
integrarse
integrity [ɪnˈtɛgrɪtɪ] n honradez f,
rectitud f
intellect [ˈɪntəlɛkt] n intelecto;
intellectual [-ˈlɛktjuəl] adj, n intelectual
mf
intelligence [ɪnˈtɛlɪdʒəns] n inteligencia
intelligent [ɪnˈtɛlɪdʒənt] adj inteligente
intend [ɪnˈtɛnd] vt (gift etc): **to ~ sth
for** destinar algo a; **to ~ to do sth** tener
intención de or pensar hacer algo

intense [ɪn'tɛns] adj intenso
intensify [ɪn'tɛnsɪfaɪ] vt intensificar; (increase) aumentar
intensity [ɪn'tɛnsɪtɪ] n (gen) intensidad f
intensive [ɪn'tɛnsɪv] adj intensivo; **intensive care** n: **to be in intensive care** estar bajo cuidados intensivos; **intensive care unit** n unidad f de vigilancia intensiva
intent [ɪn'tɛnt] n propósito; (Law) premeditación f ▷ adj (absorbed) absorto; (attentive) atento; **to all ~s and purposes** prácticamente; **to be ~ on doing sth** estar resuelto a hacer algo
intention [ɪn'tɛnʃən] n intención f, propósito; **intentional** adj deliberado
interact [ɪntər'ækt] vi influirse mutuamente; **interaction** [ɪntər'ækʃən] n interacción f, acción f recíproca; **interactive** adj (Comput) interactivo
intercept [ɪntə'sɛpt] vt interceptar; (stop) detener
interchange ['ɪntətʃeɪndʒ] n intercambio; (on motorway) intersección f
intercourse ['ɪntəkɔːs] n (sexual) relaciones fpl sexuales
interest ['ɪntrɪst] n (also Comm) interés m ▷ vt interesar; **interested** adj interesado; **to be interested in** interesarse por; **interesting** adj interesante; **interest rate** n tipo or tasa de interés
interface ['ɪntəfeɪs] n (Comput) junción f
interfere [ɪntə'fɪə*] vi: **to ~ in** entrometerse en; **to ~ with** (hinder) estorbar; (damage) estropear
interference [ɪntə'fɪərəns] n intromisión f; (Radio, TV) interferencia
interim ['ɪntərɪm] n: **in the ~** en el ínterin ▷ adj provisional
interior [ɪn'tɪərɪə*] n interior m ▷ adj interior; **interior design** n interiorismo, decoración f de interiores
intermediate [ɪntə'miːdɪət] adj intermedio
intermission [ɪntə'mɪʃən] n intermisión f; (Theatre) descanso
intern [vb ɪn'təːn, n 'ɪntəːn] (US) vt internar ▷ n interno/a
internal [ɪn'təːnl] adj (layout, pipes, security) interior; (injury, structure, memo) internal; **Internal Revenue Service** (US) n departamento de impuestos, ≈ Hacienda (SP)
international [ɪntə'næʃənl] adj internacional ▷ n (BRIT: match) partido internacional
Internet ['ɪntənɛt] n: **the ~** Internet m or f; **Internet café** n cibercafé m; **Internet Service Provider** n proveedor m de (acceso

a) Internet; **Internet user** n internauta mf
interpret [ɪn'təːprɪt] vt interpretar; (translate) traducir; (understand) entender ▷ vi hacer de intérprete; **interpretation** [ɪntəːprɪ'teɪʃən] n interpretación f; traducción f; **interpreter** n intérprete mf
interrogate [ɪn'tɛrəʊgeɪt] vt interrogar; **interrogation** [-'geɪʃən] n interrogatorio
interrogative [ɪntə'rɔgətɪv] adj interrogativo
interrupt [ɪntə'rʌpt] vt, vi interrumpir; **interruption** [-'rʌpʃən] n interrupción f
intersection [ɪntə'sɛkʃən] n (of roads) cruce m
interstate ['ɪntəsteɪt] (US) n carretera interestatal
interval ['ɪntəvl] n intervalo; (BRIT Theatre, Sport) descanso; (Scol) recreo; **at ~s** a ratos, de vez en cuando
intervene [ɪntə'viːn] vi intervenir; (event) interponerse; (time) transcurrir
interview ['ɪntəvjuː] n entrevista ▷ vt entrevistarse con; **interviewer** n entrevistador(a) m/f
intimate [adj 'ɪntɪmət, vb 'ɪntɪmeɪt] adj íntimo; (friendship) estrecho; (knowledge) profundo ▷ vt dar a entender
intimidate [ɪn'tɪmɪdeɪt] vt intimidar, amedrentar
intimidating [ɪn'tɪmɪdeɪtɪŋ] adj amedrentador, intimidante
into ['ɪntuː] prep en; (towards) a; (inside) hacia el interior de; **~ 3 pieces/French** en 3 pedazos/al francés
intolerant [ɪn'tɔlərənt] adj: **~ (of)** intolerante (con or para)
intranet ['ɪntrənɛt] n intranet f
intransitive [ɪn'trænsɪtɪv] adj intransitivo
intricate ['ɪntrɪkət] adj (design, pattern) intrincado
intrigue [ɪn'triːg] n intriga ▷ vt fascinar; **intriguing** adj fascinante
introduce [ɪntrə'djuːs] vt introducir, meter; (speaker, TV show etc) presentar; **to ~ sb (to sb)** presentar a algn (a algn); **to ~ sb to** (pastime, technique) introducir a algn a; **introduction** [-'dʌkʃən] n introducción f; (of person) presentación f; **introductory** [-'dʌktərɪ] adj introductorio; (lesson, offer) de introducción
intrude [ɪn'truːd] vi (person) entrometerse; **to ~ on** estorbar; **intruder** n intruso/a
intuition [ɪntjuː'ɪʃən] n intuición f
inundate ['ɪnʌndeɪt] vt: **to ~ with** inundar de
invade [ɪn'veɪd] vt invadir

invalid [n 'ɪnvəlɪd, *adj* ɪn'vælɪd] *n* (*Med*) minusválido/a ▷ *adj* (*not valid*) inválido, nulo

invaluable [ɪn'væljuəbl] *adj* inestimable

invariably [ɪn'veərɪəblɪ] *adv* sin excepción, siempre; **she is ~ late** siempre llega tarde

invasion [ɪn'veɪʒən] *n* invasión *f*

invent [ɪn'vɛnt] *vt* inventar; **invention** [ɪn'vɛnʃən] *n* invento; (*lie*) ficción *f*, mentira; **inventor** *n* inventor(a) *m/f*

inventory ['ɪnvəntrɪ] *n* inventario

inverted commas [ɪn'vɜːtɪd-] (*BRIT*) *npl* comillas *fpl*

invest [ɪn'vɛst] *vt* invertir ▷ *vi*: **to ~ in** (*company etc*) invertir dinero en; (*fig: sth useful*) comprar

investigate [ɪn'vɛstɪgeɪt] *vt* investigar; **investigation** [-'geɪʃən] *n* investigación *f*, pesquisa

investigator [ɪn'vɛstɪgeɪtə*] *n* investigador(a) *m/f*; **private ~** investigador(a) *m/f* privado/a

investment [ɪn'vɛstmənt] *n* inversión *f*

investor [ɪn'vɛstə*] *n* inversionista *mf*

invisible [ɪn'vɪzɪbl] *adj* invisible

invitation [ɪnvɪ'teɪʃən] *n* invitación *f*

invite [ɪn'vaɪt] *vt* invitar; (*opinions etc*) solicitar, pedir; **inviting** *adj* atractivo; (*food*) apetitoso

invoice ['ɪnvɔɪs] *n* factura ▷ *vt* facturar

involve [ɪn'vɔlv] *vt* suponer, implicar; tener que ver con; (*concern, affect*) corresponder; **to ~ sb (in sth)** comprometer a algn (con algo); **involved** *adj* complicado; **to be involved in** (*take part*) tomar parte en; (*be engrossed*) estar muy metido en; **involvement** *n* participación *f*; dedicación *f*

inward ['ɪnwəd] *adj* (*movement*) interior, interno; (*thought, feeling*) íntimo; **inward(s)** *adv* hacia dentro

iPod ® ['aɪpɔd] *n* iPod ® *m*

IQ *n abbr* (= *intelligence quotient*) cociente *m* intelectual

IRA *n abbr* (= *Irish Republican Army*) IRA *m*

Iran [ɪ'rɑːn] *n* Irán *m*; **Iranian** [ɪ'reɪnɪən] *adj, n* iraní *mf*

Iraq [ɪ'rɑːk] *n* Iraq; **Iraqi** *adj, n* iraquí *mf*

Ireland ['aɪələnd] *n* Irlanda

iris ['aɪrɪs] (*pl* ~**es**) *n* (*Anat*) iris *m*; (*Bot*) lirio

Irish ['aɪrɪʃ] *adj* irlandés/esa ▷ *npl*: **the ~** los irlandeses; **Irishman** (*irreg*) *n* irlandés *m*; **Irishwoman** (*irreg*) *n* irlandésa

iron ['aɪən] *n* hierro; (*for clothes*) plancha ▷ *cpd* de hierro ▷ *vt* (*clothes*) planchar

ironic(al) [aɪ'rɔnɪk(l)] *adj* irónico; **ironically** *adv* irónicamente

ironing ['aɪənɪŋ] *n* (*activity*) planchado; (*clothes: ironed*) ropa planchada; (: *to be ironed*) ropa por planchar; **ironing board** *n* tabla de planchar

irony ['aɪrənɪ] *n* ironía

irrational [ɪ'ræʃənl] *adj* irracional

irregular [ɪ'rɛgjulə*] *adj* irregular; (*surface*) desigual; (*action, event*) anómalo; (*behaviour*) poco ortodoxo

irrelevant [ɪ'rɛləvənt] *adj* fuera de lugar, inoportuno

irresistible [ɪrɪ'zɪstɪbl] *adj* irresistible

irresponsible [ɪrɪ'spɔnsɪbl] *adj* (*act*) irresponsable; (*person*) poco serio

irrigation [ɪrɪ'geɪʃən] *n* riego

irritable ['ɪrɪtəbl] *adj* (*person*) de mal humor

irritate ['ɪrɪteɪt] *vt* fastidiar; (*Med*) picar; **irritating** *adj* fastidioso; **irritation** [-'teɪʃən] *n* fastidio; enfado; picazón *f*

IRS (*us*) *n abbr* = **Internal Revenue Service**

is [ɪz] *vb see* **be**

ISDN *n abbr* (= *Integrated Services Digital Network*) RDSI *f*

Islam ['ɪzlɑːm] *n* Islam *m*; **Islamic** [ɪz'læmɪk] *adj* islámico

island ['aɪlənd] *n* isla; **islander** *n* isleño/a

isle [aɪl] *n* isla

isn't ['ɪznt] = **is not**

isolated ['aɪsəleɪtɪd] *adj* aislado

isolation [aɪsə'leɪʃən] *n* aislamiento

ISP *n abbr* = **Internet Service Provider**

Israel ['ɪzreɪl] *n* Israel *m*; **Israeli** [ɪz'reɪlɪ] *adj, n* israelí *mf*

issue ['ɪsjuː] *n* (*problem, subject*) cuestión *f*; (*outcome*) resultado; (*of banknotes etc*) emisión *f*; (*of newspaper etc*) edición *f* ▷ *vt* (*rations, equipment*) distribuir, repartir; (*orders*) dar; (*certificate, passport*) expedir; (*decree*) promulgar; (*magazine*) publicar; (*cheques*) extender; (*banknotes, stamps*) emitir; **at ~** en cuestión; **to take ~ with sb (over)** estar en desacuerdo con algn (sobre); **to make an ~ of sth** hacer una cuestión de algo

IT *n abbr* = **information technology**

○ KEYWORD

it [ɪt] *pron* **1** (*specific subject: not generally translated*) él (ella); (: *direct object*) lo, la; (: *indirect object*) le; (*after prep*) él (ella); (*abstract concept*) ello; **it's on the table** está en la mesa; **I can't find it** no lo (or la) encuentro; **give it to me** dámelo (or dámela); **I spoke to him about it** le hablé del asunto; **what did you learn from it?** ¿qué aprendiste de él (or ella)?; **did you go**

to it? (party, concert etc) ¿fuiste?
2 (impersonal): it's raining llueve, está
lloviendo; it's 6 o'clock/the 10th of
August son las 6/es el 10 de agosto; how far
is it? - it's 10 miles/2 hours on the train ¿a
qué distancia está? - a 10 millas/2 horas en
tren; who is it? - it's me ¿quién es? - soy yo

Italian [ɪ'tæljən] adj italiano ▷ n
italiano/a; (Ling) italiano
italics [ɪ'tælɪks] npl cursiva
Italy ['ɪtəlɪ] n Italia
itch [ɪtʃ] n picazón f ▷ vi (part of body)
picar; **to ~ to do sth** rabiar por hacer algo;
itchy adj: **my hand is itchy** me pica la
mano
it'd ['ɪtd] = **it would; it had**
item ['aɪtəm] n artículo; (on agenda)
asunto (a tratar); (also: **news ~**) noticia
itinerary [aɪ'tɪnərərɪ] n itinerario
it'll ['ɪtl] = **it will; it shall**
its [ɪts] adj su; sus pl
it's [ɪts] = **it is; it has**
itself [ɪt'sɛlf] pron (reflexive) sí mismo/a;
(emphatic) él mismo(ella misma)
ITV n abbr (BRIT: = Independent Television)
cadena de televisión comercial independiente
del Estado
I've [aɪv] = **I have**
ivory ['aɪvərɪ] n marfil m
ivy ['aɪvɪ] n (Bot) hiedra

jab [dʒæb] vt: **to ~ sth into sth** clavar algo
en algo ▷ n (inf: Med) pinchazo
jack [dʒæk] n (Aut) gato; (Cards) sota
jacket ['dʒækɪt] n chaqueta, americana
(SP), saco (LAM); (of book) sobrecubierta;
jacket potato n patata asada (con piel)
jackpot ['dʒækpɔt] n premio gordo
Jacuzzi® [dʒə'ku:zɪ] n jacuzzi® m
jagged ['dʒægɪd] adj dentado
jail [dʒeɪl] n cárcel f ▷ vt encarcelar; **jail
sentence** n pena f de cárcel
jam [dʒæm] n mermelada; (also: **traffic ~**)
embotellamiento; (inf: difficulty) apuro ▷ vt
(passage etc) obstruir; (mechanism, drawer etc)
atascar; (Radio) interferir ▷ vi atascarse,
trabarse; **to ~ sth into sth** meter algo a la
fuerza en algo
Jamaica [dʒə'meɪkə] n Jamaica
jammed [dʒæmd] adj atascado
Jan abbr (= January) ene
janitor ['dʒænɪtə*] n (caretaker) portero,
conserje m
January ['dʒænjuərɪ] n enero
Japan [dʒə'pæn] n (el) Japón; **Japanese**
[dʒæpə'ni:z] adj japonés/esa ▷ n inv
japonés/esa m/f; (Ling) japonés m
jar [dʒɑ:*] n tarro, bote m ▷ vi (sound)
chirriar; (colours) desentonar
jargon ['dʒɑ:gən] n jerga
javelin ['dʒævlɪn] n jabalina
jaw [dʒɔ:] n mandíbula
jazz [dʒæz] n jazz m
jealous ['dʒɛləs] adj celoso; (envious)
envidioso; **jealousy** n celos mpl; envidia
jeans [dʒi:nz] npl vaqueros mpl, tejanos mpl
Jello® ['dʒɛləu] n (US) gelatina
jelly ['dʒɛlɪ] n (jam) jalea; (dessert etc)
gelatina; **jellyfish** n inv medusa, aguaviva
(RPL)
jeopardize ['dʒɛpədaɪz] vt arriesgar,
poner en peligro

jerk [dʒə:k] n (jolt) sacudida; (wrench) tirón m; (inf) imbécil mf ▷ vt tirar bruscamente de ▷ vi (vehicle) traquetear

Jersey ['dʒə:zɪ] n Jersey m

jersey ['dʒə:zɪ] n jersey m; (fabric) (tejido de) punto

Jesus ['dʒi:zəs] n Jesús m

jet [dʒet] n (of gas, liquid) chorro; (Aviat) avión m a reacción; **jet lag** n desorientación f después de un largo vuelo; **jet-ski** vi practicar el motociclismo acuático

jetty ['dʒetɪ] n muelle m, embarcadero

Jew [dʒu:] n judío/a

jewel ['dʒu:əl] n joya; (in watch) rubí m; **jeweller** (us **jeweler**) n joyero/a; **jeweller's (shop)** (us **jewelry store**) n joyería; **jewellery** (us **jewelry**) n joyas fpl, alhajas fpl

Jewish ['dʒu:ɪʃ] adj judío

jigsaw ['dʒɪgsɔː] n (also: ~ **puzzle**) rompecabezas m inv, puzle m

job [dʒɔb] n (task) tarea; (post) empleo; **it's not my ~** no me incumbe a mí; **it's a good ~ that ...** menos mal que ...; **just the ~!** ¡estupendo!; **job centre** (BRIT) n oficina estatal de colocaciones; **jobless** adj sin trabajo

jockey ['dʒɔkɪ] n jockey mf ▷ vi: **to ~ for position** maniobrar para conseguir una posición

jog [dʒɔg] vt empujar (ligeramente) ▷ vi (run) hacer footing; **to ~ sb's memory** refrescar la memoria a algn; **jogging** n footing m

join [dʒɔɪn] vt (things) juntar, unir; (club) hacerse socio de; (Pol: party) afiliarse a; (queue) ponerse en; (meet: people) reunirse con ▷ vi (roads) juntarse; (rivers) confluir ▷ n juntura; **join in** vi tomar parte, participar ▷ vt fus tomar parte or participar en; **join up** vi reunirse; (Mil) alistarse

joiner ['dʒɔɪnə*] (BRIT) n carpintero/a

joint [dʒɔɪnt] n (Tech) junta, unión f; (Anat) articulación f; (Culin) pieza de carne (para asar); (inf: place) tugurio; (: of cannabis) porro ▷ adj (common) común; (combined) combinado; **joint account** n (with bank etc) cuenta común; **jointly** adv (gen) en común; (together) conjuntamente

joke [dʒəuk] n chiste m; (also: **practical ~**) broma ▷ vi bromear; **to play a ~ on** gastar una broma a; **joker** n (Cards) comodín m

jolly ['dʒɔlɪ] adj (merry) alegre; (enjoyable) divertido ▷ adv (BRIT: inf) muy, terriblemente

jolt [dʒəult] n (jerk) sacudida; (shock) susto ▷ vt (physically) sacudir; (emotionally) asustar

Jordan ['dʒɔːdən] n (country) Jordania; (river) Jordán m

journal ['dʒə:nl] n (magazine) revista; (diary) periódico, diario; **journalism** n periodismo; **journalist** n periodista mf, reportero/a

journey ['dʒə:nɪ] n viaje m; (distance covered) trayecto

joy [dʒɔɪ] n alegría; **joyrider** n gamberro que roba un coche para dar una vuelta y luego abandonarlo; **joy stick** n (Aviat) palanca de mando; (Comput) palanca de control

Jr abbr = **junior**

judge [dʒʌdʒ] n juez mf; (fig: expert) perito ▷ vt juzgar; (consider) considerar

judo ['dʒu:dəu] n judo

jug [dʒʌg] n jarra

juggle ['dʒʌgl] vi hacer juegos malabares; **juggler** n malabarista mf

juice [dʒu:s] n zumo (SP), jugo (LAM); **juicy** adj jugoso

Jul abbr (= July) jul

July [dʒu:'laɪ] n julio

jumble ['dʒʌmbl] n revoltijo ▷ vt (also: ~ up) revolver; **jumble sale** (BRIT) n venta de objetos usados con fines benéficos

● **JUMBLE SALE**
●
● Los **jumble sales** son unos mercadillos
● que se organizan con fines benéficos
● en los locales de un colegio, iglesia u
● otro centro público. En ellos puede
● comprarse todo tipo de artículos
● baratos de segunda mano, sobre
● todo ropa, juguetes, libros, vajillas o
● muebles.

jumbo ['dʒʌmbəu] n (also: ~ **jet**) jumbo

jump [dʒʌmp] vi saltar, dar saltos; (with fear etc) pegar un bote; (increase) aumentar ▷ vt saltar ▷ n salto; aumento; **to ~ the queue** (BRIT) colarse

jumper ['dʒʌmpə*] n (BRIT: pullover) suéter m, jersey m; (us: dress) mandil m

jumper cables (us) npl = **jump leads**

jump leads (BRIT) npl cables mpl puente de batería

Jun. abbr = **junior**

junction ['dʒʌŋkʃən] n (BRIT: of roads) cruce m; (Rail) empalme m

June [dʒu:n] n junio

jungle ['dʒʌŋgl] n selva, jungla

junior ['dʒu:nɪə*] adj (in age) menor, más joven; (brother/sister etc): **seven years her ~** siete años menor que ella; (position) subalterno ▷ n menor mf, joven mf; **junior high school** (us) n centro de educación

secundaria; see also **high school**; **junior
school** (BRIT) n escuela primaria
junk [dʒʌŋk] n (cheap goods) baratijas fpl;
(rubbish) basura; **junk food** n alimentos
preparados y envasados de escaso valor nutritivo
junkie ['dʒʌŋkɪ] (inf) n drogadicto/a,
yonqui mf
junk mail n propaganda de buzón
Jupiter ['dʒuːpɪtə*] n (Mythology, Astrology)
Júpiter m
jurisdiction [dʒuərɪs'dɪkʃən] n
jurisdicción f; **it falls** or **comes within/
outside our ~** es/no es de nuestra
competencia
jury ['dʒuərɪ] n jurado
just [dʒʌst] adj justo ▷ adv (exactly)
exactamente; (only) sólo, solamente; **he's ~
done it/left** acaba de hacerlo/irse; **~ right**
perfecto; **~ two o'clock** las dos en punto;
she's ~ as clever as you (ella) es tan lista
como tú; **~ as well that ...** menos mal que
...; **~ as he was leaving** en el momento en
que se marchaba; **~ before/enough** justo
antes/lo suficiente; **~ here** aquí mismo; **he
~ missed** ha fallado por poco; **~ listen to
this** escucha esto un momento
justice ['dʒʌstɪs] n justicia; (US: judge) juez
mf; **to do ~ to** (fig) hacer justicia a
justification [dʒʌstɪfɪ'keɪʃən] n
justificación f
justify ['dʒʌstɪfaɪ] vt justificar; (text)
alinear
jut [dʒʌt] vi (also: **~ out**) sobresalir
juvenile ['dʒuːvənaɪl] adj (court) de
menores; (humour, mentality) infantil ▷ n
menor m de edad

K abbr (= one thousand) mil; (= kilobyte)
kilobyte m, kiloocteto
kangaroo [kæŋgə'ruː] n canguro
karaoke [kɑːrə'əʊkɪ] n karaoke
karate [kə'rɑːtɪ] n karate m
kebab [kə'bæb] n pincho moruno
keel [kiːl] n quilla; **on an even ~** (fig) en
equilibrio
keen [kiːn] adj (interest, desire) grande,
vivo; (eye, intelligence) agudo; (competition)
reñido; (edge) afilado; (eager) entusiasta; **to
be ~ to do** or **on doing sth** tener muchas
ganas de hacer algo; **to be ~ on sth/sb**
interesarse por algo/algn
keep [kiːp] (pt, pp **kept**) vt (preserve, store)
guardar; (hold back) quedarse con; (maintain)
mantener; (detain) detener; (shop) ser
propietario de; (feed: family etc) mantener;
(promise) cumplir; (chickens, bees etc) criar;
(accounts) llevar; (diary) escribir; (prevent): **to
~ sb from doing sth** impedir a algn hacer
algo ▷ vi (food) conservarse; (remain) seguir,
continuar ▷ n (of castle) torreón m; (food
etc) comida, subsistencia; (inf): **for ~s** para
siempre; **to ~ doing sth** seguir haciendo
algo; **to ~ sb happy** tener a algn contento;
to ~ a place tidy mantener un lugar
limpio; **to ~ sth to o.s.** guardar algo para
sí mismo; **to ~ sth (back) from sb** ocultar
algo a algn; **to ~ time** (clock) mantener
la hora exacta; **keep away** vt: **to keep
sth/sb away from sb** mantener algo/a
algn apartado de algn ▷ vi: **to keep away
(from)** mantenerse apartado (de); **keep
back** vt (crowd, tears) contener; (money)
quedarse con; (conceal: information): **to keep
sth back from sb** ocultar algo a algn ▷ vi
hacerse a un lado; **keep off** vt (dog, person)
mantener a distancia ▷ vi: **if the rain keeps
off** so no lleuve; **keep your hands off!** ¡no
toques!; **"keep off the grass"** "prohibido

pisar el césped"; **keep on** vi: **to keep on doing** seguir or continuar haciendo; **to keep on (about sth)** no parar de hablar (de algo); **keep out** vi (stay out) permanecer fuera; **"keep out"** "prohibida la entrada"; **keep up** vt mantener, conservar ▷ vi. no retrasarse; **to keep up with** (pace) ir al paso de; (level) mantenerse a la altura de; **keeper** n guardián/ana m/f; **keeping** n (care) cuidado; **in keeping with** de acuerdo con
kennel ['kɛnl] n perrera; **kennels** npl residencia canina
Kenya ['kɛnjə] n Kenia
kept [kɛpt] pt, pp of **keep**
kerb [kəːb] (BRIT) n bordillo
kerosene ['kɛrəsiːn] n keroseno
ketchup ['kɛtʃəp] n salsa de tomate, catsup m
kettle ['kɛtl] n hervidor m de agua
key [kiː] n llave f; (Mus) tono; (of piano, typewriter) tecla ▷ adj (issue etc) clave inv ▷ vt (also: ~ in) teclear; **keyboard** n teclado; **keyhole** n ojo (de la cerradura); **keyring** n llavero
kg abbr (= kilogram) kg
khaki ['kɑːkɪ] n caqui
kick [kɪk] vt dar una patada or un puntapié a; (inf: habit) quitarse de ▷ vi (horse) dar coces ▷ n patada; puntapié m; (of animal) coz f; (thrill): **he does it for ~s** lo hace por pura diversión; **kick off** vi (Sport) hacer el saque inicial; **kick-off** n saque inicial; **the kick-off is at 10 o'clock** el partido empieza a las diez
kid [kɪd] n (inf: child) chiquillo/a; (animal) cabrito; (leather) cabritilla ▷ vi (inf) bromear
kidnap ['kɪdnæp] vt secuestrar; **kidnapping** n secuestro
kidney ['kɪdnɪ] n riñón m; **kidney bean** n judía, alubia
kill [kɪl] vt matar; (murder) asesinar ▷ n matanza; **to ~ time** matar el tiempo; **killer** n asesino/a; **killing** n (one) asesinato; (several) matanza; **to make a killing** (fig) hacer su agosto
kiln [kɪln] n horno
kilo ['kiːləu] n kilo; **kilobyte** n (Comput) kilobyte m, kilooccteto; **kilogram(me)** n kilo, kilogramo; **kilometre** ['kɪləmiːtə*] (US **kilometer**) n kilómetro; **kilowatt** n kilovatio
kilt [kɪlt] n falda escocesa
kin [kɪn] n see **next-of-kin**
kind [kaɪnd] adj amable, atento ▷ n clase f, especie f; (species) género; **in ~** (Comm) en especie; **a ~ of** una especie de; **to be two of a ~** ser tal para cual
kindergarten ['kɪndəgɑːtn] n jardín m

de la infancia
kindly ['kaɪndlɪ] adj bondadoso; cariñoso ▷ adv bondadosamente, amablemente; **will you ~ ...** sea usted tan amable de ...
kindness ['kaɪndnɪs] n (quality) bondad f, amabilidad f; (act) favor m
king [kɪŋ] n rey m; **kingdom** n reino; **kingfisher** n martín m pescador; **king-size(d) bed** n cama de matrimonio extragrande
kiosk ['kiːɔsk] n quiosco; (BRIT Tel) cabina
kipper ['kɪpə*] n arenque m ahumado
kiss [kɪs] n beso ▷ vt besar; **to ~ (each other)** besarse; **kiss of life** n respiración f boca a boca
kit [kɪt] n (equipment) equipo; (tools etc) (caja de) herramientas fpl; (assembly kit) juego de armar
kitchen ['kɪtʃɪn] n cocina
kite [kaɪt] n (toy) cometa
kitten ['kɪtn] n gatito/a
kiwi ['kiːwiː-] n (also: ~ fruit) kiwi m
km abbr (= kilometre) km
km/h abbr (= kilometres per hour) km/h
knack [næk] n: **to have the ~ of doing sth** tener el don de hacer algo
knee [niː] n rodilla; **kneecap** n rótula
kneel [niːl] (pt, pp **knelt**) vi (also: ~ **down**) arrodillarse
knelt [nɛlt] pt, pp of **kneel**
knew [njuː] pt of **know**
knickers ['nɪkəz] (BRIT) npl bragas fpl
knife [naɪf] (pl **knives**) n cuchillo ▷ vt acuchillar
knight [naɪt] n caballero; (Chess) caballo
knit [nɪt] vt tejer, tricotar ▷ vi hacer punto, tricotar; (bones) soldarse; **to ~ one's brows** fruncir el ceño; **knitting** n labor f de punto; **knitting needle** n aguja de hacer punto; **knitwear** n prendas fpl de punto
knives [naɪvz] npl of **knife**
knob [nɔb] n (of door) tirador m; (of stick) puño; (on radio, TV) botón m
knock [nɔk] vt (strike) golpear; (bump into) chocar contra; (inf) criticar ▷ vi (at door etc): **to ~ at/on** llamar a ▷ n golpe m; (on door) llamada; **knock down** vt atropellar; **knock off** (inf) vi (finish) salir del trabajo ▷ vt (from price) descontar; (inf: steal) birlar; **knock out** vt dejar sin sentido; (Boxing) poner fuera de combate, dejar K.O.; (in competition) eliminar; **knock over** vt (object) tirar; (person) atropellar; **knockout** n (Boxing) K.O. m, knockout m ▷ cpd (competition etc) eliminatorio
knot [nɔt] n nudo ▷ vt anudar
know [nəu] (pt **knew**, pp **known**) vt (facts) saber; (be acquainted with) conocer;

(recognize) reconocer, conocer; **to ~ how to swim** saber nadar; **to ~ about** of of sb/sth saber de algn/algo; **know-all** n sabelotodo mf; **know-how** n conocimientos mpl; **knowing** adj (look) de complicidad; **knowingly** adv (purposely) adrede; (smile, look) con complicidad; **know-it-all** (US) n = **know-all**

knowledge ['nɔlɪdʒ] n conocimiento; (learning) saber m, conocimientos mpl; **knowledgeable** adj entendido

known [nəun] pp of know ▷adj (thief, facts) conocido; (expert) reconocido

knuckle ['nʌkl] n nudillo

koala [kəu'ɑːlə] n (also: ~ bear) koala m

Koran [kɔ'rɑːn] n Corán m

Korea [kə'rɪə] n Corea; **Korean** adj, n coreano/a m/f

kosher ['kəuʃə*] adj autorizado por la ley judía

Kosovar ['kɔsəvɑ*], **Kosovan** ['kɔːsəvən] adj kosovar

Kosovo ['kɔsəvəu] n Kosovo

Kremlin ['kremlɪn] n: **the ~** el Kremlin

Kuwait [ku'weit] n Kuwait m

L (BRIT) abbr = **learner driver**

l. abbr (= litre) l

lab [læb] n abbr = **laboratory**

label ['leɪbl] n etiqueta ▷vt poner etiqueta a

labor etc ['leɪbə*] (US) = **labour** etc

laboratory [lə'bɔrətərɪ] n laboratorio

Labor Day (US) n día m de los trabajadores (primer lunes de septiembre)

labor union (US) n sindicato

labour ['leɪbə*] (US **labor**) n (hard work) trabajo; (labour force) mano f de obra; (Med): **to be in ~** estar de parto ▷vi: **to ~ (at sth)** trabajar (en algo) ▷vt: **to ~ a point** insistir en un punto; **L~, the L~ party** (BRIT) el partido laborista, los laboristas mpl; **labourer** n peón m; **farm labourer** peón m; (day labourer) jornalero

lace [leɪs] n encaje m; (of shoe etc) cordón m ▷vt (shoes: also: ~ up) atarse (los zapatos)

lack [læk] n (absence) falta ▷vt faltarle a algn, carecer de; **through** or **for ~ of** por falta de; **to be ~ing** faltar, no haber; **to be ~ing in sth** faltarle a algn algo

lacquer ['lækə*] n laca

lacy ['leɪsɪ] adj (of lace) de encaje; (like lace) como de encaje

lad [læd] n muchacho, chico

ladder ['lædə*] n escalera (de mano); (BRIT: in tights) carrera

ladle ['leɪdl] n cucharón m

lady ['leɪdɪ] n señora; (dignified, graceful) dama; **"ladies and gentlemen ..."** "señoras y caballeros ..."; **young ~** señorita; **the ladies' (room)** los servicios de señoras; **ladybird** (US **ladybug**) n mariquita

lag [læg] n retraso ▷vi (also: ~ behind) retrasarse, quedarse atrás ▷vt (pipes) revestir

lager ['lɑːgə*] n cerveza (rubia)

lagoon [lə'guːn] n laguna

laid [leɪd] *pt, pp of* **lay**; **laid back** (*inf*) *adj* relajado

lain [leɪn] *pp of* **lie**

lake [leɪk] *n* lago

lamb [læm] *n* cordero; (*meat*) (carne *f* de) cordero

lame [leɪm] *adj* cojo; (*excuse*) poco convincente

lament [lə'mɛnt] *n* quejo ▷ *vt* lamentarse de

lamp [læmp] *n* lámpara; **lamppost** (*BRIT*) *n* (poste *m* de) farol *m*; **lampshade** *n* pantalla

land [lænd] *n* tierra; (*country*) país *m*; (*piece of land*) terreno; (*estate*) tierras *fpl*, finca ▷ *vi* (*from ship*) desembarcar; (*Aviat*) aterrizar; (*fig: fall*) caer, terminar ▷ *vt* (*passengers, goods*) desembarcar; **to ~ sb with sth** (*inf*) hacer cargar a algn con algo; **landing** *n* aterrizaje *m*; (*of staircase*) rellano; **landing card** *n* tarjeta de desembarque; **landlady** *n* (*of rented house, pub etc*) dueña; **landlord** *n* propietario; (*of pub etc*) patrón *m*; **landmark** *n* lugar *m* conocido; **to be a landmark** (*fig*) marcar un hito histórico; **landowner** *n* terrateniente *mf*; **landscape** *n* paisaje *m*; **landslide** *n* (*Geo*) corrimiento de tierras; (*fig: Pol*) victoria arrolladora

lane [leɪn] *n* (*in country*) camino; (*Aut*) carril *m*; (*in race*) calle *f*

language ['læŋgwɪdʒ] *n* lenguaje *m*; (*national tongue*) idioma *m*, lengua; **bad ~** palabrotas *fpl*; **language laboratory** *n* laboratorio de idiomas; **language school** *n* academia de idiomas

lantern ['læntn] *n* linterna, farol *m*

lap [læp] *n* (*of track*) vuelta; (*of body*) regazo ▷ *vt* (*also: ~ up*) beber a lengüetadas ▷ *vi* (*waves*) chapotear; **to sit on sb's ~** sentarse en las rodillas de algn

lapel [lə'pɛl] *n* solapa

lapse [læps] *n* fallo; (*moral*) desliz *m*; (*of time*) intervalo ▷ *vi* (*expire*) caducar; (*time*) pasar, transcurrir; **to ~ into bad habits** caer en malos hábitos

laptop (computer) ['læptɔp-] *n* (ordenador *m*) portátil *m*

lard [lɑːd] *n* manteca (de cerdo)

larder ['lɑːdə*] *n* despensa

large [lɑːdʒ] *adj* grande; **at ~** (*free*) en libertad; (*generally*) en general

▌ Be careful not to translate **large** by the Spanish word *largo*.

largely *adv* (*mostly*) en su mayor parte; (*introducing reason*) en gran parte; **large-scale** *adj* (*map*) en gran escala; (*fig*) importante

lark [lɑːk] *n* (*bird*) alondra; (*joke*) broma

laryngitis [lærɪn'dʒaɪtɪs] *n* laringitis *f*

lasagne [lə'zænjə] *n* lasaña

laser ['leɪzə*] *n* láser *m*; **laser printer** *n* impresora (por) láser

lash [læʃ] *n* latigazo; (*also*: **eye~**) pestaña ▷ *vt* azotar; (*tie*): **to ~ to/together** atar a/atar; **lash out** *vi*: **to lash out (at sb)** (*hit*) arremeter (contra algn); **to lash out against sb** lanzar invectivas contra algn

lass [læs] (*BRIT*) *n* chica

last [lɑːst] *adj* último; (*end: of series etc*) final ▷ *adv* (*most recently*) la última vez; (*finally*) por último ▷ *vi* durar; (*continue*) continuar, seguir; **~ night** anoche; **~ week** la semana pasada; **at ~** por fin; **~ but one** penúltimo; **lastly** *adv* por último, finalmente; **last-minute** *adj* de última hora

latch [lætʃ] *n* pestillo; **latch onto** *vt fus* (*person, group*) pegarse a; (*idea*) agarrarse a

late [leɪt] *adj* (*far on: in time, process etc*) al final de; (*not on time*) tarde, atrasado; (*dead*) fallecido ▷ *adv* tarde; (*behind time, schedule*) con retraso; **of ~** últimamente; **~ at night** a última hora de la noche; **in ~ May** hacia fines de mayo; **the ~ Mr X** el difunto Sr X; **latecomer** *n* recién llegado/a; **lately** *adv* últimamente; **later** *adj* (*date etc*) posterior; (*version etc*) más reciente ▷ *adv* más tarde, después; **latest** ['leɪtɪst] *adj* último; **at the latest** a más tardar

lather ['lɑːðə*] *n* espuma (de jabón) ▷ *vt* enjabonar

Latin ['lætɪn] *n* latín *m* ▷ *adj* latino; **Latin America** *n* América latina; **Latin American** *adj, n* latinoamericano/a *m/f*

latitude ['lætɪtjuːd] *n* latitud *f*; (*fig*) libertad *f*

latter ['lætə*] *adj* último; (*of two*) segundo ▷ *n*: **the ~** el último, éste

laugh [lɑːf] *n* risa ▷ *vi* reír(se); (**to do sth**) **for a ~** (hacer algo) en broma; **laugh at** *vt fus* reírse de; **laughter** *n* risa

launch [lɔːntʃ] *n* lanzamiento; (*boat*) lancha ▷ *vt* (*ship*) botar; (*rocket etc*) lanzar; (*fig*) comenzar; **launch into** *vt fus* lanzarse a

launder ['lɔːndə*] *vt* lavar

Launderette® [lɔːn'drɛt] (*BRIT*) *n* lavandería (automática)

Laundromat® ['lɔːndrəmæt] (*US*) *n* = **Launderette**

laundry ['lɔːndrɪ] *n* (*dirty*) ropa sucia; (*clean*) colada; (*room*) lavadero

lava ['lɑːvə] *n* lava

lavatory ['lævətərɪ] *n* wáter *m*

lavender ['lævəndə*] *n* lavanda

lavish ['lævɪʃ] *adj* (*amount*) abundante;

(*person*): **~ with** pródigo en ▷ *vt*: **to ~ sth on sb** colmar a algn de algo

law [lɔ:] *n* ley *f*; (*Scol*) derecho; (*a rule*) regla; (*professions connected with law*) jurisprudencia; **lawful** *adj* legítimo, lícito; **lawless** *adj* (*action*) criminal

lawn [lɔ:n] *n* césped *m*; **lawnmower** *n* cortacésped *m*

lawsuit ['lɔ:su:t] *n* pleito

lawyer ['lɔ:jə*] *n* abogado/a; (*for sales, wills etc*) notario/a

lax [læks] *adj* laxo

laxative ['læksətɪv] *n* laxante *m*

lay [leɪ] (*pt, pp* **laid**) *pt of* **lie** ▷ *adj* laico; (*not expert*) lego ▷ *vt* (*place*) colocar; (*eggs, table*) poner; (*cable*) tender; (*carpet*) extender; **lay down** *vt* (*pen etc*) dejar; (*rules etc*) establecer; **to lay down the law** (*pej*) imponer las normas; **lay off** *vt* (*workers*) despedir; **lay on** *vt* (*meal, facilities*) proveer; **lay out** *vt* (*spread out*) disponer, exponer; **lay-by** *n* (*BRIT Aut*) área de aparcamiento

layer ['leɪə*] *n* capa

layman ['leɪmən] (*irreg*) *n* lego

layout ['leɪaut] *n* (*design*) plan *m*, trazado; (*Press*) composición *f*

lazy ['leɪzɪ] *adj* perezoso, vago; (*movement*) lento

lb. *abbr* = **pound** (*weight*)

lead¹ [li:d] (*pt, pp* **led**) *n* (*front position*) delantera; (*clue*) pista; (*Elec*) cable *m*; (*for dog*) correa; (*Theatre*) papel *m* principal ▷ *vt* (*walk etc in front*) ir a la cabeza de; (*guide*): **to ~ sb somewhere** conducir a algn a algún sitio; (*be leader*) dirigir; (*start, guide: activity*) protagonizar ▷ *vi* (*road, pipe etc*) conducir a; (*Sport*) ir primero; **to be in the ~** (*Sport*) llevar la delantera; (*fig*) ir a la cabeza; **to ~ the way** llevar la delantera; **lead up to** *vt fus* (*events*) conducir a; (*in conversation*) preparar el terreno para

lead² [lɛd] *n* (*metal*) plomo; (*in pencil*) mina

leader ['li:də*] *n* jefe *a m/f*, líder *mf*; (*Sport*) líder *mf*; **leadership** *n* dirección *f*; (*position*) mando; (*quality*) iniciativa

lead-free ['lɛdfri:] *adj* sin plomo

leading ['li:dɪŋ] *adj* (*main*) principal; (*first*) primero; (*front*) delantero

lead singer [li:d-] *n* cantante *mf*

leaf [li:f] (*pl* **leaves**) *n* hoja ▷ *vi*: **to ~ through** hojear; **to turn over a new ~** reformarse

leaflet ['li:flɪt] *n* folleto

league [li:g] *n* sociedad *f*; (*Football*) liga; **to be in ~ with** haberse confabulado con

leak [li:k] *n* (*of liquid, gas*) escape *m*, fuga; (*in pipe*) agujero; (*in roof*) gotera; (*in security*) filtración *f* ▷ *vi* (*shoes, ship*) hacer agua;

(*pipe*) tener (un) escape; (*roof*) gotear; (*liquid, gas*) escaparse, fugarse; (*fig*) divulgarse ▷ *vt* (*fig*) filtrar

lean [li:n] (*pt, pp* **~ed** *or* **~t**) *adj* (*thin*) flaco; (*meat*) magro ▷ *vt*: **to ~ sth on sth** apoyar algo en algo ▷ *vi* (*slope*) inclinarse; **to ~ against** apoyarse contra; **to ~ on** apoyarse en; **lean forward** *vi* inclinarse hacia adelante; **lean over** *vi* inclinarse; **leaning** *n*: **leaning (towards)** inclinación *f* (hacia)

leant [lɛnt] *pt, pp of* **lean**

leap [li:p] (*pt, pp* **~ed** *or* **~t**) *n* salto ▷ *vi* saltar

leapt [lɛpt] *pt, pp of* **leap**

leap year *n* año bisiesto

learn [lə:n] (*pt, pp* **~ed** *or* **~t**) *vt* aprender ▷ *vi* aprender; **to ~ about sth** enterarse de algo; **to ~ to do sth** aprender a hacer algo; **learner** *n* (*BRIT: also*: **learner driver**) principiante *mf*; **learning** *n* el saber *m*, conocimientos *mpl*

learnt [lə:nt] *pp of* **learn**

lease [li:s] *n* arriendo ▷ *vt* arrendar

leash [li:ʃ] *n* correa

least [li:st] *adj*: **the ~** (*slightest*) el menor, el más pequeño; (*smallest amount of*) mínimo ▷ *adv* (+ *vb*) menos; (+ *adj*): **the ~ expensive** el (la) menos costoso/a; **the ~ possible effort** el menor esfuerzo posible; **at ~** por lo menos, al menos; **you could at ~ have written** por lo menos podías haber escrito; **not in the ~** en absoluto

leather ['lɛðə*] *n* cuero

leave [li:v] (*pt, pp* **left**) *vt* dejar; (*go away from*) abandonar; (*place etc: permanently*) salir de ▷ *vi* irse; (*train etc*) salir ▷ *n* permiso; **to ~ sth to sb** (*money etc*) legar algo a algn; (*responsibility etc*) encargar a algn de algo; **to be left** quedar, sobrar; **there's some milk left over** sobra *or* queda algo de leche; **on ~** de permiso; **leave behind** *vt* (*on purpose*) dejar; (*accidentally*) dejarse; **leave out** *vt* omitir

leaves [li:vz] *npl of* **leaf**

Lebanon ['lɛbənən] *n*: **the ~** el Líbano

lecture ['lɛktʃə*] *n* conferencia; (*Scol*) clase *f* ▷ *vi* dar una clase ▷ *vt* (*scold*): **to ~ sb on** *or* **about sth** echar una reprimenda a algn por algo; **to give a ~ on** dar una conferencia sobre; **lecture hall** *n* sala de conferencias; (*Univ*) aula; **lecturer** *n* conferenciante *mf*; (*BRIT: at university*) profesor(a) *m/f*; **lecture theatre** *n* = **lecture hall**

led [lɛd] *pt, pp of* **lead¹**

ledge [lɛdʒ] *n* repisa; (*of window*) alféizar *m*; (*of mountain*) saliente *m*

leek [li:k] *n* puerro

left [lɛft] *pt, pp of* **leave** ▷ *adj* izquierdo;

(*remaining*): **there are two ~** quedan dos ▷ *n* izquierda ▷ *adv* a la izquierda; **on** *or* **to the ~** a la izquierda; **the L~** (*Pol*) la izquierda; **left-hand** *adj*: **the left-hand side** la izquierda; **left-hand drive** *adj*: **a left-hand drive car** un coche con el volante a la izquierda; **left-handed** *adj* zurdo; **left-luggage locker** *n* (BRIT) consigna *f* automática; **left-luggage (office)** (BRIT) *n* consigna; **left-overs** *npl* sobras *fpl*; **left-wing** *adj* (*Pol*) de izquierdas, izquierdista

leg [lɛg] *n* pierna; (*of animal, chair*) pata; (*trouser leg*) pernera; (*Culin: of lamb*) pierna; (: *of chicken*) pata; (*of journey*) etapa

legacy ['lɛgəsɪ] *n* herencia

legal ['liːgl] *adj* (*permitted by law*) lícito; (*of law*) legal; **legal holiday** (US) *n* fiesta oficial; **legalize** *vt* legalizar; **legally** *adv* legalmente

legend ['lɛdʒənd] *n* (*also fig: person*) leyenda; **legendary** [-ərɪ] *adj* legendario

leggings ['lɛgɪŋz] *npl* mallas *fpl*, leggins *mpl*

legible ['lɛdʒəbl] *adj* legible

legislation [lɛdʒɪs'leɪʃən] *n* legislación *f*

legislative ['lɛdʒɪslətɪv] *adj* legislativo

legitimate [lɪ'dʒɪtɪmət] *adj* legítimo

leisure ['lɛʒə*] *n* ocio, tiempo libre; **at ~** con tranquilidad; **leisure centre** (BRIT) *n* centro de recreo; **leisurely** *adj* sin prisa; lento

lemon ['lɛmən] *n* limón *m*; **lemonade** *n* (*fizzy*) gaseosa; **lemon tea** *n* té *m* con limón

lend [lɛnd] (*pt, pp* **lent**) *vt*: **to ~ sth to sb** prestar algo a algn

length [lɛŋθ] *n* (*size*) largo, longitud *f*; (*distance*): **the ~ of** todo lo largo de; (*of swimming pool, cloth*) largo; (*of wood, string*) trozo; (*amount of time*) duración *f*; **at ~** (*at last*) por fin, finalmente; (*lengthily*) largamente; **lengthen** *vt* alargar ▷ *vi* alargarse; **lengthways** *adv* a lo largo; **lengthy** *adj* largo, extenso

lens [lɛnz] *n* (*of spectacles*) lente *f*; (*of camera*) objetivo

Lent [lɛnt] *n* Cuaresma

lent [lɛnt] *pt, pp* of **lend**

lentil ['lɛntl] *n* lenteja

Leo ['liːəu] *n* Leo

leopard ['lɛpəd] *n* leopardo

leotard ['liːətɑːd] *n* mallas *fpl*

leprosy ['lɛprəsɪ] *n* lepra

lesbian ['lɛzbɪən] *n* lesbiana

less [lɛs] *adj* (*in size, degree etc*) menor; (*in quality*) menos ▷ *pron, adv* menos ▷ *prep*: **~ tax/10% discount** menos impuestos/el 10 por ciento de descuento; **~ than half** menos de la mitad; **~ than ever** menos que

nunca; **~ and ~** cada vez menos; **the ~ he works ...** cuanto menos trabaja ...; **lessen** *vi* disminuir, reducirse ▷ *vt* disminuir, reducir; **lesser** ['lɛsə*] *adj* menor; **to a lesser extent** en menor grado

lesson ['lɛsn] *n* clase *f*; (*warning*) lección *f*

let [lɛt] (*pt, pp* **~**) *vt* (*allow*) dejar, permitir; (BRIT: *lease*) alquilar; **to ~ sb do sth** dejar que algn haga algo; **to ~ sb know sth** comunicar algo a algn; **~'s go** ¡vamos!; **~ him come** que venga; **"to ~"** "se alquila"; **let down** *vt* (*tyre*) desinflar; (*disappoint*) defraudar; **let in** *vt* dejar entrar; (*visitor etc*) hacer pasar; **let off** *vt* (*culprit*) dejar escapar; (*gun*) disparar; (*bomb*) accionar; (*firework*) hacer estallar; **let out** *vt* dejar salir; (*sound*) soltar

lethal ['liːθl] *adj* (*weapon*) mortífero; (*poison, wound*) mortal

letter ['lɛtə*] *n* (*of alphabet*) letra; (*correspondence*) carta; **letterbox** (BRIT) *n* buzón *m*

lettuce ['lɛtɪs] *n* lechuga

leukaemia [luː'kiːmɪə] (US **leukemia**) *n* leucemia

level ['lɛvl] *adj* (*flat*) llano ▷ *adv*: **to draw ~ with** llegar a la altura de ▷ *n* nivel *m*; (*height*) altura ▷ *vt* nivelar; allanar; (*destroy: building*) derribar; (: *forest*) arrasar; **to be ~ with** estar a nivel de; **A ~s** (BRIT) ≈ exámenes *mpl* de bachillerato superior, B.U.P.; **AS ~** (BRIT) asignatura aprobada entre los "GCSEs" y los "A levels"; **on the ~** (*fig: honest*) serio; **level crossing** (BRIT) *n* paso a nivel

lever ['liːvə*] *n* (*also fig*) palanca ▷ *vt*: **to ~ up** levantar con palanca; **leverage** *n* (*using bar etc*) apalancamiento; (*fig: influence*) influencia

levy ['lɛvɪ] *n* impuesto ▷ *vt* exigir, recaudar

liability [laɪə'bɪlətɪ] *n* (*pej: person, thing*) estorbo, lastre *m*; (*Jur: responsibility*) responsabilidad *f*

liable ['laɪəbl] *adj* (*subject*): **~ to** sujeto a; (*responsible*): **~ for** responsable de; (*likely*): **~ to do** propenso a hacer

liaise [lɪ'eɪz] *vi*: **to ~ with** enlazar con

liar ['laɪə*] *n* mentiroso/a

liberal ['lɪbərəl] *adj* liberal; (*offer, amount etc*) generoso; **Liberal Democrat** *n* (BRIT) demócrata *m/f* liberal

liberate ['lɪbəreɪt] *vt* (*people: from poverty etc*) librar; (*prisoner*) liberar; (*country*) liberar

liberation [lɪbə'reɪʃən] *n* liberación *f*

liberty ['lɪbətɪ] *n* libertad *f*; **to be at ~** (*criminal*) estar en libertad; **to be at ~ to do** estar libre para hacer; **to take the ~ of doing sth** tomarse la libertad de hacer algo

Libra ['liːbrə] *n* Libra

librarian [laɪˈbrɛərɪən] *n* bibliotecario/a
library [ˈlaɪbrərɪ] *n* biblioteca

▌Be careful not to translate **library** by the Spanish word *librería*.

Libya [ˈlɪbɪə] *n* Libia
lice [laɪs] *npl of* **louse**
licence [ˈlaɪsəns] (*US* **license**) *n* licencia; (*permit*) permiso; (*also*: **driving ~**) carnet *m* de conducir (*SP*), licencia de manejo (*LAM*)
license [ˈlaɪsəns] *n* (*US*) = **licence** ▷ *vt* autorizar, dar permiso a; **licensed** *adj* (*for alcohol*) autorizado para vender bebidas alcohólicas; (*car*) matriculado; **license plate** (*US*) *n* placa (de matrícula); **licensing hours** (*BRIT*) *npl* horas durante las cuales se permite la venta y consumo de alcohol (*en un bar etc*)
lick [lɪk] *vt* lamer; (*inf*: *defeat*) dar una paliza a; **to ~ one's lips** relamerse
lid [lɪd] *n* (*of box, case*) tapa; (*of pan*) tapadera
lie [laɪ] (*pt* **lay**, *pp* **lain**) *vi* (*rest*) estar echado, estar acostado; (*of object*: *be situated*) estar, encontrarse; (*tell lies*: *pt, pp* **lied**) mentir ▷ *n* mentira; **to ~ low** (*fig*) mantenerse a escondidas; **lie about** *or* **around** *vi* (*things*) estar tirado; (*BRIT*: *people*) estar tumbado; **lie down** *vi* echarse, tumbarse
Liechtenstein [ˈlɪktənstaɪn] *n* Liechtenstein *m*
lie-in [laɪn] (*BRIT*) *n*: **to have a ~** quedarse en la cama
lieutenant [lɛfˈtɛnənt, *US* luːˈtɛnənt] *n* (*Mil*) teniente *mf*
life [laɪf] (*pl* **lives**) *n* vida; **to come to ~** animarse; **life assurance** (*BRIT*) *n* seguro de vida; **lifeboat** *n* lancha de socorro; **lifeguard** *n* vigilante *mf*, socorrista *mf*; **life insurance** *n* = **life assurance**; **life jacket** *n* chaleco salvavidas; **lifelike** *adj* (*model etc*) que parece vivo; (*realistic*) realista; **life preserver** (*US*) *n* cinturón *m*/chaleco salvavidas; **life sentence** *n* cadena perpetua; **lifestyle** *n* estilo de vida; **lifetime** *n* (*of person*) vida; (*of thing*) período de vida
lift [lɪft] *vt* levantar; (*end*: *ban, rule*) levantar, suprimir ▷ *vi* (*fog*) disiparse ▷ *n* (*BRIT*: *machine*) ascensor *m*; **to give sb a ~** (*BRIT*) llevar a algn en el coche; **lift up** *vt* levantar; **lift-off** *n* despegue *m*
light [laɪt] (*pt, pp* **~ed** *or* **lit**) *n* luz *f*; (*lamp*) luz *f*, lámpara; (*Aut*) faro; (*for cigarette etc*): **have you got a ~?** ¿tienes fuego? ▷ *vt* (*candle, cigarette, fire*) encender (*SP*), prender (*LAM*); (*room*) alumbrar ▷ *adj* (*colour*) claro; (*not heavy, also fig*) ligero; (*room*) con mucha

luz; (*gentle, graceful*) ágil; **lights** *npl* (*traffic lights*) semáforos *mpl*; **to come to ~** salir a luz; **in the ~ of** (*new evidence etc*) a la luz de; **light up** *vi* (*smoke*) encender un cigarrillo; (*face*) iluminarse ▷ *vt* (*illuminate*) iluminar, alumbrar; (*set fire to*) encender; **light bulb** *n* bombilla (*SP*), foco (*MEX*), bujía (*CAM*), bombita (*RPL*); **lighten** *vt* (*make less heavy*) aligerar; **lighter** *n* (*also*: **cigarette lighter**) encendedor *m*, mechero; **light-hearted** *adj* (*person*) alegre; (*remark etc*) divertido; **lighthouse** *n* faro; **lighting** *n* (*system*) alumbrado; **lightly** *adv* ligeramente; (*not seriously*) con poca seriedad; **to get off lightly** ser castigado con poca severidad
lightning [ˈlaɪtnɪŋ] *n* relámpago, rayo
lightweight [ˈlaɪtweɪt] *adj* (*suit*) ligero ▷ *n* (*Boxing*) peso ligero
like [laɪk] *vt* gustarle a algn ▷ *prep* como ▷ *adj* parecido, semejante ▷ *n*: **and the ~** y otros por el estilo; **his ~s and dislikes** sus gustos y aversiones; **I would ~, I'd ~** me gustaría; (*for purchase*) quisiera; **would you ~ a coffee?** ¿te apetece un café?; **I ~ swimming** me gusta nadar; **she ~s apples** le gustan las manzanas; **to be** *or* **look ~ sb/ sth** parecerse a algn/algo; **what does it look/taste/sound ~?** ¿cómo es/a qué sabe/ cómo suena?; **that's just ~ him** es muy de él, es característico de él; **do it ~ this** hazlo así; **it is nothing ~ ...** no tiene parecido alguno con ...; **likeable** *adj* simpático, agradable
likelihood [ˈlaɪklɪhud] *n* probabilidad *f*
likely [ˈlaɪklɪ] *adj* probable; **he's ~ to leave** es probable que se vaya; **not ~!** ¡ni hablar!
likewise [ˈlaɪkwaɪz] *adv* igualmente; **to do ~** hacer lo mismo
liking [ˈlaɪkɪŋ] *n*: **~ (for)** (*person*) cariño (a); (*thing*) afición (a); **to be to sb's ~** ser del gusto de algn
lilac [ˈlaɪlək] *n* (*tree*) lilo; (*flower*) lila
Lilo® [ˈlaɪləu] *n* colchoneta inflable
lily [ˈlɪlɪ] *n* lirio, azucena; **~ of the valley** lirio de los valles
limb [lɪm] *n* miembro
limbo [ˈlɪmbəu] *n*: **to be in ~** (*fig*) quedar a la expectativa
lime [laɪm] *n* (*tree*) limero; (*fruit*) lima; (*Geo*) cal *f*
limelight [ˈlaɪmlaɪt] *n*: **to be in the ~** (*fig*) ser el centro de atención
limestone [ˈlaɪmstəun] *n* piedra caliza
limit [ˈlɪmɪt] *n* límite *m* ▷ *vt* limitar; **limited** *adj* limitado; **to be limited to** limitarse a
limousine [ˈlɪməziːn] *n* limusina
limp [lɪmp] *n*: **to have a ~** tener cojera ▷ *vi*

cojear ▷ adj flojo; (material) fláccido

line [laɪn] n línea; (rope) cuerda; (for fishing) sedal m; (wire) hilo; (row, series) fila, hilera; (of writing) renglón m, línea; (of song) verso; (on face) arruga; (Rail) vía ▷ vt (road etc) llenar; (Sewing) forrar; **to ~ the streets** llenar las aceras; **in ~ with** alineado con; (according to) de acuerdo con; **line up** vi hacer cola ▷ vt alinear; (prepare) preparar; organizar

linear ['lɪnɪə*] adj lineal

linen ['lɪnɪn] n ropa blanca; (cloth) lino

liner ['laɪnə*] n vapor m de línea, transatlántico; (for bin) bolsa (de basura)

line-up ['laɪnʌp] n (us: queue) cola; (Sport) alineación f

linger ['lɪŋgə*] vi retrasarse, tardar en marcharse; (smell, tradition) persistir

lingerie ['lænʒəriː] n lencería

linguist ['lɪŋgwɪst] n lingüista mf; **linguistic** adj lingüístico

lining ['laɪnɪŋ] n forro; (Anat) (membrana) mucosa

link [lɪŋk] n (of a chain) eslabón m; (relationship) relación f, vínculo; (Internet) link m, enlace m ▷ vt vincular, unir; (associate): **to ~ with** or **to** relacionar con; **links** npl (Golf) campo de golf; **link up** vt acoplar ▷ vi unirse

lion ['laɪən] n león m; **lioness** n leona

lip [lɪp] n labio; **lipread** vi leer los labios; **lip salve** n crema protectora para labios; **lipstick** n lápiz m de labios, carmín m

liqueur [lɪ'kjuə*] n licor m

liquid ['lɪkwɪd] adj, n líquido; **liquidizer** [-aɪzə*] n licuadora

liquor ['lɪkə*] n licor m, bebidas fpl alcohólicas; **liquor store** (us) n bodega, tienda de vinos y bebidas alcohólicas

Lisbon ['lɪzbən] n Lisboa

lisp [lɪsp] n ceceo ▷ vi cecear

list [lɪst] n lista ▷ vt (mention) enumerar; (put on a list) poner en una lista

listen ['lɪsn] vi escuchar, oír; **to ~ to** sb/sth escuchar a algn/algo; **listener** n oyente mf; (Radio) radioyente mf

lit [lɪt] pt, pp of **light**

liter ['liːtə*] (us) n = **litre**

literacy ['lɪtərəsɪ] n capacidad f de leer y escribir

literal ['lɪtərl] adj literal; **literally** adv literalmente

literary ['lɪtərərɪ] adj literario

literate ['lɪtərət] adj que sabe leer y escribir; (educated) culto

literature ['lɪtərɪtʃə*] n literatura; (brochures etc) folletos mpl

litre ['liːtə*] (us **liter**) n litro

litter ['lɪtə*] n (rubbish) basura; (young

animals) camada, cría; **litter bin** (BRIT) n papelera; **littered** adj: **littered with** (scattered) lleno de

little ['lɪtl] adj (small) pequeño; (not much) poco ▷ adv poco; **a ~** un poco (de); **~ house/bird** casita/pajarito; **a ~ bit** un poquito; **~ by ~** poco a poco; **little finger** n dedo meñique

live¹ [laɪv] adj (animal) vivo; (wire) conectado; (broadcast) en directo; (shell) cargado

live² [lɪv] vi vivir; **live together** vi vivir juntos; **live up to** vt fus (fulfil) cumplir con

livelihood ['laɪvlɪhud] n sustento

lively ['laɪvlɪ] adj vivo; (interesting: place, book etc) animado

liven up ['laɪvn-] vt animar ▷ vi animarse

liver ['lɪvə*] n hígado

lives [laɪvz] npl of **life**

livestock ['laɪvstɔk] n ganado

living ['lɪvɪŋ] adj (alive) vivo ▷ n: **to earn** or **make a ~** ganarse la vida; **living room** n sala (de estar)

lizard ['lɪzəd] n lagarto; (small) lagartija

load [ləud] n carga; (weight) peso ▷ vt (Comput) cargar; (also: ~ up): **to ~ (with)** cargar (con or de); **a ~ of rubbish** (inf) tonterías fpl; **a ~ of, ~s of** (fig) (gran) cantidad de, montones de; **loaded** adj (vehicle): **to be loaded with** estar cargado de

loaf [ləuf] (pl **loaves**) n (barra de) pan m

loan [ləun] n préstamo ▷ vt prestar; **on ~** prestado

loathe [ləuð] vt aborrecer; (person) odiar

loaves [ləuvz] npl of **loaf**

lobby ['lɔbɪ] n vestíbulo, sala de espera; (Pol: pressure group) grupo de presión ▷ vt presionar

lobster ['lɔbstə*] n langosta

local ['ləukl] adj local ▷ n (pub) bar m; **the locals** npl los vecinos, los del lugar; **local anaesthetic** n (Med) anestesia local; **local authority** n municipio, ayuntamiento (SP); **local government** n gobierno municipal; **locally** [-kəlɪ] adv en la vecindad; por aquí

locate [ləu'keɪt] vt (find) localizar; (situate): **to be ~d in** estar situado en

location [ləu'keɪʃən] n situación f; **on ~** (Cinema) en exteriores

loch [lɔx] n lago

lock [lɔk] n (of door, box) cerradura; (of canal) esclusa; (of hair) mechón m ▷ vt (with key) cerrar (con llave) ▷ vi (door etc) cerrarse (con llave); (wheels) trabarse; **lock in** vt encerrar; **lock out** vt (person) cerrar la puerta a; **lock up** vt (criminal) meter en la cárcel; (mental patient) encerrar; (house) cerrar (con llave) ▷ vi echar la llave

locker ['lɔkə*] n casillero; **locker-room** (us) n (Sport) vestuario

locksmith ['lɔksmɪθ] n cerrajero/a

locomotive [ləukə'məutɪv] n locomotora

lodge [lɔdʒ] n casita (del guarda) ▷ vi (person): **to ~ (with)** alojarse (en casa de); (bullet, bone) incrustarse ▷ vt presentar; **lodger** n huésped mf

lodging ['lɔdʒɪŋ] n alojamiento, hospedaje m

loft [lɔft] n desván m

log [lɔg] n (of wood) leño, tronco; (written account) diario ▷ vt anotar; **log in, log on** (Comput) entrar en el sistema; **log off, log out** vi (Comput) salir del sistema

logic ['lɔdʒɪk] n lógica; **logical** adj lógico

logo ['ləugəu] n logotipo

lollipop ['lɔlɪpɔp] n pirulí m; **lollipop man/lady** (BRIT: irreg) n persona encargada de ayudar a los niños a cruzar la calle

lolly ['lɔlɪ] n (inf: ice cream) polo; (: lollipop) piruleta; (: money) guita

London ['lʌndən] n Londres; **Londoner** n londinense mf

lone [ləun] adj solitario

loneliness ['ləunlɪnɪs] n soledad f; aislamiento

lonely ['ləunlɪ] adj (situation) solitario; (person) solo; (place) aislado

long [lɔŋ] adj largo ▷ adv mucho tiempo, largamente ▷ vi: **to ~ for sth** anhelar algo; **so** or **as ~ as** mientras, con tal que; **don't be ~!** ¡no tardes!, ¡vuelve pronto!; **how ~ is the street?** ¿cuánto tiene la calle de largo?; **how ~ is the lesson?** ¿cuánto dura la clase?; **6 metres ~** que mide 6 metros, de 6 metros de largo; **6 months ~** que dura 6 meses, de 6 meses de duración; **all night ~** toda la noche; **he no ~er comes** ya no viene; **I can't stand it any ~er** ya no lo aguanto más; **~ before** mucho antes; **before ~** (+ future) dentro de poco; (+ past) poco tiempo después; **at ~ last** al fin, por fin; **long-distance** adj (race) de larga distancia; (call) interurbano; **long-haul** adj (flight) de larga distancia; **longing** n anhelo, ansia; (nostalgia) nostalgia ▷ adj anhelante

longitude ['lɔŋgɪtjuːd] n longitud f

long: long jump n salto de longitud; **long-life** adj (batteries) de larga duración; (milk) uperizado; **long-sighted** (BRIT) adj présbita; **long-standing** adj de mucho tiempo; **long-term** adj a largo plazo

loo [luː] (BRIT: inf) n wáter m

look [luk] vi mirar; (seem) parecer; (building etc): **to ~ south/on to the sea** dar al sur/al mar ▷ n (gen): **to have a ~** mirar; (glance) mirada; (appearance) aire m, aspecto; **looks** npl (good looks) belleza; **~ (here)!** (expressing annoyance etc) ¡oye!; **~!** (expressing surprise) ¡mira!; **look after** vt fus (care for) cuidar a; (deal with) encargarse de; **look around** vi echar una mirada alrededor; **look at** vt fus mirar; (read quickly) echar un vistazo a; **look back** vi mirar hacia atrás; **look down on** vt fus (fig) despreciar, mirar con desprecio; **look for** vt fus buscar; **look forward to** vt fus esperar con ilusión; (in letters): **we look forward to hearing from you** quedamos a la espera de sus gratas noticias; **look into** vt investigar; **look out** vi (beware): **to look out (for)** tener cuidado (de); **look out for** vt fus (seek) buscar; (await) esperar; **look round** vi volver la cabeza; **look through** vt fus (examine) examinar; **look up** vi mirar hacia arriba; (improve) mejorar ▷ vt (word) buscar; **look up to** vt fus admirar; **lookout** n (tower etc) puesto de observación; (person) vigía mf; **to be on the lookout for sth** estar al acecho de algo

loom [luːm] vi: **~ (up)** (threaten) surgir, amenazar; (event: approach) aproximarse

loony ['luːnɪ] (inf) n, adj loco/a m/f

loop [luːp] n lazo ▷ vt: **to ~ sth round sth** pasar algo alrededor de algo; **loophole** n escapatoria

loose [luːs] adj suelto; (clothes) ancho; (morals, discipline) relajado; **to be on the ~** estar en libertad; **to be at a ~ end** or **at ~ ends** (us) no saber qué hacer; **loosely** adv libremente, aproximadamente; **loosen** vt aflojar

loot [luːt] n botín m ▷ vt saquear

lop-sided ['lɔp'saɪdɪd] adj torcido

lord [lɔːd] n señor m; **L~ Smith** Lord Smith; **the L~** el Señor; **my ~** (to bishop) Ilustrísima; (to noble etc) Señor; **good L~!** ¡Dios mío!; **Lords** npl (BRIT: Pol): **the (House of) Lords** la Cámara de los Lores

lorry ['lɔrɪ] (BRIT) n camión m; **lorry driver** (BRIT) n camionero/a

lose [luːz] (pt, pp lost) vt perder ▷ vi perder, ser vencido; **to ~ (time)** (clock) atrasarse; **lose out** vi salir perdiendo; **loser** n perdedor(a) m/f

loss [lɔs] n pérdida; **heavy ~es** (Mil) grandes pérdidas; **to be at a ~** no saber qué hacer; **to make a ~** sufrir pérdidas

lost [lɔst] pt, pp of **lose** ▷ adj perdido; **lost property** (US lost and found) n objetos mpl perdidos

lot [lɔt] n (group: of things) grupo; (at auctions) lote m; **the ~** el todo, todos; **a ~** (large number: of books etc) muchos; (a great deal) mucho, bastante; **a ~ of, ~s**

of mucho(s) (pl); **I read a ~** leo bastante; **to draw ~s (for sth)** echar suertes (para decidir algo)

lotion ['ləʊʃən] n loción f

lottery ['lɒtəri] n lotería

loud [laʊd] adj (voice, sound) fuerte; (laugh, shout) estrepitoso; (condemnation etc) enérgico; (gaudy) chillón/ona ▷ adv (speak etc) fuerte; **out ~** en voz alta; **loudly** adv (noisily) fuerte; (aloud) en voz alta; **loudspeaker** n altavoz m

lounge [laʊndʒ] n salón m, sala (de estar); (at airport etc) sala; (BRIT: also: **~-bar**) salón-bar m ▷ vi (also: **~ about** or **around**) reposar, holgazanear

louse [laʊs] (pl **lice**) n piojo

lousy ['laʊzi] (inf) adj (bad quality) malísimo, asqueroso; (ill) fatal

love [lʌv] n (romantic, sexual) amor m; (kind, caring) cariño ▷ vt amar, querer; (thing, activity) encantarle a algn; **"~ from Anne"** (on letter) "un abrazo (de) Anne"; **to ~ to do** encantarle a algn hacer; **to be/fall in ~ with** estar enamorado/enamorarse de; **to make ~** hacer el amor; **for the ~ of** por amor de; **"15 ~"** (Tennis) "15 a cero"; **I ~ you** te quiero; **I ~ paella** me encanta la paella; **love affair** n aventura sentimental; **love life** n vida sentimental

lovely ['lʌvli] adj (delightful) encantador(a); (beautiful) precioso

lover ['lʌvə*] n amante mf; (person in love) enamorado; (amateur): **a ~ of** un(a) aficionado/a or un(a) amante de

loving ['lʌvɪŋ] adj amoroso, cariñoso; (action) tierno

low [ləʊ] adj, adv bajo ▷ n (Meteorology) área de baja presión; **to be ~ on** (supplies etc) andar mal de; **to feel ~** sentirse deprimido; **to turn (down) ~** bajar; **low-alcohol** adj de bajo contenido en alcohol; **low-calorie** adj bajo en calorías

lower ['ləʊə*] adj más bajo; (less important) menos importante ▷ vt bajar; (reduce) reducir ▷ vr: **to ~ o.s.** to (fig) rebajarse a

low-fat adj (milk, yoghurt) desnatado; (diet) bajo en calorías

loyal ['lɔɪəl] adj leal; **loyalty** n lealtad f; **loyalty card** n tarjeta cliente

L.P. n abbr (= long-playing record) elepé m

L-plates ['el-] (BRIT) npl placas fpl de aprendiz de conductor

Lt abbr (= lieutenant) Tte.

Ltd abbr (= limited company) S.A.

luck [lʌk] n suerte f; **bad ~** mala suerte; **good ~!** ¡que tengas suerte!, ¡suerte!; **bad** or **hard** or **tough ~!** ¡qué pena!; **luckily** adv afortunadamente; **lucky** adj afortunado; (at cards etc) con suerte; (object) que trae suerte

lucrative ['lu:krətɪv] adj lucrativo

ludicrous ['lu:dɪkrəs] adj absurdo

luggage ['lʌgɪdʒ] n equipaje m; **luggage rack** n (on car) baca, portaequipajes m inv

lukewarm ['lu:kwɔ:m] adj tibio

lull [lʌl] n tregua ▷ vt: **to ~ sb to sleep** arrullar a algn; **to ~ sb into a false sense of security** dar a algn una falsa sensación de seguridad

lullaby ['lʌləbaɪ] n nana

lumber ['lʌmbə*] n (junk) trastos mpl viejos; (wood) maderos mpl

luminous ['lu:mɪnəs] adj luminoso

lump [lʌmp] n terrón m; (fragment) trozo; (swelling) bulto ▷ vt (also: **~ together**) juntar; **lump sum** n suma global; **lumpy** adj (sauce) lleno de grumos; (mattress) lleno de bultos

lunatic ['lu:nətɪk] adj loco

lunch [lʌntʃ] n almuerzo, comida ▷ vi almorzar; **lunch break**, **lunch hour** n hora del almuerzo; **lunch time** n hora de comer

lung [lʌŋ] n pulmón m

lure [luə*] n (attraction) atracción f ▷ vt tentar

lurk [lə:k] vi (person, animal) estar al acecho; (fig) acechar

lush [lʌʃ] adj exuberante

lust [lʌst] n lujuria; (greed) codicia

Luxembourg ['lʌksəmbə:g] n Luxemburgo

luxurious [lʌg'zjuəriəs] adj lujoso

luxury ['lʌkʃəri] n lujo ▷ cpd de lujo

Lycra® ['laɪkrə] n licra®

lying ['laɪɪŋ] n mentiras fpl ▷ adj mentiroso

lyrics ['lɪrɪks] npl (of song) letra

m

m. _abbr_ = metre; mile; million

M.A. _abbr_ = Master of Arts

ma (_inf_) [mɑː] _n_ mamá

mac [mæk] (BRIT) _n_ impermeable _m_

macaroni [mækə'rəʊnɪ] _n_ macarrones _mpl_

Macedonia [mæsɪ'dəʊnɪə] _n_ Macedonia; **Macedonian** [-'dəʊnɪən] _adj_ macedonio ▷ _n_ macedonio/a; (Ling) macedonio

machine [mə'fiːn] _n_ máquina ▷ _vt_ (_dress etc_) coser a máquina; (_Tech_) hacer a máquina; **machine gun** _n_ ametralladora; **machinery** _n_ maquinaria; (_fig_) mecanismo; **machine washable** _adj_ lavable a máquina

macho ['mætʃəʊ] _adj_ machista

mackerel ['mækrl] _n inv_ caballa

mackintosh ['mækɪntɒʃ] (BRIT) _n_ impermeable _m_

mad [mæd] _adj_ loco; (_idea_) disparatado; (_angry_) furioso; (_keen_): **to be ~ about sth** volverle loco a algn algo

Madagascar [mædə'gæskə*] _n_ Madagascar _m_

madam ['mædəm] _n_ señora

mad cow disease _n_ encefalopatía espongiforme bovina

made [meɪd] _pt, pp of_ **make**; **made-to-measure** (BRIT) _adj_ hecho a la medida; **made-up** ['meɪdʌp] _adj_ (_story_) ficticio

madly ['mædlɪ] _adv_ locamente

madman ['mædmən] (_irreg_) _n_ loco

madness ['mædnɪs] _n_ locura

Madrid [mə'drɪd] _n_ Madrid

Mafia ['mæfɪə] _n_ Mafia

mag [mæg] _n abbr_ (BRIT _inf_) = **magazine**

magazine [mægə'ziːn] _n_ revista; (_Radio, TV_) programa _m_ magazina

maggot ['mægət] _n_ gusano

magic ['mædʒɪk] _n_ magia ▷ _adj_ mágico; **magical** _adj_ mágico; **magician** [mə'dʒɪʃən] _n_ mago/a; (_conjurer_) prestidigitador(a) _m/f_

magistrate ['mædʒɪstreɪt] _n_ juez _mf_ (municipal)

magnet ['mægnɪt] _n_ imán _m_; **magnetic** [-'nɛtɪk] _adj_ magnético; (_personality_) atrayente

magnificent [mæg'nɪfɪsənt] _adj_ magnífico

magnify ['mægnɪfaɪ] _vt_ (_object_) ampliar; (_sound_) aumentar; **magnifying glass** _n_ lupa

magpie ['mægpaɪ] _n_ urraca

mahogany [mə'hɒgənɪ] _n_ caoba

maid [meɪd] _n_ criada; **old ~** (_pej_) solterona

maiden name _n_ nombre _m_ de soltera

mail [meɪl] _n_ correo; (_letters_) cartas _fpl_ ▷ _vt_ echar al correo; **mailbox** (US) _n_ buzón _m_; **mailing list** _n_ lista de direcciones; **mailman** (US: _irreg_) _n_ cartero; **mail-order** _n_ pedido postal

main [meɪn] _adj_ principal, mayor ▷ _n_ (_pipe_) cañería maestra; (US) red _f_ eléctrica ▷ **the ~s** _npl_ (BRIT _Elec_) la red eléctrica; **in the ~** en general; **main course** _n_ (_Culin_) plato principal; **mainland** _n_ tierra firme; **mainly** _adv_ principalmente; **main road** _n_ carretera; **mainstream** _n_ corriente _f_ principal; **main street** _n_ calle _f_ mayor

maintain [meɪn'teɪn] _vt_ mantener; **maintenance** ['meɪntənəns] _n_ mantenimiento; (_Law_) manutención _f_

maisonette [meɪzə'nɛt] _n_ dúplex _m_

maize [meɪz] _n_ maíz _m_, choclo (SC)

majesty ['mædʒɪstɪ] _n_ majestad _f_; (_title_): **Your M~** Su Majestad

major ['meɪdʒə*] _n_ (_Mil_) comandante _mf_ ▷ _adj_ principal; (_Mus_) mayor

Majorca [mə'jɔːkə] _n_ Mallorca

majority [mə'dʒɒrɪtɪ] _n_ mayoría

make [meɪk] (_pt, pp_ **made**) _vt_ hacer; (_manufacture_) fabricar; (_mistake_) cometer; (_speech_) pronunciar; (_cause to be_): **to ~ sb sad** poner triste a algn; (_force_): **to ~ sb do sth** obligar a algn a hacer algo; (_earn_) ganar; (_equal_): **2 and 2 ~ 4** 2 y 2 son 4 ▷ _n_ marca; **to ~ the bed** hacer la cama; **to ~ a fool of sb** poner a algn en ridículo; **to ~ a profit/loss** obtener ganancias/sufrir pérdidas; **to ~ it** (_arrive_) llegar; (_achieve sth_) tener éxito; **what time do you ~ it?** ¿qué hora tienes?; **to ~ do with** contentarse con; **make off** _vi_ largarse; **make out** _vt_ (_decipher_) descifrar; (_understand_) entender; (_see_) distinguir; (_cheque_) extender; **make up** _vt_ (_invent_) inventar; (_prepare_) hacer; (_constitute_) constituir ▷ _vi_ reconciliarse; (_with cosmetics_) maquillarse; **make up for** _vt_

fus compensar; **makeover** ['meɪkəʊvə*]
n (*by beautician*) sesión f de maquillaje y
peluquería; (*change of image*) lavado de cara;
maker *n* fabricante *mf*; (*of film, programme*)
autor(a) *m/f*; **makeshift** *adj* improvisado;
make-up *n* maquillaje *m*

making ['meɪkɪŋ] *n* (*fig*): **in the ~** en vías
de formación; **to have the ~s of** (*person*)
tener madera de

malaria [mə'lɛərɪə] *n* malaria

Malaysia [mə'leɪzɪə] *n* Malasia, Malaysia

male [meɪl] *n* (*Biol*) macho ▷ *adj* (*sex,*
attitude) masculino; (*child etc*) varón

malicious [mə'lɪʃəs] *adj* malicioso;
rencoroso

malignant [mə'lɪgnənt] *adj* (*Med*)
maligno

mall [mɔːl] (*US*) *n* (*also*: **shopping ~**) centro
comercial

mallet ['mælɪt] *n* mazo

malnutrition [mælnjuː'trɪʃən] *n*
desnutrición f

malpractice [mæl'præktɪs] *n*
negligencia profesional

malt [mɔːlt] *n* malta; (*whisky*) whisky *m*
de malta

Malta ['mɔːltə] *n* Malta; **Maltese** [-'tiːz]
adj, n inv maltés/esa *m/f*

mammal ['mæml] *n* mamífero

mammoth ['mæməθ] *n* mamut *m* ▷ *adj*
gigantesco

man [mæn] (*pl* **men**) *n* hombre *m*;
(*mankind*) el hombre ▷ *vt* (*Naut*) tripular;
(*Mil*) guarnecer; (*operate: machine*) manejar;
an old ~ un viejo; **~ and wife** marido y
mujer

manage ['mænɪdʒ] *vi* arreglárselas,
ir tirando ▷ *vt* (*be in charge of*) dirigir;
(*control: person*) manejar; (: *ship*)
gobernar; **manageable** *adj* manejable;
management *n* dirección f; **manager** *n*
director(a) *m/f*; (*of pop star*) mánager *mf*;
(*Sport*) entrenador(a) *m/f*; **manageress**
n directora; entrenadora; **managerial**
[-ə'dʒɪərɪəl] *adj* directivo; **managing**
director *n* director(a) *m/f* general

mandarin ['mændərɪn] *n* (*also*: **~ orange**)
mandarina; (*person*) mandarín *m*

mandate ['mændeɪt] *n* mandato

mandatory ['mændətərɪ] *adj* obligatorio

mane [meɪn] *n* (*of horse*) crin f; (*of lion*)
melena

maneuver [mə'nuːvə*] (*US*) = **manoeuvre**

mangetout [mɒnʒ'tuː] *n* tirabeque *m*

mango ['mæŋgəʊ] (*pl* **-es**) *n* mango

man: manhole *n* agujero de acceso;
manhood *n* edad f viril; (*state*) virilidad f

mania ['meɪnɪə] *n* manía; **maniac**

['meɪnɪæk] *n* maníaco/a; (*fig*) maniático

manic ['mænɪk] *adj* frenético

manicure ['mænɪkjuə*] *n* manicura

manifest ['mænɪfest] *vt* manifestar,
mostrar ▷ *adj* manifiesto

manifesto [mænɪ'festəʊ] *n* manifiesto

manipulate [mə'nɪpjuleɪt] *vt* manipular

man: mankind [mæn'kaɪnd] *n*
humanidad f, género humano; **manly** *adj*
varonil; **man-made** *adj* artificial

manner ['mænə*] *n* manera, modo;
(*behaviour*) conducta, manera de ser;
(*type*): **all ~ of things** toda clase de cosas;
manners *npl* (*behaviour*) modales *mpl*; **bad**
~s mala educación

manoeuvre [mə'nuːvə*] (*US* **maneuver**)
vt, vi maniobrar ▷ *n* maniobra

manpower ['mænpauə*] *n* mano f de
obra

mansion ['mænʃən] *n* palacio, casa
grande

manslaughter ['mænslɔːtə*] *n*
homicidio no premeditado

mantelpiece ['mæntlpiːs] *n* repisa,
chimenea

manual ['mænjuəl] *adj* manual ▷ *n*
manual *m*

manufacture [mænju'fæktʃə*] *vt*
fabricar ▷ *n* fabricación f; **manufacturer** *n*
fabricante *mf*

manure [mə'njuə*] *n* estiércol *m*

manuscript ['mænjuskrɪpt] *n*
manuscrito

many ['menɪ] *adj, pron* muchos/as; **a**
great ~ muchísimos, un buen número de; **~**
a time muchas veces

map [mæp] *n* mapa *m* ▷ **to ~ out** *vt*
proyectar

maple ['meɪpl] *n* arce *m*, maple *m* (*LAM*)

Mar *abbr* (= *March*) mar

mar [mɑː*] *vt* estropear

marathon ['mærəθən] *n* maratón *m*

marble ['mɑːbl] *n* mármol *m*; (*toy*) canica

March [mɑːtʃ] *n* marzo

march [mɑːtʃ] *vi* (*Mil*) marchar;
(*demonstrators*) manifestarse ▷ *n* marcha;
(*demonstration*) manifestación f

mare [mɛə*] *n* yegua

margarine [mɑːdʒə'riːn] *n* margarina

margin ['mɑːdʒɪn] *n* margen *m*;
(*Comm*: *profit margin*) margen *m* de
beneficios; **marginal** *adj* marginal;
marginally *adv* ligeramente

marigold ['mærɪgəʊld] *n* caléndula

marijuana [mærɪ'wɑːnə] *n* marijuana

marina [mə'riːnə] *n* puerto deportivo

marinade [mærɪ'neɪd] *n* adobo

marinate ['mærɪneɪt] *vt* marinar

m

marine [məˈriːn] adj marino ▷ n soldado de marina

marital [ˈmærɪtl] adj matrimonial; **marital status** n estado m civil

maritime [ˈmærɪtaɪm] adj marítimo

marjoram [ˈmɑːdʒərəm] n mejorana

mark [mɑːk] n marca, señal f; (in snow, mud etc) huella; (stain) mancha; (BRIT Scol) nota ▷ vt marcar; manchar; (damage: furniture) rayar; (indicate: place etc) señalar; (BRIT Scol) calificar, corregir; **to ~ time** marcar el paso; (fig) marcar(se) un ritmo; **marked** adj (obvious) marcado, acusado; **marker** n (sign) marcador m; (bookmark) señal f (de libro)

market [ˈmɑːkɪt] n mercado ▷ vt (Comm) comercializar; **marketing** n márketing m; **marketplace** n mercado; **market research** n análisis m inv de mercados

marmalade [ˈmɑːməleɪd] n mermelada de naranja

maroon [məˈruːn] vt: **to be ~ed** quedar aislado; (fig) quedar abandonado ▷ n (colour) granate m

marquee [mɑːˈkiː] n entoldado

marriage [ˈmærɪdʒ] n (relationship, institution) matrimonio; (wedding) boda; (act) casamiento; **marriage certificate** n partida de casamiento

married [ˈmærɪd] adj casado; (life, love) conyugal

marrow [ˈmærəʊ] n médula; (vegetable) calabacín m

marry [ˈmærɪ] vt casarse con; (father, priest etc) casar ▷ vi (also: **get married**) casarse

Mars [mɑːz] n Marte m

marsh [mɑːʃ] n pantano; (salt marsh) marisma

marshal [ˈmɑːʃl] n (Mil) mariscal m; (at sports meeting etc) oficial m; (us: of police, fire department) jefe/a m/f ▷ vt (thoughts etc) ordenar; (soldiers) formar

martyr [ˈmɑːtə*] n mártir mf

marvel [ˈmɑːvl] n maravilla, prodigio ▷ vi: **to ~ (at)** maravillarse (de); **marvellous** (us **marvelous**) adj maravilloso

Marxism [ˈmɑːksɪzəm] n marxismo

Marxist [ˈmɑːksɪst] adj, n marxista mf

marzipan [ˈmɑːzɪpæn] n mazapán m

mascara [mæsˈkɑːrə] n rímel m

mascot [ˈmæskət] n mascota

masculine [ˈmæskjulɪn] adj masculino

mash [mæʃ] vt machacar; **mashed potato(es)** n(pl) puré m de patatas (SP) or papas (LAM)

mask [mɑːsk] n máscara ▷ vt (cover): **to ~ one's face** ocultarse la cara; (hide: feelings) esconder

mason [ˈmeɪsn] n (also: **stone~**) albañil m; (also: **free~**) masón m; **masonry** n (in building) mampostería

mass [mæs] n (people) muchedumbre f; (of air, liquid etc) masa; (of detail, hair etc) gran cantidad f; (Rel) misa ▷ cpd masivo ▷ vi reunirse; concentrarse; **the masses** npl las masas; **~es of** (inf) montones de

massacre [ˈmæsəkə*] n masacre f

massage [ˈmæsɑːʒ] n masaje m ▷ vt dar masaje en

massive [ˈmæsɪv] adj enorme; (support, changes) masivo

mass media npl medios mpl de comunicación

mass-produce [ˈmæsprəˈdjuːs] vt fabricar en serie

mast [mɑːst] n (Naut) mástil m; (Radio etc) torre f

master [ˈmɑːstə*] n (of servant) amo; (of situation) dueño, maestro; (in primary school) maestro; (in secondary school) profesor m; (title for boys): **M~ X** Señorito X ▷ vt dominar; **mastermind** n inteligencia superior ▷ vt dirigir, planear; **Master of Arts/Science** n licenciatura superior en Letras/Ciencias; **masterpiece** n obra maestra

masturbate [ˈmæstəbeɪt] vi masturbarse

mat [mæt] n estera; (also: **door~**) felpudo; (also: **table ~**) salvamanteles m inv, posavasos m inv ▷ adj = **matt**

match [mætʃ] n cerilla, fósforo; (game) partido; (equal) igual m/f ▷ vt (go well with) hacer juego con; (equal) igualar; (correspond to) corresponderse con; (pair: also: **~ up**) casar con ▷ vi hacer juego; **to be a good ~** hacer juego; **matchbox** n caja de cerillas; **matching** adj que hace juego

mate [meɪt] n (workmate) colega mf; (inf: friend) amigo/a; (animal) macho/hembra; (in merchant navy) segundo de a bordo ▷ vi acoplarse, aparearse ▷ vt aparear

material [məˈtɪərɪəl] n (substance) materia; (information) material m; (cloth) tela, tejido ▷ adj material; (important) esencial; **materials** npl materiales mpl

materialize [məˈtɪərɪəlaɪz] vi materializarse

maternal [məˈtəːnl] adj maternal

maternity [məˈtəːnɪtɪ] n maternidad f; **maternity hospital** n hospital m de maternidad; **maternity leave** n baja por maternidad

math [mæθ] (us) n = **mathematics**

mathematical [mæθəˈmætɪkl] adj matemático

mathematician [mæθəmə'tɪʃən] n matemático/a
mathematics [mæθə'mætɪks] n matemáticas fpl
maths [mæθs] (BRIT) n = **mathematics**
matinée ['mætɪneɪ] n sesión f de tarde
matron ['meɪtrən] n enfermera f jefe; (in school) ama de llaves
matt [mæt] adj mate
matter ['mætə*] n cuestión f, asunto; (Physics) sustancia, materia; (reading matter) material m; (Med: pus) pus m ▷ vi importar; **matters** npl (affairs) asuntos mpl, temas mpl; **it doesn't ~** no importa; **what's the ~?** ¿qué pasa?; **no ~ what** pase lo que pase; **as a ~ of course** por rutina; **as a ~ of fact** de hecho
mattress ['mætrɪs] n colchón m
mature [mə'tjuə*] adj maduro ▷ vi madurar; **mature student** n estudiante de más de 21 años; **maturity** n madurez f
maul [mɔːl] vt magullar
mauve [məuv] adj de color malva (SP) or guinda (LAM)
max abbr = **maximum**
maximize ['mæksɪmaɪz] vt (profits etc) llevar al máximo; (chances) maximizar
maximum ['mæksɪməm] (pl **maxima**) adj máximo ▷ n máximo
May [meɪ] n mayo
may [meɪ] (conditional **might**) vi (indicating possibility): **he ~ come** puede que venga; (be allowed to): **~ I smoke?** ¿puedo fumar?; (wishes): **~ God bless you!** ¡que Dios le bendiga!; **you ~ as well go** bien puedes irte
maybe ['meɪbiː] adv quizá(s)
May Day n el primero de Mayo
mayhem ['meɪhɛm] n caos m total
mayonnaise [meɪə'neɪz] n mayonesa
mayor [mɛə*] n alcalde m; **mayoress** n alcaldesa
maze [meɪz] n laberinto
MD n abbr = **managing director**
me [miː] pron (direct) me; (stressed, after pron) mí; **can you hear ~?** ¿me oyes?; **he heard ME** ¡me oyó a mí!; **it's ~** soy yo; **give them to ~** dámelos/las; **with/without ~** conmigo/sin mí
meadow ['mɛdəu] n prado, pradera
meagre ['miːgə*] (US **meager**) adj escaso, pobre
meal [miːl] n comida; (flour) harina; **mealtime** n hora de comer
mean [miːn] (pt, pp **~t**) adj (with money) tacaño; (unkind) mezquino, malo; (shabby) humilde; (average) medio ▷ vt (signify) querer decir, significar; (refer to) referirse a; (intend): **to ~ to do sth** pensar or

pretender hacer algo ▷ n medio, término medio; **means** npl (way) medio, manera; (money) recursos mpl, medios mpl; **by ~s of** mediante, por medio de; **by all ~s!** ¡naturalmente!, ¡claro que sí!; **do you ~ it?** ¿lo dices en serio?; **what do you ~?** ¿qué quiere decir?; **to be ~t for sb/sth** ser para algn/algo
meaning ['miːnɪŋ] n significado, sentido; (purpose) sentido, propósito; **meaningful** adj significativo; **meaningless** adj sin sentido
meant [mɛnt] pt, pp of **mean**
meantime ['miːntaɪm] adv (also: **in the ~**) mientras tanto
meanwhile ['miːnwaɪl] adv = **meantime**
measles ['miːzlz] n sarampión m
measure ['mɛʒə*] vt, vi medir ▷ n medida; (ruler) regla; **measurement** ['mɛʒəmənt] n (measure) medida; (act) medición f; **to take sb's measurements** tomar las medidas a algn
meat [miːt] n carne f; **cold ~** fiambre m; **meatball** n albóndiga
Mecca ['mɛkə] n La Meca
mechanic [mɪ'kænɪk] n mecánico/a; **mechanical** adj mecánico
mechanism ['mɛkənɪzəm] n mecanismo
medal ['mɛdl] n medalla; **medallist** (US **medalist**) n (Sport) medallista mf
meddle ['mɛdl] vi: **to ~ in** entrometerse en; **to ~ with sth** manosear algo
media ['miːdɪə] npl medios mpl de comunicación ▷ npl of **medium**
mediaeval [mɛdɪ'iːvl] adj = **medieval**
mediate ['miːdɪeɪt] vi mediar
medical ['mɛdɪkl] adj médico ▷ n reconocimiento médico; **medical certificate** n certificado m médico
medicated ['mɛdɪkeɪtɪd] adj medicinal
medication [mɛdɪ'keɪʃən] n medicación f
medicine ['mɛdsɪn] n medicina; (drug) medicamento
medieval [mɛdɪ'iːvl] adj medieval
mediocre [miːdɪ'əukə*] adj mediocre
meditate ['mɛdɪteɪt] vi meditar
meditation [mɛdɪ'teɪʃən] n meditación f
Mediterranean [mɛdɪtə'reɪnɪən] adj mediterráneo; **the ~ (Sea)** el (Mar) Mediterráneo
medium ['miːdɪəm] (pl **media**) adj mediano, regular ▷ n (means) medio; (pl **mediums**: person) médium mf; **medium-sized** adj de tamaño mediano; (clothes) de (la) talla mediana; **medium wave** n onda media
meek [miːk] adj manso, sumiso
meet [miːt] (pt, pp **met**) vt encontrar;

(*accidentally*) encontrarse con, tropezar con; (*by arrangement*) reunirse con; (*for the first time*) conocer; (*go and fetch*) ir a buscar; (*opponent*) enfrentarse con; (*obligations*) cumplir; (*encounter: problem*) hacer frente a; (*need*) satisfacer ▷ vi encontrarse; (*in session*) reunirse; (*join: objects*) unirse; (*for the first time*) conocerse; **meet up** vi: **to meet up with sb** reunirse con algn; **meet with** vt fus (*difficulty*) tropezar con; **to meet with success** tener éxito; **meeting** n encuentro; (*arranged*) cita, compromiso; (*business meeting*) reunión f; (*Pol*) mítin m; **meeting place** n lugar m de reunión or encuentro

megabyte ['mɛgəbaɪt] n (*Comput*) megabyte m, megaocteto

megaphone ['mɛgəfəun] n megáfono

megapixel ['mɛgəpɪksl] n megapíxel m

melancholy ['mɛlənkəlɪ] n melancolía ▷ adj melancólico

melody ['mɛlədɪ] n melodía

melon ['mɛlən] n melón m

melt [mɛlt] vi (*metal*) fundirse; (*snow*) derretirse ▷ vt fundir

member ['mɛmbə*] n (*gen, Anat*) miembro; (*of club*) socio/a; **Member of Congress** (*us*) n miembro mf del Congreso; **Member of Parliament** n (*BRIT*) diputado/a m/f, parlamentario/a m/f; **Member of the European Parliament** n diputado/a m/f del Parlamento Europeo, eurodiputado/a m/f; **Member of the Scottish Parliament** (*BRIT*) diputado/a del Parlamento escocés; **membership** n (*members*) número de miembros; (*state*) filiación f; **membership card** n carnet m de socio

memento [mə'mɛntəu] n recuerdo

memo ['mɛməu] n apunte m, nota

memorable ['mɛmərəbl] adj memorable

memorandum [mɛmə'rændəm] (*pl* **memoranda**) n apunte m, nota; (*official note*) acta

memorial [mɪ'mɔːrɪəl] n monumento conmemorativo ▷ adj conmemorativo

memorize ['mɛməraɪz] vt aprender de memoria

memory ['mɛmərɪ] n (*also: Comput*) memoria; (*instance*) recuerdo; (*of dead person*): **in ~ of** a la memoria de; **memory card** n (*for digital camera*) tarjeta de memoria

men [mɛn] npl of **man**

menace ['mɛnəs] n amenaza ▷ vt amenazar

mend [mɛnd] vt reparar, arreglar; (*darn*) zurcir ▷ vi reponerse ▷ n arreglo, reparación f zurcido ▷ n: **to be on the ~** ir mejorando; **to ~ one's ways** enmendarse

meningitis [mɛnɪn'dʒaɪtɪs] n meningitis f

menopause ['mɛnəupɔːz] n menopausia

men's room (*us*) n: **the ~** el servicio de caballeros

menstruation [mɛnstru'eɪʃən] n menstruación f

menswear ['mɛnzweə*] n confección f de caballero

mental ['mɛntl] adj mental; **mental hospital** n (hospital m) psiquiátrico; **mentality** [mɛn'tælɪtɪ] n mentalidad f; **mentally** adv: **to be mentally ill** tener una enfermedad mental

menthol ['mɛnθəl] n mentol m

mention ['mɛnʃən] n mención f ▷ vt mencionar; (*speak*) hablar de; **don't ~ it!** ¡de nada!

menu ['mɛnjuː] n (*set menu*) menú m; (*printed*) carta; (*Comput*) menú m

MEP n abbr = **Member of the European Parliament**

mercenary ['məːsɪnərɪ] adj, n mercenario/a

merchandise ['məːtʃəndaɪz] n mercancías fpl

merchant ['məːtʃənt] n comerciante mf; **merchant navy** (*us*), **merchant marine** n marina mercante

merciless ['məːsɪlɪs] adj despiadado

mercury ['məːkjurɪ] n mercurio

mercy ['məːsɪ] n compasión f; (*Rel*) misericordia; **at the ~ of** a la merced de

mere [mɪə*] adj simple, mero; **merely** adv simplemente, sólo

merge [məːdʒ] vt (*join*) unir ▷ vi unirse; (*Comm*) fusionarse; (*colours etc*) fundirse; **merger** n (*Comm*) fusión f

meringue [mə'ræŋ] n merengue m

merit ['mɛrɪt] n mérito ▷ vt merecer

mermaid ['məːmeɪd] n sirena

merry ['mɛrɪ] adj alegre; **M~ Christmas!** ¡Felices Pascuas!; **merry-go-round** n tiovivo

mesh [mɛʃ] n malla

mess [mɛs] n (*muddle: of situation*) confusión f; (*: of room*) revoltijo; (*dirt*) porquería; (*Mil*) comedor m; **mess about** or **around** (*inf*) vi perder el tiempo; (*pass the time*) entretenerse; **mess up** vt (*spoil*) estropear; (*dirty*) ensuciar; **mess with** (*inf*) vt fus (*challenge, confront*) meterse con (*inf*); (*interfere with*) interferir con

message ['mɛsɪdʒ] n recado, mensaje m

messenger ['mɛsɪndʒə*] n mensajero/a

Messrs abbr (*on letters*) (= *Messieurs*) Sres

messy ['mɛsɪ] adj (*dirty*) sucio; (*untidy*) desordenado

met [mɛt] *pt, pp of* **meet**
metabolism [mɛ'tæbəlɪzəm] *n*
metabolismo
metal ['mɛtl] *n* metal *m*; **metallic** [-'tælɪk] *adj* metálico
metaphor ['mɛtəfə*] *n* metáfora
meteor ['miːtɪə*] *n* meteoro; **meteorite** [-aɪt] *n* meteorito
meteorology [miːtɪɔ'rɔlədʒɪ] *n* meteorología
meter ['miːtə*] *n* (*instrument*) contador *m*; (*us: unit*) = **metre** ▷ *vt* (*us Post*) franquear
method ['mɛθəd] *n* método; **methodical** [mɪ'θɔdɪkl] *adj* metódico
meths [mɛθs] *n* (*BRIT*) alcohol *m* metilado *or* desnaturalizado
meticulous [mɛ'tɪkjʊləs] *adj* meticuloso
metre ['miːtə*] (*us* **meter**) *n* metro
metric ['mɛtrɪk] *adj* métrico
metro ['mɛtrəu] *n* metro
metropolitan [mɛtrə'pɔlɪtən] *adj* metropolitano; **the M- Police** (*BRIT*) la policía londinense
Mexican ['mɛksɪkən] *adj, n* mexicano/a, mejicano/a
Mexico ['mɛksɪkəu] *n* México, Méjico (*SP*)
mg *abbr* (= *milligram*) mg
mice [maɪs] *npl of* **mouse**
micro... [maɪkrəu] *prefix* micro...; **microchip** *n* microplaqueta; **microphone** *n* micrófono; **microscope** *n* microscopio; **microwave** *n* (*also:* **microwave oven**) horno microondas
mid [mɪd] *adj:* **in ~ May** a mediados de mayo; **in ~ afternoon** a media tarde; **in ~ air** en el aire; **midday** *n* mediodía *m*
middle ['mɪdl] *n* centro; (*half-way point*) medio; (*waist*) cintura ▷ *adj* de en medio; (*course, way*) intermedio; **in the ~ of the night** en plena noche; **middle-aged** *adj* de mediana edad; **Middle Ages** *npl:* **the Middle Ages** la Edad Media; **middle-class** *adj* de clase media; **the middle class(es)** la clase media; **Middle East** *n* Oriente *m* Medio; **middle name** *n* segundo nombre; **middle school** *n* (*us*) colegio para niños de doce a catorce años; (*BRIT*) colegio para niños de ocho o nueve a doce o trece años
midge [mɪdʒ] *n* mosquito
midget ['mɪdʒɪt] *n* enano/a
midnight ['mɪdnaɪt] *n* medianoche *f*
midst [mɪdst] *n:* **in the ~ of** (*crowd*) en medio de; (*situation, action*) en mitad de
midsummer [mɪd'sʌmə*] *n:* **in ~** en pleno verano
midway [mɪd'weɪ] *adj, adv:* **~ (between)** a medio camino (entre); **~ through** a la mitad (de)

midweek [mɪd'wiːk] *adv* entre semana
midwife ['mɪdwaɪf] (*irreg*) *n* comadrona, partera
midwinter [mɪd'wɪntə*] *n:* **in ~** en pleno invierno
might [maɪt] *vb see* **may** ▷ *n* fuerza, poder *m*; **mighty** *adj* fuerte, poderoso
migraine ['miːgreɪn] *n* jaqueca
migrant ['maɪgrənt] *n, adj* (*bird*) migratorio; (*worker*) emigrante
migrate [maɪ'greɪt] *vi* emigrar
migration [maɪ'greɪʃən] *n* emigración *f*
mike [maɪk] *n abbr* (= *microphone*) micro
mild [maɪld] *adj* (*person*) apacible; (*climate*) templado; (*slight*) ligero; (*taste*) suave; (*illness*) leve; **mildly** ['-lɪ] *adv* ligeramente; suavemente; **to put it mildly** para no decir más
mile [maɪl] *n* milla; **mileage** *n* número de millas ≈ kilometraje *m*; **mileometer** [maɪ'lɔmɪtə] *n* ≈ cuentakilómetros *m inv*; **milestone** *n* mojón *m*
military ['mɪlɪtərɪ] *adj* militar
militia [mɪ'lɪʃə] *n* milicia
milk [mɪlk] *n* leche *f* ▷ *vt* (*cow*) ordeñar; (*fig*) chupar; **milk chocolate** *n* chocolate *m* con leche; **milkman** (*irreg*) *n* lechero; **milky** *adj* lechoso
mill [mɪl] *n* (*windmill etc*) molino; (*coffee mill*) molinillo; (*factory*) fábrica ▷ *vt* moler ▷ *vi* (*also:* **~ about**) arremolinarse
millennium [mɪ'lɛnɪəm] (*pl* **~s** *or* **millennia**) *n* milenio, milenario
milli... ['mɪlɪ] *prefix:* **milligram(me)** *n* miligramo; **millilitre** (*us* **milliliter**) ['mɪlɪliːtə*] *n* mililitro; **millimetre** (*us* **millimeter**) *n* milímetro
million ['mɪljən] *n* millón *m*; **a ~ times** un millón de veces; **millionaire** [-jə'nɛə*] *n* millonario/a; **millionth** [-θ] *adj* millonésimo
milometer [maɪ'lɔmɪtə*] (*BRIT*) *n* = **mileometer**
mime [maɪm] *n* mímica; (*actor*) mimo/a ▷ *vt* remedar ▷ *vi* actuar de mimo
mimic ['mɪmɪk] *n* imitador(a) *m/f* ▷ *adj* mímico ▷ *vt* remedar, imitar
min. *abbr* = **minimum; minute(s)**
mince [mɪns] *vt* picar ▷ *n* (*BRIT Culin*) carne *f* picada; **mincemeat** *n* conserva de fruta picada; (*us: meat*) carne *f* picada; **mince pie** *n* empanadilla rellena de fruta picada
mind [maɪnd] *n* mente *f*; (*intellect*) intelecto; (*contrasted with matter*) espíritu *m* ▷ *vt* (*attend to, look after*) ocuparse de, cuidar; (*be careful*) tener cuidado con; (*object to*): **I don't ~ the noise** no me molesta el ruido; **it is on my ~** me preocupa; **to bear**

m

sth in ~ tomar or tener algo en cuenta; **to make up one's** ~ decidirse; **I don't** ~ me es igual; ~ **you ...** te advierto que ...; **never** ~! ¡es igual!, ¡no importa!; (don't worry) ¡no te preocupes!; **"~ the step"** "cuidado con el escalón"; **mindless** adj (crime) sin motivo; (work) de autómata

mine' [maɪn] pron el mío/la mía etc; **a friend of** ~ un(a) amigo/a mío/mía ▷ adj: **this book is** ~ este libro es mío

mine² [maɪn] n mina ▷ vt (coal) extraer; (bomb: beach etc) minar; **minefield** n campo de minas; **miner** n minero/a

mineral ['mɪnərəl] adj mineral ▷ n mineral m; **mineral water** n agua mineral

mingle ['mɪŋgl] vi: **to** ~ **with** mezclarse con

miniature ['mɪnətʃə*] adj (en) miniatura ▷ n miniatura

minibar ['mɪnɪbɑ:*] n minibar m

minibus ['mɪnɪbʌs] n microbús m

minicab ['mɪnɪkæb] n taxi m (que sólo puede pedirse por teléfono)

minimal ['mɪnɪml] adj mínimo

minimize ['mɪnɪmaɪz] vt minimizar; (play down) empequeñecer

minimum ['mɪnɪməm] (pl **minima**) n, adj mínimo

mining ['maɪnɪŋ] n explotación f minera

miniskirt ['mɪnɪskə:t] n minifalda

minister ['mɪnɪstə*] n (BRIT Pol) ministro/a (SP), secretario/a (LAM); (Rel) pastor m ▷ vi: **to** ~ **to** atender a

ministry ['mɪnɪstrɪ] n (BRIT Pol) ministerio, secretaría (MEX); (Rel) sacerdocio

minor ['maɪnə*] adj (repairs, injuries) leve; (poet, planet) menor; (Mus) menor ▷ n (Law) menor m de edad

Minorca [mɪ'nɔ:kə] n Menorca

minority [maɪ'nɔrɪtɪ] n minoría

mint [mɪnt] n (plant) menta, hierbabuena; (sweet) caramelo de menta ▷ vt (coins) acuñar; **the (Royal) M~**, **the (US) M~** la Casa de la Moneda; **in** ~ **condition** en perfecto estado

minus ['maɪnəs] n (also: ~ **sign**) signo de menos ▷ prep menos; **12 – 6 equals 6** 12 menos 6 son 6; ~ **24 °C** menos 24 grados

minute' ['mɪnɪt] n minuto; (fig) momento; **minutes** npl (of meeting) actas fpl; **at the last** ~ a última hora

minute² [maɪ'nju:t] adj diminuto; (search) minucioso

miracle ['mɪrəkl] n milagro

miraculous [mɪ'rækjuləs] adj milagroso

mirage ['mɪrɑ:ʒ] n espejismo

mirror ['mɪrə*] n espejo; (in car) retrovisor m

misbehave [mɪsbɪ'heɪv] vi portarse mal

misc. abbr = **miscellaneous**

miscarriage ['mɪskærɪdʒ] n (Med) aborto; ~ **of justice** error m judicial

miscellaneous [mɪsɪ'leɪnɪəs] adj varios/as, diversos/as

mischief ['mɪstʃɪf] n travesuras fpl, diabluras fpl; (maliciousness) malicia; **mischievous** [-ʃɪvəs] adj travieso

misconception [mɪskən'sepʃən] n idea equivocada; equivocación f

misconduct [mɪs'kɔndʌkt] n mala conducta; **professional** ~ falta profesional

miser ['maɪzə*] n avaro/a

miserable ['mɪzərəbl] adj (unhappy) triste, desgraciado; (unpleasant, contemptible) miserable

misery ['mɪzərɪ] n tristeza; (wretchedness) miseria, desdicha

misfortune [mɪs'fɔ:tʃən] n desgracia

misgiving [mɪs'gɪvɪŋ] n (apprehension) presentimiento; **to have ~s about sth** tener dudas acerca de algo

misguided [mɪs'gaɪdɪd] adj equivocado

mishap ['mɪshæp] n desgracia, contratiempo

misinterpret [mɪsɪn'tə:prɪt] vt interpretar mal

misjudge [mɪs'dʒʌdʒ] vt juzgar mal

mislay [mɪs'leɪ] vt extraviar, perder

mislead [mɪs'li:d] vt llevar a conclusiones erróneas; **misleading** adj engañoso

misplace [mɪs'pleɪs] vt extraviar

misprint ['mɪsprɪnt] n errata, error m de imprenta

misrepresent [mɪsreprɪ'zent] vt falsificar

Miss [mɪs] n Señorita

miss [mɪs] vt (train etc) perder; (fail to hit: target) errar; (regret the absence of): **I ~ him** (yo) le echo de menos or a faltar; (fail to see): **you can't ~ it** no tiene pérdida ▷ vi fallar ▷ n (shot) tiro fallido or perdido; **miss out** (BRIT) vt omitir; **miss out on** vt fus (fun, party, opportunity) perderse

missile ['mɪsaɪl] n (Aviat) mísil m; (object thrown) proyectil m

missing ['mɪsɪŋ] adj (pupil) ausente; (thing) perdido; (Mil): ~ **in action** desaparecido en combate

mission ['mɪʃən] n misión f; (official representation) delegación f; **missionary** n misionero/a

misspell [mɪs'spel] (pt, pp **misspelt** (BRIT) or **-ed**) vt escribir mal

mist [mɪst] n (light) neblina; (heavy) niebla; (at sea) bruma ▷ vi (eyes: also: ~ **over**, ~ **up**) llenarse de lágrimas; (BRIT: windows: also: ~

over, ~ up) empañarse
mistake [mɪs'teɪk] (vt: irreg) n error m
▷ vt entender mal; **by ~** por equivocación;
to make a ~ equivocarse; **to ~ A for B**
confundir A con B; **mistaken** pp of **mistake**
▷ adj equivocado; **to be mistaken**
equivocarse, engañarse
mister ['mɪstə*] (inf) n señor m; see **Mr**
mistletoe ['mɪsltəu] n muérdago
mistook [mɪs'tuk] pt of **mistake**
mistress ['mɪstrɪs] n (lover) amante
f; (of house) señora (de la casa); (BRIT: in
primary school) maestra; (in secondary school)
profesora; (of situation) dueña
mistrust [mɪs'trʌst] vt desconfiar de
misty ['mɪstɪ] adj (day) de niebla; (glasses
etc) empañado
misunderstand [mɪsʌndə'stænd] (irreg)
vt, vi entender mal; **misunderstanding** n
malentendido
misunderstood [mɪsʌndə'stud] pt,
pp of **misunderstand** ▷ adj (person)
incomprendido
misuse [n mɪs'juːs, vb mɪs'juːz] n mal uso;
(of power) abuso; (of funds) malversación f
▷ vt abusar de; malversar
mitt(en) ['mɪt(n)] n manopla
mix [mɪks] vt mezclar; (combine) unir ▷ vi
mezclarse; (people) llevarse bien ▷ n mezcla;
mix up vt mezclar; (confuse) confundir;
mixed adj mixto; (feelings etc) encontrado;
mixed grill n (BRIT) parrillada mixta;
mixed salad n ensalada mixta; **mixed-up**
adj (confused) confuso, revuelto; **mixer** n
(for food) licuadora; (for drinks) coctelera;
(person): **he's a good mixer** tiene don de
gentes; **mixture** n mezcla; (also: **cough
mixture**) jarabe m; **mix-up** n confusión f
ml abbr (= millilitre(s)) ml
mm abbr (= millimetre) mm
moan [məun] n gemido ▷ vi gemir;
(inf: complain): **to ~ (about)** quejarse (de)
moat [məut] n foso
mob [mɔb] n multitud f ▷ vt acosar
mobile ['məubaɪl] adj móvil ▷ n móvil m;
mobile home n caravana; **mobile phone** n
teléfono móvil
mobility [məu'bɪlɪtɪ] n movilidad f
mobilize ['məubɪlaɪz] vt movilizar
mock [mɔk] vt (ridicule) ridiculizar; (laugh
at) burlarse de ▷ adj fingido; **~ exam**
examen preparatorio antes de los exámenes
oficiales° (BRIT: Scol: inf) exámenes mpl de
prueba; **mockery** n burla
mod cons ['mɔd'kɔnz] npl abbr (= modern
conveniences) see **convenience**
mode [məud] n modo
model ['mɔdl] n modelo; (fashion model,

artist's model) modelo mf ▷ adj modelo ▷ vt
(with clay etc) modelar; (copy): **to ~ o.s. on**
tomar como modelo a ▷ vi ser modelo; **to ~
clothes** pasar modelos, ser modelo
modem ['məudəm] n modem m
moderate [adj 'mɔdərət, vb 'mɔdəreit]
adj moderado/a ▷ vi moderarse, calmarse
▷ vt moderar
moderation [mɔdə'reɪʃən] n moderación
f; **in ~** con moderación
modern ['mɔdən] adj moderno;
modernize vt modernizar; **modern
languages** npl lenguas fpl modernas
modest ['mɔdɪst] adj modesto; (small)
módico; **modesty** n modestia
modification [mɔdɪfɪ'keɪʃən] n
modificación f
modify ['mɔdɪfaɪ] vt modificar
module ['mɔdjuːl] n (unit, component,
Space) módulo
mohair ['məuhɛə*] n mohair m
Mohammed [mə'hæmɛd] n Mahoma m
moist [mɔɪst] adj húmedo; **moisture**
['mɔɪstʃə*] n humedad f; **moisturizer**
['mɔɪstʃəraɪzə*] n crema hidratante
mold etc [məuld] (US) = **mould** etc
mole [məul] n (animal, spy) topo; (spot)
lunar m
molecule ['mɔlɪkjuːl] n molécula
molest [məu'lɛst] vt importunar; (assault
sexually) abusar sexualmente de

▌ Be careful not to translate **molest** by the
▌ Spanish word molestar.

molten ['məultən] adj fundido; (lava)
líquido
mom [mɔm] (US) n = **mum**
moment ['məumənt] n momento; **at the
~** de momento, por ahora; **momentarily**
adv momentáneamente; (US: very soon)
de un momento a otro; **momentary** adj
momentáneo; **momentous** [-'mɛntəs] adj
trascendental, importante
momentum [məu'mɛntəm] n momento;
(fig) ímpetu m; **to gather ~** cobrar
velocidad; (fig) ganar fuerza
mommy ['mɔmɪ] (US) n = **mummy**
Mon abbr (= Monday) lun
Monaco ['mɔnəkəu] n Mónaco
monarch ['mɔnək] n monarca mf;
monarchy n monarquía
monastery ['mɔnəstərɪ] n monasterio
Monday ['mʌndɪ] n lunes m inv
monetary ['mʌnɪtərɪ] adj monetario
money ['mʌnɪ] n dinero; (currency)
moneda; **to make ~** ganar dinero; **money
belt** n riñonera; **money order** n giro
mongrel ['mʌŋɡrəl] n (dog) perro mestizo
monitor ['mɔnɪtə*] n (Scol) monitor m;

(also: **television ~**) receptor m de control; (of computer) monitor m ▷ vt controlar

monk [mʌŋk] n monje m

monkey ['mʌŋkɪ] n mono

monologue ['mɒnəlɒg] n monólogo

monopoly [mə'nɒpəlɪ] n monopolio

monosodium glutamate [mɒnə'səudɪəm'gluːtəmeɪt] n glutamato monosódico

monotonous [mə'nɒtənəs] adj monótono

monsoon [mɒn'suːn] n monzón m

monster ['mɒnstə*] n monstruo

month [mʌnθ] n mes m; **monthly** adj mensual ▷ adv mensualmente

monument ['mɒnjumənt] n monumento

mood [muːd] n humor m; (of crowd, group) clima m; **to be in a good/bad ~** estar de buen/mal humor; **moody** adj (changeable) de humor variable; (sullen) malhumorado

moon [muːn] n luna; **moonlight** n luz f de la luna

moor [muə*] n páramo ▷ vt (ship) amarrar ▷ vi echar las amarras

moose [muːs] n inv alce m

mop [mɒp] n fregona; (of hair) greña, melena ▷ vt fregar; **mop up** vt limpiar

mope [məup] vi estar or andar deprimido

moped ['məuped] n ciclomotor m

moral ['mɒrl] adj moral ▷ n moraleja; **morals** npl moralidad f, moral f

morale [mɒ'rɑːl] n moral f

morality [mə'rælɪtɪ] n moralidad f

morbid ['mɔːbɪd] adj (interest) morboso; (Med) mórbido

○ **KEYWORD**

more [mɔː*] adj **1** (greater in number etc) más; **more people/work than before** más gente/trabajo que antes

2 (additional) más; **do you want (some) more tea?** ¿quieres más té?; **is there any more wine?** ¿queda vino?; **it'll take a few more weeks** tardará unas semanas más; **it's 2 kms more to the house** faltan 2 kms para la casa; **more time/letters than we expected** más tiempo del que/más cartas de las que esperábamos

▷ pron (greater amount, additional amount) más; **more than 10** más de 10; **it cost more than the other one/than we expected** costó más que el otro/más de lo que esperábamos; **is there any more?** ¿hay más?; **many/much more** muchos(as)/mucho(a) más

▷ adv más; **more dangerous/easily (than)**

más peligroso/fácilmente (que); **more and more expensive** cada vez más caro; **more or less** más o menos; **more than ever** más que nunca

moreover [mɔː'rəuvə*] adv además, por otra parte

morgue [mɔːg] n depósito de cadáveres

morning ['mɔːnɪŋ] n mañana; (early morning) madrugada ▷ cpd matutino, de la mañana; **in the ~** por la mañana; **7 o'clock in the ~** las 7 de la mañana; **morning sickness** n náuseas fpl matutinas

Moroccan [mə'rɒkən] adj, n marroquí m/f

Morocco [mə'rɒkəu] n Marruecos m

moron ['mɔːrɒn] (inf) n imbécil mf

morphine ['mɔːfiːn] n morfina

Morse [mɔːs] n (also: ~ code) (código) Morse

mortal ['mɔːtl] adj, n mortal m

mortar ['mɔːtə*] n argamasa

mortgage ['mɔːgɪdʒ] n hipoteca ▷ vt hipotecar

mortician [mɔː'tɪʃən] (us) n director/a m/f de pompas fúnebres

mortified ['mɔːtɪfaɪd] adj: **I was ~** me dio muchísima vergüenza

mortuary ['mɔːtjuərɪ] n depósito de cadáveres

mosaic [məu'zeɪɪk] n mosaico

Moslem ['mɒzləm] adj, n = **Muslim**

mosque [mɒsk] n mezquita

mosquito [mɒs'kiːtəu] (pl ~es) n mosquito (SP), zancudo (LAM)

moss [mɒs] n musgo

most [məust] adj la mayor parte de, la mayoría de ▷ pron la mayor parte, la mayoría ▷ adv el más; (very) muy; **the ~** (also: + adj) el más; **~ of them** la mayor parte de ellos; **I saw the ~** yo vi el que más; **at the (very) ~** a lo sumo, todo lo más; **to make the ~ of** aprovechar (al máximo); **a ~ interesting book** un libro interesantísimo; **mostly** adv en su mayor parte, principalmente

MOT (BRIT) n abbr = **Ministry of Transport**; **the ~ (test)** inspección (anual) obligatoria de coches y camiones

motel [məu'tel] n motel m

moth [mɒθ] n mariposa nocturna; (clothes moth) polilla

mother ['mʌðə*] n madre f ▷ adj materno ▷ vt (care for) cuidar (como una madre); **motherhood** n maternidad f; **mother-in-law** n suegra; **mother-of-pearl** n nácar m; **Mother's Day** n Día m de la Madre; **mother-to-be** n futura madre f; **mother tongue** n lengua materna

motif [məʊˈtiːf] n motivo
motion [ˈməʊʃən] n movimiento; (gesture) ademán m, señal f; (at meeting) moción f ▷ vt, vi: **to ~ (to) sb to do sth** hacer señas a algn para que haga algo; **motionless** adj inmóvil; **motion picture** n película
motivate [ˈməʊtɪveɪt] vt motivar
motivation [məʊtɪˈveɪʃən] n motivación f
motive [ˈməʊtɪv] n motivo
motor [ˈməʊtə*] n motor m; (BRIT: inf: vehicle) coche m (SP), carro (LAM), automóvil m ▷ adj motor (f: motora or motriz); **motorbike** n moto f; **motorboat** n lancha motora; **motorcar** (BRIT) n coche m, carro, automóvil m; **motorcycle** n motocicleta; **motorcyclist** n motociclista mf; **motoring** (BRIT) n automovilismo; **motorist** n conductor(a) m/f, automovilista mf; **motor racing** (BRIT) n carreras fpl de coches, automovilismo; **motorway** (BRIT) n autopista
motto [ˈmɔtəʊ] (pl ~es) n lema m; (watchword) consigna
mould [məʊld] (US mold) n molde m; (mildew) moho ▷ vt moldear; (fig) formar; **mouldy** adj enmohecido
mound [maʊnd] n montón m, montículo
mount [maʊnt] n monte m ▷ vt montar, subir a; (jewel) engarzar; (picture) enmarcar; (exhibition etc) organizar ▷ vi (increase) aumentar; **mount up** vi aumentar
mountain [ˈmaʊntɪn] n montaña ▷ cpd de montaña; **mountain bike** n bicicleta de montaña; **mountaineer** n alpinista mf (SP, MEX), andinista mf (LAM); **mountaineering** n alpinismo (SP, MEX), andinismo (LAM); **mountainous** adj montañoso; **mountain range** n sierra
mourn [mɔːn] vt llorar, lamentar ▷ vi: **to ~ for** llorar la muerte de; **mourner** n doliente mf; dolorido/a; **mourning** n luto; **in mourning** de luto
mouse [maʊs] (pl mice) n (Zool, Comput) ratón m; **mouse mat** n (Comput) alfombrilla
moussaka [muˈsɑːkə] n musaca
mousse [muːs] n (Culin) crema batida; (for hair) espuma (moldeadora)
moustache [məsˈtɑːʃ] (US mustache) n bigote m
mouth [maʊθ, pl maʊðz] n boca; (of river) desembocadura; **mouthful** n bocado; **mouth organ** n armónica; **mouthpiece** n (of musical instrument) boquilla; (spokesman) portavoz mf; **mouthwash** n enjuague m
move [muːv] n (movement) movimiento; (in game) jugada; (: turn to play) turno; (change: of house) mudanza; (: of job) cambio de trabajo ▷ vt mover; (emotionally) conmover; (Pol: resolution etc) proponer ▷ vi moverse; (traffic) circular; (also: ~ house) trasladarse, mudarse; **to ~ sb to do sth** mover a algn a hacer algo; **to get a ~ on** darse prisa; **move back** vi retroceder; **move in** vi (to a house) instalarse; (police, soldiers) intervenir; **move off** vi ponerse en camino; **move on** vi ponerse en camino; **move out** vi (of house) mudarse; **move over** vi apartarse, hacer sitio; **move up** vi (employee) ser ascendido; **movement** n movimiento
movie [ˈmuːvɪ] n película; **to go to the ~s** ir al cine; **movie theater** (US) n cine m
moving [ˈmuːvɪŋ] adj (emotional) conmovedor(a); (that moves) móvil
mow [məʊ] (pt ~ed, pp mowed or mown) vt (grass, corn) cortar, segar; **mower** n (also: **lawnmower**) cortacéspedes m inv
Mozambique [məʊzæmˈbiːk] n Mozambique m
MP n abbr = **Member of Parliament**
MP3 n MP3; **MP3 player** n reproductor m (de) MP3
mpg n abbr = **miles per gallon**
m.p.h. abbr = **miles per hour** (60 m.p.h. = 96 k.p.h.)
Mr [ˈmɪstə*] (US Mr.) n: **~ Smith** (el) Sr. Smith
Mrs [ˈmɪsɪz] (US Mrs.) n: **~ Smith** (la) Sra. Smith
Ms [mɪz] (US Ms.) n = **Miss** or **Mrs**; **~ Smith** (la) Sr(t)a. Smith
MSP n abbr = **Member of the Scottish Parliament**
Mt abbr (Geo) (= mount) m
much [mʌtʃ] adj mucho ▷ adv mucho; (before pp) muy ▷ n or pron mucho; **how ~ is it?** ¿cuánto es?, ¿cuánto cuesta?; **too ~** demasiado; **it's not ~** no es mucho; **as ~ as** tanto como; **however ~ he tries** por mucho que se esfuerce
muck [mʌk] n suciedad f; **muck up** (inf) vt arruinar, estropear; **mucky** adj (dirty) sucio
mucus [ˈmjuːkəs] n mucosidad f, moco
mud [mʌd] n barro, lodo
muddle [ˈmʌdl] n desorden m, confusión f; (mix-up) embrollo, lío ▷ vt (also: ~ up) embrollar, confundir
muddy [ˈmʌdɪ] adj fangoso, cubierto de lodo
mudguard [ˈmʌdgɑːd] n guardabarros m inv
muesli [ˈmjuːzlɪ] n muesli m
muffin [ˈmʌfɪn] n panecillo dulce
muffled [ˈmʌfld] adj (noise etc) amortiguado, apagado

muffler (US) ['mʌflə*] n (Aut) silenciador m

mug [mʌg] n taza grande (sin platillo); (for beer) jarra; (inf: face) jeta ▷ vt (assault) asaltar; **mugger** ['mʌgə*] n atracador(a) m/f; **mugging** n asalto

muggy ['mʌgɪ] adj bochornoso

mule [mju:l] n mula

multicoloured ['mʌltɪkʌləd] (US), **multicolored** adj multicolor

multimedia ['mʌltɪ'mi:dɪə] adj multimedia

multinational [mʌltɪ'næfənl] n multinacional f ▷ adj multinacional

multiple ['mʌltɪpl] adj múltiple ▷ n múltiplo; **multiple choice (test)** n examen m de tipo test; **multiple sclerosis** n esclerosis f múltiple

multiplex cinema ['mʌltɪplɛks-] n multicines mpl

multiplication [mʌltɪplɪ'keɪʃən] n multiplicación f

multiply ['mʌltɪplaɪ] vt multiplicar ▷ vi multiplicarse

multistorey [mʌltɪ'stɔ:rɪ] (BRIT) adj de muchos pisos

mum [mʌm] (BRIT: inf) n mamá ▷ adj: **to keep ~** mantener la boca cerrada

mumble ['mʌmbl] vt, vi hablar entre dientes, refunfuñar

mummy ['mʌmɪ] n (BRIT: mother) mamá; (embalmed) momia

mumps [mʌmps] n paperas fpl

munch [mʌntʃ] vt, vi mascar

municipal [mju:'nɪsɪpl] adj municipal

mural ['mjuərl] n (pintura) mural m

murder ['mə:də*] n asesinato; (in law) homicidio ▷ vt asesinar, matar; **murderer** n asesino

murky ['mə:kɪ] adj (water) turbio; (street, night) lóbrego

murmur ['mə:mə*] n murmullo ▷ vt, vi murmurar

muscle ['mʌsl] n músculo; (fig: strength) garra, fuerza; **muscular** ['mʌskjulə*] adj muscular; (person) musculoso

museum [mju:'zɪəm] n museo

mushroom ['mʌfrum] n seta, hongo; (Culin) champiñón m ▷ vi crecer de la noche a la mañana

music ['mju:zɪk] n música; **musical** adj musical; (sound) melodioso; (person) con talento musical ▷ n (show) comedia musical; **musical instrument** n instrumento musical; **musician** [-'zɪʃən] n músico/a

Muslim ['mʌzlɪm] adj, n musulmán/ana m/f

muslin ['mʌzlɪn] n muselina

mussel ['mʌsl] n mejillón m

must [mʌst] aux vb (obligation): **I ~ do it** debo hacerlo, tengo que hacerlo; (probability): **he ~ be there by now** ya debe (de) estar allí ▷ n: **it's a ~** es imprescindible

mustache ['mʌstæʃ] (US) n = **moustache**

mustard ['mʌstəd] n mostaza

mustn't ['mʌsnt] = **must not**

mute [mju:t] adj, n mudo/a m/f

mutilate ['mju:tɪleɪt] vt mutilar

mutiny ['mju:tɪnɪ] n motín m ▷ vi amotinarse

mutter ['mʌtə*] vt, vi murmurar

mutton ['mʌtn] n carne f de cordero

mutual ['mju:tʃuəl] adj mutuo; (interest) común

muzzle ['mʌzl] n hocico; (for dog) bozal m; (of gun) boca ▷ vt (dog) poner un bozal a

my [maɪ] adj mi(s); **~ house/brother/ sisters** mi casa/mi hermano/mis hermanas; **I've washed ~ hair/cut ~ finger** me he lavado el pelo/cortado un dedo; **is this ~ pen or yours?** ¿es este bolígrafo mío o tuyo?

myself [maɪ'sɛlf] pron (reflexive) me; (emphatic) yo mismo; (after prep) mí (mismo); see also **oneself**

mysterious [mɪs'tɪərɪəs] adj misterioso

mystery ['mɪstərɪ] n misterio

mystical ['mɪstɪkl] adj místico

mystify ['mɪstɪfaɪ] vt (perplex) dejar perplejo

myth [mɪθ] n mito; **mythology** [mɪ'θɔlədʒɪ] n mitología

n

n/a abbr (= not applicable) no interesa
nag [næg] vt (scold) regañar
nail [neɪl] n (human) uña; (metal) clavo ▷ vt
clavar; **to ~ sth to sth** clavar algo en algo;
to ~ sb down to doing sth comprometer a
algn a que haga algo; **nailbrush** n cepillo
para las uñas; **nailfile** n lima para las uñas;
nail polish n esmalte m or laca para las
uñas; **nail polish remover** n quitaesmalte
m; **nail scissors** npl tijeras fpl para las uñas;
nail varnish (BRIT) n = **nail polish**
naïve [naɪˈiːv] adj ingenuo
naked ['neɪkɪd] adj (nude) desnudo; (flame)
expuesto al aire
name [neɪm] n nombre m; (surname)
apellido; (reputation) fama, renombre m ▷ vt
(child) poner nombre a; (criminal) identificar;
(price, date etc) fijar; **what's your ~?** ¿cómo
se llama?; **by ~** de nombre; **in the ~ of** en
nombre de; **to give one's ~ and address** dar
sus señas; **namely** adv a saber
nanny ['nænɪ] n niñera
nap [næp] n (sleep) sueñecito, siesta
napkin ['næpkɪn] n (also: **table ~**)
servilleta
nappy ['næpɪ] (BRIT) n pañal m
narcotics npl (illegal drugs)
estupefacientes mpl, narcóticos mpl
narrative ['nærətɪv] n narrativa ▷ adj
narrativo
narrator [nəˈreɪtə*] n narrador(a) m/f
narrow ['nærəʊ] adj estrecho, angosto;
(fig: majority etc) corto; (: ideas etc) estrecho
▷ vi (road) estrecharse; (diminish) reducirse;
to have a ~ escape escaparse por los pelos;
narrow down vt (search, investigation,
possibilities) restringir, limitar; (list) reducir;
narrowly adv (miss) por poco; **narrow-
minded** adj de miras estrechas
nasal ['neɪzl] adj nasal
nasty ['nɑːstɪ] adj (remark) feo; (person)

antipático; (revolting: taste, smell) asqueroso;
(wound, disease etc) peligroso, grave
nation ['neɪʃən] n nación f
national ['næʃənl] adj, n nacional m/f;
national anthem n himno nacional;
national dress n vestido nacional;
National Health Service (BRIT) n servicio
nacional de salud pública ≈ Insalud m (SP);
National Insurance (BRIT) n seguro social
nacional; **nationalist** adj, n nacionalista
mf; **nationality** [-ˈnælɪtɪ] n nacionalidad f;
nationalize vt nacionalizar; **national park**
(BRIT) n parque m nacional; **National Trust**
n (BRIT) organización encargada de preservar el
patrimonio histórico británico
nationwide ['neɪʃənwaɪd] adj en escala or
a nivel nacional
native ['neɪtɪv] n (local inhabitant) natural
mf, nacional mf ▷ adj (indigenous) indígena;
(country) natal; (innate) natural, innato; **a ~
of Russia** un(a) natural mf de Rusia; **Native
American** adj, n americano/a indígena,
amerindio/a; **native speaker** n hablante
mf nativo/a
NATO ['neɪtəʊ] n abbr (= North Atlantic
Treaty Organization) OTAN f
natural ['nætʃrəl] adj natural; **natural
gas** n gas m natural; **natural history** n
historia natural; **naturally** adv (speak etc)
naturalmente; (of course) desde luego, por
supuesto; **natural resources** npl recursos
mpl naturales
nature ['neɪtʃə*] n (also: **N~**) naturaleza;
(group, sort) género, clase f; (character)
carácter m, genio; **by ~** por or de naturaleza;
nature reserve n reserva natural
naughty ['nɔːtɪ] adj (child) travieso
nausea ['nɔːsɪə] n náuseas fpl
naval ['neɪvl] adj naval, de marina
navel ['neɪvl] n ombligo
navigate ['nævɪgeɪt] vt gobernar ▷ vi
navegar; (Aut) ir de copiloto; **navigation**
[-ˈgeɪʃən] n (action) navegación f; (science)
náutica
navy ['neɪvɪ] n marina de guerra; (ships)
armada, flota
Nazi ['nɑːtsɪ] n nazi mf
NB abbr (= nota bene) nótese
near [nɪə*] adj (place, relation) cercano;
(time) próximo ▷ adv cerca ▷ prep (also: **~
to**: space) cerca de, junto a; (: time) cerca de
▷ vt acercarse a, aproximarse a; **nearby**
[nɪəˈbaɪ] adj cercano, próximo ▷ adv cerca;
nearly adv casi, por poco; **I nearly fell** por
poco me caigo; **near-sighted** adj miope,
corto de vista
neat [niːt] adj (place) ordenado, bien
cuidado; (person) pulcro; (plan) ingenioso;

n

(spirits) solo; **neatly** adv (tidily) con esmero; (skilfully) ingeniosamente

necessarily ['nesisrili] adv necesariamente

necessary ['nesisri] adj necesario, preciso

necessity [nɪ'sesɪtɪ] n necesidad f

neck [nek] n (of person, garment, bottle) cuello; (of animal) pescuezo ▷ vi (inf) besuquearse; ~ **and** ~ parejos; **necklace** ['neklɪs] n collar m; **necktie** ['nektaɪ] n corbata

nectarine ['nektərɪn] n nectarina

need [niːd] n (lack) escasez f, falta; (necessity) necesidad f ▷ vt (require) necesitar; **I** ~ **to do it** tengo que or debo hacerlo; **you don't** ~ **to go** no hace falta que (te) vayas

needle ['niːdl] n aguja ▷ vt (fig: inf) picar, fastidiar

needless ['niːdlɪs] adj innecesario; ~ **to say** huelga decir que

needlework ['niːdlwəːk] n (activity) costura, labor f de aguja

needn't ['niːdnt] = **need not**

needy ['niːdɪ] adj necesitado

negative ['negɪtɪv] n (Phot) negativo; (Ling) negación f ▷ adj negativo

neglect [nɪ'glekt] vt (one's duty) faltar a, no cumplir con; (child) descuidar, desatender ▷ n (of house, garden etc) abandono; (of child) desatención f; (of duty) incumplimiento

negotiate [nɪ'gəuʃɪeɪt] vt (treaty, loan) negociar; (obstacle) franquear; (bend in road) tomar ▷ vi: **to** ~ **(with)** negociar (con)

negotiations [nɪgəuʃɪ'eɪʃənz] pl n negociaciones

negotiator [nɪ'gəuʃɪeɪtə*] n negociador(a) m/f

neighbour ['neɪbə*] (us **neighbor** etc) n vecino/a; **neighbourhood** n (place) vecindad f, barrio; (people) vecindario; **neighbouring** adj vecino

neither ['naɪðə*] adj ▷ conj: **I didn't move and** ~ **did John** no me he movido, ni Juan tampoco ▷ pron ninguno ▷ adv: ~ **good nor bad** ni bueno ni malo; ~ **is true** ninguno/a de los(las) dos es cierto/a

neon ['niːɔn] n neón m

Nepal [nɪ'pɔːl] n Nepal m

nephew ['nevjuː] n sobrino

nerve [nəːv] n (Anat) nervio; (courage) valor m; (impudence) descaro, frescura (nervousness) nerviosismo msg, nervios mpl; **a fit of** ~**s** un ataque de nervios

nervous ['nəːvəs] adj (anxious, Anat) nervioso; (timid) tímido, miedoso; **nervous breakdown** n crisis f nerviosa

nest [nest] n (of bird) nido; (wasps' nest) avispero ▷ vi anidar

net [net] n (gen) red f; (fabric) tul m ▷ adj (Comm) neto, líquido ▷ vt coger (SP) or agarrar (LAM) con red; (Sport) marcar; **netball** n básquet m

Netherlands ['neðələndz] npl: **the** ~ los Países Bajos

nett [net] adj = **net**

nettle ['netl] n ortiga

network ['netwəːk] n red f

neurotic [njuə'rɔtɪk] adj neurótico/a

neuter ['njuːtə*] adj (Ling) neutro ▷ vt castrar, capar

neutral ['njuːtrəl] adj (person) neutral; (colour etc, Elec) neutro ▷ n (Aut) punto muerto

never ['nevə*] adv nunca, jamás; **I** ~ **went** no fui nunca; ~ **in my life** jamás en la vida; see also **mind**; **never-ending** adj interminable, sin fin; **nevertheless** [nevəðə'les] adv sin embargo, no obstante

new [njuː] adj nuevo; (brand new) a estrenar; (recent) reciente; **New Age** n Nueva Era; **newborn** adj recién nacido; **newcomer** ['njuːkʌmə*] n recién venido/a or llegado/a; **newly** adv nuevamente, recién

news [njuːz] n noticias fpl; **a piece of** ~ una noticia; **the** ~ (Radio, TV) las noticias fpl; **news agency** n agencia de noticias; **newsagent** (BRIT) n vendedor(a) m/f de periódicos; **newscaster** n presentador(a) m/f, locutor(a) m/f; **news dealer** (US) n = **newsagent**; **newsletter** n hoja informativa, boletín m; **newspaper** n periódico, diario; **newsreader** n = **newscaster**

newt [njuːt] n tritón m

New Year n Año Nuevo; **New Year's Day** n Día m de Año Nuevo; **New Year's Eve** n Nochevieja

New Zealand [njuː'ziːlənd] n Nueva Zelanda; **New Zealander** n neozelandés/ esa m/f

next [nekst] adj (house, room) vecino; (bus stop, meeting) próximo; (following: page etc) siguiente ▷ adv después; **the** ~ **day** el día siguiente; ~ **time** la próxima vez; ~ **year** el año próximo or que viene; ~ **to** junto a, al lado de; ~ **to nothing** casi nada; ~ **please!** ¡el siguiente!; **next door** adv en la casa de al lado ▷ adj vecino, de al lado; **next-of-kin** n pariente m más cercano

NHS n abbr = **National Health Service**

nibble ['nɪbl] vt mordisquear, mordiscar

nice [naɪs] adj (likeable) simpático; (kind) amable; (pleasant) agradable;

(*attractive*) bonito, lindo (*LAM*); **nicely** *adv* amablemente; bien

niche [ni:ʃ] *n* (*Arch*) nicho, hornacina

nick [nɪk] *n* (*wound*) rasguño; (*cut, indentation*) mella, muesca ▷ *vt* (*inf*) birlar, robar; **in the ~ of time** justo a tiempo

nickel ['nɪkl] *n* níquel *m*; (*us*) moneda de 5 centavos

nickname ['nɪkneɪm] *n* apodo, mote *m* ▷ *vt* apodar

nicotine ['nɪkəti:n] *n* nicotina

niece [ni:s] *n* sobrina

night [naɪt] *n* noche *f*; (*evening*) tarde *f*; **the ~ before last** anteanoche; **at ~, by ~** de noche, por la noche; **night club** *n* cabaret *m*; **nightdress** (*BRIT*) *n* camisón *m*; **nightie** ['naɪtɪ] *n* = **nightdress**; **nightlife** *n* vida nocturna; **nightly** *adj* de todas las noches ▷ *adv* todas las noches, cada noche; **nightmare** *n* pesadilla; **night school** *n* clase(s) *f(pl)* nocturna(s); **night shift** *n* turno nocturno *or* de noche; **night-time** *n* noche *f*

nil [nɪl] (*BRIT*) *n* (*Sport*) cero, nada

nine [naɪn] *num* nueve; **nineteen** *num* diecinueve, diez y nueve; **nineteenth** [naɪn'ti:nθ] *adj* decimonoveno, decimonono; **ninetieth** ['naɪntiɪθ] *adj* nonagésimo; **ninety** *num* noventa

ninth [naɪnθ] *adj* noveno

nip [nɪp] *vt* (*pinch*) pellizcar; (*bite*) morder

nipple ['nɪpl] *n* (*Anat*) pezón *m*

nitrogen ['naɪtrədʒən] *n* nitrógeno

○ **KEYWORD**

no [nəu] (*pl* **noes**) *adv* (*opposite of "yes"*) no; **are you coming? – no (I'm not)** ¿vienes? – no; **would you like some more? – no thank you** ¿quieres más? – no gracias ▷ *adj* (*not any*): **I have no money/time/books** tengo dinero/tiempo/libros; **no other man would have done it** ningún otro lo hubiera hecho; **"no entry"** "prohibido el paso"; **"no smoking"** "prohibido fumar" ▷ *n* no *m*

nobility [nəu'bɪlɪtɪ] *n* nobleza

noble ['nəubl] *adj* noble

nobody ['nəubədɪ] *pron* nadie

nod [nɔd] *vi* saludar con la cabeza; (*in agreement*) decir que sí con la cabeza; (*doze*) dar cabezadas ▷ *vt*: **to ~ one's head** inclinar la cabeza ▷ *n* inclinación *f* de cabeza; **nod off** *vi* dar cabezadas

noise [nɔɪz] *n* ruido; (*din*) escándalo, estrépito; **noisy** *adj* ruidoso; (*child*)

escandaloso

nominal ['nɔmɪnl] *adj* nominal

nominate ['nɔmɪneɪt] *vt* (*propose*) proponer; (*appoint*) nombrar; **nomination** [nɔmɪ'neɪʃən] *n* propuesta; nombramiento; **nominee** [-'ni:] *n* candidato/a

none [nʌn] *pron* ninguno/a ▷ *adv* de ninguna manera; **~ of you** ninguno de vosotros; **I've ~ left** no me queda ninguno/a; **he's ~ the worse for it** no le ha hecho ningún mal

nonetheless [nʌnðə'lɛs] *adv* sin embargo, no obstante

non-fiction [nɔn'fɪkʃən] *n* literatura no novelesca

nonsense ['nɔnsəns] *n* tonterías *fpl*, disparates *fpl*; **~!** ¡qué tonterías!

non: non-smoker *n* no fumador(a) *m/f*; **non-smoking** *adj* (de) no fumador; **non-stick** *adj* (*pan, surface*) antiadherente

noodles ['nu:dlz] *npl* tallarines *mpl*

noon [nu:n] *n* mediodía *m*

no-one ['nəuwʌn] *pron* = **nobody**

nor [nɔ:*] *conj* = **neither** ▷ *adv* *see* **neither**

norm [nɔ:m] *n* norma

normal ['nɔ:ml] *adj* normal; **normally** *adv* normalmente

north [nɔ:θ] *n* norte *m* ▷ *adj* del norte, norteño ▷ *adv* al *or* hacia el norte; **North America** *n* América del Norte; **North American** *adj*, *n* norteamericano/a *m/f*; **northbound** ['nɔ:θbaund] *adj* (*traffic*) que se dirige al norte; (*carriageway*) de dirección norte; **north-east** *n* nor(d)este *m*; **northeastern** *adj* nor(d)este, del nor(d) este; **northern** ['nɔ:ðən] *adj* norteño, del norte; **Northern Ireland** *n* Irlanda del Norte; **North Korea** *n* Corea del Norte; **North Pole** *n* Polo Norte; **North Sea** *n* Mar *m* del Norte; **north-west** *n* nor(d) oeste *m*; **northwestern** ['nɔ:θ'westən] *adj* noroeste, del noroeste

Norway ['nɔ:weɪ] *n* Noruega; **Norwegian** [-'wi:dʒən] *adj* noruego/a ▷ *n* noruego/a; (*Ling*) noruego

nose [nəuz] *n* (*Anat*) nariz *f*; (*Zool*) hocico; (*sense of smell*) olfato ▷ *vi*: **to ~ about** curiosear; **nosebleed** *n* hemorragia nasal; **nosey** (*inf*) *adj* curioso, fisgón/ona

nostalgia [nɔs'tældʒɪə] *n* nostalgia

nostalgic [nɔs'tældʒɪk] *adj* nostálgico

nostril ['nɔstrɪl] *n* ventana de la nariz

nosy ['nəuzɪ] (*inf*) *adj* = **nosey**

not [nɔt] *adv* no; **~ that ...** no es que ...; **it's too late, isn't it?** es demasiado tarde, ¿verdad *or* no?; **~ yet/now** todavía/ahora no; **why ~?** ¿por qué no?; *see also* **all; only**

notable ['nəutəbl] *adj* notable; **notably**
adv especialmente

notch [nɔtʃ] *n* muesca, corte *m*

note [nəut] *n* (*Mus, record, letter*) nota;
(*banknote*) billete *m*; (*tone*) tono ▷ *vt*
(*observe*) notar, observar; (*write down*)
apuntar, anotar; **notebook** *n* libreta,
cuaderno; **noted** ['nəutɪd] *adj* célebre,
conocido; **notepad** *n* bloc *m*; **notepaper** *n*
papel *m* para cartas

nothing ['nʌθɪŋ] *n* nada; (*zero*) cero; **he
does** ~ no hace nada; ~ **new** nada nuevo; ~
much no mucho; **for** ~ (*free*) gratis, sin pago;
(*in vain*) en balde

notice ['nəutɪs] *n* (*announcement*) anuncio;
(*warning*) aviso; (*dismissal*) despido;
(*resignation*) dimisión *f*; (*period of time*) plazo
▷ *vt* (*observe*) notar, observar; **to bring sth
to sb's** ~ (*attention*) llamar la atención de
algn sobre algo; **to take** ~ **of** tomar nota
de, prestar atención a; **at short** ~ con poca
anticipación; **until further** ~ hasta nuevo
aviso; **to hand in one's** ~ dimitir

> ▌ Be careful not to translate **notice** by the
> Spanish word *noticia*.

noticeable *adj* evidente, obvio

notify ['nəutɪfaɪ] *vt*: **to** ~ **sb (of sth)**
comunicar (algo) a algn

notion ['nəuʃən] *n* idea; (*opinion*) opinión
f; **notions** *npl* (*us*) mercería

notorious [nəu'tɔ:rɪəs] *adj* notorio

notwithstanding [nɔtwɪθ'stændɪŋ] *adv*
no obstante, sin embargo; ~ **this** a pesar
de esto

nought [nɔ:t] *n* cero

noun [naun] *n* nombre *m*, sustantivo

nourish ['nʌrɪʃ] *vt* nutrir; (*fig*) alimentar;
nourishment *n* alimento, sustento

Nov. *abbr* (= *November*) nov

novel ['nɔvl] *n* novela ▷ *adj* (*new*) nuevo,
original; (*unexpected*) insólito; **novelist** *n*
novelista *mf*; **novelty** *n* novedad *f*

November [nəu'vɛmbə*] *n* noviembre *m*

novice ['nɔvɪs] *n* (*Rel*) novicio/a

now [nau] *adv* (*at the present time*) ahora;
(*these days*) actualmente, hoy día ▷ *conj*: ~
(that) ya que, ahora que; **right** ~ ahora
mismo; **by** ~ ya; **just** ~ ahora mismo; ~
and then, ~ **and again** de vez en cuando;
from ~ **on** de ahora en adelante; **nowadays**
['nauədeɪz] *adv* hoy (en) día, actualmente

nowhere ['nəuwɛə*] *adv* (*direction*) a
ninguna parte; (*location*) en ninguna parte

nozzle ['nɔzl] *n* boquilla

nr *abbr* (*BRIT*) = **near**

nuclear ['nju:klɪə*] *adj* nuclear

nucleus ['nju:klɪəs] (*pl* **nuclei**) *n* núcleo

nude [nju:d] *adj*, *n* desnudo/a *m/f*; **in the**
~ desnudo

nudge [nʌdʒ] *vt* dar un codazo a

nudist ['nju:dɪst] *n* nudista *mf*

nudity ['nju:dɪtɪ] *n* desnudez *f*

nuisance ['nju:sns] *n* molestia, fastidio;
(*person*) pesado, latoso; **what a** ~! ¡qué lata!

numb [nʌm] *adj*: ~ **with cold/fear**
entumecido por el frío/paralizado de miedo

number ['nʌmbə*] *n* número; (*quantity*)
cantidad *f* ▷ *vt* (*pages etc*) numerar, poner
número a; (*amount to*) sumar, ascender a; **to
be ~ed among** figurar entre; **a** ~ **of** varios,
algunos; **they were ten in** ~ eran diez;
number plate (*BRIT*) *n* matrícula, placa;
Number Ten *n* (*BRIT*: 10 Downing Street)
residencia del primer ministro

numerical [nju:'mɛrɪkl] *adj* numérico

numerous ['nju:mərəs] *adj* numeroso

nun [nʌn] *n* monja, religiosa

nurse [nə:s] *n* enfermero/a; (*also*: ~**maid**)
niñera ▷ *vt* (*patient*) cuidar, atender

nursery ['nə:sərɪ] *n* (*institution*) guardería
infantil; (*room*) cuarto de los niños; (*for
plants*) criadero, semillero; **nursery
rhyme** *n* canción *f* infantil; **nursery
school** *n* parvulario, escuela de párvulos;
nursery slope (*BRIT*) *n* (*Ski*) cuesta para
principiantes

nursing ['nə:sɪŋ] *n* (*profession*) profesión
f de enfermera; (*care*) asistencia, cuidado;
nursing home *n* clínica de reposo

nurture ['nə:tʃə*] *vt* (*child, plant*)
alimentar, nutrir

nut [nʌt] *n* (*Tech*) tuerca; (*Bot*) nuez *f*

nutmeg ['nʌtmɛg] *n* nuez *f* moscada

nutrient ['nju:trɪənt] *adj* nutritivo ▷ *n*
elemento nutritivo

nutrition [nju:'trɪʃən] *n* nutrición *f*,
alimentación *f*

nutritious [nju:'trɪʃəs] *adj* nutritivo,
alimenticio

nuts [nʌts] (*inf*) *adj* loco

NVQ *n abbr* (*BRIT*) = **National Vocational
Qualification**

nylon ['naɪlɔn] *n* nilón *m* ▷ *adj* de nilón

O

oath [əʊθ] n juramento; (swear word)
palabrota; **on** (BRIT) or **under ~** bajo
juramento

oak [əʊk] n roble m ▷ adj de roble

O.A.P. (BRIT) n, abbr = **old-age pensioner**

oar [ɔː*] n remo

oasis [əʊ'eɪsɪs] (pl **oases**) n oasis m inv

oath [əʊθ] n juramento; (swear word)
palabrota; **on** (BRIT) or **under ~** bajo
juramento

oatmeal ['əʊtmiːl] n harina de avena

oats [əʊts] npl avena

obedience [ə'biːdɪəns] n obediencia

obedient [ə'biːdɪənt] adj obediente

obese [əʊ'biːs] adj obeso

obesity [əʊ'biːsɪtɪ] n obesidad f

obey [ə'beɪ] vt obedecer; (instructions,
regulations) cumplir

obituary [ə'bɪtjʊərɪ] n necrología

object [n 'ɒbdʒɪkt, vb əb'dʒɛkt] n
objeto; (purpose) objeto, propósito; (Ling)
complemento ▷ vi: **to ~ to** estar en contra
de; (proposal) oponerse a; **to ~ that** objetar
que; **expense is no ~** no importa cuánto
cuesta; **I ~!** ¡yo protesto!; **objection**
[əb'dʒɛkʃən] n protesta; **I have no
objection to ...** no tengo inconveniente en
que ...; **objective** adj, n objetivo

obligation [ɒblɪ'geɪʃən] n obligación f;
(debt) deber m; **without ~** sin compromiso

obligatory [ə'blɪgətərɪ] adj obligatorio

oblige [ə'blaɪdʒ] vt (do a favour for)
complacer, hacer un favor a; **to ~ sb to do
sth** forzar or obligar a algn a hacer algo; **to
be ~d to sb for sth** estarle agradecido a
algn por algo

oblique [ə'bliːk] adj oblicuo; (allusion)
indirecto

obliterate [ə'blɪtəreɪt] vt borrar

oblivious [ə'blɪvɪəs] adj: **~ of** inconsciente
de

oblong ['ɒblɒŋ] adj rectangular ▷ n
rectángulo

obnoxious [əb'nɒkʃəs] adj odioso,
detestable; (smell) nauseabundo

oboe ['əʊbəʊ] n oboe m

obscene [əb'siːn] adj obsceno

obscure [əb'skjʊə*] adj oscuro ▷ vt
oscurecer; (hide: sun) esconder

observant [əb'zɜːvnt] adj observador(a)

observation [ɒbzə'veɪʃən] n observación
f; (Med) examen m

observatory [əb'zɜːvətrɪ] n observatorio

observe [əb'zɜːv] vt observar; (rule)
cumplir; **observer** n observador(a) m/f

obsess [əb'sɛs] vt obsesionar; **obsession**
[əb'sɛʃən] n obsesión f; **obsessive** adj
obsesivo; obsesionante

obsolete ['ɒbsəliːt] adj: **to be ~** estar en
desuso

obstacle ['ɒbstəkl] n obstáculo; (nuisance)
estorbo

obstinate ['ɒbstɪnɪt] adj terco, porfiado;
(determined) obstinado

obstruct [əb'strʌkt] vt obstruir; (hinder)
estorbar, obstaculizar; **obstruction**
[əb'strʌkʃən] n (action) obstrucción f;
(object) estorbo, obstáculo

obtain [əb'teɪn] vt obtener; (achieve)
conseguir

obvious ['ɒbvɪəs] adj obvio, evidente;
obviously adv evidentemente,
naturalmente; **obviously not** por supuesto
que no

occasion [ə'keɪʒən] n oportunidad
f, ocasión f; (event) acontecimiento;
occasional adj poco frecuente, ocasional;
occasionally adv de vez en cuando

occult [ɔ'kʌlt] adj (gen) oculto

occupant ['ɒkjʊpənt] n (of house)
inquilino/a; (of car) ocupante mf

occupation [ɔkjʊ'peɪʃən] n ocupación f;
(job) trabajo; (pastime) ocupaciones fpl

occupy ['ɒkjʊpaɪ] vt (seat, post, time)
ocupar; (house) habitar; **to ~ o.s. in doing**
pasar el tiempo haciendo

occur [ə'kɜː*] vi pasar, suceder; **to ~ to sb**
ocurrírsele a algn; **occurrence** [ə'kʌrəns] n
acontecimiento; (existence) existencia

ocean ['əʊʃən] n océano

o'clock [ə'klɒk] adv: **it is 5 ~** son las 5

Oct. abbr (= October) oct

October [ɔk'təʊbə*] n octubre m

octopus ['ɒktəpəs] n pulpo

odd [ɒd] adj extraño, raro; (number) impar;
(sock, shoe etc) suelto; **60 ~** 60 y pico; **at ~
times** de vez en cuando; **to be the ~ one
out** estar de más; **oddly** adv curiosamente,
extrañamente; see also **enough**; **odds** npl

(*in betting*) puntos mpl de ventaja; **it makes no odds** da lo mismo; **at odds** reñidos/as; **odds and ends** minucias fpl

odometer [ɔ'dɔmɪtə*] (*us*) n cuentakilómetros m inv

odour ['əudə*] (*us* **odor**) n olor m; (*unpleasant*) hedor m

○ KEYWORD

of [ɔv, əv] prep **1** (*gen*) de; **a friend of ours** un amigo nuestro; **a boy of 10** un chico de 10 años; **that was kind of you** eso fue muy amable por or de tu parte
2 (*expressing quantity, amount, dates etc*) de; **a kilo of flour** un kilo de harina; **there were three of them** había tres; **three of us went** tres de nosotros fuimos; **the 5th of July** el 5 de julio
3 (*from, out of*) de; **made of wood** (hecho) de madera

off [ɔf] adj, adv (*engine*) desconectado; (*light*) apagado; (*tap*) cerrado; (*BRIT: food: bad*) pasado, malo; (: *milk*) cortado; (*cancelled*) cancelado ▷ prep de; **to be ~** (*to leave*) irse, marcharse; **to be ~ sick** estar enfermo or de baja; **a day ~** un día libre or sin trabajar; **to have an ~ day** tener un día malo; **he had his coat ~** se había quitado el abrigo; **10% ~** (*Comm*) (con el) 10% de descuento; **5 km ~ (the road)** a 5 km de la carretera); **~ the coast** frente a la costa; **I'm ~ meat** (*no longer eat/like it*) paso de la carne; **on the ~ chance** por si acaso; **~ and on** de vez en cuando

offence [ə'fɛns] (*us* **offense**) n (*crime*) delito; **to take ~ at** ofenderse por

offend [ə'fɛnd] vt (*person*) ofender; **offender** n delincuente mf

offense [ə'fɛns] (*us*) n = **offence**

offensive [ə'fɛnsɪv] adj ofensivo; (*smell etc*) repugnante ▷ n (*Mil*) ofensiva

offer ['ɔfə*] n oferta, ofrecimiento; (*proposal*) propuesta ▷ vt ofrecer; (*opportunity*) facilitar; **"on ~"** (*Comm*) "en oferta"

offhand [ɔf'hænd] adj informal ▷ adv de improviso

office ['ɔfɪs] n (*place*) oficina; (*room*) despacho; (*position*) carga, oficio; **doctor's ~** (*us*) consultorio; **to take ~** entrar en funciones; **office block** (*us*), **office building** n bloque m de oficinas; **office hours** npl horas fpl de oficina; (*us Med*) horas fpl de consulta

officer ['ɔfɪsə*] n (*Mil etc*) oficial mf; (*also*: **police ~**) agente mf de policía; (*of organization*) director(a) m/f

office worker n oficinista mf

official [ə'fɪʃl] adj oficial, autorizado ▷ n funcionario/a, oficial mf

off: **off-licence** (*BRIT*) n (*shop*) bodega tienda de vinos y bebidas alcohólicas; **off-line** adj, adv (*Comput*) fuera de línea; **off-peak** adj (*electricity*) de banda económica; (*ticket*) billete de precio reducido por viajar fuera de las horas punta; **off-putting** (*BRIT*) adj (*person*) asqueroso; (*remark*) desalentador(a); **off-season** adj, adv fuera de temporada

● OFF-LICENCE

En el Reino Unido la venta de bebidas alcohólicas está estrictamente regulada y se necesita una licencia especial, con la que cuentan los bares, restaurantes y los establecimientos de **off-licence**, los únicos lugares en donde se pueden adquirir bebidas alcohólicas para su consumo fuera del local, de donde viene su nombre. También venden bebidas no alcohólicas, tabaco, chocolatinas, patatas fritas, etc. y a menudo forman parte de una cadena nacional.

offset ['ɔfsɛt] vt contrarrestar, compensar

offshore [ɔf'ʃɔ:*] adj (*breeze, island*) costera; (*fishing*) de bajura

offside ['ɔf'saɪd] adj (*Sport*) fuera de juego; (*Aut: in UK*) del lado derecho; (: *in US, Europe etc*) del lado izquierdo

offspring ['ɔfsprɪŋ] n inv descendencia

often ['ɔfn] adv a menudo, con frecuencia; **how ~ do you go?** ¿cada cuánto vas?

oh [əu] excl ¡ah!

oil [ɔɪl] n aceite m; (*petroleum*) petróleo; (*for heating*) aceite m combustible ▷ vt engrasar; **oil filter** n (*Aut*) filtro de aceite; **oil painting** n pintura al óleo; **oil refinery** n refinería de petróleo; **oil rig** n torre f de perforación; **oil slick** n marea negra; **oil tanker** n petrolero; (*truck*) camión m cisterna; **oil well** n pozo (de petróleo); **oily** adj aceitoso; (*food*) grasiento

ointment ['ɔɪntmənt] n ungüento

O.K., okay ['əu'keɪ] excl ¡O.K.!, ¡está bien!, ¡vale! (*sp*) ▷ adj bien ▷ vt dar el visto bueno a

old [əuld] adj viejo; (*former*) antiguo; **how ~ are you?** ¿cuántos años tienes?, ¿qué edad tienes?; **he's 10 years ~** tiene 10 años; **~er brother** hermano mayor; **old age** n vejez f; **old-age pension** n (*BRIT*) jubilación f, pensión f; **old-age pensioner** (*BRIT*) n jubilado/a; **old-fashioned** adj anticuado, pasado de moda; **old people's home** n (*esp BRIT*) residencia f de ancianos

olive ['ɔlɪv] n (*fruit*) aceituna; (*tree*) olivo
▷ adj (*also:* **~-green**) verde oliva; **olive oil** n
aceite m de oliva

Olympic [əu'lɪmpɪk] adj olímpico; **the ~
Games, the ~s** las Olimpiadas

omelet(te) ['ɔmlɪt] n tortilla francesa
(*SP*), omelette f (*LAM*)

omen ['əumən] n presagio

ominous ['ɔmɪnəs] adj de mal agüero,
amenazador(a)

omit [əu'mɪt] vt omitir

○ **KEYWORD**

on [ɔn] prep 1 (*indicating position*) en; sobre;
on the wall en la pared; **it's on the table**
está sobre or en la mesa; **on the left** a la
izquierda
2 (*indicating means, method, condition etc*): **on
foot** a pie; **on the train/plane** (*go*) en tren/
avión; (*be*) en el tren/el avión; **on the radio/
television/telephone** por or en la radio/
televisión/al teléfono; **to be on drugs**
drogarse; (*Med*) estar a tratamiento; **to be
on holiday/business** estar de vacaciones/
en viaje de negocios
3 (*referring to time*): **on Friday** el viernes; **on
Fridays** los viernes; **on June 20th** el 20 de
junio; **a week on Friday** del viernes en una
semana; **on arrival** al llegar; **on seeing this**
al ver esto
4 (*about, concerning*) sobre, acerca de; **a book
on physics** un libro de or sobre física
▷ adv 1 (*referring to dress*): **to have one's
coat on** tener or llevar el abrigo puesto; **she
put her gloves on** se puso los guantes
2 (*referring to covering*): **"screw the lid on
tightly"** "cerrar bien la tapa"
3 (*further, continuously*): **to walk** etc **on** seguir
caminando etc
▷ adj 1 (*functioning, in operation: machine,
radio, TV, light*) encendido/a (*SP*), prendido/a
(*LAM*); (: *tap*) abierto/a; (: *brakes*) echado/a,
puesto/a; **is the meeting still on?** (*in
progress*) ¿todavía continúa la reunión?; (*not
cancelled*) ¿va a haber reunión al fin?; **there's
a good film on at the cinema** ponen una
buena película en el cine
2 **that's not on!** (*inf: not possible*) ¡eso ni
hablar!; (: *not acceptable*) ¡eso no se hace!

once [wʌns] adv una vez; (*formerly*)
antiguamente ▷ conj una vez que; **~ he
had left/it was done** una vez que se
había marchado/se hizo; **at ~** en seguida,
inmediatamente; (*simultaneously*) a la vez;

~ a week una vez por semana; **~ more** otra
vez; **~ and for all** de una vez por todas; **~
upon a time** érase una vez

oncoming ['ɔnkʌmɪŋ] adj (*traffic*) que
viene de frente

○ **KEYWORD**

one [wʌn] num un(o)/una; **one hundred
and fifty** ciento cincuenta; **one by one**
uno a uno
▷ adj 1 (*sole*) único; **the one book which**
el único libro que; **the one man who** el
único que
2 (*same*) mismo/a; **they came in the one
car** vinieron en un solo coche
▷ pron 1 **this one** éste(ésta); **that one**
ése(ésa); (*more remote*) aquél(aquella); **I've
already got (a red) one** ya tengo uno/a
rojo/a; **one by one** uno/a por uno/a
2 **one another** os (*SP*), se (+ *el uno al otro,
unos a otros etc*); **do you two ever see one
another?** ¿vosotros dos os veis alguna vez?
(*SP*), ¿se ven ustedes dos alguna vez?; **the
boys didn't dare look at one another** los
chicos no se atrevieron a mirarse (el uno
al otro); **they all kissed one another** se
besaron unos a otros
3 (*impers*): **one never knows** nunca se sabe;
to cut one's finger cortarse el dedo; **one
needs to eat** hay que comer

one-off (*BRIT: inf*) n (*event*) acontecimiento
único

oneself [wʌn'sɛlf] pron (*reflexive*) se; (*after
prep*) sí; (*emphatic*) uno/a mismo/a; **to hurt
~** hacerse daño; **to keep sth for ~** guardarse
algo; **to talk to ~** hablar solo

one: **one-shot** [wʌn'ʃɔt] (*US*) n = **one-off**;
one-sided adj (*argument*) parcial; **one-to-
one** adj (*relationship*) de dos; **one-way** adj
(*street*) de sentido único

ongoing ['ɔngəuɪŋ] adj continuo

onion ['ʌnjən] n cebolla

on-line ['ɔnlaɪn] adj, adv (*Comput*) en línea

onlooker ['ɔnlukə*] n espectador(a) m/f

only ['əunlɪ] adv solamente, sólo ▷ adj
único, solo ▷ conj solamente que, pero; **an
~ child** un hijo único; **not ~ ... but also ...** no
sólo ... sino también ...

on-screen [ɔn'skri:n] adj (*Comput etc*) en
pantalla; (*romance, kiss*) cinematográfico

onset ['ɔnsɛt] n comienzo

onto ['ɔntu] prep = **on to**

onward(s) ['ɔnwəd(z)] adv (*move*) (hacia)
adelante; **from that time ~** desde entonces
en adelante

oops [ups] excl (*also:* **~-a-daisy!**) ¡huy!

ooze [u:z] *vi* rezumar

opaque [əu'peɪk] *adj* opaco

open ['əupn] *adj* abierto; (*car*) descubierto; (*road, view*) despejado; (*meeting*) público; (*admiration*) manifiesto ▷ *vt* abrir ▷ *vi* abrirse; (*book etc: commence*) comenzar; **in the ~ (air)** al aire libre; **open up** *vt* abrir; (*blocked road*) despejar ▷ *vi* abrirse, empezar; **open-air** *adj* al aire libre; **opening** *n* abertura; (*start*) comienzo; (*opportunity*) oportunidad *f*; **opening hours** *npl* horario de apertura; **open learning** *n* enseñanza flexible a tiempo parcial; **openly** *adv* abiertamente; **open-minded** *adj* imparcial; **open-necked** *adj* (*shirt*) desabrochado; sin corbata; **open-plan** *adj*: **open-plan office** gran oficina sin particiones; **Open University** *n* (*BRIT*) ≈ Universidad *f* Nacional de Enseñanza a Distancia, UNED *f*

- OPEN UNIVERSITY
-
- La **Open University**, fundada en
- 1969, está especializada en impartir
- cursos a distancia que no exigen una
- dedicación exclusiva. Cuenta con sus
- propios materiales de apoyo, entre
- ellos programas de radio y televisión
- emitidos por la **BBC** y para conseguir los
- créditos de la licenciatura es necesaria
- la presentación de unos trabajos y la
- asistencia a los cursos de verano.

opera ['ɔpərə] *n* ópera; **opera house** *n* teatro de la ópera; **opera singer** *n* cantante *m/f* de ópera

operate ['ɔpəreɪt] *vt* (*machine*) hacer funcionar; (*company*) dirigir ▷ *vi* funcionar; **to ~ on sb** (*Med*) operar a algn

operating room ['ɔpəreɪtɪŋ-] (*us*) *n* quirófano, sala de operaciones

operating theatre (*BRIT*) *n* sala de operaciones

operation [ɔpə'reɪʃən] *n* operación *f*; (*of machine*) funcionamiento; **to be in ~** estar funcionando *or* en funcionamiento; **to have an ~** (*Med*) ser operado; **operational** *adj* operacional, en buen estado

operative ['ɔpərətɪv] *adj* en vigor

operator ['ɔpəreɪtə*] *n* (*of machine*) maquinista *mf*, operario/a; (*Tel*) operador(a) *m/f*, telefonista *mf*

opinion [ə'pɪnɪən] *n* opinión *f*; **in my ~** en mi opinión, a mi juicio; **opinion poll** *n* encuesta, sondeo

opponent [ə'pəunənt] *n* adversario/a, contrincante *mf*

opportunity [ɔpə'tju:nɪtɪ] *n* oportunidad *f*; **to take the ~ of doing** aprovechar la ocasión para hacer

oppose [ə'pəuz] *vt* oponerse a; **to be ~d to sth** oponerse a algo; **as ~d to** a diferencia de

opposite ['ɔpəzɪt] *adj* opuesto, contrario a; (*house etc*) de enfrente ▷ *adv* en frente ▷ *prep* en frente de, frente a ▷ *n* lo contrario

opposition [ɔpə'zɪʃən] *n* oposición *f*

oppress [ə'pres] *vt* oprimir

opt [ɔpt] *vi*: **to ~ for** optar por; **to ~ to do** optar por hacer; **opt out** *vi*: **to opt out of** optar por no hacer

optician [ɔp'tɪʃən] *n* óptico *m/f*

optimism ['ɔptɪmɪzəm] *n* optimismo

optimist ['ɔptɪmɪst] *n* optimista *mf*; **optimistic** [-'mɪstɪk] *adj* optimista

optimum ['ɔptɪməm] *adj* óptimo

option ['ɔpʃən] *n* opción *f*; **optional** *adj* facultativo, discrecional

or [ɔː*] *conj* o; (*before o, ho*) u; (*with negative*): **he hasn't seen ~ heard anything** no ha visto ni oído nada; **~ else** si no

oral ['ɔːrəl] *adj* oral ▷ *n* examen *m* oral

orange ['ɔrɪndʒ] *n* (*fruit*) naranja ▷ *adj* color naranja; **orange juice** *n* jugo *m* de naranja, zumo *m* de naranja (*SP*); **orange squash** *n* naranjada

orbit ['ɔːbɪt] *n* órbita ▷ *vt, vi* orbitar

orchard ['ɔːtʃəd] *n* huerto

orchestra ['ɔːkɪstrə] *n* orquesta; (*US: seating*) platea

orchid ['ɔːkɪd] *n* orquídea

ordeal [ɔː'diːl] *n* experiencia horrorosa

order ['ɔːdə*] *n* orden *m*; (*command*) orden *f*; (*good order*) buen estado; (*Comm*) pedido ▷ *vt* (*also*: **put in ~**) arreglar, poner en orden; (*Comm*) pedir; (*command*) mandar, ordenar; **in ~** orden; (*of document*) en regla; **in (working) ~** en funcionamiento; **in ~ to do/that** para hacer/que; **on ~** (*Comm*) pedido; **to be out of ~** estar desordenado; (*not working*) no funcionar; **to ~ sb to do sth** mandar a algn hacer algo; **order form** *n* hoja de pedido; **orderly** *n* (*Mil*) ordenanza *m*; (*Med*) enfermero/a (auxiliar) ▷ *adj* ordenado

ordinary ['ɔːdnrɪ] *adj* corriente, normal; (*pej*) común y corriente; **out of the ~** fuera de lo común

ore [ɔː*] *n* mineral *m*

oregano [ɔrɪ'gɑːnəu] *n* orégano

organ ['ɔːgən] *n* órgano; **organic** [ɔː'gænɪk] *adj* orgánico; **organism** *n* organismo

organization [ɔːgənaɪ'zeɪʃən] *n* organización *f*

organize ['ɔːgənaɪz] *vt* organizar;

organized ['ɔːɡənaizd] adj organizado;
organizer n organizador(a) m/f
orgasm ['ɔːɡæzəm] n orgasmo
orgy ['ɔːdʒɪ] n orgía
oriental [ɔːrɪ'ɛntl] adj oriental
orientation [ɔːrɪen'teiʃən] n orientación f
origin ['ɔrɪdʒɪn] n origen m
original [ə'rɪdʒɪnl] adj original; (first)
primero; (earlier) primitivo ⊳ n original m;
originally adv al principio
originate [ə'rɪdʒɪneɪt] vi: **to ~ from, to ~
in** surgir de, tener su origen en
Orkneys ['ɔːknɪz] npl: **the ~** (also: **the
Orkney Islands**) las Orcadas
ornament ['ɔːnəmənt] n adorno; (trinket)
chuchería; **ornamental** [-'mɛntl] adj
decorativo, de adorno
ornate [ɔː'neɪt] adj muy ornado, vistoso
orphan ['ɔːfn] n huérfano/a
orthodox ['ɔːθədɔks] adj ortodoxo
orthopaedic [ɔːθə'piːdɪk] (us **orthopedic**)
adj ortopédico
osteopath ['ɔstɪəpæθ] n osteópata mf
ostrich ['ɔstrɪtʃ] n avestruz m
other ['ʌðə*] adj otro ⊳ pron: **the ~ (one)**
el(la) otro/a ⊳ adv: **~ than** aparte de;
otherwise adv de otra manera ⊳ conj (if
not) si no
otter ['ɔtə*] n nutria
ouch [autʃ] excl ¡ay!
ought [ɔːt] (pt ~) aux vb: **I ~ to do it** debería
hacerlo; **this ~ to have been corrected**
esto debiera haberse corregido; **he ~ to win**
(probability) debe or debiera ganar
ounce [auns] n onza (28.35g)
our ['auə*] adj nuestro; see also **my**; **ours**
pron (el) nuestro/(la) nuestra etc; see also
mine[1]; **ourselves** pron pl (reflexive, after
prep) nosotros; (emphatic) nosotros mismos;
see also **oneself**
oust [aust] vt desalojar
out [aut] adv fuera, afuera; (not at home)
fuera (de casa); (light, fire) apagado; **~ there**
allí (fuera); **he's ~** (absent) no está, ha salido;
to be ~ in one's calculations equivocarse
(en sus cálculos); **to run ~** salir corriendo;
~ loud en alta voz; **~ of** (outside) fuera
de; (because of: anger etc) por; **~ of petrol**
sin gasolina; **"~ of order"** "no funciona";
outback n interior m; **outbound** adj
(flight) de salida; (flight: not return) de ida;
outbreak n (of war) comienzo; (of disease)
epidemia; (of violence etc) ola; **outburst** n
explosión f, arranque m; **outcast** n paria
mf; **outcome** n resultado; **outcry** n
protestas fpl; **outdated** adj anticuado,
fuera de moda; **outdoor** adj exterior, de
aire libre; (clothes) de calle; **outdoors** adv

al aire libre
outer ['autə*] adj exterior, externo; **outer
space** n espacio exterior
outfit ['autfɪt] n (clothes) conjunto
out: outgoing adj (character) extrovertido;
(retiring: president etc) saliente; **outgoings**
(BRIT) npl gastos mpl; **outhouse** n
dependencia
outing ['autɪŋ] n excursión f, paseo
out: outlaw n proscrito ⊳ vt proscribir;
outlay n inversión f; **outlet** n salida;
(of pipe) desagüe m; (us Elec) toma de
corriente; (also: **retail outlet**) punto de
venta; **outline** n (shape) contorno, perfil m;
(sketch, plan) esbozo ⊳ vt (plan etc) esbozar;
in outline (fig) a grandes rasgos; **outlook** n
(fig: prospects) perspectivas fpl; (: for weather)
pronóstico; **outnumber** vt superar
en número; **out-of-date** adj (passport)
caducado; (clothes) pasado de moda; **out-of-
doors** adv al aire libre; **out-of-the-way** adj
apartado; **out-of-town** adj (shopping centre
etc) en las afueras; **outpatient** n paciente
mf externo/a; **outpost** n puesto avanzado;
output n (volumen m de) producción m,
rendimiento; (Comput) salida
outrage ['autreɪdʒ] n escándalo; (atrocity)
atrocidad f ⊳ vt ultrajar; **outrageous**
[-'reɪdʒəs] adj monstruoso
outright [adv aut'raɪt, adj 'autraɪt]
adv (ask, deny) francamente; (refuse)
rotundamente; (win) de manera absoluta;
(be killed) en el acto ⊳ adj franco; rotundo
outset ['autsɛt] n principio
outside [aut'saɪd] n exterior m ⊳ adj
exterior, externo ⊳ adv fuera ⊳ prep fuera
de; (beyond) más allá de; **at the ~** (fig) a lo
sumo; **outside lane** n (Aut: in Britain) carril
m de la derecha; (: in US, Europe etc) carril m
de la izquierda; **outside line** n (Tel) línea
(exterior); **outsider** n (stranger) extraño,
forastero
out: outsize adj (clothes) de talla grande;
outskirts npl alrededores mpl, afueras fpl;
outspoken adj muy franco; **outstanding**
adj excepcional, destacado; (remaining)
pendiente
outward ['autwəd] adj externo; (journey)
de ida; **outwards** adv (esp BRIT) = **outward**
outweigh [aut'weɪ] vt pesar más que
oval ['əuvl] adj ovalado ⊳ n óvalo
ovary ['əuvərɪ] n ovario
oven ['ʌvn] n horno; **oven glove** n
guante m para el horno, manopla para el
horno; **ovenproof** adj resistente al horno;
oven-ready adj listo para el horno
over ['əuvə*] adv encima, por encima
⊳ adj or adv (finished) terminado; (surplus)

o

de sobra ▷ *prep* (por) encima de; (*above*) sobre; (*on the other side of*) al otro lado de; (*more than*) más de; (*during*) durante; **~ here** (por) aquí; **~ there** (por) allí *or* allá; **all ~** (*everywhere*) por todas partes; **~ and ~ (again)** una y otra vez; **~ and above** además de; **to ask sb ~** invitar a algn a casa; **to bend ~** inclinarse

overall [*adj, n* 'əʊvərɔ:l, *adv* əʊvə'rɔ:l] *adj* (*length etc*) total; (*study*) de conjunto ▷ *adv* en conjunto ▷ *n* (BRIT) guardapolvo; **overalls** *npl* (*boiler suit*) mono (SP) *or* overol *m* (LAM) (de trabajo)

overboard *adv* (Naut) por la borda

overcame [əʊvə'keɪm] *pt of* **overcome**

overcast ['əʊvəkɑ:st] *adj* encapotado

overcharge [əʊvə'tʃɑ:dʒ] *vt*: **to ~ sb** cobrar un precio excesivo a algn

overcoat ['əʊvəkəʊt] *n* abrigo, sobretodo

overcome [əʊvə'kʌm] *vt* vencer; (*difficulty*) superar

over: overcrowded *adj* atestado de gente; (*city, country*) superpoblado; **overdo** (*irreg*) *vt* exagerar; (*overcook*) cocer demasiado; **to overdo it** (*work etc*) pasarse; **overdone** [əʊvə'dʌn] *adj* (*vegetables*) recocido; (*steak*) demasiado hecho; **overdose** *n* sobredosis *f inv*; **overdraft** *n* saldo deudor; **overdrawn** *adj* (*account*) en descubierto; **overdue** *adj* retrasado; **overestimate** *vt* sobreestimar

overflow [*vb* əʊvə'fləʊ, *n* 'əʊvəfləʊ] *vi* desbordarse ▷ *n* (*also*: **~ pipe**) (cañería de) desagüe *m*

overgrown [əʊvə'grəʊn] *adj* (*garden*) invadido por la vegetación

overhaul [*vb* əʊvə'hɔ:l, *n* 'əʊvəhɔ:l] *vt* revisar, repasar ▷ *n* revisión *f*

overhead [*adv* əʊvə'hɛd, *adj, n* 'əʊvəhɛd] *adv* por arriba *or* encima ▷ *adj* (*cable*) aéreo ▷ *n* (US) = **overheads**; **overhead projector** *n* retroproyector; **overheads** *npl* (*expenses*) gastos *mpl* generales

over: overhear (*irreg*) *vt* oír por casualidad; **overheat** *vi* (*engine*) recalentarse; **overland** *adj, adv* por tierra; **overlap** [əʊvə'læp] *vi* traslaparse; **overleaf** *adv* al dorso; **overload** *vt* sobrecargar; **overlook** *vt* (*have view of*) dar a, tener vistas a; (*miss: by mistake*) pasar por alto; (*excuse*) perdonar

overnight [əʊvə'naɪt] *adv* durante la noche; (*fig*) de la noche a la mañana ▷ *adj* de noche; **to stay ~** pasar la noche; **overnight bag** *n* fin *m* de semana, neceser *m* de viaje

overpass (US) ['əʊvəpɑ:s] *n* paso superior

overpower [əʊvə'paʊə*] *vt* dominar; (*fig*) embargar; **overpowering** *adj* (*heat*) agobiante; (*smell*) penetrante

over: overreact [əʊvəri'ækt] *vi* reaccionar de manera exagerada; **overrule** *vt* (*decision*) anular; (*claim*) denegar; **overrun** (*irreg*) *vt* (*country*) invadir; (*time limit*) rebasar, exceder

overseas [əʊvə'si:z] *adv* (*abroad: live*) en el extranjero; (*travel*) al extranjero ▷ *adj* (*trade*) exterior; (*visitor*) extranjero

oversee [əʊvə'si:] (*irreg*) *vt* supervisar

overshadow [əʊvə'ʃædəʊ] *vt*: **to be ~ed by** estar a la sombra de

oversight ['əʊvəsaɪt] *n* descuido

oversleep [əʊvə'sli:p] (*irreg*) *vi* quedarse dormido

overspend [əʊvə'spɛnd] (*irreg*) *vi* gastar más de la cuenta; **we have overspent by 5 pounds** hemos excedido el presupuesto en 5 libras

overt [əʊ'və:t] *adj* abierto

overtake [əʊvə'teɪk] (*irreg*) *vt* sobrepasar; (BRIT Aut) adelantar

over: overthrow (*irreg*) *vt* (*government*) derrocar; **overtime** *n* horas *fpl* extraordinarias

overtook [əʊvə'tuk] *pt of* **overtake**

over: overturn *vt* volcar; (*fig: plan*) desbaratar; (*: government*) derrocar ▷ *vi* volcar; **overweight** *adj* demasiado gordo *or* pesado; **overwhelm** *vt* aplastar; (*emotion*) sobrecoger; **overwhelming** *adj* (*victory, defeat*) arrollador(a); (*feeling*) irresistible

ow [aʊ] *excl* ¡ay!

owe [əʊ] *vt*: **to ~ sb sth, to ~ sth to sb** deber algo a algn; **owing to** *prep* debido a, por causa de

owl [aʊl] *n* búho, lechuza

own [əʊn] *vt* tener, poseer ▷ *adj* propio; **a room of my ~** una habitación propia; **to get one's ~ back** tomar revancha; **on one's ~** solo, a solas; **own up** *vi* confesar; **owner** *n* dueño/a; **ownership** *n* posesión *f*

ox [ɔks] (*pl* **~en**) *n* buey *m*

Oxbridge ['ɔksbrɪdʒ] *n* universidades de Oxford y Cambridge

oxen ['ɔksən] *npl of* **ox**

oxygen ['ɔksɪdʒən] *n* oxígeno

oyster ['ɔɪstə*] *n* ostra

oz. *abbr* = **ounce(s)**

ozone ['əʊzəʊn] *n* ozono; **ozone friendly** *adj* que no daña la capa de ozono; **ozone layer** *n* capa *f* de ozono

p

p [pi:] abbr = **penny; pence**

P.A. n abbr = **personal assistant; public address system**

p.a. abbr = **per annum**

pace [peɪs] n paso ▷vi: **to ~ up and down** pasearse de un lado a otro; **to keep ~ with** llevar el mismo paso que; **pacemaker** n (Med) regulador m cardíaco, marcapasos m inv; (Sport: also: **pacesetter**) liebre f

Pacific [pə'sɪfɪk] n: **the ~ (Ocean)** el (Océano) Pacífico

pacifier ['pæsɪfaɪə*] (US) n (dummy) chupete m

pack [pæk] n (packet) paquete m; (of hounds) jauría; (of people) manada, bando; (of cards) baraja; (bundle) fardo; (US: of cigarettes) paquete m; (back pack) mochila ▷vt (fill) llenar; (in suitcase etc) meter, poner; (cram) llenar, atestar; **to ~ (one's bags)** hacerse la maleta; **to ~ sb off** despachar a algn; **pack in** vi (watch, car) estropearse ▷vt (inf) dejar; **pack it in!** ¡para!, ¡basta ya!; **pack up** vi (inf: machine) estropearse; (person) irse ▷vt (belongings, clothes) recoger; (goods, presents) empaquetar, envolver

package ['pækɪdʒ] n paquete m; (bulky) bulto; (also: **~ deal**) acuerdo global; **package holiday** n vacaciones fpl organizadas; **package tour** n viaje m organizado

packaging ['pækɪdʒɪŋ] n envase m

packed [pækt] adj abarrotado; **packed lunch** n almuerzo frío

packet ['pækɪt] n paquete m

packing ['pækɪŋ] n embalaje m

pact [pækt] n pacto

pad [pæd] n (of paper) bloc m; (cushion) cojinete m; (inf: home) casa ▷vt rellenar; **padded** adj (jacket) acolchado; (bra) reforzado

paddle ['pædl] n (oar) canalete m; (US: for table tennis) paleta ▷vt impulsar con canalete ▷vi (with feet) chapotear; **paddling pool** (BRIT) n estanque m de juegos

paddock ['pædək] n corral m

padlock ['pædlɔk] n candado

paedophile ['pi:dəʊfaɪl] (US **pedophile**) adj de pedófilos ▷n pedófilo/a

page [peɪdʒ] n (of book) página; (of newspaper) plana; (also: **~ boy**) paje m ▷vt (in hotel etc) llamar por altavoz a

pager ['peɪdʒə*] n (Tel) busca m

paid [peɪd] pt, pp of **pay** ▷adj (work) remunerado; (holiday) pagado; (official etc) a sueldo; **to put ~ to** (BRIT) acabar con

pain [peɪn] n dolor m; **to be in ~** sufrir; **to take ~s to do sth** tomarse grandes molestias en hacer algo; **painful** adj doloroso; (difficult) penoso; (disagreeable) desagradable; **painkiller** n analgésico; **painstaking** ['peɪnzteɪkɪŋ] adj (person) concienzudo, esmerado

paint [peɪnt] n pintura ▷vt pintar; **to ~ the door blue** pintar la puerta de azul; **paintbrush** n (of artist) pincel m; (of decorator) brocha; **painter** n pintor(a) m/f; **painting** n pintura

pair [pɛə*] n (of shoes, gloves etc) par m; (of people) pareja; **a ~ of scissors** unas tijeras; **a ~ of trousers** unos pantalones, un pantalón

pajamas [pə'dʒɑːməz] (US) npl pijama m

Pakistan [pɑːkɪ'stɑːn] n Paquistán m; **Pakistani** adj, n paquistaní m/f

pal [pæl] (inf) n compinche mf, compañero/a

palace ['pæləs] n palacio

pale [peɪl] adj (gen) pálido; (colour) claro ▷n: **to be beyond the ~** pasarse de la raya

Palestine ['pælɪstaɪn] n Palestina; **Palestinian** [-'tɪnɪən] adj, n palestino/a m/f

palm [pɑːm] n (Anat) palma; (also: **~ tree**) palmera, palma ▷vt: **to ~ sth off on sb** (inf) encajar algo a algn

pamper ['pæmpə*] vt mimar

pamphlet ['pæmflət] n folleto

pan [pæn] n (also: **sauce~**) cacerola, cazuela, olla; (also: **frying ~**) sartén f

pancake ['pænkeɪk] n crepe f

panda ['pændə] n panda m

pane [peɪn] n cristal m

panel ['pænl] n (of wood etc) panel m; (Radio, TV) panel m de invitados

panhandler ['pænhændlə*] (US) n (inf) mendigo/a

panic ['pænɪk] n terror m pánico ▷vi dejarse llevar por el pánico

panorama [pænə'rɑːmə] n panorama m

pansy ['pænzɪ] n (Bot) pensamiento; (inf,

pej) maricón *m*
pant [pænt] *vi* jadear
panther ['pænθə*] *n* pantera
panties ['pæntɪz] *npl* bragas *fpl*, pantis *mpl*
pantomime ['pæntəmaɪm] (*BRIT*) *n*
revista musical representada en Navidad, basada
en cuentos dehadas

● **PANTOMIME**
●
●
● En época navideña se ponen en escena
● en los teatros británicos las llamadas
● **pantomimes**, que son versiones libres
● de cuentos tradicionales como Aladino
● o El gato con botas. En ella nunca faltan
● personajes como la dama ("dame"),
● papel que siempre interpreta un actor,
● el protagonista joven ("principal boy"),
● normalmente interpretado por una
● actriz, y el malvado ("villain"). Es un
● espectáculo familiar en el que se anima
● al público a participar y aunque va
● dirigido principalmente a los niños,
● cuenta con grandes dosis de humor para
● adultos.

pants [pænts] *n* (*BRIT: underwear: woman's*)
bragas *fpl*; (: *man's*) calzoncillos *mpl*;
(*US: trousers*) pantalones *mpl*
paper ['peɪpə*] *n* papel *m*; (*also:* **news~**)
periódico, diario; (*academic essay*) ensayo;
(*exam*) examen *m* ▷ *adj* de papel ▷ *vt*
empapelar, tapizar (*MEX*); **papers** *npl*
(*also:* **identity ~s**) papeles *mpl*, documentos
mpl; **paperback** *n* libro en rústica; **paper**
bag *n* bolsa de papel; **paper clip** *n* clip *m*;
paper shop (*BRIT*) *n* tienda de periódicos;
paperwork *n* trabajo administrativo
paprika ['pæprɪkə] *n* pimentón *m*
par [pɑ:*] *n* par *f*; (*Golf*) par *m*; **to be on a ~**
with estar a la par con
paracetamol [pærə'si:təmɔl] (*BRIT*) *n*
paracetamol *m*
parachute ['pærəʃu:t] *n* paracaídas *m inv*
parade [pə'reɪd] *n* desfile *m* ▷ *vt* (*show*)
hacer alarde de ▷ *vi* desfilar; (*Mil*) pasar
revista
paradise ['pærədaɪs] *n* paraíso
paradox ['pærədɔks] *n* paradoja
paraffin ['pærəfɪn] (*BRIT*) *n* (*also:* **~ oil**)
parafina
paragraph ['pærəgrɑ:f] *n* párrafo
parallel ['pærəlɛl] *adj* en paralelo; (*fig*)
semejante ▷ *n* (*line*) paralela; (*fig, Geo*)
paralelo
paralysed ['pærəlaɪzd] *adj* paralizado
paralysis [pə'rælɪsɪs] *n* parálisis *f inv*
paramedic [pærə'mɛdɪk] *n* auxiliar *m/f*

sanitario/a
paranoid ['pærənɔɪd] *adj* (*person, feeling*)
paranoico
parasite ['pærəsaɪt] *n* parásito/a
parcel ['pɑ:sl] *n* paquete *m* ▷ *vt* (*also:* **~**
up) empaquetar, embalar
pardon ['pɑ:dn] *n* (*Law*) indulto ▷ *vt*
perdonar; **~ me!, I beg your ~!** (*I'm sorry!*)
¡perdone usted!; **(I beg your) ~?, ~ me?**
(*US: what did you say?*) ¿cómo?
parent ['pɛərənt] *n* (*mother*) madre *f*;
(*father*) padre *m*; **parents** *npl* padres *mpl*
▌ Be careful not to translate **parent** by the
▌ Spanish word *pariente*.
parental [pə'rɛntl] *adj* paternal/maternal
Paris ['pærɪs] *n* París
parish ['pærɪʃ] *n* parroquia
Parisian [pə'rɪzɪən] *adj, n* parisiense *mf*
park [pɑ:k] *n* parque *m* ▷ *vt* aparcar,
estacionar ▷ *vi* aparcar, estacionarse
parking ['pɑ:kɪŋ] *n* aparcamiento,
estacionamiento; **"no ~"** "prohibido
estacionarse"; **parking lot** (*US*) *n* parking
m; **parking meter** *n* parquímetro; **parking**
ticket *n* multa de aparcamiento
parkway ['pɑ:kweɪ] (*US*) *n* alameda
parliament ['pɑ:ləmənt] *n* parlamento;
(*Spanish*) Cortes *fpl*; **parliamentary**
[-'mɛntərɪ] *adj* parlamentario

● **PARLIAMENT**
●
● El Parlamento británico (**Parliament**)
● tiene como sede el palacio de
● Westminster, también llamado "Houses
● of Parliament" y consta de dos cámaras.
● La Cámara de los Comunes ("House
● of Commons"), compuesta por 650
● diputados (**Members of Parliament**)
● elegidos por sufragio universal en su
● respectiva circunscripción electoral
● (constituency), se reúne 175 días al año
● y sus sesiones son moderadas por el
● Presidente de la Cámara (**Speaker**). La
● cámara alta es la Cámara de los Lores
● ("House of Lords") y está formada por
● miembros que han sido nombrados
● por el monarca o que han heredado su
● escaño. Su poder es limitado, aunque
● actúa como tribunal supremo de
● apelación, excepto en Escocia.

Parmesan [pɑ:mɪ'zæn] *n* (*also:* **~ cheese**)
queso parmesano
parole [pə'rəul] *n*: **on ~** libre bajo palabra
parrot ['pærət] *n* loro, papagayo
parsley ['pɑ:slɪ] *n* perejil *m*
parsnip ['pɑ:snɪp] *n* chirivía

parson ['pɑːsn] n cura m
part [pɑːt] n (gen, Mus) parte f; (bit) trozo; (of machine) pieza; (Theatre etc) papel m; (of serial) entrega; (us: in hair) raya ▷ adv = **partly** ▷ vt separar ▷ vi (people) separarse; (crowd) apartarse; **to take ~ in** tomar parte or participar en; **to take sth in good ~** tomar algo en buena parte; **to take sb's ~** defender a algn; **for my ~** por mi parte; **for the most ~** en su mayor parte; **to ~ one's hair** hacerse la raya; **part with** vt fus ceder, entregar; (money) pagar; **part of speech** n parte f de la oración, categoría f gramatical
partial ['pɑːʃl] adj parcial; **to be ~ to** ser aficionado a
participant [pɑːˈtɪsɪpənt] n (in competition) concursante mf; (in campaign etc) participante mf
participate [pɑːˈtɪsɪpeɪt] vi: **to ~ in** participar en
particle ['pɑːtɪkl] n partícula; (of dust) grano
particular [pəˈtɪkjulə*] adj (special) particular; (concrete) concreto; (given) determinado; (fussy) quisquilloso; (demanding) exigente; **in ~** en particular; **particularly** adv (in particular) sobre todo; (difficult, good etc) especialmente; **particulars** npl (information) datos mpl; (details) pormenores mpl
parting ['pɑːtɪŋ] n (act) separación f; (farewell) despedida; (BRIT: in hair) raya ▷ adj de despedida
partition [pɑːˈtɪʃən] n (Pol) división f; (wall) tabique m
partly ['pɑːtlɪ] adv en parte
partner ['pɑːtnə*] n (Comm) socio/a; (Sport, at dance) pareja; (spouse) cónyuge mf; (lover) compañero/a; **partnership** n asociación f; (Comm) sociedad f
partridge ['pɑːtrɪdʒ] n perdiz f
part-time ['pɑːt'taɪm] adj, adv a tiempo parcial
party ['pɑːtɪ] n (Pol) partido; (celebration) fiesta; (group) grupo; (Law) parte f interesada ▷ cpd (Pol) de partido
pass [pɑːs] vt (time, object) pasar; (place) pasar por; (overtake) rebasar; (exam) aprobar; (approve) aprobar ▷ vi pasar; (Scol) aprobar, ser aprobado ▷ n (permit) permiso; (membership card) carnet m; (in mountains) puerto, desfiladero; (Sport) pase m; (Scol: also: ~ mark): **to get a ~ in** aprobar en; **to ~ sth through sth** pasar algo por algo; **to make a ~ at sb** (inf) hacer proposiciones a algn; **pass away** vi fallecer; **pass by** vi pasar ▷ vt (ignore) pasar por alto; **pass on** vt transmitir; **pass out** vi desmayarse;

pass over vi, vt omitir, pasar por alto; **pass up** vt (opportunity) renunciar a; **passable** adj (road) transitable; (tolerable) pasable
passage ['pæsɪdʒ] n (also: ~way) pasillo; (act of passing) tránsito; (fare, in book) pasaje m; (by boat) travesía; (Anat) tubo
passenger ['pæsɪndʒə*] n pasajero/a, viajero/a
passer-by [pɑːsə'baɪ] n transeúnte mf
passing place n (Aut) apartadero
passion ['pæʃən] n pasión f; **passionate** adj apasionado; **passion fruit** n fruta de la pasión, granadilla
passive ['pæsɪv] adj (gen, also Ling) pasivo
passport ['pɑːspɔːt] n pasaporte m; **passport control** n control m de pasaporte; **passport office** n oficina de pasaportes
password ['pɑːswɜːd] n contraseña
past [pɑːst] prep (in front of) por delante de; (further than) más allá de; (later than) después de ▷ adj pasado; (president etc) antiguo ▷ n (time) pasado; (of person) antecedentes mpl; **he's ~ forty** tiene más de cuarenta años; **ten/quarter ~ eight** las ocho y diez/cuarto; **for the ~ few/3 days** durante los últimos días/últimos 3 días; **to run ~ sb** pasar a algn corriendo
pasta ['pæstə] n pasta
paste [peɪst] n pasta; (glue) engrudo ▷ vt pegar
pastel ['pæstl] adj pastel; (painting) al pastel
pasteurized ['pæstəraɪzd] adj pasteurizado
pastime ['pɑːstaɪm] n pasatiempo
pastor ['pɑːstə*] n pastor m
past participle [-'pɑːtɪsɪpl] n (Ling) participio m (de) pasado or (de) pretérito or pasivo
pastry ['peɪstrɪ] n (dough) pasta; (cake) pastel m
pasture ['pɑːstʃə*] n pasto
pasty¹ ['pæstɪ] n empanada
pasty² ['peɪstɪ] adj (complexion) pálido
pat [pæt] vt dar una palmadita a; (dog etc) acariciar
patch [pætʃ] n (of material: eye patch) parche m; (mended part) remiendo; (of land) terreno ▷ vt remendar; **(to go through) a bad ~** (pasar por) una mala racha; **patchy** adj desigual
pâté ['pæteɪ] n paté m
patent ['peɪtnt] n patente f ▷ vt patentar ▷ adj patente, evidente
paternal [pəˈtɜːnl] adj paternal; (relation) paterno
paternity leave [pəˈtɜːnɪtɪ-] n permiso m

por paternidad, licencia por paternidad

path [pɑ:θ] n camino, sendero; (trail, track) pista; (of missile) trayectoria

pathetic [pəˈθetɪk] adj patético, lastimoso; (very bad) malísimo

pathway [ˈpɑ:θweɪ] n sendero, vereda

patience [ˈpeɪʃns] n paciencia; (BRIT Cards) solitario

patient [ˈpeɪʃnt] n paciente mf ▷ adj paciente, sufrido

patio [ˈpætɪəʊ] n patio

patriotic [pætrɪˈɒtɪk] adj patriótico

patrol [pəˈtrəʊl] n patrulla ▷ vt patrullar por; **patrol car** n coche m patrulla

patron [ˈpeɪtrən] n (in shop) cliente mf; (of charity) patrocinador(a) m/f; **~ of the arts** mecenas m

patronizing [ˈpætrənaɪzɪŋ] adj condescendiente

pattern [ˈpætən] n (Sewing) patrón m; (design) dibujo; **patterned** adj (material) estampado

pause [pɔ:z] n pausa ▷ vi hacer una pausa

pave [peɪv] vt pavimentar; **to ~ the way for** preparar el terreno para

pavement [ˈpeɪvmənt] (BRIT) n acera, banqueta (MEX), andén m (CAM), vereda (SC)

pavilion [pəˈvɪlɪən] n (Sport) caseta

paving [ˈpeɪvɪŋ] n pavimento, enlosado

paw [pɔ:] n pata

pawn [pɔ:n] n (Chess) peón m; (fig) instrumento ▷ vt empeñar; **pawn broker** n prestamista mf

pay [peɪ] (pt, pp **paid**) n (wage etc) sueldo, salario ▷ vt pagar ▷ vi (be profitable) rendir; **to ~ attention (to)** prestar atención (a); **to ~ sb a visit** hacer una visita a algn; **to ~ one's respects to sb** presentar sus respetos a algn; **pay back** vt (money) reembolsar; (person) pagar; **pay for** vt fus pagar; **pay in** vt ingresar; **pay off** vt saldar ▷ vi (scheme, decision) dar resultado; **pay out** vt (money) gastar, desembolsar; **pay up** vt pagar (de mala gana); **payable** adj: **payable to** pagadero a; **pay day** n día m de paga; **pay envelope** (US) n = **pay packet**; **payment** n pago; **monthly payment** mensualidad f; **payout** n pago; (in competition) premio en metálico; **pay packet** (BRIT) n sobre m (de paga); **pay phone** n teléfono público; **payroll** n nómina; **pay slip** n recibo de sueldo; **pay television** n televisión f de pago

PC n abbr = **personal computer**; (BRIT) (= police constable) policía mf ▷ adv abbr = **politically correct**

p.c. abbr = **per cent**

PDA n abbr (= personal digital assistant)

agenda electrónica

PE n abbr (= physical education) ed. física

pea [pi:] n guisante m (SP), arveja (LAM), chícharo (MEX, CAM)

peace [pi:s] n paz f; (calm) paz f, tranquilidad f; **peaceful** adj (gentle) pacífico; (calm) tranquilo, sosegado

peach [pi:tʃ] n melocotón m (SP), durazno (LAM)

peacock [ˈpi:kɔk] n pavo real

peak [pi:k] n (of mountain) cumbre f, cima; (of cap) visera; (fig) cumbre f; **peak hours** npl horas fpl punta

peanut [ˈpi:nʌt] n cacahuete m (SP), maní m (LAM), cacahuate m (MEX); **peanut butter** n manteca de cacahuete or maní

pear [pɛə*] n pera

pearl [pə:l] n perla

peasant [ˈpeznt] n campesino/a

peat [pi:t] n turba

pebble [ˈpebl] n guijarro

peck [pɛk] vt (also: ~ at) picotear ▷ n picotazo; (kiss) besito; **peckish** (BRIT: inf) adj: **I feel peckish** tengo ganas de picar algo

peculiar [pɪˈkju:lɪə*] adj (odd) extraño, raro; (typical) propio, característico; **~ to** propio de

pedal [ˈpedl] n pedal m ▷ vi pedalear

pedalo [ˈpedələu] n patín m a pedal

pedestal [ˈpedəstl] n pedestal m

pedestrian [pɪˈdestrɪən] n peatón m, peatón/ona m/f ▷ adj pedestre; **pedestrian crossing** (BRIT) n paso de peatones; **pedestrianized** adj: **a pedestrianized street** una calle peatonal; **pedestrian precinct** (US **pedestrian zone**) n zona peatonal

pedigree [ˈpedɪgri:] n genealogía; (of animal) raza, pedigrí m ▷ cpd (animal) de raza, de casta

pedophile [ˈpi:dəufaɪl] (US) n = **paedophile**

pee [pi:] (inf) vi mear

peek [pi:k] vi mirar a hurtadillas

peel [pi:l] n piel f; (of orange, lemon) cáscara; (: removed) peladuras fpl ▷ vt pelar ▷ vi (paint etc) desconcharse; (wallpaper) despegarse, desprenderse; (skin) pelar

peep [pi:p] n (BRIT: look) mirada furtiva; (sound) pío ▷ vi (BRIT: look) mirar furtivamente

peer [pɪə*] vi: **to ~ at** esudriñar ▷ n (noble) par m; (equal) igual m; (contemporary) contemporáneo/a

peg [peg] n (for coat etc) gancho, colgadero; (BRIT: also: **clothes ~**) pinza

pelican [ˈpelɪkən] n pelícano; **pelican crossing** (BRIT) n (Aut) paso de peatones señalizado

pelt [pɛlt] vt: **to ~ sb with sth** arrojarle algo a algn ▷ vi (*rain*) llover a cántaros; (*inf: run*) correr ▷ n pellejo

pelvis ['pɛlvɪs] n pelvis f

pen [pɛn] n (*fountain pen*) pluma; (*ballpoint pen*) bolígrafo; (*for sheep*) redil m

penalty ['pɛnltɪ] n (*gen*) pena; (*fine*) multa

pence [pɛns] npl of **penny**

pencil ['pɛnsl] n lápiz m; **pencil in** vt (*appointment*) apuntar con carácter provisional; **pencil case** n estuche m; **pencil sharpener** n sacapuntas m inv

pendant ['pɛndnt] n pendiente m

pending ['pɛndɪŋ] prep antes de ▷ adj pendiente

penetrate ['pɛnɪtreɪt] vt penetrar

penfriend ['pɛnfrɛnd] (BRIT) n amigo/a por carta

penguin ['pɛŋgwɪn] n pingüino

penicillin [pɛnɪ'sɪlɪn] n penicilina

peninsula [pə'nɪnsjulə] n península

penis ['piːnɪs] n pene m

penitentiary [pɛnɪ'tɛnʃərɪ] (US) n cárcel f, presidio

penknife ['pɛnnaɪf] n navaja

penniless ['pɛnɪlɪs] adj sin dinero

penny ['pɛnɪ] n (pl **pennies** or **pence**) (BRIT) n penique m; (US) centavo

penpal ['pɛnpæl] n amigo/a por carta

pension ['pɛnʃən] n (*state benefit*) jubilación f; **pensioner** (BRIT) n jubilado/a

pentagon ['pɛntəgən] (US) n: **the P~** (Pol) el Pentágono

penthouse ['pɛnthaus] n ático de lujo

penultimate [pɛ'nʌltɪmət] adj penúltimo

people ['piːpl] npl gente f; (*citizens*) pueblo, ciudadanos mpl; (Pol): **the ~** el pueblo ▷ n (*nation, race*) pueblo, nación f; **several ~ came** vinieron varias personas; **~ say that ...** dice la gente que ...

pepper ['pɛpə*] n (*spice*) pimienta; (*vegetable*) pimiento ▷ vt: **to ~ with** (*fig*) salpicar de; **peppermint** n (*sweet*) pastilla de menta

per [pə:*] prep por; **~ day/~son** por día/ persona; **~ annum** al año

perceive [pə'siːv] vt percibir; (*realize*) darse cuenta de

per cent n por ciento

percentage [pə'sɛntɪdʒ] n porcentaje m

perception [pə'sɛpʃən] n percepción f; (*insight*) perspicacia; (*opinion etc*) opinión f

perch [pə:tʃ] n (*fish*) perca; (*for bird*) percha ▷ vi: **to ~ (on)** (*bird*) posarse (en); (*person*) encaramarse (en)

percussion [pə'kʌʃən] n percusión f

perfect [adj, n 'pə:fɪkt, vb pə'fɛkt] adj perfecto ▷ n (*also: ~ tense*) perfecto ▷ vt perfeccionar; **perfection** [pə'fɛkʃən] n perfección f; **perfectly** ['pə:fɪktlɪ] adv perfectamente

perform [pə'fɔːm] vt (*carry out*) realizar, llevar a cabo; (Theatre) representar; (*piece of music*) interpretar ▷ vi (*well, badly*) funcionar; **performance** n (*of a play*) representación f; (*of actor, athlete etc*) actuación f; (*of car, engine, company*) rendimiento; (*of economy*) resultados mpl; **performer** n (*actor*) actor m, actriz f

perfume ['pə:fjuːm] n perfume m

perhaps [pə'hæps] adv quizá(s), tal vez

perimeter [pə'rɪmɪtə*] n perímetro

period ['pɪərɪəd] n período; (Scol) clase f; (*full stop*) punto; (Med) regla ▷ adj (*costume, furniture*) de época; **periodical** [pɪərɪ'ɔdɪkl] n periódico; **periodically** adv de vez en cuando, cada cierto tiempo

perish ['pɛrɪʃ] vi perecer; (*decay*) echarse a perder

perjury ['pə:dʒərɪ] n (Law) perjurio

perk [pə:k] n extra m

perm [pə:m] n permanente f

permanent ['pə:mənənt] adj permanente; **permanently** adv (*lastingly*) para siempre, de modo definitivo; (*all the time*) permanentemente

permission [pə'mɪʃən] n permiso

permit [n 'pə:mɪt, vt pə'mɪt] n permiso, licencia ▷ vt permitir

perplex [pə'plɛks] vt dejar perplejo

persecute ['pə:sɪkjuːt] vt perseguir

persecution [pə:sɪ'kjuːʃən] n persecución f

persevere [pə:sɪ'vɪə*] vi persistir

Persian ['pə:ʃən] adj, n persa mf; **the ~ Gulf** el Golfo Pérsico

persist [pə'sɪst] vi: **to ~ (in doing sth)** persistir (en hacer algo); **persistent** adj persistente; (*determined*) porfiado

person ['pə:sn] n persona; **in ~** en persona; **personal** adj personal; individual; (*visit*) en persona; **personal assistant** n ayudante mf personal; **personal computer** n ordenador m personal; **personality**

[-'næltti] n personalidad f; **personally** adv personalmente; (in person) en persona; **to take sth personally** tomarse algo a mal; **personal organizer** n agenda; **personal stereo** n Walkman® m

personnel [pɜ:sə'nɛl] n personal m

perspective [pə'spɛktɪv] n perspectiva

perspiration [pɜ:spɪ'reɪʃən] n transpiración f

persuade [pə'sweɪd] vt: **to ~ sb to do sth** persuadir a algn para que haga algo

persuasion [pə'sweɪʒən] n persuasión f; (persuasiveness) persuasiva

persuasive [pə'sweɪsɪv] adj persuasivo

perverse [pə'vɜ:s] adj perverso; (wayward) travieso

pervert [n 'pɜ:vɜ:t, vb pə'vɜ:t] n pervertido/a ▷ vt pervertir; (truth, sb's words) tergiversar

pessimism ['pɛsɪmɪzəm] n pesimismo

pessimist ['pɛsɪmɪst] n pesimista mf; **pessimistic** [-'mɪstɪk] adj pesimista

pest [pɛst] n (insect) insecto nocivo; (fig) lata, molestia

pester ['pɛstə*] vt molestar, acosar

pesticide ['pɛstɪsaɪd] n pesticida m

pet [pɛt] n animal m doméstico ▷ cpd favorito ▷ vt acariciar; **teacher's ~** favorito/a (del profesor); **~ hate** manía

petal ['pɛtl] n pétalo

petite [pə'ti:t] adj chiquita

petition [pə'tɪʃən] n petición f

petrified ['pɛtrɪfaɪd] adj horrorizado

petrol ['pɛtrəl] (BRIT) n gasolina

petroleum [pə'trəʊliəm] n petróleo

petrol: petrol pump (BRIT) n (in garage) surtidor m de gasolina; **petrol station** (BRIT) n gasolinera; **petrol tank** (BRIT) n depósito (de gasolina)

petticoat ['pɛtɪkəʊt] n enaguas fpl

petty ['pɛtɪ] adj (mean) mezquino; (unimportant) insignificante

pew [pju:] n banco

pewter ['pju:tə*] n peltre m

phantom ['fæntəm] n fantasma m

pharmacist ['fɑ:məsɪst] n farmacéutico/a

pharmacy ['fɑ:məsɪ] n farmacia

phase [feɪz] n fase f; **phase in** vt introducir progresivamente; **phase out** vt (machinery, product) retirar progresivamente; (job, subsidy) eliminar por etapas

Ph.D. abbr = **Doctor of Philosophy**

pheasant ['fɛznt] n faisán m

phenomena [fə'nɒmɪnə] npl of **phenomenon**

phenomenal [fɪ'nɒmɪnl] adj fenomenal, extraordinario

phenomenon [fə'nɒmɪnən] (pl **phenomena**) n fenómeno

Philippines ['fɪlɪpi:nz] npl: **the ~** las Filipinas

philosopher [fɪ'lɒsəfə*] n filósofo/a

philosophical [fɪlə'sɒfɪkl] adj filosófico

philosophy [fɪ'lɒsəfɪ] n filosofía

phlegm [flɛm] n flema

phobia ['fəʊbjə] n fobia

phone [fəʊn] n teléfono ▷ vt telefonear, llamar por teléfono; **to be on the ~** tener teléfono; (be calling) estar hablando por teléfono; **phone back** vt, vi volver a llamar; **phone up** vt, vi llamar por teléfono; **phone book** n guía telefónica; **phone booth** n cabina telefónica; **phone box** (BRIT) n = **phone booth**; **phone call** n llamada (telefónica); **phonecard** n teletarjeta; **phone number** n número de teléfono

phonetics [fə'nɛtɪks] n fonética

phoney ['fəʊnɪ] adj falso

photo ['fəʊtəʊ] n foto f; **photo album** n álbum m de fotos; **photocopier** n fotocopiadora; **photocopy** n fotocopia ▷ vt fotocopiar

photograph ['fəʊtəgrɑ:f] n fotografía ▷ vt fotografiar; **photographer** [fə'tɒgrəfə*] n fotógrafo; **photography** [fə'tɒgrəfɪ] n fotografía

phrase [freɪz] n frase f ▷ vt expresar; **phrase book** n libro de frases

physical ['fɪzɪkl] adj físico; **physical education** n educación f física; **physically** adv físicamente

physician [fɪ'zɪʃən] n médico/a

physicist ['fɪzɪsɪst] n físico/a

physics ['fɪzɪks] n física

physiotherapist [fɪzɪəʊ'θɛrəpɪst] n fisioterapeuta

physiotherapy [fɪzɪəʊ'θɛrəpɪ] n fisioterapia

physique [fɪ'zi:k] n físico

pianist ['pi:ənɪst] n pianista mf

piano [pɪ'ænəʊ] n piano

pick [pɪk] n (tool: also: **~-axe**) pico, piqueta ▷ vt (select) elegir, escoger; (gather) coger (SP), recoger; (remove, take out) sacar, quitar; (lock) abrir con ganzúa; **take your ~** escoja lo que quiera; **the ~ of** lo mejor de; **to ~ one's nose/teeth** hurgarse las narices/limpiarse los dientes; **to ~ a quarrel with sb** meterse con algn; **pick on** vt fus (person) meterse con; **pick out** vt escoger; (distinguish) identificar; **pick up** vi (improve: sales) ir mejor; (: patient) reponerse; (Finance) recobrarse ▷ vt recoger; (learn) aprender; (Police: arrest) detener; (person: for sex) ligar; (Radio) captar; **to pick up speed**

acelerarse; **to pick o.s. up** levantarse
pickle ['pɪkl] n (also: **~s**: as condiment)
escabeche m; (fig: mess) apuro ▷ vt encurtir
pickpocket ['pɪkpɔkɪt] n carterista mf
pick-up ['pɪkʌp] n (also: **~ truck**)
furgoneta, camioneta
picnic ['pɪknɪk] n merienda ▷ vi ir de
merienda; **picnic area** n zona de picnic;
(Aut) área de descanso
picture ['pɪktʃə*] n cuadro; (painting)
pintura; (photograph) fotografía; (TV)
imagen f; (film) película; (fig: description)
descripción f; (: situation) situación f ▷ vt
(imagine) imaginar; **pictures** npl: **the ~s**
(BRIT) el cine; **picture frame** n marco;
picture messaging n (envío de) mensajes
con imágenes
picturesque [pɪktʃə'rɛsk] adj pintoresco
pie [paɪ] n pastel m; (open) tarta; (small: of
meat) empanada
piece [piːs] n pedazo, trozo; (of cake) trozo;
(item): **a ~ of clothing/furniture/advice**
una prenda (de vestir)/un mueble/un
consejo ▷ vt: **to ~ together** juntar; (Tech)
armar; **to take to ~s** desmontar
pie chart n gráfico de sectores or tarta
pier [pɪə*] n muelle m, embarcadero
pierce [pɪəs] vt perforar; **pierced** adj: **I've
got pierced ears** tengo los agujeros hechos
en las orejas
pig [pɪg] n cerdo, chancho (LAM); (pej: unkind
person) asqueroso; (: greedy person) glotón/
ona m/f
pigeon ['pɪdʒən] n paloma; (as food)
pichón m
piggy bank ['pɪgɪ-] n hucha (en forma de
cerdito)
pigsty ['pɪgstaɪ] n pocilga
pigtail (girl's) trenza
pike [paɪk] n (fish) lucio
pilchard ['pɪltʃəd] n sardina
pile [paɪl] n montón m; (of carpet, cloth)
pelo; **pile up** vi +adv (accumulate: work)
amontonarse, acumularse ▷ vt +adv (put
in a heap: books, clothes) apilar, amontonar;
(accumulate) acumular; **piles** npl (Med)
almorranas fpl, hemorroides mpl; **pile-up** n
(Aut) accidente m múltiple
pilgrimage ['pɪlgrɪmɪdʒ] n peregrinación
f, romería
pill [pɪl] n píldora; **the ~** la píldora
pillar ['pɪlə*] n pilar m
pillow ['pɪləu] n almohada; **pillowcase**
n funda
pilot ['paɪlət] n piloto ▷ cpd (scheme etc)
piloto ▷ vt pilotar; **pilot light** n piloto
pimple ['pɪmpl] n grano
PIN n abbr (= personal identification number)
número personal
pin [pɪn] n alfiler m ▷ vt prender (con
alfiler); **~s and needles** hormigueo; **to ~
sb down** (fig) hacer que algn concrete; **to ~
sth on sb** (fig) colgarle a algn el sambenito
de algo
pinafore ['pɪnəfɔː*] n delantal m
pinch [pɪntʃ] n (of salt etc) pizca ▷ vt
pellizcar; (inf: steal) birlar; **at a ~** en caso
de apuro
pine [paɪn] n (also: **~ tree**) pino ▷ vi: **to ~
for** suspirar por
pineapple ['paɪnæpl] n piña, ananás m
ping [pɪŋ] n (noise) sonido agudo; **ping-
pong®** n pingpong m
pink [pɪŋk] adj rosado, (color de) rosa ▷ n
(colour) rosa; (Bot) clavel m, clavellina
pinpoint ['pɪnpɔɪnt] vt precisar
pint [paɪnt] n pinta (BRIT = 568cc, US =
473cc); (BRIT: inf: of beer) pinta de cerveza ≈
jarra (SP)
pioneer [paɪə'nɪə*] n pionero/a
pious ['paɪəs] adj piadoso, devoto
pip [pɪp] n (seed) pepita; **the ~s** (BRIT) la
señal
pipe [paɪp] n tubo, caño; (for smoking) pipa
▷ vt conducir en cañerías; **pipeline** n (for
oil) oleoducto; (for gas) gasoducto; **piper** n
gaitero/a
pirate ['paɪərət] n pirata mf ▷ vt (cassette,
book) piratear
Pisces ['paɪsiːz] n Piscis m
piss [pɪs] (inf!) vi mear; **pissed** (inf!) adj
(drunk) borracho
pistol ['pɪstl] n pistola
piston ['pɪstən] n pistón m, émbolo
pit [pɪt] n hoyo; (also: **coal ~**) mina; (in
garage) foso de inspección; (also: **orchestra
~**) platea ▷ vt: **to ~ one's wits against sb**
medir fuerzas con algn
pitch [pɪtʃ] n (Mus) tono; (BRIT Sport)
campo, terreno; (fig) punto; (tar) brea ▷ vt
(throw) arrojar, lanzar ▷ vi (fall) caer(se); **to
~ a tent** montar una tienda (de campaña);
pitch-black adj negro como boca de lobo
pitfall ['pɪtfɔːl] n riesgo
pith [pɪθ] n (of orange) médula
pitiful ['pɪtɪful] adj (touching) lastimoso,
conmovedor(a)
pity ['pɪtɪ] n compasión f, piedad f ▷ vt
compadecer(se de); **what a ~!** ¡qué pena!
pizza ['piːtsə] n pizza
placard ['plækɑːd] n letrero; (in march etc)
pancarta
place [pleɪs] n lugar m, sitio; (seat) plaza,
asiento; (post) puesto; (home): **at/to his ~**
en/a su casa; (role: in society etc) papel m ▷ vt
(object) poner, colocar; (identify) reconocer;

P

to take ~ tener lugar; **to be ~d** (in race, exam) colocarse; **out of ~** (not suitable) fuera de lugar; **in the first ~** en primer lugar; **to change ~s with sb** cambiarse de sitio con algn; **~ of birth** lugar m de nacimiento; **place mat** n (wooden etc) salvamanteles m inv; (linen etc) mantel m individual; **placement** n (positioning) colocación f; (at work) emplazamiento

placid ['plæsɪd] adj apacible

plague [pleɪg] n plaga; (Med) peste f ▷ vt (fig) acosar, atormentar

plaice [pleɪs] n inv platija

plain [pleɪn] adj (unpatterned) liso; (clear) claro, evidente; (simple) sencillo; (not handsome) poco atractivo ▷ adv claramente ▷ n llano, llanura; **plain chocolate** n chocolate m amargo; **plainly** adv claramente

plaintiff ['pleɪntɪf] n demandante mf

plait [plæt] n trenza

plan [plæn] n (drawing) plano; (scheme) plan m, proyecto ▷ vt proyectar, planificar ▷ vi hacer proyectos; **to ~ to do** pensar hacer

plane [pleɪn] n (Aviat) avión m; (Math, fig) plano; (also: **~ tree**) plátano; (tool) cepillo

planet ['plænɪt] n planeta m

plank [plæŋk] n tabla

planning ['plænɪŋ] n planificación f; **family ~** planificación familiar

plant [plɑ:nt] n planta; (machinery) maquinaria; (factory) fábrica ▷ vt plantar; (field) sembrar; (bomb) colocar

plantation [plæn'teɪʃən] n plantación f; (estate) hacienda

plaque [plæk] n placa

plaster ['plɑ:stə*] n (for walls) yeso; (also: **~ of Paris**) yeso mate, escayola (SP); (BRIT: also: **sticking ~**) tirita (SP), curita (LAM) ▷ vt enyesar; (cover): **to ~ with** llenar or cubrir de; **plaster cast** n (Med) escayola; (model, statue) vaciado de yeso

plastic ['plæstɪk] n plástico ▷ adj de plástico; **plastic bag** n bolsa de plástico; **plastic surgery** n cirujía plástica

plate [pleɪt] n (dish) plato; (metal, in book) lámina; (dental plate) placa de dentadura postiza

plateau ['plætəʊ] (pl **~s** or **~x**) n meseta, altiplanicie f

platform ['plætfɔ:m] n (Rail) andén m; (stage, BRIT: on bus) plataforma; (at meeting) tribuna; (Pol) programa m (electoral)

platinum ['plætɪnəm] adj, n platino

platoon [plə'tu:n] n pelotón m

platter ['plætə*] n fuente f

plausible ['plɔ:zɪbl] adj verosímil; (person) convincente

play [pleɪ] n (Theatre) obra, comedia ▷ vt (game) jugar; (compete against) jugar contra; (instrument) tocar; (part: in play etc) hacer el papel de; (tape, record) poner ▷ vi jugar; (band) tocar; (tape, record) sonar; **to ~ safe** ir a lo seguro; **play back** vt (tape) poner; **play up** vi (cause trouble to) dar guerra; **player** n jugador(a) m/f; (Theatre) actor(actriz) m/f; (Mus) músico/a; **playful** adj juguetón/ona; **playground** n (in school) patio de recreo; (in park) parque m infantil; **playgroup** n jardín m de niños; **playing card** n naipe m, carta; **playing field** n campo de deportes; **playschool** n = **playgroup**; **playtime** n (Scol) recreo; **playwright** n dramaturgo/a

plc abbr (= public limited company) ≈ S.A.

plea [pli:] n súplica, petición f; (Law) alegato, defensa

plead [pli:d] vt (Law): **to ~ sb's case** defender a algn; (give as excuse) poner como pretexto ▷ vi (Law) declararse; (beg): **to ~ with sb** suplicar or rogar a algn

pleasant ['plɛznt] adj agradable

please [pli:z] excl ¡por favor! ▷ vt (give pleasure to) dar gusto a, agradar ▷ vi (think fit): **do as you ~** haz lo que quieras; **~ yourself!** (inf) ¡haz lo que quieras!, ¡como quieras! **pleased** adj (happy) alegre, contento; **pleased (with)** satisfecho (de); **pleased to meet you** ¡encantado!, ¡tanto gusto!

pleasure ['plɛʒə*] n placer m, gusto; **"it's a ~"** "el gusto es mío"

pleat [pli:t] n pliegue m

pledge [plɛdʒ] n (promise) promesa, voto ▷ vt prometer

plentiful ['plɛntɪful] adj copioso, abundante

plenty ['plɛntɪ] n: **~ of** mucho(s)/a(s)

pliers ['plaɪəz] npl alicates mpl, tenazas fpl

plight [plaɪt] n situación f difícil

plod [plɒd] vi caminar con paso pesado; (fig) trabajar laboriosamente

plonk [plɒŋk] (inf) n (BRIT: wine) vino peleón ▷ vt: **to ~ sth down** dejar caer algo

plot [plɒt] n (scheme) complot m, conjura; (of story, play) argumento; (of land) terreno ▷ vt (mark out) trazar; (conspire) tramar, urdir ▷ vi conspirar

plough [plaʊ] (us **plow**) n arado ▷ vt (earth) arar; **to ~ money into** invertir dinero en; **ploughman's lunch** (BRIT) n almuerzo de pub a base de pan, queso y encurtidos

plow [plaʊ] (us) = **plough**

ploy [plɔɪ] n truco, estratagema

pluck [plʌk] vt (fruit) coger (SP), recoger (LAM); (musical instrument) puntear; (bird) desplumar; (*eyebrows*) depilar; **to ~ up courage** hacer de tripas corazón

plug [plʌg] *n* tapón *m*; (*Elec*) enchufe *m*, clavija; (*Aut: also:* **spark(ing) ~**) bujía ▷ *vt* (*hole*) tapar; (*inf: advertise*) dar publicidad a; **plug in** *vt* (*Elec*) enchufar; **plughole** *n* desagüe *m*

plum [plʌm] *n* (*fruit*) ciruela

plumber ['plʌmə*] *n* fontanero/a (*SP, CAM*), plomero/a (*LAM*)

plumbing ['plʌmɪŋ] *n* (*trade*) fontanería, plomería; (*piping*) cañería

plummet ['plʌmɪt] *vi:* **to ~ (down)** caer a plomo

plump [plʌmp] *adj* rechoncho, rollizo ▷ *vi:* **to ~ for** (*inf: choose*) optar por

plunge [plʌndʒ] *n* zambullida ▷ *vt* sumergir, hundir ▷ *vi* (*fall*) caer; (*dive*) saltar; (*person*) arrojarse; **to take the ~** lanzarse

plural ['pluərl] *adj* plural ▷ *n* plural *m*

plus [plʌs] *n* (*also:* **~ sign**) signo más ▷ *prep* más, y, además de; **ten/twenty ~** más de diez/veinte

ply [plaɪ] *vt* (*a trade*) ejercer ▷ *vi* (*ship*) ir y venir ▷ *n* (*of wool, rope*) cabo; **to ~ sb with drink** insistir en ofrecer a algn muchas copas; **plywood** *n* madera contrachapada

P.M. *n abbr* = **Prime Minister**

p.m. *adv abbr* (= *post meridiem*) de la tarde *or* noche

PMS *n abbr* (= *premenstrual syndrome*) SPM *m*

PMT *n abbr* (= *premenstrual tension*) SPM *m*

pneumatic drill [nju:'mætɪk-] *n* martillo neumático

pneumonia [nju:'məunɪə] *n* pulmonía

poach [pəutʃ] *vt* (*cook*) escalfar; (*steal*) cazar (*or pescar*) en vedado ▷ *vi* cazar (*or* pescar) en vedado; **poached** *adj* escalfado

P.O. Box *n abbr* (= *Post Office Box*) apdo., aptdo.

pocket ['pɔkɪt] *n* bolsillo; (*fig: small area*) bolsa ▷ *vt* meter en el bolsillo; (*steal*) embolsar; **to be out of ~** (*BRIT*) salir perdiendo; **pocketbook** (*US*) *n* cartera; **pocket money** *n* asignación *f*

pod [pɔd] *n* vaina

podiatrist [pɔ'di:ətrɪst] (*US*) *n* pedicuro/a

podium ['pəudɪəm] *n* podio

poem ['pəuɪm] *n* poema *m*

poet ['pəuɪt] *n* poeta *m/f*; **poetic** [-'ɛtɪk] *adj* poético; **poetry** *n* poesía

poignant ['pɔɪnjənt] *adj* conmovedor(a)

point [pɔɪnt] *n* punto; (*tip*) punta; (*purpose*) fin *m*, propósito; (*use*) utilidad *f*; (*significant part*) lo significativo; (*moment*) momento; (*Elec*) toma (de corriente); (*also:* **decimal ~**): **2 ~ 3 (2.3)** dos coma tres (2,3) ▷ *vt* señalar; (*gun etc*): **to ~ sth at sb** apuntar

algo a algn ▷ *vi:* **to ~ at** señalar; **points** *npl* (*Aut*) contactos *mpl*; (*Rail*) agujas *fpl*; **to be on the ~ of doing sth** estar a punto de hacer algo; **to make a ~ of** poner empeño en; **to get/miss the ~** comprender/no comprender; **to come to the ~** ir al meollo; **there's no ~ (in doing)** no tiene sentido (hacer); **point out** *vt* señalar; **point-blank** *adv* (*say, refuse*) sin más hablar; (*also:* **at point-blank range**) a quemarropa; **pointed** *adj* (*shape*) puntiagudo, afilado; (*remark*) intencionado; **pointer** *n* (*needle*) aguja, indicador *m*; **pointless** *adj* sin sentido; **point of view** *n* punto de vista

poison ['pɔɪzn] *n* veneno ▷ *vt* envenenar; **poisonous** *adj* venenoso; (*fumes etc*) tóxico

poke [pəuk] *vt* (*jab with finger, stick etc*) empujar; (*put*): **to ~ sth in(to)** introducir algo en; **poke about** *or* **around** *vi* fisgonear; **poke out** *vi* (*stick out*) salir

poker ['pəukə*] *n* atizador *m*; (*Cards*) póker *m*

Poland ['pəulənd] *n* Polonia

polar ['pəulə*] *adj* polar; **polar bear** *n* oso polar

Pole [pəul] *n* polaco/a

pole [pəul] *n* palo; (*fixed*) poste *m*; (*Geo*) polo; **pole bean** (*us*) *n* ≈ judía verde; **pole vault** *n* salto con pértiga

police [pə'li:s] *n* policía ▷ *vt* vigilar; **police car** *n* coche-patrulla *m*; **police constable** (*BRIT*) *n* guardia *m*, policía *m*; **police force** *n* cuerpo de policía; **policeman** (*irreg*) *n* policía *m*, guardia *m*; **police officer** *n* guardia *m*, policía *m*; **police station** *n* comisaría; **policewoman** (*irreg*) *n* mujer *f* policía

policy ['pɔlɪsɪ] *n* política; (*also:* **insurance ~**) póliza

polio ['pəulɪəu] *n* polio *f*

Polish ['pəulɪʃ] *adj* polaco ▷ *n* (*Ling*) polaco

polish ['pɔlɪʃ] *n* (*for shoes*) betún *m*; (*for floor*) cera (de lustrar); (*shine*) brillo, lustre *m*; (*fig: refinement*) educación *f* ▷ *vt* (*shoes*) limpiar; (*make shiny*) pulir, sacar brillo a; **polish off** *vt* (*food*) despachar; **polished** *adj* (*fig: person*) elegante

polite [pə'laɪt] *adj* cortés, atento; **politeness** *n* cortesía

political [pə'lɪtɪkl] *adj* político; **politically** *adv* políticamente; **politically correct** políticamente correcto

politician [pɔlɪ'tɪʃən] *n* político/a

politics ['pɔlɪtɪks] *n* política

poll [pəul] *n* (*election*) votación *f*; (*also:* **opinion ~**) sondeo, encuesta ▷ *vt* encuestar; (*votes*) obtener

pollen ['pɒlən] n polen m

polling station ['pəulɪŋ-] n centro electoral

pollute [pə'luːt] vt contaminar

pollution [pə'luːʃən] n polución f, contaminación f del medio ambiente

polo ['pəuləu] n (sport) polo; **polo-neck** adj de cuello vuelto ▷ n (sweater) suéter m de cuello vuelto; **polo shirt** n polo, niqui m

polyester [pɒlɪ'estə*] n poliéster m

polystyrene [pɒlɪ'staɪriːn] n poliestireno

polythene ['pɒlɪθiːn] (BRIT) n politeno; **polythene bag** n bolsa de plástico

pomegranate ['pɒmɪgrænɪt] n granada

pompous ['pɒmpəs] adj pomposo

pond [pɒnd] n (natural) charca; (artificial) estanque m

ponder ['pɒndə*] vt meditar

pony ['pəunɪ] n poni m; **ponytail** n coleta; **pony trekking** (BRIT) n excursión f a caballo

poodle ['puːdl] n caniche m

pool [puːl] n (natural) charca; (also: **swimming ~**) piscina, alberca (MEX), pileta (RPL); (fig: of light etc) charco; (Sport) chapolín m ▷ vt juntar; **pools** npl quinielas fpl

poor [puə*] adj pobre; (bad) de mala calidad ▷ npl: **the ~** los pobres; **poorly** adj mal, enfermo ▷ adv mal

pop [pɒp] n (sound) ruido seco; (Mus) (música) pop m; (inf: father) papá m; (drink) gaseosa ▷ vt (put quickly) meter (de prisa) ▷ vi reventar; (cork) saltar; **pop in** vi entrar un momento; **pop out** vi salir un momento; **popcorn** n palomitas fpl

poplar ['pɒplə*] n álamo

popper ['pɒpə*] (BRIT) n automático

poppy ['pɒpɪ] n amapola

Popsicle® ['pɒpsɪkl] (US) n polo

pop star n estrella del pop

popular ['pɒpjulə*] adj popular; **popularity** [pɒpju'lærɪtɪ] n popularidad f

population [pɒpju'leɪʃən] n población f

pop-up ['pɒpʌp] (Comput) adj (menu, window) emergente ▷ n ventana emergente, (ventana f) pop-up f

porcelain ['pɔːslɪn] n porcelana

porch [pɔːtʃ] n pórtico, entrada; (US) veranda

pore [pɔː*] n poro ▷ vi: **to ~ over** engolfarse en

pork [pɔːk] n carne f de cerdo or (LAM) chancho; **pork chop** n chuleta de cerdo; **pork pie** n (BRIT: Culin) empanada de carne de cerdo

porn [pɔːn] adj (inf) porno inv ▷ n porno; **pornographic** [pɔːnə'græfɪk] adj pornográfico; **pornography** [pɔː'nɒgrəfɪ]

n pornografía

porridge ['pɒrɪdʒ] n gachas fpl de avena

port [pɔːt] n puerto; (Naut: left side) babor m; (wine) vino de Oporto; **~ of call** puerto de escala

portable ['pɔːtəbl] adj portátil

porter ['pɔːtə*] n (for luggage) maletero; (doorkeeper) portero/a, conserje m/f

portfolio [pɔːt'fəuliəu] n cartera

portion ['pɔːʃən] n porción f; (of food) ración f

portrait ['pɔːtreɪt] n retrato

portray [pɔː'treɪ] vt retratar; (actor) representar

Portugal ['pɔːtjugl] n Portugal m

Portuguese [pɔːtju'giːz] adj portugués/esa ▷ n inv portugués/esa m/f; (Ling) portugués m

pose [pəuz] n postura, actitud f ▷ vi (pretend) **to ~ as** hacerse pasar por ▷ vt (question) plantear; **to ~ for** posar para

posh [pɒʃ] (inf) adj elegante, de lujo

position [pə'zɪʃən] n posición f; (job) puesto; (situation) situación f ▷ vt colocar

positive ['pɒzɪtɪv] adj positivo; (certain) seguro; (definite) definitivo; **positively** adv (affirmatively, enthusiastically) de forma positiva; (inf: really) absolutamente

possess [pə'zes] vt poseer; **possession** [pə'zeʃən] n posesión f; **possessions** npl (belongings) pertenencias fpl; **possessive** adj posesivo

possibility [pɒsɪ'bɪlɪtɪ] n posibilidad f

possible ['pɒsɪbl] adj posible; **as big as ~** lo más grande posible; **possibly** adv posiblemente; **I cannot possibly come** me es imposible venir

post [pəust] n (BRIT: system) correos mpl; (BRIT: letters, delivery) correo; (job, situation) puesto; (pole) poste m ▷ vt (BRIT: send by post) echar al correo; (BRIT: appoint): **to ~ to** enviar a; **postage** n porte m, franqueo; **postal** adj postal, de correos; **postal order** n giro postal; **postbox** (BRIT) n buzón m; **postcard** n tarjeta postal; **postcode** (BRIT) n código postal

poster ['pəustə*] n cartel m

postgraduate ['pəust'grædjuət] n posgraduado/a

postman ['pəustmən] (BRIT: irreg) n cartero

postmark ['pəustmɑːk] n matasellos m inv

post-mortem [-'mɔːtəm] n autopsia

post office n (building) (oficina de) correos m; (organization): **the Post Office** Correos m inv (SP), Dirección f General de Correos (LAM)

postpone [pəs'pəun] vt aplazar

posture ['pɒstʃə*] n postura, actitud f
postwoman ['pəustwumən] (BRIT: irreg) n cartera
pot [pɒt] n (for cooking) olla; (teapot) tetera; (coffeepot) cafetera; (for flowers) maceta; (for jam) tarro, pote m; (inf: marijuana) chocolate m ▷ vt (plant) poner en tiesto; **to go to ~** (inf) irse al traste
potato [pə'teɪtəu] (pl **-es**) n patata (SP), papa (LAM); **potato peeler** n pelapatatas m inv
potent ['pəutnt] adj potente, poderoso; (drink) fuerte
potential [pə'tɛnʃl] adj potencial, posible ▷ n potencial m
pothole ['pɒthəul] n (in road) bache m; (BRIT: underground) gruta
pot plant ['pɒtplɑ:nt] n planta de interior
potter ['pɒtə*] n alfarero/a ▷ vi: **to ~ around** or **about** (BRIT) hacer trabajitos; **pottery** n cerámica; (factory) alfarería
potty ['pɒtɪ] n orinal m de niño
pouch [pautʃ] n (Zool) bolsa; (for tobacco) petaca
poultry ['pəultrɪ] n aves fpl de corral; (meat) pollo
pounce [pauns] vi: **to ~ on** precipitarse sobre
pound [paund] n libra (weight = 453g or 16oz; money = 100 pence) ▷ vt (beat) golpear; (crush) machacar ▷ vi (heart) latir; **pound sterling** n libra esterlina
pour [pɔ:*] vt echar; (tea etc) servir ▷ vi correr, fluir; **to ~ sb a drink** servirle a algn una copa; **pour in** vi (people) entrar en tropel; **pour out** vi salir en tropel ▷ vt (drink) echar, servir; (fig): **to pour out one's feelings** desahogarse; **pouring** adj: **pouring rain** lluvia torrencial
pout [paut] vi hacer pucheros
poverty ['pɒvətɪ] n pobreza, miseria
powder ['paudə*] n polvo; (also: **face ~**) polvos mpl ▷ vt polvorear; **to ~ one's face** empolvarse la cara; **powdered milk** n leche f en polvo
power ['pauə*] n poder m; (strength) fuerza; (nation, Tech) potencia; (drive) empuje m; (Elec) fuerza, energía ▷ vt impulsar; **to be in ~** (Pol) estar en el poder; **power cut** (BRIT) n apagón m; **power failure** n = **power cut**; **powerful** adj poderoso; (engine) potente; (speech etc) convincente; **powerless** adj: **powerless (to do)** incapaz (de hacer); **power point** (BRIT) n enchufe m; **power station** n central f eléctrica
p.p. abbr (= per procurationem); **p.p. J. Smith** p.p. (por poder de) J. Smith; (= pages) págs
PR n abbr = **public relations**

practical ['præktɪkl] adj práctico; **practical joke** n broma pesada; **practically** adv (almost) casi
practice ['præktɪs] n (habit) costumbre f; (exercise) práctica, ejercicio; (training) adiestramiento; (Med: of profession) práctica, ejercicio; (Med, Law: business) consulta ▷ vt, vi (US) = **practise**; **in ~** (in reality) en la práctica; **out of ~** desentrenado
practise ['præktɪs] (US **practice**) vt (carry out) practicar; (profession) ejercer; (train at) practicar ▷ vi ejercer; (train) practicar; **practising** adj (Christian etc) practicante; (lawyer) en ejercicio
practitioner [præk'tɪʃənə*] n (Med) médico/a
pragmatic [præg'mætɪk] adj pragmático
prairie ['prɛərɪ] n pampa
praise [preɪz] n alabanza(s) f(pl), elogio(s) m(pl) ▷ vt alabar, elogiar
pram [præm] (BRIT) n cochecito de niño
prank [præŋk] n travesura
prawn [prɔ:n] n gamba; **prawn cocktail** n cóctel m de gambas
pray [preɪ] vi rezar; **prayer** [preə*] n oración f, rezo; (entreaty) ruego, súplica
preach [pri:tʃ] vi predicar; **preacher** n predicador(a) m/f
precarious [prɪ'kɛərɪəs] adj precario
precaution [prɪ'kɔ:ʃən] n precaución f
precede [prɪ'si:d] vt, vi preceder; **precedent** ['prɛsɪdənt] n precedente m; **preceding** [prɪ'si:dɪŋ] adj anterior
precinct ['pri:sɪŋkt] n recinto
precious ['prɛʃəs] adj precioso
precise [prɪ'saɪs] adj preciso, exacto; **precisely** adv precisamente, exactamente
precision [prɪ'sɪʒən] n precisión f
predator ['prɛdətə*] n depredador m
predecessor ['pri:dɪsɛsə*] n antecesor(a) m/f
predicament [prɪ'dɪkəmənt] n apuro
predict [prɪ'dɪkt] vt pronosticar; **predictable** adj previsible; **prediction** [-'dɪkʃən] n predicción f
predominantly [prɪ'dɔmɪnəntlɪ] adv en su mayoría
preface ['prɛfəs] n prefacio
prefect ['pri:fɛkt] (BRIT) n (in school) monitor(a) m/f
prefer [prɪ'fə:*] vt preferir; **to ~ doing** or **to do** preferir hacer; **preferable** ['prɛfrəbl] adj preferible; **preferably** ['prɛfrəblɪ] adv de preferencia; **preference** ['prɛfrəns] n preferencia; (priority) prioridad f
prefix ['pri:fɪks] n prefijo
pregnancy ['prɛgnənsɪ] n (of woman) embarazo; (of animal) preñez f

pregnant ['pregnant] adj (woman)
embarazada; (animal) preñada
prehistoric ['pri:his'tɒrik] adj
prehistórico
prejudice ['predʒudɪs] n prejuicio;
prejudiced adj (person) predispuesto
preliminary [prɪ'lɪmɪnərɪ] adj preliminar
prelude ['prelju:d] n preludio
premature ['premətʃuə*] adj prematuro
premier ['premɪə*] adj primero, principal
▷ n (Pol) primer(a) ministro/a
première ['premɪeə*] n estreno
Premier League [premɪə'li:g] n primera
división
premises ['premɪsɪz] npl (of business etc)
local m; **on the ~** en el lugar mismo
premium ['pri:mɪəm] n premio;
(insurance) prima; **to be at a ~** ser muy
solicitado
premonition [premə'nɪʃən] n
presentimiento
preoccupied [pri:'ɒkjupaɪd] adj
ensimismado
prepaid [pri:'peɪd] adj porte pagado
preparation [prepə'reɪʃən] n preparación
f; **preparations** npl preparativos mpl
preparatory school [prɪ'pærətərɪ-] n
escuela preparatoria
prepare [prɪ'peə*] vt preparar, disponer;
(Culin) preparar ▷ vi: **to ~ for** (action)
prepararse or disponerse para; (event) hacer
preparativos para; **~d to** dispuesto a; **~d for**
listo para
preposition [prepə'zɪʃən] n preposición f
prep school [prep-] n = **preparatory
school**
prerequisite [pri:'rekwɪzɪt] n requisito
preschool ['pri:sku:l] adj preescolar
prescribe [prɪ'skraɪb] vt (Med) recetar
prescription [prɪ'skrɪpʃən] n (Med) receta
presence ['prezns] n presencia; **in sb's ~**
en presencia de algn; **~ of mind** aplomo
present [adj, n 'preznt, vb prɪ'zent]
adj (in attendance) presente; (current)
actual ▷ n (gift) regalo; (actuality): **the ~**
la actualidad, el presente ▷ vt (introduce,
describe) presentar; (expound) exponer; (give)
presentar, dar, ofrecer; (Theatre) representar;
to give sb a ~ regalar algo a algn; **at ~**
actualmente; **presentable** [prɪ'zentəbl]
adj: **to make o.s. presentable** arreglarse;
presentation [-'teɪʃən] n presentación f;
(of report etc) exposición f; (formal ceremony)
entrega de un regalo; **present-day** adj
actual; **presenter** [prɪ'zentə*] n (Radio, TV)
locutor(a) m/f; **presently** adv (soon) dentro
de poco; (now) ahora; **present participle** n
participio (de) presente

preservation [prezə'veɪʃən] n
conservación f
preservative [prɪ'zə:vətɪv] n
conservante m
preserve [prɪ'zə:v] vt (keep safe) preservar,
proteger; (maintain) mantener; (food)
conservar ▷ n (for game) coto, vedado; (often
pl: jam) conserva, confitura
preside [prɪ'zaɪd] vi presidir
president ['prezɪdənt] n presidente m/f;
presidential [-'denʃl] adj presidencial
press [pres] n (newspapers): **the P~** la
prensa; (printer's) imprenta; (of button)
pulsación f ▷ vt empujar; (button etc)
apretar; (clothes: iron) planchar; (put
pressure on: person) presionar; (insist): **to ~
sth on sb** insistir en que algn acepte algo
▷ vi (squeeze) apretar; (pressurize): **to ~ for**
presionar por; **we are ~ed for time/money**
estamos apurados de tiempo/dinero; **press
conference** n rueda de prensa; **pressing**
adj apremiante; **press stud** (BRIT) n botón
m de presión; **press-up** (BRIT) n plancha
pressure ['preʃə*] n presión f; **to put ~
on sb** presionar a algn; **pressure cooker**
n olla a presión; **pressure group** n grupo
de presión
prestige [pres'ti:ʒ] n prestigio
prestigious [pres'tɪdʒəs] adj prestigioso
presumably [prɪ'zju:məblɪ] adv es de
suponer que, cabe presumir que
presume [prɪ'zju:m] vt: **to ~ (that)**
presumir (que), suponer (que)
pretence [prɪ'tens] (US **pretense**) n
fingimiento; **under false ~s** con engaños
pretend [prɪ'tend] vt, vi (feign) fingir
▌ Be careful not to translate **pretend** by the
▌ Spanish word pretender.
pretense [prɪ'tens] (US) n = **pretence**
pretentious [prɪ'tenʃəs] adj presumido;
(ostentatious) ostentoso, aparatoso
pretext ['pri:tekst] n pretexto
pretty ['prɪtɪ] adj bonito, lindo (LAM) ▷ adv
bastante
prevail [prɪ'veɪl] vi (gain mastery)
prevalecer; (be current) predominar;
prevailing adj (dominant) predominante
prevalent ['prevələnt] adj (widespread)
extendido
prevent [prɪ'vent] vt: **to ~ sb from doing
sth** impedir a algn hacer algo; **to ~ sth
from happening** evitar que ocurra algo;
prevention [prɪ'venʃən] n prevención f;
preventive adj preventivo
preview ['pri:vju:] n (of film) preestreno
previous ['pri:vɪəs] adj previo, anterior;
previously adv antes
prey [preɪ] n presa ▷ vi: **to ~ on** (feed on)

alimentarse de; **it was ~ing on his mind** le preocupaba, le obsesionaba

price [praɪs] n precio ▷ vt (goods) fijar el precio de; **priceless** adj que no tiene precio; **price list** n tarifa

prick [prɪk] n (sting) picadura ▷ vt pinchar; (hurt) picar; **to ~ up one's ears** aguzar el oído

prickly ['prɪklɪ] adj espinoso; (fig: person) enojadizo

pride [praɪd] n orgullo; (pej) soberbia ▷ vt: **to ~ o.s. on** enorgullecerse de

priest [priːst] n sacerdote m

primarily ['praɪmərɪlɪ] adv ante todo

primary ['praɪmərɪ] adj (first in importance) principal ▷ n (us Pol) elección f primaria; **primary school** (BRIT) n escuela primaria

prime [praɪm] adj primero, principal; (excellent) selecto, de primera clase ▷ n: **in the ~ of life** en la flor de la vida ▷ vt (wood: fig) preparar; **~ example** ejemplo típico; **Prime Minister** n primer(a) ministro/a

primitive ['prɪmɪtɪv] adj primitivo; (crude) rudimentario

primrose ['prɪmrəʊz] n primavera, prímula

prince [prɪns] n príncipe m

princess [prɪnˈsɛs] n princesa

principal ['prɪnsɪpl] adj principal, mayor ▷ n director(a) m/f; **principally** adv principalmente

principle ['prɪnsɪpl] n principio; **in ~** en principio; **on ~** por principio

print [prɪnt] n (footprint) huella; (fingerprint) huella dactilar; (letters) letra de molde; (fabric) estampado; (Art) grabado; (Phot) impresión f ▷ vt imprimir; (cloth) estampar; (write in capitals) escribir en letras de molde; **out of ~** agotado; **print out** vt (Comput) imprimir; **printer** n (person) impresor(a) m/f; (machine) impresora; **printout** n (Comput) impresión f

prior ['praɪə*] adj anterior, previo; (more important) más importante; **~ to** antes de

priority [praɪˈɒrɪtɪ] n prioridad f; **to have ~ (over)** tener prioridad (sobre)

prison ['prɪzn] n cárcel f, prisión f ▷ cpd carcelario; **prisoner** n (in prison) preso/a; (captured person) prisionero; **prisoner-of-war** n prisionero de guerra

pristine ['prɪstiːn] adj pristino

privacy ['prɪvəsɪ] n intimidad f

private ['praɪvɪt] adj (personal) particular; (property, industry, discussion etc) privado; (person) reservado; (place) tranquilo ▷ n soldado raso; **"~"** (on envelope) "confidencial"; (on door) "prohibido el paso";

in ~ en privado; **privately** adv en privado; (in o.s.) en secreto; **private property** n propiedad f privada; **private school** n colegio particular

privatize ['praɪvɪtaɪz] vt privatizar

privilege ['prɪvɪlɪdʒ] n privilegio; (prerogative) prerrogativa

prize [praɪz] n premio ▷ adj de primera clase ▷ vt apreciar, estimar; **prize-giving** n distribución f de premios; **prizewinner** n premiado/a

pro [prəʊ] n (Sport) profesional mf ▷ prep a favor de; **the ~s and cons** los pros y los contras

probability [prɒbəˈbɪlɪtɪ] n probabilidad f; **in all ~** con toda probabilidad

probable ['prɒbəbl] adj probable

probably ['prɒbəblɪ] adv probablemente

probation [prəˈbeɪʃən] n: **on ~** (employee) a prueba; (Law) en libertad condicional

probe [prəʊb] n (Med, Space) sonda; (enquiry) encuesta, investigación f ▷ vt sondar; (investigate) investigar

problem ['prɒbləm] n problema m

procedure [prəˈsiːdʒə*] n procedimiento; (bureaucratic) trámites mpl

proceed [prəˈsiːd] vi (do afterwards): **to ~ to do sth** proceder a hacer algo; (continue): **to ~ (with)** continuar or seguir (con); **proceedings** npl acto(s) (pl); (Law) proceso; **proceeds** ['prəʊsiːdz] npl (money) ganancias fpl, ingresos mpl

process ['prəʊsɛs] n proceso ▷ vt tratar, elaborar

procession [prəˈsɛʃən] n desfile m; **funeral ~** cortejo fúnebre

proclaim [prəˈkleɪm] vt (announce) anunciar

prod [prɒd] vt empujar ▷ n empujón m

produce [n 'prɒdjuːs, vt prəˈdjuːs] n (Agr) productos mpl agrícolas ▷ vt producir; (play, film, programme) presentar; **producer** n productor(a) m/f; (of film, programme) director(a) m/f; (of record) productor(a) m/f

product ['prɒdʌkt] n producto; **production** [prəˈdʌkʃən] n producción f; (Theatre) presentación f; **productive** [prəˈdʌktɪv] adj productivo; **productivity** [prɒdʌkˈtɪvɪtɪ] n productividad f

Prof. [prɒf] abbr (= professor) Prof

profession [prəˈfɛʃən] n profesión f; **professional** adj profesional ▷ n profesional mf; (skilled person) perito

professor [prəˈfɛsə*] n (BRIT) catedrático/a; (us, CANADA) profesor(a) m/f

profile ['prəʊfaɪl] n perfil m

profit ['prɒfɪt] n (Comm) ganancia ▷ vi: **to ~ by or from** aprovechar or sacar provecho

de; **profitable** adj (Econ) rentable
profound [prə'faund] adj profundo
programme ['prəugræm] (us **program**) n
programa m ▷ vt programar; **programmer**
(us **programer**) n programador(a)
m/f; **programming** (us **programing**) n
programación f
progress [n 'prəugres, vi prə'gres]
n progreso; (development) desarrollo
▷ vi progresar, avanzar; **in** ~ en curso;
progressive [-'gresiv] adj progresivo;
(person) progresista
prohibit [prə'hibit] vt prohibir; **to** ~ **sb**
from doing sth prohibir a algn hacer algo
project [n 'prɔdʒekt, vb prə'dʒekt] n
proyecto ▷ vt proyectar ▷ vi (stick out) salir,
sobresalir; **projection** [prə'dʒekʃən]
n proyección f; (overhang) saliente m;
projector [prə'dʒektə*] n proyector m
prolific [prə'lɪfɪk] adj prolífico
prolong [prə'lɔn] vt prolongar, extender
prom [prɔm] n abbr = **promenade** (us: ball)
baile m de gala; **the P~s** ver abajo

> ● **PROM**
> ●
> ● El ciclo de conciertos de música clásica
> ● más conocido de Londres es el llamado
> ● **the Proms** (promenade concerts),
> ● que se celebra anualmente en el Royal
> ● Albert Hall. Su nombre se debe a que
> ● originalmente el público paseaba
> ● durante las actuaciones, costumbre que
> ● en la actualidad se mantiene de forma
> ● simbólica, permitiendo que parte de
> ● los asistentes permanezcan de pie. En
> ● Estados Unidos se llama **prom** a un
> ● baile de gala en un centro de educación
> ● secundaria o universitaria.

promenade [prɔmə'nɑːd] n (by sea) paseo
marítimo
prominent ['prɔmɪnənt] adj (standing out)
saliente; (important) eminente, importante
promiscuous [prə'mɪskjuəs] adj
(sexually) promiscuo
promise ['prɔmɪs] n promesa ▷ vt, vi
prometer; **promising** adj prometedor(a)
promote [prə'məut] vt (employee)
ascender; (product, pop star) hacer
propaganda por; (ideas) fomentar;
promotion [-'məuʃən] n (advertising
campaign) campaña f de promoción; (in rank)
ascenso
prompt [prɔmpt] adj rápido ▷ adv: **at 6
o'clock** ~ a las seis en punto ▷ n (Comput)
aviso ▷ vt (urge) mover, incitar; (when
talking) instar; (Theatre) apuntar; **to** ~ **sb to**

do sth instar a algn a hacer algo; **promptly**
adv rápidamente; (exactly) puntualmente
prone [prəun] adj (lying) postrado; ~ **to**
propenso a
prong [prɔn] n diente m, punta
pronoun ['prəunaun] n pronombre m
pronounce [prə'nauns] vt pronunciar
pronunciation [prənʌnsɪ'eɪʃən] n
pronunciación f
proof [pruːf] n prueba ▷ adj: ~ **against** a
prueba de
prop [prɔp] n apoyo; (fig) sostén m
accesorios mpl, at(t)rezzo msg; **prop up**
vt (roof, structure) apuntalar; (economy)
respaldar
propaganda [prɔpə'gændə] n
propaganda
propeller [prə'pelə*] n hélice f
proper ['prɔpə*] adj (suited, right) propio;
(exact) justo; (seemly) correcto, decente;
(authentic) verdadero; (referring to place): **the
village** ~ el pueblo mismo; **properly** adv
(adequately) correctamente; (decently)
decentemente; **proper noun** n nombre
m propio
property ['prɔpətɪ] n propiedad f;
(personal) bienes mpl muebles
prophecy ['prɔfɪsɪ] n profecía
prophet ['prɔfɪt] n profeta m
proportion [prə'pɔːʃən] n proporción
f; (share) parte f; **proportions** npl
(size) dimensiones fpl; **proportional**
adj: **proportional (to)** en proporción (con)
proposal [prə'pəuzl] n (offer of marriage)
oferta de matrimonio; (plan) proyecto
propose [prə'pəuz] vt proponer ▷ vi
declararse; **to** ~ **to do** tener intención de
hacer
proposition [prɔpə'zɪʃən] n propuesta
proprietor [prə'praɪətə*] n propietario/a,
dueño/a
prose [prəuz] n prosa
prosecute ['prɔsɪkjuːt] vt (Law) procesar;
prosecution [-'kjuːʃən] n proceso, causa;
(accusing side) acusación f; **prosecutor** n
acusador(a) m/f; (also: **public prosecutor**)
fiscal mf
prospect [n 'prɔspekt, vb prə'spekt]
n (possibility) posibilidad f; (outlook)
perspectiva ▷ vi: **to** ~ **for** buscar; **prospects**
npl (for work etc) perspectivas fpl;
prospective [prə'spektɪv] adj futuro
prospectus [prə'spektəs] n prospecto
prosper ['prɔspə*] vi prosperar;
prosperity [-'sperɪtɪ] n prosperidad f;
prosperous adj próspero
prostitute ['prɔstɪtjuːt] n prostituta;
(male) hombre que se dedica a la prostitución

protect [prə'tɛkt] vt proteger; **protection** [-'tɛkʃən] n protección f; **protective** adj protector(a)

protein ['prəutiːn] n proteína

protest [n 'prəutɛst, vb prə'tɛst] n protesta ▷ vt (insist): **to ~ about** or **at/against** protestar de/contra ▷ vt (insist): **to ~ (that)** insistir en (que)

Protestant ['prɔtɪstənt] adj, n protestante mf

protester [prə'tɛstə*] n manifestante mf

protractor [prə'træktə*] n (Geom) transportador m

proud [praud] adj orgulloso; (pej) soberbio, altanero

prove [pruːv] vt probar; (show) demostrar ▷ vi: **to ~ (to be) correct** resultar correcto; **to ~ o.s.** probar su valía

proverb ['prɔvəːb] n refrán m

provide [prə'vaɪd] vt proporcionar, dar; **to ~ sb with sth** proveer a algn de algo; **provide for** vt fus (person) mantener a; (problem etc) tener en cuenta; **provided** conj: **provided (that)** con tal de que, a condición de que; **providing** [prə'vaɪdɪŋ] conj: **providing (that)** a condición de que, con tal de que

province ['prɔvɪns] n provincia; (fig) esfera; **provincial** [prə'vɪnʃəl] adj provincial; (pej) provinciano

provision [prə'vɪʒən] n (supplying) suministro, abastecimiento; (of contract etc) disposición f; **provisions** npl (food) comestibles mpl; **provisional** adj provisional

provocative [prə'vɔkətɪv] adj provocativo

provoke [prə'vəuk] vt (cause) provocar, incitar; (anger) enojar

prowl [praul] vi (also: ~ about, ~ around) merodear ▷ n: **on the ~** de merodeo

proximity [prɔk'sɪmɪtɪ] n proximidad f

proxy ['prɔksɪ] n: **by ~** por poderes

prudent ['pruːdənt] adj prudente

prune [pruːn] n ciruela pasa ▷ vt podar

pry [praɪ] vi: **to ~ (into)** entrometerse (en)

PS n abbr (= postscript) P.D.

pseudonym ['sjuːdənɪm] n seudónimo

PSHE (BRIT: Scol) n abbr (= personal, social and health education) formación social y sanitaria

psychiatric [saɪkɪ'ætrɪk] adj psiquiátrico

psychiatrist [saɪ'kaɪətrɪst] n psiquiatra mf

psychic ['saɪkɪk] adj (also: ~al) psíquico

psychoanalysis [saɪkəuə'nælɪsɪs] n psicoanálisis m inv

psychological [saɪkə'lɔdʒɪkl] adj psicológico

psychologist [saɪ'kɔlədʒɪst] n psicólogo/a

psychology [saɪ'kɔlədʒɪ] n psicología

psychotherapy [saɪkəu'θɛrəpɪ] n psicoterapia

pt abbr = pint(s); point(s)

PTO abbr (= please turn over) sigue

pub [pʌb] n abbr (= public house) pub m, bar m

puberty ['pjuːbətɪ] n pubertad f

public ['pʌblɪk] adj público ▷ n: **the ~** el público; **in ~** en público; **to make ~** hacer público

publication [pʌblɪ'keɪʃən] n publicación f

public: public company n sociedad f anónima; **public convenience** (BRIT) n aseos mpl públicos (SP), sanitarios mpl (LAM); **public holiday** n (día m de) fiesta (SP), (día m) feriado (LAM); **public house** (BRIT) n bar m, pub m

publicity [pʌb'lɪsɪtɪ] n publicidad f

publicize ['pʌblɪsaɪz] vt publicitar

public: public limited company n sociedad f anónima (S.A.); **publicly** adv públicamente, en público; **public opinion** n opinión f pública; **public relations** n relaciones fpl públicas; **public school** n (BRIT) escuela privada; (US) instituto; **public transport** n transporte m público

publish ['pʌblɪʃ] vt publicar; **publisher** n (person) editor(a) m/f; (firm) editorial f; **publishing** n (industry) industria del libro

pub lunch n almuerzo que se sirve en un pub; **to go for a ~** almorzar o comer en un pub

pudding ['pudɪŋ] n pudín m; (BRIT: dessert) postre m; **black ~** morcilla

puddle ['pʌdl] n charco

Puerto Rico [pwɛː'təu'riːkəu] n Puerto Rico

puff [pʌf] n soplo; (of smoke, air) bocanada; (of breathing) resoplido ▷ vt: **to ~ one's pipe** chupar la pipa ▷ vi (pant) jadear; **puff pastry** n hojaldre m

pull [pul] n (tug) **to give sth a ~** dar un tirón a algo ▷ vt tirar de; (press: trigger) apretar; (haul) tirar, arrastrar; (close: curtain) echar ▷ vi tirar; **to ~ to pieces** hacer pedazos; **not to ~ one's punches** no andarse con bromas; **to ~ one's weight** hacer su parte; **to ~ o.s. together** sobreponerse; **to ~ sb's leg** tomar el pelo a algn; **pull apart** vt (break) romper; **pull away** vi (vehicle: move off) salir, arrancar; (draw back) apartarse bruscamente; **pull back** vt (lever etc) tirar hacia sí; (curtains) descorrer ▷ vi (refrain) contenerse; (Mil: withdraw) retirarse; **pull down** vt (building) derribar; **pull in** vi (car etc) parar (junto a la acera); (train) llegar a la estación; **pull off** vt (deal etc) cerrar; **pull out** vi (car, train etc) salir ▷ vt sacar, arrancar; **pull over** vi (Aut) hacerse a un lado; **pull up** vi (stop) parar ▷ vt (raise) levantar; (uproot) arrancar, desarraigar

pulley ['puli] n polea

pullover ['pulǝuvǝ*] n jersey m, suéter m

pulp [pʌlp] n (of fruit) pulpa

pulpit ['pulpit] n púlpito

pulse [pʌls] n (Anat) pulso; (rhythm) pulsación f; (Bot) legumbre f; **pulses** pl n legumbres

puma ['pju:mǝ] n puma m

pump [pʌmp] n bomba; (shoe) zapatilla ▷ vt sacar con una bomba; **pump up** vt inflar

pumpkin ['pʌmpkɪn] n calabaza

pun [pʌn] n juego de palabras

punch [pʌntʃ] n (blow) golpe m, puñetazo; (tool) punzón m; (drink) ponche m ▷ vt (hit): **to ~ sb/sth** dar un puñetazo or golpear a algn/algo; **punch-up** (BRIT: inf) n riña

punctual ['pʌŋktjuǝl] adj puntual

punctuation [pʌŋktju'eɪʃǝn] n puntuación f

puncture ['pʌŋktʃǝ*] (BRIT) n pinchazo ▷ vt pinchar

punish ['pʌnɪʃ] vt castigar; **punishment** n castigo

punk [pʌŋk] n (also: ~ rocker) punki mf; (also: ~ rock) música punk; (US: inf: hoodlum) rufián m

pup [pʌp] n cachorro

pupil ['pju:pl] n alumno/a; (of eye) pupila

puppet ['pʌpɪt] n títere m

puppy ['pʌpɪ] n cachorro, perrito

purchase ['pǝ:tʃɪs] n compra ▷ vt comprar

pure [pjuǝ*] adj puro; **purely** adv puramente

purify ['pjuǝrɪfaɪ] vt purificar, depurar

purity ['pjuǝrɪtɪ] n pureza

purple ['pǝ:pl] adj purpúreo; morado

purpose ['pǝ:pǝs] n propósito; **on ~** a propósito, adrede

purr [pǝ:*] vi ronronear

purse [pǝ:s] n monedero; (US: handbag) bolso (SP), cartera (LAM), bolsa (MEX) ▷ vt fruncir

pursue [pǝ'sju:] vt seguir

pursuit [pǝ'sju:t] n (chase) caza; (occupation) actividad f

pus [pʌs] n pus m

push [puʃ] n empuje m, empujón m; (of button) presión f; (drive) empuje m ▷ vt empujar; (button) apretar; (promote)

promover ▷ vi empujar; (demand): **to ~ for** luchar por; **push in** vi colarse; **push off** (inf) vi largarse; **push on** vi seguir adelante; **push over** vt (cause to fall) hacer caer, derribar; (knock over) volcar; **push through** vi (crowd) abrirse paso a empujones ▷ vt (measure) despachar; **pushchair** (BRIT) n sillita de ruedas; **pusher** n (drug pusher) traficante mf de drogas; **push-up** (US) n plancha

pussy(-cat) ['pusɪ-] (inf) n minino (inf)

put [put] (pt, pp ~) vt (place) poner, colocar; (put into) meter; (say) expresar; (a question) hacer; (estimate) estimar; **put aside** vt (lay down: book etc) dejar o poner a un lado; (save) ahorrar; (in shop) guardar; **put away** vt (store) guardar; **put back** vt (replace) devolver a su lugar; (postpone) aplazar; **put by** vt (money) guardar; **put down** vt (on ground) poner en el suelo; (animal) sacrificar; (in writing) apuntar; (revolt etc) sofocar; (attribute): **to put sth down to** atribuir algo a; **put forward** vt (ideas) presentar, proponer; **put in** vt (complaint) presentar; (time) dedicar; **put off** vt (postpone) aplazar; (discourage) desanimar; **put on** vt ponerse; (light etc) encender; (play etc) presentar; (gain): **to put on weight** engordar; (brake) echar; (record, kettle etc) poner; (assume) adoptar; **put out** vt (fire, light) apagar; (rubbish etc) sacar; (cat etc) echar; (one's hand) alargar; (inf: person): **to be put out** alterarse; **put through** vt (Tel) poner; (plan etc) hacer aprobar; **put together** vt unir, reunir; (assemble: furniture) armar, montar; (meal) preparar; **put up** vt (raise) levantar, alzar; (hang) colgar; (build) construir; (increase) aumentar; (accommodate) alojar; **put up with** vt fus aguantar

putt [pʌt] n putt m, golpe m corto; **putting green** n green m; minigolf m

puzzle ['pʌzl] n rompecabezas m inv; (also: **crossword ~**) crucigrama m; (mystery) misterio ▷ vt dejar perplejo, confundir ▷ vi: **to ~ over sth** devanarse los sesos con algo; **puzzled** adj perplejo; **puzzling** adj misterioso, extraño

pyjamas [pɪ'dʒɑ:mǝz] (BRIT) npl pijama m

pylon ['paɪlǝn] n torre f de conducción eléctrica

pyramid ['pɪrǝmɪd] n pirámide f

q

quack [kwæk] n graznido; (pej: doctor) curandero/a

quadruple [kwɔ'druːpl] vt, vi cuadruplicar

quail [kweɪl] n codorniz f ▷ vi: **to ~ at** or **before** amedrentarse ante

quaint [kweɪnt] adj extraño; (picturesque) pintoresco

quake [kweɪk] vi temblar ▷ n abbr = **earthquake**

qualification [kwɔlɪfɪ'keɪʃən] n (ability) capacidad f; (often pl: diploma etc) título; (reservation) salvedad f

qualified ['kwɔlɪfaɪd] adj capacitado; (professionally) titulado; (limited) limitado

qualify ['kwɔlɪfaɪ] vt (make competent) capacitar; (modify) modificar ▷ vi (in competition): **to ~ (for)** calificarse (para); (pass examination(s)): **to ~ (as)** calificarse (de), graduarse (en); (be eligible): **to ~ (for)** reunir los requisitos (para)

quality ['kwɔlɪtɪ] n calidad f; (of person) cualidad f

qualm [kwɑːm] n escrúpulo

quantify ['kwɔntɪfaɪ] vt cuantificar

quantity ['kwɔntɪtɪ] n cantidad f; **in ~** en grandes cantidades

quarantine ['kwɔrəntiːn] n cuarentena

quarrel ['kwɔrl] n riña, pelea ▷ vi reñir, pelearse

quarry ['kwɔrɪ] n cantera

quart [kwɔːt] n ≈ litro

quarter ['kwɔːtə*] n cuarto, cuarta parte f; (us: coin) moneda de 25 centavos; (of year) trimestre m; (district) barrio ▷ vt dividir en cuartos; (Mil: lodge) alojar; **quarters** npl (barracks) cuartel m; (living quarters) alojamiento; **a ~ of an hour** un cuarto de hora; **quarter final** n cuarto de final; **quarterly** adj trimestral ▷ adv cada 3 meses, trimestralmente

quartet(te) [kwɔː'tɛt] n cuarteto

quartz [kwɔːts] n cuarzo

quay [kiː] n (also: **~side**) muelle m

queasy ['kwiːzɪ] adj: **to feel ~** tener náuseas

queen [kwiːn] n reina; (Cards etc) dama

queer [kwɪə*] adj raro, extraño ▷ n (inf: highly offensive) maricón m

quench [kwɛntʃ] vt: **to ~ one's thirst** apagar la sed

query ['kwɪərɪ] n (question) pregunta ▷ vt dudar de

quest [kwɛst] n busca, búsqueda

question ['kwɛstʃən] n pregunta; (doubt) duda; (matter) asunto, cuestión f ▷ vt (doubt) dudar de; (interrogate) interrogar, hacer preguntas a; **beyond ~** fuera de toda duda; **out of the ~** imposible; ni hablar; **questionable** adj dudoso; **question mark** n punto de interrogación; **questionnaire** ['nɛə*] n cuestionario

queue [kjuː] (BRIT) n cola ▷ vi (also: **~ up**) hacer cola

quiche [kiːʃ] n quiche m

quick [kwɪk] adj rápido; (agile) ágil; (mind) listo ▷ n: **cut to the ~** (fig) herido en lo vivo; **be ~!** ¡date prisa!; **quickly** adv rápidamente, de prisa

quid [kwɪd] (BRIT: inf) n inv libra

quiet ['kwaɪət] adj (voice, music etc) bajo; (person, place) tranquilo; (ceremony) íntimo ▷ n silencio; (calm) tranquilidad f ▷ vt, vi (us) = **quieten**

⬛ Be careful not to translate **quiet** by the Spanish word quieto.

quietly adv tranquilamente; (silently) silenciosamente

quilt [kwɪlt] n edredón m

quirky ['kwɜːkɪ] adj raro, estrafalario

quit [kwɪt] (pt, pp = or ~ted) vt dejar, abandonar; (premises) desocupar ▷ vi (give up) renunciar; (resign) dimitir

quite [kwaɪt] adv (rather) bastante; (entirely) completamente; **that's not ~ big enough** no acaba de ser lo bastante grande; **~ a few of them** un buen número de ellos; **~ (so)!** ¡así es!, ¡exactamente!

quits [kwɪts] adj: **~ (with)** en paz (con); **let's call it ~** dejémoslo en tablas

quiver ['kwɪvə*] vi estremecerse

quiz [kwɪz] n concurso ▷ vt interrogar

quota ['kwəutə] n cuota

quotation [kwəu'teɪʃən] n cita; (estimate) presupuesto; **quotation marks** npl comillas fpl

quote [kwəut] n cita; (estimate) presupuesto ▷ vt citar; (price) cotizar ▷ vi: **to ~ from** citar de; **quotes** npl (inverted commas) comillas fpl

q

r

rabbi ['ræbaɪ] *n* rabino

rabbit ['ræbɪt] *n* conejo

rabies ['reɪbiːz] *n* rabia

RAC (*BRIT*) *n abbr* (= *Royal Automobile Club*) ≈ RACE *m*

rac(c)oon [rə'kuːn] *n* mapache *m*

race [reɪs] *n* carrera; (*species*) raza ⊳ *vt* (*horse*) hacer correr; (*engine*) acelerar ⊳ *vi* (*compete*) competir; (*run*) correr; (*pulse*) latir a ritmo acelerado; **race car** (*US*) *n* = **racing car; racecourse** *n* hipódromo; **racehorse** *n* caballo de carreras; **racetrack** *n* pista; (*for cars*) autódromo

racial ['reɪʃl] *adj* racial

racing ['reɪsɪŋ] *n* carreras *fpl*; **racing car** (*BRIT*) *n* coche *m* de carreras; **racing driver** (*BRIT*) *n* piloto *mf* de carreras

racism ['reɪsɪzəm] *n* racismo; **racist** [-sɪst] *adj, n* racista *mf*

rack [ræk] *n* (*also*: **luggage ~**) rejilla; (*shelf*) estante *m*; (*also*: **roof ~**) baca, portaequipajes *m inv*; (*dish rack*) escurreplatos *m inv*; (*clothes rack*) percha ⊳ *vt* atormentar; **to ~ one's brains** devanarse los sesos

racket ['rækɪt] *n* (*for tennis*) raqueta; (*noise*) ruido, estrépito; (*swindle*) estafa, timo

racquet ['rækɪt] *n* raqueta

radar ['reɪdɑː*] *n* radar *m*

radiation [reɪdɪ'eɪʃən] *n* radiación *f*

radiator ['reɪdɪeɪtə*] *n* radiador *m*

radical ['rædɪkl] *adj* radical

radio ['reɪdɪəu] *n* radio *f*; **on the ~** por radio; **radioactive** *adj* radioactivo; **radio station** *n* emisora

radish ['rædɪʃ] *n* rábano

RAF *n abbr* (= *Royal Air Force*) las Fuerzas Aéreas Británicas

raffle ['ræfl] *n* rifa, sorteo

raft [rɑːft] *n* balsa; (*also*: **life ~**) balsa salvavidas

rag [ræg] *n* (*piece of cloth*) trapo; (*torn cloth*) harapo; (*pej: newspaper*) periodicucho; (*for charity*) actividades estudiantiles benéficas; **rags** *npl* (*torn clothes*) harapos *mpl*

rage [reɪdʒ] *n* rabia, furor *m* ⊳ *vi* (*person*) rabiar, estar furioso; (*storm*) bramar; **it's all the ~** (*very fashionable*) está muy de moda

ragged ['rægɪd] *adj* (*edge*) desigual, mellado; (*appearance*) andrajoso, harapiento

raid [reɪd] *n* (*Mil*) incursión *f*; (*criminal*) asalto; (*by police*) redada ⊳ *vt* invadir, atacar; asaltar

rail [reɪl] *n* (*on stair*) barandilla, pasamanos *m inv*; (*on bridge, balcony*) pretil *m*; (*of ship*) barandilla; (*also*: **towel ~**) toallero; **railcard** *n* (*BRIT*) tarjeta para obtener descuentos en el tren; **railing(s)** *n(pl)* vallado; **railroad** (*US*) *n* = **railway; railway** (*BRIT*) *n* ferrocarril *m*, vía férrea; **railway line** (*BRIT*) *n* línea (de ferrocarril); **railway station** (*BRIT*) *n* estación *f* de ferrocarril

rain [reɪn] *n* lluvia ⊳ *vi* llover; **in the ~** bajo la lluvia; **it's ~ing** llueve, está lloviendo; **rainbow** *n* arco iris; **raincoat** *n* impermeable *m*; **raindrop** *n* gota de lluvia; **rainfall** *n* lluvia; **rainforest** *n* selvas *fpl* tropicales; **rainy** *adj* lluvioso

raise [reɪz] *n* aumento ⊳ *vt* levantar; (*increase*) aumentar; (*improve: morale*) subir; (*: standards*) mejorar; (*doubts*) suscitar; (*a question*) plantear; (*cattle, family*) criar; (*crop*) cultivar; (*army*) reclutar; (*loan*) obtener; **to ~ one's voice** alzar la voz

raisin ['reɪzn] *n* pasa de Corinto

rake [reɪk] *n* (*tool*) rastrillo; (*person*) libertino ⊳ *vt* (*garden*) rastrillar

rally ['rælɪ] *n* (*Pol etc*) reunión *f*, mitin *m*; (*Aut*) rallye *m*; (*Tennis*) peloteo ⊳ *vt* reunir ⊳ *vi* recuperarse

RAM [ræm] *n abbr* (= *random access memory*) RAM *f*

ram [ræm] *n* carnero; (*also*: **battering ~**) ariete *m* ⊳ *vt* (*crash into*) dar contra, chocar con; (*push: fist etc*) empujar con fuerza

Ramadan [ræmə'dæn] *n* ramadán *m*

ramble ['ræmbl] *n* caminata, excursión *f* en el campo ⊳ *vi* (*pej: also*: **~ on**) divagar; **rambler** *n* excursionista *mf*; (*Bot*) trepadora; **rambling** *adj* (*speech*) inconexo; (*house*) laberíntico; (*Bot*) trepador(a)

ramp [ræmp] *n* rampa; **on/off ~** (*us Aut*) vía de acceso/salida

rampage [ræm'peɪdʒ] *n*: **to be on the ~** desmandarse ⊳ *vi*: **they went rampaging through the town** recorrieron la ciudad armando alboroto

ran [ræn] *pt of* **run**

ranch [rɑːntʃ] *n* hacienda, estancia

random ['rændəm] adj fortuito, sin
orden; (Comput, Math) aleatorio ▷ n: **at ~**
al azar

rang [ræŋ] pt of **ring**

range [reɪndʒ] n (of mountains) cadena de
montañas, cordillera; (of missile) alcance m;
(of voice) registro; (series) serie f; (of products)
surtido; (Mil: also: **shooting ~**) campo de
tiro; (also: **kitchen ~**) fogón m ▷ vt (place)
colocar; (arrange) arreglar ▷ vi: **to ~ over**
(extend) extenderse por; **to ~ from ... to ...**
oscilar entre ... y ...

ranger ['reɪndʒə*] n guardabosques mf inv

rank [ræŋk] n (row) fila; (Mil) rango;
(status) categoría; (BRIT: also: **taxi ~**) parada
de taxis ▷ vi: **to ~ among** figurar entre ▷ adj
fétido, rancio; **the ~ and file** (fig) la base

ransom ['rænsəm] n rescate m; **to hold to
~** (fig) hacer chantaje a

rant [rænt] vi divagar, desvariar

rap [ræp] vt golpear, dar un golpecito en
▷ n (music) rap m

rape [reɪp] n violación f; (Bot) colza ▷ vt
violar

rapid ['ræpɪd] adj rápido; **rapidly** adv
rápidamente; **rapids** npl (Geo) rápidos mpl

rapist ['reɪpɪst] n violador m

rapport [ræ'pɔ:*] n simpatía

rare [rɛə*] adj raro, poco común;
(Culin: steak) poco hecho; **rarely** adv pocas
veces

rash [ræʃ] adj imprudente, precipitado ▷ n
(Med) sarpullido, erupción f (cutánea); (of
events) serie f

rasher ['ræʃə*] n lonja

raspberry ['rɑ:zbərɪ] n frambuesa

rat [ræt] n rata

rate [reɪt] n (ratio) razón f; (price) precio;
(: of hotel etc) tarifa; (of interest) tipo; (speed)
velocidad f ▷ vt (value) tasar; (estimate)
estimar; **rates** npl (BRIT: property tax)
impuesto municipal; (fees) tarifa; **to ~ sth/
sb as** considerar algo/a algn como

rather ['rɑ:ðə*] adv: **it's ~ expensive** es
algo caro; (too much) es demasiado caro; (to
some extent) más bien; **there's ~ a lot** hay
bastante; **I would** or **I'd ~ go** preferiría ir; **or
~** mejor dicho

rating ['reɪtɪŋ] n tasación f; (score) índice
m; (of ship) clase f; **ratings** npl (Radio, TV)
niveles mpl de audiencia

ratio ['reɪʃɪəu] n razón f; **in the ~ of 100 to
1** a razón de 100 a 1

ration ['ræʃən] n ración f ▷ vt racionar;
rations npl víveres mpl

rational ['ræʃənl] adj (solution, reasoning)
lógico, razonable; (person) cuerdo, sensato

rattle ['rætl] n golpeteo; (of train etc)

traqueteo; (for baby) sonaja, sonajero
▷ vi castañetear; (car, bus): **to ~ along**
traquetear ▷ vt hacer sonar agitando

rave [reɪv] vi (in anger) encolerizarse; (with
enthusiasm) entusiasmarse; (Med) delirar,
desvariar ▷ n (inf: party) rave m

raven ['reɪvən] n cuervo

ravine [rə'vi:n] n barranco

raw [rɔ:] adj crudo; (not processed) bruto;
(sore) vivo; (inexperienced) novato, inexperto;
~ materials materias primas

ray [reɪ] n rayo; **~ of hope** (rayo de)
esperanza

razor ['reɪzə*] n (open) navaja; (safety razor)
máquina de afeitar; (electric razor) máquina
(eléctrica) de afeitar; **razor blade** n hoja
de afeitar

Rd abbr = **road**

RE n abbr (BRIT) = **religious education**

re [ri:] prep con referencia a

reach [ri:tʃ] n alcance m; (of river etc)
extensión f entre dos recodos ▷ vt alcanzar,
llegar a; (achieve) lograr ▷ vi extenderse;
within ~ al alcance (de la mano); **out of
~** fuera del alcance; **reach out** vt (hand)
tender ▷ vi: **to reach out for sth** alargar or
tender la mano para tomar algo

react [ri:'ækt] vi reaccionar; **reaction**
[-'ækʃən] n reacción f; **reactor** [ri:'æktə*]
n (also: **nuclear reactor**) reactor m (nuclear)

read [ri:d, pt, pp red] (pt, pp ~) vi leer ▷ vt
leer; (understand) entender; (study) estudiar;
read out vt leer en alta voz; **reader** n
lector(a) m/f; (BRIT: at university) profesor(a)
m/f adjunto/a

readily ['redɪlɪ] adv (willingly) de buena
gana; (easily) fácilmente; (quickly) en seguida

reading ['ri:dɪŋ] n lectura; (on instrument)
indicación f

ready ['redɪ] adj listo, preparado;
(willing) dispuesto; (available) disponible
▷ adv: **~-cooked** listo para comer ▷ n: **at
the ~** (Mil) listo para tirar ▷ **to get ~** vi
prepararse ▷ **to get ~** vt preparar; **ready-
made** adj confeccionado

real [rɪəl] adj verdadero, auténtico; **in
~ terms** en términos reales; **real ale** n
cerveza elaborada tradicionalmente;
real estate n bienes mpl raíces; **realistic**
[-'lɪstɪk] adj realista; **reality** [ri:'ælɪtɪ] n
realidad f; **reality TV** n telerrealidad f

realization [rɪəlaɪ'zeɪʃən] n comprensión
f; (fulfilment, Comm) realización f

realize ['rɪəlaɪz] vt (understand) darse
cuenta de

really ['rɪəlɪ] adv realmente; (for emphasis)
verdaderamente; (actually): **what ~
happened** lo que pasó en realidad; **~?** ¿de

veras?; **~!** (annoyance) ¡vamos!, ¡por favor!

realm [rɛlm] n reino; (fig) esfera

realtor ['rɪəltɔː*] (US) n agente mf inmobiliario/a

reappear [riːə'pɪə*] vi reaparecer

rear [rɪə*] adj trasero ▷ n parte f trasera ▷ vt (cattle, family) criar ▷ vi (also: **~ up**: animal) encabritarse

rearrange [riːə'reɪndʒ] vt ordenar or arreglar de nuevo

rear: rear-view mirror n (Aut) (espejo) retrovisor m; **rear-wheel drive** n tracción f trasera

reason ['riːzn] n razón f ▷ vi: **to ~ with sb** tratar de que algn entre en razón; **it stands to ~ that ...** es lógico que ...; **reasonable** adj razonable; (sensible) sensato; **reasonably** adv razonablemente; **reasoning** n razonamiento, argumentos mpl

reassurance [riːə'ʃuərəns] n consuelo

reassure [riːə'ʃuə*] vt tranquilizar, alentar; **to ~ sb that ...** tranquilizar a algn asegurando que ...

rebate ['riːbeɪt] n (on tax etc) desgravación f

rebel [n 'rɛbl, vi rɪ'bɛl] n rebelde mf ▷ vi rebelarse, sublevarse; **rebellion** [rɪ'bɛljən] n rebelión f, sublevación f; **rebellious** [rɪ'bɛljəs] adj rebelde; (child) revoltoso

rebuild [riː'bɪld] vt reconstruir

recall [vb rɪ'kɔːl, n 'rɪːkɔl] vt (remember) recordar; (ambassador etc) retirar ▷ n recuerdo; retirada

rec'd abbr (= received) rbdo

receipt [rɪ'siːt] n (document) recibo; (for parcel etc) acuse m de recibo; (act of receiving) recepción f; **receipts** npl (Comm) ingresos mpl

▌Be careful not to translate **receipt** by the Spanish word receta.

receive [rɪ'siːv] vt recibir; (guest) acoger; (wound) sufrir; **receiver** n (Tel) auricular m; (Radio) receptor m; (of stolen goods) perista mf; (Comm) administrador m jurídico

recent ['riːsnt] adj reciente; **recently** adv recientemente; **recently arrived** recién llegado

reception [rɪ'sɛpʃən] n recepción f; (welcome) acogida; **reception desk** n recepción f; **receptionist** n recepcionista mf

recession [rɪ'sɛʃən] n recesión f

recharge [riː'tʃɑːdʒ] vt (battery) recargar

recipe ['rɛsɪpɪ] n receta; (for disaster, success) fórmula

recipient [rɪ'sɪpɪənt] n recibidor(a) m/f; (of letter) destinatario/a

recital [rɪ'saɪtl] n recital m

recite [rɪ'saɪt] vt (poem) recitar

reckless ['rɛkləs] adj temerario, imprudente; (driving, driver) peligroso

reckon ['rɛkən] vt calcular; (consider) considerar; (think): **I ~ that ...** me parece que ...

reclaim [rɪ'kleɪm] vt (land, waste) recuperar; (land: from sea) rescatar; (demand back) reclamar

recline [rɪ'klaɪn] vi reclinarse

recognition [rɛkəg'nɪʃən] n reconocimiento; **transformed beyond ~** irreconocible

recognize ['rɛkəgnaɪz] vt: **to ~ (by/as)** reconocer (por/como)

recollection [rɛkə'lɛkʃən] n recuerdo

recommend [rɛkə'mɛnd] vt recomendar; **recommendation** [rɛkəmɛn'deɪʃən] n recomendación f

reconcile ['rɛkənsaɪl] vt (two people) reconciliar; (two facts) compaginar; **to ~ o.s. to sth** conformarse a algo

reconsider [riːkən'sɪdə*] vt repensar

reconstruct [riːkən'strʌkt] vt reconstruir

record [n, adj 'rɛkɔːd, vt rɪ'kɔːd] n (Mus) disco; (of meeting etc) acta; (register) registro, partida; (file) archivo; (also: **criminal ~**) antecedentes mpl; (written) expediente m; (Sport, Comput) récord m ▷ adj récord, sin precedentes ▷ vt registrar; (Mus: song etc) grabar; **in ~ time** en un tiempo récord; **off the ~** adj no oficial ▷ adv confidencialmente; **recorded delivery** (BRIT) n (Post) entrega con acuse de recibo; **recorder** n (Mus) flauta de pico; **recording** n (Mus) grabación f; **record player** n tocadiscos m inv

recount [rɪ'kaunt] vt contar

recover [rɪ'kʌvə*] vt recuperar ▷ vi (from illness, shock) recuperarse; **recovery** n recuperación f

recreate [riːkrɪ'eɪt] vt recrear

recreation [rɛkrɪ'eɪʃən] n recreo; **recreational vehicle** (US) n caravan or rulota pequeña; **recreational drug** droga recreativa

recruit [rɪ'kruːt] n recluta mf ▷ vt reclutar; (staff) contratar; **recruitment** n reclutamiento

rectangle ['rɛktæŋgl] n rectángulo; **rectangular** [-'tæŋgjulə*] adj rectangular

rectify ['rɛktɪfaɪ] vt rectificar

rector ['rɛktə*] n (Rel) párroco

recur [rɪ'kəː*] vi repetirse; (pain, illness) producirse de nuevo; **recurring** adj (problem) repetido, constante

recyclable [riː'saɪkləbl] adj reciclable

recycle [riː'saɪkl] vt reciclar

recycling [ri:'saɪklɪŋ] n reciclaje
red [rɛd] n rojo ▷ adj rojo; (hair) pelirrojo; (wine) tinto; **to be in the ~** (account) estar en números rojos; (business) tener un saldo negativo; **to give sb the ~ carpet treatment** recibir a algn con todos los honores; **Red Cross** n Cruz f Roja; **redcurrant** n grosella roja
redeem [rɪ'di:m] vt redimir; (promises) cumplir; (sth in pawn) desempeñar; (fig, also Rel) rescatar
red: red-haired adj pelirrojo; **redhead** n pelirrojo/a; **red-hot** adj candente; **red light** n: **to go through a red light** (Aut) pasar la luz roja; **red-light district** n barrio chino
red meat n carne f roja
reduce [rɪ'dju:s] vt reducir; **to ~ sb to tears** hacer llorar a algn; **"~ speed now"** (Aut) "reduzca la velocidad"; **reduced** adj (decreased) reducido, rebajado; **at a reduced price** con rebaja or descuento; **"greatly reduced prices"** "grandes rebajas"; **reduction** [rɪ'dʌkʃən] n reducción f; (of price) rebaja; (discount) descuento; (smaller-scale copy) copia reducida
redundancy [rɪ'dʌndənsɪ] n (dismissal) despido; (unemployment) desempleo
redundant [rɪ'dʌndnt] adj (BRIT: worker) parado, sin trabajo; (detail, object) superfluo; **to be made ~** quedar(se) sin trabajo
reed [ri:d] n (Bot) junco, caña; (Mus) lengüeta
reef [ri:f] n (at sea) arrecife m
reel [ri:l] n carrete m, bobina; (of film) rollo; (dance) baile escocés ▷ vt (also: ~ up) devanar; (also: ~ in) sacar ▷ vi (sway) tambalear(se)
ref [rɛf] (inf) n abbr = **referee**
refectory [rɪ'fɛktərɪ] n comedor m
refer [rɪ'fə:*] vt (send: patient) referir; (: matter) remitir ▷ vi: **to ~ to** (allude to) referirse a, aludir a; (apply to) relacionarse con; (consult) consultar
referee [rɛfə'ri:] n árbitro; (BRIT: for job application): **to be a ~ for sb** proporcionar referencias a algn ▷ vt (match) arbitrar en
reference ['rɛfrəns] n referencia; (for job application: letter) carta de recomendación; **with ~ to** (Comm: in letter) me remito a; **reference number** n número de referencia
refill [vt ri:'fɪl, n 'ri:fɪl] vt rellenar ▷ n repuesto, recambio
refine [rɪ'faɪn] vt refinar; **refined** adj (person) fino; **refinery** n refinería
reflect [rɪ'flɛkt] vt reflejar ▷ vi (think) reflexionar, pensar; **it ~s badly/well on him** le perjudica/le hace honor; **reflection** [-'flɛkʃən] n (act) reflexión f; (image) reflejo;

(criticism) crítica; **on reflection** pensándolo bien
reflex ['ri:flɛks] adj, n reflejo
reform [rɪ'fɔ:m] n reforma ▷ vt reformar
refrain [rɪ'freɪn] vi: **to ~ from doing** abstenerse de hacer ▷ n estribillo
refresh [rɪ'frɛʃ] vt refrescar; **refreshing** adj refrescante; **refreshments** npl refrescos mpl
refrigerator [rɪ'frɪdʒəreɪtə*] n frigorífico (SP), nevera (SP), refrigerador m (LAM), heladera (RPL)
refuel [ri:'fjuəl] vi repostar (combustible)
refuge ['rɛfju:dʒ] n refugio, asilo; **to take ~ in** refugiarse en; **refugee** [rɛfju'dʒi:] n refugiado/a
refund [n 'ri:fʌnd, vb rɪ'fʌnd] n reembolso ▷ vt devolver, reembolsar
refurbish [ri:'fə:bɪʃ] vt restaurar, renovar
refusal [rɪ'fju:zəl] n negativa; **to have first ~ on** tener la primera opción a
refuse¹ ['rɛfju:s] n basura
refuse² [rɪ'fju:z] vt rechazar; (invitation) declinar; (permission) denegar ▷ vi: **to ~ to do sth** negarse a hacer algo; (horse) rehusar
regain [rɪ'geɪn] vt recobrar, recuperar
regard [rɪ'gɑ:d] n mirada; (esteem) respeto; (attention) consideración f ▷ vt (consider) considerar; **to give one's ~s to** saludar de su parte a; **"with kindest ~s"** "con muchos recuerdos"; **as ~s, with ~ to** con respecto a, en cuanto a; **regarding** prep con respecto a, en cuanto a; **regardless** adv a pesar de todo; **regardless of** sin reparar en
regenerate [rɪ'dʒenəreɪt] vt regenerar
reggae ['rɛgeɪ] n reggae m
regiment ['rɛdʒɪmənt] n regimiento
region ['ri:dʒən] n región f; **in the ~ of** (fig) alrededor de; **regional** adj regional
register ['rɛdʒɪstə*] n registro ▷ vt registrar; (birth) declarar; (car) matricular; (letter) certificar; (instrument) marcar, indicar ▷ vi (at hotel) registrarse; (as student) matricularse; (make impression) producir impresión; **registered** adj (letter, parcel) certificado
registrar ['rɛdʒɪstrɑ:*] n secretario/a (del registro civil)
registration [rɛdʒɪs'treɪʃən] n (act) declaración f; (Aut: also: ~ number) matrícula
registry office ['rɛdʒɪstrɪ-] (BRIT) n registro civil; **to get married in a ~** casarse por lo civil
regret [rɪ'grɛt] n sentimiento, pesar m ▷ vt sentir, lamentar; **regrettable** adj lamentable
regular ['rɛgjulə*] adj regular; (soldier)

profesional; (*usual*) habitual; (: *doctor*) de cabecera ▷ *n* (*client etc*) cliente/a *m/f* habitual; **regularly** *adv* con regularidad; (*often*) repetidas veces

regulate ['rɛgjuleɪt] *vt* controlar; **regulation** [-'leɪʃən] *n* (*rule*) regla, reglamento

rehabilitation ['ri:əbɪlɪ'teɪʃən] *n* rehabilitación *f*

rehearsal [rɪ'hə:səl] *n* ensayo

rehearse [rɪ'hə:s] *vt* ensayar

reign [reɪn] *n* reinado; (*fig*) predominio ▷ *vi* reinar; (*fig*) imperar

reimburse [ri:ɪm'bə:s] *vt* reembolsar

rein [reɪn] *n* (*for horse*) rienda

reincarnation [ri:ɪnkɑ:'neɪʃən] *n* reencarnación *f*

reindeer ['reɪndɪə*] *n inv* reno

reinforce [ri:ɪn'fɔ:s] *vt* reforzar; **reinforcements** *npl* (*Mil*) refuerzos *mpl*

reinstate [ri:ɪn'steɪt] *vt* reintegrar; (*tax, law*) reinstaurar

reject [*n* 'ri:dʒɛkt, *vb* rɪ'dʒɛkt] *n* (*thing*) desecho ▷ *vt* rechazar; (*suggestion*) descartar; (*coin*) expulsar; **rejection** [rɪ'dʒɛkʃən] *n* rechazo

rejoice [rɪ'dʒɔɪs] *vi*: **to ~ at** *or* **over** regocijarse *or* alegrarse de

relate [rɪ'leɪt] *vt* (*tell*) contar, relatar; (*connect*) relacionar ▷ *vi* relacionarse; **related** *adj* afín; (*person*) emparentado; **related to** (*subject*) relacionado con; **relating to** *prep* referente a

relation [rɪ'leɪʃən] *n* (*person*) familiar *mf*, pariente *mf*; (*link*) relación *f*; **relations** *npl* (*relatives*) familiares *mpl*; **relationship** *n* relación *f*; (*personal*) relaciones *fpl*; (*also:* **family relationship**) parentesco

relative ['rɛlətɪv] *n* pariente *mf*, familiar *mf* ▷ *adj* relativo; **relatively** *adv* (*comparatively*) relativamente

relax [rɪ'læks] *vi* descansar; (*unwind*) relajarse ▷ *vt* (*one's grip*) soltar, aflojar; (*control*) relajar; (*mind, person*) descansar; **relaxation** [ri:læk'seɪʃən] *n* descanso; (*of rule, control*) relajamiento; (*entertainment*) diversión *f*; **relaxed** *adj* relajado; (*tranquil*) tranquilo; **relaxing** *adj* relajante

relay ['ri:leɪ] *n* (*race*) carrera de relevos ▷ *vt* (*Radio, TV*) retransmitir

release [rɪ'li:s] *n* (*liberation*) liberación *f*, (*from prison*) puesta en libertad; (*of gas etc*) escape *m*; (*of film etc*) estreno; (*of record*) lanzamiento ▷ *vt* (*prisoner*) poner en libertad; (*gas*) despedir, arrojar; (*from wreckage etc*) soltar; (*catch, spring etc*) desenganchar; (*film*) estrenar; (*book*) publicar; (*news*) difundir

relegate ['rɛləgeɪt] *vt* relegar; (*BRIT Sport*): **to be ~d to** bajar a

relent [rɪ'lɛnt] *vi* ablandarse; **relentless** *adj* implacable

relevant ['rɛləvənt] *adj* (*fact*) pertinente; **~ to** relacionado con

reliable [rɪ'laɪəbl] *adj* (*person, firm*) de confianza, de fiar; (*method, machine*) seguro; (*source*) fidedigno

relic ['rɛlɪk] *n* (*Rel*) reliquia; (*of the past*) vestigio

relief [rɪ'li:f] *n* (*from pain, anxiety*) alivio; (*help, supplies*) socorro, ayuda; (*Art, Geo*) relieve *m*

relieve [rɪ'li:v] *vt* (*pain*) aliviar; (*bring help to*) ayudar, socorrer; (*take over from*) sustituir; (: *guard*) relevar; **to ~ sb of sth** quitar algo a algn; **to ~ o.s.** hacer sus necesidades; **relieved** *adj*: **to be relieved** sentir un gran alivio

religion [rɪ'lɪdʒən] *n* religión *f*

religious [rɪ'lɪdʒəs] *adj* religioso; **religious education** *n* educación *f* religiosa

relish ['rɛlɪʃ] *n* (*Culin*) salsa; (*enjoyment*) entusiasmo ▷ *vt* (*food etc*) saborear; (*enjoy*): **to ~ sth** hacerle mucha ilusión a algn algo

relocate [ri:ləu'keɪt] *vt* cambiar de lugar, mudar ▷ *vi* mudarse

reluctance [rɪ'lʌktəns] *n* renuencia

reluctant [rɪ'lʌktənt] *adj* renuente; **reluctantly** *adv* de mala gana

rely on [rɪ'laɪ-] *vt fus* depender de; (*trust*) contar con

remain [rɪ'meɪn] *vi* (*survive*) quedar; (*be left*) sobrar; (*continue*) quedar(se), permanecer; **remainder** *n* resto; **remaining** *adj* que queda(n); (*surviving*) restante(s); **remains** *npl* restos *mpl*

remand [rɪ'mɑ:nd] *n*: **on ~** detenido (bajo custodia) ▷ *vt*: **to be ~ed in custody** quedar detenido bajo custodia

remark [rɪ'mɑ:k] *n* comentario ▷ *vt* comentar; **remarkable** *adj* (*outstanding*) extraordinario

remarry [ri:'mærɪ] *vi* volver a casarse

remedy ['rɛmədɪ] *n* remedio ▷ *vt* remediar, curar

remember [rɪ'mɛmbə*] *vt* recordar, acordarse de; (*bear in mind*) tener presente; (*send greetings to*): **~ me to him** dale recuerdos de mi parte; **Remembrance Day** *n* ≈ día en que se recuerda a los caídos en las dos guerras mundiales

● **REMEMBRANCE DAY**
●
● En el Reino Unido el domingo más

próximo al 11 de noviembre se conoce como **Remembrance Sunday** o **Remembrance Day**, aniversario de la firma del armisticio de 1918 que puso fin a la Primera Guerra Mundial. Ese día, a las once de la mañana (hora en que se firmó el armisticio), se recuerda a los que murieron en las dos guerras mundiales con dos minutos de silencio ante los monumentos a los caídos. Allí se colocan coronas de amapolas, flor que también se suele llevar prendida en el pecho tras pagar un donativo destinado a los inválidos de guerra.

remind [rɪ'maɪnd] vt: **to ~ sb to do sth** recordar a algn que haga algo; **to ~ sb of sth** (of fact) recordar algo a algn; **she ~s me of her mother** me recuerda a su madre; **reminder** n notificación f; (memento) recuerdo

reminiscent [remɪ'nɪsnt] adj: **to be ~ of sth** recordar algo

remnant ['remnənt] n resto; (of cloth) retal m

remorse [rɪ'mɔːs] n remordimientos mpl

remote [rɪ'məut] adj (distant) lejano; (person) distante; **remote control** n telecontrol m; **remotely** adv remotamente; (slightly) levemente

removal [rɪ'muːvəl] n (taking away) el quitar; (BRIT: from house) mudanza; (from office: dismissal) destitución f; (Med) extirpación f; **removal man** (irreg) n (BRIT) mozo de mudanzas; **removal van** (BRIT) n camión m de mudanzas

remove [rɪ'muːv] vt quitar; (employee) destituir; (name: from list) tachar, borrar; (doubt) disipar; (abuse) suprimir, acabar con; (Med) extirpar

Renaissance [rɪ'neɪsɑ̃s] n: **the ~** el Renacimiento

rename [riː'neɪm] vt poner nuevo nombre a

render ['rendə*] vt (thanks) dar; (aid) proporcionar, prestar; (make): **to ~ sth useless** hacer algo inútil

rendezvous ['rɔndɪvuː] n cita

renew [rɪ'njuː] vt (resume) reanudar; (loan etc) prorrogar

renovate ['renəveɪt] vt renovar

renowned [rɪ'naund] adj renombrado

rent [rent] n (for house) arriendo, renta ▷ vt alquilar; **rental** n (for television, car) alquiler m

reorganize [riː'ɔːgənaɪz] vt reorganizar

rep [rep] n abbr = **representative**

repair [rɪ'peə*] n reparación f, compostura ▷ vt reparar, componer; (shoes) remendar; **in good/bad ~** en buen/mal estado; **repair kit** n caja de herramientas

repay [riː'peɪ] vt (money) devolver, reembolsar; (person) pagar; (debt) liquidar; (sb's efforts) devolver, corresponder a; **repayment** n reembolso, devolución f; (sum of money) recompensa

repeat [rɪ'piːt] n (Radio, TV) reposición f ▷ vt repetir ▷ vi repetirse; **repeatedly** adv repetidas veces; **repeat prescription** n (BRIT) receta renovada

repellent [rɪ'pelənt] adj repugnante ▷ n: **insect ~** crema or loción f anti-insectos

repercussions [riːpə'kʌʃənz] npl consecuencias fpl

repetition [repɪ'tɪʃən] n repetición f

repetitive [rɪ'petɪtɪv] adj repetitivo

replace [rɪ'pleɪs] vt (put back) devolver a su sitio; (take the place) reemplazar, sustituir; **replacement** n (act) reposición f; (thing) recambio; (person) suplente mf

replay ['riːpleɪ] n (Sport) desempate m; (of tape, film) repetición f

replica ['replɪkə] n copia, reproducción f (exacta)

reply [rɪ'plaɪ] n respuesta, contestación f ▷ vi contestar, responder

report [rɪ'pɔːt] n informe m; (Press etc) reportaje m; (BRIT: also: **school ~**) boletín m escolar; (of gun) estallido ▷ vt informar de; (Press etc) hacer un reportaje sobre; (notify: accident, culprit) denunciar ▷ vi (make a report) presentar un informe; (present o.s.): **to ~ (to sb)** presentarse (ante algn); **report card** n (US, SCOTTISH) cartilla escolar; **reportedly** adv según se dice; **reporter** n periodista mf

represent [reprɪ'zent] vt representar; (Comm) ser agente de; (describe): **to ~ sth as** describir algo como; **representation** [-'teɪʃən] n representación f; **representative** n representante mf; (US Pol) diputado/a m/f ▷ adj representativo

repress [rɪ'pres] vt reprimir; **repression** [-'preʃən] n represión f

reprimand ['reprɪmɑːnd] n reprimenda ▷ vt reprender

reproduce [riːprə'djuːs] vt reproducir ▷ vi reproducirse; **reproduction** [-'dʌkʃən] n reproducción f

reptile ['reptaɪl] n reptil m

republic [rɪ'pʌblɪk] n república; **republican** adj, n republicano/a m/f

reputable ['repjutəbl] adj (make etc) de renombre

reputation [repju'teɪʃən] n reputación f

request [rɪ'kwest] n petición f; (formal)

solicitud f ▷ vt: **to ~ sth of** or **from sb** solicitar algo a algn; **request stop** (BRIT) n parada discrecional

require [rɪˈkwaɪə*] vt (need: person) necesitar, tener necesidad de; (: thing, situation) exigir; (want) pedir; **to ~ sb to do sth** pedir a algn que haga algo; **requirement** n requisito; (need) necesidad f

resat [riːˈsæt] pt, pp of **resit**

rescue [ˈrɛskjuː] n rescate m ▷ vt rescatar

research [rɪˈsəːtʃ] n investigaciones fpl ▷ vt investigar

resemblance [rɪˈzɛmbləns] n parecido

resemble [rɪˈzɛmbl] vt parecerse a

resent [rɪˈzɛnt] vt tomar a mal; **resentful** adj resentido; **resentment** n resentimiento

reservation [rɛzəˈveɪʃən] n reserva; **reservation desk** (US) n (in hotel) recepción f

reserve [rɪˈzəːv] n reserva; (Sport) suplente mf ▷ vt (seats etc) reservar; **reserved** adj reservado

reservoir [ˈrɛzəvwɑː*] n (artificial lake) embalse m, tank; (small) depósito

residence [ˈrɛzɪdəns] n (formal: home) domicilio; (length of stay) permanencia; **residence permit** (BRIT) n permiso de permanencia

resident [ˈrɛzɪdənt] n (of area) vecino/a; (in hotel) huésped mf ▷ adj (population) permanente; (doctor) residente; **residential** [-ˈdɛnʃəl] adj residencial

residue [ˈrɛzɪdjuː] n resto

resign [rɪˈzaɪn] vt renunciar a ▷ vi dimitir; **to ~ o.s. to** (situation) resignarse a; **resignation** [rɛzɪɡˈneɪʃən] n dimisión f; (state of mind) resignación f

resin [ˈrɛzɪn] n resina

resist [rɪˈzɪst] vt resistir, oponerse a; **resistance** n resistencia

resit [ˈriːsɪt] (BRIT) (pt, pp **resat**) vt (exam) volver a presentarse a; (subject) recuperar, volver a examinarse de (SP)

resolution [rɛzəˈluːʃən] n resolución f

resolve [rɪˈzɔlv] n resolución f ▷ vt resolver ▷ vi: **to ~ to do** resolver hacer

resort [rɪˈzɔːt] n (town) centro turístico; (recourse) recurso ▷ vi: **to ~ to** recurrir a; **in the last ~** como último recurso

resource [rɪˈsɔːs] n recurso; **resourceful** adj despabilado, ingenioso

respect [rɪsˈpɛkt] n respeto ▷ vt respetar; **respectable** adj respetable; (large: amount) apreciable; (passable) tolerable; **respectful** adj respetuoso; **respective** adj respectivo; **respectively** adv respectivamente

respite [ˈrɛspaɪt] n respiro

respond [rɪsˈpɔnd] vi responder; (react) reaccionar; **response** [-ˈpɔns] n respuesta; reacción f

responsibility [rɪspɔnsɪˈbɪlɪtɪ] n responsabilidad f

responsible [rɪsˈpɔnsɪbl] adj (character) serio, formal; (job) de confianza; (liable): **~ (for)** responsable (de); **responsibly** adv con seriedad

responsive [rɪsˈpɔnsɪv] adj sensible

rest [rɛst] n descanso, reposo; (Mus: pause) pausa, silencio; (support) apoyo; (remainder) resto ▷ vi descansar; (be supported): **to ~ on** descansar sobre ▷ vt: **to ~ sth on/against** apoyar algo en or sobre/contra; **the ~ of them** (people, objects) los demás; **it ~s with him to ...** depende de él el que ...

restaurant [ˈrɛstərɔŋ] n restaurante m; **restaurant car** (BRIT) n (Rail) coche-comedor m

restless [ˈrɛstlɪs] adj inquieto

restoration [rɛstəˈreɪʃən] n restauración f; devolución f

restore [rɪˈstɔː*] vt (building) restaurar; (sth stolen) devolver; (health) restablecer; (to power) volver a poner a

restrain [rɪsˈtreɪn] vt (feeling) contener, refrenar; (person): **to ~ (from doing)** disuadir (de hacer); **restraint** n (restriction) restricción f; (moderation) moderación f; (of manner) reserva

restrict [rɪsˈtrɪkt] vt restringir, limitar; **restriction** [-kʃən] n restricción f, limitación f

rest room (US) n aseos mpl

restructure [riːˈstrʌktʃə*] vt reestructurar

result [rɪˈzʌlt] n resultado ▷ vi: **to ~ in** terminar en, tener por resultado; **as a ~ of** a consecuencia de

resume [rɪˈzjuːm] vt reanudar ▷ vi comenzar de nuevo

■ Be careful not to translate **resume** by the Spanish word resumir.

résumé [ˈreɪzjuːmeɪ] n resumen m; (US) currículum m

resuscitate [rɪˈsʌsɪteɪt] vt (Med) resucitar

retail [ˈriːteɪl] adj, adv al por menor; **retailer** n detallista mf

retain [rɪˈteɪn] vt (keep) retener, conservar

retaliation [rɪtælɪˈeɪʃən] n represalias fpl

retarded [rɪˈtɑːdɪd] adj retrasado

retire [rɪˈtaɪə*] vi (give up work) jubilarse; (withdraw) retirarse; (go to bed) acostarse; **retired** adj (person) jubilado; **retirement** n (giving up work: state) retiro; (: act) jubilación f

retort [rɪ'tɔ:t] *vi* contestar

retreat [rɪ'tri:t] *n* (*place*) retiro; (*Mil*) retirada ▷ *vi* retirarse

retrieve [rɪ'tri:v] *vt* recobrar; (*situation, honour*) salvar; (*Comput*) recuperar; (*error*) reparar

retrospect ['rɛtrəspɛkt] *n*: **in ~** retrospectivamente; **retrospective** [-'spɛktɪv] *adj* retrospectivo; (*law*) retroactivo

return [rɪ'tə:n] *n* (*going or coming back*) vuelta, regreso; (*of sth stolen etc*) devolución *f*; (*Finance: from land, shares*) ganancia, ingresos *mpl* ▷ *cpd* (*journey*) de regreso; (*BRIT: ticket*) de ida y vuelta; (*match*) de vuelta ▷ *vi* (*person etc: come or go back*) volver, regresar; (*symptoms etc*) reaparecer; (*regain*): **to ~ to** recuperar ▷ *vt* devolver; (*favour, love etc*) corresponder a; (*verdict*) pronunciar; (*Pol: candidate*) elegir; **returns** *npl* (*Comm*) ingresos *mpl*; **in ~ (for)** a cambio (de); **by ~ of post** a vuelta de correo; **many happy ~s (of the day)!** ¡feliz cumpleaños!; **return ticket** *n* (*esp BRIT*) billete *m* (*SP*) *or* boleto *m* (*LAM*) de ida y vuelta, billete *m* redondo (*MEX*)

reunion [ri:'ju:nɪən] *n* (*of family*) reunión *f*; (*of two people, school*) reencuentro

reunite [ri:ju:'naɪt] *vt* reunir; (*reconcile*) reconciliar

revamp [ri:'væmp] *vt* renovar

reveal [rɪ'vi:l] *vt* revelar; **revealing** *adj* revelador(a)

revel ['rɛvl] *vi*: **to ~ in sth/in doing sth** gozar de algo/con hacer algo

revelation [rɛvə'leɪʃən] *n* revelación *f*

revenge [rɪ'vɛndʒ] *n* venganza; **to take ~ on** vengarse de

revenue ['rɛvənju:] *n* ingresos *mpl*, rentas *fpl*

Reverend ['rɛvərənd] *adj* (*in titles*): **the ~ John Smith** (*Anglican*) el Reverendo John Smith; (*Catholic*) el Padre John Smith; (*Protestant*) el Pastor John Smith

reversal [rɪ'və:sl] *n* (*of order*) inversión *f*; (*of direction, policy*) cambio; (*of decision*) revocación *f*

reverse [rɪ'və:s] *n* (*opposite*) contrario; (*back: of cloth*) revés *m*; (: *of coin*) reverso; (: *of paper*) dorso; (*Aut: also: ~ gear*) marcha atrás, revés *m* ▷ *adj* (*order*) inverso; (*direction*) contrario; (*process*) opuesto ▷ *vt* (*decision, Aut*) dar marcha atrás a; (*position, function*) invertir ▷ *vi* (*BRIT Aut*) dar marcha atrás; **reverse-charge call** (*BRIT*) *n* llamada a cobro revertido; **reversing lights** (*BRIT*) *npl* (*Aut*) luces *fpl* de retroceso

revert [rɪ'və:t] *vi*: **to ~ to** volver a

review [rɪ'vju:] *n* (*magazine, Mil*) revista; (*of book, film*) reseña; (*US: examination*) repaso, examen *m* ▷ *vt* repasar, examinar; (*Mil*) pasar revista a; (*book, film*) reseñar

revise [rɪ'vaɪz] *vt* (*manuscript*) corregir; (*opinion*) modificar; (*price, procedure*) revisar ▷ *vi* (*study*) repasar; **revision** [rɪ'vɪʒən] *n* corrección *f*; modificación *f*; (*for exam*) repaso

revival [rɪ'vaɪvəl] *n* (*recovery*) reanimación *f*; (*of interest*) renacimiento; (*Theatre*) reestreno; (*of faith*) despertar *m*

revive [rɪ'vaɪv] *vt* resucitar; (*custom*) restablecer; (*hope*) despertar; (*play*) reestrenar ▷ *vi* (*person*) volver en sí; (*business*) reactivarse

revolt [rɪ'vəʊlt] *n* rebelión *f* ▷ *vi* rebelarse, sublevarse ▷ *vt* dar asco a, repugnar; **revolting** *adj* asqueroso, repugnante

revolution [rɛvə'lu:ʃən] *n* revolución *f*; **revolutionary** *adj, n* revolucionario/a *m/f*

revolve [rɪ'vɒlv] *vi* dar vueltas, girar; (*life, discussion*): **to ~ (a)round** girar en torno a

revolver [rɪ'vɒlvə*] *n* revólver *m*

reward [rɪ'wɔ:d] *n* premio, recompensa ▷ *vt*: **to ~ (for)** recompensar *or* premiar (por); **rewarding** *adj* (*fig*) valioso

rewind [ri:'waɪnd] *vt* rebobinar

rewritable [ri:'raɪtəbl] *adj* (*CD, DVD*) reescribible

rewrite [ri:'raɪt] (*pt* **rewrote**, *pp* **rewritten**) *vt* reescribir

rheumatism ['ru:mətɪzəm] *n* reumatismo, reúma *m*

rhinoceros [raɪ'nɒsərəs] *n* rinoceronte *m*

rhubarb ['ru:ba:b] *n* ruibarbo

rhyme [raɪm] *n* rima; (*verse*) poesía

rhythm ['rɪðm] *n* ritmo

rib [rɪb] *n* (*Anat*) costilla ▷ *vt* (*mock*) tomar el pelo a

ribbon ['rɪbən] *n* cinta; **in ~s** (*torn*) hecho trizas

rice [raɪs] *n* arroz *m*; **rice pudding** *n* arroz *m* con leche

rich [rɪtʃ] *adj* rico; (*soil*) fértil; (*food*) pesado; (: *sweet*) empalagoso; (*abundant*): **~ in** (*minerals etc*) rico en

rid [rɪd] (*pt, pp* **~**) *vt*: **to ~ sb of sth** librar a algn de algo; **to get ~ of** deshacerse *or* desembarazarse de

riddle ['rɪdl] *n* (*puzzle*) acertijo; (*mystery*) enigma *m*, misterio ▷ *vt*: **to be ~d with** ser lleno *or* plagado de

ride [raɪd] (*pt* **rode**, *pp* **ridden**) *n* paseo; (*distance covered*) viaje *m*, recorrido ▷ *vi* (*as sport*) montar; (*go somewhere: on horse, bicycle*) dar un paseo, pasearse; (*travel: on bicycle, motorcycle, bus*) viajar ▷ *vt* (*a horse*)

r

montar a; (a bicycle, motorcycle) andar en;
(distance) recorrer; **to take sb for a ~** (fig)
engañar a algn; **rider** n (on horse) jinete
mf; (on bicycle) ciclista mf; (on motorcycle)
motociclista mf

ridge [rɪdʒ] n (of hill) cresta; (of roof)
caballete m; (wrinkle) arruga

ridicule ['rɪdɪkjuːl] n irrisión f, burla ▷ vt
poner en ridículo, burlarse de; **ridiculous**
[-'dɪkjuləs] adj ridículo

riding ['raɪdɪŋ] n equitación f; **I like ~** me
gusta montar a caballo; **riding school** n
escuela de equitación

rife [raɪf] adj: **to be ~** ser muy común; **to be
~ with** abundar en

rifle ['raɪfl] n rifle m, fusil m ▷ vt saquear

rift [rɪft] n (in clouds) claro;
(fig: disagreement) desavenencia

rig [rɪg] n (also: **oil ~**: at sea) plataforma
petrolera ▷ vt (election etc) amañar

right [raɪt] adj (correct) correcto, exacto;
(suitable) indicado, debido; (proper)
apropiado; (just) justo; (morally good)
bueno; (not left) derecho ▷ n bueno;
(title, claim) derecho; (not left) derecha
▷ adv bien, correctamente; (not left) a la
derecha; (exactly): **~ now** ahora mismo ▷ vt
enderezar; (correct) corregir ▷ excl ¡bueno!,
¡está bien!; **to be ~** (person) tener razón;
(answer) ser correcto; **is that the ~ time?**
(of clock) ¿es esa la hora buena?; **by ~s** en
justicia; **on the ~** a la derecha; **to be in
the ~** tener razón; **~ away** en seguida; **~
in the middle** exactamente en el centro;
right angle n ángulo recto; **rightful** adj
legítimo; **right-hand** adj: **right-hand drive**
conducción f por la derecha; **the right-hand
side** derecha; **right-handed** adj diestro;
rightly adv correctamente, debidamente;
(with reason) con razón; **right of way** n (on
path etc) derecho de paso; (Aut) prioridad f;
right-wing adj (Pol) derechista

rigid ['rɪdʒɪd] adj rígido; (person, ideas)
inflexible

rigorous ['rɪgərəs] adj riguroso

rim [rɪm] n borde m; (of spectacles) aro; (of
wheel) llanta

rind [raɪnd] n (of bacon) corteza; (of lemon
etc) cáscara; (of cheese) costra

ring [rɪŋ] n (pt **rang**, pp **rung**) n (of metal)
aro; (on finger) anillo; (of people) corro; (of
objects) círculo; (gang) banda; (for boxing)
cuadrilátero; (of circus) pista; (bull ring)
ruedo, plaza; (sound of bell) toque m ▷ vi
(on telephone) llamar por teléfono; (bell)
repicar; (doorbell, phone) sonar; (also: **~ out**)
sonar; (ears) zumbar ▷ vt (BRIT Tel) llamar,
telefonear; (bell etc) hacer sonar; (doorbell)

tocar; **to give sb a ~** (BRIT Tel) llamar or
telefonear a algn; **ring back** (BRIT) vt, vi
(Tel) devolver la llamada; **ring off** (BRIT) vi
(Tel) colgar, cortar la comunicación; **ring up**
(BRIT) vt (Tel) llamar, telefonear; **ringing
tone** n (Tel) tono de llamada; **ringleader**
n (of gang) cabecilla m; **ring road** (BRIT) n
carretera periférica or de circunvalación;
ringtone n (on mobile) tono de llamada

rink [rɪŋk] n (also: **ice ~**) pista de hielo

rinse [rɪns] n aclarado; (dye) tinte m ▷ vt
aclarar; (mouth) enjuagar

riot ['raɪət] n motín m, disturbio ▷ vi
amotinarse; **to run ~** desmandarse

rip [rɪp] n rasgón m, rasgadura ▷ vt rasgar,
desgarrar ▷ vi rasgarse, desgarrarse; **rip
off** vt (inf: cheat) estafar; **rip up** vt hacer
pedazos

ripe [raɪp] adj maduro

rip-off ['rɪpɔf] n (inf): **it's a ~!** ¡es una
estafa!, ¡es un timo!

ripple ['rɪpl] n onda, rizo; (sound)
murmullo ▷ vi rizarse

rise [raɪz] (pt **rose**, pp **risen**) n (slope)
cuesta, pendiente f; (hill) altura; (BRIT: in
wages) aumento; (in prices, temperature)
subida; (fig: to power etc) ascenso ▷ vi
subir; (waters) crecer; (sun, moon) salir;
(person: from bed etc) levantarse; (also: **~
up**: rebel) sublevarse; (in rank) ascender;
to give ~ to dar lugar or origen a; **to ~ to
the occasion** ponerse a la altura de las
circunstancias; **risen** ['rɪzn] pp of **rise**;
rising adj (increasing: number) creciente;
(: prices) en aumento or alza; (tide) creciente;
(sun, moon) naciente

risk [rɪsk] n riesgo, peligro ▷ vt arriesgar;
(run the risk of) exponerse a; **to take** or **run
the ~ of doing** correr el riesgo de hacer; **at
~** en peligro; **at one's own ~** bajo su propia
responsabilidad; **risky** adj arriesgado,
peligroso

rite [raɪt] n rito; **last ~s** exequias fpl

ritual ['rɪtjuəl] adj ritual ▷ n ritual m, rito

rival ['raɪvl] n rival mf; (in business)
competidor(a) m/f ▷ adj rival, opuesto ▷ vt
competir con; **rivalry** n competencia

river ['rɪvə*] n río ▷ cpd (port) de río;
(traffic) fluvial; **up/down ~** río arriba/abajo;
riverbank n orilla (del río)

rivet ['rɪvɪt] n roblón m, remache m ▷ vt
(fig) captar

road [rəud] n camino; (motorway etc)
carretera; (in town) calle f ▷ cpd (accident) de
tráfico; **major/minor ~** carretera principal/
secundaria; **roadblock** n barricada; **road
map** n mapa m de carreteras; **road rage**
n agresividad en la carretera; **road safety** n

seguridad f vial; **roadside** n borde m (del camino); **roadsign** n señal f de tráfico; **road tax** n (BRIT) impuesto m de rodaje; **roadworks** npl obras fpl

roam [rəum] vi vagar

roar [rɔː*] n rugido; (of vehicle, storm) estruendo; (of laughter) carcajada ▷ vi rugir; hacer estruendo; **to ~ with laughter** reírse a carcajadas; **to do a ~ing trade** hacer buen negocio

roast [rəust] n carne f asada, asado ▷ vt asar; (coffee) tostar; **roast beef** n rosbif m

rob [rɔb] vt robar; **to ~ sb of sth** robar algo a algn; (fig: deprive) quitar algo a algn; **robber** n ladrón/ona m/f; **robbery** n robo

robe [rəub] n (for ceremony etc) toga; (also: **bath~**) albornoz m

robin ['rɔbɪn] n petirrojo

robot ['rəubɔt] n robot m

robust [rəu'bʌst] adj robusto, fuerte

rock [rɔk] n roca; (boulder) peña, peñasco; (US: small stone) piedrecita; (BRIT: sweet) ≈ pirulí ▷ vt (swing gently: cradle) balancear, mecer; (: child) arrullar; (shake) sacudir ▷ vi mecerse, balancearse; sacudirse; **on the ~s** (drink) con hielo; (marriage etc) en ruinas; **rock and roll** n rocanrol m; **rock climbing** n (Sport) escalada

rocket ['rɔkɪt] n cohete m; **rocking chair** ['rɔkɪŋ-] n mecedora

rocky ['rɔkɪ] adj rocoso

rod [rɔd] n vara, varilla; (also: **fishing ~**) caña

rode [rəud] pt of **ride**

rodent ['rəudnt] n roedor m

rogue [rəug] n pícaro, pillo

role [rəul] n papel m; **role-model** n modelo a imitar

roll [rəul] n rollo; (of bank notes) fajo; (also: **bread ~**) panecillo; (register, list) lista, nómina; (sound of drums etc) redoble m ▷ vt hacer rodar; (also: **~ up**: string) enrollar; (cigarette) liar; (also: **~ out**: pastry) aplanar; (flatten: road, lawn) apisonar ▷ vi rodar; (drum) redoblar; (ship) balancearse; **roll over** vi dar una vuelta; **roll up** vi (inf: arrive) aparecer ▷ vt (carpet) arrollar; (: sleeves) arremangar; **roller** n rodillo; (wheel) rueda; (for road) apisonadora; (for hair) rulo; **Rollerblades®** npl patines mpl en línea; **roller coaster** n montaña rusa; **roller skates** npl patines mpl de rueda; **roller-skating** n patinaje sobre ruedas; **to go roller-skating** ir a patinar (sobre ruedas); **rolling pin** n rodillo (de cocina)

ROM [rɔm] n abbr (Comput: = read only memory) ROM f

Roman ['rəumən] (irreg) adj romano/a;

Roman Catholic (irreg) adj, n católico/a m/f (romano/a)

romance [rə'mæns] n (love affair) amor m; (charm) lo romántico; (novel) novela de amor

Romania etc [ruː'meɪnɪə] n = **Rumania** etc

Roman numeral n número romano

romantic [rə'mæntɪk] adj romántico

Rome [rəum] n Roma

roof [ruːf] (pl **~s**) n techo; (of house) techo, tejado ▷ vt techar, poner techo a; **the ~ of the mouth** el paladar; **roof rack** n (Aut) baca, portaequipajes m inv

rook [ruk] n (bird) graja; (Chess) torre f

room [ruːm] n cuarto, habitación f; (also: **bed~**) dormitorio, recámara (MEX), pieza (SC); (in school etc) sala; (space, scope) sitio, cabida; **roommate** n compañero/a de cuarto; **room service** n servicio de habitaciones; **roomy** adj espacioso; (garment) amplio

rooster ['ruːstə*] n gallo

root [ruːt] n raíz f ▷ vi arraigarse

rope [rəup] n cuerda; (Naut) cable m ▷ vt (tie) atar or amarrar con (una) cuerda; (climbers: also: **~ together**) encordarse; (an area: also: **~ off**) acordonar; **to know the ~s** (fig) conocer los trucos (del oficio)

rose [rəuz] pt of **rise** ▷ n rosa; (shrub) rosal m; (on watering can) roseta

rosé ['rəuzeɪ] n vino rosado

rosemary ['rəuzmərɪ] n romero

rosy ['rəuzɪ] adj rosado, sonrosado; **a ~ future** un futuro prometedor

rot [rɔt] n podredumbre f; (fig: pej) tonterías fpl ▷ vt pudrir ▷ vi pudrirse

rota ['rəutə] n (sistema m de) turnos m

rotate [rəu'teɪt] vt (revolve) hacer girar, dar vueltas a; (jobs) alternar ▷ vi girar, dar vueltas

rotten ['rɔtn] adj podrido; (dishonest) corrompido; (inf: bad) pocho; **to feel ~** (ill) sentirse fatal

rough [rʌf] adj (skin, surface) áspero; (terrain) quebrado; (road) desigual; (voice) bronco; (person, manner) tosco, grosero; (weather) borrascoso; (treatment) brutal; (sea) picado; (town, area) peligroso; (cloth) basto; (plan) preliminar; (guess) aproximado ▷ n (Golf): **in the ~** en las hierbas altas; **to ~ it** vivir sin comodidades; **to sleep ~** (BRIT) pasar la noche al raso; **roughly** adv (handle) torpemente; (make) toscamente; (speak) groseramente; (approximately) aproximadamente

roulette [ruː'let] n ruleta

round [raund] adj redondo ▷ n círculo; (BRIT: of toast) rebanada; (of policeman) ronda; (of milkman) recorrido; (of doctor) visitas *fpl*; (*game: of cards, in competition*) partida; (*of ammunition*) cartucho; (*Boxing*) asalto; (*of talks*) ronda ▷ *vt* (*corner*) doblar ▷ *prep* alrededor de; (*surrounding*): **~ his neck/the table** en su cuello/alrededor de la mesa; (*in a circular movement*): **to move ~ the room/sail ~ the world** dar una vuelta a la habitación/circunnavigar el mundo; (*in various directions*): **to move ~ a room/house** moverse por toda la habitación/casa; (*approximately*) alrededor de ▷ *adv*: **all ~** por todos lados; **the long way ~** por el camino menos directo; **all (the) year ~** durante todo el año; **it's just ~ the corner** (*fig*) está a la vuelta de la esquina; **~ the clock** *adv* las 24 horas; **to go ~ to sb's (house)** ir a casa de algn; **to go ~ the back** pasar por atrás; **enough to go ~** bastante (para todos); **a ~ of applause** una salva de aplausos; **a ~ of drinks/sandwiches** una ronda de bebidas/bocadillos; **round off** *vt* (*speech etc*) acabar, poner término a; **round up** *vt* (*cattle*) acorralar; (*people*) reunir; (*price*) redondear; **roundabout** (*BRIT*) *n* (*Aut*) isleta; (*at fair*) tiovivo ▷ *adj* (*route, means*) indirecto; **round trip** *n* viaje *m* de ida y vuelta; **roundup** *n* rodeo; (*of criminals*) redada; (*of news*) resumen *m*

rouse [rauz] *vt* (*wake up*) despertar; (*stir up*) suscitar

route [ruːt] *n* ruta, camino; (*of bus*) recorrido; (*of shipping*) derrota

routine [ruːˈtiːn] *adj* rutinario ▷ *n* rutina; (*Theatre*) número

row¹ [rəu] *n* (*line*) fila, hilera; (*Knitting*) pasada ▷ *vi* (*in boat*) remar ▷ *vt* conducir remando; **4 days in a ~** 4 días seguidos

row² [rau] *n* (*racket*) escándalo; (*dispute*) bronca, pelea; (*scolding*) regaño ▷ *vi* pelear(se)

rowboat [ˈrəubəut] (*US*) = **rowing boat**

rowing [ˈrəuɪŋ] *n* remo; **rowing boat** (*BRIT*) *n* bote *m* de remos

royal [ˈrɔɪəl] *adj* real; **royalty** *n* (*royal persons*) familia real; (*payment to author*) derechos *mpl* de autor

rpm *abbr* (= *revs per minute*) r.p.m.

R.S.V.P. *abbr* (= *répondez s'il vous plaôt*) SRC

Rt. Hon. *abbr* (*BRIT*) (= *Right Honourable*) título honorífico de diputado

rub [rʌb] *vt* frotar; (*scrub*) restregar ▷ *n*: **to give sth a ~** frotar algo; **to ~ sb up** *or* **~ sb** (*US*) **the wrong way** entrarle a algn por mal ojo; **rub in** *vt* (*ointment*) aplicar frotando; **rub off** *vi* borrarse; **rub out** *vt* borrar

rubber [ˈrʌbə*] *n* caucho, goma; (*BRIT: eraser*) goma de borrar; **rubber band** *n* goma, gomita; **rubber gloves** *npl* guantes

mpl de goma

rubbish [ˈrʌbɪʃ] (*BRIT*) *n* basura; (*waste*) desperdicios *mpl*; (*fig: pej*) tonterías *fpl*; (*junk*) pacotilla; **rubbish bin** (*BRIT*) *n* cubo *or* bote *m* (*MEX*) *or* tacho (*SC*) de la basura; **rubbish dump** (*BRIT*) *n* vertedero, basurero

rubble [ˈrʌbl] *n* escombros *mpl*

ruby [ˈruːbɪ] *n* rubí *m*

rucksack [ˈrʌksæk] *n* mochila

rudder [ˈrʌdə*] *n* timón *m*

rude [ruːd] *adj* (*impolite: person*) mal educado; (*: word, manners*) grosero; (*crude*) crudo; (*indecent*) indecente

ruffle [ˈrʌfl] *vt* (*hair*) despeinar; (*clothes*) arrugar; **to get ~d** (*fig: person*) alterarse

rug [rʌg] *n* alfombra; (*BRIT: blanket*) manta

rugby [ˈrʌgbɪ] *n* rugby *m*

rugged [ˈrʌgɪd] *adj* (*landscape*) accidentado; (*features*) robusto

ruin [ˈruːɪn] *n* ruina ▷ *vt* arruinar; (*spoil*) estropear; **ruins** *npl* ruinas *fpl*, restos *mpl*

rule [ruːl] *n* (*norm*) norma, costumbre *f*; (*regulation, ruler*) regla; (*government*) dominio ▷ *vi* gobernar; (*Law*) fallar; **as a ~** por regla general; **rule out** *vt* excluir; **ruler** *n* (*sovereign*) soberano; (*for measuring*) regla; **ruling** *adj* (*party*) gobernante; (*class*) dirigente ▷ *n* (*Law*) fallo, decisión *f*

rum [rʌm] *n* ron *m*

Rumania [ruːˈmeɪnɪə] *n* Rumanía; **Rumanian** *adj* rumano/a ▷ *n* rumano/a *m/f*; (*Ling*) rumano

rumble [ˈrʌmbl] *n* (*noise*) ruido sordo ▷ *vi* retumbar, hacer un ruido sordo; (*stomach, pipe*) sonar

rumour [ˈruːmə*] (*US* **rumor**) *n* rumor *m* ▷ *vt*: **it is ~ed that ...** se rumorea que ...

rump steak *n* filete *m* de lomo

run [rʌn] (*pt* **ran**, *pp* **run**) *n* (*fast pace*): **at a ~** corriendo; (*Sport, in tights*) carrera; (*outing*) paseo, excursión *f*; (*distance travelled*) trayecto; (*series*) serie *f*; (*Theatre*) temporada; (*Ski*) pista ▷ *vt* correr; (*operate: business*) dirigir; (*: competition, course*) organizar; (*: hotel, house*) administrar, llevar; (*Comput*) ejecutar; (*pass: hand*) pasar; (*Press: feature*) publicar ▷ *vi* correr; (*work: machine*) funcionar, marchar; (*bus, train: operate*) circular, ir; (*: travel*) ir; (*continue: play*) seguir; (*contract*) ser válido; (*flow: river*) fluir; (*colours, washing*) desteñirse; (*in election*) ser candidato; **there was a ~ on** (*meat, tickets*) hubo mucha demanda de; **in the long ~** a la larga; **on the ~** en fuga; **I'll ~ you to the station** te llevaré a la estación (en coche); **to ~ a risk** correr un riesgo; **to ~ a bath** llenar la bañera; **run after** *vt fus* (*to* catch up) correr tras; (chase) perseguir; **run away** vi huir; **run down** vt (production) ir reduciendo; (factory) ir restringiendo la producción en; (car) atropellar; (criticize) criticar; **to be run down** (person: tired) estar debilitado; **run into** vt fus (meet: person, trouble) tropezar con; (collide with) chocar con; **run off** vt (water) dejar correr; (copies) sacar ▷ vi huir corriendo; **run out** vi (person) salir corriendo; (liquid) irse; (lease) caducar, vencer; (money etc) acabarse; **run out of** vt fus quedar sin; **run over** vt (Aut) atropellar ▷ vt fus (revise) repasar; **run through** vt fus (instructions) repasar; **run up** vt (debt) contraer; **to run up against** (difficulties) tropezar con; **runaway** adj (horse) desbocado; (truck) sin frenos; (child) escapado de casa

rung [rʌŋ] pp of **ring** ▷ n (of ladder) escalón m, peldaño

runner ['rʌnə*] n (in race: person) corredor(a) m/f; (: horse) caballo; (on sledge) patín m; **runner bean** (BRIT) n = judía verde; **runner-up** n subcampeón/ona m/f

running ['rʌnɪŋ] n (sport) atletismo; (of business) administración f ▷ adj (water, costs) corriente; (commentary) continuo; **to be in/out of the ~ for sth** tener/no tener posibilidades de ganar algo; **6 days ~** 6 días seguidos

runny ['rʌnɪ] adj fluido; (nose, eyes) gastante

run-up ['rʌnʌp] n: **~ to** (election etc) período previo a

runway ['rʌnweɪ] n (Aviat) pista de aterrizaje

rupture ['rʌptʃə*] n (Med) hernia ▷ vt: **to ~ o.s** causarse una hernia

rural ['ruərl] adj rural

rush [rʌʃ] n ímpetu m; (hurry) prisa; (Comm) demanda repentina; (current) corriente f fuerte; (of feeling) torrente m; (Bot) junco ▷ vt apresurar; (work) hacer de prisa ▷ vi correr, precipitarse; **rush hour** n horas fpl punta

Russia ['rʌʃə] n Rusia; **Russian** adj ruso/a ▷ n ruso/a m/f; (Ling) ruso

rust [rʌst] n herrumbre f, moho ▷ vi oxidarse

rusty ['rʌstɪ] adj oxidado

ruthless ['ru:θlɪs] adj despiadado

RV (US) n abbr = **recreational vehicle**

rye [raɪ] n centeno

S

Sabbath ['sæbəθ] n domingo; (Jewish) sábado

sabotage ['sæbətɑ:ʒ] n sabotaje m ▷ vt sabotear

saccharin(e) ['sækərɪn] n sacarina

sachet ['sæʃeɪ] n sobrecito

sack [sæk] n (bag) saco, costal m ▷ vt (dismiss) despedir; (plunder) saquear; **to get the ~** ser despedido

sacred ['seɪkrɪd] adj sagrado, santo

sacrifice ['sækrɪfaɪs] n sacrificio ▷ vt sacrificar

sad [sæd] adj (unhappy) triste; (deplorable) lamentable

saddle ['sædl] n silla (de montar); (of cycle) sillín m ▷ vt (horse) ensillar; **to be ~d with sth** (inf) quedar cargado con algo

sadistic [sə'dɪstɪk] adj sádico

sadly ['sædlɪ] adv lamentablemente; **to be ~ lacking in** estar por desgracia carente de

sadness ['sædnɪs] n tristeza

s.a.e. abbr (= stamped addressed envelope) sobre con las propias señas de uno y con sello

safari [sə'fɑ:rɪ] n safari m

safe [seɪf] adj (out of danger) fuera de peligro; (not dangerous, sure) seguro; (unharmed) ileso ▷ n caja de caudales, caja fuerte; **~ and sound** sano y salvo; **(just) to be on the ~ side** para mayor seguridad; **safely** adv seguramente, con seguridad; **to arrive safely** llegar bien; **safe sex** n sexo seguro or sin riesgo

safety ['seɪftɪ] n seguridad f; **safety belt** n cinturón m (de seguridad); **safety pin** n imperdible m, seguro (MEX), alfiler m de gancho (SC)

saffron ['sæfrən] n azafrán m

sag [sæg] vi aflojarse

sage [seɪdʒ] n (herb) salvia; (man) sabio

Sagittarius [sædʒɪ'tɛərɪəs] n Sagitario

Sahara [sə'hɑ:rə] n: **the ~ (Desert)** el

(desierto del) Sáhara

said [sɛd] *pt, pp of* **say**

sail [seɪl] *n* (*on boat*) vela; (*trip*): **to go
for a ~** dar un paseo en barco ▷ *vt* (*boat*)
gobernar ▷ *vi* (*travel: ship*) navegar; (*Sport*)
hacer vela; (*begin voyage*) salir; **they ~ed
into Copenhagen** arribaron a Copenhague;
sailboat (*us*) *n* = **sailing boat**; **sailing** *n*
(*Sport*) vela; **to go sailing** hacer vela; **sailing
boat** *n* barco de vela; **sailor** *n* marinero,
marino

saint [seɪnt] *n* santo

sake [seɪk] *n*: **for the ~ of** por

salad ['sæləd] *n* ensalada; **salad cream**
(*BRIT*) *n* (especie f de) mayonesa; **salad
dressing** *n* aliño

salami [sə'lɑːmɪ] *n* salami *m*, salchichón *m*

salary ['sælərɪ] *n* sueldo

sale [seɪl] *n* venta; (*at reduced prices*)
liquidación f, saldo; (*auction*) subasta;
sales *npl* (*total amount sold*) ventas *fpl*,
facturación f; **"for ~"** "se vende"; **on ~** en
venta; **on ~ or return** (*goods*) venta por
reposición; **sales assistant** (*us*), **sales
clerk** *n* dependiente/a *m/f*; **salesman/
woman** (*irreg*) *n* (*in shop*) dependiente/a
m/f; **salesperson** (*irreg*) *n* vendedor(a)
m/f, dependiente/a *m/f*; **sales rep** *n*
representante *mf*, agente *mf* comercial

saline ['seɪlaɪn] *adj* salino

saliva [sə'laɪvə] *n* saliva

salmon ['sæmən] *n inv* salmón *m*

salon ['sælɔn] *n* (*hairdressing salon*)
peluquería; (*beauty salon*) salón *m* de belleza

saloon [sə'luːn] *n* (*us*) bar *m*, taberna;
(*BRIT Aut*) coche *m* (de) turismo; (*ship's
lounge*) cámara, salón *m*

salt [sɔlt] *n* sal f ▷ *vt* salar; (*put salt on*)
poner sal en; **saltwater** *adj* de agua salada;
salty *adj* salado

salute [sə'luːt] *n* saludo; (*of guns*) salva
▷ *vt* saludar

salvage ['sælvɪdʒ] *n* (*saving*) salvamento,
recuperación f; (*things saved*) objetos *mpl*
salvados ▷ *vt* salvar

Salvation Army [sæl'veɪʃən-] *n* Ejército
de Salvación

same [seɪm] *adj* mismo ▷ *pron*: **the ~** el(la)
mismo/a, los(las) mismos/as; **the ~ book
as** el mismo libro que; **at the ~ time** (*at the
same moment*) al mismo tiempo; (*yet*) sin
embargo; **all** *or* **just the ~** sin embargo, aun
así; **to do the ~ (as sb)** hacer lo mismo (que
algn); **the ~ to you!** ¡igualmente!

sample ['sɑːmpl] *n* muestra ▷ *vt* (*food*)
probar; (*wine*) catar

sanction ['sæŋkʃən] *n* aprobación f ▷ *vt*
sancionar; aprobar; **sanctions** *npl* (*Pol*)
sanciones *fpl*

sanctuary ['sæŋktjuərɪ] *n* santuario;
(*refuge*) asilo, refugio; (*for wildlife*) reserva

sand [sænd] *n* arena; (*beach*) playa ▷ *vt*
(*also: ~ down*) lijar

sandal ['sændl] *n* sandalia

sand: sandbox (*us*) *n* = **sandpit**;
sandcastle *n* castillo de arena; **sand dune**
n duna; **sandpaper** *n* papel *m* de lija;
sandpit *n* (*for children*) cajón *m* de arena;
sands *npl* playa *sg* de arena; **sandstone**
['sændstəun] *n* piedra arenisca

sandwich ['sændwɪtʃ] *n* sandwich *m* ▷ *vt*
intercalar; **~ed between** apretujado entre;
cheese/ham ~ sandwich de queso/jamón

sandy ['sændɪ] *adj* arenoso; (*colour*) rojizo

sane [seɪn] *adj* cuerdo; (*sensible*) sensato

⬛ Be careful not to translate **sane** by the
Spanish word *sano*.

sang [sæŋ] *pt of* **sing**

sanitary towel (*us* **sanitary napkin**) *n*
paño higiénico, compresa

sanity ['sænɪtɪ] *n* cordura; (*of judgment*)
sensatez f

sank [sæŋk] *pt of* **sink**

Santa Claus [sæntə'klɔːz] *n* San Nicolás,
Papá Noel

sap [sæp] *n* (*of plants*) savia ▷ *vt* (*strength*)
minar, agotar

sapphire ['sæfaɪə*] *n* zafiro

sarcasm ['sɑːkæzm] *n* sarcasmo

sarcastic [sɑː'kæstɪk] *adj* sarcástico

sardine [sɑː'diːn] *n* sardina

SASE (*us*) *n abbr* (= *self-addressed stamped
envelope*) sobre con las propias señas de uno y
con sello

Sat. *abbr* (= *Saturday*) sáb

sat [sæt] *pt, pp of* **sit**

satchel ['sætʃl] *n* (*child's*) mochila, cartera
(*SP*)

satellite ['sætəlaɪt] *n* satélite *m*; **satellite
dish** *n* antena de televisión por satélite;
satellite television *n* televisión f vía
satélite

satin ['sætɪn] *n* raso ▷ *adj* de raso

satire ['sætaɪə*] *n* sátira

satisfaction [sætɪs'fækʃən] *n*
satisfacción f

satisfactory [sætɪs'fæktərɪ] *adj*
satisfactorio

satisfied ['sætɪsfaɪd] *adj* satisfecho; **to be
~ (with sth)** estar satisfecho (de algo)

satisfy ['sætɪsfaɪ] *vt* satisfacer; (*convince*)
convencer

Saturday ['sætədɪ] *n* sábado

sauce [sɔːs] *n* salsa; (*sweet*) crema; jarabe
m; **saucepan** *n* cacerola, olla

saucer ['sɔːsə*] *n* platillo; **Saudi Arabia** *n*

Arabia Saudí or Saudita
sauna ['sɔ:nə] n sauna
sausage ['sɒsɪdʒ] n salchicha; **sausage roll** n empanadita de salchicha
sautéed ['səuteɪd] adj salteado
savage ['sævɪdʒ] adj (cruel, fierce) feroz, furioso; (primitive) salvaje ▷ n salvaje mf ▷ vt (attack) embestir
save [seɪv] vt (rescue) salvar, rescatar; (money, time) ahorrar; (put by, keep: seat) guardar; (Comput) salvar (y guardar); (avoid: trouble) evitar; (Sport) parar ▷ vi (also: ~ up) ahorrar ▷ n (Sport) parada ▷ prep salvo, excepto
savings ['seɪvɪŋz] npl ahorros mpl; **savings account** n cuenta de ahorros; **savings and loan association** (us) n sociedad f de ahorro y préstamo
savoury ['seɪvərɪ] (us **savory**) adj sabroso; (dish: not sweet) salado
saw [sɔ:] (pt **~ed**, pp **~ed** or **~n**) pt of **see** ▷ n (tool) sierra ▷ vt serrar; **sawdust** n (a) serrín m
sawn [sɔ:n] pp of **saw**
saxophone ['sæksəfəun] n saxófono
say [seɪ] (pt, pp **said**) n: **to have one's ~** expresar su opinión ▷ vt decir; **to have a** or **some ~ in sth** tener voz or tener que ver en algo; **to ~ yes/no** decir que sí/no; **could you ~ that again?** ¿podría repetir eso?; **that is to ~** es decir; **that goes without ~ing** ni que decir tiene; **saying** n dicho, refrán m
scab [skæb] n costra; (pej) esquirol m
scaffolding ['skæfəldɪŋ] n andamio, andamiaje m
scald [skɔ:ld] n escaldadura ▷ vt escaldar
scale [skeɪl] n (gen, Mus) escala; (of fish) escama; (of salaries, fees etc) escalafón m ▷ vt (mountain) escalar; (tree) trepar; **scales** npl (for weighing: small) balanza; (: large) báscula; **on a large ~** en gran escala; **~ of charges** tarifa, lista de precios
scallion ['skæljən] (us) n cebolleta
scallop ['skɒləp] n (Zool) venera; (Sewing) festón m
scalp [skælp] n cabellera ▷ vt escalpar
scalpel ['skælpl] n bisturí m
scam [skæm] n (inf) estafa, timo
scampi ['skæmpɪ] npl gambas fpl
scan [skæn] vt (examine) escudriñar; (glance at quickly) dar un vistazo a; (TV, Radar) explorar, registrar ▷ n (Med): **to have a ~** pasar por el escáner
scandal ['skændl] n escándalo; (gossip) chismes mpl
Scandinavia [skændɪ'neɪvɪə] n Escandinavia; **Scandinavian** adj, n escandinavo/a m/f

scanner ['skænə*] n (Radar, Med) escáner m
scapegoat ['skeɪpgəut] n cabeza de turco, chivo expiatorio
scar [skɑ:] n cicatriz f; (fig) señal f ▷ vt dejar señales en
scarce [skɛəs] adj escaso; **to make o.s. ~** (inf) esfumarse; **scarcely** adv apenas
scare [skɛə*] n susto, sobresalto; (panic) pánico ▷ vt asustar, espantar; **to ~ sb stiff** dar a algn un susto de muerte; **bomb ~** amenaza de bomba; **scarecrow** n espantapájaros m inv; **scared** adj: **to be scared** estar asustado
scarf [skɑ:f] (pl **~s** or **scarves**) n (long) bufanda; (square) pañuelo
scarlet ['skɑ:lɪt] adj escarlata
scarves [skɑ:vz] npl of **scarf**
scary ['skɛərɪ] (inf) adj espeluznante
scatter ['skætə*] vt (spread) esparcir, desparramar; (put to flight) dispersar ▷ vi desparramarse; dispersarse
scenario [sɪ'nɑ:rɪəu] n (Theatre) argumento; (Cinema) guión m; (fig) escenario
scene [si:n] n (Theatre, fig etc) escena; (of crime etc) escenario; (view) panorama m; (fuss) escándalo; **scenery** n (Theatre) decorado; (landscape) paisaje m

> ⏹ Be careful not to translate **scenery** by the Spanish word escenario.

scenic adj pintoresco
scent [sɛnt] n perfume m, olor m; (fig: track) rastro, pista
sceptical ['skɛptɪkl] adj escéptico
schedule ['ʃɛdju:l] (us) ['skɛdju:l] n (timetable) horario; (of events) programa m; (list) lista ▷ vt (visit) fijar la hora de; **to arrive on ~** llegar a la hora debida; **to be ahead of/behind ~** estar adelantado/en retraso; **scheduled flight** n vuelo regular
scheme [ski:m] n (plan) plan m, proyecto; (plot) intriga; (arrangement) disposición f; (pension scheme etc) sistema m ▷ vi (intrigue) intrigar
schizophrenic [skɪtzə'frɛnɪk] adj esquizofrénico
scholar ['skɒlə*] n (pupil) alumno/a; (learned person) sabio/a, erudito/a; **scholarship** n erudición f; (grant) beca
school [sku:l] n escuela, colegio; (in university) facultad f ▷ cpd escolar; **schoolbook** n libro de texto; **schoolboy** n alumno; **school children** npl alumnos mpl; **schoolgirl** n alumna; **schooling** n enseñanza; **schoolteacher** n (primary) maestro/a; (secondary) profesor(a) m/f
science ['saɪəns] n ciencia; **science**

fiction n ciencia-ficción f; **scientific**
[-'tıfık] adj científico; **scientist** n
científico/a
sci-fi ['saıfaı] n abbr (inf) = **science fiction**
scissors ['sızəz] npl tijeras fpl; **a pair of ~**
unas tijeras
scold [skəuld] vt regañar
scone [skɔn] n pastel de pan
scoop [sku:p] n (for flour etc) pala; (Press)
exclusiva
scooter ['sku:tə*] n moto f; (toy) patinete
m
scope [skəup] n (of plan) ámbito; (of
person) competencia; (opportunity) libertad
f (de acción)
scorching ['skɔ:tʃıŋ] adj (heat, sun)
abrasador(a)
score [skɔ:*] n (points etc) puntuación f;
(Mus) partitura; (twenty) veintena ▷ vt (goal,
point) ganar; (mark) rayar; (achieve: success)
conseguir ▷ vi marcar un tanto; (Football)
marcar (un) gol; (keep score) llevar el tanteo;
~s of (lots of) decenas de; **on that ~** en lo
que se refiere a eso; **to ~ 6 out of 10** obtener
una puntuación de 6 sobre 10; **score out** vt
tachar; **scoreboard** n marcador m; **scorer**
n marcador m; (keeping score) encargado/a
del marcador
scorn [skɔ:n] n desprecio
Scorpio ['skɔ:pıəu] n Escorpión m
scorpion ['skɔ:pıən] n alacrán m
Scot [skɔt] n escocés/esa m/f
Scotch tape® (us) n cinta adhesiva, celo,
scotch® m
Scotland ['skɔtlənd] n Escocia
Scots [skɔts] adj escocés/esa; **Scotsman**
(irreg) n escocés; **Scotswoman** (irreg) n
escocesa; **Scottish** ['skɔtıʃ] adj escocés/
esa; **Scottish Parliament** n Parlamento
escocés
scout [skaut] n (Mil: also: **boy ~**)
explorador m; **girl ~** (us) niña exploradora
scowl [skaul] vi fruncir el ceño; **to ~ at sb**
mirar con ceño a algn
scramble ['skræmbl] n (climb) subida
(difícil); (struggle) pelea ▷ vi: **to ~ through/
out** abrirse paso/salir con dificultad; **to ~
for** pelear por; **scrambled eggs** npl huevos
mpl revueltos
scrap [skræp] n (bit) pedacito; (fig) pizca;
(fight) riña, bronca; (also: **~ iron**) chatarra,
hierro viejo ▷ vt (discard) desechar,
descartar ▷ vi reñir, armar una bronca;
scraps npl (waste) sobras fpl, desperdicios
mpl; **scrapbook** n álbum m de recortes
scrape [skreıp] n: **to get into a ~** meterse
en un lío ▷ vt raspar; (skin etc) rasguñar;
(scrape against) rozar ▷ vi: **to ~ through**

(exam) aprobar por los pelos; **scrap paper** n
pedazos mpl de papel
scratch [skrætʃ] n rasguño; (from claw)
arañazo ▷ vt (paint, car) rayar; (with claw,
nail) rasguñar, arañar; (rub: nose etc) rascarse
▷ vi rascarse; **to start from ~** partir de cero;
to be up to ~ cumplir con los requisitos;
scratch card n (BRIT) tarjeta f de "rasque
y gane"
scream [skri:m] n chillido ▷ vi chillar
screen [skri:n] n (Cinema, TV) pantalla;
(movable barrier) biombo ▷ vt (conceal)
tapar; (from the wind etc) proteger; (film)
proyectar; (candidates etc) investigar a;
screening n (Med) investigación f médica;
screenplay n guión m; **screen saver** n
(Comput) protector m de pantalla
screw [skru:] n tornillo ▷ vt (also: **~
in**) atornillar; **screw up** vt (paper etc)
arrugar; **to screw up one's eyes** arrugar el
entrecejo; **screwdriver** n destornillador m
scribble ['skrıbl] n garabatos mpl ▷ vt, vi
garabatear
script [skrıpt] n (Cinema etc) guión m;
(writing) escritura, letra
scroll [skrəul] n rollo
scrub [skrʌb] n (land) maleza ▷ vt fregar,
restregar; (inf: reject) cancelar, anular
scruffy ['skrʌfı] adj desaliñado, piojoso
scrum(mage) ['skrʌm(mıdʒ)] n (Rugby)
melée f
scrutiny ['skru:tını] n escrutinio, examen
m
scuba diving ['sku:bə'daıvıŋ] n
submarinismo
sculptor ['skʌlptə*] n escultor(a) m/f
sculpture ['skʌlptʃə*] n escultura
scum [skʌm] n (on liquid) espuma;
(pej: people) escoria
scurry ['skʌrı] vi correr; **to ~ off**
escabullirse
sea [si:] n mar m ▷ cpd de mar, marítimo;
by ~ (travel) en barco; **on the ~** (boat) en el
mar; (town) junto al mar; **to be all at ~** (fig)
estar despistado; **out to ~, at ~** en alta
mar; **seafood** n mariscos mpl; **sea front** n
paseo marítimo; **seagull** n gaviota
seal [si:l] n (animal) foca; (stamp) sello ▷ vt
(close) cerrar; **seal off** vt (area) acordonar
sea level n nivel m del mar
seam [si:m] n costura; (of metal) juntura;
(of coal) veta, filón m
search [sə:tʃ] n (for person, thing) busca,
búsqueda; (Comput) búsqueda; (inspection: of
sb's home) registro ▷ vt (look in) buscar en;
(examine) examinar; (person, place) registrar
▷ vi: **to ~ for** buscar; **in ~ of** en busca de;
search engine n (Comput) buscador m;

search party n pelotón m de salvamento
sea: seashore n playa, orilla del mar;
seasick adj mareado; **seaside** n playa,
orilla del mar; **seaside resort** n centro
turístico costero

season ['si:zn] n (of year) estación f;
(sporting etc) temporada; (of films etc)
ciclo ▷vt (food) sazonar; **in/out of ~** en
sazón/fuera de temporada; **seasonal** adj
estacional; **seasoning** n condimento,
aderezo; **season ticket** n abono

seat [si:t] n (in bus, train) asiento; (chair)
silla; (Parliament) escaño; (buttocks) culo,
trasero; (of trousers) culera ▷vt sentar;
(have room for) tener cabida para; **to be
~ed** sentarse; **seat belt** n cinturón m de
seguridad; **seating** n asientos mpl

sea: sea water n agua del mar; **seaweed** n
alga marina

sec. abbr = **second(s)**

secluded [sɪ'klu:dɪd] adj retirado

second ['sɛkənd] adj segundo ▷adv en
segundo lugar ▷n segundo; (Aut: also:
~ gear) segunda; (Comm) artículo con
algún desperfecto; (BRIT Scol: degree) título
de licenciado con calificación de notable
▷vt (motion) apoyar; **secondary** adj
secundario; **secondary school** n escuela
secundaria; **second-class** adj de segunda
clase ▷adv (Rail) en segunda; **secondhand**
adj de segunda mano, usado; **secondly**
adv en segundo lugar; **second-rate** adj de
segunda categoría; **second thoughts: to
have second thoughts** cambiar de
opinión; **on second thoughts** or **thought**
(US) pensándolo bien

secrecy ['si:krəsɪ] n secreto

secret ['si:krɪt] adj, n secreto; **in ~** en
secreto

secretary ['sɛkrətərɪ] n secretario/a; **S~
of State (for)** (BRIT Pol) Ministro (de)

secretive ['si:krətɪv] adj reservado,
sigiloso

secret service n servicio secreto

sect [sɛkt] n secta

section ['sɛkʃən] n sección f; (part) parte f;
(of document) artículo; (of opinion) sector m;
(cross-section) corte m transversal

sector ['sɛktə*] n sector m

secular ['sɛkjulə*] adj secular, seglar

secure [sɪ'kjuə*] adj seguro; (firmly fixed)
firme, fijo ▷vt (fix) asegurar, afianzar; (get)
conseguir

security [sɪ'kjuərɪtɪ] n seguridad f; (for
loan) fianza; (: object) prenda; **securities** npl
(Comm) valores mpl, títulos mpl; **security
guard** n guardia m/f de seguridad

sedan [sɪ'dæn] (US) n (Aut) sedán m

sedate [sɪ'deɪt] adj tranquilo ▷vt tratar
con sedantes

sedative ['sɛdɪtɪv] n sedante m, sedativo

seduce [sɪ'dju:s] vt seducir; **seductive**
[-'dʌktɪv] adj seductor(a)

see [si:] (pt **saw**, pp **seen**) vt ver;
(accompany): **to ~ sb to the door** acompañar
a algn a la puerta; (understand) ver,
comprender ▷vi ver ▷n (arz)obispado; **to
~ that** (ensure) asegurar que; **~ you soon!**
¡hasta pronto!; **see off** vt despedir; **see
out** vt (take to the door) acompañar hasta la
puerta; **see through** vt fus (fig) calar ▷vt
(plan) llevar a cabo; **see to** vt fus atender a,
encargarse de

seed [si:d] n semilla; (in fruit) pepita;
(fig: gen pl) germen m; (Tennis etc)
preseleccionado/a; **to go to ~** (plant)
granar; (fig) descuidarse

seeing ['si:ɪŋ] conj: **~ (that)** visto que, en
vista de que

seek [si:k] (pt, pp **sought**) vt buscar; (post)
solicitar

seem [si:m] vi parecer; **there ~s to
be ...** parece que hay ...; **seemingly** adv
aparentemente, según parece

seen [si:n] pp of **see**

seesaw ['si:sɔ:] n subibaja

segment ['sɛgmənt] n (part) sección f; (of
orange) gajo

segregate ['sɛgrɪgeɪt] vt segregar

seize [si:z] vt (grasp) agarrar, asir;
(take possession of) secuestrar; (: territory)
apoderarse de; (opportunity) aprovecharse de

seizure ['si:ʒə*] n (Med) ataque m; (Law: of
power) incautación f

seldom ['sɛldəm] adv rara vez

select [sɪ'lɛkt] adj selecto, escogido
▷vt escoger, elegir; (Sport) seleccionar;
selection n selección f, elección f; (Comm)
surtido; **selective** adj selectivo

self [sɛlf] (pl **selves**) n uno mismo; **the
~** el yo ▷prefix auto...; **self-assured** adj
seguro de sí mismo; **self-catering** (BRIT)
adj (flat etc) con cocina; **self-centred** (US
self-centered) adj egocéntrico; **self-
confidence** n confianza en sí mismo;
self-confident adj seguro de sí (mismo),
lleno de confianza en sí mismo; **self-
conscious** adj cohibido; **self-contained**
(BRIT) adj (flat) con entrada particular;
self-control n autodominio; **self-defence**
(US **self-defense**) n defensa propia; **self-
drive** adj (BRIT) sin chofer or (SP) chófer;
self-employed adj que trabaja por cuenta
propia; **self-esteem** n amor m propio;
self-indulgent adj autocomplaciente;
self-interest n egoísmo; **selfish** adj

egoísta; **self-pity** n lástima de sí mismo;
self-raising [sɛlf'reɪzɪŋ] (US **self-rising**)
adj: **self-raising flour** harina con levadura;
self-respect n amor m propio; **self-service**
adj de autoservicio
sell [sɛl] (pt, pp **sold**) vt vender ▷ vi
venderse; **to ~ at** or **for £10** venderse a 10
libras; **sell off** vt liquidar; **sell out** vi: **to
sell out of tickets/milk** vender todas las
entradas/toda la leche; **sell-by date** n
fecha de caducidad; **seller** n vendedor(a)
m/f
Sellotape® ['sɛləʊteɪp] (BRIT) n celo (SP),
cinta Scotch® (LAM) or Dúrex® (MEX, ARG)
selves [sɛlvz] npl of **self**
semester [sɪ'mɛstə*] (US) n semestre m
semi... [sɛmɪ] prefix semi..., medio...;
semicircle n semicírculo; **semidetached
(house)** n (casa) semiseparada; **semi-final**
n semi-final m
seminar ['sɛmɪnɑ:*] n seminario
semi-skimmed [sɛmɪ'skɪmd] adj
semidesnatado; **semi-skimmed (milk)** n
leche semidesnatada
senate ['sɛnɪt] n senado; **the S~** (US) el
Senado; **senator** n senador(a) m/f
send [sɛnd] (pt, pp **sent**) vt mandar, enviar;
(signal) transmitir; **send back** vt devolver;
send for vt fus mandar traer; **send in** vt
(report, application, resignation) mandar; **send
off** vt (goods) despachar; (BRIT Sport: player)
expulsar; **send on** vt (letter, luggage)
remitir; (person) mandar; **send out** vt
(invitation) mandar; (signal) emitir; **send up**
vt (person, price) hacer subir; (BRIT: parody)
parodiar; **sender** n remitente mf; **send-off**
n: **a good send-off** una buena despedida
senile ['si:naɪl] adj senil
senior ['si:nɪə*] adj (older) mayor, más
viejo; (: on staff) de más antigüedad; (of
higher rank) superior; **senior citizen** n
persona de la tercera edad; **senior high
school** (US) n ≈ instituto de enseñanza
media; see also **high school**
sensation [sɛn'seɪʃən] n sensación f;
sensational adj sensacional
sense [sɛns] n (faculty, meaning) sentido;
(feeling) sensación f; (good sense) sentido
común, juicio ▷ vt sentir, percibir; **it
makes ~** tiene sentido; **senseless** adj
estúpido, insensato; (unconscious) sin
conocimiento; **sense of humour** (BRIT) n
sentido del humor
sensible ['sɛnsɪbl] adj sensato; (reasonable)
razonable, lógico

▌ Be careful not to translate **sensible** by
the Spanish word sensible.

sensitive ['sɛnsɪtɪv] adj sensible; (touchy)

susceptible
sensual ['sɛnsjʊəl] adj sensual
sensuous ['sɛnsjʊəs] adj sensual
sent [sɛnt] pt, pp of **send**
sentence ['sɛntns] n (Ling) oración f; (Law)
sentencia, fallo ▷ vt: **to ~ sb to death/
to 5 years (in prison)** condenar a algn a
muerte/a 5 años de cárcel
sentiment ['sɛntɪmənt] n sentimiento;
(opinion) opinión f; **sentimental** [-'mɛntl]
adj sentimental
Sep. abbr (= September) sep., set.
separate [adj 'sɛprɪt, vb 'sɛpəreɪt] adj
separado; (distinct) distinto ▷ vt separar;
(part) dividir ▷ vi separarse; **separately**
adv por separado; **separates** npl (clothes)
coordinados mpl; **separation** [-'reɪʃən] n
separación f
September [sɛp'tɛmbə*] n se(p)tiembre
m
septic ['sɛptɪk] adj séptico; **septic tank** n
fosa séptica
sequel ['si:kwl] n consecuencia,
resultado; (of story) continuación f
sequence ['si:kwəns] n sucesión f, serie f;
(Cinema) secuencia
sequin ['si:kwɪn] n lentejuela
Serb [sə:b] adj, n = **Serbian**
Serbian ['sə:bɪən] adj serbio ▷ n serbio/a;
(Ling) serbio
sergeant ['sɑ:dʒənt] n sargento
serial ['sɪərɪəl] n (TV) telenovela, serie
f televisiva; (Book) serie f; **serial killer** n
asesino/a múltiple; **serial number** n
número de serie
series ['sɪəri:s] n inv serie f
serious ['sɪərɪəs] adj serio; (grave) grave;
seriously adv en serio; (ill, wounded etc)
gravemente
sermon ['sə:mən] n sermón m
servant ['sə:vənt] n servidor(a) m/f; (house
servant) criado/a
serve [sə:v] vt servir; (customer) atender;
(train) pasar por; (apprenticeship) hacer;
(prison term) cumplir ▷ vi (at table) servir;
(Tennis) sacar; **to ~ as/for/to do** servir de/
para/para hacer ▷ n (Tennis) saque m; **it ~s
him right** se lo tiene merecido; **server** n
(Comput) servidor m
service ['sə:vɪs] n servicio; (Rel) misa;
(Aut) mantenimiento; (dishes etc) juego
▷ vt (car etc) revisar; (: repair) reparar; **to be
of ~ to sb** ser útil a algn; **~ included/not
included** servicio incluido/no incluido
(Econ: tertiary sector) sector m terciario or
(de) servicios; (BRIT: on motorway) área de
servicio; (Mil): **the S~s** las fuerzas armadas;
service area n (on motorway) área de

servicio; **service charge** (BRIT) n servicio; **serviceman** (irreg) n militar m; **service station** n estación f de servicio

serviette [sə:vɪˈɛt] (BRIT) n servilleta

session [ˈsɛʃən] n sesión f; **to be in ~** estar en sesión

set [sɛt] (pt, pp ~) n juego; (Radio) aparato; (TV) televisor m; (of utensils) batería; (of cutlery) cubierto; (of books) colección f; (Tennis) set m; (group of people) grupo; (Cinema) plató m; (Theatre) decorado; (Hairdressing) marcado ▷ adj (fixed) fijo; (ready) listo ▷ vt (place) poner, colocar; (fix) fijar; (adjust) ajustar, arreglar; (decide: rules etc) establecer, decidir ▷ vi (sun) ponerse; (jam, jelly) cuajarse; (concrete) fraguar; (bone) componerse; **to be ~ on doing sth** estar empeñado en hacer algo; **to ~ to music** poner música a; **to ~ on fire** incendiar, poner fuego a; **to ~ free** poner en libertad; **to ~ sth going** poner algo en marcha; **to ~ sail** zarpar, hacerse a la vela; **set aside** vt poner aparte, dejar de lado; (money, time) reservar; **set down** vt (bus, train) dejar; **set in** vi (infection) declararse; (complications) comenzar; **the rain has set in for the day** parece que va a llover todo el día; **set off** vi partir ▷ vt (bomb) hacer estallar; (events) poner en marcha; (show up well) hacer resaltar; **set out** vi partir ▷ vt (arrange) disponer; (state) exponer; **to set out to do sth** proponerse hacer algo; **set up** vt establecer; **setback** n revés m, contratiempo; **set menu** n menú m

settee [sɛˈtiː] n sofá m

setting [ˈsɛtɪŋ] n (scenery) marco; (position) disposición f; (of sun) puesta; (of jewel) engaste m, montadura

settle [ˈsɛtl] vt (argument) resolver; (accounts) ajustar, liquidar; (Med: calm) calmar, sosegar ▷ vi (dust etc) depositarse; (weather) serenarse; **to ~ for sth** convenir en aceptar algo; **to ~ on sth** decidirse por algo; **settle down** vi (get comfortable) ponerse cómodo, acomodarse; (calm down) calmarse, tranquilizarse; (live quietly) echar raíces; **settle in** vi instalarse; **settle up** vi: **to settle up with sb** ajustar cuentas con algn; **settlement** n (payment) liquidación f; (agreement) acuerdo, convenio; (village etc) pueblo

setup [ˈsɛtʌp] n sistema m; (situation) situación f

seven [ˈsɛvn] num siete; **seventeen** num diez y siete, diecisiete; **seventeenth** [sɛvnˈtiːnθ] adj decimoséptimo; **seventh** num séptimo; **seventieth** [ˈsɛvntɪɪθ] adj septuagésimo; **seventy** num setenta

sever [ˈsɛvə*] vt cortar; (relations) romper

several [ˈsɛvərl] adj, pron varios/as m/fpl, algunos/as m/fpl; **~ of us** varios de nosotros

severe [sɪˈvɪə*] adj severo; (serious) grave; (hard) duro; (pain) intenso

sew [səu] (pt ~ed, pp ~n) vt, vi coser

sewage [ˈsuːɪdʒ] n aguas fpl residuales

sewer [ˈsuːə*] n alcantarilla, cloaca

sewing [ˈsəuɪŋ] n costura; **sewing machine** n máquina de coser

sewn [səun] pp of **sew**

sex [sɛks] n sexo; (lovemaking): **to have ~** hacer el amor; **sexism** [ˈsɛksɪzəm] n sexismo; **sexist** adj, n sexista mf; **sexual** [ˈsɛksjuəl] adj sexual; **sexual intercourse** n relaciones fpl sexuales; **sexuality** [sɛksjuˈælɪtɪ] n sexualidad f; **sexy** adj sexy

shabby [ˈʃæbɪ] adj (person) desharrapado; (clothes) raído, gastado; (behaviour) ruin inv

shack [ʃæk] n choza, chabola

shade [ʃeɪd] n sombra; (for lamp) pantalla; (for eyes) visera; (of colour) matiz m, tonalidad f; (small quantity): **a ~ (too big/more)** un poquitín (grande/más) ▷ vt dar sombra a; (eyes) proteger del sol; **in the ~** en la sombra; **shades** npl (sunglasses) gafas fpl de sol

shadow [ˈʃædəu] n sombra ▷ vt (follow) seguir y vigilar; **shadow cabinet** (BRIT) n (Pol) gabinete paralelo formado por el partido de oposición

shady [ˈʃeɪdɪ] adj sombreado; (fig: dishonest) sospechoso; (: deal) turbio

shaft [ʃɑːft] n (of arrow, spear) astil m; (Aut, Tech) eje m, árbol m; (of mine) pozo; (of lift) hueco, caja; (of light) rayo

shake [ʃeɪk] (pt shook, pp shaken) vt sacudir; (building) hacer temblar; (bottle, cocktail) agitar ▷ vt (tremble) temblar; **to ~ one's head** (in refusal) negar con la cabeza; (in dismay) mover or menear la cabeza, incrédulo; **to ~ hands with sb** estrechar la mano a algn; **shake off** vt sacudirse; (fig) deshacerse de; **shake up** vt agitar; (fig) reorganizar; **shaky** adj (hand, voice) trémulo; (building) inestable

shall [ʃæl] aux vb: **~ I help you?** ¿quieres que te ayude?; **I'll buy three, ~ I?** compro tres, ¿no te parece?

shallow [ˈʃæləu] adj poco profundo; (fig) superficial

sham [ʃæm] n fraude m, engaño

shambles [ˈʃæmblz] n confusión f

shame [ʃeɪm] n vergüenza ▷ vt avergonzar; **it is a ~ that/to do** es una lástima que/hacer; **what a ~!** ¡qué lástima!; **shameful** adj vergonzoso; **shameless** adj desvergonzado

shampoo [ʃæmˈpuː] n champú m ▷ vt

lavar con champú

shandy [ˈʃændɪ] *n mezcla de cerveza con gaseosa*

shan't [ʃɑːnt] = **shall not**

shape [ʃeɪp] *n* forma ▷ *vt* formar, dar forma a; (*sb's ideas*) formar; (*sb's life*) determinar; **to take ~** tomar forma

share [ʃeə*] *n* (*part*) parte *f*, porción *f*; (*contribution*) cuota; (*Comm*) acción *f* ▷ *vt* dividir; (*have in common*) compartir; **to ~ out (among** *or* **between)** repartir (entre); **shareholder** (BRIT) *n* accionista *mf*

shark [ʃɑːk] *n* tiburón *m*

sharp [ʃɑːp] *adj* (*blade, nose*) afilado; (*point*) puntiagudo; (*outline*) definido; (*pain*) intenso; (*Mus*) desafinado; (*contrast*) marcado; (*voice*) agudo; (*person: quick-witted*) astuto; (: *dishonest*) poco escrupuloso ▷ *n* (*Mus*) sostenido ▷ *adv*: **at 2 o'clock ~** a las 2 en punto; **sharpen** *vt* afilar; (*pencil*) sacar punta a; (*fig*) agudizar; **sharpener** *n* (*also*: **pencil sharpener**) sacapuntas *m inv*; **sharply** *adv* (*turn, stop*) bruscamente; (*stand out, contrast*) claramente; (*criticize, retort*) severamente

shatter [ˈʃætə*] *vt* hacer añicos or pedazos; (*fig: ruin*) destruir, acabar con ▷ *vi* hacerse añicos; **shattered** *adj* (*grief-stricken*) destrozado, deshecho; (*exhausted*) agotado, hecho polvo

shave [ʃeɪv] *vt* afeitar, rasurar ▷ *vi* afeitarse, rasurarse ▷ *n*: **to have a ~** afeitarse; **shaver** *n* (*also*: **electric shaver**) máquina de afeitar (eléctrica)

shavings [ˈʃeɪvɪŋz] *npl* (*of wood etc*) virutas *fpl*

shaving cream [ˈʃeɪvɪŋ-] *n* crema de afeitar

shaving foam *n* espuma de afeitar

shawl [ʃɔːl] *n* chal *m*

she [ʃiː] *pron* ella

sheath [ʃiːθ] *n* vaina; (*contraceptive*) preservativo

shed [ʃed] (*pt, pp ~*) *n* cobertizo ▷ *vt* (*skin*) mudar; (*tears, blood*) derramar; (*load*) derramar; (*workers*) despedir

she'd [ʃiːd] = **she had; she would**

sheep [ʃiːp] *n inv* oveja; **sheepdog** *n* perro pastor; **sheepskin** *n* piel *f* de carnero

sheer [ʃɪə*] *adj* (*utter*) puro, completo; (*steep*) escarpado; (*material*) diáfano ▷ *adv* verticalmente

sheet [ʃiːt] *n* (*on bed*) sábana; (*of paper*) hoja; (*of glass, metal*) lámina; (*of ice*) capa

sheik(h) [ʃeɪk] *n* jeque *m*

shelf [ʃelf] (*pl* **shelves**) *n* estante *m*

shell [ʃel] *n* (*on beach*) concha; (*of egg, nut etc*) cáscara; (*explosive*) proyectil *m*,

obús *m*; (*of building*) armazón *f* ▷ *vt* (*peas*) desenvainar; (*Mil*) bombardear

she'll [ʃiːl] = **she will; she shall**

shellfish [ˈʃelfɪʃ] *n inv* crustáceo; (*as food*) mariscos *mpl*

shelter [ˈʃeltə*] *n* abrigo, refugio ▷ *vt* (*aid*) amparar, proteger; (*give lodging to*) abrigar ▷ *vi* abrigarse, refugiarse; **sheltered** *adj* (*life*) protegido; (*spot*) abrigado

shelves [ʃelvz] *npl of* **shelf**

shelving [ˈʃelvɪŋ] *n* estantería

shepherd [ˈʃepəd] *n* pastor *m* ▷ *vt* (*guide*) guiar, conducir; **shepherd's pie** (BRIT) *n pastel de carne y patatas*

sheriff [ˈʃerɪf] (US) *n* sheriff *m*

sherry [ˈʃerɪ] *n* jerez *m*

she's [ʃiːz] = **she is; she has**

Shetland [ˈʃetlənd] *n* (*also*: **the ~s, the ~ Isles**) las Islas de Zetlandia

shield [ʃiːld] *n* escudo; (*protection*) blindaje *m* ▷ *vt*: **to ~ (from)** proteger (de)

shift [ʃɪft] *n* (*change*) cambio; (*at work*) turno ▷ *vt* trasladar; (*remove*) quitar ▷ *vi* moverse

shin [ʃɪn] *n* espinilla

shine [ʃaɪn] (*pt, pp* **shone**) *n* brillo, lustre *m* ▷ *vi* brillar, relucir ▷ *vt* (*shoes*) lustrar, sacar brillo a; **to ~ a torch on sth** dirigir una linterna hacia algo

shingles [ˈʃɪŋglz] *n* (*Med*) herpes *mpl or fpl*

shiny [ˈʃaɪnɪ] *adj* brillante, lustroso

ship [ʃɪp] *n* buque *m*, barco ▷ *vt* (*goods*) embarcar; (*send*) transportar or enviar por vía marítima; **shipment** *n* (*goods*) envío; **shipping** *n* (*act*) embarque *m*; (*traffic*) buques *mpl*; **shipwreck** *n* naufragio ▷ *vt*: **to be shipwrecked** naufragar; **shipyard** *n* astillero

shirt [ʃəːt] *n* camisa; **in (one's) ~ sleeves** en mangas de camisa

shit [ʃɪt] (*inf!*) *excl* ¡mierda! (!)

shiver [ˈʃɪvə*] *n* escalofrío ▷ *vi* temblar, estremecerse; (*with cold*) tiritar

shock [ʃɔk] *n* (*impact*) choque *m*; (*Elec*) descarga (eléctrica); (*emotional*) conmoción *f*; (*start*) sobresalto, susto; (*Med*) postración *f* nerviosa ▷ *vt* dar un susto a; (*offend*) escandalizar; **shocking** *adj* (*awful*) espantoso; (*outrageous*) escandaloso

shoe [ʃuː] (*pt, pp* **shod**) *n* zapato; (*for horse*) herradura ▷ *vt* (*horse*) herrar; **shoelace** *n* cordón *m*; **shoe polish** *n* betún *m*; **shoeshop** *n* zapatería

shone [ʃɔn] *pt, pp of* **shine**

shook [ʃʊk] *pt of* **shake**

shoot [ʃuːt] (*pt, pp* **shot**) *n* (*on branch, seedling*) retoño, vástago ▷ *vt* disparar; (*kill*) matar a tiros; (*wound*) pegar un tiro; (*execute*)

fusilar; (film) rodar, filmar ▷ vi (Football)
chutar; **shoot down** vt (plane) derribar;
shoot up vi (prices) dispararse; **shooting**
n (shots) tiros mpl; (Hunting) caza con escopeta
shop [ʃɔp] n tienda; (workshop) taller m
▷ vi (also: **go ~ping**) ir de compras; **shop
assistant** (BRIT) n dependiente/a m/f;
shopkeeper n tendero/a; **shoplifting** n
mechería; **shopping** n (goods) compras
fpl; **shopping trolley** n bolsa (de compras);
shopping centre (US **shopping center**) n
centro comercial; **shopping mall** n centro
comercial; **shopping trolley** n (BRIT)
carrito de la compra; **shop window** n
escaparate m (SP), vidriera (LAM)
shore [ʃɔ:*] n orilla ▷ vt: **to ~ (up)** reforzar;
on ~ en tierra
short [ʃɔ:t] adj corto; (in time) breve, de
corta duración; (person) bajo; (curt) brusco,
seco; (insufficient) insuficiente; **(a pair of) ~s**
(unos) pantalones mpl cortos; **to be ~ of sth**
estar falto de algo; **in ~** en pocas palabras; **~
of doing ...** fuera de hacer ...; **it is ~ for** es la
forma abreviada de; **to cut ~** (speech, visit)
interrumpir, terminar inesperadamente;
everything ~ of ... todo menos ...; **to fall
~ of** no alcanzar; **to run ~ of** quedarle a
algn poco; **to stop ~** parar en seco; **to stop
~ of** detenerse antes de; **shortage** n: **a
shortage of** una falta de; **shortbread**
n especie de mantecada; **shortcoming**
n defecto, deficiencia; **short(crust)
pastry** (BRIT) n pasta quebradiza;
shortcut n atajo; **shorten** vt acortar;
(visit) interrumpir; **shortfall** n déficit m;
shorthand (BRIT) n taquigrafía; **short-
lived** adj efímero; **shortly** adv en breve,
dentro de poco; **shorts** npl pantalones mpl
cortos; (US) calzoncillos mpl; **short-sighted**
(BRIT) adj miope; (fig) imprudente; **short-
sleeved** adj de manga corta; **short story**
n cuento; **short-tempered** adj enojadizo;
short-term adj (effect) a corto plazo
shot [ʃɔt] pt, pp of **shoot** ▷ n (sound) tiro,
disparo; (try) tentativa; (injection) inyección
f; (Phot) toma, fotografía; **to be a good/
poor ~** (person) tener buena/mala puntería;
like a ~ (without any delay) como un rayo;
shotgun n escopeta
should [ʃud] aux vb: **I ~ go now** debo irme
ahora; **he ~ be there now** debe de haber
llegado (ya); **I ~ go if I were you** yo en tu
lugar me iría; **I ~ like to** me gustaría
shoulder ['ʃəuldə*] n hombro ▷ vt (fig)
cargar con; **shoulder blade** n omóplato
shouldn't ['ʃudnt] = should not
shout [ʃaut] n grito ▷ vt gritar ▷ vi gritar,
dar voces

shove [ʃʌv] n empujón m ▷ vt empujar;
(inf: put): **to ~ sth in** meter algo a
empellones
shovel ['ʃʌvl] n pala; (mechanical)
excavadora ▷ vt mover con pala
show [ʃəu] (pt **~ed**, pp **~n**) n (of emotion)
demostración f; (semblance) apariencia;
(exhibition) exposición f; (Theatre) función
f, espectáculo; (TV) show m ▷ vt mostrar,
enseñar; (courage etc) mostrar, manifestar;
(exhibit) exponer; (film) proyectar ▷ vi
mostrarse; (appear) aparecer; **for ~** para
impresionar; **on ~** (exhibits etc) expuesto;
show in vt (person) hacer pasar; **show off**
(pej) vi presumir ▷ vt (display) lucir; **show
out** vt: **to show sb out** acompañar a algn a
la puerta; **show up** vi (stand out) destacar;
(inf: turn up) aparecer ▷ vt (unmask)
desenmascarar; **show business** n mundo
del espectáculo
shower ['ʃauə*] n (rain) chaparrón m,
chubasco; (of stones etc) lluvia; (for bathing)
ducha, regadera (MEX) ▷ vi llover ▷ vt
(fig): **to ~ sb with sth** colmar a algn de algo;
to have a ~ ducharse; **shower cap** n gorro
de baño; **shower gel** n gel m de ducha
showing ['ʃəuɪŋ] n (of film) proyección f
show jumping n hípica
shown [ʃəun] pp of **show**
show: show-off (inf) n (person)
presumido/a; **showroom** n sala de muestras
shrank [ʃræŋk] pt of **shrink**
shred [ʃred] n (gen pl) triza, jirón m ▷ vt
hacer trizas; (Culin) desmenuzar
shrewd [ʃru:d] adj astuto
shriek [ʃri:k] n chillido ▷ vi chillar
shrimp [ʃrɪmp] n camarón m
shrine [ʃraɪn] n santuario, sepulcro
shrink [ʃrɪŋk] (pt **shrank**, pp **shrunk**) vi
encogerse; (be reduced) reducirse; (also: **~
away**) retroceder ▷ vt encoger ▷ n (inf,
pej) loquero/a; **to ~ from (doing) sth** no
atreverse a hacer algo
shrivel ['ʃrɪvl] (also: **~ up**) vt (dry) secar
▷ vi secarse
shroud [ʃraud] n sudario ▷ vt: **~ed in
mystery** envuelto en el misterio
Shrove Tuesday ['ʃrəuv-] n martes m de
carnaval
shrub [ʃrʌb] n arbusto
shrug [ʃrʌg] n encogimiento de
hombros ▷ vt, vi: **to ~ (one's shoulders)**
encogerse de hombros; **shrug off** vt negar
importancia a
shrunk [ʃrʌŋk] pp of **shrink**
shudder ['ʃʌdə*] n estremecimiento,
escalofrío ▷ vi estremecerse
shuffle ['ʃʌfl] vt (cards) barajar ▷ vi: **to ~**

(one's feet) arrastrar los pies
shun [ʃʌn] vt rehuir, esquivar
shut [ʃʌt] (pt, pp **~**) vt cerrar ▷ vi
cerrarse; **shut down** vt, vi cerrar; **shut
up** vi (inf: keep quiet) callarse ▷ vt (close)
cerrar; (silence) hacer callar; **shutter** n
contraventana; (Phot) obturador m
shuttle [ʃʌtl] n lanzadera; (also: **~ service**)
servicio rápido y continuo entre dos puntos;
(Aviat) puente m aéreo; **shuttlecock** n
volante m
shy [ʃaɪ] adj tímido
sibling [ˈsɪblɪŋ] n (formal) hermano/a
Sicily [ˈsɪsɪlɪ] n Sicilia
sick [sɪk] adj (ill) enfermo; (nauseated)
mareado; (humour) negro; (vomiting): **to be
~** (BRIT) to **feel ~** tener náuseas;
to be ~ of (fig) estar harto de; **sickening**
adj (fig) asqueroso; **sick leave** n baja por
enfermedad; **sickly** adj enfermizo; (smell)
nauseabundo; **sickness** n enfermedad f,
mal m; (vomiting) náuseas fpl
side [saɪd] n (gen) lado; (of body) costado;
(of lake) orilla; (of hill) ladera; (team) equipo
▷ adj (door, entrance) lateral ▷ vi: **to ~ with
sb** tomar el partido de algn; **by the ~ of** al
lado de; **~ by ~** juntos/as; **from ~ to ~** de un
lado para otro; **from all ~s** de todos lados;
to take ~s (with) tomar partido (con);
sideboard n aparador m; **sideboards**
(BRIT) npl **=sideburns; sideburns** npl
patillas fpl; **sidelight** n (Aut) luz f lateral;
sideline n (Sport) línea de banda; (fig)
empleo suplementario; **side order** n plato
de acompañamiento; **side road** n (BRIT)
calle f lateral; **side street** n calle f lateral;
sidetrack vt (fig) desviar (de su propósito);
sidewalk (US) n acera; **sideways** adv de
lado
siege [siːdʒ] n cerco, sitio
sieve [sɪv] n colador m ▷ vt cribar
sift [sɪft] vt cribar; (fig: information)
escudriñar
sigh [saɪ] n suspiro ▷ vi suspirar
sight [saɪt] n (faculty) vista; (spectacle)
espectáculo; (on gun) mira, alza ▷ vt divisar;
in ~ a la vista; **out of ~** fuera de (la) vista;
on ~ (shoot) sin previo aviso; **sightseeing** n
excursionismo, turismo; **to go sightseeing**
hacer turismo
sign [saɪn] n (with hand) señal f, seña;
(trace) huella, rastro; (notice) letrero; (written)
signo ▷ vt firmar; (Sport) fichar; **to ~ sth
over to sb** firmar el traspaso de algo a algn;
sign for vt fus (item) firmar el recibo de;
sign in vi firmar el registro (al entrar); **sign
on** vi (BRIT: as unemployed) registrarse como
desempleado; (for course) inscribirse ▷ vt

(Mil) alistar; (employee) contratar; **sign up**
vi (Mil) alistarse; (for course) inscribirse ▷ vt
(player) fichar
signal [ˈsɪgnl] n señal f ▷ vi señalizar ▷ vt
(person) hacer señas a; (message) comunicar
por señales
signature [ˈsɪgnətʃə*] n firma
significance [sɪgˈnɪfɪkəns] n (importance)
trascendencia
significant [sɪgˈnɪfɪkənt] adj
significativo; (important) trascendente
signify [ˈsɪgnɪfaɪ] vt significar
sign language n lenguaje m para
sordomudos
signpost [ˈsaɪnpəʊst] n indicador m
Sikh [siːk] adj, n sij mf
silence [ˈsaɪlns] n silencio ▷ vt acallar;
(guns) reducir al silencio
silent [ˈsaɪlnt] adj silencioso; (not speaking)
callado; (film) mudo; **to remain ~** guardar
silencio
silhouette [sɪluˈɛt] n silueta
silicon chip [ˈsɪlɪkən-] n plaqueta de
silicio
silk [sɪlk] n seda ▷ adj de seda
silly [ˈsɪlɪ] adj (person) tonto; (idea) absurdo
silver [ˈsɪlvə*] n plata; (money) moneda
suelta ▷ adj de plata; (colour) plateado;
silver-plated adj plateado
similar [ˈsɪmɪlə*] adj: **~ (to)** parecido
or semejante (a); **similarity** [-ˈlærɪtɪ] n
semejanza; **similarly** adv del mismo modo
simmer [ˈsɪmə*] vi hervir a fuego lento
simple [ˈsɪmpl] adj (easy) sencillo;
(foolish, Comm: interest) simple; **simplicity**
[-ˈplɪsɪtɪ] n sencillez f; **simplify** [ˈsɪmplɪfaɪ]
vt simplificar; **simply** adv (live, talk)
sencillamente; (just, merely) sólo
simulate [ˈsɪmjuːleɪt] vt fingir, simular
simultaneous [sɪməlˈteɪnɪəs] adj
simultáneo; **simultaneously** adv
simultáneamente
sin [sɪn] n pecado ▷ vi pecar
since [sɪns] adv desde entonces, después
▷ prep desde ▷ conj (time) desde que;
(because) ya que, puesto que; **~ then, ever ~**
desde entonces
sincere [sɪnˈsɪə*] adj sincero; **sincerely**
adv: **yours sincerely** (in letters) le saluda
atentamente
sing [sɪŋ] (pt **sang**, pp **sung**) vt, vi cantar
Singapore [sɪŋəˈpɔː*] n Singapur m
singer [ˈsɪŋə*] n cantante mf
singing [ˈsɪŋɪŋ] n canto
single [ˈsɪŋgl] adj único, solo; (unmarried)
soltero; (not double) simple; **~ ticket** n
(BRIT: also: **~ ticket**) billete m sencillo;
(record) sencillo, single m; **singles** npl

(*Tennis*) individual *m*; **single out** *vt* (*choose*)
escoger; **single bed** *n* cama individual;
single file *n*: **in single file** en fila de uno;
single-handed *adv* sin ayuda; **single-
minded** *adj* resuelto, firme; **single parent**
n padre *m* soltero, madre *f* soltera (*o
divorciado etc*); **single parent family** familia
monoparental; **single room** *n* cuarto
individual

singular ['sɪŋgjulə*] *adj* (*odd*) raro,
extraño; (*outstanding*) excepcional ▷ *n*
(*Ling*) singular *m*

sinister ['sɪnɪstə*] *adj* siniestro

sink [sɪŋk] (*pt* sank, *pp* sunk) *n* fregadero
▷ *vt* (*ship*) hundir, echar a pique;
(*foundations*) excavar ▷ *vi* hundirse; **to ~
sth into** hundir algo en; **sink in** *vi* (*fig*)
penetrar, calar

sinus ['saɪnəs] *n* (*Anat*) seno

sip [sɪp] *n* sorbo ▷ *vt* sorber, beber a
sorbitos

sir [sə*] *n* señor *m*; **S~ John Smith** Sir John
Smith; **yes ~** sí, señor

siren ['saɪərn] *n* sirena

sirloin ['sə:lɔɪn] *n* (*also*: **~ steak**) solomillo

sister ['sɪstə*] *n* hermana; (*BRIT: nurse*)
enfermera jefe; **sister-in-law** *n* cuñada

sit [sɪt] (*pt, pp* **sat**) *vi* sentarse; (*be sitting*)
estar sentado; (*assembly*) reunirse; (*for
painter*) posar ▷ *vt* (*exam*) presentarse a;
sit back *vi* (*in seat*) recostarse; **sit down**
vi sentarse; **sit on** *vt fus* (*jury, committee*)
ser miembro de, formar parte de; **sit up** *vi*
incorporarse; (*not go to bed*) velar

sitcom ['sɪtkɔm] *n abbr* (= *situation comedy*)
comedia de situación

site [saɪt] *n* sitio; (*also*: **building ~**) solar
m ▷ *vt* situar

sitting ['sɪtɪŋ] *n* (*of assembly etc*) sesión
f; (*in canteen*) turno; **sitting room** *n* sala
de estar

situated ['sɪtjueɪtɪd] *adj* situado

situation [sɪtju'eɪʃən] *n* situación *f*; **"~s
vacant"** (*BRIT*) "ofrecen trabajo"

six [sɪks] *num* seis; **sixteen** *num* diez y
seis, dieciséis; **sixteenth** [sɪks'tiːnθ] *adj*
decimosexto; **sixth** [sɪksθ] *num* sexto;
sixth form *n* (*BRIT*) clase *f* de alumnos del
sexto año (*de 16 a 18 años de edad*); **sixth-
form college** *n* instituto *m* para alumnos
de 16 a 18 años; **sixtieth** ['sɪkstɪɪθ] *adj*
sexagésimo; **sixty** *num* sesenta

size [saɪz] *n* tamaño; (*extent*) extensión *f*;
(*of clothing*) talla; (*of shoes*) número; **sizeable**
adj importante, considerable

sizzle ['sɪzl] *vi* crepitar

skate [skeɪt] *n* patín *m*; (*fish: pl inv*) raya
▷ *vi* patinar; **skateboard** *n* monopatín *m*;

skateboarding *n* monopatín *m*; **skater**
n patinador(a) *m/f*; **skating** *n* patinaje *m*;
skating rink *n* pista de patinaje

skeleton ['skɛlɪtn] *n* esqueleto; (*Tech*)
armazón *f*; (*outline*) esquema *m*

skeptical ['skɛptɪkl] (*us*) = **sceptical**

sketch [skɛtʃ] *n* (*drawing*) dibujo; (*outline*)
esbozo, bosquejo; (*Theatre*) sketch *m* ▷ *vt*
dibujar; (*plan etc: also*: **~ out**) esbozar

skewer ['skjuːə*] *n* broqueta

ski: [skiː] *n* esquí *m* ▷ *vi* esquiar; **ski boot**
n bota de esquí

skid [skɪd] *n* patinazo ▷ *vi* patinar

ski: skier *n* esquiador(a) *m/f*; **skiing** *n*
esquí *m*

skilful ['skɪlful] (*us* **skillful**) *adj* diestro,
experto

ski lift *n* telesilla *m*, telesquí *m*

skill [skɪl] *n* destreza, pericia; técnica;
skilled *adj* hábil, diestro; (*worker*)
cualificado

skim [skɪm] *vt* (*milk*) desnatar; (*glide over*)
rozar, rasar ▷ *vi*: **to ~ through** (*book*) hojear;
skimmed milk (*us* **skim milk**) *n* leche *f*
desnatada

skin [skɪn] *n* piel *f*; (*complexion*) cutis *m*
▷ *vt* (*fruit etc*) pelar; (*animal*) despellejar;
skinhead *n* cabeza *m/f* rapada, skin(head)
m/f; **skinny** *adj* flaco

skip [skɪp] *n* brinco, salto; (*BRIT: container*)
contenedor *m* ▷ *vi* brincar; (*with rope*) saltar
a la comba ▷ *vt* saltarse

ski: ski pass *n* forfait *m* (de esquí); **ski pole**
n bastón *m* de esquiar

skipper ['skɪpə*] *n* (*Naut, Sport*) capitán *m*

skipping rope ['skɪpɪŋ-] (*us* **skip rope**)
n comba

skirt [skə:t] *n* falda, pollera (*sc*) ▷ *vt* (*go
round*) ladear

skirting board ['skə:tɪŋ-] (*BRIT*) *n* rodapié
m

ski slope *n* pista de esquí

ski suit *n* traje *m* de esquiar

skull [skʌl] *n* calavera; (*Anat*) cráneo

skunk [skʌŋk] *n* mofeta

sky [skaɪ] *n* cielo; **skyscraper** *n*
rascacielos *m inv*

slab [slæb] *n* (*stone*) bloque *m*; (*flat*) losa;
(*of cake*) trozo

slack [slæk] *adj* (*loose*) flojo; (*slow*) de poca
actividad; (*careless*) descuidado; **slacks** *npl*
pantalones *mpl*

slain [sleɪn] *pp of* **slay**

slam [slæm] *vt* (*throw*) arrojar
(violentamente); (*criticize*) criticar
duramente ▷ *vi* (*door*) cerrarse de golpe; **to
~ the door** dar un portazo

slander ['slɑːndə*] *n* calumnia,

difamación f

slang [slæŋ] n argot m; (jargon) jerga

slant [slɑːnt] n sesgo, inclinación f; (fig) interpretación f

slap [slæp] n palmada; (in face) bofetada ▷ vt dar una palmada or bofetada a; (paint etc): **to ~ sth on sth** embadurnar algo con algo ▷ adv (directly) exactamente, directamente

slash [slæʃ] vt acuchillar; (fig: prices) fulminar

slate [sleɪt] n pizarra ▷ vt (fig: criticize) criticar duramente

slaughter ['slɔːtə*] n (of animals) matanza; (of people) carnicería ▷ vt matar; **slaughterhouse** n matadero

Slav [slɑːv] adj eslavo

slave [sleɪv] n esclavo/a ▷ vi (also: ~ away) sudar tinta; **slavery** n esclavitud f

slay [sleɪ] (pt **slew**, pp **slain**) vt matar

sleazy ['sliːzɪ] adj de mala fama

sled [sled] (US) = **sledge**

sledge [sledʒ] n trineo

sleek [sliːk] adj (shiny) lustroso; (car etc) elegante

sleep [sliːp] (pt, pp **slept**) n sueño ▷ vi dormir; **to go to ~** quedarse dormido; **sleep in** vi (oversleep) quedarse dormido; **sleep together** vi (have sex) acostarse juntos; **sleeper** n (person) durmiente mf; (BRIT Rail: on track) traviesa f; (: train) coche-cama m; **sleeping bag** n saco de dormir; **sleeping car** n coche-cama m; **sleeping pill** n somnífero; **sleepover** n: **we're having a sleepover at Jo's** nos vamos a quedar a dormir en casa de Jo; **sleepwalk** vi caminar dormido; (habitually) ser sonámbulo; **sleepy** adj soñoliento; (place) soporífero

sleet [sliːt] n aguanieve f

sleeve [sliːv] n manga; (Tech) manguito; (of record) portada; **sleeveless** adj sin mangas

sleigh [sleɪ] n trineo

slender ['slendə*] adj delgado; (means) escaso

slept [slept] pt, pp of **sleep**

slew [sluː] pt of **slay** ▷ vi (BRIT: veer) torcerse

slice [slaɪs] n (of meat) tajada; (of bread) rebanada; (of lemon) rodaja; (utensil) pala ▷ vt cortar (en tajos), rebanar

slick [slɪk] adj (skilful) hábil, diestro; (clever) astuto ▷ n (also: **oil ~**) marea negra

slide [slaɪd] (pt, pp **slid**) n (movement) descenso; (in playground) tobogán m; (Phot) diapositiva; (BRIT: also: **hair ~**) pasador m ▷ vt correr, deslizar ▷ vi

(slip) resbalarse; (glide) deslizarse; **sliding** adj (door) corredizo

slight [slaɪt] adj (slim) delgado; (frail) delicado; (pain etc) leve; (trivial) insignificante; (small) pequeño ▷ n desaire m ▷ vt (insult) ofender, desairar; **not in the ~est** en absoluto; **slightly** adv ligeramente, un poco

slim [slɪm] adj delgado, esbelto; (fig: chance) remoto ▷ vi adelgazar; **slimming** n adelgazamiento

slimy ['slaɪmɪ] adj cenagoso

sling [slɪŋ] (pt, pp **slung**) n (Med) cabestrillo; (weapon) honda ▷ vt tirar, arrojar

slip [slɪp] n (slide) resbalón m; (mistake) descuido; (underskirt) combinación f; (of paper) papelito ▷ vt (slide) deslizar ▷ vi deslizarse; (stumble) resbalar(se); (decline) decaer; (move smoothly): **to ~ into/out of** (room etc) introducirse en/salirse de; **to give sb the ~** eludir a algn; **a ~ of the tongue** un lapsus; **to ~ sth on/off** ponerse/quitarse algo; **slip up** vi (make mistake) equivocarse; meter la pata

slipper ['slɪpə*] n zapatilla, pantufla

slippery ['slɪpərɪ] adj resbaladizo; **slip road** (BRIT) n carretera de acceso

slit [slɪt] (pt, pp **~**) n raja; (cut) corte m ▷ vt rajar; cortar

slog [slɔg] (BRIT) vi sudar tinta; **it was a ~** costó trabajo (hacerlo)

slogan ['sləʊgən] n eslogan m, lema m

slope [sləʊp] n (up) cuesta, pendiente f; (down) declive m; (side of mountain) falda, vertiente m ▷ vi: **to ~ down** estar en declive; **to ~ up** inclinarse; **sloping** adj en pendiente; en declive; (writing) inclinado

sloppy ['slɔpɪ] adj (work) descuidado; (appearance) desaliñado

slot [slɔt] n ranura ▷ vt: **to ~ into** encajar en; **slot machine** n (BRIT: vending machine) distribuidor m automático; (for gambling) tragaperras m inv

Slovakia [sləʊ'vækɪə] n Eslovaquia

Slovene [sləʊ'viːn] adj esloveno ▷ n esloveno/a; (Ling) esloveno; **Slovenia** [sləʊ'viːnɪə] n Eslovenia; **Slovenian** adj, n = **Slovene**

slow [sləʊ] adj lento; (not clever) lerdo; (watch): **to be ~** atrasar ▷ adv lentamente, despacio ▷ vt, vi retardar; "**~**" (road sign) "disminuir velocidad"; **slow down** vi reducir la marcha; **slowly** adv lentamente, despacio; **slow motion** n: **in slow motion** a cámara lenta

slug [slʌg] n babosa; (bullet) posta; **sluggish** adj lento; (person) perezoso

slum [slʌm] n casucha
slump [slʌmp] n (economic) depresión f
▷ vi hundirse; (prices) caer en picado
slung [slʌŋ] pt, pp of **sling**
slur [slə:*] n: **to cast a ~ on** insultar ▷ vt
(speech) pronunciar mal
sly [slaɪ] adj astuto; (smile) taimado
smack [smæk] n bofetada ▷ vt dar con la
mano a; (child, on face) abofetear ▷ vi: **to ~ of**
saber a, oler a
small [smɔ:l] adj pequeño; **small ads**
(BRIT) npl anuncios mpl por palabras; **small
change** n suelto, cambio
smart [smɑ:t] adj elegante; (clever) listo,
inteligente; (quick) rápido, vivo ▷ vi escocer,
picar; **smartcard** n tarjeta inteligente
smash [smæʃ] n (also: **~-up**) choque m;
(Mus) exitazo ▷ vt (break) hacer pedazos;
(car etc) estrellar; (Sport: record) batir
▷ vi hacerse pedazos; (against wall etc)
estrellarse; **smashing** (inf) adj estupendo
smear [smɪə*] n mancha; (Med) frotis m inv
▷ vt untar; **smear test** n (Med) citología,
frotis m inv (cervical)
smell [smɛl] (pt, pp **smelt** or **~ed**) n olor
m; (sense) olfato ▷ vt, vi oler; **smelly** adj
maloliente
smelt [smɛlt] pt, pp of **smell**
smile [smaɪl] n sonrisa ▷ vi sonreír
smirk [smə:k] n sonrisa falsa or afectada
smog [smɔg] n esmog m
smoke [sməuk] n humo ▷ vi fumar;
(chimney) echar humo ▷ vt (cigarettes)
fumar; **smoke alarm** n detector m de
humo, alarma contra incendios; **smoked**
adj (bacon, glass) ahumado; **smoker** n
fumador(a) m/f; (Rail) coche m fumador;
smoking n: **"no smoking"** "prohibido
fumar"

▌Be careful not to translate **smoking** by
the Spanish word smoking.

smoky adj (room) lleno de humo; (taste)
ahumado
smooth [smu:ð] adj liso; (sea) tranquilo;
(flavour, movement) suave; (sauce) fino;
(person: pej) meloso ▷ vt (also: **~ out**) alisar;
(creases, difficulties) allanar
smother ['smʌðə*] vt sofocar; (repress)
contener
SMS n abbr (= short message service) (servicio)
SMS; **SMS message** n (mensaje m) SMS
smudge ['smʌdʒ] n mancha ▷ vt manchar
smug [smʌg] adj presumido; orondo
smuggle ['smʌgl] vt pasar de
contrabando; **smuggling** n contrabando
snack [snæk] n bocado; **snack bar** n
cafetería
snag [snæg] n problema m

snail [sneɪl] n caracol m
snake [sneɪk] n serpiente f
snap [snæp] n (sound) chasquido;
(photograph) foto f ▷ adj (decision)
instantáneo ▷ vt (break) quebrar; (fingers)
castañetear ▷ vi quebrarse; (fig: speak
sharply) contestar bruscamente; **to ~ shut**
cerrarse de golpe; **snap at** vt fus (dog)
intentar morder; **snap up** vt agarrar;
snapshot n foto f (instantánea)
snarl [snɑ:l] vi gruñir
snatch [snætʃ] n (small piece) fragmento
▷ vt (snatch away) arrebatar; (fig) agarrar; **to
~ some sleep** encontrar tiempo para dormir
sneak [sni:k] (pt (us) **snuck**) vi: **to ~ in/out**
entrar/salir a hurtadillas ▷ n (inf) soplón/
ona m/f; **to ~ up on sb** aparecérsele de
improviso a algn; **sneakers** npl zapatos
mpl de lona
sneer [snɪə*] vi reír con sarcasmo;
(mock): **to ~ at** burlarse de
sneeze [sni:z] vi estornudar
sniff [snɪf] vi sollozar ▷ vt husmear, oler;
(drugs) esnifar
snigger ['snɪgə*] vi reírse con disimulo
snip [snɪp] n tijeretazo; (BRIT: inf: bargain)
ganga ▷ vt tijeretear
sniper ['snaɪpə*] n francotirador(a) m/f
snob [snɔb] n (e)snob mf
snooker ['snu:kə*] n especie de billar
snoop [snu:p] vi: **to ~ about** fisgonear
snooze [snu:z] n siesta ▷ vi echar una
siesta
snore [snɔ:*] n ronquido ▷ vi roncar
snorkel ['snɔ:kl] n (tubo) respirador m
snort [snɔ:t] n bufido ▷ vi bufar
snow [snəu] n nieve f ▷ vi nevar;
snowball n bola de nieve ▷ (fig)
agrandirse, ampliarse; **snowstorm** n
nevada, nevasca
snub [snʌb] vt (person) desairar ▷ n
desaire m, repulsa
snug [snʌg] adj (cosy) cómodo; (fitted)
ajustado

○ KEYWORD

so [səu] adv **1** (thus, likewise) así, de este
modo; **if so** de ser así; **I like swimming – so
do I** a mí me gusta nadar – a mí también;
I've got work to do – so has Paul tengo
trabajo que hacer – Paul también; **it's 5
o'clock – so it is!** son las cinco – ¡pues es
verdad!; **I hope/think so** espero/creo que
sí; **so far** hasta ahora; (in past) hasta este
momento
2 (in comparisons etc: to such a degree) tan;
so quickly (that) tan rápido (que); **so big**

(that) tan grande (que); **she's not so clever as her brother** no es tan lista como su hermano; **we were so worried** estábamos preocupadísimos
3: so much adj, adv tanto; **so many** tantos/as
4 (phrases): **10 or so** unos 10, 10 o así; **so long!** (inf: goodbye) ¡hasta luego!
▷ conj **1** (expressing purpose): **so as to do** para hacer; **so (that)** para que +subjun
2 (expressing result) así que; **so you see, I could have gone** así que ya ves, (yo) podría haber ido

soak [səuk] vt (drench) empapar; (steep in water) remojar ▷ vi remojarse, estar a remojo; **soak up** vt absorber; **soaking** adj (also: **soaking wet**) calado or empapado (hasta los huesos or el tuétano)
so-and-so ['səuənsəu] n (somebody) fulano/a de tal
soap [səup] n jabón m; **soap opera** n telenovela; **soap powder** n jabón m en polvo
soar [sɔː*] vi (on wings) remontarse; (rocket: prices) dispararse; (building etc) elevarse
sob [sɔb] n sollozo ▷ vi sollozar
sober ['səubə*] adj (serious) serio; (not drunk) sobrio; (colour, style) discreto; **sober up** vt quitar la borrachera
so-called ['səu'kɔːld] adj así llamado
soccer ['sɔkə*] n fútbol m
sociable ['səuʃəbl] adj sociable
social ['səuʃl] adj social ▷ n velada, fiesta; **socialism** n socialismo; **socialist** adj, n socialista mf; **socialize** vi: **to socialize (with)** alternar (con); **social life** n vida social; **socially** adv socialmente; **social security** n seguridad f social; **social services** npl servicios mpl sociales; **social work** n asistencia social; **social worker** n asistente/a m/f social
society [sə'saɪətɪ] n sociedad f; (club) asociación f; (also: **high ~**) alta sociedad
sociology [səusɪ'ɔlədʒɪ] n sociología
sock [sɔk] n calcetín m
socket ['sɔkɪt] n cavidad f; (BRIT Elec) enchufe m
soda ['səudə] n (Chem) sosa; (also: **~ water**) soda; (US: also: **~ pop**) gaseosa
sodium ['səudɪəm] n sodio
sofa ['səufə] n sofá m; **sofa bed** n sofá-cama m
soft [sɔft] adj (lenient, not hard) blando; (gentle, not bright) suave; **soft drink** n bebida no alcohólica; **soft drugs** npl drogas fpl blandas; **soften** ['sɔfn] vt

ablandar; suavizar; (effect) amortiguar ▷ vi ablandarse; suavizarse; **softly** adv suavemente; (gently) delicadamente, con delicadeza; **software** n (Comput) software m
soggy ['sɔgɪ] adj empapado
soil [sɔɪl] n (earth) tierra, suelo ▷ vt ensuciar
solar ['səulə*] adj solar; **solar power** n energía solar; **solar system** n sistema m solar
sold [səuld] pt, pp of **sell**
soldier ['səuldʒə*] n soldado; (army man) militar m
sold out adj (Comm) agotado
sole [səul] n (of foot) planta; (of shoe) suela; (fish: pl inv) lenguado ▷ adj único; **solely** adv únicamente, sólo, solamente; **I will hold you solely responsible** le consideraré el único responsable
solemn ['sɔləm] adj solemne
solicitor [sə'lɪsɪtə*] (BRIT) n (for wills etc) ≈ notario/a; (in court) ≈ abogado/a
solid ['sɔlɪd] adj sólido; (gold etc) macizo ▷ n sólido
solitary ['sɔlɪtərɪ] adj solitario, solo
solitude ['sɔlɪtjuːd] n soledad f
solo ['səuləu] n solo ▷ adv (fly) en solitario; **soloist** n solista m/f
soluble ['sɔljuːbl] adj soluble
solution [sə'luːʃən] n solución f
solve [sɔlv] vt resolver, solucionar
solvent ['sɔlvənt] adj (Comm) solvente ▷ n (Chem) solvente m
sombre ['sɔmbə*] (US **somber**) adj sombrío

○ **KEYWORD**

some [sʌm] adj **1** (a certain amount or number): **some tea/water/biscuits** té/agua/(unas) galletas; **there's some milk in the fridge** hay leche en el frigo; **there were some people outside** había algunas personas fuera; **I've got some money, but not much** tengo algo de dinero, pero no mucho
2 (certain: in contrasts) algunos/as; **some people say that ...** hay quien dice que ...; **some films were excellent, but most were mediocre** hubo películas excelentes, pero la mayoría fueron mediocres
3 (unspecified): **some woman was asking for you** una mujer estuvo preguntando por ti; **he was asking for some book (or other)** pedía un libro; **some day** algún día; **some day next week** un día de la semana que viene

▷ pron **1** (a certain number): **I've got some**
(books etc) tengo algunos/as
2 (a certain amount) algo; **I've got some**
(money, milk) tengo algo; **could I have some**
of that cheese? ¿me puede dar un poco de
ese queso?; **I've read some of the book** he
leído parte del libro
▷ adv: **some 10 people** unas 10 personas,
una decena de personas

some: somebody ['sʌmbədɪ] pron =
someone; somehow adv de alguna
manera; (for some reason) por una u otra
razón; **someone** pron alguien; **someplace**
(US) adv = **somewhere; something** pron
algo; **would you like something to eat/**
drink? ¿te gustaría cenar/tomar algo?;
sometime adv (in future) algún día, en
algún momento; (in past): **sometime last**
month durante el mes pasado; **sometimes**
adv a veces; **somewhat** adv algo;
somewhere adv (be) en alguna parte, (go) a
alguna parte; **somewhere else** (be) en otra
parte; (go) a otra parte
son [sʌn] n hijo
song [sɒŋ] n canción f
son-in-law ['sʌnɪnlɔː] n yerno
soon [suːn] adv pronto, dentro de poco;
~ afterwards poco después; see also **as**;
sooner adv (time) antes, más temprano;
(preference: rather): **I would sooner do that**
preferiría hacer eso; **sooner or later** tarde
o temprano
soothe [suːð] vt tranquilizar; (pain) aliviar
sophisticated [sə'fɪstɪkeɪtɪd] adj
sofisticado
sophomore ['sɒfəmɔː*] (US) n estudiante
mf de segundo año
soprano [sə'prɑːnəu] n soprano f
sorbet ['sɔːbeɪ] n sorbete m
sordid ['sɔːdɪd] adj (place etc) sórdido;
(motive etc) mezquino
sore [sɔː*] adj (painful) doloroso, que duele
▷ n llaga
sorrow ['sɒrəu] n pena, dolor m
sorry ['sɒrɪ] adj (regretful) arrepentido;
(condition, excuse) lastimoso; **~!** ¡perdón!,
¡perdone!; **~?** ¿cómo?; **to feel ~ for sb**
tener lástima a algn; **I feel ~ for him** me da
lástima
sort [sɔːt] n clase f, género, tipo; **sort out**
vt (papers) clasificar; (organize) ordenar,
organizar; (resolve: problem, situation etc)
arreglar, solucionar
SOS n SOS m
so-so ['səusəu] adv regular, así así
sought [sɔːt] pt, pp of **seek**
soul [səul] n alma

sound [saund] n (noise) sonido, ruido;
(volume: on TV etc) volumen m; (Geo) estrecho
▷ adj (healthy) sano; (safe, not damaged)
en buen estado; (reliable: person) digno de
confianza; (sensible) sensato, razonable;
(secure: investment) seguro ▷ adv: **~ asleep**
profundamente dormido ▷ vt (alarm) sonar
▷ vi sonar, resonar; (fig: seem) parecer; **to ~**
like sonar a; **soundtrack** n (of film) banda
sonora
soup [suːp] n (thick) sopa; (thin) caldo
sour ['sauə*] adj agrio; (milk) cortado; **it's ~**
grapes (fig) están verdes
source [sɔːs] n fuente f
south [sauθ] n sur m ▷ adj del sur,
sureño ▷ adv al sur, hacia el sur; **South**
Africa n África del Sur; **South African**
adj, n sudafricano/a m/f; **South America**
n América del Sur, Sudamérica; **South**
American adj, n sudamericano/a m/f;
southbound adj (con) rumbo al sur;
southeastern [sauθ'iːstən] adj sureste,
del sureste; **southern** ['sʌðən] adj del sur,
meridional; **South Korea** n Corea del Sur;
South Pole n Polo Sur; **southward(s)** adv
hacia el sur; **south-west** n suroeste m;
southwestern [sauθ'westən] adj suroeste
souvenir [suːvə'nɪə*] n recuerdo
sovereign ['sɒvrɪn] adj, n soberano/a m/f
sow¹ [səu] (pt ~ed, pp sown) vt sembrar
sow² [sau] n cerda, puerca
soya ['sɔɪə] (BRIT) n soja
spa [spɑː] n balneario
space [speɪs] n espacio; (room) sitio
▷ cpd espacial ▷ vt (also: **~ out**) espaciar;
spacecraft n nave f espacial; **spaceship** n
= **spacecraft**
spacious ['speɪʃəs] adj amplio
spade [speɪd] n (tool) pala, laya; **spades** npl
(Cards: British) picas fpl; (: Spanish) espadas fpl
spaghetti [spə'getɪ] n espaguetis mpl,
fideos mpl
Spain [speɪn] n España
spam [spæm] n (junk e-mail) spam m
span [spæn] n (of bird, plane) envergadura;
(of arch) luz f; (in time) lapso ▷ vt extenderse
sobre, cruzar; (fig) abarcar
Spaniard ['spænjəd] n español(a) m/f
Spanish ['spænɪʃ] adj español(a) ▷ n
(Ling) español m, castellano; **the Spanish**
npl los españoles
spank [spæŋk] vt zurrar
spanner ['spænə*] (BRIT) n llave f (inglesa)
spare [speə*] adj de reserva; (surplus)
sobrante, de más ▷ n = **spare part** ▷ vt (do
without) pasarse sin; (refrain from hurting)
perdonar; **to ~** (surplus) sobrante, de sobra;
spare part n pieza de repuesto; **spare**

room n cuarto de los invitados; **spare time** n tiempo libre; **spare tyre** (US **spare tire**) n (Aut) neumático or llanta (LAM) de recambio; **spare wheel** n (Aut) rueda de recambio

spark [spɑːk] n chispa; (fig) chispazo; **spark(ing) plug** n bujía

sparkle ['spɑːkl] n centelleo, destello ⊳ vi (shine) relucir, brillar

sparrow ['spærəu] n gorrión m

sparse [spɑːs] adj esparcido, escaso

spasm ['spæzəm] n (Med) espasmo

spat [spæt] pt, pp of **spit**

spate [speɪt] n (fig): **a ~ of** un torrente de

spatula ['spætjulə] n espátula

speak [spiːk] (pt **spoke**, pp **spoken**) vt (language) hablar; (truth) decir ⊳ vi hablar; (make a speech) intervenir; **to ~ to sb/of** or **about sth** hablar con algn/de or sobre algo; **~ up!** ¡habla fuerte!; **speaker** n (in public) orador(a) m/f; (also: **loudspeaker**) altavoz m; (for stereo etc) bafle m; (Pol): **the Speaker** (BRIT) el Presidente de la Cámara de los Comunes; (US) el Presidente del Congreso

spear [spɪə*] n lanza ⊳ vt alancear

special ['speʃl] adj especial; (edition etc) extraordinario; (delivery) urgente; **special delivery** n (Post): **by special delivery** por entrega urgente; **special effects** npl (Cine) efectos mpl especiales; **specialist** n especialista mf; **speciality** [speʃɪ'ælɪtɪ] (BRIT) n especialidad f; **specialize** vi: **to specialize (in)** especializarse (en); **specially** adv sobre todo, en particular; **special needs** npl (BRIT): **children with special needs** niños que requieren una atención diferenciada; **special offer** n (Comm) oferta especial; **special school** n (BRIT) colegio m de educación especial; **specialty** (US) n = **speciality**

species ['spiːʃiːz] n inv especie f

specific [spə'sɪfɪk] adj específico; **specifically** adv específicamente

specify ['spesɪfaɪ] vt, vi especificar, precisar

specimen ['spesɪmən] n ejemplar m; (Med: of urine) espécimen m; (: of blood) muestra

speck [spek] n grano, mota

spectacle ['spektəkl] n espectáculo; **spectacles** npl (BRIT: glasses) gafas fpl (SP), anteojos mpl; **spectacular** [-'tækjulə*] adj espectacular; (success) impresionante

spectator [spek'teɪtə*] n espectador(a) m/f

spectrum ['spektrəm] (pl **spectra**) n espectro

speculate ['spekjuleɪt] vi: **to ~ (on)** especular (en)

sped [sped] pt, pp of **speed**

speech [spiːtʃ] n (faculty) habla; (formal talk) discurso; (spoken language) lenguaje m; **speechless** adj mudo, estupefacto

speed [spiːd] n velocidad f; (haste) prisa; (promptness) rapidez f; **at full** or **top ~** a máxima velocidad; **speed up** vi acelerarse ⊳ vt acelerar; **speedboat** n lancha motora; **speeding** n (Aut) exceso de velocidad; **speed limit** n límite m de velocidad, velocidad f máxima; **speedometer** [spɪ'dɔmɪtə*] n velocímetro; **speedy** adj (fast) veloz, rápido; (prompt) pronto

spell [spel] (pt, pp **spelt** (BRIT) or **~ed**) n (also: **magic ~**) encanto, hechizo; (period of time) rato, período ⊳ vt deletrear; (fig) anunciar, presagiar; **to cast a ~ on sb** hechizar a algn; **he can't ~** pone faltas de ortografía; **spell out** vt (explain): **to spell sth out for sb** explicar algo a algn en detalle; **spellchecker** ['speltʃekə*] n corrector m ortográfico; **spelling** n ortografía

spelt [spelt] pt, pp of **spell**

spend [spend] (pt, pp **spent**) vt (money) gastar; (time) pasar; (life) dedicar; **spending** n: **government spending** gastos mpl del gobierno

spent [spent] pt, pp of **spend** ⊳ adj (cartridge, bullets, match) usado

sperm [spəːm] n esperma

sphere [sfɪə*] n esfera

spice [spaɪs] n especia ⊳ vt condimentar

spicy ['spaɪsɪ] adj picante

spider ['spaɪdə*] n araña

spike [spaɪk] n (point) punta; (Bot) espiga

spill [spɪl] (pt, pp **spilt** or **~ed**) vt derramar, verter ⊳ vi derramarse; **to ~ over** desbordarse

spin [spɪn] (pt, pp **spun**) n (Aviat) barrena; (trip in car) paseo (en coche); (on ball) efecto ⊳ vt (wool etc) hilar; (ball etc) hacer girar ⊳ vi girar, dar vueltas

spinach ['spɪnɪtʃ] n espinaca; (as food) espinacas fpl

spinal ['spaɪnl] adj espinal

spin doctor n informador(a) parcial al servicio de un partido político etc

spin-dryer (BRIT) n secador m centrífugo

spine [spaɪn] n espinazo, columna vertebral; (thorn) espina

spiral ['spaɪərl] n espiral f ⊳ vi (fig: prices) subir desorbitadamente

spire ['spaɪə*] n aguja, chapitel m

spirit ['spɪrɪt] n (soul) alma; (ghost) fantasma m; (attitude, sense) espíritu m; (courage) valor m, ánimo; **spirits** npl (drink) licor(es) m(pl); **in good ~s** alegre, de buen ánimo

spiritual ['spɪrɪtjuəl] *adj* espiritual ▷ *n* espiritual *m*

spit [spɪt] (*pt, pp* **spat**) *n* (*for roasting*) asador *m*, espetón *m*; (*saliva*) saliva ▷ *vi* escupir; (*sound*) chisporrotear; (*rain*) lloviznar

spite [spaɪt] *n* rencor *m*, ojeriza ▷ *vt* causar pena a, mortificar; **in ~ of** a pesar de, pese a; **spiteful** *adj* rencoroso, malévolo

splash [splæʃ] *n* (*sound*) chapoteo; (*of colour*) mancha ▷ *vt* salpicar ▷ *vi* (*also:* **~ about**) chapotear; **splash out** (*inf*) *vi* (BRIT) derrochar dinero

splendid ['splendɪd] *adj* espléndido

splinter ['splɪntə*] *n* (*of wood etc*) astilla; (*in finger*) espigón *m* ▷ *vi* astillarse, hacer astillas

split [splɪt] (*pt, pp* **~**) *n* hendedura, raja; (*fig*) división *f*; (*Pol*) escisión *f* ▷ *vt* partir, rajar; (*party*) dividir; (*share*) repartir ▷ *vi* dividirse, escindirse; **split up** *vi* (*couple*) separarse; (*meeting*) acabarse

spoil [spɔɪl] (*pt, pp* **~t** *or* **~ed**) *vt* (*damage*) dañar; (*mar*) estropear; (*child*) mimar, consentir

spoilt [spɔɪlt] *pt, pp of* **spoil** ▷ *adj* (*child*) mimado, consentido; (*ballot paper*) invalidado

spoke [spəʊk] *pt of* **speak** ▷ *n* rayo, radio

spoken ['spəʊkn] *pp of* **speak**

spokesman ['spəʊksmən] (*irreg*) *n* portavoz *m*

spokesperson ['spəʊkspəːsn] (*irreg*) *n* portavoz *m/f*, vocero/a (LAM)

spokeswoman ['spəʊkswʊmən] (*irreg*) *n* portavoz *f*

sponge [spʌndʒ] *n* esponja; (*also:* **~ cake**) bizcocho ▷ *vt* (*wash*) lavar con esponja ▷ *vi*: **to ~ off** *or* **on sb** vivir a costa de algn; **sponge bag** (BRIT) *n* esponjera

sponsor ['spɒnsə*] *n* patrocinador(a) *m/f* ▷ *vt* (*applicant, proposal etc*) proponer; **sponsorship** *n* patrocinio

spontaneous [spɒn'teɪnɪəs] *adj* espontáneo

spooky ['spuːkɪ] (*inf*) *adj* espeluznante, horripilante

spoon [spuːn] *n* cuchara; **spoonful** *n* cucharada

sport [spɔːt] *n* deporte *m*; (*person*): **to be a good ~** ser muy majo ▷ *vt* (*wear*) lucir, ostentar; **sport jacket** (US) *n* = **sports jacket**; **sports car** *n* coche *m* deportivo; **sports centre** (BRIT) *n* polideportivo; **sports jacket** (BRIT) *n* chaqueta deportiva; **sportsman** (*irreg*) *n* deportista *m*; **sports utility vehicle** *n* todoterreno *m inv*;

sportswear *n* trajes *mpl* de deporte *or* sport; **sportswoman** (*irreg*) *n* deportista; **sporty** *adj* deportista

spot [spɒt] *n* sitio, lugar *m*; (*dot: on pattern*) punto, mancha; (*pimple*) grano; (*Radio*) cuña publicitaria; (*TV*) espacio publicitario; (*small amount*): **a ~ of** un poquito de ▷ *vt* (*notice*) notar, observar; **on the ~** allí mismo; **spotless** *adj* perfectamente limpio; **spotlight** *n* foco, reflector *m*; (*Aut*) faro auxiliar

spouse [spauz] *n* cónyuge *mf*

sprain [spreɪn] *n* torcedura ▷ *vt*: **to ~ one's ankle/wrist** torcerse el tobillo/la muñeca

sprang [spræŋ] *pt of* **spring**

sprawl [sprɔːl] *vi* tumbarse

spray [spreɪ] *n* rociada; (*of sea*) espuma; (*container*) atomizador *m*; (*for paint etc*) pistola rociadora; (*of flowers*) ramita ▷ *vt* rociar; (*crops*) regar

spread [spred] (*pt, pp* **~**) *n* extensión *f*; (*for bread etc*) pasta para untar; (*inf: food*) comilona ▷ *vt* extender; (*butter*) untar; (*wings, sails*) desplegar; (*work, wealth*) repartir; (*scatter*) esparcir ▷ *vi* (*also:* **~ out**: *stain*) extenderse; (*news*) diseminarse; **spread out** *vi* (*move apart*) separarse; **spreadsheet** *n* hoja electrónica *or* de cálculo

spree [spriː] *n*: **to go on a ~** ir de juerga

spring [sprɪŋ] (*pt* **sprang**, *pp* **sprung**) *n* (*season*) primavera; (*leap*) salto, brinco; (*coiled metal*) resorte *m*; (*of water*) fuente *f*, manantial *m* ▷ *vi* saltar, brincar; **spring up** *vi* (*thing: appear*) aparecer; (*problem*) surgir; **spring onion** *n* cebolleta

sprinkle ['sprɪŋkl] *vt* (*pour: liquid*) rociar; (: *salt, sugar*) espolvorear; **to ~ water etc on, ~ with water etc** rociar *or* salpicar de agua *etc*

sprint [sprɪnt] *n* esprint *m* ▷ *vi* esprintar

sprung [sprʌŋ] *pp of* **spring**

spun [spʌn] *pt, pp of* **spin**

spur [spəː*] *n* espuela; (*fig*) estímulo, aguijón *m* ▷ *vt* (*also:* **~ on**) estimular, incitar; **on the ~ of the moment** de improviso

spurt [spəːt] *n* chorro; (*of energy*) arrebato ▷ *vi* chorrear

spy [spaɪ] *n* espía *mf* ▷ *vi*: **to ~ on** espiar a ▷ *vt* (*see*) divisar, lograr ver

sq. *abbr* = **square**

squabble ['skwɒbl] *vi* reñir, pelear

squad [skwɒd] *n* (*Mil*) pelotón *m*; (*Police*) brigada; (*Sport*) equipo

squadron ['skwɒdrn] *n* (*Mil*) escuadrón *m*; (*Aviat, Naut*) escuadra

s

squander ['skwɔndə*] vt (money) derrochar, despilfarrar; (chances) desperdiciar

square [skwɛə*] n cuadro; (in town) plaza; (inf: person) carca m/f ▷ adj cuadrado; (inf: ideas, tastes) trasnochado ▷ vt (arrange) arreglar; (Math) cuadrar; (reconcile) compaginar; **all ~** igual(es); **to have a ~ meal** comer caliente; **2 metres ~** 2 metros en cuadro; **2 ~ metres** 2 metros cuadrados; **square root** n raíz f cuadrada

squash [skwɔʃ] n (BRIT: drink): **lemon/ orange ~** zumo (SP) or jugo (LAM) de limón/ naranja; (US Bot) calabacín m; (Sport) squash m ▷ vt aplastar

squat [skwɔt] adj achaparrado ▷ vi (also: **~ down**) agacharse, sentarse en cuclillas; **2 ~ metres** 2 metros ▷ n okupa mf (SP)

squeak [skwiːk] vi (hinge) chirriar, rechinar; (mouse) chillar

squeal [skwiːl] vi chillar, dar gritos agudos

squeeze [skwiːz] n presión f; (of hand) apretón m; (Comm) restricción f ▷ vt (hand, arm) apretar

squid [skwɪd] n inv calamar m; (Culin) calamares mpl

squint [skwɪnt] vi bizquear, ser bizco ▷ n (Med) estrabismo

squirm [skwəːm] vi retorcerse, revolverse

squirrel ['skwɪrəl] n ardilla

squirt [skwəːt] vi salir a chorros ▷ vt chiscar

Sr abbr = **senior**

Sri Lanka [srɪ'læŋkə] n Sri Lanka m

St abbr = **saint; street**

stab [stæb] n (with knife) puñalada; (of pain) pinchazo; (inf: try): **to have a ~ at (doing) sth** intentar (hacer) algo ▷ vt apuñalar

stability [stə'bɪlɪtɪ] n estabilidad f

stable ['steɪbl] adj estable ▷ n cuadra, caballeriza

stack [stæk] n montón m, pila ▷ vt amontonar, apilar

stadium ['steɪdɪəm] n estadio

staff [stɑːf] n (work force) personal m, plantilla; (BRIT Scol) cuerpo docente ▷ vt proveer de personal

stag [stæg] n ciervo, venado

stage [steɪdʒ] n escena; (point) etapa; (platform) plataforma; (profession): **the ~** el teatro ▷ vt (play) poner en escena, representar; (organize) montar, organizar; **in ~s** por etapas

stagger ['stægə*] vi tambalearse ▷ vt (amaze) asombrar; (hours, holidays) escalonar; **staggering** adj asombroso

stagnant ['stægnənt] adj estancado

stag night, stag party n despedida de soltero

stain [steɪn] n mancha; (colouring) tintura ▷ vt manchar; (wood) teñir; **stained glass** n vidrio m de color; **stainless steel** n acero inoxidable

staircase ['stɛəkeɪs] n = **stairway**

stairs [stɛəz] npl escaleras fpl

stairway ['stɛəweɪ] n escalera

stake [steɪk] n estaca, poste m; (Comm) interés m; (Betting) apuesta ▷ vt (money) apostar; (life) arriesgar; (reputation) poner en juego; (claim) presentar una reclamación; **to be at ~** estar en juego

stale [steɪl] adj (bread) duro; (food) pasado; (smell) rancio; (beer) agrio

stalk [stɔːk] n tallo, caña ▷ vt acechar, cazar al acecho

stall [stɔːl] n (in market) puesto; (in stable) casilla (de establo) ▷ vt (Aut) calar; (fig) dar largas a ▷ vi (Aut) calarse; (fig) andarse con rodeos

stamina ['stæmɪnə] n resistencia

stammer ['stæmə*] n tartamudeo ▷ vi tartamudear

stamp [stæmp] n sello (SP), estampilla (LAM), timbre m (MEX); (mark) marca, huella; (on document) timbre m ▷ vi (also: **~ one's foot**) patear ▷ vt (mark) marcar; (letter) franquear; (with rubber stamp) sellar; **stamp out** vt (fire) apagar con el pie; (crime, opposition) acabar con; **stamped addressed envelope** n (BRIT) sobre m sellado con las señas propias

stampede [stæm'piːd] n estampida

stance [stæns] n postura

stand [stænd] (pt, pp **stood**) n (position) posición f, postura; (for taxis) parada; (hall stand) perchero; (music stand) atril m; (Sport) tribuna; (at exhibition) stand m ▷ vi (be) estar, encontrarse; (be on foot) estar de pie; (rise) levantarse; (remain) quedar en pie; (in election) presentar candidatura ▷ vt (place) poner, colocar; (withstand) aguantar, soportar; (invite to) invitar; **to make a ~** (fig) mantener una postura firme; **to ~ for parliament** (BRIT) presentarse (como candidato) a las elecciones; **stand back** vi retirarse; **stand by** vi (be ready) estar listo ▷ vt fus (opinion) aferrarse a; (person) apoyar; **stand down** vi (withdraw) ceder el puesto; **stand for** vt fus (signify) significar; (tolerate) aguantar, permitir; **stand in for** vt fus suplir a; **stand out** vi destacarse; **stand up** vi levantarse, ponerse de pie; **stand up for** vt fus defender; **stand up to** vt fus hacer frente a

standard ['stændəd] n patrón m, norma; (level) nivel m; (flag) estandarte m ▷ adj (*size etc*) normal, corriente; (*text*) básico; **standards** npl (*morals*) valores mpl morales; **standard of living** n nivel m de vida

standing ['stændɪŋ] adj (*on foot*) de pie, en pie; (*permanent*) permanente ▷ n reputación f; **of many years'** que lleva muchos años; **standing order** (BRIT) n (*at bank*) orden f de pago permanente

stand: standpoint n punto de vista; **standstill** n: **at a standstill** (*industry, traffic*) paralizado; (*car*) parado; **to come to a standstill** quedar paralizado; pararse

stank [stæŋk] pt of **stink**

staple ['steɪpl] n (*for papers*) grapa ▷ adj (*food etc*) básico ▷ vt grapar

star [stɑː*] n estrella; (*celebrity*) estrella, astro ▷ vt (*Theatre, Cinema*) ser el/la protagonista de; **the stars** npl (*Astrology*) el horóscopo

starboard ['stɑːbəd] n estribor m

starch [stɑːtʃ] n almidón m

stardom ['stɑːdəm] n estrellato

stare [stɛə*] n mirada fija ▷ vi: **to ~ at** mirar fijo

stark [stɑːk] adj (*bleak*) severo, escueto ▷ adv: **~ naked** en cueros

start [stɑːt] n principio, comienzo; (*departure*) salida; (*sudden movement*) salto, sobresalto; (*advantage*) ventaja ▷ vt empezar, comenzar; (*cause*) causar; (*found*) fundar; (*engine*) poner en marcha ▷ vi comenzar, empezar; (*with fright*) asustarse, sobresaltarse; (*train etc*) salir; **to ~ doing** or **to do sth** empezar a hacer algo; **start off** vi empezar, comenzar; (*leave*) salir, ponerse en camino; **start out** vi (*begin*) empezar; (*set out*) partir, salir; **start up** vi comenzar; (*car*) ponerse en marcha ▷ vt comenzar; poner en marcha; **starter** n (*Aut*) botón m de arranque; (*Sport: official*) juez mf de salida; (BRIT *Culin*) entrante m; **starting point** n punto de partida

startle ['stɑːtl] vt asustar, sobrecoger; **startling** adj alarmante

starvation [stɑː'veɪʃən] n hambre f

starve [stɑːv] vi tener mucha hambre; (*to death*) morir de hambre ▷ vt hacer pasar hambre

state [steɪt] n estado ▷ vt (*say, declare*) afirmar; **the S~s** los Estados Unidos; **to be in a ~** estar agitado; **statement** n afirmación f; **state school** n escuela or colegio estatal; **statesman** (*irreg*) n estadista m

static ['stætɪk] n (*Radio*) parásitos mpl ▷ adj estático

station ['steɪʃən] n estación f; (*Radio*) emisora; (*rank*) posición f social ▷ vt

colocar, situar; (*Mil*) apostar

stationary ['steɪʃnərɪ] adj estacionario, fijo

stationer's (shop) (BRIT) n papelería

stationery [-nərɪ] n papel m de escribir, artículos mpl de escritorio

station wagon (US) n ranchera

statistic [stə'tɪstɪk] n estadística; **statistics** n (*science*) estadística

statue ['stætjuː] n estatua

stature ['stætʃə*] n estatura; (*fig*) talla

status ['steɪtəs] n estado; (*reputation*) estatus m; **status quo** n (e)statu quo m

statutory ['stætjutrɪ] adj estatutario

staunch [stɔːntʃ] adj leal, incondicional

stay [steɪ] n estancia ▷ vi quedar(se); (*as guest*) hospedarse; **to ~ put** seguir en el mismo sitio; **to ~ the night/5 days** pasar la noche/estar 5 días; **stay away** vi (*from person, building*) no acercarse; (*from event*) no acudir; **stay behind** vi quedar atrás; **stay in** vi quedarse en casa; **stay on** vi quedarse; **stay out** vi (*of house*) no volver a casa; (*on strike*) permanecer en huelga; **stay up** vi (*at night*) velar, no acostarse

steadily ['stɛdɪlɪ] adv constantemente; (*firmly*) firmemente; (*work, walk*) sin parar; (*gaze*) fijamente

steady ['stɛdɪ] adj (*firm*) firme; (*regular*) regular; (*person, character*) sensato, juicioso; (*boyfriend*) formal; (*look, voice*) tranquilo ▷ vt (*stabilize*) estabilizar; (*nerves*) calmar

steak [steɪk] n filete m; (*beef*) bistec m

steal [stiːl] (pt **stole**, pp **stolen**) vt robar ▷ vi robar; (*move secretly*) andar a hurtadillas

steam [stiːm] n vapor m; (*mist*) vaho, humo ▷ vt (*Culin*) cocer al vapor ▷ vi echar vapor; **steam up** vi (*window*) empañarse; **to get steamed up about sth** (*fig*) ponerse negro por algo; **steamy** adj (*room*) lleno de vapor; (*window*) empañado; (*heat, atmosphere*) bochornoso

steel [stiːl] n acero ▷ adj de acero

steep [stiːp] adj escarpado, abrupto; (*stair*) empinado; (*price*) exorbitante, excesivo ▷ vt empapar, remojar

steeple ['stiːpl] n aguja

steer [stɪə*] vt (*car*) conducir (SP), manejar (LAM); (*person*) dirigir ▷ vi conducir, manejar; **steering** n (*Aut*) dirección f; **steering wheel** n volante m

stem [stɛm] n (*of plant*) tallo; (*of glass*) pie m ▷ vt detener; (*blood*) restañar

step [stɛp] n paso; (*on stair*) peldaño, escalón m ▷ vi: **to ~ forward/back** dar un paso adelante/hacia atrás; **steps** npl (BRIT) = **stepladder**; **in/out of ~ (with)** acorde/en disonancia (con); **step down**

vi (fig) retirarse; **step in** vi entrar; (fig) intervenir; **step up** vt (increase) aumentar; **stepbrother** n hermanastro; **stepchild** (pl **stepchildren**) n hijastro/a m/f; **stepdaughter** n hijastra; **stepfather** n padrastro; **stepladder** n escalera doble or de tijera; **stepmother** n madrastra; **stepsister** n hermanastra; **stepson** n hijastro

stereo ['stɛrɪəu] n estéreo ▷ adj (also: ~phonic) estéreo, estereofónico

stereotype ['stɪərɪətaɪp] n estereotipo ▷ vt estereotipar

sterile ['stɛraɪl] adj estéril; **sterilize** ['stɛrɪlaɪz] vt esterilizar

sterling ['stə:lɪŋ] adj (silver) de ley ▷ n (Econ) libras fpl esterlinas fpl; **one pound ~** una libra esterlina

stern [stə:n] adj severo, austero ▷ n (Naut) popa

steroid ['stɪərɔɪd] n esteroide m

stew [stju:] n estofado, guiso ▷ vt estofar, guisar; (fruit) cocer

steward ['stju:əd] n camarero; **stewardess** n (esp on plane) azafata

stick [stɪk] (pt, pp **stuck**) n palo; (of dynamite) barreno; (as weapon) porra; (also: **walking ~**) bastón m ▷ vt (glue) pegar; (inf: put) meter; (: tolerate) aguantar, soportar; (thrust); **to ~ sth into** clavar or hincar algo en ▷ vi pegarse; (be unmoveable) quedarse parado; (in mind) quedarse grabado; **stick out** vi sobresalir; **stick up** vi sobresalir; **stick up for** vt fus defender; **sticker** n (label) etiqueta engomada; (with slogan) pegatina; **sticking plaster** n esparadrapo; **stick shift** (us) n (Aut) palanca de cambios

sticky ['stɪkɪ] adj pegajoso; (label) engomado; (fig) difícil

stiff [stɪf] adj rígido, tieso; (hard) duro; (manner) estirado; (difficult) difícil; (person) inflexible; (price) exorbitante ▷ adv: **scared/bored ~** muerto de miedo/aburrimiento

stifling ['staɪflɪŋ] adj (heat) sofocante, bochornoso

stigma ['stɪgmə] n (fig) estigma m

stiletto [stɪ'lɛtəu] (BRIT) n (also: ~ **heel**) tacón m de aguja

still [stɪl] adj inmóvil, quieto ▷ adv todavía; (even) aun; (nonetheless) sin embargo, aun así

stimulate ['stɪmjuleɪt] vt estimular

stimulus ['stɪmjuləs] (pl **stimuli**) n estímulo, incentivo

sting [stɪŋ] (pt, pp **stung**) n picadura; (pain) escozor m, picazón f; (organ) aguijón m ▷ vt, vi picar

stink [stɪŋk] (pt **stank**, pp **stunk**) n hedor m, tufo ▷ vi heder, apestar

stir [stə:*] n (fig: agitation) conmoción f ▷ vt (tea etc) remover; (fig: emotions) provocar ▷ vi moverse; **stir up** vt (trouble) fomentar; **stir-fry** vt sofreír removiendo ▷ n plato preparado sofriendo y removiendo los ingredientes

stitch [stɪtʃ] n (Sewing) puntada; (Knitting) punto; (Med) punto (de sutura); (pain) punzada ▷ vt coser; (Med) suturar

stock [stɔk] n (Comm: reserves) existencias fpl, stock m; (: selection) surtido; (Agr) ganado, ganadería; (Culin) caldo; (descent) raza, estirpe f; (Finance) capital m ▷ adj (fig: reply etc) clásico ▷ vt (have in stock) tener existencias de; **~s and shares** acciones y valores; **in ~** en existencia or almacén; **out of ~** agotado; **to take ~ of** (fig) asesorar, examinar; **stockbroker** ['stɔkbrəukə*] n agente m/or corredor m/f de bolsa(a); **stock cube** (BRIT) n pastilla de caldo; **stock exchange** n bolsa; **stockholder** ['stɔkhəuldə*] (us) n accionista m/f

stocking ['stɔkɪŋ] n media

stock market n bolsa (de valores)

stole [stəul] pt of **steal** ▷ n estola

stolen ['stəuln] pp of **steal**

stomach ['stʌmək] n (Anat) estómago; (belly) vientre m ▷ vt tragar, aguantar; **stomachache** n dolor m de estómago

stone [stəun] n piedra; (in fruit) hueso (= 6.348 kg; 14 libras) ▷ adj de piedra ▷ vt apedrear; (fruit) deshuesar

stood [stud] pt, pp of **stand**

stool [stu:l] n taburete m

stoop [stu:p] vi (also: ~ **down**) doblarse, agacharse; (also: **have a ~**) ser cargado de espaldas

stop [stɔp] n parada; (in punctuation) punto ▷ vt parar, detener; (break) suspender; (block: pay) suspender; (: cheque) invalidar; (also: **put a ~ to**) poner término a ▷ vi pararse, detenerse; (end) acabarse; **to ~ doing sth** dejar de hacer algo; **stop by** vi pasar por; **stop off** vi interrumpir el viaje; **stopover** n parada; (Aviat) escala; **stoppage** n (strike) paro; (blockage) obstrucción f

storage ['stɔ:rɪdʒ] n almacenaje m

store [stɔ:*] n (stock) provisión f; (depot) (BRIT: large shop) almacén m; (us) tienda; (reserve) reserva, repuesto ▷ vt almacenar; **stores** npl víveres mpl; **to be in ~ for sb** (fig) esperarle a algn; **storekeeper** (us) n tendero/a

storey ['stɔ:rɪ] (us **story**) n piso

storm [stɔ:m] n tormenta; (fig: of

applause) salva; (: *of criticism*) nube f ▷ *vi* (*fig*) rabiar ▷ *vt* tomar por asalto; **stormy** *adj* tempestuoso

story ['stɔːrɪ] *n* historia; (*lie*) mentira; (*us*) = **storey**

stout [staʊt] *adj* (*strong*) sólido; (*fat*) gordo, corpulento; (*resolute*) resuelto ▷ *n* cerveza negra

stove [stəʊv] *n* (*for cooking*) cocina; (*for heating*) estufa

straight [streɪt] *adj* recto, derecho; (*frank*) franco, directo; (*simple*) sencillo ▷ *adv* derecho, directamente; (*drink*) sin mezcla; **to put** or **get sth ~** dejar algo en claro; **~ away**, **~ off** en seguida; **straighten** *vt* (*also*: **straighten out**) enderezar, poner derecho ▷ *vi* (*also*: **straighten up**) enderezarse, ponerse derecho; **straightforward** *adj* (*simple*) sencillo; (*honest*) honrado, franco

strain [streɪn] *n* tensión f; (*Tech*) presión f; (*Med*) torcedura; (*breed*) tipo, variedad f ▷ *vt* (*back etc*) torcerse; (*resources*) agotar; (*stretch*) estirar; (*food, tea*) colar; **strained** *adj* (*muscle*) torcido; (*laugh*) forzado; (*relations*) tenso; **strainer** *n* colador m

strait [streɪt] *n* (*Geo*) estrecho (*fig*): **to be in dire ~s** estar en un gran apuro

strand [strænd] *n* (*of thread*) hebra; (*of hair*) trenza; (*of rope*) ramal m; **stranded** *adj* (*person: without money*) desamparado; (: *without transport*) colgado

strange [streɪndʒ] *adj* (*not known*) desconocido; (*odd*) extraño, raro; **strangely** *adv* de un modo raro; **stranger** *n* desconocido/a; (*from another area*) forastero/a

■ Be careful not to translate **stranger** by the Spanish word *extranjero*.

strangle ['stræŋgl] *vt* estrangular

strap [stræp] *n* correa; (*of slip, dress*) tirante m

strategic [strə'tiːdʒɪk] *adj* estratégico

strategy ['strætɪdʒɪ] *n* estrategia

straw [strɔː] *n* paja; (*drinking straw*) caña, pajita; **that's the last ~!** ¡eso es el colmo!

strawberry ['strɔːbərɪ] *n* fresa, frutilla (*sc*)

stray [streɪ] *adj* (*animal*) extraviado; (*bullet*) perdido; (*scattered*) disperso ▷ *vi* extraviarse, perderse

streak [striːk] *n* raya; (*in hair*) raya ▷ *vt* rayar ▷ *vi*: **to ~ past** pasar como un rayo

stream [striːm] *n* riachuelo, arroyo; (*of people, vehicles*) riada, caravana; (*of smoke, insults etc*) chorro ▷ *vt* (*Scol*) dividir en grupos por habilidad ▷ *vi* correr, fluir; **to ~ in/out** (*people*) entrar/salir en tropel

street [striːt] *n* calle f; **streetcar** (*us*) *n* tranvía m; **street light** *n* farol m (*LAM*), farola (*sp*); **street map** *n* plano (de la ciudad); **street plan** *n* plano

strength [streŋθ] *n* fuerza; (*of girder, knot etc*) resistencia; (*fig: power*) poder m; **strengthen** *vt* fortalecer, reforzar

strenuous ['strenjʊəs] *adj* (*energetic, determined*) enérgico

stress [stres] *n* presión f; (*mental strain*) estrés m; (*accent*) acento ▷ *vt* subrayar, recalcar; (*syllable*) acentuar; **stressed** *adj* (*tense*) estresado, agobiado; (*syllable*) acentuado; **stressful** *adj* (*job*) estresante

stretch [stretʃ] *n* (*of sand*) trecho ▷ *vi* estirarse; (*extend*): **to ~ to** or **as far as** extenderse hasta ▷ *vt* extender, estirar; (*make demands*) exigir el máximo esfuerzo a; **stretch out** *vi* tenderse ▷ *vt* (*arm etc*) extender; (*spread*) estirar

stretcher ['stretʃə*] *n* camilla

strict [strɪkt] *adj* severo; (*exact*) estricto; **strictly** *adv* severamente; estrictamente

stride [straɪd] (*pt* **strode**, *pp* **stridden**) *n* zancada, tranco ▷ *vi* dar zancadas, andar a trancos

strike [straɪk] (*pt, pp* **struck**) *n* huelga; (*of oil etc*) descubrimiento; (*attack*) ataque m ▷ *vt* golpear, pegar; (*oil etc*) descubrir; (*bargain, deal*) cerrar ▷ *vi* declarar la huelga; (*attack*) atacar; (*clock*) dar la hora; **on ~** (*workers*) en huelga; **to ~ a match** encender un fósforo; **striker** *n* huelguista mf; (*Sport*) delantero; **striking** *adj* llamativo

string [strɪŋ] (*pt, pp* **strung**) *n* cuerda; (*row*) hilera ▷ *vt*: **to ~ together** ensartar; **to ~ out** extenderse; **the strings** *npl* (*Mus*) los instrumentos de cuerda; **to pull ~s** (*fig*) mover palancas

strip [strɪp] *n* tira; (*of land*) franja; (*of metal*) cinta, lámina ▷ *vt* desnudar; (*paint*) quitar; (*also*: **~ down**: *machine*) desmontar ▷ *vi* desnudarse; **strip off** *vt* (*paint etc*) quitar ▷ *vi* (*person*) desnudarse

stripe [straɪp] *n* raya; (*Mil*) galón m; **striped** *adj* a rayas, rayado

stripper ['strɪpə*] *n* artista mf de striptease

strip-search ['strɪpsəːtʃ] *vt*: **to ~ sb** desnudar y registrar a algn

strive [straɪv] (*pt* **strove**, *pp* **striven**) *vi*: **to ~ for sth/to do sth** luchar por conseguir/ hacer algo

strode [strəʊd] *pt of* **stride**

stroke [strəʊk] *n* (*blow*) golpe m; (*Swimming*) brazada; (*Med*) apoplejía; (*of paintbrush*) toque m ▷ *vt* acariciar; **at a ~** de un solo golpe

stroll [strəul] n paseo, vuelta ▷ vi dar un paseo or una vuelta; **stroller** (us) n (for child) sillita de ruedas

strong [strɔŋ] adj fuerte; **they are 50 ~** son 50; **stronghold** n fortaleza; (fig) baluarte m; **strongly** adv fuertemente, con fuerza; (believe) firmemente

strove [strəuv] pt of **strive**

struck [strʌk] pt, pp of **strike**

structure ['strʌktʃə*] n estructura; (building) construcción f

struggle ['strʌgl] n lucha ▷ vi luchar

strung [strʌŋ] pt, pp of **string**

stub [stʌb] n (of ticket etc) talón m; (of cigarette) colilla; **to ~ one's toe on sth** dar con el dedo (del pie) contra algo; **stub out** vt apagar

stubble ['stʌbl] n rastrojo; (on chin) barba (incipiente)

stubborn ['stʌbən] adj terco, testarudo

stuck [stʌk] pt, pp of **stick** ▷ adj (jammed) atascado

stud [stʌd] n (shirt stud) corchete m; (of boot) taco; (earring) pendiente m (de bolita); (also: ~ **farm**) caballeriza; (also: ~ **horse**) caballo semental ▷ vt (fig): **~ded with** salpicado de

student ['stju:dənt] n estudiante mf ▷ adj estudiantil; **student driver** (us) n conductor(a) mf en prácticas; **students' union** (building) centro de estudiantes; (BRIT: association) federación f de estudiantes

studio ['stju:dɪəu] n estudio; (artist's) taller m; **studio flat** n estudio

study ['stʌdɪ] n estudio ▷ vt estudiar; (examine) examinar, investigar ▷ vi estudiar

stuff [stʌf] n materia; (substance) material m, sustancia; (things) cosas fpl ▷ vt llenar; (Culin) rellenar; (animals) disecar; (inf: push) meter; **stuffing** n relleno; **stuffy** adj (room) mal ventilado; (person) de miras estrechas

stumble ['stʌmbl] vi tropezar, dar un traspié; **to ~ across, ~ on** (fig) tropezar con

stump [stʌmp] n (of tree) tocón m; (of limb) muñón m ▷ vt: **to be ~ed for an answer** no saber qué contestar

stun [stʌn] vt dejar sin sentido

stung [stʌŋ] pt, pp of **sting**

stunk [stʌŋk] pp of **stink**

stunned [stʌnd] adj (dazed) aturdido, atontado; (amazed) pasmado; (shocked) anonadado

stunning ['stʌnɪŋ] adj (fig: news) pasmoso; (: outfit etc) sensacional

stunt [stʌnt] n (in film) escena peligrosa; (publicity stunt) truco publicitario

stupid ['stju:pɪd] adj estúpido, tonto; **stupidity** [-'pɪdɪtɪ] n estupidez f

sturdy ['stə:dɪ] adj robusto, fuerte

stutter ['stʌtə*] n tartamudeo ▷ vi tartamudear

style [staɪl] n estilo; **stylish** adj elegante, a la moda; **stylist** n (hair stylist) peluquero/a

sub... [sʌb] prefix sub...; **subconscious** adj subconsciente

subdued [səb'dju:d] adj (light) tenue; (person) sumiso, manso

subject [n 'sʌbdʒɪkt, vb səb'dʒɛkt] n súbdito; (Scol) asignatura; (matter) tema m; (Grammar) sujeto ▷ vt: **to ~ sb to sth** someter a algn a algo; **to be ~ to** (law) estar sujeto a; (person) ser propenso a; **subjective** [-'dʒɛktɪv] adj subjetivo; **subject matter** (content) contenido

subjunctive [səb'dʒʌŋktɪv] adj, n subjuntivo

submarine [sʌbmə'ri:n] n submarino

submission [səb'mɪʃən] n sumisión f

submit [səb'mɪt] vt someter ▷ vi: **to ~ to sth** someterse a algo

subordinate [sə'bɔ:dɪnət] adj, n subordinado/a m/f

subscribe [səb'skraɪb] vi suscribir; **to ~ to** (opinion, fund) suscribir, aprobar; (newspaper) suscribirse a

subscription [səb'skrɪpʃən] n abono; (to magazine) subscripción f

subsequent ['sʌbsɪkwənt] adj subsiguiente, posterior; **subsequently** adv posteriormente, más tarde

subside [səb'saɪd] vi hundirse; (flood) bajar; (wind) amainar

subsidiary [səb'sɪdɪərɪ] adj secundario ▷ n sucursal f, filial f

subsidize ['sʌbsɪdaɪz] vt subvencionar

subsidy ['sʌbsɪdɪ] n subvención f

substance ['sʌbstəns] n sustancia

substantial [səb'stænʃl] adj sustancial, sustancioso; (fig) importante

substitute ['sʌbstɪtju:t] n (person) suplente mf; (thing) sustituto ▷ vt: **to ~ A for B** sustituir A por B, reemplazar B por A; **substitution** n sustitución f

subtle ['sʌtl] adj sutil

subtract [səb'trækt] vt restar, sustraer

suburb ['sʌbə:b] n barrio residencial; **the ~s** las afueras (de la ciudad); **suburban** [sə'bə:bən] adj suburbano; (train etc) de cercanías

subway ['sʌbweɪ] n (BRIT) paso subterráneo or inferior; (us) metro

succeed [sək'si:d] vi (person) tener éxito; (plan) salir bien ▷ vt suceder a; **to ~ in**

doing lograr hacer

success [sək'sɛs] n éxito

▎Be careful not to translate **success** by the Spanish word *suceso*.

successful adj exitoso; (business) próspero; **to be successful (in doing)** lograr (hacer); **successfully** adv con éxito

succession [sək'sɛʃən] n sucesión f, serie f

successive [sək'sɛsɪv] adj sucesivo, consecutivo

successor [sək'sɛsə*] n sucesor(a) m/f

succumb [sə'kʌm] vi sucumbir

such [sʌtʃ] adj tal, semejante; (of that kind): **~ a book** tal libro; (so much): **~ courage** tanto valor ▷ adv tan; **~ a long trip** un viaje tan largo; **~ a lot of** tanto/a(s); **~ as** (like) tal como; **as ~** como tal; **such-and-such** adj tal o cual

suck [sʌk] vt chupar; (bottle) sorber; (breast) mamar

Sudan [su'dæn] n Sudán m

sudden ['sʌdn] adj (rapid) repentino, súbito; (unexpected) imprevisto; **all of a ~** de repente; **suddenly** adv de repente

Sunday [su:] vt demandar

suede [sweɪd] n ante m, gamuza

suffer ['sʌfə*] vt sufrir, padecer; (tolerate) aguantar, soportar ▷ vi sufrir; **to ~ from** (illness etc) padecer; **suffering** n sufrimiento

suffice [sə'faɪs] vi bastar, ser suficiente

sufficient [sə'fɪʃənt] adj suficiente, bastante

suffocate ['sʌfəkeɪt] vi ahogarse, asfixiarse

sugar ['ʃugə*] n azúcar m ▷ vt echar azúcar a, azucarar

suggest [sə'dʒɛst] vt sugerir; **suggestion** [-'dʒɛstʃən] n sugerencia

suicide ['suɪsaɪd] n suicidio; (person) suicida mf; see also **commit**; **suicide attack** n atentado suicida; **suicide bomber** n terrorista mf suicida; **suicide bombing** n atentado suicida

suit [su:t] n (man's) traje m; (woman's) conjunto; (Law) pleito; (Cards) palo ▷ vt convenir; (clothes) sentar a, ir bien a; (adapt): **to ~ sth to** adaptar or ajustar algo a; **well ~ed** (well matched: couple) hecho el uno para el otro; **suitable** adj conveniente; (apt) indicado; **suitcase** n maleta, valija (RPL)

suite [swi:t] n (of rooms, Mus) suite f; (furniture): **bedroom/dining room ~** (juego de) dormitorio/comedor; see also **three-piece suite**

sulfur ['sʌlfə*] (US) n = **sulphur**

sulk [sʌlk] vi estar de mal humor

sulphur ['sʌlfə*] (US sulfur) n azufre m

sultana [sʌl'tɑːnə] n (fruit) pasa de Esmirna

sum [sʌm] n suma; (total) total m; **sum up** vt resumir ▷ vi hacer un resumen

summarize ['sʌməraɪz] vt resumir

summary ['sʌmərɪ] n resumen m ▷ adj (justice) sumario

summer ['sʌmə*] n verano ▷ cpd de verano; **in ~** en verano; **summer holidays** npl vacaciones fpl de verano; **summertime** n (season) verano

summit ['sʌmɪt] n cima, cumbre f; (also: **~ conference**, **~ meeting**) (conferencia) cumbre f

summon ['sʌmən] vt (person) llamar; (meeting) convocar; (Law) citar

Sun. abbr (= Sunday) dom

sun [sʌn] n sol m; **sunbathe** vi tomar el sol; **sunbed** n cama solar; **sunblock** n filtro solar; **sunburn** n (painful) quemadura; (tan) bronceado; **sunburned, sunburnt** adj (painfully) quemado por el sol; (tanned) bronceado

Sunday ['sʌndɪ] n domingo

sunflower ['sʌnflauə*] n girasol m

sung [sʌŋ] pp of **sing**

sunglasses ['sʌnglɑːsɪz] npl gafas fpl (SP) or anteojos fpl (LAM) de sol

sunk [sʌŋk] pp of **sink**

sun: sunlight n luz f del sol; **sun lounger** n tumbona, perezosa (LAM); **sunny** adj soleado; (day) de sol; (fig) alegre; **sunrise** n salida del sol; **sun roof** n (Aut) techo corredizo; **sunscreen** n protector m solar; **sunset** n puesta del sol; **sunshade** n (over table) sombrilla; **sunshine** n sol m; **sunstroke** n insolación f; **suntan** n bronceado; **suntan lotion** n bronceador m; **suntan oil** n aceite m bronceador

super ['su:pə*] (inf) adj genial

superb [su:'pə:b] adj magnífico, espléndido

superficial [su:pə'fɪʃəl] adj superficial

superintendent [su:pərɪn'tɛndənt] n director(a) m/f; (Police) subjefe/a m/f

superior [su'pɪərɪə*] adj superior; (smug) desdeñoso ▷ n superior m

superlative [su'pə:lətɪv] n superlativo

supermarket ['su:pəmɑːkɪt] n supermercado

supernatural [su:pə'nætʃərəl] adj sobrenatural ▷ n: **the ~** lo sobrenatural

superpower ['su:pəpauə*] n (Pol) superpotencia

superstition [su:pə'stɪʃən] n superstición f

superstitious [su:pə'stɪʃəs] adj supersticioso

S

superstore ['su:pəstɔ:*] n (BRIT)
hipermercado

supervise ['su:pəvaiz] vt supervisar;
supervision [-'vɪʒən] n supervisión f;
supervisor n supervisor(a) m/f

supper ['sʌpə*] n cena

supple ['sʌpl] adj flexible

supplement [n 'sʌplɪmənt, vb sʌplɪ'mɛnt]
n suplemento ▷ vt suplir

supplier [sə'plaɪə*] n (Comm)
distribuidor(a) m/f

supply [sə'plaɪ] vt (provide) suministrar;
(equip): **to ~ (with)** proveer (de) ▷ n
provisión f; (of gas, water etc) suministro;
supplies npl (food) víveres mpl; (Mil)
pertrechos mpl

support [sə'pɔ:t] n apoyo; (Tech) soporte
m ▷ vt apoyar; (financially) mantener;
(uphold, Tech) sostener

▌ Be careful not to translate **support** by
the Spanish word soportar.

supporter n (Pol etc) partidario/a; (Sport)
aficionado/a

suppose [sə'pəuz] vt suponer; (imagine)
imaginarse; (duty): **to be ~d to do sth** deber
hacer algo; **supposedly** [sə'pəuzɪdlɪ] adv
según cabe suponer; **supposing** conj en
caso de que

suppress [sə'prɛs] vt suprimir; (yawn)
ahogar

supreme [su'pri:m] adj supremo

surcharge ['sə:tʃɑ:dʒ] n sobretasa,
recargo

sure [ʃuə*] adj seguro; (definite, convinced)
cierto; **to make ~ of sth/that** asegurarse
de algo/asegurar que; **~!** (of course) ¡claro!,
¡por supuesto!; **~ enough** efectivamente;
surely adv (certainly) seguramente

surf [sə:f] n olas fpl ▷ vt: **to ~ the Net**
navegar por Internet

surface ['sə:fɪs] n superficie f ▷ vt (road)
revestir ▷ vi salir a la superficie; **by ~ mail**
por vía terrestre

surfboard ['sə:fbɔ:d] n tabla (de surf)

surfer ['sə:fə*] n (in sea) surfista mf; **web** or
net ~ internauta mf

surfing ['sə:fɪŋ] n surf m

surge [sə:dʒ] n oleada, oleaje m ▷ vi (wave)
romper; (people) avanzar en tropel

surgeon ['sə:dʒən] n cirujano/a

surgery ['sə:dʒərɪ] n cirugía; (BRIT: room)
consultorio

surname ['sə:neɪm] n apellido

surpass [sə:'pɑ:s] vt superar, exceder

surplus ['sə:pləs] n excedente m; (Comm)
superávit m ▷ adj excedente, sobrante

surprise [sə'praɪz] n sorpresa ▷ vt
sorprender; **surprised** adj (look, smile) de

sorpresa; **to be surprised** sorprenderse;
surprising adj sorprendente; **surprisingly**
adv: **it was surprisingly easy** me etc
sorprendió lo fácil que fue

surrender [sə'rɛndə*] n rendición f,
entrega ▷ vi rendirse, entregarse

surround [sə'raund] vt rodear,
circundar; (Mil etc) cercar; **surrounding**
adj circundante; **surroundings** npl
alrededores mpl, cercanías fpl

surveillance [sə:'veɪləns] n vigilancia

survey [n 'sə:veɪ, vb sə:'veɪ] n inspección
f, reconocimiento; (inquiry) encuesta ▷ vt
examinar, inspeccionar; (look at) mirar,
contemplar; **surveyor** n agrimensor(a) m/f

survival [sə'vaɪvl] n supervivencia

survive [sə'vaɪv] vi sobrevivir; (custom
etc) perdurar ▷ vt sobrevivir a; **survivor** n
superviviente mf

suspect [adj, n 'sʌspɛkt, vb səs'pɛkt] adj, n
sospechoso/a m/f ▷ vt (person) sospechar
de; (think) sospechar

suspend [səs'pɛnd] vt suspender;
suspended sentence n (Law) libertad f
condicional; **suspenders** npl (BRIT) ligas
fpl; (us) tirantes mpl

suspense [səs'pɛns] n incertidumbre f,
duda; (in film etc) suspense m; **to keep sb in
~** mantener a algn en suspense

suspension [səs'pɛnʃən] n (gen, Aut)
suspensión f; (of driving licence) privación f;
suspension bridge n puente m colgante

suspicion [səs'pɪʃən] n sospecha; (distrust)
recelo; **suspicious** adj receloso; (causing
suspicion) sospechoso

sustain [səs'teɪn] vt sostener, apoyar;
(suffer) sufrir, padecer

SUV (esp us) n abbr (= sports utility vehicle)
todoterreno m inv, 4x4 m

swallow ['swɒləu] n (bird) golondrina ▷ vt
tragar; (fig.: pride) tragarse

swam [swæm] pt of **swim**

swamp [swɒmp] n pantano, ciénaga
▷ vt (with water etc) inundar; (fig) abrumar,
agobiar

swan [swɒn] n cisne m

swap [swɒp] n canje m, intercambio
▷ vt: **to ~ (for)** cambiar (por)

swarm [swɔ:m] n (of bees) enjambre
m; (fig) multitud f ▷ vi (bees) formar un
enjambre; (people) pulular; **to be ~ing with**
ser un hervidero de

sway [sweɪ] vi mecerse, balancearse ▷ vt
(influence) mover, influir en

swear [swɛə*] (pt swore, pp sworn) vi
(curse) maldecir; (promise) jurar ▷ vt jurar;
swear in vt: **to be sworn in** prestar
juramento; **swearword** n taco, palabrota

sweat [swɛt] n sudor m ▷ vi sudar
sweater ['swɛtə*] n suéter m
sweatshirt ['swɛtʃəːt] n suéter m
sweaty ['swɛtɪ] adj sudoroso
Swede [swiːd] n sueco/a
swede [swiːd] (BRIT) n nabo
Sweden ['swiːdn] n Suecia; **Swedish**
['swiːdɪʃ] adj sueco ▷ n (Ling) sueco
sweep [swiːp] (pt, pp **swept**) n (act)
barrido; (also: **chimney ~**) deshollinador(a)
m/f ▷ vt barrer; (with arm) empujar; (current)
arrastrar ▷ vi barrer; (arm etc) moverse
rápidamente; (wind) soplar con violencia
sweet [swiːt] n (candy) dulce m, caramelo;
(BRIT: pudding) postre m ▷ adj dulce;
(fig: kind) dulce, amable; (: attractive) mono;
sweetcorn n maíz m; **sweetener**
['swiːtnə*] n (Culin) edulcorante m;
sweetheart n novio/a; **sweetshop** n
(BRIT) confitería, bombonería
swell [swɛl] (pt **-ed**, pp **swollen** or
-ed) n (of sea) marejada, oleaje m ▷ adj
(us: inf: excellent) estupendo, fenomenal ▷ vt
hinchar, inflar ▷ vi (also: **~ up**) hincharse;
(numbers) aumentar; (sound, feeling) ir
aumentando; **swelling** n (Med) hinchazón f
swept [swɛpt] pt, pp of **sweep**
swerve [swəːv] vi desviarse bruscamente
swift [swɪft] n (bird) vencejo ▷ adj rápido,
veloz
swim [swɪm] (pt **swam**, pp **swum**) n: **to go
for a ~** ir a nadar or a bañarse ▷ vi nadar;
(head, room) dar vueltas ▷ vt nadar; (the
Channel etc) cruzar a nado; **swimmer** n
nadador(a) m/f; **swimming** n natación f;
swimming costume (BRIT) n bañador m,
traje m de baño; **swimming pool** n piscina,
alberca (MEX), pileta (RPL); **swimming
trunks** npl bañador m (de hombre);
swimsuit n =**swimming costume**
swing [swɪŋ] (pt, pp **swung**) n (in
playground) columpio; (movement) balanceo,
vaivén m; (change of direction) viraje m;
(rhythm) ritmo ▷ vt balancear; (also: **~
round**) voltear, girar ▷ vi balancearse,
columpiarse; (also: **~ round**) dar media
vuelta; **to be in full ~** estar en plena marcha
swipe card [swaɪp-] n tarjeta magnética
deslizante, tarjeta swipe
swirl [swəːl] vi arremolinarse
Swiss [swɪs] adj, n inv suizo/a m/f
switch [swɪtʃ] n (for light etc) interruptor
m; (change) cambio ▷ vt (change) cambiar
de; **switch off** vt apagar; (engine) parar;
switch on vt encender (SP), prender (LAM);
(engine, machine) arrancar; **switchboard** n
(Tel) centralita (SP), conmutador m (LAM)
Switzerland ['swɪtsələnd] n Suiza

swivel ['swɪvl] vi (also: **~ round**) girar
swollen ['swəʊlən] pp of **swell**
swoop [swuːp] n (by police etc) redada ▷ vi
(also: **~ down**) calarse
swop [swɔp] = **swap**
sword [sɔːd] n espada; **swordfish** n pez
m espada
swore [swɔː*] pt of **swear**
sworn [swɔːn] pp of **swear** ▷ adj
(statement) bajo juramento; (enemy)
implacable
swum [swʌm] pp of **swim**
swung [swʌŋ] pt, pp of **swing**
syllable ['sɪləbl] n sílaba
syllabus ['sɪləbəs] n programa m de
estudios
symbol ['sɪmbl] n símbolo; **symbolic(al)**
[sɪm'bɔlɪk(l)] adj simbólico; **to be
symbolic(al) of sth** simbolizar algo
symmetrical [sɪ'mɛtrɪkl] adj simétrico
symmetry ['sɪmɪtrɪ] n simetría
sympathetic [sɪmpə'θɛtɪk] adj
(understanding) comprensivo; (showing
support): **~ to(wards)** bien dispuesto hacia
  Be careful not to translate **sympathetic**
  by the Spanish word simpático.
sympathize ['sɪmpəθaɪz] vi: **to ~ with**
(person) compadecerse de; (feelings)
comprender; (cause) apoyar
sympathy ['sɪmpəθɪ] n (pity) compasión f
symphony ['sɪmfənɪ] n sinfonía
symptom ['sɪmptəm] n síntoma m,
indicio
synagogue ['sɪnəgɔg] n sinagoga
syndicate ['sɪndɪkɪt] n sindicato; (of
newspapers) agencia (de noticias)
syndrome ['sɪndrəʊm] n síndrome m
synonym ['sɪnənɪm] n sinónimo
synthetic [sɪn'θɛtɪk] adj sintético
Syria ['sɪrɪə] n Siria
syringe [sɪ'rɪndʒ] n jeringa
syrup ['sɪrəp] n jarabe m; (also: **golden ~**)
almíbar m
system ['sɪstəm] n sistema m; (Anat)
organismo; **systematic** [-'mætɪk] adj
sistemático, metódico; **systems analyst** n
analista mf de sistemas

ta [tɑː] (BRIT: inf) excl ¡gracias!
tab [tæb] n lengüeta; (label) etiqueta; **to keep ~s on** (fig) vigilar
table ['teɪbl] n mesa; (of statistics etc) cuadro, tabla ▷ vt (BRIT: motion etc) presentar; **to lay** or **set the ~** poner la mesa; **tablecloth** n mantel m; **table d'hôte** [tɑːbl'dəut] adj del menú; **table lamp** n lámpara de mesa; **tablemat** n (for plate) posaplatos m inv; (for hot dish) salvamantel m; **tablespoon** n cuchara de servir; (also: **tablespoonful**: as measurement) cucharada
tablet ['tæblɪt] n (Med) pastilla, comprimido; (of stone) lápida
table tennis n ping-pong m, tenis m de mesa
tabloid ['tæblɔɪd] n periódico popular sensacionalista

⬤ **TABLOID PRESS**
⬤
⬤ El término **tabloid press** o **tabloids**
⬤ se usa para referirse a la prensa
⬤ popular británica, por el tamaño más
⬤ pequeño de los periódicos. A diferencia
⬤ de los de la llamada **quality press**,
⬤ estas publicaciones se caracterizan
⬤ por un lenguaje sencillo, una
⬤ presentación llamativa y un contenido
⬤ sensacionalista, centrado a veces en los
⬤ escándalos financieros y sexuales de los
⬤ famosos, por lo que también reciben el
⬤ nombre peyorativo de "gutter press".

taboo [tə'buː] adj, n tabú m
tack [tæk] n (nail) tachuela; (fig) rumbo ▷ vt (nail) clavar con tachuelas; (stitch) hilvanar ▷ vi virar
tackle ['tækl] n (fishing tackle) aparejo (de pescar); (for lifting) aparejo ▷ vt (difficulty) enfrentarse con; (challenge: person) hacer

frente a; (grapple with) agarrar; (Football) cargar; (Rugby) placar
tacky ['tækɪ] adj pegajoso; (pej) cutre
tact [tækt] n tacto, discreción f; **tactful** adj discreto, diplomático
tactics ['tæktɪks] npl táctica
tactless ['tæktlɪs] adj indiscreto
tadpole ['tædpəul] n renacuajo
taffy ['tæfɪ] (US) n melcocha
tag [tæg] n (label) etiqueta
tail [teɪl] n cola; (of shirt, coat) faldón m ▷ vt (follow) vigilar a; **tails** npl (formal suit) levita
tailor ['teɪlə*] n sastre m
Taiwan [taɪ'wɑːn] n Taiwán m; **Taiwanese** [taɪwə'niːz] adj, n taiwanés/esa m/f
take [teɪk] (pt **took**, pp **taken**) vt tomar; (grab) coger (SP), agarrar (LAM); (gain: prize) ganar; (require: effort, courage) exigir; (tolerate: pain etc) aguantar; (hold: passengers etc) tener cabida para; (accompany, bring, carry) llevar; (exam) presentarse a; **to ~ sth from** (drawer etc) sacar algo de; (person) quitar algo a; **I ~ it that ...** supongo que ...; **take after** vt fus parecerse a; **take apart** vt desmontar; **take away** vt (remove) quitar; (carry) llevar; (Math) restar; **take back** vt (return) devolver; (one's words) retractarse de; **take down** vt (building) derribar; (letter etc) apuntar; **take in** vt (deceive) engañar; (understand) entender; (include) abarcar; (lodger) acoger, recibir; **take off** vi (Aviat) despegar ▷ vt (remove) quitar; **take on** vt (work) aceptar; (employee) contratar; (opponent) desafiar; **take out** vt sacar; **take over** vt (business) tomar posesión de; (country) tomar el poder ▷ vi: **to take over from sb** reemplazar a algn; **take up** vt (a dress) acortar; (occupy: time, space) ocupar; (engage in: hobby etc) dedicarse a; (accept): **to take sb up on** aceptar algo de algn; **takeaway** (BRIT) adj (food) para llevar ▷ n tienda or restaurante m de comida para llevar; **taken** pp of **take**; **takeoff** n (Aviat) despegue m; **takeout** (US) n = **takeaway**; **takeover** n (Comm) absorción f; **takings** npl (Comm) ingresos mpl
talc [tælk] n (also: **~um powder**) (polvos de) talco
tale [teɪl] n (story) cuento; (account) relación f; **to tell ~s** (fig) chivarse
talent ['tælnt] n talento; **talented** adj de talento
talk [tɔːk] n charla; (conversation) conversación f; (gossip) habladurías fpl, chismes mpl ▷ vi hablar; **talks** npl (Pol etc) conversaciones fpl; **to ~ about** hablar de; **to ~ sb into doing sth** convencer a algn para que haga algo; **to ~ sb out of doing sth**

disuadir a algn de que haga algo; **to ~ shop** hablar del trabajo; **talk over** vt discutir; **talk show** n programa m de entrevistas

tall [tɔːl] adj alto; (object) grande; **to be 6 feet ~** (person) ≈ medir 1 metro 80

tambourine [tæmbə'riːn] n pandereta

tame [teɪm] adj domesticado; (fig) mediocre

tamper ['tæmpə*] vi: **to ~ with** tocar, andar con

tampon ['tæmpən] n tampón m

tan [tæn] n (also: **sun~**) bronceado ▷ vi ponerse moreno ▷ adj (colour) marrón

tandem ['tændəm] n tándem m

tangerine [tændʒə'riːn] n mandarina

tangle ['tæŋgl] n enredo; **to get in(to) a ~** enredarse

tank [tæŋk] n (water tank) depósito, tanque m; (for fish) acuario; (Mil) tanque m

tanker ['tæŋkə*] n (ship) buque m, cisterna; (truck) camión m cisterna

tanned [tænd] adj (skin) moreno

tantrum ['tæntrəm] n rabieta

Tanzania [tænzə'nɪə] n Tanzania

tap [tæp] n (BRIT: on sink etc) grifo (SP), llave f, canilla (RPL); (gas tap) llave f; (gentle blow) golpecito ▷ vt (hit gently) dar golpecitos en; (resources) utilizar, explotar; (telephone) intervenir; **on ~** (fig: resources) a mano; **tap dancing** n claqué m

tape [teɪp] n (also: **magnetic ~**) cinta magnética; (cassette) cassette f, cinta; (sticky tape) cinta adhesiva; (for tying) cinta ▷ vt (record) grabar (en cinta); (stick with tape) pegar con cinta adhesiva; **tape measure** n cinta métrica, metro; **tape recorder** n grabadora

tapestry ['tæpɪstrɪ] n (object) tapiz m; (art) tapicería

tar [tɑː] n alquitrán m, brea

target ['tɑːgɪt] n blanco

tariff ['tærɪf] n (on goods) arancel m; (BRIT: in hotels etc) tarifa

tarmac ['tɑːmæk] n (BRIT: on road) asfaltado; (Aviat) pista (de aterrizaje)

tarpaulin [tɑː'pɔːlɪn] n lona impermeabilizada

tarragon ['tærəgən] n estragón m

tart [tɑːt] n (Culin) tarta; (BRIT: inf: prostitute) puta ▷ adj agrio, ácido

tartan ['tɑːtn] n tejido escocés m

tartar(e) sauce ['tɑːtə-] n salsa tártara

task [tɑːsk] n tarea; **to take to ~** reprender

taste [teɪst] n (sense) gusto; (flavour) sabor m; (sample): **have a ~!** ¡prueba un poquito!; (fig) muestra, idea ▷ vi: **to ~ of** or **like** (fish, garlic etc) saber a; **you can ~ the garlic (in it)** se nota el sabor a ajo; **in**

good/bad ~ de buen/mal gusto; **tasteful** adj de buen gusto; **tasteless** adj (food) soso; (remark etc) de mal gusto; **tasty** adj sabroso, rico

tatters ['tætəz] npl: **in ~** hecho jirones

tattoo [tə'tuː] n tatuaje m; (spectacle) espectáculo militar ▷ vt tatuar

taught [tɔːt] pt, pp of **teach**

taunt [tɔːnt] n burla ▷ vt burlarse de

Taurus ['tɔːrəs] n Tauro

taut [tɔːt] adj tirante, tenso

tax [tæks] n impuesto ▷ vt gravar (con un impuesto); (fig: memory) poner a prueba; (: patience) agotar; **tax-free** adj libre de impuestos

taxi ['tæksɪ] n taxi m ▷ vi (Aviat) rodar por la pista; **taxi driver** n taxista mf; **taxi rank** (BRIT) n = **taxi stand**; **taxi stand** n parada de taxis

tax payer n contribuyente mf

TB n abbr = **tuberculosis**

tea [tiː] n té m; (BRIT: meal) ≈ merienda (SP); cena; **high ~** (BRIT) merienda-cena (SP); **tea bag** n bolsita de té; **tea break** (BRIT) n descanso para el té

teach [tiːtʃ] (pt, pp taught) vt: **to ~ sb sth, ~ sth to sb** enseñar algo a algn ▷ vi (be a teacher) ser profesor(a), enseñar; **teacher** n (in secondary school) profesor(a) m/f; (in primary school) maestro/a, profesor(a) de EGB; **teaching** n enseñanza

tea: tea cloth n (BRIT) paño de cocina, trapo de cocina (LAM); **teacup** n taza para el té

tea leaves npl hojas de té

team [tiːm] n equipo; (of horses) tiro; **team up** vi asociarse

teapot ['tiːpɔt] n tetera

tear¹ [tɪə*] n lágrima; **in ~s** llorando

tear² [tɛə*] (pt tore, pp torn) n rasgón m, desgarrón m ▷ vt romper, rasgar ▷ vi rasgarse; **tear apart** vt (also fig) hacer pedazos; **tear down** vt +adv (building, statue) derribar; (poster, flag) arrancar; **tear off** vt (sheet of paper etc) arrancar; (one's clothes) quitarse a tirones; **tear up** vt (sheet of paper etc) romper

tearful ['tɪəfəl] adj lloroso

tear gas ['tɪə-] n gas m lacrimógeno

tearoom ['tiːruːm] n salón m de té

tease [tiːz] vt tomar el pelo a

tea: teaspoon n cucharita; (also: **teaspoonful**: as measurement) cucharadita; **teatime** n hora del té; **tea towel** (BRIT) n paño de cocina

technical ['teknɪkl] adj técnico

technician [tek'nɪʃn] n técnico/a

technique [tek'niːk] n técnica

technology [tek'nɔlədʒɪ] n tecnología

teddy (bear) ['tɛdɪ-] n osito de felpa
tedious ['tiːdɪəs] adj pesado, aburrido
tee [tiː] n (Golf) tee m
teen [tiːn] adj =**teenage** ▷ n (us)=
  teenager
teenage ['tiːneɪdʒ] adj (fashions etc)
  juvenil; (children) quinceañero; **teenager** n
  adolescente mf
teens [tiːnz] npl: **to be in one's ~** ser
  adolescente
teeth [tiːθ] npl of **tooth**
teetotal ['tiːtəʊtl] adj abstemio
telecommunications
  [tɛlɪkəmjuːnɪ'keɪʃənz] n
  telecomunicaciones fpl
telegram ['tɛlɪgræm] n telegrama m
telegraph pole ['tɛlɪgrɑːf-] n poste m
  telegráfico
telephone ['tɛlɪfəun] n teléfono ▷ vt
  llamar por teléfono, telefonear; (message)
  dar por teléfono; **to be on the ~** (talking)
  hablar por teléfono; (possessing telephone)
  tener teléfono; **telephone book** n guía f
  telefónica; **telephone booth, telephone
  box** (BRIT) n cabina telefónica; **telephone
  call** n llamada (telefónica); **telephone
  directory** n guía (telefónica); **telephone
  number** n número de teléfono
telesales ['tɛlɪseɪlz] npl televenta(s) f(pl)
telescope ['tɛlɪskəup] n telescopio
televise ['tɛlɪvaɪz] vt televisar
television ['tɛlɪvɪʒən] n televisión f; **on ~**
  en la televisión; **television programme** n
  programa m de televisión
tell [tɛl] (pt, pp **told**) vt decir; (relate: story)
  contar; (distinguish): **to ~ sth from**
  distinguir algo de ▷ vi (talk): **to ~ (of)**
  contar; (have effect) tener efecto; **to ~ sb to
  do sth** mandar a algn hacer algo; **tell off**
  vt: **to tell sb off** regañar a algn; **teller** n (in
  bank) cajero/a
telly ['tɛlɪ] (BRIT: inf) n abbr (= television)
  tele f
temp [tɛmp] n abbr (BRIT) (= temporary)
  temporero/a
temper ['tɛmpə*] n (nature) carácter m;
  (mood) humor m; (bad temper) (mal) genio;
  (fit of anger) acceso de ira ▷ vt (moderate)
  moderar; **to be in a ~** estar furioso; **to lose
  one's ~** enfadarse, enojarse
temperament ['tɛmprəmənt] n
  (nature) temperamento; **temperamental**
  [tɛmprə'mɛntl] adj temperamental
temperature ['tɛmprətʃə*] n
  temperatura; **to have** or **run a ~** tener fiebre
temple ['tɛmpl] n (building) templo; (Anat)
  sien f
temporary ['tɛmpərərɪ] adj provisional;

(passing) transitorio; (worker) temporero;
  (job) temporal
tempt [tɛmpt] vt tentar; **to ~ sb into
  doing sth** tentar or inducir a algn a hacer
  algo; **temptation** n tentación f; **tempting**
  adj tentador(a); (food) apetitoso/a
ten [tɛn] num diez
tenant ['tɛnənt] n inquilino/a
tend [tɛnd] vt cuidar ▷ vi: **to ~ to do sth**
  tener tendencia a hacer algo; **tendency**
  ['tɛndənsɪ] n tendencia
tender ['tɛndə*] adj (person, care) tierno,
  cariñoso; (meat) tierno; (sore) sensible ▷ n
  (Comm: offer) oferta; (money): **legal ~** moneda
  de curso legal ▷ vt ofrecer
tendon ['tɛndən] n tendón m
tenner ['tɛnə*] n (inf) (billete m de) diez
  libras m
tennis ['tɛnɪs] n tenis m; **tennis ball** n
  pelota de tenis; **tennis court** n cancha de
  tenis; **tennis match** n partido de tenis;
  tennis player n tenista mf; **tennis racket**
  n raqueta de tenis
tenor ['tɛnə*] n (Mus) tenor m
tenpin bowling ['tɛnpɪn-] n (juego de
  los) bolos
tense [tɛns] adj (person) nervioso; (moment,
  atmosphere) tenso; (muscle) tenso, en tensión
  ▷ n (Ling) tiempo
tension ['tɛnʃən] n tensión f
tent [tɛnt] n tienda (de campaña) (SP),
  carpa (LAM)
tentative ['tɛntətɪv] adj (person, smile)
  indeciso; (conclusion, plans) provisional
tenth [tɛnθ] num décimo
tent: tent peg n clavija, estaca; **tent pole**
  n mástil m
tepid ['tɛpɪd] adj tibio
term [təːm] n (word) término; (period)
  período; (Scol) trimestre m ▷ vt llamar;
  terms npl (conditions, Comm) condiciones
  fpl; **in the short/long ~** a corto/largo plazo;
  to be on good ~s with sb llevarse bien con
  algn; **to come to ~s with** (problem) aceptar
terminal ['təːmɪnl] adj (disease) mortal;
  (patient) terminal ▷ n (Elec) borne m;
  (Comput) terminal m; (also: **air ~**) terminal f;
  (BRIT: also: **coach ~**) estación f terminal f
terminate ['təːmɪneɪt] vt terminar
termini ['təːmɪnaɪ] npl of **terminus**
terminology [təːmɪ'nɔlədʒɪ] n
  terminología
terminus ['təːmɪnəs] n (pl **termini**) n
  término, (estación f) terminal f
terrace ['tɛrəs] n terraza; (BRIT: row of
  houses) hilera de casas adosadas; **the ~s**
  (BRIT Sport) las gradas fpl; **terraced** adj
  (garden) en terrazas; (house) adosado

terrain [tɛ'reɪn] n terreno

terrestrial [tɪ'rɛstrɪəl] adj (life) terrestre; (BRIT: channel) de transmisión (por) vía terrestre

terrible ['tɛrɪbl] adj terrible, horrible; (inf) atroz; **terribly** adv terriblemente; (very badly) malísimamente

terrier ['tɛrɪə*] n terrier m

terrific [tə'rɪfɪk] adj (very great) tremendo; (wonderful) fantástico, fenomenal

terrified ['tɛrɪfaɪd] adj aterrorizado

terrify ['tɛrɪfaɪ] vt aterrorizar; **terrifying** adj aterrador(a)

territorial [tɛrɪ'tɔːrɪəl] adj territorial

territory ['tɛrɪtərɪ] n territorio

terror ['tɛrə*] n terror m; **terrorism** n terrorismo; **terrorist** n terrorista mf; **terrorist attack** n atentado (terrorista)

test [tɛst] n (gen, Chem) prueba; (Med) examen m; (Scol) examen m, test m; (also: **driving ~**) examen m de conducir ▷ vt probar, poner a prueba; (Med, Scol) examinar

testicle ['tɛstɪkl] n testículo

testify ['tɛstɪfaɪ] vi (Law) prestar declaración; **to ~ to sth** atestiguar algo

testimony ['tɛstɪmənɪ] n (Law) testimonio

test: test match n (Cricket, Rugby) partido internacional; **test tube** n probeta

tetanus ['tɛtənəs] n tétano

text [tɛkst] n; (on mobile phone) mensaje m de texto ▷ vt: **to ~ sb** (inf) enviar un mensaje (de texto) or un SMS a algn; **textbook** n libro de texto

textile ['tɛkstaɪl] n textil m, tejido

text message n mensaje m de texto

text messaging [-'mɛsɪdʒɪŋ] n (envío de) mensajes mpl de texto

texture ['tɛkstʃə*] n textura

Thai [taɪ] adj, n tailandés/esa m/f

Thailand ['taɪlænd] n Tailandia

than [ðæn] conj (in comparisons): **more ~ 10/once** más de 10/una vez; **I have more/less ~ you/Paul** tengo más/menos que tú/Paul; **she is older ~ you think** es mayor de lo que piensas

thank [θæŋk] vt dar las gracias a, agradecer; **~ you (very much)** muchas gracias; **~ God!** ¡gracias a Dios! ▷ excl (also: **many ~s, ~s a lot**) ¡gracias! ▷ **~s to** prep gracias a; **thanks** npl gracias fpl; **thankfully** adv (fortunately) afortunadamente; **Thanksgiving (Day)** n día m de Acción de Gracias

○ **KEYWORD**

that [ðæt] (pl **those**) adj (demonstrative) ese/a; (pl) esos/as; (more remote) aquel(aquélla); (pl) aquellos/as; **leave those books on the table** deja esos libros sobre la mesa; **that one** ése(ésa); (more remote) **that one over there** ése(ésa) de ahí; aquél(aquélla) de allí ▷ pron **1** (demonstrative) ése/a; (pl) ésos/as; (neuter) eso; (more remote) aquél(aquélla); (pl) aquéllos/as; (neuter) aquello; **what's that?** ¿qué es eso (or aquello)?; **who's that?** ¿quién es ése/a (or aquél (aquella))?; **is that you?** ¿eres tú?; **will you eat all that?** ¿vas a comer todo eso?; **that's my house** ésa es mi casa; **that's what he said** eso es lo que dijo; **that is (to say)** es decir

2 (relative: subject, object) que; (with preposition) (el (la)) que etc, el(la) cual etc; **the book (that) I read** el libro que leí; **the books that are in the library** los libros que están en la biblioteca; **all (that) I have** todo lo que tengo; **the box (that) I put it in** la caja en la que or donde lo puse; **the people (that) I spoke to** la gente con la que hablé **3** (relative: of time) que; **the day (that) he came** el día (en) que vino

▷ conj que; **he thought that I was ill** creyó que yo estaba enfermo

▷ adv (demonstrative): **I can't work that much** no puedo trabajar tanto; **I didn't realise it was that bad** no creí que fuera tan malo; **that high** así de alto

thatched [θætʃt] adj (roof) de paja; (cottage) con tejado de paja

thaw [θɔː] n deshielo ▷ vi (ice) derretirse; (food) descongelarse ▷ vt (food) descongelar

○ **KEYWORD**

the [ðiː, ðə] def art **1** (gen) el f, la pl, los fpl, las (NB 'el' immediately before f n beginning with stressed (h)a; a+ el =al; de + el = del); **the boy/girl** el chico/la chica; **the books/flowers**

los libros/las flores; **to the postman/from the drawer** al cartero/del cajón; **I haven't the time/money** no tengo tiempo/dinero **2** (+adj to form n) los; lo; **the rich and the poor** los ricos y los pobres; **to attempt the impossible** intentar lo imposible **3** (in titles): **Elizabeth the First** Isabel primera; **Peter the Great** Pedro el Grande **4** (in comparisons): **the more he works the more he earns** cuanto más trabaja más gana

theatre ['θɪətə*] (us **theater**) n teatro; (also: **lecture ~**) aula; (Med: also: **operating ~**) quirófano

theft [θɛft] n robo

their [ðɛə*] adj su; **theirs** pron (el) suyo((la) suya etc); see also **my; mine¹**

them [ðɛm, ðəm] pron (direct) los/las; (indirect) les; (stressed, after prep) ellos(ellas); see also **me**

theme [θi:m] n tema m; **theme park** n parque de atracciones (en torno a un tema central)

themselves [ðəm'sɛlvz] pl pron (subject) ellos mismos(ellas mismas); (complement) se; (after prep) sí (mismos(as)); see also **oneself**

then [ðɛn] adv (at that time) entonces; (next) después; (later) luego, después; (and also) además ▷ conj (therefore) en ese caso, entonces ▷ adj: **the ~ president** el entonces presidente; **by ~** para entonces; **from ~ on** desde entonces

theology [θɪ'ɔlədʒɪ] n teología

theory ['θɪərɪ] n teoría

therapist ['θɛrəpɪst] n terapeuta mf

therapy ['θɛrəpɪ] n terapia

○ **KEYWORD**

there [ðɛə*] adv **1 there is, there are** hay; **there is no-one here/no bread left** no hay nadie aquí/no queda pan; **there has been an accident** ha habido un accidente **2** (referring to place) ahí; (distant) allí; **it's there** está ahí; **put it in/on/up/down there** ponlo ahí dentro/encima/arriba/abajo; **I want that book there** quiero ese libro de ahí; **there he is!** ¡ahí está! **3** there, there (esp to child) ea, ea

there: thereabouts adv por ahí; **thereafter** adv después; **thereby** adv así, de ese modo; **therefore** adv por lo tanto; **there's = there is; there has**

thermal ['θə:ml] adj termal; (paper) térmico

thermometer [θə'mɔmɪtə*] n termómetro

thermostat ['θə:məustæt] n termostato

these [ði:z] pl adj estos/as ▷ pl pron éstos/as

thesis ['θi:sɪs] (pl **theses**) n tesis f inv

they [ðeɪ] pl pron ellos(ellas); (stressed) ellos (mismos)(ellas (mismas)); **~ say that ...** (it is said that) se dice que ...; **they'd = they had; they would; they'll = they shall; they will; they're = they are; they've = they have**

thick [θɪk] adj (in consistency) espeso; (in size) grueso; (stupid) torpe ▷ n: **in the ~ of the battle** en lo más reñido de la batalla; **it's 20 cm ~** tiene 20 cm de espesor; **thicken** vi espesarse ▷ vt (sauce etc) espesar; **thickness** n espesor m; grueso

thief [θi:f] (pl **thieves**) n ladrón/ona m/f

thigh [θaɪ] n muslo

thin [θɪn] adj (person, animal) flaco; (in size) delgado; (in consistency) poco espeso; (hair, crowd) escaso ▷ vt: **to ~ (down)** diluir

thing [θɪŋ] n cosa; (object) objeto, artículo; (matter) asunto; (mania): **to have a ~ about sb/sth** estar obsesionado con algn/algo; **things** npl (belongings) efectos mpl (personales); **the best ~ would be to ...** lo mejor sería ...; **how are ~s?** ¿qué tal?

think [θɪŋk] (pt, pp **thought**) vi pensar ▷ vt pensar, creer; **what did you ~ of them?** ¿qué te parecieron?; **to ~ about sth/sb** pensar en algo/algn; **I'll ~ about it** lo pensaré; **to ~ of doing sth** pensar en hacer algo; **I ~ so/not** creo que sí/no; **to ~ well of sb** tener buen concepto de algn; **think over** vt reflexionar sobre, meditar; **think up** vt (plan etc) idear

third [θə:d] adj (before n) tercer(a); (following n) tercero/a ▷ n tercero/a; (fraction) tercio; (BRIT Scol: degree) título de licenciado con calificación de aprobado; **thirdly** adv en tercer lugar; **third party insurance** (BRIT) n seguro contra terceros; **Third World** n Tercer Mundo

thirst [θə:st] n sed f; **thirsty** adj (person, animal) sediento; (work) que da sed; **to be thirsty** tener sed

thirteen ['θə:'ti:n] num trece; **thirteenth** [-'ti:nθ] adj decimotercero

thirtieth ['θə:tɪəθ] adj trigésimo

thirty ['θə:tɪ] num treinta

○ **KEYWORD**

this [ðɪs] (pl **these**) adj (demonstrative) este a pl; estos/as; (neuter) esto; **this man/woman** este hombre(esta mujer); **these children/flowers** estos chicos/estas flores;

this one (here) éste/a, esto (de aquí) ▷ *pron (demonstrative)* éste/a *pl*, éstos/as; *(neuter)* esto; **who is this?** ¿quién es éste/ésta?; **what is this?** ¿qué es esto?; **this is where I live** aquí vivo; **this is what he said** esto es lo que dijo; **this is Mr Brown** *(in introductions)* le presento al Sr. Brown; *(photo)* éste es el Sr. Brown; *(on telephone)* habla el Sr. Brown ▷ *adv (demonstrative)*: **this high/long** *etc* así de alto/largo *etc*; **this far** hasta aquí

thistle ['θɪsl] *n* cardo
thorn [θɔ:n] *n* espina
thorough ['θʌrə] *adj (search)* minucioso; *(wash)* a fondo; *(knowledge, research)* profundo; *(person)* meticuloso; **thoroughly** *adv (search)* minuciosamente; *(study)* profundamente; *(wash)* a fondo; *(utterly: bad, wet etc)* completamente, totalmente
those [ðəuz] *pl adj* esos(esas); *(more remote)* aquellos/as
though [ðəu] *conj* aunque ▷ *adv* sin embargo
thought [θɔ:t] *pt, pp of* **think** ▷ *n* pensamiento; *(opinion)* opinión *f*; **thoughtful** *adj* pensativo; *(serious)* serio; *(considerate)* atento; **thoughtless** *adj* desconsiderado
thousand ['θauzənd] *num* mil; **two ~** dos mil; **~s of** miles de; **thousandth** *num* milésimo
thrash [θræʃ] *vt* azotar; *(defeat)* derrotar
thread [θrɛd] *n* hilo; *(of screw)* rosca ▷ *vt (needle)* enhebrar
threat [θrɛt] *n* amenaza; **threaten** *vi* amenazar ▷ *vt*: **to threaten sb with/ to do** amenazar a algn con/con hacer; **threatening** *adj* amenazador(a), amenazante
three [θri:] *num* tres; **three-dimensional** *adj* tridimensional; **three-piece suite** *n* tresillo; **three-quarters** *npl* tres cuartas partes; **three-quarters full** tres cuartas partes lleno
threshold ['θrɛʃhəuld] *n* umbral *m*
threw [θru:] *pt of* **throw**
thrill [θrɪl] *n (excitement)* emoción *f*; *(shudder)* estremecimiento ▷ *vt* emocionar; **to be ~ed** *(with gift etc)* estar encantado; **thrilled** *adj*: **I was thrilled** Estaba emocionada; **thriller** *n* novela (*or* obra *or* película) de suspense; **thrilling** *adj* emocionante
thriving ['θraɪvɪŋ] *adj* próspero
throat [θrəut] *n* garganta; **to have a sore ~** tener dolor de garganta
throb [θrɔb] *vi* latir; dar punzadas; vibrar

throne [θrəun] *n* trono
through [θru:] *prep* por, a través de; *(time)* durante; *(by means of)* por medio de, mediante; *(owing to)* gracias a ▷ *adj (ticket, train)* directo ▷ *adv* completamente, de parte a parte; *de principio a fin*; **to put sb ~ to sb** *(Tel)* poner *or* pasar a algn con algn; **to be ~** *(Tel)* tener comunicación; *(have finished)* haber terminado; **"no ~ road"** (BRIT) "calle sin salida"; **throughout** *prep (place)* por todas partes de, por todo; *(time)* durante todo ▷ *adv* por *or* en todas partes
throw [θrəu] *(pt* **threw**, *pp* **thrown**) *n* tiro; *(Sport)* lanzamiento ▷ *vt* tirar, echar; *(Sport)* lanzar; *(rider)* derribar; *(fig)* desconcertar; **to ~ a party** dar una fiesta; **throw away** *vt* tirar; *(money)* derrochar; **throw in** *vt (Sport: ball)* sacar; *(include)* incluir; **throw off** *vt* deshacerse de; **throw out** *vt* tirar; *(person)* echar; expulsar; **throw up** *vi* vomitar
thru [θru:] *(US)* = **through**
thrush [θrʌʃ] *n* zorzal *m*, tordo
thrust [θrʌst] *(pt, pp ~)* *vt* empujar con fuerza
thud [θʌd] *n* golpe *m* sordo
thug [θʌg] *n* gamberro/a
thumb [θʌm] *n (Anat)* pulgar *m*; **to ~ a lift** hacer autostop; **thumbtack** *(US) n* chincheta *(SP)*
thump [θʌmp] *n* golpe *m*; *(sound)* ruido seco *or* sordo ▷ *vt* golpear ▷ *vi (heart etc)* palpitar
thunder ['θʌndə*] *n* trueno ▷ *vi* tronar; *(train etc)*: **to ~ past** pasar como un trueno; **thunderstorm** *n* tormenta
Thur(s). *abbr (= Thursday)* juev
Thursday ['θə:zdɪ] *n* jueves *m inv*
thus [ðʌs] *adv* así, de este modo
thwart [θwɔ:t] *vt* frustrar
thyme [taɪm] *n* tomillo
Tibet [tɪ'bɛt] *n* el Tibet
tick [tɪk] *n (sound: of clock)* tictac *m*; *(mark)* palomita; *(Zool)* garrapata; *(BRIT: inf)*: **in a ~** en un instante ▷ *vi* hacer tictac ▷ *vt* marcar; **tick off** *vt* marcar; *(person)* reñir
ticket ['tɪkɪt] *n* billete *m (SP)*, boleto *(LAM)*; *(for cinema etc)* entrada; *(in shop: on goods)* etiqueta; *(for raffle)* papeleta; *(for library)* tarjeta; *(parking ticket)* multa de aparcamiento *(SP)* or por estacionamiento *(indebido)* *(LAM)*; **ticket barrier** *n (BRIT: Rail)* barrera más allá de la cual se necesita billete/boleto; **ticket collector** *n* revisor(a) *m/f*; **ticket inspector** *n* revisor(a) *m/f*, inspector(a) *m/f* de boletos *(LAM)*; **ticket machine** *n* máquina de billetes *(SP)* or boletos *(LAM)*; **ticket office** *n*

t

(*Theatre*) taquilla (*SP*), boletería (*LAM*); (*Rail*)
mostrador *m* de billetes (*SP*) or boletos (*LAM*)

tickle ['tɪkl] *vt* hacer cosquillas a ▷ *vi*
hacer cosquillas; **ticklish** *adj* (*person*)
cosquilloso; (*problem*) delicado

tide [taɪd] *n* marea; (*fig: of events etc*) curso,
marcha

tidy ['taɪdɪ] *adj* (*room etc*) ordenado; (*dress,
work*) limpio; (*person*) (bien) arreglado ▷ *vt*
(*also:* **~ up**) poner en orden

tie [taɪ] *n* (*string etc*) atadura; (*BRIT: also:*
neck~) corbata; (*fig: link*) vínculo, lazo; (*Sport
etc: draw*) empate *m* ▷ *vt* atar ▷ *vi* (*Sport etc*)
empatar; **to ~ in a bow** atar con un lazo; **to
~ a knot in sth** hacer un nudo en algo; **tie
down** *vt* (*fig: person: restrict*) atar; (*: to price,
date etc*) obligar a; **tie up** *vt* (*dog, person*)
atar; (*arrangements*) concluir; **to be tied up**
(*busy*) estar ocupado

tier [tɪə*] *n* grada; (*of cake*) piso

tiger ['taɪgə*] *n* tigre *m*

tight [taɪt] *adj* (*rope*) tirante; (*money*)
escaso; (*clothes*) ajustado; (*bend*) cerrado;
(*shoes, schedule*) apretado; (*budget*) ajustado;
(*security*) estricto; (*inf: drunk*) borracho ▷ *adv*
(*squeeze*) muy fuerte; (*shut*) bien; **tighten** *vt*
(*rope*) estirar; (*screw, grip*) apretar; (*security*)
reforzar ▷ *vi* estirarse; apretarse; **tightly**
adv (*grasp*) muy fuerte; **tights** (*BRIT*) *npl*
panti *mpl*

tile [taɪl] *n* (*on roof*) teja; (*on floor*) baldosa;
(*on wall*) azulejo

till [tɪl] *n* caja (registradora) ▷ *vt* (*land*)
cultivar ▷ *prep, conj* = **until**

tilt [tɪlt] *vt* inclinar ▷ *vi* inclinarse

timber ['tɪmbə*] *n* (*material*) madera

time [taɪm] *n* tiempo; (*epoch: often pl*)
época; (*by clock*) hora; (*moment*) momento;
(*occasion*) vez *f*; (*Mus*) compás *m* ▷ *vt*
calcular or medir el tiempo de; (*race*)
cronometrar; (*remark, visit etc*) elegir el
momento para; **a long ~** mucho tiempo; **4
at a ~** de 4 en 4; 4 a la vez; **for the ~ being**
de momento, por ahora; **from ~ to ~** de vez
en cuando; **at ~s** a veces; **in ~** (*soon enough*)
a tiempo; (*after some time*) con el tiempo;
(*Mus*) al compás; **in a week's ~** dentro de
una semana; **in no ~** en un abrir y cerrar de
ojos; **any ~** cuando sea; **on ~** a la hora; **5 ~s 5**
5 por 5; **what ~ is it?** ¿qué hora es?; **to have
a good ~** pasarlo bien, divertirse; **time limit**
n plazo; **timely** *adj* oportuno; **timer** *n* (*in
kitchen etc*) programador *m* horario; **time-
share** *n* apartamento (or casa) a tiempo
compartido; **timetable** *n* horario; **time
zone** *n* huso horario

timid ['tɪmɪd] *adj* tímido

timing ['taɪmɪŋ] *n* (*Sport*) cronometraje *m*;

the ~ of his resignation el momento que
eligió para dimitir

tin [tɪn] *n* estaño; (*also:* **~ plate**) hojalata;
(*BRIT: can*) lata; **tinfoil** *n* papel *m* de estaño

tingle ['tɪŋgl] *vi* (*person*): **to ~ (with)**
estremecerse (de); (*hands etc*) hormiguear

tinker ['tɪŋkə*]: **~ with** *vt fus* jugar con,
tocar

tinned [tɪnd] (*BRIT*) *adj* (*food*) en lata, en
conserva

tin opener [-əupnə*] (*BRIT*) *n* abrelatas
m inv

tint [tɪnt] *n* matiz *m*; (*for hair*) tinte *m*;
tinted *adj* (*hair*) teñido; (*glass, spectacles*)
ahumado

tiny ['taɪnɪ] *adj* minúsculo, pequeñito

tip [tɪp] *n* (*end*) punta; (*gratuity*) propina;
(*BRIT: for rubbish*) vertedero; (*advice*) consejo
▷ *vt* (*waiter*) dar una propina a; (*tilt*)
inclinar; (*empty: also:* **~ out**) vaciar, echar;
(*overturn: also:* **~ over**) volcar; **tip off** *vt*
avisar, poner sobre aviso a

tiptoe ['tɪptəu] *n*: **on ~** de puntillas

tire ['taɪə*] *n* (*US*) = **tyre** ▷ *vt* cansar ▷ *vi*
cansarse; (*become bored*) aburrirse; **tired**
adj cansado; **to be tired of sth** estar harto
de algo; **tire pressure** (*US*) = **tyre pressure**;
tiring *adj* cansado

tissue ['tɪʃuː] *n* tejido; (*paper handkerchief*)
pañuelo de papel, kleenex® *m*; **tissue paper**
n papel *m* de seda

tit [tɪt] *n* (*bird*) herrerillo común; **to give ~
for tat** dar ojo por ojo

title ['taɪtl] *n* título

T-junction ['tiː:dʒʌŋkʃən] *n* cruce *m* en T

TM *abbr* = **trademark**

○ **KEYWORD**

to [tuː, tə] *prep* **1** (*direction*) a; **to go to
France/London/school/the station** ir a
Francia/Londres/al colegio/a la estación;
to go to Claude's/the doctor's ir a casa de
Claude/al médico; **the road to Edinburgh**
la carretera de Edimburgo
2 (*as far as*) hasta, a; **from here to London**
de aquí a or hasta Londres; **to count to 10**
contar hasta 10; **from 40 to 50 people** entre
40 y 50 personas
3 (*with expressions of time*): **a quarter/
twenty to 5** las 5 menos cuarto/veinte
4 (*for, of*): **the key to the front door** la llave
de la puerta principal; **she is secretary to
the director** es la secretaría del director;
a letter to his wife una carta a or para su
mujer
5 (*expressing indirect object*) a; **to give sth to
sb** darle algo a algn; **to talk to sb** hablar con

algn; **to be a danger to sb** ser un peligro para algn; **to carry out repairs to sth** hacer reparaciones en algo

6 (*in relation to*): **3 goals to 2** 3 goles a 2; **30 miles to the gallon** ≈ 94 litros a los cien (kms)

7 (*purpose, result*): **to come to sb's aid** venir en auxilio *or* ayuda de algn; **to sentence sb to death** condenar a algn a muerte; **to my great surprise** con gran sorpresa mía

▷ with vb **1** (*simple infin*): **to go/eat** ir/comer **2** (*following another vb*): **to want/try/start to do** querer/intentar/empezar a hacer **3** (*with vb omitted*): **I don't want to** no quiero **4** (*purpose, result*) para; **I did it to help you** lo hice para ayudarte; **he came to see you** vino a verte

5 (*equivalent to relative clause*): **I have things to do** tengo cosas que hacer; **the main thing is to try** lo principal es intentarlo **6** (*after adj etc*): **ready to go** listo para irse; **too old to ...** demasiado viejo (como) para ...

▷ *adv*: **pull/push the door to** tirar de/ empujar la puerta

toad [təud] *n* sapo; **toadstool** *n* hongo venenoso

toast [təust] *n* (*Culin*) tostada; (*drink, speech*) brindis *m* ▷ *vt* (*Culin*) tostar; (*drink to*) brindar por; **toaster** *n* tostador *m*

tobacco [tə'bækəu] *n* tabaco

toboggan [tə'bɔgən] *n* tobogán *m*

today [tə'deɪ] *adv*, *n* (*also fig*) hoy *m*

toddler ['tɔdlə*] *n* niño/a (que empieza a andar)

toe [təu] *n* dedo (del pie); (*of shoe*) punta; **to ~ the line** (*fig*) conformarse; **toenail** *n* uña del pie

toffee ['tɔfɪ] *n* toffee *m*

together [tə'geðə*] *adv* juntos; (*at same time*) al mismo tiempo, a la vez; **~ with** junto con

toilet ['tɔɪlət] *n* inodoro; (*BRIT: room*) (cuarto de) baño, servicio ▷ *cpd* (*soap etc*) de aseo; **toilet bag** *n* neceser *m*, bolsa de aseo; **toilet paper** *n* papel *m* higiénico; **toiletries** *npl* artículos *mpl* de tocador; **toilet roll** *n* rollo de papel higiénico

token ['təukən] *n* (*sign*) señal *f*, muestra; (*souvenir*) recuerdo; (*disc*) ficha ▷ *adj* (*strike, payment etc*) simbólico; **book/record ~** (*BRIT*) vale *m* para comprar libros/discos; **gift ~** (*BRIT*) vale-regalo

Tokyo ['təukjəu] *n* Tokio, Tókio

told [təuld] *pt*, *pp of* **tell**

tolerant ['tɔlərnt] *adj*: **~ of** tolerante con

tolerate ['tɔləreɪt] *vt* tolerar

toll [təul] *n* (*of casualties*) número de víctimas; (*tax, charge*) peaje *m* ▷ *vi* (*bell*) doblar; **toll call** *n* (*us Tel*) conferencia, llamada interurbana; **toll-free** (*us*) *adj*, *adv* gratis

tomato [tə'mɑ:təu] (*pl* **~es**) *n* tomate *m*; **tomato sauce** *n* salsa de tomate

tomb [tu:m] *n* tumba; **tombstone** *n* lápida

tomorrow [tə'mɔrəu] *adv*, *n* (*also: fig*) mañana; **the day after ~** pasado mañana; **~ morning** mañana por la mañana

ton [tʌn] *n* tonelada (*BRIT* = 1016 kg; *us* = 907 kg); (*metric ton*) tonelada métrica; **~s of** (*inf*) montones de

tone [təun] *n* tono ▷ *vi* (*also: ~ in*) armonizar; **tone down** *vt* (*criticism*) suavizar; (*colour*) atenuar

tongs [tɔŋz] *npl* (*for coal*) tenazas *fpl*; (*curling tongs*) tenacillas *fpl*

tongue [tʌŋ] *n* lengua; **~ in cheek** irónicamente

tonic ['tɔnɪk] *n* (*Med*) tónico; (*also: ~ water*) (agua) tónica

tonight [tə'naɪt] *adv*, *n* esta noche; esta tarde

tonne [tʌn] *n* tonelada (métrica) (1.000kg)

tonsil ['tɔnsl] *n* amígdala; **tonsillitis** [-'laɪtɪs] *n* amigdalitis *f*

too [tu:] *adv* (*excessively*) demasiado; (*also*) también; **~ much** demasiado; **~ many** demasiados/as

took [tuk] *pt of* **take**

tool [tu:l] *n* herramienta; **tool box** *n* caja de herramientas; **tool kit** *n* juego de herramientas

tooth [tu:θ] (*pl* **teeth**) *n* (*Anat, Tech*) diente *m*; (*molar*) muela; **toothache** *n* dolor *m* de muelas; **toothbrush** *n* cepillo de dientes; **toothpaste** *n* pasta de dientes; **toothpick** *n* palillo

top [tɔp] *n* (*of mountain*) cumbre *f*, cima; (*of tree*) copa; (*of head*) coronilla; (*of ladder, page*) lo alto; (*of table*) superficie *f*; (*of cupboard*) parte *f* de arriba; (*lid: of box*) tapa; (: *of bottle, jar*) tapón *m*; (*of list etc*) cabeza; (*toy*) peonza; (*garment*) blusa; camiseta ▷ *adj* de arriba; (*in rank*) principal, primero; (*best*) mejor ▷ *vt* (*exceed*) exceder; (*be first in*) encabezar; **on ~ of** (*above*) sobre, encima de; (*in addition to*) además de; **from ~ to bottom** de pies a cabeza; **top up** *vt* llenar; (*mobile phone*) recargar (el saldo de); **top floor** *n* último piso; **top hat** *n* sombrero de copa

topic ['tɔpɪk] *n* tema *m*; **topical** *adj* actual

topless ['tɔplɪs] *adj* (*bather, bikini*) topless *inv*

topping ['tɔpɪŋ] *n* (*Culin*): **with a ~ of**

cream con nata por encima
topple ['tɒpl] vt derribar ▷ vi caerse
top-up card n (for mobile phone) tarjeta prepago
torch [tɔːtʃ] n antorcha; (BRIT: electric) linterna
tore [tɔː*] pt of **tear²**
torment [n 'tɔːmɛnt, vt tɔː'mɛnt] n tormento ▷ vt atormentar; (fig: annoy) fastidiar
torn [tɔːn] pp of **tear²**
tornado [tɔː'neɪdəu] (pl ~es) n tornado
torpedo [tɔː'piːdəu] (pl ~es) n torpedo
torrent ['tɒrnt] n torrente m; **torrential** [tɒ'rɛnʃl] adj torrencial
tortoise ['tɔːtəs] n tortuga
torture ['tɔːtʃə*] n tortura ▷ vt torturar; (fig) atormentar
Tory ['tɔːrɪ] (BRIT) adj, n (Pol) conservador(a) m/f
toss [tɒs] vt tirar, echar; (one's head) sacudir; **to ~ a coin** echar a cara o cruz; **to ~ up for sth** jugar a cara o cruz algo; **to ~ and turn** (in bed) dar vueltas
total ['təutl] adj total, entero; (emphatic: failure etc) completo, total ▷ n total m, suma ▷ vt (add up) sumar; (amount to) ascender a
totalitarian [təutælɪ'tɛərɪən] adj totalitario
totally ['təutəlɪ] adv totalmente
touch [tʌtʃ] n tacto; (contact) contacto ▷ vt tocar; (emotionally) conmover; **a ~ of** (fig) un poquito de; **to get in ~ with sb** ponerse en contacto con algn; **to lose ~** (friends) perder contacto; **touch down** vi (on land) aterrizar; **touchdown** n aterrizaje m; (on sea) amerizaje m; (us Football) ensayo; **touched** adj (moved) conmovido; **touching** adj (moving) conmovedor(a); **touchline** n (Sport) línea de banda; **touch-sensitive** adj sensible al tacto
tough [tʌf] adj (material) resistente; (meat) duro; (problem etc) difícil; (policy, stance) inflexible; (person) fuerte
tour ['tuə*] n viaje m, vuelta; (also: **package ~**) viaje m todo comprendido; (of town, museum) visita; (by band etc) gira ▷ vt recorrer, visitar; **tour guide** n guía mf turístico/a
tourism ['tuərɪzm] n turismo
tourist ['tuərɪst] n turista mf ▷ cpd turístico; **tourist office** n oficina de turismo
tournament ['tuənəmənt] n torneo
tour operator n touroperador(a) m/f, operador(a) m/f turístico/a
tow [təu] vt remolcar; **"on** or **in** (us) **~"**

(Aut) "a remolque"; **tow away** vt llevarse a remolque
toward(s) [tə'wɔːd(z)] prep hacia; (attitude) respecto a, con; (purpose) para
towel ['tauəl] n toalla; **towelling** n (fabric) felpa
tower ['tauə*] n torre f; **tower block** (BRIT) n torre f (de pisos)
town [taun] n ciudad f; **to go to ~** ir a la ciudad; (fig) echar la casa por la ventana; **town centre** (BRIT) n centro de la ciudad; **town hall** n ayuntamiento
tow truck (us) n camión m grúa
toxic ['tɒksɪk] adj tóxico
toy [tɔɪ] n juguete m; **toy with** vt fus jugar con; (idea) acariciar; **toyshop** n juguetería
trace [treɪs] n rastro ▷ vt (draw) trazar, delinear; (locate) encontrar; (follow) seguir la pista de
track [træk] n (mark) huella, pista; (path: gen) camino, senda; (: of bullet etc) trayectoria; (: of suspect, animal) pista, rastro; (Rail) vía; (Sport) pista; (on tape, record) canción f ▷ vt seguir la pista de; **to keep ~ of** mantenerse al tanto de, seguir; **track down** vt (prey) seguir el rastro de; (sth lost) encontrar; **tracksuit** n chándal m
tractor ['træktə*] n tractor m
trade [treɪd] n comercio; (skill, job) oficio ▷ vi negociar, comerciar ▷ vt (exchange): **to ~ sth (for sth)** cambiar algo (por algo); **trade in** vt (old car etc) ofrecer como parte del pago; **trademark** n marca de fábrica; **trader** n comerciante mf; **tradesman** (irreg) n (shopkeeper) tendero; **trade union** n sindicato
trading ['treɪdɪŋ] n comercio
tradition [trə'dɪʃən] n tradición f; **traditional** adj tradicional
traffic ['træfɪk] n (gen, Aut) tráfico, circulación f ▷ vi: **to ~ in** (pej: liquor, drugs) traficar en; **traffic circle** (us) n isleta; **traffic island** n refugio, isleta; **traffic jam** n embotellamiento; **traffic lights** npl semáforo; **traffic warden** n guardia mf de tráfico
tragedy ['trædʒədɪ] n tragedia
tragic ['trædʒɪk] adj trágico
trail [treɪl] n (tracks) rastro, pista; (path) camino, sendero; (dust, smoke) estela ▷ vt (drag) arrastrar; (follow) seguir la pista de ▷ vi arrastrar; (in contest etc) ir perdiendo; **trailer** n (Aut) remolque m; (caravan) caravana; (Cinema) trailer m, avance m
train [treɪn] n tren m; (of dress) cola; (series) serie f ▷ vt (educate, teach skills to) formar; (sportsman) entrenar; (dog) adiestrar; (point: gun etc): **to ~ on** apuntar

a ▷ vi (Sport) entrenarse; (learn a skill): **to ~ as a teacher** etc estudiar para profesor etc; **one's ~ of thought** el razonamiento de algn; **trainee** [treɪ'niː] n aprendiz(a) m/f; **trainer** n (Sport: coach) entrenador(a) m/f; (of animals) domador(a) m/f; **trainers** npl (shoes) zapatillas fpl (de deporte); **training** n formación f; entrenamiento; **to be in training** (Sport) estar entrenando; **training course** n curso de formación; **training shoes** npl zapatillas fpl (de deporte)

trait [treɪt] n rasgo

traitor ['treɪtə*] n traidor(a) m/f

tram [træm] (BRIT) n (also: **~car**) tranvía m

tramp [træmp] n (person) vagabundo/a; (inf: pej: woman) puta

trample ['træmpl] vt: **to ~ (underfoot)** pisotear

trampoline ['træmpəliːn] n trampolín m

tranquil ['træŋkwɪl] adj tranquilo; **tranquillizer** (US **tranquilizer**) n (Med) tranquilizante m

transaction [træn'zækʃən] n transacción f, operación f

transatlantic ['trænzət'læntɪk] adj transatlántico

transcript ['trænskrɪpt] n copia

transfer [n 'trænsfə:*, vb træns'fə:*] n (of employees) traslado; (of money, power) transferencia; (Sport) traspaso; (picture, design) calcomanía ▷ vt trasladar; transferir; **to ~ the charges** (BRIT Tel) llamar a cobro revertido

transform [træns'fɔ:m] vt transformar; **transformation** n transformación f

transfusion [træns'fju:ʒən] n transfusión f

transit ['trænzɪt] n: **in ~** en tránsito

transition [træn'zɪʃən] n transición f

transitive ['trænzɪtɪv] adj (Ling) transitivo

translate [trænz'leɪt] vt traducir; **translation** [-'leɪʃən] n traducción f; **translator** n traductor(a) m/f

transmission [trænz'mɪʃən] n transmisión f

transmit [trænz'mɪt] vt transmitir; **transmitter** n transmisor m

transparent [træns'pærnt] adj transparente

transplant ['trænsplɑ:nt] n (Med) transplante m

transport [n 'trænspɔ:t, vt træns'pɔ:t] n transporte m; (car) coche m (SP), carro (LAM), automóvil m ▷ vt transportar; **transportation** [-'teɪʃən] n transporte m

transvestite [trænz'vɛstaɪt] n travestí mf

trap [træp] n (snare, trick) trampa; (carriage) cabriolé m ▷ vt coger (SP) o agarrar (LAM) (en una trampa); (trick) engañar; (confine) atrapar

trash [træʃ] n (rubbish) basura; (nonsense) tonterías fpl; (pej): **the book/film is ~** el libro/la película no vale nada; **trash can** (US) n cubo or bote m (MEX) or tacho (SC) de la basura

trauma ['trɔːmə] n trauma m; **traumatic** [trɔː'mætɪk] adj traumático

travel ['trævl] n el viajar ▷ vi viajar ▷ vt (distance) recorrer; **travel agency** n agencia de viajes; **travel agent** n agente mf de viajes; **travel insurance** n seguro de viaje; **traveller** (US **traveler**) n viajero/a; **traveller's cheque** (US **traveler's check**) n cheque m de viajero; **travelling** (US **traveling**) n los viajes, el viajar; **travel-sick** adj: **to get travel-sick** marearse al viajar; **travel sickness** n mareo

tray [treɪ] n bandeja; (on desk) cajón m

treacherous ['trɛtʃərəs] adj traidor, traicionero; (dangerous) peligroso

treacle ['triːkl] (BRIT) n melaza

tread [trɛd] (pt **trod**, pp **trodden**) n (step) paso, pisada; (sound) ruido de pasos; (of stair) escalón m; (of tyre) banda de rodadura ▷ vi pisar; **tread on** vt fus pisar

treasure ['trɛʒə*] n tesoro ▷ vt (value: object, friendship) apreciar; (: memory) guardar; **treasurer** n tesorero/a

treasury ['trɛʒərɪ] n: **the T~** el Ministerio de Hacienda

treat [triːt] n (present) regalo ▷ vt tratar; **to ~ sb to sth** invitar a algn a algo; **treatment** n tratamiento

treaty ['triːtɪ] n tratado

treble ['trɛbl] adj triple ▷ vt triplicar ▷ vi triplicarse

tree [triː] n árbol m; **~ trunk** tronco (de árbol)

trek [trɛk] n (long journey) viaje m largo y difícil; (tiring walk) caminata

tremble ['trɛmbl] vi temblar

tremendous [trɪ'mɛndəs] adj tremendo, enorme; (excellent) estupendo

trench [trɛntʃ] n zanja

trend [trɛnd] n (tendency) tendencia; (of events) curso; (fashion) moda; **trendy** adj de moda

trespass ['trɛspəs] vi: **to ~ on** entrar sin permiso en; **"no ~ing"** "prohibido el paso"

trial ['traɪəl] n (Law) juicio, proceso; (test: of machine etc) prueba; **trial period** n periodo de prueba

triangle ['traɪæŋgl] n (Math, Mus) triángulo

t

triangular [traɪˈæŋɡjʊlə*] *adj* triangular

tribe [traɪb] *n* tribu *f*

tribunal [traɪˈbjuːnl] *n* tribunal *m*

tribute [ˈtrɪbjuːt] *n* homenaje *m*, tributo;
to pay ~ to rendir homenaje a

trick [trɪk] *n* (*skill, knack*) tino, truco;
(*conjuring trick*) truco; (*joke*) broma; (*Cards*)
baza ▷ *vt* engañar; **to play a ~ on sb** gastar
una broma a algn; **that should do the ~** a
ver si funciona así

trickle [ˈtrɪkl] *n* (*of water etc*) goteo ▷ *vi*
gotear

tricky [ˈtrɪkɪ] *adj* difícil; delicado

tricycle [ˈtraɪsɪkl] *n* triciclo

trifle [ˈtraɪfl] *n* bagatela; (*Culin*) dulce de
bizcocho borracho, gelatina, fruta y natillas
▷ *adv*: **a ~ long** un poquito largo

trigger [ˈtrɪɡə*] *n* (*of gun*) gatillo

trim [trɪm] *adj* (*house, garden*) en buen
estado; (*person, figure*) esbelto ▷ *n* (*haircut
etc*) recorte *m*; (*on car*) guarnición *f* ▷ *vt*
(*neaten*) arreglar; (*cut*) recortar; (*decorate*)
adornar; (*Naut: a sail*) orientar

trio [ˈtriːəʊ] *n* trío

trip [trɪp] *n* viaje *m*; (*excursion*) excursión *f*;
(*stumble*) traspié *m* ▷ *vi* (*stumble*) tropezar;
(*go lightly*) andar a paso ligero; **on a ~** de
viaje; **trip up** *vi* tropezar, caerse ▷ *vt* hacer
tropezar or caer

triple [ˈtrɪpl] *adj* triple

triplets [ˈtrɪplɪts] *npl* trillizos/as *mpl/fpl*

tripod [ˈtraɪpɔd] *n* trípode *m*

triumph [ˈtraɪʌmf] *n* triunfo ▷ *vi*: **to ~
(over)** vencer; **triumphant** [traɪˈʌmfənt]
adj (*team etc*) vencedor(a); (*wave, return*)
triunfal

trivial [ˈtrɪvɪəl] *adj* insignificante;
(*commonplace*) banal

trod [trɔd] *pt of* **tread**

trodden [ˈtrɔdn] *pp of* **tread**

trolley [ˈtrɔlɪ] *n* carrito; (*also:* **~ bus**)
trolebús *m*

trombone [trɔmˈbəʊn] *n* trombón *m*

troop [truːp] *n* grupo, banda; **troops** *npl*
(*Mil*) tropas *fpl*

trophy [ˈtrəʊfɪ] *n* trofeo

tropical [ˈtrɔpɪkl] *adj* tropical

trot [trɔt] *n* trote *m* ▷ *vi* trotar; **on the ~**
(*BRIT: fig*) seguidos/as

trouble [ˈtrʌbl] *n* problema *m*, dificultad
f; (*worry*) preocupación *f*; (*bother, effort*)
molestia, esfuerzo; (*unrest*) inquietud
f; (*Med*): **stomach** *etc* **~** problemas *mpl*
gástricos *etc* ▷ *vt* (*disturb*) molestar; (*worry*)
preocupar, inquietar ▷ *vi*: **to ~ to do sth**
molestarse en hacer algo; **troubles** *npl* (*Pol
etc*) conflictos *mpl*; (*personal*) problemas *mpl*;
to be in ~ estar en un apuro; **it's no ~!** ¡no

es molestia (ninguna)!; **what's the ~?** (*with
broken TV etc*) ¿cuál es el problema?; (*doctor
to patient*) ¿qué pasa?; **troubled** *adj* (*person*)
preocupado; (*country, epoch, life*) agitado;
troublemaker *n* agitador(a) *m/f*; (*child*)
alborotador *m*; **troublesome** *adj* molesto

trough [trɔf] *n* (*also:* **drinking ~**)
abrevadero; (*also:* **feeding ~**) comedero;
(*depression*) depresión *f*

trousers [ˈtraʊzəz] *npl* pantalones *mpl*;
short ~ pantalones *mpl* cortos

trout [traʊt] *n inv* trucha

trowel [ˈtraʊəl] *n* (*of gardener*) palita; (*of
builder*) paleta

truant [ˈtruənt] *n*: **to play ~** (*BRIT*) hacer
novillos

truce [truːs] *n* tregua

truck [trʌk] *n* (*lorry*) camión *m*; (*Rail*) vagón
m; **truck driver** *n* camionero

true [truː] *adj* verdadero; (*accurate*) exacto;
(*genuine*) auténtico; (*faithful*) fiel; **to come
~** realizarse

truly [ˈtruːlɪ] *adv* (*really*) realmente;
(*truthfully*) verdaderamente;
(*faithfully*): **yours ~** (*in letter*) le saluda
atentamente

trumpet [ˈtrʌmpɪt] *n* trompeta

trunk [trʌŋk] *n* (*of tree, person*) tronco;
(*of elephant*) trompa; (*case*) baúl *m*; (*us Aut*)
maletero; **trunks** *npl* (*also:* **swimming ~s**)
bañador *m* (de hombre)

trust [trʌst] *n* confianza; (*responsibility*)
responsabilidad *f*; (*Law*) fideicomiso ▷ *vt*
(*rely on*) tener confianza en; (*hope*) esperar;
(*entrust*): **to ~ sth to sb** confiar algo a algn;
to take sth on ~ fiarse de algo; **trusted** *adj*
de confianza; **trustworthy** *adj* digno de
confianza

truth [truːθ, *pl* truːðz] *n* verdad *f*; **truthful**
adj veraz

try [traɪ] *n* tentativa, intento; (*Rugby*)
ensayo ▷ *vt* (*attempt*) intentar; (*test: also:* **~
out**) probar, someter a prueba; (*Law*) juzgar,
procesar; (*strain: patience*) hacer perder ▷ *vi*
probar; **to have a ~** tener suerte; **to ~ to
do sth** intentar hacer algo; **~ again!** ¡vuelve
a probar!; **~ harder!** ¡esfuérzate más!; **well, I
tried** al menos lo intenté; **try on** *vt* (*clothes*)
probarse; **trying** *adj* (*experience*) cansado; (*person*) pesado

T-shirt [ˈtiːʃəːt] *n* camiseta

tub [tʌb] *n* cubo (*SP*), cubeta (*SP, MEX*),
balde *m* (*LAM*); (*bath*) bañera (*SP*), tina (*LAM*),
bañadera (*RPL*)

tube [tjuːb] *n* tubo; (*BRIT: underground*)
metro; (*for tyre*) cámara de aire

tuberculosis [tjʊbəːkjuˈləʊsɪs] *n*
tuberculosis *f inv*

tube station (BRIT) n estación f de metro

tuck [tʌk] vt (put) poner; **tuck away** vt (money) guardar; (building): **to be tucked away** esconderse, ocultarse; **tuck in** vt meter dentro; (child) arropar ▷ vi (eat) comer con apetito; **tuck shop** n (Scol) tienda ≈ bar m (del colegio) (SP)

Tue(s). abbr (= Tuesday) mart

Tuesday ['tju:zdɪ] n martes m inv

tug [tʌg] n (ship) remolcador m ▷ vt tirar de

tuition [tju:'ɪʃən] n (BRIT) enseñanza; (: private tuition) clases fpl particulares; (US: school fees) matrícula

tulip ['tju:lɪp] n tulipán m

tumble ['tʌmbl] n (fall) caída ▷ vi caer; **to ~ to sth** (inf) caer en la cuenta de algo; **tumble dryer** (BRIT) n secadora

tumbler ['tʌmblə*] n (glass) vaso

tummy ['tʌmɪ] (inf) n barriga, tripa

tumour ['tju:mə*] (US **tumor**) n tumor m

tuna ['tju:nə] n inv (also: ~ **fish**) atún m

tune [tju:n] n melodía ▷ vt (Mus) afinar; (Radio, TV, Aut) sintonizar; **to be in/out of ~** (instrument) estar afinado/desafinado; (singer) cantar afinadamente/desafinar; **to be in/out of ~ with** (fig) estar de acuerdo/en desacuerdo con; **tune in** vi: **to tune in (to)** (Radio, TV) sintonizar (con); **tune up** vi (musician) afinar (su instrumento)

tunic ['tju:nɪk] n túnica

Tunisia [tju:'nɪzɪə] n Túnez m

tunnel ['tʌnl] n túnel m; (in mine) galería ▷ vi construir un túnel/una galería

turbulence ['tə:bjuləns] n (Aviat) turbulencia

turf [tə:f] n césped m; (clod) tepe m ▷ vt cubrir con césped

Turk [tə:k] n turco/a

Turkey ['tə:kɪ] n Turquía

turkey ['tə:kɪ] n pavo

Turkish ['tə:kɪʃ] adj, n turco; (Ling) turco

turmoil ['tə:mɔɪl] n: **in ~** revuelto

turn [tə:n] n turno; (in road) curva; (of mind, events) rumbo; (Theatre) número; (Med) ataque m ▷ vt girar, volver; (collar, steak) dar la vuelta a; (page) pasar; (change): **to ~ sth into** convertir algo en ▷ vi volver; (person: look back) volverse; (reverse direction) dar la vuelta; (milk) cortarse; (become): **to ~ nasty/forty** ponerse feo/cumplir los cuarenta; **a good ~** un favor; **it gave me quite a ~** me dio un susto; **"no left ~"** (Aut) "prohibido girar a la izquierda"; **it's your ~** te toca a ti; **in ~** por turnos; **to take ~s (at)** turnarse (en); **turn around** vi (person) volverse, darse la vuelta ▷ vt (object) dar la vuelta a, voltear (LAM); **turn away** vi

apartar la vista ▷ vi rechazar; **turn back** vi volverse atrás ▷ vt hacer retroceder; (clock) retrasar; **turn down** vt (refuse) rechazar; (reduce) bajar; (fold) doblar; **turn in** vi (inf: go to bed) acostarse ▷ vt (fold) doblar hacia dentro; **turn off** vi (from road) desviarse ▷ vt (light, radio etc) apagar; (tap) cerrar; (engine) parar; **turn on** vt (light, radio etc) encender (SP), prender (LAM); (tap) abrir; (engine) poner en marcha; **turn out** vt (light, gas) apagar; (produce) producir ▷ vi (voters) concurrir; **to turn out to be ...** resultar ser ...; **turn over** vi (person) volverse ▷ vt (object) dar la vuelta a; (page) volver; **turn round** vi volverse; (rotate) girar; **turn to** vt fus: **to turn to sb** acudir a algn; **turn up** vi (person) llegar, presentarse; (lost object) aparecer ▷ vt (gen) subir; **turning** n (in road) vuelta; **turning point** n (fig) momento decisivo

turnip ['tə:nɪp] n nabo

turn: turnout n concurrencia; **turnover** n (Comm: amount of money) volumen m de ventas; (: of goods) movimiento; **turnstile** n torniquete m; **turn-up** (BRIT) n (on trousers) vuelta

turquoise ['tə:kwɔɪz] n (stone) turquesa ▷ adj color turquesa

turtle ['tə:tl] n galápago; **turtleneck (sweater)** n jersey m de cuello vuelto

tusk [tʌsk] n colmillo

tutor ['tju:tə*] n profesor(a) m/f; **tutorial** [-'tɔ:rɪəl] n (Scol) seminario

tuxedo [tʌk'si:dəu] (US) n smóking m, esmoquin m

TV [ti:'vi:] n abbr (= television) tele f

tweed [twi:d] n tweed m

tweezers ['twi:zəz] npl pinzas fpl (de depilar)

twelfth [twelfθ] num duodécimo

twelve [twelv] num doce; **at ~ o'clock** (midday) a mediodía; (midnight) a medianoche

twentieth ['twentɪɪθ] adj vigésimo

twenty ['twentɪ] num veinte

twice [twaɪs] adv dos veces; **~ as much** dos veces más

twig [twɪg] n ramita

twilight ['twaɪlaɪt] n crepúsculo

twin [twɪn] adj, n gemelo/a m/f ▷ vt hermanar; **twin(-bedded) room** n habitación f doble; **twin beds** npl camas fpl gemelas

twinkle ['twɪŋkl] vi centellear; (eyes) brillar

twist [twɪst] n (action) torsión f; (in road, coil) vuelta; (in wire, flex) doblez f; (in story) giro ▷ vt torcer; (weave) trenzar; (roll around) enrollar; (fig) deformar ▷ vi serpentear

t

twit [twɪt] (*inf*) *n* tonto

twitch [twɪtʃ] *n* (*pull*) tirón *m*; (*nervous*) tic *m* ▷ *vi* crisparse

two [tu:] *num* dos; **to put ~ and ~ together** (*fig*) atar cabos

type [taɪp] *n* (*category*) tipo, género; (*model*) tipo; (*Typ*) tipo, letra ▷ *vt* (*letter etc*) escribir a máquina; **typewriter** *n* máquina de escribir

typhoid ['taɪfɔɪd] *n* tifoidea

typhoon [taɪ'fu:n] *n* tifón *m*

typical ['tɪpɪkl] *adj* típico; **typically** *adv* típicamente

typing ['taɪpɪŋ] *n* mecanografía

typist ['taɪpɪst] *n* mecanógrafo/a

tyre ['taɪə*] (*us* **tire**) *n* neumático, llanta (*LAM*); **tyre pressure** (*BRIT*) *n* presión *f* de los neumáticos

UFO ['ju:fəu] *n abbr* (= *unidentified flying object*) OVNI *m*

Uganda [ju:'gændə] *n* Uganda

ugly ['ʌglɪ] *adj* feo; (*dangerous*) peligroso

UHT *abbr* (= *UHT milk*) leche *f* UHT, leche *f* uperizada

UK *n abbr* = **United Kingdom**

ulcer ['ʌlsə*] *n* úlcera; (*mouth ulcer*) llaga

ultimate ['ʌltɪmət] *adj* último, final; (*greatest*) máximo; **ultimately** *adv* (*in the end*) por último, al final; (*fundamentally*) a or en fin de cuentas

ultimatum [ʌltɪ'meɪtəm] (*pl ~s or* **ultimata**) *n* ultimátum *m*

ultrasound ['ʌltrəsaund] *n* (*Med*) ultrasonido

ultraviolet ['ʌltrə'vaɪəlɪt] *adj* ultravioleta

umbrella [ʌm'brɛlə] *n* paraguas *m inv*; (*for sun*) sombrilla

umpire ['ʌmpaɪə*] *n* árbitro

UN *n abbr* (= *United Nations*) NN. UU.

unable [ʌn'eɪbl] *adj*: **to be ~ to do sth** no poder hacer algo

unacceptable [ʌnək'sɛptəbl] *adj* (*proposal, behaviour, price*) inaceptable; **it's ~ that** no se puede aceptar que

unanimous [ju:'nænɪməs] *adj* unánime

unarmed [ʌn'ɑ:md] *adj* (*defenceless*) inerme; (*without weapon*) desarmado

unattended [ʌnə'tɛndɪd] *adj* desatendido

unattractive [ʌnə'træktɪv] *adj* poco atractivo

unavailable [ʌnə'veɪləbl] *adj* (*article, room, book*) no disponible; (*person*) ocupado

unavoidable [ʌnə'vɔɪdəbl] *adj* inevitable

unaware [ʌnə'wɛə*] *adj*: **to be ~ of** ignorar; **unawares** *adv*: **to catch sb unawares** pillar a algn desprevenido

unbearable [ʌn'bɛərəbl] *adj* insoportable

unbeatable [ʌn'bi:təbl] *adj* (*team*)

invencible; (*price*) inmejorable; (*quality*) insuperable

unbelievable [ʌnbɪ'liːvəbl] *adj* increíble

unborn [ʌn'bɔːn] *adj* que va a nacer

unbutton [ʌn'bʌtn] *vt* desabrochar

uncalled-for [ʌn'kɔːldfɔː*] *adj* gratuito, inmerecido

uncanny [ʌn'kænɪ] *adj* extraño

uncertain [ʌn'sɜːtn] *adj* incierto; (*indecisive*) indeciso; **uncertainty** *n* incertidumbre *f*

unchanged [ʌn'tʃeɪndʒd] *adj* igual, sin cambios

uncle ['ʌŋkl] *n* tío

unclear [ʌn'klɪə*] *adj* poco claro; **I'm still ~ about what I'm supposed to do** todavía no tengo muy claro lo que tengo que hacer

uncomfortable [ʌn'kʌmfətəbl] *adj* incómodo; (*uneasy*) inquieto

uncommon [ʌn'kɔmən] *adj* poco común, raro

unconditional [ʌnkən'dɪʃənl] *adj* incondicional

unconscious [ʌn'kɔnʃəs] *adj* sin sentido; (*unaware*): **to be ~ of** no darse cuenta de ▷ *n*: **the ~** el inconsciente

uncontrollable [ʌnkən'trəuləbl] *adj* (*child etc*) incontrolable; (*temper*) indomable; (*laughter*) incontenible

unconventional [ʌnkən'venʃənl] *adj* poco convencional

uncover [ʌn'kʌvə*] *vt* descubrir; (*take lid off*) destapar

undecided [ʌndɪ'saɪdɪd] *adj* (*character*) indeciso; (*question*) no resuelto

undeniable [ʌndɪ'naɪəbl] *adj* innegable

under ['ʌndə*] *prep* debajo de; (*less than*) menos de; (*according to*) según, de acuerdo con; (*sb's leadership*) bajo ▷ *adv* debajo, abajo; **~ there** allí abajo; **~ repair** en reparación; **undercover** *adj* clandestino; **underdone** *adj* (*Culin*) poco hecho; **underestimate** *vt* subestimar; **undergo** (*irreg*) *vt* sufrir; (*treatment*) recibir; **undergraduate** *n* estudiante *mf*; **underground** *n* (BRIT: *railway*) metro; (*Pol*) movimiento clandestino ▷ *adj* (*car park*) subterráneo ▷ *adv* (*work*) en la clandestinidad; **undergrowth** *n* maleza; **underline** *vt* subrayar; **undermine** *vt* socavar, minar; **underneath** [ʌndə'niːθ] *adv* debajo ▷ *prep* debajo de, bajo; **underpants** *npl* calzoncillos *mpl*; **underpass** (BRIT) *n* paso subterráneo; **underprivileged** *adj* desposeído; **underscore** *vt* subrayar; **undershirt** (US) *n* camiseta; **underskirt** (BRIT) *n* enaguas *fpl*

understand [ʌndə'stænd] *vt, vi* entender, comprender; (*assume*) tener entendido; **understandable** *adj* comprensible; **understanding** *adj* comprensivo ▷ *n* comprensión *f*, entendimiento *n*; (*agreement*) acuerdo

understatement ['ʌndəsteɪtmənt] *n* modestia (excesiva); **that's an ~!** ¡eso es decir poco!

understood [ʌndə'stud] *pt, pp of* **understand** ▷ *adj* (*agreed*) acordado; (*implied*): **it is ~ that** se sobreentiende que

undertake [ʌndə'teɪk] (*irreg*) *vt* emprender; **to ~ to do sth** comprometerse a hacer algo

undertaker ['ʌndəteɪkə*] *n* director(a) *m/f* de pompas fúnebres

undertaking ['ʌndəteɪkɪŋ] *n* empresa; (*promise*) promesa

under: underwater *adv* bajo el agua ▷ *adj* submarino; **underway** *adj*: **to be underway** (*meeting*) estar en marcha; (*investigation*) estar llevándose a cabo; **underwear** *n* ropa interior; **underwent** *vb see* **undergo**; **underworld** *n* (*of crime*) hampa, inframundo

undesirable [ʌndɪ'zaɪrəbl] *adj* (*person*) indeseable; (*thing*) poco aconsejable

undisputed [ʌndɪ'spjuːtɪd] *adj* incontestable

undo [ʌn'duː] (*irreg*) *vt* (*laces*) desatar; (*button etc*) desabrochar; (*spoil*) deshacer

undone [ʌn'dʌn] *pp of* **undo** ▷ *adj*: **to come ~** (*clothes*) desabrocharse; (*parcel*) desatarse

undoubtedly [ʌn'dautɪdlɪ] *adv* indudablemente, sin duda

undress [ʌn'dres] *vi* desnudarse

unearth [ʌn'ɜːθ] *vt* desenterrar

uneasy [ʌn'iːzɪ] *adj* intranquilo, preocupado; (*feeling*) desagradable; (*peace*) inseguro

unemployed [ʌnɪm'plɔɪd] *adj* parado, sin trabajo ▷ *npl*: **the ~** los parados

unemployment [ʌnɪm'plɔɪmənt] *n* paro, desempleo; **unemployment benefit** *n* (BRIT) subsidio de desempleo *or* paro

unequal [ʌn'iːkwəl] *adj* (*unfair*) desigual; (*size, length*) distinto

uneven [ʌn'iːvn] *adj* desigual; (*road etc*) lleno de baches

unexpected [ʌnɪk'spektɪd] *adj* inesperado; **unexpectedly** *adv* inesperadamente

unfair [ʌn'feə*] *adj*: **~ (to sb)** injusto (con algn)

unfaithful [ʌn'feɪθful] *adj* infiel

unfamiliar [ʌnfə'mɪlɪə*] *adj* extraño, desconocido; **to be ~ with** desconocer

u

unfashionable [ʌnˈfæʃnəbl] *adj* pasado or fuera de moda

unfasten [ʌnˈfɑːsn] *vt* (*knot*) desatar; (*dress*) desabrochar; (*open*) abrir

unfavourable [ʌnˈfeɪvərəbl] (*us* **unfavorable**) *adj* desfavorable

unfinished [ʌnˈfɪnɪʃt] *adj* inacabado, sin terminar

unfit [ʌnˈfɪt] *adj* bajo de forma; (*incompetent*): ~ **(for)** incapaz (de); ~ **for work** no apto para trabajar

unfold [ʌnˈfəuld] *vt* desdoblar ▷ *vi* abrirse

unforgettable [ʌnfəˈgetəbl] *adj* inolvidable

unfortunate [ʌnˈfɔːtʃnət] *adj* desgraciado; (*event, remark*) inoportuno; **unfortunately** *adv* desgraciadamente

unfriendly [ʌnˈfrɛndlɪ] *adj* antipático; (*behaviour, remark*) hostil, poco amigable

unfurnished [ʌnˈfəːnɪʃt] *adj* sin amueblar

unhappiness [ʌnˈhæpɪnɪs] *n* tristeza, desdicha

unhappy [ʌnˈhæpɪ] *adj* (*sad*) triste; (*unfortunate*) desgraciado; (*childhood*) infeliz; ~ **about/with** (*arrangements etc*) poco contento con, descontento de

unhealthy [ʌnˈhɛlθɪ] *adj* (*place*) malsano; (*person*) enfermizo; (*fig: interest*) morboso

unheard-of [ʌnˈhəːdɔv] *adj* inaudito, sin precedente

unhelpful [ʌnˈhɛlpful] *adj* (*person*) poco servicial; (*advice*) inútil

unhurt [ʌnˈhəːt] *adj* ileso

unidentified [ʌnaɪˈdɛntɪfaɪd] *adj* no identificado, sin identificar; *see also* **UFO**

uniform [ˈjuːnɪfɔːm] *n* uniforme *m* ▷ *adj* uniforme

unify [ˈjuːnɪfaɪ] *vt* unificar, unir

unimportant [ʌnɪmˈpɔːtənt] *adj* sin importancia

uninhabited [ʌnɪnˈhæbɪtɪd] *adj* desierto

unintentional [ʌnɪmˈtɛnʃənəl] *adj* involuntario

union [ˈjuːnjən] *n* unión *f*; (*also*: **trade** ~) sindicato ▷ *cpd* sindical; **Union Jack** *n* bandera del Reino Unido

unique [juːˈniːk] *adj* único

unisex [ˈjuːnɪsɛks] *adj* unisex

unit [ˈjuːnɪt] *n* unidad *f*; (*section: of furniture etc*) elemento; (*team*) grupo; **kitchen** ~ módulo de cocina

unite [juːˈnaɪt] *vt* unir ▷ *vi* unirse; **united** *adj* unido; (*effort*) conjunto; **United Kingdom** *n* Reino Unido; **United Nations (Organization)** *n* Naciones *fpl* Unidas; **United States (of America)** *n* Estados *mpl* Unidos

unity [ˈjuːnɪtɪ] *n* unidad *f*

universal [juːnɪˈvəːsl] *adj* universal

universe [ˈjuːnɪvəːs] *n* universo

university [juːnɪˈvəːsɪtɪ] *n* universidad *f*

unjust [ʌnˈdʒʌst] *adj* injusto

unkind [ʌnˈkaɪnd] *adj* poco amable; (*behaviour, comment*) cruel

unknown [ʌnˈnəun] *adj* desconocido

unlawful [ʌnˈlɔːful] *adj* ilegal, ilícito

unleaded [ʌnˈlɛdɪd] *adj* (*petrol, fuel*) sin plombo

unleash [ʌnˈliːʃ] *vt* desatar

unless [ʌnˈlɛs] *conj* a menos que; ~ **he comes** a menos que venga; ~ **otherwise stated** salvo indicación contraria

unlike [ʌnˈlaɪk] *adj* (*not alike*) distinto de or a; (*not like*) poco propio de ▷ *prep* a diferencia de

unlikely [ʌnˈlaɪklɪ] *adj* improbable; (*unexpected*) inverosímil

unlimited [ʌnˈlɪmɪtɪd] *adj* ilimitado

unlisted [ʌnˈlɪstɪd] (*us*) *adj* (*Tel*) que no consta en la guía

unload [ʌnˈləud] *vt* descargar

unlock [ʌnˈlɔk] *vt* abrir (con llave)

unlucky [ʌnˈlʌkɪ] *adj* desgraciado; (*object, number*) que da mala suerte; **to be** ~ tener mala suerte

unmarried [ʌnˈmærɪd] *adj* soltero

unmistak(e)able [ʌnmɪsˈteɪkəbl] *adj* inconfundible

unnatural [ʌnˈnætʃrəl] *adj* (*gen*) antinatural; (*manner*) afectado; (*habit*) perverso

unnecessary [ʌnˈnɛsəsərɪ] *adj* innecesario, inútil

UNO [ˈjuːnəu] *n abbr* (= *United Nations Organization*) ONU *f*

unofficial [ʌnəˈfɪʃl] *adj* no oficial; (*news*) sin confirmar

unpack [ʌnˈpæk] *vi* deshacer las maletas ▷ *vt* deshacer

unpaid [ʌnˈpeɪd] *adj* (*bill, debt*) sin pagar, impagado; (*Comm*) pendiente; (*holiday*) sin sueldo; (*work*) sin pago, voluntaria

unpleasant [ʌnˈplɛznt] *adj* (*disagreeable*) desagradable; (*person, manner*) antipático

unplug [ʌnˈplʌg] *vt* desenchufar, desconectar

unpopular [ʌnˈpɔpjulə*] *adj* impopular, poco popular

unprecedented [ʌnˈprɛsɪdəntɪd] *adj* sin precedentes

unpredictable [ʌnprɪˈdɪktəbl] *adj* imprevisible

unprotected [ˈʌnprəˈtɛktɪd] *adj* (*sex*) sin protección

unqualified [ʌnˈkwɔlɪfaɪd] *adj* sin título, no cualificado; (*success*) total

unravel [ʌnˈrævl] vt desenmarañar
unreal [ʌnˈrɪəl] adj irreal; (extraordinary) increíble
unrealistic [ʌnrɪəˈlɪstɪk] adj poco realista
unreasonable [ʌnˈriːznəbl] adj irrazonable; (demand) excesivo
unrelated [ʌnrɪˈleɪtɪd] adj sin relación; (family) no emparentado
unreliable [ʌnrɪˈlaɪəbl] adj (person) informal; (machine) poco fiable
unrest [ʌnˈrest] n inquietud f, malestar m; (Pol) disturbios mpl
unroll [ʌnˈrəʊl] vt desenrollar
unruly [ʌnˈruːlɪ] adj indisciplinado
unsafe [ʌnˈseɪf] adj peligroso
unsatisfactory [ˈʌnsætɪsˈfæktərɪ] adj poco satisfactorio
unscrew [ʌnˈskruː] vt destornillar
unsettled [ʌnˈsetld] adj inquieto, intranquilo; (weather) variable
unsettling [ʌnˈsetlɪŋ] adj perturbador(a), inquietante
unsightly [ʌnˈsaɪtlɪ] adj feo
unskilled [ʌnˈskɪld] adj (work) no especializado; (worker) no cualificado
unspoiled [ˈʌnˈspɔɪld], **unspoilt** [ˈʌnˈspɔɪlt] adj (place) que no ha perdido su belleza natural
unstable [ʌnˈsteɪbl] adj inestable
unsteady [ʌnˈstedɪ] adj inestable
unsuccessful [ʌnsəkˈsesful] adj (attempt) infructuoso; (writer, proposal) sin éxito; **to be ~** (in attempting sth) no tener éxito, fracasar
unsuitable [ʌnˈsuːtəbl] adj inapropiado; (time) inoportuno
unsure [ʌnˈʃʊə*] adj inseguro, poco seguro
untidy [ʌnˈtaɪdɪ] adj (room) desordenado; (appearance) desaliñado
untie [ʌnˈtaɪ] vt desatar
until [ənˈtɪl] prep hasta ▷ conj hasta que; **~ he comes** hasta que venga; **~ now** hasta ahora; **~ then** hasta entonces
untrue [ʌnˈtruː] adj (statement) falso
unused [ʌnˈjuːzd] adj sin usar
unusual [ʌnˈjuːʒəl] adj insólito, poco común; (exceptional) inusitado; **unusually** adv (exceptionally) excepcionalmente; **he arrived unusually early** llegó más temprano que de costumbre
unveil [ʌnˈveɪl] vt (statue) descubrir
unwanted [ʌnˈwɒntɪd] adj (clothing) viejo; (pregnancy) no deseado
unwell [ʌnˈwel] adj: **to be/feel ~** estar indispuesto/sentirse mal
unwilling [ʌnˈwɪlɪŋ] adj: **to be ~ to do sth** estar poco dispuesto a hacer algo
unwind [ʌnˈwaɪnd] (irreg) vt desenvolver ▷ vi (relax) relajarse

unwise [ʌnˈwaɪz] adj imprudente
unwittingly [ʌnˈwɪtɪŋlɪ] adv inconscientemente, sin darse cuenta
unwrap [ʌnˈræp] vt desenvolver
unzip [ʌnˈzɪp] vt abrir la cremallera de; (Comput) descomprimir

○ **KEYWORD**

up [ʌp] prep: **to go/be up sth** subir/estar subido en algo; **he went up the stairs/ the hill** subió las escaleras/la colina; **we walked/climbed up the hill** subimos la colina; **they live further up the street** viven más arriba en la calle; **go up that road and turn left** sigue por esa calle y gira a la izquierda
▷ adv 1 (upwards, higher) más arriba; **up in the mountains** en lo alto (de la montaña); **put it a bit higher up** ponlo un poco más arriba or alto; **up there** ahí or allí arriba; **up above** en lo alto, por encima, arriba
2: **to be up** (out of bed) estar levantado; (prices, level) haber subido
3: **up to** (as far as) hasta; **up to now** hasta ahora or la fecha
4: **to be up to: it's up to you** (depending on) depende de ti; **he's not up to it** (job, task etc) no es capaz de hacerlo; **his work is not up to the required standard** su trabajo no da la talla; (inf: be doing): **what is he up to?** ¿que estará tramando?
▷ n: **ups and downs** altibajos mpl

up-and-coming [ʌpəndˈkʌmɪŋ] adj prometedor(a)
upbringing [ˈʌpbrɪŋɪŋ] n educación f
update [ʌpˈdeɪt] vt poner al día
upfront [ʌpˈfrʌnt] adj claro, directo ▷ adv a las claras; (pay) por adelantado; **to be ~ about sth** admitir algo claramente
upgrade [ʌpˈgreɪd] vt (house) modernizar; (employee) ascender
upheaval [ʌpˈhiːvl] n trastornos mpl; (Pol) agitación f
uphill [ʌpˈhɪl] adj cuesta arriba; (fig: task) penoso, difícil ▷ adv: **to go ~** ir cuesta arriba
upholstery [ʌpˈhəʊlstərɪ] n tapicería f
upmarket [ʌpˈmɑːkɪt] adj (product) de categoría
upon [əˈpɒn] prep sobre
upper [ˈʌpə*] adj superior, de arriba ▷ n (of shoe: also: ~s) empeine m; **upper-class** adj de clase alta
upright [ˈʌpraɪt] adj derecho; (vertical) vertical; (fig) honrado
uprising [ˈʌpraɪzɪŋ] n sublevación f
uproar [ˈʌprɔː*] n escándalo

upset [n 'ʌpsɛt, vb, adj ʌp'sɛt] n (to plan etc) revés m, contratiempo; (Med) trastorno ▷ vt irreg (glass etc) volcar; (plan) alterar; (person) molestar, disgustar ▷ adj molesto, disgustado; (stomach) revuelto
upside-down [ʌpsaɪd'daun] adv al revés; **to turn a place ~** (fig) revolverlo todo
upstairs [ʌp'stɛəz] adv arriba ▷ adj (room) de arriba ▷ n el piso superior
up-to-date ['ʌptə'deɪt] adj al día
uptown ['ʌptaun] (US) adv hacia las afueras ▷ adj exterior, de las afueras
upward ['ʌpwəd] adj ascendente; **upward(s)** adv hacia arriba; (more than): **upward(s) of** más de
uranium [juə'reɪnɪəm] n uranio
Uranus [juə'reɪnəs] n Urano
urban ['ə:bən] adj urbano
urge [ə:dʒ] n (desire) deseo ▷ vt: **to ~ sb to do sth** animar a algn a hacer algo
urgency ['ə:dʒənsɪ] n urgencia
urgent ['ə:dʒənt] adj urgente; (voice) perentorio
urinal ['juərɪnl] n (building) urinario; (vessel) orinal m
urinate ['juərɪneɪt] vi orinar
urine ['juərɪn] n orina, orines mpl
US n abbr (= United States) EE. UU.
us [ʌs] pron nos; (after prep) nosotros/as; see also **me**
USA n abbr (= United States (of America)) EE.UU.
use [n ju:s, vb ju:z] n uso, empleo; (usefulness) utilidad f ▷ vt usar, emplear; **she ~d to do it** (ella) solía or acostumbraba hacerlo; **in ~** en uso; **out of ~** en desuso; **to be of ~** servir; **it's no ~** (pointless) es inútil; (not useful) no sirve; **to be ~d to** estar acostumbrado a, acostumbrar; **use up** vt (food) consumir; (money) gastar; **used** [ju:zd] adj (car) usado; **useful** adj útil; **useless** adj (unusable) inservible; (pointless) inútil; (person) inepto; **user** n usuario/a; **user-friendly** adj (computer) amistoso
usual ['ju:ʒuəl] adj normal, corriente; **as ~** como de costumbre; **usually** adv normalmente
utensil [ju:'tɛnsl] n utensilio; **kitchen ~s** batería de cocina
utility [ju:'tɪlɪtɪ] n utilidad f; (public utility) (empresa de) servicio público
utilize ['ju:tɪlaɪz] vt utilizar
utmost ['ʌtməust] adj mayor ▷ n: **to do one's ~** hacer todo lo posible
utter ['ʌtə*] adj total, completo ▷ vt pronunciar, proferir; **utterly** adv completamente, totalmente
U-turn ['ju:'tə:n] n viraje m en redondo

v. abbr = **verse; versus;** (= volt) v; (= vide) véase
vacancy ['veɪkənsɪ] n (BRIT: job) vacante f; (room) habitación f libre; **"no vacancies"** "completo"
vacant ['veɪkənt] adj desocupado, libre; (expression) distraído
vacate [və'keɪt] vt (house, room) desocupar; (job) dejar (vacante)
vacation [və'keɪʃən] n vacaciones fpl; **vacationer** (US **vacationist**) n turista m/f
vaccination [væksɪ'neɪʃən] n vacunación f
vaccine ['væksi:n] n vacuna
vacuum ['vækjum] n vacío; **vacuum cleaner** n aspiradora
vagina [və'dʒaɪnə] n vagina
vague [veɪg] adj vago; (memory) borroso; (ambiguous) impreciso; (person: absent-minded) distraído; (: evasive): **to be ~** no decir las cosas claramente
vain [veɪn] adj (conceited) presumido; (useless) vano, inútil; **in ~** en vano
Valentine's Day ['væləntaɪnzdeɪ] n día de los enamorados
valid ['vælɪd] adj válido; (ticket) valedero; (law) vigente
valley ['vælɪ] n valle m
valuable ['væljuəbl] adj (jewel) de valor; (time) valioso; **valuables** npl objetos mpl de valor
value ['vælju:] n valor m; (importance) importancia ▷ vt (fix price of) tasar, valorar; (esteem) apreciar; **values** npl (principles) principios mpl
valve [vælv] n válvula
vampire ['væmpaɪə*] n vampiro
van [væn] n (Aut) furgoneta, camioneta
vandal ['vændl] n vándalo/a; **vandalism** n vandalismo; **vandalize** vt dañar, destruir
vanilla [və'nɪlə] n vainilla

vanish ['vænɪʃ] vi desaparecer
vanity ['vænɪtɪ] n vanidad f
vapour ['veɪpə*] (us **vapor**) n vapor m; (on breath, window) vaho
variable ['vɛərɪəbl] adj variable
variant ['vɛərɪənt] n variante f
variation [vɛərɪ'eɪʃən] n variación f
varied ['vɛərɪd] adj variado
variety [və'raɪətɪ] n (diversity) diversidad f; (type) variedad f
various ['vɛərɪəs] adj (several: people) varios/as; (reasons) diversos/as
varnish ['vɑːnɪʃ] n barniz m; (nail varnish) esmalte m ▷ vt barnizar; (nails) pintar (con esmalte)
vary ['vɛərɪ] vt variar; (change) cambiar ▷ vi variar
vase [vɑːz] n jarrón m
▌Be careful not to translate **vase** by the Spanish word **vaso**.
Vaseline® ['væsɪliːn] n vaselina®
vast [vɑːst] adj enorme
VAT [væt] (BRIT) n abbr (= value added tax) IVA m
vault [vɔːlt] n (of roof) bóveda; (tomb) panteón m; (in bank) cámara acorazada ▷ vt (also: **~ over**) saltar (por encima de)
VCR n abbr = **video cassette recorder**
VDU n abbr (= visual display unit) UPV f
veal [viːl] n ternera
veer [vɪə*] vi (vehicle) virar; (wind) girar
vegan ['viːgən] n vegetariano/a estricto/a, vegetaliano/a
vegetable ['vɛdʒtəbl] n (Bot) vegetal m; (edible plant) legumbre f, hortaliza ▷ adj vegetal
vegetarian [vɛdʒɪ'tɛərɪən] adj, n vegetariano/a m/f
vegetation [vɛdʒɪ'teɪʃən] n vegetación f
vehicle ['viːɪkl] n vehículo; (fig) medio
veil [veɪl] n velo ▷ vt velar
vein [veɪn] n vena; (of ore etc) veta
Velcro® ['vɛlkrəu] n velcro® m
velvet ['vɛlvɪt] n terciopelo
vending machine ['vɛndɪŋ-] n distribuidor m automático
vendor ['vɛndə*] n vendedor(a) m/f; **street ~** vendedor(a) m/f callejero/a
vengeance ['vɛndʒəns] n venganza; **with a ~** (fig) con creces
venison ['vɛnɪsn] n carne f de venado
venom ['vɛnəm] n veneno; (bitterness) odio
vent [vɛnt] n (in jacket) respiradero; (in wall) rejilla (de ventilación) ▷ vt (fig: feelings) desahogar
ventilation [vɛntɪ'leɪʃən] n ventilación f
venture ['vɛntʃə*] n empresa ▷ vt

(opinion) ofrecer ▷ vi arriesgarse, lanzarse; **business ~** empresa comercial
venue ['vɛnjuː] n lugar m
Venus ['viːnəs] n Venus m
verb [vəːb] n verbo; **verbal** adj verbal
verdict ['vəːdɪkt] n veredicto, fallo; (fig) opinión f, juicio
verge [vəːdʒ] (BRIT) n borde m; **"soft ~s"** (Aut) "arcén m no asfaltado"; **to be on the ~ of doing sth** estar a punto de hacer algo
verify ['vɛrɪfaɪ] vt comprobar, verificar
versatile ['vəːsətaɪl] adj (person) polifacético; (machine, tool etc) versátil
verse [vəːs] n poesía; (stanza) estrofa; (in bible) versículo
version ['vəːʃən] n versión f
versus ['vəːsəs] prep contra
vertical ['vəːtɪkl] adj vertical
very ['vɛrɪ] adv muy ▷ adj: **the ~ book which** el mismo libro que; **the ~ last** el último de todos; **at the ~ least** al menos; **~ much** muchísimo
vessel ['vɛsl] n (ship) barco; (container) vasija; see **blood**
vest [vɛst] n (BRIT) camiseta; (US: waistcoat) chaleco
vet [vɛt] vt (candidate) investigar ▷ n abbr (BRIT) = **veterinary surgeon**
veteran ['vɛtərn] n excombatiente mf, veterano/a
veterinary surgeon ['vɛtrɪnərɪ-] (US **veterinarian**) n veterinario/a m/f
veto ['viːtəu] (pl **~es**) n veto ▷ vt prohibir, poner el veto a
via ['vaɪə] prep por, por medio de
viable ['vaɪəbl] adj viable
vibrate [vaɪ'breɪt] vi vibrar
vibration [vaɪ'breɪʃən] n vibración f
vicar ['vɪkə*] n párroco (de la Iglesia Anglicana)
vice [vaɪs] n (evil) vicio; (Tech) torno de banco; **vice-chairman** (irreg) n vicepresidente m
vice versa ['vaɪsɪ'vəːsə] adv viceversa
vicinity [vɪ'sɪnɪtɪ] n: **in the ~ (of)** cercano (a)
vicious ['vɪʃəs] adj (attack) violento; (words) cruel; (horse, dog) resabido
victim ['vɪktɪm] n víctima
victor ['vɪktə*] n vencedor(a) m/f
Victorian [vɪk'tɔːrɪən] adj victoriano
victorious [vɪk'tɔːrɪəs] adj vencedor(a)
victory ['vɪktərɪ] n victoria
video ['vɪdɪəu] n vídeo (SP), video (LAM); **video call** n videollamada; **video camera** n videocámara, cámara de vídeo; **video (cassette) recorder** n vídeo (SP), video (LAM); **video game** n videojuego;

videophone n videoteléfono; **video shop** n videoclub m; **video tape** n cinta de vídeo

vie [vaɪ] vi: **to ~ (with sb for sth)** competir (con algn por algo)

Vienna [vɪˈenə] n Viena

Vietnam [vjɛtˈnæm] n Vietnam m; **Vietnamese** [-nəˈmiːz] n inv, adj vietnamita mf

view [vjuː] n vista; (outlook) perspectiva; (opinion) opinión f, criterio ▷ vt (look at) mirar; (fig) considerar; **on ~** (in museum etc) expuesto; **in full ~ (of)** en plena vista (de); **in ~ of the weather/the fact that** en vista del tiempo/del hecho de que; **in my ~** en mi opinión; **viewer** n espectador(a) m/f; (TV) telespectador(a) m/f; **viewpoint** n (attitude) punto de vista; (place) mirador m

vigilant [ˈvɪdʒɪlənt] adj vigilante

vigorous [ˈvɪɡərəs] adj enérgico, vigoroso

vile [vaɪl] adj vil, infame; (smell) asqueroso; (temper) endemoniado

villa [ˈvɪlə] n (country house) casa de campo; (suburban house) chalet m

village [ˈvɪlɪdʒ] n aldea; **villager** n aldeano/a

villain [ˈvɪlən] n (scoundrel) malvado/a; (in novel) malo; (BRIT: criminal) maleante mf

vinaigrette [vɪneɪˈɡrɛt] n vinagreta

vine [vaɪn] n vid f

vinegar [ˈvɪnɪɡə*] n vinagre m

vineyard [ˈvɪnjɑːd] n viña, viñedo

vintage [ˈvɪntɪdʒ] n (year) vendimia, cosecha ▷ cpd de época

vinyl [ˈvaɪnl] n vinilo

viola [vɪˈəʊlə] n (Mus) viola

violate [ˈvaɪəleɪt] vt violar

violation [vaɪəˈleɪʃən] n violación f; **in ~ of sth** en violación de algo

violence [ˈvaɪələns] n violencia

violent [ˈvaɪələnt] adj violento; (intense) intenso

violet [ˈvaɪələt] adj violado, violeta ▷ n (plant) violeta

violin [vaɪəˈlɪn] n violín m

VIP n abbr (= very important person) VIP m

virgin [ˈvɜːdʒɪn] n virgen f

Virgo [ˈvɜːɡəʊ] n Virgo

virtual [ˈvɜːtjʊəl] adj virtual; **virtually** adv prácticamente; **virtual reality** n (Comput) mundo or realidad f virtual

virtue [ˈvɜːtjuː] n virtud f; (advantage) ventaja; **by ~ of** en virtud de

virus [ˈvaɪərəs] n (also Comput) virus m inv

visa [ˈviːzə] n visado (SP), visa (LAM)

vise [vaɪs] (US) n (Tech) = **vice**

visibility [vɪzɪˈbɪlɪtɪ] n visibilidad f

visible [ˈvɪzəbl] adj visible

vision [ˈvɪʒən] n (sight) vista; (foresight, in dream) visión f

visit [ˈvɪzɪt] n visita ▷ vt (person (US: also: ~ with) visitar, hacer una visita a; (place) ir a, (ir a) conocer; **visiting hours** npl (in hospital etc) horas fpl de visita; **visitor** n (in museum) visitante mf; (invited to house) visita; (tourist) turista mf; **visitor centre** (US **visitor center**) n centro m de información

visual [ˈvɪzjʊəl] adj visual; **visualize** vt imaginarse

vital [ˈvaɪtl] adj (essential) esencial; (dynamic) dinámico; (organ) vital

vitality [vaɪˈtælɪtɪ] n energía, vitalidad f

vitamin [ˈvɪtəmɪn] n vitamina

vivid [ˈvɪvɪd] adj (account) gráfico; (light) intenso; (imagination, memory) vivo

V-neck [ˈviːnɛk] n cuello de pico

vocabulary [vəʊˈkæbjʊlərɪ] n vocabulario

vocal [ˈvəʊkl] adj vocal; (articulate) elocuente

vocational [vəʊˈkeɪʃənl] adj profesional

vodka [ˈvɒdkə] n vodka m

vogue [vəʊɡ] n: **in ~** en boga

voice [vɔɪs] n voz f ▷ vt expresar; **voice mail** n fonobuzón m

void [vɔɪd] n vacío; (hole) hueco ▷ adj (invalid) nulo, inválido; (empty): **~ of** carente or desprovisto de

volatile [ˈvɒlətaɪl] adj (situation) inestable; (person) voluble; (liquid) volátil

volcano [vɒlˈkeɪnəʊ] (pl **~es**) n volcán m

volleyball [ˈvɒlɪbɔːl] n vol(e)ibol m

volt [vəʊlt] n voltio; **voltage** n voltaje m

volume [ˈvɒljuːm] n (gen) volumen m; (book) tomo

voluntarily [ˈvɒləntrɪlɪ] adv libremente, voluntariamente

voluntary [ˈvɒləntərɪ] adj voluntario

volunteer [vɒlənˈtɪə*] n voluntario/a ▷ vt (information) ofrecer ▷ vi ofrecerse (de voluntario); **to ~ to do** ofrecerse a hacer

vomit [ˈvɒmɪt] n vómito ▷ vt, vi vomitar

vote [vəʊt] n voto; (votes cast) votación f; (right to vote) derecho de votar; (franchise) sufragio ▷ vt (chairman) elegir; (propose): **to ~ that** proponer que ▷ vi votar, ir a votar; **~ of thanks** voto de gracias; **voter** n votante mf; **voting** n votación f

voucher [ˈvaʊtʃə*] n (for meal etc) vale m

vow [vaʊ] n voto ▷ vt: **to ~ to do/that** jurar hacer/que

vowel [ˈvaʊəl] n vocal f

voyage [ˈvɔɪɪdʒ] n viaje m

vulgar [ˈvʌlɡə*] adj (rude) ordinario, grosero; (in bad taste) de mal gusto

vulnerable [ˈvʌlnərəbl] adj vulnerable

vulture [ˈvʌltʃə*] n buitre m

W

waddle ['wɔdl] vi anadear

wade [weɪd] vi: **to ~ through** (water) vadear; (fig: book) leer con dificultad

wafer ['weɪfə*] n galleta, barquillo

waffle ['wɔfl] n (Culin) gofre m ▷ vi dar el rollo

wag [wæg] vt menear, agitar ▷ vi moverse, menearse

wage [weɪdʒ] n (also: **~s**) sueldo, salario ▷ vt: **to ~ war** hacer la guerra

wag(g)on ['wægən] n (horse-drawn) carro; (BRIT Rail) vagón m

wail [weɪl] n gemido ▷ vi gemir

waist [weɪst] n cintura, talle m; **waistcoat** (BRIT) n chaleco

wait [weɪt] n (interval) pausa ▷ vi esperar; **to lie in ~ for** acechar a; **I can't ~ to** estoy deseando; **to ~ for** esperar (a); **wait on** vt fus servir a; **waiter** n camarero; **waiting list** n lista de espera; **waiting room** n sala de espera; **waitress** ['weɪtrɪs] n camarera

waive [weɪv] vt suspender

wake [weɪk] n (pt woke or ~d, pp woken or ~d) vt (also: **~ up**) despertar ▷ vi (also: **~ up**) despertarse ▷ n (for dead person) vela, velatorio; (Naut) estela

Wales [weɪlz] n País m de Gales; **the Prince of ~** el príncipe de Gales

walk [wɔːk] n (stroll) paseo; (hike) excursión f a pie, caminata; (gait) paso, andar m; (in park etc) paseo, alameda ▷ vi andar, caminar; (for pleasure, exercise) pasear ▷ vt (distance) recorrer a pie, andar; (dog) pasear; **10 minutes' ~ from here** a 10 minutos de aquí andando; **people from all ~s of life** gente de todas las esferas; **walk out** n (audience) salir; (workers) declararse en huelga; **walker** n (person) paseante mf, caminante mf; **walkie-talkie** ['wɔːkɪ'tɔːkɪ] n walkie-talkie m; **walking**

n el andar; **walking shoes** npl zapatos mpl para andar; **walking stick** n bastón m; **Walkman®** n Walkman® m; **walkway** n paseo

wall [wɔːl] n pared f; (exterior) muro; (city wall etc) muralla

wallet ['wɔlɪt] n cartera, billetera

wallpaper ['wɔːlpeɪpə*] n papel m pintado ▷ vt empapelar

walnut ['wɔːlnʌt] n nuez f; (tree) nogal m

walrus ['wɔːlrəs] (pl ~ or **~es**) n morsa

waltz [wɔːlts] n vals m ▷ vi bailar el vals

wand [wɔnd] n (also: **magic ~**) varita (mágica)

wander ['wɔndə*] vi (person) vagar; deambular; (thoughts) divagar ▷ vt recorrer, vagar por

want [wɔnt] vt querer, desear; (need) necesitar ▷ n: **for ~ of** por falta de; **wanted** adj (criminal) buscado; **"wanted"** (in advertisements) "se busca"

war [wɔː*] n guerra; **to make ~ (on)** declarar la guerra (a)

ward [wɔːd] n (in hospital) sala; (Pol) distrito electoral; (Law: child: also: **~ of court**) pupilo/a

warden ['wɔːdn] n (BRIT: of institution) director(a) m/f; (of park, game reserve) guardián/ana m/f; (BRIT: also: **traffic ~**) guardia mf

wardrobe ['wɔːdrəub] n armario, ropero; (clothes) vestuario

warehouse ['wɛəhaus] n almacén m, depósito

warfare ['wɔːfɛə*] n guerra

warhead ['wɔːhɛd] n cabeza armada

warm [wɔːm] adj caliente; (thanks) efusivo; (clothes etc) abrigado; (welcome, day) caluroso; **it's ~** hace calor; **I'm ~** tengo calor; **warm up** vi (room) calentarse; (person) entrar en calor; (athlete) hacer ejercicios de calentamiento ▷ vt calentar; **warmly** adv afectuosamente; **warmth** n calor m

warn [wɔːn] vt avisar, advertir; **warning** n aviso, advertencia; **warning light** n luz f de advertencia

warrant ['wɔrnt] n autorización f; (Law: to arrest) orden f de detención; (: to search) mandamiento de registro

warranty ['wɔrənti] n garantía

warrior ['wɔriə*] n guerrero/a

Warsaw ['wɔːsɔː] n Varsovia

warship ['wɔːʃɪp] n buque m or barco de guerra

wart [wɔːt] n verruga

wartime ['wɔːtaɪm] n: **in ~** en tiempos de guerra, en la guerra

wary ['wɛərɪ] adj cauteloso

was [wɔz] *pt of* **be**
wash [wɔʃ] *vt* lavar ▷ *vi* lavarse; *(sea etc)*: **to ~ against/over sth** llegar hasta/cubrir algo ▷ *n (clothes etc)* lavado; *(of ship)* estela; **to have a ~** lavarse; **wash up** *vi (BRIT)* fregar los platos; *(US)* lavarse; **washbasin** *(US)* *n* lavabo; **wash cloth** *(US)* *n* manopla; **washer** *n (Tech)* arandela; **washing** *n (dirty)* ropa sucia; *(clean)* colada; **washing line** *n* cuerda de (colgar) la ropa; **washing machine** *n* lavadora; **washing powder** *(BRIT)* *n* detergente *m* (en polvo)
Washington ['wɔʃɪŋtən] *n* Washington *m*
wash: washing-up *(BRIT)* *n* fregado, platos *mpl* (para fregar); **washing-up liquid** *(BRIT)* *n* líquido lavavajillas; **washroom** *(US)* *n* servicios *mpl*
wasn't ['wɔznt] = **was not**
wasp [wɔsp] *n* avispa
waste [weɪst] *n* derroche *m*, despilfarro; *(of time)* pérdida; *(food)* sobras *fpl*; *(rubbish)* basura, desperdicios *mpl* ▷ *adj (material)* de desecho; *(left over)* sobrante; *(land)* baldío, descampado ▷ *vt* malgastar, derrochar; *(time)* perder; *(opportunity)* desperdiciar; **waste ground** *(BRIT)* *n* terreno baldío; **wastepaper basket** *n* papelera
watch [wɔtʃ] *n (also:* **wrist ~**) reloj *m*; *(Mil: group of guards)* centinela *m*; *(act)* vigilancia; *(Naut: spell of duty)* guardia ▷ *vt (look at)* mirar, observar; *(: match, programme)* ver; *(spy on, guard)* vigilar; *(be careful of)* cuidarse de, tener cuidado de ▷ *vi* ver, mirar; *(keep guard)* montar guardia; **watch out** *vi* cuidarse, tener cuidado; **watchdog** *n* perro guardián; *(fig)* persona u organismo encargado de asegurarse de que las empresas actúan dentro de la legalidad; **watch strap** *n* pulsera (de reloj)
water ['wɔːtə*] *n* agua ▷ *vt (plant)* regar ▷ *vi (eyes)* llorar; *(mouth)* hacerse la boca agua; **water down** *vt (milk etc)* aguar; *(fig: story)* dulcificar, diluir; **watercolour** *(US* **watercolor**) *n* acuarela; **watercress** *n* berro; **waterfall** *n* cascada, salto de agua; **watering can** *n* regadera; **watermelon** *n* sandía; **waterproof** *adj* impermeable; **water-skiing** *n* esquí *m* acuático
watt [wɔt] *n* vatio
wave [weɪv] *n (of hand)* señal *f* con la mano; *(on water)* ola; *(Radio, in hair)* onda; *(fig)* oleada ▷ *vi* agitar la mano; *(flag etc)* ondear ▷ *vt (handkerchief, gun)* agitar; **wavelength** *n* longitud *f* de onda
waver ['weɪvə*] *vi (voice, love etc)* flaquear; *(person)* vacilar
wavy ['weɪvɪ] *adj* ondulado
wax [wæks] *n* cera ▷ *vt* encerar ▷ *vi*

(moon) crecer
way [weɪ] *n* camino; *(distance)* trayecto, recorrido; *(direction)* dirección *f*, sentido; *(manner)* modo, manera; *(habit)* costumbre *f*; **which ~? - this ~** ¿por dónde? *or* ¿en qué dirección? - por aquí; **on the ~** *(en route)* en (el) camino; **to be on one's ~** estar en camino; **to be in the ~** bloquear el camino; *(fig)* estorbar; **to go out of one's ~ - to do sth** desvivirse por hacer algo; **under ~** en marcha; **to lose one's ~** extraviarse; **in a ~** en cierto modo *or* sentido; **no ~!** *(inf)* ¡de eso nada!; **by the ~ ...** a propósito ...; **"~ in"** *(BRIT)* "entrada"; **"~ out"** *(BRIT)* "salida"; **the ~ back** el camino de vuelta; **"give ~"** *(BRIT Aut)* "ceda el paso"
W.C. *n (BRIT)* váter *m*
we [wiː] *pl pron* nosotros/as
weak [wiːk] *adj* débil, flojo; *(tea etc)* claro; **weaken** *vi* debilitarse; *(give way)* ceder ▷ *vt* debilitar; **weakness** *n* debilidad *f*; *(fault)* punto débil; **to have a weakness for** tener debilidad por
wealth [welθ] *n* riqueza; *(of details)* abundancia; **wealthy** *adj* rico
weapon ['wepən] *n* arma; **~s of mass destruction** armas de destrucción masiva
wear [weə*] *(pt* **wore**, *pp* **worn**) *n (use)* uso; *(deterioration through use)* desgaste *m* ▷ *vt (clothes)* llevar; *(shoes)* calzar; *(damage: through use)* gastar, usar ▷ *vi (last)* durar; *(rub through etc)* desgastarse; **evening ~** ropa de etiqueta; **sports~/ baby~** ropa de deportes/de niños; **wear off** *vi (pain etc)* pasar, desaparecer; **wear out** *vt* desgastar; *(person, strength)* agotar
weary ['wɪərɪ] *adj* cansado; *(dispirited)* abatido ▷ *vi*: **to ~ of** cansarse de
weasel ['wiːzl] *n (Zool)* comadreja
weather ['weðə*] *n* tiempo ▷ *vt (storm, crisis)* hacer frente a; **under the ~** *(fig: ill)* indispuesto, pachucho; **weather forecast** *n* boletín *m* meteorológico
weave [wiːv] *(pt* **wove**, *pp* **woven**) *vt (cloth)* tejer; *(fig)* entretejer
web [web] *n (of spider)* telaraña; *(on duck's foot)* membrana; *(network)* red *f*; **the (World Wide) W~** la Red; **web address** *n* dirección *f* de Internet; **webcam** *n* webcam *f*; **web page** *n* (página) web *m or f*; **website** *n* sitio web
Wed. *abbr (= Wednesday)* miérc
wed [wed] *(pt, pp* **~ded**) *vt* casar ▷ *vi* casarse
we'd [wiːd] = **we had**; **we would**
wedding ['wedɪŋ] *n* boda, casamiento; **silver/golden ~ (anniversary)** bodas *fpl* de plata/de oro; **wedding anniversary** *n*

aniversario de boda; **wedding day** n día m de la boda; **wedding dress** n traje m de novia; **wedding ring** n alianza

wedge [wɛdʒ] n (of wood etc) cuña; (of cake) trozo ▷vt acuñar; (push) apretar

Wednesday ['wɛdnzdɪ] n miércoles m inv

wee [wiː] (scottish) adj pequeñito

weed [wiːd] n mala hierba, maleza ▷vt escardar, desherbar; **weedkiller** n herbicida m

week [wiːk] n semana; **a ~ today/ on Friday** de hoy/del viernes en ocho días; **weekday** n día m laborable; **weekend** n fin m de semana; **weekly** adv semanalmente, cada semana ▷adj semanal ▷n semanario

weep [wiːp] (pt, pp **wept**) vi, vt llorar

weigh [weɪ] vt, vi pesar; **to ~ anchor** levar anclas; **weigh up** vt sopesar

weight [weɪt] n peso; (metal weight) pesa; **to lose/put on ~** adelgazar/engordar; **weightlifting** n levantamiento de pesas

weir [wɪə*] n presa

weird [wɪəd] adj raro, extraño

welcome ['wɛlkəm] adj bienvenido ▷n bienvenida ▷vt dar la bienvenida a; (be glad of) alegrarse de; **thank you - you're ~** gracias – de nada

weld [wɛld] n soldadura ▷vt soldar

welfare ['wɛlfɛə*] n bienestar m; (social aid) asistencia social; **welfare state** n estado del bienestar

well [wɛl] n fuente f, pozo ▷adv bien ▷adj: **to be ~** estar bien (de salud) ▷excl ¡vaya!, ¡bueno!; **as ~** también; **as ~ as** además de; **~ done!** ¡bien hecho!; **get ~ soon!** ¡que te mejores pronto!; **to do ~** (business) ir bien; (person) tener éxito

we'll [wiːl] = we will; we shall

well: well-behaved adj bueno; **well-built** adj (person) fornido; **well-dressed** adj bien vestido

wellies ['wɛlɪz] (inf) npl (BRIT) botas de goma

well: well-known adj (person) conocido; **well-off** adj acomodado; **well-paid** [wel'peɪd] adj bien pagado, bien retribuido

Welsh [wɛlʃ] adj galés/esa ▷n (Ling) galés m; **Welshman** (irreg) n galés m; **Welshwoman** (irreg) n galesa

went [wɛnt] pt of **go**

wept [wɛpt] pt, pp of **weep**

were [wəː*] pt of **be**

we're [wɪə*] = we are

weren't [wəːnt] = were not

west [wɛst] n oeste m ▷adj occidental, del oeste ▷adv al or hacia el oeste; **the W~** el Oeste, el Occidente; **westbound** ['wɛstbaund] adj (traffic, carriageway) con rumbo al oeste; **western** adj occidental ▷n (Cinema) película del oeste; **West Indian** adj, n antillano/a m/f

wet [wɛt] adj (damp) húmedo; (soaked) **~ through** mojado; (rainy) lluvioso ▷n (BRIT: Pol) conservador(a) m/f moderado/a; **to get ~** mojarse; **"~ paint"** "recién pintado"; **wetsuit** n traje m térmico

we've [wiːv] = we have

whack [wæk] vt dar un buen golpe a

whale [weɪl] n (Zool) ballena

wharf [wɔːf] (pl **wharves**) n muelle m

○ KEYWORD

what [wɔt] adj **1** (in direct/indirect questions) qué; **what size is he?** ¿qué talla usa?; **what colour/shape is it?** ¿de qué color/forma es? **2** (in exclamations): **what a mess!** ¡qué desastre!; **what a fool I am!** ¡qué tonto soy! ▷pron **1** (interrogative) qué; **what are you doing?** ¿qué haces or estás haciendo?; **what is happening?** ¿qué pasa or está pasando?; **what is it called?** ¿cómo se llama?; **what about me?** ¿y yo qué?; **what about doing ...?** ¿qué tal si hacemos ...? **2** (relative) lo que; **I saw what you did/was on the table** vi lo que hiciste/había en la mesa ▷excl (disbelieving) ¡cómo!; **what, no coffee!** ¡que no hay café!

whatever [wɔt'ɛvə*] adj: **~ book you choose** cualquier libro que elijas ▷pron: **do ~ is necessary** haga lo que sea necesario; **~ happens** pase lo que pase; **no reason ~ or whatsoever** ninguna razón sea la que sea; **nothing ~** nada en absoluto

whatsoever [wɔtsəu'ɛvə*] adj see **whatever**

wheat [wiːt] n trigo

wheel [wiːl] n rueda; (Aut: also: **steering ~**) volante m; (Naut) timón m ▷vt (pram etc) empujar ▷vi (also: **~ round**) dar la vuelta, girar; **wheelbarrow** n carretilla; **wheelchair** n silla de ruedas; **wheel clamp** n (Aut) cepo

wheeze [wiːz] vi resollar

○ KEYWORD

when [wɛn] adv cuando; **when did it happen?** ¿cuándo ocurrió?; **I know when it happened** sé cuándo ocurrió ▷conj **1** (at, during, after the time that) cuando; **be careful when you cross the road** ten cuidado al cruzar la calle; **that**

was when I needed you fue entonces que te necesité

2 (*on, at which*): **on the day when I met him** el día en qué le conocí

3 (*whereas*) cuando

whenever [wɛn'ɛvə*] *conj* cuando; (*every time that*) cada vez que ▷ *adv* cuando sea

where [wɛə*] *adv* dónde ▷ *conj* donde; **this is ~** aquí es donde; **whereabouts** *adv* dónde ▷ *n*: **nobody knows his whereabouts** nadie conoce su paradero; **whereas** *conj* visto que, mientras; **whereby** *pron* por lo cual; **wherever** *conj* dondequiera que; (*interrogative*) dónde

whether ['wɛðə*] *conj* si; **I don't know ~ to accept or not** no sé si aceptar o no; **~ you go or not** vayas o no vayas

O **KEYWORD**

which [wɪtʃ] *adj* **1** (*interrogative: direct, indirect*) qué; **which picture(s) do you want?** ¿qué cuadro(s) quieres?; **which one?** ¿cuál?

2 in which case en cuyo caso; **we got there at 8 pm, by which time the cinema was full** llegamos allí a las 8, cuando el cine estaba lleno

▷ *pron* **1** (*interrogative*) cual; **I don't mind which** el/la que sea

2 (*relative: replacing noun*) que; (: *replacing clause*) lo que; (: *after preposition*) (el(la)) que etc el/la cual etc; **the apple which you ate/which is on the table** la manzana que comiste/que está en la mesa; **the chair on which you are sitting** la silla en la que estás sentado; **he said he knew, which is true/I feared** dijo que lo sabía, lo cual *or* lo que es cierto/me temía

whichever [wɪtʃ'ɛvə*] *adj*: **take ~ book you prefer** coja (*SP*) el libro que prefiera; **~ book you take** cualquier libro que coja

while [waɪl] *n* rato, momento ▷ *conj* mientras; (*although*) aunque; **for a ~** durante algún tiempo

whilst [waɪlst] *conj* = **while**

whim [wɪm] *n* capricho

whine [waɪn] *n* (*of pain*) gemido; (*of engine*) zumbido; (*of siren*) aullido ▷ *vi* gemir; zumbar; (*fig: complain*) gimotear

whip [wɪp] *n* látigo; (*Pol: person*) encargado de la disciplina partidaria en el parlamento ▷ *vt* azotar; (*Culin*) batir; (*move quickly*): **to ~ sth out/off** sacar/quitar algo de un tirón; **whipped cream** *n* nata *or* crema montada

whirl [wə:l] *vt* hacer girar, dar vueltas

a ▷ *vi* girar, dar vueltas; (*leaves etc*) arremolinarse

whisk [wɪsk] *n* (*Culin*) batidor *m* ▷ *vt* (*Culin*) batir; **to ~ sb away** *or* **off** llevar volando a algn

whiskers ['wɪskəz] *npl* (*of animal*) bigotes *mpl*; (*of man*) patillas *fpl*

whiskey ['wɪskɪ] (*US, IRELAND*) *n* = **whisky**

whisky ['wɪskɪ] *n* whisky *m*

whisper ['wɪspə*] *n* susurro ▷ *vi, vt* susurrar

whistle ['wɪsl] *n* (*sound*) silbido; (*object*) silbato ▷ *vi* silbar

white [waɪt] *adj* blanco; (*pale*) pálido ▷ *n* blanco; (*of egg*) clara; **whiteboard** *n* pizarra blanca; **interactive whiteboard** pizarra interactiva; **White House** (*US*) *n* Casa Blanca; **whitewash** *n* (*paint*) jalbegue *m*, cal *f* ▷ *vt* blanquear

whiting ['waɪtɪŋ] *n inv* (*fish*) pescadilla

Whitsun ['wɪtsn] *n* pentecostés *m*

whittle ['wɪtl] *vt*: **to ~ away**, **~ down** ir reduciendo

whizz [wɪz] *vi*: **to ~ past** *or* **by** pasar a toda velocidad

O **KEYWORD**

who [hu:] *pron* **1** (*interrogative*) quién; **who is it?**, **who's there?** ¿quién es?; **who are you looking for?** ¿a quién buscas?; **I told her who I was** le dije quién era yo

2 (*relative*) que; **the man/woman who spoke to me** el hombre/la mujer que habló conmigo; **those who can swim** los que saben *or* sepan nadar

whoever [hu:'ɛvə*] *pron*: **~ finds it** cualquiera *or* quienquiera que lo encuentre; **ask ~ you like** pregunta a quien quieras; **~ he marries** no importa con quién se case

whole [həul] *adj* (*entire*) todo, entero; (*not broken*) intacto ▷ *n* todo; (*all*): **the ~ of the town** toda la ciudad, la ciudad entera ▷ *n* (*total*) total *m*; (*sum*) conjunto; **on the ~**, **as a ~** en general; **wholefood(s)** *n(pl)* alimento(s) *m(pl)* integral(es); **wholeheartedly** [həul'ha:tɪdlɪ] *adv* con entusiasmo; **wholemeal** *adj* integral; **wholesale** *n* venta al por mayor ▷ *adj* al por mayor; (*fig: destruction*) sistemático; **wholewheat** *adj* = **wholemeal**; **wholly** *adv* totalmente, enteramente

O **KEYWORD**

whom [hu:m] *pron* **1** (*interrogative*): **whom did you see?** ¿a quién viste?; **to**

whom did you give it? ¿a quién se lo diste?; **tell me from whom you received it** dígame de quién lo recibió
2 (*relative*) que; **to whom** a quien(es); **of whom** de quien(es), del/de la que *etc*; **the man whom I saw/to whom I wrote** el hombre que vi/a quien escribí; **the lady about/with whom I was talking** la señora de (la) que/con quien *or* (la) que hablaba

whore [hɔ:*] (*inf, pej*) n puta

○ **KEYWORD**

whose [hu:z] adj
1 (*possessive: interrogative*): **whose book is this?, whose is this book?** ¿de quién es este libro?; **whose pencil have you taken?** ¿de quién es el lápiz que has cogido?; **whose daughter are you?** ¿de quién eres hija?
2 (*possessive: relative*) cuyo/a, *pl* cuyos/as; **the man whose son you rescued** el hombre cuyo hijo rescataste; **those whose passports I have** aquellas personas cuyos pasaportes tengo; **the woman whose car was stolen** la mujer a quien le robaron el coche ▷ *pron* de quién; **whose is this?** ¿de quién es esto?; **I know whose it is** sé de quién es

○ **KEYWORD**

why [waɪ] adv por qué; **why not?** ¿por qué no?; **why not do it now?** ¿por qué no lo haces (*or* hacemos *etc*) ahora? ▷ *conj*: **I wonder why he said that** me pregunto por qué dijo eso; **that's not why I'm here** no es por eso (por lo) que estoy aquí; **the reason why** la razón por la que
▷ *excl* (*expressing surprise, shock, annoyance*) ¡hombre!, ¡vaya!; (*explaining*): **why, it's you!** ¡hombre, eres tú!; **why, that's impossible** ¡pero sí eso es imposible!

wicked ['wɪkɪd] adj malvado, cruel
wicket ['wɪkɪt] n (*Cricket: stumps*) palos *mpl*; (*: grass area*) terreno de juego
wide [waɪd] adj ancho; (*area, knowledge*) vasto, grande; (*choice*) amplio ▷ *adv*: **to open ~** abrir de par en par; **to shoot ~** errar el tiro; **widely** adv (*travelled*) mucho; (*spaced*) muy; **it is widely believed/known that ...** mucha gente piensa/sabe que ...; **widen** vt ensanchar; (*experience*) ampliar ▷ *vi* ensancharse; **wide open** adj abierto de par en par; **widespread** adj extendido, general

widow ['wɪdəu] n viuda; **widower** n viudo
width [wɪdθ] n anchura; (*of cloth*) ancho
wield [wi:ld] vt (*sword*) blandir; (*power*) ejercer
wife [waɪf] (*pl* **wives**) n mujer f, esposa
wig [wɪg] n peluca
wild [waɪld] adj (*animal*) salvaje; (*plant*) silvestre; (*person*) furioso, violento; (*idea*) descabellado; (*rough: sea*) bravo; (*: land*) agreste; (*: weather*) muy revuelto; **wilderness** ['wɪldənɪs] n desierto; **wildlife** n fauna; **wildly** adv (*behave*) locamente; (*lash out*) a diestro y siniestro; (*guess*) a lo loco; (*happy*) a más no poder

○ **KEYWORD**

will [wɪl] aux vb **1** (*forming future tense*): **I will finish it tomorrow** lo terminaré *or* voy a terminar mañana; **I will have finished it by tomorrow** lo habré terminado para mañana; **will you do it? – yes I will/no I won't** ¿lo harás? – sí/no
2 (*in conjectures, predictions*): **he will** *or* **he'll be there by now** ya habrá *or* debe (de) haber llegado; **that will be the postman** será *or* debe ser el cartero
3 (*in commands, requests, offers*): **will you be quiet!** ¿quieres callarte?; **will you help me?** ¿quieres ayudarme?; **will you have a cup of tea?** ¿te apetece un té?; **I won't put up with it!** ¡no lo soporto! ▷ *vt* (*pt, pp* **willed**): **to will sb to do sth** desear que algn haga algo; **he willed himself to go on** con gran fuerza de voluntad, continuó
▷ *n* voluntad f; (*testament*) testamento

willing ['wɪlɪŋ] adj (*with goodwill*) de buena voluntad; (*enthusiastic*) entusiasta; **he's ~ to do it** está dispuesto a hacerlo; **willingly** adv con mucho gusto
willow ['wɪləu] n sauce m
willpower ['wɪlpauə*] n fuerza de voluntad
wilt [wɪlt] vi marchitarse
win [wɪn] (*pt, pp* **won**) n victoria, triunfo ▷ *vt* ganar; (*obtain*) conseguir, lograr ▷ *vi* ganar; **win over** vt convencer a
wince [wɪns] vi encogerse
wind¹ [wɪnd] n viento; (*Med*) gases *mpl* ▷ *vt* (*take breath away from*) dejar sin aliento a
wind² [waɪnd] (*pt, pp* **wound**) vt enrollar; (*wrap*) envolver; (*clock, toy*) dar cuerda a ▷ *vi* (*road, river*) serpentear; **wind down** vt (*car window*) bajar; (*fig: production, business*) disminuir; **wind up** vt (*clock*) dar cuerda a; (*debate, meeting*) concluir, terminar

w

windfall | 428

windfall ['wɪndfɔ:l] n golpe m de
suerte

winding ['waɪndɪŋ] adj (road) tortuoso;
(staircase) de caracol

windmill ['wɪndmɪl] n molino de viento

window ['wɪndəu] n ventana; (in car, train)
ventanilla; (in shop etc) escaparate m (SP),
vidriera (LAM); **window box** n jardinera
de ventana; **window cleaner** n (person)
limpiacristales mf inv; **window pane** n
cristal m; **window seat** n asiento junto a la
ventana; **windowsill** n alféizar m, repisa

windscreen ['wɪndskri:n] (US **windshield**)
n parabrisas m inv; **windscreen wiper** (US
windshield wiper) n limpiaparabrisas
m inv

windsurfing ['wɪndsə:fɪŋ] n windsurf m

windy ['wɪndɪ] adj de mucho viento; **it's**
~ hace viento

wine [waɪn] n vino; **wine bar** n enoteca;
wine glass n copa (para vino); **wine list** n
lista de vinos; **wine tasting** n degustación
f de vinos

wing [wɪŋ] n ala; (Aut) aleta; **wing mirror**
n (espejo) retrovisor m

wink [wɪŋk] n guiño, pestañeo ▷ vi
guiñar, pestañear

winner ['wɪnə*] n ganador(a) m/f

winning ['wɪnɪŋ] adj (team) ganador(a);
(goal) decisivo; (smile) encantador(a)

winter ['wɪntə*] n invierno ▷ vi invernar;
winter sports npl deportes mpl de
invierno; **wintertime** n invierno

wipe [waɪp] n: **to give sth a ~** pasar un
trapo sobre algo ▷ vt limpiar; (tape) borrar;
wipe out vt (debt) liquidar; (memory) borrar;
(destroy) destruir; **wipe up** vt limpiar

wire [waɪə*] n alambre m; (Elec) cable m
(eléctrico); (Tel) telegrama m ▷ vt (house)
poner la instalación eléctrica en;
(also: **~ up**) conectar; (person: telegram)
telegrafiar

wiring ['waɪərɪŋ] n instalación f
eléctrica

wisdom ['wɪzdəm] n sabiduría, saber
m; (good sense) cordura; **wisdom tooth** n
muela del juicio

wise [waɪz] adj sabio; (sensible) juicioso

wish [wɪʃ] n deseo ▷ vt querer; **best ~es**
(on birthday etc) felicidades fpl; **with best**
~es (in letter) saludos mpl, recuerdos mpl; **to**
~ sb goodbye despedirse de algn; **he ~ed**
me well me deseó mucha suerte; **to ~ to**
do/sb to do sth querer hacer/que algn haga
algo; **to ~ for** desear

wistful ['wɪstful] adj pensativo

wit [wɪt] n ingenio, gracia; (also: **~s**)
inteligencia; (person) chistoso/a

witch [wɪtʃ] n bruja

○ **KEYWORD**

with [wɪð, wɪθ] prep **1** (accompanying, in
the company of) con (con +mí, ti, sí = conmigo,
contigo, consigo); **I was with him** estaba con
él; **we stayed with friends** nos quedamos
en casa de unos amigos; **I'm (not) with you**
(don't understand) (no) te entiendo; **to be**
with it (inf: person: up-to-date) estar al tanto;
(: alert) ser despabilado

2 (descriptive, indicating manner etc) con; de;
a room with a view una habitación con
vistas; **the man with blue eyes** el hombre
de los ojos azules; **red with anger** rojo de
ira; **to shake with fear** temblar de miedo;
to fill sth with water llenar algo de agua

withdraw [wɪθ'drɔ:] vt retirar, sacar ▷ vi
retirarse; **to ~ money (from the bank)**
retirar fondos (del banco); **withdrawal** n
retirada; (of money) reintegro; **withdrawn**
pp of **withdraw** ▷ adj (person) reservado,
introvertido

withdrew [wɪθ'dru:] pt of **withdraw**

wither ['wɪðə*] vi marchitarse

withhold [wɪθ'həuld] vt (money) retener;
(decision) aplazar; (permission) negar;
(information) ocultar

within [wɪð'ɪn] prep dentro de ▷ adv
dentro; **~ reach (of)** al alcance (de); **~ sight**
(of) a la vista (de); **~ the week** antes de
acabar la semana; **~ a mile (of)** a menos de
una milla (de)

without [wɪð'aut] prep sin; **to go ~ sth**
pasar sin algo

withstand [wɪθ'stænd] vt resistir a

witness ['wɪtnɪs] n testigo mf ▷ vt
(event) presenciar; (document) atestiguar
la veracidad de; **to bear ~ to** (fig) ser
testimonio de

witty ['wɪtɪ] adj ingenioso

wives [waɪvz] npl of **wife**

wizard ['wɪzəd] n hechicero

wk abbr = **week**

wobble ['wɔbl] vi temblar; (chair) cojear

woe [wəu] n desgracia

woke [wəuk] pt of **wake**

woken ['wəukən] pp of **wake**

wolf [wulf] n lobo

woman ['wumən] (pl women) n mujer f

womb [wu:m] n matriz f, útero

won [wʌn] pt, pp of **win**

wonder ['wʌndə*] n maravilla, prodigio;
(feeling) asombro ▷ vi: **to ~ whether/why**
preguntarse si/por qué; **to ~ at** asombrarse
de; **to ~ about** pensar sobre or en; **it's no**

~ (that) no es de extrañarse (que +*subjun*);
wonderful *adj* maravilloso
won't [wəʊnt] = **will not**
wood [wʊd] *n* (*timber*) madera; (*forest*)
bosque *m*; **wooden** *adj* de madera;
woodwind *n* (*Mus*) instrumentos *mpl*
de viento de madera; **woodwork** *n*
carpintería
wool [wʊl] *n* lana; **to pull the ~ over sb's
eyes** (*fig*) engatusar a algn; **woollen** (*us*
woolen) *adj* de lana; **woolly** (*us* **wooly**) *adj*
lanudo, de lana; (*fig: ideas*) confuso
word [wəːd] *n* palabra; (*news*) noticia;
(*promise*) palabra (de honor) ▷ *vt* redactar;
in other ~s en otras palabras; **to break/
keep one's ~** faltar a la palabra/cumplir la
promesa; **to have ~s with sb** reñir con algn;
word processing *n* proceso de textos;
word processor *n* procesador *m* de textos
wore [wɔː*] *pt of* **wear**
work [wəːk] *n* trabajo; (*job*) empleo,
trabajo; (*Art, Literature*) obra ▷ *vi* trabajar;
(*mechanism*) funcionar, marchar; (*medicine*)
ser eficaz, surtir efecto ▷ *vt* (*shape*)
trabajar; (*stone etc*) tallar; (*mine etc*) explotar;
(*machine*) manejar, hacer funcionar ▷ *npl*
(*of clock, machine*) mecanismo; **to be out
of ~** estar parado, no tener trabajo; **to ~
loose** (*part*) desprenderse; (*knot*) aflojarse;
works *n* (*BRIT: factory*) fábrica; **work out**
vi (*plans etc*) salir bien, funcionar; **works**
vt (*problem*) resolver; (*plan*) elaborar;
it works out at £100 suma 100 libras;
worker *n* trabajador(a) *m/f*, obrero/a;
work experience *n* **I'm going to do my
work experience in a factory** voy a hacer
las prácticas en una fábrica; **workforce**
n mano de obra; **working class** *n* clase
f obrera ▷ *adj*; **working-class** obrero;
working week *n* semana laboral;
workman (*irreg*) *n* obrero; **work of art** *n*
obra de arte; **workout** *n* (*Sport*) sesión *f*
de ejercicios; **work permit** *n* permiso de
trabajo; **workplace** *n* lugar *m* de trabajo;
worksheet *n* (*Scol*) hoja de ejercicios;
workshop *n* taller *m*; **work station** *n*
puesto *or* estación *f* de trabajo; **work
surface** *n* encimera; **worktop** *n* encimera
world [wəːld] *n* mundo ▷ *cpd* (*champion*)
del mundo; (*power, war*) mundial; **to think
the ~ of sb** (*fig*) tener un concepto muy alto
de algn; **World Cup** *n* (*Football*): **the World
Cup** el Mundial, los Mundiales; **world-wide**
adj mundial, universal; **World-Wide Web**
n: **the World-Wide Web** el World Wide Web
worm [wəːm] *n* (*also: **earth ~***) lombriz *f*
worn [wɔːn] *pp of* **wear** ▷ *adj* usado;
worn-out *adj* (*object*) gastado; (*person*)

rendido, agotado
worried ['wʌrɪd] *adj* preocupado
worry ['wʌrɪ] *n* preocupación *f* ▷ *vt*
preocupar, inquietar ▷ *vi* preocuparse;
worrying *adj* inquietante
worse [wəːs] *adj, adv* peor ▷ *n* lo peor;
a change for the ~ un empeoramiento;
worsen *vt, vi* empeorar; **worse off** *adj*
(*financially*): **to be worse off** tener menos
dinero; (*fig*): **you'll be worse off this way**
de esta forma estarás peor que nunca
worship ['wəːʃɪp] *n* adoración *f* ▷ *vt*
adorar; **Your W~** (*BRIT: to mayor*) señor
alcalde; (*: to judge*) señor juez
worst [wəːst] *adj, adv* peor ▷ *n* lo peor; **at
~** en lo peor de los casos
worth [wəːθ] *n* valor *m* ▷ *adj*: **to be ~**
valer; **it's ~ it** vale *or* merece la pena; **to be ~
one's while (to do)** merecer la pena (hacer);
worthless *adj* sin valor; (*useless*) inútil;
worthwhile *adj* (*activity*) que merece la
pena; (*cause*) loable
worthy ['wəːðɪ] *adj* respetable; (*motive*)
honesto; **~ of** digno de

○ **KEYWORD**

would [wʊd] *aux vb* **1** (*conditional tense*): **if
you asked him he would do it** si se lo
pidieras, lo haría; **if you had asked him
he would have done it** si se lo hubieras
pedido, lo habría *or* hubiera hecho
2 (*in offers, invitations, requests*): **would you
like a biscuit?** ¿quieres una galleta?; (*formal*)
¿querría una galleta?; **would you ask him
to come in?** ¿quiere hacerle pasar?; **would
you open the window please?** ¿quiere *or*
podría abrir la ventana, por favor?
3 (*in indirect speech*): **I said I would do it** dije
que lo haría
4 (*emphatic*): **it WOULD have to snow today!**
¡tenía que nevar precisamente hoy!
5 (*insistence*): **she wouldn't behave** no
quiso comportarse bien
6 (*conjecture*): **it would have been midnight**
sería medianoche; **it would seem so** parece
ser que sí
7 (*indicating habit*): **he would go there on
Mondays** iba allí los lunes

wouldn't ['wʊdnt] = **would not**
wound¹ [wuːnd] *n* herida ▷ *vt* herir
wound² [waʊnd] *pt, pp of* **wind²**
wove [wəʊv] *pt of* **weave**
woven ['wəʊvən] *pp of* **weave**
wrap [ræp] *vt* (*also: **~ up***) envolver;
(*gift*) envolver, abrigar ▷ *vi* (*dress warmly*)
abrigarse; **wrapper** *n* (*on chocolate*) papel

w

m; (*BRIT: of book*) sobrecubierta; **wrapping**
n envoltura, envase *m*; **wrapping paper**
n papel *m* de envolver; (*fancy*) papel *m* de
regalo

wreath [riːθ, *pl* riːðz] *n* (*funeral wreath*)
corona

wreck [rɛk] *n* (*ship: destruction*) naufragio;
(*: remains*) restos *mpl* del barco; (*pej: person*)
ruina ▷ *vt* (*car etc*) destrozar; (*chances*)
arruinar; **wreckage** *n* restos *mpl*; (*of
building*) escombros *mpl*

wren [rɛn] *n* (*Zool*) reyezuelo

wrench [rɛntʃ] *n* (*Tech*) llave *f* inglesa; (*tug*)
tirón *m*; (*fig*) dolor *m* ▷ *vt* arrancar; **to ~
sth from sb** arrebatar algo violentamente
a algn

wrestle ['rɛsl] *vi*: **to ~ (with sb)** luchar (con
or contra algn); **wrestler** *n* luchador(a) *m/f*
(de lucha libre); **wrestling** *n* lucha libre

wretched ['rɛtʃɪd] *adj* miserable

wriggle ['rɪgl] *vi* (*also: ~ about*) menearse,
retorcerse

wring [rɪŋ] (*pt, pp* **wrung**) *vt* retorcer;
(*wet clothes*) escurrir; (*fig*): **to ~ sth out of sb**
sacar algo por la fuerza a algn

wrinkle ['rɪŋkl] *n* arruga ▷ *vt* arrugar ▷ *vi*
arrugarse

wrist [rɪst] *n* muñeca

writable ['raɪtəbl] *adj* (*CD, DVD*) escribible

write [raɪt] (*pt* **wrote**, *pp* **written**) *vt*
escribir; (*cheque*) extender ▷ *vi* escribir;
write down *vt* escribir; (*note*) apuntar;
write off *vt* (*debt*) borrar (como
incobrable); (*fig*) desechar por inútil; **write
out** *vt* escribir; **write-off** *n* siniestro total;
writer *n* escritor(a) *m/f*

writing ['raɪtɪŋ] *n* escritura; (*hand-writing*)
letra; (*of author*) obras *fpl*; **in ~** por escrito;
writing paper *n* papel *m* de escribir

written ['rɪtn] *pp of* **write**

wrong [rɒŋ] *adj* (*wicked*) malo; (*unfair*)
injusto; (*incorrect*) equivocado, incorrecto;
(*not suitable*) inoportuno, inconveniente;
(*reverse*) del revés ▷ *adv* equivocadamente
▷ *n* injusticia ▷ *vt* ser injusto con; **you
are ~ to do it** haces mal en hacerlo; **you
are ~ about that, you've got it ~** en eso
estás equivocado; **to be in the ~** no tener
razón, tener la culpa; **what's ~?** ¿qué pasa?;
to go ~ (*person*) equivocarse; (*plan*) salir
mal; (*machine*) estropearse; **wrongly** *adv*
mal, incorrectamente; (*by mistake*) por
error; **wrong number** *n* (*Tel*): **you've got
the wrong number** se ha equivocado de
número

wrote [rəut] *pt of* **write**

wrung [rʌŋ] *pt, pp of* **wring**

WWW *n abbr* (= *World Wide Web*) WWW *m*

XL *abbr* = **extra large**

Xmas ['ɛksməs] *n abbr* = **Christmas**

X-ray ['ɛksreɪ] *n* radiografía ▷ *vt*
radiografiar, sacar radiografías de

xylophone ['zaɪləfəun] *n* xilófono

yacht [jɔt] n yate m; **yachting** n (sport) balandrismo

yard [jɑːd] n patio; (measure) yarda; **yard sale** n (US) n venta de objetos usados (en el jardín de una casa particular)

yarn [jɑːn] n hilo; (tale) cuento, historia

yawn [jɔːn] n bostezo ▷ vi bostezar

yd. abbr (= yard) yda

yeah [jɛə] (inf) adv sí

year [jɪə*] n año; **to be 8 ~s old** tener 8 años; **an eight-~-old child** un niño de ocho años (de edad); **yearly** adj anual ▷ adv anualmente, cada año

yearn [jəːn] vi: **to ~ for sth** añorar algo, suspirar por algo

yeast [jiːst] n levadura

yell [jɛl] n grito, alarido ▷ vi gritar

yellow ['jɛləu] adj amarillo; **Yellow Pages®** npl páginas fpl amarillas

yes [jɛs] adv sí ▷ n sí m; **to say/answer ~** decir/contestar que sí

yesterday ['jɛstədɪ] adv ayer ▷ n ayer m; **~ morning/evening** ayer por la mañana/tarde; **all day ~** todo el día de ayer

yet [jɛt] adv ya; (negative) todavía ▷ conj sin embargo, a pesar de todo; **it is not finished ~** todavía no está acabado; **the best ~** el/la mejor hasta ahora; **as ~** hasta ahora, todavía

yew [juː] n tejo

Yiddish ['jɪdɪʃ] n yiddish m

yield [jiːld] n (Agr) cosecha; (Comm) rendimiento ▷ vt ceder; (results) producir, dar; (profit) rendir ▷ vi rendirse, ceder; (US Aut) ceder el paso

yob(bo) ['jɔb(bəu)] n (BRIT inf) gamberro

yoga ['jəugə] n yoga m

yog(h)ourt ['jəugət] n yogur m

yog(h)urt ['jəugət] n = **yog(h)ourt**

yolk [jəuk] n yema (de huevo)

○ **KEYWORD**

you [juː] pron **1** (subject: familiar) tú; (pl) vosotros/as (SP), ustedes (LAM); (polite) usted; (pl) ustedes; **you are very kind** eres/es etc muy amable; **you Spanish enjoy your food** a vosotros (or ustedes) los españoles os (or les) gusta la comida; **you and I will go** iremos tú y yo

2 (object: direct: familiar) te; (pl) os (SP), les (LAM); (polite) le; (pl) les; (f) la; (pl) las; **I know you** te/le etc conozco

3 (object: indirect: familiar) te; (pl) os (SP), les (LAM); (polite) le; (pl) les; **I gave the letter to you yesterday** te/os etc di la carta ayer

4 (stressed): **I told you to do it** te dije a ti que lo hicieras, es a ti a quien dije que lo hicieras; see also **3; 5**

5 (after prep: NB: con +ti = contigo: familiar) ti; (pl) vosotros/as (SP), ustedes (LAM); (: polite) usted; (pl) ustedes; **it's for you** es para ti/vosotros etc

6 (comparisons: familiar) tú; (pl) vosotros/as (SP), ustedes (LAM); (: polite) usted; (pl) ustedes; **she's younger than you** es más joven que tú/vosotros etc

7 (impersonal one): **fresh air does you good** el aire puro (te) hace bien; **you never know** nunca se sabe; **you can't do that!** ¡eso no se hace!

you'd [juːd] = **you had; you would**

you'll [juːl] = **you will; you shall**

young [jʌŋ] adj joven ▷ npl (of animal) cría; (people): **the ~ los** jóvenes, la juventud; **youngster** n joven mf

your [jɔː*] adj tu; (pl) vuestro; (formal) su; see also **my**

you're [juə*] = **you are**

yours [jɔːz] pron tuyo (pl), vuestro; (formal) suyo; see also **faithfully; mine¹** see also **sincerely**

yourself [jɔːˈsɛlf] pron tú mismo; (complement) te; (after prep) tí (mismo); (formal) usted mismo; (: complement) se; (: after prep) sí (mismo); **yourselves** pl pron vosotros mismos; (after prep) vosotros (mismos); (formal) ustedes (mismos); (: complement) se; (: after prep) sí mismos; see also **oneself**

youth [pl juːðz] n juventud f; (young man) joven m; **youth club** n club m juvenil; **youthful** adj juvenil; **youth hostel** n albergue m de juventud

you've [juːv] = **you have**

Z

zeal [ziːl] *n* celo, entusiasmo

zebra ['ziːbrə] *n* cebra; **zebra crossing** (*BRIT*) *n* paso de peatones

zero ['zɪərəu] *n* cero

zest [zɛst] *n* ánimo, vivacidad *f*; (*of orange*) piel *f*

zigzag ['zɪgzæg] *n* zigzag *m* ▷ *vi* zigzaguear, hacer eses

Zimbabwe [zɪm'bɑːbwɪ] *n* Zimbabwe *m*

zinc [zɪŋk] *n* cinc *m*, zinc *m*

zip [zɪp] *n* (*also*: **~ fastener,** (*US*) **~per**) cremallera (*SP*), cierre (*AM*) *m*, zíper *m* (*MEX, CAM*) ▷ *vt* (*also*: **~ up**) cerrar la cremallera de; (*file*) comprimir; **zip code** (*US*) *n* código postal; **zip file** *n* (*Comput*) archivo comprimido; **zipper** (*US*) *n* cremallera

zit [zɪt] *n* grano

zodiac ['zəudɪæk] *n* zodíaco

zone [zəun] *n* zona

zoo [zuː] *n* (jardín *m*) zoo *m*

zoology [zu'ɔlədʒɪ] *n* zoología

zoom [zuːm] *vi*: **to ~ past** pasar zumbando; **zoom lens** *n* zoom *m*

zucchini [zuː'kiːnɪ] (*US*) *n*(*pl*) calabacín(ines) *m*(*pl*)